DICTIONARY OF NORTH CAROLINA BIOGRAPHY

EDITED BY
WILLIAM S. POWELL
VOLUME 1 A–C

DICTIONARY OF NORTH CAROLINA BIOGRAPHY

EDITED BY WILLIAM S. POWELL
VOLUME 1 A–C

The University of North Carolina Press *Chapel Hill*

© 1979 The University of North Carolina Press
All rights reserved
Manufactured in the United States of America
ISBN 0-8078-1329-X
Library of Congress Catalog Card Number 79-10106

Library of Congress Cataloging in Publication Data

Main entry under title:

Dictionary of North Carolina biography.

  Includes bibliographies.
  1. North Carolina—Biography.   I. Powell,
William Stevens, 1919–
CT252.D5   920′.0756   79-10106
ISBN 0-8078-1329-X

16 Jan '80

IN MEMORY OF   **Gordon Heath**
14 November 1918—28 November 1942

Banks Poston
14 July 1919—3 June 1944

Ira Royster
3 December 1917—19 February 1945

William Waller
17 June 1918—25 June 1943

whose youthful promise was sacrificed in World War II

Preface

The *Dictionary of North Carolina Biography* is a cooperative work in the fullest sense. Hundreds of people have been involved in its planning and production. My role has been that of planner and mover of others. From my knowledge of the names of North Carolinians of some importance, I drew up a list of possible subjects for inclusion in the present work. On it, as a matter of course, were all governors and members of congress from North Carolina, as well as a number of notable people whose roles were quite varied: authors, clergymen, military men, newspaper editors, physicians, teachers, and leaders in government at various levels. This list was circulated to many North Carolinians whose advice I sought, especially the members of the Historical Society of North Carolina, a small organization of professional historians, librarians, archivists, and writers. With the generous and frank recommendations of these people, the list was revised and further circulated both within and beyond the state. Names were deleted and names were added.

I then began to look at the various roles played by the people of North Carolina over the years, to consider fields of endeavor, contributions, or notoriety. Once again the list was revised to include artists, composers, outstanding printers, inventors, pioneer explorers, engineers, architects, builders, and others who might have been overlooked. I even ventured to include noted pirates, a few criminals whose names were once widely known, people involved in landmark judicial cases, and persons who were noted for their physical characteristics, such as size, height, advanced age, or, for example, because they were Siamese twins. Even a hermit whose good advice was sought by leaders of the state seemed worthy of inclusion.

Several questions that were raised during this time were easily resolved. It was decided that no living person should be included. Nor did the definition of a North Carolinian cause any trouble.

I adopted the definition followed by the North Carolina Collection at The University of North Carolina Library. A North Carolinian is anyone born in the colony or state without regard to where he later lived; further, a North Carolinian is anyone, no matter where born, who lived in North Carolina and did something worthy of note while there. There are, however, a few people included who do not precisely fit this definition since they were neither born in North Carolina nor did they live there. Their close association with the colony or state, nevertheless, was such that they could not reasonably be omitted. Sir Walter Raleigh is such an example, as are some of the early proprietors, explorers of the region, cartographers, and naturalists.

Volunteers willing to undertake serious research and to write biographies according to specific directions were then sought. The refined list of potential subjects to be included in the *Dictionary of North Carolina Biography* was circulated to hundreds of people, many already known to me and others who had been suggested to me as capable biographers. My instructions indicated that each biography should contain certain vital information arranged in a standard form, including an account of the subject's role or contribution. Biographers were instructed to be objective in dealing with the subject and to avoid such terms as "noted," "outstanding," "first," and "prominent." Each author was also expected to undertake fresh research in primary sources whenever possible. Each fact in a biography was to be checked against a second source and all questionable data was to be verified. Finally a concise bibliography of consulted sources was to be prepared. Each sketch is signed by its author, but I have exercised an editor's prerogative in several cases.

All of the approximately seven hundred contributors to this work have volunteered their services. No one was pressed into agreeing to write biographies although it is possible that some will say I coerced them into completing their work. I regret that it has not been possible to reimburse biographers for their work. The *Dictionary of North Carolina Biography* is a labor of love, of pride in North Carolina, and of deep interest in the subject of the biography. Included among the authors are noted scholars in many fields—professors and teachers, attorneys, clergymen, physicians, archivists, librarians, newspaper editors and reporters. Equally active and thorough in their work have been a great many students, both undergraduate and graduate, housewives, genealogists, and others, including a bus driver and a deputy sheriff.

In all honesty I must add that the work of some authors of biographies was not equal to their interest and enthusiasm; in these cases I revised their work myself, advised the author concerning revisions, or sought another author.

When more than one person volunteered to write a specific biography, I attempted to select the one who, in my judgment, best knew the subject or had most ready access to the sources. In some cases I discovered that one person knew something special about a particular subject, so I occasionally arranged for two people to collaborate on a single biography. In the case of one North Carolinian—who as an adult moved to South Carolina and afterwards to Georgia—three people, one from each state, contributed to the biography.

Not infrequently authors discovered that subjects proposed for inclusion in the dictionary did not actually represent persons whose contributions were outstanding. They suggested that these names be deleted and I often took that advice. On the other hand, while engaged in research, biographers sometimes discovered another person who deserved inclusion. The list also underwent changes for this reason.

Authors at times were unable to discover adequate information for a well-rounded biography; this was particularly true for subjects who lived in the seventeenth and early eighteenth centuries. I made the decision to include a number of less-than-complete biographies in the belief that whatever could be found would be of some use and that future research might be based upon what had been presented here.

Chapel Hill   WILLIAM S. POWELL
17 February 1979

Acknowledgments

I am indebted to the Research Council of The University of North Carolina at Chapel Hill for grants to cover some of the costs of mimeographing and mailing and for the services of a student assistant who compiled the initial list of governors, senators, and congressmen. Contributors to this fund are countless loyal alumni of The University of North Carolina whose generosity to Alumni Annual Giving makes possible much of the research on this campus. Dr. Claiborne T. Smith, Jr., Dr. Oliver H. Orr, and Mrs. Clara Flannagan also provided funds for mimeographing and postage when the Research Council grants were exhausted.

The North Carolina American Revolution Bicentennial Commission made a grant to The University of North Carolina Press to assist with the publication costs of volume one.

My wife, Virginia Waldrop Powell, has aided me with the *Dictionary of North Carolina Biography* by hours and hours of alphabetizing and filing, by checking the thoroughness of the biographies, and by diligently reading proof. Beyond this she has listened with real (or expertly feigned) enthusiasm to my reports of exciting new information discovered by an author, and she has patiently and with genuine sympathy heard my complaints of distress over authors who ignored deadlines. She has also sought answers to specific questions that I have raised about many biographies but, alas, I have not succeeded in persuading her to become a contributor of biographies.

I cannot adequately express my gratitude and satisfaction for the excellent work done by the contributors to this volume. The time and expense that so many of them have invested in their work will, I trust, be readily apparent to the reader. A number of authors have undertaken travel to libraries and archives at home and abroad entirely at their own expense.

Faults will surely be found and I beg the indulgence of those who find them. What we have jointly accomplished will surely be of sufficient merit to deserve an occasional pardon.

The staff of The University of North Carolina Press, notably the editorial and production departments, have been especially kind. Their eagerness to make this work a model in every way has been a source of inspiration. The keen editorial eye of Janice Bolster improved the manuscript immeasurably.

Finally, I should like to reiterate that the *Dictionary of North Carolina Biography* is the cooperative work of nearly a thousand people: biographers; advisors who helped prepare the list of subjects; librarians and archivists who aided many of the biographers; and those responsible for the physical production of this volume. In these days of large grants for research into almost every imaginable area, it is with considerable satisfaction that I thank everyone associated with the *Dictionary of North Carolina Biography* for this demonstration that something worthwhile can be produced without such a subsidy.

Dictionary of North Carolina Biography

Abbot(t), Henry *(ca. 1740–May 1791)*, Baptist minister and revolutionary patriot, was born in London. His father was the Reverend John Abbot, a minor or petty canon of St. Paul's Cathedral and rector of the city church of St. Michael in London. The younger Abbot was baptized in the Anglican church, received a "tolerable" education, and in the 1750s migrated to America "without the consent or knowledge of his parents."

Henry Abbot settled in Camden (until 1777 Pasquotank) County, occupying himself first as a schoolmaster. In 1758 he embraced the General Baptist faith and was baptized by Elder Joseph Parker. Shortly thereafter, however, like many others in his region, Abbot switched from the General to the more Calvinistic Particular Baptists. He was ordained by Elders Charles Daniel and James Gamewell and began a lifelong effort to spread the gospel along the Pasquotank River. From 1758 until about 1764 Abbot was a traveling evangelist and undoubtedly became well known to congregations on both sides of the river. He served briefly as minister for a group at Tar River and in 1764 or 1765 accepted an invitation to become pastor of Shiloh Church in Pasquotank County, following the death of the previous minister, John Burgess.

Organized in 1729, Shiloh was the first permanent Baptist church in North Carolina. Forty years after its founding, Shiloh, with Abbot as pastor, participated in the formation of the historic Kehukee Baptist Association. Within five years, however, a dispute over the association's proper relationship with the Separate Baptists, who had spread south from New England, led to division and gave rise to a fundamental reevaluation of qualifications for church membership. Formerly, a mere desire for baptism was deemed sufficient evidence of salvation, but a new wave of religious fervor produced in many churches a purge of members who by their own admission had been baptized prior to conversion. One who made this confession was the Reverend Henry Abbot, and consequently, Abbot had to be baptized for a third time in about 1779, before his church could be admitted formally to the reformed Kehukee Association.

While distinguishing himself as a minister, Henry Abbot did not ignore political developments within the colonies. During his gubernatorial administration, William Tryon had made no effort to conceal a personal dislike for North Carolina Baptists; when a later governor, Josiah Martin, initiated a conciliatory policy regarding the Regulators, Abbot and another Baptist minister presented the governor with a letter of commendation from the Kehukee Association for his spirit of toleration.

In 1776 Abbot and four other men were chosen to represent Pasquotank County in the provincial congress that met at Halifax and endorsed American independence. At this gathering the minister from Shiloh Church actively participated in the work of at least four committees, including one delegated to "take into consideration the defence and the state of the Sea coast," another (the Committee of Privileges and Elections) empowered to "send for Persons, Papers and Records"and report to the congress, and a third requested to "devise a more effectual way for apprehending deserters." Undoubtedly one of Abbot's most important contributions came with his service on the committee that drafted a constitution and bill of rights for North Carolina.

Henry Abbot had an interest not only in political guarantees but in religious liberties as well. Under colonial rule only the established church was authorized to perform the marriage ceremony, and this privilege was extended to dissenting sects only after ties with the mother country had been severed. Near the conclusion of the last session of 1776, Abbot, quick to take advantage of the move toward independence, introduced a resolution providing that ministers of all denominations might perform the marriage rite. Although passed in a slightly amended form, this resolution was the forerunner of a state law approved by the legislature some fifteen months later.

During the American Revolution, Abbot served as recruiting officer for Pasquotank County and held a seat on the three-member Salt Commission for Edenton (Port Roanoke). His interest in affairs of state continued after the war. In 1788 he was one of Camden's representatives at the Hillsborough Convention that rejected the proposed United States Constitution and suggested written assurance of certain individual liberties. A year later, when a second convention gathered in Fayetteville, he was again a delegate and voted with the majority to ratify the historic document.

Abbot was a peer of the most learned men in North Carolina. He is generally recognized as author of the nineteenth article of the state constitution, which made formal acknowledgement that "all men have natural and inalienable rights to worship almighty God according to the dictates of their own conscience." Variously described as an "elegant gentleman" and "popular idol," Abbot came to exercise an influence hardly equaled by ministers from his area before or since.

At his death he possessed six slaves and resided on a three- or four-hundred-acre estate in Camden County. Between 1766 and 1772, he married Mariam Caroon Lurry Wilson, and although there were no children by this union, Abbot's wife had two sons, William and Thomas, by the first of her two previous marriages. The Reverend Henry Abbot died after a short but "violent" illness and was possibly buried at a now obliterated site on his plantation northeast of Shiloh.

SEE: C. T. Bailey, ed., *North Carolina Baptist Almanac* (1883); Lemuel Burkitt and Jesse Read, *A Concise History of the Kehukee Baptist Association* (1850); Walter Clark, ed.,

State Records of North Carolina, 16 vols. (1886–1907);
Maloy Alton Huggins, *A History of North Carolina
Baptists, 1727–1932* (1967); London *Daily Advertiser*, 30
Jan. 1744; George Washington Paschal, *History of North
Carolina Baptists*, 2 vols. (1930); Jesse Forbes Pugh, *Three
Hundred Years along the Pasquotank* (1957); William L.
Saunders, ed., *Colonial Records of North Carolina*, 10 vols.
(1886–90).

JERRY W. COTTEN

Abbott, Joseph Carter *(15 July 1825–8 Oct. 1881)*,
Union general, United States senator, political lobbyist,
newspaper editor, and manufacturer, was born a son of
Aaron Abbott in Concord, N.H. He had two brothers
and six sisters. Upon graduation from Phillips Academy,
Andover, Mass., in 1846, Abbott returned to Concord,
undertook the study of law, and was admitted to the
New Hampshire bar in 1852. While maintaining a law
practice at Concord, he served as editor of the
Manchester (N.H.) *Daily American* (1851–57) and as
editor and owner of the Boston *Atlas and Bee* (1859–61).

Meanwhile, Abbott had become active in the Whig
party. Though the party soon disappeared, the Whig
ideal of nationalism and concern for economic growth
remained with Abbott all his life. With the disintegration
of the Whig organization, Abbott joined the short-lived
Know Nothing party, which was transformed into the
"Fremont clubs" in 1856 and absorbed into the
Republican party shortly thereafter. His political
activities won for him political appointments: he was
adjutant general of the New Hampshire militia (1855–61)
and served on the commission that surveyed the
boundary between New Hampshire and Canada.

With the outbreak of the Civil War, Abbott dropped all
other activities to organize the Seventh Regiment of
New Hampshire Volunteers, an achievement that
entitled him to serve as its commanding officer with the
rank of colonel. He yielded the position, however, to
H. S. Putnam, who had more military experience, and
served instead as lieutenant colonel and second in
command, in Florida and South Carolina. In 1863
Putnam was killed during an attack on Battery Wagner,
near Charleston, and Abbott assumed command and the
rank of colonel. On 15 Jan. 1865 he was promoted to
brigadier general for "gallant and meritorious service"
during the federal storming of Fort Fisher.

Abbott also took part in the capture of Wilmington and
for more than three months was the commander of the
Port of Wilmington. The assignment was a difficult one.
Because of the influx of refugees and freed prisoners of
war, the population of the city increased two and a half
times within a few days of the federal occupation. Food
and sanitary facilities were inadequate, and disease
broke out. Abbott's wife came to Wilmington to join him
and do relief work in the refugee camps but caught
typhoid fever and died.

Yet it was in the chaos and misery of postwar
Wilmington that Abbott came to the decision that the
city would be his permanent home. Perhaps he was
influenced by the public recognition given to him and
his wife for their work in cleaning up the signs of war.
He certainly made many friends at this time. He may
also have become aware of exceptional business
opportunities then existing in southeastern North
Carolina.

For whatever reasons, in September 1865, after being
mustered out of the army and settling his business
affairs in New England, Abbott returned at the age of
forty to Wilmington, which would remain his home for
the rest of his life. The financial resources of the former

lawyer and newspaperman went a long way in a region
where the money supply had largely vanished with the
Confederacy. With business partners, several of whom
were also newcomers, he formed the Cape Fear Building
Company and bought three thousand acres of pine
forest in Bladen County on the Wilmington, Charlotte
and Rutherfordton Railroad, fifty miles west of
Wilmington. From the throngs of unemployed refugees
the partners recruited a work force that eventually
numbered 150 and built a sawmill and woodworking
plant that produced railroad cars, laths, fence pickets,
broom handles, and the parts for prefabricated houses.
Some of these products were marketed as far away as
Cuba. Abbott and his associates also laid out the town of
Abbottsburg.

Even Abbott's enemies would often cheerfully
concede that Abbottsburg was perhaps the most
promising economic development in southeastern North
Carolina. The New Englander's politics were quite a
different matter. Elected to the North Carolina
Constitutional Convention of 1868, Abbott emerged as
one of the most influential delegates present, partly
because the convention had been elected in such a way
as to exclude most of the established political leadership
of antebellum North Carolina. Few of the delegates had
any political experience at all. Rare indeed was the
delegate who could match the political resources that
Abbott brought, with his legal training, newspaper
background, and experience of political, military, and
business leadership.

But Abbott's influence was not entirely a matter of
political know-how. He also had at least $20,000,
contributed by railroad owner George Swepson, which
he used to win passage of measures providing for state
aid to railroads. Subsequent investigations have shown
that much of this money was used for bribes, for
which Abbott was roundly condemned by both
contemporary newspapers and later historians. Rarely
have his critics overlooked his New England origin; and,
generally speaking, the corrupting influence of Abbott
and other carpetbaggers has attracted more attention
than has that of the native-born members of the same
lobby

It is significant, however, that from his own
constituency in southeastern North Carolina there has
been virtually no condemnation of Abbott for his
activities on behalf of the railroads, from either his fellow
Republicans or his Democratic opponents. The future
prosperity of the area depended so heavily upon
completion of the WC&R that both parties took a
permissive view of the tactics Abbott used to win
appropriations for it. Most people in the section to some
degree benefited from his impropriety, though few more
than Abbott himself, with his three thousand acres of
land along the favored line.

Following the convention Abbott was elected to the
legislature which chose him for the United States
Senate. He immediately became the chief spokesman for
another special interest group, this time the Wilmington
port lobby, which, like the WC&R Railroad, was so
closely linked to the prosperity and economic
development of the region that it enjoyed the local
support of both parties. The arguments Abbott
presented to the Senate for federally financed harbor
improvements were based on carefully researched
studies made by engineers and local leaders of the
Wilmington area, who were often Democrats. As a result
of local bipartisan cooperation to bring about the
completion of the WC&R and the improvement of the
harbor, both of which owed much to Abbott's efforts,

honest and otherwise, Wilmington emerged at the end of the century as an important port for cotton exports.

Abbott's later years were clearly unhappy ones. His Cape Fear Building Company was ruined by two converging developments: first he and some competing lumbermen exhausted the forest resources in easy reach of Abbottsburg; and then, before he could relocate his plant, the panic of 1873 struck and caused a $100,000 contraction in his assets. He became bankrupt and Abbotsburg a ghost town.

He still had political influence and was able to obtain political jobs; he was collector of the Wilmington Customs House from 1874 until 1878. But failure dogged his heels in politics as well as in business. As a result of the disputed election of 1876, Rutherford B. Hayes won the presidency by making an arrangement with his Democratic opponents at the expense of many of his former friends in the South. Like many southern Republicans, Abbott suffered from the bargain. He was dropped from the Republican National Committee, though Hayes gave him a minor job as inspector of ports.

Abbottsburg, once the symbol of progress in southeastern North Carolina, fell into decay, slowly throttled by the relentless encroachment of a second-growth scrub forest. Its founder, hounded by creditors and abandoned by many of his friends on the Potomac as well as on the Cape Fear, spent his last years brooding in his home in Wilmington. His one outside interest appears to have been the activities of the Presbyterian church. He died at the age of fifty-six and was buried in Valley Cemetery, Manchester, N.H. He was survived by his third wife, the former Ellen C. Tasker of Providence, R.I. He had no children.

SEE: *Biog. Dir. Am. Cong.* (1950); W. McKee Evans, *Ballots and Fence Rails: Reconstruction on the Lower Cape Fear* (1967); *Report of the Commission to Investigate Fraud and Corruption Under Act of Assembly Session 1870–1872* (Shipp Report, 1872); *Report of the Railroad Investigation Commission* (Bragg Report, 1871).

WILLIAM MCKEE EVANS

Abercromby (or Abercrombie), James *(1707–1775)*, colonial agent and member of Parliament, was born in Tullibody, Clackmannanshire, Scotland. He was the third son of Alexander Abercromby, M.P. There were many branches of the Abercromby family of Clackmannanshire in the eighteenth century, all noted for their wealth, legal training, military careers, and staunch Whiggish leanings. Following preparatory training at Westminster in London, James Abercromby attended Leyden University in Holland from 1724 to 1726. In the latter year he returned to London, entering Lincoln's Inn to study law. He was admitted to the bar in 1728. However, as was the case with many who studied at Lincoln's Inn, Abercromby chose a career in public service rather than law.

In 1730 Abercromby left England for South Carolina, having received an appointment as attorney general for the colony. He held this position for fifteen years and, during the period from 1739 to 1760, also served as a member of the South Carolina assembly. He was one of the South Carolina commissioners appointed to run the boundary line between that colony and North Carolina in 1735 and 1736. During the French and Indian War (1754–63) James Abercromby held two positions: from 1757 to 1765 deputy auditor general for plantations and from 1758 to 1764 agent for the Royal American Regiment, which was commanded by a cousin also named James Abercromby. In 1760 Abercromby returned to England and a year later, through attachment to Thomas Pelham-Holles, Duke of Newcastle, gained the seat for Clackmannan and Kinross in Parliament. However, he did not join Newcastle's open opposition to the Lord Bute government, as expected, choosing instead to support the 1762 Anglo-French peace negotiations that led to the Peace of Paris, 1763. Later he rejoined the Newcastle Whigs in opposing repeal of the Stamp Act in 1766 and passage of William Pitt's land tax bill in 1767.

The following year Abercromby retired from Parliament. He returned to Clackmannanshire where, until his death seven years later, he lived on a small parliamentary pension awarded in 1764.

Abercromby is best remembered for his contributions as colonial agent. During his career in this capacity he served three colonies: South Carolina from 1742 to 1757, Virginia from 1754 to 1774, and North Carolina from 1759 to 1763. Although a staunch Whig, Abercromby as an agent was in no way a proponent of colonial self-reliance or self-determinism. In fact, he was outspokenly in favor of colonial subservience and strict enforcement of mercantilist trade regulations. While these views can be seen in his opposition to repeal of the Stamp Act in 1766, they are expressed most clearly in a treatise submitted in 1752 to Robert D'Arcy, the Earl of Holderness and secretary of state for the North, under the title *An Examination of the Acts of Parliament Relative to the Trade and Government of Our American Colonies: Also the Different Constitutions of Government in those Colonies Considered with Remarks by way of a Bill for Amendment of the Laws of this Kingdom in relation to the Government and Trade of those Colonies: Which Bill is Humbly Submitted to the Consideration of His Majesty's Ministers of State, more particularly those in Office, before whom the Several Matters herein Treated are properly Cognizable: And for whose Use this Performance is intended*. While as verbose in content as in title, the pamphlet has been characterized by the historian Charles M. Andrews as the best available eighteenth-century presentation of the mercantilist system. The main points of Abercromby's argument were that the colonies were founded to benefit England and that it was solely Parliament's responsibility to enforce this relationship by statute. Should Parliament not move to assume its responsibility, Abercromby predicted that the American colonies, while in 1752 still divided in interest and action, would eventually realize their common concerns and unite as an independent confederation. To prevent this occurrence, Abercromby urged the passage of a statute clearly stating and providing for the firm enforcement of colonial subservience to the mother country. Thereby, he argued, colonial self-assertiveness would be stemmed and the growing population and prosperity of America could be channeled to the best interests of Britain and the British people.

With such ideas, it is not surprising that Abercromby was a strong supporter of the royal governor and the "prerogative party" in contests with the colonial assembly. As agent for the Virginia colony in the late 1750s, he uncompromisingly supported Governor Robert Dinwiddie in his dispute with the House of Burgesses over the pistole fee. When Dinwiddie's successor, Francis Fauquier, attempted to cool the burgesses' anger by allowing the lower house to appoint its own agent, Abercromby was bitter in his denunciation of the governor for such a show of weakness. Thereafter he did little for the colony. While his devotion to duty can be documented by his frequent attendance at sessions of the board of trade, his actions were often at odds with the best interests of the colony he represented. The principles of colonial subservience and mercantilism held priority in his mind. As agent for South Carolina, his efforts before the board of trade on the salt monopoly and on colonial defense clearly reveal his devotion to England's best interests. In his service to North Carolina, Abercromby was exhaustive in his aid to Governor Gabriel Johnston against assembly criticism of the latter's "tyranny" in the passage of the 1746 representation act. Likewise, he provided Governor Arthur Dobbs with unqualified aid during the quitrent controversy of the 1750s. These actions raised the ire of the North Carolina lower house, and renewal of Abercromby's appointment was hotly contested before it was passed in 1758. Ironically, the council objected to his reappointment as North Carolina agent in 1760, labeling him "a tool of the Assembly cabal."

By 1760 Abercromby's usefulness as a colonial agent had begun to decline. The rising tide of colonial "independency" ran counter to all the ideals he held dear. While he continued as North Carolina's agent until 1763 and as Virginia's until 1774, he was agent in name only, for the representation of these colonies had passed to men whose ideas were more compatible with the interests of the lower houses.

Due possibly to the travel required by his service as agent for three colonies, Abercromby never married. At his death he was buried in the Abercromby family graveyard in Clackmannan. It is perhaps fortunate that he did not live to see the final repudiation of his ideas on colonial policy in the American Revolution.

SEE: James Abercromby Letter Book (Virginia State Library, Richmond); Charles M. Andrews, *Colonial Period of American History*, vol. 4, *England's Commercial and Colonial Policy* (1938); Ella Lonn, *The Colonial Agents of the Southern Colonies* (1945); Charles F. Mullett, "James Abercromby and French Encroachments in America," *Canadian Historical Review* 26 (1945); Louis Namier, *England in the Age of the American Revolution* (1930); William Saunders and Walter Clark, eds., *Colonial and State Records of North Carolina*, 26 vols. (1886–1905); Jack M. Sosin, *Agents and Merchants* (1965); Alan Valentine, ed., *The British Establishment, 1760–1784*, 2 vols. (1970).

MICHAEL G. MARTIN, JR.

Abernethy, Arthur Talmage *(1872–15 May 1956)*, author, minister, and educator, was born of Scottish and German ancestry in the town of Rutherford College. His father, a Methodist minister and the founder and president of Rutherford College, was Robert Laban Abernethy; his mother was Mary Ann Hayes. A cousin, Charles Laban Abernethy, was a member of Congress for twelve years. Arthur Abernethy was graduated from Rutherford College at fourteen; he received his master's degree from Trinity College (now Duke University) and his doctorate from Johns Hopkins University. A Latin and Greek scholar at seventeen, he taught for seven years at Rutherford College as one of the youngest professors in the nation.

Seeking a change from teaching, Abernethy began a long journalistic career when he became secretary to the publisher of the *Philadelphia Record*. He worked there for seventeen years, frequently writing editorials. In Philadelphia he also served as business manager of the Philadelphia College of Commerce; there he met his wife, the former Mrs. Edna Beatty Lachot of

Philadelphia, who was a graduate of the college. Later he became feature editor and Sunday editor of the *Pittsburgh Post*, columnist for the *Milwaukee Sentinel*, and feature writer and drama critic for the *New York Tribune*. Throughout his life he contributed to the *Charlotte Observer* and other North Carolina papers.

Abernethy is perhaps best known for his writing, which ranged from novels and poems to collections of sermons and factual works of a speculative nature. He was the author of more than fifty books, in which his sense of humor and his strong southern orientation, an inheritance from his father, are prominent. His religious writings, usually evangelical rather than descriptive, include *The Apostles' Creed: A Romance in Religion*, *Center-Shots at Sin*, and *Christian's Treasure Island: A Restoration Romance*. His interest in historical and anthropological subjects is represented in numerous works ranging from a three-volume *History of New York* to such pamphlets as *The Jew a Negro* and *Did Washington Aspire to be King?* He is perhaps best known, however, for his regional stories, novels, and sketches including *Moonshine, Being Appalachia's Arabian Nights*, a collection of sketches dealing with mountain people and the manufacture of "moonshine" liquor. One of his historical romances, *A Royal Southern Family*, is autobiographical, drawing on the history of his family from its origins in Scotland and, particularly, upon the character of his great-grandmother, Fanny Wetner (or Whitener), who traced her lineage back to a member of the royal Wedner family of Saxe-Coburg-Gotha.

In November 1948 Governor R. Gregg Cherry named Abernethy poet laureate of North Carolina for the remainder of his administration which ended the following January. It was only in 1953, however, that a successor poet laureate was named.

Abernethy had long wanted to enter the ministry, as his father and two brothers—the Reverend John Turner Abernethy and the Reverend Will Abernethy—had done. A third brother, Dr. Logan Berge Abernethy, like his father became a college president, first at Weaver College and then at Mt. City College. Late in his life A. T. Abernethy realized this ministerial ambition, serving first for four years as pastor of the First Methodist Church in Belmont, N.Y., then for a number of years as pastor of a large Christian church in Cincinnati, Ohio. For the last two years before his retirement he was pastor at the Asheville Christian Church. During retirement he served a term as mayor of the town of Rutherford College, acted for several years as magistrate, and occasionally preached in local churches. The last of his family, he died at the age of eighty-three and was buried in Rutherford College Cemetery.

SEE: *Asheville Citizen-Times*, 29 Apr. 1951; Jerome Dowd, *Sketches of Prominent Living North Carolinians* (1888); R. Gatewood, ed., *A Rockett/Abernethy Genealogy* (1969); Mabel B. McClure, *The Abernethys* (1934); Raleigh *News and Observer*, 17 May 1956; W. L. Sherrill, *Annals of Lincoln County* (1937).

PETER L. ABERNETHY

Abernethy, Charles Laban *(18 Mar. 1872–23 Feb. 1955)*, congressman and lawyer, was born in the town of Rutherford College, Burke County. His father, John Turner Abernethy, was the son of Robert L. Abernethy, the founder of Rutherford College. His mother was the former Martha Scott. After attending public elementary schools and Mount Olive High School, he entered his grandfather's college where he prepared for a law course at The University of North Carolina. In 1893 he founded a weekly newspaper, the *Beaufort Herald*, which he published until he decided to concentrate more fully on the practice of law. After being admitted to the bar in 1895, he opened a law office in Beaufort and for many years was the only lawyer in Carteret County. He served as city attorney for two years. A member of the state executive committee of the Democratic party from 1898 to 1900, he was a presidential elector in 1900 on the Democratic ticket of Bryan and Stevenson, at that time the youngest person ever to have sat in the electoral college. He was an elector again in 1904 on the ticket of Parker and Davis. Upon being appointed solicitor of the third (later the fifth) judicial district, he moved to New Bern in 1913. He served as solicitor for twelve years and then practiced law until elected in 1922 to fill the unexpired House of Representatives term of Sam M. Brinson, who had died in office. He was reelected to a full term in the Sixty-eighth Congress and to five additional terms, until defeated by Graham A. Barden in 1934. He resumed the practice of law in New Bern in 1935 and unsuccessfully tried to regain his seat in Congress in the elections of 1936, 1938, and 1940. Retiring from his law firm in 1938, he remained a resident of New Bern until his death.

Abernethy's greatest contribution was his early and persistent advocacy of an inland waterway. Laboring long and hard for his project, he was one of the principal spokesmen for the Intracoastal Waterway that was eventually established. His article "Has North Carolina Kept the Pace?" published in the August 1927 *Southern Advertising and Publishing*, promoted the waterway and included numerous statistics indicating the economic and industrial growth his state was then experiencing. He was instrumental, as well, in having Fort Macon returned to the people of North Carolina. Then Abernethy, as a member of the House Appropriations Committee, secured funds for the construction of a federal building to house several government agencies with offices in New Bern. His success in raising the funds was seen as a major victory accomplished despite the opposition of President Hoover's Republican administration and the onset of the Depression; hailing the funding as a notable political feat, Will Rogers commented that his home town of Claremore, Okla. could also get a building costing $3,000,000 if Abernethy were its representative. New Bern further profited from Abernethy's influence when he persuaded the government to locate a customs office there.

Abernethy was a member of numerous fraternal orders, including the Elks, Odd Fellows, Red Men, Woodmen of the World, Kiwanis, and Knights of Pythias. He was master of the Franklin Masonic Lodge in Beaufort, a Knight Templar, and a member of the Sudan Shrine Temple in New Bern. An active Methodist layman, he organized the Deems Bible Class of Centenary Methodist Church in New Bern and often commuted from Washington to conduct the class on Sundays.

Abernethy suffered several nervous breakdowns and was hospitalized first in 1920 and intermittently thereafter until 1942, when he became a patient in the state mental hospitals of North Carolina until shortly before his death. His condition, which prevented him from attending the Democratic convention in Chicago in 1932, was made worse in the following months by the special session of Congress called to consider economic conditions at the height of the Depression and by the heavy workload he carried as a member of the appropriations committee at this time of economic crisis. His failure to regain his seat in Congress also contributed

to the increasing mental instability that eventually resulted in his commitment to state institutions in Raleigh and Butner. After his release, he returned to New Bern and lived quietly for two years until his death.

Married to the former Minnie M. May of Pitt County on 19 Dec. 1895, Abernethy had one son, Charles Laban, Jr., a lawyer in New Bern who became his father's legal guardian. Abernethy is buried in Cedar Grove Cemetery in New Bern. A portrait, presented by his daughter-in-law, has been placed in the courtroom of the superior court of the district where he served.

SEE: Charles Laban Abernethy MSS (Manuscript Department, Library, Duke University, Durham); *Biog. Dir. Am. Cong.* (1950); Raleigh *News and Observer*, 24 Feb. 1955, 31 May 1970; *Southern Advertising and Publishing* 2 (1927).

PAUL I. CHESTNUT

Abington, Thomas (d. *November or December 1707*), attorney and colonial official of North Carolina, took oath as attorney general 25 Feb. 1695/96. He was replaced in that office 3 Oct. 1696, apparently because of poor health. He subsequently served as clerk of Pasquotank Precinct court (October 1699, or earlier, until his death), clerk of the general court (1706–7), clerk of the council and court of chancery (ca. 1706–7), and clerk of the lower house of the assembly (November 1707).

Abington lived in Pasquotank Precinct, where he held at least 445 acres of land at his death. It is not known whether he married.

Abington died between 13 Nov. 1707, when he made his will, and 28 Dec. 1707, when the will was proved. He apparently became ill during or soon after the assembly session and died at the house of John Hecklefield on Little River, where the session had been held. The legatees named in his will included Mary Tully, a goddaughter; Mrs. Elizabeth Hecklefield, who was bequeathed a sum for her "care and trouble" during his illness; Tobias Knight, secretary of the colony, who was one of the executors; and several others who apparently were friends. No legatees were identified as relatives.

SEE: J. Bryan Grimes, ed., *Abstract of North Carolina Wills* (1910); J. R. B. Hathaway, ed., *North Carolina Historical and Genealogical Register*, 3 vols. (1900–1903); Abington's will and various documents from Albemarle County Papers, 1678–1714 (North Carolina State Archives, Raleigh); Mattie Erma Edwards Parker, ed., *North Carolina Higher-Court Records, 1670–1696* and *1697–1701* (1968 and 1971); William S. Price, Jr., ed., *North Carolina Higher-Court Records, 1702–1708* (1974).

MATTIE ERMA E. PARKER

Adair, James Robert (ca. *1709–ca. 1787*), author, planter, and Indian trader, eldest son of Thomas Adair, was born in County Antrim, Ireland. With his father and three brothers he came to the colonies in 1730, settling first in Pennsylvania near the present town of Chester. In Charleston, S.C., five years later, he became a partner to Indian trader George Galphin. In the first decade of his perilous career, he traded with the Catawbas and Cherokees. In 1744 he first traded with the Chickasaws; in 1747, at the behest of Governor James Glenn of South Carolina, he went on an expedition to open trade with the Choctaws. Although Adair escaped from many types of imprisonment, his most difficult escape came when he was taken by the French who had controlled

Choctaw trade until Adair interfered. He was scheduled to be hanged, but managed an escape, the details of which are not known. Governor Glenn, meantime, sent out an expedition to gain control of Adair's Chickasaw trade and then refused to pay the £2,200 Adair had spent on his expedition to the Choctaw country. Adair never forgave Glenn.

After Adair broke with Glenn in 1750, he moved to Johnston (later Dobbs, now Greene) County in North Carolina at the invitation of Governor Dobbs, his personal friend. He settled at Fairfields, a plantation home on Great Contentnea Creek named for Fairfield, Connecticut, the birthplace of his first wife, Ann McCarty, whom he had married on 18 Oct. 1744. They had three daughters, Saranna (m. William McTyer), Elizabeth (m. John Cade), and Agnes (m. John Gibson). Adair resumed his travels and in the 1750s was trading among the Indians of the Carolinas. In the Cherokee war of 1760, Adair received a captain's commission and led the Chickasaws against the Cherokees.

Throughout his years among the Indians, Adair kept notes. There is no record of his education, but he practiced medicine among the Indians. He wrote that he was "well acquainted with near 2,000 miles of the American continent," mostly in what is now the southern and southeastern United States. He was Dr. James Adair but, informally, "Robert" or "Robin."

In 1763 he went back to England. Legend has it that through his gallantry he became acquainted with a wealthy lady in whose London home he met Lady Caroline Keppel, daughter of the Earl of Albemarle. They fell in love, and her family, although objecting to the marriage, permitted the wedding in 1759 after a separation proved to affect Lady Caroline's health. During this separation from him she wrote the ballad, "Robin Adair." Three children were born to the couple (one son named Robert became a member of Parliament), and George III gave Adair an appointment in the field of medicine. Although Adair returned to America, he supposedly made trips back to England. Lady Caroline died in 1769 at the age of thirty-two.

For two or three years after 1765 Adair was in America trading with the Chickasaws and Choctaws out of Mobile. Late in 1768, he was in New York trying unsuccessfully to find a publisher for his book, *History of American Indians*, in which he tried to prove his theory that the Indians were the lost tribes of Israel; the book was published in London in 1775. In 1770 Adair removed his family from Dobbs to Bladen (now Robeson) County, where he purchased a large plantation that he named Patcherly. Tradition has it that he served as physician with Francis Marion during the American Revolution; he lived in a Whig area where Marion often conducted military operations.

The most notable Whig of south Robeson, Archibald McKissack, witnessed Adair's will. Although by some reports Adair was buried in England in 1790, his will was probated in Bladen County in 1787. In it he left an inheritance to Robert Adair of County Antrim. The North Carolina Society of Colonial Dames was responsible for a granite shaft erected to honor him in August 1934 near Ashpole Presbyterian Church (Robeson County).

SEE: James Robert Adair, *History of American Indians* (1775); Arthur Collins, *Peerage of England* (1812), vol. 3; Margaret McMahan, "Robert Adair, Man of Legend Ended Wanderings in Robeson," Lumberton *Robesonian*, 8 Oct. 1972; "Memorial Shaft Set in Honor of Adair," *Robesonian*, special ed., 29 Nov. 1937; Robeson County Medical Auxiliary, *Our Medical Heritage* (1951);

"Romantic Adventurer, Indian Trader, Writer 'Robin' Adair Left Descendants in Rowland Area," *Robesonian*, historical ed., 26 Feb. 1951.

MAUD THOMAS SMITH

Adair, John (*1732–24 Feb. 1827*), pioneer settler and local official, usually identified as "The Entry Taker," was born in County Antrim, Northern Ireland. He married Ellen Crawford and had at least one son, John Jr., and one daughter, Mary or Maria. He is to be distinguished from General John Adair (1757–1840), who was born in Chester County, S.C., and who later moved to Kentucky, where he became the eighth governor of that state and died at White Hall, Mercer County. General John Adair lived in North Carolina for only a year or two when he attended school in Charlotte.

John Adair, the Entry Taker, is also to be distinguished from his son, John, Jr., born in Ireland in 1754, who, though not so well known, served his country well in defending the frontier while living with his parents in Sullivan County, then North Carolina, but afterward Tennessee. He moved to Knox County in 1791, and lived there for fourteen years before moving to Wayne County, Kentucky, where he died.

John Adair, the Entry Taker, brought his family to America about 1767, landing in Baltimore. He lived in Maryland and Pennsylvania, about a year in each colony, before moving to Sullivan County in 1772. There he acquired four hundred acres on the north side of the Holston River on both sides of the main wagon road. In 1779 he was appointed entry taker for Sullivan County; in 1780 he was drafted for military service, but his son served as his substitute.

In 1781, before the Battle of King's Mountain, Adair released state funds for arms and supplies to Colonel Isaac Shelby and Colonel John Sevier, both of whom he knew well. Without funds, they had turned for a loan to him as land agent. Adair's reply to the request was: "I have no authority in law to make that disposition of this money. It belongs to the impoverished treasury of North Carolina, and I dare not appropriate a cent of it to any purpose, but if our country is overrun by the British our liberties are gone. Let the money go, too. Take it. If the enemy, by its use, is driven from the country, I can trust that country to justify and vindicate my conduct, so take it." The loan amounted to $12,735. Shelby and Sevier pledged themselves to see it refunded, or the act of the Entry Taker legalized.

A group of western Virginians and Carolinians submitted a document read in Congress 13 Jan. 1785, asking for the establishment of an independent government to be known as the State of Franklin; John Adair was one of the four residents of Sullivan County to sign the petition.

In 1787 Hawkins County was formed from Sullivan and Adair was appointed commissary agent. In 1788 he was also named commissary agent for the route through the Cumberland Gap that was the passageway for travelers through the wilderness to the Cumberland Plateau. In that same year he built Fort Adair on the Broadway Road, which was the Indian path to the Clinch River.

In 1790 North Carolina ceded land to be known as the Territory South of the Ohio; it remained so designated until 1 June 1796, when Tennessee became the sixteenth state. During those six years Adair took several public actions. In 1790 he was appointed to serve as justice of the peace of Hawkins County. In 1791 he was one of the first to buy a lot in Knoxville. In that same year the legislature of North Carolina granted him a 640-acre section of land four and a half miles north of Knoxville in the Beaverdam Basin. He built his home, called Adair Station, on Adair Creek. In 1792 Adair was appointed a justice of the peace and a member of the court of common pleas and quarter sessions for Knox County. Two years later, when Blount College, now the University of Tennessee, was established, he was named a trustee. In 1796 Adair was a member of the constitutional commission that wrote the constitution for the State of Tennessee. In this same year Knoxville was founded by Adair's close friend and contemporary Hugh Lawson White of Iredell County, who named Adair a commissioner. Adair also served as a trustee of Hampden-Sydney Academy and as an elder in the First Presbyterian Church of Knoxville, established in 1793. He was a presidential elector from the Hamilton district from 1796 to 1800.

Adair died at his residence.

SEE: James Barnett Adair, *Adair History and Genealogy* (1924); John Preston Arthur, *Western North Carolina* (1914); Lyman Chalkley, comp., *Chronicles of the Scotch-Irish Settlement . . . from the . . . Records of Augusta County, Virginia, 1745–1800*, vols. 1–3 (1912–13); Lyman G. Draper, *King's Mountain and Its Heroes* (1929); General Services Administration, Veterans Records (Washington, D.C.); *Knoxville Register*, 28 Mar. 1827; Allan L. Poe, correspondence (August 1974) and personal interview (18 May 1975); J. G. M. Ramsey, *The Annals of Tennessee to the End of the Eighteenth Century* (1853); Worth Ray, *Tennessee Cousins* (1950); Tennessee and King's Mountain Papers (State Historical Society of Wisconsin, Madison); *Tennessee History Magazine* 8 (1924); Tennessee Land Entries (Tennessee State Library and Archives, Nashville); Samuel Cole Williams, *History of the Lost State of Franklin* (1924).

MARY ADAIR EDWARDS PHIFER

Adams, Donald Keith (*6 Mar. 1902–20 May 1971*), educator and psychologist, was born in Orville, Ohio, the son of John F. and Elizabeth Taylor Adams. His preparatory education was completed at the local high school in 1919, and he entered Pennsylvania State University, University Park, that fall. He was graduated with a B.A. in 1923. The next year he taught in the high school at Donora, Pa., and then went to Harvard University, where he earned the M.A. degree in 1925. From Harvard he went to Yale University for two subsequent years, receiving the degree of Ph.D. there in 1927 in psychology, with a special emphasis in social psychology.

The following year he was a Sterling Fellow at Yale, after which he joined the faculty of Wesleyan University, Middletown, Conn. In 1929 he taught at Iowa State University, Ames, and then spent two years as a Fellow of the National Research Council in Berlin, Germany. When he returned to the United States in 1931, he accepted an invitation to join the faculty of Duke University as professor of psychology, a post he held until his retirement in 1967.

For three successive summers he taught special classes, first at the University of California, Berkeley, in 1948; then at Cornell University, Ithaca, N.Y., in 1949 and the following summer at Salzburg, Austria, where he conducted a seminar in American Studies. As at Duke, he proved a popular and stimulating teacher in those special assignments and commanded great respect in his field around the world.

He used his several sabbaticals from his work at Duke for special teaching, research, and writing. With a Guggenheim Fellowship, he spent 1937–38 divided between lecturing and studying at Geneva, Switzerland, and lecturing at Swarthmore College, Swarthmore, Pa. During another session, 1958–59, he held a Fulbright Scholarship at the Max-Planck-Institut, Seewiesen/Starnberg.

On military leave from Duke, Adams spent 1943–45 in Washington, London, Paris, and Wiesbaden in assessment research for the Office of Strategic Services. The following year he was sent to Japan with the United States Strategic Bombing Service, and then, from 1946 to 1948, he was chief psychologist in the Veterans Administration in Atlanta and Richmond. He returned to Duke and served as chairman of the Department of Psychology from 1947 to 1951.

Adams's scholarly writings included: *Experimental Studies of Adaptive Behavior* (Baltimore, 1929); the translation, with K. E. Zener, of K. Levin's *Dynamic Theory of Personality* (New York, 1935); *The Anatomy of Personality* (New York, 1954); and *Learning Theory, Personality Theory and Clinical Research* (New York, 1954). In addition he contributed many articles to a long list of academic and professional journals. Among these was his classic "Restatement of the Problem of Learning," published in the *British Journal of Psychology* (1932).

Through the years he held membership in numerous organizations: American Psychological Association (fellow); American Association for the Advancement of Science (fellow); American Association of University Professors; American Board of Examiners in Clinical Psychology (diplomate); Southeastern Psychological Association; North Carolina Psychological Association (president, 1954–55); and Sigma Xi, scientific fraternity.

Adams's teaching, lecturing, and writing covered a broad spectrum of interests. He was a recognized authority on animal behavior and comparative psychology, but throughout his career at Duke, his scholarly interests ranged further, into the fields of development, personality, and social psychology.

Adams was married on 27 July 1927 to Naomi Quinter Holsepple. They had one daughter, Nancy Quinter (Mrs. Robert Malone). Adams died at Duke Hospital, Durham.

SEE: Data Files (Office of Information Services, Duke University, Durham).

C. SYLVESTER GREEN

Adams, John Hampton (*1875–31 Jan. 1935*), a pioneer in the High Point textile industry, was born on a plantation near Adamsville, Marlboro County, S.C., the son of Jonathan and Mary Jane Newton Adams. Jonathan Adams was a prosperous planter whose successes were interrupted by the Civil War, during which he served in the Confederate Army and by the establishment of a free labor system.

John H. Adams, the only son in a family of ten children, attended the Palmetto High School, Adamsville, and the Oak Ridge Institute, Guilford County, N.C. He first entered business in South Carolina as a bookkeeper with W. B. Adams and Company and later held a similar position with F. P. Tatum of McColl, S.C. In 1900 Adams settled in High Point, where he was to pioneer the manufacture of hosiery. He became an associate of J. Henry Millis, himself a pioneer High Point industrialist and businessman. After an apprenticeship as bookkeeper, he joined Millis in organizing and then actively managing a business to manufacture pants and overalls. In marketing the products, he provided his salesmen with a complementary line of hosiery manufactured by a small Randleman mill. Both lines prospered, and soon Adams and Millis decided to expand their operation to include the manufacture of hosiery. In 1904 they, with eleven other investors, organized the High Point Hosiery Mill. Adams induced one of the investors, Charles C. Robbins of Asheboro, a man experienced in the hosiery textile industry, to join in the management of the company. The hosiery operation subsequently proved so lucrative that it displaced the parent line; Adams devoted his full attention to the manufacture of hosiery. The business grew so rapidly that the capacity of the plant was substantially increased. The Adams and Millis interests organized other manufacturing concerns, including the Piedmont Mills, the Kernersville Knitting Company, the Pioneer Hosiery Company, and the Consolidated Mills Company. Soon allied industries were launched to facilitate hosiery production by this sprawling complex of companies. The Highland Cotton Mills and the Cloverdale Dye Works were founded to supply the ever-increasing need for yarn.

After the death of J. H. Millis in 1914, Adams was the president and manager of this industrial empire. In 1927 a consolidation of the various enterprises resulted in the organization of the Adams-Millis Corporation. This firm which was guided by Adams, its first president, until his death, was destined to become one of the nation's leading hosiery firms and to be listed on the New York Stock Exchange. Before 1927 the Adams-Millis interests specialized in lower-priced seamless hosiery (at one time being the world's leading producer), but in 1929 they opened a modern full-fashioned hosiery mill. Thereafter they were among the leading producers of both hosiery styles.

Adams's influence on the hosiery industry reached beyond his own companies. He frequently advised and invested in other manufacturing enterprises in High Point and throughout North Carolina. In addition to his business activities Adams was a director of the Wachovia Bank and Trust Company, a trustee of the Oak Ridge Institute, and a steward and trustee of Wesley Memorial Methodist Church, of which he was a dedicated member.

J. H. Adams was married on 14 June 1906 to Elizabeth Barnes of Bennettsville, S.C. She and two daughters, Martha Ellen (Nell) and Elizabeth, survived him. Adams was buried in Oakwood Cemetery in High Point.

SEE: J. J. Farriss, *High Point, North Carolina*, 7th ed. (n.d.); *High Point Enterprise*, 1 Feb. 1935; *Pioneer Days and Progress of High Point, N.C., 1859–1948* (1948); Marjorie W. Young, ed., *Textile Leaders of the South* (1963).

MAX R. WILLIAMS

Adams, Junius Greene (8 Feb. 1884–4 Jan. 1962), attorney and cattleman, was born in Statesville, the son of Joseph Shephard Adams and Sallie Greene Adams, a native of Greensboro. They were descendants of a long line of English and Scottish forebears, some of whom settled in the Piedmont section when it was being taken up by the first pioneers. The elder Adams, a successful lawyer and jurist, died in 1911 while presiding at a term of the superior court at Warrenton.

Junius G. Adams was educated in the public schools of Asheville, at Mooresville High School, and at The University of North Carolina, where he studied law. He was admitted to the North Carolina bar in 1906 and began to practice in Asheville in the firm of Adams and

Adams with his father and brother, John S. Adams. From 1910 through 1914 Adams served as judge of the Asheville police court. Four years later his practice in Asheville was interrupted when, during World War I, he joined the army. From 1918 to 1919 he served as a judge advocate, and later as legal adviser to the director of Purchase, Storage, and Traffic Division of the General Staff, and later still as executive secretary and counsel of the U.S. Liquidation Commission in Paris and special commissioner for the liquidation of the Third Army in Coblentz. Returning to active practice as a member of the Asheville bar in 1920, he became known as a lawyer of unusual and outstanding ability, particularly in business law and civil actions.

Adams played a vital role in the growth and development of the economic, social, and cultural life of the western North Carolina mountain region. He was closely identified with the activities of two outstanding benefactors who contributed greatly to the economic progress of the area: the family of George W. Vanderbilt, the owners and developers of the vast and multiple interests of the Biltmore Estate (when Adams first became associated with the Vanderbilt Estate, Biltmore House and Gardens were relatively unknown); and E. W. Grove, the owner and builder of Grove Park Inn and Grove Park, an outstanding residential area, and of many of Asheville's commercial structures. Adams also served as counsel for the Buncombe County Sinking Fund Commission from its organization in 1937 until his death. The objective of this body was the long-term funding of the Asheville and Buncombe County bond indebtedness brought into default by the depression of the 1930s.

Adams was nationally known in agricultural activities. He was president of the American Jersey and Cattle Club from 1943 to 1946 and headed the Purebred Dairy and Cattle Association in 1949–50. As a result of his interest in dairying, Adams in 1952 was awarded an honorary Doctor of Agriculture degree by North Carolina State University at Raleigh, at the same time that Dr. Carl A. Schenck, founder of America's first forestry school, at the Biltmore Estate, was presented the honorary degree of Doctor of Forestry.

In Asheville Adams was a founder and first president of the Civitan Club and a member of the Masonic Order and the Biltmore Forest Country Club. He held membership in the Southen Society of New York, in the Army and Navy Club of Washington, D.C., and in the Dairy Shrine Club of Biltmore. He was a vestryman of All Souls Episcopal Church at Biltmore and a trustee of the Asheville School for Boys. He belonged to the American Bar Association, the American Judicature Society, and the Lawyers' Club of New York.

Adams married Helen Barber of Galena, Ill., in 1907. They had three sons, two of whom survived him. Junius G., Jr., and Joel B. Adams were long associated as members of the North Carolina bar, while the third son, Stephen S., lived for some time in Atlanta. Junius G. Adams, Sr., died of a heart attack at the age of 77, and after services at All Souls Episcopal Church at Biltmore, his body was taken for burial to the cemetery of the Calvary Episcopal Church at Fletcher.

A portrait of Judge Adams was commissioned by the Dairy Shrine Club of Waterloo, Iowa, in honor of his work and outstanding leadership in the dairy industry and in connection with the "Hall of Fame" award in that state. Another large portrait was commissioned for Junius G. Adams, Jr., and hangs in his home.

SEE: Junius G. Adams, Jr., personal recollections (2 Jan. 1975); *Asheville Citizen-Times*, 19 July 1959, 29 July 1959,

5 Jan. 1962, 24 Sept. 1962, 28 Sept. 1962; Francis J. Hazel, "A Eulogy on Judge Junius G. Adams at Meeting of the Buncombe County Bar Association, October 1, 1962" (North Carolina Room, Pack Memorial Library, Asheville).

ARTUS MONROE MOSER

Adams, Spencer Bell (15 Oct. 1860–12 Jan. 1943), lawyer, judge, and Republican party leader, was born near Dobson, in Surry County, the son of John A. and Sara A. Adams, who came to North Carolina from Pittsylvania County, Va., in 1857 and purchased an estimated eleven thousand acres of land. The Adams family owned a large number of slaves but in politics opposed secession, supported the Whig party, and in 1860 endorsed the Constitutional Union party led by John Bell of Tennessee. After the outbreak of the Civil War, however, John A. Adams and his family supported the Confederate cause. Spencer Bell Adams's father died in 1862, his mother in 1873. Thrown upon his own resources at an early age, Adams attended school at Riceville, Va., later enrolling in the Booneville Academy in Yadkin County and subsequently in a private school in Rockingham County. In 1881 he entered the Dick and Dillard law school in Greensboro. In February 1882 he completed legal studies and was licensed to practice in the state courts.

Adams commenced his law practice in Yanceyville, Caswell County. As a Republican party stalwart, he was elected clerk of the superior court and probate judge for Caswell County in 1882 and reelected in 1886, 1890, and 1894. In 1896 he resigned this office and was elected judge of the superior court. In this latter capacity, Adams handed down a notable decision in the case of *Wood* v. *Bellamy*, involving efforts of the Fusionists (the coalition of Republicans and Populists) to abolish state institutional offices, recharter eleemosynary institutions under different names, and fill the vacated positions with political appointees. This action, Adams maintained, would subject state institutions to undue political pressure and interference; his decision was subsequently upheld by the state supreme court. In 1898 Adams resigned as superior court judge to run for Congress in the fifth district, a Democratic party stronghold. In this contest he was defeated by his Democratic opponent, William Walton Kitchin. In the same year Adams moved to Greensboro to practice law. He was chosen by Republicans as secretary and treasurer of the North Carolina Railroad, a position he filled from 1899 to 1901.

In May 1900 the Republican state convention nominated Adams as its gubernatorial candidate to oppose Charles B. Aycock. The Republican losses of 1898 and the volatile issues of white supremacy and the suffrage amendment presaged defeat. However, Adams's receipt of over 125,000 votes and his successful pressure on Aycock to take a more forthright stand on the issue of public education indicate that he managed a creditable campaign. President Theodore Roosevelt appointed Adams chief judge of the Choctaw and Chickasaw Citizenship Court in the Indian Territory in July 1902. This court completed its work at the end of 1904, and Adams returned to Greensboro to resume his legal practice.

In 1905 Adams became involved in a bitter factional dispute in Republican ranks that involved state chairman Thomas S. Rollins and former United States Senator Marion Butler, who were pitted against Congressman Edmond Spencer Blackburn. The strategy of the Rollins, Butler, and Adams faction involved the resignation of Rollins as state chairman and his replacement by Adams. Subsequently, Adams was chosen over Spencer Blackburn as state chairman in the 1906 Republican state convention in Greensboro. The faction to which Adams belonged was believed to represent the established leadership of the party and was strongly endorsed by the *Daily Industrial News* of Greensboro. Adams maintained that as chairman he augmented party membership, and the congressional and state races of 1908 attested to formidable gains in the Republican vote. In 1910 Adams was replaced as Republican state chairman by John Motley Morehead of Charlotte. Presumably Morehead's election represented a change from the old office broker leadership to the new business and industrial spokesman. Adams was a North Carolina delegate in the Republican National Convention of 1900 and served as a delegate-at-large and member of the platform committee in the 1908 national convention.

Adams continued to practice law in Greensboro. His colleagues took note that during a long career as attorney he frequently represented the oppressed and underprivileged.

Adams combined an interest in farming with his professional and political activities. For many years he operated a stock farm in eastern Guilford County. In 1917 he sold this farm and purchased another near Whitsett, known as Wildwood Stock Farm, where he raised shorthorn cattle and Berkshire hogs.

In 1894 Adams married Lizzie L. Swift. Six children, four daughters and two sons, were born to this union. When Adams died, he was survived by three daughters. He was buried on 15 Jan. 1943 in Green Hill Cemetery in Greensboro.

SEE: Samuel A. Ashe, ed., *Biographical History of North Carolina*, vol. 5 (1906); *Charlotte Observer*, 13, 14, Jan. 1943; Raleigh *News and Observer*, 14 Jan. 1943; *North Carolina: The Old North State and the New*, vol. 5 (1941); *Proceedings of the Forty-Fifth Annual Session of the North Carolina Bar Association* (1943), 41; David C. Roller, "Republican Factionalism in North Carolina, 1904–1906," *North Carolina Historical Review*, 42 (1965); Theodore Roosevelt Papers (Library of Congress, Washington, D.C.); Joseph F. Steelman, "The Progressive Era in North Carolina, 1884–1917" (Ph.D. diss., University of North Carolina, 1955); Joseph F. Steelman, "Republican Party Politics in North Carolina, 1902; Factions, Leaders, and Issues," East Carolina College, *Publications in History*, 3 (1966); Joseph F. Steelman, "Republicanism in North Carolina: John Motley Morehead's Campaign to Revive a Moribund Party, 1908–1910," *North Carolina Historical Review* 42 (1965).

JOSEPH F. STEELMAN

Akehurst (Ackhust, Acorst, Akust), Daniel (ca. 1653–ca. Dec. 1699), colonial official, was born in England, probably in Sussex. He settled in North Carolina in the early 1680s. Akehurst was a devout Quaker and served as a minister much of his life. In 1671 he was seized at a Quaker meeting in Hastings, Sussex, and was fined and imprisoned in "a nasty hole called the Darkhouse" for participating in the meeting. In 1675 he made a missionary trip to New England. Akehurst's permanent removal to America was associated with his appointment to the North Carolina council as proprietor's deputy by a fellow Quaker, John Archdale, who had recently bought a proprietorship in Carolina. The appointment was made 26 Mar. 1681.

Akehurst arrived in North Carolina at some date before December 1684, by which time he owned a plantation in Pasquotank Precinct. His official position was then only nominal, for John Archdale also had come to the colony and was himself performing the governmental duties he had delegated to Akehurst. It is not certain that Akehurst actively served as council member at any time in the 1680s, although Archdale returned to England in 1686. Of the sparse surviving records of that decade, only one, a will proved before him in 1688, indicates that Akehurst held an office of any sort. His earliest service on the council for which there is clear evidence was in January 1693/94.

At some time after 1 Sept. 1688, Akehurst moved to Warwick County, Va., probably because of the disorders attending the banishment of Governor Seth Sothel. Although Akehurst subsequently returned to North Carolina in active official service, he claimed Warwick County as his residence the remainder of his life.

In early December 1693 Akehurst was at his Virginia plantation preparing to return to North Carolina. By that time the Carolina proprietors were reorganizing the government of their colonies and making other reforms to alleviate the grievances that had led to the earlier disorders. Akehurst was to be secretary of the colony as well as council member in the reorganized government.

By January 1693/94 Akehurst was in North Carolina serving as secretary and council member, positions in which he was active until his death. There is indication, but no clear evidence, that he also served as acting chief executive for brief intervals in early 1694, when Philip Ludwell, then acting governor, was frequently absent from the colony.

As member of the council, Akehurst was *ex officio* justice of the general court until the fall of 1697, when the composition of the court was changed. He was *ex officio* justice of the court of chancery throughout his tenure as council member. In 1695 he was appointed deputy collector of customs for Pasquotank and Little River District. In 1696, and probably other years, he was escheator for the colony. In the spring of 1699, he and Henderson Walker were sent to Virginia to settle the long-standing boundary dispute, but the mission failed, when Virginia officials refused to recognize the commissions held by the North Carolina agents. Later that year Akehurst served on a commission to investigate a charge of murder, subsequently found false, brought against a group of Indians.

In private life Akehurst was a planter and attorney. He owned plantations in both Virginia and North Carolina. In the 1690s, however, he did not live on his Pasquotank property but made his North Carolina home on a plantation, leased from John Archdale, on New Begun Creek.

Akehurst was John Archdale's personal attorney as well as his governmental deputy. He not only handled legal matters for Archdale but also managed the proprietor's North Carolina properties. Other clients included residents of Virginia, Pennsylvania, and Bermuda as well as North Carolinians.

Akehurst was active in Quaker affairs in both Virginia and North Carolina. He was associated with the Little River Monthly Meeting in North Carolina and with the Warwick River meetings in Virginia. In 1698 and 1699 he entertained Thomas Story, the English missionary, in his Virginia home, where Story preached several times. He accompanied Story on visits to other Virginia meetings, to a number of which Akehurst himself had preached. North Carolina Quakers, in recording Akehurst's death, paid tribute to the fervor of his ministry among them.

There are minor discrepancies in the records about the date of Akehurst's death, but it seems clear that he died in Virginia in November or December 1699 or January 1700. Akehurst was survived by his wife, Ann, and a daughter, Philochrista (Filiachristy, Filia). There are indications that Ann was Akehurst's second wife, but the records are not clear. His first wife may have been a Mary Akehurst who, like Philochrista, was listed without identification among Akehurst's "transports" when he proved his headrights. No other reference to Mary Akehurst has been found in North Carolina records. Ann, whose name does not appear among the "transports," seems to have lived chiefly on the Virginia plantation, which appears to have been her own property before her marriage to Akehurst. Philochrista was in North Carolina with her father much of the time. By July 1699 she had married a North Carolinian, Joseph Jordan.

Akehurst bequeathed his North Carolina property to Philochrista and his Virginia property to his wife. For some years after her father's death, Philochrista and her husband lived on the plantation that Akehurst had rented from John Archdale. Ann continued to live on her Warwick River plantation.

SEE: Joseph Besse, *A Collection of the Sufferings of the People Called Quakers . . . ,* 2 vols. (1753); J. Bryan Grimes, ed., *Abstract of North Carolina Wills* (1910); J. R. B. Hathaway, ed., *North Carolina Historical and Genealogical Register,* 3 vols. (1900–1903); William Wade Hinshaw, comp., *Encyclopedia of American Quaker Genealogy,* vols. 1 and 6 (1936, 1950); "Isle of Wight County Records," *Virginia Historical Magazine* 7 (1899); North Carolina State Archives (Raleigh), for the Albemarle Book of Warrants and Surveys (1681–1706), Council Minutes, Wills, Inventories (1677–1701), and a certified copy of Akehurst's will (filed in Chowan County Wills); Mattie Erma Edwards Parker, ed., *North Carolina Higher-Court Records, 1670–1696* and *1697–1701* (1968 and 1971); William S. Price, Jr., ed., *North Carolina Higher-Court Records, 1702–1708* (1794); Records of the Little River and Symons Creek Monthly Meeting (Quaker Collection, Guilford College Library, Greensboro); William L. Saunders, ed., *The Colonial Records of North Carolina,* vols. 1–2 (1886); John Smith, "The Lives of the Ministers of the Gospel Among the People Called Quakers" (MS, ca. 1770) and "Dictionary of Quaker Biography" (typescript; both in the Quaker Collection, Haverford College Library, Haverford, Pa.); Thomas Story, *Journal of the Life of Thomas Story* (1747).

MATTIE ERMA E. PARKER

Akerman, Amos Tappan (*23 Feb. 1821–21 Dec. 1880*), lawyer, and U.S. attorney general, was born in Portsmouth, N.H., the son of Benjamin and Olive Meloon Akerman. He was educated at Phillips Exeter Academy and Dartmouth College, being graduated from the latter in 1842. His first employment was as headmaster of a boys' academy in Murfreesboro, where his students included Pulaski Cowper, later private secretary to Governor Thomas Bragg and General Lawrence S. Baker of Gates County. Years afterward, Cowper and Baker remembered schoolmaster Akerman as one who, "with a too painful frequency, exemplified the proverb of not 'sparing the rod,' and not 'spoiling the child.'"

Following a term in Murfreesboro, Akerman in 1846 found employment as a private tutor with John McPherson Berrien of Savannah, Ga. Akerman studied law under Berrien, was licensed to practice, and settled at Clarksville, Ga. Initially an opponent of secession, he accepted the fact of disunion and served first with Toombs's brigade and later with the quartermaster department. After the war he served in Georgia's state constitutional convention of 1868 and was appointed attorney general by President Grant in 1870. An opponent of the vast claims to land sought by major railroad interests, Akerman was attacked by Huntington, Gould, and other magnates, who were successful in persuading Grant to remove him from office at the end of 1871. He resumed his law practice in Georgia and continued with it until his death a decade later, at Cartersville.

Akerman married Martha Rebecca Galloway shortly after first moving to Georgia.

SEE: *DAB*, vol. 1 (1928); *Nat. Cyc. Am. Biog.*, vol. 4 (1899 [portrait]); *Raleigh Observer*, 17 Aug. 1877.

THOMAS C. PARRAMORE

Alderman, Edwin Anderson (*15 May 1861–29 Apr. 1931*), educator, orator, university president, was born in Wilmington as the third surviving child and only son of James and Susan Jane Corbett Alderman. His ancestors on both sides had been residents of North Carolina for several generations, although his paternal line has been traced to William Alderman, born in Massachusetts in 1640. His mother's family, of mixed English, French, and Scottish blood, was descended from Thomas Corbett, who migrated from France to England before 1692. Alderman's father, by occupation an inspector of lumber, was an officer of the First Presbyterian Church of Wilmington during the time when Woodrow Wilson's father, Joseph Ruggles Wilson, was minister there. Young Alderman received his early education in private schools in Wilmington and for two years attended the Bethel Military Academy, Warrenton, Va. He enrolled in 1878 at The University of North Carolina, where he was graduated in 1882 with the Ph.B. degree, receiving honors in English and Latin. He also won the coveted Mangum Medal for oratory.

Following graduation, he accepted a teaching position in the Goldsboro public schools and came under the influence of Edward P. Moses, who infected him with the zeal for public education that thereafter characterized Alderman's career. He succeeded Moses as super-intendent of the Goldsboro schools in 1885 and remained in that position until the summer of 1889, when Alderman and Charles D. McIver were appointed by the North Carolina Superintendent of Public Instruction Sidney M. Finger to conduct teachers' institutes throughout the state. For more than three years Alderman and McIver toured the state bringing to ill-prepared teachers a measure of pedagogical instruction and endeavoring against numerous obstacles to arouse support for the public schools. Although their success was far from spectacular, they probably helped to prepare the ground for the educational renaissance that occurred under the leadership of Governor Charles B. Aycock a decade later.

In June 1891 Alderman was named professor and McIver was elected president of the State Normal and Industrial School, now The University of North Carolina at Greensboro, an establishment then recently authorized by the General Assembly for the education of young women. In October 1892 the school was opened, enrolling approximately two hundred students during its first year.

In 1893 Alderman became professor of the history and philosophy of education at The University of North

Carolina and was assigned additional teaching duties in the history department. He is credited with introducing to the university broad, survey-type courses on the history of Western civilization. During 1895 and 1896 Alderman supervised the research and writing of the first thesis ever accepted by The University of North Carolina for the master's degree in history: J. A. Moore's "History of the Public School System in North Carolina." Alderman also acquired some reputation for his own research in local history. In 1896 he was elected president of the university. During the four years of his presidency enrollment increased steadily; but the university continued to be plagued by financial problems, its annual income during Alderman's tenure never amounting to more than $50,000.

In 1900 Alderman became president of Tulane University. During his four years there he emphasized closer relations with the public schools and the opening of educational opportunities to all worthy students. His presidency was marked by a significant increase in enrollment and some expansion of the physical plant. Although he met with moderate success in his efforts to expand the university's financial resources, his appeals to private philanthropy did not evoke the response he had expected. His most effective service was publicizing the institution and strengthening its connection with the public schools. In this work he made effective use of the Southern Education Board, an institution established in 1901 of which Alderman was a member until its dissolution in 1914 (although his most effective services were rendered before 1907).

Alderman was elected first president at the University of Virginia in 1904, all previous administrative heads of the eighty-five-year-old institution having held the office of chairman of the faculty. Although he met with some opposition, Alderman succeeded in tying the university to the movement for democratizing education, of which he was a principal leader. With the willing support of the faculty, he was able during the first decade of his administration to move the traditional, conservative institution into the mainstream of modern academic life and to make it the apex of the commonwealth's system of public schools. He secured state appropriations and led a successful campaign to increase the university's endowment by soliciting private contributions. He cooperated with the faculty in reorganizing the undergraduate curriculum to bring it more in line with the conventional academic pattern. He emphasized the development of the professional schools of law, engineering, and especially medicine but— apparently believing that the time for detailed research had not yet arrived in the South—placed significantly less emphasis upon the graduate school and the library. Although the natural sciences made considerable gains in both equipment and faculty during Alderman's presidency, history and the social sciences lagged. During the decade 1904 to 1914, the university faculty doubled in size while the student body increased by less than 50 percent, in part because of the raising of admission requirements at Alderman's insistence.

The remaining seventeen years of Alderman's presidency were marked by diverse advances. He lost a controversy with the alumni, however, resulting from his recommendation of the establishment of a coordinate college for women, although a modified form of coeducation was instituted at Virginia after World War I. But Alderman more than regained any popularity he had forfeited in this battle when he succeeded in 1922 in preventing the removal of the medical department from Charlottesville to Richmond; he emerged from the struggle a local hero. By the end of Alderman's first twenty-five years as president of the university (1904–29), the student body had quadrupled and the endowment had grown from $350,000 to $10,000,000; and there were to be additional increases in both students and endowment before Alderman's death two years later. Alderman's personal prestige was much enhanced by a memorial address on Woodrow Wilson delivered in Washington, D.C., before the assembled dignitaries of the nation on 15 Dec. 1924.

Meanwhile, Alderman's health had become a matter of prime concern to him. As early as 1906 he had received ominous warnings that he was not an entirely well man. On 24 Nov. 1912, shortly after Wilson's election to the presidency and just as Alderman was being publicly discussed as a possible candidate for an important diplomatic post under the new administration, he was admitted as a patient at Lake Saranac, N.Y., with tuberculosis of the larynx and complications in both lungs. Although he was released in the spring of 1914, he never regained his former vigor, and his later years were marked by increasingly poor health complicated by numerous ailments. On 29 Apr. 1931, while on his way to deliver an address at the inauguration of Harry Woodburn Chase, recently of The University of North Carolina, as president of the University of Illinois, Alderman suffered a stroke of apoplexy. Taken from the train at Connellsville, Pa., and rushed to the state hospital, he died a few hours later without ever regaining consciousness. His funeral was held in the little Gothic chapel on the University of Virginia campus, and his body was interred in the university cemetery. The University of Virginia possesses both an oil portrait of Alderman, showing him in academic attire, painted by Eugene Edward Speicher and presented to the university in 1922, and a bust by Sergei Konenkov presented in 1930.

Alderman was married to Emma Groves, a sister of Professor Ralph Henry Groves of The University of North Carolina and one of the belles of the state, on 29 Dec. 1885 at Chapel Hill. Their three children all died in early childhood, and Emma herself died of tuberculosis in 1896. On 10 Feb. 1904, Alderman married Bessie Green Hearn of New Orleans, several years his junior. Both she and their only child, Edwin Anderson Alderman, Jr., survived Alderman.

SEE: Alderman Library, University of Virginia, Charlottesville; W. Conard Gass, "Kemp Plummer Battle and the Development of Historical Instruction at the University of North Carolina," *North Carolina Historical Review* 45 (1968); Rose H. Holder, *McIver of North Carolina* (1957); Dumas Malone, *Edwin A. Alderman* (1940); Minutes of the Board of Trustees (1893–1904) and Minutes of the Faculty of The University of North Carolina (1893–1904) (Library, University of North Carolina, Chapel Hill).

W. CONARD GASS

Alderman, John Thomas (26 June 1853–11 Apr. 1932), educator, Baptist historian, and Mason, was born in Salemburg, Sampson County. His father was Amariah Biggs Alderman (1819–89), a Baptist minister in Sampson and adjoining counties; his mother was Penelope Eliza Howard. His primary and secondary education was obtained at home under the direction of his parents. He attended Wake Forest College in 1872–73 and in 1873 began his career in education by teaching in a local school. He returned to Wake Forest College in 1876 and was graduated with an A.B. degree in June

1880. Alderman taught school at Newton Grove until 1881. From 1882 to 1891 he was principal of Fork Academy, Davie County, and from 1883 to 1891 he served as superintendent of the Davie County schools. He was superintendent of the Reidsville schools, 1892–94, and in 1894 became superintendent of schools in Talapoosa, Ga. After a year there he went on to become principal of City High School, Columbus, Ga. In 1899 he returned to Henderson, N.C., where he organized the school system and served as superintendent of schools until his retirement in 1923. Alderman also served as principal of the state school for the blind in Raleigh from January to August of 1918, after the death of J. E. Ray; he served on the school's board of directors for sixteen years. He conducted many teachers' institutes and wrote articles on educational subjects throughout his career.

Alderman was elected to the North Carolina Senate in 1925 and 1929.

One of the leading Baptist laymen in North Carolina, Alderman served at the Henderson First Baptist Church as, among many other things, deacon and Sunday school superintendent. He acted for the Tar River Baptist Association as moderator, 1922–23, 1928–30; as a member of the executive committee, 1922–26; and as historian, 1926–31.

In 1921 Alderman was appointed to the historical commission of the Baptist State Convention of North Carolina, the function of which was to encourage research and collect historical materials for the Baptist Historical Collection, Wake Forest College. Alderman was elected chairman on 13 June 1922 and continued to serve until his death. As chairman, he developed a biographical questionnaire sent to all North Carolina Baptist ministers in 1923–24. His card file of information on deceased Baptist ministers and his other notes were the basis for the biography file now in the E. T. Crittenden Collection in Baptist History, Z. Smith Reynolds Library, Wake Forest University. In 1923 Alderman began writing a history of the Sandy Creek Baptist Association, and in 1925 he and the other members of the historical commission were authorized to select an individual to write a history of North Carolina Baptists. Dr. George Washington Paschal of Wake Forest College was selected, and in 1930 his *History of North Carolina Baptists, Volume I, 1663–1805* was released. As chairman of the historical commission, Alderman attended the two hundredth anniversary of Shiloh Baptist Church, Camden County, and in 1927 addressed the centennial meeting of the Eastern Baptist Association.

Alderman was regular correspondent of the *Charity and Children* (Thomasville), the *Gold Leaf* (Henderson), and the *Biblical Recorder* (Raleigh). In 1923 the *Biblical Recorder* published a series of his biographical sketches of North Carolina Baptist ministers. He also wrote articles for the *North Carolina Booklet* and the *North Carolina Baptist Historical Papers*.

Alderman was also one of the outstanding Masons in North Carolina. He was initiated into the order in Mingo Lodge, Sampson County, in November 1874. In 1900 he was admitted to the Henderson Lodge and served as commander of the Henderson Commandery, Knights Templar, from 1905 to 1909. He coauthored the *Masonic Code of North Carolina*. In 1912 he was the grand master of the Grand Council and advanced through the various offices of the Grand Lodge of North Carolina, becoming grand high priest of the Grand Royal Arch Chapter and in 1914 grand master of the Grand Lodge of North Carolina.

Alderman married Lillian Frances Watson of Warrenton on 22 Aug. 1894. They had two children, John Thomas, Jr., and Virginia (Mrs. James Merrill Peace).

SEE: John Thomas Alderman Papers (Baptist Historical Collection, Wake Forest University, Winston-Salem); *North Carolina Baptist State Convention Annual, 1932* [photograph]; *North Carolina: The Old North State and the New*, vol. 3 (1941); Raleigh *News and Observer*, 13 Apr. 1932.

JOHN R. WOODARD, JR.

Alexander, Annie Lowrie (*10 Jan. 1864–15 Oct. 1929*), physician, teacher, and philanthropist, was born near the town of Cornelius in Mecklenburg County of Scotch-Irish ancestry. Her father was Dr. John Brevard Alexander (1834–1911), a physician and author. She was also descended from two famous Revolutionary patriots: the Reverend Alexander Craighead and the Reverend David Caldwell. Dr. Annie Lowrie Alexander's mother was Ann Wall Lowrie (1834–93).

Miss Alexander, following early education under a private tutor and her father, entered Woman's Medical College in Philadelphia, from which institution she was graduated in 1884. After a year as intern at her alma mater, she became an assistant teacher of anatomy in the Woman's Medical College of Baltimore, Md., while at the same time practicing medicine privately. In 1887 she returned to North Carolina to become the first woman to practice medicine in the South, having obtained her license in 1885 from the Maryland Board of Medical Examiners (in a class of one hundred candidates, in which she was the only woman, she made the highest grade). Later she did postgraduate work in the New York Polyclinic. She continued to practice her profession until her death, serving on the staffs of the Presbyterian and St. Peter's hospitals of Charlotte and acting for twenty-three years as physician for the Presbyterian College for Women (later Queens College).

In 1890 Miss Alexander's parents moved to Charlotte and established their home with their daughter at 410 North Tryon St.

During the occupancy of Camp Greene in Charlotte during World War I, Miss Alexander was appointed acting assistant surgeon, her principal work being the medical inspection of thousands of school children. Along with her medical practice, she performed social welfare work, especially among women and girls; for many years she was on the board of managers of the Charlotte YWCA, and later she was a trustee and the examining physician for the physical education department of the YWCA. She was physician and board member of the Florence Crittendon Home and a board member of the Associated Charities and of the Cooperative Nursing Association.

Miss Alexander was noted for her femininity, gentle manners, and cultured womanhood. Baptized in childhood in the Bethel Presbyterian Church, she later became a loyal member of the First Presbyterian Church of Charlotte. She was a member of the Daughters of the American Revolution, the United Daughters of the Confederacy, and the Charlotte Woman's Club. She was an honorary member of the North Carolina Medical Society and of the Southern Medical Society. She served as president of the Mecklenburg Medical Society and as a vice-president of the Women's Physicians of the Southern Medical Association.

She died of pneumonia in Charlotte, after four days of illness, and was buried there in Elmwood Cemetery.

SEE: John B. Alexander, *History of Mecklenburg County from 1740 to 1900* (1902); *Charlottte Observer*, 16 Oct. 1929, 21 Jan. 1940 ("Old Times Recall Dr. Annie Lowrie Alexander"); Delta Kappa Gamma Society of North Carolina, comp., *Some Pioneer Teachers of North Carolina* (1955); Raleigh *News and Observer*, 16 Oct. 1929; Mrs. W. R. Stowe, correspondence (1960); Charles M. Strong, *History of Mecklenburg County Medicine* (1929).

HAROLD J. DUDLEY

Alexander, Eben (*9 Mar. 1851–11 Mar. 1910*), teacher, administrator, and diplomat, was born in Knoxville, Tenn., son of Ebenezer and Margaret McClung Alexander. His father was judge of the second circuit of Tennessee, and his grandfather, Adam Rankin Alexander, had been a member of the United States House of Representatives, from 1823 to 1827. Eben Alexander entered Yale in 1869 after preparatory work at East Tennessee University, later the University of Tennessee. At Yale he distinguished himself through membership in Psi Upsilon, Skull and Bones, and Phi Beta Kappa. After graduation in 1873 he accepted a position as instructor in ancient languages at East Tennessee. In 1874 he married Marion Howard-Smith, with whom he later had two sons, Eben and John Howard, and two daughters, Eleanor and Margaret McClung. During thirteen years on the faculty Alexander acquired teaching and administrative experience as professor of Greek, president of the Tennessee State Teachers' Association, and chairman of the faculty when the institution was without a president in 1885–86. Maryville College conferred the Ph.D. degree upon him in 1886.

Although Alexander was considered for the post of president of East Tennessee, he was not selected, most probably because of his reluctance to go along with a movement to de-emphasize the classics. After some resulting controversy, he resigned from the faculty of East Tennessee, accepted a professorship of Greek at The University of North Carolina, and moved to Chapel Hill in 1886. In his first six years there he continued to show a strong interest in teaching, evidence of which may be seen in several articles in the *North Carolina Teacher* between 1889 and 1892, as well as in comments, written with George T. Winston, in the "Classical Department" of that journal. In 1893 the university conferred upon Alexander the degree of LL.D.

Also in 1893 Grover Cleveland appointed Alexander minister to Greece, Romania, and Serbia. During his term of service the Olympic Games were revived (in 1896), and according to *Harper's Weekly* (28 Sept. 1895), the first contribution was from Alexander. While in Athens he became good friends with Stephen and Cora Crane, both of whom were war correspondents in the Greco-Turkish War. Crane's novel *Active Service* was dedicated to Alexander.

Upon his return to Chapel Hill in 1897, Alexander was asked to take an active role in the administration of the university. He was named dean of the faculty in 1900 by President Venable and became chief administrative officer of the College of Liberal Arts and graduate studies, as well as supervisor of the library. He helped to establish the Order of the Golden Fleece (1903), a chapter of Phi Beta Kappa (1904), and *Studies in Philology* (1906), the official journal of the Philological Club, of which he was a charter member (1893). He also participated significantly in the effort to obtain a $50,000 (later $55,000) grant from Andrew Carnegie to build a library (1905).

Because of poor health Alexander was forced to take a

leave of absence in 1909; in the following year he died in Knoxville, Tenn.

SEE: Eben Alexander Papers (Southern Historical Collection, University of North Carolina, Chapel Hill); Samuel A. Ashe, ed., *Biographical History of North Carolina*, vol. 3 (1905); Stanley J. Folmsbee, *Tennessee Establishes a State University* (1961); Lillian Gilkes, *Cora Crane* (1960); E. W. Knight and Agatha B. Adams, *The Graduate School* (1946); *Nat. Cyc. Am. Biog.*, vol. 12 (1904); Louis R. Wilson, *The University of North Carolina, 1900–1930* (1957).

GARY R. KEARNEY

Alexander, Evan Shelby *(1767–28 Oct. 1809)*, lawyer and legislator from Salisbury, was born in Mecklenburg County, probably in the Clear Creek Township area, where his father owned a plantation. He was the son of Colonel Adam Alexander and Mary Shelby and a cousin of Nathaniel Alexander. Evan Shelby Alexander was graduated from Princeton University in 1787. His father had intended that he should enter the ministry, but he preferred the law. He was admitted to the bar and set up practice in Salisbury. He served three terms in the North Carolina House of Commons between 1796 and 1803, and two years later he was chosen to finish the congressional term of his cousin Nathaniel, who had become governor of the state. He was reelected as a representative to the Tenth Congress and served from 24 Feb. 1806 until 3 Mar. 1809. He also served as a trustee of The University of North Carolina from 1799 to 1809.

Alexander never married. Dying in Salisbury, he was buried there in the old Lutheran Cemetery.

SEE: *Biog. Dir. Am. Cong.* (1950); Alvah Stafford, comp. Alexander Notebooks (Public Library of Charlotte and Mecklenburg County, Charlotte); *Who Was Who in America, 1607–1896*.

EVA MURPHY

Alexander, Hezekiah *(1728–16 July 1801)*, Revolutionary statesman, was born in Cecil County, Md., of Scotch-Irish ancestry. His grandfather, Joseph Alexander, a tanner, is thought to be one of seven brothers who migrated to Somerset County, Md., sometime prior to 1670. His father, James Alexander, moved to Cecil County where he became a magistrate and an elder in the Presbyterian church. His mother, Margaret McKnitt, the daughter of John McKnitt and Jane Wallace, was James Alexander's first wife.

A member of a large family, Hezekiah Alexander learned the blacksmith's trade and then moved to Cumberland (now Franklin) County on the Pennsylvania frontier. On 12 June 1752 he married Mary Sample; they settled on a small tract purchased the previous year. When the outbreak of the French and Indian War opened the area to severe Indian attacks, Alexander's family was forced to flee. By 1764 Alexander was buying land near the Catawba River in Piedmont, North Carolina, an area where many of his relatives had settled. He rose to become, with Thomas Polk, one of the most influential men in Mecklenburg County. He was an elder of the Sugar Creek Presbyterian Church, where preached the fiery Alexander Craighead. In 1768 Governor William Tryon appointed him a county magistrate. Three years later, as treasurer and trustee, he played a prominent part in the creation of Queens College, the first college chartered south of Virginia and the only school for the training of Presbyterian ministers south of Nassau Hall in New Jersey.

From the first, the largely Presbyterian settlers of Mecklenburg were at odds with the Crown. They opposed the land claims of Governor Arthur Dobbs and George Selwyn in "the war of Sugar Creek." Also deeply resented were laws placing restrictions on Presbyterian ministers and taxing the inhabitants for the support of the Anglican church. A petition to the governor in 1769 warned that there were in the county over a thousand members of the Church of Scotland "able to bear arms," who "shall ever be more ready to support that government under which they find the most liberty." The levying of new restrictions on America by Parliament and the king's veto of the Queens College charter in 1773 led Alexander to give his support to the actions of the Continental Congress and to become a member of Mecklenburg's Committee of Safety. An effective public speaker, he was active in a series of public meetings held by the committee during the winter and spring of 1774–75. Following the outbreak of fighting at Lexington, he took part in the adoption of the Mecklenburg Resolves of May 31, 1775, which declared all British laws and authority to be henceforth null and void. The royal governor wrote England that these were the most "treasonable publications" that "this continent have yet produced." Captain James Jack, who carried a copy of the resolves to the North Carolina delegation in Congress, later remembered Hezekiah as chairman of that May meeting; others thought it might have been Abraham or Adam Alexander, who were his cousins. Chairman or not, he played a major role in bringing about the break with Great Britain.

In September the Patriots organized a council and six District Committees of Safety to oversee the town and county committees of the province, and named Hezekiah Alexander to the Salisbury district committee. In December of 1775 this committee sent a military expedition to western South Carolina, which crushed the Scovellite Tories there. Alexander outfitted and supplied the expedition as its commissary. In May 1776, when the district committees were abolished and virtual dictatorial powers were given to the council, he was selected to be one of its thirteen members. With his colleagues in this office, he saw to the raising, provisioning, and financing of the patriot forces, served as the highest judicial body, and determined civilian and military policy in the province. The Tory threat in the east was suppressed by the Battle of Moore's Creek Bridge, and an expedition sent against the Cherokees ended that threat to the west. The actions taken by the council in these first years of conflict were crucial in determining the success of the Revolution in North Carolina.

Following the Declaration of Independence, the council called for a congress to meet at Halifax in November to establish a permanent government for the state. Hezekiah was subsequently elected a delegate to this congress. He was a champion of the democratic forces in Mecklenburg, against the conservatives led by Thomas Polk. In all his actions, his chief lieutenants were Waightstill Avery, an attorney who boarded in his home, and Alexander's younger brother, John McKnitt Alexander. At Halifax, because of his council reputation, he was placed on the committees that drafted the bill of rights and the constitution. His influence helped make the North Carolina constitution, second only to Pennsylvania's, the most democratic of those then drawn.

With this, his major work, accomplished, his remaining years were spent in Mecklenburg with his family of seven sons and three daughters. He continued to play a leading role in the affairs of his church and served wisely and conscientiously as county magistrate until 1794. His stone house still stands in Charlotte and he was buried in the cemetery of the Sugar Creek Presbyterian Church.

SEE: Account Book of William Sample Alexander (possession of Osmund Barringer, Rocky Mount); John B. Alexander, *History of Mecklenburg County from 1740 to 1900* (1902); Samuel P. Bates and J. Fraise Richard, *History of Franklin County, Pennsylvania* (1887); Deeds, Births, Marriages, and Wills (Hall of Records, Annapolis, Md.; Cecil County Courthouse, Elkton, Md.; Historical Society of Pennsylvania, Philadelphia; Mecklenburg County Courthouse, Charlotte); *First Census of the U.S. 1790* (1908); William Henry Foote, *Sketches of North Carolina, Historical and Biographical* (1846); John G. Herndon, "John McKnitt (ca. 1660–1714) and Some of His Kinsfolk: Alexanders, Brevards, Dales," *Pennsylvania Genealogical Magazine* 16 (1948); Mecklenburg County Court Minutes (North Carolina State Archives, Raleigh); "A Modern Poem by The Mecklenburg Censor" (1777, Library, Charleston, S.C.); William L. Saunders, ed., *Colonial Records of North Carolina*, vols. 6–10 (1888–90).

NORRIS W. PREYER

Alexander, John (*ca. 1738–1799*), Anglican clergyman, was a native of Northern Ireland. He was educated at the grammar school in Shrewsbury, England, and was received about 1760 into the ministry of the Presbyterian church in Ireland. In 1762 he received from his church permission to go as a missionary to the colony of North Carolina, and later that year he began preaching to congregations in what is now Pitt County.

Not long after coming to the colony, Alexander was converted to the Church of England and applied for ordination. Upon the receipt of adverse reports about him, the church denied his application, and Alexander moved southward in hopes of finding support for his ambition. He made his residence at Sunbury, Ga., among a settlement of Puritans from New England and a handful of Anglicans. Sunbury Anglicans assisted Alexander in a new application for orders, and in 1766 he went to London and received ordination and a promise of support from the Society for the Propagation of the Gospel in Foreign Parts (SPG). He returned to Sunbury for two years but became embroiled in personal difficulties, lost his income from the SPG, and was in 1768 obliged to leave Sunbury in search of more hospitable churchmen.

After an unsuccessful effort to locate at Purrysburg, S.C., Alexander continued northward to Hertford County, N.C., where St. Barnabas parish, created coterminously with the county in 1759, had been without a minister since that time. An application to Governor William Tryon, then working to strengthen the Anglican position in the colony, procured the parish for Alexander; he appears to have settled on glebe land near the chapel of St. John's. His difficulties with congregations, perhaps brought on by what was described as "an over temper," continued to plague him in St. Barnabas and were compounded by the vestry's increasing balkiness in paying his salary. He may have continued to preach for a time during the Revolution, but by the 1780s he had given up trying to hold together the disintegrating Anglican congregations under his charge and had retired from the ministry. In 1786 he

acquired a farm in adjacent Bertie County and moved there to spend the remainder of his life.

Alexander would have nothing to do with the struggling new Protestant Episcopal Church in the years following the war. He wrote into his will of 1799 a bitter indictment of the decline of "the Manly, Masculine Voice of Orthodoxy" and "the senseless Rant of Whining Fanaticism." He left behind a reputation for being, in Governor Tryon's words, "a sensible excentrical Genius"; long years after his death it was observed by Duncan C. Winston that the parson had been "a prominent man in his day and of some peculiar characteristics."

The name of his wife, who appears to have preceded him to the grave, is not known, but he had daughters named Elizabeth, Martha, and Rachel.

SEE: Thomas C. Parramore, "John Alexander, Anglican Missionary," *North Carolina Historical Review* 43 (1966).

THOMAS C. PARRAMORE

Alexander, John Brevard (*27 May 1834–24 June 1911*), physician, historian, and churchman, was born in Lemley's Township, Mecklenburg County. Of Scotch-Irish ancestry, he was the son of Robert Davidson Alexander, grandson of William B. Alexander, and great-grandson of John McKnitt Alexander. His mother was Abigail Bain Caldwell, daughter of Samuel Craighead Caldwell, granddaughter of David Caldwell, and great-granddaughter of Alexander Craighead. In 1850 young Alexander entered Davidson College from Alexandrianna and there joined the Masonic fraternity. He was graduated in 1852 with high honors and afterward began a course of study at the Medical College of South Carolina, from which he was graduated in 1855 at the top of his class.

During the Civil War Alexander served in Company C, Thirty-seventh North Carolina Infantry, first as a private (1861–62) and then as a surgeon (1862–65). After the war he returned to his home county to resume his medical practice. In 1890 he and his family moved to North Tryon Street in Charlotte. He managed a drugstore in connection with his profession throughout his career until 1898, when his health declined.

On 18 May 1858 Alexander was married to Annie Wall Lowrie, the granddaughter of Superior Court Judge Samuel Lowrie. They had six children: Robert D. (d. 1901); Dixie (d. 1909); Annie Lowrie, M.D., one of the earliest women from the South to be graduated from the Woman's Medical College, Philadelphia (1884); Lucy (d. December 1919), wife of J.H. Halliburton; Samuel Lowrie (d. 1887); and James Houston, a farmer at Goldston, Chatham County.

Alexander wrote three books, *Biographical Sketches of the Early Settlers of the Hopewell Section* (1898), *The History of Mecklenburg County from 1740 to 1900* (1902), and *Reminiscences of the Past Sixty Years* (1908). He also compiled a sketch of local church history, "Presbyterianism, How and Where It Was First Planted in Mecklenburg County."

He was an elder of the Bethel Presbyterian Church for thirty-five years, and after moving to Charlotte he was active in the First Presbyterian Church there. He died at his home in Charlotte and was buried in Elmwood Cemetery.

SEE: Alexander's own books (cited in the text); *Charlotte News*, 25 June 1911; *Davidson College Alumni Catalogue* (1924); *North Carolina: Rebuilding an Ancient Common-wealth*, vol. 4 (1929); Charles L. Van Noppen,

"Biographical Sketch of John Brevard Alexander, M.D." (Manuscript Department, Library, Duke University, Durham).

EVA MURPHY

Alexander, Joseph *(ca. 1735–30 June 1809)*, clergyman and educator, born in Cecil County, Md., was the son of Theophilus and Catherine Alexander and grandson of James and Margaret McKnitt Alexander. His mother's maiden name is believed to have been Wallis. He had a brother, George, and five sisters, Margaret, Sophia, Heziah, Ann and Catrine. Theophilus was an affluent blacksmith who reared and educated his children in the strict Calvinist tradition. Joseph was sent to Nottingham Academy at Colora, Md., where in 1759 he, Thomas Ruston, and Benjamin Rush were recommended by the head of the school for entrance to Nassau Hall (later Princeton University). At Nassau, from which Alexander was graduated in the class of 1760, he met and married Martha Esther Davies, daughter of Samuel Davies, the president of the college. For the next several years he applied himself to the study of theology, having chosen the Presbyterian ministry as a profession, and in 1767 he was licensed by Newcastle Presbytery. In the same year he moved to North Carolina in the wake of the Nottingham Colony, which had originated near his Maryland home. He transferred his ecclesiastical affiliation to the Presbytery of Hanover, as did David Caldwell, whom he had known at Princeton; John McKnitt Alexander, a cousin; and other relatives. On 4 Mar. 1768 "Father" Henry Pattillo ordained both Caldwell and Alexander in the same ceremony, and the latter accepted the pastorate of the Sugar (Sugaw) Creek Presbyterian Church in Mecklenburg County.

Within a short time after his ordination, Alexander opened an academy, with provisions for boarding students. One pupil was Thomas Reese, who later became an eminent clergyman in the Carolinas. On 15 Jan. 1771, as a result of the success of the academy, the General Assembly of North Carolina authorized the opening of Queens College in Charlotte, with Joseph Alexander as a fellow and trustee. When Crown disapproval forced the college to close, Alexander moved to the Bullock's Creek Presbyterian Church, in present York County, S.C. where he continued to conduct his own school. The students at the new location included an eventual South Carolina governor, David Johnson; William H. Crawford, who became a candidate for the presidency of the United States; Andrew Jackson, later the seventh president of the United States; and James McRee, R. B. Walker, John B. Davies, and Thomas Neely, who became Presbyterian ministers. In 1797 the South Carolina General Assembly authorized the founding of Alexandria College, named in honor of the clergyman-educator, but the school never materialized. In 1807 the College of South Carolina recognized Alexander's contribution to education by conferring the D.D. degree upon him.

Alexander participated prominently in the expansion of the organization of the Presbyterian church, being an original member of the Presbytery of Orange (created in 1770), the Presbytery of South Carolina (1784), the Synod of the Carolinas (1788), and the General Assembly of the Presbyterian Church in the United States (1789). He held various official positions in these organizations, including the office of moderator of Hanover Presbytery (1770) and the Synod of the Carolinas (1791). In addition to his regular pastorate, Alexander preached at Nazareth, in present-day Spartanburg, from 1774 to 1776; at Thicketty Creek, in Union County, in 1775; and at Beersheba, from 1775 to 1780.

During the American Revolution Alexander was an enthusiastic patriot. Particularly influential was a meeting at his church after the Battle of Camden, at which he encouraged the patriots to continue their efforts to win independence. Alexander was closely related to the men in his first parish who drafted the Mecklenburg Resolves, and he became so aggressive in his encouragement of the Revolution that the male members of his church brought rifles to Sabbath services to guard the minister and his congregation.

After the war, a controversy over hymn singing split the membership in Alexander's church, and in 1801 the pastor resigned to devote his remaining years to the supervision of his school and farm.

Alexander was buried in the cemetery at Bullock's Creek Church. He was survived by two sons, Samuel Davies and George Baldwin, and by his daughters: Sarah, widow of Joseph Barnett; Editha, wife of Robert S. Walker; Ann, wife of James Garrison; Margaret, wife of Abner McJunkin; and Martha, Esther, and Judah, married to men named Byers, King, and Bankhead respectively. He willed his two slaves and considerable real and personal property to his family.

Alexander's only known publication is *Eight Sermons on Important Subjects; By the Reverend Joseph Alexander, D.D. In the District of York, South Carolina* (Charleston, 1807).

SEE: William Henry Foote, *Sketches of North Carolina, Historical and Biographical* (1846); Hanover Presbytery Minutes, 1755–1812 (Library, Union Theological Seminary, Richmond, Va.); George Howe, *History of the Presbyterian Church in South Carolina*, 2 vols., (1870); *Princeton University General Biographical Catalogue 1746–1906* (1908); "Records of the Presbyterian Church, and the Presbyterian Church in the United States of America" (Presbyterian Historical Society, Philadelphia, Pa.); York County Deeds (York County Courthouse, York, S.C.), for Will Book A.

DURWARD T. STOKES

Alexander, Julia McGehee *(14 Jan. 1876–23 Feb. 1957)*, attorney, author, legislator, and historian, was born of Scotch-Irish ancestry at Enderly, her father's plantation, three miles north of Charlotte in Mecklenburg County. Her father, Captain Sydenham B. Alexander, a U.S. congressman who also served five terms in the North Carolina Senate, was one of the chief advocates for the establishment of North Carolina State College and was the author of the first good roads law for the state. He was a direct descendant of Major General Joseph Alexander, revolutionary hero of the Battle of Charlotte, and also of John McKnitt Alexander. Julia Alexander's mother was Pauline Violet Nicholson.

Miss Alexander was the second woman to be licensed to practice law in North Carolina, the first woman to enter independent law practice in the state, and the first woman to serve as a representative in the North Carolina House of Representatives. Following graduation from Mary Baldwin College, Staunton, Va., she studied law at The University of North Carolina where she was president of her class, then at the University of Michigan, and still later at Columbia University Law School in New York. After her admission to the North Carolina bar in 1914, she practiced in Charlotte. She served as a representative in the North Carolina legislature from 1925 to 1927. She was a vice-president of both the Mecklenburg Bar Association and the American Bar Association, and in 1924 she represented the National Bar Association as a guest of the British bar (while in London was entertained at Buckingham Palace by Queen Mary). Her chief legislative interests were taxes and agriculture.

Alexander was elected the first president of the North Carolina Federation of Business and Professional Women in 1919. The first regent of the Mecklenburg chapter of the Daughters of the American Revolution (1912), she was also lifetime president of the Stonewall Jackson chapter of the United Daughters of the Confederacy. She had a charter membership in the American Legion Auxiliary of Hornet's Nest, Post 9. As the official Mecklenburg county historian, she was partly instrumental in having the historic U.S. Mint rebuilt as the Mint Museum. She helped organize the Charlotte Humane Society, and served as its first president. In 1932 she chaired the George Washington Bi-Centennial Commission for Charlotte. She was an active member of the First Presbyterian Church and engaged in various philanthropic causes.

Miss Alexander was author of *Charlotte in Picture and Prose, A Short History of Mecklenburg County*, and *Mothers of Great Men*. Her hobbies included historical research, sports, and travel.

She was buried in Elmwood Cemetery, Charlotte.

SEE: *American Women*, vol. 2 (1939–40); *Charlotte Observer*, 23 Feb. 1957; *North Carolina Manual* (1925); *North Carolina Presbyterian News*, October 1965; Presbyterian Church in the U.S., *Minutes of the Sessions*, North Carolina Synod (1909); Raleigh *News and Observer*, 21 Dec. 1924.

HAROLD J. DUDLEY

Alexander, Mark (*7 Feb. 1792–6 July 1883*), lawyer, gentleman farmer, and politician, was born at the family home, Salem, Mecklenburg County, Va., the son of Mark and Lucy Bugg Alexander. His ancestors, Scotch-Irish Presbyterians, had settled in Mecklenburg County, N.C. An uncle, Nathaniel, was governor of North Carolina and a United States congressman. As a young man, Mark Alexander's father moved to Mecklenburg County, Va.; he later served in the Virginia House of Delegates.

Alexander's education began in a local school. In 1805 he entered an academy in Louisburg, N.C., and in 1807 he matriculated at The University of North Carolina, where he was in attendance until 1810. Three years later he obtained a license to practice law in Virginia.

His career as a politician began in 1815 with his election to the Virginia House of Delegates. He was a member of the legislature until 1819, when he was elected to the United States House of Representatives. Ideologically an Old Republican, he believed in state supremacy, strict construction, and a laissez-faire economy. He served in the House until he declined reelection in 1833. While in Congress, he acted as chairman of the Committee on the District of Columbia for several sessions and was also a member of the Ways and Means Committee. He was also a delegate to the Virginia Constitutional convention of 1829–30. In 1845 he returned to the Virginia House of Delegates for one term.

During his political career and afterward, Alexander continued his law practice; he became a gentleman farmer, at one time owning approximately three thousand acres and a hundred slaves. He was also a devoted family man. On 1 June 1831 he married Sally

Park Turner, daughter of ex-Senator and Governor James and Betsy Park Turner of Bloomsburg, Warren County. Most of the Alexanders' married life was spent at their home, Park Forest, in Mecklenburg County, Va. Five of their children lived to maturity: James T., Betty P., Robert Park, Mark T., and Mary Rebecca.

A portrait by Chester Harding supports the opinion of Alexander's contemporaries, one of whom (Hugh Blair Grigsby) said that he was "one of the most graceful men of his generation." Among his many friends were Virginia statesman Littleton Waller Tazewell and arch-conservative John Randolph of Roanoke.

Because of poor business judgment and lingering problems caused by the Civil War, Alexander lost Park Forest in 1882. He and his wife then moved to Scotland Neck to live with their daughter Rebecca and her husband, Norfleet Smith. There Mark Alexander, at the time supposedly the country's oldest living ex-congressman, died in 1883. He was buried in the cemetery at Trinity Episcopal Church in Scotland Neck.

SEE: Baskerville Papers (Virginia Historical Society, Richmond), for Mark Alexander, license to practice law in Virginia; *Debates and Proceedings of the Congress of the United States*, Sixteenth-eighteenth Congresses, 1855–56; Gravestones of Mark and Sallie P. Alexander, Trinity Episcopal Church, Scotland Neck; Hugh Blair Grigsby Papers (Virginia Historical Society, Richmond), for diaries, 20 May 1876–14 Dec. 1877 and (no. 16) 15 Dec. 1877–7 Jan. 1879, and letters from Mark Alexander to Hugh Blair Grigsby, n.d.-30 June 1877 and 18 Sept. 1877–1 Sept. 1880; *Journal of the House of Delegates of the Commonwealth of Virginia* (1815–18, 1845); Mecklenburg County Census Schedules (1850, Virginia State Library, Richmond); Mecklenburg County Land Books (1809–32, 1835, 1840, 1845, 1850, 1855, 1860, 1866, 1870, 1873, 1875, 1877–83, County Clerk's Office, Boydton, Va.); Mecklenburg County Personal Property Books (1811–12, 1814, 1816–31, 1835, 1840, 1845, 1850, 1855, 1860, 1863, 1867, 1875, 1880, Virginia State Library, Richmond); *Proceedings and Debates of the Virginia State Convention of 1829–30* (1830); *Register of Debates in Congress*, 19th-22nd Congresses; *Richmond Daily Dispatch*, 11 July 1883 (Virginia State Library, Richmond); Norman K. Risjord, *The Old Republicans* (1965); Warren County Marriage Bonds.

SUSAN L. BRACEY

Alexander, Nathaniel (*5 Mar. 1756–6 Mar. 1808*), physician, congressman, and governor, was born in Mecklenburg County, the oldest child of the six children of Moses and Sarah Alexander. Moses Alexander was an influential citizen of the colony; he held the rank of lieutenant colonel and served in the Cherokee boundary expedition and in both of Governor Tryon's campaigns against the Regulators.

Nathaniel got his early education in a nearby log school. He was graduated from Princeton University at the age of twenty. An interest in medicine was awakened at Princeton and further cultivated, and in 1778 he was commissioned a surgeon in a North Carolina regiment of the Continental army; he served until the end of hostilities, working under great difficulties because of the scarcity of medicine and hospital supplies.

After the war Alexander practiced medicine for a few years at High Hills of Santee, S.C., and then returned to his home state and practiced his profession in or near Charlotte. He became interested in the Masonic Order and was among those who petitioned the Grand Lodge to authorize a lodge in Charlotte. He became a charter member when the petition resulted in the establishment there of Phalanx Lodge 31 in 1797. The following year he was named junior warden, in 1802 senior warden, and in 1806 grand marshal. On one or more occasions he represented Phalanx Lodge 31 in the Grand Lodge, and shortly before his death he was named senior grand marshal of the Charlotte lodge.

Politically, Alexander became identified with the Jeffersonian Republicans. In 1797 he was elected to represent Mecklenburg County in the North Carolina House of Commons; in 1801 and again in 1802 he served in the state senate. He was then elected to both the Eighth and the Ninth Congresses, serving from March 1803 until November 1805. He resigned to become governor of North Carolina, succeeding Governor James Turner, who had been elected by the legislature to the U.S. Senate. Alexander's cousin, Evan Shelby Alexander, also served in Congress.

As governor, Alexander proved forward-looking and generally popular. Even the Federalists admitted that he was "an ornament to the predominant party and, like few of them, a scholar and a true patriot." With the support of discerning Federalists, he was reelected for a second one-year term.

Alexander took an enlightened stand on such public issues as internal improvements, reorganization of the court system, and popular education. In recognition of his leadership in education, he was elected president of the board of trustees of The University of North Carolina, in the days before the governor automatically held this position ex officio. He seems to have grasped the fundamental and indispensable place of education in a democracy, and later historians have acclaimed him as the forerunner of the series of educational statesmen that included Calvin H. Wiley, Charles D. McIver, Edwin A. Alderman, and Charles B. Aycock.

Unhappily for the state, a career marked by brilliance and unstinting service to his fellowmen and still full of promise was cut short less than a year after Alexander left the governorship. He died in Salisbury and was buried in the Old Cemetery of the First Presbyterian Church in Charlotte.

As a young man Alexander married a daughter of Colonel Thomas Polk, Mecklenburg patriot and revolutionary officer. No children were born of the union.

SEE: Samuel A. Ashe, ed., *Biographical History of North Carolina*, vol. 1 (1905); Earley Winfred Bridges, *The Masonic Governors of North Carolina* (1937); Beth G. Crabtree, *North Carolina Governors, 1585 to 1958* (1958); *Bio. Dir. Am. Cong.* (1961); Archibald Henderson, Newspaper clippings on North Carolina history and biography; Hugh T. Lefler and Albert R. Newsome, *North Carolina: The History of a Southern State* (1954); Mrs. W. S. Stewart and Mrs. Eugene N. Davis, *Markers Placed by Daughters of the American Revolution, 1900–1940* (1940).

PAUL W. WAGER

Alexander, Sydenham Benoni (8 Dec. 1840–14 June 1921), agriculturist and legislator, was born at Rosedale, a Mecklenburg County farm ten miles north of Charlotte. His father was Dr. Moses Winslow Alexander, first a physician and later a farmer, and his mother was Violet Graham, a sister of Governor William A. Graham. Young Syd and his eleven brothers and sisters descended from several generations of Scotch-Irish Presbyterians.

After preparatory schooling at Rocky River Academy

in Cabarrus County and Wadesboro Institute in Anson, County, Alexander enrolled at The University of North Carolina, being graduated in 1860. When the Civil War erupted the following April, he enlisted in the First North Carolina Regiment. In August he became drillmaster of the Twenty-eighth Regiment, and during 1862 he was chosen first lieutenant and then captain of Company K of the Forty-second Regiment. Late in the war he was detailed as inspector general on the staff of General Robert F. Hoke, but he returned to his old command before the Confederate surrender. He received special commendation for his actions in one of the engagements around Petersburg.

By 1877 Captain Alexander had gained recognition both for his accomplishments as a farmer and for his concern with broad agricultural issues. He was elected that year as master of the Grange in North Carolina and as ex officio member of the state board of agriculture. He strongly supported the newly created state department of agriculture and its energetic commissioner, L. L. Polk. The board as a whole, however, was conservative and lethargic. When the frustrated commissioner resigned, Alexander was offered the job but quickly declined it. He operated a model farm, read widely, and wrote several articles on cattle raising.

Alexander's family connections, education, war service, and personal qualities combined to make him an attractive political candidate. A Democrat, he won election to the General Assembly of 1879 as a state senator from the twenty-ninth district. In that session he forcefully advocated, and saw enacted, a road improvement law and a stock fencing law. That these laws necessitated additional taxation angered so many of his constituents that he was denied reelection. But within a few years the merits of these measures, and especially the appearance of macadamized roads in Mecklenburg County, vindicated the senator. His people gladly sent him to the legislatures of 1883, 1885, 1887, and 1901. Agriculture, finance, and education were his principal committee and floor interests. During the eighties he opposed the railroads' free pass evil and discriminatory freight rates and favored an effective state railroad commission. He added influence to the struggle to establish a land-grant institution separate from the university, and in 1887 the legislature chartered the North Carolina College of Agriculture and Mechanic Arts, located it at Raleigh, and named Alexander to the first board of trustees. He was instrumental in bringing the first president and two other faculty members to Raleigh, and he sent two of his sons to the college. Shortly after the fight for the "farmer boys' school" was won, the conscientious captain, pondering an appointment to the board of agriculture, confided in a letter to a friend: ". . . the more I think of it the more I think I ought to accept, for if any damn thing ever needed a friend, it does now." He accepted, as he did at various times the presidency of the Mecklenburg County Fair, the North Carolina State Fair, and the North Carolina Railroad.

The Farmers' Alliance, representing nationwide agrarian discontent, entered the state in 1887, and he became its first president. Alliance leaders backed him for the Democratic nomination for governor in 1888, but he lost to the candidate of the conservative business interests, Daniel G. Fowle. As a consolation prize to the farmers, the nomination for lieutenant governor was offered to Alexander, who declined it. Ironically, Fowle died in office. Alexander continued as an Alliance leader, successfully running for Congress from the Sixth District in 1890 and again in 1892. He served on the

House agriculture committee in both the Fifty-second and Fifty-third Congresses. He voiced opposition to placing wool on the tariff's free list and support for issuing fractional currency for the convenience of persons who lived from 3 to 25 miles from a post office. His longest speech, delivered 21 Aug. 1893, was applauded as an analysis of "the present panic" and a statement of the "necessity for immediate relief" through "more currency in circulation as proposed by the Sherman [Silver Purchase] Act." Notably, he introduced the measure to "extend to Alaska the benefit of . . . instruction in agriculture and the mechanic arts." Republican-Populist fusion dominated the state between 1894 and 1900. In the Democratic return to power, Alexander, then of the twenty-fifth district, regained his congressional seat and joined his colleagues in 1901 to appropriate $200,000 for the public schools.

Enderly, Alexander's rural Mecklenburg estate immediately west of Charlotte, had long been his home and refuge, but in 1906 he moved into the city. After that point, except for leadership in the 1909 campaign of the American Cotton Association "to put in the hands of the farmer the control of his crop," he lived mostly in retirement. He was a genial, solid man in health, but during his last six years, he was an invalid.

Alexander married Emma Pauline Nicholson, of Halifax County, on 20 June 1872. They became the parents of three sons (Sydenham Brevard, a merchant; Thomas Willis, a lawyer, and Emory Graham, a surgeon) and three daughters (Pattie Thorne; Violet Graham; and Julia McGehee, the second licensed woman attorney in North Carolina). Emma died in 1880, and on 16 Sept 1885, in Louisburg, he married Louise Perry of Franklin County. They had no children; she died in 1890.

SEE: *Alumni News*, North Carolina State College, January 1930; *Charlotte Observer*, 30 Apr. 1916, 15 and 16 June 1921; *Congressional Record*, 1891–95; *Nat. Cyc. Am. Biog.*, vol. 33 (1947 [portrait]); S. Noblin, *L. L. Polk* (1949); *North Carolina Senate Journal*, 1879, 1883–87, 1901; R. W. Winston, *It's a Far Cry* (1937).

STUART NOBLIN

Alexander, William Julius (*March 1797–15 Feb. 1857*), speaker of the North Carolina House of Commons, solicitor, and superintendent of the Charlotte branch of the U.S. Mint, was born in Salisbury, the son of William Alexander. He attended Poplar Tent Academy under the direction of a Reverend Dr. Robinson and was graduated from The University of North Carolina in 1816. After serving an apprenticeship under Archibald Henderson in Salisbury, Alexander was admitted to the bar in 1818. He married Catharine Wilson, daughter of Joseph Wilson, solicitor of the Sixth Circuit.

In 1826 Alexander entered public life as a Democratic representative from Mecklenburg County in the North Carolina House of Commons. He served five consecutive terms from 1826 to 1831 and two additional terms in 1833–34 and 1834–35. He was speaker in 1829–30, 1833–34, and 1834–35. He also served as a trustee of The University of North Carolina from 1827 until 1856. Following the death of his father-in-law in August 1829, he was appointed solicitor in his stead; he resigned in 1833. In 1835 he was defeated by Romulus M. Saunders for a seat on the superior court. In 1846 President James K. Polk, a fellow alumnus of the university and member of the same campus literary society, appointed Alexander superintendent of the U.S. branch mint in Charlotte, succeeding Greene W. Caldwell, who volunteered to fight in the war with

Mexico. Alexander held this position as late as 1851. At his retirement he moved to Lincolnton, where he died.

SEE: Kemp P. Battle, *History of the University of North Carolina*, 2 vols. (1907–1912); Daniel Lindsey Grant, *Alumni History of the University of North Carolina* (1924); Henry T. Shanks, ed., *The Papers of Willie Person Mangum*, 5 vols. (1950–1956); William L. Sherrill, *Annals of Lincoln County, North Carolina* (1937); John H. Wheeler, *Historical Sketches of North Carolina* (1851); John H. Wheeler, *Reminiscences and Memoirs of North Carolina and Eminent North Carolinians* (1884).

ROGER N. KIRKMAN

Allen, Arch Turner (*10 Jan. 1875–20 Oct. 1934*), educator, writer, and North Carolina state superintendent of public instruction at the beginning of the Great Depression, was born in Hiddenite, the sixth of seven children of George James Allen (1824–1911) and Mary Elizabeth Campbell Allen (1838–1911). His grandfather, Robert Allen, had been a prosperous farmer, a prominent community leader, and one of the founding settlers of Alexander County in the mid-nineteenth century.

Allen received his early schooling in a one-room rural school at Rocky Spring. He studied briefly under the highly respected academy organizer and Methodist minister Brantley York and then prepared for college at Morganton and Vashti academies. In 1897 Allen was graduated from The University of North Carolina, where he studied mathematics and served as a laboratory assistant in the department of physics; he was elected treasurer of Phi Beta Kappa and president of the Dialectic Literary Society. In later years, Allen did further study at The University of North Carolina, the University of Tennessee, and Columbia University. He was awarded honorary degrees by Elon College (D.C.L., 1924) and The University of North Carolina (LL.D., 1927).

Allen began his career in 1897 as Statesville school principal and eighth-grade teacher under the guidance of Superintendent D. Matt Thompson. From 1904 to 1905 he was principal in Washington, and from 1905 to 1907 he was principal of Dilworth School in Charlotte. In 1907 he became superintendent of Graham schools; three years later he assumed the superintendency of the Salisbury public schools, where he remained until 1917. Allen served in the state department of education from 1917 to 1923, during the administrations of Superintendents James Yadkin Joyner and Eugene Clyde Brooks. From 1917 to 1921 he was a member of the State Board of Examiners and Institute Conductors, and from 1921 to 1923 he was director of teacher training. In 1923 Allen was elected to the presidency of Cullowhee State Normal School, but before he could assume the position, he was appointed to fill Brooks's unexpired term.

Allen took office as state superintendent of public instruction in June 1923 and directed the state's school policy until his death. Major issues of his administration included consolidation, teacher certification, curriculum revision, longer school terms, high schools, school finance, public opinion, and state educational responsibility. Initially, Allen's primary goal was to raise the quality of the rural elementary schools. He sought to create a system that would offer "equal educational advantages to all children—rich and poor alike—rural and city." Convinced that consolidation was the best means of equalizing opportunities, Allen advocated a county plan of taxation, organization, and administration that would decrease the number of school districts, provide school transportation, make rural buildings larger and more adequate, and establish a universal eight-month term in rural as well as urban areas. Not until the economy drive of the depression added the needed incentive were these goals achieved.

Economic conditions took a serious turn in 1930, and the schools began to come under attack as a waste of money. Many counties were unable to collect local school taxes, and there were demands that schools be limited to seven grades or closed entirely. Then the old doctrine that primary responsibility lay with the county was replaced with a new philosophy in school maintenance and support: education was a state function and the state must support it. In 1933 the legislature decided on complete support. It set up a state-wide and state-supported eight-month term, greatly reduced the number of school districts, provided for state-operated transportation, and based support on income and sales taxes rather than on property taxes. Although Allen termed the state appropriation "very skimpy," he was convinced that the legislature had provided a firm foundation on which to build a good system of schools when conditions improved.

Allen saw the key issue of his day as broader and far more basic than finance. The attack on schools was more than just a drive against taxes; it was a questioning of the value of public education. Schools could recover from economic loss, but not, Allen warned, from the loss of public good will. He advised the formulation of a new philosophy that would be in spirit with the times and would appeal to the common man. He envisioned a democratic school system based upon universal opportunity and dedicated to equality and to the preservation of individual rights. The modern school, said Allen, should rest upon "the philosophy of individual freedom and the concomitant of individual responsibility." The school should not indoctrinate or manufacture people; it should help children develop personalities of their own and promote the ability for analysis, self-direction, and cooperation.

Allen's accomplishments as an educator gained him inclusion in the North Carolina Educational Hall of Fame. He had contributed to his calling not only through his work as state superintendent but also by serving as president of numerous professional organizations: the North Carolina City Superintendents' Association, the North Carolina Teachers' Assembly, the National Council of State Superintendents and Commissioners, and the Division of Superintendents of Public Instruction of the National Educational Association.

In addition to his professional activities, Allen was involved throughout his lifetime in community affairs. He was a member of the Methodist church, the Kiwanis Club, the Junior Order of United American Mechanics, the Watauga Club, the Raleigh History Club, and the Democratic party.

Allen was married to Claribell McDowell of Charlotte, daughter of John McDowell and an alumna of Queens College. They were married on 19 June 1909 amd were the parents of Arch Turner, Jr. (b. 13 Sept. 1910), and Elizabeth McDowell (b. 26 Sept. 1914).

Arch Turner Allen died in Raleigh after a lengthy illness. The funeral was held at Edenton Street Methodist Church and interment took place at Montlawn Memorial Park

As a spokesman for education in North Carolina, Allen wrote numerous newspaper articles and presented a series of school talks on radio station WPTF. He wrote articles for such magazines as the *High School Journal*, *School Life*, and the *Journal of the National Educational*

Association; and he presented speeches before the North Carolina Teachers' Assembly and the Southern Conference on Education. He published studies for the department of education and contributed an informative chapter, "A State System of Schools in North Carolina," to *State Centralization in North Carolina*, edited by Paul Betters and published by the Brookings Institution in 1932.

SEE: Arch T. Allen Private Papers (North Carolina State Archives, Raleigh [pictures], and Southern Historical Collection, University of North Carolina, Chapel Hill); *Asheville Citizen*, 23 Oct. 1934; Raleigh *News and Observer*, 13 Dec. 1923, 21, 22 Oct. 1934; *High School Journal*, 17 (Nov. 1934); *Biennial Reports*, of the State Superintendent of Public Instruction, 1922–34; *North Carolina, Rebuilding an Ancient Commonwealth*, vol. 3 (1929); *North Carolina: the Old North State and the New*, vol. 5 (1941); *North Carolina Education*, February 1936; *State School Facts* (1928–34); State Superintendent of Public Instruction Papers (North Carolina State Archives, Raleigh); *Who Was Who*, vol. 1 (1943).

GEORGE-ANNE WILLARD

Allen, Eleazer *(1692–7 Jan. 1750)*, colonial official, was born in Massachusetts to the former Mary Anna Bendall and Daniel Allen, a Harvard M.A. and librarian of the college. After the death of his father sometime before 1720, young Allen went to Charleston, S.C., and became a merchant, apparently interrupting his college studies to do so; in about 1726 he returned to Massachusetts briefly and was graduated from Harvard. About 1722 he married Sarah Rhett, the eldest daughter of William Rhett, a leading figure in South Carolina society and business. Another of Rhett's daughters married Roger Moore, and through this family connection, Allen became interested in the lower Cape Fear region of North Carolina, where Roger Moore and his brother Maurice were among the principal landowners. In 1725, when Governor George Burrington, during his proprietary administration of North Carolina, began making large land grants to encourage settlement in the lower Cape Fear, Allen was a leading beneficiary. At some time between 1725 and his permanent move to North Carolina in 1734, Allen constructed a plantation just north of Roger Moore's Orton. He named his home Lilliput for the imaginary country in *Gulliver's Travels*.

When George Burrington was chosen as first royal governor of North Carolina in 1730, he nominated Eleazer Allen to a council seat. Although confirmed by the Privy Council in London, Allen did not accept his mandamus as a councillor during Burrington's administration (1731–34). He was serving as clerk of the lower house of assembly in South Carolina at the time and chose not to leave.

Allen was also named as a councilor in Gabriel Johnston's royal instructions, and he attended Johnston's swearing in as governor of North Carolina on 2 Nov. 1734 at Brunswick. The new chief executive then administered the oaths of a councilor to Allen. This early association with Johnston and dissociation from the controversial Burrington, combined with his social position, wealth, and intelligence, made Allen a favorite with the governor even though the two men had not known each other previously. On 6 Mar. 1735 Johnston and the council appointed Allen receiver general of quitrents for the colony, one of the most lucrative offices in the province. Although there was already a receiver general for North Carolina holding a Crown commission, he resided in South Carolina, and Johnston was anxious to have such an important officer in close proximity. The board of trade would ultimately commend the governor's move. As was often the case in colonial America, appointment to one office led to others. Almost as soon as he had arrived in North Carolina, Allen was made a justice of the peace for New Hanover County. He served on the commission that settled the boundary between North and South Carolina, and all of the commissioners from both colonies met at Lilliput on 23 Apr. 1735 to establish guidelines for the survey. In March 1736 Allen became precinct treasurer of New Hanover; by October he was a judge of the court of oyer and terminer.

As the lower Cape Fear region began to burgeon into the trade center of the colony, Governor Johnston became increasingly disaffected with the leading landowners there, especially the Moores and their allies (called "the Family" by some historians, since most of its members were related by birth or marriage). Relations between the governor and Allen, a leading "Family" figure, became strained. By early 1740 Allen was allying himself with some of his fellow councilors, Nathaniel Rice, Edward Moseley, and Roger Moore, to oppose Johnston's efforts to shift the center of activity in the lower Cape Fear from "the Family"-dominated town of Brunswick to Newton (later Wilmington). Governor Johnston was eventually successful, and by May 1742 Allen had patched up his quarrel with the governor and accepted a royal commission under the sign manual as receiver general. In November 1743 he was named a surveying officer in the mapping of the Granville District. In March of the following year Receiver General Allen laid before his fellow councilors his complaints about quitrent collections in North Carolina. He objected primarily to the lack of currency in the colony, which forced him to accept commodities as payment. Although the governor and council ruled that quitrents would be payable in the future only in specie, there was little machinery for enforcing such a decree.

Whatever problems Allen may have had with certain of his duties, his career continued to prosper. In March 1748 he was made an associate justice of the general court, which was, for all practical purposes, the highest criminal and civil court in North Carolina. During his last year of life, Allen held two of the most important offices in the province. In October 1749 he succeeded the deceased Edward Moseley as public treasurer for the southern counties, an office to which he was elected by the General Assembly. Later in 1749 Allen was elevated to the chief justiceship of the general court, upon the death of Enoch Hall.

At the time of his death the following year, Allen was a wealthy man who owned 1,285 acres of land and 50 slaves. The inventory of his estate showed sizeable holdings of silver and china, but most impressive was a library containing more than two hundred English and fifty French titles. Reflecting his interests as a man of culture and a provincial officer, Allen owned such books as Plutarch's *Lives*, Ovid's *Metamorphoses*, several navigation and surveying manuals, Fielding's *Tom Jones*, and Locke's *Essay Concerning Human Understanding*.

SEE: Samuel A. Ashe, ed., *Biographical History of North Carolina*, vol. 5 (1906); Estate Inventories, 1753 (Secretary of State Papers, North Carolina State Archives, Raleigh), for a manuscript inventory of Allen's library; Lawrence Lee, *The Lower Cape Fear in Colonial Days* (1965); William S. Price, Jr., "'Men of Good Estates': Wealth among North Carolina's Royal Councillors," *North Carolina Historical Review* 49 (1972); William L. Saunders,

ed., *Colonial Records of North Carolina*, vols. 3–4 (1886).

WILLIAM S. PRICE, JR.

Allen, Fulton (10 July 1907–12 Feb. 1941), better known as Negro blues singer and guitarist Blind Boy Fuller, was born in Wadesboro of poor rural parents, Calvin Allen and Mary Jane Walker. He was one of ten children. His family was not markedly musical, but his sister Ethel was reputedly a fine guitar player. Allen was little interested in playing as a young man and had few musical skills when he began to lose his sight in 1926. He moved the following year to Winston-Salem, where his brother Milton lived. Allen worked as a laborer in a coal yard while living on Vine Street, close to the tobacco factories and warehouses around which he soon began earning a scanty living playing guitar and singing. He lost his vision totally in 1927 and had as his only means of support the occasional income from playing for the migrant work force of the tobacco town. He listened carefully to phonograph records of such popular Negro blues artists as Blind Blake and Big Bill Broonzy and drew skillfully and eclectically from their resources, welding them onto a technically distinctive Carolinas—or Piedmont—style blues to produce his own infectious style, which both characterized the gentle, finger-picked guitar style of the East Coast and gave rise to a whole new generation of younger bluesmen who modelled their own styles upon Fuller's. In this manner he epitomized a gradual evolution in this aspect of black secular music in the 1930s.

Having spent a brief period in Danville, Va., Fuller settled in Durham in 1929. He seldom moved far from there, although he sometimes played at gatherings of seasonal tobacco workers, as in the market area in Raleigh, or at country parties in and around Durham and Orange counties. He had direct influence on only a few friends among younger musicians in and around Durham.

Fuller became the most prolific of all East Coast blues recording artists, and his records sold in large quantities. Through his records the gentle blues of the Piedmont were heard throughout the southern states, and in postwar years the recordings of other musicians from New York to California reflected Fuller's influence. In 1935 he was led to the shop of recording agent J. B. Long, who had already taken "race" artists, as they were called in the phonograph trade of the thirties, to record for the American Recording Company. In July 1935 Fuller made his first trip to New York to record in the company of Blind Gary Davis, from whom he learned much of his guitar-playing proficiency. Further trips to record took Fuller to Columbia, S.C., Memphis, and Chicago. On many of his recordings he was accompanied by his own guitar only, but on some he used a blind harmonica player, Sonny Terry, and sometimes a washboard player named George Washington, both from Durham, or guitarist Floyd Council from nearby Chapel Hill. All of his secular material was released under the name Blind Boy Fuller, although some religious songs were issued as by Brother George and his Sanctified Singers. His success was such that he had recorded 135 numbers by the time of his last session in June 1940.

As least as early as 1937 he was suffering from serious kidney trouble, and a doctor's report for the welfare department showed that the restoration of his vision was impossible. Despite increasingly serious illness, there was no evident decline in Fuller's recording talents, and certainly not in his output. He moved to live on Massey Avenue close to the hospital, to which he made frequent trips. Nevertheless, he was still recording within eight months of his death. He died in Durham and was buried there at Grove Hill Cemetery.

He was married in 1926 to Cora Mae Martin in Bennettsville, S.C. There were no children.

SEE: Bruce Bastin, *Crying for the Carolines* (1971 [portraits]); John Godrich and Robert M. W. Dixon, *Blues and Gospel Records 1902–1941* (1969); *Mebane Enterprise-Journal*, 13 Sept. 1973.

BRUCE BASTIN

Allen, George Venable (3 Nov. 1903–11 July 1970), diplomat and association executive, was born in Durham of French, English, Scotch-Irish, and Dutch ancestry. He was the son of Thomas Ellis and Harriet Moore Allen and one of six children. His secondary education was completed at Durham High School; he received the A.B. degree at Duke University in 1924 and the M.A. degree in International Relations at Harvard University in 1929. In later years, Allen, a member of Phi Beta Kappa and Tau Kappa Alpha, received honorary degrees from several institutions of higher education, including Duke University and High Point College. On 2 Oct. 1934, he married Katharine (Kitty) Thaxter Martin from Chevy Chase, Md.; they had three sons: George Venable, Jr., Jack Martin, and Richard Allison.

In 1919, Allen served in the Student Army Service Corps. After graduation from Duke, he taught school and was a principal in the public schools of Buncombe County from 1924 to 1928. During the period 1925 to 1929, he was at various times a newspaper reporter for the *Asheville Times* and the *Durham Herald-Sun*. Allen became a clerk in the Census Bureau in Washington, D.C., in 1930 but within a year began his diplomatic career by accepting the post of American vice-consul at Kingston, Jamaica.

As a member of the U.S. Foreign Service, Allen spent three decades in various positions both within the country and overseas. In 1931 he became vice-consul in Shanghai, China, where he remained until he accepted, in 1934, a similar post in Patras, Greece. Two years later he received a promotion to consul and diplomatic secretary in Cairo, Egypt. He returned to Washington in 1938 to work in the Middle Eastern Division, Department of State. Allen's first ambassadorial appointment was to Iran in 1946; he later served as U.S. ambassador to Yugoslavia (1950–53), India and Nepal (1953–55), and Greece (1956–57). These appointments placed him at critical junctures, where he ably represented the United States. He participated in several major conferences of the forties, including the Moscow Conference, the Cairo Conference, the U.N. Conference in San Francisco, and the Potsdam Conference. In 1948 he chaired the U.S. delegation to the UNESCO Conference in Beirut. Allen was assistant secretary of state for public affairs from 1948 to 1950 and assistant secretary of the Bureau of Near Eastern, South Asian, and African Affairs in 1955 and 1956. From 1957 to 1960 he served as director of the U.S. Information Agency.

In 1960 Allen left the Foreign Service to become president of the Tobacco Institute, Inc. Six years later he became director general of the Foreign Service Institute, a training center for diplomats sponsored by the U.S. State Department. His government career ended in a retirement ceremony in November 1968.

Allen served his alma mater as vice-chairman of the Duke University Board of Trustees and general chairman of the Duke Fifth Decade Program.

Throughout his career, Allen wrote for publication and spoke before various organizations. In 1929 he won the Charles Sumner Prize for "The Effect of the League of Nations upon the Execution of the Treaty of Versailles," written under the pseudonym C. Adolphus, Jr. He was the recipient of the Robert Woods Bliss Essay Award for Foreign Service Officers in 1935. Two government publications bear his name, *The President's Point Four Program* (1949) and *Report on India* (1954). He contributed a section to Richard F. Boyce's *Diplomatic and Consular Officers, Retired, Inc.* (1969), and also left a book manuscript on his experiences as ambassador to Iran. Various journals contain his articles on such topics as propaganda, diplomacy, tobacco, democracy, Iran, the U.S. Information Agency, and the U.S. Foreign Service and foreign policy. From 1941 to 1943, he served as a lecturer at American University; although favorite topics were the Foreign Service and foreign policy, he also spoke on peace, the space race, the tobacco industry, India, Iran, Russia, and UNESCO.

Other organizations that claimed his time included the International Association of Students in Economics and Commerce; the American Association for the United Nations; the Institute of International Education in Washington; the President's Committee on Employ-ment of the Physically Handicapped; the Meridian House, Washington; the United States National Commission for UNESCO; the American Farm School, Salonika, Greece; the Foreign Students Service Council in Washington; the Federal Union; and the Diplomatic and Consular Officers, Retired. He belonged to Delta Sigma Phi, the Metropolitan Club in Washington, the Chevy Chase Club in Maryland, and the Lotus Club and the Brook in New York. Allen was a Democrat and Methodist church member; he enjoyed playing golf and tennis.

At the time of his death, Allen was chairman of the People-to-People Program of the federal government. He died at his farm home near Bahama and was buried in Rock Creek Cemetery in Washington, D.C.

SEE: Allen-Angier Family Papers (Manuscript Depart-ment, Library, Duke University, Durham); William S. Powell, ed., *North Carolina Lives* (1962); Laurence Adolph Steinhardt Papers (Manuscript Division, Library of Congress, Washington, D.C.); Harry S. Truman Papers (White House Files, Truman Library, Independence, Mo.); *Who Was Who in America*, vol. 5 (1973).

SHARON E. KNAPP

Allen, Nathaniel (ca. 1755–1805), planter, promoter, and legislator, was a resident of Edenton and an owner of property in Chowan and Tyrrell counties. A nephew of Joseph Hewes—a North Carolina signer of the Declaration of Independence and naval promoter during the Revolutionary War—Allen owned his uncle's former home on West King Street in Edenton from 1794 to his death. In 1788 he was elected to the North Carolina convention to consider ratification of the federal Constitution. In 1795 the General Assembly chose him to be councilor of state for a one-year term, and he returned to Raleigh once more in 1802 as a member of the House of Commons from Edenton. Although Allen was nominally an Episcopalian, the Reverend Charles Pettigrew once referred to him as an unbeliever. It is not known how he acquired the excellent education and the scientific knowledge displayed in his letters. That he was a civic-minded leader of Edenton is demonstrated by his support of a fire company in 1791 and an academy in 1800.

His most outstanding achievement was the development of Tyrrell County, a swampy area lying across Albemarle Sound from Edenton. Through the medium of the Lake Company, Allen and his partners, Josiah Collins and Samuel and Luther Dickinson, began in about 1785 to secure land grants and purchase other lands around Lake Phelps and north to the sound, until they held more than fifty thousand acres. A survey of this land revealed great resources of timber and rich soil if the swamp could be drained. The Lake Company imported a hundred slaves from Guinea in 1786 to dig, from the lake to the Scuppernong River, a seven-mile canal that when completed afforded drainage, transportation, and power for mills. To induce settlement, the company persuaded a clergyman, Charles Pettigrew, to move there in 1789. The culture of rice flourished around Lake Phelps for some years, together with that of wheat and forest products. The rice was shipped to New York and the West Indies directly from the mouth of the Scuppernong River. The county grew so rapidly in population and wealth that in 1802 it was divided in two, Tyrrell and Washington. As an example of the company's rapidly accumulating wealth, by 1799 it rented to three tenants and owned two barns, a stable, a machine house, a sawmill, a gristmill, a warehouse, and two dwelling houses.

Allen was married prior to May 1791, at which time Charles Pettigrew congratulated him and his wife on the birth of a daughter. In 1805, Allen became incapacitated from rheumatism; he died shortly after 11 Nov. His wife had died earlier, for his will names only a daughter, Mary; two sisters; Hannah Gill of Philadelphia and Mary Davis of Alexandria; and three sons, Francis, Bonaparte, and William. After a small house on his town lot was left to a female slave, half of the estate went to his daughter and the other half was divided among his three sons. He acknowledged his sons as "natural sons . . . begotton on the body of . . . Fanny Coulston," and to her he left a portion of his household and kitchen furniture.

SEE: Chowan and Tyrrell County Records (North Carolina State Archives, Raleigh); S. M. Lemmon, ed., *The Pettigrew Papers*, vol. 1, *1685–1818* (1971).

SARAH MC CULLOH LEMMON

Allen, Richard, Sr. *(26 Nov. 1741–10 Oct. 1832)*, Revolutionary War captain and public official, was born in Baltimore County, Md. At the age of twenty-one, Allen moved to Frederick County, Va., where he spent seven years before settling in Rowan County, N.C., in 1770. In less than a year Surry County was formed from part of Rowan, including that section in which Allen lived. Through purchases of adjoining lands, he amassed a large estate along Big Bugaboo Creek.

When fighting with England broke out, Allen volunteered for six months' service in Captain Jesse Walton's company of minutemen, the first such unit raised in Surry County. As a first sergeant he marched with his company to Salisbury and underwent sixteen days of training and exercising. Early in 1776, Allen began a long series of frustrating military campaigns.

Upon learning that Loyalists under General Donald MacDonald were gathering at Cross Creek for a march to the coast, Captain Walton and his company set out on 13 Feb. to offer assistance to the Whig forces. They arrived at Cross Creek only to find that the Loyalists had been defeated at Moore's Creek Bridge the previous day. Allen and his companions missed their first chance to do battle, but Walton's company was given the honor of returning the captured prisoners to Hillsborough. Before

they reached Hillsborough, however, they were met by two companies of mounted troops under Captains Robert Mebane and Abraham Shephard, who took charge of the prisoners. Walton and his company subsequently were discharged from service. Allen returned home; a few months later his six-months' term expired.

Not long after the expiration of this first term, Allen became an ensign in a company commanded by Captain Benjamin Cleveland. The company soon received orders to pursue Colonel [James?] Roberts and his Tory brigade in western North Carolina. Cleveland and his men took up the chase and followed Roberts well into Virginia but were unable to overtake the elusive Tories. After three weeks they learned to their dismay that Roberts had disbanded his forces and sent them home. Early in 1778, Cleveland was promoted to lieutenant colonel; Allen succeeded him and continued as captain of the company until the close of the war.

In late 1779, the Americans expected a British attack on Charleston, and Captain Allen's company was ordered to assist in Charleston's defense. On 13 Jan. 1780 they began their march. Upon reaching Charleston, they rendezvoused with the Third Regiment of North Carolina Militia, under the command of Colonel Andrew Hampton. Allen and his men were among the troops occupying the town for several weeks in preparation for the anticipated sea approach of the British. Clinton's assault did not come as early as expected, however, and Allen's term of service expired before the major battle began. He and his men were discharged and sent home. Returning to Wilkes County (formed from Surry in 1777, effective 1778), Allen led his men in a series of campaigns against the Tories from April to September 1780. The most notable skirmishes involved the well-known Tory leader Colonel Samuel Bryan.

In September 1780, Colonel Cleveland called out all the troops in Wilkes County to march against Colonel Patrick Ferguson's army of British regulars and Tories. Allen and his men quickly volunteered for service, but Allen was denied the opportunity to meet the British at Kings Mountain. Although Allen had a horse and was eager to ride with the mounted troops, Colonel Cleveland ordered him to take charge of the infantry units and bring up a rear guard. As Allen's units neared Kings Mountain, they met American soldiers returning from battle with their prisoners; once more Allen had arrived at the scene of battle too late to be a participant.

Allen's final expectation of action came in January 1781, when express brought word that Cornwallis was approaching from South Carolina. After marching back and forth between Salem and Hillsborough trying to contact other American units, Allen's company finally joined General Nathanael Greene's army at High Rock Ford in Guilford County, where they were recuperating from the Battle at Guilford Courthouse. After a few days, Allen and his men were discharged and returned to Wilkes County.

Captain Allen was in almost continuous service from 1775 to 1781. He was ordered to the scene of most of the major battles in the Carolinas: Moore's Creek Bridge, Charleston, Kings Mountain, and Guilford Courthouse. Yet he took no active role in any of them. It is ironic that at a time when numbers of Americans were deserting the battlefields, a man who wanted to meet the British in major conflict was never able to do so.

In the midst of the Revolutionary War, Richard Allen, Sr., became in 1778 the first sheriff of the newly created Wilkes County; except for two years, he held the office until 1790. While county sheriff in 1788, Allen was elected to attend the convention in Hillsborough to vote on the proposed federal Constitution. The delegation was headed by William Lenoir, whose antipathy to the proposed Constitution influenced the voting pattern of his colleagues. Politics was not Allen's favorite venture, but he agreed to serve one term in the House of Commons of the 1793 General Assembly. For several years afterward he enjoyed the peace and quiet of his plantation on Big Bugaboo Creek; but in 1798, at the age of fifty-seven, he was called out of retirement to resume the office of sheriff. Upon completion of this service in 1804, Allen retired permanently.

At some time after the Revolution, Allen was given the rank of colonel of the Wilkes County Militia; though he was long known as Colonel Richard Allen, Sr., the promotion may have been an honorary one.

A devoted Baptist, Allen helped to establish Briar Creek Church in 1783 and was chosen as its first clerk, beginning forty-one years of faithful service to the church. By 1824 the advancing infirmities of old age reduced Allen to a virtual invalid, forcing his resignation of this office. He spent the remaining years of his life in the custody and care of his son, Richard, Jr., and his daughter-in-law, Margaret Hampton Allen. When he died at the age of ninety-one, Richard Allen, Sr., was survived by five sons and three daughters: Richard, Jr., Thomas, Jesse, James, William, Mary Kimbrough, Sarah Baugust, and Elizabeth Walsh.

SEE: John L. Cheney, Jr., ed., *North Carolina Government 1585–1974* (1975); Walter Clark, ed., *State Records of North Carolina*, vols. 21–22 (1903–7); A. B. Cox, *Footprints on the Sands of Time* (1900); Deeds, Estate Papers, and Wills (State Archives, Raleigh; Wilkes County Courthouse, Wilkesboro); *First Census of the U.S. 1790* (1908); Johnson J. Hayes, *Land of Wilkes* (1962); Katherine Keogh White, *The King's Mountain Men* (1924).

JERRY L. CROSS

Allen, William (*fl.* 1677–95), colonial official of North Carolina, was in Albemarle by 9 June 1677, when he witnessed the signatures on two bills of debt to New England traders.

In November 1681, Allen was a member of the council and ex officio justice of the general court. That he held his council seat by vote of the assembly indicates that he was also a member of the assembly. In April 1695 he was the presiding justice of Currituck Precinct Court. Because of the sparseness of surviving records of the period, his tenure in these offices cannot be determined.

Allen had at least 450 acres of land, apparently in Currituck Precinct. Seven of his headrights were assigned him by a New England trader, Mordecai Bowden; he may have had business connections with Bowden. Nothing more is known of his private life.

SEE: Albemarle Book of Warrants and Surveys, 1681–1706 (North Carolina State Archives, Raleigh), for proof of Allen's headrights; J. R. B. Hathaway, ed., *North Carolina Historical and Genealogical Register*, 3 vols. (1900–3); Mattie Erma Edwards Parker, ed., *North Carolina Higher-Court Records, 1670–1696* (1968).

MATTIE ERMA E. PARKER

Allen, William (18 Dec. 1803–11 July 1879), congressman, governor of Ohio, lawyer, and nationally prominent Democratic leader, was born in Edenton, one of three natural sons of Nathaniel Allen (ca. 1755–1805) and Fanny Coulston. Nathaniel had been a member of the North Carolina convention that rejected the federal

Constitution in 1788, and in 1802 he had represented Edenton in the state's House of Commons. Orphaned when young, William relied upon his half sister, Mary Granberry Allen Thurman, whose husband, the Reverend Pleasant Thurman, ministered to Methodist churches at Edenton until 1811, at Lynchburg, Va., until 1819, and at Chillicothe, Ohio, for years thereafter.

The facts of William's early schooling are obscure. He recalled in later life that he left an apprenticeship in Lynchburg to follow the Thurmans to Ohio, where he attended Chillicothe Academy and developed his lifelong interest in books. Located on the Scioto River in south central Ohio, Chillicothe had been the capital of the Northwest Territory and had served as the first capital of Ohio; it remained the courthouse town of Ross County. The Scioto Valley merited William Allen's toast as "the granary of the state, the stock-yard of the West."

Allen passed the examination for the Ohio bar at the age of twenty-one. He may have begun professional training under the lawyer Gustavus Scott, but he refined his legal knowledge and undertook active practice in and from the Chillicothe office of Rufus King's son, Edward (1795–1836). Edward King was captain of the local militia company, the Chillicothe Blues, which Allen joined in 1825. Allen's performances in the Fourth of July programs at Chillicothe in 1829 and 1830 brought him to widening public notice, and when King was commissioned a major general in 1831 and removed to Cincinnati, Allen was chosen to command the Blues.

Allen's patriotic oration of 1829 was printed in Chillicothe's influential Whig weekly, the *Scioto Gazette*; but politically both he and the nephew he brought into law partnership with him, Allen Granberry Thurman (1813–95), proved staunch proponents of Jacksonian Democracy. During the Civil War, the pair stood out as antiwar Democrats. In 1831 Captain Allen ran unsuccessfully for the Ohio legislature. On 22 Oct. 1831, when Chillicothe was celebrating the opening of navigation on the Ohio Canal to Lake Erie, Allen, as commander of the Blues, rendered formal military honors to Ohio's Whig governor, Duncan McArthur, a Chillicothe pioneer who had become a militia general before the War of 1812 and had improved the fine local estate known as Fruit Hill.

When the Jacksonian Democrats of Ohio's Seventh Congressional District selected Allen in the fall of 1831 to try for the district seat in the U.S. House of Representatives, the Whigs prevailed upon Governor McArthur to run against him. In the ensuing contested election, Allen was declared the winner by a single vote, 3738 to 3737. He sat in the Twenty-third Congress, 4 Mar. 1833–4 Mar. 1835.

In his campaign for reelection to the House, Allen was defeated by William K. Bond. In January 1837, however, there was enough Van Buren sentiment in the Ohio legislature to put Allen into the U.S. Senate (on a vote of 55 to 52) to replace the respected incumbent, Thomas Ewing. Six years later the legislature voted to retain Allen in the Senate for another term. This son of North Carolina thus represented Ohio in the Senate at Washington in the Twenty-fifth through the Thirtieth congresses, 4 Mar. 1837–3 Mar. 1849. Cooperation of Democrats and Free Soilers in 1849 led to the replacing of Allen with Salmon P. Chase.

Allen rightly sensed in 1846 that his own course in the Twenty-ninth Congress would gain him more favor with the people than all his past life together. As chairman of the Senate Committee on Foreign Relations he shared in the expansionist triumphs of a Democratic administration headed by President James K. Polk. In particular,

Allen's stand on Oregon brought national notice, including wry mention in a chapter of Herman Melville's fanciful *Mardi*, published in 1849.

Senator Allen opposed the extension of slavery but abhorred abolitionism. In other respects, even his successor, Senator Chase, could write from Washington in 1854: "Your general course in Congress, as a Senator from Ohio had my entire approval and that feeling has been increased by the more intimate knowledge of it which I have gained from the *Congressional Globe* since I have been here. The firmness with which you opposed the schemes of corruptionists, the steadiness with which you insisted on the rights of the U. States in our controversies with England, your advocacy of publicity in Executive Proceedings of the Senate especially commend my admiration."

During Allen's first term in the U.S. Senate he was married to Effie McArthur Coones, only daughter and considerable heiress of Duncan McArthur of Fruit Hill. She died at Washington, D.C., 3 Mar. 1847, leaving a young daughter, Effie, Allen's only child. Effie grew up to become the wife of David H. Scott, M.D. Allen had the Scotts and their children live with him at Fruit Hill, where after his Washington years he cherished books and practiced farming and stock-raising. During the 1850s and 1860s, though he did not aggressively seek office, he continued a party asset, and both he and his kinsman Thurman emerged politically during the Reconstruction era, Thurman as U.S. Senator from Ohio, 1869–81, and Allen as the septuagenarian governor of Ohio, 1874–76. His service at Columbus was so creditable that Democrats, especially in Ohio, wanted him to seek further preferment.

William Allen died at Fruit Hill and was buried at Grandview Cemetery, Chillicothe. The State of Ohio commissioned the sculptor Charles H. Niehaus to carve the white marble statue of Allen that graces Statuary Hall in the Capitol at Washington.

SEE: William Allen Papers (Manuscript Division, Library of Congress, Washington, D.C.); Chillicothe, Ohio, *Scioto Gazette* (microfilm, Library of Congress, Washington, D.C.); *DAB*, vol. 1 (1928); Reginald C. McGrane, *William Allen: A Study in Frontier Democracy* (1925); Ross County Historical Society (Chillicothe, Ohio), for Allen memorabilia; "William Allen, of Ohio," *New York Times*, 30 June 1879.

H. B. FANT

Allen, William Cola (13 Dec. 1859–25 Oct. 1952), educator and historian, was born in Halifax of Scottish ancestry. His father was James V. Allen, the leading merchant in Halifax County and a major of the local regiment of Home Guards during the Civil War. His mother was Maria Aaron, his father's second wife and Allen was the fourth of their five children. His great-great-grandfather James Allen moved from Prince Edward County, Va., to what is now Halifax County and established himself as the first of three generations of planters and slaveholders. His great-grandfather, also named James Allen, and his grandfather John Allen both fought in the Continental Army during the American Revolution, the former attaining the rank of colonel.

Allen attended private schools in Halifax County and was graduated from Wake Forest College in 1885. During his long and distinguished career as an educator, he served as principal of the Pantego Male and Female Academy of Beaufort County, 1885–87; founder and superintendent of the Scotland Neck Military Academy, 1887–92; principal of the Wilson High School, 1892–97; principal of the Reidsville High School, 1897–99;

superintendent of the city schools of Waynesville, 1899–1914; superintendent of the schools of Weldon, 1914–19; superintendent of the schools of Canton, 1919–22; and training director of the U.S. Veterans' Administration Vocational School in Waynesville, 1922–25. In April 1925 he was elected superintendent of public instruction of Haywood County, and continued as superintendent and as a teacher in Waynesville High School until his retirement in 1942.

As a historian and author, Allen was interested in county and state history. Among his writings were newspaper articles and five books. His first book, *North Carolina History Stories* (Richmond: Johnson Publishing Co.), written for children, appeared in 1901. *Centennial of Haywood County*, his next work, was published on the hundredth anniversary of the establishment of Haywood County. *The History of Halifax* (Boston: Cornhill Co.), another county history, was published in 1918; it was followed by *The Annals of Haywood County* in 1935. In 1942 Allen's last book, *The Story of Our State, North Carolina*, was published.

During World War I, Allen was field director of the Red Cross in the government vocational school located at Sulphur Springs in Waynesville.

Allen was a lifelong Democrat and an active member of the First Baptist Church in Waynesville. He was superintendent of the Sunday school for thirty years and deacon and deacon emeritus for sixty; he was also, for a number of years, treasurer of the church. He belonged to both the Odd Fellows and Knights of Pythias fraternities and held professional memberships with the North Carolina Educational Association and the National Educational Association.

Allen met Cottie Wilkinson, daughter of Jordan and Mary Jane Windley Wilkinson of Beaufort County, when he was principal at the Pantego Male and Female Academy and she a teacher at the Pantego Male and Female Academy. They were married on 20 Dec. 1887 and had two children, William C., Jr., and Lillian May (Mrs. Humes H. W.) Hart. Allen's wife predeceased him on 22 Feb. 1948.

SEE: *Asheville Citizen-Times*, 16 Dec. 1949, 26 Oct. 1952; *Greensboro Daily News*, 24 Jan. 1943; *North Carolina: Rebuilding an Ancient Commonwealth*, vol. 4 (1929); *Waynesville Mountaineer*, 16 Dec. 1937, 24 Feb. 1948, 30 July 1948.

SAMUEL M. GAINOR

Allen, William Reynolds (26 Mar. 1860–8 Sept. 1921), lawyer and associate justice of the North Carolina supreme court, was born at Kenansville, Duplin County. His father was William A. Allen, lawyer, state senator, and lieutenant colonel in the Fifty-first North Carolina Regiment during the Civil War; his mother was Maria Goodwin Hicks of Oxford.

Allen received his education at R. W. Millard's and Samuel Clements's schools in Kenansville and at Trinity College, 1876–77; he left Trinity at the end of his junior year and taught school for a year or two at Auburn in Wake County. Upon returning to Kenansville, he read law with his father and passed his bar examination in the spring of 1881.

Soon after entering into a partnership with his father, Allen moved with his family to Goldsboro. There, in 1884, he became a member of the firm of Faircloth and Allen. In 1889 he was the senior partner of the firm of Allen and Dortch (his colleague's father was William T. Dortch).

A confirmed Democrat, Allen was elected a representative to the General Assembly in 1893, 1899, and

1901. During these terms he was chairman of the Judiciary Committee and of the Committee on Railroads and Railroad Commissioners and was a strong advocate of the repeal of tax exemption for corporations in the state. He was coauthor of a bill dividing murder into two degrees, and he helped establish the North Carolina Corporation Commission.

Among the more controversial issues he supported was the establishment of suffrage upon a basis of universal educational requirements, with its "Grandfather Clause." During his last term of office, he was chairman of the board dealing with the impeachment of two judges, a *cause célèbre* of the time that arose out of conflicts in the shellfish industry. The result was an acquittal, but the airing was believed to have had a salutary effect.

During the years 1894 and 1903–11, Allen was a judge of the superior court and held hearings in every county of the state. He was elected an associate justice of the supreme court and took office in 1911.

Allen published his "Annotations" on court matters in the 164th *Report* for the bar and his "Tables of Cases, Overruled, Modified or Reversed" in the 171st issue of the same publication. The University of North Carolina conferred upon him the degree of LL.D., and in the summers of 1920 and 1921 he delivered a series of lectures before the university law school.

Judge Allen was a member of the Methodist Episcopal Church South, served on the board of trustees for the Methodist Orphanage in Raleigh, and was chairman of the board of education for Wayne County. On 3 Nov. 1886 he married Mattie M. Moore, daughter of Dr. Matt Moore and Martha Middleton Moore, the former a wealthy planter of Duplin County. Their surviving children were Mary Moore, William R., Elizabeth H. Roper, Oliver H., and Dorothy S. Duncan.

A portrait of the late Judge Allen was presented to the supreme court at a ceremony held on 6 Sept. 1922.

SEE: *North Carolina Bar Association Report of 1922, North Carolina Bar Association Proceedings, 1899–1948; North Carolina Manuals; North Carolina Supreme Court Reports*, vol. 184; *North Carolina: The Old North State and the New*, vol. 4 (1941); Raleigh *News and Observer*, 7 Sept. 1922; *Trinity Alumni Register*, vol. 2 (1916).

JOHN MACFIE

Alley, Felix Eugene (*5 July 1873–7 Jan. 1957*), attorney, superior court judge, and author, was born in Whiteside Cove, Jackson County, youngest son of John E. Alley and Sarah Whiteside Norton Alley. Both were pioneer settlers of the area. Young Alley was graduated from Cullowhee High School in 1896 and studied law at The University of North Carolina, 1897–98. In 1898 he was elected clerk of superior court in his native county; he continued to study law privately. Admitted to the bar in 1903, he established a practice in Webster and represented Jackson County in the General Assembly of 1905. He was solicitor of the Twentieth Judicial District, 1910–14; afterward, he removed to Waynesville as an attorney and remained there the rest of his life. At various times he served as county attorney for Haywood, Jackson, and Swain counties and for the town of Waynesville. In 1933 he was appointed judge of the superior court, a post he held until his retirement in 1948. He was awarded the honorary LL.D. degree by Western Carolina College in 1952.

As a young man, Alley was a noted banjo player; he wrote the ballad "Kidder Cole" at the age of sixteen. He

was the author of two books, *Random Thoughts and Musings of a Mountaineer* (1941) and *What Think Ye of Christ?* (1946).

In 1899, Alley married Mary Elvira Hayes. They were the parents of two sons and a daughter: Felix E., Jr., John Hayes, and Edna Louise (Mrs. J. Willford Ray).

SEE: *Asheville Citizen*, 29 June 1952, 7 Jan. 1957.

ROBERT O. CONWAY

Allison, Benjamin (*1717–63*), physician and member of Parliament, was a native of Sutton-cum-Lound, England. He was educated at East Retford Free Grammar School and trained with Joseph Bright, a surgeon of Retford. Settling in medical practice in Retford, he was elected junior bailiff of the borough in 1747. He was twice elected to one of Retford's seats in Parliament, elected alderman in 1750, and elected senior bailiff at Retford in 1751. Allison was regarded as an outstanding physician but a difficult man; he was frequently at odds with fellow officials. He resigned from Retford's municipal government in 1756 and is believed to have emigrated in that year to America. After several years in Philadelphia, Allison moved to Edenton, where a mercantile firm in which he had become a partner had large warehouses. He was appointed justice of the peace in Chowan County in 1760 but died in the fall of 1763, leaving his American property to his six children and to friends and relatives in England. His wife, the former Elizabeth Bayles of Andover, England, died at Philadelphia in 1760. His American estate remained unsettled at the opening of the Revolution, was confiscated, and in 1791, was advertised for sale at Edenton.

SEE: *East Retford* (England) *Advertiser*, December 1854; Edenton *State Gazette of North-Carolina*, 23 Sept. 1791; J. R. B. Hathaway, ed., *North Carolina Historical and Genealogical Register*, vol. 1 (1900); William L. Saunders, ed., *Colonial Records of North Carolina*, vol. 6 (1888).

THOMAS C. PARRAMORE

Alspaugh, John Wesley (*22 July 1831–4 Nov. 1912*), banker, editor, and lawyer, was born in Forsyth County, one of ten children of John and Elizabeth Lashmit Alspaugh. He was the grandson of Henry Alspaugh, who came from Germany about the time of the Revolutionary War and settled in the Moravian community of Salem. Alspaugh's father was minister for nearly fifty-six years of the Methodist Episcopal Church in Winston. Alspaugh spent his early years on the family farm and there received his only education prior to entering Trinity College in 1850. After graduation in 1855, Alspaugh moved to Greensboro to study law under Judge Robert Dick. Obtaining his license to practice law in 1857, Alspaugh opened an office in Winston. Because of financial need, he was forced to take a position with a newspaper, the weekly *Western Sentinel*. Within a year, Alspaugh had become coeditor and by 1859 was editor and proprietor. The newspaper staunchly supported the South and the Democratic party during this crucial period, favoring Breckinridge in the presidential campaign of 1860.

Following the siege of Fort Sumter, the *Sentinel* ardently favored North Carolina's joining the Confederacy and attacked the "John Brown Administration" in Washington. Alspaugh continued to support the Southern Democratic position through his newspaper until retiring as editor in 1872.

In 1858, Alspaugh was elected chief clerk of the North Carolina Senate. He originally intended to serve only one term but was reelected and stayed in office until the end of the Civil War.

After retiring as editor of the *Western Sentinel*, Alspaugh devoted himself to the practice of law and to business and civic affairs. In 1876 he was one of the primary organizers of the First National Bank of Winston. He was cashier until 1892, when he became president.

From the 1870s until his death, Alspaugh had three main interests: the industrial and civic progress of Winston, the development of Trinity College, and the work of the Christian churches. He promoted the progress of Winston through his capacity as banker and businessman, by aiding in the development of manufactures and greater railroad facilities for his community. He was mayor of Winston from 1871 to 1876 and town commissioner from 1886 to 1893.

Alspaugh helped develop Trinity from a small and nearly bankrupt college in the 1870s and 1880s to a successful institution at the time of his death. He served as a trustee from 1869 until his death and was president of the board of trustees from 1880 until 1897. In 1884, when Trinity nearly closed its doors for lack of money, Alspaugh and two other men formed a committee of management, which completely controlled the college for two years. This service, along with liberal financial contributions and solicitation of contributions from others, enabled Trinity to survive.

To promote his third interest, Alspaugh, a member of Centenary Methodist Church and a deeply religious man, contributed a great deal of money for the building of churches in Winston.

Alspaugh was married in 1861 to Olivia Stedman, who died in 1869; he was married again in 1872, to Celeste Tucker. He had no children by his first wife and two daughters and one son by his second wife: Emma Celeste, John Wesley, Jr., and Violet G. He died after a stroke of paralysis and was interred at Mt. Tabor Methodist Church Cemetery.

SEE: Samuel A. Ashe, ed., *Biographical History of North Carolina*, vol. 8 (1917 [portrait]); Samuel A. Ashe, *Cyclopedia of Eminent and Representative Men of the Carolinas of the Nineteenth Century* (1892); Nora C. Chaffin, *Trinity College, 1839–1892* (1950); Winston *Western Sentinel*, 1857–72.

THOMAS W. AUSTIN, JR.

Alston, John (1653–1758), early settler, is remembered more as the progenitor of a family whose members have played significant political and social roles in North Carolina than as an important figure in his own right. He was born in Bedfordshire, England, where his family in 1640 had acquired the castle at Odell, after having been seated at Saxham Hall in Norfolk since the Middle Ages. The founder of the North Carolina Alstons was the third in succession to bear the name John; the founder of the South Carolina family, another John Alston, was his first cousin. John of North Carolina was the son of Ann, daughter of the celebrated John Wallis, Savilian professor of geometry and archivist of Oxford University. John Alston was baptized on 5 Dec. 1673 in the parish church at Felmersham, a village that lies almost in sight of Odell and Pavenham, the other two Bedford villages closely associated with the Alstons.

Alston may have emigrated to the West Indies or possibly to South Carolina before moving to Virginia, whence he entered North Carolina; he was thirty-eight years old when his name first appeared in the Albemarle Book of Warrants and Surveys in 1711, at which time he was named as grantee of land on the northwest side of Bennett's Creek in that part of Chowan (now Gates) County that lay in the territory in dispute between Virginia and North Carolina. Unlike other settlers in this area, Alston does not appear in the fragmentary records of Nansemond, the adjacent Virginia county. William Byrd, in his account of surveying the dividing line between the two colonies in 1728, mentioned dining with Major Alston at the home of Thomas Speight in Perquimans on 19 Mar. 1728. On 24 Mar. he wrote: "This being Sunday the People flock't from all parts partly out of Curiosity, & partly out of Devotion. Among the Female part of our Congregation, there was not much Beauty, the most fell to Majr. Alston's daughter, who is said to be no niggard of it. . . . Major Alston & Captain Baker dined with us. . . ."

From 1711 throughout the remaining forty-seven years of his life, John Alston continued to acquire and to assist his children to acquire land in the expanding areas of Bertie, Edgecombe, Granville, and Orange. Like his sons, he seems consciously to have determined to establish his descendants as landholders. In much the same pattern, Alston held public positions comparable to those his family had held at home; in 1720 he became a justice of the peace for Chowan, continuing in that post until he was commissioned assistant justice of the court of oyer and terminer in 1724, in which office he served for five years. In 1725 he became collector of revenue for the colony. In 1738 Alston was elected to the vestry of St. Paul's Parish, Edenton; he continued as a vestryman until he was named sheriff in Chowan in 1746 at the age of seventy-three. In the colonial militia, Alston is recorded as captain before 1724; in 1725 he became a major; and in 1729 he was designated colonel.

About 1700, John Alston was married to Mary, daughter of John Clark of Pasquotank and niece of Chief Justice John Palin. His wife's Quaker ancestry may account for the biblical names found among the early North Carolina Alstons, names not so prevalent among their South Carolina kinsmen. The list of John and Mary Clark Alston's children and their places of residence illustrates how the children of settlers in the Albemarle quickly expanded their land holdings and moved to developing areas inland: Joseph John (ca. 1702–81) of Edgecombe (later Halifax) County; Mary, who married first Henry Guston of Bertie County and second William Seward of Isle of Wight County, Va.; Solomon (ca. 1707–84) of Bute (later Warren) County; Sarah (b. ca. 1709), who married Thomas Kearney of Edgecombe (later Halifax) County; Elizabeth (b. ca. 1711) married to Samuel Williams of Edgecombe County; William (ca. 1714–ca. 1743) of Edgecombe County; Charity (b. ca. 1718), who married first Robert Hilliard and second John Dawson, both of Northampton County; Philip (ca. 1723–83) of Bute (later Warren) County; James (d. 1761) of Orange County; and Martha, married to Lemuel Wilson of Norfolk County, Va.

Unlike many of the early colonists, John Alston lived a long life, surviving two of his children. On 17 Sept. 1754, at the age of eighty-one, he began writing his will; he finished and dated it 20 Feb. 1755. Three years later he died at his residence on Bennet's Creek; his will was probated in Chowan County.

SEE: William K. Boyd, ed., *William Byrd's Histories of the Dividing Line betwixt Virginia and North Carolina* (1929); Deeds of the counties of Bertie, Edgecombe, Chowan, and Granville (North Carolina State Archives, Raleigh);

J. Bryan Grimes, ed., *Abstract of North Carolina Wills* (1910); Joseph A. Groves, *The Alstons and Allstons of North and South Carolina* (1901).

CLAIBORNE T. SMITH, JR.

Alston, Lemuel James *(1760–1836)*, U.S. congressman and jurist, was the son of Solomon, Jr., and Sarah Alston of Granville (now Warren) County. His great-grandfather John Alston had emigrated from Bedfordshire, England, by 1711; he founded one of the two colonial branches of Alstons in the Carolinas. Solomon Alston died by the time his son was eleven years old, but nothing else is known of Lemuel's boyhood. Shortly after the Revolutionary War, Lemuel moved to Greens Mill, S.C., where he invested in real estate and established a law practice.

In 1786, Alston received at least one grant of 418 acres of land in the vicinity of Greens Mill from South Carolina Governor William Moultrie. Within a short time, he acquired several other tracts, securing the most extensive landholdings in the area. His division of property into lots for resale, "Alston's Plat," became the basis for the city of Greenville.

As a lawyer and one of the area's leading citizens, he won election to the U.S. House of Representatives in 1806 and reelection two years later. In the national capital he boarded with a distant cousin, Willis Alston, a long-term North Carolina congressman. Both tended to support the Jeffersonian majority, but Lemuel retained enough independence to vote against that majority and against his more powerful cousin on some issues. The South Carolina representative's career in the House was undistinguished. He abstained from active participation in floor debate. Like most Jeffersonians, he voted for the Embargo Act of 1807, the Nonintercourse Act of 1809, and Macon's Bill No. 2 in 1810, dependably supporting their basic propositions through all phases of debate. His voting record indicates a willingness to uphold most measures designed to maintain and occasionally increase U.S. defenses, but he seems to have refrained from belligerent hostility to either Great Britain or France. On one other significant issue, southwestward expansion, Alston's position suggests that he personally was already casting a longing eye toward expansion: he consistently supported the organization of Orleans Territory for statehood. In his only vote against expansionism, he opposed agreement with a Senate proposal restricting the rights of free blacks in Orleans Territory. His attitude toward blacks may have been ambivalent, however; when the vote was retaken, he reversed his position.

After serving his second term he lost his seat to his immediate predecessor, Elias Earle, in 1810. Five years later, by rumor still rancorous over his constituents' rejection, Alston sold his remaining 11,028 acres of Greenville real estate to another North Carolina native son, Vardry McBee, and moved southwest, relocating in Grove Hill in the Alabama Territory. He immediately assumed prominence there, presiding over both the Clarke County orphans' court and the county court from 1816 to 1821. After 1821 he withdrew from public life, retiring to Alston Place in Clarke County, where he died at the age of seventy-six.

Alston was married twice, first to Elizabeth Williams, and then, after her death, to another Elizabeth Williams, the widow of his first wife's half brother, Joseph Williams. He fathered eight children, all by the second Elizabeth; only four survived infancy. His only direct descendants were born to his son William Williams.

SEE: *Annals of Congress*, 1807–11; *Biog. Dir. Am. Cong.* (1961); S. S. Gitterden, *The Greenville Century Book* (1903); Joseph A. Groves, *The Alstons and Allstons of North and South Carolina* (1901); *Who Was Who in America, 1607–1896*.

TIMOTHY J. WIEST

Alston, Louis Watson *(28 June 1884–18 Jan. 1960)*, philanthropist, was born at Maple Cottage in the southeastern part of Warren County, known from early times as "the Fork." The youngest of the eight children of Philip Guston Alston and his wife, Jane Crichton, he grew up on inherited lands that his ancestor, Philip Alston, son of the immigrant John Alston of Chowan, began purchasing in 1760, part of the "Clun Seat" tract of ten thousand acres. Succeeding generations of the Alston family had made this a thickly settled rural neighborhood with a web of interlocking relationships. Before the Civil War, it was one of the most opulent sections of the state. Post-Reconstruction poverty was accordingly more marked here, and Louis Alston often spoke of those difficult times.

The boy's mother died when he was nine years old, and he then made his home with his oldest sister, Mrs. Archibald Davis Williams, at Linwood in Franklin County. His father married as his second wife Mrs. Lucy McColl Roper and moved to Marlboro County, S.C. Louis Alston attended the famous Graham School in Warrenton and then was graduated from the Atlanta Dental College.

Influenced by his father's residence in South Carolina, Dr. Alston settled in Camden, S.C., to practice. Here he met and married Charlotte Niven McKinney, member of a wealthy Binghamton, N.Y., family. Her parents, William Allison McKinney and Mary Elizabeth Niven, had wintered in Camden for many years.

After marriage in 1913, the Alstons went to live in Savannah. In 1916 they moved to Morganton, N.C., where Dr. Alston practiced his profession and began to raise flowers commercially. As time passed, he devoted less and less time to dentistry. Mrs. Alston eventually inherited a large estate, and as a consequence Dr. Alston found himself increasingly involved in business affairs. Twins were born to the Alstons, one of whom, Robert Niven, died in infancy. As the surviving child, Mary Niven, grew older, her parents spent the winters in Baltimore, both to be near her school and to provide her with the stimulus of urban life. The pattern thus established lasted the rest of their lives; they lived in an apartment in Baltimore in winter and in their Morganton house in summer.

Throughout his life, Alston was a devoted communicant of the Episcopal church. As a boy living in the country and later as a student, Emmanuel Church in Warrenton came to be the focus of his religious life. In Baltimore, he attended the Cathedral of the Incarnation both because it was near his apartment and also because, being near Johns Hopkins, the parish had developed a ministry to college students and faculty in which he had a particular interest. The church was a major recipient of Alston's philanthropy. The Baltimore cathedral, Grace Church, in Morganton and his childhood parish in Warrenton received substantial help from him.

There are numerous examples of Alston's personal and often, as befitted a modest man, anonymous philanthropy. During World War II, he was profoundly troubled by the privations of the English clergy. He had read some of the works of Dr. S. C. Carpenter, dean of Exeter, and admired them, and he made the dean a number of practical gifts designed to make life a bit easier during the war years. For a long period, Alston saw to it that certain elderly and impecunious persons whom he had known as a child were provided with funds for some of the comforts as well as the necessities of life.

No doubt influenced by boyhood instruction from his sister, Alston maintained a lifelong interest in nature and the cultivation of the soil. He once commented to a friend that the only two worthwhile occupations were medicine and farming, in the sense of improving the land. His knowledge of botany was vast, especially of the trees, shrubs, and flowers of his native North Carolina. He was also interested in birds, and his library contained a complete set of Audubon's *Birds of America*, the earlier works of Alexander Wilson, and a fine set of the works of the eighteenth-century Englishman John Albin.

Alston died in Baltimore. By his will the bulk of his estate was divided into five equal parts among the University of the South and the dioceses of North Carolina, East Carolina, Western North Carolina, and Central New York. In each instance the principal of the gift was to be invested, and Alston specified the uses to which the income was to be put. In the case of the University of the South, the income was to be used for its School of Theology. The diocesan bequests stipulated that the income be used for theological education, work among college students, and supplementation to the salaries of the lower paid clergy. The diocese of Western North Carolina was also required to provide assistance to the aged and infirm.

Alston's daughter, a musician and novelist (under the penname Marian Niven), resides in New York.

SEE: Columbia, S.C., *State*, 2 Mar. 1960; Morganton *News-Herald*, 29 Feb. 1960; Edward W. Phifer, "In Memoriam: Louis Watson Alston," Morganton *News-Herald*, 16 Feb. 1960; W. Rhodes Weaver, *Greensboro Daily News*, 28 Feb. 1960; Mary Lewis Williams and Henry W. Lewis, personal interviews (1974).

                                                         CLAIBORNE T. SMITH, JR.

Alston, Philip (ca. 1745–91), revolutionary patriot, was born in Halifax County, the son of Joseph John Alston and his first wife, Elisabeth Chancy. In 1772 he bought four thousand acres of land in a horseshoe-shaped bend in the Deep River in Cumberland (later Moore) County. He moved to this tract and is thought to have built the fine colonial house, called "The House in the Horseshoe," yet standing there. Alston began to purchase more land and by 1777 appeared on the tax lists with sixty-five hundred acres. He achieved prominence in his new home; with the onset of the Revolution in 1775, he was appointed second major of the Cumberland Militia. In 1776 he was appointed a justice of the county court and promoted to lieutenant colonel of the militia. Elected to the House of Commons as a representative from Cumberland in the fall of 1777, Alston was granted a leave of absence in December to give full time to military affairs. In 1778, after controversy, he was promoted to colonel. Little is known of his actual military service, but in March of 1779 General John Ashe reported that Colonel Alston had been taken prisoner at Briar Creek in Georgia. On his release he was involved in local skirmishes with David Fanning, the notorious Tory marauder of nearby Chatham County. Tradition says that, in 1781, Fanning trapped Alston in his home. As Fanning began setting

fire to the house, Mrs. Alston emerged with a flag of truce and her husband was led away captive.

With the formation of Moore County in 1784, Philip Alston was appointed justice and became the first clerk of court. Having been elected to the state senate, he resigned the clerkship on 23 Feb. 1785, "promising that George Glascock should act as deputy until James Alston (his son) comes of age"; the court appointed James Alston clerk. Philip Alston was elected to the senate again the following year.

The records reveal a dark side to Alston's character. Even before the Revolution, Philip Alston, styled "gunsmith," was accused of counterfeiting. In September 1777, Colonel Robert Rowan, a prominent patriot in Cumberland, wrote Governor Richard Caswell, criticizing Alston's political activities in the county and stating that "he seems to rule them all, and a greater tyrant is not upon the face of the earth according to his power" and that "about two or three years ago no gentleman with the least regard for his character would have kept this hectoring, domineering person company." In December 1785 testimony was presented to the assembly that Alston had murdered one Thomas Taylor. As Taylor had been a Tory and Alston was commanding a corps of militia in the service of the state at the time of Taylor's death, the committee of the assembly thought he should not be tried for murder. He was accordingly pardoned by Governor Richard Caswell.

In a few months there was further evidence of the colonel's violent nature. According to the court minutes of Moore County, on 20 Feb. 1786, "Philip Alston in a very abusive manner treated George Glascock, he the said Alston then sitting as Justice, on a bench." Glascock, a native of Virginia and first cousin to George Washington, had been appointed deputy clerk of court when Alston resigned. Deep-seated enmity developed between the two men. Glascock contested Alston's reelection to the senate in 1786 but lost. In May 1787 a number of citizens from Moore, probably led by Glascock, successfully petitioned the assembly to have Alston removed as justice of the peace; three months later Glascock was murdered. Evidence suggested that Alston ordered his slave Dave to commit the crime. Dave was seized, imprisoned, and released on bond; on 21 Aug. 1787, Alston forfeited a £250 bail when Dave failed to appear. That Alston himself was imprisoned for his part in the murder is attested by a note in the *Fayetteville Gazette* of 1 Dec. 1790: "Broke gaol on the 5th instant, Philip Alston, late of Moore County, committed as an accessory to the murder of George Glascock." In less than a year, Alston himself was dead; on 24 Nov. 1791 his son James qualified as administrator of his estate. Tradition says he fled to Tennessee and was there murdered by the runaway Dave.

Before leaving Halifax County, Philip Alston married Temperance, the second daughter of Drew Smith of the Scotland Neck section. In his will in 1762, Smith entailed a tract of land of four hundred acres on the Roanoke to his daughter Temperance. The Alstons sold this land in 1789, and James Alston, "eldest son and heir, joined to break the entail." James Alston married Mary Wilcox of Fayetteville and represented Chatham County in the legislature in 1800. Later he moved to Telfair County, Ga. According to family records, Philip Alston and his wife had three other sons and a daughter. John, the second son, who was mentioned in the will of his grandfather in Halifax county in 1778, moved to Fairfield County, S.C., where he left descendants. Philip, Jr., moved to Jackson, Tenn. There is no record of the fourth son, Drew. The only daughter, Mary Drew (b. 12 Jan. 1784), married in 1799 William Carroll. After he died without issue, she married William Harris and had with him three children, one of whom, Sarah, in 1832 married Albert Pickett, the historian of Alabama.

SEE: The Deeds and Wills of the County of Halifax (North Carolina State Archives, Raleigh); Joseph A. Groves, *The Alstons and Allstons of North and South Carolina* (1901); Blackwell P. Robinson, *A History of Moore County, N.C.* (1956).

CLAIBORNE T. SMITH, JR.

Alston, Willis *(1769–10 Apr. 1837)*, congressman, was born at the family plantation on Fishing Creek, near Littleton, in Halifax County. His parents were John Alston (1740–84) and Ann Hunt Macon, daughter of Gideon and Priscilla Jones Macon and sister of Nathaniel Macon. The interrelated Alston, Seawell, Jones, Hawkins, and Macon families furnished many political leaders to Halifax and Warren counties.

At twenty-one, after attending Princeton, Willis was elected to the House of Commons and served from 1790 to 1792. He was elected to the state senate in 1794 and served two years. In 1798 he defeated Thomas Blount for the seat in Congress from Halifax and Tar River District. He served in the Sixth and seven succeeding congresses (March 1799 to March 1815).

Alston and Blount were opposed again in 1800; Alston kept his seat by 638 votes. Former Governor William R. Davie lost to Alston in 1803 by 823 votes. Alston went on to defeat John Binford in 1804, William Cherry in 1806, Daniel Mason in 1808, and Joseph H. Bryan in 1810. In 1813, Daniel Mason opposed Alston a second time, offering himself as a "peace candidate," because Alston had voted for war the year before. By the end of the War of 1812 Alston had decided not to run again and did not run in 1815.

When Alston first went to Congress, while John Adams was still president, sessions were held in Philadelphia. There Alston roomed at the same place as his uncle, Nathaniel Macon, and another freshman congressman, John Randolph. The alliance did not last long. After the government moved to Washington and Jefferson became president, Randolph and Macon became disillusioned with Jefferson's leadership and parted company with Alston. Early in 1804 and again in 1811, Alston and Randolph came to physical violence over differences. Alston became the most influential Jeffersonian supporter in the North Carolina delegation between 1807 and 1815, serving most of the time on the powerful Ways and Means Committee and becoming a friend of John C. Calhoun and the War Hawks during the War of 1812.

After his return home in 1815 Alston continued to be active in politics and was elected to commons each year between 1819 and 1824. He supported funds for internal improvements, led a movement to investigate the accounts of state treasurer John Haywood, launched a campaign to make state banks redeem their notes in specie, and became an active supporter of Calhoun for the presidency. It was during this period that he married for the second time, on 29 May 1817, and four of his five children were born.

In 1824, Hutchins G. Burton resigned his Halifax District seat in Congress to become governor. Willis Alston and George Outlaw, supported by W. H. Crawford forces, entered a special election for the position, Outlaw winning by about two hundred votes.

Outlaw soon became ill, however, and in 1825, Alston regained his old seat. This time he served three terms (March 1825 to March 1831), opposing the tariff and staunchly supporting Calhoun. In 1828 he supported the Jackson-Calhoun ticket and was suggested by the Calhoun forces in the North Carolina assembly as their choice for governor. After Jackson's term began, Alston became chairman of the House Elections Committee; but with the split between Jackson and the Calhoun forces in 1831, Alston decided to give up his seat from Halifax in favor of his friend, John Branch, late secretary of the navy. During the 1832 presidential campaign, Alston was an elector on the ticket supporting Philip P. Barbour for vice-president against Jackson's candidate, Martin Van Buren; during the Nullification controversy, he was vocal in his support of South Carolina.

Alston was married twice, first to Pattie Moore of Halifax County and second to Sarah (Sallie) Madeline Potts of Wilmington. There were no children of the first marriage, but five were born of the second union: Charles; Ariellah, who married James B. Hawkins; Leonidas; Missouri, who married Archibald Davis Alston; and Edgar. Alston died in Halifax and was buried in the private burying ground at his plantation Butterwood, not far from where he was born.

SEE: *Biog. Dir. Am. Cong.* (1971); D. H. Gilpatrick, *Jeffersonian Democracy in North Carolina* (1931); Perry M. Goldman and James S. Young, *The United States Congressional Directories, 1789–1840* (1973); Joseph A. Groves, *The Alstons and Allstons of North and South Carolina* (1901); W. S. Hoffmann, *Andrew Jackson and North Carolina Politics* (1971); J. W. Moore, "Early Baptist Laymen in North Carolina," Raleigh *Biblical Recorder*, 14 Jan. 1891; *North Carolina Manual* (1913).

DANIEL M. MCFARLAND

Amadas, Philip *(ca. 1565–?)*, naval commander and explorer, was the son of John and Jane Amadas of Plymouth, England. In his youth he released his estate in the manors of Trethake, Penkelewe, to Sir Walter Raleigh and became a member of his household. It is from this association that he was sent in 1584, at age nineteen, to explore the coast of America for a suitable site for Raleigh's proposed colony. Amadas, like Arthur Barlowe, was captain of his own flagship, the *Bark Ralegh*, with Simon Fernandez as master and pilot. On 13 July 1584 they arrived at an inlet leading to an island named Roanoke by the natives. This inlet they named Port Ferdinando after the pilot, who was the first to discover it. For six weeks, Amadas and Barlowe explored and traded, visiting chief Wingina on Roanoke Island, before returning to England with the Indians Manteo and Wanchese on board.

The next year, 1585, Amadas, now given the title Admiral of Virginia and second in naval command to Sir Richard Grenville, sailed again for the New World on the *Tiger*. He remained on Roanoke Island under the governance of Sir Ralph Lane for a year and possibly served as both admiral and colonel. He may also have been leader of the Chesapeake Bay expedition and was perhaps instrumental in making entrenchments for the Roanoke Island fort. In June 1586, Amadas and his fellow colonists left for England in Sir Francis Drake's ships. From that time on, nothing further is known of Philip Amadas.

SEE: David B. Quinn, ed., *The Roanoke Voyages, 1584–1590*, vols. 1–2 (1955).

JOHN W. SHIRLEY

Ammons, Elias Milton *(28 July 1860–20 May 1925)*, rancher, legislator, and Colorado governor, was born in Macon County. His parents, Jehu R. Ammons and Margaret C. Brendle, both traced the American origins of their families to the colonial period. When Elias was eleven, the family migrated westward, settling in Denver, Colo. There the boy found it necessary to work for four years as a spindle feeder in the Denver Woolen Mills, as a teamster in a lumber camp, and as a lamplighter, before completing his education at East Denver High School. After his graduation in 1880, he secured a job with the *Denver Times*, where he worked for four and a half years. He progressed steadily in journalistic ability and responsibility, rising to an assistant editorship, but failing eyesight forced him to turn to another profession. He chose cattle ranching.

Within a few years, having established himself as a rancher, the young man turned to politics as an additional outlet for his energies. His first political post was a minor one, clerk of the district court of Douglas County in 1890. That same year, running as a Republican, Ammons won election to the Colorado House of Representatives, so he resigned the clerkship. He served four years in the house, the last two as speaker. With the emergence of the free silver question on the national scene, he grew disaffected with the Republican leadership's espousal of the gold standard. Joining a group of similarly disenchanted Republicans led by Senator Henry Teller, he ran for election to the state senate as a Silver Republican and won. Two years later he was reelected. Increasingly finding his views incompatible with his original party affiliation, he left the Republicans entirely and enrolled in the more amenable Democratic party.

In both 1904 and 1906 the physically frail and almost blind Ammons campaigned for state-wide office. Both years he ran for lieutenant governor on a ticket with Alva Adams as the gubernatorial candidate; both years he lost. The 1904 verdict proved particularly bitter when an apparent Democratic victory was reversed by the revelation of electoral frauds in the Denver area.

By 1912, however, Ammons soared to the peak of his political career. Aided by the division of the normal Republican vote between a regular party nominee and a Progressive candidate, the rancher glided to victory in the race for governor on a forty-nine thousand vote cushion. His term in office began routinely. He sponsored legislation to improve laws governing public utilities, insurance, and banking; to revise the tax system; to provide for coal mine inspection; and to prepare a more comprehensive plan for state highway development. As he had done throughout his public career, he spoke out against federal conservation measures that in his opinion deprived the states of their rights to develop their natural resources as they saw fit. After September 1913, most of his remaining year and a half as governor was occupied by a massive, disruptive coal strike.

Following a long series of sporadic attempts to unionize the Colorado mine fields, John R. Lawson led an all-out United Mine Workers' effort to organize the state's southern coal mining region. When strikers physically resisted the operators' use of scabs, the owners appealed to Ammons for assistance in maintaining production. The governor ordered the state militia to their aid. Soldiers and miners scuffled repeatedly during the protracted struggle. Finally, on 20 Apr. 1914, after another confrontation, militiamen drove miners and their families from their tent camps at Ludlow and burned the camps. In the ensuing melee,

five miners and one soldier were killed and two women and eleven children burned or suffocated in the fire. The incident fused a ten-day outbreak of violence characterized by burnings, dynamitings, and murders. Ammons and the state troops were unable to control the situation; U.S. troops were called in to restore order. The federal soldiers quelled the violence, but the strike continued. The governor was subject to virulent public condemnation. Legislators called for his impeachment. Although a motion introduced in the legislature demanding his resignation was quashed by a vote of 26 to 4, Governor Ammons's reelection hopes were shattered. When the Democratic party met to nominate candidates for the 1914 campaign, he was completely ignored. The coal strike dragged on until December, and the governor played no significant role in its final settlement.

At the expiration of his term, Ammons returned to his ranching and business enterprises. Since 1886 he had worked actively in the interests of Colorado farmers, holding membership in the Grange, the Farmers' Union, and the state board of agriculture and assisting in the establishment of the Colorado Cattle and Horse Growers' Association and the National Western Stock Show at Denver. He continued his activity as president of both the Farmers' Life Insurance Company and the Middle Park Land and Livestock Company and as vice-president of the agricultural board. In addition, he remained active in other civic affairs, serving, for instance, in the closing years of his life, as president of the Denver Chamber of Commerce and of the State Historical and Natural History Society.

Ammons was survived by his wife of thirty-six years, Elizabeth Fleming Ammons.

SEE: *DAB*, vol. 1 (1928); Percy S. Fritz, *Colorado: The Centennial State* (1941); W. F. Stone, *History of Colorado*, vol. 2 (1918); Carl Ubbelohde, *A Colorado History* (1965); *Who Was Who in America*, vol. 1 (1943).

                                                                                TIMOTHY J. WIEST

Ammons, John *(4 July 1831–9 Sept. 1914)*, Western North Carolina Baptist leader, was born in the Gabriel's Creek community of present Madison County, the oldest child of Stephen and Lovada M. Ammons.

With only a meager education gained in old field schools, Ammons was in 1854 licensed to preach by the East Fork of Bull Creek Baptist Church. Soon he became well known in Madison and other nearby counties as both evangelist and pastor. At the age of twenty-seven, by which time he had a wife and three children, Ammons entered Mars Hill College as a student. Two years later, at the Burnsville Academy in Yancey County, he launched a career as a schoolmaster. During the Civil War Ammons served as a missionary to Confederate troops in Western North Carolina and taught in various schools. From 1866 until 1868 he was president of Mars Hill College, a position made especially difficult from the fact that both sides in the recent war were well represented in the student body. His report to the Western Baptist Convention in 1867 declared that the institution, with an enrollment surpassing one hundred, was prospering.

From Mars Hill, Ammons moved to his small, recently purchased farm at Morgan Hill in Buncombe County. Though continuing to do some teaching and farming, he became largely engaged in his work as pastor, serving more than twenty churches during the next three decades. Before the close of this period he returned to Madison, where he was for a short time county superintendent of public instruction. He held other positions, including an appointment by the Sunday School Association (Raleigh) as Sunday school missionary in Western North Carolina and election by the Western Baptist Convention as corresponding secretary of its mission board. His public debates with representatives of the Campbellite Christian and Methodist denominations attracted considerable attention and were a particular source of pleasure to Ammons. Contemporary Baptists in Western North Carolina "had come to regard him as the greatest exponent of their faith."

Previously a Democrat, Ammons was caught up in the political upheaval of the 1890s and changed his party affiliation to Fusionist. He became chairman of the 1894 Populist convention of the Ninth Congressional District and the party's candidate for the state senate. The Democratic *Asheville Daily Citizen* made merry over an opposition ticket consisting of Republican James M. Moody, a "Haywood Radical," and Populist Ammons, a "Madison Minister." There were references to "Profane and Dirty Utterances" in the convention that selected them. Ammons was quoted as saying that he "had been born in a Democratic family, nursed at a Democratic breast, rocked in a Democratic gum [cradles were unknown then] and for more than 40 years had voted the straight Democratic ticket. But once he had made up his mind to change, all the powers of the eternal pit could not swerve him." A *Citizen* reporter referred to Spring Creek as the home of Jeter C. Pritchard and "the burial place of the Rev. Ammons." Despite such dire predictions, Ammons and Moody were elected, even though by small majorities, and represented the Thirty-third Senatorial District in the 1895 legislature. Ammons's recorded votes were all with the Fusionist majority.

Although respected in Baptist circles throughout his long period of service, Ammons was not always popular. A recent writer points out that he tended to be "long-winded, intolerant toward those who opposed him, and somewhat bitter toward younger men who had supplanted him." Frequent long absences from home helped limit his effectiveness as a farmer and were an imposition on his family. A contemporary wrote of Ammons, "The small remuneration that he received from his churches deprived his children, to a very great extent, from being educated. He seemed almost a stranger to his children."

Sallie E. Jervis, whom he had married in 1850, survived him. Ammons was buried at Gabriel's Creek Baptist Church burying ground near his home. His *Outlines of History* contains a reproduction of his portrait.

SEE: John Ammons, *Outlines of History of the French Broad Association and Mars Hill College* (ca. 1907); *Asheville Daily Citizen*, 10 Sept.–16 Nov. 1894; John Angus McLeod, *From These Stones: Mars Hill College* (1955); *Minutes of the One Hundred and Eighth Annual Session of the French Broad Baptist Association*, 1915; *North Carolina Senate Journal*, 1895; Raleigh *Biblical Recorder*, 16 Sept. 1914, 14 Apr. 1915.

HENRY S. STROUPE

Anderson, Albert (18 Oct. 1859–16 Oct. 1932), physician and superintendent of the state mental hospital at Raleigh, was born near Eagle Rock. His father, Jesse Anderson, worked a small farm during the difficult times of Reconstruction, and young Anderson witnessed the destructive march of Sherman's army through the Eagle Rock area. His mother was Mary

Tucker. Anderson attended local schools a few months each year with his younger brothers, "stopping off for foddering time" and other farm chores as the occasion demanded. Subsequently, he attended the Raleigh Male Academy and at the age of nineteen entered Trinity College, doing odd jobs to help cover costs; he was graduated in 1883 with an M.A. degree. From 1883 to 1887 he was an instructor at and the principal of the small Middleburg Male Academy in Vance County, of which he is said to have been the founder. While at Middleburg an interest in the sciences led him to the study of medicine under private instruction, probably with a doctor attached to the Middleburg medical school, which was reputed to be the first in the state. Anderson then attended the University of Virginia for one year, passing his finals there in 1888 and, soon after, the examination of the North Carolina State Board of Medical Examiners.

He immediately began a general practice in Wilson, taking time off as the opportunity arose to do postgraduate work at New York Polyclinic and other medical schools in the North. In 1892 the state board of health selected him as one of two North Carolinians to attend special courses offered to boards of health by the U.S. government. Six years later he was appointed a member of the state board of medical examiners.

Anderson was described as tall and slightly stout, well built, clean shaven, conservatively dressed, and almost clerical in appearance, yet a charming conversationalist. He was an excellent speaker, always logical and convincing, and addressed many medical gatherings. His persuasiveness was a chief factor in his ability to organize others. In 1898 he and Dr. E. C. Moore were responsible for the construction of a first-class hospital at Wilson, one of the best in that area of North Carolina. He was the chief supporter of a plan to make the county medical society a basic unit of government, an enterprise that required prospective members of the state society to enroll in their home county units; he himself was made councilor for an eight-county unit of the Wilson area.

Probably in recognition of his ability to combine medicine with business, the Jefferson Standard Life Insurance Company of Raleigh made him its medical director in 1907, a position he held for five years until the company moved to Greensboro. In 1913, Governor Locke Craig appointed Anderson superintendent of the state hospital for the mentally ill. It stood on Dix Hill, named for Dorothea Dix, pioneer in the care of the emotionally disturbed. Anderson was without training or substantial experience in mental health, but he immediately set himself to transform the "asylum" into a modern hospital; his approach included "remolding the attitude of hospital personnel toward the so-called insane." He expanded the premises and instituted a training school for nurses, so that they could better deal with "that part of the public which still retained crude ideas of the nature of mental illness." In an age before the general use of tranquilizers, he stressed occupational therapy for those able to accept it. Through his efforts, the mental hygiene exhibit, sponsored by the National Committee on Mental Hygiene, was held in Raleigh for three years.

During the years following his start at Wilson, Anderson held many positions. He was president of the Seaboard Medical Society and the Tri-State Medical Society, as well as a delegate to meetings of the American Medical Association. He was a director of the Raleigh branch of the North Carolina Bank and Trust Company and a trustee on the board of directors at Duke University. He was a charter member of the Junior

Order of United American Mechanics and a member of the Tar Heel and Watauga clubs. A member of the Jenkins Memorial Methodist Church, he taught Sunday school for some years. On 12 Dec. 1888 he married Pattie Rountree Woodard, a sister of Mrs. Charles B. Aycock, wife of the governor. There were no children.

SEE: Samuel A. Ashe, ed., *Biographical History of North Carolina*, vol. 2 (1905); *History of North Carolina*, vol. 4 (1919); *North Carolina: Rebuilding an Ancient Commonwealth*, vol. 3 (1928); Raleigh *News and Observer*, 17 Oct. 1932; *Southern Medicine and Surgery* 94 (1932); *Trinity Alumni Register*, vols. 1 and 2 (1915–1917); *Who's Who in Raleigh*, 1916; *Who's Who in the South*, 1927.

JOHN MACFIE

Anderson, Edwin Alexander (*16 July 1860–23 Sept. 1933*), rear admiral of the U.S. Navy and winner of the Congressional Medal of Honor, was born at Masonboro Sound near Wilmington. He was the son of Dr. Edwin Alexander Anderson (1815–94), who married in 1842 Mary Coit Lillington (1823–97), daughter of Major John A. and Mary Hill Lillington. In an adventurous career that spanned five decades, Anderson was thrice decorated for gallantry and became one of the nation's best-known naval figures.

In 1878 he was appointed by Alfred M. Waddell to the Naval Academy and was graduated in 1882. Over the next fifteen years he advanced to the rank of lieutenant, serving on vessels that took him to all parts of the world. He witnessed a revolution in Haiti, when he was invalided there with pneumonia, and served for three years on ships protecting the sealing trade in the Bering Sea and along the Alaskan coast. In 1891 he took part in a scientific expedition in the Pacific waters around the Galápagos Islands. He served aboard the steamer *Albatross* when it made the first survey of a cable route between California and Honolulu.

At the outbreak of the Spanish-American War in 1897, he was ordered to the *Marblehead*, a ship then blockading the port of Havana. This vessel was later blockading the port of Cienfuegos when it engaged and captured a Spanish steamer, the *Argorata*. On 11 May 1898, while in an open boat and exposed to very heavy shore fire, he successfully cut the submarine cable lines in the port of Cienfuegos. For this act he was advanced in rank and won a medal of honor from President McKinley. He also saw action in the blockade of Guantánamo Bay and in engagements with other Spanish ships.

After the war he served for a time in China, where he took part in quelling the Boxer Rebellion of 1900. He later served with the American fleet in Panama and was honored by that republic for his meritorious service. In 1915, with the rank of captain, he commanded the *New Hampshire* during the occupation of Veracruz in Mexico. He went ashore in command of a regiment of Blue Jackets and Marines and for extraordinary heroism in this engagement was awarded the Congressional Medal of Honor.

During World War I he served as brevet admiral of the American Patrol in European waters and was awarded the Distinguished Service Medal. After the war he was named commander in chief of the Eastern Fleet, with the full rank of rear admiral. At the time, this was the highest military rank ever achieved by a North Carolinian in the service of the United States.

His fame reached its height during the terrible earthquakes that devastated Japan in 1923. As Eastern Fleet commander, Anderson ordered his ships quickly into Japanese ports and assisted the stunned Japanese with food and supplies. He personally directed the distribution of $5 million in emergency supplies to the Japanese nation, an act which brought world acclaim and helped save many lives. Each year thereafter, the government of Japan bestowed on him a special gift or memento at Christmas as an expression of gratitude.

In 1888 he married Mertie Mosely Lorain, of Baltimore, Md. Their only child, Lorain Anderson, also a Navy officer, rose to the rank of lieutenant commander.

In 1926, Anderson retired from naval service to his home near Wilmington. In his late years he was an honored figure and often a guest speaker at local or state functions. He died at James Walker Memorial Hospital in Wilmington following a major operation there and was buried at Arlington National Cemetery, Washington, D.C.

SEE: *Charlotte Observer*, 27 Apr. 1900, 24 Sept. 1933; *Greensboro Daily News*, 24 Feb. 1963; Raleigh *News and Observer*, 7 June 1932, 24 Sept. 1933; *Who Was Who*, vol. 1 (1943).

JAMES MEEHAN

Anderson, George Burgwyn (*12 Apr. 1831–16 Oct. 1862*), Confederate soldier, was born near Hillsborough of Scotch-Irish ancestry. His father was William E. Anderson; his mother, Eliza Burgwyn. At an early age, Anderson demonstrated marked intellectual abilities that enabled him to enter The University of North Carolina at age sixteen. After one year there, he received an appointment to West Point, where he was graduated in 1852, standing ninth in a class of forty-one. Anderson was appointed brevet second lieutenant in the Second Dragoons and, following a brief tour in California, joined the regiment at Fort Chadbourne, Tex. Promoted to first lieutenant on 13 Dec. 1855, he served as regimental adjutant for over a year. With the regiment, Anderson witnessed the civil strife and violence engulfing Kansas during this period and marched under Albert Sidney Johnston to settle the Mormon problems in Utah. In the fall of 1859 he was detached on recruiting duties to Louisville, Ky. He remained on this duty until the firing on Fort Sumter, when he tendered his resignation (25 Apr. 1861) to offer his services to his native state.

Within a month, Anderson was appointed colonel of the Fourth North Carolina Volunteers. Organizing, equipping, and training the recruits occupied Anderson for two months. At the end of July, the regiment moved to Manassas Junction, Va., where Anderson assumed command of the post until the spring of 1862, when the Confederate army withdrew to the Peninsula. Anderson's first real action came at Seven Pines or Fair Oaks on 31 May. Temporarily commanding a brigade in D. H. Hill's division, he led a charge down the Williamsburg road. The attack stalled until Anderson, seizing the flag of the Twenty-seventh Georgia, personally led the brigade in the capture of Federal breastworks. His display of courage and leadership prompted President Jefferson Davis to promote him on 9 June to brigadier general.

Anderson assumed command of four North Carolina regiments, Second, Fourth, Fourteenth, and Thirtieth, a brigade whose combat record would be equalled by few others. In the Seven Days, he commanded the brigade with skill and conspicuousness, being wounded in the hand at Malvern Hill. His next battle was at South Mountain, Md., where Hill's division alone stubbornly resisted the Federal attacks for a full day on 14 Sept.

Three days later, Anderson's brigade held the right of the Confederate line in the bloody lane at the Battle of Sharpsburg. The Confederate soldiers repulsed three concerted Federal attacks, until a mistake in orders caused one brigade to withdraw, resulting in a collapse of the line. Anderson, while standing on a knoll rallying his men, was hit in the ankle by a minie ball. Though the wound was painful, it was not considered serious, and Anderson was sent home to Raleigh to recover. The wound failed to heal, however; an amputation was performed, but he never fully responded and died on 16 Oct. He was buried with full military ceremony in Oakwood Cemetery at Raleigh.

Anderson married Mildred Ewing, 8 Nov. 1859; they were the parents of two children, one of whom, George B., Jr., lived to adulthood.

SEE: Samuel A. Ashe, ed., *Biographical History of North Carolina*, vol. 4 (1906); Walter Clark, ed., *Histories of the Several Regiments and Battalions From North Carolina, in the Great War 1861–65*, vols. 1 and 4 (1901); Clement A. Evans, ed., *Confederate Military History*, vol. 4 (1899); Douglas S. Freeman, *Lee's Lieutenants: A Study in Command*, vol. 1 (1942); Louis H. Manarin, ed., *North Carolina Troops, 1861–1865: A Roster*, vol. 4 (1973); A. M. Waddell, "General George Burgwyn Anderson," *Southern Historical Society Papers*, 14 (1886); Ezra J. Warner, *Generals in Gray: Lives of the Confederate Commanders* (1959).

JEFFRY D. WERT

Anderson, Robert Burton (8 Jan. 1833–3 Dec. 1899), Presbyterian minister, Confederate chaplain, and teacher, the son of James and Eliza Williams Burton Anderson, was born in Williamsboro, Vance (then Granville) County. His father had come to America from his native Kilmarnock, Scotland, at the age of twenty-one. Soon after the birth of Robert, the family moved to Lincoln County; there Robert attended a small local school, before enrolling in the Caldwell Institute in Hillsborough. Later he entered Princeton University and was graduated in 1854. Apprenticed to William Murphy of Salisbury to learn the mercantile business, he was forced by poor health to change his occupation and turned to teaching for a time.

In September 1856, at Popular Tent Church (Presbyterian) in Cabarrus County, he felt called upon to prepare himself for the ministry, and he subsequently enrolled in the Columbian Theological Seminary, Columbia, S.C. Following his graduation in 1859, he was licensed by the Presbyterian church and served in Mecklenburg County until October 1863, when he joined the Fourth North Carolina Regiment as chaplain. Because of ill health, he resigned in August 1864; after regaining his health, he served the Presbyterian church in Concord for a time. In January 1867 he removed to Yorkville, S.C., took charge of the Yorkville Institute for Young Ladies, and also served a local church. After three years the school was sold, and poor health prevented Anderson's acceptance of a call to the local church. Instead, he returned to North Carolina and began in 1871, on a part-time basis, to serve churches in the vicinity of Morganton and Newton. In 1875 he was installed as the regular minister of the church in Morganton, where he remained for the rest of his life.

In 1881, Southwestern University awarded Anderson an honorary D.D. degree. He served as a trustee of Davidson College from 1863 until 1869 and again from 1884 until his death. For two years during the latter period, he was president of the board of trustees.

Anderson was married to Jennie H. Thornwell in 1860, and they were the parents of two sons and a daughter: James Henley, Thornwell, and Nancy Thornwell. Anderson died in Morganton.

SEE: Alfred Nevin, *Encyclopedia of the Presbyterian Church in the U.S.A.* (1884); Presbyterian Church, Synod of North Carolina, *Minutes* (1890); Ernest C. Scott, *Ministerial Directory of the Presbyterian Church, United States, 1861–1941* (1942).

JEAN A. BERNHARDT

Anderson, Robert Campbell, Jr. (26 July 1864–20 Feb. 1955), Presbyterian minister and son of the Reverend Robert Campbell and Justina Caroline Armistead Anderson, was born near Martinsville, Va. He was graduated from Hampden-Sydney College in 1887 and from Union Theological Seminary in Virginia in 1890. Licensed by Roanoke Presbytery of the Presbyterian Church, U.S., on 26 Apr. of the same year, and ordained to the ministry by the Presbytery of Central Texas on the thirtieth of the following August, he held the pastorate of the San Angelo, Tex., Presbyterian church from 1890 until 1892. He served as pastor of the Second Presbyterian Church of Roanoke, Va., from 1892 to 1897, with the exception of the academic year 1895–96, which he spent in study at Edinburgh, Scotland. He was pastor of the Shelbyville, Tenn., Presbyterian church, from 1898 to 1905 and of the First Presbyterian Church of Gastonia from 1905 to 1911.

In 1911 he became president of the Mountain Retreat Association of Montreat, an office he held until his retirement in 1946. From 1921 to 1947 he was also president of the Montreat Normal School for Young Women, which he had founded in 1916, and of its successor, Montreat College. In 1959 the latter institution was renamed Montreat-Anderson College in honor of Dr. and Mrs. Anderson. Davidson College conferred the D.D. degree upon Anderson in 1923, and in 1939 Hampden-Sydney College honored him with its Algernon Sydney Sullivan Award.

On 30 Dec. 1890 he married Katie P. Walker of Richmond, Va., who died in 1892. On 11 Nov. 1896 he and Sadie Kelly Gaither of Charlotte were married. Dr. and Mrs. Anderson established the Robert C. and Sadie G. Anderson Foundation for the advancement of the work of the Presbyterian Church in the U.S. Anderson wrote *The Story of Montreat from Its Beginning, 1897–1947* (1949); he became widely known as the developer and builder of Montreat as a conference center for his denomination. The Historical Foundation and the library of Montreat-Anderson College, both at Montreat, have portraits of him. He died at Montreat and was buried in Elmwood Cemetery, Charlotte.

SEE: Robert Campbell Anderson, Jr., *The Story of Montreat from Its Beginning* (1949); Robert Campbell Anderson, Jr., Papers (Historical Foundation, Montreat); Henry Dendy, in Presbyterian Church in the U.S., *Minutes*, Synod of Appalachia (1955); "Facts of the Life of Dr. R. C. Anderson" (evidently autobiographical MS, Anderson Papers).

THOMAS H. SPENCE, JR.

Andrews, Alexander Boyd (23 July 1841–17 Apr. 1915), railroad executive and construction engineer, was born near Franklinton, the son of William J. Andrews, a small planter, and his wife, Virginia Hawkins, daughter of Colonel John D. Hawkins.

After his mother's death in 1852 and his father's the

following year, Andrews passed under the guardianship of his uncle, Philemon B. Hawkins, a railroad developer. In 1859, at the age of seventeen, he left Henderson Male Academy to join Hawkins as a clerk on a contract construction project on the Blue Ridge Railway near Pendleton, S.C. Almost immediately, the young man demonstrated exceptional ability; within six months he was promoted to become general superintendent, purchasing agent, and paymaster, positions he held until the Civil War interrupted construction.

Andrews enlisted in Company E, Ninth North Carolina Regiment (afterward the First North Carolina Cavalry), and was elected second lieutenant on 16 May 1861. In September he was promoted to first lieutenant and transferred to Company B; in July 1862 he was promoted to captain and placed in command of the company. Shortly thereafter, on 9 July 1862, while patrolling the Roanoke River near Hamilton, he participated in one of the more bizarre skirmishes of the war. Encountering three lightly armed Federal gunboats sailing upriver to attack the railroad bridge at Weldon, his cavalry command attacked and repulsed the enemy with rifle fire, in a rare instance of combat between cavalry and naval units.

Andrews, with the rest of his regiment, was later attached to the Army of Northern Virginia and fought in most of the campaigns of 1862 and 1863. On 22 Sept. 1863 he was shot through the left lung in a skirmish at Jack's Shop; the wound left him convalescent for months and forced his retirement from the army in 1864.

After the war, almost penniless, Andrews borrowed one hundred dollars to lease and equip a ferry that he personally operated across the Roanoke River at Weldon, under contract with the Petersburg Railroad; ironically, he replaced the demolished railroad bridge he had once defended. Then, in July 1867, partly through family contacts, he became superintendent of the Raleigh and Gaston Railroad and, in the following year, of the Chatham Railroad. In this capacity, he again proved his competence, rapidly repairing war damage and completing fifty-six miles of new construction. On 1 Nov. 1875 he left the Raleigh and Gaston to join the rapidly growing Richmond and Danville Railroad as superintendent of its North Carolina Railroad line from Charlotte to Goldsboro, which it was leasing from the state on a thirty-year contract. His reputation was further enhanced in this position; from 1878 to 1880 he also served as superintendent of the Atlantic and North Carolina Railroad (another state-owned, privately leased line), and by the 1880s he was supervising all Richmond and Danville operations in the state.

This high reputation also earned Andrews considerable influence in state Democratic administrations. Under Governor Zebulon B. Vance, he served as a military aide with the rank of colonel; under Governor Thomas Jordan Jarvis, he was a close advisor on railroad affairs. It was in this role that Andrews entered "the great North Carolina Railroad War" over the fate of the Western North Carolina Railroad.

Chartered in 1855 by the General Assembly, the W.N.C.R.R. was intended to complete the antebellum vision of a "North Carolina system," a trunk line of railways connecting the western portions of the state with the eastern ports. Joining the North Carolina Railroad at Salisbury, the line was intended to run to Asheville, with branches extending to Paint Rock, Tenn., and through Murphy to Ducktown, Tenn. The Civil War, however, halted construction, and economic depression, combined with rough terrain, hindered postwar expansion. In 1872 the company went bankrupt; in June

1875 the state bought the road outright but was unable to progress rapidly. By 1880 the line still had not reached Asheville, and easterners (such as Walter Clark in his "Mud Cut" letters) attacked the project as a costly, unproductive boondoggle.

Then an Irish entrepreneur, William J. Best, approached Governor Jarvis in early 1880 with a proposal that he and three other New York financiers (James D. Fish, William R. Grace, and J. Nelson Tappan) purchase the W.N.C.R.R. In return, Best would legally bind himself to complete the extension to Asheville and would further agree (in an informal, nonbinding arrangement) to complete the Paint Rock and Ducktown branches.

Believing Best's offer the most satisfactory answer to the state's dilemma, Jarvis quickly called a special session of the General Assembly, which approved the sale on 20 Mar. 1880 under two conditions: the purchasers would have to reorganize the company and pay off its floating debt (about $30,000), and they would have to complete construction of the main and branch lines according to a fixed schedule concluding with the opening of the Ducktown line by 1 Jan. 1885. Only when these conditions were met could the deed to the railroad be transferred.

All seemed well until mid-May 1880, when Best's associates suddenly refused to pay the floating debt and withdrew from the transaction. Best was left stranded; the sale act required that he pay the loan and reorganize the company by 29 May 1880 or forfeit control of the road. At once Jarvis and Vance (now a U.S. senator), acting as state commissioners in the sale, authorized Andrews to go to New York and help Best arrange for new financial backing. Andrews did so; three directors of the Richmond and Danville extended Best a ninety-day loan of $50,000, in return for half the W.N.C.R.R.'s stock. On 29 May, the last possible day before forfeiture, Andrews returned to North Carolina, paid off the floating debt, and assumed control of the railroad as president, while maintaining his positions with the Richmond and Danville. Two months later, the badly overextended Best, unable to raise cash to repay the loan, signed over a controlling share of the stock to the Richmond and Danville, and on 31 July 1880 the W.N.C.R.R passed entirely under R. & D. control.

Vance and most eastern members of the legislature were furious. "The monopoly [the Richmond and Danville]," Vance wrote, "is seeking to enrich the people and cities of other states at the expense of sacrificing the only hope of obtaining the long cherished idea of a central trunk line." On 19 June 1880 the Raleigh *Observer* reprinted a story from the *New York Times* that reported the organization of a "vast railroad combination" including both the R. & D. and the W.N.C.R.R.; the paper speculated further that most of the North Carolina road's freight traffic would be diverted to Virginia, rather than North Carolina, ports. Andrews was personally blamed in many eastern newspapers as the agent of a conspiracy of out-of-state capitalists consciously subverting the best interests of the state; together with Best and Buford, the president of the Richmond and Danville, he was subjected to close, hostile questioning by the state senate Committee on Internal Improvements during public hearings in Raleigh, 16–19 Feb. 1881.

Undeterred by criticism, Andrews proceeded vigorously with plans to complete the Western North Carolina's construction. Facing exceptionally difficult terrain and chronic labor shortages, he completed the line to Asheville by October 1880 and to Paint Rock by

January 1882. At the same time, through careful lobbying with Jarvis and state treasurer John Milton Worth, two of the state's three W.N.C.R.R. commissioners, he was able to obtain necessary extensions of building deadlines as well as extra contingents of convict laborers. Attempts by Vance (the third commissioner) and other eastern interests to declare the Richmond and Danville's lease forfeit and to reassign it to Best (who had meanwhile formed a new syndicate leasing the Atlantic and North Carolina Railroad) failed when Jarvis and Worth effectively vetoed the plan at a commissioners' meeting, 17 Nov. 1881. Finally, in 1884, Andrews liquidated the Richmond and Danville's debt to North Carolina with a single payment of $600,000, relieving the state of levying any public taxes in that year; and in January 1891 the W.N.C.R.R. at last reached Ducktown, an engineering achievement unparalleled in the state's history at that time.

Although completion of the Western North Carolina was Andrews's best-known achievement, he also constructed numerous shorter railroads in the state during this period, most notably the North Carolina Midland Railroad from Winston-Salem to Mooresville; the Yadkin Railroad; the High Point, Randleman, Asheboro, and Southern Railroad; the Statesville and Western Railroad from Statesville to Taylorsville; and the Northwestern North Carolina Railroad. At the same time, he continued to advance rapidly in the Richmond and Danville management, as assistant to the president (1883–86), third vice-president (1886–89), and second vice-president (1889–94). When the Richmond and Danville declared bankruptcy in 1892, Andrews became general agent of its receivers, a position he held until 1894; and when the R. & D.'s holdings were reorganized within the Southern Railway Company, he joined the new firm as director (1894–1915), second vice-president (1894–95), and first vice-president (1895–1915). Reportedly, he declined the presidency of the Southern at one point, because he would have had to move his residence from Raleigh to Washington, D.C.

In addition, Andrews served as president of several semidependent rail lines within the state, including the Charlotte, Columbia, and Augusta Railroad; the Columbia, Oxford, and Henderson Railroad; the Atlantic, Tennessee, and Ohio Railroad; the Statesville and Western Railroad; and the Piedmont Railroad. All these roads were absorbed into the overall Seaboard system in 1894. He was also president of the Danville and Western Railway, the Blue Ridge Railway, the Augusta and Southern Railway, the Tallulah Falls Railway, and the Hartwell Railway; and first vice-president of the Mobile and Ohio Railroad and Alabama and Great Southern Railroad.

In 1886, at the request of President Grover Cleveland, he made a tour of inspection of the Northern Pacific Railroad on behalf of the federal government.

A Democrat and close friend of governors Jarvis and Elias Carr, Andrews nevertheless broke publicly with the party to vote for William McKinley in 1896. Although his sole experiences in public life were services as alderman in Henderson and Raleigh, he remained for over thirty years a significant and controversial figure in state politics by virtue of his position as a lobbyist for railroad interests. Josephus Daniels repeatedly charged that Andrews misused his powers to issue railroad passes and his position as a social arbiter and member of the Raleigh Capital Club to influence state legislators unduly. Walter Clark, in a letter to a political associate, wrote angrily: "Andrews is a corrupter of young men,"

in response to the latter's machinations regarding one controversial piece of rail legislation. Andrews, for his part, helped to underwrite the Raleigh *Morning Post* and the *Raleigh Daily Tribune*, a Fusionist newspaper, as competition for Daniels's *News and Observer*. Andrews's private railway car, when parked in Raleigh, was reputedly the scene of frequent gatherings of pro-railroad legislators and state officials. In July 1897 it was revealed that Andrews owned a half interest in Round Knob Hotel, a popular rail stop, with Major James W. Wilson, then chairman of the State Railroad Commission, and that the hotel was operated by S. Otho Wilson, also a member of the commission. These revelations led Governor Daniel Russell to dismiss both commissioners; Andrews himself had eight separate civil actions, each for five thousand dollars, brought against him for failure to testify about the affair before the State Corporation Commission.

In addition to his rail interests, Andrews was a director (1871–1915) and vice-president (1890–1915) of Citizens' National Bank and also a director of the Raleigh Savings Bank and Trust Company, the Jefferson Standard Life Insurance Company, the North Carolina Home Insurance Company, and the Sloss-Sheffield Steel and Iron Company of Birmingham, Ala. A trustee of The University of North Carolina (1885–1915) and founder and president (1891–1915) of the Home for Confederate Veterans in Raleigh, he also served as state commissioner and fifth vice-president for the Columbian Exposition of Chicago in 1893.

On 1 Sept. 1869, Andrews married Julia Martha Johnston, daughter of Colonel William Johnston of Charlotte. The couple had five children: William J., manager of the Raleigh Electric Company; Alexander Boyd, Jr., a Raleigh attorney, amateur historian, and state Masonic official; Jane Hawkins (Mrs. William M. Marks); John Harris; and Graham Harris, a banker and long-time mayor of Raleigh.

Andrews was Episcopalian and a member of the Church of the Good Shepherd in Raleigh. He died at his home at 407 North Blount Street and was buried with Masonic rites at Oakwood Cemetery in Raleigh.

SEE: Alexander Boyd Andrews Papers (Southern Historical Collection, University of North Carolina, Chapel Hill); Samuel A. Ashe, ed., *Biographical History of North Carolina*, vol. 1 (1905), and *Cyclopedia of Eminent and Representative Men of the Carolinas of the Nineteenth Century*, vol. 2 (1892); Walter Clark, *Histories of the Several Regiments and Battalions from North Carolina in the Great War, 1861–1865* (1901); Josephus Daniels, *Editor in Politics* (1941), and *Tar Heel Editor* (1939); Hugh T. Lefler and Albert Ray Newsome, eds., *The Papers of Walter Clark*, 2 vols. (1948–50); Margaret W. Morris, "The Completion of the Western North Carolina Railroad," *North Carolina Historical Review* 52 (1975); W. Buck Yearns, ed., *The Papers of Thomas Jordan Jarvis*, vol. 1, *1869–1882* (1969).

BENNETT L. STEELMAN

Andrews, Alexander Boyd, Jr. *(2 Feb. 1873–21 Oct. 1946)*, attorney, Masonic official, and amateur historian, was born in Henderson, the second son of Alexander Boyd Andrews, senior vice-president of the Southern Railroad, and his wife, Julia Martha Johnston. After studying at the Raleigh Male Academy, he entered The University of North Carolina, where he was a member of the Dialectic Literary Society, Sigma Alpha Epsilon fraternity, and the Order of the Gimghouls. After being graduated in 1893 with a Litt. B. degree, he studied law at the university for a year and was admitted to the bar in September 1894.

Andrews commenced practice in Raleigh and remained there for the rest of his life. A president of the Wake County Bar Association in 1928 and 1929 and of the state bar association at the same time, he also served on the American Bar Association's Committee on Legal Education and, from 1922 to 1943, its Committee on Judicial Salaries, chairing the latter committee from 1922 to 1935. He was a member of the Raleigh Board of Aldermen from 1900 to 1904 and briefly acted as mayor *pro tempore*. In 1930 he chaired the executive committee of the state advisory committee for Furnifold M. Simmons's unsuccessful campaign for renomination to the U.S. Senate.

Most of Andrews's activities, however, were devoted to private charitable pursuits. A member and past master of the William G. Hill Lodge, he attained the Thirty-third Degree in the Scottish rite, served as state grand commander in the Knights Templar in 1906 and in 1908 was grand high priest of the state Grand Royal Arch Chapter. In 1916 he was elected grand master of the Grand Lodge of North Carolina. While in office, he was instrumental in arranging Masonic loan funds at several North Carolina colleges and in obtaining dispensation for a state temple of the Ancient Arabic Order, Nobles of the Mystic Shrine. When the Sudan Temple was instituted at New Bern on 26 Sept. 1917, Andrews was elected its first illustrious potentate. He was also an exalted ruler of the Raleigh Elks Lodge and a president of the Raleigh Kiwanis Club.

A devoted student of North Carolina history and lore, Andrews amassed an enormous collection of historical pamphlets and documents. In 1928 he published and distributed thousands of copies of the state anthem at his own expense. At his death, his collection went to The University of North Carolina, East Carolina Teacher's College, and the New Bern Public Library. He wrote numerous articles on Masonic and Episcopal church history, including a digest of Masonic law and an unpublished biographical sketch of William Joseph Williams (1759–1823), the North Carolina artist and Mason. His "Richard Dobbs Speight" (*North Carolina Historical Review* 1 [April 1924]) is considered a model of objective scholarship and attention to detail. A member of the American Statistical Association and an accomplished amateur statistician, Andrews regularly, on his own volition, issued statistical reports on various aspects of public policy. Some of these, such as his 1942 census of graduate degrees held by state college instructors, which indicated a marked inequality in the staffs of white and Negro institutions, excited considerable controversy.

A trustee of The University of North Carolina from 1927 to 1946 and a secretary to the board, Andrews also served on the board of trustees of East Carolina Teacher's College (1919–46) and of Oxford Orphanage (1917–43). From 1927 to 1929 he was president of The University of North Carolina Alumni Association. A devout Episcopalian and a member of the Church of the Good Shepherd in Raleigh, he was a member of the house of deputies at its triennial general convention (1931–43) and chairman of its committee on canons (1940–43). From 1934 until his death, he was chancellor of the Diocese of North Carolina. Personally generous, he endowed loan funds in honor of his father and wife as gifts to his diocese, to St. Mary's College in Raleigh, to The University of North Carolina, to East Carolina Teacher's College, and to North Carolina State College in Raleigh. Among his other pursuits, he was a member of the original board of trustees of the Roanoke Island Historical Association.

On 5 Nov. 1908 Andrews married Mary Helen Sharples, of Media, Pa. The couple had no children. Andrews died at his home in Raleigh and was buried in Oakwood Cemetery.

SEE: "Alexander Boyd Andrews," North Carolina Bar Association, *Proceedings* 30 (1928); Alexander Boyd Andrews, Jr., collection of pamphlets (North Carolina Collection, University of North Carolina, Chapel Hill); Alexander Boyd Andrews, Jr., Papers (Southern Historical Collection, University of North Carolina, Chapel Hill); Tom Bost, "With Us Tar Heels," *Greensboro Daily News*, 24 Oct. 1946; Gertrude S. Carraway, *Crown of Life: History of Christ Church, New Bern* (1940), and *Years of Light: History of St. John's Lodge* (1944); Walter Klein, "The Andrews Census," *Carolina Magazine*, May 1942; Paul Morris, "Thirty Years of the New History," *North Carolina Historical Review* 32 (1955).

BENNETT L. STEELMAN

Andrews, Robert Macon (*18 Aug. 1870–10 Mar. 1947*), Methodist Protestant minister, educator, and administrator, was the first president of High Point College. He was born near Chapel Hill, the son of Manly and Martha Cheek Andrews, and was educated in the public schools of Orange and Alamance counties, at Yadkin College, and at the Yale Divinity School. In 1896 he was admitted on trial into the North Carolina Annual Conference of the Methodist Protestant Church and served on the Roanoke circuit, in the Halifax County area, until 1898, when he was ordained an elder and elected into full membership in the conference. He was assigned that year to the Asheville and Swannanoa mission, and from then until 1900 he worked under the direction of the board of missions and church extension, making surveys in the interest of establishing churches. After 1900, Andrews served appointments on the Granville circuit; Grace Church, Greensboro (twice); Mebane; Henderson; Charlotte; and the West End and Bethel Battleground churches in Greensboro. Following his retirement in 1942, he served as the supply pastor of Mount Pleasant Church in the Greensboro district.

This succession of appointments was interrupted by six positions of high leadership in the Methodist Protestant Church. He twice served as president of the North Carolina annual conference (1917–21 and 1932–36); he was the field agent for the promotion of High Point College for two years and was immediately elected the first president of the college when it opened in 1924. From 1936 to 1939 he served as the editor of the *Methodist Protestant Herald*, published in Greensboro.

Andrews was eight times a delegate to the General Conference of the Methodist Protestant Church. He was also a delegate to the Uniting Conference of the Methodist Church in Kansas City in 1939. He was awarded the D.D. degree in June 1919 by Adrian College in Michigan.

Andrews married Olive Harris, a member of a prominent Methodist Protestant family in Henderson, on 15 Dec. 1909. His death occurred in Greensboro, and he was buried in the Mount Pleasant Cemetery there. Mrs. Andrews died on 25 May 1969.

SEE: J. Elwood Carroll, *History of the North Carolina Annual Conference of the Methodist Protestant Church* (1939); *Journal of the North Carolina Annual Conference of the Methodist Protestant Church*, scattered issues; Emmett

K. McLarty, Jr., *Memorial Service* (1947).

RALPH HARDEE RIVES

Andrews, Samuel (*fl. 1775–89*), a Loyalist leader during the Revolution, left his home in New Bern for Governor Josiah Martin's protection after the latter fled to the Cape Fear estuary in 1775. Commissioned a lieutenant by the governor, he fought at Moore's Creek Bridge and was taken prisoner to Halifax. He was released in October 1776 after taking the state oath of allegiance before the committee of safety. In 1781, Andrews raised a militia company in Bladen County and joined Cornwallis's forces. Part of the time he served under David Fanning, specializing in rescuing Loyalist prisoners and conducting them to the British areas. In 1782 he was in Charles Town as a major in Hector McNeill's regiment of the North Carolina militia.

At the evacuation of Charles Town, he went to East Florida, taking his wife, four children, and four slaves with him. There they lived on Doctor's Lagoon. Meanwhile, in North Carolina, Andrews was specifically excluded from the 1783 Act of Pardon and Oblivion. He reluctantly decided to go to Nova Scotia. In 1784 he told the Spanish authorities that he had not decided whether to remain in East Florida or to go with the British. He was in Shelburne, Nova Scotia, in 1785, and in 1788 he received 250 acres on the nearby Tusket River. He was living in the Shelburne area in 1789.

SEE: Walter Clark, ed., *State Records of North Carolina*, vol. 16 (1907); East Florida Papers, Bundle 323 A (Manuscript Division, Library of Congress, Washington, D.C.), for the 1784 census; Marion Gilroy, *Loyalists and Land Settlement in Nova Scotia* (1937); Public Archives of Nova Scotia, vol. 213 (Halifax, N.S.); Public Record Office, A.O., 13:138, for the Joseph Mercer claim, and T., 50:5; Lorenzo Sabine, *Biographical Sketches of Loyalists in the American Revolution* (1864; reprint ed., 1966); William L. Saunders, ed., *Colonial Records of North Carolina*, vol. 10 (1890).

CAROLE WATTERSON TROXLER

Anthony, Graham Hudson (*2 Apr. 1892–25 Dec. 1967*), industrialist, was born in Shelby, where his father, J. A. Anthony, was a lawyer. He received a B.E. in mechanical engineering from North Carolina State College in 1914 and an honorary Doctor of Engineering degree 3 Oct. 1942, for his contributions to the university. A big man, "Aus" played football, was active in campus affairs, and was popular with his classmates. After his graduation from college, he was employed by various manufacturing firms in New England; he finally settled in West Hartford, Conn., where he accomplished his most outstanding work in the computer industry. He was president and board chairman of the Veeder-Root Company (now Veeder Industries), a multimillion dollar firm manufacturing computer and machine parts. He was on the boards of ten other banking, insurance, and industrial firms and held the presidency of Colt's Patent Fire Arms Manufacturing Company (now Colt's, Inc.) from 1944 to 1949. He also served on the National War Labor Board during World War II and was a member of the board of the National Association of Manufacturers from 1936 to 1943.

His first wife, Elizabeth Johnson Anthony, daughter of a former mayor of Raleigh, James Iredell Johnson, died in 1953, leaving a son, James I. In 1954 he married Mrs. Mary Alice Stevens Kaiser, who had two sons from her previous marriage. Graham H. Anthony died in

Lancaster, Pa., while visiting his son for Christmas. He was outlived by two brothers, Oliver S. Anthony of Shelby and John A. Anthony of Norfolk, Va., and three sisters, Margaret Meagher, Mary Woodson, and Elizabeth Hauser of Shelby. His body was returned to West Hartford for funeral services and burial in the city's Fairview Cemetery.

SEE: *New York Times*, 29 Dec. 1967 (obit.). North Carolina State College *Agromeck* (1914); Raleigh *News and Observer*, 4 July 1943, 27 Dec. 1967 (obit.); Student Records, University of North Carolina Archives (Library, University of North Carolina, Chapel Hill).

D. A. YANCHISIN

Archdale, John (*ca. 5 May 1642–ca. 1710*), colonial governor and proprietary shareholder of Carolina, was born in England, the son of Thomas and Mary Nevill Archdale and the grandson of Richard Archdale, a London merchant. Archdale's first connection with America came through the marriage of his sister Mary to Ferdinando Gorges the younger, one of the heirs to the proprietorship of Maine. Claim to the proprietary was contested by the Massachusetts government, which annexed Maine in 1652 and governed the province until the restoration of Charles II, when Gorges moved to make good his claim. Gorges ordered Charles II proclaimed in the province, commissioned civil officers in opposition to the Massachusetts ones, and appealed to the Privy Council for confirmation of his proprietary rights. When, in 1664, Gorges received confirmation of his title to Maine, he sent Archdale to make good his claim against Massachusetts and to settle the government of Maine on a sure foundation under authority of his charter. Archdale's visit, however, coincided with the visit of the Crown's commissioners for the reduction of New Netherlands and for the investigation of the New England governments. The Crown commissioners disallowed both the Massachusetts and the Gorges claims to the civil government of Maine and established a government directly responsible to the Crown. Archdale returned to England in 1665; in 1677, Gorges sold to Massachusetts his proprietary title to the soil of Maine.

In December 1673, Archdale married Ann Dobson Cary, a widow whose son by her previous marriage, Thomas Cary, was subsequently deputy governor of North Carolina. The Archdales had by this marriage one son, Thomas, and a daughter, Mary.

Archdale's conversion to Quakerism occurred some time after 1674. In 1678 he bought the Berkeley of Stratton share in the proprietary of Carolina, though he subsequently made over the title to his infant son, Thomas. In 1682 Archdale made plans to visit Carolina on behalf of the proprietors in order to collect quitrents and to help quiet the disturbances in the colony. He arrived in the fall of 1683 and remained for about three years, during which period he acted intermittently as governer of North Carolina.

In July 1694, Thomas Smith, governor of the southern part of Carolina, requested that the proprietors send out a new governor with full powers to deal with the unrest and dissension among the colonists. The proprietors commissioned Archdale governor of both halves of Carolina, and he made a tour of the English colonies on his way to assume the government of the proprietary. He landed in Maine early in 1695 and traveled south, visiting every colony en route to Charleston, which he reached in August 1695. Once in Charleston he set about "to allay the heates" of the people, to moderate the differences between Dissenters and Churchmen, and to choose a council and call an assembly. At this time he appointed as deputy governor of South Carolina Joseph Blake, who was to carry out in that province many of Archdale's plans for the colony; his deputy governor for North Carolina was Thomas Harvey, who was also sympathetic to Archdale's program of reforms and who carried on his program there. Archdale tried to deal fairly with Huguenot settlers in the face of hostility from the English-speaking settlers in South Carolina.

During Archdale's tenure as governor, the South Carolina assembly passed a number of important acts, since known as Archdale's Laws. A poor law, a comprehensive slave law, and in recognition of Archdale's Quaker principles, a law exempting conscientious objectors from military duty were enacted. In both Carolinas compromises were reached over quitrents and land sales. Archdale is credited by some with introducing to the Carolinas seed-rice from Madagascar. He oversaw the construction of improved public roads and (in South Carolina) military fortifications, and he showed great tact in his dealings with the Spanish governor of St. Augustine.

In return for his outstanding services to the two provinces, Archdale received votes of thanks from both the North and South Carolina assemblies. In 1696 Archdale's son, Thomas, sold the Berkeley of Stratton share in the proprietary of Carolina to Joseph Blake, and Archdale returned to England. In 1698, Archdale was elected to the House of Commons as member for Wycombe. However, when Archdale offered to affirm rather than swear the oath required of members, the House refused to seat him. A by-election was held, and his brother Thomas was elected to fill the vacant seat.

Archdale purchased the Sir William Berkeley share of Carolina in 1705 and for three years took an active part as a member of the proprietary board. On 22 Oct. 1708 he sold his proprietary share to his son-in-law and daughter, John and Mary Danson, and died "a year or two" afterward, according to contemporary testimony by Maurice Ashley, a fellow proprietor of Carolina.

Archdale wrote a short article, undated but probably after 1702, entitled "Weighty Considerations," and presented it to the House of Commons for its consideration. In 1707 he published a short tract entitled *A New Description of that Fertile and Pleasant Province of Carolina with a Brief Account of Its Discovery and Settling and the Government thereof to this Time, with Several Remarkable Passages of Divine Providence during my Time.*

SEE: Archdale MSS (Manuscript Division, Library of Congress, Washington, D.C.); Samuel A. Ashe, ed., *Biographical History of North Carolina*, vol. 1 (1905); Henry G. Hood, Jr., *The Public Career of John Archdale (1642–1717)* (1976); William L. Saunders, ed., *Colonial Records of North Carolina*, vols. 1, 2, 4, 5 (1886–1887).

HENRY G. HOOD, JR.

Arderne, John (*d. ca. 1710*), first appears in the records of North Carolina in October 1701, acting as an attorney for his kinsman, the wealthy planter and former councilor William Duckenfield. At some time in 1702, Duckenfield conveyed to Arderne Salmon Creek Plantation, a four-thousand-acre tract formerly owned by Seth Sothel, the controversial proprietary governor. Arderne had come to North Carolina without any "visible estate," and Duckenfield agreed to sell him Salmon Creek Plantation for two hundred pounds, to advance his kinsman in the community. However,

Arderne never paid any portion of the two hundred pound price.

During 1703, Arderne served in the lower house of the assembly, but his activities there are not recorded. Deputy Governor Thomas Cary chose Arderne to sit on his Anglican-dominated council in March 1705; he was still there through October 1706 but does not appear in council records after that date.

Arderne served as a churchwarden and vestry member of St. Paul's Parish in Chowan Precinct during 1708 and was replaced in February 1709. At his death, which occurred sometime between early 1709 and early 1712, Arderne bequeathed his North Carolina property and his holdings in England to William Duckenfield. His will also refers to a brother living in "Clayton bridge house" in Lancashire, Manchester Parish, England. It seems likely that the house was Arderne's ancestral home.

SEE: Chancery Court Minutes for May 1713 (Secretary of State Papers 878, North Carolina State Archives, Raleigh); J. Bryan Grimes, ed., *Abstract of North Carolina Wills* (1910); J. R. B. Hathaway, ed., *North Carolina Historical and Genealogical Register*, vol. 2 (1901); William S. Price, Jr., ed., *North Carolina Higher-Court Records, 1702–1708* and *1709–1723* (1974 and [1977]); William L. Saunders, ed., *Colonial Records of North Carolina*, vol. 1 (1886).

WILLIAM S. PRICE, JR.

Arends, John Godfrey (*11 Dec. 1740–9 July 1807*), pioneer Lutheran minister, Revolutionary War patriot, and founding father and first president of the North Carolina Synod of the Lutheran Church, was born near Göttingen, Germany. Although little is known of Arends's personal history before he left Germany, upon his arrival in North Carolina, his life was recorded with dependable certainty. In 1772 the newly organized Lutheran congregations of North Carolina determined to send to Europe for a pastor and schoolmaster, as none could be obtained in America. The Lutheran delegation applied to the Consistory Council of Hanover. As Hanover at that time was an electorate of the Holy Roman Empire under the British ruling house, the delegation first sought the approval of the English throne. George III granted the delegation its petition for a schoolmaster, as well as a minister, and when Arends left for North Carolina, he took with him both his diploma from the Teachers' Seminary in Hanover and a personal recommendation and certification to teach from King George.

Arriving in 1773, Arends settled near Organ Church in Rowan County and began immediately to serve the congregation as schoolmaster. The Reverend Adolph Nussmann, who had accompanied him from Hanover, served as minister to the Organ Church for only one year before moving to Cabarrus, leaving his former congregation without a regular pastor. Realizing that it would be impossible to serve the needs of all the area Lutheran churches without another minister, the church turned to Arends, as he was the only other well-educated man in the vicinity. On 28 Aug. 1775, Arends was publicly examined and ordained into the ministry by the Reverend Joachim Buelow of South Carolina, and thus, Arends became the first man to be ordained a Lutheran minister in North Carolina.

For the next decade of his life, Arends served as itinerant minister in a vast area that today includes the counties of Rowan, Cabarrus, Iredell, Catawba, Lincoln,

Davidson, Guilford, Stokes, and others. According to
recent historian Carl Hammer, Jr., he "traveled long
distances on horseback in all kinds of weather, over bad
roads and forest paths, to spread the Gospel among
people who had long been without pastoral care." Before
his death in 1807, Arends had served nineteen churches
in the area, helping to found most of them.

Even though Arends's congregations received
financial assistance from territory under the rule of
George III, and though Arends, as a minister, was often
harassed, persecuted, and at times in danger of his life,
he took up the cause of American independence,
defying both British soldiers and American Tories.

In 1785, Arends moved to Lincoln County. In all, he
either helped organize, or was the first regular minister
of, nine churches in the Catawba Valley. These years
were spent busily ministering to the needs of his many
congregations. He traveled by horseback from one
church to the next, often as far as fifty miles a day,
preaching, baptizing, and confirming his parishioners.
At the same time, he was also a gentleman planter.

In the years 1800–1801, there occurred a phenomenon
that spurred Arends to perhaps his most notable
historical accomplishment. In these years, the so-called
Great Revival, which had begun in Kentucky, spread
into the Carolinas, bringing with it a kind of religious
hysteria involving "convulsions, prostrations, the
involuntary gnashing of teeth, strange exercises," and
the "jerks." As the official U.S. Lutheran history
indicates, because of their concern over this "outburst of
intensive religious activity" and the "alarming
deterioration of both faith and morals" among the
general populace, the Lutheran ministers of North
Carolina saw "the need for some authoritative
organization."

Hence, on 2 May 1803, Arends and three fellow
ministers met at St. John's Church in Salisbury with
fourteen lay delegates from various Lutheran
congregations and organized the North Carolina Synod
of the Lutheran Church. Arends was elected the first
president. The North Carolina Synod was the third
Lutheran synod to be founded in America, following
those in Pennsylvania (1748) and New York (1786).

In 1776, Arends married pioneer Michael Rudisill's
daughter, Hannah; they had eight children, the
descendants of whom are prominent today in western
North Carolina. The graves of the Reverend and Mrs.
Arends were moved in 1920 to the cemetery adjoining
the original Old White Church, which burned in 1893.
To commemorate the two-hundredth anniversary of
Arends's arrival in North Carolina from Germany, a
special celebration was held at Organ Church near
Salisbury in 1973, at which time a statue of the pioneer
minister was unveiled.

Arends's last years were spent in blindness. He died
in 1807 and was buried beneath the pulpit of the Old
White Church in Lincolnton.

SEE: Austin Allran, "John Godfrey Arends" (North
Carolina Collection, University of North Carolina,
Chapel Hill); G. D. Bernheim and George H. Cox,
*History of the Evangelical Lutheran Synod and Ministerium
of North Carolina* (1902); Carl Hammer, Jr., *Rhinelanders
on the Yadkin* (1965); Jacob L. Morgan et al., eds.,
History of the Lutheran Church in North Carolina (1953).

AUSTIN ALLRAN

Argo, Thomas Munro *(30 Apr. 1841–14 Jan. 1909)*,
Confederate officer, attorney, solicitor, and legislator,

was born in Weteumpka, Ala. A few years later, his
family moved to McMinville, Tenn., where young Argo
lived during his boyhood and obtained his early
education. He was the eldest of seven children of
William Hammond Argo and Julia Cain. His parents
were originally from North Carolina, and his father was
of French Huguenot extraction. From Tennessee, Argo
moved to North Carolina in 1860 to enter the university.
He was graduated with honors in the class of 1863.
Following graduation, he immediately entered the
Confederate Army, enlisting in the First North Carolina
Heavy Artillery, and was commissioned second
lieutenant of Company D by Governor Zebulon B.
Vance. He was wounded and captured in the defense of
Fort Fisher in January 1865 and remained a prisoner until
the end of the hostilities. He returned to Chapel Hill in
1865 and studied law under William A. Battle and S. F.
Phillips. He received the LL.B. degree and was admitted
to practice law in 1867, beginning his profession in
Chapel Hill. In 1868 and 1870 he was elected from
Orange County to the legislature as a Democrat (at that
time called a Conservative). His ability was quickly
recognized by his associates, and he was an active
representative, although the Republican was the
dominant party of that day. He figured prominently in
the fight to drive the carpetbaggers from the state.

Argo removed to Raleigh in 1872, where he resided
and continued to pursue his legal profession for the
remainder of his life. In 1884 he was a leader in the
formation of the state bar association, serving as
secretary of the organization for some time. In 1886 he
was elected solicitor of the fourth judicial district, an
office he held until 1891. Running as an independent
candidate against the regular Democratic nominee, he
won by a wide majority. During his term, he was
connected with much of the important litigation in the
courts of Wake and the adjacent counties and frequently
acted as leading counsel. Among his prominent cases
was that of Samuel Coley against the Southern Railway.
He also prosecuted the famous case *State* v. *Cross and
White*; Cross and White were officials of the State
National Bank in Raleigh who had wrecked the
institution and fled to Canada. Argo had decided
political convictions and was for many years a
conservative Republican on the national level. In state
and local issues he was an independent. His political
affiliation, as may be surmised, restricted his career to
some extent, in a community so largely Democratic and
characterized in former years more conspicuously than
in later years by political intolerance.

Legal activities did not prevent Argo from taking part
in civic and local affairs. He served as a member of the
board of directors and of the executive committee of the
insane asylum. He was a member of the William G. Hill
Masonic Lodge No. 214. An Episcopalian, he was one of
twenty-two men who signed a petition to form a second
white Episcopal church in Raleigh. He was a charter
member of the Church of the Good Shepherd, organized
in 1874.

Argo was married first in 1864, to Mattie Hubbard; to
them was born one son, Fordyce M. Following his first
wife's death, Argo married Mrs. Kate Baker in 1876; she
died in 1886. On 4 June 1893 he married Mrs. Ernestine
Spears Perry. To this union were born three children,
Thomas, Ruth, and Laura. In 1908 it became apparent
that Argo's health was failing, but until this last illness
he was an active member of the Raleigh bar. He died at
the age of sixty-eight and was buried in Raleigh's
Oakwood Cemetery.

SEE: Samuel A. Ashe, ed., *Biographical History of North Carolina*, vol. 3 (1905); Carrie L. Broughton, ed., *Marriage and Death Notices* (n.d.), for 1867–93; Ernest Haywood, ed., *Some Notes in Regard to the Eminent Lawyers* (1936); W. S. O'Brien, *North Carolina Bar Association Report of 1909, North Carolina Bar Association Proceedings, 1899–1948*; Raleigh *News and Observer*, 14 Jan. 1909; *Raleigh Times*, 14 Jan. 1909; LaRene R. Ward, ed., *Therefore with Angels and Archangels, 1874–1974* (1974).

ELIZABETH E. NORRIS

Armfield, Eugene Morehead (*12 Apr. 1904–23 Nov. 1953*), writer, teacher, and translator, was born in Thomasville, the son of Jesse L. Armfield, first cashier of the Bank of Thomasville, and Dion Griffith Armfield, whose parents for many years operated the Thomasville Hotel. After high school, Armfield attended Culver Military Academy, Culver, Ind., for two years and then came home to enter The University of North Carolina. His major was French and the romance languages, and as an undergraduate instructor during his senior year he taught several classes in French. After being graduated with the class of 1925, he went to Harvard for further study, with the intention of becoming a teacher of languages. He earned his master's degree the following year and at this point went to France to study for a time at the Sorbonne. While there, he had a hand in compiling two textbooks that found limited use in the study of the French language.

Armfield returned to Harvard, where he continued and completed the academic work for the doctorate except for the required dissertation. His enthusiasm for a teaching career was, in fact, beginning to wane and was being superseded by a strong urge to write. Leaving Harvard, he secured a position with *Publishers' Weekly* in New York City, where, as an associate editor, he had ample opportunity to write articles on books, authors, and related topics. Dozens of his short stories were published in the little magazines of the time, and one published in Henry Mencken's *American Mercury* gave him his first national audience.

Soon thereafter, *Story Magazine* published Armfield's "Little Acorns," a tale of life in a military school stemming from his experiences at Culver Military Academy. This narrative contained elements of excellence that attracted the attention of editors, making it easier for him to find a publisher for his first (and only) novel, half finished at the time. *Where the Weak Grow Strong* was published by Covoci Friede in 1936. In it Armfield described a series of incidents in a small southern town in the fall of 1912, allowing the reader to peer behind the window curtains and between the sheets of families in social strata ranging from the factory environment to the most exalted social level. That the locale was his native Thomasville was shortly made manifest by anguished cries of outrage from his fellow townspeople. The identification of characters in *Where the Weak Grow Strong* with a number of Thomasville families was evidently not difficult.

Eugene Armfield was never married, but he found considerable time to give attention to women. Not actually estranged from his family, he nevertheless went his own way and maintained a lifestyle foreign to the conventional ways of his southern kin. At the time of his death, he was living with a devoted woman of some means on Long Island, and there he was buried.

SEE: Eugene Morehead Armfield, *Where the Weak Grow Strong* (1936); Henry M. Armfield and Lucille Armfield Bruton, personal interviews (1974); M. Jewell Sink and Mary Green Matthews, *Pathfinders Past and Present* (1972); *State Magazine* 30 (26 Dec. 1936).

WILLIAM UNDERWOOD

Armfield, Joseph Franklin (*24 Jan. 1862–10 Oct. 1910*), colonel of a regiment of North Carolina troops in the Spanish-American War and later brigadier general and adjutant general of the North Carolina State Guard, was born at Yadkinville, son of Robert F. Armfield, well-known legislator and criminal attorney, and Mary Ann Denny Armfield. His father was at one time president of the North Carolina Senate, later a representative in the U.S. House of Representatives from the North Carolina Seventh District, and finally a superior court judge.

Armfield spent most of his life in Statesville, where his father moved in 1870, and was educated there in the common schools and at the Statesville Male Academy. Primarily, he was a farmer, but he was best known in his military career. When a young man, he enlisted in the Iredell Blues, the local military company that had been reorganized after the Civil War. He rose quickly to the captaincy of the Blues and after about six years in that position was elected colonel of his regiment, then the Fourth Regiment of the North Carolina State Guard.

At the outbreak of the war with Spain in 1898, his regiment volunteered; after being mustered in, in May, it was reorganized as the First North Carolina Regiment, with Armfield as its colonel. As the war progressed, it was stationed at Jacksonville, Fla.; after the surrender of the Spanish forces, it was the only North Carolina regiment to be sent to Cuba. In April 1899 it was brought home and disbanded after about eleven months of service. Much of that time, Armfield was acting brigadier general in the absence of the regular general. At the beginning of the administration of Governor Charles B. Aycock in 1901, he was appointed brigadier general of the North Carolina State Guard. He held that position until he was appointed adjutant general of the guard by Governor W. W. Kitchen in 1909.

Armfield spent the latter part of his life at the old Armfield homestead in Statesville, with a married sister and her husband, Dr. and Mrs. W. J. Hill. He came home in early October of 1910, suffering from Bright's disease, and died soon after. He was buried with full military honors, with most of the state's dignitaries attending, in Oakwood Cemetery in Statesville.

SEE: Statesville *Landmark*, 1898–99, 14 Oct. 1910.

HOMER M. KEEVER

Armfield, Robert Franklin (*9 July 1829–9 Nov. 1898*), attorney, legislator, and judge, was born in Guilford County, west of Greensboro, near the present-day Pomona. He was the third son of Robert Armfield of an old Quaker family, whose ancestor, John Armfield, had led a band of settlers to the section in about 1765.

At the age of fourteen, Robert Franklin Armfield began attending Union Institute in Randolph County, the school that, after a series of metamorphoses, became Duke University. At the time, it was an academy under the control of Braxton Craven. Until he was twenty, Armfield alternated between study at Union Institute and teaching in public schools. Then he read law under John A. Gilmer, was licensed, and settled in the newly created town of Yadkinville to practice his profession.

In 1861 he was elected from Yadkin County to the secession convention and signed the Ordinance of

Secession. In February of 1862 he enlisted in Company B, Thirty-eighth Regiment of North Carolina troops, as first lieutenant. When the regiment was reorganized, he was elected lieutenant colonel. He was involved in the Seven Days fighting around Richmond and was wounded at Shephardstown in October. While he was at home on furlough, he was appointed solicitor of the Sixth Judicial District by the legislature, resigned from the army, and held the office of solicitor until he was removed by President Andrew Johnson at the end of the war.

In the summer of 1865 he moved to Wilkesboro and from there, in the fall of 1870, to Statesville, where he spent the remainder of his life. Statesville at the time was the hub of an eleven-county congressional district including Wilkes, Yadkin, and Rowan. In 1874 he considered running for the U.S. House of Representatives, but when a survey showed the popularity of the incumbent, W. M. Robbins, his fellow townsman of Statesville, Armfield withdrew and accepted the nomination to the North Carolina Senate. He was elected and was chosen president pro tem when the senate organized. Since Lieutenant Governor Curtis H. Brogden had been elevated to the governorship by the death of Governor Tod R. Caldwell, Armfield became next in line for the governorship and acquired the sobriquet Governor Armfield.

In 1878, in what Robbins considered a "rump convention," Armfield received the Democratic nomination for the House, and with the backing of Robbins he was elected. A split developed in the Democratic party between the supporters of Armfield, mainly from Wilkes and Yadkin counties, and those of Robbins, primarily from Rowan, where Robbins was living when first elected to Congress. That factionalism finally cost Statesville and the Democrats the representation in Congress. In 1880 the fight for the nomination was hard, with Armfield winning in the convention and easily defeating his fellow townsman, David Furches, in the election. Two years later, Robbins won the nomination but was defeated in the election by Dr. Tyre York, Democrat turned Republican from Wilkes County. In 1884, Armfield made a good fight for the nomination in a new district that still included Iredell, Rowan, and Yadkin counties, but not Wilkes; he lost, nonetheless, and the congressional seat went back to Rowan.

In January 1889, Governor Alfred M. Scales appointed Armfield a judge of the superior court, and in 1890 he was elected to fill the unexpired term of the man he replaced. He retired from the bench 1 Jan. 1895 and died at his home in Statesville several years later.

It was as a criminal lawyer that Armfield won his reputation. In one of his better known cases, he cooperated with Zebulon B. Vance to defend Tom Dula for the murder of Laura Foster during Reconstruction days.

On 13 Jan. 1857, Armfield married Mary Ann Denny of Guilford County. One of their sons, C. H. Armfield, became a prominent lawyer in Statesville. Another, Joseph Franklin, was a leader in the North Carolina militia and brigadier general of the North Carolina State Guard.

SEE: *Biog. Dir. Am. Cong.* (1950); Statesville *Landmark*, 11 Nov. 1898.

HOMER M. KEEVER

Armfield, Wyatt Jackson (*25 Nov. 1843–12 Oct. 1933*), banker and businessman, was born near High Point on

the Armfield family plantation, the son of Richard Beeson Armfield and Annie Chipman Armfield. The family was originally from England and of Quaker stock.

Armfield grew up on his father's farm and enrolled at Oak Ridge Institute just before the Civil War. When the war forced the school to close, he went into the quartermaster corps of the Confederate army and worked in the Jamestown Woolen Mill, which had contracted to supply the gray uniforms for Confederate soldiers. The mill was burned by Stoneman's Raiders in the closing days of the war.

No sooner had smoke cleared from the battlefields than Armfield set out for the West and obtained employment in sales with a nursery at Knightstown, Ind. He built a sales organization for the firm and traveled extensively throughout the eastern half of the nation, selling fruit trees and shrubbery. By the 1880s he returned to North Carolina.

On 20 Dec. 1866, Armfield married Jennie Britt, daughter of J. O. Britt, a large landowner and peanut grower of Britt's Landing in Perry County, Tenn. She died in 1918, after many years of presiding over the stately mansion, Brittania, at High Point, where Armfield had built an extensive banking empire reaching through most of central Carolina.

Armfield was instrumental in the establishment of the first national bank in Greensboro, known at the time as the National Bank of Greensboro. With associates, he set up the National Bank of High Point in 1886 and, when the cashier returned to his Wilmington home, installed as cashier his son, Eugene, who had just been graduated from The University of North Carolina. Others of his sons, W. J., Jr., Frank, and Jesse, were placed in various of the branch banks Armfield set up in Asheboro, Thomasville, Madison, Graham, Troy, Mocksville, and other places in the state.

Rechartered after twenty years, the bank in High Point was liquidated in 1908, paying all depositors in full and providing stockholders 111 percent on their investment. Armfield retired from active banking and enjoyed gathering his children and grandchildren about him at his home, one of the finest in High Point. On Deep River near High Point, his descendants continue to hold land that has been in the family since 1795.

Armfield saw High Point grow from a water tank village to an industrial and furniture-marketing center. As one of the state's pioneer bankers, he knew both depressions and booms and bore an equal contempt for each.

During his lifetime, Armfield took an avid interest in numerous civic and educational enterprises, including founding of the High Point Public Library.

Armfield's children, in addition to those mentioned as banking and business associates, included Mrs. Rupert T. Pickens of High Point and Mrs. Frank Armfield of Concord.

Upon Armfield's death, his body was placed in the family mausoleum at Oakwood Cemetery in High Point.

SEE: Manuscript sketches written for an additional volume of Samuel A. Ashe, ed., *Biographical History of North Carolina* (Library, Duke University, Durham).

HOLT MCPHERSON

Armistead, Lewis Addison (*18 Feb. 1817–3 July 1863*), Confederate general, was born in New Bern, while his mother, Elizabeth Stanly, wife of army officer Walter Keith Armistead, was visiting her parents, former Congressman John Stanly (1775–1833), son of John

Wright Stanly, and Elizabeth Frank Stanly, daughter of Martin Frank (Franck) of Jones County.

The Armisteads had been in America since William Armistead came from Yorkshire, England, about 1735, to Virginia. William's grandson Henry resided in Gloucester County and married Martha Burwell. Their grandson John and his wife, Mary Baylor, were the parents of the "Military Armisteads."

Walter Keith Armistead (1785–1845), youngest son of John and Mary Armistead, was in military service, as were his four brothers. A member of the second graduating class at the U.S. Military Academy, West Point, he took part in the War of 1812 and the Seminole War, became the army's chief engineer, and at the time of his death, with the rank of brevet brigadier general, was second in command of the army. One of Walter's brothers, Major George A. Armistead (1780–1818), was known as "the hero of Fort McHenry." He commanded the fort in September 1814, when, during its bombardment by the British Fleet, Francis Scott Key wrote "The Star-Spangled Banner," designated by Congress in 1931 as the national anthem. After the battle, Major Armistead was breveted to lieutenant colonel, retroactive to 12 Sept. 1814.

Lewis Armistead, desiring to follow his father and uncles in an army career, was admitted 1 Sept. 1834 to the military academy. An untoward incident prevented his completing its courses. Another cadet, Jubal A. Early, later "a fire-eating soldier" for the Confederacy, is reported to have "insulted" him on the parade ground. At mess, in retaliation, Armistead cracked Early over the head with a plate and was, as a result, dismissed 15 Feb. 1836.

Still determined to carry on the family profession, he was graduated from a military school in North Carolina and on 10 July 1839 became a second lieutenant in the Sixth Regiment, U.S. Infantry, commanded by Zachary Taylor. He fought against the Seminoles under General Taylor and also under his father, and in 1844 he was promoted to first lieutenant.

During the Mexican War he led the storming party at Chapultepec, participated in other battles, and won a reputation for bravery and aggressive fighting. After the war he served fourteen years on the western frontier. In 1855 he was breveted captain and then promoted to major.

In the summer of 1860 he told a disconsolate friend, "I know but one country and one flag. Let me sing you a song and drive away your gloom." He sang "The Star-Spangled Banner." However, when the necessity for choice came, he did not hesitate to prefer the Confederacy. At Los Angeles he presented his major's uniform to a friend, Winfield Scott Hancock, then a captain and brevet major, with the remark, "Some day you may need this." They met later at Gettysburg.

Resigning from the U.S. Army on 26 May 1861, Armistead joined General Albert Sidney Johnston and other officers who had resigned and journeyed with them across the continent from Vallecito to San Antonio, New Orleans, and Richmond. He entered Confederate service as a colonel at Richmond. On 1 Apr. 1862 he was commissioned brigadier general.

Displaying conspicuous gallantry, bravery, and coolness under fire at Seven Pines, Malvern Hill, Second Manassas, and Sharpsburg, he was appointed provost marshal of the Confederate army. General Robert E. Lee personally thanked him for the ability and efficiency with which he discharged the duties of that position.

On 3 July 1863, the third day of the Battle of Gettysburg, the guiding point for the Confederate charge was a clump of trees just beyond a low stone wall. Putting his hat on the point of his sword, Armistead mounted his horse and called in stentorian tones for the men of his brigade to follow him through a rain of shot and shell toward the Union position on Cemetery Hill. General George E. Pickett, who directed the charge from a nearby house, was not present to lead his division. Two other generals were put out of action. Armistead automatically assumed leadership. His horse was shot from under him, but he dashed forward on foot and was the first to leap over the stone wall. Some thirty-odd yards beyond the wall, he laid his hand on a cannon, with the proud announcement, "This cannon is mine." But he was then riddled with bullets and fell, mortally wounded. Within a few minutes he died, at the "high-water mark" of the Confederacy.

His body was buried in a vault in St. Paul's cemetery at Baltimore, Md. A memorial plaque was dedicated there in recent years by the General Lewis Addison Armistead Chapter, United Daughters of the Confederacy, of Washington, D.C.

General Armistead was married to Cecelia Lee Love, daughter of Richard H. Love of Fairfax County, Va; they had one son, Walker Keith, who married the granddaughter of Daniel Webster.

SEE: G. S. Carraway, *The Stanly Family* (1969); *DAB*, vol. 1 (1928); *The War of the Rebellion: A Compilation of the Official Records of the Union and Confederate Armies*, series 1, vols. 6, 9–12, 18, 19, 21, 27, 29, 30, 33, 36, 50, 51 (1881–97); *William and Mary Quarterly* 6 (Jan. 1898).

GERTRUDE S. CARRAWAY

Armstrong, Frank Alton, Jr. (*24 May 1902–20 Aug. 1969*), air force officer, was born in Hamilton, the son of Frank Alton and Annie Elizabeth Hobbs Armstrong. Upon the completion of high school and preparatory school, Armstrong entered Wake Forest College, where he played varsity football and baseball for five years. He received the LL.B. degree in 1922 and the B.S. degree in 1925. Following graduation, he played professional baseball for a Sarasota, Fla., minor league team before enlisting as a flying cadet with the U.S. Army in 1928.

Following cadet training at Brooks Field, Tex., Armstrong was commissioned a second lieutenant in the U.S. Army Air Corps. Between 1930 and 1934 he served as a flying instructor at various air bases in the United States and in 1934 was assigned to air mail duty, flying domestic mail between Burbank, Calif., and Las Vegas, Nev. From 1935 to 1938 he was stationed in the Panama Canal Zone, with pursuit and observation squadrons operating out of Albrook Field.

After returning to the United States, Armstrong assumed command of the Thirteenth Bombardment Squadron. In October 1940 he was selected to visit England as an American military observer. During his three months in war-torn London, Armstrong witnessed the German blitz bombing of England and marveled at the determination of the British people. His observations and reports became vital for planning American air operations in Europe once the United States entered World War II late in 1941. By February of 1942, he was back in England as Operations Officer for the U.S. Army Air Corps Bomber Command. As lieutenant colonel and then as colonel, Armstrong served as bombardment group commander, wing commander, and ultimately division commander of the Eighth Bomber Command. On 17 Aug. 1942, Armstrong led the first U.S. daylight bombing raid over enemy territory, striking targets at

Rouen-Cotteville, France. In December 1942 he was promoted to brigadier general and given command of the 306th Heavy Bombardment Group. On 27 Jan. 1943 he commanded the first U.S. heavy bombing raid over Germany, which bombed Wilhelmshaven. Armstrong's experiences in Europe during this period became the basis for the successful book and motion picture *Twelve O'Clock High*.

After returning to the United States in August 1943, he commanded Air Corps training at Colorado Springs, Colo., and became commanding general of the 315th Bombardment Wing (Very Heavy). The 315th, which was to see action in the Pacific Theater of Operations, was provided with the new B-29 bomber, rather than the B-17 Flying Fortress bombers used against Germany. The planes were equipped with a new "Eagle" airborne radar for precision night bombing, and all guns except the tail guns had been removed to permit heavier bomb loads. The 315th was transferred to Guam during May 1945, and for three months it devastated Japanese petroleum refineries and storage centers. On 15 Aug. 1945 Armstrong commanded the longest and last nonstop combat flight of World War II, flying round trip from Guam to Honshu, Japan. When the war ended, Armstrong flew the first nonstop flight from Japan (Hokkaido) to Washington, D.C.

After spending 1946 as chief of staff for Operations of the Pacific Air Command, Armstrong returned to the United States as senior air advisor at the Armed Forces Staff College, Norfolk, Va. In May 1948 he was ordered to Alaska as chief of staff of the Alaskan Air Command. While in Alaska, in September 1949, Armstrong and other members of the Air Command pioneered an air route from Alaska across the North Pole to Norway and from Norway to New York.

After returning to the mainland in 1950, Armstrong was promoted to major general. He became a part of the Strategic Air Command at McDill Air Force Base, and in October 1952 he took command of the Second Air Force at Barksdale Air Force Base, La. In July 1956 he returned to Alaska to head the Alaskan Air Command, becoming two months later commander in chief, Alaska, with the rank of lieutenant general. Armstrong was deeply disturbed over the inadequate defense of Alaska. On numerous occasions he urged the deployment of intermediate range ballistic missles (IRBMs) in Alaska as a vital link in the American defense system. His contention that Alaska was a logical debarkation point for a Russian attack upon the United States failed to rally support from a Cold War administration married to the "Fortress America" concept of defense. On several occasions his views brought him in sharp conflict with the chairman of the Joint Chiefs of Staff and the secretary of defense. Armstrong retired from the air force in July 1961 after thirty-three years of service.

Among the many decorations Armstrong received for his services were the Distinguished Flying Cross with four Oak Leaf Clusters; the Distinguished Service Medal with Oak Leaf Cluster; the Silver Star; the British Distinguished Flying Cross (first British air medal awarded to a U.S. airman during World War II); the Gold Medal of the Aero Club of Norway (the highest civil award of Norway); Belgium's Croix de Guerre with palm; and the U.S. Conservation Service Award for leadership in wildlife conservation in Alaska.

In 1929, Armstrong married Vernelle Lloyd (Fluffy) Hudson of Richmond, Va., who died in February 1962. He married again; his second wife, Mrs. Peggy Jenison Lippe, died in April 1973. Armstrong's only son, Major

Frank A. Armstrong, III, was killed in action over Vietnam in 1967.

General Armstrong died at his home in Tampa, Fla., and was buried in Arlington Cemetery.

SEE: Frank A. Armstrong, Jr., Papers (East Carolina Manuscript Collection, Greenville); W. F. Craven and J. L. Cate, eds., *The Army Air Forces in World War II* (1948–58); Raleigh *News and Observer*, 21 Aug. 1969 (obit.); *Who Was Who in America*, vol. 5 (1973).

DONALD R. LENNON

Armstrong, James (*d. 1794*), revolutionary officer, was a resident of Pitt County during the Revolution and until his death. Little is known of his ancestry or his family, but he was apparently a well-to-do planter and leader in his community. He was elected a major in the Pitt County militia in September 1775. On 30 Nov. 1776 he was appointed colonel of the Eighth Regiment of North Carolina Continental troops. He was also a member of the Pitt County Committee of Safety in 1776. In September 1777 he led his troops in the Battle of Brandywine, near Philadelphia, and his regiment suffered such casualties that it was dissolved and its remnants combined with the Second North Carolina Continentals. Following this battle, Armstrong presided over a court of inquiry into the conduct of another North Carolina officer, Colonel Gideon Lamb, in which the latter was acquitted. On 1 June 1778, Armstrong resigned from the Continental forces; he later became a colonel in the North Carolina militia. In this capacity he took part in the Battle of Stono Ferry, S.C., 20 June 1779, where he was wounded. In 1780 he was in charge of recruiting for the North Carolina forces in the eastern part of the state and on 6 Feb. 1781 was made brigadier general of the militia in the New Bern area. Shortly afterward, he retired at half pay; he later received for his military services a grant of 7,200 acres of land in Tennessee.

In 1782, Armstrong became Commissioner of Confiscated Property for the District of New Bern and in 1784 a member of the North Carolina Governor's Council of State. From 1788 to 1790 he served in the state legislature. In November 1789 he represented Pitt County at the convention in Fayetteville, when North Carolina ratified the Constitution of the United States.

James Armstrong died late in 1794, and his descendants subsequently left the area. According to the census of 1790, he owned ten slaves at that time and may have had as many as four sons and two daughters.

SEE: Henry T. King, *Sketches of Pitt County . . . 1704–1910* (1911); Hugh F. Rankin, *The North Carolina Continentals* (1971); William L. Saunders and Walter Clark, eds., *Colonial and State Records of North Carolina*, 26 vols. (1886–1907).

ELMER D. JOHNSON

Armstrong, John (*27 Nov. 1798–15 Sept. 1844*), Baptist minister and educator, was born in Philadelphia, Pa., the son of Robert and Mary Armstrong. His early life was spent in poverty, and he served an apprenticeship as a tinker. Before he was sixteen years old, however, he was converted and felt called to preach the Gospel. Armstrong placed himself under the care of the Reverend William Staughton, who directed his education, first in the Institute in Philadelphia and later at Columbian College, Washington, D.C. He was graduated with a B.A. degree in 1825 and moved to Nashville, N.C., as headmaster of a school. Within two years he was recognized as one of the most prominent Baptists in the state and was named director of the North Carolina Baptist Benevolent Society at its first meeting on 10 Feb. 1829.

A new epoch in Armstrong's life began with the organization of the Baptist State Convention at Greenville, 26 Mar. 1830. He was one of the seventeen men who inaugurated this enterprise and was elected the first corresponding secretary of the convention, a place he held during his remaining seven and a half years in North Carolina.

In 1830, Samuel Wait resigned the New Bern pastorate to become the agent of the Baptist State Convention. Armstrong was called to fill the vacancy in April 1830 and served the church until May 1834.

Armstrong's interest in ministerial education was manifested as early as 1831, when he proposed to the Baptist State Convention to give free instruction to any young ministers that the convention would send him. His greatest work in North Carolina was in connection with Wake Forest College. His labors for Wake Forest began as soon as its establishment was proposed and continued with enthusiasm as long as he remained in the state. As corresponding secretary of the convention, he had the chief direction of the plans for its opening. He was a charter member of the board of trustees and a member of the committee that chose Samuel Wait as the first president. Armstrong was a very persuasive advocate of the manual labor feature of the Wake Forest Institute and on 19 Jan. 1833 delivered a lecture in Raleigh on this subject.

The board of trustees decided in May 1834 to erect a large college building to house both dormitories and classrooms. The cost of this structure would be ten thousand dollars, and the trustees asked Armstrong to go into the field and raise the money. Though he had traveled in only five counties in eastern North Carolina, he had already raised more than $13,500 when the convention met in November of that year. Before the first of February 1835, he had increased subscriptions to $17,000. Of this amount, more than $13,500 was collected. This accomplishment will appear more remarkable when it is realized that there were at that time not more than thirteen thousand Baptists in North Carolina.

As a college professor, Armstrong had a brief but most eventful career. Though elected to the chair of ancient languages at Wake Forest earlier, he did not enter upon its duties until the opening of the second session in February 1835. He made out the first course of studies for Wake Forest, and although the school was only a manual labor institute, his faith in the future of the school was such that he planned a college program. To Armstrong, Wake Forest owes the beginnings of its library; he served as first librarian of the school. Each of the literary societies had its own library, but the selection and purchase of books was under the care of Armstrong. He also had a leading role in the organization of the two literary societies. He had been at the institution only two weeks when, on 14 Feb. 1835, he delivered an address to the students on "The Value of Polemic Studies." At its conclusion, the Philomathesian and Euzelian societies were formed. Dr. G. W. Paschal credits Armstrong with the writing of both society constitutions and the adoption of parliamentary procedures. In addition to the orations and other exercises of the societies, the students gave a play written by Armstrong, concerning the rescue of a maiden captured by the Indians. The play, which

Paschal credits as being the first college play ever written and performed in North Carolina, was presented at night in a hollow north of the campus.

Armstrong was full of devices for the physical, moral, and spiritual improvement of the students. When he had been at Wake Forest for only a month, he lectured the students on the evils of coffee. As a result the students pledged themselves to substitute molasses and water for coffee for a space of three months; ten students "formed a society for the use of pure water." Later, under Armstrong's influence, nearly every student in the institution resolved to abstain from the use of tobacco.

Armstrong was a leader in religious activities at Wake Forest. It was said of him, "In the pulpit, in the prayer meeting, in the student Society of Inquiry, in Bible classes, in a special theological class for young ministers, in special addresses, in ordinary times and times of revival, he was indefatigable in his religious zeal and work." When the Wake Forest Baptist Church was organized on 30 Aug. 1835, he was most active and served, with Samuel Wait, as assistant pastor. The diaries of W. T. Brooks, a student, contain the texts of many of Armstrong's sermons and lectures, which demonstrate that during his tenure at Wake Forest he was possessed with a passion to provide the Baptists of North Carolina with an educated ministry.

In July 1837, Armstrong was granted a leave of absence for two years to study in Europe. On 17 July 1837 he embarked at New York for Havre. For two years in France and Italy he pursued a course of reading and visiting places of historical interest. In a series of letters published in the *Biblical Recorder*, he left a most interesting account of his observations from 30 Dec. 1837, when he was in Lyons, France, until he reached Geneva on 5 Apr. 1838. In not twice as many days, Armstrong wrote forty-eight letters of an average length of about three thousand words. He kept a journal of his notes and studies and even prepared a manuscript volume of his travels, but many travel books were appearing at this time and he hesitated to publish his. After his death the journals and manuscripts were lost. When he returned to Wake Forest, he found that his place had been filled during his absence. Armstrong appeared before the trustees in the fall of 1839 and offered his resignation. The trustees refused it, but he insisted and was released at a later board meeting. "Wake Forest never received a greater blow," according to a later historian.

He received an invitation from the church at Columbus, Miss., and began his work there in the spring of 1840. He led the church in paying off its heavy debt and increased the church membership. He moved to Noxubee County, Miss., in the spring of 1843 and lived on one of the plantations belonging to his wife. He continued to preach in the neighborhood and instructed a number of scholars in the classics. He attended the meetings of the Mississippi Baptist Convention and was moderator of the Columbus Association in 1843.

Armstrong married Mrs. Pamela Pouncy, a member of the Columbus, Miss., Baptist Church, in July 1842. There apparently were no children. In 1844 Armstrong contracted a fever that, taking a severe form, brought him to his death.

SEE: W. T. Brooks, MS diaries (Baptist Historical Collection, Wake Forest University, Winston-Salem); Hight C. Moore, "A Century of Service" (typescript, 13 Nov. 1934, Baptist Collection, Wake Forest University, Winston-Salem); George W. Paschal,

Wake Forest Student, 46 (May 1929); Raleigh *Biblical Recorder*, 5 and 19 Oct. 1844, 3 May 1845; William B. Sprague, *Annals of the American Pulpit*, vol. 6 (1860).

JOHN R. WOODARD

Armstrong, Martin *(ca. 1739–1808)*, Revolutionary War soldier, surveyor, and politician, was born in Augusta County, Va., the fourth son of James and Jean Armstrong, previously of Lancaster County, Pa. About 1750, the Armstrongs moved from Virginia to Anson County, N.C., and settled on the banks of the Catawba River. In time, the family spread south, but Martin Armstrong settled in Surry County, where more than fifty land patents were issued in his name. Land speculation, furthered by his craft as a surveyor, seems to have been his main activity.

In 1770 he was appointed commissioner to run the dividing line between Rowan and the new county of Surry and to lay out and sell lots for building the town of Richmond. Rival factions had struggled over the location of the county seat; the Armstrong brothers, Martin and John, eventually won through unscrupulous maneuvers. Later, when the town of Clarksville in Davidson County was formed, Martin Armstrong was appointed to lay it out. Both towns were situated on land owned by either Martin or John Armstrong, whose careers in politics, soldiering, and land-dealing were strikingly parallel.

In 1782, noticing that accelerated settlement in the region beyond the mountains was preempting the most desirable land in an area the state had intended for use as bounty land payments for Revolutionary War service, Armstrong wrote to General Jethro Sumner to urge that steps be taken to secure the area for bounty land. As a result, Armstrong was appointed entry taker and surveyor of the military lands and put in charge of an office in Nashville (Tennessee then being a part of North Carolina). At the same time, his brother John was made entry taker for lands in eastern Tennessee, a powerful combination of strategic positions that led to abuses and fraud.

On a tip from Andrew Jackson, Governor Samuel Ashe of North Carolina forced an investigation into the land office operations and found proof of extensive frauds in which not only the Armstrongs but also others of higher office and greater repute were implicated. Though desperate measures (fire and theft) were plotted to prevent discovery of the frauds, they were uncovered in time to thwart the destruction of the records holding the proof. Despite evidence of criminal action, no trial or conviction ever took place, presumably because Governor John Sevier of the newly created State of Tennessee was himself implicated and refused to extradite the other men involved.

Martin Armstrong was relieved of his appointment by an act of the North Carolina legislature, though he stoutly maintained his innocence of any wrongdoing and refused to relinquish the records of his office, a stand that was heartily endorsed by the government of Tennessee, where he ended his career as surveyor general of the state.

While land was Martin Armstrong's livelihood, he wielded power in both the local militia and politics. He was appointed colonel of the Surry Militia in 1776 at the outbreak of the Revolutionary War, but he had already gained military experience as an Indian fighter on both the Virginia and North Carolina frontiers. In 1773 he had raised troops to aid the settlers then being harassed by the Indians at the instigation of the British government. He was sent to General Griffith Rutherford's aid in 1776 to fight the Cherokees. His final military action came at the Battle of Kings Mountain, where he marched his regiment to oppose Colonel Patrick Ferguson instead of joining General Horatio Gates as he had been ordered. After the battle, on his own initiative, he released or allowed to escape some five hundred prisoners of war, frustrating General Nathanael Greene's plan to exchange them for Americans captured by the British, including General Rutherford.

Because of these actions, parts of a pattern of insubordination, Martin Armstrong was stripped of his command in 1781. He nevertheless maintained his position in the local militia and ended his military career as a brigadier general of the Eighth Brigade of North Carolina Militia.

As a power in the local government of Surry County, he held a variety of public offices: justice of the peace, sheriff, tax collector, delegate to the provincial congress of 1775, and senator for Surry in 1783; finally, despite dishonor in both military and governmental service, he was in 1779 once more returned to the General Assembly to represent Surry County.

He married Mary Tate in 1766; she died in Davidson County, Tenn., in 1836. Five of their children are known: Thomas Temple (b. 1770), who married Mary McMurry; Jane (b. ca. 1773), who married first William Hewlett and second John Evans; Mary Ann Elizabeth (b. 1775), married to Alexander McCall; John Barclay (b. ca. 1777); and Joseph. Martin Armstrong died in Nashville, Tenn.

SEE: Thomas P. Abernethy, *From Frontier to Plantation in Tennessee* (1932); Martin Armstrong Papers (Southern Historical Collection, University of North Carolina, Chapel Hill); Kemp P. Battle, *History of the University of North Carolina*, vol. 1 (1907); Walter Clark, ed., *State Records of North Carolina*, vols. 11, 12, 14, 15, 16, 17, 18, 19, 23, 24 (1886–1907); "Correspondence between William Christmas and Martin Armstrong," *Nashville Tennessee Gazette*, 16 Apr. 1800 (Tennessee State Library and Archives, Nashville); Adelaide L. Fries, ed., *Records of the Moravians in North Carolina*, vols. 1–2 (1922); Glasgow Land Frauds (Secretary of State Papers, General Records [1663–1959], boxes 753–56, North Carolina State Archives, Raleigh); Governors' Papers, vol. 21, and Legislative Papers, 1797, 1798 (Department of Cultural Resources, North Carolina State Archives, Raleigh); J. G. Hollingsworth, *History of Surry County, North Carolina* (1935); William L. Saunders, ed., *Colonial Records of North Carolina*, vols. 9–10; Ethel S. Updike, ed., *Armstrong, Branyon, Bryson and Allied Families of the South* (1967); H. M. Wagstaff, ed., *Papers of John Steele*, vols. 1–2 (1924).

JEAN BRADLEY ANDERSON

Arnett, Alex Mathews *(13 Feb. 1888–7 Aug. 1945)*, historian and teacher, was born near Sylvania, Ga., the fourth son in a family of six children. His father, Hamilton John Arnett, was well known in Sylvania for his work as schoolteacher, Baptist pastor, tax collector, and county superintendent of schools. Less is known of Alex's mother, Georgia Anne Dixon Arnett, who shared in her husband's religious endeavors and was active in the Baptist Women's Missionary Society. She died when Alex was only seven years old, and his father married Joanna O. Ennis in 1897.

None of Hamilton Arnett's children followed him into the ministry. Alex, however, like his father became a teacher. In 1908 he received his B.A. degree from Baptist-sponsored Mercer University in Macon, Ga., where his father had studied thirty-five years earlier. From 1908 to 1912 he taught English and history in high schools in Millen and Americus, Ga.

The next two years were turning points in Arnett's career. In 1912 he accepted a position teaching history at Shorter College in Rome, Ga., and in 1913 he received his M.A. degree from Columbia University. While at Shorter, he met Ethel Stephens of Ball Ground, Ga., and they were married in 1916. They had two daughters, Georgia Anne and Dorothy Stephens.

Arnett stayed at Shorter until 1917, when he accepted a position as instructor in history at Columbia and began work on his doctorate. He received his Ph.D. in 1922. He then taught for a year at Furman University in Greenville, S.C. From 1923 until his death he taught at North Carolina College for Women in Greensboro.

Arnett's years at Columbia were important in his professional career and intellectual growth. He developed a close friendship with his mentor, Benjamin Burks Kendrick, a fellow Georgian. Arnett decided to leave Furman for the Women's College partly because Kendrick had decided to teach there. They worked closely together and coauthored *The South Looks at Its Past* (1935). Arnett's approach to American history, like Kendrick's, was deeply influenced by the work of Charles Beard. Although Beard left Columbia in 1917 in protest against wartime infringements on academic freedom, his influence on his colleagues and students remained strong. Beard's writings were one of the cornerstones of the progressive interpretation that dominated studies in American history until after World War II. Each of Arnett's studies reflects the pervasive influence and basic assumptions of the progressive view—the emphasis on economic factors in determining behavior and on the conflicts between haves and have-nots, between capitalists and agrarians, as the source of historical change. In addition, Arnett and his fellow progressive historians thought that out of this conflict would emerge a more egalitarian and democratic America. Arnett's *Populist Movement in Georgia: A View of The "Agrarian Crusade" in the Light of Solid South Politics* (1922), *The South Looks at Its Past* (1935), and *Claude Kitchin and the Wilson War Policies* (1937) were all written within the progressive framework. They also reflect Arnett's special interest in the South, its history and problems, its identity and character.

The Populist Movement in Georgia was a pioneering work in the field. Earlier studies had viewed populism with more hostility than scholarship and identified it almost exclusively with the western states. Thus, Arnett's study was more than a narrow monograph; it was the first balanced study of populism. Despite some notable attempts to revise historical opinion of the Populists, Arnett's work, although enlarged upon, has not been substantially challenged.

The South Looks at Its Past was written in collaboration with Kendrick as a historical preface for the regional studies done under the direction of Howard Odum at The University of North Carolina. The book reflects the mature interpretations of these two scholars, rather than original research. The study is divided into two parts and it seems likely that Arnett was responsible for the period since 1875. He developed further several of the basic premises of *The Populist Movement in Georgia* and also reviewed the social, political, and economic weaknesses of the twentieth-century South, while noting areas of progress. For Arnett, there was a major break between the Old and the New South. However, he almost totally ignored southern thought, religion,

mores, and racial attitudes, all areas where other scholars would find significant continuity.

In *Claude Kitchin and the Wilson War Policies*, Arnett confronted one of the great tragedies of the twentieth century. World War I constituted a formidable challenge to the liberal gospel of progress. The war fought to end all wars, to secure self-determination of peoples, and to make the world safe for democracy did none of these things and brought instead death and destruction on a scale that had once been unimaginable. Arnett, however, wrote not of tragedy and defeat but of the "good" Kitchin and the "evil" Wilson. The book was Arnett's weakest work. His analyses were superficial, and he failed to relate Kitchen either to agrarian reform or to his southern background. The book did, however, reflect an attitude toward U.S. participation in the war that was widely shared at the time it was published. Arnett's own opposition to American entry in the war evidently developed after the fact, since in 1917 he was an instructor in the Student Army Training Corps at Columbia.

In various ways, Arnett served his profession, college, and community. As a member of the American Historical Association, the Southern Historical Association, and the North Carolina Literary and Historical Association, he worked for the advancement of the historical profession at the national, regional, and state levels. He contributed numerous articles and book reviews to scholarly journals. In *The Story of North Carolina* (1933), he tried to explain the state's history to young readers. Beyond his duties as professor, Arnett served on faculty committees concerned with such diverse interests as the college library, interdepartmental majors, and the campus radio station. He took an active interest in the development of Greensboro's public libraries; from 1932 until his death he was a member of the Greensboro Public Library Board.

Arnett had an artistic bent that perhaps was never fully realized. He enjoyed painting and writing. In collaboration with his wife he wrote a detective story, never published.

Arnett was buried at Double Head's Baptist Church in Screven County, Ga., where his father had been a pastor for over fifty years.

SEE: Ethel Stephens Arnett, file of clippings and personal interview; Clipping files (North Carolina Collection, University of North Carolina, Chapel Hill; Library, University of North Carolina, Greensboro; Greensboro Public Library), for obituaries, reviews of Arnett's books, and a guide to materials on Arnett; *Directory of American Scholars* (1942); *Nat. Cyc. Am. Biog.*, vol. 36 (1950); *North Carolina: The Old North State and the New*, vol. 3 (1941); *Who's Who in America*, 1944–45; *Who's Who in American Education*, 1944–45; *Who Was Who in America*, vol. 2 (1950); Leslie S. Williams, *The Life and Ministry of Hamilton John Arnett* (1935).

JERROLD M. HIRSCH

Arnett, Silas W. *(fl. 1783–1806),* was a printer in New Bern as early as 12 Dec. 1783, for the senate on that date rejected a House of Commons resolution to name the firm of Arnett and Hodge the public printers. The senate action proposed to award the contract to Martin and Company, but the journal does not report further action on the matter. Two years later, on 28 Dec. 1785, the General Assembly elected Arnett and Hodge the public printers. They were the first to be chosen by an election, rather than by special resolution, in both houses. In November 1785, Arnett and Hodge also began publishing the *State Gazette of North Carolina* at New Bern. In 1787, Andrew Blanchard replaced Arnett as Abraham Hodge's partner in the printing and publishing firm.

An attorney, Arnett pursued a career of public service during the remainder of his life. In November 1789 he was a delegate from Beaufort County to the constitutional convention at Fayetteville and voted with the majority to approve the ratification of the U.S. Constitution, already in force in all states except North Carolina and Rhode Island. Although he did not have to live in Beaufort County in order to represent it, the 1790 census does list a Silas W. Arnett in Beaufort County. In the Pitt County court records for 1790, a Silas White Arnett, Esq., is listed as an attorney for the defense. An 1803 document from the Craven County court lists a W. Arnett as clerk of the superior court and an 1804 document lists S. W. Arnett as the clerk. It is definitely known that Silas Arnett was clerk of this court between 1805 and 1806; his term probably began as early as 1803.

Arnett was also active in state Masonic affairs. He may have lived in Windsor, N.C., at some time during his life, because in December 1788 the minutes of the New Bern St. John's Lodge, No. 3, reported that Arnett, "of Royal Edwin Lodge of Windsor," came to New Bern as grand junior warden of the North Carolina Grand Lodge. The New Bern lodge minutes refer to Arnett again in December 1789, as "the Right Worshipful Senior Grand Warden" of the state lodge. Shortly thereafter, he transferred his membership to the New Bern lodge, and lodge members officiated at his funeral on 31 May 1806.

He married twice: to Susanna Davis in Craven County on 14 June 1785 and to Elizabeth Latchmore on 23 Sept. 1793.

SEE: Clarence S. Brigham, *History and Bibliography of American Newspapers, 1690–1820* (1947); Gertrude S. Carraway, *Years of Light: History of St. John's Lodge* (1944); Walter Clark, ed., *The State Records of North Carolina*, 16 vols. (1886–1907); Elizabeth Moore, *Records of Craven County, North Carolina* (1960).

THOMAS A. BOWERS
GERTRUDE S. CARRAWAY

Arrington, Archibald Hunter (*13 Nov. 1809–20 July 1872*), planter, lawyer, and representative in the U.S. Congress and the Congress of the Confederate States of America, was born at the family home in Hilliardston on Swift Creek, about fifteen miles north of Nashville in Nash County. His mother, Elizabeth Nicholson, was the widow of Thomas Mann; his father, John Arrington, was an influential and wealthy planter of Nash County who had served in the state senate and who, on his death in 1830, willed his three children, Samuel Lewis, Elizabeth Ann Williams, and Archibald Hunter, over sixty slaves and extensive property and money. A namesake and nephew, Archibald Hunter Arrington Williams, was a prominent figure in the state during the latter part of the century. Arrington—"Baldy," as he was affectionately called by friends and constitutents—was educated in the local schools of Nash County and at Bobbit's celebrated Louisburg Academy; he read law under Judge William H. Battle.

Although Arrington became involved in politics, his primary interest was the management of his estates and related commercial activities. While he remained in North Carolina to develop the family fortune, his older brother, Samuel Lewis, moved to Alabama, where the Arringtons had substantial interests. The two brothers remained confidants, regularly corresponding about business affairs, politics, family, and friends, and Arrington often made extended visits to Alabama to look after his interests there. His activities so enlarged the fortune left by his father that his estate was valued at over $300,000 in the 1860 census; he was one of the few agricultural entrepreneurs in antebellum North Carolina to possess over a hundred slaves. His personal life, characterized by a hospitable and industrious nature, a passion for blooded horses, and a strong consciousness of family ties, was typical of his class.

Even Arrington's engagement in government reflected an elitist sense of responsibility. While his legislative career was undistinguished, essentially passive and negative, he was an extremely able campaigner. Standing as a staunch Democrat when that party was very much in the minority in the state, he was elected to the Twenty-seventh and Twenty-eighth Congresses, 4 Mar. 1841–3 Mar. 1845. In 1840 he defeated the incumbent, General M. T. Hawkins of Warren County, in the Sixth Congressional District, and in a memorable campaign of 1842, he was successful against the seemingly invincible Edward Stanley. His bid to the Twenty-ninth Congress, after redistricting, was thwarted by J. R. J. Daniel in 1844. There was an attempt in 1858 to bring him into the gubernatorial election, but, following his own inclination and the advice of his nephew, Jonathan A. Williams, Jr., he demurred in favor of Duncan K. McRae. McRae, despite Arrington's counsel, was bested by John W. Ellis. Always a defender of southern rights, Arrington was a member of the state's secession convention. In 1861 he was elected to the First Confederate Congress for the Fifth District and performed workmanlike service on the Committee for Indian Affairs; he was defeated for reelection in 1863 by the belligerent antisecessionist Josiah Turner. His last major political service was performed as a delegate to the Union National Convention of 1866. Locally prominent, he was long the presiding justice for the court of pleas and quarter sessions in his county, and he was appointed a county commissioner following the 16 May 1868 act to better govern the former rebel areas.

Arrington's family ties attached both him and his brother closely to their Mann half-relations and extended into the Battle, Cooper, Drake, Williams, and Wimberly families of North Carolina. Arrington's first wife, Mary Jones Arrington (1820–51), was the daughter of Peter Arrington (1768–1837), purportedly the richest man in Nash County, and the mother of Mary Arrington Thorpe (d. 1883) and John Peter (b. 1851). Arrington's second wife, Kate Wimberly (1834–71), who was the daughter of Robert D. Wimberly of Edgecombe County, bore him nine children, of whom six sons lived to maturity.

Arrington was interred in the family burial plot at his plantation in Hilliardston. Presumably, his family still owns the portrait or copies mentioned in a will he prepared in 1858.

SEE: Thomas B. Alexander and Richard E. Beringer, *The Anatomy of the Confederate Congress* (1972); A. H. Arrington Papers (Southern Historical Collection, University of North Carolina, Chapel Hill); *Biog. Dir. Am. Cong.* (1971); Joseph G. de R. Hamilton, *Party Politics in North Carolina, 1835–1860* (1916); *Journal of the Confederate Congress* (1905); North Carolina Collection (University of North Carolina, Chapel Hill), for Arrington's electioneering statements: *To the Freemen of the Eighth Congressional District of North Carolina* (Hilliardston, 1843), *To the Voters of the Fifth Congressional District of North Carolina* . . . (Hilliardston, 1863), and

Address of Hon. A. H. Arrington (printed as an extra to the Battleboro *Advance*, 1871); Charles L. Van Noppen Papers (Manuscript Department, Library, Duke University, Durham); W. Buck Yearns, *The Confederate Congress* (1960).

D. A. YANCHISIN

Arrington, Katherine Clark Pendleton *(12 Apr. 1876–12 Apr. 1955)*, art patron and civic leader, was born in Warrenton, the daughter of Major Arthur Sylbert Pendleton, a businessman connected with Hooks Smelting Co. of Philadelphia, dealers in railroad equipment. Her mother, Victoria Louise Clark Pendleton, was the daughter of James Sampson and Martha A. Lanier Clark of Pitt County. Through her maternal connections, Mrs. Arrington was related to a number of distinguished Virginia families, including the Lees. She had two brothers, Milo M. and Arthur S., an army doctor who retired to Raleigh. After Milo's death, she raised his daughter, Katherine Clark Pendleton II, as her own.

Mrs. Arrington was graduated from Hollins College in 1896. Shortly afterwards, she married Peter Arrington of Petersburg, Va., son of Samuel Peter and Hannah Bolton White Arrington. The couple traveled widely in Europe and the Orient where he developed the China market for the British-American Tobacco Co. He became a director and head of both the export and manufacturing departments of British-American before his death in 1916.

After her husband's death, Mrs. Arrington became deeply committed to a number of civic projects. She was probably most prominently involved with spreading an appreciation of fine art throughout the state. In 1933 she presented two gargoyles and a bishop in his niche from the Westminster clock tower (Big Ben) to The University of North Carolina, as a memorial to her brother Milo; the figures were installed on the south side of Person Hall Art Gallery. Also during the 1930s she helped establish the Mint Museum of Art in Charlotte. Her favorite project was the North Carolina State Art Society; she was its sponsor and prime force, acting as vice-president in the first year of its existence and as president every year thereafter until shortly before her death. For many years, she used her considerable means and connections to sponsor exhibitions throughout the state and to make many gifts. The State Art Museum in Raleigh stands as a monument to her energies and talents.

Mrs. Arrington had many other interests and was very active in community and historical projects. One of the founders of the Warren County Red Cross Auxiliary, she volunteered to go to France as an ambulance driver, but armistice was declared before she was to leave. She was a member of the state Democratic party executive committee from 1924 to 1928 and was active in the North Carolina Symphony Society. Maternal family ties led her to participate in the restoration of Stratford Hall in Virginia, making gifts and raising funds. In 1932 she was a member of the George Washington Bicentennial Commission. She was also an active member of many patriotic societies: Barons of Runnymeade, Americans of Royal Descent, Descendants of Knights of the Garter, North Carolina and National Colonial Dames of America, and Women Descendants of the Ancient and Honorable Artillery Company of the State of New York.

Mrs. Arrington served as a trustee of The University of North Carolina from 1936 until her death and was awarded an honorary LL.D. by the university in 1947. In 1950 she was recognized by Chi Omega Sorority,

receiving its first annual Distinguished Service Award for Women in North Carolina. Her house, containing both family heirlooms and many pieces acquired during her travels, became almost a museum itself.

She was buried in Fairview Cemetery, Warrenton.

SEE: Katherine Clark Pendleton Arrington Papers (North Carolina State Art Museum, Raleigh); *Asheville Citizen*, 15 Apr. 1955; *Durham Morning Herald*, 14 Apr. 1955; Carl Goerch, *Characters . . . Always Characters* (1945); *Greensboro Daily News*, 14 Apr. 1955; *North Carolina: The Old North State and the New*, vol. 5 (1941); Raleigh *News and Observer*, 10 Dec. 1933, 6 Apr. 1950, 13 and 29 Apr. 1955.

WILLIAM T. MOYE

Arthur, John Preston *(24 Oct. 1851–6 Dec. 1916)*, teacher, lawyer, orator, and writer, was born in Columbia, S.C. His father was Edward John Arthur, newpaperman and cartoonist, whose home was the first in the town to be burned by Sherman's army. His mother was Martha Ann Henry; her father, Robert Henry, had been wounded at the age of fourteen in the Battle of Kings Mountain. Henry settled in Buncombe County and became the county's most outstanding citizen.

Arthur enrolled at the Virginia Military Institute in 1866 and was graduated in 1871. He studied at the University of South Carolina from December 1871 until May 1872, when he was granted an LL.B. degree. A few years later he was admitted to practice before the South Carolina Supreme Court, having already been admitted to the state bar.

Arthur taught school in Columbia from 1873 to 1875 and was adjutant of the Palmetto regiment in 1881. He worked in the office of attorney W. H. Phelp, in New York City from December 1881 to September 1884 and in that of attorney J. H. Hubbell from December 1884 to August 1887; he was admitted to the New York state bar in February 1885. He removed to Asheville in August 1887 and was made secretary of the Asheville Street Railway Co., later serving as superintendent and general manager until 1894. In that year he was admitted to the North Carolina state bar; he practiced in Asheville until 1898.

For several years after giving up law, Arthur seems to have drifted considerably, drinking heavily. Rather early in the 1900s he began work on his *Western North Carolina: A History, 1730–1913*, a 710-page volume on which he labored for about ten years. It was published in 1914. In 1912 he left Asheville for Boone, where he lived at the Blair Hotel for the remainder of his life. Soon after reaching Boone, he was engaged by twenty-two citizens of the community to write the *History of Watauga County, North Carolina*, published in 1915.

The revenue from his books was small, and by 1916 Arthur's financial situation had become acute. In one of his last letters he stated that he was digging potatoes and gathering apples at fifty cents a day and was looking for a job of any kind. He applied for a job at the local livery stable and was turned down. He died in utter poverty. Friends gave him a decent burial, and a marker was set up at his grave.

He was an Episcopalian and never married.

SEE: Boone *Watauga Democrat*, 10 Dec. 1916; Owen Gudger and Mrs. E. L. Gaston, Asheville, personal contacts; Pack Memorial Library (Asheville), for a very few newspaper clippings.

O. LESTER BROWN

Artom, Camillo *(5 June 1893–3 Feb. 1970),* internationally recognized scientist and head of the department of biochemistry at Bowman Gray School of Medicine of Wake Forest University, was born in Asti, Italy, of a Jewish family prominent in business and politics. His father, Victor Artom, was a banker. His brother, Eugenio Artom, who served in the Italian Senate, was a lawyer and professor of history in Florence, Italy. Beginning the study of medicine at the University of Rome, Camillo Artom received an M.D. degree at the University of Padua in 1917. Following World War I service with the Italian Alpine troops, in which he earned a lieutenant's rank and two decorations, he returned to the laboratory and classroom and was awarded a Ph.D. in physiology by the University of Messina in 1923 and a Ph.D. in biochemistry by the University of Palermo in 1926. After further studies at the universities of Amsterdam and Frankfurt, he received appointments as chairman of the department of biochemistry, first at the University Cagliari and in 1935 at the University of Palermo.

The Mussolini government imposed increasing restrictions on Italian Jews, and in 1939 Artom migrated to Wake Forest as professor of biochemistry and chairman of the department in the School of Medical Sciences at Wake Forest College, bringing with him a reputation as "the outstanding biochemist that Italy has produced in the present generation." In 1941, Artom became head of the department of biochemistry at the Bowman Gray School of Medicine at Winston-Salem. In this position he continued until 1961; in 1963 he became professor emeritus, and he continued his research there until his death in 1970.

Artom's more than two hundred papers, mostly dealing with body fats, were published in the most prestigious of scientific journals, including *Nature* and the *Annual Review of Biochemistry*. One paper, published in 1939, was the first publication on the use of a radioisotope in the study of intermediary metabolism. His special field was lipid metabolism, dealing with the absorption of fat in food through its metabolism in the liver to its appearance in arterial walls. Especially important was his investigation of the synthesis of phospho-lipids in the liver and his interest in the formation of lecithin in the liver. Artom's studies have had an important bearing on modern understanding of arteriosclerosis; he also did significant work on the incorporation of amino acids into fat-soluble compounds.

Artom was regarded as a fine teacher, and in 1963 the senior class of Bowman Gray dedicated to him their yearbook, *The Gray Matter*. In 1968 he was awarded the first Medallion of Merit of Wake Forest University. He died in Winston-Salem and was buried in Asti, Italy.

In 1929 he married Bianca Ara of Venice, Italy. They had one son, George Victor. Artom was naturalized as a U.S. citizen in 1946.

SEE: *American Men of Science*, 11th ed., vol. 1 (1965); Irving E. Carlyle to Mrs. Albert D. Lasker, letter (23 Mar. 1966, copy in the possession of Mrs. Artom); Dr. L. Emmett Holt to Dr. Coy C. Carpenter, letter (19 Oct. 1938, original in the possession of Dr. Carpenter but quoted in Carlyle to Lasker, above); *Who's Who in America*, 1960–71; *Who Was Who in America*, vol. 5 (1973); *Winston-Salem Journal-Sentinel*, 9 May 1948, 24 Sept. 1967; Winston-Salem *Twin-City Sentinel*, 1 Feb. 1968.

PETER W. HAIRSTON

Asbury, Daniel *(18 Feb. 1762–15 Apr. 1825),* pioneer Methodist preacher, was born in Fairfax County, Va., the son of Thomas and Pettie Jennings Asbury. At the age of sixteen he went to Kentucky, where he was captured by a band of Shawnee Indians while transporting provisions to a frontier army post. He was taken first to the West and then into Canada and finally became a prisoner of the British during the Revolutionary War. Upon release from a Detroit prison, he found his way back to his father's home in Virginia. There he was converted, entered the traveling ministry of the Methodist Episcopal Church in 1786, and was appointed to serve the Amelia Circuit in Virginia. The following year he was sent to North Carolina, where he served for most of the remaining years of his life. In Lincoln County he met and married Nancy L. Morris; they were the parents of eleven children: Franklin, Pettie (m. Robert Abernethy), Susanna L. (m. James Wilkerson), James Thomas, Henry, Lettie (m. William Cornelius), Daniel, Wesley, Hiram, William, and Fletcher.

Some years after his marriage, Asbury temporarily left the traveling ministry, although he continued to serve as a local preacher. Then in 1803 he returned to the itinerant ranks, and in 1806 was appointed presiding elder of the Swanino (Swannanoa) district. He served a total of fourteen years as a presiding elder. In 1808 he was elected one of eleven representatives of the South Carolina Conference (which included the western half of North Carolina) to the first delegated General Conference of the Methodist Episcopal Church.

Although Daniel Asbury was not related to Bishop Francis Asbury, they were close friends and colaborers, and the bishop visited Daniel's home on numerous occasions. Daniel was considered one of the most important of the early Methodist leaders in the state and personally established numerous preaching places and circuits.

When the annual conference met at Fayetteville in January 1825, Daniel Asbury sought and was granted the superannuate relation. He died at his home and was buried at Rehoboth Church, Catawba County.

SEE: Daniel Asbury Papers (Folder 1, Commission on Archives and History, United Methodist Church, Lake Junaluska); Elmer T. Clark et al., *The Journal and Letters of Francis Asbury*, 3 vols. (1958); Nolan B. Harmon, *Encyclopedia of World Methodism* (1974); *Minutes of the Annual Conference*, Methodist Episcopal Church, 1786–1825.

LOUISE L. QUEEN

Asbury, Francis *(20/21 Aug. 1745–31 Mar. 1816),* first bishop of American Methodism, was born in Handsworth, Birmingham, England, the only son of Joseph and Elizabeth Asbury. He completed only eight years of formal education. At the age of twelve, in his words, "the Spirit of God strove frequently and powerfully" over him. When he was between seventeen and eighteen, he began to exhort and preach; he traveled in Staffordshire, Gloucestershire, Bedfordshire, Sussex, Northampton, and Wilshire.

Asbury, a lay preacher, went to America for missionary work in 1771 at the assignment of John Wesley (1703–91), founder of Methodism. For the next half century, he traveled 270,000 miles, preached 16,425 sermons, presided over 224 conferences, ordained 4,000 preachers, and helped Methodism outstrip the growth of population five to one. Francis Asbury, "the Prophet of the Long Road," traveled some six thousand miles annually, ever extending the boundaries of his labors, until they reached from Maine to Georgia and westward to Ohio. He was one of the best-known men of his day and one of the most often seen. His almost ceaseless, though not haphazard, activity earned him the epithet "Bishop of North America."

In 1951, the National Historical Publications Commission of the U.S. government included Asbury among the sixty-six great Americans whose works the body recommended for proper editing and publication, along with Washington, Jefferson, and Adams. His letters and his journal, begun in 1771 and ended in 1815, have been published in three volumes.

At the Christmas conference—the organizational meeting of the Methodist Episcopal Church in America—held on 24 Dec. 1784 at Lovely Lane Chapel in Baltimore, Asbury, then thirty-nine years old, was ordained first deacon, then elder, and then bishop in three consecutive days. He was the first bishop to be consecrated in the new denomination in America. Bishop Thomas Coke, appointed by Wesley, shared the leadership, but he gave his efforts primarily to other fields. Among other duties, Asbury and Coke called on Washington soon after his election to the presidency.

Asbury went to North Carolina first in 1780 and last in 1816. The celebrated circuit rider visited the state seventy-two times but left no account of his final visit. Some visits were for a few days, although others lasted several weeks. Seldom did he travel alone; traveling companions appointed by the conferences included Henry Boehm, John Wesley Bond, John Crawford, Tobias Gibson, Henry Hill, Hope Hull, Jesse Lee, Stith Mead, Thomas Morrell, Joel Smith, Nicholas Snethen, and Humphrey Wood. Bishops Thomas Coke, Richard Whatcoat, and William McKendree each made some visits with him. In North Carolina he traveled by horseback and by wheeled contrivances: carriages, a little Jersey, wagon, chaise, and gig; there are no references to stagecoaches.

Asbury lifted up "the trumpet of the Lord" in a great variety of places. Congregations ranged from small to very large; at the conference in Raleigh in 1811 some two thousand were present. He preached in the courthouses of Anson, Beaufort, Buncombe, Camden, Chowan, Edgecombe, Gates, Hertford, Lenoir, Martin, Northampton, Pasquotank, and Sampson counties. He also presided at quarterly meetings, societies, and classes, encouraged Bible reading and study, held watch-night services and love feasts, baptized converts, and recruited men into the itinerant ministry. From his saddlebags he constantly distributed books and pamphlets to encourage education in the wilderness.

Asbury never retired, never returned to his native land and, because of the nature of his itinerant work, never married. He died in Spotsylvania County, Va., and was interred there. Soon thereafter, his body was removed to the vault at Eutaw Street Church in Baltimore, virtual headquarters of American Methodism. In 1854 his body was reinterred in the Lord's Acre in Mt. Olivet Cemetery in Baltimore, near the graves of Robert Strawbridge, Reuben Ellis, Wilson Lee, John Haggerty and Bishops Beverly Waugh and Enoch George.

SEE: Grady L. E. Carroll, *Francis Asbury in North Carolina* (1965); Elmer T. Clark, *An Album of Methodist History* (1952), and *Francis Asbury's Last Journey* (ca. 1960); Elmer T. Clark et al., *The Journal and Letters of Francis Asbury*, 3 vols. (1958); J. Manning Potts, *Selections from the Journal of Francis Asbury* (ca. 1960).

GRADY L. E. CARROLL

Ashe, John *(24 Mar. 1725–24 Oct. 1781)*, colonial legislator, Stamp Act patriot, and army officer, was born at Grovely in New Hanover, now Brunswick County, the son of Elizabeth Swann and John Baptista Ashe. His father was a native of England, a lawyer, who settled in the Cape Fear region and served as a member of the governor's council. The elder Ashe, who died in 1734, provided in his will for a sound, liberal education, including Latin, Greek, and French, for his son. The son, a member of the Harvard class of 1746, although he did not graduate, entered professional life and settled on the Northeast Cape Fear River; there he built a fine plantation house, Green Hill, in which he had an excellent library. He served as colonel of the militia and in 1752 was elected to the assembly; in 1762 he became speaker of the house. He was described as an eloquent speaker, patriotic, and strong willed. A staunch patriot, he was a member of the committee of correspondence and of the committee of safety.

When the outraged citizens of Wilmington were ordered by Great Britain to accept the Stamp Act, Ashe took a strong stand in opposition. He resigned his royal commission, was elected to the same rank by the people of New Hanover County, and became the first to accept a military commission at the hands of the people. Later, on the eve of the American Revolution, colonial Governor Josiah Martin took refuge in Fort Johnston on the Cape Fear. Rumor spread that the governor was preparing to reinforce Fort Johnston, whereupon Colonel Ashe sought to raise a regiment by the force of his character and by pledging his estate, which meant that the recruits took his promissory notes instead of pay. At the head of five hundred men, he attacked the fort and on 17 July 1775 reduced it to ashes. In this affair, he took the full responsibility upon himself and with his own hands applied the torch that burned the fort.

The council of safety met in October of 1775 and appointed Ashe, his brother Samuel, and Cornelius Harnett to speak to the people and explain to them the need for the military organization requested by the provincial congress. Ashe's rally to this cause was so creditable and successful that, for this and other services, the congress that met in Halifax on 4 Apr. 1776 promoted him to the rank of brigadier general.

Ashe's strength seems to have been in parliamentary debate and in the force of his eloquence, but the warmth of feeling and imagination required for the orator were unfavorable to the cool calculation and cautious observance of detail required by a sound military commander. So it is unfortunate that his name is most often connected with an affair showing his lack of skill and experience in military command, rather than with one portraying the patriotic oratory for which he was so well educated and adapted. Early in 1779 he was sent to Georgia with a large command by which Governor Richard Caswell hoped to reinforce General Benjamin Lincoln, then in the command of the Southern Army. Lincoln planned an all-out attack against the British and ordered Ashe to pursue the English leader, Colonel William Campbell, below the Savannah River and, deploying the whole army, to secure Georgia for the Continentals. It was necessary that Ashe hold his position in the sweeping attack. He crossed the river 25 Feb. 1779 and headed for Briar Creek, about forty-five miles below Augusta. He reached Briar Creek on the twenty-seventh and found the bridge destroyed by the enemy. Vast swamps surrounding the bridge area made this a most untenable position for Ashe. Before the bridge was repaired, the enemy sent a detachment back across the creek and circled to the rear of Ashe's troops. Some of his troops discovered the British about eight miles away and sent a message to warn Ashe, but it was intercepted. Delay in repairing the bridge, with unorganized observation parties and poorly armed troops, made retreat virtually impossible for the militia and Continentals under Ashe. The defeat was total and gave Georgia to the enemy. General Ashe was disgraced; his case was tried by a court martial at his own request. He was found free of any display of cowardice but was censured for his lack of foresight.

After his surprise and defeat, he made his way home. Two of his sons, Samuel and William, had been taken prisoner, and Wilmington had become a British garrison. In 1781, while in hiding, Ashe was betrayed to the enemy. He was made a prisoner in Wilmington at a place called Craig's "bull-pen," suffered a long confinement, and contracted smallpox. Paroled because of his extreme illness, he began to make his way to join his family at Hillsborough. He got no farther than Sampson Hall, the residence of Colonel John Sampson of Sampson County, where he died and was buried in an unmarked grave.

Ashe was married to his cousin, Rebecca Moore, sister of Judge Maurice Moore and General James Moore. To them were born four sons—William, Samuel, John, and A'Court, none of whom left children—and three daughters—Harriet, Eliza (whose husband, William H. Hill, was U.S. district attorney), and Mary (who married an Alston and whose son, Joseph, was governor of South Carolina from 1812 to 1814 and husband of Theodosia, the daughter of Aaron Burr).

SEE: Samuel A. Ashe, ed., *Biographical History of North Carolina*, vol. 4 (1906); E. W. Caruthers, *Revolutionary Incidents* (1854); William S. Powell, James K. Huhta, and Thomas J. Farnham, eds., *The Regulators in North Carolina* (1971); James Sprunt, *Chronicles of the Cape Fear River* (1914); John H. Wheeler, *Historical Sketches of North Carolina* (1851).

HEUSTIS P. WHITESIDE

Ashe, John Baptist (1748–27 Nov. 1802), Continental and U.S. congressman, soldier, and tobacco grower, was born in the Rocky Point district of New Hanover County, presumably at his father's residence, The Neck, on Northeast Cape Fear River. His father, of Wiltshire, England ancestry, was Samuel Ashe, future governor of the state and brother to militia Brigadier General John Ashe. His mother was Mary Porter, cousin to her husband and his first wife. Two younger sons were Samuel, Jr., a captain of dragoons during the Revolution, and Cincinnatus, lost at sea while serving aboard a privateer. Ostensibly christened for John Baptista Ashe, *pater familias* in Carolina, the grandson elected to drop the final *a* from his middle name.

J. B. Ashe's emergence into history occurred during the Regulator uprising, when, in May 1771, as a lieutenant in a detachment of New Hanover militia, he and a man named Walker were surprised by the insurgents, tied to a tree, and "most severely whipt with small Hickory Sticks." Ashe served in Colonel Alexander Lillington's militia battalion at the Moore's Creek victory over the loyalists, 27 Feb. 1776, and thereafter he saw continuous service until about a month before Yorktown. He was appointed captain, Sixth Regiment, North Carolina Continental Line, on 16 Apr. 1776, promoted to major of the same regiment on 26 Jan. 1777, and transferred to the First Regiment on 1 June 1778; by January 1780, he was referred to as lieutenant colonel.

His commission as major, First Regiment, was signed by John Jay, president of the Congress, in 1779.

Ashe presumably shared the agony of the Valley Forge encampment during the winter of 1777–78. In January 1780 he was the only Continental officer at Wilmington, where he was engaged in assisting brigade chaplain Adam Boyd in procuring shoes for the rank and file. In February 1781, Brigadier General Jethro Sumner gave Ashe the command of a regiment in support of the militia. In the spring and summer of that year he was operating in the Salisbury area under Sumner, who in late July detached him, commanding three hundred newly armed troops, to join Major General Nathanael Greene's forces in South Carolina. On 8 Sept. some four hundred unwillingly conscripted Continentals under Ashe "behaved to admiration at Eutaw, where they almost annihilated a British Regiment," according to Colonel William R. Davie.

At this point, Ashe resigned from active duty, but the demeanor of a soldier never deserted him. In due course, Military Land Warrant 495 allotted him 4,457 acres on the basis of 65 months' service. He became a charter member of the North Carolina Society of the Cincinnati, founded at Hillsborough in October 1783, with Jethro Sumner as first president. On Sumner's death in March 1785, Ashe was elected to succeed him and presumably held the post until his own demise. An executor of the general's estate, he also acted as guardian, with James Gray, of Sumner's younger children, Jackie S. and McKinney Hurst. On 19 Dec. 1789 the General Assembly appointed Ashe colonel of artillery for the state.

Ashe's entry into state politics began with three terms as a member of the House of Commons for Halifax County, 1784–86. In December 1785 he was appointed chairman of the committee of the whole. In November 1786 he was unanimously chosen speaker on the proposal of William R. Davie, from which it may be inferred that Ashe was of a more conservative cast than the majority of his family. In August of that year, however, James Iredell had deemed him anti-Federalist.

Ashe was nominated a delegate to the Continental Congress in December 1785 but failed of election. On 16 Dec. 1786 he was elected to Congress for the one-year term, along with Timothy Bloodworth, William Blount, Benjamin Hawkins, Alexander Martin, and Thomas Polk. He was in attendance in New York City from 28 Mar. to 10 May and from 13 Aug. to 29 Oct. 1787. His few recorded domestic concerns were the nature of the defenses against the Indians in Davidson County specifically and the western boundaries of North Carolina in general, with special reference to the Hopewell Treaty, and efforts to procure proper duplication of the muster rolls of the North Carolina Line. Foreign matters discussed included the question of American prisoners in Algiers, the affairs of France, and infractions of the peace treaty with Great Britain. His bill to the state for attendance at the Congress is dated Halifax, 30 Nov. 1787. Though named as a state delegate for the congressional sessions beginning in November 1788, he chose not to accept.

At the Fayetteville convention to debate the Constitution of the new United States, in November 1789, Ashe represented Halifax County. When the delegates went into committee of the whole to consider adoption, Ashe presided as chairman, 18–20 Nov. and joined the majority in favoring adoption. He also represented Halifax in the senate in 1789 and on 25 Nov. was appointed speaker pro tem. Five days later he chaired the Finance Committee and in early December signed its recommendation against a bill that would have paid the state's certificates of indebtedness at about one-fifth their face value.

Following North Carolina's admission to the federal union, Ashe was elected to the First Congress as a Republican, or anti-Federalist, representative from Halifax District. His earliest recorded vote at New York came in the second session on 31 May 1790, on the question where to locate the national capital. On 10 Feb. 1791 he wrote from Philadelphia, the new seat of Congress, to his friend Reading Blount, of Beaufort County, that he was opposed to the excise tax on liquor then being discussed. He added that the land office bill also under debate was but a vast lobbying business. Reelected to the Second Congress, Ashe first voted on record during the first session, 14 Mar. 1792. He remained in Philadelphia until at least mid-November that year.

In 1795, the first year of his father's governorship, Ashe represented the town of Halifax in the House of Commons.

On 20 Nov. 1802, Ashe was chosen governor of North Carolina by a large majority in the legislature. When a committee of that body arrived at his Halifax home to declare its action, they found him ill; he died soon after. When his death was formally announced to the senate on 29 Nov., his successor in office, James Turner of Warren County, proposed a thirty-day period of mourning that was unanimously adopted.

On 7 Oct. 1779, Ashe married Elizabeth (26 Feb. 1762–ca. 1 Sept. 1812), daughter of the late Joseph Montfort of Halifax, one-time provincial grand master of Masons in North America, and older sister to Mary Montfort, who became Mrs. Willie Jones. Henceforth, the couple made their home on the southern outskirts of Halifax. Elizabeth became her husband's sole administratrix upon his death.

As of 1785, Ashe owned forty-eight slaves; by the time of the federal census of 1790, the total had risen to sixty-three. The Ashes had one child, Samuel Porter (b. 17 July 1791), who married first Jane Puckett of Henderson, Ky., in 1811, and then Mary, daughter of militia Colonel William Shepperd of Hillsborough; with Mary, he removed to Fayetteville, where he represented Cumberland County in the General Assembly of 1823–25. The couple had two sons and a daughter and eventually settled at Brownsville, Tenn.

Ashe and his wife are thought to be buried in unmarked graves just south of Halifax, possibly in the private burial ground at White Hall (now Glen Ivy) estate. Because they were married by a priest of the Church of England, their religious persuasion was presumably Episcopalian. Portraits of both, miniatures on ivory by an unknown artist, are in possession of Ashe's descendant, Mrs. L. Watson Hall of Little Rock, Ark. Both likenesses were engraved by the Philadelphia lithographer Albert Rosenthal about 1885 and were first reproduced by C. W. Bowman.

Ashe's name is commemorated by Ashe's Island, off Onslow County.

SEE: W. C. Allen, *History of Halifax County* (1918); Samuel A. Ashe, ed., *Biographical History of North Carolina*, vol. 8 (1917); C. W. Bowen, *The History of the Centennial Celebration of the Inauguration of George Washington* (1892); Edmund C. Burnett, ed., *Letters of Members of the Continental Congress*, vol. 8 (1936); Walter Clark, ed., *State Records of North Carolina*, vols. 17–21 (1899–1903); Clements Library (University of Michigan, Ann Arbor), for MSS; Curtis C. Davis, *Revolution's Godchild* (1976); C. L. Davis and H. H. Bellas, *A Brief History of the North Carolina Troops . . . in the War of the Revolution* (1896); Elizabeth F. Ellett, *Women of the American Revolution*, 2nd ed., vol. 2 (1848); Emmett Collection (New York Public Library, New York City, for MSS); J. C. Fitzpatrick, ed., *Diaries of George Washington*, vol. 4 (1925); General Society of the Cincinnati Archives (Library of Congress), for the North Carolina folder; M. De Lancey Haywood, "Mrs. Elizabeth Montfort Ashe," Raleigh *North Carolina Review*, 4 Aug. 1912; Stan V. Henkels, Catalogue 1074, pt. 3 (11–12 Dec. 1913); Historical Society of Pennsylvania (Philadelphia), for MSS; Alice B. Keith, ed., *J. G. Blount Papers* (1952–59); "Letter-Book of Lt. Enos Reeves," *Pennsylvania Magazine of History and Biography* 21 (1897); G. J. McRee, *Life of James Iredell* (1857–58); Annie B. Morecock, "Elizabeth Montfort Ashe" (typescript, possession of Curtis Carroll Davis, Halifax); National Archives, Washington, D.C., for MSS; North Carolina State Archives (Raleigh), for Bennehan, Blount, and Rev. Mil. papers; *Raleigh Register*, 30 Nov. 1802; Southern Historical Collection (University of North Carolina, Chapel Hill), for Caswell and Sumner papers; W. C. Watson, ed., *Men and Times of the Revolution*, 2nd ed. (1857); *Wilmington Gazette*, 9 Dec. 1802.

CURTIS CARROLL DAVIS

Ashe, John Baptista (d. October 1734), colonial official, was the son of John Ashe, who had settled in South Carolina after emigrating from Wiltshire, England, in about 1700. The elder Ashe served as an assemblyman and died in London in 1703 while on a mission petitioning for relief for South Carolina religious dissenters. About 1718, John Baptista Ashe settled in the Albemarle region of North Carolina and the following year married Elizabeth Swann, daughter of Samuel Swann. Allied by this match with some of the leading families in the province, the Lillingtons, Moseleys, and Moores, Ashe became a part of the social and political elite of the colony.

Ashe was elected to the lower house of the assembly from Beaufort Precinct in 1723 and served through 1727. During sessions in 1725 and 1726, he was speaker of the assembly. Identified during the proprietary governorship of George Burrington in 1724–25 as one of that controversial executive's confederates, Ashe was elevated to the council when Burrington returned to North Carolina as the first royal governor in February 1731. Appointments to other lucrative offices ensued when Ashe moved southward to the lower Cape Fear area, which the governor was interested in developing. By April 1731 he was public treasurer of New Hanover Precinct and later in the year, deputy surveyor "for all the new Cape Fear lands." Yet by the spring of 1732, Ashe and the governor had become enemies; Ashe joined with Chief Justice William Smith and Secretary Nathaniel Rice in opposing the hot-tempered Burrington. By October 1732, Burrington had jailed Ashe briefly on a libel charge.

It is difficult to understand why Ashe broke with Burrington, but there are at least two possible reasons. Burrington's violent conduct was earning him many enemies in North Carolina and in England, and Ashe undoubtedly foresaw problems for those identified with the governor. Also, Smith and Rice were personal friends of Martin Bladen, a member of Parliament and a leading figure on the board of trade, which was charged with the overall administration of the colonies; by allying with these men, Ashe could hope to profit from Burrington's inevitable fall. Ashe consistently opposed the governor on all substantive issues during the remainder of his service on the council.

Before Burrington was relieved as governor in November 1734, Ashe died, probably late in October. He had not been active in politics during the preceding summer and possibly was in a deteriorating physical state. Ashe was buried on his plantation, Grovely, near Brunswick. His considerable estate, including at least 5,000 acres of land was left to two sons and a daughter, who had married George Moore of the eminent lower Cape Fear family. Ashe's sons, John and Samuel, were respectively a revolutionary general and a governor of the state.

SEE: Samuel A. Ashe, ed., *Biographical History of North Carolina*, vol. 4 (1906); J. Bryan Grimes, ed., *Abstract of North Carolina Wills* (1910); William S. Price, Jr., "'Men of Good Estates': Wealth among North Carolina's Royal Councillors," *North Carolina Historical Review* 49 (1972), and "A Palace Revolution? A Strange Incident in George Burrington's Royal Governorship," *North Carolina Historical Review* (forthcoming); William L. Saunders, ed., *Colonial Records of North Carolina*, vols. 2–3 (1886).

WILIAM S. PRICE, JR.

Ashe, Samuel (*1725–3 Feb. 1813*), judge and governor, was born near Bath, where his father, John Baptista Ashe, was speaker in the assembly, representing the Beaufort Precinct. His father and his mother, Elizabeth Swann, moved to the Cape Fear region, where Samuel's brother John, later general, Stamp Act patriot, soldier, and colonial legislator, was born. Samuel's parents died before he was ten and he was raised by his uncle, Sam Swann, head of the Popular party and speaker of the assembly.

After being educated in law, Ashe returned to the Wilmington district and became assistant attorney for the Crown. Notwithstanding this close British alliance, he was one of the first prominent men to become a zealous patriot, organizing revolutionary groups as early as 1774, when the colonial governor refused to convene the legislature. Ashe and seven others were appointed by the people to prepare a notice urging that the counties elect delegates to meet 20 Aug. at Johnston Court House, in what became the first revolutionary convention held in the state. The next January, Ashe was made a member of New Hanover's committee of safety. Later that year he became a member of the provincial congress. In August 1776, as president of the council of safety, he organized an expedition under General Griffith Rutherford against the Indians. At the Halifax congress of 13 Nov. 1776, Ashe was appointed to the committee to frame the North Carolina Constitution. One of the first acts of Governor Richard Caswell, once the constitution was adopted, was to appoint Ashe as judge to hold the first court under the authority of the State of North Carolina.

The first legislature under the new constitution elected Ashe speaker of the senate; that legislature also made him presiding judge of the state court. He served in this capacity until 1795, when he was elected governor, and held the governorship for three terms. It is interesting to note that just as Samuel was the first judge to hold court in North Carolina by popular decree, his brother, General John Ashe, was the first to receive a military commission at the hands of the people.

Although early in life he was a strong Federalist, Ashe later stood warmly for states' rights and became ardently Jeffersonian. Always interested in education, he served

on the board of Innes Academy in Wilmington and was president of the board of trustees of The University of North Carolina. Ashe married first a cousin, Mary Porter, to whom were born three sons, John Baptista, Cincinnatus, and Samuel. John Baptista, after a distinctive military career, was speaker of the house and a member of the Continental and U.S. Congresses; he was elected governor but died before being inaugurated. After the death of his first wife, Ashe married Mrs. Elizabeth Merrick, by whom he had several children; only one, Thomas, lived to maturity.

Although no portrait is known to exist, Samuel Ashe is described by James Sprunt, in a quotation from G. J. McRee, as being "of stalwart frame, endowed with practical good sense, a profound knowledge of human nature, and an energy that eventually raised him to the bench and the post of governor." Asheville (previously Morristown), Asheboro, and Ashe County were named in his honor. He died at Rocky Point, Pender County, where his grave is well marked and kept in the cemetery of his once lovely plantation, The Neck.

SEE: *Appleton's Cyclopedia of American Biography*, vol. 1 (1887); Samuel A. Ashe, ed., *History of North Carolina*, vol. 1 (1908); *Asheville Citizen*, 6 Mar. 1936; R. D. W. Connor, *History of North Carolina* (1919); *DAB*, vol. 1 (1928); John H. Wheeler, *Reminiscences and Memoirs of North Carolina* (1883–84).

HEUSTIS P. WHITESIDE

Ashe, Samuel A'Court (*13 Sept. 1840–31 Aug. 1938*), soldier, lawyer, politician, historian, journalist, and editor, was born at Wrightsville Sound, near Wilmington. His parents were William Shepperd Ashe of Rocky Point and Sarah Ann Green. His distinguished ancestry and relatives included John Baptista Ashe, colonial official; John Baptist Ashe, governor-elect; John Ashe, revolutionary general; Samuel Ashe, judge and governor; William Shepperd Ashe, judge; and Thomas S. Ashe, congressman and supreme court justice.

As a boy, Ashe lived at his father's plantation at Rocky Point. There he received an elementary education from private tutors and traveling teachers. In 1849 he was enrolled in boarding school at Macon, Ga., leaving there after six months to enter Abbott's Academy at Georgetown, D.C. The year 1852 brought him to Rugby Academy at Washington, D.C., where he studied until moving to Oxford Military Academy in Oxford, Md., in 1854. He was by then preparing for the U.S. Naval Academy at Annapolis, which he entered in 1855; he rose to be second in his class. At this time, also, he began a lifelong friendship with Alfred Thayer Mahan, the noted naval theorist. Ashe resigned from the naval academy, however, in 1858, returning to his father's home at Rocky Point. Here he began reading law, first on his own, then under the direction of William Ruffin.

With the bombardment of Fort Sumter and the opening of the Civil War, Ashe followed his native state, first as an engineer with the unofficial commission of lieutenant. This commission was regularized in January 1862, when he was assigned to Charleston. In June of that year he was commissioned a captain and assigned, as assistant adjutant general, to General William D. Pender, then participating in the campaign against Union General John Pope. After Second Manassas, Ashe was captured and confined at Washington, D.C. Paroled after a few weeks, he returned to Wilmington; his formal exchange took place in November, and he then resumed his captain's commission on the staff of General

Thomas L. Clingman. The following summer (1863), he was assigned as an engineer to Battery Wagner at Charleston and was given responsibility for nightly repairs of damages from Federal fire. When the fort was abandoned, Ashe returned to Fayetteville, where he served as assistant commanding officer of the arsenal until the close of the war.

After the war, Ashe found himself in very reduced circumstances: his father's property had been dispersed by the upheavals of the war and its aftermath. He therefore accepted a position as a conductor on the Wilmington and Weldon Railroad in January 1866. He was, however, able to renew his law education by private study and was admitted to the North Carolina bar in December 1866. His retirement from the railroad on 1 Dec. and the subsequent opening of his practice were made possible by a gift of five hundred dollars from his old Annapolis friend, Alfred Mahan.

Soon after Ashe began his practice in Wilmington, he became interested and involved in politics, as a partisan of the forces opposed to the coalition of blacks and northern sympathizers then controlling the state legislature under the patronage of the occupying forces and the Republican party. Until 1870 Ashe simply made speeches supporting candidates of his views, in what was then an overwhelmingly Republican area. In 1870, however, the Republicans split and proposed two slates of candidates. This split made it possible for Ashe's party, campaigning under the Conservative label, to send one member each to the state house and senate, the former being Ashe himself.

Because the statewide Conservative movement had achieved a majority in the legislature, Ashe was enabled to play a significant role, serving notably as chairman of the Finance Committee and as a member of the Judiciary Committee. During the disruption attending the impeachment of Governor W. W. Holden, Ashe took a leading part in house legislation, proposing a reform of the state's tax laws and fiscal system that was passed by the house but not the senate. A similar plan was adopted by a later legislature. While in the house, Ashe moved his law practice to Raleigh.

Ashe was not returned to the house in 1872, but did, in the course of the campaign, gain his first experience in publishing, issuing in partnership with John Spellman a campaign paper entitled *Blasting Powder*. After the election, he entered into a law partnership with U.S. Senator Augustus H. Merrimon and Thomas Fuller, later a U.S. judge, which continued from January 1873 to July 1879. He also spent the year 1874 as editor of the *Evening Crescent*, a daily paper supporting the Democrats, as the conservatives were by then called. He continued active in the Democratic party, serving on the state executive committee and as its chairman from 1877 to 1880.

In 1879 he withdrew from his law partnership to purchase the newly defunct Raleigh *Observer*, which he resuscitated and published until merging it in 1881 with the Raleigh *Daily News*, to form the *News and Observer*. Under his management, the paper became quite prosperous. In 1885 he was appointed postmaster of Raleigh, a post he held until 1889. By this time, however, the *News and Observer* had engendered several competitors, and in the ensuing period of intense competition, the paper barely managed to survive. In 1893 it purchased the last competitor, the *Chronicle*, and Ashe published the combined papers as the *News-Observer-Chronicle*. Ashe no longer held a majority interest in this expanded concern, and his association with it ended when his partners elected to sell the paper in 1894.

After attempting for two years, unsuccessfully, to reestablish his law practice, Ashe accepted a post as cashier under the then collector of internal revenue and later U.S. senator, Furnifold M. Simmons. He served as the president of Willard Manufacturing Company from 1896 to 1906 and as vice-president of the Raleigh Hosiery Company from 1900 to 1907, before becoming, again under the patronage of Simmons, an expert employee of the U.S. Senate Finance Committee from 1912 to 1917 and clerk of the U.S. District Court at Raleigh from 1918 to 1936. These activities by no means constituted his whole employment during the period, as he remained active in the Democratic party and a constant author and editor for Charles L. Van Noppen Publishers and other firms.

At his death at the age of ninety-seven, he was buried in Oakwood Cemetery, Raleigh. A memorial in his honor was unveiled on Capitol Square in Raleigh on 13 Sept. 1940.

Ashe was married to Hannah Emerson Willard on 10 Aug. 1871. He was a member of the Episcopal church, belonging to St. John's Church at Wilmington and Christ Church in Raleigh and serving as vestryman of each.

Ashe was a prolific author and editor. He edited the *Biographical History of North Carolina* (1905–17) and the *Cyclopedia of Eminent and Representative Men of the Carolinas* (1892). He wrote a two-volume *History of North Carolina* (1908–25) and numerous other shorter works, from analysis of aspects of the Civil War, such as *The Charge at Gettysburg* (1902), to such commemorative writings as *Centennial Ceremonies Held in Christ Church, Raleigh, N.C.* (1921), to works on political issues, such as *A Day with the Professor and his Friends: Familiar Chats on Free Coinage . . .* (1895). He was, in addition, a regular contributor to the *Confederate Veteran* during 1926–32.

SEE: Samuel A. Ashe, articles in the *Confederate Veteran*, and, ed., *Biographical History of North Carolina*, vol. 1 (1905); Heriot Clarkson, *Memorial to Captain Samuel A'Court Ashe* (ca. 1941); Alfred Thayer Mahan Papers (Manuscript Division, Library of Congress, Washington, D.C.); North Carolina State Archives (Raleigh), for the Alexander Boyd Andrews, Samuel A'Court Ashe, William H. S. Burgwyn, John C. B. Ehringhaus, Jane S. McKimmon, and David Paton collections; Manuscript Department, Library (Duke University, Durham), for the Samuel A'Court Ashe [photographs], Corneille Ashe Little, Thomas M. Pittman, and Furnifold M. Simmons collections; Thomas Merritt Pittman Papers (Southern Historical Collection, University of North Carolina, Chapel Hill); William James Rivers Papers (South Caroliniana Library, University of South Carolina, Columbia); *Who Was Who in America*, vol. 1 (1943).

DAVID WILLIAM BROWN

Ashe, Thomas Samuel (*19 July 1812–4 Feb. 1887*), congressman and state supreme court justice, was born at The Hawfields, his maternal grandfather's home near Graham in Alamance County, then part of Orange County. The Ashe family had been prominent in sixteenth- and seventeenth-century Wiltshire, England, and had given North Carolina many distinguished citizens since early colonial days. Thomas's parents were Pasquale Paoli Ashe and Elizabeth Shepherd Strudwick, and as as a boy he lived at The Neck, the Ashe home on the Cape Fear River in New Hanover, now Pender, County. When Thomas was about twelve, the family moved to Alabama, but he returned to North Carolina to attend the Bingham School in Orange County. He then entered The University of North Carolina and was graduated third in his class in 1832. He declined a university tutorship in order to begin studying law in Hillsborough, under Chief Justice Thomas Ruffin, and began practicing in Wadesboro in 1836. In the next year he married Carolyn Burgwin of New Hanover County, a granddaughter of Governor Abner Nash.

Ashe was elected as a Whig for a term in the House of Commons in 1842 and for a term in the senate in 1854. From 1848 to 1852 he served as his district's solicitor. In 1859 he declined his party's nomination for Congress, even though his district was Whig and he surely would have been elected. Meanwhile, he had bought and was managing a small plantation in Anson County.

In February 1861 the legislature submitted to the people the question of a constitutional convention and called for an election of delegates to it. Ashe was chosen as a Unionist delegate, but the voters rejected the call for the convention and the delegates never assembled. After Lincoln's call for volunteers in April, however, North Carolina quickly called a convention, and this time Ashe was elected to it as an immediate secessionist. In November 1861 he was elected a representative to the Confederate Congress.

In this Congress, Ashe was a member of the Committee on the Judiciary. During his two years' service he quietly but firmly opposed every major effort made there to enlarge the powers of the central government at the expense of the states or of individuals. He apparently believed, however, that the Confederacy could win its independence without such legislation and deplored the peace agitation that developed during 1863. In 1863, Ashe campaigned for reelection on these terms and lost to an avowed peace man. In December 1864 he was elected to the Confederate Senate over Edwin G. Reade, but the war ended before his term began.

In 1868, after both Zebulon B. Vance and Augustas H. Merrimon had declined the nomination, Ashe agreed to become the Conservative party candidate for governor, even though General Edward Canby's orders prevented him from voting at that time. Ashe campaigned vigorously against the ratification of the constitution proposed by the Convention of 1868, but he was defeated by W. W. Holden by a vote of 92,235 to 73,594.

In 1872, Ashe was elected to the U.S. House of Representatives as a Conservative. He served on the Committee on Coinage, Weights, and Measures, and his only speech of importance was one urging the continuance of the mint at Charlotte. Ashe was reelected in 1874 and this time was on the prestigious Committee on the Judiciary. He participated in preparing impeachment charges against Secretary of War W. W. Belknap and in framing the resolution providing for an electoral commission to decide the disputed election of 1876. He also participated in the investigation of James G. Blaine in the Mulligan Letters scandal. The principle of rotation in office then operating in North Carolina ruled that representatives should serve only two terms, and Ashe was not a candidate for reelection.

In 1878 the Democratic Party secured Ashe's election as associate justice of the state supreme court, where he was a dependable, conservative judge. In *J. M. Worth, Treasurer* v. *Petersburg Railroad Company* (89 N.C. 301), he ruled that the general assembly could in no way circumvent a charter exempting a company from paying taxes. And in *William Horne* v. *The State of North Carolina* (84 N.C. 362), he decided that the constitutional amendment of 1879 removed his court's jurisdiction from claims against the state involving Reconstruction

bonds. He was reelected to the court until his death at home. He was buried in East View Cemetery, Wadesboro.

In addition to his public career, Ashe was a trustee of The University of North Carolina for thirty years and vestryman in the Calvary Episcopal Church of Wadesboro for thirty-one. Ashe was survived by an unmarried daughter, Josephine; five married daughters, Mrs. Richard H. Battle, Mrs. A. J. Hines, Mrs. J. A. Lockhart, Mrs. James McNair, and Mrs. James C. Marshall; and by a son, Samuel T. Ashe.

SEE: Samuel A. Ashe, ed., *Biographical History of North Carolina*, vol. 8 (1917 [portrait]); Kemp P. Battle, *History of the University of North Carolina*, 2 vols. (1907–12); Charlotte *Daily Chronicle*, 5 Feb. 1887 (obit.); *Congressional Record*, 1873–74; *DAB*, vol. 1 (1928); *Journal of the Confederate Congress*, 1905; *Journal of the General Assembly*, 1842–43, 1844–45; *North Carolina Reports*, vols. 80–96.

BUCK YEARNS

Ashe, William Shepperd (*14 Sept. 1814–14 Sept. 1862*), lawyer, rice planter, state senator, congressman, and railroad president, was born in the Lower Cape Fear plantation community of Rocky Point, the third son of Samuel and Elizabeth Shepperd Ashe, both members of prominent planting families, and grandson of Samuel Ashe, governor of North Carolina and judge. Following a course in classical studies at Washington (later Trinity) College in Hartford, Conn., Ashe read law in the office of North Carolina Judge John de Rossett Toomen. He was admitted to the state bar only two or three days after his marriage to Sarah Ann Green of Brunswick County, in January 1836.

Shortly thereafter, he was elected county solicitor on the Democratic ticket for the four counties of the Lower Cape Fear, a position he seems to have held only briefly, for, as noted later by his son, Samuel A. Ashe, "his planting interests and his social disposition, which was at variance with the exactions of a professional life, led him . . . to abandon the practice of law." Then, doubtless with more leisure time on his rice plantation for reading and thinking, he kept well abreast of the political questions and happenings of the day and apparently remained quite active in the Democratic party. In 1844 he was selected a presidential elector on the Democratic ticket of Polk and Dallas.

In 1846, Ashe won election from New Hanover County to the state senate. In this body, he concerned himself principally with appropriations for railroad building and, more especially, with where these railways would be built. Feeling that railroads from the western part of the state should lead to the state's ports in the east, especially Wilmington, rather than connecting with lines that served the ports of South Carolina or Virginia, he advocated the construction of a railroad from Charlotte to Goldsboro, there to connect with the Wilmington-Weldon line for passage of goods to and from the port city of Wilmington. Mainly through his influence, this railroad ultimately materialized in the North Carolina Railroad, despite advocacy of other routes by such distinguished figures as governors John M. Morehead and William A. Graham.

In the election of 1848, Ashe won not only reelection to the state senate but also a seat in the U.S. Congress, which he entered in December 1849, as a freshman member of the body that would pass the Compromise of 1850. He contributed little to the compromise efforts, however, choosing rather to side with southern extremists to the extent of advocating secession as the proper course for the South. In the Congress, where he would serve two terms, his principal interests, as in the state senate, concerned internal improvements, especially the securing of federal appropriations for improving the channels of the rivers of North Carolina. Finding the Democratic members, who held the majority, opposed on principle to such appropriations, Ashe was able to persuade a good number of them to leave the chamber long enough to allow the Whigs, who had not earlier gone on public record as opposed to such measures, to pass his bill.

In 1854, Ashe became president of the Wilmington and Weldon Railroad, a fitting office in the light of his earlier legislation, which had done so much to promote the railroad, and one that he would hold for the rest of his life. He immediately set about promoting for the railroad a new era of progress and profits, concluding in England a very advantageous arrangement on the road's bonded debt, developing a large Florida travel for the line, arranging through freight trains to Charlotte via the North Carolina Railroad, and perhaps most interestingly, establishing regular steamship connections with the line in Wilmington and New York. In 1858, Ashe once again became a state senator, in order to help thwart former Governor Morehead's plan to pass legislation providing for a railroad from Greensboro to Danville, which would have cut the state in two and directed half the state's traffic away from Ashe's line.

At the Charleston convention in 1860, to which Ashe was a delegate, leading North Carolina Democrats, including Governor John W. Ellis, tried unsuccessfully to present Ashe's name for nomination for vice-president. In 1861, Ashe served in the state convention, where, in addition to being one of the most vocal spokesmen for secession, he strongly supported a constitutional amendment allowing Jews in the state to hold public office. He further advocated that the state cooperate wherever possible to promote the Confederate cause. Because of this stance, he was asked in the summer of 1861 by President Jefferson Davis, a long-time friend, to assume control of the Confederate government's transportation between New Orleans and Richmond. He accordingly took a position in the quartermaster's department, first as a major and then as a colonel, for a year.

By the spring of 1862, however, with the eastern part of the state under armed invasion, Ashe was anxious to become more directly involved in the military aspects of the war. President Davis responded to his desires, first by asking him to collect guns from the citizens for the soldiers until the blockade runners could provide the needed rifles, and then by commissioning him as colonel in the field with the authority to raise his own legion of infantry, artillery, and cavalry. Hardly had he launched this latter project when fate, ironically at the hands of his own railroad, cut short his plans. In September 1862, when returning from the salt works at Wrightsville Sound that he and others had started, he received word that one of his two sons, both soldiers in General Lee's army, had been captured. Quickly commandeering a hand car, he hastened home in the hope of obtaining more information about his son's fate. During the trip, his car was struck in the darkness by an unlighted train. Ashe was mortally injured and died three days later. He was interred in the family cemetery at The Neck, near Rocky Point. Of the two sons who survived him, Major John G. Ashe moved on to Texas after the war, where he died in 1867, leaving descendants; Samuel A. Ashe

would become one of North Carolina's most distinguished historians.

SEE: Samuel A. Ashe, ed., *Biographical History of North Carolina*, vol. 8 (1917); *Biog. Dir. Am. Cong.* (1928); R. D. W. Connor, *History of North Carolina* (1919); *DAB*, vol. 1 (1928); Hugh T. Lefler and Albert R. Newsome, *North Carolina: The History of a Southern State*, rev. ed. (1963); U. B. Phillips, *History of Transportation in the Eastern Cotton Belt to 1860* (1908).

JAMES M. CLIFTON

Ashe, William Willard (*4 June 1872–18 Mar. 1932*), forester, dendrologist, and conservationist, was born at Elmwood, the family home in Raleigh. The oldest of nine children of Samuel A'Court Ashe and Hannah Emerson Willard Ashe, he was a descendant of Samuel Ashe, North Carolina governor from 1795 to 1798, and the grandson of William Shepperd Ashe, U.S. congressman from 1849 to 1855. After being tutored by his mother and great-aunt, he entered Raleigh Male Academy at the age of twelve. At The University of North Carolina, he joined the SAE fraternity and was graduated in 1891 with the degree B.Litt; he received the M.S. degree from Cornell University in 1892. He concentrated his studies in botany and geology and pursued an interest in ornithology, creating an unusually large collection of bird eggs and stuffed birds. He later formed extensive herbariums in Raleigh and in Washington, D.C.

In 1892 he was appointed forester in the North Carolina Geological Survey. Ashe and the other members of this select group made North Carolina the pioneer state in southern conservation. As part of their campaign to advertise the state's resources and encourage efficient use and long-range planning, Ashe and Gifford Pinchot surveyed the state's forests; the surveyors published their report in 1897 as *Timber Trees and Forests of North Carolina*. While secretary-treasurer of the first North Carolina Forestry Association, Ashe campaigned to reduce forest fire destruction and emphasized the economic value of the state's forests.

In 1905 he joined the U.S. Forest Service, holding successively the ranks of forest expert and forest assistant, assistant district forester, and senior forest inspector. Participating in the government's purchase of Forest Reserve lands under the Weeks Act of 1911, he became perhaps the most skilled appraiser of the value of eastern timber lands, by one estimate saving the government over a million dollars. At the time of his death he was chief of the Forest Service's land acquisition force for the national forest region of the eastern and southern states. His studies in logging and lumbering resulted in extensive savings in this southern industry. He was among the first to call for the preservation of wilderness areas, in a 1922 article "Reserved Areas Of Principal Forest Types As a Guide in Developing an American Silviculture," *Journal of Forestry* 20:276–83.

Impressive scientific achievements mark his work in forestry and botany, despite the time he gave to administrative duties. His experiments with the cup and gutter system of turpentine gathering contributed to the later adoption of this more efficient and less destructive technique. He perfected the method of commercial growing of longleaf pines. His writings include 167 titles in such fields as forest economics, influences, legislation, management, and research; land acquisition for public forest and parks; systematic botany and dendrology; and soil erosion. Ashe published 510 new botanical names, mostly southeastern, in 35 genera, including many new species. Over a dozen species and varieties commemorate his or his wife's name.

Ashe was a member of the Torrey Botanical Club and of the Society of American Foresters, serving as the society's vice-president in 1919. He served the National Forest Reservation Commission as secretary and editor from 1918 to 1924. He was appointed to the Forest Service Tree Name Committee in 1928 and was its chairman from 1930 until his death.

Ashe was a Democrat and an Episcopalian. He married his widowed distant cousin, Mrs. Margaret Henry Wilcox, in 1906; they had no children, although his wife had children by her previous marriage. Ashe died in Washington, D.C., following the third operation for a hernia contracted on a field trip. He was buried in Oakwood Cemetery in Raleigh.

SEE: *American Men of Science*, 1st and 3rd eds. (1906, 1927); William Willard Ashe Papers (Southern Historical Collection, University of North Carolina, Chapel Hill); Hannah Willard Ashe Bason (Raleigh), personal contact; William A. Dayton, *William Willard Ashe* (1936 [portrait and bibliography]); *Journal of Forestry* 30 (1932); 44 (1946 [portrait]); Raleigh *News and Observer*, 19 and 21 Mar. 1932.

FRANK BEDINGFIELD VINSON

Ashley, Samuel Stanford (12 May 1819–5 Oct. 1887), minister, educator, and missionary, was the eldest of eleven children born to Samuel and Lydia Franklin Olney Ashley in Cumberland, R.I. Ashley's father came from Hampton, Conn., was educated at Brown College, and practiced law in Ashford, Conn., from 1817 to 1828 and in Providence from 1828 until his death in 1855; a lifetime of ill health prevented him from attaining fame or fortune in his practice, but he was noted for high moral character, an admiration of Louis Kossuth, and a study of Swedenborg. Ashley's mother was the daughter of James Marony and Abby Newell Olney of Olneyville, R.I.

Samuel Stanford Ashley spent his youth and early manhood in Ashford and Providence. He attended the Providence public schools and, from 1837 to 1840, Oberlin College; halfway through his junior year, ill health compelled him to withdraw. He returned to Providence to organize temperance societies, edit a newspaper, the *Samaritan*, and become principal of the Meeting Street School from 1843 to 1846. On 5 May 1842, Ashley married Mary E. Eells, daughter of Waterman and Luthenia Tomlinson Eells of Bridgeport. From this marriage came two children, Mary Augusta (3 Feb. 1843–14 May 1914) and Edgar Samuel Stanford (24 Dec. 1850–12 Oct. 1928), neither of whom married. In June 1846, Ashley returned to Oberlin and entered the theological department; he was graduated in 1849.

Upon his ordination as a Congregational minister on 1 Aug. 1849, in Wakeman, Ohio, Ashley became acting pastor of the Evangelical Congregational Church of Globe Village, Fall River, Mass. He held this position until 16 June 1852, when he was installed as pastor of the Congregational church at Northborough, Mass. While in these pastorates, Ashley demonstrated his strong anti-slavery feeling through support of the American Missionary Association. Eager to become involved with Union troops during the Civil War, he secured dismissal from his Northborough pastorate on 21 Sept. 1864, to join with S. W. Alvord in evangelical service with the

United States Christian Commission at City Point and Fortress Monroe, Va. His military superiors regarded him as "intelligent, sagacious, and honorable."

Toward the end of the war, Ashley became greatly interested in the welfare of the freedmen and decided that it was his duty to minister to them. He was employed by the Freedmen's Bureau before May 1865 to assist in educating the freedmen. In September 1865 the American Missionary Association appointed him a missionary to evangelize and educate the freedmen in and around Wilmington, N.C. Simultaneously, the Freedmen's Bureau appointed him assistant super-intendent of education for the Wilmington District, in which position he served without pay. The bureau agreed, however, to provide him transportation in the discharge of his A.M.A. duties. Ashley worked aggressively to establish freedmen's schools in Wilmington, Fayetteville, Bladenboro, Goldsboro, and Brunswick County and to establish Brewer Orphan Asylum near Wilmington. Ashley's ten schools, at their height, had as many as eighteen hundred pupils enrolled, and the blacks hailed him as the pioneer of Negro education in North Carolina.

Ashley's efforts to educate and uplift the freedmen resulted in his entry into North Carolina politics. He became convinced that the freedmen must have political equality to enable them to escape the oppression of native whites. Regarding Congressional Reconstruction as a righteous cause, he joined the Republican Association in Wilmington, helped to establish the *Wilmington Post*, spoke at political rallies, and was elected a delegate to the North Carolina Constitutional Convention of 1868. In the convention, Ashley was dismayed that Republican politicians would sacrifice what he regarded as the true interests of the freedmen to their own personal needs. He spoke little but, as chairman of the Committee on Education, helped to draft the article that for the first time provided for the public education of blacks. This article was most bitterly attacked by the Conservatives because it did not provide for segregated schools, although the Republicans had no plans to integrate the schools. In 1868, Ashley was elected superintendent of public instruction under the new constitution, and under his leadership the public school system, which had ceased during the war, was revived. In 1870 the Conservatives gained control of the legislature and began cutting education appropriations. Believing that these cuts were aimed at him personally, Ashley resigned in the fall of 1871, rather than see the whole school system destroyed.

Under the auspices of the A.M.A., Ashley then went as a professor to Straight University in New Orleans, where he was shortly afterward appointed acting president. He served simultaneously as the head of the A.M.A. mission in southern Louisiana and as pastor of Morris Brown Congregational Church in New Orleans. Contracting the dengue and yellow fever in the summer and fall of 1873, Ashley was so weakened that he returned to Northborough to recuperate.

The A.M.A. called him to serve again from 1874 to 1878 as head of the mission in Atlanta. His major achievements there were his pastorate of the First Congregational Church of Atlanta, the establishment of a church at Marietta, his preservation of the A.M.A. school in Atlanta, and his promotion of Atlanta University.

Ashley retired in 1878 to his small farm in Northborough, but he remained active in public affairs. He was chairman of the town school committee, actively supported the library, and served as postmaster of Northborough from 1883 to 1885. Ashley died of heart disease and was buried in Providence.

SEE: American Missionary Association Archives (Amistad Research Center, Dillard University, New Orleans, La.); Samuel Stanford Ashley Collection (Northborough Historical Society, Northborough, Mass. [portrait]); *Congregational Yearbook* (1888); *North Carolina Reports of the State Superintendent of Public Instruction* (1868–71); Oberlin College Archives (Oberlin, Ohio), for a biographical sketch; Francis Bacon Trowbridge, *The Ashley Genealogy* (1896 [portrait]); *Wilmington Post*, 3 May 1868.

JOHN L. BELL, JR.

Atkins, James, Jr. *(18 Apr. 1850–5 Dec. 1923)*, Methodist clergyman, was born at Knoxville, Tenn., the son of a Methodist preacher who served his church almost half a century and was elected a delegate to the general conference six times. After Atkins's education was interrupted by the Civil War, he received the M.A. degree from Emory and Henry College and later the D.D. degree from Trinity College (now Duke University).

Atkins served his church in several capacities. In 1872 he was admitted on trial in the Holston Conference of the Methodist Episcopal Church, South, and was appointed to Morristown and Mossy Creek. Between 1873 and 1878 he served Jonesboro, Abingdon, and Asheville as pastor. In 1879 he served as president of Asheville Female College, which closed permanently in 1901, and in 1889 he became president of Emory and Henry College. In 1893 he returned to the Asheville Female College and remained there three years. In 1896 he was elected general secretary of the Sunday school board and editor of Sunday school literature, serving with distinction for ten years. He wrote a notable book, entitled *The Kingdom in the Cradle*, which advanced the concept of training young people into the Christian life without the radical conversion experience that had been regarded as essential. It had far-reaching influence across the denomination; revivals gave way to "preaching missions" for spiritual growth of church members.

In 1906, Atkins was elected a bishop at the General Conference of the Methodist Episcopal Church, South, in Birmingham, Ala. He exercised supervision over conferences across the country, including the Pacific Coast, always maintaining Waynesville as his home. In 1918–19 he was chairman of the Centenary Commission and helped raise $50 million for home and foreign missions. As a result of this effort, missions were established in Belgium, Poland, and Czechoslovakia. For four years he supervised work in these fields.

In 1913, Atkins was instrumental in establishing the Southern Assembly and choosing Lake Junaluska, near Waynesville, as its site. He was the first chairman of the board of trustees and erected two houses at the site. His son operated the institution from 1933 to 1938, when the indebtedness was paid, and the assembly was accepted as the property of the Methodist Episcopal Church, South.

In 1876 he married Ella M. Branner by whom he had four children; after her death he married Eva Rhodes in 1921. Bishop Atkins was buried at Waynesville.

SEE: Western N.C. Conference, *Minutes* (1924).

GRADY L. E. CARROLL

Atkins, Robert *(ca. 1695–1731)*, adventurer, trader, and land developer, of unknown origin, arrived in Bath County in 1715, just after the close of the Tuscarora Indian War, which had reduced Bath County's powerful Tuscarora tribes to insignificance. Most of their remnants had fled to New York, leaving the vast and virtually uninhabited Neuse River basin, their former domain, open to explorers, prospectors, adventurers, and eventually settlers.

Atkins soon became engaged in the small craft commerce conducted by boats in the coastal sounds and rivers too shallow, too sparsely settled, or too uncharted to be served by ships. He acquired an interest in trading posts at Bath, New Bern, and Core Sound (later Beaufort).

In 1718, Atkins moved to his trading post at New Bern. The following year, he began a major new venture by entering a tract of 609 acres up the Neuse River, some 40 miles farther west than the closest settlers on the river above New Bern. His plan was to prove the superiority for cultivation of the lands far inland, to acquire large grants of choice lands for himself, and to establish a river transportation service that would develop with the influx of new settlers moving into the abandoned back country.

During the period 1719 to 1722, Atkins steadily built his reputation as a businessman and planter and developed improvements of his upstream plantation, which prospered and became known as Atkins's Bank. He was contemplating marriage and was well received among the leading families of New Bern and Craven Precinct. Then, rather suddenly, his situation was changed. Some said that misfortune struck him, and others, that his sins had found him out; these paraphrased the dying declaration of a murdered missionary, according to gossip darkly whispered door to door at New Bern.

The Reverend Ebenezer Taylor, an aging, dedicated, moderately wealthy Anglican missionary, had come to serve in Bath County, declaring to the tithe-resenting populace that he would accept no support other than voluntary contributions. The Reverend Mr. Taylor found it convenient to travel by Atkins's boat lines on his circuit through the Neuse River and Core Sound settlements. In February 1720, "while in the course of his Mission traveling by Water from Bath Towne to Core Sound he fell sick and Dyed and not without Suspicion of some foule Practices of one Daniel McDaniel and others who transported him. . . ." Most responsible among the others was Robert Atkins. They left their passenger, a person of advanced years and rather delicate health, to maintain camp for himself for ten days in an open boat on the beach of Harbor Island in the mouth of Neuse River, while the crew hunted wild hogs. After Taylor died of exposure, a chest belonging to him was broken open and the contents appropriated. A witness claimed that the dying man had raised a trembling hand, pointed a quivering finger, and cried out, in agony, "Be sure your Sins will find you out!" Investigation tended to show criminal negligence and robbery. The accusing finger pointed at Atkins. He was arrested and bound over to court on a felony charge. However, he and McDaniel jumped bail and left the province for two years. Atkins returned in 1724 and contemptuously resisted arrest. Though eventually arrested, he was convicted only of contempt. Nevertheless, his reputation was ruined. His fortunes declined, and so did his character and health.

Before he died in 1731, most of his estate had been dissipated. On 16 December 1729, he was at long last issued royal grants for the two partly cleared tracts of land at Atkins's Bank. The two adjoining tracts each comprised 640 acres and covered in shape and area a square mile. These lands he soon assigned as part payment to his lawyer, William Heritage, whose political star and prestige at the bar were then ascending.

Atkins died young, quite unexpectedly and without a will. In fact, he appears to have been killed. His last attorney, Martin Franck—a German Palatine and noted leader of the de Graffenried colonists at New Bern—took his corpse to Atkins's Bank for burial and administered his estate. The Neuse River settlement and development plans of Atkins were adopted and carried out with great success by William Heritage. During the eight-year period from 1731 to 1739, settlers spread up the Neuse basin to the borders of present Wake County.

SEE: Bath County land grants (Office of the Secretary of State, Raleigh); Craven County records, especially court minutes and deeds, N.C. Council Journals, 1712–28, and N.C. Estate Inventories and Settlements (North Carolina State Archives, Raleigh); William L. Saunders, ed., *Colonial Records of North Carolina*, vol. 2 (1886); Talmage C. Johnson and Charles R. Holloman, *The Story of Kinston and Lenoir County* (1954).

CHARLES R. HOLLOMAN

Atkins, Simon Green (11 June 1863–28 June 1934), educator and founder of Winston-Salem State University, was born in Haywood, Chatham County. His parents were Allen and Eliza Atkins, farmers.

Atkins received his early schooling in Haywood. He was an astute student and progressed to teaching in the town school before he enrolled in St. Augustine's Normal Collegiate Institute, now St. Augustine's College, in 1880. After graduating from college, he took a teaching position in Chatham County. His aptitude was recognized, and he was brought to Livingstone College in Salisbury in the fall of 1884 by Dr. J. C. Price. There Atkins served as head of the grammar school department for six years and also, during the last two years, acted as the treasurer of the college. While associated with Livingstone College, Atkins spent his summers conducting institutes for black teachers in various North Carolina counties.

In 1890 the city of Winston offered Atkins the position of principal of the public school for blacks, and he accepted. Soon after arriving in Winston, he initiated a project to develop Columbian Heights, a neglected section of town, in order to provide blacks with better housing conditions and ownership of their homes. He himself moved to this development in 1892 and started a school there the same year. In 1895 he resigned from his position with the public school to work full time with his school, which by then was called the Slater Normal and Industrial School. It came under state supervision that year and received a legislative charter in 1897. The school grew rapidly and expanded under Atkins's leadership, until the state bought the property in 1905 and took full control.

During the following years, the curriculum of the school, under the guidance of the state board of education, was upgraded from high school level to include a two-year post-high school program. In 1925 the North Carolina General Assembly rechartered the school as the Winston-Salem Teachers' College, extending its curriculum to four years of college work and limiting its function to the training of teachers, supervisors, and principals for the black elementary

schools of the state. Atkins continued as president of the college until retiring at the end of the spring term in 1934, because of poor health. After his death, his son, Francis L. Atkins, was elected his successor by the board of trustees.

Atkins was a member of the African Methodist Episcopal Zion church for fifty years. During twenty of these, he served as the church's secretary. He represented the church at three successive ecumenical conferences: 1901 in London, 1911 in Toronto, and 1921 in London.

Atkins was one of the founders of the North Carolina Negro Teachers' Association, organized in 1881. He served this organization for several terms as secretary and as president (ending in 1927).

Atkins married Oleona Pegram of New Bern on 3 Sept. 1889. Educated at Scotia Woman's College in Concord, she was a teacher.

SEE: A. B. Caldwell, ed., *History of the American Negro*, vol. 4, *North Carolina Edition* (1921 [photograph]); C. H. Hamlin, *Ninety Bits of North Carolina Biography* (1946); N. C. Newbold, ed., *Five North Carolina Negro Educators* (1939 [photograph]).

SAMUEL M. GAINOR

Atkinson, Henry (1782–14 June 1842), military officer, born into a locally prominent family in Caswell, now Person, County. His father, John Atkinson, received land grants from the colonial government in 1748 and 1750. By 1785, his landholdings totaled 6,100 acres in the present Person and Caswell counties. Henry Atkinson's mother, about whom little is known, died shortly after his birth, leaving six children, and John soon afterward married Francis Dickens. When John Atkinson died in 1792, he left two more children, 3,665 acres, and seventeen slaves.

John and his sons Edward and Richard all engaged actively in local and state politics. During the Revolution, John served as a delegate to the Hillsborough provincial congress (August 1775), a member of the Hillsborough Committee of Safety, and, at three different times, a member of the House of Commons. In 1781 he became the new state's tobacco purchasing agent. In addition, he was a justice of the peace in Orange County from 1776 to 1788. Edward served as county sheriff and state legislator before his death in 1797. Richard sat in the House of Commons and the state senate.

At the age of eighteen, Henry Atkinson inherited a thousand acres in Caswell County. Two years later he was among the ten trustees who obtained the charter for Caswell Academy, a local free school. He became clerk and then treasurer of the school's board of trustees. In 1804–5 he ventured into commerce, establishing a small store, but the business failed. Whether his agricultural enterprises failed similarly or whether he merely felt disinclined to continue the life of a planter is uncertain, but in either case, Atkinson entered the U.S. Army on 1 July 1808 as a captain in the Third Infantry.

Atkinson spent his first five years of military service in routine duties along the Lower Mississippi River and the Gulf Coast. His activities there presaged much of his later career. Although Atkinson rose to become one of the senior commanders in the West after the War of 1812, he was rarely involved in combat; most of his life was devoted to the historically unspectacular but nonetheless vital administration of a frontier army in times of relative peace.

One year after the outbreak of the war with Britain,

Atkinson was appointed brevet colonel and inspector general in the Ninth Military District. His new assignment took him to the Northeast, where he remained for five years. Although the New York-Vermont theater of war was more explosive than the Gulf theater at the time of Atkinson's transfer, the young officer led no troops in battle. He did receive his first command, the Thirty-seventh Infantry, in April 1814, after a one-week paper command of the Forty-seventh. His task, however, was to provide for the coastal defense of Connecticut. With the Thirty-seventh in the New London area and, after the war, with the Sixth Infantry at Plattsburgh, N.Y., he concentrated on drilling, fort-building, and road construction, activities that were to consume much of his time on the western frontier.

In 1818, Atkinson was placed in command of the military district consisting of Kentucky, Tennessee, and the Missouri Territory, and he and the Sixth moved west. Although the territory underwent frequent nominal changes and his own supervision varied from a *de jure* to a *de facto* one, this vast frontier area was to be Atkinson's predominant domain until his death in 1842.

The colonel's first major undertaking was leading one column of a three-pronged exploratory expedition initiated by Secretary of War John C. Calhoun. He progressed as far as Council Bluffs, where he constructed an outpost that Calhoun later named Fort Atkinson, before Congress terminated funding for the project in the wake of the Panic of 1819.

In the army reorganization of 1821, Atkinson lost his district command, but his friends in Washington helped him retain his colonelcy and his post as head of the Sixth Infantry. Although subordinate to General Edmund Gaines, Atkinson continued to oversee his old area of jurisdiction, now placed in his charge as the Right Wing. His leadership in securing the frontier lasted until the mid-1830s.

Atkinson's primary responsibility in the 1820s was negotiation with the Indians, who called him "White Beaver." He showed a certain conciliation and finesse in these dealings. Until the Black Hawk uprising, he avoided physical conflict between the army and the Indians through effective manipulation of a show of force in conjunction with negotiation. One of his premier accomplishments was his leadership of an expedition from St. Louis to the mouth of the Yellowstone River in 1825. He negotiated twelve treaties with sixteen bands of Indians and, using paddle wheel keelboats for the first time on a military venture, suffered no serious damages to the boats and lost no men.

In the next two years, under directions from Gaines, he selected the site for and supervised the construction of a new army infantry school, over which he was to exercise personal control, at Jefferson Barracks, Mo. From that time on, Jefferson Barracks was his home, and he divided his time between frontier problems and infantry instruction.

His sole command of troops in combat came in 1832. The Sauks under Black Hawk tried to recross the Mississippi River to lands in Illinois they had surrendered to the United States in the Corn Treaty of 1831. Atkinson apparently overemphasized the dangers inherent in the situation. He prompted Illinois's Governor John Reynolds to call out an undisciplined militia and refused to parlay with the Indians. His cautious pursuit of Black Hawk evoked criticism from Washington, and General Winfield Scott was ordered to assume command with fresh troops. However, Scott's men were stricken by an epidemic of Asiatic cholera before departure and so Atkinson was left to conduct the campaign. After two months of exasperating, unrewarding marching, Atkinson caught up with the Sauks and soundly defeated them at Bad Axe, Wisc., on 2 Aug.

During July, Atkinson had been forced to encamp and await provisions. At the juncture of the Bark and Rock rivers, his troops constructed a shelter for the sick and supply base, christened Fort Coshconong. After the campaign, the fort was given to friendly Potawatomies, who maintained it for less than a year before being forced to sell all their eastern lands. Within a few years, white settlers occupied the site and constructed the town of Fort Atkinson, Wisc.

The last ten years of Atkinson's life were frustrating ones. Young officers superseded him in the actual command of the expanding frontier. He became chiefly a paper-shuffling intermediary. He grew irascible and evinced signs of approaching senility. In 1838, President Martin Van Buren offered him the first governorship of the new Iowa Territory, but the colonel immediately spurned the appointment without specifying reasons. His last important military achievement was the supervision of the westward removal of the Winnebago Indians to northern Iowa in 1840. In the process, he established the last of three Fort Atkinsons, this one built for the protection of the Sauks and Foxes about thirty-five miles west of Prairie du Chien.

Atkinson married Mary Ann Bullitt in Christ Episcopal Church, Louisville, Ky., on 15 Jan. 1826; a son, Henry, Jr., was born to them the following February. George Catlin painted a portrait of Atkinson in 1824.

Atkinson died of dysentery in his home in 1842 and was buried at Jefferson Barracks. Some time later, his body was reinterred in the Bullitt-Gwathmey family lot in Cave Hill Cemetery in Louisville.

SEE: *DAB*, vol. 1 (1928); Roger L. Nichols, *General Henry Atkinson* (1965); Mrs. George Swart, ed., *Footsteps of Our Founding Fathers* (1964); *Who Was Who in America, 1607–1896*.

TIMOTHY J. WIEST

Atkinson, James Oscar (20 Apr. 1867–2 July 1940), editor and religious leader, was one of six sons born to George Washington and Mary Elizabeth Jones Atkinson in Wake County. He received the M.A. degree from Wake Forest College in 1890 and the same degree from Harvard College in 1893. Although he was reared a Baptist and attended a Baptist college, James O. Atkinson was troubled by the denomination's practice of closed communion. He joined the Christian church and preached his first sermon as a college student at Catawba Springs Christian Church.

When the Southern Convention of the Christian Church established Elon College in 1890, Atkinson was appointed the first professor of sociology and psychology. He earned a reputation as an excellent teacher and served Elon College in other ways: dean from 1903 to 1905, lecturer when he was no longer on the faculty, and a trustee from 1914 to 1940. He was also pastor of the Elon College Community Church from 1897 to 1917.

Atkinson served his church in several capacities. In 1900 the Southern Convention of the Christian Church appointed him editor of its official publication, the weekly *Christian Sun*, published in North Carolina since 1844, except for the period from 1863 to 1867. He served until 1916 and then was reappointed in 1924 to serve until 1936. From 1919 to 1940, Atkinson was mission secretary to the southern convention, in which position he continued to organize women to support missions. His great desire was to establish a college like Elon in China, but the convention's resources would permit support only of its existing missions in Puerto Rico and Japan. At one time, Atkinson was president of the board of control of the Franklinton Christian College for Negroes in North Carolina, and this contact afforded him numerous opportunities to speak in black churches. When the Seattle Council met in 1931 to plan the merger of the Christian and Congregational churches, Atkinson aided this union through work on the committee on union. Because of his commitment to the Christian church's goal of uniting all Christians, he was elected to the General Council of Congregational Christian Churches. Atkinson considered his service as trustee of The University of North Carolina, president of the North Carolina Press Association, and trustee of the North Carolina School for the Deaf as extensions of his church work.

Atkinson married one of his students, Emma Williamson of Driver, Va., who was graduated in 1895. Willis John Lee, a trustee of Elon, and his wife, Mary Jennet, had reared Emma on their Town Point estate on the James River near Suffolk. Emma and James Oscar had three daughters and one son. Atkinson died in Greensboro and was interred at Magnolia Cemetery at Elon College.

SEE: *Christian Sun*, 11 July 1940, 26 Apr. 1956; John Leslie Lobingier, *Pilgrims and Pioneers in the Congregational Christian Tradition* (1965); Raleigh *News and Observer*, 3 July 1940 (photograph).

JOHN L. BELL, JR.

Atkinson, Joseph Mayo (*7 Jan. 1820–6 Mar. 1891*), Presbyterian clergyman in Raleigh for thirty-five years, was one of the eleven children of Robert and Mary Tabb Mayo Atkinson of Mansfield, Dinwiddie County, Va., and one of four brothers who became clergymen. An elder brother, Thomas, became the third Episcopal bishop of North Carolina. Another, John Mayo, served as president of Hampden-Sydney College, Va., from 1857 to 1883. After following briefly in the steps of his brothers at Hampden-Sydney College, Joseph transferred to the College of New Jersey, now Princeton, from which he was graduated in 1841. He entered Princeton Theological Seminary and completed his studies in 1843.

Although his father and elder brothers remained Episcopalians, Joseph joined in the growing influence of the Presbyterian church over all things religious in the South. He was licensed to preach by the Winchester Presbytery in 1843 and ordained elder by the same body two years later. From 1843 until 1849, he served as pastor of small churches in Sheperdstown and Smithfield, Va. In 1849, however, he moved to a much larger church in Frederick, Md. His successes in Maryland and the presence of his brother Thomas as resident Episcopal bishop in Raleigh paved the way for his election as pastor of First Presbyterian in Raleigh in 1855. In that important pastorate he succeeded Drury Lacy, who had just been elected president of Davidson College. After twenty years at First Presbyterian, Atkinson's health gave way, forcing him into the semiretired life of a high school teacher. By 1877 he was sufficiently recovered to take on the pastorate of the Second Presbyterian Church in Raleigh, where he remained until 1890. Following a year of retirement, Atkinson died at Warrenton.

Like his brother Thomas, Joseph Mayo Atkinson disliked slavery and dreaded southern secession. Yet, also like his brother, once the Civil War began, he came to the defense of slavery and the Confederacy. In one of the most ringing sermons heard in Civil War North Carolina, Atkinson on 18 Sept. 1862 celebrated Confederate military successes by declaring, "Never in the history of mankind has the wonder-working providence of God been more strikingly manifest than in the successive phases of this contest." Among those who convinced southerners that they were fighting a war of self-defense, Atkinson argued that the South "is now making for herself a name which shall be gratefully and admiringly murmured wherever freedom has a friend or the God of Providence a worshipper." In addition to stirring up the home front, Atkinson wrote tracts for the consumption of the southern soldiery. He had already demonstrated an interest in guiding the lives of young men with his 1860 publication of a series of lectures entitled *The True Path*.

In 1843, Atkinson married Sally Page Wellford of Fredericksburg, Va.

SEE: M. De Lancey Haywood, *Lives of the Bishops of North Carolina* (1910); E. C. Scott, comp., *Ministerial Directory of the Presbyterian Church, U.S.* (1942).

LARRY EDWARD TISE

Atkinson, Thomas (*6 Aug. 1807–4 Jan. 1881*), third Episcopal bishop of North Carolina, was one of eleven children of Robert and Mary Tabb Mayo Atkinson of Mansfield, Dinwiddie County, Va., and one of four brothers who became Episcopal or Presbyterian clergymen. A younger brother, Joseph Mayo, entered the Presbyterian ministry and followed Thomas to North Carolina.

Born on his father's plantation and educated in local schools, Atkinson entered Yale College at age fourteen. During his junior year, following a student spree on which he refused to serve as informant, he was forced to leave or be expelled. He then entered Hampden-Sydney College, from which he was graduated in 1825 with top honors of his class. After three years of study under Judge Henry St. George Tucker of Winchester, Va., Atkinson was licensed to practice law, a vocation he pursued successfully for eight years. Following the course of many another lawyer during his lifetime, Atkinson decided to enter the ministry in 1836. Ordained a deacon on 18 Nov. by William Meade, assistant bishop of Virginia, he served one year as assistant rector of Christ Church, Norfolk. Upon his advancement to the priesthood on 7 May 1837 by Richard Channing Moore, bishop of Virginia, he became rector of St. Paul's Church, Norfolk. During the next sixteen years he served successfully as rector of St. Paul's, Norfolk (1837–39); St. Paul's, Lynchburg (1839–43); St. Peters, Baltimore (1843–50); and Grace Church, Baltimore, a church he organized (1850–53).

During his tenure in Baltimore, Atkinson was twice elected bishop of Indiana (1843, 1846), an honor that on both occasions he declined. Although in 1843 he rejected the election on the grounds that he was ill-prepared for the office of bishop, three years later he declined because he did not wish to live in a community inflamed with hatred for slavery and slaveholders. Despite the fact that he disliked abolitionism, he had years earlier freed his own slaves and expressed a preference for living in the slave South in order to serve as a meliorating influence. When he was nominated in 1853 to become bishop of

South Carolina, his prompt expression of opposition to slavery cooled South Carolinians toward his election. In May of the same year, however, he was elected bishop of North Carolina, following thirty ballotings by a sharply divided North Carolina diocesan convention. On 17 Oct. 1853, Atkinson was consecrated at the General Convention of the Protestant Episcopal Church in New York. Succeeding Levi S. Ives, who renounced his episcopate to become a Roman Catholic, Atkinson remained North Carolina's Episcopal bishop for twenty-eight turbulent years.

As the Civil War approached, Atkinson provided enlightened and moderate leadership for North Carolina's Episcopalians. He promoted education by founding a church school for boys in Raleigh and the Ravenscroft School in Asheville. He urged the religious instruction of slaves throughout the state. He argued effectively against using theories of Negro racial inferiority as a basis for defending slavery. Until Lincoln's call for southern troops to suppress the rebellious South, Atkinson opposed secession in word and deed. Thereafter, however, he put the Episcopal church in North Carolina in the service of the Confederacy. While he was initially opposed to a similar severing of the Protestant Episcopal Church, by October 1861 he came to support southern moves to erect a Protestant Episcopal Church in the Confederate States of America. At the conclusion of the war, he continued his moderation by becoming one of only two southern bishops to attend the Philadelphia general convention in October 1865 and to participate in plans for the reunification of the church. Soon thereafter, Atkinson announced his intentions to make North Carolina a model for dealing with the problem of freed blacks. In 1866 he placed the operation of black Episcopal churches fully in the hands of black clergymen. Two years later he led the move to open the Episcopal school for blacks near Raleigh that eventually became St. Augustine's College.

When his health failed in 1866, Atkinson traveled widely in America and Europe to recover the vibrancy of his earlier years. Such travels brought him to the international Anglican conference at York, England, in 1866; the First Lambeth Conference at Lambeth Palace in 1867; and to Cambridge University, where he received an honorary doctoral degree, also in 1867. Atkinson's health continuing to decline, Theodore Benedict Lyman was elected his assistant bishop in 1873. Atkinson died in Wilmington, where he had made his home since 1855. He was survived by Josepha Gwinn Wilder, daughter of John Wilder of Petersburg, Va., whom he had married in 1828 and by whom he had three children.

SEE: J. B. Cheshire, *The Church in the Confederate States* (1912); M. De Lancey Haywood, *Lives of the Bishops of North Carolina* (1910); Joseph Jones Papers (Manuscript Department, Library, Duke University, Durham); Lewis N. Whittle Papers (Southern Historical Collection, University of North Carolina, Chapel Hill).

LARRY EDWARD TISE

Attakullakulla *(1705–79)*, a Cherokee warrior and statesman—known to the English as The Little Carpenter, because his name meant "wood leaning up" and therefore suggested house-building—became the most prominent Cherokee of the third quarter of the eighteenth century. Of prestigious birth, he was destined to high position from youth and on maturity was chosen to the office of second or right-hand man, the executive arm to the first man or priestly Ulustuli of the Overhill Cherokees and hence of the Cherokee nation. His home was at Tuskeegee on the Little Tennessee, a few miles from Chota, the Cherokee capital, in present Monroe County, Tenn. (North Carolina at that time). Attakullakulla first appears in the records at about age thirty, when he was one of six Cherokee ambassadors chosen in 1730 to go to England to make a treaty of trade and alliance. In 1739 he was captured by the Caughnawagas (Canadian Iroquois) and carried to Canada, where he was adopted into the family of the principal Caughnawaga chief. In Canada he became acquainted with French officers, traders, and priests and met the French governor. He developed an awareness of the Iroquois tactic of playing the French against the English to obtain security and trade concessions. Cherokee security and a plentiful trade were to be his lifetime objectives after he returned to the Cherokee country as a result of the 1742 Cherokee peace with the Iroquois.

After 1745, when the Cherokees were engaged in bitter war with the Creek Indians, Attakullakulla was instrumental in bringing Iroquois into the Cherokee country to aid against the Creeks. When, in 1751, because of disturbances attendant upon the Iroquois presence in the Cherokee country, South Carolina embargoed the Cherokee trade, Attakullakulla went to Williamsburg to seek a Virginia trade. This effort failing, he went to the Ohio to contact Pennsylvania traders. Governor James Glen of South Carolina then sought to have him apprehended as an enemy. When finally Glen decided to mediate a peace between the Creeks and the Cherokees and to lift the embargo, Attakullakulla, to cement Carolina-Cherokee friend-ship, led a war party against French convoys on the Mississippi.

In 1753, after Glen had opened official correspondence with the Overhill leadership at Chota, Attakullakulla went as emissary to Charleston and there, with threats of competition from Virginia, Pennsylvania, or even the French, forced Glen to provide better terms in the trade. Nevertheless, mindful of the disastrous embargo of 1751, Attakullakulla determined to undermine the South Carolina trade monopoly. For favoring an effort to open trade with the French, however, his life was threatened by the pro-English headmen of the nation; they forcibly reminded him that, as the only living signer of the Treaty of 1730 with the English, he must hold to the sanctity of his word. Thenceforward, he opposed overtures of any sort to the French but pushed strongly for a Virginia trade.

Fear of Attakullakulla's interest in Virginia led Governor Glen in 1753 to build Fort Prince George at Keowee among the Lower Cherokees. In 1755, the interest of the Virginians in the Cherokees, from whom they desired assistance against the French in the Ohio Valley, brought Glen to Saluda, S.C., in May, where Attakullakulla and Old Hop, the Cherokee first man, obtained trade concessions and the promise of a fort for the Overhill Cherokees, in return for ceding to the British overlordship of the lands all the way to the mouth of the Tennessee River.

Continuing Virginia efforts to obtain Cherokee help and the slowness of South Carolina in implementing Glen's Saluda promises brought Attakullakulla and other Cherokees to Broad River, N.C., to make a treaty for Virginia trade and a Virginia fort among the Overhills. In return, Cherokee warriors would operate against the French on the Virginia frontier. At this time, Attakullakulla and others consented to the building of Fort Dobbs, twenty miles west of Salisbury. Delays in implementing the Broad River treaty led the Overhills to disillusionment with the English and with Attakullakulla's diplomacy. When finally, in late 1756, South Carolina did build Fort Loudoun near Chota, Attakullakulla led Cherokees against the French on the Mississippi. Relatively few Overhills went to Virginia, that frontier being left to the Lower Cherokees to defend.

When in 1758 friction between Cherokee horse stealers and Virginia frontiersmen and scalp hunters caused the death of a score of Cherokees in Virginia, the Cherokees demanded war on the English. Attakullakulla stood for peace and, stalling a declaration of war, went to Virginia to seek Virginia reparation and a Virginia trade. In the latter effort he was successful, but before he could return, Cherokee vengeance seekers had murdered a score of frontiersmen in North Carolina. He still strove for peace. In October 1759 a delegation of Cherokee peacemakers, including Oconostota, the Great Warrior, went to Charlestown, but there they were seized by Governor William Lyttelton as hostages for the surrender of those Cherokees who had murdered North Carolinians. Lyttelton marched a South Carolina army to Fort Prince George to enforce his demands. Attakullakulla conducted negotiations for the Cherokees and managed to free Oconostota and three others by promising to surrender four of the murderers, but the Cherokees refused to honor the promise and went to war against South Carolina. Attakullakulla refused to participate in the war or in the councils of the Cherokee nation and withdrew with his family into the woods. In 1760, when the Overhills captured Fort Loudoun and massacred the officers, Attakullakulla rescued Captain John Stuart, who had befriended him in Charlestown, and sent him off to Virginia. After British armies had twice devastated the Cherokee country, Oconostota called on Attakullakulla to enter into peace negotiations with South Carolina. Attakullakulla effected the peace in December 1761.

Early in 1763 he opposed Creek efforts to involve the Cherokees in war with the English, and he led war parties against the Iroquois, who in 1761 had warred against the Cherokees as allies of the English. He was probably instrumental in the murder of Iroquois deputies who came to broach a peace to avert an all-Indian uprising against the English.

In November 1763, as the agent of Oconostota, he attended the great conference of southern governors with the southern Indians at Augusta, called by John Stuart, then his majesty's superintendent for the southern Indians, to settle trade and boundary problems. Attakullakulla spoke strongly for trade and peace and against white encroachments in the valley of the Kanawha and urged the fixing of boundaries to protect the Indian country from trespass.

In June 1765 he went to Virginia to demand reparation for recent Virginia murders of Cherokees and to ask for a Virginia trade. The Virginians agreed but were so slow in implementing their promises that Attakullakulla had great difficulty in frustrating Cherokee demands for war. Finally he proposed that war be delayed while he and Oconostota went to England for redress. Stuart rejected this plan but agreed to help the Cherokees obtain peace with the Iroquois and promised a quick survey of the boundary. He sent Attakullakulla and Oconostota to New York to make peace with the Iroquois. From November 1767 until the following April, they were at Johnson Hall in the Mohawk country making the peace.

With the Iroquois war settled, Attakullakulla attempted to make peace with the Wabash River Indians

north of the Ohio, who had been inveterate enemies. After failing to do so, he led a war party against these Indians to avenge the deaths of relatives.

After 1769, Attakullakulla was associated with land deals that brought the whites ever nearer the Cherokee country. These were efforts to legitimize the inevitable and thus avoid war. Goods shortages occasioned by repeated colonial nonimportation agreements in the struggle of the colonists with the Crown made the quantities of goods and ammunition received in these deals attractive. The 1769 treaty with James Robertson leased the Watauga lands to North Carolina settlers for eight years.

In October 1770, Attakullakulla attended the conference at Lochaber, S.C., at which the Cherokees ceded the land east of a line from six miles east of the Long Island of the Holston to the mouth of the Kanawha in the Ohio. During the survey he altered the line to extend westward along the east bank of the Kentucky River. The new line violated the treaty of Lochabar, and its generosity has been attributed to the gifts he received. In the autumn of 1774, despite Lord Dartmouth's prohibition on sales west of the Lochabar line, Attakullakulla was engaged in negotiation with Richard Henderson of North Carolina for the sale of all lands between the mountains and the Cumberland River. He went to North Carolina with Henderson to determine the quantity and types of goods to be given the Cherokees for the sale. The Cherokees received $10,000 in goods at the ratification of the sale at the Treaty of Sycamore Shoals, 14–17 Mar. 1775. Though the quantity of goods seemed large, when they were distributed among the Cherokees, each man received much less than he could make in a year hunting the same territory. Many Cherokees were dissatisfied, and soon there were clashes with whites settled on the Watauga lands and elsewhere. Attakullakulla's influence began to wane. In May and June of 1776, Attakullakulla supported Stuart's efforts to keep the Cherokees from going to war before the British were ready to attack the South, but neither he nor the other elder headmen could prevent the young Cherokee warriors from going to war. Attakullakulla then went to Pensacola to demand that the British supply the Cherokees with a trade.

Retaliation from North Carolina, South Carolina, and Virginia resulted in destruction of most of the Cherokee towns. The recalcitrants fled to the Chickamauga region of northwest Georgia, where they could maintain contact with the British. Attakullakulla and Oconostota then made peace overtures to the Americans, which resulted in the Treaty of Fort Patrick Henry in April 1777, wherein the chiefs agreed to neutrality in the war between the British and the Americans. This treaty, however, did not prevent the Chickamauga dissidents from continuing the war. Few American traders went to the Cherokee country, and the neutral towns were denied a British trade. In February 1778, Attakullakulla visited Pensacola, where he professed friendship to the English and applied to Stuart for renewal of trade. Unsuccessful in this bid, in September he visited Fort Rutledge in South Carolina on a similar mission and professed friendship for the Americans. The effort failed, and he died shortly afterward.

After 1753, Attakullakulla consistently opposed war with the colonists and the English and sought by every means to increase the flow of trade goods to the Cherokee country. Although he is accused of having taken bribes while promoting these policies, it must be borne in mind that it was the immemorial custom of all eastern Indian diplomats to expect presents from opposing negotiators on successful completion of a treaty.

Attakullakulla had an English-style frame house at Tuskeegee, and he once asked Governor Glen to give him slaves to help his wife. His demand went unfulfilled because of a South Carolina law forbidding slave ownership by Indians. Though thoroughly Indian and a conscientious practioner of Indian mores, he enjoyed the amenities of the white man's way and sought peace and economic prosperity for his people.

SEE: John R. Alden, *John Stuart and the Southern Colonial Frontier* (1944); David H. Corkran, *The Cherokee Frontier* (1962); Thomas Gage Papers (Clements Library, University of Michigan, Ann Arbor); William L. McDowell, Jr., ed., *Documents Relating to Indian Affairs*, 2 vols. (1958–70); South Carolina Council Minutes (South Carolina Archives Department, Columbia).

D. H. CORKRAN

Atwater, John Wilbur (27 Dec. 1840–4 July 1910), U.S. congressman, state senator, and farmer, was born in the community of Farrington in eastern Chatham County, the son of Jahaza Atwater and Sally Stone. His grandfather, Moses Atwater, a saddler by trade, lived in southern Bingham Township of Orange County but had extensive holdings in Baldwin and Williams townships of Chatham. Atwater genealogical records indicate that the progenitor of this family was David Atwater, one of the first planters of New Haven, Conn. He originally lived at Royton in the county of Kent, England, where the Atwaters had resided for generations. David came to New England in 1637 at the age of twenty-two and married Damaris Syare of Southampton, L.I. He occupied seat three of the First Church of Christ in New Haven. Its first building is said to have been erected on land once owned by Joshua Atwater, David's brother. According to family tradition, a direct descendant, Enos, left the Atwaters of New England for unknown reasons and settled in southern Orange County, where a son, Titus, father of Moses, purchased land in 1794 and 1796.

John W. Atwater attended local schools, including William Close Academy, and was about to enter college when the Civil War broke out. He enlisted in the Confederate army and served in Company D, First Regiment, North Carolina Volunteer Infantry; he was with General Robert E. Lee until the surrender at Appomattox. He then returned to his farm. However, agriculture had fallen into a state of severe stagnation. The confiscation of livestock, emancipation of labor, low prices, and the crop-lien system led to a sense of despair that eventually culminated in the formation of the Populist party.

This was essentially an agrarian revolt against the restrictive credit policies of the times. The Populists had been preceded by the National Grange, which came to North Carolina in 1873, and which supported cooperative ventures and educational and social activities. It was followed by the Farmers' Alliance, with aims similar to those of the Grange but without the Grange's reluctance to enter political activity to get support in the legislature. Atwater joined the Alliance in 1887 and served two terms as president of the Chatham chapter. In 1890 he was elected a state senator as an Alliance Democrat. The radical wing of the Alliance, which included Atwater, subsequently became disillusioned and, abandoning all hope of support from the Democrats and the Republicans, formed the People's or Populist party in 1892. At a convention held in

August, 72 counties were represented by 495 delegates. They won three seats in each house. Among those elected to the senate was Atwater; he was reelected in 1896 and in 1898 was elected by the Populists to the U.S. Congress, where he served from March 1899 to March 1901. He was an unsuccessful candidate for reelection in 1900 and returned to farming.

Atwater was married first, in 1861, to Eugenia E. Farrington. Five children were born to them: Alfred Sidney, John Bunyan, Harriet Lee, Addie Susan, and William M. In 1883, Atwater married Alice Farrington; daughter, Lillian, died in infancy. In 1899, Atwater and Sophrina J. Baldwin were married.

Something of an omnivorous reader, Atwater gave most of his library to the public shortly before his death. He was a Methodist and Sunday school superintendent of the Mt. Pleasant Church of Chatham County and was interred in its cemetery.

SEE: *Biographical Directory of the American Congress* (1961); Wade H. Hadley et al., *Chatham County, 1771–1971* (1976); Dewitt C. Mangum, *Biographical Sketches of Members of the Legislature of North Carolina, Session 1897* (1897); W. F. Tomlinson, *Biography of the State Officers and the Members of the General Assembly, 1893* (1893); *Who Was Who in America*, vol. 4 (1968).

JOHN MACFIE
NELL ATWATER

Autry, Micajah (1794 or 1795–March 1836), western pioneer and soldier, was born in Sampson County, the son of Theophilus and Elizabeth Crumpler Autry. When he was six years old, his family moved to Cumberland County, where his parents lived until their death.

Young Micajah showed an early interest both in books and in warfare. Volunteering when eighteen or nineteen for military duty during the War of 1812, he served as a private in Captain William Lord's company, which marched to the defense of Wilmington when it was threatened by the British. He served for the duration of the war.

According to family tradition, Autry returned home stricken with chills and fever. Unable to farm, he prepared himself as a teacher. By 1823, however, he was drawn westward to begin his career as one of the frontier adventurers who went to Texas to aid in the struggle for separation from Mexico.

First settling in Hayesboro in middle Tennessee, he taught and studied law there. In 1824 he married Mrs. Martha Wyche Putney Wilkinson, the prosperous widow of a doctor, by whom she had one daughter, Amelia. Of the several children born to Martha and Micajah, two lived to maturity: Mary became Mary Autry Greer of Beaumont, Tex. and James died in the first battle of Murfreesboro at the head of a Texas regiment during the Civil War.

According to his daughter, Micajah Autry was an intelligent and sensitive individual who liked to sing, especially the song of the "Good Old North State." He also enjoyed playing the violin, painting, and writing poetry, although he apparently did not pursue any of these interests seriously.

Ambition and circumstances continued to draw Autry westward. While in Hayesboro, near Nashville, he apparently became acquainted with Andrew Jackson and other Tennessee politicians. His daughter later claimed that Autry knew Sam Houston well and voted for him as governor of Tennessee. He moved his family and slaves westward to Jackson, Tenn., in 1831. While there, he joined in law practice with Andrew L. Martin.

Although they prospered in law, their attempt to establish a store failed. In an attempt to recoup his losses, Autry decided to investigate Texas as a possible place to resettle his family.

While in Jackson, Autry became acquainted with David Crockett, who, after being defeated by a Jacksonian politician, had become disillusioned with Tennessee politics. Some evidence indicates that Autry admired Crockett and may have been influenced by him in deciding to explore Texas.

In late 1835, Autry set out for Texas, stopping first at Memphis, Tenn., and then at Natchitoches, La., sending letters of his travels to his wife from both places. He traveled from Memphis down the Mississippi and up the Red River to Natchitoches on the steamboat *Pacific*. Unsure of the conditions that existed in Texas, he and a companion made a side trip from Natchitoches to New Orleans to inquire about events in Texas and to check on the best route. Autry then walked the 115 miles from Natchitoches, La., to Nacogdoches, Tex., where the Texas frontier apparently captured his enthusiasm. He wrote to his wife, "I go whole Hog in the cause of Texas. . . . There is not so fair a portion of the earth's surface warmed by the sun." Autry also revealed in the letter one of his motives for going to Texas and serving in the army; such service, he believed, would entitle him to 640 acres of land, with an additional 4,444 acres if he settled his family in Texas. His heirs eventually received 3,840 acres, given in two grants, 1839 and 1846, for Autry's service in the cause of the Texas revolution.

The trip to Nacogdoches proved fateful for Autry. At San Augustine he joined a company led by Captain H. S. Kimble from Clarksville, Tenn. After arriving in Nacogdoches, Autry was sworn in as a member of the Volunteer Auxiliary Corps for six months. Although his name was misspelled on the muster roll (M. Authey), his heirs were granted land donations partly on the basis of that list.

Autry indicated that he planned to proceed with the company to Washington-on-the-Brazos. Whether he did so is unknown; the next news of him was of his death at the Alamo. A postscript to his last letter from Nacogdoches reads, "Col. Crockett has joined our company." Autry apparently was pleased, and tradition has it that Autry served with Crockett's brigade at the Alamo. Given his prior acquaintance with Crockett and his association with other Tennesseans in the trek to Texas, he probably was indeed part of Crockett's defense of the south wall of the Alamo. If so, he was among the first to die when the Mexicans swarmed over that wall of the mission-fortress on 6 Mar. 1836. His name stands fourth in the alphabetical listing on the monument to those who died in defense of the Alamo. He is among those whom Texans honor today in celebrating the Texas revolution.

SEE: Micajah Autry, letters, 7 and 13 Dec. 1835, 13 Jan. 1836 (possession of James L. Autry); Mary Autry Greer (Beaumont, Tex.), reminiscences; Adele B. Looscan, "Micajah Autry, A Soldier of the Alamo," *Quarterly of the Texas State Historical Association* 14 (1910–11); Thomas Lloyd Miller, *Bounty and Donation Land Grants of Texas, 1835–1888* (1967).

J. B. SMALLWOOD, JR.

Avery, Alphonso Calhoun (*11 Sept. 1835–13 June 1913*), Confederate officer and judge, was born at Swan Ponds in Burke County, the fifth son of Isaac Thomas and Harriet Erwin Avery. While his father was a wealthy man, he believed that his sons should know farming thoroughly and raised them to follow the plow for at least one season. Once this training was over, young Avery was prepared for college at the Bingham School in Oaks, Orange County, and then entered The University of North Carolina; he was graduated with the A.B. degree in 1857, excelling in Latin and mathematics and standing first in his class.

Avery spent the next two years in Yancey, now Mitchell, County, in charge of a grass and stock farm for his father. He began to study law under the well-known teacher Richmond Pearson, later chief justice, at Logtown and within a year, in June 1860, was licensed to practice in the county courts. He was preparing to stand for his examination for license to appear before the superior court when the war intervened. On 27 Feb. 1861, he married Susan Washington Morrison, daughter of the Reverend R. H. Morrison of Lincoln County and granddaughter of General Joseph Graham of Lincoln County. The Reverend Mr. Morrison was a Presbyterian minister and the first president of Davidson College.

Three months later, Avery was helping his brother Isaac Erwin raise a company in the Sixth Regiment, North Carolina troops, and was granted a commission as first lieutenant in the same regiment. As a lieutenant in Company F, commanded by his brother, Captain I. E. Avery, he saw action in the battles of First Manassas and Seven Pines. After the Battle of Seven Pines, Captain Avery was placed in command of the Sixth Regiment, and shortly thereafter, A. C. Avery was promoted to captain and became the commander of Company E, Sixth Regiment. With his keen mind and legal education, however, he was considered to be of more value at headquarters than in the field and consequently was transferred to the staff of his brother-in-law, Major General Daniel Harvey Hill, in December 1862. There he was promoted to major and served for some time as assistant inspector general of Hill's division in the Army of Northern Virginia. In 1864 he went with the ill-fated Hill to the Army of the West, where his brother-in-law served for a time as a corps commander. When General Hill returned to Richmond, after a disagreement with General Braxton Bragg, Major Avery remained in the West, serving on the staffs of generals John C. Breckenridge, Thomas C. Hindman, and John B. Hood; he was with Hood in the retreat from Dalton to the Chattahoochee River.

Because his three older brothers had already been killed in action and his father was dying, Major Avery was granted a leave of absence by General Hood in the summer of 1864; within a month or so he was transferred to the Department of North Carolina. In the fall of that year, at the suggestion of the adjutant general of Western North Carolina District, he was authorized to organize a battalion that was subsequently enlarged to a regiment and used for the protection of the northwestern frontier of North Carolina. For a few months, Avery's battalion served a useful purpose, but it was unable to cope with the large Federal force that was moved to East Tennessee in the spring of 1865. At this time, Major General George Stoneman, with a division of Federal cavalry, moved into western North Carolina on a mammoth raid, and Major Avery was captured while doing military business at the Confederate army headquarters in Salisbury. With other captured prisoners, he was marched back to Tennessee and confined at Camp Chase until August 1865, at which time he was paroled.

Avery returned to Swan Ponds to begin the practice of law in Morganton. However, he was in no way returning to the life he had left. Led since childhood to believe that he would assume a favored position in the community, he was profoundly disillusioned to learn that in the ferment following the war years, his economic status had abruptly changed. There developed for him and others like him a ceaseless struggle against the blight of poverty and the crush of debt. Families were as large as ever and as demanding as ever, but money was almost nonexistent and the people were in no position to pay for services. As soon as he returned home, he became actively engaged in politics and in 1866 was elected to the state senate from a district composed of Burke, Caldwell, and McDowell counties. During his tenure of office, he originated and secured the passage of an act implementing the extension of the Western North Carolina Railroad to Old Fort. With the passage of the Reconstruction Act by the U.S. Congress in 1867, however, the Conservative Democrats were swept out of office and the Republican party was formed and took over. Composed of blacks, die-hard Unionists, disaffected Confederates, carpetbaggers, and scalawags, it ruled the state in a tempestuous fashion until 1877, a period of almost ten years.

With this turn of events, Avery joined an underground resistance movement instituted by the Conservative politicians of the state. A leader in the organization of the Ku Klux Klan in western North Carolina, he rode with the vigilantes. The Klan was a powerful resistance movement against the Republican party, its principles, and its policies. Confederate soldiers and respected citizens manned its ranks. It functioned actively and effectively during the late sixties and early seventies and promptly disbanded when it was no longer needed. There was no resemblance between it and subsequent organizations of the same name.

Avery was elected a Conservative delegate to the North Carolina Constitutional Convention of 1875. This body revised the state constitution, which had been rewritten by the Republicans in 1868. In 1876 he was a Democratic presidential elector. In 1878, with the return of the Democrats to power, he was elected a judge of the superior court of North Carolina. The same year he professed his faith and became a member of the First Presbyterian Church at Morganton. On 2 Nov. 1879 he was ordained and installed as a ruling elder in this church, an office that he fulfilled in an exemplary manner for more than twenty-five years. In 1886 his wife died, and three years later he married Sara Love Thomas, daughter of Colonel W. H. Thomas, a prominent political figure in western North Carolina. In 1889, Trinity College conferred on him the M.A. degree, and in the same year, The University of North Carolina honored him with the LL.D. degree.

Avery rode the circuits as a superior court judge for ten years and in 1888 was elected an associate justice of the Supreme Court of North Carolina. He served on the supreme court for eight years and during this time filed more than five hundred opinions, in which he displayed an absorbing passion for the rights of man. In 1892, the year Trinity College was moved to Durham, he assumed the burden of its struggling law school as dean and teacher, serving in this capacity for more than a year.

After his retirement from the bench in 1897, Avery conducted a private law practice in the courts of western North Carolina and also taught a law class in Morganton. He was a member of the Southern Historical Society and a prolific writer, not only on legal matters, but also on historical and biographical subjects. His *Life and Character of General D. H. Hill* has been recognized as the best sketch of this famous Confederate officer. At the time of his death he had just completed a *History of the Presbyterian Churches at Quaker Meadows and Morganton* but never had the opportunity to proofread it.

Avery had eleven children, among them Isaac Erwin Avery, the local editor of the *Charlotte Observer* whose untimely death in 1904 shortened what might have been a brilliant career in writing. Other children of Avery and his first wife, Susan Washington Morrison, were Harriet Eloise, Morrison Robert, Susan Washington, Alphonso Calhoun, and Alfred Lee. Avery's children with his second wife, Sallie Love Thomas, were Lenoir, Gladys (Mrs. Charles Tillett, a special representative of the United States to the United Nations), and Edith.

SEE: Samuel A. Ashe, ed., *Biographical History of North Carolina*, vol. 7 (1908); Alphonso Calhoun Avery, *History of the Presbyterian Churches* (1913); Elroy McKendree Avery and Catharine Hitchcock (Tilden) Avery, *The Groton Avery Clan*, vol. 1 (1912); Walter Clark, ed., *Histories of the Several Regiments and Battalions from North Carolina in the Great War, 1861–1865* (1909); Edward W. Phifer, "Saga of a Burke County Family," *North Carolina Historical Review* 39 (1962).

ISAAC THOMAS AVERY, JR.

Avery, Clark Moulton (3 Oct. 1819–18 June 1864), Confederate officer, was the second child of Isaac Thomas and Harriet Erwin Avery of Burke County. He was graduated from The University of North Carolina in 1839 with a B.A. degree. On 23 June 1841 he married Elizabeth Tilghman Walton, daughter of Thomas and Martha McEntire Walton.

The newly married couple seemed to be in no financial want, and in 1847 Avery acquired from his father-in-law 915 acres of farm land and a brick house several miles southwest of Morganton. This house, called Magnolia, still stands.

For twenty years, Avery occupied himself with the peaceful and pleasant, though not necessarily profitable, pursuits of a slaveholding planter; and although he took an active part in local politics, he did not seek public office. He was prevailed upon by his friends to run for the proposed state convention in an election on 28 Feb. 1861 and was elected a delegate by an overwhelming majority over one of the most popular Unionists in the county. The delegates did not meet, however, because a small majority of the electors of the state voted "no convention."

Avery reacted vigorously when the institution of slavery came under attack; he became a fiery secessionist and soon was willing to maintain the righteousness of his convictions by force if necessary. On 12 Apr. 1861, hostilities began at Charleston, and on 15 Apr. Lincoln issued his "Proclamation for Coercion," calling on all states to furnish troops to fight to preserve the Union. For North Carolina, this was the last straw, and on 17 Apr. Governor John W. Ellis issued his rejoinder, calling the General Assembly into special session on 1 May; on the same date, the companies of the First Regiment of the North Carolina troops volunteered and by 16 May were formed into a regiment at the state capitol by order of the adjutant general. They called themselves the First North Carolina Volunteers and signed up to serve six months. Company G, the Burke Rifles, was one of the ten companies of this regiment, and Captain Clark Moulton Avery was the company commander. Colonel Daniel Harvey Hill was regimental commander. The entire regiment reached Richmond by 21 May and after camping there for several days, on 24 May moved by rail and steamboat to Yorktown on the peninsula between the York and the James rivers.

On 10 June, Colonel Hill's troops, with several Virginia companies, were attacked by a Union force of about 4,400 men at Big Bethel Church. In this small battle the Federal forces were defeated and driven from the field within a few hours. Wrote D. H. Hill in his official report: "Captain Avery Company G displayed great coolness, judgment and efficiency in the battle of Bethel." After that time this regiment was known as "The Bethel Regiment." While the regiment was still at Yorktown, an order received from the adjutant general of North Carolina changed its designation from the First to the Nineteenth Regiment; the officers held a meeting and adopted resolutions opposing the change in a most vehement manner. On 12 Nov. 1861, the regiment was mustered out of service in Richmond; it returned to North Carolina the following day and disbanded. Appointed lieutenant colonel of the Thirty-third Regiment of North Carolina troops, which was in the process of organizing and training at the old fairground in Raleigh (later at Camp Mangum), Avery was promoted to colonel as of 17 Jan. 1862.

He instituted a rigorous training program for his regiment, and their later brilliant record is evidence of the value of such training.

In an action near New Bern, Avery was captured when the Thirty-third and Twenty-sixth North Carolina regiments, after making a valiant stand, were surrounded and overrun by the enemy. He was transported to Old Fort Columbus on Governor's Island, N.Y., and moved to Johnson's Island, Ohio, during the summer of 1862. Here, although the housing conditions were very crowded, the prisoners were furnished sufficient food to keep them from starving. After seven months' imprisonment, Avery was released by exchange. His health had been undermined by the imprisonment, but he would take only a short leave from his troops before returning; he returned to active duty in the late fall of 1862. In December, his regiment played a vital role at the Battle of Fredericksburg in closing the gap between the troops of generals James H. Lane and James J. Archer. Avery received his first disabling wound of the war at the Battle of the Orange Plank Road in May 1863. Soon returning to his troops, he was again wounded at Gettysburg.

After a short time with his family, Avery was again leading his forces at the Battle of the Wilderness, where they were under attack by Grant's troops. He was struck in the right thigh by a bullet and later, while lying on a litter, was again hit in the body and neck, and his left arm was shattered by a minié ball. His left arm was amputated, and he was moved to the Orange County Courthouse, where he was nursed by the women of the community; six weeks later he died from an infection in the leg wound.

A daughter, Laura Pairo, was born to Colonel and Mrs. Avery on 27 May 1864, shortly after he was fatally wounded; she was named for the woman who nursed Avery until his death. He was first buried in Virginia, but his wife, a short while later, took a servant and rode on horseback to Virginia to return his body to Morganton for permanent burial. They both lie now in the church yard of the First Presbyterian Church, Morganton.

Avery was survived by four children: Martha Matilda, who married George Phifer; Harriet Eloise, who married the Reverend James Colton; Isaac Thomas; and Laura Pairo, who married the Reverend John A. Gilmer.

SEE: Samuel A. Ashe, ed., *Biographical History of North Carolina*, vol. 7 (1908); Isaac Thomas Avery, personal recollections; Elroy McKendree Avery and Catharine Hitchcock (Tilden) Avery, *The Groton Avery Clan*, vol. 1 (1912); Edward W. Phifer, "Saga of a Burke County Family," *North Carolina Historical Review* 39 (1962); John H. Wheeler, *Historical Sketches of North Carolina* (1851).

ISAAC THOMAS AVERY, JR.

Avery, Isaac Erwin (20 Dec. 1828–3 July 1863), Confederate officer, fourth son of Isaac Thomas and Harriet Erwin Avery, was born at Swan Ponds in Burke County. He grew up on the family plantation and entered The University of North Carolina in 1847, but he attended for only one year. He then assisted his father in the operation of the plantation and managed a large farm in Yancey County. When the Western North Carolina Railroad was chartered in 1854, plans were soon completed to build a road from Salisbury to Morganton and eventually to Asheville. Avery entered into a business relationship with Charles F. Fisher of Salisbury and Samuel McDowell Tate of Morganton, and they contracted to participate in the building of the road. When the eruption of war in 1861 interrupted work on the road, it had been completed to within three miles of Morganton.

Avery undertook to raise a company as soon as his friend Colonel Charles Fisher was appointed by the governor to organize the Sixth North Carolina Regiment of state troops. With the assistance of his brother, A. C. Avery, he enlisted the largest company in the regiment, the enlistees agreeing to serve for three years or the duration of the war. Avery commanded E Company. After a period of training at Company Shops, now Burlington, the regiment was sent to Virginia and placed in the brigade of General Barnard Bee. As a detached regiment, it participated in the Battle of First Manassas and gave a good account of itself in this first great battle of the war. Avery was promoted to lieutenant colonel after the Battle of Seven Pines; and on 18 June 1862, he was promoted to colonel. His regiment participated in all of Lee's great campaigns of the summer and fall of 1862. Avery was seriously wounded at Gaines' Farm in 1862 and was out of action until the fall. After he returned to the regiment, Colonel Robert H. Chilton wrote in an inspection report: "The Sixth North Carolina Regiment, Co. Avery: Arms mixed, but in fine order, although two-thirds of the regiment are badly shod and clad, and 20 barefoot, the regiment shows high character of its officers in its superior neatness, discipline and drill."

As senior colonel, Avery was in command at Gettysburg of what had been known as Hoke's Brigade, composed of the Sixth, Twenty-first, Fifty-fourth and Fifty-seventh North Carolina regiments. On the second day of the battle he was called upon to lead two regiments in an attack on an enemy position on Cemetery Hill. The attack was made, even though one of the two regiments had been detached from Avery's force.

The attack commenced a little before dusk in smoke so thick that the oncoming figures were sometimes obscured. Avery was in front of the brigade on a white horse, the only mounted man of the command. A ball struck him at the base of his neck on the right side and the impact knocked him from the saddle. The missile had found a vital spot. He was stunned by the fall, his right arm went limp, and he began to bleed. His brigade moved on to storm the heights, and to cling there precariously for a time in a desperate hand-to-hand fight but, because no support came, eventually was forced to withdraw. Colonel Avery died there on the field of battle. As he lay among the wounded and dying, he brought out paper and pencil and wrote in uncertain letters, as his aide, Captain J. A. McPherson reported, "Major, tell my father I died with my face to the enemy, I. E. Avery." The original note is now in the State Archives in Raleigh.

The regimental historian of the Fifty-seventh Regiment commented, "the writer supposes that others will write the story of Colonel Avery's military life, or perhaps have done so, but I cannot forbear to say here that he was a gallant soldier, a very efficient brigade commander, and had he lived, would have doubtless risen rapidly in rank." His dying message has been widely noted.

Avery's body was brought by his faithful servant, Elijah Avery, in a cart to Williamsport, where it was buried. Some overzealous Confederates, after the war, had it disinterred and removed to a Confederate cemetery. His friends tried without success to trace the removing party so that his remains might be returned to North Carolina for final burial, but he lies, instead, in an unknown grave.

Colonel Isaac Erwin Avery never married.

SEE: Samuel A. Ashe, ed., *Biographical History of North Carolina*, vol. 7 (1908); Elroy McKendree Avery and Catharine Hitchcock (Tilden) Avery, *The Groton Avery Clan*, vol. 1 (1912); Walter Clark, ed., *Histories of the Several Regiments and Battalions from North Carolina in the Great War, 1861–1865* (1909); *The War of the Rebellion: A Compilation of the Official Records of the Union and Confederate Armies*, ser. 1, vol. 11, pt. 3 (1884); Edward W. Phifer, "Saga of a Burke County Family," *North Carolina Historical Review* 39 (1962); John H. Wheeler, *Historical Sketches of North Carolina* (1851).

ISAAC THOMAS AVERY, JR.

Avery, Isaac Erwin (*1 Dec. 1871–2 Apr. 1904*), Foreign Service officer and newspaperman, was born at Swan Ponds, Burke County, the second son of Alphonso Calhoun and Susan Morrison Avery. His parents moved to Morganton when he was very young, and there he attended primary schools. He was prepared for college by the Reverend John A. Gilmer at the academy in Morganton and might have entered college at the age of sixteen, but he chose to remain at home for a while, devoting most of his time to reading. He entered the sophomore class of Trinity College, then located in Randolph County, which later moved to Durham and is now Duke University. At Trinity he displayed a fondness for history and literature, was an excellent football player, and was universally liked by faculty and students. During his senior year he read law under his father, who was teaching law at Trinity; he was licensed in September 1893.

While he was regarded by all who knew him as possessing a mind especially fitted for the law, his tastes and talents constantly drove him toward newspaper and more general literary work. He was editor of the *Trinity Archive* at college, and correspondent for several newspapers in the state. The first contribution that earned him money was a paragraph of about thirty lines sent to "Town Topics," without expectation of payment, during the Christmas vacation of 1892, for which he received ten dollars.

After being licensed to practice law, Avery returned to Morganton, where he was employed by W. C. Erwin as associate editor of the *Morganton Herald*. He attracted much outside attention by his original methods and the excellent humor in many of his articles. He accepted an

appointment as secretary to the consul general at Shanghai from President Cleveland and left for China in March 1894. In less than a year he was appointed vice-consul general at Shanghai, an office he filled until the spring of 1898, when a new consul general was named by President McKinley. In China he was a regular contributor to the *North China Daily News*, the leading English paper in the Orient.

A few months after his return to North Carolina, Avery took up active newspaper work, reporting the proceedings of the state senate of 1899. About 1 May 1899 he moved to Greensboro and established a news bureau, representing a number of leading papers in North Carolina and elsewhere. Through his activities as a reporter his reputation grew, and on 1 Jan. 1900 he became city editor of the *Charlotte Observer*, a position he held until his death.

As city editor, he was free to criticize or commend the public acts of men who came under his observation, and he became widely known for the way he handled stories of human interest, either pathetic or humorous. As a miscellaneous news-gatherer he was also highly successful. He was regarded as a masterful interviewer and was in demand for meetings and news events.

More significant than his work as reporter, interviewer, or editorial writer was his "Variety of Idle Comments," a department of the *Observer* that appeared on Monday mornings; upon this department his fame largely rests. A collection of his writings was published in book form, the year following his death, under the title *Idle Comments*.

Avery never married but was engaged at the time of his death, which apparently was by suicide. Contemporary rumor said that there was a "Madame Butterfly" in his past and that a friend of his was to tell his fiancée of the past prior to the marriage.

SEE: Samuel A. Ashe, ed., *Biographical History of North Carolina*, vol. 7 (1908); Elroy McKendree Avery and Catharine Hitchcock (Tilden) Avery, *The Groton Avery Clan*, vol. 2 (1912); Isaac Erwin Avery, Preface to *Idle Comments* (1905).

ISAAC THOMAS AVERY, JR.

Avery, Isaac Thomas (*22 Sept. 1785–31 Dec. 1864*), politician, planter, and banker, only son of Waightstill Avery and Leah Probart Avery, was born at Swan Ponds, Burke County. He had little formal education: he received an adequate education in the classics and some knowledge of science under Samuel Doak at Washington College near Jonesboro in Washington County, Tenn., but he left the college at the age of sixteen when his father, Waightstill Avery, became incapacitated. He returned home to shoulder the responsibilities for the family's prospering estate and slaves as well as to accompany his father as he continued the practice of law.

The young Avery showed an early interest in politics, representing Burke County in the legislature for the first time in 1809 at the age of twenty-four and returning to the lower house in 1810 and 1811. After that time he never again sought public office but continued to be a formidable figure in western North Carolina politics as an advisor to the governor, being three times appointed to the governor's council. In 1824 he was a presidential elector from North Carolina, at which time he initially supported Calhoun, who championed internal improvements. When Calhoun's star faded, however, he reluctantly supported Andrew Jackson over William H. Crawford. He was also a presidential elector for John Quincy Adams in 1828.

In 1815 he married Harriet Eloise Erwin, daughter of William Willoughby and Matilda Sharpe Erwin, both members of prominent families. Mrs. Erwin was a daughter of William Sharpe, a Salisbury lawyer who served on the Holston River Treaty Commission with Waightstill Avery. Isaac Thomas and Harriet Erwin Avery had twelve sons and four daughters, six of whom died in infancy or childhood.

In 1829, Avery was appointed head of the Morganton branch of the North Carolina State Bank, a position he held for thirty years. At this time, gold mines at Brindletown in southern Burke County were producing profitably, and Avery was extremely optimistic about the future of this industry in western North Carolina. However, because of the lack of transportation, it was extremely difficult for any enterprise other than agriculture to prosper in Burke County. It was almost impossible to get the products out of the county.

Avery was a member of the board of internal improvements from 1821 to 1822 and was for many years president of the Catawba Navigation Company, which attempted to make this river navigable from its upper reaches to the South Carolina line. The project was unsuccessful, apparently because of inadequate capitalization, incompetent technical assistance, and the eventual development of the steam locomotive as a more efficient mode of transportation.

As the Avery family grew, the old brick house that Waightstill Avery had built became inadequate, and a new and larger house was erected in 1848. Isaac Avery of necessity administered large agricultural holdings, but he was considered a man of culture and learning and, like his father, primarily a classical scholar. He collected copies of the works of the Latin writers, as well as Shakespeare, and is reported to have read Latin easily even in his advanced years.

Four of his sons served in the Confederate army, three of them as colonels. Three were killed during the Civil War on the field of battle, and the fourth son died shortly afterward as a result of wounds received during the war.

Avery was buried in the family burial ground at Swan Ponds. A grandson said he seemed to give up his will to live when a servant returned with news of the death of his third son in battle.

SEE: Samuel A. Ashe, ed., *Biographical History of North Carolina*, vol. 7 (1908); Elroy McKendree Avery and Catharine Hitchcock (Tilden) Avery, *The Groton Avery Clan*, vol. 1 (1912); Edward W. Phifer, "Saga of a Burke County Family," *North Carolina Historical Review* 39 (1962); John H. Wheeler, *Historical Sketches of North Carolina* (1851).

ISAAC THOMAS AVERY, JR.

Avery, Waightstill (10 May 1741–13 Mar. 1821), first attorney general of North Carolina, represented Burke County in the House of Commons for five years and in the senate for one.

The first Avery to settle in this country was Christopher Avery, who, with his young son James, came from England in the ship *Arabella* and landed at Boston in 1631. James Avery married Johanna Greenslade. The youngest of ten children of this marriage was Samuel (b. 14 Aug. 1664), who married Susanna Palmes, daughter of William Palmes of the Province of Munster, Ireland, on 27 Oct. 1686. Humphrey Avery, sixth child of Samuel and Susanna Palmes Avery, was born 4 July 1699, married Jerusha Morgan, and had twelve children. The tenth son was Waightstill Avery, born in Groton, Conn.

Waightstill Avery and his younger brother, Isaac, were prepared for college by the Reverend Samuel Seabury. Waightstill Avery was graduated from Princeton, then called the College of New Jersey, in 1766; awarded first honors in his class, he delivered the Latin salutatory. He taught at the college for a year and then read law with Lyttleton Dennis, a prominent Maryland lawyer. Moving to North Carolina in 1769, he entered the colony at Edenton, where he had letters of introduction to such prominent people as James Iredell and Joseph Hewes. He was admitted to practice in the colonies on 4 Feb. 1769 and lived in Salisbury a year; he then moved to Charlotte, where he lived and boarded at the house of Hezekiah Alexander. During this period he renewed contacts with Ephraim Brevard, Adlai Osborne, and others from his Princeton years. While in Charlotte in 1772, he was elected a member of the provincial assembly and appointed attorney general for the Crown. In May 1775 he was a member of the committee that passed the famous Mecklenburg Resolves and was among the signers of that document. In August he became a delegate to the provincial congress held at Hillsborough, which placed the state under a military organization. In September he was appointed one of the thirteen members of the provincial council, which had been given great powers by the provincial congress. On 10 May 1776 he resigned his commission as attorney general. He was a member of the congress that met at Halifax on 12 Nov. 1776 and served on the committee that drew up and reported the first North Carolina Constitution. Governor David L. Swain said later that an examination of the records would indicate that more of the constitution of 1776 was in the handwriting of Waightstill Avery than was in that of any other member of the committee.

After the formation of the state government, Waightstill Avery was elected to the first General Assembly, which met at New Bern in 1777; by that body he was named the first attorney general of North Carolina.

He married, on 3 Oct. 1778 at New Bern, Mrs. Leah Probart Francks, daughter of Captain Yelverton Peyton Probart of Snow Hill, Md. Mrs. Francks had a large farm in Jones County, where they settled.

Avery was made one of the governor's council on 26 Oct. 1779, and in 1779 he resigned the office of attorney general to become colonel of the militia of Jones County in place of Nathan Bryan, who resigned. In this capacity he was engaged for more than two years.

In the meantime, he had purchased Swans Pond plantation in Burke County and sent his wife, two young daughters, and his slaves there; he joined his family there late in 1781, when it became apparent that independence had been won.

In 1780, while occupying Charlotte, Cornwallis ordered the burning of Avery's office; of his books and papers, only those stored in the house of his friend Hezekiah Alexander were saved. This evidence of displeasure was visited only upon those whom Cornwallis considered leading offenders.

Avery was elected by Burke County to the House of Commons in 1782, 1783, 1784, 1785, and 1793 and to the senate in 1796. In 1801 he was rendered helpless in his lower limbs by paralysis, but he continued to practice his profession from Raleigh to Jonesboro, Tenn., until a few years before his death in 1821.

Avery, an avowed Presbyterian of puritan extraction, accepted a challenge to a duel from Andrew Jackson, then a young lawyer at Jonesboro court, as a result of a courtroom incident. In a criminal case before the court,

Avery had been severe in his comments on some of the legal positions taken by young Jackson. Family stories handed down for generations state that it was Avery's custom to refer to Bacon, the noted English jurist, and then to pull his copy of Bacon's reports from his saddlebags to bolster his opinions. Jackson, in playing a prank on him, substituted a side of bacon for Bacon's book and caused Avery much embarrassment. Avery took Jackson to task for such levity in the court, and Jackson, of a certainty, replied with a challenge to a duel. Avery accepted the challenge saying, "This evening after Court is adjourned," and they went on the field. Jackson fired first, with no effect, and Avery fired in the air; then Avery walked up to Jackson and delivered him a lecture. They left the grounds very good friends.

Avery was a gentlemen of the old school and until his death wore knee britches, powdered wigs, and full dress of the times of Washington. He was a man of great dignity and demeanor but was remarkably courteous in his language and manner, even toward young people.

Colonel Avery had three daughters and a son. His daughter Elizabeth married William Lenoir and settled at Lenoir City, Tenn. Louisa married Thomas Lenoir, another son of his old friend General William Lenoir, and settled first at Pigeon River in Haywood County and afterward at Fort Defiance, the old Lenoir homestead. The third daughter married first a Mr. Pore and then a Mr. Summey and lived on Mills River in Henderson County. Avery's son, Isaac Thomas, married Harriet Eloise Erwin.

Avery died at Morganton and was buried in a family graveyard near there.

SEE: Samuel A. Ashe, ed., *Biographical History of North Carolina*, vol. 7 (1908); Elroy McKendree Avery and Catharine Hitchcock (Tilden) Avery, *The Groton Avery Clan*, vol. 1 (1912).

ISAAC THOMAS AVERY, JR.

Avery, William Waightstill (*25 May 1816–3 July 1864*), Confederate congressman and army officer, was born at Swan Ponds, his father's plantation in Burke County. He was the oldest son of Isaac Thomas Avery, planter, slaveholder, and cashier of the Morganton branch of the state bank, and of Harriet Eloise Erwin, the daughter of William Willoughby Erwin.

After growing up in Burke County, Avery entered The University of North Carolina in 1833. Although inadequate preparation forced him to study during vacations, he was graduated with highest honors and gave the valedictory address in 1837. He then studied law under Judge William Gaston, was licensed to practice in 1839, and entered politics in 1840 as an unsuccessful Democratic candidate for the state House of Commons. Two years later, however, he was elected and served one term as representative from Burke County. Between 1842 and 1850, Avery devoted himself to his law practice in Morganton, but in 1850 and 1852 he again represented Burke County in the House of Commons.

In the session of 1850 he supported a bill amending the state constitution to remove freehold qualifications for electors of the state senate. At the same time he opposed the calling of a special convention to approve this amendment, on the grounds that such a convention might proceed to attack the federal basis of representation, reopening animosity between eastern and western sections of the state and drawing undesirable attention to the whole question of the

political representation of slaves. In the same session, when the legislature established a joint select committee on Negro slavery to consider resolves related to the Compromise of 1850, Avery reported to the House of Commons for the minority of the committee. The minority resolutions defined the Union as a compact among sovereign states and affirmed North Carolina's right to secede if the people, in a special convention, believed secession necessary to the protection of their rights. Although the legislature failed to adopt any of the proposed resolutions, Avery had clearly taken his place as a states' rights Democrat.

While defending slavery and southern rights and gradually moving toward active support for secession by 1860, Avery also became one of a group of leaders who, in the 1840s and 1850s, demanded progress for North Carolina. After his appointment as a trustee of the university in 1850, Avery delivered a commencement address to the two student societies in 1851 on the theme of state pride. Reminding his listeners of North Carolina's contributions to the American Revolution, he urged them to overcome the backwardness of recent decades by building ports and factories, improving the state's schools, producing a state literature, and ending emigration from the state. On a practical level, he took an active part in the organization of the Western North Carolina Railroad, of which he became a director in 1857.

In November 1851, as he left the courthouse at Marion, Avery was hit with a rock and then beaten with a cowhide by Samuel Fleming, a participant in a suit in which Avery was involved as legal counsel. Two weeks later, when Fleming walked into Judge William Horn Battle's courtroom in Morganton, Avery shot him through the heart. Tried for murder before Judge Battle, Avery was acquitted on the grounds of extreme provocation leading to temporary insanity, with the jury deliberating for only ten minutes.

In spite of some criticism, especially in the Whig press, of the laxity of the law in this case, the incident appears to have had little effect on Avery's political career. He was reelected to the House of Commons in 1852, led the delegation from North Carolina to the Democratic National Convention that nominated James Buchanan in 1856, and in the latter year was elected to the state senate, of which he was chosen speaker. In 1858 he ran for the congressional seat vacated when the legislature appointed Thomas L. Clingman to the U.S. Senate, but conflict between Avery and David Coleman, another Democrat, resulted in the election of the Whig candidate, Zebulon Baird Vance.

Again in 1860, Avery was chairman of the state's delegation to the Democratic National Convention in Charleston, S.C. As chairman of the committee on resolutions, he favored the majority report denying the right of Congress or territorial legislatures to prohibit slavery in the territories, demanding federal protection for all property in those territories, upholding the Fugitive Slave Act, and advocating the acquisition of Cuba from Spain as soon as practicable. The North Carolina delegation did not walk out when the convention adopted instead the committee's minority report, supporting popular sovereignty in the territories and the platform of 1856. In the subsequent convention in Baltimore, however, the denial of seats to those southerners who had walked out in Charleston led Avery and the majority of the North Carolina delegation to leave and, with other southerners, nominate John C. Breckinridge of Kentucky. Accused in North Carolina of Disunionism, Avery insisted in a debate in Charlotte that he was merely protecting southern rights and was no more a Disunionist than presidents Franklin Pierce and James Buchanan.

After Lincoln's election, however, Avery apparently decided that secession could no longer be avoided. He was reelected to the state senate in 1860 and, in December of that year, presented resolutions from a nonpartisan group of his Burke County constituents advocating the call for a secession convention in North Carolina. While the state's voters rejected such a convention in February 1861, despite the continuing efforts of Avery and other secessionists, Burke County supported it by a vote of 718 to 273.

After North Carolina finally seceded on 20 May 1861, Avery was chosen by the secession convention to represent the state in the provisional Confederate Congress, where he served as chairman of the committee on military affairs. Failing to win appointment to the Confederate Senate in 1861, he returned to Burke County with Jefferson Davis's authorization to raise a regiment for the Confederate Army; there, however, the protests of his father and the fact that his four younger brothers were already serving convinced him that family obligations demanded his presence at home. Nevertheless, he died in Morganton from wounds received when he and Colonel T. G. Walton led a company of Burke County militia against a party of Tennessee Unionists, who had marched into the state and captured several conscripts in training near Morganton. Avery was buried in the cemetery of the First Presbyterian Church in Morganton.

In May 1846, Avery married Mary Corinna Morehead, the daughter of John Motley Morehead, Whig governor of North Carolina from 1841 to 1845. They had two sons: John Morehead, who became a lawyer in Dallas, Tex.; and William Waightstill of Mitchell County. They also had three daughters: Annie Harriet, who married Joseph H. Scales of Patrick, Va.; Corinna Iredell, who married George P. Erwin of Morganton; and Adelaide Matilda, who married John J. Hemphill of South Carolina.

SEE: Samuel A. Ashe, ed., *Biographical History of North Carolina*, vol. 7 (1908); Elroy McKendree Avery and Catharine Hitchcock (Tilden) Avery, *The Groton Avery Clan*, 2 vols. (1912); Waightstill Avery Papers (Southern Historical Collection, University of North Carolina, Chapel Hill); W. W. Avery, *Address Delivered before the Two Literary Societies of the University* (1851); and *Speech upon the Subject of Constitutional Reform* (1850); W. W. Avery and M. Erwin, *Address to the People of the 46th and 49th Senatorial Districts* (1861); Charleston Democratic Convention Papers, 1860 (Library, Duke University, Durham); *Charlotte Observer*, 30 Sept. 1928; *DAB*, vol. 1 (1928); *Greensboro Daily News*, 18 July 1926; *North Carolina Manual* (1913); O. M. Peterson, "W. W. Avery in the Democratic National Convention of 1860," *North Carolina Historical Review* 31 (1954); Edward W. Phifer, "Saga of a Burke County Family: Conclusion," *North Carolina Historical Review* 39 (1962); Raleigh *North Carolina Standard*, 8 Dec. 1860; Salisbury *Carolina Watchman*, 20 and 27 Nov. 1851, 4 Dec. 1851; J. C. Sitterson, *The Secession Movement in North Carolina* (1939).

ELGIVA D. WATSON

Avery, Willoughby Francis (*7 May 1843–24 Nov. 1876*), journalist, was born at Swan Ponds, Burke County, the youngest of the sixteen children born of Isaac Thomas and Harriet Erwin Avery. He was the "Benjamin" of a large family. Fifteen years old at the time of his mother's death, he grew up a jolly, carefree boy and entered The University of North Carolina in the

fall of 1860. At the university he stood first in a large class but left to volunteer in the Confederate Army.

Avery's first service was as a lieutenant in a company of cavalry raised in Burke County by Colonel T. G. Walton, which became Company F, Forty-third North Carolina or Third Cavalry. In 1862 he was transferred to the Thirty-third Regiment, which was commanded by his older brother, Colonel Clark Moulton Avery. He served as a second lieutenant in Company C, was later promoted to captain and transferred to Company I, and served in this capacity until the end of the war. He was wounded first at the Battle of Sharpsburg and again at Gettysburg; finally, in May 1864, in the Wilderness of Spotsylvania, he was so dangerously wounded that his life was saved only by a very skillful operation. When the war ended in 1865, he was twenty-two years old and had already endured more physical and emotional anguish than most men are called upon to tolerate in a lifetime. Plagued by crippling wounds of the flesh and of the spirit, he survived the war only eleven years.

On 7 Nov. 1866 he married Martha Caroline Jones; she died in less than two years, as did their infant daughter.

Avery chose journalism as a vocation and edited newspapers in Asheville and Charlotte before returning to his native county and establishing a newspaper at Morganton, which he called the *Blue Ridge Blade*. In February 1875 he married Laura Atkinson of Johnston County, a stepdaughter of W. S. Smith. They had one son, Willoughby Moulton Avery, who later married Emma Sharpe of Greensboro, a granddaughter of Judge Thomas Settle.

Willoughby Avery died when his son was only seven months old; he was buried in the churchyard of the First Presbyterian Church at Morganton, where he had been a member since 1 Aug. 1867. This grave has since been moved to the lawn at the new church site in Morganton.

SEE: Samuel A. Ashe, ed., *Biographical History of North Carolina*, vol. 7 (1908); Alphonso Calhoun Avery, *History of the Presbyterian Churches* (1913); Elroy McKendree Avery and Catharine Hitchcock (Tilden) Avery, *The Groton Avery Clan*, vol. 1 (1912); Walter Clark, ed., *Histories of the Several Regiments and Battalions from North Carolina in the Great War, 1861–1865* (1901); Edward W. Phifer, "Saga of a Burke County Family," *North Carolina Historical Review* 39 (1962).

ISAAC THOMAS AVERY, JR.

Avirett, James Battle (*12 Mar. 1835–16 Feb. 1912*), Episcopal priest, author, and Confederate chaplain, the son of Serena Thomas and John Alfred Averitt, was born on the Averitt plantation near New River Chapel and the present town of Richlands. Avirett, who adopted this spelling of the name, was a student at The University of North Carolina from 1850 through 1852. In 1861 he was ordained to the diaconate by Bishop William Meade. When the Seventh Virginia Cavalry was organized on 17 June 1861, Avirett was named chaplain to this unit, which came to be known as Ashby's Cavalry. When Avirett died he was reputed to have been the last surviving Confederate chaplain.

From 1865 until 1871, Avirett conducted Dunbar Institute, an Episcopal seminary for young ladies in Winchester, Va.; afterward, he was rector of churches at Sligo, Silver Spring, and Upper Marlboro, and at Waterville, N.Y. In 1894 he became rector of St. Paul's Church, Louisburg, N.C., where he served until his retirement in 1899. During the period from 1867 to 1901, Avirett wrote four published works. *The Memoirs of General Turner Ashby and His Compeers* was published in

1867. *Watchman, What of the Night? or The Causes Affecting Church Growth* was published in May 1897 by St. James's Church, Kittrell, and St. Paul's Church, Louisburg, both served by Avirett. The text of the pamphlet was the sermon he preached before the Eighty-first Annual Convention of the Diocese of North Carolina. In September 1897 he published another pamphlet, *Who Was the Rebel?* his 17 Sept. oration at the foundation stone ceremony for the North Carolina Plot in the Stonewall Cemetery, Winchester, Va. Avirett's fourth published work was the book *The Old Plantation: How We Lived in Great House and Cabin before the War*, which appeared in 1901.

Avirett married Mary Louise Dunbar Williams of Winchester, Va., and they were the parents of two sons, John Williams and Phillip Williams. John W. Avirett became editor of the *Cumberland* (Md.) *Evening Times*, and when James Avirett retired, he went to Cumberland to live with his son and often contributed articles to John's newspaper. Avirett died in Cumberland and was buried in Winchester.

SEE: James Battle Avirett's own works; *Clerical Directory of the Protestant Episcopal Church in the United States of America*; *The Episcopal Church Annual*; D. L. Grant, *Alumni History of the University of North Carolina* (1924); Zae H. Gwynn, *Abstracts of the Records of Onslow County, North Carolina* (1961); *Journals of the* [Episcopal] *Diocese of North Carolina*.

TUCKER REED LITTLETON

Aycock, Charles Brantley (1 Nov. 1859–4 Apr. 1912), governor of North Carolina, was born on a farm near Fremont in the broad, flat valley of the Neuse River. Ancestors of his father, Benjamin Aycock, and his mother, Serena Hooks, had come to the valley from England during the colonial period. Benjamin and Serena Aycock were industrious, thrifty, and pious, and both had a good sense of management. About 1840 they settled in a house on 50 acres of land. By 1860 they had accumulated 1,036 acres, and in 1863 they owned 13 slaves. Benjamin Aycock participated avidly in the Primitive Baptist church and the Democratic party. He served in the North Carolina Senate from 1863 to 1866 and for eight years was clerk of court of Wayne County. In the senate he distinguished himself by his willingness to centralize power in the Confederate government and his unwillingness to elevate the status of the Negro.

The youngest of ten children, Charles B. Aycock attended private schools in Fremont and Wilson. At the age of sixteen, he taught in the public school in Fremont for one term. After preparing himself further for college by an additional year of study at a private academy in Kinston, he enrolled at The University of North Carolina in 1877. Ambitious and energetic, he read widely, became a student leader in oratorical and literary activities, worked with the Young Men's Christian Association, and taught a Sunday school class for boys in a rural congregation. He joined the Missionary Baptist Church, a denomination to which he belonged for the rest of his life. In the summers of 1878 and 1879 he attended the university's normal school. In 1879, in Durham County, he delivered an address on education, apparently his first public performance apart from teaching. For three months he edited the *Chapel Hill Ledger*, a small weekly newspaper. In the spring of 1880 he took an extracurricular course in law and completed the requirements for a degree. Being graduated after only three years, he won commencement awards for oratory and English composition.

Aycock apprenticed himself to the law office of A. K. Smedes in Goldsboro, received a license to practice in January 1881, and formed a partnership in Goldsboro with Frank Arthur Daniels. The two men became, and remained, general practitioners of the law. In 1880, Aycock delivered campaign speeches for the Democratic party; he continued to do so in every election year for the rest of his life. In 1882 he was conspicuous in county and district conventions. He joined with Joseph E. Robinson and William C. Munroe to establish a Democratic newspaper, the *Goldsboro Daily Argus*, in 1885. In the next year he was a delegate to the Democratic State Convention, and in 1888 he served as district presidential elector and made numerous speeches in behalf of Grover Cleveland.

In 1890, Aycock sought the Democratic nomination to the U.S. House of Representatives in the Third Congressional District. Many voters had joined the Farmers' Alliance. Although Aycock expressed his approval of Alliance demands, he was handicapped by being neither a farmer nor an Alliance member. Nonetheless, at the district convention, he contended strongly against four other candidates and received a plurality on numerous ballots. Distressed by the continued deadlock, he withdrew as a candidate in order to make nomination possible.

During the same years in which he was building a law practice and a political reputation, Aycock was also working vigorously in behalf of the public schools. In 1881 he campaigned for a special tax to support a graded school in Goldsboro; it was approved in a referendum on 2 May. Under the provisions of the statute, the revenues collected from white citizens were applied to the schools for white children, and the revenues collected from Negroes were applied to Negro schools. In June, Aycock was chosen by Wayne County officials to be county superintendent of public instruction, a part-time position that he held until the summer of 1882, at which time he resigned in order to devote more attention to his law practice. In 1886 the state supreme court ruled that separate taxes for the races were unconstitutional. Aycock joined a campaign to raise an emergency fund to keep the Goldsboro schools operating until the adoption of a new tax, uniform and nondiscriminatory, to support schools for both races for nine-month terms. The act authorizing the referendum on the tax also named a board of trustees for the entire city system. Aycock was one of the members, and as long as he lived in Goldsboro he served on the board, often as chairman. Also in 1887, Aycock was selected as a member both of the committee of a Wayne County Negro school district and of the board of directors of the State Normal School for Negroes in Goldsboro.

At the Democratic State Convention in 1892, Aycock helped Elias Carr, a Farmers' Alliance leader, win the nomination for governor and was himself chosen presidential elector-at-large. Carr lacked oratorical skill, and Aycock became the party's chief stump speaker in the eastern half of the state. As a reward for his services, he was selected by President Cleveland to be the U.S. attorney for the eastern district of North Carolina, a position he held from 1893 to 1897.

The Populists and Republicans won a majority of seats in the General Assembly in 1894, and Aycock's rise to eminence slowed perceptibly. In 1895 the General Assembly removed him from the board of trustees of the State Normal School for Negroes in Goldsboro. In 1896 he was recommended for the gubernatorial nomination by the Democratic convention in his congressional district, but he declined to be a candidate against the strong Populist and Republican forces, by then loosely united in a "Fusion Party." Nonetheless, prior to the elections of that year, he campaigned for Democratic presidential nominee William Jennings Bryan and substituted for Democratic gubernatorial candidate Cyrus Watson in a series of speaking engagements. In 1897 he cooperated with Fusion leaders in a state-wide effort to persuade voters in local school districts to adopt school taxes.

The Fusion-dominated legislatures of 1895 and 1897 and Republican Governor Daniel L. Russell encouraged an enlarged political role for Negroes, who voted in great numbers and held a variety of public offices. Many white people, Democratic and Fusionist, were unprepared for the abrupt change. Imbued with the white supremacy traditions of his family and sensitive to the growing social and racial tensions under the Fusion administration, Aycock stressed, early in the campaign of 1898, that the Democrats must adopt a platform emphasizing white supremacy and appealing to all classes of white people. Foremost among a large group of able Democratic orators who spoke throughout the state, Aycock represented the party in debates with Cyrus Thompson, Populist secretary of state. Racial tensions were heightened by the anti-Negro sentiments expressed in the campaign, and weapons were displayed at some political gatherings. Aycock argued that a Democratic administration could restore white supremacy and peace.

In the elections of 1898, the Democratic party won a large majority of seats in both houses of the General Assembly. In 1899, Aycock worked closely with the Democratic legislators, who proposed an amendment to the state constitution requiring the electorate to pass a literacy test before registering and to pay a poll tax before voting. Through a "grandfather clause," the amendment exempted from the literacy test all men who were qualified voters on or before 1 Jan. 1867 or who were lineal descendants of such voters. The exemption was limited to 1 Dec. 1908. Any man who registered before that date would be validly registered for the rest of his life; any man who applied for registration after that date would have to pass the literacy test. The legislature also provided that $100,000 would be appropriated annually for distribution among the public schools. Intended to assist the schools in preparing young men to pass the literacy test after 1908, this appropriation was the first direct legislative appropriation for the public schools in thirty years and the first in the history of the state to be paid.

The proposed constitutional amendment was especially significant for Aycock. It enabled him to imbue the campaign of 1900 with a sense of dignity and noble purpose that the campaign of 1898 had lacked. His views and personal attractiveness appealed to so many delegates at the Democratic State Convention in April 1900 that he was unopposed for the gubernatorial nomination. In the campaign, he pledged to devote his four-year term as governor to improving the public school system. He stressed the importance of the suffrage amendment as a device for eliminating the race problem in politics, compelling educational advancement, and preparing the way for Negroes to participate fully in politics when they were literate. In the elections in August 1900, the amendment was approved by a large majority, and Aycock was elected by an even greater majority. His inaugural address in January 1901 emphasized education and the race problem. He promised that universal suffrage would return as a consequence of universal education and that the rights of Negroes would be protected.

In his first year in office, Aycock staged a one-man crusade for education, speaking at local rallies held in behalf of school taxes and bonds, addressing audiences at private schools and at colleges, and whenever possible turning additional public appearances into pleas for educational progress. After his first year in office, he broadened the crusade, utilizing funds provided by the Southern Education Board. An Association for the Promotion of Public Education in North Carolina was organized, and speakers were sent to rallies throughout the state. Aycock himself attended as many as time and energy permitted. He remained loyal to his pledge to work for universal education. When two bills to enable white people to tax themselves to improve schools for white children without improving schools for Negro children were introduced in the legislature in 1901, Aycock stated that he would resign if they were adopted. Both bills died in committee.

Under Aycock's leadership, the appropriations for the public schools and the state's colleges were increased, teaching standards were raised, state adoption of textbooks replaced the more expensive system of local adoption, 877 libraries were established in rural schools, and hundreds of schoolhouses were built. The enrollment of white children rose 11 percent, and the average length of the school term increased from seventy-three days to eighty-five days. Local expenditures for Negro schools did not increase at the same rate as expenditures for white schools, but the enrollment of Negro children rose 10 percent and the average length of the school term increased from sixty-three days to eighty days. Teachers organized into associations for the promotion of their profession, teacher pay went up, and compensation for county superintendents doubled. Local school taxes were being collected in 229 districts in 1904, compared to 30 in 1900. In the same period, 37 new municipal graded schools were established. On the basis of the amount of money spent for public education as a percentage of wealth, North Carolina moved in rank among the states from thirty-second in 1900 to twenty-first in 1904.

Also under Aycock's leadership, a temperance law and a child labor law were enacted, taxes on businesses and corporations were increased, the good roads movement was encouraged, and new regulations were imposed on the railroads. When private entrepreneurs tried to use the courts to seize control of the Atlantic and North Carolina Railroad, Aycock thwarted them with charges of conspiracy to injure state property. In an effort to save money that could be diverted to schools and charities, he expanded the program of leasing convicts to private enterprise. He followed a generous clemency policy, granting more full pardons than any other governor in North Carolina history, before or since. Eleven lynchings occurred during his administration. He called out the militia on several occasions to protect prisoners, offered rewards for the apprehension of lynchers, and urged, without success, the adoption of an anti-lynch law by the legislature. He supported efforts to study and protect land and wildlife. The activities of the state geological board were broadened, and the department of agriculture was enlarged. The Audubon Society of North Carolina was empowered to enforce the bird and game laws, thus becoming the first state game commission in the South.

After leaving the governorship, Aycock returned to Goldsboro and resumed his law practice with Frank A.

Daniels. In 1909 he moved to Raleigh and formed a partnership with Robert W. Winston. In 1911 he yielded to numerous requests that he become a candidate for the Democratic nomination to the U.S. Senate, but on 4 Apr. 1912, before he had begun an active campaign, he died while addressing the Alabama Educational Association in Birmingham. His heart suddenly failed; the last word the audience heard him speak as he collapsed on the platform was "education." He was buried in Oakwood Cemetery in Raleigh. As a sponsor of education, he perhaps has had no peer among state governors in American history.

Aycock married Varina Woodard on 25 May 1881, and the couple had three children: Ernest, Charles Brantley, Jr., and Alice. In January 1891, after Varina's death in 1889, Aycock married her sister, Cora. This marriage produced seven children: William Benjamin, Mary Lily, Connor Woodard, John Lee, Louise Rountree, Frank Daniels, and Brantley (Charles Brantley, Jr., had died in 1901).

Portraits of Aycock are located in the North Carolina State Capitol, the Governor's Mansion, and the Wake County Courthouse in Raleigh. Statues stand on Capitol Square in Raleigh and in the U.S. Capitol in Washington, D.C.

SEE: Bibliography in Oliver H. Orr, Jr., *Charles Brantley Aycock* (1961).

OLIVER H. ORR, JR.

Ayllón, Lucas Vásquez de (*ca. 1480–18 Oct. 1526*), explorer, was the son of Judge Juan Ayllón, head of a noble and rich family of Toledo, Spain, which probably originated in the province of Segovia. Ayllón was educated in civil law, probably at the University of Salamanca. His fondness for adventure explains his reluctance to remain in Toledo and enjoy the position and wealth of his family. Consequently, he was sent to Santo Domingo by Cardinal Jiménez de Cisneros—founder of the University of Alcalá and adviser to Queen Isabel and King Ferdinand—as one of three justices of the supreme court. The party, including three Hieronymite monks, arrived in the island in 1516.

For several years, Ayllón had no unusual experiences in his position as judge. However, after the arrival of Cortés in Mexico, the situation changed abruptly. Both Diego Velázquez, the governor, and Rodrigo de Narváez were jealous of the newcomer and the success he seemed to have in New Spain. They decided to send a force to stop him. Some time later, Ayllón was given the difficult assignment of attempting to dissuade them from interfering with Cortés. The authorities did not relish the possibility of the natives of New Spain witnessing what would amount to civil war between two factions of the invading Christians. For his efforts, Ayllón got a very rude reception from both Velázquez and Narváez, and also a short period of imprisonment. Cortés continued to be master of the situation in Mexico.

Ayllón was intrigued by the colorful stories brought to Santo Domingo by Francisco Gordillo, who had sailed along the coast of Florida as far as latitude 33°30'. With a slave trader, Gordillo had captured some seventy Indians. Ayllón ordered the Indians released, but he could not forget the stories told of Florida; he finally decided to go to Spain with a request for permission to explore the coast of Chicora. The permission was granted, and at the same time the Emperor Charles V made Ayllón a Knight of the Order of Santiago, the highest Spanish military order. The historian Oviedo, who was in Spain at the same time, says that he passed by the famous Hieronymite Monastery of Nuestra Señora de Guadalupe, a mecca for returning voyagers after Columbus's visit there in 1493, where he saw Ayllón, just honored by the emperor.

Ayllón returned to Santo Domingo in June 1526 and immediately made plans to send an expedition to Florida with [Diego?] Miruelo as chief pilot. The expedition, financed by Ayllón, sailed with three ships: *La Bretona*, the flagship; and two smaller vessels, *Santa Catalina* and *Chorruca*; as well as a smaller boat to be used in exploring inland waters. With more than five hundred men, women, and children, black slaves, and several friars of the Order of Preachers, they sailed to latitude 33°40', to an area that had been called Chicora and to a stream called the River Jordan. The whole area was marshy, infested with mosquitoes, and obviously not suitable for the establishment of their new utopia. The expedition sailed about 150 miles to the southwest, perhaps to the Cape Fear River. The Indians of the area, aware that the newcomers had suffered a setback to the north, attacked almost immediately. And as so often happened to Spain in America, dissension arose among Ayllón's followers. Ayllón and many others became seriously ill of a fever. He died on St. Luke's day. One contemporaneous report says that his body was thrown into the sea. The rest of the party, now numbering fewer than 150, returned with the one remaining ship to Santo Domingo.

Ayllón was a pioneer in introducing sugar into the New World and with one Francisco de Ceballos built a fine sugar mill on the north coast some forty-five leagues from Santo Domingo, an enterprise that was managed by his heirs after his death. Ayllón had at least two children, including a son who in 1562 requested and received permission to establish a colony in Chicora, where his father had failed and died, but who himself died before he could put his plan into operation. Ayllón's daughter, Doña Inés de Villalobos, married Juan de Junco, a captain who had sailed with Sebastian Cabot. Ayllón had at least one brother, Perálvarez, also a member of the Order of Santiago, who fought with Caesar Borgia in Italy and who was both a poet and a dramatist.

After Ayllón's failure to etablish a colony in Chicora, the emperor never again turned his eyes to the northern latitudes of North America, leaving that area to the English and the French.

Ayllón was a most unusual man to be interested in establishing a colony in the wilderness. Rich, noble, well educated, he offered a strong contrast to most of the *conquistadores*. He used his own resources to finance the expedition, asking the emperor only for permission. In some measure he resembles Sir Walter Raleigh. There is one big difference: Walter Raleigh never came close to the shores of North Carolina.

SEE: Edward G. Bourne, *Spain in America: 1450–1580* (1904); Hernán Cortés, *Cartas de relación al Emperador Carlos V* (1866); Bernal Díaz del Castillo, *Historia verdadera de la conquista de México*, ed. Joaquín Ramírez Cabañas (1939); *Encyclopedia universal illustrada, Espasa-Calpe*, vol. 67; Gonzalo Fernández de Oviedo, *Historia general y natural de las Indias*, ed. Pérez de Tudela, 5 vols. (1959); Henry Harrisse, *The Discovery of North America*, facsimile ed. (1931); Antonio de Herrera y Tordesillas, *Décadas*, ed. A. Ballesteros (1934); Hugh T. Lefler, "Explorations and Attempts at Settlement," in Blackwell P. Robinson, ed., *The North Carolina Guide* (1955); Hugh T. Lefler and Albert R. Newsome, *North Carolina: The History of a Southern State* (1954); Salvador de Madariaga, *Hernán*

Cortés, Conquest of Mexico (1958); Mapa Oficial Española, 1527, and Map of Diego Rivero, 1529, in Johann George Kohl, ed., *Die Beiden Altesten General-Karten von Amerika Ausgfuhrt in Jahren 1527. un 1529 auf befehl Kaiser Karls V.* (1860); Samuel Eliot Morison, *The European Discovery of America: The Northern Voyages, 500–1600* (1971); John Gilmary Shea, *Narratives and Critical History of America,* ed. Justin Winsor (n.d.); Garcilaso de la Vega, *La Florida del Inca* (1956).

STERLING STOUDEMIRE

Babcock, Charles Henry *(25 Sept. 1899–13 Dec. 1967),* investment banker and counselor and philanthropist, was born the son of Charles Henry and Ella Park Babcock in Lafayette, Ind. Graduated from the University of Pennsylvania with a B.S. degree in 1920, he worked first with Guaranty Trust of New York in New York City (1920–23); he then was vice-president of the Mah-Jongg Corportion of America, San Francisco, in 1923 and 1924 and of Guaranty Trust of New York in Philadelphia from 1924 to 1931. He established his own brokerage firm in 1931, Reynolds and Company of New York (now Reynolds Security, Inc.), of which he was senior partner until his death.

Babcock served as a private in the U.S. Army in World War I. A major in World War II, he was chief financial officer of the American Headquarters of the European Theater of Operations.

He lived in Greenwich, Conn., until 1949, when he moved to Winston-Salem, the early home of his wife, Mary Reynolds (the daughter of R. J. Reynolds), whom he had married on 16 Dec. 1929. He enjoyed entertaining friends in his home. He was also an avid traveler and made himself familiar with all parts of the United States and many foreign countries.

In Winston-Salem, Babcock became active in many community, cultural, and business activities, all of which he pursued in a self-effacing manner. He was a director of the Piedmont Publishing Company (newspapers), R. J. Reynolds Tobacco Company, and Security Life and Trust Company, now Integon Corporation (life insurance). He served as commisioner of public housing for Winston-Salem and was president-treasurer of the Mary Reynolds Babcock Foundation (established with $12 million from his first wife's estate) and vice-president and treasurer of the Z. Smith Reynolds Foundation. An active churchman, he belonged to Centenary Methodist Church, Winston-Salem.

His philanthropies included a major contribution to the relocation of Wake Forest College (now University) in Winston-Salem in 1956. In addition, through the two foundations, he was a prime influence in multiple projects in education, the arts, health and welfare, the restoration of Old Salem and Bethabara, and the establishment of Piedmont University Center at Reynolda (the home of the Reynolds family) and of the North Carolina Fund, a private interest organization designed to fight poverty.

One of Babcock's educational interests was the Asian Studies Program, a joint effort of Wake Forest University, Salem College, and Winston-Salem State University, established to introduce international and intercultural dimensions in educational curricula.

In New York, he was a member of the Grolier Society, Alpha Chi Rho, the Down Town Association, and the University and Bankers Club. In Winston-Salem, he was a member of the Twin City Club, Forsyth Country Club, and the Old Town Club.

By his first wife, Babcock had four children, Mary Katherine (Mrs. Kenneth Mountcastle, Jr.), Charles Henry, Barbara Frances (Mrs. Frederick H. Lassiter), and Betsy Main. Mary Reynolds Babcock died in 1953. On 8 Sept. 1954, Babcock married Mrs. Winifred Penn Knies.

Babcock's funeral service was conducted in the Chapel of Wake Forest University on 15 Dec. 1967, with interment in Salem Cemetery.

SEE: Raleigh *News and Observer,* 14 Dec. 1967; *Who's Who in America,* 1968–69; *Who Was Who in America,* vol. 5 (1973); *Winston-Salem Journal,* 14 and 15 Dec. 1967 and, for letters to the editor, 20 and 28 Dec. 1967.

C. SYLVESTER GREEN

Babcock, Mary Reynolds *(8 Aug. 1908–17 July 1953),* philanthropist, was born in Winston of Scottish ancestry. Her father was R. J. Reynolds, founder of R. J. Reynolds Tobacco Company; her mother was Mary Smith Reynolds. As a young girl, she attended a private school at Reynolda, the family estate. She later attended Salem Academy and Miss Wright's School in Bryn Mawr, Pa. After her graduation she spent several months in Paris studying art. On 16 Dec. 1929 she married Charles Henry Babcock, an investment banker from Philadelphia. They lived for a time in Greenwich, Conn., but moved to Winston-Salem in 1934 when she acquired Reynolda.

In 1936, when Mrs. Babcock inherited $30 million from her father, she was described as one of the richest women in the world. Her primary interest was in helping others, and she contributed generously to many worthwhile causes. In 1951 she and her husband gave three hundred acres at Reynolda to Wake Forest College, and the college moved from Wake County to Winston-Salem, where a completely new campus was built. Her will provided $12 million for a charitable trust, and the Mary Reynolds Babcock Foundation was established at Reynolda with her husband as the first chairman of the board. Since 1954, the foundation has contributed generously to Wake Forest University and to other organizations, particularly those concerned with private higher education, social welfare, and the arts.

Mary Reynolds Babcock was shy and retiring. She enjoyed a limited circle of friends and delighted in collecting recipes and growing flowers, but her primary interest was philanthropy.

She was the mother of Mary Katherine, Barbara, Betsy Main, and Charles Henry, Jr. One portrait of her hangs in Babcock Dormitory, Salem College, and another in the offices of the Mary Reynolds Babcock Foundation at Reynolda. She died in New York City and was buried in Winston-Salem.

SEE: Mary Reynolds Babcock Foundation Annual Report, 1973; *New York Times,* 18 and 19 July 1953, 19 Aug. 1953; *Winston-Salem Journal,* 18 July 1953; Winston-Salem *Twin City Sentinel,* 18 July 1953.

HUBERT K. WOOTEN

Bachelder, Oscar Louis *(14 July 1852–26 June 1935),* master potter, was born in Menasha, Wis., the son of Hannah Tipley Bodwell (or Bothwell) and Calvin B. Bachelder. He came from many generations of potters on both sides, and his father worked in the noted potteries at Bennington, Vt. Bachelder moved from Wisconsin to North Carolina in 1911 and established the Omar Khayyám Pottery at Luther, west of Asheville. Initially, he made such practical pieces as jugs, churns, and crocks, but later he switched to artistically designed work, explaining: "I wanted to create beauty unmarred by the hand of commerce." An advertising card that he distributed asserted: "Each article has merit and individuality. No replicas. O. L. Bachelder, artist."

In 1919 he won the Logan Prize awarded by the Chicago Art Institute, where his pottery was displayed. Bachelder's work was also exhibited in New York, Philadelphia, Boston, Detroit, Buffalo, and Paris.

Called "a dreamer, philosopher, artist, and lover of nature," Bachelder died in 1935 at the age of eighty-two, survived by his widow, Mrs. Pink Bachelder.

SEE: *Antiques Journal*, September 1974; *Asheville Citizen*, 23 Dec. 1928, 27 Oct. 1929, 26 June 1935.

ROBERT O. CONWAY

Backhouse, John (*d. 1784 or 1785*), legislator, planter, mariner, and salt maker, first appeared in Carteret County records about 1758. That same year, he became a justice of the peace for Carteret County. In four deeds dated from 1758 to 1774, he is listed as a mariner; four other deeds executed between 1763 and 1775 list him as a planter or farmer. At first, Backhouse appears to have lived on Houston's (Holston's) Creek, a part of Carteret County that is now in Jones County. His last residence was on Pettiver's (Pettiford) Creek in Carteret County near the mouth of the White Oak River, where it is presumed he was buried.

Backhouse represented Carteret County in the North Carolina House of Commons during the third, fourth, and fifth assemblies under Governor Arthur Dobbs, 1761–62. In the fifth assembly, he served on the Committee of Propositions and Grievances and on a special committee to prepare a bill for amending and continuing the act for the inspection of tar, pitch, turpentine, beef, pork, and so on.

In 1772, Backhouse is mentioned as owning a lot in the town later named Swansboro, but no further deed record can be found for his town lot or his disposition of it. In 1776 he represented Carteret County in the fourth provincial congress, after which he appears to have dropped out of public life and perhaps to have entered into a period of steadily declining health. His will was made in 1782. In 1783 he patented two tracts of land adjoining his plantation. His will, as recorded, evidences some copying inaccuracies but seems to indicate that he was the owner of two salt works or of one large operation with two pans or vats at the time of his death. One portion of his river shore land still bears the name Salt Works Point.

Backhouse first married Elizabeth Dudley, widow of the Thomas Dudley who resided on White Oak River and died there in 1753. Elizabeth was the daughter of John (d. 1745) and Katherine Jarratt. Elizabeth Jarratt Dudley Backhouse died on 30 May 1767 in her fifty-ninth year and was buried beside a son, Abraham Dudley, in the Houston Cemetery (north side of Holston's Creek, a tributary of White Oak River, in Jones County). By his first wife, Backhouse had one son, Allen.

Backhouse was married again, to Mary Williams, daughter of Colonel John Pugh Williams of Fort Barnwell in Craven County. The bond for this marriage was dated 31 Dec. 1768. By this union, Backhouse appears to have had four children: John Pugh, who died intestate before 1815, when Allen Backhouse claimed to be his sole surviving heir; Sarah; Mary; and Catherine ("Kitty").

Backhouse evidently died late in 1784 or extemely early in 1785. His will was probated in March 1785; but by that time his widow was already remarried to her neighbor, Guillaume (William) Ferrand, who together with her was granted administration of Backhouse's estate.

Allen Backhouse, John's eldest son, married first Elizabeth Starkey, a daughter of John Starkey, Jr., on 13 July 1796. She appears to have died before January 1797. Allen's second wife was Ruth Wilson, widow of James Wilson of New Bern. Their marriage occurred on 5 Aug. 1809, while Allen was the postmaster of Swansboro and a merchant there. By 1811, however, he was listed as a merchant of New Bern, where in 1838 he was also operating a boarding house. Through Allen, John Backhouse had a grandson, John Allen, who became a well-educated and well-known minister. John Allen Backhouse is also listed in a deed of 1837 as the publisher of the *Carolina Sentinel* of New Bern. Another grandson, Benjamin Williams Backhouse, was a student at The University of North Carolina from 1830 to 1833 and was on the way to becoming a prominent lawyer when he died in July 1836, at the age of twenty-two.

On 4 Nov. 1804, Kitty Backhouse married Samuel Chapman of New Bern, a clerk of Craven County Court. Their son, Samuel Edward Chapman, became a physician; his uncle, Dr. Stephen Lee Ferrand, bequeathed all his medical books and equipment to him.

By her second husband, William Ferrand, Mary Williams Backhouse Ferrand had two sons, Dr. Stephen Lee and William Pugh, Sr. She died in August 1796 and was buried on the Backhouse-Ferrand Plantation on Pettiver's Creek, not far from the town of Swansboro, where she died.

SEE: William L. Saunders, ed., *Colonial Records of North Carolina*, vols. 5–6 (1887–88).

TUCKER REED LITTLETON

Bacon, Henry, Jr. (*28 Nov. 1866–16 Feb. 1924*), architect of the Lincoln Memorial, Washington, D.C., was born in Watseka, Ill., one of seven children of Henry (1822–91) and Elizabeth (1831–1912) Bacon of Massachusetts. Henry Bacon, Sr., an engineer, worked with the development of the Illinois Central Railroad before moving to the Wilmington office of the U.S. Engineer Department. The Bacon family lived in Southport (then Smithville) from 1876 to 1880, nearer the site of Bacon's work than the Wilmington office, but in 1880 they moved to Wilmington.

The elder Bacon was in charge of the construction of a barrier dam across New Inlet, near the mouth of the Cape Fear River. New Inlet, cut by a severe storm in 1761, formed a second mouth to the Cape Fear. Young Henry's interest in engineering and architecture must have been stimulated by his father's work. His later understanding of the engineering problems of anchoring the Lincoln Memorial in fill land reclaimed from the Potomac River and his success with this difficult problem probably owe much to his knowledge of the work of Henry Bacon, Sr., on the Cape Fear River.

Henry Bacon, Jr., was probably already attending school in Wilmington in 1880 when his family moved there from Southport. He went to study at Chauncey Hall School in Boston in 1881, at the age of fifteen, but returned to Wilmington, where he was graduated from Tileston High School in 1884. The same year he entered the University of Illinois; after one year he left to take a position as draftsman for the architectural firm of Chamberlain and Whidden in Boston.

In 1885, Bacon moved to New York to work with the

firm of McKim, Mead and White, probably the most prestigious and innovative architectural firm of its era. In 1889 he won the coveted Rotch Travelling Scholarship. By that time he had so thoroughly established himself at the McKim firm that his winning seems to have been a foregone conclusion.

With the award, Bacon began two years of travel, study, and sketching in Europe. His scrapbooks and drawings from the era cover architectural details and motifs viewed in France, Italy, Greece, and Turkey. During his study, Bacon visited the archeological site at Assos, Turkey, near Troy. An older brother, Francis H. Bacon (1856–1940), had worked there from 1881 to 1883 as chief draftsman for the Harvard archeological expeditions. When the expedition findings were published in 1902 and 1921, Francis was given credit not only for the editing and writing of the explanatory notes, but for most of the plans, elevations, details, and restoration drawings. Included among the drawings was one for the Tomb of Publius Varius by Henry Bacon. Francis later became a furniture designer and maker in Boston, and Henry used his products in furnishing several of the buildings he designed.

It was during the time spent in Assos that Henry met Laura Calvert, daughter of the British consul at the Dardanelles, near Assos. They were married, and another Calvert daughter became Francis's wife.

Henry Bacon returned to employment with McKim, Mead and White in 1891 and the following year spent six months in Chicago as McKim's personal representative at the World's Columbian Exposition. While working for McKim, Bacon designed the exposition's Pennsylvania Railroad Building (1891), his first independent commission.

Bacon continued to work with the McKim firm until 1897; at that time he went into partnership with James Brite, who had traveled in Europe with him during part of the Rotch Scholarship study. Brite and Bacon maintained their partnership until 1903, when the firm was dissolved, and each established his own practice.

In 1911, Bacon was appointed architect for the Lincoln Memorial in Washington. His design was accepted in 1912, and the work was completed between 1913 and 1922, when the memorial was dedicated.

Bacon had been sought by McKim in 1901 to work with the McMillan Commission in evolving a new plan for Washington. Because he was then involved in competition for the design of a new Department of Agriculture building, he could not accept the task. He remained the prime choice of McKim, Daniel Burnam, and Augustus Saint-Gaudens, all members of the McMillan Commission. After winning the Lincoln Memorial design commission, he worked with Burnam and others in designing the Reflecting Pool (ca. 1922) between the Washington Monument and the Lincoln Memorial. He also designed a street lighting system for the city (1923); the light standards used throughout most of Washington today are from his design. Bacon seems also to have been the commission choice for other Washington buildings, but he died before he could undertake other jobs.

The Lincoln Memorial design won Bacon national renown and a gold medal from the American Institute of Architects, the highest honor the organization could bestow. A superb engineering and architectural feat, the design, featuring a Greek temple with Roman attic, is generally considered the most successful of the Washington Mall monuments.

In announcing the gold medal, the AIA noted that "for the third time in its history the institute will present the gold medal to one of its members." Only Charles F. McKim in 1909 and George B. Post had received it previously. For the presentation to Bacon, during the 1923 AIA Annual Meeting, the institute devised a pageant unequaled before or since in its history. On a rainy April night, Bacon rode from the Washington Monument end of the Tidal Basin to the Lincoln Memorial end on a specially constructed barge. Special lighting had been devised for the barge and for architectural students who pulled it. At the end of the barge ride, Bacon was greeted by Chief Justice of the Supreme Court William H. Taft and escorted to the memorial, where President Warren G. Harding presented the medal amid appropriate music and speeches.

During the last ten years of Bacon's life, even while he was at work on the Lincoln Memorial and other projects, he was employed in campus planning and building design at Wesleyan University, Middletown, Conn. The university awarded him an honorary M.A. in 1920 and today displays a large collection of his work in the several campus buildings he designed. The university also houses his library and the largest single collection of his drawings, plans, elevations, sketches, scrapbooks, and letters.

Throughout his life, Bacon maintained close contact with family and friends in Wilmington. In 1923 he spent Christmas with his family there and then returned to New York, where, in February, he entered the hospital for an intestinal cancer operation and died a few days later.

By the time of his death, Bacon was one of the best-known architects of his era. He was a member of the National Commission of Fine Arts, Washington; the American Academy of Arts and Letters; the National Academy of Design; the National Sculpture Society; the Century Association; and the Architectural League of New York. He was a Fellow of the American Institute of Architects.

Bacon's body was returned to Wilmington for family burial there in Oakdale Cemetery. His grave marker is a design from his drawing (1907) of a stele from the Troad, now in the Boston Museum of Fine Arts.

In Wilmington, Bacon designed the shingle-style Donald MacRae Residence (1902) at South Third and Dock Streets, now the church offices of St. James Episcopal Church. In 1903 he remodeled the Hugh MacRae residence (now demolished) on Market Street. The Boney or Confederate Monument (1924) at Dock and South Third, by F. H. Packer, was designed in collaboration with Bacon, though it was erected after his death.

The Walter Parsley Residence (1915), Live Oaks, on Masonboro Sound in New Hanover County survives, as does All Saint's Episcopal Church (ca. 1910) in Linville, Avery County. The church seems to have set the design for other buildings nearby, which show Bacon's obvious influence. On Capitol Square in Raleigh, Bacon was the architect for the Women of the Confederacy Monument (1913), for which Augustus Lukeman was sculptor.

Bacon was not particularly interested in residential design. He designed Chesterwood (1900), Stockbridge, Mass., for his friend and fellow worker Daniel Chester French. The North Carolina residences were also for family or friends. He designed few other dwellings.

That there is not more work by Bacon in North Carolina reflects not so much a lack of recognition by the state he considered his home as his working methods. He seemed reluctant to seek commissions and maintained only a small office, preferring to supervise personally the commissions he undertook.

In addition to the works already mentioned, Bacon's designs included: Hall of History (Hurst Hall) (1897), American University, Washington, D.C.; Hanna Mausoleum (1904), Cleveland, Ohio; Eben Richards House, Carter Hall, Tuxedo Park, N.Y. (remodeling, 1904); Parnell Monument (1905), Dublin, Ireland (with Saint-Gaudens); Danforth Memorial Library (1906), Patterson, N.J.; Dresden Madison Nursing Home (1906) and Union Square Savings Bank (1907), Manhattan, N.Y.; Magee Memorial (1907), Pittsburgh, Pa. (with Saint-Gaudens); Marshall Field Monument (1909), Chicago, Ill. (with French); Lincoln Memorial (1909), Lincoln, Neb. (with French); Carl Schurz Monument (1910), Morningside, N.Y. (with sculptor Karl Bitter); Exeter Bandstand (1913), Exeter, N.H.; Court of the Seasons (1915), Panama-Pacific Exposition, San Francisco, Calif.; Lafayette Monument (1916), Prospect Park, Brooklyn, N.Y. (with French); Dupont Memorial Fountain (1921), Washington, D.C. (with French); Roosevelt Memorial (1923), Santiago, Cuba (with French); Citizens and Manufacturers National Bank (1923), Waterbury, Conn.

SEE: Francis H. Bacon, "Archaeological Investigations at Assos," *Art and Archaeology* 12 (1921), and *Investigations at Assos* (1902); Leslie N. Boney, Jr., Ida Brooks Kellam, Augustus Moore, Jr., Janet Seapker, and the U.S. Army Corps of Engineers, personal communications; *DAB*, vol. 1 (1928); Aymar Embury, "Henry Bacon," *Architectural Record* 55 (1924); *Journal of the American Institute of Architects* 11 (1923), 12 (1924); North Carolina State Archives (Raleigh); Ruth Ryley Selden, "Henry Bacon and His Work at Wesleyan University" (M.A. thesis, University of Virginia, 1974); Henry F. Withey, *Biographical Dictionary of American Architects* (1956).

TONY P. WREN

Badger, George Edmund (17 Apr. 1795–11 May 1866), superior court judge, secretary of the navy, and U.S. senator, was born in New Bern, the son of Thomas and Lydia Cogdell Badger. His father was a native of Windham, Conn., who removed to New Bern when a young man. In 1793, Thomas married the daughter of Richard Cogdell of New Bern, and George Edmund was the eldest of three children. He received his secondary education in New Bern. In 1810 he entered Yale College, where he remained for only two years because of a lack of funds. Returning to New Bern, he studied law under his maternal cousin, John Stanley, and was licensed to practice in 1815.

Throughout his life, Badger was a devoted member of the Episcopal church. From 1825 until his death he was an active member of Christ Church, Raleigh, frequently serving on its vestry and several times representing the parish in diocesan conventions.

Badger served as a trustee of The University of North Carolina from 1818 to 1844. One of his important accomplishments as a trustee was the introduction of a resolution calling for the establishment of a chair of modern languages. As a result of the resolution, a professor of modern languages was employed in 1826. In appreciation of his services to the university and in recognition of his intellectual attainments, the university conferred on him the LL.D. degree in 1834. His alma mater, Yale College, awarded him the LL.D. in 1848.

Badger was elected a member of the House of Commons from the borough of New Bern in 1816. Four years later he was elected a judge of the superior

court, serving in this office until he resigned in 1825 to practice law in Raleigh; there he made his home until his death. His first active participation in national politics was in the presidential campaign of 1828, when he supported the candidacy of Andrew Jackson. He was a member of the state Central Jackson Committee, writing the two most important pamphlets it issued in Jackson's interest. In recognition of his work, the Democratic party of North Carolina nominated Badger as its choice for the cabinet post of attorney general. The party's recommendation was passed over by Jackson, who instead appointed John Branch of North Carolina, then serving in the Senate, as secretary of the navy. A few years later, Badger broke with Jackson on the question of the recharter of the Bank of the United States and aligned himself with the newly formed Whig party, whose advocacy of internal improvements and a strong central government met with his hearty approval.

Badger played an active role in the presidential election of 1840. On 3 Mar. he delivered a speech in Granville County that was recognized as the platform of the Whig party of North Carolina. He also delivered the keynote address at the Whig state convention. In recognition of his work in the campaign of 1840, President-elect William Henry Harrison appointed him secretary of the navy; his appointment was confirmed by the Senate on 6 Mar.

After a careful study of the needs of the navy, Badger made a report to Congress recommending the establishment of a home squadron for the protection of the nation's coastline. This recommendation was enacted into law in July 1841, creating the nucleus of what was later the Atlantic fleet. In his second report on the navy, also accepted by Congress, Badger advocated the increase of naval ordnance as well as a fund for experimenting with and testing the value of improved ordnance. During his brief period as secretary of the navy, he encouraged new inventions for the improvement, especially in speed, of war vessels. In summing up his work in the Navy Department, the editor of the *Philadelphia Inquirer and Daily Courier* wrote: "We have been called upon by a number of officers of the Navy, as far as it has been ascertained, that never was the Department characterized by more efficiency, vigor, and ability than during the brief but brilliant administration of the Hon. Geo. E. Badger."

One month after his inauguration, President Harrison died. He was succeeded in office by Vice-President John Tyler. On 11 Sept. Badger and the other members of the cabinet, with the exception of Secretary of State Daniel Webster, resigned their posts because of Tyler's position on the establishment of a national bank: Tyler vetoed two different bills passed by Congress creating a national bank, one of the cherished measures of the Whig party. Senator William A. Graham of North Carolina wrote a friend that the secretaries had not deserted the president on account of a mere disagreement, "but for trifling and treachery towards them."

In 1846 the North Carolina legislature elected Badger to the U.S. Senate to fill the unexpired term of William H. Haywood, Jr. Two years later he was reelected for a regular six-year term. In the course of his senatorial career, Badger opposed the Mexican War and the Wilmot Proviso, supported the Compromise of 1850, worked actively for the passage of the Kansas-Nebraska bill, and sponsored measures for the improvement of the merchant marine. He was recognized in the Senate as a consistent defender of the constitution and an advocate of a strong central government.

In January 1853, President Fillmore nominated Badger as an associate justice of the U.S. Supreme Court to fill the vacancy caused by the death of Justice John McKinley, who had presided over the Southwestern Circuit. The nomination aroused much hostile criticism from the Democrats, particularly from those of the lower South, who distrusted Badger's views on slavery and on centralized government. Badger was refused confirmation by a party vote of twenty-six to twenty-five; the single most important factor in the rejection was his residence outside the district. The senators from Alabama, Louisiana, and Mississippi were bitter in their opposition to the nomination.

In the fall of 1854, Badger was defeated for reelection to a legislature controlled by the Democrats. On the eve of his departure, 3 Mar. 1855, the Senate unanimously passed a resolution introduced by a Democrat expressing its appreciation ". . . for his uniform courtesy, ability, liberality, and valuable services during his long and distinguished career in this body." Such a tribute was unique at that time in the annals of the Senate.

From the time of his retirement from the Senate until 1860, Badger devoted most of his energy to the practice of law. Before leaving Washington he formed a law partnership with J. M. Carlisle, for the purpose of participating in cases before the court of claims and the U.S. Supreme Court. Upon returning to Raleigh in 1855, he was elected one of the county magistrates, an office he held for the next six years.

Badger's last appearances in public life were as an elector at large on the Bell and Everett ticket in the election of 1860 and as a delegate from Wake County to the Secession Convention of 1861. Throughout the sectional controversies of 1860 and early 1861, Badger maintained his position as a Union man, but when Lincoln called for volunteers for the invasion of the South, he joined with those favoring separation. When the convention met in Raleigh on 20 May 1861, Badger introduced "An Ordinance Declaring the Separation of North Carolina from the United States of America." The ordinance was based upon the right of revolution, carefully avoiding any reference to the theory of secession, a political concept he never acknowledged. Badger's proposal was rejected by the convention, which adopted a simple ordinance of secession from the Union introduced by Burton Craige.

Badger was first married in 1818 to Rebecca Turner, daughter of Governor James Turner. She died six years later without issue. In 1826 he married Mary Polk, daughter of Colonel William Polk, by whom he had two children: Catherine (b. 1827) and Sarah (b. 1833). Mary Polk Badger died in 1834. In 1836, Badger married a widow, Mrs. Delia Haywood Williams, daughter of Sherwood Haywood. They had seven children: Mary Rose (b. 1836), George Edmund (b. 1838), Richard C. (b. 1839), Annie H. (b. 1841), Thomas (b. 1843), Sherwood (b. 1844), and Edmund S. (b. 1846).

SEE: G. E. Badger MSS (North Carolina State Archives, Raleigh; Library, University of North Carolina, Chapel Hill; Library, Duke University, Durham; Archives of the Navy Department); G. E. Badger, *Speech Delivered at the Great Whig Meeting in the County of Granville* (1840); *Congressional Globe*, 1841, 1846–55; William A. Graham, *Discourse in Memory of the Life and Character of the Honorable George E. Badger* (1866); L. F. London, "George Edmund Badger, Member of the Harrison-Tyler Cabinet, 1841," *South Atlantic Quarterly* 37 (1938), and "The Public Career of George Edmund Badger" (Ph.D. diss., University of North Carolina, 1936); H. D. Pegg, "The Whig Party in North Carolina, 1834–1861" (Ph.D. diss., University of North Carolina, 1932); Raleigh *North Carolina Standard*, 1840–66; *Raleigh Register*, 1816–61; David Schenck, *Personal Sketches of Distinguished Delegates of the State Convention, 1861–62* (1885); Washington, D.C., *National Intelligencer*, 1841–61, 1846–55; P. M. Wilson, "George Edmund Badger, Secretary of the United States Navy," in *North Carolina Booklet*, vol. 15 (1916).

LAWRENCE F. LONDON

Bagge, Traugott *(26 June 1729–16 Apr. 1800)*, Moravian leader, was born in Gothenburg, Sweden, the fourteenth and youngest child of merchant Lorenz Bagge and Anna Margaretha Calms. He was educated in the town schools and trained by his father in the trade of merchant. In 1775, Bagge joined the Unity of the Brethren (Moravians); he was called to service in England in 1759. There he met Rachel Nikelson, and they were married in 1767. A year later, Bagge and his wife answered a call to go to Wachovia and the Moravian settlement in North Carolina. They arrived in Bethabara on 14 Feb. 1768 and immediately became important members of the Wachovia community. Early in 1772, Bagge became the chairman of the first Aufseher Collegium and also took charge of the community store, first at Bethabara and later at Salem. During the following years, Bagge's duties and responsibilities increased: in addition to charge of all store books and accounts, supervision of all trade and commerce of the community, and travel as far away as Charleston, S.C., and Philadelphia, Pa., on store business, Bagge managed to hold several local civic offices and serve as a member of the North Carolina assembly.

Bagge was active in governmental affairs; in 1778 he presented to the assembly in Hillsborough a petition concerning the Moravian position during the Revolutionary War. Since bearing arms was against Moravian policy, Bagge was highly praised for his instrumental role in lowering the fines for abstention from military service. Bagge also presented to the assembly the brethren's petitions asking that Dobbs Parish remain undivided by county lines, protesting the Oath of Affirmation and Abjuration, and asking for protection from the Confiscation Act. In 1782, Bagge became a justice of the peace, was elected to the North Carolina assembly, and was appointed auditor for Surry County.

The onset of the Revolutionary War was a difficult time for the Moravians in America. Not only did they object to bearing arms, they owed a proprietary quitrent for the Wachovia tract and a debt of gratitude to the Crown: Religious exiles from several European countries, they had been aided and encouraged by the English government to settle in the American colonies. When the revolutionary factions required an oath of allegiance to the new state and a renunciation of all allegiance to England and her government, the Moravian colonists found a difficult choice. Although Bagge's petitions achieved little success, through his letters and papers he at least brought to public view the causes of the Moravians' uncertainty.

Despite his enthusiastic civic activity, Bagge was efficient in his own business. As manager of the *Gemein* or church-owned store, he maintained a balance in imports and exports and kept the books in order and the accounts financially sound. Although he was apparently a choleric individual at times (he was constantly at odds with his apprentices), his excellent business sense and training made the store a success. He operated the store until his death.

By 1793, Bagge was the leading layman in financial matters in Wachovia. His mercantile policies resulted in a vast trading network including the whole eastern part of the country from New England to Georgia, as well as trade with several European countries. During the Revolution he acted as an important supplier for the Continental forces.

Bagge translated many Moravian papers from German into English, including the "History of the Brethren." He also wrote an unpublished narrative history describing the American Moravians' tribulations during the Revolution.

Bagge married only once and had four children: Anna Elisabeth, Maria Rachel, Benjamin Samuel, and Charles Frederick. Charles alone outlived his father; he helped operate the store temporarily after his father's death. Bagge died in Salem; his death was felt keenly in Wachovia and around the state and country.

SEE: Moravian Church Archives (Winston-Salem), for Aufseher Collegium Minutes, Bagge Papers (including Bagge's will and a personal memoir), Diacony Conference Minutes, Elders' Conference Minutes, Helpers' Conference Minutes, Salem Diary, and Wachovia Diary.

JAN HIESTER

Bagley, Dudley Warren (18 Apr. 1889–27 Oct. 1964), experimental farmer; state legislator; civic, educational, and farm leader; and assistant comptroller general of the United States, was born in Moyock, Currituck County, to Raleigh Old and Eva Berryman Dudley Bagley. His father, who had been reared as an orphan, had become a leading progressive farmer in Currituck County. His brother, Charles, was a Rhodes Scholar and professor of Romance Languages at Dartmouth College.

Bagley was educated at Trinity Park School (1906–8) and Trinity College (1909–10). He entered the University of Virginia in 1912 with the intention of pursuing a career in engineering but had to leave school because of ill health. He returned to the family farm in Moyock and developed a renowned truck and seed farm at Highland Farm, which he operated with his father. To compete with the tenant farmers nearby, he began to specialize and to experiment with improved varieties of corn and soybeans. He developed a business of growing crops for seeds, the only farm in North Carolina to do so.

During World War I, he enlisted in the army and rose to the rank of lieutenant as a machine gun instructor, though he did not see action abroad.

In 1930 he helped found the Currituck Mutual Exchange, a cooperative in which farmers pooled their resources to obtain credit and market advantages. He was also active in the North Carolina Farmers' Cooperative Exchange and was a vice-president and director of the National Fruit and Vegetable Exchange from 1932 to 1936.

As a member of the state senate from 1933 to 1935, Bagley gave particular support to education programs including opposition to a reduction in the school term and in teacher salaries. He helped to found the North Carolina Rural Electrification Association and was appointed its director by Governor J. C. B. Ehringhaus; he held the post from 1935 to 1940. A close associate of Lindsay C. Warren, member of the U.S. House of Representatives, Bagley was made his assistant when Warren accepted the post of comptroller general of the United States. As Warren's assistant from 1940 to 1946,

he ran the internal affairs of the comptroller's office, especially the work of the General Accounting Office. He studied accounting at night in order better to supervise the operations of the office and made an important contribution by improving its auditing.

His interest in education and progressive farming made him a strong supporter of North Carolina State College, of which he was a trustee from 1923 to 1932. After it merged into the Consolidated University of North Carolina, Bagley was a university trustee (1932–40).

After his retirement from Washington on 30 June 1946, Bagley returned to Highland Farm, where he continued his agricultural experiments and his activities in state affairs. He was a member of a commission appointed by Governor Gregg Cherry to study conditions in the public schools. The commission produced a report in 1948, *Education in North Carolina—Today and Tomorrow*. He also served on a later commission to study higher education, which produced a report in 1955.

Bagley's other activities included service as trustee of the North Carolina Institute of Fisheries Research (1948–53), trustee of Elizabeth City State College (1953–55), and director of the Rural Rehabilitation Corporation (1952–62).

In 1917, Bagley married Ida Frost Bray, a native of Sligo and an active participant in Democratic party politics and philanthropic activities. Mrs. Bagley was a trustee of the Knapp Foundation, an agent for the Knapp philanthropies, and chairman of the Currituck County Board of Charities and Public Welfare. The Bagleys had no children.

Bagley died at Moyock and was buried in the Bagley Memorial Cemetery there. The Bagley papers are a rich deposit in the Southern Historical Collection at the Library of The University of North Carolina.

SEE: Charles R. Bagley, *Dudley Warren Bagley* (1959); *North Carolina: The Old North State and the New*, vol. 3 (1941); William S. Powell, ed., *North Carolina Lives* (1962); Raleigh *News and Observer*, 29 Oct. 1964.

THOMAS S. MORGAN

Bagley, Worth (6 Apr. 1874–11 May 1898), naval officer, was born in Raleigh, the son of Major William Henry Bagley (5 July 1833–21 Feb. 1886) of Perquimans County, attorney, editor of the Elizabeth City *Sentinel*, soldier, state senator, private secretary to Governor Jonathan Worth, and marshal of the North Carolina Supreme Court. His mother was Adelaide Worth, Governor Worth's daughter. His sister and brother were Addie Worth (1869–1943), wife of editor and politician Josephus Daniels, and Admiral David Worth, who was commander of a destroyer in World War I. Worth received his education at the Centennial Graded School and at the Raleigh Male Academy, under schoolmasters Hugh Morson and Captain Claude B. Denson. He was appointed by Congressman D. H. Bunn from the Fourth District to the U.S. Naval Academy, from which he was graduated in June 1895.

Bagley spent the succeeding two years on several vessels of the North Atlantic Squadron and, after final examination, was commissioned as ensign on 1 July 1897. He served on the *Indiana* and the *Maine* and was invited to become executive officer on the *Winslow*, a torpedo boat. Following destruction of the *Maine*, the *Winslow* proceeded to Key West. On 11 May 1898, as the *Winslow* was engaged in a battle in the harbor of Cardenas, Cuba, Bagley and two other sailors were killed in the performance of duty. On 13 May funeral services were held in Key West. On arrival in Raleigh, Bagley's body lay in state in the Capitol. The funeral was held in the south end of Capitol Square, and he was interred with the honors of a brigadier general in Oakwood Cemetery in Raleigh, near the graves of his father, his mother, and Governor Worth.

The North Carolina General Assembly directed that a suitable spot on Capitol Square be set aside for a permanent monument to Bagley. Captain N. W. West suggested contributions for a monument in a letter to the Raleigh *Morning Post*. Citizens of North Carolina provided the funds, and F. Packer was the sculptor of the statue. On 20 May 1907 the statue to the memory to the only American naval officer killed in the Spanish-American War was unveiled, and two other heroes of the war, Victor Blue and Richmond Pearson Hobson, grandson of North Carolina Chief Justice Richmond Pearson, made tributes.

SEE: Beth G. Crabtree, *North Carolina Governors, 1585 to 1958* (1958); Josephus Daniels, *Editor in Politics* (1941); *North Carolina Journal of Education*, 3 (Apr., May 1900); Records of Oakwood Cemetery, Raleigh; *State Magazine* 9 (6 Dec. 1941); Gary Trawick and Paul Wyche, *One Hundred Years, One Hundred Men* (1971); Richard L. Zuber, *Jonathan Worth* (1965).

GRADY L. E. CARROLL

Bahnson, Agnew Hunter (*10 Mar. 1886–21 Mar. 1966*), textile manufacturer, was born in Salem, the son of Dr. Henry Theodore and Emma Fries Bahnson. His grandfather, George Frederic Bahnson, moved to Salem in 1849 from Lancaster, Pa., to become minister of the Home Moravian Church. Bahnson was educated at Salem Boys' School and at The University of North Carolina, from which he was graduated in 1906. He spent the next fourteen months traveling in Europe and Egypt and, when he returned, began work in his family's textile mills. He was employed first as an apprentice in the Mayo Mills in Mayodan and afterward as a loom fixer in the Loray Mills in Gastonia. In 1909 he became superintendent of the Pomona Mills in Greensboro and in 1911 agent for the Washington Mills Company in Fries, Va. He became secretary and treasurer of the Arista Mills in 1912 and after three years became president, succeeding his uncle, John W. Fries. In 1921 he became secretary and treasurer of the Washington Mills, and in 1923, he developed the Mayo Sales Corporation. In the same year he became president of the Washington Mills, with which the Mayo Mills had recently consolidated.

Bahnson and his brother, Frederic Fries Bahnson, formed the Normalair Company in 1915, to manufacture humidifiers for textile mills. The name was changed to the Bahnson Company in 1929, and in 1940 Agnew acquired Frederic's interest in the firm. In 1947, Agnew Hunter Bahnson, Jr., succeeded as president of the company. At the time of his death, the elder Bahnson was chairman of the boards of Washington Mills, the Bahnson Company, Arista Mills Company, and the Mayo Sales Corporation.

Bahnson was a Moravian and made substantial contributions to the Moravian church and to Salem College. In 1941 the Moravian College in Bethlehem, Pa., awarded him an honorary LL.D. degree.

Bahnson was married to Elizabeth Moir Hill on 18 Nov. 1914, and they were the parents of Agnew Hunter, Jr., and Elizabeth Hill. He was buried in the Salem Moravian Cemetery.

SEE: *Who's Who in America*, 1936–37; *Winston-Salem Journal*, 22 Mar. 1966; Winston-Salem *Twin City Sentinel*, 21 Mar. 1966.

HUBERT K. WOOTEN

Bahnson, Frederic Fries (*6 Mar. 1876–18 Mar. 1944*), engineer and manufacturer, was born in Salem, the son of Dr. Henry Theodore and Emma Fries Bahnson. He was educated at the Salem Boys' School and was graduated from The University of North Carolina in 1896. He began the study of medicine at the University of Pennsylvania but, because of poor eyesight, was forced to give it up after a year and a half. In accordance with both medical advice to work outdoors and his own natural inclination for engineering, in 1897 he began work as an engineer for Fries Manufacturing and Power Company. He later worked as an engineer for Stanley Electric Company in Pittsfield, Mass., and for the Florida East Coast Railway Company. He returned to Salem in 1905 and assisted his uncle, John W. Fries, in experiments on textile humidification. In 1915 he and his brother, Agnew Hunter Bahnson, acquired the rights to the Fries humidifier and formed the Normalair Company. The firm became the Bahnson Company in 1929, and in 1940 Frederic sold his interest in it to Agnew.

In 1929, Bahnson founded the Southern Steel Stamping Company to make furniture hardware. At the time of his death he was president of the company and consulting engineer for the Bahnson Company. During the course of his work, Bahnson acquired several patents in humidification and in furniture hardware design. His diversions included photography and work with precious metals.

On 14 Apr. 1910, Bahnson was married to Bleeker Reid of Charlotte; they were the parents of four children: Frederic, Jr., Reid, Henry, and Alex. Bahnson was buried in the Salem Moravian Cemetery.

SEE: *Winston-Salem Journal*, 19 Mar. 1944; Winston-Salem *Twin City Sentinel*, 18 Mar. 1944.

HUBERT K. WOOTEN

Bahnson, Henry Theodore (*4 Mar. 1845–16 Jan. 1917*), surgeon and cattle breeder, was born in Lancaster, Pa., where his father, George Frederick Bahnson, was the minister of the Moravian church. In 1849 the senior Bahnson moved his family to Salem, where he had been called to the pastorate of the Home Moravian Church. He later became the bishop for the southern province of the *Unitas Fratrum* (Moravian denomination). Henry Bahnson's mother was Anna Gertrude Pauline Conrad. Young Henry began his education at Salem Boys' School, transferred in 1858 to Nazareth Hall, the Moravian boarding school in Nazareth, Pa., and then entered Moravian College and Theological Seminary in Bethlehem, Pa.

His schooling was interrupted in 1862, when he enlisted in the Confederate Army as a private in Company G, Second North Carolina Infantry Battalion. He was captured at the Battle of Gettysburg and held in prison in Baltimore City jail and then at Point Lookout, Md., for six months. In January 1864 he was exchanged and transferred to Company B, First North Carolina Battalion of Sharpshooters, where he gained a reputation in keeping with the designation of the group. He was with General Robert E. Lee's troops at Appomattox and had been promoted to the rank of captain, but the surrender came before his commission could be delivered. In later life, Bahnson enjoyed referring to himself as "the only surviving private in the Civil War." He walked home from Appomattox, living on roots and berries, and was in such bad condition when he finally got home that his mother did not recognize him. For the rest of his life he could not bear to see any food left on a plate or wasted in any way. He hated all he had seen during his three years of war service and could scarcely ever be persuaded to talk about his experiences. When he did discuss the war, it was with great sympathy for all who had suffered on both sides of the conflict.

After a short rest at home, Bahnson went to Philadelphia to study medicine at the University of Pennsylvania. Thus began a lifelong friendship with the famous surgeon Dr. D. Hayes Agnew, his teacher, whom he revered so much that he named one of his sons for him. After graduation in Practical and Surgical Anatomy in 1867, Bahnson went to Europe to continue his studies at the universities of Berlin, Prague, and Utrecht. Returning home, he secured his license in May 1869 and began his long practice of medicine, treating patients in Salem and even journeying into Virginia when he was needed. His fame as a surgeon and especially as a diagnostician was widespread, but equally renowned were his kindness and thoughtfulness and his way with people, according to many anecdotes told by his grateful patients.

Soon after he began his practice, Bahnson bought the house where he and his second wife would rear their children, just two doors north of the Home Moravian Church in Salem. The previous owner, also a physician, was known for a flower garden made of terraces on the steep hillside that fell from the back of the house down to a little creek. Dr. and Mrs. Bahnson further developed this garden, and Bahnson dammed up the creek to make a pond, where he grew not only water lilies of his own hybridizing but also Egyptian lotus and, for the first time ever in the United States outside a greenhouse, the Victoria Regia water lily. In *Old Salem North Carolina*, facing page 130, there is a picture of a young girl sitting in the center of one of these large, rimmed lily pads, while Dr. Bahnson, in waders, stands nearby in the pond.

Another hobby of Bahnson's was his farm, for which in 1882 he bought the first Guernsey cattle owned in North Carolina. The first Guernsey registered by the American Guernsey Cattle Club from the State of North Carolina was born on Bahnson's farm on 6 May 1884. One of Bahnson's bulls, Squire of Salem 1451, was dropped 18 Nov. 1886; through two cows sired by this bull, the strain was transmitted to every part of the United States. Bahnson helped five of the earliest Guernsey breeders in the state establish their herds by selling them some of his stock.

Physician, botanist, and cattle breeder, Bahnson still found time to devote to his church. During the Civil War he had read the New Testament through in Greek; while he was a medical student, he was confirmed on 29 July 1866, in the First Moravian Church in Philadelphia. He moved his membership to the Home Moravian Church in Salem and served his church well as a member of various committees and boards, including the Board of Trustees of Moravian College and Seminary, Bethlehem, Pa. For many years he was the college physician for Salem Academy and College, and the Bahnson infirmary (1925) was named in his honor.

Bahnson died in Salem after a long illness and was buried in the Moravian graveyard in Salem. At his death he was president of the Board of Surgeons of the Southern Railway system and chief surgeon to the Southbound Railroad. He had served as president of the North Carolina Medical Society; president of the North Carolina Board of Health; secretary of the North Carolina Board of Medical Examiners; and member of the Board of Directors of the State Hospital at Morganton. He belonged to the American Public Health Association and the Tri-state Medical Association; was an honorary member of the Virginia and other medical societies, and had been nominated for membership in the National Board of United States Surgeons. He was a Mason and Knight Templar.

Bahnson was married twice: on 3 Nov. 1870 to Adelaide de Schweinitz, who died 3 Aug. 1871, and then to Emma Caroline Fries on 14 Apr. 1874. To this second union were born six children: Henry T., Jr., and Carrie, who died early; Frederick Fries, Agnew Hunter, Mary Louise, and Pauline Conrad. Mrs. James A. Gray, Sr., (Pauline Bahnson) left a portrait of her father to her children.

SEE: Henry T. Bahnson, MS describing his Civil War experiences (possession of Mrs. Archie K. Davis, Winston-Salem); K. G. Hamilton, ed., *The Records of the Moravians in North Carolina*, vol. 11 (1969); "Memoir of Henry T. Bahnson" (MS, Moravian Church Archives, Winston-Salem); D. R. Nifong, *Brethren With Stethoscopes* (1965 [photograph]); M. B. Owen, ed., *Old Salem North Carolina* (1941); J. W. Pou, ed., *North Carolina Guernsey History* (1972); E. Rondthaler, *The Memorabilia of Fifty Years, 1877 to 1927* (1928).

ANNA WITHERS BAIR

Bailey, Christopher Thomas (*24 Oct. 1835–5 June 1895*), editor and clergyman, was one of ten children born to William Moody and Alice Clarke Bailey of James City County, Va. His parents were of Scottish and Welsh descent, the elder Bailey's father, Anselm J. Bailey, having settled on Virginia's eastern shore in the late eighteenth century. William Moody Bailey was a successful farmer before removing to Williamsburg for the sake of the education of his younger children.

Bailey completed his preparatory education at Williamsburg Academy and then entered the College of William and Mary, intent upon pursuing the legal profession. But frequent attendance at religious services of a group of blacks in the community, where he was often called upon to read the Scriptures for the illiterate pastor of the congregation, had made a deep impression upon him. Accordingly, he transferred to Richmond College in 1856 to study for the work of the ministry and remained a student there until the summer of 1859.

The Sunday School and Publication Board of the Baptist General Association of Virginia employed young Bailey as a colporteur for a few months in 1858–59. He was ordained to the full work of the ministry upon being called to the pastoral care of Moore's Swamp Baptist Church, Surry County, Va., in 1859. Although exempt from military obligation, Bailey spent a good portion of the Civil War years with the Sixteenth Virginia Infantry and Thirteenth Virginia Cavalry, while performing occasional pastoral functions for Baptist churches in Surry and Sussex counties.

In late 1865, Bailey became assistant principal of the Reynoldson Academy, Gates County, but he remained at this post for less than two years. He was pastor of Middle Swamp Baptist Church, Gates County, from 1866 to 1867 and, subsequently, of Edenton Baptist Church (1868–71), Hertford Baptist Church (1868–70), and Warrenton Baptist Church (1871–76).

In July 1875, Bailey purchased the interest of A. F.

Redd in the *Biblical Recorder*, the Baptist weekly published in Raleigh, of which he was later to become both editor and sole proprietor. This work occupied his remaining days and elicited his most significant work. Under his management, the circulation of the *Biblical Recorder* rose from less than two thousand subscribers to almost seven thousand. His editorial policy was ably expressed in the issue for 11 Aug. 1880, when he wrote: "In our editorials we have sought to be practical and have written on those subjects which bear on Christian conduct, Christian character and growth in grace and usefulness. We have not introduced into our column's [*sic*] those subjects which are calculated to engender unending controversies." Accordingly, Bailey generally addressed his editorial comments to some subject designed to encourage growth in faith and piety, to some particular tenet of the Baptist denomination warranting explanation or defense, or to matters of church polity and practice. Nevertheless, he sometimes placed the weight of his editorial opinion behind measures of more general appeal and interest. Thus, one finds occasional editorials calling for the election of legislators committed to enlarging and strengthening the free school system (8 Aug. 1880), favoring the Prohibition Bill of 1881 (1 May 1881), opposing a free tuition plan for The University of North Carolina (25 Feb. 1885, and 11 Mar. 1885), and opposing state aid to higher education (24 Oct. 1894).

He took an interest in all the affairs of the North Carolina Baptist State Convention and of the larger Baptist denomination. He served as president of the Baptist State Convention (1885–86) and as a trustee of Wake Forest College (1877–95). He was instrumental in the formation of the North Carolina Ministers' Life Association in 1883, the earliest effort of Baptists in North Carolina to make adequate provision for aged or indigent ministers and their families. As editor and publisher of the annual *North Carolina Baptist Almanac* (1882–92), he was instrumental in collecting and preserving much valuable biographical and historical data concerning the denomination. Wake Forest College recognized Bailey's work by awarding him the D.D. degree in 1884.

On 21 Nov. 1865, Bailey was married to Annie Sarah Bailey, daughter of the Reverend Josiah Clanton Bailey, Greensville County, Va. To their union were born five children: Sallie, who married Wesley Norwood Jones; Christopher Thomas; Josiah William, later U.S. senator from North Carolina; Edmund Lamar; and Bayard Yates, who died in infancy.

Stricken with a partial paralysis while preaching at the Fayetteville Street Baptist Church, Raleigh, on 6 Mar. 1892, Bailey suffered a decline in health that left him unable to return to his office after 1 Nov. 1894. He died several months later and was interred in Oakwood Cemetery, Raleigh. Columbus Durham, writing in the pages of the *Biblical Recorder* for 12 June 1895, called him the "most successful editor the Baptists of North Carolina ever had."

SEE: Samuel A. Ashe, ed., *Cyclopedia of Eminent and Representative Men of the Carolinas of the Nineteenth Century*, vol. 2 (1892); Josiah W. Bailey, "Dr. C. T. Bailey," Raleigh *Biblical Recorder*, 2 Jan. 1935; Foy Johnson Farmer, *Sallie Bailey Jones* (1949); Raleigh *Biblical Recorder*, editorial pp., 28 July 1875 ff.

R. HARGUS TAYLOR

Bailey, Josiah William *(14 Sept. 1873–15 Dec. 1946)*, U.S. senator, was born in Warrenton, the second son

and third of five children of Christopher Thomas and Annie Sarah (Bailey) Bailey. He grew up in Raleigh, where his father edited the *Biblical Recorder*, the official weekly newspaper of the North Carolina Baptist Convention. He received his education in the Raleigh Township Graded Schools (1880–87), the Raleigh Male Academy (1887–89), and Wake Forest College (1889–93), where he was graduated with the B.A. degree. He assisted his father with the *Recorder* for two years and, following his father's death in June 1895, became official editor of the *Recorder*. Holding this position until 1907, Bailey not only ably expressed his views on religious, moral, and social issues but also involved the *Recorder* and himself in political conflicts and reform crusades, most notably for improvements in North Carolina's elementary and secondary school system.

While such educational reformers as Charles D. McIver and Edwin A. Alderman favored financing educational improvements through local taxation, Bailey led in advocating direct appropriations by the General Assembly. In 1898 he allied with Furnifold M. Simmons, the state Democratic chairman, and Charles B. Aycock, the prospective Democratic nominee for governor, in the "white supremacy" campaign that broke the control of the fusion of Populists, Negroes, and Republicans over state government. As part of this "bargain," Simmons and Aycock in 1899 won legislative approval of a law securing a four-month school term and supporting the principle of direct appropriations to public schools with a grant of $100,000 annually. State responsibility for public education was, thereby, firmly established.

As chairman of the Anti-Saloon League in North Carolina between 1903 and 1907, Bailey campaigned extensively and successfully for local option. He resigned in 1907, however, when the league declared for state prohibition and leaned toward national prohibition, which Bailey considered unfeasible. He also resigned as editor of the *Biblical Recorder* in 1907, and in 1908 he secured admittance to the state bar. In the forefront of the state's progressive movement, he advocated the initiative and referendum, ballot reform, a commission form of government for Raleigh, liquidation of the officers' fee system in Wake County, and abolishment of franchise politics in Raleigh. In 1913, President Woodrow Wilson appointed Bailey to the office of collector of internal revenue for the eastern district of North Carolina (consolidated in 1919 to cover the whole state). Holding this post until 1921, Bailey reorganized the collecting and accounting systems and reduced the cost of collections by 65 percent.

Bailey's marriage, on 16 Aug. 1916, to Edith Pou of Raleigh allied him to one of the state's most influential families.

Bailey served in 1913 on the North Carolina Constitution Commission, created by Governor Locke Craig, which included among its recommendations reform of the revenue and taxation system and requirement of a six-month public school term. Bailey not only fought for these proposed constitutional amendments but, with Clarence Poe, editor of the *Progressive Farmer*, sponsored a broad progressive program for the Democratic State Convention in 1914. The latter called for a state-wide primary and corrupt-practices act, tax revision, an elastic judicial circuit system, enlarged state aid to public health and education, just freight and insurance rates, rural credit facilities for farmers, and an improved child labor law. Neither the proposed constitutional amendments nor the program to revitalize the Democratic party won acceptance from the conservatively controlled

Democratic party machinery in North Carolina. However, Bailey continued the battle and based his independent, but unsuccessful, campaign for the Democratic gubernatorial nomination in 1924 squarely upon the 1914 platform.

Breaking with the political organization of Senator Simmons in 1922–23, Bailey determined to seek the Democratic gubernatorial nomination. He lost the 1924 contest to Angus W. McLean, but created for himself both a state-wide image as a social and political reformer and a strong nucleus of loyal supporters and dependable organizers. In the presidential campaign of 1928, North Carolina Democrats divided bitterly over support for Alfred E. Smith. While Simmons bolted the party to back Herbert Hoover, Bailey, now a "regular" Democrat, spoke extensively throughout the state in defense of religious freedom and in loyal support of Smith. Attacking Simmons's "irregularity" and "disloyalty," Bailey in 1930 defeated Simmons for the Democratic senatorial nomination and then triumphed over his Republican opponent, George M. Pritchard, to win the office of U.S. senator.

Attaining his first and only elective office at the age of fifty-six, Bailey remained in the Senate until his death fifteen years later. He gave his personal loyalty to Franklin D. Roosevelt but opposed much of the New Deal legislation. His opposition votes rested upon conviction that many New Deal measures gave special privilege to special interests, encouraged unsound financial and economic practices, violated trusted constitutional principles, involved unwise centralization of power, or tended toward collectivist regimentation. His pro-business and anti-organized labor bias was revealed in his support of such measures as the National Industrial Recovery Act (1933) and his opposition to such measures as the National Labor Relations Act (1935) and the Fair Labor Standards Act (1938). He played a major role among Democratic senators in defeating Roosevelt's "court-packing" plan in 1937. In 1938 he joined with Senator Arthur H. Vandenberg (R., Mich.) to draft a "conservative manifesto" that sought to rally popular support for conservative financial practices and to influence Roosevelt to turn to the political right.

As chairman of the powerful Senate Commerce Committee (1938–46), Bailey frequently attempted to restrain New Deal spending, but when confronted by the threat of war in Europe he used his office to support Roosevelt's policy of preparedness. He joined the president in urging repeal of the arms embargo and in passage of the Neutrality Act of 1939, which opened the arsenal of the United States to Great Britain and France. He fought for both increased defense expenditures, especially for the navy, and the Selective Service Act in 1940. Speaking for the Lend-Lease Bill in early 1941, Bailey declared himself for intervention in the European conflict. During World War II, he worked closely with Roosevelt and with Rear Admiral Emory S. Land, chairman of the Maritime Commission and administrator of the War Shipping Administration. The Senate Commerce Committee dealt with such problems as buying and leasing foreign merchant vessels for national defense and deciding transportation priorities. Bailey disagreed, however, with Roosevelt's economic stabilization policies, which he considered too soft, and with organized labor's threat to industrial mobilization. He repeatedly backed anti-strike legislation and promoted a "work-or-fight" law to draft civilians into essential war industries. As early as 1942, Bailey recorded himself in favor of the establishment of the United Nations Organization.

After the summer of 1945, Bailey was frequently absent from the Senate because of illness. He died of a cerebral hemorrhage at his home in Raleigh and was buried in Raleigh's Oakwood Cemetery. He was survived by his wife and their five chilren: James Hinton Pou, Annie Elizabeth, Josiah William, Edith Pou, and Sallie.

SEE: Josiah William Bailey Papers (Manuscript Department, Library, Duke University, Durham); John Robert Moore, *Senator Josiah William Bailey of North Carolina* (1968 [photographs]); James T. Patterson, *Congressional Conservatism and the New Deal* (1967); Elmer L. Puryear, *Democratic Party Dissension in North Carolina, 1928–1936* (1962); Joseph F. Steelman, "The Progressive Democratic Convention of 1914 in North Carolina," *North Carolina Historical Review* 46 (1969); Richard L. Watson, Jr., "A Southern Democratic Primary," ibid. 42 (1965).

JOHN ROBERT MOORE

Bailey, William Henry (*22 Jan. 1831–13 June 1925*), lawyer, attorney general, code commissioner, county attorney, and state representative, was born at Mt. Pleasant on Little River, Pasquotank County, the son of Judge John Lancaster and Priscilla Brownrigg Bailey. In the early 1840s the family moved to Hillsborough, where the elder Bailey began the practice of law. The son attended William Bingham's school and Caldwell Institute in Hillsborough and was licensed by the county court in 1851 to practice law. He joined his father's firm briefly but moved to Yanceyville in 1852. There, on 20 Oct. of that year, he was married to Annie Chamberlayne Howerton. In December 1856 he was appointed attorney general of the state to fill an unexpired term extending through 1857. He was elected county attorney for Caswell County in 1858, but in 1860 he removed to Black Mountain and taught law there briefly. On 24 Apr. 1861, he enlisted for six months as a private in the Bethel Regiment, First North Carolina Volunteers. He later returned to his law practice and toward the end of the war moved to Salisbury, where he joined the firm of Boyden and Blackman. In 1870 he moved to Charlotte and formed a partnership with Judge William M. Shipp.

Bailey was made code commissioner of North Carolina in August 1870 and served until the commission was abolished in 1873. In 1882 he was elected to the state house of representatives from Mecklenburg County and appointed to the Judiciary Committee. In the legislature, he was considered a liberal and an independent, although he most often voted Democratic.

Bailey was noted as a humorist and played the banjo. An active Mason, he was master of Eagle Lodge No. 71 and of Fulton Lodge No. 99. In 1885, Rutherford College bestowed upon him the LL.D. degree.

He was the author of a number of books and articles, including *The Effect of the Civil War upon the Rights of Persons and Property* (1867); *The Onus Probandi, Preparation for Trial and the Right to Open and Conclude* (1868); "Provincial Reminiscences of Colonel Benjamin Hill, . . . , John Campbell, . . . , Joseph Montfort, . . . , the Montfort Family and Alexander McCulloch" (1889–90); "The State of Religion in the Province of North Carolina" (1890); "Battle of Great Bethel Church" (1895); *The Detective Faculty, As Illustrated from Judicial Records and the Actualities of Experience* (1896); "The Regulators of North Carolina" (1895, 1896); and *The Genealogy of the Latham, Hill, Montford, Littlejohn, McCulloch, Campbell and Brownrigg Families* (1899). He was also editor of *Fifth North Carolina Digest* (1897), a continuation of W. H. Battle's *Digest* (1866).

Bailey removed to Houston, Texas, in 1891, where he spent the remainder of his life.

SEE: William Henry Bailey, *Genealogy of the Latham, Hill, Montfort . . . Families* (1899); Charlotte City Directory, 1891/92; Jerome Dowd, *Sketches of Prominent Living North Carolinians* (1888); J. S. Tomlinson, *Assembly Sketch-Book, Session 1883* (1883); *Who's Who in America*, 1901–1902 and 1908–1909.

SUZY MAYNARD

Baily, Dykeman Waldron (*1 July 1871–21 Apr. 1953*), sportsman, businessman, and novelist, was born in Mt. Kisco, N.Y. His father was Elbert Todd Baily, local politician and son of Benjamin Baily, personal attorney to Cornelius Vanderbilt. His mother was Deborah Lawrence Holmes, related to the prominent New England family of that name and to the Winston Churchill family of England. He received his education at the Mt. Kisco Academy and in 1888–89 took a "special Latin class" at St. John's College (Fordham University). For two years he studied law with his uncle, W. F. Baily, in Eau Claire, Wis., but seems to have spent more time hunting and fishing in the Wisconsin wilds than studying. After returning to New York State, he was variously employed and was married to Marie Antoinette Dearborn.

In 1894, on the advice of a friend, he ventured to Taylorsville, N.C., and bought a small plant engaged in manufacturing insulator pins from mountain locust for the Niagara Falls Power Company. Thereafter, he moved to Elkin and made almost daily forays into the surrounding hills searching for the valued locust. On these trips he became familiar with the mountain people and ways later described in his first novel, *Heart of the Blue Ridge* (1915). He built a number of small houses along the Yadkin River for laborers in his sawmill and, with an associate, organized a baseball club for the town. At the turn of the century he was mayor of Elkin. In about 1904, business affairs took him to New Bern and then on to Beaufort, where he lived next door to writer Irving Bacheller.

For the next fifteen years he was again in the New York area, employed as a real estate agent and traveling bookseller. Alexander Grosset, of the publishing firm Grosset and Dunlap, encouraged him to write his first novel. From it the motion picture *Heart of the Blue Ridge*, starring Clara Kimball Young, was shot at Chimney Rock. Baily's three other novels were *The Homeward Trail* (1916), a love story of the Croatan Indians; *When the Cock Crows* (1918), published by himself, a romantic story with scenes in Beaufort, on Cedar Island, and the Core Banks; and *June Gold* (1922), a yarn of rumrunning days near Bogue Inlet.

In the mid-1920s, Baily settled in Morehead City as salesman for the Hickory Chair Company, which was owned by an uncle. With his nephew, John Fox II, he purchased the hunting tracts of Piney Island and Raccoon Key in northern Carteret County, an area "about the size of the main island of Bermuda," he wrote. The depression terminated his salesmanship days, and he turned completely to his cherished sports of hunting and fishing. He became manager of Camp Bryan, an exclusive hunting club in the forests between New Bern and Morehead City, where pheasants, turkeys, deer, and bear were plentiful. At the club, patronized by the wealthy and famous, baseball star Babe Ruth and humorist Irvin S. Cobb became his friends.

Baily's last years were spent in writing lyrics set to music by others, but songs like "Old North State—The Happy Land" (1941) were not commercially successful. He published *The Autobiography of Waldron Baily* in 1958. His six children were Natalie Marie (Mrs. Bert Graham), DeWitt Dearborn, Dykeman Waldron, Jr., Frances Irene (Mrs. Abbott Morris), Margaret Virginia (Mrs. T. Elwood Butt), and Josephine Holmes (Mrs. Hal Alford). Baily was an Episcopalian and a Democrat. He died in Morehead City and was buried in the Bonnerton Cemetery at Aurora.

SEE: *The Autobiography of Waldron Baily* (1958); Mrs. Abbott Morris, interview (5 July 1973, Morehead City); Raleigh *News and Observer*, 24 Apr. 1953 (obit.); *State Magazine* 32 (19 December 1964).

RICHARD WALSER

Bain, Donald William (*2 Apr. 1841–17 Nov. 1892*), state treasurer, was one of five children born to William T. Bain and Martha A. Hill of Raleigh. He was a descendant of mid-eighteenth century Scotch-Irish immigrants who settled in the Wilmington area, and he was linked with the Huguenots through his paternal grandmother, Frances Hall. His father was a prominent Mason, serving as secretary of the Grand Lodge of North Carolina all but four years between 1836 and his death in 1867.

Bain received his education at South Lowell and Pittsboro high schools and at Lovejoy Academy. At age sixteen he embarked upon what proved to be two of three lifelong careers. In search of a profession, he obtained a position as the youngest clerk in the state comptroller's office, beginning thirty-five years of service in the state financial organization. The same year, he was welcomed into membership in the Edenton Street Methodist Church in Raleigh, where he had attended since boyhood and participated actively throughout his life. He inaugurated his third career in 1867, succeeding his father as grand secretary of the North Carolina Masons.

Bain cultivated industrious work habits and a love for finance in the comptroller's office throughout the Civil War years, and, in July 1865, he accepted an appointment as chief clerk of the North Carolina Treasury Department. He held the post just seven months less than twenty years. One of the pressing issues confronting the state during Bain's head clerkship was the settlement of an attempted repudiation of the state debt in the 1870s. In the last year of the decade, he served as a commissioner for the adjustment and renewal of special tax railroad bonds as part of the final settlement. Five years later, following the resignation of the incumbent, the Democratic party presented Bain to the electorate as their candidate for treasurer, and he won a four-year term. In 1888 and again in 1892, the party renominated him by acclamation. He served North Carolina as a hard-working, conscientious steward of finances until his death from heart disease nine days after his third electoral victory. In the course of his public service, he earned a reputation for devotion to duty, comprehensive knowledge of the financial system, sincerity, and upstanding Christian character.

His church and Masonic careers were almost as important to him as his political career. He held numerous positions in the Edenton Street Church and wrote a pamphlet history of it in 1881. Beyond his local involvement, however, he was active and influential in both the state and national Methodist Episcopal organizations. Yearly, the Raleigh district chose him to represent it at the North Carolina Annual Conference of the Methodist Episcopal Church, South, and in 1883 he became the first layman ever elected secretary of the conference. He held the post until 1892. Twice he represented the state church at national conferences: in Richmond in 1886 and in St. Louis four years later. In the Masonic Lodge he was secretary of the Grand Royal Arch chapter, recorder of the Grand Council, grand commander of the Knights Templar for North Carolina from 1885 to 1887, and, for twenty-five years, grand secretary of the North Carolina Masons. As a member of the Scottish Rite, he held thirty-two of a possible thirty-three degrees.

On 26 Jan. 1865, Bain married Adelaide V. Hill, the daughter of a Raleigh physician. Of their four children, only William H., Ernest B., and Adelaide V. survived Donald. Throughout the summer of 1892, Bain was unwell. By fall, he knew he had an incurable heart disorder, but he stood for reelection anyway. He died in Raleigh at the age of fifty-two and was buried there.

SEE: Samuel A. Ashe, ed., *Cyclopedia of Eminent and Representative Men of the Carolinas of the Nineteenth Century*, vol. 2 (1892); Donald W. Bain, *Edenton St. Sunday School of the Methodist Episcopal Church, South* (1881); John C. Bain, *The Bain Family* (n.d.); John J. Lafferty, *Sketches and Portraits of the General Conference of the Methodist Episcopal Church South* (1886 [photograph]); Raleigh *News and Observer*, 17 Nov. 1892; Raleigh *North Carolinian*, 18 Nov. 1892; F. L. Reid, *Journal of the North Carolina Conference of the Methodist Episcopal Church South, 1892*.

TIMOTHY J. WIEST

Baity, Herman Glenn (2 Sept. 1895–6 Apr. 1975), sanitary engineer and educator, was born in Clarksville Township, Davie County, to George Wesly and Sallie Sprinkle Baity. He was educated in public schools in Iredell County and was graduated from Harmony High School in 1913. He then entered The University of North Carolina and in 1917 received his A.B. Upon his graduation from the university, he became a first lieutenant with the Allied Expeditionary Force in France until 1919, serving through the St. Mihiel and Argonne offensives. He attended the Sorbonne, University of Paris, in 1919.

Upon returning to the United States, he became the superintendent of schools in Ronda for a year. He left this post to take a position as instructor and student at his alma mater, from which he received a B.S. degree in 1922. While a student at Chapel Hill, he was editor of the *Tar Heel* and a member of both Di Society and Phi Beta Kappa.

After receiving his B.S., Baity served as assistant sanitary engineer of the state board of health from 1922 to 1924. In 1924 he entered Harvard University on a Rockefeller Foundation grant, winning his M.S. degree in 1925; he completed resident study requirements for his doctorate in 1926 and submitted his thesis for and received the first doctorate in the field of sanitary engineering in 1928. During this period at Harvard, he won the Clemens Herschel Prize for the most outstanding work done in America in the field of sanitation, achieving the most brilliant record made in the Harvard Engineering School. He was invited to join the Harvard faculty but refused and returned to The University of North Carolina.

From 1926 until 1929 he served as associate professor of sanitary engineering at the university and, until 1931,

as associate engineer for the state board of health. During this period he helped promote the rebuilding of water works and sewage disposal facilities throughout the state.

Baity was the head of the sanitary engineering department from 1928 until 1936 and dean of the School of Engineering from 1930 until 1936, when the department was included in the School of Public Health. He remained department chairman until his retirement in 1955.

During the depression, he served as the director of the branch of the state federal Public Works Administration in the early 1930s and took an absence from teaching to devote full time to the organization from 1934 to 1936.

From 1937 to 1943, Baity acted as consultant to the National Resources Planning Board in addition to his teaching; he was special consultant to the U.S. Public Health Service from 1941 until 1949. During this period he spent a good deal of time in South America, helping to develop sanitary installations in Brazil, Uruguay, Bolivia, Peru, and elsewhere.

In the 1946–47 school term he was acting dean of the School of Public Health, and on 12 Mar. 1952 he became the chief engineer and director of sanitary engineering for the World Health Organization in Geneva, Switzerland. In this position, he played a major role in developing sanitation facilities throughout the world. In 1962, Baity returned to his home in Chapel Hill; he nonetheless maintained an active role as international consultant to the World Health Organization, and in 1964–65 he served as visiting professor of sanitary engineering at the University of Teheran.

Baity was a frequent contributor to publications, particularly the *American Journal of Public Health*. He is credited with membership in the Society for Promotion of Engineering Education, North Carolina Academy of Science, American Public Health Association, and the British Association of Municipal Workers. He was given a life membership award in the American Society of Engineers and the Hemisphere Award of the Inter-American Association of Sanitary Engineers; he was president of the latter organization in 1954.

In 1930, Baity married Elizabeth Chesley; two sons, William and Philip, were born to them.

Baity's body was cremated, and the ashes were divided between the old Chapel Hill Cemetery and his garden in France.

SEE: *Chapel Hill Newspaper*, 7 and 8 Apr. 1975; *Chapel Hill Weekly*, *Durham Sun*, and Raleigh *News and Observer*, scattered issues; "Faculty of the University of North Carolina, 1795–1945" (typescript, North Carolina Collection, University of North Carolina, Chapel Hill); D. L. Grant, *Alumni History of the University of North Carolina* (1924).

TYNDALL P. HARRIS, JR.

Baker, Archibald (10 Dec. 1812–2 Oct. 1878), minister and educator, was born in Marion County, S.C. At an early age, he moved with his parents, Archibald (1769–1842) and Catherine McCallum Baker (1777–1859), to Robeson County, where he grew up. He attended Jackson College, Columbia, Tenn., and in 1837 enrolled in Union Theological Seminary, Richmond, Va. Following his graduation, he was licensed by the Fayetteville presbytery on 17 Oct. 1840.

Ordained by the same presbytery on 15 May 1841, he began his career as a Presbyterian minister at the church in Laurel Hill. From 1841 until 1845 he served the churches on the Ashpole circuit as well as his own. In 1848 he became pastor of the church in Salisbury, which added 156 communicants to its roll during his eleven years there.

While in Salisbury, he took an active part in the affairs of the North Carolina Synod. He chaired the committee on colportage in 1849 and 1858 and served on the committee on devotional exercises in 1852 and 1857. Elected moderator in 1851, he preached his valedictory sermon in 1852 on Psalm 48. In 1852, the synod named Baker its first agent for foreign missions, a post he held for seven years. In 1855 he succeeded Drury Lacy as stated clerk of the synod.

Baker's paramount interest was education, particularly higher education. Elected to the Synodical Board of Education in 1848, he served as its secretary in 1850. He represented the synod on the board of directors of Union Theological Seminary and was chosen second vice-president of the board in 1854. The Salisbury Academy, sponsored by his church, achieved a state-wide reputation for excellence under the guidance of Baker and its board of trustees, which included Maxwell Chambers. Chambers, whose wife, Catherine, was a member of Baker's congregation, shared another interest with Baker: Davidson, the college established by the synod in 1835. Baker addressed the fledgling college's literary societies in 1845 and conducted the sale of Davidson scholarships in Concord presbytery. Chambers, a member of the building committee, loaned $5,000 to the hard-pressed institution in 1852.

When he died, Chambers left substantial sums to every member of Baker's family and his library to Baker himself. He bequeathed the bulk of his estate, over $250,000, to Davidson. This gift, which put the college on firm financial footing, has been attributed to Baker's advice and influence. In 1858, Davidson's trustees placed a history of the college, written by Baker at their request, and a copy of Chambers's will in the cornerstone of the first building erected with the endowment.

One year later, Baker left North Carolina for a church in Fernandina, Fla. In 1873 he returned to assume the presidency of Floral College and a pastorate at Centre Church in Robeson County. After more than three years' service, he resigned the presidency but continued as Centre's minister and a leader in the synod Sunday School Association. While addressing an association convention, held in his church, he was stricken by paralysis and died.

Baker and his first wife, Sarah James (d. 1856), had five children: Hinton J., Catherine, Laura, Archibald Hinton, and Annie. In 1861, Baker married Mary Elizabeth Gilchrist (1832–1904).

SEE: Last Will of Maxwell Chambers (North Carolina Collection, University of North Carolina, Chapel Hill); Presbyterian Church in the U.S., *Minutes of the Sessions*, North Carolina Synod; Jethro Rumple, *The History of Presbyterianism in North Carolina* (1966), and *A History of Rowan County* (1881); E. C. Scott, comp., *Ministerial Directory of the Presbyterian Church, U.S.* (1942).

ELLEN BARRIER NEAL

Baker, Blake (*ca. 1730–69*), lawyer and legislator, was born in Chowan County, the son of Henry Baker and his second wife, Ruth Chancey. Henry Baker had served as sheriff, captain in the militia, burgess, justice, and surveyor in Nansemond County, Va. When the dividing line between North Carolina and Virginia was established in 1728, the family's lands fell into North Carolina. Henry is perhaps the Mr. Baker mentioned several times in William Byrd's account of running the dividing line.

The name Blake came from Baker's paternal grandmother, Mary Blake, and was continued in the family for at least four generations. Blake Baker's wife apparently was Mary Kinchen McKinne, widow of Richard McKinne, who died in 1755. They had two daughters, Mary Blake and Elizabeth, and one son, Blake.

Though trained as a cabinetmaker, Baker studied law and became active in the assembly as a representative from Halifax County, which he first represented in 1760. He was still serving in the assembly at the time of his death. He served on the Committee of Privileges and Elections, on the Committee to Settle and Allow Public Claims, and on a committee to "fix the seat of government."

SEE: Simon Jones Baker Papers (Southern Historical Collection, University of North Carolina, Chapel Hill); Bryan Papers, Charles Holloman Papers (North Carolina State Archives, Raleigh); William L. Saunders and Walter Clark, eds., *Colonial and State Records of North Carolina*, vols. 6, 8, 23, 25 (1886–1914); *Raleigh Register*, 13 and 20 Nov. 1818.

SUE DOSSETT SKINNER

Baker, Blake, Jr. (*ca. 1755–11 Oct. 1818*), attorney general, was the son of Blake Baker (d. 1769) and the grandson of Henry Baker of Chowan County (d. 1739). His mother, Mary, was probably a Kinchen: the 1758 will of William Kinchen of Edgecombe County refers to Blake Baker, Sr., as a brother. The elder Blake Baker, an attorney, was a member of the assembly from Halifax County from 1760 until his death in 1769.

Little is known of the early life of the second Blake Baker. He removed his residence to Warren County. He is said to have been a lawyer of ability and experience, and he succeeded Judge Haywood as attorney general of North Carolina in 1794, serving until 1803. In this capacity he drew up the indictment for the state in the 1800 trial against James Glasgow, secretary of state of North Carolina, who was found guilty of fraud in his handling of lands belonging to the State of Tennessee. Governor David Lowry Swain, in an account of the Glasgow trial in his "Tucker Hall" address, gave the impression that Attorney General Baker was not effective in the prosecution of the case and that the state relied more on Edward Jones, the solicitor general. Bishop Cheshire, in his chapter on the Glasgow trial in *Nonnulla*, supported Baker and questioned Swain on this point.

In 1807, Baker represented Warren County in the House of Commons. In 1808 he was appointed a judge of the superior court in the eastern district for a year. Again appointed superior court judge in 1818, he died the following October while holding court in Moore County. A relative, Dr. Simmons Baker, said of him, "He was bred for the law and by dint of hard labor, for he was not brilliant, he came to be considered very safe counsel."

Blake Baker married first Ann Clark of Tarboro; she died without issue. He married secondly a cousin, Ann Bullock Allen, by whom he had an only son, Blake. In the nineteenth century, "Blake Baker" was used as a given name by many families in Eastern North Carolina.

SEE: Simmons Jones Baker Papers (Southern Historical Collection, University of North Carolina, Chapel Hill); Simmons Jones Baker, "Recollections of the Baker Family" (MS, 1847); Joseph B. Cheshire, *Nonnulla* (1930);

John H. Wheeler, *Historical Sketches of North Carolina* (1851).

CLAIBORNE T. SMITH, JR.

Baker, James McNair (*20 July 1821–20 June 1892*), Confederate senator, circuit judge, and justice of the Supreme Court of Florida, was born in Robeson County, the tenth and youngest child of Archibald (1769–1842) and Catherine McCallum Baker (1777–1859). His grandfather, Daniel McCallum, had emigrated from Argyllshire, Scotland, in 1770 and settled in Robeson County, where he married Isabel Sellars, also from Argyllshire. Baker's other grandfather was John Baker of Moore County. One of James McNair Baker's five brothers was the Reverend Archibald Baker (10 Dec. 1810–2 Oct. 1878), who was the president of Floral College, North Carolina, and held pastorates at Ashpole Church, Robeson County, Rockingham, Laurel Hill, Philadelphus, and Salisbury.

Archibald Baker having died, James McNair Baker's brother, Angus Sellars, sent James to Davidson College, where he specialized in law and was graduated in 1844. He began a law practice at Lumberton, but it was terminated when an attack of typhoid fever left him in a weakened condition, and his physician recommended a sojourn in Florida. He rode on horseback to Florida in 1847 and in that year was admitted to the bar at Madison. He began practice at old Columbus, the head of navigation of the Suwannee River, but shortly moved to Alligator, the name of which he was instrumental in having changed to Lake City.

In 1852 he became state's attorney for the Suwannee Circuit. In that same year he was made a delegate to the Whig National Convention in Baltimore, where, with the rest of the Florida delegation, he opposed the nomination of Winfield Scott. Scott's nomination turned Florida against the Whig party, and Baker was unsuccessful when, in 1856, he resigned his position, accepted the Whig nomination for Congress, and stumped the entire state on horseback. After the Civil War, Baker became a staunch Democrat.

In 1859, even though the Suwanee circuit was Democratic, Baker was elected judge as the Whig candidate by a very large majority.

Although Baker was opposed to secession in 1860 and supported the Bell and Everett ticket, after Florida seceded his allegiance was given to the Confederacy. In 1861 he was elected by the legislature to represent Florida in the Confederate Senate; he was reelected in 1863 and served throughout the war, living in Richmond.

Baker returned to Florida at the close of the war and established his home in Jacksonville, where he resided the rest of his life. In 1866 he was appointed associate justice of the Florida Supreme Court by Governor David S. Walker, but, in 1868, upon the ratification of the new constitution and the beginning of Reconstruction, he retired from public office and began the practice of law again. He earned his greatest professional reputation at this time, through his connection with litigation concerning the disposition of the lands of the internal improvement fund of Florida and the bonds and indebtedness contracted by the railroads built under the terms of the act of 1855 creating that fund.

In 1876 he became a member of the state Democratic executive committee and worked hard and successfully to redeem the state from the misgovernment of the Reconstruction period. He gained his greatest respect,

perhaps, as a defender of southern rights during the carpetbagger era.

In 1881, at the almost unanimous request of the bar, he accepted from Govenor William Bloxham the appointment of judge of the fourth judicial circuit, to which position he was reappointed in 1885 by Governor Edward Perry. Failing health caused his resignation in August 1890. He died at his home and was interred in Evergreen Cemetery in Jacksonville, where also are buried his wife, two of their sons, and some grandchildren.

For a great many years, Baker was a ruling elder of the Presbyterian church and often attended the church councils. In 1885 he represented the Synod of South Georgia and Florida at the Pan-Presbyterian Council in Philadelphia.

On 9 Aug. 1859, Baker was married in Fayetteville to Fanny Perry Gilchrist (1838–1901), only surviving child of the Reverend Adam and Mary Blaine Gilchrist. The bride's father, long-time pastor of the Fayetteville Presbyterian Church, performed the ceremony. Their seven children, two of whom died in infancy, were Susan Gilchrist (Jones), Fanny James (Stockton), Adam Gilchrist, James McCallum, William Hoge, James Duncan, and Robert Alexander.

Baker County, Fla., was named in his honor.

SEE: Family Bible of Mrs. James McNair Baker (possession of Mrs. William T. Stockton, Jacksonville, Fla.); Louis Farrell and Flora Janie Hamer Hooker, *Robesonian McCallums and Collateral Families* (1946); Pleasant Daniel Gold, *History of Duval County, Florida* (1928); Jacksonville *Florida Times-Union*, 7 May 1961; *Memoirs of Florida* (1902); Tombstone inscriptions in Evergreen Cemetery, Jacksonville, Fla.

MRS. A. WALDO JONES

Baker, Joseph Henry (*25 Dec. 1831–12 Feb. 1902*), physician and surgeon, was born in Edgecombe County. His father was William S. Baker, a physician and farmer who had been a county representative in 1838 and 1840. His grandfather was Moses Baker, owner of an extensive plantation employing many slaves. Moses represented the county in the House of Commons several times between 1819 and 1829. Moses Baker's father was Jonathan Baker, a native of England who first settled in Nansemond or adjacent Isle of Wight County, Va. It is possible that the Bakers of England were among the gentry, because there is evidence of an old Virginia deed stamped with a wax seal bearing a coat of arms. Joseph H. Baker's mother was Julia Shirley or Shurley, daughter of Henry and Elizabeth Davis Shurley.

Baker attended schools in Tarboro and entered The University of North Carolina in 1850, but after two years he transferred to the University of Pennsylvania. He obtained his M.D. degree in 1854 and entered into a practice with Dr. J. Lawrence, an elderly physician. In April 1861 he joined the Edgecombe Guards, afterward Company A, First North Carolina Regiment of Volunteers. While stationed at Yorktown, Va., he was surgeon in charge of the regiment, which disbanded in November of that year. He then returned to Tarboro and, in time, built up a substantial practice. Baker was president of the county board of health, twice vice-president of the Medical Society of North Carolina, and a member of the Edgecombe Medical Association. At a meeting of the latter in 1880, Baker was a committee member entrusted to convey a petition to the state medical society, requesting (1) that legal steps be taken to protect physicians and patients from "ignorant and incompetent druggists," by having druggists licensed through the state board of medical examiners, and (2) that, in an age when the family doctor spent hours in his horse and buggy, despite "the proverbial unwillingness of a large portion of our patients to pay the physician, even when able," a statutory lien be made legal for recovery of medical claims.

Baker was several times an alderman of Tarboro and twice its mayor. As a Democrat, he was elected to the state legislature in 1866–67, and in 1868 he was a delegate, with Henry C. Cherry, a black, to attend the convention under the Reconstruction Act to form a new state constitution. He was a member of the Odd Fellows and in 1870 was elected grand master of Grand Lodge. He was a member of the American Legion of Honor and also a director of various banking, building and loan, and agriculture associations. His first wife was Susan A. Foxhall of Edgecombe County. They had four sons, Frank S., Thomas A., Joseph H., Jr., and Julian M. His second wife was Ida Manly, daughter of Governor Charles Manly of Raleigh. To them were born a son and a daughter. Baker was a member of the Protestant Episcopal Church of Tarboro and was buried in the cemetery of Calvary Church.

SEE: Samuel A. Ashe, ed., *Biographical History of North Carolina*, vol. 8 (1917 [portrait]); D. L. Grant, *Alumni History of the University of North Carolina* (1924); *Makers of America*, vol. 2 (1916); *North Carolina Medical Journal* 6 (1880); *Transactions of the Medical Society* (1902).

JOHN MACFIE

Baker, Julian Meredith *(26 Oct. 1857–19 Oct. 1935)*, physician and surgeon, was born in Tarboro of English and French Huguenot background. His father, Joseph Henry Baker, was also a physician in Tarboro; his mother, Susan Foxhall, was descended from the D'Ancie or Dancy family of Edgecombe County, who were established on a plantation well before 1765.

Baker received his elementary education at the Tarboro Male Academy and later attended the Horner and Graves School (formerly known as the Hillsboro Military Academy). After spending two years at the University of Illinois, Baker attended The University of North Carolina, from which he was graduated in 1877 with a B.S. degree. Though short in stature, Baker "was noted for his vigorous, active frame and he excelled in athletics, and gymnasium work particularly." He was captain of the baseball team and first president of the university's athletic association, as well as a member of the Phi Kappa Sigma fraternity. He spent a year at the Bellevue Hospital Medical College in New York and a similar term at the University of Maryland, from which he received his M.D. degree in 1879.

Baker then returned to Tarboro, where he opened general practice that soon became substantial. Beginning in 1906, he specialized in surgery and gynecology and established a reputation throughout the entire South. Through the years, he did postgraduate work at New York Polyclinic, the Chicago Medical School, and the Mayo Brothers' Clinic, among other places. Despite the demands of his practice, he wrote articles for numerous medical journals, which were noted for their careful research. He was awarded the Pittman prize by the Medical Society of North Carolina in 1887 for an essay on malarial haematuria.

In 1910, Baker retired from general practice and surgery and began to treat cancer patients with X-rays and radium; he was considered a pioneer in this field at the time. He was the organizer of the Pittman Sanitarium, which later became the Edgecombe General Hospital, the first in the county, of which he became chief of staff.

Baker was chairman of the county board of commissioners, was the first public health officer of the county, and was chairman of both the board of education and the local chapter of the Red Cross. He was also president of the state board of medical examiners, president of the state medical society, and a member of the American Medical Association. He was a Democrat, yet he was tolerant of those who entertained different views. He was a member of the Presbyterian church, past master of Concord Lodge 58 A.F. and A.M., and a thirty-second degree Mason.

The Baker residence, in which he maintained his office, was within the town of Tarboro. Baker was also a large landowner, raising cotton, peanuts, corn, and fine stock. One of his largest farms was Foxhall, part of the original grant from Earl Granville to the Dancys and said to have remained in the family for two hundred years.

Baker married Elizabeth Jiggitts Howard on 17 June 1884. She was born at Milton on 30 Aug. 1863 and was a daughter of George Howard, lawyer and judge of Tarboro, and Anna Stamp Howard. Elizabeth H. Baker was educated at Peace Institute in Raleigh and the Mary Baldwin College of Staunton, Va. The Bakers had three daughters, all of whom married: Anna H. Fenner and Sue Foxhall Green, both of Tarboro, and Elizabeth H. Sprague of Flushing, N.Y.

Baker's burial was at Greenwood Cemetery, Tarboro.

SEE: Samuel A. Ashe, ed., *Biographical History of North Carolina*, vol. 8 (1917); D. L. Grant, *Alumni History of the University of North Carolina* (1924); *Makers of America*, vol. 2 (1916, [portrait]); *Transactions of the Medical Society of the State of North Carolina* (1936); *North Carolina Medical Journal* 20 (1959); *North Carolina: Rebuilding an Ancient Commonwealth*, vol. 3 (1929); *North Carolina: The Old North State and the New*, vol. 5 (1941).

JOHN MACFIE

Baker, Laurence *(1745–1805)*, Revolutionary War patriot, was born at Buckland, the estate of his parents, Henry Baker and Catherine Booth. The first of his family in America was Henry Baker, who settled Buckland in what was then Nansemond County, Va., in the seventeenth century. When the line was surveyed between Virginia and North Carolina in 1728, Buckland fell in Chowan County in the latter colony. Henry Baker II, realizing that his plantation would be in North Carolina, made a present to William Byrd, chief of the Virginia Line Commissioners, in the hope that Byrd would help him retain the surveyorship of Nansemond County. Later county divisions placed Buckland in Hertford County in 1759 and finally in Gates County in 1779. An old armorial seal given to Laurence Baker by his kinsman, Laurence Baker of "Shoal Bay," Isle of Wight County, Va., bears the arms of the Bakers of County Kent. The seal was brought to America by the immigrant ancestor of the Bakers, and, as Buckland is the name of a parish in Kent near Dover, it is plausible that Henry named his new home after his old parish in England.

There is little information available regarding the early life of Laurence Baker. His father died in 1770, and his brother William, having inherited Buckland, resettled on a plantation called Coles Hill not far away. Laurence did not appear in public life until the Revolution. He was a delegate to the Hillsborough convention, 21 Aug. 1775, and was appointed a member of the safety committee for the Edenton District. He was a delegate to the Halifax congress, April 1776, and was appointed major in the Continental Army. Hertford again sent him as delegate to the Halifax convention in November 1776, but he resigned to prepare for active military service. According to his son, he served as a colonel under Colonel Jonas Johnston and General Benjamin Lincoln at the Battle of Stono, where he "acquitted himself like a brave man."

After the war, Baker served for a time as general of state troops. In 1778 he was a member of a commission to mark the site for a court house in the proposed new county of Gates; he served as clerk of court for Gates until his death. In 1801 he was the winner of the lottery held by The University of North Carolina to raise funds for the completion of South Building.

Baker first married Anne Jones, the daughter of Albridgeton Jones of Southampton County, Va., and his wife, Elizabeth, daughter of John Simmons. Anne Jones Baker died about the time Baker left for active service during the war. Later, he married Anna Maria Burgess, the daughter of the Reverend Thomas Burgess, the last Church of England clergyman in Halifax County. By his first wife, Baker fathered three children: Simmons J.; Elizabeth, the wife of Joseph Harvey; and Agatha, who never married. Three more children were born to the second marriage: John Burgess, member of the legislature from Hertford and later Gates; Maria, wife of Richard Smith of Scotland Neck; and Martha, who married Dr. Cary Whitaker of Enfield.

Baker's will, dated 6 Sept. 1805, was probated in Gates County in 1807.

SEE: Simmons Jones Baker, "Recollections of the Baker Family" (MS, 1847); William Byrd, *History of the Dividing Line* (1866); William L. Saunders and Walter Clark, eds., *Colonial and State Records of North Carolina*, 30 vols. (1886–1914); Southern Historical Collection (University of North Carolina, Chapel Hill); Benjamin B. Winborne, *The Colonial and State Political History of Hertford County* (1906).

CLAIBORNE T. SMITH, JR.

Baker, Laurence Simmons (15 May 1830–10 Apr. 1907), Confederate soldier, farmer, insurance agent, and railroad agent, was born at Coles Hill, Gates County. (Through a clerical error in the War Department records, his name frequently appears as "Lawrence.") Baker's family was of English descent; the American branch was founded by Henry Baker, who came to Virginia from England in the seventeenth century. From him descended Major Laurence Baker, a leader in the Revolution. Major Baker's son was Dr. John Burgess Baker, physician and legislator from Gates County and father of Laurence Simmons Baker. Laurence S. Baker's mother was Mary Wynn Baker. Young Baker was educated in North Carolina and at Norfolk Academy. He entered West Point and was graduated in the class of 1851. Commissioned a second lieutenant in the Third U.S. Cavalry (Mounted Rifles), he attained the rank of captain and served on the frontier.

Although opposed to secession, Baker threw his lot with North Carolina when it seceded from the Union in 1861, resigning his commission on 10 May. He was promoted to lieutenant colonel of the Confederate cavalry, dating from 16 Mar. 1861, and on 8 May he was appointed lieutenant colonel of the First North Carolina

Cavalry (Ninth North Carolina Regiment), of which Robert Ransom was colonel and James B. Gordon major. This regiment was to prove one of the finest cavalry regiments in Confederate service and was to distinguish itself on many fields of battle. Upon the completion of its organization, the regiment was sent to Virginia and there, on 26 Nov. 1861, participated in its first military engagement at Vienna. In the spring of 1862, Colonel Ransom transferred from command of the regiment to the infantry, and Baker succeeded to his place, becoming colonel on 1 Mar. 1862. Later that month, Baker and the regiment were sent back to North Carolina to help stem the advance of Burnside's Union forces. In June, however, Baker's command was ordered to return to Virginia to help Lee's army repel McClellan's forces in front of Richmond. Serving in the cavalry brigade of General Jeb Stuart, Baker's regiment patrolled the right flank of Lee's army east of Richmond during the great Seven Days battles. On 29 June 1862, during this campaign, the First North Carolina Cavalry was ordered to make a reconnaissance of the position of the retreating Union army on Willis Church Road, southeast of Richmond. Baker led his regiment into action, driving back Union cavalry until Union infantry support forced him to retire. In the reorganization of Stuart's cavalry following the Seven Days battles, Baker's regiment was placed in General Wade Hampton's cavalry brigade; it served under Hampton in the battles of Second Manassas, South Mountain, Sharpsburg, Williamsport, Fredericksburg, and Chancellorsville. In the bloody battle of Brandy Station, 9 June 1863, the First North Carolina Cavalry did admirable service in helping to throw back the advance of Union cavalry. At Upperville, Union cavalry again attacked, and Hampton turned to Baker for help. "First N.C., follow me," yelled Baker, and the Union cavalry were handsomely repulsed.

In the Gettysburg campaign, the regiment accompanied Stuart on his controversial raid around the Union army. In the cavalry action on 3 July 1863, in the rear of the Union army, General Hampton was wounded, and Baker succeeded to the command of the brigade. In this capacity he handled well the difficult job of covering the retreat of the army back to Virginia, fighting at Hagerstown and Falling Waters. Once back in Virginia, Baker continued in command of the brigade, picketing the Potomac from Falling Waters to Hedgeville. During this time, there were frequent skirmishes with Union cavalry, until at last Baker's brigade was drawn back to the line of the Rappahannock River. Here, on 31 July 1863, Union cavalry again advanced on Brandy Station, and Baker's men resisted. General Stuart, Baker's superior, reported to General Lee: "Hampton's brigade behaved with its usual gallantry and was skillfully handled by Colonel Baker. . . ." Lee recommended Baker for promotion that same day; he was made brigadier general, dating from 23 July (confirmed 16 Feb. 1864), and assigned to command an exclusive brigade of North Carolina cavalry containing the First, Second, Third and Fifth North Carolina cavalry regiments. Baker had been badly wounded in the right arm during the action at Brandy Station, however, to the extent that the arm was shattered and unusable. Unfit for active field service, he yielded command of his new brigade to James B. Gordon.

In May 1864, when General Hampton became the chief of cavalry in Lee's army after Stuart's death, Hampton requested Baker for division command with the rank of major general. Baker's wound prevented acceptance of this offer, and on 9 June 1864 he was assigned instead to command the Second North

Carolina Military District, with headquarters at Goldsboro. In this quieter departmental command, Baker had charge of Confederate troops at Goldsboro, Kinston, Wilmington, Plymouth, and Weldon. In particular, he had to protect the Weldon Railroad, a major lifeline to Richmond and Petersburg, from the forays of Union forces. Baker was wounded again in a skirmish on 22 Sept., but he returned to duty in time to help confront Sherman's Union army near Savannah and Augusta, Ga. Recalled back to service in North Carolina by General Braxton Bragg, Baker was put in charge of the First Brigade of North Carolina Junior Reserves, a brigade consisting of boys younger than eighteen, in Hoke's division. In March 1865, Baker led this brigade in the Battle of Bentonville, a last desperate effort to stop Sherman's advance into North Carolina. In April, Baker's command was detached from Johnston's main army to hold open the Weldon Railroad. Upon learning of the surrender of Lee's army, Baker sought to rejoin Johnston with his command but was unable to do so. Johnston surrendered on 26 Apr. 1865, and Baker gave up the struggle.

He was paroled at Raleigh on 8 May 1865 and began a struggle probably more difficult for him than the war had been. Having had all his previous training and experience in the military, he had somehow to fit into civilian life. He lived at New Bern for some time, engaging in farming. Then he moved to Norfolk, Va., carrying on a trucking business, only to return to North Carolina to engage in insurance until 1877. He was then offered a position as agent of the Seaboard Air Line Railroad at Suffolk, Va. He accepted it and served there until his death.

Baker was also a member of the Tom Smith Camp, United Confederate Veterans, at Suffolk. He worked diligently to keep alive comradeship among his soldiers and survivors of the war.

In 1855, Baker married Elizabeth E. Henderson, daughter of Dr. Alexander Henderson of Salisbury. They had three children: Alexander, sheriff of Nansemond County, Va.; Stuart; and Elizabeth E.

One of the last surviving Confederate generals, Baker was buried at Cedar Hill Cemetery, Suffolk, Va.

SEE: Mrs. John H. Anderson, "The Confederate Generals of the Old North State" (typescript, North Carolina Collection, University of North Carolina, Chapel Hill); Walter Clark, ed., *Histories of the Several Regiments and Battalions from North Carolina in the Great War, 1861–1865* (1901); *DAB*, vol. 1 (1928); C. A. Evans, *Confederate Military History*, vol. 4 (1899); Douglas Freeman, *Lee's Lieutenants*, vol. 3 (1944); Ezra Warner, *Generals in Gray* (1970); Marcus J. Wright, *General Officers of the Confederate Army* (1911).

PAUL BRANCH

Baker, Simmons Jones (*15 Feb. 1775–18 Aug. 1853*), physician and legislator, was born in Hertford County, the son of Laurence Baker and his first wife Anne Jones, daughter of Albridgeton Jones and Elizabeth Simmons. Baker's mother died when he was young, and he lived for seven years with his maternal aunt, Sarah Burgess, in southeastern Virginia; there he attended the school run by her husband, the Reverend Henry John Burgess. In 1793 he went to Europe and attended lectures at the medical school in Edinburgh, then the most celebrated in the world. There is no record that he was graduated, but in that day few physicians took a degree.

After his return home, he married, on 24 Oct. 1795, Polly Smith, the daughter of Turner and Bettie Edwards

Smith of Scotland Neck, Halifax County. The Bakers settled on a Halifax County plantation given Polly by her grandfather, James Smith, and in 1796 they built a house called Greenwood. Greenwood is now the southern end of the present town of Scotland Neck.

When Baker went to England in 1793, he carried with him an old armorial seal that had passed down in the family and took it to the Herald's College in London to find out if any Baker still lived in England with the same coat of arms. He found that Sir George Baker, then physician to King George III, was the only such person. He made a second trip to Europe shortly after his marriage to consult this Dr. Baker about a personal illness. The trip was successful, and in gratitude he included the name "George" in the name of his firstborn son.

In 1800, Baker sold Greenwood and moved several miles east to Palmyra, in what was then Martin County. He became politically active and represented the county in the House of Commons in 1814 and 1815 and in the senate from 1816 to 1818. In 1828, Baker moved to Jackson County, Fla., where he remained for several years, acquiring large tracts of land near the present town of Marianna and around St. Andrews Bay. His plantation in Florida was Buckland Place. For the next decade he lived in Florida intermittently; then he returned to Raleigh, where he resided until shortly before his death.

Tradition says that Baker was a competent and learned physician, but little information is available about this important facet of his life. In a published article, Dr. Jeremiah Battle referred to notes from Baker on a severe type of malaria prevalent on the Roanoke, and mention is made of dissections performed on victims dying of the disease. As was the custom of the day, Baker undoubtedly trained many young physicians in his home, but no names are known. Two sons-in-law were physicians, and they, with his ward, Dr. Albridgeton S. N. Burgess, were probably of the number. He does not appear to have participated in the first attempt to form the North Carolina Medical Society in 1799. After 1849, when the society was finally organized on a sound basis, Baker was listed as an honorary member.

Baker was interested in education all his life. He was a trustee of the Vine Hill Academy in Scotland Neck when it was chartered by the legislature in 1809. Vine Hill was influential in Eastern North Carolina for a hundred years. He was a trustee of The University of North Carolina from 1812 until his death in 1853, and it appears that he took this duty seriously. On 22 June 1831, during the commencement activities at Chapel Hill, friends of education organized the North Carolina Institute of Education, and Baker was unanimously elected president.

An active layman of the Episcopal church, Baker was one of the churchmen who organized Trinity Church, Scotland Neck, in February 1833. On 7 Mar. 1838, Baker and several other physicians founded St. Luke's Church in Marianna, Fla., and he served as the first senior warden.

Baker was grand master of the Masons in North Carolina in 1832 and again in 1840 and in that capacity laid the cornerstone of the present capitol building in Raleigh, 4 July 1833.

Describing Baker as a man of liberal education, very lively and intelligent in his conversation, Elisha Mitchell commented, "He sets a higher value on the 'Amor Patriae' than any man I've ever known."

Polly, Baker's first wife, died in 1812, after the birth of her eighth child. In 1814, Baker married Ann Cleverius

Seawell, widow of Henry Hunter of Williamston. She died in Raleigh in 1843, leaving one surviving child, Elizabeth, who married William H. Dudley, of Wilmington. By his first marriage, Baker had two sons and five daughters who reached maturity. The oldest son, James Laurence George, was a member of the legislature from Martin in 1832. James and Simmons, Jr., eventually moved to Florida; the town of Greenwood there was named for the old home in Halifax County. Of the daughters, Emily married Dr. Benjamin B. Hunter of Tarboro; Mary Eliza married William Armistead of Bertie; Anna Maria married Dr. William Hunter of Raleigh; Ann Jones married Gabriel Long Stewart of Martin; and Laura married the Reverend Joseph H. Saunders.

Baker died in Raleigh. An obituary in the *Raleigh Register* stated: "During his long and valuable life, he enjoyed the respect and esteem of all who came into association with him—he was a true specimen of that excellent race of men—now nearly extinct, the old school gentleman." A portrait of Dr. Baker, in profile with white wig and queue, hangs in the Masonic Temple in Raleigh. He was buried in a private cemetery near Scotland Neck, Halifax County, where a large central monument records the ages of Baker, his wives, and their progeny.

SEE: Jeremiah Battle, "Edgecombe County in 1811," *North Carolina Historical Review* 6 (1929); Kemp P. Battle, *History of the University of North Carolina*, vol. 1 (1907); Deeds and Wills of the Counties of Martin and Halifax (North Carolina State Archives, Raleigh); Stuart Hall Smith and Claiborne T. Smith, Jr., *The History of Trinity Parish* (1955); J. Randall Stanley, *History of Jackson County* (1950).

CLAIBORNE T. SMITH, JR.

Balch, Hezekiah James *(1745–76)*, Presbyterian clergyman and revolutionary leader, was born at Deer Creek, Hartford County, Md., the son of James and Ann Goodwin (or Goodwine) Balch. His brothers were the Reverend Steven B. Balch of Georgetown; the Reverend James Balch (25 Dec. 1750–12 Jan. 1821), whose ministry was mainly in Tennessee; and William Balch of Georgia. His cousin, the Reverend Hezekiah Balch (1741–1810), was a Hopkinsian whose ministry was spent in several states, including Tennessee. The parents of Hezekiah James Balch moved to Mecklenburg County about 1751. Young Balch was graduated from Nassau Hall (now Princeton) in 1766 in the same class with Waightstill Avery. The Donegal Presbytery in Pennsylvania licensed him to preach and sent him as a missionary to Virginia and North Carolina in 1768. In June 1769 he presented a call to Donegal Presbytery from Rocky River and Poplar Tent congregations in what was then Mecklenburg County. Balch was ordained and transferred to Orange Presbytery when the Carolinas were separated from Virginia's Hanover Presbytery in May 1770. Balch served as pastor of the two congregations until his death early in 1776. He conducted a school at his home and was a member of the board of trustees of Queens College in Charlotte, chartered in 1771.

According to local tradition, Balch married Martha Sconnel (McConnel or McCandless), and they had two children. In March 1769, Balch purchased land between English Buffalo and Coddle creeks about four miles from the present city of Concord. He built his home on this or on an adjoining tract purchased later.

Balch was an active supporter of the revolutionary movement in Mecklenburg County, was a member of the Mecklenburg Resolves convention of 31 May 1775, and signed the resolves.

He is said to have served briefly as captain of a Maryland company in the Continental Army, but he died early in 1776 and was buried in Poplar Tent Church cemetery. The grave site was unmarked until 1847, when funds were raised to erect a monument, and a local resident who had been present at the burial pointed out the location of the grave. Balch's widow married George Marlin McWhorter and moved to Tennessee.

The date of Balch's death has been questioned, but he has been confused with two other Presbyterian ministers who served in both North Carolina and Tennessee, one of whom was his brother, James. It is clear that Hezekiah James Balch died in 1776, because the Mecklenburg County court minutes of June 1777 note the appointment of his wife and two members of his family to administer his estate.

SEE: Galusha B. Balch, *Genealogy of the Balch Families in America* (1897); W. Hamilton Eubank, *Historical Sketch of Poplar Tent Church* (1924); William Henry Foote, *Sketches of North Carolina, Historical and Biographical* (1846); Luther Thompson Hartsell, "Mecklenburg Records Prove Balch Died in 1776," *Uplift* 21 (1941); Thomas H. Spence, Jr., *The Presbyterian Congregation on Rocky River* (1954).

H. J. DUDLEY
GEORGE TROXLER

Baldwin, Alice Mary *(24 Jan. 1879–12 Oct. 1960)*, educator, was born in Lewiston, Me., where her father was head of the Latin School. She was the eldest of the five children of the Reverend Fritz Walter and Sarah Bingham Lyman Baldwin. Coming from a long line of congregational ministers and educators, she grew up in a family environment of strong religious, moral, and educational principles. When she was nine years old, her father accepted the pastorate of Trinity Congregational Church in East Orange, N.J., where he served until his retirement in 1915.

Following her graduation from a private school in East Orange, Miss Baldwin entered Bates College in 1896 and won first prize in the freshman class for scholarship. After that year, she transferred to Cornell University, being graduated in 1900 with a degree in history and membership in Phi Beta Kappa. During the next two years she was a graduate student and assistant in history at Cornell. After receiving her M.A. degree in June 1902, she went on a traveling fellowship to Europe for study at the Sorbonne and research in Sweden. In December 1903 she began teaching French, German, and English at the Glen Ridge (N.J.) High School. The following year she went to Fargo College, Fargo, N.D., as dean of women and instructor in history, but she also taught American literature and German. She became instructor of history at the Baldwin School, Bryn Mawr, Pa., in 1906 and was appointed head of the history department in 1912. During these years she also studied in the graduate schools of Bryn Mawr College, Columbia University, the University of Pennsylvania, and the Teachers College of Columbia University. She served as trustee of the Baldwin School from 1919 to 1921, when she took a leave of absence and entered the University of Chicago as a fellow in history, to study toward the Ph.D. degree. She became an assistant to Professor Andrew C. McLaughlin, who directed her dissertation. In her second year there she was president of the Graduate Club. In 1923 she went to Trinity College in Durham,

N.C., as acting dean of women for the summer. She had been given a teaching assistantship in the history department at the University of Chicago for the coming year, but while she was at Trinity, President William P. Few invited her to accept the postion of dean of women and assistant professor of history. McLaughlin would have preferred her to become a permanent member of the history department at the University of Chicago, but because he saw no possibility of a woman being added to the departmental faculty in the foreseeable future, he encouraged her to accept Few's offer. She worked out an arrangement with the University of Chicago that permitted her to return to Trinity after teaching only one semester on her assistantship. In January 1924 she assumed her new duties at Trinity as the first woman to have full faculty status there. She finished her dissertation on the New England clergy and the American Revolution and graduated *magna cum laude* in 1926.

After Miss Baldwin returned to Trinity College, James B. Duke signed the indenture that provided for the expansion of Trinity into Duke University. It was decided that a coordinate college for women would be among the several colleges of the university, and Miss Baldwin was named dean of the Women's College in 1926. She held that post until her retirement in 1947. More than any other person, she deserves credit for the standards of excellence that have characterized the college.

Believing that the position of dean was strengthened by classroom and faculty experience, Miss Baldwin continued to teach history until her other responsibilities made it necessary for her to stop. She continued to hold faculty status, though, and in 1939 she became a full professor. She served on many local, state, and national committees dealing with education and held membership in a large number of professional and civic organizations. During the Second World War she served with seven other distinguished women educators on the Educational Advisory Council that worked with the Bureau of Naval Personnel in organizing and directing the WAVES. She was a Daughter of the American Revolution, a Colonial Dame, a Congregationalist, and a Democrat.

The writings of Miss Baldwin include *The New England Clergy and the American Revolution*, "The Clergy of Connecticut in Revolutionary Days," "The Development and Place of the Coordinate College," "College Bound," "The Woman's College As I Remember It," "History of the North Carolina Division of AAUW, 1947–1957," and contributions to various magazines. She was coeditor of *North Carolina Occupations* and at the time of her death had almost completed a study of the reading interests of women in the American colonies before 1750.

As a tribute to her untiring efforts in promoting higher education for women and in recognition of her many achievements, the class of 1943 of the Woman's College established the annual Alice M. Baldwin Scholarship Fund. In 1946 she was awarded the LL.D. degree by the Woman's College of The University of North Carolina, and, two years after she retired, Duke University bestowed the same honor upon her. In 1958 she was presented the ninth annual North Carolina Distinguished Service Award for Women by The University of North Carolina's chapter of the Chi Omega sorority. In 1964 the auditorium of the Duke Woman's College was named in her honor, and her portrait hangs in the Union Building at Duke.

In retirement, Miss Baldwin continued to live in Durham. After her death a memorial service was conducted in the Duke University Chapel, and her ashes were buried in the family plot at Lenox, Mass.

SEE: Alice Mary Baldwin Papers (Duke University Archives, Durham); Julia R. Grout, personal contact; *Who Was Who in America*, vol. 4 (1968).

MATTIE U. RUSSELL

Balfour, Andrew (1737–10 Mar. 1782), Revolutionary War leader, officer in the North Carolina militia, and one of Randolph County's first representatives, was born in Edinburgh, Scotland, to Andrew and Margaret Robertson Balfour. His father was an Edinburgh Burgess and guildbrother with an estate known as Braidwood in the parish of Temple. There is no record of the son's date of birth, but the parish register for Temple shows that Andrew, Jr., was baptized on 23 Feb. 1737, and that other children followed thereafter: Margaret, Isabel, and John. Andrew married Janet Mackormick (McCormick) in Temple on 14 Apr. 1768 and in the proclamation of the banns immediately preceding the ceremony was described as an Edinburgh merchant. Balfour left Scotland in 1772, sailing from Greenock on 20 May and arriving in Boston on 18 July; he left behind his wife and infant daughter Isabel (Tibbie). His wife died 17 July 1773, and Balfour later married Elizabeth Dayton of Newport, R.I. Failing to achieve business success in the North, Balfour moved to Charleston, S.C., where he engaged in salt manufacturing while living with his younger brother, John, a Charleston merchant and planter. In 1778 he moved to Rowan County, North Carolina, where he purchased a plantation on the Bettie McGhee Creek. After building his first house, Balfour sent for his daughter in Scotland; she traveled to the new home with Balfour's sister Margaret, and together the three established permanent housekeeping arrangements on the plantation.

With the formation of Randolph County, Balfour served as one of the county's first justices of the peace and also as an elected representative in the House of Commons. He was always recognized as a man of superior intelligence, high moral character, and unflinching courage. From the beginning of the revolutionary movement, Balfour served as a leading advocate and activist in the American cause. At the first outbreak of fighting he offered his services to George Washington and served with distinction in the Continental Army. According to the David Fanning narrative, Balfour declared that there should be no resting place for a Tory's foot upon American soil. During his military career he was a close and personal friend of Washington's but was engaged primarily in the battles in Georgia and the Carolinas. In 1780 he was captured by Tories, but he escaped with the aid of local Whigs.

While home on leave, Balfour was surprised one Sunday morning by David Fanning and his band of marauding Tories, who were scouting in the Haw River country. He was killed by Fanning on the front porch of his residence in the presence of his sister and daughter. Fanning escaped punishment for the deed, but one Frederick Smith of Randolph County was charged with the murder and hanged in 1783. Balfour was buried in the family graveyard on the plantation. The cemetery has been restored and maintained by the Andrew Balfour Chapter of the DAR in Asheboro. The local Masonic lodge, a school, and a residential surburb have been named in Balfour's honor.

Elizabeth Balfour and two young children, Andrew, Jr., and Margaret, who remained in Connecticut until after her husband's death, moved to Salisbury in December 1784. Later, when her financial affairs became difficult, mutual friends informed President Washington, who appointed her postmistress at Salisbury on 31 Mar. 1796. She was the first woman to receive such appointment in the new nation, and she held the post for twenty-six years (1796–1822). Upon retirement, she moved to Randolph County, where her son, Andrew Balfour, Jr., and grandson, John Balfour Troy, had large landholdings, and lived there until her death. She was buried in the Balfour family cemetery.

SEE: Samuel A. Ashe, ed., *Biographical History of North Carolina*, vol. 2 (1905); Eli W. Caruthers, *Revolutionary Incidents . . . Chiefly in the "Old North State"* (1854); W. E. Hennessee, "The First Postmistress," *State Magazine* 7 (17 February 1940); Scottish Record Office and Scottish Registrar-General's Department (Edinburgh, Scotland), for files of the Balfour family and Temple parish registers.

HORACE W. RAPER

Barden, Graham Arthur *(26 Sept. 1896–29 Jan. 1967)*, congressman, was born in Turkey Township, Sampson County, the son of James Jefferson Barden and Mary Robinson James. He grew up in Pender County, served as a seaman in the navy during 1918 and 1919, was graduated in law from The University of North Carolina in 1920, and that same year began practice in New Bern. There, he also taught in high school and was a colorful and popular football coach.

At the university, he played in the first football game he ever witnessed with the first football he had ever seen. He starred as a varsity regular. He later coached New Bern teams to championship finals in football, baseball, and basketball, although he was familiar only with football. College teammates said no scrimmage got rough enough for him, no score one-sided enough, to ruffle the happy-go-lucky disposition that earned him the nickname "Happy."

His disposition made him a natural vote-getter, and "Hap" Barden progressed from Craven County judge (1920–24) to state legislator (1933) to congressman (3 Jan. 1935). In the General Assembly, he successfully sponsored a bill making salary payments standard for teachers, regardless of race.

When he announced that he would retire as of 3 Jan. 1961, after a career during which he headed the Education and Labor Committee for a decade, more than one hundred colleagues in the House of Representatives met together to beg him to reconsider his decision and remain in Congress. Distinguished Americans from every area of the nation joined in this plea, but to no avail: although he did not reveal it at that time, ill health had dictated his decision.

One of his accomplishments was preparation of legislation expanding the vocational education program throughout the nation. He also was instrumental in the passage of the Barden-La Follette Act, which makes vocational training possible for all types of physically handicapped people. Barden led in the passage of the Taft-Hartley Act and the Landrum-Griffin Act, designed to control corruption in labor unions. He was author of Section 14 (b), the "Right-to Work" provision, of the Taft-Hartley Act, which barely survived one of the bitterest assaults ever to explode in Congress.

For years, Barden stoutly resisted federal intrusion into public schools and predicted, accurately, that federal aid would lead to federal control of education. In 1949 his proposal to aid public education while

specifically excluding parochial and private schools embroiled him in a quarrel with Cardinal Spellman, who called him "a new apostle of bigotry." Barden found his outstanding defender in this instance in the liberal wing of the party. She was Mrs. Franklin Delano Roosevelt. Time and the courts supported his position.

Lawmakers who clamored for instant cures to social issues often charged Barden with being ultra-conservative, anti-union, and lazy. He replied, in a favorite quotation, that he "never knew the Republic to be endangered by a bill that was not passed." Labor lobbyists found him amiable, if not cooperative; and perceiving the wisdom of not overstraining his "happy" nature, they usually refrained from criticizing him and bided their time.

Homefolks who appreciated his stances elected him to Congress for thirteen terms with virtually no campaigning on his part. The district benefited. Camp Davis was established there as a temporary army base during World War II; and his district attracted three of the four major military bases in North Carolina; Camp Lejeune for Marines in Onslow County, the Cherry Point Marine Air Station in Craven County, and SAC's Seymour Johnson Air Force Base in Wayne County.

Those who enjoyed the hospitality of the Barden home along the Trent River near New Bern, where he and Agnes Foy Barden raised a son, Dr. Graham A., Jr., and a daughter, Mrs. David S. Sabiston, revel in recollections of his disposition. The Trent River was his fishing ground, offering release from congressional pressures.

Barden died after seven quiet years of retirement and was buried in Cedar Grove Cemetery, near the New Bern First Presbyterian Church, where funeral rites were held.

The idea of the Barden Chair of Government at Campbell College won wide editorial endorsement. The *Goldsboro News-Argus* observed: "The committee organized to raise the needed funds is comprised of men of all faiths, and particularly of men who appreciate the sound government principles which Graham Barden followed all his life. This type of memorial is most fitting for Graham Barden."

SEE: *Biog. Dir. Am. Cong.* (1971); *Congressional Directory*, (1935–61); *Congressional Record*, (1935–61); New Bern *Sun-Journal*, 30 Jan. 1967.

JACK RILEY

Barker, Penelope *(1728–96)*, revolutionary patriot, was born in Edenton, Chowan County. Her parents were Samuel Padgett, physician and planter, and Elizabeth Blount, daughter of the prominent Chowan planter and political leader James Blount. Penelope had two sisters: Elizabeth, who married John Hodgson, a noted Edenton attorney; and Sarah, who married Joseph Eelbeck, a physician. While still in her teens, Penelope was shaken by a series of tragic blows. Within a year, death claimed her father and her sister Elizabeth. She quickly learned the meaning of responsibility, for the Hodgson household and Elizabeth's children, Isabella, John, and Robert, were placed in her care. In 1745, John Hodgson and Penelope Padgett were married. Two sons, Samuel (1746–55) and Thomas (1747–72), were born of this union. The marriage was a short one, however, for in 1747, Hodgson died.

Again Penelope was forced to assume heavy burdens: the care of five children and the management of the Hodgson plantations. A most eligible widow at nineteen, she soon attracted the attention of James

Craven, local planter and political leader, and they were married in 1751. While no children were born of this union, the marriage did result in a sizeable increase in Penelope's wealth. When Craven died in 1755, his extensive estate passed entirely into her hands.

Penelope was only twenty-seven when James Craven died, and her beauty, coupled with her great wealth, attracted many suitors. One of the most prominent of these was widower Thomas Barker (1713–89), Edenton attorney and member of the assembly, who married Penelope in 1757. Three children were born to the Barkers, none of whom lived to reach the age of one year: little Penelope survived less than two months, Thomas less than nine, and Nathaniel less than ten. In 1761, Penelope was left to manage the household and plantations alone, for in that year Thomas Barker sailed for London to serve as agent for the North Carolina colony. As a result of the American Revolution and the British blockade of American ports, he was forced to remain in England until early September 1778.

In contrast to most colonial wives, Penelope Barker was well accustomed to single-handedly managing her household and lands. Her character had been tempered by tragedy. She had borne five children and mothered her husbands' four others by previous marriages. By 1761 seven of these children had died, and in 1772 her son Thomas Hodgson died at the early age of twenty-five. The lone surviving child, Betsy Barker, also left Penelope's care through marriage to Colonel William Tunstall, a prominent planter of Pittsylvania County, Va.

As the colonial independence movement grew in intensity, with an increase in riots and other extralegal activities in opposition to British taxation, Penelope, because of her husband's position, probably realized as much as any other person in North Carolina the potential costs of such actions. Thus, her leadership of fifty-one Edenton women, on 25 Oct. 1774, in open opposition to Parliament's Tea Act of 1773 must have been well considered. The choice of a tea party as the form for such an action is not surprising. The tea party was in the colonies, as in Britain, the most socially acceptable of gatherings, often including both men and women. Meeting at the home of Elizabeth King, wife of an Edenton merchant, with Penelope Barker presiding, the ladies signed the following resolve: "We the Ladyes of Edenton, do hereby solemnly engage not to conform to ye pernicious Custom of Drinking Tea, or that we, the aforesaid Ladyes, will not promote ye wear of any manufacture from England, until such time that all Acts which tend to enslave this our Native Country shall be repealed." This episode might well have passed unnoticed by history if a caricature depicting the "Edenton Tea Party" had not appeared in the *Morning Chronicle and London Advertiser* on 16 Jan. 1775.

Following the Revolution, Penelope led a more subdued life in Edenton, finally welcoming the return of her husband in 1778 and mourning his passing in 1789. She outlived Barker another seven years and in 1796 was buried beside him in the Johnston family graveyard at Hayes Plantation, near Edenton. The only known portrait of Penelope Barker hangs in the Cupola House, Edenton.

SEE: Hayes Collection, 1748–1806 (Southern Historical Collection, University of North Carolina, Chapel Hill); James C. Moore, comp., *North Carolina Heroines of the American Revolution* (1972); Lou Rogers, "Penelope Barker," *We the People of North Carolina*, vol. 2 (Nov. 1944), and *Tar Heel Women* (1949).

MICHAEL G. MARTIN, JR.

Barker, Thomas *(1713–89)*, lawyer and political leader, was born in the colony of Rhode Island. Little is known of his ancestry or life before he moved to North Carolina. He received legal training in Rhode Island, and, before immigrating to North Carolina, he was associated with a Boston mercantile house. Arthur Dobbs, royal governor of North Carolina from 1754 to 1765, stated that Barker came to the colony "as the skipper of a New England bark." In all probability, Barker was serving as the on-board factor for a New England commercial firm, sailing with a cargo to supervise its sale and to oversee the purchase of goods for the firm.

Barker arrived in Edenton in 1735 and immediately entered upon a career in public service. In September 1736 he received an appointment as clerk to the lower house committees on Grievance and Propositions and on Public Claims. In April 1741 he secured from Governor Gabriel Johnston a six-hundred-acre land grant in Bertie County and soon thereafter crossed the Roanoke River from Edenton to take possession of this land. Early in 1742, having settled his plantation, he married Pheribee Pugh (née Savage), widow of Francis Pugh, wealthy planter, shipowner, and member of the governor's council. To this marriage one daughter, Betsy, was born.

In March 1742, Barker was elected a member of the assembly from Bertie County. Early recognized for his legal and business abilities, he was chosen to draft bills regulating the colony's general and county courts and to be a member of the Committee on Public Accounts. Reelected in 1746, he was chosen as a commissioner to revise and print the laws of the province. With the creation of the position of public treasurer for the northern district in 1748, Barker was selected to fill the post. He held this office until 1764.

During the representation controversy arising over Governor Johnston's efforts to break the northern counties' control of the assembly, Barker served as the agent for the northern counties in their appeal to the board of trade. Early in the 1750s, following his wife's death, he reestablished his residence in Edenton and was elected as that borough's representative to the assembly in 1754, beginning almost a decade of continuous service in the lower house. As during his earlier tenure there, his main efforts were directed toward financial and judicial reform. He was a constant member of the joint assembly-council committee that examined the accounts of the colony's treasurers. He tackled the thorny problem of North Carolina's court system by submitting bills to establish supreme, superior, and inferior courts; to define the duties of the chief justice and attorney general; to expand the right of jury trial; and to regulate the fees assessed by the courts. As a staunch supporter of the Church of England, he authored bills calling for the establishment and support of new vestries. His devotion to his constituents in Edenton was evidenced by his bills to improve the inspection of exports at the port, to confirm existing land patents in the area, to repair the county's courthouse, and to erect St. Paul's Church in the parish. Barker's high standing in the assembly is best shown by his repeated selection to chair the committee of the whole and by his appointment as a member of the Committee of Correspondence in December 1758.

Barker's prominence among assembly leaders singled him out for criticism by the royal governor when the latter and the assembly were at cross purposes. Such was the case from 1757 through 1760, during the struggle over the emission of paper money and payment of the governor's salary. In various letters to the board of trade, Governor Arthur Dobbs accused Barker of bribery, election fraud, and misuse of provincial funds to continue the power of the opposition clique in the assembly. These charges were directed more against a faction of the assembly than against Barker personally, for in 1757 Dobbs recommended him to the board of trade for membership on the council, stating that Barker had "promoted His Majesty's interest in the Assembly."

By the late 1750s, Barker had established himself as a successful attorney in Edenton and a political leader of prominence throughout the colony. In Edenton, a thriving commercial center during the 1750s, Barker met and was attracted to Penelope Craven, a widow since 1755. In 1757 they were married. Of the three children born of this marriage, none survived to reach the age of one year. The grief over these losses was softened somewhat by the happy marriage of Betsy, Barker's daughter by previous marriage, to Colonel William Tunstall, a wealthy planter of Pittsylvania County, Virginia.

In the early 1760s a controversy erupted between the assembly and Governor Dobbs over the selection of an agent to represent the colony in London. Barker was the overwhelming choice of the lower house, while the governor and council countered with Samuel Smith. Efforts at compromise proved futile. The council refused to approve Barker as agent, and the assembly blocked all appropriations for Smith's salary. Thus, in 1761, both men sailed for London—Smith to represent the council and Barker the assembly. Once in London, Barker appears to have served as an aide to James Abercromby, who had held the North Carolina agency since 1749. Barker is not recorded as having appeared before the board of trade until after Abercromby's death in 1775. The period must have proved a trying one for Barker, separated from his wife and friends in a strange land.

No record exists of Barker's work and life in London prior to 1774. In that year, however, he was officially appointed as special agent, with Alexander Elmsley, to represent North Carolina in the court and attachment controversy before the board of trade. He submitted a memorial to the board on this subject in March 1775 and attended sessions of the body during May of that year, when the memorial was discussed. As the Anglo-American problems deepened and the movement toward open colonial rebellion accelerated, Barker's role in London became increasingly more difficult, just as his concern for his wife and friends in North Carolina grew more acute. In June 1775, Barker and Elmsley achieved for North Carolina an exemption from the Trade Restraining Act, which had been passed by Parliament two months earlier. However, news of this exemption was received with hostility by North Carolinians, who had forced the flight of Governor Josiah Martin and who had recently heard of the opening skirmish of the Revolution at Lexington and Concord. No doubt disillusioned by the totally unexpected, bitter denunciations of his efforts and deeply concerned about his wife's welfare, Barker in 1776 wanted only to return to America. However, the outbreak of open warfare in the colonies and the British blockade of America made his immediate return impossible. In late spring of 1778, he was able to leave England for France and on 8 July sailed from Nantes for North Carolina.

Early in September 1778, Barker arrived in Edenton and was reunited with his wife after a separation of seventeen years. However, because of his prolonged absence from the state, he was not considered a North Carolina citizen. If judged a Loyalist, he would forfeit his property to the state; he moved quickly to avert this possibility and took the prescribed oath of allegiance before an Edenton justice of the peace on the day following his return. On 20 Jan. 1779, the grant of citizenship was formalized by act of the state senate. The following month, Barker was nominated in the General Assembly as a delegate to the Continental Congress. While he did not win election, his nomination reveals that he was still held in high esteem. Following his return to Edenton, Barker, sixty-five years old, retired from public service to enjoy the comforts of his home and friends. At his death, he was buried in the Johnston family graveyard on the grounds of Hayes Plantation, near Edenton. The only known portrait of Thomas Barker, an oil attributed to Sir Joshua Reynolds, was painted in about 1771 while Barker was living in London and is part of the Hayes collection at Hayes Plantation.

SEE: Hayes Collection, 1748–1806 (Southern Historical Collection, University of North Carolina, Chapel Hill); Ella Lonn, *The Colonial Agents of the Southern Colonies* (1945); William L. Saunders and Walter Clark, eds., *Colonial and State Records of North Carolina*, 30 vols. (1886–1914).

MICHAEL G. MARTIN, JR.

Barlowe, Arthur (*fl. 1584*), explorer, is remembered today for his entertaining report to Sir Walter Raleigh describing the experiences of the 1584 Virginia expedition, of which he was a member. This report has been called "one of the clearest contemporary pictures of the contact of Europeans with North American Indians." In his narrative, Barlowe describes the four-month expedition (27 Apr. to mid-September 1584) in glowing terms. The savages are "most gentle, loving and faithfull, void of all guile, and treason, and such as lived after the manner of the golden age." A detailed picture of their generous hospitality is given, as well as the manner of making boats, warfare among the tribes, and the type of food grown and its preparation. The soil was the "most plentifull, sweete, fruitfull, and wholsome of all the world," and English peas planted by the voyagers grew fourteen inches in ten days. There are omissions in Barlowe's report, however, and it is thought that the omitted material was suppressed deliberately, for propaganda purposes.

Nothing is known of Barlowe personally except that, like Philip Amadas, he was part of Raleigh's household in his early years. On the Virginia expedition he was second captain to Amadas and accompanied him on the visit to Chief Wingina's village on Roanoke Island. On the return to England in September, they took with them two Indians, Manteo and Wanchese, who were taught English and served as propaganda agents for a second voyage.

There is no certain evidence that Barlowe returned to Virginia on the 1585 expedition, although Amadas did. His name is listed only in the Holinshed account of the 1585 expedition, and that reference cannot be trusted. He is not listed in the *Tiger* journal, and, although it is possible that Barlowe kept the journal himself and forgot to include his own name, the report is not written in his style. Like his friend Amadas, Barlowe dropped out of sight after his return to England.

SEE: John Aubrey, *Brief Lives*, ed. Andrew Clark, 2 vols. (1898); David B. Quinn, ed., *The Roanoke Voyages, 1584–1590*, vol. 1 (1955).

JOHN W. SHIRLEY

Barnes, David Alexander *(1819–24 June 1892)*, judge and legislator, was born in Northampton County, the son of Collin W. Barnes and Collin's second wife and cousin Louisa Barnes. Collin Barnes, a native of Nansemond County, Va., had settled in Northampton and become a successful planter; he represented the county in the North Carolina Senate in 1829 and 1830.

Following graduation from The University of North Carolina in 1840, David Barnes entered politics and represented Northampton County in the House of Commons in 1844, 1846, and 1850. A member of the Secession Convention in 1861, he was during the war a member of the military council of Governor Zebulon Vance. In 1866, Barnes was appointed provisional judge of the superior court of the First Judicial District by Governor W. W. Holden; he served until 1868. The same governor appointed him trustee of The University of North Carolina in 1868. In 1872, Barnes moved to Murfreesboro; in 1873 he was a candidate for Congress but was defeated by C. L. Cobb. In July 1873, at the instance of the state board of education, a state educational convention was held under the presidency of B. F. Moore. Barnes was one of the vice-presidents of the convention, which met to discuss the reopening of the university. While still living in Jackson, Barnes was one of the thirteen persons who organized the Church of the Saviour in 1851 and later served on the vestry. He was well-regarded by his fellow citizens for his general manners and acquirements.

In 1872, Barnes married Bettie Vaughan, the daughter of Colonel Uriah Vaughan, a well-to-do merchant in Murfreesboro. They had one son, David Collin, and three daughters.

SEE: Kemp P. Battle, *History of the University of North Carolina*, 2 vols. (1907–12); D. L. Grant, *Alumni History of the University of North Carolina* (1924); John H. Wheeler, *Reminiscences and Memoirs of North Carolina* (1883–84); Benjamin B. Winborne, *The Colonial and State Political History of Hertford County* (1906).

CLAIBORNE T. SMITH, JR.

Barnes, Joshua *(15 June 1813–13 Oct. 1890)*, justice, militia officer, and legislator, was born in Edgecombe County. His parents were Jesse Barnes and Edith Jordan, both from families long established in that area. He was educated at Benjamin Sumner's Academy at Arcadia in Person County, after which he became a planter. Within a few years, he had entered public life as a justice of the peace and a captain in the Edgecombe County Militia. His appointment to the rank of lieutenant colonel was dated 19 Mar. 1839, and he was soon afterward elected brigadier general of the North Carolina militia in the counties of Edgecombe, Martin, Northampton, and Halifax. He resigned from this position several years before the Civil War.

Throughout his life, Barnes was a prominent supporter of local education. He was an incorporator of the Toisnot Male Academy on 18 Jan. 1847 and of the Wilson Female Seminary on 16 Feb. 1859. He also took an active part in the incorporation of the town of Wilson on 29 Jan. 1849, and he was probably the only man in the state who was a commissioner of a town of which he was not a resident. As chairman of the board, he was technically the first mayor of Wilson, serving until 14 Sept. 1850.

Barnes represented Edgecombe County in the North Carolina General Assembly in the sessions of 1840, 1842, 1844, 1850, and 1854. He was state senator from Wilson County in 1868 and served on the important Military Committee. Wilson County was established under his leadership, despite long and vigorous opposition, by an act of the General Assembly ratified on 15 Feb. 1855; it embraced portions of the counties of Edgecombe, Nash, Johnston, and Wayne. He also served as chairman of the first session of the Wilson County court, held on 1 June 1857.

On 24 Sept. 1874, about one year after suffering the first of two crippling strokes, Barnes joined the Wilson Primitive Baptist Church, of which he was soon afterward elected a deacon. He was very faithful in his church attendance and the performance of all business obligations. He died in Wilson and was buried in Maplewood Cemetery.

On 16 May 1843, Barnes married Matilda Bynum (21 May 1819–5 Dec. 1883), daughter of Turner Bynum and Nancy Jenkins of Edgecombe County. They had only two children, Nannie (12 Apr. 1884–19 July 1901), who married Alpheus Branch, founder of the Branch Banking and Trust Company; and Louis Dicken Wilson (21 Dec. 1846–16 Nov. 1856), named for his father's distinguished friend General Louis D. Wilson, for whom Wilson County also was named.

SEE: *History of North Carolina*, vol. 4 (1919); *Wilson Times*, 11 and 13 Dec. 1951.

HUGH B. JOHNSTON, JR.

Barnhill, Maurice Victor *(5 Dec. 1887–12 Oct. 1963)*, lawyer and chief justice of the North Carolina Supreme Court, had the distinction of being the first honor law student at The University of North Carolina. He was the son of Martin VanBuren Barnhill and Mary Dawes Barnhill and was born near Enfield in Halifax County. His parents were affiliated with the Methodist Protestant church and worshiped at the historic old Bradford's Church located near their home. Barnhill attended the Elm City Academy and was graduated from The University of North Carolina School of Law.

He was admitted to the bar in 1909 and practiced law in Raleigh for a year before moving to Rocky Mount, where he lived and practiced law for the next twenty-seven years. He became a superior court judge in June 1924 and was appointed associate justice on the state supreme court on 1 July 1937. He became chief justice of the supreme court on 1 Feb. 1951, a position he occupied until his retirement. On 30 Apr. 1946, The University of North Carolina awarded him the honorary LL.D. degree.

As a superior court judge, Barnhill presided over two trials that attracted world-wide attention. The more famous of the two involved the murder of Gastonia's police chief. There was a suspicion of Communist activity connected with this murder, and, during the course of the trial, a "Kangaroo Jury" sat in the balcony of the courthouse to return its own verdict. The trial received international publicity, including an article in *Time* magazine complimentary to Barnhill's handling of it. The other case involved a man named Luke Lea, who was some $1 million overdrawn at an Asheville bank during the depression.

When a portrait of Chief Justice Barnhill was unveiled in the Justice Building in Raleigh in March 1966, U.S. Senator Sam Ervin stated: "Graced with sophistication in knowledge of many subjects, he yet retained that simplicity of manner and firmness of conviction that comes with self-knowledge, belief in God, and an awareness of man's place in the universe."

Barnhill married Nannie Rebecca Cooper of Rocky

Mount on 5 June 1912. To their union were born two children, a son and a daughter. Barnhill was buried in Raleigh.

SEE: M. V. Barnhill, Jr., to Ralph Hardee Rives, letter (22 Apr. 1975); *Enfield Progress*, Raleigh *News and Observer*, and Rocky Mount *Telegram*, scattered issues.

RALPH HARDEE RIVES

Barringer, Daniel Laurens (*1 Oct. 1788–16 Oct. 1852*), lawyer and congressman, was born at Poplar Grove in Cabarrus County. He was the son of John Paul Barringer (1721–1807) and Catherine Blackwelder. His father emigrated from Germany (where the family name was Behringer) to Pennsylvania in 1743 and about 1750 moved on to the Mount Pleasant community on Dutch Buffalo Creek (near the later Concord). John Paul was a militia captain in the Revolution and also served in the North Carolina assembly.

After studying law, Daniel Laurens moved to the state capital to practice. There, in July 1811, he married Nancy (or Ann) White, a granddaughter of Governor Richard Caswell and daughter of William White, North Carolina secretary of state from 1778 to 1811. Barringer represented Wake County in the House of Commons in 1813, 1819, 1820, 1821, and 1822 and was active during this period in the militia affairs of his county.

In 1823, Barringer opposed Willie Person Mangum for a seat in Congress but was defeated, 2,523 to 1,729. Three years later Mangum resigned to accept an appointment to the state court, and Barringer, running against James Mebane, won the seat in a special election by a scant twenty-one votes. The following year he won a full term by narrowly defeating Archibald D. Murphey.

In 1829, claiming to be an independent, he defeated two Jackson partisans, and in 1831 his seat was not contested. By 1833, Barringer's opposition to Jackson began to tell against him, and he was returned by a margin of just sixty-one votes. In 1835, listed with the Whigs, he lost his seat to Dr. William Montgomery, 2,706 to 2,416. While in Congress, from December 1826 to March 1835, he served on the Territories, Expenditures in the Treasury, and Revolutionary Pensions committees, and in the Twenty-second Congress he was chairman of the Select Committee on the Militia.

Soon after returning to Raleigh, Barringer decided to move to Shelbyville, county seat of Bedford County, Tenn. There he continued to practice law and was a Whig leader in campaigns against James K. Polk, governor of Tennessee from 1839 to 1841 and president from 1845 to 1849. Barringer was a member and speaker of the lower house of the Tennessee assembly from 1843 to 1845 and a Whig elector in 1844, supporting Henry Clay against Polk. Barringer died in Shelbyville and was buried in the Willow Mount Cemetery.

SEE: *Biog. Dir. Am. Cong.* (1971); W. S. Hoffmann, *Andrew Jackson and North Carolina Politics* (1971); *North Carolina Manual* (1913).

DANIEL M. MCFARLAND

Barringer, Daniel Moreau (*30 July 1806–1 Sept. 1873*), lawyer, congressman, and minister to Spain, was born at Poplar Grove in Cabarrus County, the oldest child of Paul Barringer and Elizabeth Brandon and the grandson of John Paul Barringer, a German immigrant who became a prominent citizen of Cabarrus County. His uncle was congressman Daniel Laurens Barringer, and his brothers were Rufus and Victor Clay Barringer. He

signed his name Daniel M. or, more often, D. M., but he was called Moreau by family and friends.

Barringer was prepared for college by the Reverend John Robinson of Cabarrus County; he enrolled at The University of North Carolina in January 1824 with advanced standing, entering the second term of the sophomore year. After graduation as an honor student in June 1826, he remained at the university for a few months, after which he began the study of law in Hillsborough with Thomas Ruffin. He was admitted to the bar early in 1829 and began practice in Concord in his home county, speedily attaining success in his profession.

Barringer was elected to the House of Commons in 1829 and in the six succeeding annual elections. He was active as a committee member and served as chairman of the Committee on the Judiciary. In the session of 1834–35 he was a member of two successive committees on a bill to provide for amending the state constitution, a measure that he and other representatives of western counties had been advocating for some time. The reform movement resulted in the call of the constitutional convention of 1835. Barringer again represented his county and served as a member of important committees, but illness led him to request leave of absence before the convention adjourned. He went immediately to Philadelphia for medical treatment, but his recovery was so slow that for several years he refrained from public activity. In 1840 and 1842 he returned to the legislature, which then met biennially.

In 1843, Barringer ran for Congress in a district formerly represented by a Democrat and won by more than 350 votes after a hard campaign. He was reelected in 1845, defeating veteran Democratic politician Charles Fisher by a narrow margin. In his third election, in 1847, no candidate was nominated in opposition to him. He was an early and active supporter of Zachary Taylor's 1848 presidential campaign, but he did not run for reelection to Congress. Instead, he sought a diplomatic appointment, soliciting the post of minister to Spain in spite of the opposition of the North Carolina senators, who, though both Whigs, were supporting other candidates. Barringer was appointed on 18 June 1849, spent some time in Washington for briefing, and reached Madrid in time for presentation to Queen Isabella II on 24 Oct. 1849. Confirmation of his appointment was delayed until September 1850, through the influence of one of the disgruntled North Carolina senators.

Unlike the preceding and succeeding Democratic administrations, the Whig administration of Taylor and his successor Fillmore, who reappointed Barringer, made no effort to acquire Cuba from Spain. Barringer was instructed instead to seek adjustment of the discriminatory customs duties and other restrictions on the trade of the United States with Cuba and Puerto Rico. Such peaceful aims were hampered by the strained relations that resulted from several filibustering expeditions to Cuba, launched from the United States by Narciso Lopez and other refugee Spaniards, with the support and participation of American citizens. The first expedition was prevented from sailing by the federal government, but two more reached Cuba and were defeated there. Prisoners were taken both times, and, after the second defeat, Lopez and a number of others were executed. Receipt in New Orleans of news of the execution of several Americans precipitated an anti-Spanish riot and the wrecking of the Spanish consulate. The surviving captives were sent to prison in Spain, where many appealed to Barringer for aid. He was diligent in his efforts in their behalf, even though he did not approve of the expeditions and doubted that all of the claims to American citizenship were valid. The State Department in Washington and Barringer in Spain worked to maintain peaceful relations, to resist threatened guarantees of Spanish possession of Cuba by Great Britain and France, and to procure the release of the prisoners. They were ultimately successful in these aims, although the pardon of the prisoners was delayed until Congress voted reparations for the wrecking of the consulate in New Orleans. In spite of the problems related to Cuba that dominated his ministry, Barringer managed to maintain cordial personal relationships in Spain, where he and his attractive young wife were popular in diplomatic and court circles.

Mrs. Barringer was the former Elizabeth Wethered, daughter of Lewin Wethered, prominent Quaker merchant of Baltimore, and sister of former Whig congressman John Wethered. She and Barringer were married on 15 Aug. 1848, when Barringer was forty-two and she was twenty-six. In the interval between their marriage and the departure for Spain, they did not establish a residence, and they were slow to do so when Barringer's ministry ended. He was not replaced immediately by the Democratic administration of Franklin Pierce, but he resigned and left Spain in September 1853, traveling in Europe with his wife and two young children, who had been born in Spain, before returning to the United States in May 1854. Mrs. Barringer spent much of the time in the next few years with her family in Baltimore, while Barringer went back and forth between Baltimore and North Carolina. They usually spent summers at watering places in Virginia.

Barringer renewed his political connections in Cabarrus County immediately on his return and was again elected to the House of Commons for the session of 1854–55. He was nominated for election to the U.S. Senate, but the Whig party was declining and a Democrat was elected. Perhaps because of the party situation, perhaps because of his unsettled residence, Barringer did not serve again in the legislature. He opposed the principles of the American party and in 1856 affiliated with the Democrats.

Barringer's inheritance from his father, including lands in Mississippi, and the sucessful investment of the proceeds of his early law practice, furnished ample means for a comfortable life. When he established residence in Raleigh in 1858, he became a member of the Raleigh bar but did not engage in active practice. He bought and renovated a home near the governor's "palace," and he and his wife became prominent Raleigh residents. Barringer was busy with service on the board of trustees of The University of North Carolina, the board of directors of the North Carolina Railroad, and other public affairs, but did not seek elective office. The Buchanan administration offered him appointment as minister to Costa Rica and Nicaragua, but he declined. By 1860 he had become a leader in the Democratic party and a member of the state executive committee. He and Lincoln had been fellow-Whigs in the Thirtieth Congress, and, according to family tradition, had been seat mates and friends, but in 1860 Barringer urged North Carolina Democrats to agree on one slate of electors pledged to vote for the Democratic candidate most likely to defeat Lincoln. When his efforts to unite the two opposing factions of the party failed, he supported the Breckinridge-Lane ticket. After the election, he was chosen by the legislature to be a member of North Carolina's delegation to the 1861 Peace Convention in Washington and served conscientiously, despite his doubt that the body could reconcile

conflicting viewpoints. When North Carolina seceded, he supported his friend Governor John W. Ellis. In 1862 he was appointed an aide, with the rank of colonel, to Ellis's successor, Henry T. Clark.

For the remainder of the war years, Barringer and his family lived quietly in Raleigh, saddened by the enforced separation from Mrs. Barringer's family in Baltimore and grief-stricken by the deaths in 1864 of two children. In March 1865, Barringer fell while dismounting from a railroad car in Salisbury and sustained a badly broken leg, which recovered slowly and remained permanently shortened. Investment in Confederate, state, and railroad stocks and bonds caused heavy losses, but Barringer's financial circumstances at the end of the war still compared favorably with those of most North Carolinians. New grief came, however, when Mrs. Barringer developed cancer in 1866. She went for treatment first to Baltimore and then to New York, where she died on 4 June 1867 after prolonged illness. Barringer's chief concern thereafter became the care and education of the remaining children, one a boy only seven years old.

Despite family anxieties, Barringer did not entirely lose interest in politics. He was a delegate to the Union Convention in Philadelphia in 1866, and in April 1867, in a letter widely published in the newspapers, he urged cooperation with congressional Reconstruction. By 1868, however, he was actively supporting the Conservative presidential campaign. In 1872 he was a delegate to the Baltimore convention of the Democratic party and chairman of the state Democratic-Conservative executive committee.

Barringer died at the White Sulphur Springs, Greenbrier, W.Va., and was buried in Greenmount Cemetery in Baltimore. He was baptized a Lutheran, and his wife had been a member of a Quaker family, but in Raleigh they both became members of the Protestant Episcopal church. Barringer was survived by two sons, Lewin Wethered, then a young lawyer, and Daniel Moreau, Jr.

SEE: Ackland Art Center (Chapel Hill), for a portrait by Federico do Madrazo; Samuel A. Ashe, ed., *Biographical History of North Carolina*, vol. 1 (1905); Brandon Barringer and L. Wethered Barroll, *The Wethered Book* (1967); Daniel Moreau Barringer Papers (Southern Historical Collection, University of North Carolina, Chapel Hill); French Ensor Chadwick, *The Relations of the United States and Spain* (1909); William R. Manning, ed., *Diplomatic Correspondence of the United States* (1939); *Proceedings and Debates of the Convention of North-Carolina, Called to Amend the Constitution* (1836); Basil Rauch, *American Interest in Cuba* (1948).

CAROLYN A. WALLACE

Barringer, Daniel Moreau, Jr. (*25 May 1860–30 Nov. 1929*), lawyer, sportsman, mineralogist, consulting engineer, and geologist, the son of Elizabeth Wethered, of Baltimore, and Daniel Moreau Barringer, was born in Raleigh. He was educated in local schools, at Bingham's Military Academy in Alamance County, at the Penn Lucy School near Baltimore, and at Princeton, from which he was graduated in 1879. He was graduated in law from the University of Pennsylvania in 1882, the year in which he also received the M.A. degree from Princeton. For several years he was associated with his older brother, Lewin Wethered, in the practice of law in Philadelphia, but the practice did not hold his interest. In 1889 he entered Harvard University to study economic geology, and afterward, at the University of Virginia, he studied mineralogy. He worked briefly with the Arkansas Geological Survey but soon began traveling widely to examine mining property around the world. He assisted in developing the Hanover Mine at Fierro, N.M., which produced iron and copper for more than sixty years. In 1896 he and two partners discovered and soon began mining an immensely rich silver deposit in Arizona. There he met and married Margaret Bennett of Phoenix in 1897; they were the parents of nine children, eight of whom survived: Brandon, Daniel Moreau, Sarah, John Paul, Elizabeth Wethered, Lewin Bennett, Richard Wethered, and Philip Ellicott.

Barringer was the author of *A Description of Minerals of Commercial Value* (New York, 1893) and, with John Stokes Adams, of *The Laws of Mines and Mining in the United States*, 2 vols. (Boston, 1897–1911). He also wrote a number of scientific papers. He lived in Philadelphia when not traveling throughout the country and abroad on business, and he also owned an estate in Delaware County, Pa., on which he built a house modeled after his grandfather's plantation-style house in North Carolina. Barringer was one of the most influential proponents of the Roosevelt Dam in Arizona, forerunner of western reservoir projects. He was active in securing the nomination of his Princeton classmate, Woodrow Wilson, for president in 1912 and was an advocate of "preparedness," although he was opposed to the League of Nations. He held a long-distance swimming record, was an avid hunter and an ardent conservationist, and, with Theodore Roosevelt and Owen Wister, formed the Boone and Crockett Club for big-game hunters. He also invented and patented a rifle sight.

For a number of years, Barringer was interested in various craters in the West, particularly Meteor Crater in northern Arizona. He acquired title to it and undertook to find the meteor that he was convinced had formed the depression, six hundred feet deep and nearly a mile across. The site was developed commercially, and revenue from it was used to support the study of meteorites.

Barringer was a member of the North Carolina Battle Monument Commission in 1928, and it was he who suggested to Gutzon Borglum, the sculptor, the idea of the representation of Pickett's charge at Gettysburg. The statue is startlingly like that of the Marines raising the flag at Iwo Jima twenty years later.

Barringer died of a heart attack in Philadelphia.

SEE: Brandon Barringer and L. Wethered Barroll, *The Wethered Book* (1967).

WILLIAM S. POWELL

Barringer, Paul (26 Sept. 1778–20 June 1844), businessman, member of the North Carolina House of Commons and Senate, and brigadier general in the War of 1812, was born at the family homeplace, Poplar Grove, in southeastern Cabarrus County. He was the eldest child of John Paul Barringer, founder of the Barringer family in North Carolina, who emigrated from Germany to Pennsylvania in 1743. John Paul's second wife, Catherine Blackwelder, was Paul's mother. Since his father spoke only German, young Paul's early education was conducted mainly in the German language, but at the age of eighteen he was sent to an English classical school, where he remained for three years. He spoke and wrote both English and German fluently.

When he was twenty-one years old, he moved to Concord and, with his father's help, became a successful planter and merchant. Later he helped to organize the first cotton mill in Cabarrus County and became its first president. He also subscribed $2,000 toward the construction of North Carolina's first railroad, the Raleigh to Gaston Railroad. Not only did he support this railroad financially, but he was one of a small group that worked to make the idea of such an undertaking a reality.

In 1805, Barringer married Elizabeth Brandon of Rowan County, daughter of Matthew Brandon, an enthusiastic supporter of the American Revolution. Barringer's father died in 1807; a few years later, the young couple moved back to the family home. There they had a family of eleven children, two of whom died in early childhood: Daniel Moreau, U.S. minister to Spain under presidents Taylor and Fillmore; Margaret, married first to John Boyd and second to Andrew Grier; Paul Brandon, one of the first settlers in the "Chickasaw Purchase" at Pontotoc, Miss.; Mary Ann; Matthew; William; Elizabeth; Alfred; Rufus, a general in the Confederate Army; Catherine, who married W. C. Means; and Victor, lawyer, professor at Davidson College, state senator, and U.S. representative at the International Court at Alexandria, Egypt, from 1874 to 1894.

A handsome man nearly six feet tall, Barringer was quiet and unassuming. He preferred a simple life as a planter and merchant and close relationships with his family, church, and community. Underneath his quiet dignity, however, was a leader and a man of integrity. Because his associates recognized his leadership and respected his integrity, he was elected to represent his county for twelve years in the North Carolina Assembly, where he performed admirably and won the esteem of his fellow legislators. He was a member of the Federalist party until he later joined the Whig party. In 1823 he refused to run for reelection, claiming that his business interests—three plantations, two stores, a tannery, and a cotton mill—needed his guidance. Because he felt it necessary to locate nearer his enterprises, he moved his family in 1838 from Poplar Grove to a location two and a half miles west of Concord and built a home called Bellevue.

Like many others of German descent who had suffered hardship in Germany, Barringer was not in favor of slavery. He did for a time own about fifteen slaves; these he later gave to his son Paul Brandon to take to Mississippi, saying he did not believe the practice was moral or economically sound and that he did not wish to own them any longer.

He was opposed to the War of 1812, but when the war broke out, he quickly volunteered and was commissioned a brigadier general of volunteers, a position he held throughout the war.

Like his father before him, Barringer was a deeply religious man. He held office in St. John's Lutheran Church, for the building of which his father had given the land and most of the money. Paul, too, was a generous financial and spiritual supporter of this church.

Barringer was buried in the then new Lutheran Cemetery in Concord.

SEE: Samuel A. Ashe, ed., *Biographical History of North Carolina*, vol. 1 (1905); Smith Barrier, "Deutschland in Piedmont North Carolina," *Uplift* 25 (9, 16, 23 Jan. 1937); *Concord Daily Tribune*, 29 Aug. 1934; Tombstones, St. John's Lutheran Churchyard, Cabarrus County, and Lutheran Graveyard, Concord; John H. Wheeler, *Historical Sketches of North Carolina* (1964).

MARY RICHMOND KEATING

Barringer, Paul Brandon (*13 Feb. 1857–9 Jan. 1941*), physician and educator. born in Concord, was the son of Rufus Barringer, a general in the Confederate Army, and Eugenia Morrison Barringer, whose father, the Reverend Robert Hall Morrison, was the first president of Davidson College. His grandfather, General Paul Barringer, served in the U.S. Army during the War of 1812. His mother's sisters were married to General Thomas J. ("Stonewall") Jackson and General Daniel H. Hill of the Confederate Army. Following his early education at Bingham School in North Carolina and Kenmore School in Virginia, he enrolled in the University of Virginia, where he studied chemistry, agriculture, and mechanical drawing before receiving a medical degree in 1877. He received his M.D. from the University of the City of New York in 1878 and returned to Dallas, N.C., where he practiced for three years. From 1881 to 1884 he studied in clinics in London, Paris, and Vienna.

In 1886, Barringer became the attending physician at Davidson College. There he taught anatomy, physiology, and histology and established a medical preparatory school, which became the North Carolina Medical College, the first medical school chartered in the state. In 1889 he was appointed professor of physiology and surgery at the University of Virginia, where he subsequently taught medicine, ophthalmology, and dermatology; he served as chairman of the medical faculty from 1891 to 1895 and as chairman of the university faculty from 1895 to 1903. From 1907 to 1912 he was president of Virginia A & M College, later known as Virginia Polytechnic Institute. During World War I he worked for the federal government, supervising public health measures in American coal mining areas.

Barringer published a variety of scientific papers dealing with cholera, syphilis, and typhoid fever. He was a recognized authority on venomous reptiles and wrote extensively on the subject. He authored a series of studies of the American Negro between 1896 and 1901. Barringer was a member of the American Medical Association, Southern Tri-State Medical Association, and North Carolina Medical Society and was president of the Medical Society of Virginia. He served on the Virginia Board of Health and Board of Agriculture and was president of the Albemarle County Red Cross. He was a member of Zeta Psi social fraternity, Nu Sigma Nu medical fraternity, and the North Carolina Academy of Science and was honorary president of the University of Virginia Alumni Association. In recognition of his contributions to education and medicine, he received honorary LL.D. degrees from the University of South Carolina and Davidson College.

Barringer married Nannie Irene Hannah in 1882; the couple had seven children. He died in Charlottesville, Va., and was buried there in University Cemetery. He was an active member of the Presbyterian church.

SEE: R. H. Lafferty, *The North Carolina Medical College* (1946 [portrait]).

MARCUS B. SIMPSON, JR.

Barringer, Rufus Clay (*2 Dec. 1821–3 Feb. 1895*), Confederate Army officer and legislator, was a descendant of French Huguenots who left France during the early seventeenth century for England and Germany. Barringer's grandfather, John Paul, known as "Pioneer Paul," was born in the Duchy of Württemberg on 4 June 1721. He left Germany on the ship *Phoenix* and arrived in Philadelphia on 30 Sept. 1743. He and his first wife, Anna Eliza Eisman, originally settled in the Wyoming Valley of Pennsylvania. In 1753 they migrated to Dutch Buffalo Creek, now part of Cabarrus County. Anna Barringer died in 1777, leaving two children, John Paul and Catherine. John Paul later married Catherine Blackwelder, and this marriage produced seven children. Paul, the eldest, served in the state legislature, as a Concord magistrate, and as a general in the War of 1812. He was a prosperous planter and a successful merchant. His marriage to Elizabeth Brandon, daughter of a distinguished North Carolina family, produced ten children.

Rufus Clay Barringer, their ninth child, was born in Cabarrus County. He was graduated from The University of North Carolina in 1842 and studied law with his brother, Daniel Moreau, a law partner of Chief-Justice Richmond M. Pearson. After completing the bar requirements, Rufus Barringer settled in Concord and, from 1848 to 1850, represented Cabarrus County in the House of Commons. In 1854, at the age of thirty-three, he married Eugenia Morrison, his first wife. She died in 1858, and in the winter of 1861 while serving with the Confederate forces he married Rosalie Chunn of Charlotte.

Politically, Rufus Barringer was a Whig who favored Negro suffrage. Although he was devoted to the Union and the Constitution, he placed North Carolina's interests first. He urged the North Carolina Assembly to arm the state, and, when North Carolina seceded from the Union, he was among the first to volunteer. On 16 May 1861, Barringer became captain of Company F, First North Carolina Cavalry. He was promoted to major on 26 Aug. 1863 and to lieutenant colonel in November of that year. In June 1864 he was commissioned brigadier general and took over command of North Carolina's cavalry brigade, which consisted of the First, Second, Third, and Fifth Regiments. Barringer fought in seventy-six actions and was wounded three times. He was cited for gallantry at the battles of Willis' Church, Brandy Station, Auburn Mills, Buckland Races, Davis' Farm, Reams' Station (where he commanded a division), and Chamberlain Run, which was the last decisive Confederate victory in Virginia. Barringer was captured on 3 Apr. 1865 at Namozine Church. While confined at City Point prison, he met President Lincoln, in Lincoln's first encounter with a Confederate general.

After the war, Barringer returned to politics and advocated North Carolina's acceptance of the Reconstruction Acts of 1867. He served in the 1875 North Carolina Constitutional Convention but was defeated in 1880 when he ran for lieutenant governor. In 1865, Barringer moved to Charlotte. He maintained law offices there and in Concord until his retirement from the bar in 1884 and was a key figure in establishing North Carolina's rail system. Barringer devoted the later part of his life to detailing a series of cavalry sketches that described the significant battles in which he had participated. Before he died, he completed a history of the Ninth Regiment. His third wife, Margaret Long of Orange County, and three sons survived him.

SEE: R. W. Allison, "History of Cabarrus County and Concord" (MS, Concord Public Library); Paul Barringer, *The Natural Bent* (1949); Cabarrus County Court House (Concord), for Rufus Barringer's will and land transfers; *Charlotte Democrat*; C. A. Evans, ed., *Confederate Military History*, vol. 4 (1899); Marvin Krieger, "Warren Clay Coleman" (M.A. thesis, Wake Forest University, 1969).

MARVIN KRIEGER

Barringer, Victor Clay (*29 Mar. 1827–27 May 1896*), lawyer, state senator, professor, and U.S. representative to the International Court in Egypt, was born at the family home, Poplar Grove, in Cabarrus County, near Concord. Of German and English ancestry, he was the youngest child of Paul Barringer, prominent business-man and state legislator, and Elizabeth Brandon, the daughter of Matthew Brandon of Rowan County. He was baptized Victor in St. John's Lutheran Church, which had been founded by his grandfather, John Paul Barringer. He adopted Clay as his middle name after hearing a speech by Henry Clay, while visiting an older brother who was a U.S. congressman.

Barringer was educated in Concord and attended Gettysburg College in Pennsylvania. He later entered The University of North Carolina, from which he was graduated in 1848. While there, he served as president of the Dialectic Society, and his farewell address before the society was acclaimed as a remarkable example of public speaking. Following his graduation, he began the study of law with his congressman brother, Daniel Moreau, but his study was interrupted when Daniel was appointed U.S. minister to Spain in 1849. Victor accompanied his brother to Spain and served as his private secretary for five years. During his stay there he wrote a series of articles entitled "Letters From Spain," which were published in the *Pilot*, a Concord paper.

In 1854, Barringer returned to Concord and resumed his practice of law. This was interrupted again when he accepted an offer to become professor of belles lettres at Davidson College. He resigned from the college faculty in 1860 to serve as a senator in the North Carolina legislature and was one of several state senators who urged that a state convention be called to deal with the impending crisis of the Civil War. When North Carolina seceded in 1861, he accepted a commission as a major in the First North Carolina Cavalry. He served with this regiment for only a few weeks, however, mostly in battles around Petersburg, Va. Forced to resign because of poor health, he returned to Concord and remained there for the duration of the war, practicing law when his health permitted.

Following Lee's surrender to Grant in April 1865, Jefferson Davis, president of the Confederacy, moved south with his cabinet from the Confederate capital at Richmond. Davis knew Barringer's brothers Daniel and Rufus, a general in the Confederate Army, and when he reached Concord, he sent a message requesting permission to spend the night at Barringer's home. The Barringers were pleased to open their home to him, and Davis stayed at least one night, possibly two. Just before his arrival, the Barringers had heard rumors of President Lincoln's assassination; and Barringer discussed the matter with Davis, who had not heard the rumors. After Davis left Concord, Barringer learned that the assassination stories were true and rode to Charlotte to inform Davis, fearing that Lincoln's murder would increase the danger to the Confederate president.

In 1868, Barringer was appointed by the governor to serve on the Code Commission of North Carolina, whose function was to adjust the state laws to the code of civil procedure under the new state constitution. Barringer was one of three authors of the first Code of Civil Procedure for North Carolina. A few years later, he was appointed by President Grant to be one of the commissioners responsible for condensing the U.S. statutes into the present *Revised Statutes of the United States*.

In 1874, the khedive of Egypt requested President Grant to appoint an able jurist to serve as the U.S. representative to the International Court at Alexandria, Egypt, and Grant appointed Barringer. The purpose of this court was to hear cases involving foreigners in Egypt. During his stay in Egypt, the Arabi Pasha Rebellion destroyed the Barringer home in Alexandria, Barringer's collection of oriental art, and his nearly completed manuscript entitled "The Relation of the Mussulmen and the Roman Law." He never tried to reproduce his work.

After serving two ten-year terms on the International Court, Barringer returned to the United States in 1894. When he left Egypt, he was awarded the Order of the Osmanieh, the highest decoration given by the khedive. A former U.S. consul general to Egypt said of him: "Justice Barringer lived in Egypt for twenty years, and during that time enjoyed the confidence and had the appreciation of all those with whom he came in contact. . . . He was a jurist of high ability, a scholar of considerable attainments, an entertaining conversationalist, and above all a loyal, intense American, who dignified the position he held, and his decisions were always regarded with respect."

Victor married Maria Massey of North Carolina; they had no children. Following their return from Egypt, the Barringers settled in Washington, D.C., and lived there until Victor's death at age sixty-nine. He was buried in the Rock Creek Cemetery, Washington.

SEE: Samuel A. Ashe, ed., *Biographical History of North Carolina*, vol. 1 (1905); Smith Barrier, "Deutschland in Piedmont North Carolina," *Uplift* 25 (9, 16, 23 Jan. 1937); *Concord Daily Tribune*, 29 Aug. 1934, 20 Aug. 1961; *Nat. Cyc. Am. Biog.*, vol. 13 (1906).

MARY RICHMOND KEATING

Barrow (Barro, Barrows), John (*ca. 1643–10 June 1718*), colonial official, moved to Albemarle in 1662 or earlier, probably from Virginia.

Barrow was a member of the council of the Albemarle colony and ex officio justice of the courts held by the council (1689–91). He was justice of the county court of Albemarle (1692–94) and justice of Perquimans Precinct court (1689–90 and 1697–1703). In 1708 he was a member of the lower house of the assembly.

Barrow lived in Perquimans Precinct, where he held at least three hundred acres of land on Yawpim Creek. He was a Quaker and an active member of the Perquimans Monthly Meeting, which occasionally met at his house.

Barrow married Sarah Sutton on 1 Feb. 1668/69. The couple had nine children: Johannah, Elizabeth, Ann, Sarah, William, John, Jr., George, James, and Joseph. Johannah married Jenkin Williams, and Ann married John Bently, son of Richard Bently. All the sons lived to adulthood and married. William's wife was Elizabeth Cook, widow of John Cook. The first wife of John, Jr., was named Sarah; the second was Rachel Larance, daughter of William Larance. Joseph was also married twice, first to Jane (or Jean) Nicholson and second to Sarah Peirce. James, like his father and two of his brothers, chose a wife named Sarah, whose maiden name is not known. George married Elizabeth Turner.

Two of Barrow's sons died about a week after he did—John, Jr., on 15 June and James on 18 June 1718. The records indicate that Johannah and Joseph were the only children surviving past June.

SEE: J. Bryan Grimes, ed., *Abstract of North Carolina Wills* (1910); Guilford College Library (Greensboro), for MS Quaker records; J. R. B. Hathaway, ed., *North Carolina Historical and Genealogical Register*, 3 vols. (1900–

1903); William Wade Hinshaw, comp., *Encyclopedia of American Quaker Genealogy*, vol. 1 (1936); North Carolina State Archives (Raleigh), for Albemarle Book of Warrants and Surveys (1681–1706), Albemarle County Papers (1678–1714), Perquimans Births, Marriages, Deaths and Flesh Marks (1659–1739, 1701–1820, 2 vols.), and Perquimans Precinct Court Minutes (1688–93, 1698–1706, 2 vols.); Mattie Erma Edwards Parker, ed., *North Carolina Higher-Court Records, 1670–1696* and *1697–1701* (1968, 1971); William S. Price, Jr., ed., *North Carolina Higher-Court Records, 1702–1708* (1974); William L. Saunders, ed., *Colonial Records of North Carolina*, vol. 1 (1886); Ellen Goode Winslow, *History of Perquimans County* (1931).

MATTIE ERMA E. PARKER

Barrow, Robert Ruffin *(1798–27 July 1875)*, planter, was born in Halifax County, the eldest child of Bartholomew Barrow and his first wife, Ascension Slatter, daughter of James Slatter and Charity Cotten. He was reared in North Carolina a few miles east of Enfield and accompanied his father to Louisiana in 1820. He settled in Terrebonne Parish in 1829 and called his home Residence. Before the Civil War, he built an agricultural empire equaled by few planters of the antebellum South. At the time of the war, he owned sixteen plantations in three Louisiana parishes, large land holdings in Texas, and over seven hundred slaves. Barrow did not confine his interests solely to planting but was deeply concerned with the political issues of his day and the gathering storms of the Civil War. He wrote and published many pamphlets on national and regional matters, several of which have survived. In a twenty-page pamphlet, *On the Political Parties Of the Country*, he decried secession as a means of settling the South's problems.

When war came, Barrow was sixty-three years old and did not serve in the Confederate Army. He did support the southern cause, however, by financing the construction of the *Pioneer*, one of the first submarines ever designed. The builder of the *Pioneer* was Captain Horace Hunley, Barrow's brother-in-law. The boat was launched on Lake Pontchartrain near New Orleans in February 1862 and was demonstrated with partial success. It sank on one of its early trials, however, and was raised, only to be immersed again to prevent its capture by Admiral Farragut of the Union navy. After the war it was recovered from the bottom of Lake Pontchartrain and was exhibited in Jackson Square, New Orleans. Later in the war, Hunley built other submarines, one of which, the *Hunley*, sank the Federal warship *Housatonic* at Charleston, S.C.

In 1850, at the age of fifty-two, Barrow married Volumnia Washington Hunley of Smith County, Tenn. They made their home at Residence, near Houma, La., and had two children, Roberta and Robert R., Jr., who both married and left descendants. Barrow died in New Orleans and was first buried in Girod Cemetery there; his remains were later removed to Magnolia Cemetery at Houma.

SEE: William Barrow Floyd, *The Barrow Family of Old Louisiana* (1963).

CLAIBORNE T. SMITH, JR.

Barrow, William *(26 Feb. 1765–19 Nov. 1823)*, Louisiana pioneer, was born in Halifax County, the son of William Barrow and his wife, Olivia, who was the daughter of Robert Ruffin of Northampton County. His grandfather

William had moved from Southampton County, Va., to North Carolina in 1747. His father having died in 1787, William Barrow, with his mother, his brother Robert, and his sister Mary and her husband, David Lane, moved to the Southwest in 1797. They eventually settled in West Feliciana, then under the dominion of Spain, where they were joined by another sister, Sarah, and her husband, John Dawson. The family prospered in Louisiana, and twenty years later the two brothers who had remained in North Carolina, Bennett and Bartholomew, joined them also.

William Barrow settled the Highland plantation in 1801. As settlement progressed, the Felicianans became concerned about their status as citizens of Spain. The Louisiana Purchase of 1803 did not include what was then called West Florida, which included Feliciana County and four other districts in Louisiana. In June 1810, five hundred citizens of Feliciana set up a revolutionary government, and Barrow was active in this movement. In September 1810 the insurrectionists captured Baton Rouge and proclaimed West Florida an independent state. A constitution was adopted and application made for admission to the United States. Barrow was one of the five members of the provisional government of the new nation. Shortly thereafter, President Madison proclaimed West Florida part of the United States, and, on 7 Dec. 1810, Governor William C. Claiborne of Louisiana raised the American flag in the village of St. Francisville. Barrow later saw active service during the War of 1812.

Barrow died in Washington, D.C., and was buried there. His remains were later returned to Louisiana and buried at Highland. He left an estate of 7,160 arpents of land and 348 slaves. In 1792, before leaving North Carolina, he had married Pheraby, the daughter of Robert Hillard of Northampton County. They were survived by six children. A son, William Ruffin, built the beautiful Greenwood Plantation, considered by many architects the epitome of Greek revival plantation houses. Another son, Bennett Hillard, inherited Highland and was the author of a well-known plantation diary, edited by Edwin A. Davis as *Plantation Life in the Florida Parishes of Louisiana, 1836–1846*.

SEE: William Barrow Floyd, *The Barrow Family of Old Louisiana* (1963); Harnett Kane, *Plantation Parade* (1945).

CLAIBORNE T. SMITH, JR.

Barry, John Decatur *(21 June 1839–24 Mar. 1867)*, Confederate officer and newspaper editor, was born at Wilmington, the son of John A. Barry, a native of Philadelphia, who was a graduate of the U.S. Naval Academy and, later in life, a member of the firm Barry and Bryant at Wilmington. Barry's mother was the former Mary Owen, daughter of General James Owen, brother of Governor John Owen of Bladen County. Barry had an older brother, James, and two younger sisters, Eliza and Mary. Young Barry attended The University of North Carolina from 1856 to 1859. In November 1861, at the outbreak of the Civil War, he enlisted in the Wilmington Rifle Guards at Coosawhatchie as a private. This company subsequently became Company I of the Eighteenth North Carolina Regiment, which in March of 1862 was attached to the brigade of Brigadier General Lawrence O'B. Branch at Kinston. On 24 Apr. 1862, the regiment was reorganized, and Private Barry was elected captain of Company I. Barry served in this capacity for the next six months, accompanying his regiment to Virginia in the first week of May 1862 and fighting at

Hanover Court House, the Seven Days' campaign, Cedar Mountain, Second Manassas, Harper's Ferry, and Sharpsburg. In October 1862 the Eighteenth North Carolina was reorganized, and Barry was elected major of the regiment. At this new rank he served in the battles of Fredericksburg and Chancellorsville.

At Chancellorsville, the Eighteenth North Carolina had the misfortune of firing the shots that mortally wounded Confederate General Stonewall Jackson. This incident occurred on the night of 2 May 1863, during the battle. Unknown to the men of the Eighteenth, Jackson and a party of staff officers had ridden in front of the Confederate lines to reconnoiter the Union position. Upon returning to their lines, this party of horsemen was mistaken by the Eighteenth in the darkness and confusion of battle for Union cavalry. Shots rang out, and some of Jackson's party shouted that they were friends and called for the firing to stop. Barry suspected this to be a ruse and, the regiment having orders to shoot anything at its front, called on his men to open fire. The shooting started again, and by the time the error had been discovered, Jackson had been mortally wounded. Jackson's loss was irreplaceable, but the army never blamed the Eighteenth North Carolina for following its orders.

When the battle of Chancellorsville ended, Barry was the only one of thirteen regimental officers in James Lane's brigade not killed or wounded. The Eighteenth's colonel, Thomas Purdie, having been killed and its lieutenant colonel wounded, Barry took over command of the regiment with the rank of colonel. He led the regiment with distinction at Gettysburg, Mine Run, and the Wilderness campaigns in the summer and winter of 1863 and the spring of 1864. On 2 June 1864, at the battle of Cold Harbor, a few miles from Richmond, Lane was severely wounded by a Union sharpshooter and Barry succeeded to the command of the brigade. In this capacity he led the brigade throughout the balance of the battle of Cold Harbor and the opening of the siege of Petersburg. So impressive was Barry's leadership that his division commander, Major General Cadmos Wilcox, recommended him for promotion even though he was one of the younger officers in the army. Accordingly, on 8 Aug. 1864, Barry was appointed temporary brigadier general, dating from 3 Aug., under the new Confederate law authorizing officers of temporary rank to fill the place of a regular commander temporarily incapacitated. A few days afterward, however, Barry was himself painfully wounded by a Union sharpshooter while on a reconnoitering tour. Because he was disabled for some time, and because Lane returned to the command of the brigade during his absence, Barry's temporary appointment to brigadier general was canceled. He returned to command the Eighteenth North Carolina at his regular grade of colonel. However, his wound and impaired health soon rendered him unfit for active field service, and he sought duty in some less active capacity. Upon the recommendation of a board of surgeons, he was retired from active field service and assigned to departmental duty in North Carolina, leaving his regiment in late March 1865. There he served out the balance of the war.

Barry's postwar years were marked by a downhill struggle with failing health. Returning to Wilmington, he went into partnership with Major William H. Bernard and founded the Wilmington *Dispatch*, a morning daily newspaper and one of the leading newspapers of the state Democratic party. Publication was begun on 1 Oct. 1865. The partnership with Bernard lasted but a few months, however, and the firm soon dissolved, each

partner assuming his part of the obligations. Barry continued publication of the paper for several years but then suspended it. Only a few more years of broken health remained to him, and he finally died at his mother's house in Wilmington. He was buried in Oakdale Cemetery.

In 1863, Barry married Fannie Jones of Hampton, Va., sister of Pembroke Jones of the U.S. Navy and Tom Jones of the U.S. Army.

SEE: Walter Clark, ed., *Histories of the Several Regiments and Battalions from North Carolina in the Great War, 1861–1865*, vols. 2, 4, 5 (1901); C. A. Evans, *Confederate Military History*, vol. 4 (1899); Mrs. Karen E. Gottovi, Wilmington Public Library, personal assistance; North Carolina Census (1850); James Sprunt, *Chronicles of the Cape Fear River* (1914); Ezra Warner, *Generals in Gray* (1959); Wilmington *Daily Journal*, 26 Mar. 1867; Marcus J. Wright, *General Officers of the Confederate Army* (1911).

PAUL BRANCH

Barton, Stephen, Jr. *(1806–10 Mar. 1865),* manufacturer and brother of Clara Barton, was born at Oxford, Mass., the son of Stephen and Sarah Stone Barton. As a young man, he joined with a brother in the lumber business and founded a mill town—North Oxford—around the sawmill and other facilities connected with their business. Stephen enjoyed a special relationship with his younger sister Clara and provided her first employment in his cloth factory when she was seventeen years old. In 1856 he purchased a tract of timberland and a steam sawmill on the Chowan River in Hertford County. At this site, about two miles north of the mouth of Meherrin River, Barton and a crew of New England artisans, including several members of his family, erected another mill town, this one called Bartonsville. A post office was established there, along with wharves, lumberyards, a gristmill, warehouses, and other facilities. In 1860 he acquired North Carolina rights to machinery for making plow-handles and plow-beams, and he had produced many thousands by the time the Civil War broke out in the spring of 1861. Caught with most of his manufactures in storage, Barton sent his crew north and determined to sit out the war at Bartonsville in order to protect his investment.

Although Barton opposed both slavery and secession, he maintained a neutral position in the war and local Confederate garrisons, respecting his position, left him alone. Union gunboat officers operating on the Chowan also understood Barton's situation and did not annoy him, although they were sometimes able to deliver to him mail or news from his friends and relations in the North. In the meantime, his relations, particularly his sister Clara, plotted scheme after scheme for bringing him out of North Carolina, only to be blocked by his determination to maintain his lonely vigil at Bartonsville.

In 1864, with the families of Confederate soldiers in Hertford, as elsewhere in the South, beginning to suffer from want of supplies, Barton and a few sympathetic friends arranged to bring supplies from Norfolk in exchange for their own cotton. With a pass from Union officers who controlled the eastern side of the Chowan, Barton himself made several trips by wagon into Pasquotank County, where Union agents purchased his cotton and gave him bacon and other commodities for distribution to the poor of Hertford County. On one such mission, Barton was arrested by Union authorities on suspicion of being a Confederate agent, imprisoned at Norfolk, and mistreated by prison officials. His health broke, and, by the time Clara was able to learn of his condition and have him freed, he was near death. He joined her at a field hospital near Richmond, and the two of them went to her home in Washington, D.C., where he died. His sister accompanied the remains to Oxford, Mass., where Stephen was buried in the Barton family cemetery. Three weeks later, on 1 Apr., a Union cavalry patrol arrived at Bartonsville and, on the assumption that it was Confederate property, burned the entire establishment.

Stephen Barton was married to Elizabeth Rich of Charleston, Mass., and by her had one son, Samuel R. Barton, who assisted him in creating the mill town at Bartonsville.

SEE: Samuel R. Barton Papers (Manuscript Division, Library of Congress, Washington, D.C.); Stephen Barton Papers (Manuscript Department, Library, Duke University, Durham); Thomas C. Parramore, "The Bartons of Bartonsville," *North Carolina Historical Review* 51 (1974 [photograph]).

THOMAS C. PARRAMORE

Bartram, William (*9 Feb. 1739–22 July 1823*), naturalist, was the son of John Bartram, an eminent naturalist, and his wife, Ann Mendenhall Bartram. He was born near Philadelphia, where his gifts as an artist brought him in his youth to the attention of Benjamin Franklin. Franklin proposed that William become an engraver, but he was apprenticed instead to a Philadelphia merchant in 1756. In 1761, his apprenticeship completed, William moved to Bladen County, where his uncle William had a large plantation and considerable property on the Cape Fear River. Here the nephew opened a store and spent the next four years alternately occupied with his business and investigating the flora and fauna of the Cape Fear region.

The Bartram family was established in the Cape Fear country by the early eighteenth century, when Bartram's grandfather, the first William Bartram, settled at Whitoc plantation. There he was attacked and killed by local Indians, and his wife and sons, William and John, were taken captive. Mrs. Bartram was subsequently able to return to Philadelphia with her sons. John remained in Philadelphia, but William later returned to North Carolina to resume control of their father's estate. He became a man of considerable influence as a colonel of militia and was for many years a representative in the colonial legislature of North Carolina. White Lake in Bladen County was known as Lake Bartram when he owned much land in the vicinity. Colonel Bartram also had a son named William, first cousin of the naturalist, and it was this household that the naturalist joined in 1761. The two cousins were often companions on botanical and zoological jaunts in the vicinity of Ashwood, Bartram's plantation.

The mercantile venture of William Bartram did not prosper in Bladen. John Bartram, newly appointed as botanist to King George III, stopped by Ashwood in 1765 on a mission to Florida; he took his son with him on the trip, and afterward the two returned to Philadelphia. William tried for three more years to find success as a merchant in Philadelphia, but by 1770 he was almost bankrupt and disillusioned with the effort. He returned to Ashwood, where, during the next two years, Colonel Bartram, his wife, and their son, Dr. William Bartram, all died. Leaving Ashwood in the latter part of 1772 and returning once more to Philadelphia, Bartram in the following spring set forth on his famous "travels," outlined in the volume *Travels through North and South*

Carolina, Georgia, etc., which he brought out in 1791. Chiefly through the fine reception accorded to the book, Bartram became an established member of the international literary and scientific community and a member of many American and foreign learned societies. A Quaker by upbringing, Bartram became an ardent deist.

Bartram visited Ashwood, apparently for the last time, late in 1776. He always held Ashwood in affectionate regard as a place where he and his cousins had engaged in "pastimes . . . of the most Innocent and simple nature such as amuse Brothers, Sisters and Friends." At least one biographer has suggested that William had a brief love affair with one of Colonel Bartram's daughters, but the naturalist was never married.

SEE: *DAB*, vol. 2 (1929); Ernest Earnest, *John and William Bartram* (1940); Francis Harper, *Travels of William Bartram*, naturalists' ed. (1958).

THOMAS C. PARRAMORE

Baskerville, Charles (*18 July 1870–28 Jan. 1922*), chemist and college professor, was born in Deerbrook, Noxubel County, Miss., the son of Charles Baskerville, a physician and former Confederate Army captain, and his wife, Augusta Johnson. The family traced its origins to Charles Baskerville of Mecklenburg County, Va., a Continental army officer during the American Revolution. A cousin, William W. Baskerville (1850–99), was a noted professor of English at Vanderbilt University (1881–89).

Baskerville's father distinguished himself in treating the sick during the yellow fever epidemics at Memphis, Tenn., in 1876 and 1879; he died of pneumonia contracted in the course of the latter epidemic. Baskerville grew up in his maternal grandparents' home in Columbus, Miss., where he worked part-time as a printer's devil. After a varied academic career, including studies in local Columbus schools, two years at the University of Mississippi, and specialty courses at the University of Virginia (1890) and Vanderbilt (1890–91), he entered The University of North Carolina, from which he was graduated with a B.S. degree in 1892.

Baskerville's undergraduate record at Chapel Hill was brilliant. A member of Phi Beta Kappa, the Gimghouls, and Delta Kappa Epsilon Fraternity, he was also president of the powerful University Athletic Association and first editor of the student newspaper, the *Tar Heel*. In his spare time he was fullback and manager of the Carolina football squads of 1892, 1893, and 1894.

After an intensive summer course in chemistry at the University of Berlin (1893), Baskerville returned to Chapel Hill to complete his graduate work under Francis Preston Venable; in 1894 he received a doctorate for his dissertation, *A Comparison of the Methods of Estimation and Separation of Zinc*. Within the next decade, he advanced rapidly in the university hierarchy, serving successively as assistant in the chemical laboratory (1891–93), instructor in chemistry (1893–94), assistant professor of chemistry (1894–98), and associate professor of chemistry (1898–1900). In 1900, upon Venable's succession to the presidency, Baskerville became chairman of the chemistry department, Smith Professor of General and Analytic Chemistry (after 1902, Smith Professor of General and Industrial Chemistry), and director of the chemical laboratory, all of which positions he held until 1904. From 1901 onward, he was also staff chemist for the North Carolina State Geological Survey.

During this period, Baskerville continued his research,

concentrating on a study of the rare earths thorium, lanthanum, praseodymium, and neodymium and the rare metals titanium and zirconium. This work was climaxed in 1903, when Baskerville announced the discovery of two previously unknown chemical elements, which he named "carolinium" and "berzelium." Though refuted by later research, these claims were sufficiently respected by his contemporaries to earn him an invitation to join the faculty of the City College of New York, which he accepted in 1904.

From 1904 onward, Baskerville served as professor of chemistry at City College and as director of its chemical laboratories, succeeding D. O. Doremus. In these capacities, he completely reorganized his department, designed new laboratory facilities, and acted as a consultant to the city, state, and federal governments in such fields as wood alcohol regulation and school and factory ventilation. At the same time, his personal research shifted from pure science to such applied fields as the manufacture and use of surgical anaesthetics, refinement of vegetable oil, recovery of shale oil, and recycling of paper. As chairman of the American Chemical Society's Committee on Occupational Diseases, he was among the first scientists to study seriously the problem of industry-related illnesses.

A member (1894) and fellow (1898) of the American Association for the Advancement of Science, Baskerville served as secretary of its chemical section (1898), secretary of the association's council (1899), and vice-president and section secretary (1903); he was also a member of the American Institute of Chemical Engineers, the American Electrochemical Society, the Washington Academy of Science, the New York Academy of Science, the Franklin Institute, and several other scientific associations.

The author of six books and over two hundred scientific papers, Baskerville also wrote extensively on scientific topics for such popular journals as *Science* and *Review of Reviews*.

On 24 Apr. 1895, Baskerville married Mary Boykin Shaw (1872–1957) of Raleigh. The couple had two children: Charles, Jr. (b. 1896), a popular New York commercial artist, portrait-painter, and muralist; and Elizabeth Snow.

Baskerville died at his home in New York and was buried at Oakwood Cemetery in Raleigh.

SEE: J. H. Barnhardt and Francis Preston Venable, MSS written for Samuel A. Ashe, ed., *Biographical History of North Carolina* (Library, Duke University, Durham); Charles Baskerville, *Aids to Teachers of School Chemistry* (1899); *A Course in Qualitative Analysis* (1910, with L. J. Curtman); "The Elements," *Science* 19 (1904); "The Function of the University," *University of Virginia Alumni Bulletin*, August 1910; *Radium and Radio-active Substances* (1905); and, ed., *Anaesthesia* (1914, with T. J. Gwathney); and *Municipal Chemistry* (1911); Kemp P. Battle, *History of the University of North Carolina*, vol. 2 (1912); "Charles Baskerville," *Science* 5 (1922); *DAB*, vol. 2 (1929).

BENNETT L. STEELMAN

Bassett, John Spencer (10 Sept. 1867–27 Jan. 1928), historian, was born at Tarboro, the second child of Richard Baxter Bassett and Mary Jane Wilson Bassett. His father had come from Virginia to eastern North Carolina as a builder and contractor shortly before the Civil War; his mother was the daughter of a Maine millwright who had moved to North Carolina a generation earlier. Richard Bassett enlisted in the

Edgecombe Guards, First North Carolina Regiment, at the beginning of the Civil War, but after the Battle of Big Bethel he was transferred to the commissary department and engaged in the production of military supplies.

Bassett's education began in the public schools of Richlands and Goldsboro and was continued at the Jefferson Davis Military Academy at LaGrange. He entered Trinity College, then in Randolph County, as a junior in 1886 and was graduated in 1888. After teaching two years in the Durham public schools, he returned to Trinity as instructor in English and principal of the preparatory department. In 1891, partly under the influence of Stephen B. Weeks, a recent graduate of Johns Hopkins University and a professor at Trinity, he entered Hopkins and became a member of the famed Herbert Baxter Adams seminar. He was a Scholar and Fellow at Hopkins and was graduated in 1894 with a dissertation entitled *The Constitutional Beginnings of North Carolina, 1663–1729*. He returned to Trinity, by then removed to Durham, where he began a dozen active years of teaching, writing, and collecting southern Americana, following the practice of his predecessor, Weeks, who had organized the Trinity College Historical Society. Through the society, public appeals, and personal efforts, he began to build the resources of the library, of which he became the "manager" in 1900.

He encouraged his students to publish and sought a means of publication. In 1895 he arranged with the editor of the student publication, the *Archive*, to furnish reprints of historical articles; these were bound and in 1897 became the *Historical Papers* of the Trinity College Historical Society, the only such publication in North Carolina. Bassett himself was building a reputation as a productive scholar. He was necessarily limited in his sources, though he had the advantage of the *Colonial Records of North Carolina*, published between 1886 and 1890. He published "Regulators of North Carolina, 1765–1771" (American Historical Association, 1895), *Slavery and Servitude in the Colony of North Carolina* (Johns Hopkins Studies, 1896), *Anti-Slavery Leaders in North Carolina* (ibid., 1898), *Slavery in the State of North Carolina* (ibid., 1899), *The Writings of Colonel William Byrd* (New York, 1901), and in the American Nation Series *The Federalist System* (1906).

Drawbacks at Trinity, besides a small salary and limited opportunity for research, included what Bassett saw as an intellectual environment restricted by a lack of trained scholars, by political partisanship, by a narrow clergy, and by a public motivated more by patriotic bias than by objective attitudes. As an instructor in 1890, he had helped to organize a secret society for upperclassmen, "an assembly for the development of mankind in all relations to society." It was a scholarship society known as the "9019," and it was this organization that initially sponsored the *South Atlantic Quarterly* (1902–), which was to "be devoted to the literary, historical, and social development of the South." Bassett, the editor, intended to publish "sober and instructive articles" designed for "serious minded" southerners. During the forty months that he edited the journal, he attacked various facets of southern provincialism. It was not until the issue of October 1903, however, which carried his article "Stirring Up the Fires of Race Antipathy," that "a storm of protest from North Carolina conservatives" brought demands that he resign as editor and be removed from the faculty of Trinity. His earlier studies of slavery in the state had been written with sympathy and understanding for both races, and he recognized the complexities of the system. His father and grandfather had owned slaves, never many, and with some reluctance, but they had taken no part in antislavery agitation. Bassett himself was a steady liberal, and he was unhappy about the recent disfranchisement of the black man in North Carolina by constitutional amendment (1900). In the *South Atlantic Quarterly* he had already written of the contrasting views on education of the two Negro leaders, Booker T. Washington and W. E. B. Du Bois. Washington advocated a practical, vocational type of education for the black; Du Bois rejected industrial training in favor of higher learning of a more classical sort. Bassett thought that there was room for both but that, under existing conditions, Washington's view was more applicable to the great majority of the black race.

The public seemed to be unaware of the discussions in the *South Atlantic* until his controversial article appeared. It has been described as "for the most part a dispassionate discussion of the race problem in the South." It suggested that some blacks had made progress since emancipation and that many had not, but that of Booker T. Washington there could be no doubt: "Now Washington is a great and good man, a Christian statesman, and take him all in all the greatest man, save General Lee, born in the South in a hundred years; but he is not a typical negro." This sentence in particular, inserted as an afterthought, "to counteract the reactionary feeling in the Southern press," was not written "with the idea of raising a controversy"; yet he came to think that "the affair cleared the atmosphere to some extent with regard to the negro question. I think it showed some people in North Carolina that they were likely to get into trouble by cultivating the anti-negro spirit." Whatever the intention, a storm of protest followed. His explanation in the press that he had no thought of trying to bridge the gulf between the races, that he had "no thought of social equality," and that he was "thinking only of the industrial and civic outlook of the negro race" went unheeded. Led by Josephus Daniels, who reprinted the entire article in the Raleigh *News and Observer*, most of the press denounced Bassett in choice epithets and demanded that he be fired. For some time there had been a rivalry between state and private educational institutions in North Carolina, and an effort was made by some of the friends of state-supported schools to attack Trinity through Bassett. Daniels asserted his friendship for Trinity but denounced President John C. Kilgo, who had made "blunder after blunder," had "exhibited a spirit of venom," and had "shown contempt for tradition." Under the circumstances, Bassett offered to resign if the trustees requested it. Walter Hines Page, a former Trinity student, pointed out to B. N. Duke that the issue of freedom of thought and expression was involved, not the correctness of Bassett's opinion. Other leaders of opinion came to the support of Bassett, and when the trustees met, on 1 Dec. 1903, Kilgo made a plea in behalf of academic freedom. Unknown to the trustees, Kilgo had prepared a letter of resignation to be presented in case of an adverse decision, and he had received similar letters from the faculty. The trustees declined to accept Bassett's offer of resignation. Instead, they presented a strong statement in behalf of academic freedom, a statement prepared by Dean William P. Few with the assistance of William Garrott Brown, a visiting friend of both Few and Bassett. The episode put Trinity in a good light, for, as Page remarked, it presented "a chance to show the whole world that there is at least one institution in the South and in North Carolina that is free."

Already Bassett was recognized outside the South as a productive scholar, and when the opportunity came in 1906 to go to Smith College with a higher salary, a lighter teaching load, and more opportunity for research, he accepted. Another reason for leaving Trinity was the conviction that he "could not write history and direct public sentiment" at the same time, and he was also afraid that he might be the cause of dissension on the faculty. He wrote Boyd, "I merely wanted a peaceful atmosphere." He continued to have a warm interest in Trinity and in the promotion of historical activities in the South, but his own writing shifted largely to other fields.

The Federalist System was published shortly before he left Trinity. It was a sound and readable volume, produced in a remarkably short time, though without recourse to manuscript sources, and it was well received. His next significant work was a two-volume biography of Andrew Jackson, begun in a preliminary way at Trinity but not published until 1911. A massive work, although not lively, it was probably important in preparing the way for broader studies of the Jackson era, as was his six-volume edition of the *Correspondence of Andrew Jackson* (1926–35). In 1915 he began the *Smith College Studies in History*, "the first learned publication of that college," and in volume 6 (1921) he published "The Westover Journal of John A. Selden, Esqr., 1838–1862," owner of a plantation once owned by the Byrds. His last significant volume touching the South, *The Plantation Overseer as Revealed in His Letters*, followed in 1925. These letters, from overseers in the James K. Polk plantation in Mississippi, showed the practical problems of plantation management, the actual workings of the slave system, and the limitations of most of the overseers.

Perhaps Bassett's most famous book, and the most rewarding financially, was *A Short History of the United States* (1913), which went into many editions and was extensively used as a college text. He wrote *Expansion and Reform, 1889–1926* (1926) for a series, and he contributed a volume to the *Pageant of America: A Pictorial History of the United States* (1928). Several of his works touched on historians and historiography; in *The Middle Group of American Historians* (1917) were essays on Jared Sparks, George Bancroft, William H. Prescott, John L. Motley, and Peter Force. He later edited some correspondence of Sparks and Bancroft and also letters of Parkman to Pierre Margry; both were published in the *Smith College Studies in History* (1917, 1923). He edited *The Writing of History* (1926), to which he contributed an essay, "The Present State of History Writing." Events of World War I diverted him to international affairs, and he subsequently published *The Lost Fruits of Waterloo* (1918), *Our War with Germany* (1919), and *The League of Nations: A Chapter in World Politics* (1928).

Although many of his writings have been superseded, he was a notable pioneer in American historiography. He became increasingly influential in the councils of the American Historical Association, and in 1919 he was elected secretary; he soon became active in a movement to endow the organization. He remained secretary until his death, which resulted from a street accident in Washington, D.C., while he was on his way to a meeting of the American Council of Learned Societies.

He was married on 19 Aug. 1892 to Jessie Lewellyn of Durham; they were the parents of a son, Richard Horace, and a daughter, Margaret Byrd.

SEE: Nora C. Chaffin, *Trinity College, 1839–1892* (1950); *DAB*, vol. 2 (1929); Wendell H. Stephenson, *Southern History in the Making* (1964); *Who's Who in America*, 1926–27; Robert H. Woody, ed., *The Papers and Addresses of William P. Few* (1951).

ROBERT H. WOODY

Battle, Cullen Andrews (*1 June 1829–8 Apr. 1905*), lawyer, politician, and Confederate general, was born in Powelton, Ga., but removed with his parents to Irwinton, Ala., in 1836. His father, Dr. Cullen Battle, was a native of Edgecombe County, and his mother, Jane Andrews Lamon, was a native of Wake County. After graduation from the University of Alabama, he read law with his brother-in-law, John Gill Shorter, later to be war governor of Alabama. Battle in 1851 married Georgia Florida Williams of La Grange, Ga. Beginning the practice of law at Tuskegee in 1852, he became active in politics, serving as a presidential elector and delivering many political addresses throughout the country.

When his state seceded from the Union in 1861, he raised a company of volunteers at Tuskegee and joined the Third Alabama Regiment, of which Tennant Lomax became colonel and Battle lieutenant colonel. At Boonsboro, Md., he was wounded, and at Fredericksburg he was injured when his horse fell on him. He was on the command staff at Chancellorsville. For conspicuous gallantry at Gettysburg, he was promoted to brigadier general. In many other campaigns and battles he played a leading role. At Cedar Creek, Va., he was wounded and permanently disabled. On 19 Oct. 1864 he was commissioned major general, but because of his wounds he was never active in this rank.

During the last part of the war, Battle appeared before each regiment of his brigade, appealing to the men to reenlist unconditionally for the remainder of the conflict. His soldiers were the first to do so, and he was warmly praised by his superior officers and by the Confederate Congress.

After the war, Battle resumed his law practice at Tuskegee. He was elected to Congress, but Republicans refused to seat him or other Southern Democrats disfranchised for their parts in the Civil War. When his son, Henry Wilson, was pastor of the First Baptist Church at New Bern, from January 1888 to December 1890, Battle moved there and was warmly welcomed by numerous former war comrades from Craven and adjoining counties.

Battle for a short time edited the *New Bern Journal*. Without soliciting the office or even receiving advance notice, he was elected mayor by New Bern councilmen on 8 May 1890; he served in that office with great honor and distinction. His address on Confederate Memorial Day, 10 May 1890, is regarded as one of the most eloquent speeches ever heard in the town, and occasionally he spoke at other North Carolina cities.

He died in Greensboro while his son was the Baptist pastor there and was buried at Petersburg, Va. In addition to his son, Battle was also survived by a daughter, Jennie. A grandson, John, born while the Reverend Henry Wilson Battle and his wife (formerly a Miss Stewart from Clinton) lived in New Bern, became governor of Virginia.

A new temporary army camp for guard duty along the North Carolina coast was opened in January 1942, during World War II, at Glenburnie Park, two miles up the Neuse River from New Bern. Lieutenant Colonel Wilson H. Stephenson, the second commanding officer, named it Camp Battle for General Battle, with the assertion that the designation was doubly appropriate for a modern war post, although he hoped that it would always be called Camp Battle and never Battle Camp.

SEE: G. S. Carraway, *First Baptist Church, New Bern* (1942); New Bern City Records (New Bern); New Bern *Sun-Journal*, 2 May 1942; Raleigh *News and Observer*, 1 Mar. 1942.

GERTRUDE S. CARRAWAY

Battle, Elisha (*9 Jan. 1723–6 Mar. 1799*), planter, revolutionary patriot, and state legislator, was born in Nansemond County, Va. He was the fifth child and third son of William and Sarah Hunter Battle. Earlier paternal and maternal ancestors had emigrated from Yorkshire, England, in the mid-seventeenth century, his grandfather, John Battle, settling on a two-hundred-acre estate on the west bank of Nansemond River in Nansemond County, Va. In 1663 this same John Battle obtained a royal patent for 640 acres of land on Pasquotank River in North Carolina. Here Elisha Battle's father, William, was born in 1682. In 1690, upon the death of his father, William returned to Nansemond County, where he continued to reside until his death in 1749.

By deed of record dated 17 Aug. 1747, Elisha Battle purchased four hundred acres on the north side of Tar River, in Edgecombe County, from Samuel Holliman. This purchase formed the nucleus of Cool Spring Plantation, near the present town limits of Rocky Mount, to which Battle moved with his family in late 1747 or early 1748. Subsequent purchases made Battle a large and prosperous landholder. He soon gained a reputation as a man of honest conviction, sound judgment, and considerable native ability.

According to an early biographer, Battle was appointed justice of the peace in about 1756, retaining this position until the infirmities of old age forced him to relinquish it in 1795. By 1759 he was serving as a justice for Edgecombe county court (later the inferior court of pleas and quarter sessions). He was one of five commissioners appointed in 1760 to "found and lay out" the town of Tarboro.

The same early biographer indicates that Battle was elected to represent Edgecombe in the colonial House of Commons as early as 1771, though his first recorded appearance there is during the assembly that convened in New Bern, 4–21 Dec. 1773. With the threat of impending warfare, Battle was named chairman of Edgecombe's committee of safety (1774–75). He also represented his county in the provincial congresses that met in Halifax in April 1776 and in November 1776.

With the establishment of an independent state government, Elisha Battle was elected to represent Edgecombe County in the state senate, 1777–81, 1783, and 1785–87. He served as chairman of the committee of the whole during much of the session of the constitutional convention, convened in Hillsborough in July 1788. With the majority of the delegates, Battle held that it would be too dangerous to adopt the proposed federal constitution without amendments to reserve and secure certain rights to the individual states. Accordingly, he voted to postpone adoption until such amendments were effected.

In 1742, Battle married Elizabeth Sumner, a first cousin to Brigadier General Jethro Sumner, who served in the Continental Army under Washington. To their union were born eight children: Sarah, who married Jacob Hilliard and, afterward, Henry Horn; John, who married Frances Davis; Elizabeth, who married Josiah Crudup, Jr.; Elisha, who married Sarah Bunn; William, who married Charity Horn; Dempsey, who married Jane Andrews; Jacob, who married Penelope Edwards; and Jethro, who married Martha Lane.

Battle united with the Falls of Tar River Baptist Church in 1764, attaining prominence in the affairs of his local congregation and the larger denomination. He served as a deacon and as a clerk at Falls of Tar River. He was also instrumental in the organization of the Kehukee Baptist Association in 1769, serving that body occasionally as moderator and as clerk.

He was buried on the family plantation.

SEE: Samuel A. Ashe, ed., *Biographical History of North Carolina*, vol. 6 (1907); H. B. Battle et al., *The Battle Book* (1930); Lemuel Burkitt and Jesse Read, *A Concise History of the Kehukee Baptist Association* (1803); William L. Saunders and Walter Clark, eds., *Colonial and State Records of North Carolina*, 30 vols. (1886–1914); J. Kelly Turner and J. L. Bridgers, Jr., *History of Edgecombe County* (1920).

R. HARGUS TAYLOR

Battle, Ephraim (*d. 1798*), farmer, patriot, and local official, was born in the part of Edgecombe County that is now Nash. He was the son of the Thomas Battle, who died in Onslow County in 1769, and a grandson of John Battle II, who died in January 1774.

He first appeared in the Onslow County records in 1769 and had evidently settled on the upper New River near the present town of Richlands. He emerged as a leader in Onslow County about the time of the Revolution and remained such until his death. On 11 June 1776, Battle was appointed the captain of a company of militia from Onslow County. On 31 July 1776 he was listed as the captain of the largest company in the camp at Wilmington in the battalion commanded by Colonel Thomas Brown and in the brigade under command of General John Ashe.

The treasurer's and comptroller's records reveal that Battle was the commissioner of Onslow County for the years 1781, 1782, and 1784. His duties as commissioner seem to have been to procure supplies for the military forces in the county and to oversee their distribution, rendering account therefore to the state treasurer/comptroller.

Following the Revolution, Battle acquired substantial landholdings in Onslow County and was evidently a prosperous farmer and businessman. In 1795, a deed giving land for public use for a "Meeting house of Religion" designated Ephraim Battle as one of four "commissioners of the town and county of Onslow." This deed apparently conveyed land at the town of Onslow Court House, the earlier name for present-day Jacksonville.

Battle died sometime between 15 Mar. and the April term of court, 1798. Reputedly married twice, he was survived by eight children: Lott, Abner, William (who died single), Thomas, Frederick (who died single), James, Sarah Williams, and Mary.

SEE: H. B. Battle et al., *The Battle Book* (1930); Zae H. Gwynn, *Abstracts of the Records of Onslow County, North Carolina* (1961); William L. Saunders, ed., *Colonial Records of North Carolina*, vol. 10 (1890); Sons of the American Revolution, North Carolina Society, *Lineage Book of Past and Present Members* (1951).

TUCKER REED LITTLETON

Battle, George Gordon (*26 Oct. 1868–29 Apr. 1949*), leading Democrat and one of New York City's outstanding lawyers, was born at Cool Spring Plantation near Rocky Mount in Edgecombe County, the son of Captain Turner Westray Battle and Lavinia Bassett Daniel Battle of Halifax, daughter of Joseph J. Daniel, associate justice of the North Carolina Supreme Court. George Gordon's father was a cotton planter, whose forebears in 1747 immigrated to Edgecombe County on the Tar River from Nansemond County, Va., where Battles from England had settled in 1653 and 1654.

Battle's youth was spent on the plantation. At the age of thirteen, he was sent to The University of North Carolina, which he attended for a year and a half in 1881–82. From 1883 to 1886 he studied at Hanover Academy in Virginia; in 1889 he received his M.A. from the University of Virginia. While in Virginia he began studying law, and after graduation he continued in the office of his oldest brother, Judge Jacob Battle, in Rocky Mount. However, a short while later he decided to enter law school at Columbia University in New York City.

He was a brilliant student at Columbia, with an aptitude for the framing of indictments that won him a post with District Attorney De Lancey Nicoll, who had asked the law faculty to recommend an assistant. He served in the district attorney's office for five years, from 1892 to 1897, resigning to enter private practice. Twice in later years he served as special assistant district attorney to investigate crime and corruption in New York, in 1911 and again in 1919.

Among the better-known lawsuits in which he was engaged as counsel was one brought by George H. Carle, later governor of Pennsylvania, as receiver for the Pennsylvania Sugar Refining Company, against the American Sugar Refining Company for violation of the Sherman Anti-Trust Act. In another important suit, he was counsel for the minority stockholders of the Houston Central Railway, who, after litigation lasting thirty-five years, finally won a decision from the U.S. Supreme Court upholding a $6,600,000 verdict. Battle was defense attorney for Earl Browder, then general secretary of the Communist party in the United States. He represented such concerns as the Diamond Match Company and was attorney in many prominent will suits.

Battle raised money for such diverse beneficiaries as the Salvation Army, Sweet Briar College, the Passion Players from Oberammergau, the Royal Arch Masons, and the Sesquicentennial Celebration of the American Revolution in Philadelphia. He was executive chairman of the Community Council of National Defense for the City of New York, secretary of the Committee on Educational Publicity in Interests of World Peace, and chairman of the Committee on Psychiatric Work for the Girls Service League of America. On several occasions he arbitrated major labor disputes, and he was chairman of the National Committee on Prison Labor Reform.

As president of New York City's Parks and Playgrounds Association, he was an ardent fighter against encroachments upon park property, especially Central Park, which he felt should be kept as rural as possible. Himself childless, he continually sought more city playgrounds.

While campaigning for Al Smith in 1928, he began fighting anti-Semitism; later he served on several Jewish committees. An editorial in the *American Hebrew* hailed him as one of the most effective espousers of the cause of Jewry among New York gentiles, and he was awarded the American Hebrew medal for keeping "the flame of religious hatred from searing American Democracy."

He was married in Richmond, Va., 12 Apr. 1898, to Martha Burrell Dabney Bagby, the daughter of George William Bagby, for many years state librarian of Virginia, and Lucy Parke Chamberlayne. Both the Battles were devoted members of the Episcopal church.

Battle suffered a fatal heart attack while on his way to his country home in Orange County, Va., and was buried in Hollywood Cemetery, Richmond, Va. Three portraits exist: one in his law office in New York, one in the Nash County Courthouse in Nashville, and another with a niece in Rocky Mount.

SEE: H. B. Battle et al., *The Battle Book* (1930); Geoffrey Hellman, profiles in *New Yorker*, 1 Mar. 1933; *New York Times*, 30 Apr.–1 May 1949; *Who's Who in America*, 1938–39.

DOROTHY B. WILKINSON

Battle, Herbert Bemerton (29 May 1862–3 July 1929), chemist and industrialist, was the fourth child and third son of Kemp Plummer Battle, president of The University of North Carolina (1876–91), and Martha Ann Battle Battle (his parents were distant cousins). He was born at Chapel Hill in the cottage of his paternal grandfather, while Raleigh, where his parents then maintained their residence, was believed to be under threat of attack by Federal troops. His paternal grandfather, William Horn Battle, was a distinguished judge and law professor. His maternal grandfather was James Smith Battle, a planter and textile manufacturer of Edgecombe and Nash counties. His brothers were Kemp Plummer, Jr., Thomas Hall, and William James. His sister, Nellie, married Dr. Richard Henry Lewis II.

Battle received his preparatory education at the Lovejoy Academy, Raleigh. He early evidenced a strong interest in the sciences, especially chemistry. Following his graduation from The University of North Carolina with the B.S. degree (1881), he served from 1881 to 1887 as assistant chemist at the North Carolina Agricultural Experiment Station. In 1887 he was awarded his Ph.D. by the university and became state chemist and director of the Agricultural Experiment Station. He served there until the Republican administration of Governor Daniel L. Russell abolished his position (he being a Democrat) and assigned his duties to the Agricultural and Mechanical College. Battle then organized and became president and manager of the Southern Chemical Company, Winston, which manufactured agricultural fertilizers. Following the company's sale to the Virginia-Carolina Chemical Company in 1901, he joined in 1902 the Southern Cotton Oil Company of Savannah, Ga., and Montgomery, Ala. In 1906 he organized at Montgomery the Battle Laboratory, of which he became president, a position he retained until his death at Montgomery. He was buried in Oakwood Cemetery in Raleigh.

A member of several professional organizations, he contributed numerous articles to scientific journals and coauthored (with F. B. Dancy) *Chemical Conversion Tables* (1885) and (with W. J. Gascoyne) *Chemical Conversion Tables* (1909). He was a charter member of the North Carolina Sons of the Revolution and was active in the promotion of various civic causes. A devout Episcopalian, he attended the services of his church regularly, gave liberally to its financial support, and participated in its activities. On 25 Nov. 1885, he married Alice Matilda Wilson, a native of Statesville and at the time a resident of Morganton. She was a daughter of James W. Wilson, chairman of the North Carolina Railroad Commission and president of the Western North Carolina Railroad. Herbert and Alice Battle were the parents of James Wilson and Nellie Lewis, wife of John Manning Booker. Mrs. Battle died in 1919.

A photograph of Herbert Bemerton Battle serves as the frontispiece of *The Battle Book: A Genealogy of the Battle Family in America . . .* (1930), which he "planned and in great part executed." At the time of his death, a tribute in the *Montgomery Advertiser* (8 July 1929) described him as a "citizen who builded up his town" and predicted, "Montgomery will miss Dr. Herbert B. Battle, but it will not forget him, for his memory will ever abide as a strengthening and comforting influence."

SEE: Battle Family Papers and John Bryan Grimes Papers (Southern Historical Collection, University of North Carolina, Chapel Hill); H. B. Battle et al., *The Battle Book* (1930); Kemp P. Battle, *Memories of an Old-Time Tar Heel* (1945); D. L. Grant, *Alumni History of the University of North Carolina* (1924); University of North Carolina Faculty Journal (University Archives, Library, University of North Carolina, Chapel Hill); *Who's Who in America*, 1927–28.

W. CONARD GASS

Battle, Jacob (16 Jan. 1852–12 Dec. 1916), lawyer, state senator, and superior court judge, was born at the Falls of Tar River in Nash County. He was the eldest son of Turner Westray Battle and Lavinia Bassett Daniel Battle, daughter of Joseph John Daniel, associate justice of the North Carolina Supreme Court. Jacob Battle's father was a planter of Edgecombe County, who took a deep interest in public affairs. At the beginning of the Civil War he formed a company, the Confederate Guards, with which he served as captain.

At the age of eleven Jacob became a pupil of Ralph H. Graves, the elder, under whom he studied for two years at Belmont School, Granville County; he then spent one session at St. Timothy's Hall at Catonsville, Md. In 1866 he entered The University of North Carolina, remaining there until the university closed its doors in 1868 and then transferring to the University of Virginia, where he received his undergraduate degree and his M.A. in 1872. Determined to follow the legal profession, he studied under private instructors and took a summer course in law at the University of Virginia, acquiring his license from the state supreme court in 1876.

He opened a law office in Rocky Mount and soon established a flourishing practice. In 1892 he was elected state senator. Because of a keen interest in education, he was made chairman of the Committee on Education and thereby helped to stimulate a sentiment favorable to the diffusion of education throughout the state. Governor Elias Carr selected him to fill a vacancy on the superior court in his district in 1893. The Democratic convention nominated him to succeed himself, but a fusion between Populist and Republican parties resulted in the defeat of the state Democratic ticket. At the expiration of his term he returned to his law practice in Rocky Mount.

It is interesting to note that the bill to adopt North Carolina's state motto, *esse quam videri*, which passed unanimously in 1893, was introduced by Battle at the request of Judge (later Chief Justice) Walter Clark. It is a tribute to Battle's impartiality and knowledge of the law that very few of the cases he decided as a superior court judge were appealed to the supreme court and that those few had an exceptionally high record of affirmance.

He was married twice: in 1874 to Iva Isabella Steele of Yorkville, S.C., who died in 1894, and in 1896 to Nell Gupton of Rocky Mount. From his first marriage was born a son, Jacob, Jr., who predeceased his father, and from his second another son, Turner Westray III, and two daughters, Dorothy and Mary Long Gordon.

Battle was a member of the Episcopal church and for many years served as senior warden and treasurer of the Church of the Good Shepherd. He died at his home in Rocky Mount and was buried in the old family burying ground near Cool Spring Plantation at Old Town. There are several portraits of him, one in the Nash County Courthouse, Nashville, one with each daughter, and another with the descendants of his son Turner.

SEE: Samuel A. Ashe, quoted in Rocky Mount *Evening Telegram*, 12 Dec. 1916; H. B. Battle et al., *The Battle Book* (1930); Kemp D. Battle, Address on presentation of portrait to Nash County Courthouse (1 Mar. 1933, in the possession of the author); Resolutions Commemorative of Late Jacob Battle, Esq. (24 Jan. 1917, in the possession of the author); *State* 32 (26 Oct. 1963).

DOROTHY B. WILKINSON

Battle, James Smith *(25 June 1786–18 July 1854),* planter, judge, and manufacturer, was born at Cool Spring Plantation, Edgecombe County, the son of Penelope Langley Edwards and Jacob Battle. He entered The University of North Carolina in 1802 but was not graduated. On New Year's Day, 1812, he married Mrs. Temperance Fort; she died in 1814, leaving a son, James Marmaduke. On 2 Dec. 1822, Battle married Sally Harriet, daughter of Samuel Westray of Nash County. They were the parents of William Smith, who married Elizabeth Dancy; Cornelia Viola, who married John Dancy; Turner Westray, married to Lavinia Daniel; Mary Eliza, married first to William Dancy and second to Dr. Newsom Pittman; Penelope Bradford, who married William Ruffin Cox; and Martha Ann, married to Kemp P. Battle.

Battle was a justice of the peace and judge of the court of pleas and quarter sessions, Edgecombe County. He was an active and faithful member of the Kehukee Baptist Church at the Falls of Tar River near Rocky Mount. A large planter through much of his life, he owned about twenty thousand acres of rich river land and several hundred slaves at the time of his death. In 1847 he purchased the Rocky Mount Mill, a cotton factory, and operated it with his son William Smith until his death. He contracted to build and with his own slaves completed many miles of the Raleigh and Wilmington Railroad.

A slave on one of Battle's plantations became embroiled in an unfortunate quarrel with an overseer, as a result of which the overseer, a white man, was stabbed by the slave and died. After a careful investigation of the circumstances, Battle was convinced that the slave had acted in self-defense under extreme provocation. Battle therefore was determined to see that the slave received justice and thereby became perhaps the first slave owner in the South to defend a slave in court against the charge of murdering a white man. Battle engaged two leading members of the North Carolina bar to represent the slave, and to one of them he is said to have paid the very substantial fee of a thousand dollars. When the accused was judged guilty in a primary court and sentenced to death, an appeal was carried to the state supreme court, where the decision was reversed. The opinion of the Supreme Court of North Carolina in *State* vs. *Will* (18 N.C. *Reports* 121) is a landmark in southern jurisprudence.

Battle died at Westray, Nash County. A portrait of him by Sully is owned by a descendant.

SEE: H. B. Battle et al., *The Battle Book* (1930); Kemp P. Battle, *Memories of an Old-Time Tar Heel* (1945); *Rocky Mount Mills* (1943).

ELIZABETH D. BATTLE

Battle, Joel *(16 May 1779–25 Aug. 1829),* planter, merchant, militia colonel, and cotton manufacturer, was one of the three children of William Butler and Charity Horn Battle. He was one of the founders of the Rocky Mount Mills at the falls of the Tar River in Nash County, the second textile mill to begin operation in North Carolina and the oldest mill still in operation at its original site.

Few details are known of Battle's life. He attended The University of North Carolina from 1798 to 1800. On 9 Apr. 1801, he married Mary Palmer ("Polly") Johnston (14 Jan. 1786–23 Feb. 1866), and shortly afterward they moved to Shell Bank Plantation on the Tar River.

In 1816, Battle, along with his brother-in-law Peter Evans, Henry A. Donaldson, and John Hogan, began buying land around the Falls of Tar River. Hogan sold his share to Battle in 1817. A stone mill was constructed at the falls in 1816 or 1817 and expanded in 1819. By 1820, Battle and his partners owned the entire area, and the mill was in full operation. In that year they got a license to build a dam at the falls. Dissension among the partners in the 1820s led to Donaldson's buying Evans's interest in 1821 and then, in 1828, selling his share to Battle. The Battle family continued to control the mills for a number of years.

Joel and Mary Battle had eleven children, nine of whom lived to adulthood: William Horn, Amos Johnston, Richard Henry, Catharine Anne, Benjamin Dossey, Christopher Columbus, Isaac Luther, Susan Esther, and Laura Carolina. Battle was buried at the Oaks, his Edgecombe County home, but in 1872 his remains, along with those of his wife, were moved to Oakwood Cemetery in Raleigh.

SEE: Herbert B. Battle, *The Battle Book* (1930); Battle Family Papers (Southern Historical Collection, University of North Carolina, Chapel Hill); Daniel L. Grant, *Alumni History of the University of North Carolina* (1924); *Raleigh Register*, 4 Sept. 1829.

ANASTATIA SIMS

Battle, John Thomas Johnson *(14 Apr. 1859–29 Sept. 1940),* physician, was born in Wake Forest. His father, John Applewhite Battle, was a farmer. His mother was Anne Mariah Capell. Battle attended Wake Forest College from 1872 to 1879, graduating in 1879 with an M.A. From 1879 to 1882 he was a medical student at Earpsboro, probably under his brother Adolphus James, who had attended Wake Forest College and was a doctor in Earpsboro. He received his M.D. from the College of Physicians and Surgeons, Baltimore, Md., in 1884 and took postgraduate courses at Johns Hopkins and New York Polyclinic. He returned to North Carolina and practiced medicine in Wadesboro from 1894 to 1898.

Battle served his profession as a member of the state board of medical examiners from 1902 to 1908 and of the Guilford County Board of Health from 1911 to the time of his death. He was responsible for the hiring of the first full-time county health officer in North Carolina. He was a member of the American Medical Association, the North Carolina Medical Society, and the Association of Life Insurance Directors of America; in May 1939 he was elected president of the Wake Forest Medical alumni. Battle was also a pioneer in the organization of the American Life Convention. At a meeting held in St. Louis, Mo., in January 1905, he was appointed to the committee on organization, and his committee recommended that a permanent organization be effected. Almost singlehandedly, he checked an epidemic of typhoid fever afflicting over one hundred of the children in the Baptist Orphanage at Thomasville in 1904–5; he responded to a phone call after two children had died and, leaving everything in Greensboro, moved to Thomasville and worked for almost two months until the disease was under control. Battle continuously stressed the need for public health measures and waged a relentless war against the fly.

Battle was a firm believer in the importance of a Christian education. He assisted many students to obtain educations at Woman's College, at Southern Baptist Theological Seminary, Louisville, Ky., at Wake Forest College, at Hartford Seminary Foundation in Connecticut, and, especially, at Meredith College in Raleigh. Battle served as trustee at Wake Forest from 1904 to 1927 and at Meredith College from 1911 to 1940. He was an active participant in the establishment of Bowman Gray School of Medicine in Winston-Salem. He gave $10,250 to Meredith for scholarships in 1937, and, at his death, benefits to the college totaled $30,000. He gave many of his books to the Bowman Gray Medical Library and $17,000 in stock to Wake Forest College. Meredith College honored Battle by naming a gymnasium for him.

Battle was a Baptist and joined the First Baptist Church of Greensboro when he moved there in 1898. In 1907 he transferred to Forest Avenue, now College Park Baptist Church. He served the church as deacon, Sunday school superintendent, chairman of the board of trustees, and chairman of the building committee for a new church edifice. While at Forest Avenue Baptist Church, Battle organized, and was scoutmaster for, one of Greensboro's first Boy Scout troops. His will left the church $5,000 in cash and several lots in the Greensboro area.

Battle was also active in civic endeavors. He was chairman of the Guilford County Draft Board and the Ninth District Selective Service Advisory Board during World War I, after trying to enlist at the age of fifty-eight. He was a lifelong Democrat, a Mason, and a loyal member of the Sons of the American Revolution.

Battle was best known for his activities as medical director of the Jefferson Standard Life Insurance Company of Greensboro. From 1912 until 1918 he was medical director for Southern Life and Trust Company, predecessor of the present-day Pilot Life. In 1918, at the insistence of Julian Price, he took the position of associate medical director for the Jefferson Standard, which he held until elected medical director upon the death of Dr. J. P. Turner.

Battle married Dora L. Burne from Wadesboro in 1896. She died on 14 Feb. 1936. They had no children, and Battle had no close relatives when he died. He was buried in Wake Forest.

SEE: Baptist Historical Collection (Wake Forest University, Winston-Salem); [Walter C. Jackson], *John Thomas Battle, M.D.* (1945); *Jeffersonian*, October 1940.

JOHN R. WOODARD

Battle, Kemp Davis (9 Oct. 1888–5 July 1973), lawyer, was born in Rocky Mount. His grandfather, Kemp Plummer Battle, served as president and historian of The University of North Carolina. On his maternal side, he was a descendant of James Davis, the first printer and the first newspaper editor in North Carolina. He was the son of Thomas Hall Battle, the chief executive officer of Rocky Mount Mills, and Elizabeth Mershon Davis Battle.

Two years after he was born his mother died, and he went to Chapel Hill to live with his grandparents while his grandfather was serving as president of the university. Before entering college, he attended the John Graham Preparatory School for Boys located at Warrenton. At the age of seventeen, Battle entered The University of North Carolina, where his leadership ability soon became evident. There he developed strong friendships with Frank Porter Graham, Charles W. Tillett, Jr., and Francis E. Winslow. The four, who enjoyed an interest in debating, became known as the "Pin Point Discussion Club." Battle was graduated from the university in 1909, winning the prestigious Willie P. Mangum Medal for excellence in oratory. He was

admitted to the North Carolina Bar Association in 1910, having combined his first year in the two-year law school program with his last year as an undergraduate. He went to Rocky Mount to begin practicing law but then, because of tuberculosis, went to Dr. Trudeau's Sanitarium at Saranac Lake, N.Y., to receive treatment. In 1911 his friend Francis E. Winslow joined him in forming the firm of Battle and Winslow. From 1912 to 1915 he received treatment and attended the University of Denver, where he received his LL.B. degree in 1914. Winslow continued as his law partner for a period of nearly sixty-two years. From 1918 until 1920, Battle served as a judge in the Rocky Mount Municipal Court. His law firm grew and became Battle, Winslow, Merrell, Scott, and Wiley. On several occasions he was a contributor to the *North Carolina Law Review*, and periodically he served as a lecturer at the law school. He was a member of the American Bar Association. During his tenure as president of the North Carolina Bar Association in 1932 and 1933, he was influential in gaining the passage of a bill that transferred the control on admission and disbarment of lawyers from the state supreme court to the state bar. He served on the council of the state bar from 1933 to 1941.

A many-faceted individual, Battle was active in business, serving for fifty-five years in the capacities of legal counsel, vice-president, or chairman of the board of directors of Rocky Mount Mills and serving on the board of directors of Carolina Telephone and Telegraph Company.

Battle was very active in the Church of the Good Shepherd in Rocky Mount, where he acted as a vestryman and a senior warden. He was a delegate to the triennial Convention of the Episcopal Church, a member of the executive committee of the Diocese of North Carolina, and chancellor from 1954 to 1957. In 1966, Bishop Thomas A. Fraser of North Carolina presented to him the Bishop's Award, "for devoted and untiring service to the church."

Battle, like his grandfather, had an interest in history and a large personal library. After leaving the university, he wrote "Life and Services of Colonel Jonas Johnston" for the *North Carolina Booklet*, a publication dealing with North Carolina history. He recorded the minutes of the North Carolina state bar from 1936 to 1941 in the *North Carolina Law Review*. With other relatives, he served on the publishing committee for *The Battle Book: A Genealogy of the Battle Family in America*, to which he contributed "A History of the Rocky Mount Mills."

In 1925, Battle was elected president of the Rocky Mount Kiwanis Club, of which he was a charter member. Through his leadership this club worked to fight the dreaded disease of tuberculosis. He served as president of the North Carolina Tuberculosis Association in 1949 and became a member of the board of directors as well as secretary and vice-president of the National Tuberculosis Association. For his dedicated work he received from the National Tuberculosis Association in 1956 the Will Ross Medal, the highest award the national association presents to a layman.

In the 1930s he served as general chairman of the Committee for a Revised Constitution for North Carolina; parts of the proposed revision were passed.

A strong interest in education was evidenced by Battle's service as a trustee of the Rocky Mount Public Schools from 1923 to 1944 and as a member of the board of directors of the Braswell Memorial Library in Rocky Mount from 1925 to 1940. He aided in the founding of the North Carolina Wesleyan College in Rocky Mount and dedicated himself to bettering The University of North

Carolina. In 1927 he demonstrated a strong belief in the importance of preserving freedom when he expressed opposition to the controversial "Monkey Bill," which would have disallowed the teaching of evolution in the North Carolina public schools and colleges; at the age of seventy-six, he made a widely acclaimed speech advocating the repeal of the "Speaker Ban Law." For many years he served as chairman of the Committee on Honorary Degrees at the university and as a member of the trustees' executive committee. In 1959 he declined reelection to the latter, ending over 120 consecutive years during which a Battle had been a member of The University of North Carolina Board of Trustees. In 1960 he was awarded the LL.D. degree by his alma mater.

Partly through Battle's influence, the Rocky Mount Mills donated the Lewis House, built in 1830 by the ancestors of Battle's wife, to the Nash County Historical Association for historic preservation. He was also interested in Rocky Mount Mills' donation of the land known as Battle Park to create a public recreational area. He served as a member of the board of directors of Park View Hospital Association, Inc., and played a key role in the organization and establishment in 1971 of the $12 million Nash General Hospital.

Battle married Laura Maud Bunn on 30 Oct. 1917; they had two children, Elizabeth Mershon Grossberg and Laura Winstead. The family lived near Rocky Mount in a home designed by Arthur C. Nash.

Battle remained remarkably active in mind and body until his death. He was buried in the family plot at Pineview Cemetery in Rocky Mount.

SEE: H. B. Battle et al., *The Battle Book* (1930); Kemp D. Battle, "High Adventure" (Honor Awards Convocation Address, North Carolina Wesleyan College, 15 May 1962); "Life and Services of Colonel Jonas Johnston," *North Carolina Booklet*, vol. 18 (1919); and "Statement Presented to the Speaker Ban Study Commission," *Friends of the University*, 9 Sept. 1965; *Chapel Hill Newspaper*, 11 and 15 July 1973; Rocky Mount *Evening Telegram*, 5 June 1942, 22 Apr. 1959, 7 June 1960, 14 Aug. 1968, 25 Jan. 1973, 6, 9, 24, and 25 July 1973; Rocky Mount *Telegram*, 27 Apr. 1952, 9 June 1960, 7 and 15 July 1973; Francis E. Winslow, *Kemp Davis Battle* (1973); *Yackety-Yack* (1906–11).

B. W. C. ROBERTS

Battle, Kemp Plummer *(19 Dec. 1831–4 Feb. 1919)*, lawyer, railroad president, university president, educator, and historian, was born at Louisburg. He was the fourth child and third son of William Horn Battle, a distinguished North Carolina jurist, and Lucy Martin Plummer Battle. He was a great-grandson of Elisha Battle, a native of Nansemond County, Va., who in 1748 moved to the Tar River country of North Carolina and became a prominent member of the Baptist denomination and a civic and political leader. Two of Kemp Battle's brothers, Julian (b. 1826) and Thomas Devereaux (b. 1837), died in infancy. His remaining five brothers, like Kemp himself, were graduates of The University of North Carolina. His two youngest brothers, Wesley Lewis (1843–63) and Junius Cullen (1841–62), both died of battle wounds during the Civil War. His older brother, Joel (b. 1828), studied medicine for one year with a maternal uncle and then attended the University of Pennsylvania, from which he received the M.D. degree. He entered practice with a fair prospect of success but was forced by ill health to abandon medicine for the less demanding occupation of country merchant. He died in 1858. A younger brother, William Horn, Jr. (1833–93),

also became a physician. After receiving his M.D. from the Medical College of South Carolina, he practiced medicine for many years at Lilesville. A third brother, Richard Henry (1835–1912), practiced law in Raleigh after a brief period of practice in Wadesboro. Kemp's older sister, Susan Catharine (1830–67), died unmarried 22 years after a fall from a runaway horse had left her an invalid for life. His younger sister, Mary Johnston (b. 1840), who married William Van Wyck II of New York, died unexpectedly in 1865, leaving a one-day-old daughter.

Battle received his early training in private schools in Louisburg, Raleigh, and Chapel Hill. He entered The University of North Carolina as a freshman in 1845 and was graduated with first honors as valedictorian of his class in 1849. During 1849–50 he served as tutor of Latin in the university, and for the following four years he was tutor of mathematics, meanwhile studying law with his father. He was admitted to the bar in 1854 and entered the practice of law in Raleigh. The following year he was married to his distant cousin, Martha Ann ("Pattie") Battle, daughter of James S. Battle of Edgecombe County, planter and cotton manufacturer. In 1857 he was named a director of the newly rechartered Bank of North Carolina. In 1861 he was chosen a delegate from Wake County to the Secession Convention and signed the Ordinance of Secession, though he had been a strong Union man prior to Lincoln's call for troops to coerce the seceding states. During the Civil War he served as president of the Chatham Railroad, which was organized to haul coal from the coal fields of Chatham County to the Confederate armament factories.

In 1862 the legislature made Battle a trustee of The University of North Carolina, a position he held until the entire board was discharged by the Reconstruction General Assembly of 1868. Renamed to the board in 1874, he served through successive reappointments until his death. He was elected state treasurer in 1866, but the U.S. military authorities removed him from office in 1868 in the process of carrying out congressional Reconstruction. From 1869 to 1871 he served as president of the State Fair Association at Raleigh, and he was for many years a member of the state board of agriculture. In 1875 he was active in the reopening of The University of North Carolina, closed since 1871. He personally solicited funds for the repair of campus buildings and was one of the leaders in persuading the legislature to grant the state's income from the Morrill Land Grant Act of 1862 to the university. These funds, which the university continued to receive until 1887, made possible the resumption of classes.

Named president of the university in 1876, Battle served until 1891, when he resigned to become Alumni Professor of History; he hoped thenceforth to devote his energies to teaching history by "the modern methods of instruction in the use of original sources to produce monographs of great men, institutions, and the progress of national questions." Toward this end, he worked, with little immediate success, to accumulate an adequate collection of historical works in the university library and to procure a "historical museum under a salaried curator, in a fire-proof building," where he could display manuscripts, other valuable papers, and relics, including those collected by the North Carolina Historical Society, which were then in the university's safekeeping, though the society retained legal title to them.

The society, founded in 1844 by David L. Swain, then president of The University of North Carolina, had declined rapidly in membership and influence after Swain's death in 1868. Battle's attempts to revive the society as a state-wide organization met with little success, and it became in effect a subsidiary of the university, with its membership virtually limited to the university faculty and student body. Under Battle's leadership, the society collected by 1900 a good deal of material for the university library.

Battle also instituted graduate study in history at the university. Much of the research done by his students was of potential value to the public, but the university had no funds to publish most of it. Although a partial solution to the problem was provided by the *University Magazine,* which printed many biographical sketches and narratives of past events, there remained a need for the occasional publication of monographs "in a more compact and convenient shape." Beginning in 1900, this need was met by the *James Sprunt Historical Monographs.* Endowed by James Sprunt, a Wilmington businessman, and published under the auspices of the department of history, the monographs provided a convenient medium of publication for some of the research done by the faculty and students. As a condition of the endowment, Battle was made editor of the monographs during his tenure at the university. Consequently, he edited and prepared for publication the first seven numbers of the series.

Battle contributed to the dissemination of historical information in a number of other ways. He gave lectures on historical subjects, especially the United States and North Carolina, before various types of groups throughout the state. He was a founder of the short-lived but influential Southern History Association and served throughout the eleven years of the organization's existence (1896–1907) as a member of its administrative council.

Despite the various demands upon his time, Battle was a productive historian. He wrote seven numbers of the *North Carolina Booklets,* a series dealing with the history of the state that was published by the North Carolina Society of the Daughters of the Revolution, and wrote numerous historical articles for the periodical press as well as a number of sketches for Ashe's *Biographical History of North Carolina.* His major work was the *History of the University of North Carolina* in two volumes, still in 1965 considered a "significant study." This work excepted, Battle's personal contributions to historical literature, like those of most of his generation of history professors, were based on scanty sources and consequently were narrow in conception and shallow in interpretation.

Kemp Plummer Battle was the father of three daughters and four sons. His first child, Cornelia Viola (1857–86), married Richard H. Lewis II, a Raleigh physician. His two younger daughters were Susan Martin (1864–70) and Penelope Bradford (1866–68). His second child and first son, Kemp Plummer, Jr. (1859–1922), became a physician and medical school professor. His second son, Thomas Hall (1860–1936), practiced law in Tarboro and Rocky Mount and served for several years as president of the Bank of Rocky Mount and treasurer and general manager of the Rocky Mount Mills. The third son, Herbert Bemerton (1862–1929), received the Ph.D. degree in chemistry from The University of North Carolina and served for several years as director of the North Carolina Agricultural Experiment Station. Battle's youngest child was William James (1870–1955); after taking the A.B. (1888) and the A.M. (1889) degrees at The University of North Carolina, he undertook graduate work at Harvard, where he was awarded the Ph.D. in 1893. He taught the classical languages at the universities of Chicago,

Cincinnati, and Texas and served for many years as dean of the latter school and for a time as its acting president.

In politics, Battle was an antebellum Whig and a postbellum Democrat. In religion he was an Episcopalian. Numerous photographs survive, several of which have been reproduced in his published memoirs, *Memories of an Old-Time Tar Heel,* and in his *History of the University of North Carolina,* vol. 2.

SEE: Battle Family Papers and Cornelia (Phillips) Spencer Papers (Southern Historical Collection, University of North Carolina, Chapel Hill); Kemp P. Battle, *History of the University of North Carolina,* 2 vols. (1907–12), and *Memories of an Old-Time Tar Heel* (1945); George A. Beebe, "One Hundred Years of History in the University of North Carolina" (M.A. thesis, University of North Carolina, 1946); W. Conard Gass, "Kemp Plummer Battle and the Development of Historical Instruction at the University of North Carolina," *North Carolina Historical Review* 45 (1968); J. M. Heck Collection, Bryan Grimes Papers, Mrs. Cornelia Phillips Spencer Papers, Walter Clark Papers, Samuel A'Court Ashe Papers (North Carolina State Archives, Raleigh).

W. CONARD GASS

Battle, Kemp Plummer, Jr. *(9 Mar. 1859–23 Mar. 1922),* physician and professor, was born in Raleigh of English, Welsh, and Scottish ancestry. He was the eldest son of Kemp Plummer Battle, who served with distinction as president of The University of North Carolina (1876–91), and Martha Ann Battle, a distant cousin of his father. At age twelve he entered the Bingham School in Mebane. Entering The University of North Carolina in 1875, he was graduated with honors in 1879 and studied medicine there for one year. He received his M.D. degree from the University of Virginia in 1881 and, the following year, a second degree in medicine at the Bellevue Medical College in New York City. Two years of internship followed; the first in Charity Hospital, Blackwell's Island, N.Y., and the second in Blackwell's Island Insane Asylum. Through competitive examination he secured a position as assistant surgeon in the U.S. Marine Service, but he relinquished it in 1885 to take special studies in London, England, in diseases of the eye, ear, nose, and throat.

Three letters addressed to the editor of the *North Carolina Medical Journal* and published during Battle's sojourn in London and Paris, 1885–86, afford insight on the professional orientation that was to enhance his future career as an American pioneer teacher in the emerging surgical specialties of ophthalmology and oto-laryngology. He began attendance in May 1886 at Moorsfields, the hospital named for that old part of London where the Royal London Ophthalmic Hospital, founded in 1804, was situated. Patients were assigned to students in open clinics under supervision of many of the great teachers of the day: Warren Tay, Sir John Tweedy, Andrew Lang, Sir Jonathan Hutchinson, Landolt, and Galezowski. The broadest range of eye ailments was provided, and students were required to become proficient in the use of the ophthalmoscope and retinoscope. Practical courses in operative surgery were offered in the postmortem rooms of St. Thomas' Hospital; there the student was exposed to the most advanced techniques of cataract extraction. Afternoons were spent in Sir Morell MacKenzie's Throat Hospital in Golden Square, where basic principles of laryngology and rhinology were given upon a firm literary expression.

Nor were Battle's interests confined to his specialty

studies. He attended a session of the British Medical Association at Brighton and recorded personal vignettes and professional opinions of Lawson Tait, Sir Spenser Welles, Sir Henry Thompson, and American guests: Dr. Frank Billings, Dr. Nathan Smith Davis, and Dr. Graham Lusk. He regularly attended meetings of the Ophthalmological Society of the United Kingdom, where he was further privileged to hear lectures and discussions of Jonathan Hutchinson and of Dr. John Hughlings Jackson, who introduced "use of the ophthalmoscope in the diagnosis of brain disease." Visiting the wards of King's College Hospital, he was welcomed to accompany Sir Joseph Lister when he "walked the wards" and to witness Lister's operations, where he could observe "the antiseptic method" of surgery and sense the evolution of this technique since its inception in 1867. The Hunterian Museum was a favorite haunt, and the graphic resumé of his impressions is impeccable. The highlight of his stay in Paris was a visit to Pasteur's laboratory in the Rue d'Ulm. In two pages he records a vivid and concise description of Pasteur's research on rabies.

Returning to Raleigh, Battle entered practice with Dr. Richard Henry Lewis II, the husband of his oldest sister, Cornelia ("Nellie") Viola. This association continued for twenty-eight years. Dr. John B. Wright joined the partnership in 1914 and Dr. Vonnie M. Hicks in 1921. From 1885 to 1913, Battle was professor of physiology in the Leonard Medical School of Shaw University in Raleigh and, from 1903 until 1910, professor of diseases of the ear, nose, and throat in the Raleigh branch of the Medical Department of The University of North Carolina.

From 1886 through 1907, Battle produced eighteen publications emphasizing his specialty of otolaryngology; legislative support for preventive and restorative measures for children prone to eye, ear, nose, and throat ailments; and improved communication between family physician and specialist. He was conversant with scientific progress at home and abroad and introduced diagnostic criteria, techniques, and instruments, some of which bear his name.

In private life his intellectual acumen made him valuable as a manuscript editor and proofreader. He paid frequent visits to the clinics of professional colleagues in the East and Midwest. An experienced Appalachian mountain climber, he was a substantial supporter of his university's first gymnasium, built in 1885.

Battle was one of the first three ear, eye, nose, and throat practitioners in North Carolina. He was a member of the state board of medical examiners from 1897 to 1900, was president of the Wake County Medical Society in 1913 and belonged to the Raleigh Academy of Medicine and the American Academy of Ophthalmology and Laryngology. He was ophthalmologist of the North Carolina School for the Blind, visiting oculist and aurist of Rex and St. Agnes' hospitals, and regional oculist of Seaboard Airline Railroad. He served as secretary-treasurer of the board of trustees of St. Mary's School, vestryman of the Church of the Good Shepherd and director of the Mechanics Savings Bank.

Battle was married first, on 4 Feb. 1890, to Eliza N. McKee of Raleigh, a sister of Dr. James McKee; she died on 12 Apr. 1919. His second marriage was to Mrs. Sally Hall Strong of Raleigh, who survived him. There were no offspring from either marriage.

Battle died in the Chestnut Hill Hospital of Philadelphia, following an illness of seven months, and was buried in Oakwood Cemetery in Raleigh.

SEE: Kemp P. Battle, *History of the University of North Carolina*, vol. 2 (1912), and *Memories of an Old-Time Tar Heel* (1945); F. H. Garrison, *History of Medicine*, 4th ed. (1929); *Medicine in North Carolina*, vol. 2 (1972); *North Carolina Medical Journal*, 18–56 (1886–1907); [Hubert A. Royster], *Historical Sketch of the University of North Carolina Medical Department at Raleigh* (1941); *Transactions of the Medical Society* (Apr. 1922).

WARNER WELLS

Battle, Richard Henry (*3 Dec. 1835–19 May 1912*), attorney and civic leader, was born in Louisburg, Franklin County, the son of William Horn and Lucy Martin Plummer Battle. His father was a justice of the North Carolina Supreme Court. He was descended from Elisha Battle, a member of the conventions that adopted the 1776 constitution and the federal Constitution. His maternal grandfather was Kemp Plummer, a lawyer. A brother, Kemp Plummer Battle, was president of The University of North Carolina.

Following his education at Mrs. Eliza Taylor's school in Raleigh and the preparatory school at The University of North Carolina, Battle entered the university. In June 1854 he was granted his A.B.; in 1858 he received the LL.B. Years later, in 1895, his alma mater honored him with an LL.D.

Battle served as tutor of mathematics and Greek from 1854 to 1858. During this time he read law with his father, who was professor of law in Chapel Hill. Battle was licensed to practice law and opened his office in Wadesboro in December 1858.

Battle entered the Civil War first as a lieutenant in Company I, Forty-third Regiment, North Carolina Troops, becoming quartermaster of the regiment in 1862, with the rank of captain. He resigned to join the staff of Zebulon B. Vance as private secretary, a position he held until August 1864. From then until 1865 he was auditor for the state.

Battle practiced law after the war, first forming a partnership with Samuel H. Phillips, with whom he practiced until December 1868. He, his father, and his brother next formed a partnership under the firm name W. H. Battle and Sons. Still later, in January 1876, he and Samuel F. Mordecai practiced together under the partnership name Battle and Mordecai.

During the administration of Governor Alfred M. Scales, Battle was urged to accept appointment as a superior court judge, an offer he declined. He was a member of the constitutional convention of 1875 and of the state house of representatives in 1880. He was a member of the state democratic executive committee serving as chairman from 1884 to 1888, and was an alderman of the city of Raleigh in 1880.

In addition to political posts, Battle assumed many civic responsibilities. From 1879 to 1912 he was a trustee of The University of North Carolina; in 1891 he was secretary-treasurer of the board. He was noted for work leading to the establishment of Rex Hospital and for his service as president of its board of trustees. Battle also was a long-time president of the Board of Trustees of the Olivia Raney Library in Raleigh; president of the trustees of the Raleigh Cemetery Association, which established Oakwood Cemetery; president of the trustees of Raleigh Associated Charities; a trustee of both St. Mary's and St. Augustine's schools in Raleigh; and both president and vice-president of the advisory board of the North Carolina Agricultural Society.

When the bronze statue of Zebulon B. Vance was unveiled in Capitol Square in Raleigh in 1900, Battle delivered the address. The cornerstone of the "new" Rex Hospital on South Street was laid in January 1909 with Battle the featured speaker. He prepared several sketches for Ashe's *Biographical History of North Carolina*.

A member of the Protestant Episcopal church, Battle was a regular and faithful communicant, serving as a vestryman of the Chapel of the Cross in Chapel Hill from 1855 to 1858, of Calvary Church in Wadesboro from 1861 to 1862, and of Christ Church in Raleigh from 1863 to 1874; he was elected senior warden of the Church of the Good Shepherd in Raleigh on 26 Feb. 1874, having been one of the leaders in its establishment. For many years he served as deputy to the General Convention of the Episcopal Church in the United States.

Battle married Annie Ruffin Ashe, daughter of Confederate Senator Thomas S. Ashe, on 28 Nov. 1860; she predeceased him by nearly nineteen years. The Battles had ten children, four of whom survived him.

Several weeks before his death, Battle suffered a slight stroke; he was hospitalized in Rex Hospital for ten days preceding his death. His funeral was conducted at the Church of the Good Shepherd in Raleigh, with burial in Oakwood Cemetery. Through provisions of his will, Battle continued his expression of loyalty to the Church of the Good Shepherd, The University of North Carolina, and the Olivia Raney Library.

SEE: D. L. Grant, *Alumni History of the University of North Carolina* (1924); *North Carolina Manual* (1911); Raleigh *News and Observer*, 21 May 1912; Will of Richard H. Battle and PC 310, Richard H. Battle (North Carolina State Archives, Raleigh).

MEMORY F. MITCHELL

Battle, Samuel Westray (4 Aug. 1854–29 Apr. 1927), surgeon in the U.S. Navy, was born in Nash County and died in Raleigh. His father was William S. Battle, planter and owner of Rocky Mount Mills during the Civil War. His mother was Elizabeth Dancy of Tarboro. He was educated at Horner School in Oxford and Bellevue Hospital Medical College. From 1875 to 1884 he was a surgeon in the U.S. Navy, and from 1879 to 1883 he was in charge of the U.S. Naval Hospital, Pensacola, Fla. He retired from active naval service in 1884 because of serious injury to his left wrist and hand during a collision at sea.

From 1884 until his death he practiced medicine in Asheville and for many years lived in the old Biltmore Hotel in the center of town. He was medical director of Clarence Barker Memorial Hospital in nearby Biltmore. During this period, he served as major and assistant surgeon general of the North Carolina State Guard and as a member of the American Medical Association, Mississippi Valley Medical Association, Tri-State Medical Association, American Climatological Association, Association of Military Surgeons, North Carolina Board of Health, Medical Corps of the U.S. Navy, and Naval Order of the United States. He was president of Buncombe County Medical Society; fellow of the Rhinological, Otological, and Laryngological societies; and a member of the North Carolina Society of the Cincinnati. It was while attending a meeting of this last society in Raleigh that he suffered a stroke and died.

His wife, Alice Maude Belknap, was born in Newport, N.H., 29 Apr. 1863, and died in Asheville on 29 Oct. 1899. She was the daughter of Rear Admiral George E. Belknap and Ellen Deborah Read. The children of Samuel and Alice Battle were Madelon Belknap, Maude Dancy, Samuel Westray, and Belknap.

Samuel Westray Battle remarried in New York City on 7 Feb. 1918. His second wife was Mrs. Jane Hall Liddell of Charlotte, born in Ridgeway, Pa., on 31 Mar. 1866; she died in Asheville.

SEE: H. B. Battle et al., *The Battle Book* (1930); Samuel Westray Battle to William S. Battle, letters (Southern Historical Collection, University of North Carolina Library, Chapel Hill).

MARGARET B. LEWIS

Battle, Thomas Hall (2 Aug. 1860–23 Jan. 1936), banker, industrialist, attorney, and educator, was born in Raleigh, a descendant of a long line of jurists and educators. His father was Kemp P. Battle, president of The University of North Carolina. He spent his early life in Raleigh, attended school there, and enrolled in The University of North Carolina, graduating at the head of his class in 1880. He taught school and traveled briefly before reading law at the university under Dr. John Manning. After gaining his law license in 1882, he moved to Tarboro, practiced law briefly, and became a solicitor of the court in Edgecombe County. Three years later he moved to Rocky Mount and practiced law, but there he became involved in corporate business with the Rocky Mount Mills, first as a director, later for twelve years as president, and finally as treasurer.

As a financial leader, he organized the Bank of Rocky Mount in 1889, serving later as its president. He also helped organize and headed the Rocky Mount Savings and Loan Company and the Rocky Mount Insurance and Investment Company. As early as 1892 he urged the formation of a state banking association, which was created when the North Carolina Bankers Association was organized at Morehead City in July of 1897, with Battle as the first president.

He was a leader in the Episcopal church, serving as senior warden. First elected mayor of Rocky Mount in 1886, he served a decade in that post. He helped organize the Rocky Mount Graded School and was chairman of its board of trustees; he also was chairman of the Rocky Mount Board of Education for thirty-four consecutive years.

Born in war and educated during Reconstruction, Battle became a symbol of the group of North Carolina leaders who contributed importantly to the rebuilding of the state after the ravages of war.

Battle was married three times: in 1887 to Bettie Davis of Wilson, who died in 1890; in 1895 to Sallie G. Hyman of Tarboro, who died in 1917; and in 1920 to Mary Weddell of Tarboro. There were six children: Kemp Davis, Hyman L., Ethel, Josephine, Martha Ann, and Mary Thomas. Portraits of Battle are in various places, including the North Carolina Bankers Association.

SEE: Samuel A. Ashe, ed., *Biographical History of North Carolina*, vol. 6 (1907); Raleigh *News and Observer*, 24 Jan. 1936; *Tarheel Banker* 14 (1936); *Who Was Who in America*, vol. 1 (1943).

T. HARRY GATTON

Battle, Turner Westray (3 June 1899–1 Jan. 1944), assistant to the U.S. secretary of labor, was born in Rocky Mount, the son of Jacob and Nell Gray Gupton Battle. The third Turner Westray Battle, he was a student at Staunton Military Academy from 1913 to 1916 and was graduated from the U.S. Naval Academy in 1919.

He served in the Pacific Fleet first as assistant engineer officer on the U.S.S. *Arkansas*, then as chief engineer of the U.S.S. *Meyer*, and then as commanding officer of the U.S.S. *Duncan*. After resigning from the Navy in 1921, he became associated with the Socony Burner Corporation. He later was made a district manager of the International Combustion Engineering Corporation of New York.

In 1933, Battle was appointed executive assistant in the Department of Labor under Frances Perkins. Among his other assignments there, he served as president of the U.S. Housing Corporation, the representative of the secretary of labor on the Special Board for Public Works, a member of the Interdepartmental Shipping Policy Committee, a member of the Committee to Designate Airports of Entry, and the representative of the Labor Department on the Works Progress Board.

However, soon after Pearl Harbor, he enlisted in the Marine Corps and early in 1942 was commissioned first lieutenant. He saw active duty in the South Pacific; while there, he was promoted to the rank of captain. He died at Camp Lejeune and was interred in the old Battle burial ground near Cool Spring Plantation in Edgecombe County.

Battle was married twice. His first marriage, on 6 Nov. 1920, was to Helen Staats of Pasadena, Calif., daughter of William Richardson and Isabelle Lawton Staats. They had one son, Turner Westray Battle IV. Battle married, second, Mary Patton of Huntsville, Ala., on 9 Aug. 1936. He was a lifelong Episcopalian and Democrat.

SEE: H. B. Battle et al., *The Battle Book* (1930); Rocky Mount *Evening Telegram*, 3 Jan. 1944; *Southern Churchman*, February 1944; *Who's Who in America*, 1940–41.

DOROTHY BATTLE WILKINSON

Battle, William Horn (17 Oct. 1802–4 Mar. 1879), lawyer, legislator, and jurist, was born in Edgecombe County. His father was Joel Battle, cofounder of one of the first cotton mills in the Southeast; his mother was Mary P. Johnston. Battle entered the sophomore class of The University of North Carolina and was graduated two years later, in 1820, second in his class. He then studied law for three years at Williamsboro in the office of Chief Justice Leonard Henderson of the state supreme court. He was admitted to the bar in 1824. The following year he married Lucy Martin Plummer of Warrenton and entered upon the practice of law at Louisburg. He was an unsuccessful candidate for the lower house of the General Assembly in 1831 and 1832 but represented Franklin County in the House of Commons in the legislative sessions of 1833–34 and 1834–35. From 1834 to 1839 he served jointly with Thomas P. Devereaux as reporter to the state supreme court. Upon Devereaux's resignation in 1839, he was made sole reporter and moved his residence from Louisburg to Raleigh.

In 1833, Battle was named one of a commission of three charged with the responsibility of revising the statutory laws of the state, and in 1837 he was one of two commissioners to see the revised statutes through the press. In 1839 he was a delegate to the Whig National Convention that nominated William Henry Harrison for the presidency. In 1840 he was appointed a superior court judge, and in 1843 he moved his family to Chapel Hill to educate his sons at the university. Becoming professor of law in The University of North Carolina in 1845, he served continuously in the position until 1868. In 1848 he was given an interim appointment to the state supreme court, but the legislature did not confirm him in the position. He was, however, reelected a superior court judge. In 1852 he received a permanent appointment as a justice of the North Carolina Supreme Court; he served until his removal by the Reconstruction Act of March 1867. In 1868 he moved to Raleigh to practice law in partnership with two of his sons.

The General Assembly of 1871–72 appointed Battle sole commissioner to revise the North Carolina statutes, and the legislature of 1872–73 authorized the publication of the result as *Battle's Revisal*. For several years at this period of his life, Battle served as president of the Raleigh National Bank. His wife died in 1874, and in 1876 he returned to Chapel Hill with his son Kemp, who had been elected president of the reopened University of North Carolina. He again served as professor of law in the university until his death at Chapel Hill in 1879. Burial was in Oakwood Cemetery, Raleigh. His portrait was presented to the North Carolina Supreme Court in 1892.

In addition to his work as reviser of the state's statutory law, Battle edited several of the early volumes of the North Carolina *Reports* and in 1865 prepared a digest of the decisions of the North Carolina Supreme Court, which he published in three volumes at his own expense. He was a charter member of the antebellum North Carolina Historical Society; prior to the Civil War he wrote for the *University of North Carolina Magazine* biographical sketches of early justices of the state supreme court and short articles on the early history of The University of North Carolina. Although he was reared in a Baptist family, he did not affiliate with any church until middle life, when he joined the Episcopal church, his wife's denomination. He was for many years a vestryman of the Chapel of the Cross, the Episcopal parish church of Chapel Hill, and for thirty-five consecutive years was lay delegate to the denomination's general convention. Before the Civil War he was a Whig and during Reconstruction a Conservative. Although he supported the Confederate cause once North Carolina had seceded, he considered secession unwise and deplored the Civil War.

Battle was the father of ten children, two of whom, Julian and Thomas Devereaux, died in infancy. The six sons who reached adulthood were all graduates of The University of North Carolina: Joel, Junius Cullen, Wesley Lewis, Kemp Plummer, William Horn, Jr., and Richard Henry. Battle's oldest daughter, Susan Catharine, who never married, was long an invalid. His youngest daughter, Mary, married William Van Wyck II.

SEE: Joseph B. Batchelor, "Address at Presentation of Portrait to Supreme Court," 90 *N.C. Reports*; Battle Family Papers, David Lowry Swain Papers, and Charles Phillips Papers (Southern Historical Collection, University of North Carolina, Chapel Hill); Kemp P. Battle, *History of the University of North Carolina*, 2 vols. (1907–12), and *Memories of an Old-Time Tar Heel* (1945); *Obituaries, Funeral, and Proceedings of Bar in Memory of W. H. Battle* (1879); Raleigh *Observer*, 15 Mar. 1879.

W. CONARD GASS

Battle, William Smith (4 Oct. 1823–10 Nov. 1915), planter and manufacturer, was born in Edgecombe County, the son of Sally Harriet Westray and James Smith Battle. He began his education at Stony Hill and Louisburg academies and was graduated from The University of North Carolina in 1844. Battle soon was occupied in the management of a very large plantation devoted to the production of cotton. He also owned and operated the Rocky Mount Cotton Mill and a grist mill and within a few years was probably the wealthiest man in the county. In 1858 he began the construction of a large brick home in Tarboro and in 1860 moved his family there.

He was a delegate to the convention of 1861 and voted for secession from the Union. His cotton mills thereafter produced cloth for uniforms and yarn for socks for the Confederate Army. His plantations supplied meat and corn, and he invested heavily in Confederate bonds. His activity apparently attracted the attention of Federal officials: in the summer of 1863, a raiding party of Union troops was dispatched from New Bern to destroy his industrial enterprise. At great sacrifice, Battle rebuilt the cotton mill, the grist mill, and a cotton gin. The end of the war found him in extreme financial straits. The cotton mill burned again and was rebuilt with money borrowed at a staggering rate of interest. Land was sold to repay loans, but the Panic of 1873 brought utter ruin. In 1890, Battle turned over his remaining property to his creditors and retired to a farm in his wife's name in Edgecombe County, where he farmed for many years.

On 25 June 1845, Battle married Elizabeth Mary Dancy, daughter of Charlotte Sessums and Francis Little Dancy of Tarboro. They were the parents of nine sons and a daughter: James Smith II, who married John Anna Somerville; Frank Dancy, married to Emily Semple; William Smith II; John Dancy, who married Mary Fremont; Samuel Westray, married to Alice Belknap; Camillus Little; Elisha; Octavius, married to Margaret Maud Anthony; Marmaduke; and Elizabeth Dancy.

Although he belonged to no church, Battle was buried in the Calvary Episcopal churchyard in Tarboro.

SEE: H. B. Battle et al., *The Battle Book* (1930); Kemp P. Battle, *Memories of an Old-Time Tar Heel* (1945); *Rocky Mount Mills* (1943).

ELIZABETH DANCY BATTLE

Batts, Nathaniell (*ca. 1620–ca. 1679*), fur trader, explorer, and early settler, was by 1655 operating a fur trading post in what would be North Carolina.

There seems to be little doubt that Batts was part of the group employed in 1653 and 1654 by Francis Yeardley, prominent planter of Lynnhaven, Va., to establish a fur trade with the Indians to the southward and to explore that region in detail. In 1655, Yeardley sent Robert Bodnam, a carpenter, to the south to build a house twenty feet square (containing two rooms and a chimney) for Batts to live in while he traded with the Indians. The house was erected beside Salmon (then Fletts) Creek at the western end of Albemarle (then Roanoke) Sound. This trading post appears on the Nicholas Comberford map of 1657, entitled "The South Part of Virginia," with the legend "Batts House."

The Comberford map may well reflect the exploration undertaken by the Yeardley group, and much of the information it contains may have come from Batts's explorations. Certainly the frequent appearance of his name on geographical features of the area would so indicate. In 1657 the Virginia General Court acknowledged the great pains and trouble he had taken in his discovery of an inlet to the southward. His discoveries were incorporated in the Comberford map produced in that same year by a well-known member of the "Thames School" of London mapmakers. It was this map that was used by the Lords Proprietors of Carolina in 1663 to delineate the northern boundaries of their province.

For nearly a quarter of a century after the erection of Batts's fur trading post, he divided his time and interest between Carolina and Virginia. On 25 May 1656 he married Mary Woodhouse, a widow with some property; they lived in Lower Norfolk County on the Woodhouse plantation, Roede, which eventually came to be called "Batts Quarters." During the 1650s and probably for a much longer period he was plagued by large debts. When he married Mary Woodhouse, he signed a marriage settlement in which he acknowledged that he was "indebted to some men in Virginia" and promised not to use his wife's property to satisfy any of his debts. In the following year the Virginia General Court gave him as his reward for the discovery of an inlet protection "from all his Creditors within this County for one year & a day." Batts was "frequently involved in litigation over the non-payment of his debts and other matters." Despite his financial problems, he acquired nine hundred acres of land in Nansemond County from Samuel Stephens and later sold the land to Colonel Thomas Francis.

Along with his important interests in Virginia, Batts continued to be heavily involved in Carolina. On 24 Sept. 1660 he purchased from Kiscutanewh, king of the Yeopim Indians, all the land on the west bank of the Pasquotank River from its mouth to the head of New Begin Creek. This transaction, which survives in the records of Lower Norfolk County, Va., is the oldest known surviving North Carolina land deed. Batts also held land in Chowan Precinct on which he lived for a time. His best-known holding was Heriots Island at the mouth of Yeopim River in the Albemarle Sound, which by 1672 was called Batts Island and by the 1690s, Batts Grave.

In 1672, George Fox, founder of the Quaker sect, visited Carolina, met Batts, and visited him at his Chowan plantation. Fox reported that Batts "had been a rude, desperate man" but that he attended some of Fox's meetings and seemed interested in healing by means of prayer. Fox says that Batts "had been Governor of Roanoke" and refers to him as "the Old Governor." No other known source supports such a title, although the possibility that the Virginia government may have placed him in charge of the settlements about Albemarle Sound before 1664 cannot be altogether dismissed.

SEE: *American Historical Review* 45 (1939); W. P. Cumming, *North Carolina in Maps* (1966); *Imago Mundi* 24 (1970); *North Carolina Historical Review* 43 (1966); *Rebel* 3 (Spring 1960); *Virginia Magazine of History and Biography* 79 (1971).

ELIZABETH G. MCPHERSON
HERBERT R. PASCHAL

Bauer, Adolphus Gustavus (*4 Dec. 1858–14 May 1898*), architect, was born in Martinsburg, West Virginia, of German parents from Brunswick and Hanover. He graduated from Bethany College, W.Va., in June 1879 and later studied portrait painting at an art school in Cincinnati. In 1881 he joined Samuel Sloan, well-known Philadelphia architect, as chief draftsman. Bauer went to Raleigh, N.C., with Sloan in 1883 and lived there until his death. From 1880 to 1889 his work took him to nearly every state west of the Mississippi and south of New England. In the fall of 1889 and the following spring, Bauer traveled abroad, visiting Scotland, England, France, Germany, Italy, Spain, and the northern coast of Africa.

Sloan designed some of the finest public buildings in the country and was particularly noted for his work on mental hospitals. Bauer worked with him on numerous projects, including the state hospitals at Morganton and at Columbia. A number of buildings in Raleigh were designed by Sloan—a Gothic two-story structure at St. Mary's, a building at St. Augustine's Normal School, an addition to Peace College and the Centennial Graded School. Bauer was credited with making specifications for the main exhibition building at the North Carolina State Exposition.

One of the most distinctive buildings by Sloan and Bauer was the Governor's Mansion in Raleigh. Sloan died in 1884 before completion of the house, and Bauer continued his work. In his extension of the Agriculture Building, Bauer was complimented for an interior "admirable with ample space and light" and was recognized as "one who has much taste and ability in such matters." He was appointed architect for an opera house planned by the city. Among other buildings designed by Bauer was the Baptist Female Seminary (Meredith College), located on the block south of the executive mansion and similar to it in design. Bauer advertised as draftsman and consulting architect for buildings of every description throughout the state. Included were cottages, villas, city dwellings, churches, schools, banks, hotels, railroad depots, county jails and courthouses, stores, opera houses, farmhouses, factories, small barns, and stables—from the most artistic and costly to the plainest and cheapest. He also designed machinery; iron, stone, or wooden bridges; monuments; and furniture.

Bauer committed suicide in May 1898. His death followed a deep depression after the death of his wife. Another contributing factor, according to an account in the local newspaper, was a head injury sustained two years previously, when he was struck by a train while crossing railroad tracks at the depot in Durham. His injury led to brief confinements in a mental hospital. He evidently recognized his periods of melancholia, stating in a suicide note: "I wish to say that if I, by violence to myself should die, I wish to be buried by the side of my wife, in Raleigh, N.C., where I have so long sojourned and among the Southern people I have liked so well." He was buried in Oakwood Cemetery next to the monument erected to Rachel Blythe Bauer.

In June 1895, Bauer married Rachel Blythe of the Cherokees of Swain County. Her family were leaders of the tribe, but Rachel was educated at an orphanage and later studied stenography at the Baptist Institute (Meredith College). She was a stamp clerk at the Raleigh Post Office. Rachel joined the First Presbyterian Church, and the couple lived near the corner of North Wilmington and Jones streets. The Bauers had two children, the youngest five years old when his mother died. The eldest, a daughter, was raised by her father's family in Belleair, Ohio, and the boy, Fred, was sent to the Cherokee reservation. He became vice-chief of the tribe and led the opposition when the Skyline Highway threatened to run through Indian territory. He was a World War I veteran and district president of the American Indian Federation; his wife served as secretary.

SEE: *Orphan's Friend*, 1 Sept. 1916; Raleigh *News and Observer*, 13 May 1898, 6 Mar. 1938, 8 July 1962; *Raleigh Times*, 22 July 1963.

BETH CRABTREE

Baxter, Elisha (*1 Sept. 1827–31 May 1899*), governor of Arkansas and a protagonist in the Brooks-Baxter War there, was born in Rutherford County, the seventh of eight children of William and Catherine Lee Baxter. He was a brother of John Baxter and an uncle of Plato Durham. Elisha received only a rudimentary schooling and turned down a West Point appointment at the insistence of his aged father. At the age of twenty he went into the mercantile business in Rutherfordton with his brother-in-law, Spencer Eaves. In 1849 he married Harriet Patton of Rutherford County, who bore him six children: Millard P., Edward A., Catherine M., George E., Hattie O., and Fannie E.

Baxter moved to Arkansas in 1852 and settled at Batesville, where he opened a general store the next year in partnership with his brother, Taylor Baxter. The business failed in 1855, and he went to work in the printing office of the *Independent Balance*. At the same time he read law; he was admitted to the bar and began practice in 1856.

The business failure may have resulted from Baxter's growing preoccupation with politics. A Whig, he was elected mayor of Batesville in 1853, the year after he moved there, and he was sent to the state house of representatives in 1854 and 1858. He opposed secession and, when it came about, tried to remain neutral, refusing either to support the Confederacy or to take up arms against his friends and neighbors. In 1862 he turned down a Federal colonelcy, but his neutral stance made his personal and professional life so difficult that he took his family to Missouri for safety. Nevertheless, Confederate cavalry captured him there in 1863 and sent him back to Arkansas to face charges of treason. Baxter escaped from prison in Little Rock before his case came to trial. Stung by charges of disloyalty and cowardice, he made his way to Batesville, raised a regiment of Arkansas Federals, and became its colonel.

In the spring of 1864, Baxter was elected to the state supreme court under the new Unionist government of Isaac Murphy. He had scarcely assumed this office when the legislature elected him to the U.S. Senate. Owing to congressional dissatisfaction with presidential Reconstruction, Baxter and his colleagues were not seated, and he returned to his law practice in Batesville. When the Republican Reconstruction regime was organized in 1868, Governor Powell Clayton appointed Baxter a circuit judge. He served as judge (and also federal register in bankruptcy) until the Republicans nominated him for governor in 1872.

Baxter's reputation was that of a political moderate, affiliated with the Republican party but not closely associated with its leadership or the alleged improprieties of radical rule. Nevertheless, it was the Clayton ("Minstrel") leadership that secured his gubernatorial nomination; the rival "Brindletail" faction named Joseph Brooks, a northern native, whom the Democrats also endorsed. After a heated campaign marked by many irregularities, Baxter was declared elected by a slim margin of 2,919 votes and took office on 6 Jan. 1873. As governor, he supported financial economies and a return of voting privileges to disfranchised ex-Confederates; he appointed a number of Democrats to office. These policies brought a reversal of political alignments. Democrats generally came around to Baxter's support, abandoning Brooks's efforts to gain the governorship by court action on grounds of fraud. Republicans for the most part switched to Brooks by the spring of 1874.

The state supreme court, under Republican control, then ruled in Brooks's favor, whereupon he went to the capitol building with a few supporters and ejected Baxter from the governor's office. Baxter refused to yield and set up headquarters in a building nearby. Both claimants appealed to Washington and called out the militia for support. As rival forces converged on Little Rock, an armed outbreak seemed imminent, but nothing of consequence occurred. The national administration refused to choose between Brooks and Baxter, holding that it was up to the state legislature to decide. As a result of many vacancies and special elections that Republicans refused to contest, legislative control had passed to the Democrats, and the legislature declared for Baxter. Brooks retired from the field, but Baxter's term was cut short by the adoption of a new Democratic-sponsored constitution calling for a gubernatorial election in 1874. Democrats offered Baxter the nomination for a full new term, but he declined rather than incur the charge of having sold out to them for a longer lease on the governorship. On 12 Nov. 1874 he retired to his home at Batesville, where he practiced law and farmed until his death.

SEE: "Elisha Baxter's Autobiography," ed. Ted R. Worley, *Arkansas Historical Quarterly* 14 (1955); *DAB*, vol. 2 (1929); Clarence W. Griffin, *History of Old Tryon and Rutherford Counties* (1937); John M. Harrell, *The Brooks and Baxter War* (1893).

ALLEN W. TRELEASE

Baxter, John (5 Mar. 1819–2 Apr. 1886), lawyer, legislator, southern Unionist, and U.S. circuit court judge, was the son of Irish immigrants, Catherine Lee and William Baxter, who had settled in Rutherford County. He was a brother of Elisha Baxter and an uncle of Plato Durham. Baxter's early education was confined to the rural schools of Rutherford County. After a try at business, he read law and was admitted to the bar in 1840. In 1842 he married Orra Alexander of Buncombe County and in the same year was elected to the House of Commons as a Whig from Rutherford County. In 1844 he was a presidential elector on the Henry Clay ticket. Moving to Henderson County in 1845, he was elected to the legislature there the next year and sponsored the act chartering the town of Hendersonville. Elected to three more successive terms, beginning in 1852, he served as speaker during the first of them. Baxter was an outspoken supporter of Western sectional interests within the state, including legislative reapportionment, and also of increased industrialization.

In 1857, Baxter moved to Knoxville, Tenn., in order to further his legal career. Within a short time he was reputed to be the highest paid lawyer in East Tennessee.

During the secession controversy, Baxter was an ardent Unionist, along with most other prominent East Tennesseans. In January 1861 he was elected as a Unionist to the state's proposed secession convention, which never met, being voted down by a popular referendum. Later that year he went to Richmond, Va., where he persuaded Confederate authorities, including President Davis, to refrain from widespread arrests of East Tennessee Unionists. At about the same time, Baxter was himself persuaded by Zebulon B. Vance of North Carolina to cooperate with the Confederacy in order to prevent Rebel excesses against Tennessee Unionists. Late in 1861 he ran for the Confederate Congress but was soundly defeated by an ardent secessionist in an election that most Unionists boycotted. In the spring of 1862, Baxter went on private business to Memphis, where he was briefly arrested as an enemy of the South. After this incident he drifted back toward his original Unionism. In 1864 he and other Unionists reacted to the Emancipation Proclamation by supporting McClellan and the national Democratic party.

After the war, Baxter was a vocal opponent of William G. Brownlow's Radical Republican administration. In 1870, when the Conservatives regained power, Baxter was elected to the new constitutional convention and was chosen by the members as chairman of the judiciary committee. In 1872 he joined with Thomas A. R. Nelson and Joseph S. Fowler in an effort to establish the Liberal Republican party in Tennessee and participated in the Cincinnati convention, which nominated Horace Greeley for president. With the failure of that movement, Baxter returned to the Republican party and supported Rutherford B. Hayes for president in 1876. The next year, Hayes appointed him judge of the circuit court for the Sixth Circuit, which included the states of Tennessee, Kentucky, Ohio, and Michigan. On the bench, Baxter was characterized as a knowledgeable student of the law, who could grasp the sense of a case without tarrying over technicalities.

In 1879, Baxter became a trustee of the University of Tennessee. In that capacity he advocated the admission of black students, provided they lived in separate dormitories.

Baxter died in Hot Springs, Ark., where he had gone for relief of an arthritic condition. He was survived by five children, including George W. Baxter, a governor of Wyoming Territory. He was buried in Old Gray Cemetery in Knoxville.

SEE: Thomas B. Alexander, *Political Reconstruction in Tennessee* (1950), and *Thomas A. R. Nelson of East Tennessee* (1956); J. P. Arthur, *Western Carolina* (1914); John Baxter, "Speech Made in Reply to Hon. T. L. Clingman at Rutherfordton" and "To the Voters of Henderson County [1854, *Messages, Speeches, etc.*]" (North Carolina Collection, University of North Carolina, Chapel Hill); *DAB*, vol. 2 (1929); Stanley J. Folmsbee, *Tennessee Establishes a State University* (1961); John Welb Green, *Bench and Bar of Knox County, Tennessee* (1947 [portrait]); *Knoxville* (Tennessee) *Daily American*, 3 Apr. 1886 (obit.); *Nashville* (Tennessee) *Daily American*, 3 Apr. 1886 (obit.); Oliver Perry Temple, *Notable Men of Tennessee* (1912).

CHARLES A. NEWELL, JR.

Bayard, Elizabeth Cornell (1761/62–17 Jan. 1854), the plaintiff in the North Carolina Superior Court case *Bayard* v. *Singleton* (1787), was the daughter of Samuel Cornell (1731–81) and Susannah Mabson (1736/37–10 Feb. 1778). The Cornell family lived in New Bern, where Samuel Cornell was a member of Christ Church. After 1777, however, most of the family resided in Flushing, N.Y. The family included four other daughters: Susannah, who married Captain Henry Chad (or Chads) in 1783; Sarah (1761–2 June 1803), who married Matthew Clarkson on 14 Feb. 1792; Hannah (d. 1818), who married New Yorker Herman LeRoy on 19 Oct. 1786 at William Bayard's house; and Mary (d. 1813), who married Isaac Edwards, Governor William Tryon's secretary and aide-de-camp. In 1783, Elizabeth married William Bayard, Jr. (1761–18 Sept. 1826), a New York merchant and Herman LeRoy's business partner. Elizabeth died at the age of ninety-two in Albany, N.Y., at the home of one of her sons-in-law, Stephen Van Rensselaer. It was at the Bayards' home in New York City that Alexander Hamilton died, on 12 July 1804.

The court case involving the Bayards concerned the property of Loyalist Samuel Cornell. Cornell transferred a share of the property to his daughter Elizabeth when in December 1777 he refused to take the oath of allegiance to the state. Cornell then removed his family to New York. By an act of the legislature passed in 1779 and considered retroactive to 1776, all of his property was confiscated. Elizabeth's portion was acquired by Spyres Singleton. She filed suit against him in November 1784, but it was three years before the case came to trial. In 1787 the court upheld the Confiscation Acts of 1779 and 1785 and awarded the property to the defendant.

The children of Elizabeth and William Bayard numbered seven. Catharine (1786–1813) married Duncan P. Campbell. Susan (1787–11 Oct. 1814) married Benjamin Woolsey Rogers on 10 Dec. 1807. William

(1788–9 Mar. 1875) married Catharine Hammond in 1812.
Maria (1789–23 Oct. 1875) married Duncan P. Campbell,
her brother-in-law, in 1817. Justine (b. 1793) married
Joseph Blackwell in 1811. Robert (b. 1797) married
Elizabeth McEvers in 1820. On 2 Jan. 1817, Harriet
Elizabeth (12 Feb. 1799–19 July 1875) married General
Stephen Van Rensselaer, eldest son of Stephen Van
Rensselaer (the last Patroon) and Margaret Schuyler.

SEE: Gertrude S. Carraway, *Crown of Life: History of Christ
Church, New Bern* (1940); John Cornell, *Genealogy of the
Cornell Family* (1901); S. Cornell, "Law Case: Tried and
Determined," *American Museum* 6 (1789); Quinton
Holton, "History of the Case of Bayard vs. Singleton"
(M.A. thesis, University of North Carolina, 1948);
Elizabeth Moore, *Records of Craven County, North Carolina*
(1960); New York Public Library, Papers Relating to
Samuel Cornell, North Carolina Loyalist (1913); North
Carolina State Archives (Raleigh), for Superior Court
Records. New Bern District, "Superior Court Minutes,
Craven Co., 1787–1794" (D.C.R. 9.002); *Who Was Who in
America, 1607–1896.*

EVA BURBANK MURPHY

Beach, Charles Maynard *(1 Jan. 1876–18 Aug. 1959)*,
educator, was born in Caldwell County, near Lenoir, the
son of Joseph Lawson and Anne Shuford Beach. He
attended schools in the community, including Hibriten
Academy, and was graduated from Taylorsville
Collegiate Institute in 1897. For two years he taught in a
small, local school known as Beach School; in 1899 he
entered Wake Forest College, from which he was
graduated with both the B.A. and the M.A. degrees in
1902.

In the summer of 1902 he went to Delway to organize a
projected elementary and high school. Although he was
encouraged by many community leaders, he performed
an indescribable amount of hard work in order to bring
into being the Dell School. He became the first principal,
responsible not only for administration but for soliciting
students and raising money to erect needed buildings,
both of which he did with marked success.

Beach left Dell School in 1914 to become principal of
the reopened Leaksville-Spray Institute, Leaksville. The
school closed again after two years. He then became
principal of the Spray High School and superintendent
of the Spray graded school system, where he served with
effectiveness and efficiency for three years.

Beach accepted a call to become head of the Wingate
School, Wingate, in the summer of 1919. In early 1923
the Wingate School became Wingate Junior College, and
Beach became its first president. Later that year, his
health had so deteriorated that he asked to be relieved of
administrative responsibilities. In early manhood, he
had developed an extreme nervous condition, sometimes described as palsy, and although he did not allow
his condition to deter him in his work, he became
increasingly conscious of the affliction. He remained at
Wingate until 1934, teaching Bible and related subjects in
the college. He lived in Cary for three years and then in
1937 returned to Leaksville, where he built a home and
lived out his years in fruitful service to the community
through many avenues of interest and responsibility,
limited only by his health.

Although not an ordained minister, Beach was always
active as a lay preacher and speaker at all kinds of
religious groups. For a time he served as religious
activities director of the Spray YMCA. He was active in
his local church as a deacon, Sunday school teacher, and
for a time interim pastor of the Spray Baptist Church. An
article in the *Biblical Recorder* in early 1953 noted
affectionately that he was "Mr. Chips" to hundreds of
his former students, many of whom had recently
attended a celebration in his honor.

In 1938, Beach proposed a vast program of
supplementary education, of which he became the
director, under the aegis of the Leaksville Township
public schools. This attack on adult illiteracy was highly
successful, so much so that he was described as having
"banished illiteracy from Rockingham County." At its
peak, the program had twelve teachers and offered a
wide range of subjects to more than nine hundred adults
each year.

On 23 Dec. 1902, Beach married Bessie Claudine
Hagwood of Wake County, daughter of William Henry
and Charity Helen Mitchell Hagwood. The Beaches had
three sons: Joseph W. of Raleigh, James L. of Sarasota,
Fla., and Clarence M. of Eden. Beach died at Leaksville
and was interred in the Leaksville cemetery.

SEE: Catalog, Wingate College, 1951; Frank C. Cowan,
Historical Sketch of the Spray Baptist Church (1954); H. I.
Hester, *The Wingate College Story* (1972); *Leaksville News*,
24 Aug. 1959; E. I. Olive, *Alumni Directory, Wake Forest
College* (1959); Raleigh *Biblical Recorder*, January 1953;
Raleigh *News and Observer*, 19 Aug. 1959.

C. SYLVESTER GREEN

Beal, Fred Erwin *(1896–15 Nov. 1954)*, union organizer
for the National Textile Workers' Union and leader of the
Gastonia strikes of 1929, introduced Communism to
North Carolina. He was born in Lawrence, Mass., a
textile town to which his parents moved when their farm
could no longer support them. There young Beal went to
work in a mill at age fourteen, changing bobbins on
spinning machines. Very early he became susceptible to
radical ideas. At a time when the labor movement was
beginning to blossom, Beal quickly joined those calling
for better working conditions, shorter hours, and higher
wages; when eighteen years old he participated in a
strike over a wage cut in the Pacific Mills in Lawrence. He
continued strike activities, changing jobs several times,
and came to associate with Socialist party union
members. Soon it appeared to him that the American
Communist party was more active than any other on the
workers' behalf; and in 1928 a strike in New Bedford,
Mass., which brought out some thirty thousand
workers, brought Beal into the party. His work in New
Bedford earned him a reputation as a good organizer.

The following year, Beal went south to Charlotte,
where he represented the Communist-run National
Textile Workers' Union. An extremely skilled organizer,
he was able to overcome the distrust many workers felt
toward the northerner. Taking advantage of the
extremely harsh working conditions and playing down
his Communist association, Beal soon organized a local
in Gastonia. This was one of the earliest unions at a
textile mill in North Carolina and was the first
Communist-backed one. Soon a cause developed around
which the union was able to take root. At the Loray mills,
where the small secret local was organized, five
employees were discovered to be party members and
were discharged. Beal was able to rally two hundred mill
workers to strike against this action. Through hard work,
he spread the activity to other mills in the area. Five
companies of North Carolina National Guard were called
out to control the disorder.

Finally, in an atmosphere of mounting pressure,
shooting broke out between strikers and Gastonia police,
and Chief O. F. Aderholt was killed. With

anti-Communist sentiment growing, Beal and six others were found guilty, in an emotion-charged courtroom, of conspiracy to murder. As strike leader, Beal received a sentence of sixteen to twenty years. While on bail he slipped out of the country to visit the Soviet Union. With dreams of "the workers' fatherland" in his mind, he was eager to see the grand Communist experiment before he began serving his sentence. Although Beal was disappointed in what he saw, after he came home he decided to give the Soviet Union another chance. Skipping bail, he went back for three years, working in several capacities, but became convinced that Soviet workers were worse off than their American counterparts. Not only were conditions bad, but he also missed freedoms he had known in the United States.

Back in the United States again, Beal wrote *Proletarian Journey* to expose the actual conditions of workers in the Soviet Union. Then, in 1938, he turned himself over to North Carolina authorities and began serving his sentence. After almost four years he was paroled because of both good behavior and popular sentiment that his trial had not been a fair one. Governor Melville Broughton authorized the parole on 9 Jan. 1942. Six years later, on 20 May 1948, Beal's American citizenship was restored, as he totally renounced Communism. He worked for a textile company in New York for a while, quietly pursuing union activities and lecturing in opposition to Communism. He died of a heart attack in Lawrence, Mass.

SEE: Fred E. Beal, "I was a Communist Martyr," *American Mercury* 42 (Sept. 1937), and *Proletarian Journey* (1937); *Greensboro Daily News*, and Raleigh *News and Observer*, scattered issues; *Life*, 7 June 1948; *New York Times*, 16 Nov. 1954.

                                                                                                    R. VETO

Beal, Helen Marjorie (*30 Mar. 1887–27 July 1965*), librarian, was born in Oneida, N.Y., the daughter of Joseph and Helen Clark Beal. She attended Syracuse University and was graduated from the Carnegie Institute Library School, Pittsburgh. She held positions in public libraries in New York City, Eau Claire and Madison, Wis., and Kenwood, N.Y., and was librarian of the Stout Institute, Menomonie, Wis., and assistant supervisor of school libraries and public library organizer for the State of New York before coming to North Carolina in 1930. She became secretary and director of the North Carolina Library Commission in 1930 and served in that capacity until her retirement on 30 June 1950. She died in Raleigh.

As executive officer for the state library commission, Miss Beal was instrumental in extending public library service to rural North Carolina. Under her jurisdiction, North Carolina had more bookmobiles than any other state and more counties with county-wide library service than any other southeastern state. When she came to North Carolina in 1930, only 38 percent of the population of the state had any access to a public library; when she retired in 1950, 95 percent of all North Carolinians had access to free public library service. Speaking to all kinds of groups around the state, Miss Beal was able to arouse interest in and enthusiasm for public library service. This popular support resulted in the first State Aid to Public Libraries Act, passed by the General Assembly and ratified on 8 Mar. 1941. For the first time, the state declared its policy "to promote the establishment and development of public library service throughout all sections of the State." One hundred thousand dollars

was provided in 1941–42 "for promoting, aiding and equalizing public library service."

Working with agricultural extension, Miss Beal helped to plan the Home Demonstration Reading Program, still in existence, and provided the annually revised reading lists for the clubs. In recognition of her contribution to rural cultural life, Miss Beal was named by the *Progressive Farmer* in 1943 as "the Woman of the Year in Service to Rural North Carolina because of her outstanding service to farm families of North Carolina in helping to provide every family of every county in the State with an opportunity to know good books." The announcement of the award in the January 1944 issue of the *Progressive Farmer* cited the increase in bookmobiles from three in 1930 to thirty-nine in 1944. By 1950, North Carolina had eighty-eight bookmobiles serving ninety of the one hundred counties. The choice of Miss Beal as "Woman of the Year" was lauded in several newspapers. In the 2 Jan. 1944 *News and Observer*, Nell Battle Lewis wrote, "No nicer person than Miss Beal lives in this State, and it rejoices me to see her more generally appreciated." A *Greensboro Daily News* editorial on 5 Jan. 1944 cited progress in library services and stated, "All this improvement is due in large part to Miss Beal's common sense, tact, energy, knowledge of her job and devotion to it."

Miss Beal was an active and contributing member of the North Carolina, Southeastern, and American Library associations. She twice served as chairman of the Library Extension Board of the American Library Association, as well as a member of its governing council. She was a charter member of the Tennessee Valley Library Council. She was president of the Southeastern Library Association from 1938 to 1940; served on the Advisory Committee for the Southeastern Library Survey, 1946–48; and edited the North Carolina Survey returns that were published in 1948 as "Libraries in North Carolina, a Survey, 1946–47." She was the author (with R. A. Felton) of *Library of the Open Road* (1929) and contributor to professional journals. Miss Beal was also a member of the North Carolina Literary and Historical Association, the North Carolina Conference for Social Service, the Daughters of the American Revolution, and Christ Episcopal Church, Raleigh.

SEE: North Carolina State Library (Raleigh), for MSS; *Progressive Farmer* and Raleigh *News and Observer*, scattered issues; *Public Laws of North Carolina*, Session 1941, chap. 93; *Who's Who in Library Service*, 1943–44.

                                                                                   ELAINE VON OESEN

Beard, John, Jr. (*1797–15 July 1876*), newspaper editor and politician, was born in Salisbury, the son of Lewis and Susan Dunn Beard. He was graduated from Yale University and was elected to the House of Commons from Salisbury in 1818 shortly after his graduation. An ardent Federalist, he represented Federalist views in declining to call for a constitutional convention in 1818. He served in the state senate in 1826–27 and 1833–34. Changing his political stand and becoming a follower of Jeffersonian principles, he was again elected to the state senate, over the popular Thomas G. Polk, in 1834.

While he was in the senate, the constitutional convention question again arose and he was appointed chairman of the committee to which the question was referred. Beard's report for a convention to change the outmoded 1776 state constitution was carried, and the convention was subsequently called.

In local affairs, Beard was no less active. He was

appointed in 1824 one of the commissioners to build a bridge across the South Yadkin River; he was elected secretary of the Rowan Agricultural Society in 1826 and was a member of the building committee for Saint Luke's Episcopal Church in 1827. He was elected county trustee in 1828.

In 1833, Beard purchased the *Western Carolinian* from Burton Craige. After three years of giving journalistic support to John C. Calhoun and later the Whig party and Senator Willie P. Mangum, he relinquished the paper to John W. Hampton in 1835. He was in this year unsuccessful in his attempt to purchase half interest in the Raleigh *Star*.

In the last issue of the *Carolinian*, Beard took leave of his readers by announcing his intention of removing to the Southwest. He first went to Missouri and then in 1838 moved to St. Augustine, Fla. Between 1838 and 1845 he held the offices of clerk of the U.S. Court and U.S. marshal.

After Florida became a state in 1845, he was elected registrar of public lands and moved to Tallahassee, the new state capital. His bid for Congress in 1850 was not successful because of his opposition to the admission of California as a "Free State." Following this attempt, he was elected comptroller of the state but resigned in 1854 to accept the agency of the Appalachicola Land Company.

A member of the Florida Secession Convention of 1861 he later did all in his power for the cause of the South. After the war he was appointed again to the comptroller's office.

In 1869, Beard was attacked by vertigo and gave up his position. He died in Tallahassee.

Beard first married Maria Kelley, who died in 1830. There were nine children of the marriage. In 1838 he married Maria William Anderson, daughter of George Anderson of St. Augustine, Fla.

SEE: James S. Brawley, *The Rowan Story* (1953); William S. Powell, *St. Luke's Episcopal Church* (1953); Jethro Rumple, *A History of Rowan County* (1881); Salisbury *Western Carolinian*, 25 May 1824, 17 Oct. 1826, 16 Jan. 1827, 27 May 1828, 12 Oct. 1830, 10 June 1833, 12 Aug. 1833, 28 Feb. 1835, 22 June 1838, 17 and 24 Aug. 1876; H. T. Shanks, *The Papers of Willie Pearson Mangum*, 5 vols. (1950–56).

JAMES S. BRAWLEY

Beard, Lewis (1754–11 Dec. 1820), county and state official, was born in Salisbury of German ancestry. His father, John Lewis Beard, was born in Germany but immigrated to Philadelphia as a young man. John Lewis Beard was naturalized in Salisbury in 1755 and, unlike most of his fellow countrymen in Rowan County, took an active and leading role in the affairs of his county and town. He was by trade a butcher, a tanner, an innkeeper, and a large land owner. During the Revolution he supplied the Continental Army with shoes. Lewis Beard's mother was Christine Snapp, daughter of Lawrence Snapp, a German immigrant who owned a plantation on the Yadkin River seven miles from Salisbury.

Lewis Beard added to the family possessions, subsequently acquiring thirteen lots in Salisbury and almost fifteen thousand acres in Rowan, Montgomery, and Burke counties, some of it in ore properties. He operated a large store on the town square and lived in his home on the present site of the post office. He had two large plantations on the Yadkin River and thirty slaves. In 1818 he secured from the legislature the right to erect a bridge over the stream on his own lands. He employed

Ithiel Town, noted builder and architect, to design the bridge, which cost $30,000; its pier can still be observed upstream from Interstate 85. This bridge, the first across the Yadkin, attracted wide attention and was used as a model for future bridges erected in North and South Carolina.

One of the county's wealthiest inhabitants, Beard gained the confidence of his countrymen and was frequently called to important trusts, which he "executed with zeal, integrity and ability." In 1786 he was appointed assessor of the town lands, and on 2 Aug. 1796 he was named public treasurer of the county, a position he held for life. In 1800, as treasurer, he let the contract for the building of a new brick courthouse on the square to replace the original wooden one. He was appointed high sheriff of Rowan and served from 1787 until 1791. He represented Salisbury in the House of Commons in 1791–92 and Rowan in the senate in 1793. In 1808 he was named a director of the Salisbury branch of the Bank of Cape Fear on the recommendation of his friend and neighbor, General John Steele.

Beard married Susan Dunn, daughter of John Dunn, in 1785; they were the parents of one son, John Beard, Jr., and two daughters. One daughter, Christine, married Charles Fisher; another, Mary, married Moses A. Locke.

Beard was buried in the family plot in the old Lutheran Cemetery in Salisbury. His widow died in 1840.

SEE: James S. Brawley, *The Rowan Story* (1953); Marriage Records of Rowan County (North Carolina State Archives, Raleigh); Rowan County Court Minutes, 1780–1800 (North Carolina State Archives, Raleigh); Jethro Rumple, *A History of Rowan County* (1881); Salisbury *North Carolina Mercury and Salisbury Advertiser*, 23 Jan. 1800; Salisbury *Western Carolinian*, 19 Dec. 1820, 4 Oct. 1825, 7 Aug. 1840; United States Census (1810); H. M. Wagstaff, ed., *The Papers of John Steele*, 2 vols. (1924).

JAMES S. BRAWLEY

Beasley, Frederic (1777–1 Nov. 1845), Episcopal clergyman and philosopher, was born near Edenton, the son of John Beasley and Elizabeth Blount Beasley. His mother was a sister of James Blount, owner of Mulberry Hill, and a member of the wealthy Blount family of Eastern Carolina; his aunt Mary "Polly" Blount married the Reverend Charles Pettigrew, first bishop-elect of the Protestant Episcopal Diocese of North Carolina. Beasley's older brother John became a physician and practiced in Edenton for many years; he also had a sister, Martha, and four other siblings.

After a local education, Beasley entered the College of New Jersey at Princeton, probably in the late fall of 1795. His correspondence with his uncle Pettigrew reveals him as an extremely serious young man, concerned about atheism and alcoholism. He rejected law as a career, saying that "L stood for lawyer and L for liar." Instead, after reading a formidable list of theological and philosophical books recommended by his uncle, he began to express a desire to attain "perfection in religion." Although he considered teaching classical languages at The University of North Carolina following his graduation in 1797, he remained at Princeton as a tutor for two years while pursuing studies in theology. At this time he began a lifelong friendship with John Henry Hobart, later a bishop of the Diocese of New York.

In 1800, Beasley became a lay reader at Christ Church, New Brunswick, N.J.; he was ordained deacon in 1801 and priest in 1802. He began his parish ministry at St. John's Church, Elizabeth, N.J., where he remained only a few months before being called to St. Peter's Church,

Albany. In 1809 he moved to Baltimore, Md., where he was associate rector of St. Paul's Church. His opening sermon was so well received that the vestry ordered it printed.

His interest in education continuing, however, he accepted the post of provost of the University of Pennsylvania at Philadelphia in 1813. For fifteen years he served both as administrator and as professor of moral philosophy. Although no longer a parish priest, he was active in the affairs of the Diocese of Pennsylvania, serving numerous terms on the standing committee, where he labored to raise the level of literary and theological attainment of candidates for holy orders. He was a close associate of Bishop William White, the dean of American bishops. In 1815, Beasley received the D.D. degree from Columbia College and also from the University of Pennsylvania.

Resigning in 1828, he traveled briefly to Kentucky and then became rector of St. Michael's Church, Trenton, N.J. He had never been strong, even as a college student; his health gradually declined, and he retired to Elizabeth in 1836. He died of "dropsy in the chest" and was buried at St. John's Church in Elizabeth.

Beasley was one of the four most prominent exponents of natural realism as taught and disseminated by the College of New Jersey at Princeton, ranking in company with John Witherspoon; Samuel Stanhope Smith, who had taught him; and Samuel Miller. The Princeton "school" opposed agnosticism, materialism, and idealism. It was dualistic: in its cosmology, it counterposed world and deity; in psychology, soul and body; in epistemology, subject and object. Beasley adhered strongly to this school, displaying a particular dualism; he attacked Hume and Berkeley in his most noted work, *A Search of Truth in the Science of the Human Mind* (1822); truth was not to be found by intuition, but by a slow process of trial and error. In his analysis of perception by the senses, he approached a modern psychological explanation of obsessions and *idées fixes* that long went unrecognized. Other published works included *A Sermon on Duelling* (1811); *American Dialogues of the Dead* (1815); *A Vindication of the Argument a priori in Proof of the Being and Attributes of God, from the Objections of Dr. Waterland* (1825); *A Vindication of the Fundamental Principles of Truth and Order in the Church of Christ, from the Allegations of the Rev. William E. Channing, D.D.* (1830); and *An Examination of No. 90 of the Tracts for the Times* (1842). He also wrote extensively for periodicals and at one point was involved in the Tractarian dispute.

He was married on 22 Aug. 1803 to Susan W. Dayton by whom he had one daughter. After her death, he married Mary [Maria] Williamson, by whom he had nine children, seven of whom lived to maturity. One son, Frederick W., became a clergyman, and a second entered law. His second wife survived him, dying on 2 July 1852.

SEE: *Annals of the American Pulpit*, vol. 5 (1859); *Appleton's Cyclopedia of American Biography*, vol. 1 (1887); *Correspondence of John Henry Hobart*, vol. 3 (1911–12); Joseph Hooper, *A History of Saint Peter's Church in the City of Albany* (1900); I. Woodbridge Riley, *American Philosophy: The Early Schools* (1907).

SARAH MCCULLOH LEMMON

Bechtler, Christopher (1782–ca. December 1842), metallurgist, goldsmith, jeweler, and coiner, was born in the Grand Duchy of Baden in Germany, probably to an insignificant family of the peasantry or middle class. Nothing is known of his education. It is likely that his father was a skilled artisan, for Bechtler became a

gunmaker and goldsmith of some repute in his neighborhood and passed the craft on to his son, Augustus.

These talented and successful craftsmen might have been forgotten long ago had they not decided to emigrate to the United States. Apparently leaving part of his family behind in Germany and bringing one or two sons and perhaps a nephew with him, the middle-aged Bechtler traveled to New York by way of Havre, landing in October 1829. Moving south immediately, he stopped briefly in Philadelphia to begin naturalization procedures and most likely arrived within a few months in Rutherford County, N.C., which would be his home for the remainder of his life. Bechtler shortly established himself in a shop in Rutherfordton as a jeweler and maker of clocks and watches. Although an alien legally unable to hold land, he made arrangements through a trustee to purchase a farm in mid-1830.

Bechtler did some gold mining on his farm, and it was the Carolina gold rush, then rapidly flowering, that brought him a new and noteworthy career. By 1830, much of Western and Piedmont North Carolina was caught up in the quest for gold, which increasingly became a medium of exchange in the absence of plentiful hard currency. Yet citizens wanted standard gold coinage, and some miners resorted to the arduous, dangerous trip to the U.S. Mint in Philadelphia to exchange their precious metal for specie. Other citizens, including a majority of the General Assembly, began a prolonged battle to persuade Congress to establish branch mints in the southern gold region. Meanwhile, Templeton Reid in Georgia began the private coinage of domestic gold on a limited scale, an undertaking perhaps not known to the Bechtlers.

By this time, production of gold in North Carolina, much of it mined near Rutherfordton, had reached an annual volume of $500,000. In 1831 local leaders convinced Bechtler, who already assayed gold, to begin coinage of the metal and create a sound regional currency. Bechtler had theretofore experimented with coining gold pieces valued at $2.50 and $5.00, and he set out to enlarge the business. Once his local reputation for integrity spread to other areas, he was eminently successful. During the first four years of his new endeavor, Bechtler minted $109,000 worth of gold. In the following single year, he produced nearly $700,000 in private coinage. Throughout the first nine years of his operation, Bechtler was to coin some $2,241,840 in gold and flux (melt) an additional $1,384,000 worth of bullion. Toward the end of the period, the federal government finally began operation of a branch mint in nearby Charlotte, but Bechtler continued his decreased, although still substantial, business.

Bechtler's minting venture succeeded because his coins, available in several varieties, filled a need for a circulating medium in Western North Carolina, as well as neighboring states, and because he maintained a personal reputation for honesty in transactions. He charged a 2½ percent fee for coinage of bullion and turned out gold pieces in several varieties but only three denominations. Besides the $2.50 and $5.00 gold coins, he produced in 1832 the first gold dollar minted in the nation, a coin not made by the federal mints for nearly two decades thereafter. Generally his products bore his name, their weight in gold, and their place of origin or manufacture stamped upon them. Bechtler himself designed and fabricated all of the hand-operated equipment with which he produced his coins.

Establishing his mint after an already successful career as a goldsmith and jeweler, Bechtler obviously continued his other interests An expert creator of various golden trinkets, he was also a clever gunsmith. In 1832, the Bechtlers had invented a device for accurately firing a rifle at the then rapid rate of eight rounds per minute. Christopher Bechtler evidenced his concern for religion when he became a charter member of the Rutherfordton Presbyterian Church in 1835.

Bechtler apparently died in or near Rutherfordton. His death signaled the incipient end of the mint that had supplied much of the circulating medium of the region and the nation's first gold dollar. After his demise, his son and assistant Augustus Bechtler briefly managed the mint, before Christopher Bechtler, Jr., a nephew, assumed responsibility for the enterprise. He was reportedly a man of questionable scruples. The insignificant remaining operations ceased within a few years, and Christopher, Jr., moved away. Nevertheless, Bechtler coins continued to circulate freely in the region for many years and have since become rare prizes for collectors.

Bechtler's will revealed that he had a wife and five children, but his wife and most of the offspring apparently never came to North Carolina. Bechtler's remains were removed from Rutherfordton to the North several decades after his demise.

SEE: Thomas Featherstonhaugh, "A Private Mint in North Carolina," Southern History Association *Publications* 10 (1906); Clarence Griffin, *The Bechtlers and Bechtler Coinage* (1929 [portrait]); Rutherford County Records (Rutherfordton), for court minutes, deeds, and estates records; Rutherfordton *North Carolina Spectator and Western Advertiser*, 1830–35.

RICHARD F. KNAPP

Beckwith, John (*31 July 1785–8 May 1870*), physician and surgeon, was born in Poughkeepsie, N.Y., the son of Elizabeth Dart and John Beckwith, a Revolutionary War veteran of New York. The younger Beckwith was admitted to the practice of medicine at New London, Conn. He went south for his health and while in North Carolina visited a friend at New Bern. There he attended a "large entertainment" and met Margaret Cogdell Stanly (26 May 1787–7 Jan. 1864), daughter of Ann Cogdell and John Wright Stanly. Tradition relates that Miss Stanly was ashamed of her party dress because of its cut, but Beckwith asked to be introduced to the young lady in the white silk dress with high neck and long lace sleeves. He fell in love with her, and they were married in New Bern, 3 Dec. 1807.

Beckwith served as a surgeon with New York forces during the War of 1812 and afterwards moved to North Carolina. The exact sequence of his moves within the state is not clear, and he apparently lived in several places more than once. He probably lived first in New Bern, then in Salisbury, and finally in Raleigh. He was also in Hillsborough and Fayetteville for some time. His skill in medicine and surgery, particularly in eye operations, was widely known and highly praised. One of the earliest cataract operations is reported to have been performed by him. A Rowan County farmer felt compelled to bring the surgeon's work to the attention of the public in a letter to the editor of the *Western Carolinian* in Salisbury in January 1822. Isaac Wiseman wrote that Dr. Beckwith performed an operation on his wife's right eye that did not give her more pain than bleeding, and in a week she could see well enough to walk. The same operation was performed on her left eye with equal success.

In March 1823, Beckwith operated successfully on a nineteen-year-old youth who had been blind from birth. After the operation the patient's eyes were able to distinguish minute objects and were reported to be "daily acquiring strength. The operation was performed with little pain and succeeded by no inflammation." The *Western Carolinian* concluded that the "success which has attended the various cases operated on by Dr. Beckwith, [is] we believe, unparalleled; and the spirit of kindness and benevolence he has manifested toward those who were laboring under the complicated evils of poverty and blindness, we trust, will bring upon him the blessings of those who were ready to perish." The *Raleigh Register* referred with pride to his operations for the relief of blindness, declaring that he had as few instances of failure as the more famed doctors in the North. In Salem, the Moravian journal for 1 June 1823 recorded: "Our Br. Kramsch went to Salisbury on the 19th of last month at the invitation of Dr. Beckwith, a well-known eye doctor there. He returned today after a successful operation on the eye on which no previous operation had been performed, and had the joy of again being able to see his family and friends."

Beckwith was the author of "A Memoir on the Natural Walls, or Solid Dykes in the State of North-Carolina, about which there have been debates, whether they were basaltic, or of some other formation," published in the *American Journal of Science and Arts* 5 (1822): 1–7. This natural formation in Rowan County, believed to have been of prehistoric construction, long attracted the attention of scientists.

Beckwith moved to Raleigh in 1823, where he remained until moving in January 1845 to Petersburg, Va.; there Mrs. Beckwith died. The Beckwiths were the parents of John Watrus, who became the Episcopal Bishop of Georgia; Thomas Stanly, who practiced medicine in Petersburg; James, who died when a student at the Salisbury Academy in 1821; Cornelia; Nancy; and Katherine. Thomas Stanly married Agnes, daughter of Edmund Ruffin of Virginia; their son, Charles Minnigerode (1851–1928), at one time an instructor at the University of the South, Sewanee, Tenn., was consecrated Bishop of Alabama in 1902.

After his wife's death, Beckwith moved to Riverdale (now in the Bronx), N.Y., to live with his daughter, Katherine (Mrs. Henry F. Spaulding), and it was there that he died.

SEE: James D. Beckwith (Raleigh), family records; G. S. Carraway, *The Stanly (Stanley) Family* (1969); Adelaide L. Fries, ed., *Records of the Moravians in North Carolina*, vol. 8 (1954); Susan Nye Hutchison, diary (Southern Historical Collection, University of North Carolina, Chapel Hill); Guion Johnson, *Ante-Bellum North Carolina* (1937); Salisbury *Western Carolinian*, 30 Oct. 1821, 22 Jan. 1822, 4 and 17 Feb. 1823, 8 Nov. 1834.

GERTRUDE S. CARRAWAY
JAMES S. BRAWLEY

Beckwith, John Watrus (*1 Feb. 1831–23 Nov. 1890*), Episcopal bishop, was born in Raleigh, the son of Margaret Stanly and John Beckwith. In 1852 he was graduated from Trinity College, Hartford, Conn., and a short while later was admitted a candidate for holy orders in North Carolina. Ordained to the diaconate by Bishop Thomas Atkinson in May 1854, he was assigned to Calvary Church, Wadesboro. A year later he was advanced to the priesthood and soon moved to Anne Arundell County, Md. After serving parishes in Mississippi and Alabama, he became a chaplain in the Confederate Army, serving for a time on the staff of

General Leonidas Polk, who had been bishop of Louisiana. By his eloquence, Beckwith is said to have exerted great influence over the soldiers who came in contact with him. In 1865 he became rector of Trinity Church, New Orleans, where he was serving when elected bishop of Georgia in 1868. He was consecrated on 2 Apr. at St. John's Church, Savannah, and later in the year both his alma mater and the University of Georgia conferred upon him the degree of Doctor of Sacred Theology. A conservative churchman, he was described as "one of the most eminent men the Protestant Episcopal Church in the South has produced." He was a modest man and is said to have declined to preach before Queen Victoria on one occasion and on another to have declined an invitation to preach in Westminster Abbey. He frequently visited his native state and often preached there, however.

He married Ella Brockinborough of Virginia, and they were the parents of John F., Ella, and Bessie. He was buried in Oakland Cemetery, Atlanta.

SEE: B. C. Beckwith, *John Bailey Beckwith, M.D.* (1893); Paul Beckwith, *The Beckwiths* (1891); *New York Times*, 24 Nov. 1890.

WILLIAM S. POWELL

Beddingfield, Eugene Crocker (10 Oct. 1862–19 Mar. 1926), farmer, legislator, and railroad commissioner, was born in Wake County to Alexander Hanson and Palmyra La Fayette Chappell Beddingfield. His mother's original ancestor in America was Thomas Chappell, who in 1635 settled near the site of Petersburg, Va. Several members of Palmyra Chappell's family were Revolutionary War soldiers; her grandfather Samuel Chappell joined the Continental Army before the Battle of Trenton in 1776, was wounded and captured during the course of the war, but served until Cornwallis's surrender at Yorktown. His son Edward, grandfather of E. C. Beddingfield, served as a soldier during the War of 1812.

Military service was not limited to the maternal line. Beddingfield's father, born in Wake County, enlisted as a Confederate soldier but died of pneumonia at Gordonsville, Va., on 17 Nov. 1863. Responsibility for the care of his thirteen-month-old son fell to his widow and her father, Edward Chappell, then seventy-five years old. Growing up on his grandfather's small farm, where life during the postbellum period was hard, young Beddingfield engaged in strenuous manual labor. He cut ditches, split rails, built fences, and performed other chores.

Eugene Beddingfield's educational opportunities were restricted. He attended a subscription school for a few months each year. At the age of fourteen he enrolled for one year in the Forestville Academy, whose principal was Dr. Richard H. Lewis II, an outstanding educator. Even this limited formal education necessitated sacrifices on his family's part, and Beddingfield was largely self-educated. His thirst for knowledge led him to fill his spare moments reading books, especially histories and biographies. A country doctor reported to his son, Hubert A. Royster, that the youth was often seen with a book resting on the plow handles. He borrowed books from friends, including Josephus Daniels. At about age seventeen, Beddingfield began teaching school a few months each year and spending the other months engaged in farming.

Religion, as well as education, was an important factor in his life. At age fifteen he united with the Midway Missionary Baptist Church. Always a faithful member, he moved with the church to Millbrook where his membership continued until his death. He also became a Mason and held all the elective positions in his lodge, Neuse Lodge No. 97, except that of treasurer.

On Thanksgiving Day, 24 Nov. 1881, Beddingfield married Nancy Peebles. The couple had eight children: Alexander Edward (1882–1943), Eugene Thomas (1884–1954), Charles Amos (1886–1938), Rebecca Jane (1887–1918), Leroy Chappell (1891–1969), Louise Wilson (1893–), Charles Lemuel (1895–1973), and an infant son who died at birth in 1889.

Interest in the welfare of the farming class led Beddingfield into politics. In 1888 he was nominated by the Democratic County Convention to the state house of representatives and subsequently elected. He served during the session of 1889.

In January 1890 he succeeded Leonidas L. Polk as secretary of the North Carolina State Farmers' Alliance. An energetic and aggressive Allianceman, he was an active campaigner in 1890 and later. He played a decisive role in pressing Alliance demands on candidates for public office, including Senator Zebulon B. Vance. A supporter of Vance, he insisted nevertheless that the senator demonstrate concern for the farmer. Beddingfield had no sympathy with the Bourbon element in the Democratic party and was strong in his advocacy of Alliance reforms, but he opposed the formation of the Populist party. He was especially interested in the Alliance proposal of legislation to create a railroad commission.

The legislature of 1891 created the Railroad Commission, and Beddingfield was elected one of the three commissioners for a term of six years. He resigned as secretary of the Alliance on 28 Mar. 1891, in order to take the new post. He was not reelected in 1897 by the Fusionist legislature. Nevertheless, when the Democrats regained control of the General Assembly in 1899 and replaced the Railroad Commission with the Corporation Commission, Beddingfield was chosen to the newly created commission. The Republican he displaced challenged the Beddingfield appointment, and the North Carolina Supreme Court in *Abbott* v. *Beddingfield* (125 N.C. Reports 256) decided for the plaintiff.

In 1900, Beddingfield was again elected a state representative from Wake County. He served on the Corporation Commission from April 1903 to January 1909. In a letter to the editor of the *News and Observer*, dated 9 Mar. 1908, he announced his intention of retiring from the commission when his term expired. Resuming his political career in 1918, he was elected to the state senate and served one term.

He also served on the Board of Commissioners of Wake County. He was appointed by Governor Angus W. McLean to the Board of Trustees of East Carolina Teacher's College in Greenville for a four-year term beginning in April 1925.

Beddingfield died at Rex Hospital in Raleigh; he was buried in the family cemetery in the Millbrook Community of Wake County with full Masonic honors.

SEE: *Annual Reports of the North Carolina Corporation Commission, 1903–1908; Annual Reports of the North Carolina Railroad Commission, 1891–1897;* Eugene C. Beddingfield Papers and Elias Carr Papers (East Carolina University Manuscript Collection, Greenville); *Charlotte Observer,* 20 and 21 Mar. 1926; Clinton *Caucasian,* 2 June 1892; Josephus Daniels, *Tar Heel Editor* (1939); Farmers' State Alliance Papers (North Carolina State Archives, Raleigh); *North Carolina House Journal,* 1889, 1901; *North Carolina Manual* (1919); *North Carolina Senate Journal,* 1919; *North Carolina Year Book* (1901); Raleigh *Biblical Recorder,*

14 Apr. 1926; Raleigh *News and Observer*, 29 July 1900, 3 Aug. 1900, 10 Mar. 1908; Raleigh *State Chronicle*, 1 Apr. 1891; Zebulon B. Vance Papers (Southern Historical Collection, University of North Carolina, Chapel Hill); Charles L. Van Noppen Papers (Manuscript Department, Library, Duke University, Durham), for a MS biography of Beddingfield.

LALA CARR STEELMAN

Beeman, Joseph Henry *(17 Nov. 1833–31 July 1909)*, Confederate officer and congressman, was born in Gates County. He moved with his parents to Morgan County, Ala., in 1847 and then to Mississippi in 1849. Brought up on a farm, he received an academic education and for a time worked as a teacher and merchant. During the Civil War he served as a lieutenant in the Confederate Army. He spent most of his life, however, as a farmer in Scott County, Miss.

When discontented farmers, trapped between rising production costs and falling cotton prices, formed a state Alliance to improve agricultural conditions, Beeman became a founding member. In 1888 he served on a committee that urged Alliancemen to boycott jute bagging, "to maintain the contest being waged against the bagging trust," and recommended the establishment of a cotton bagging factory in the state as soon as possible. He also chaired the state executive committee for a time.

Similar discontent with economic conditions had fueled earlier successful Independent, Greenbacker, and Fusion movements in Mississippi, and Beeman moved easily from his prominent position in the Alliance into state politics. He attended local and state Democratic conventions and in 1883 was chosen to represent Scott County in the state house of representatives, an office he held until 1891.

Beeman, who listed himself in the house directory as married, a Democrat, and a member of the Methodist church, served in 1884 and 1886 on the committees on Claims and Corporations. In 1888 he was appointed to the more prestigious committees on Agriculture and Ways and Means and chaired the Claims Committee.

By 1890, Beeman had risen to a position of power in the house. He chose his seat before the general drawing, an honor usually reserved for the floor leaders of the dominant faction, and nominated the successful candidate for speaker. He served on the Rules Committee as well as the Ways and Means and continued as chairman of the Claims Committee. The most controversial issue before the legislature was a bill to call a constitutional convention, a proposal strongly supported by the Alliance. Beeman twice led the fight to defeat a substitute bill that called instead for a referendum on the proposal, and then successfully sponsored an amendment to the original bill that established a more democratic system of representation in the convention.

In August 1890 the Fifth District Democratic convention nominated Beeman for Congress on the 320th ballot. He campaigned on a platform stressing Republican hostility to the South (exemplified in the Force Bill) and the harmful effects of Republican economic policies (especially the McKinley tariff) on "agriculturalists and consumers." His off-year election campaign, in which the Alliance sub-treasury plan was the most absorbing issue, attracted less attention than the constitutional convention then meeting in Jackson.

On 4 Nov. 1890, the day after the convention adjourned, Beeman and one other Alliance candidate won election to the House. On 4 Mar. 1891, Beeman took his seat in the Fifty-second Congress, where he served on the committees on Manufactures and Education. While in Congress he introduced petitions from farm organizations in Mississippi in support of pure food laws, extension of rural mail service, currency expansion, and suppression of speculation in farm products.

At the end of his term in 1893 he returned to his home in Ely and engaged in agricultural pursuits until his death in Lena in adjacent Leake County. He was buried in the Beeman family cemetery in Lena.

SEE: *Biog. Dir. Am. Cong.* (1971); Jackson (Miss.) *Clarion Ledger*, scattered issues; *Mississippi House of Representatives Journal*, 1884–90; Dunbar Rowland, ed., *Encyclopedia of Mississippi History*, vol. 1 (1907).

ELLEN BARRIER NEAL

Belk, Henry *(8 May 1898–20 Oct. 1972)*, newspaper editor and civic leader, was born in Monroe, the son of Robert Lee and Lula Rape Belk. Henry Belk was graduated from Monroe High School and received an A.B. degree from Trinity College in 1923. While in high school Belk was a reporter for the Monroe *Journal*. As a student at Trinity he was director of the college news bureau (1920–23) and was the first to publicize the term "Blue Devils" as the nickname of the college football team. After graduation he served for two years as director of the news bureau and instructor in journalism and English at Wake Forest College. In the academic year 1925–26 he lectured in journalism at New Rochelle College, New Rochelle, N.Y., while enrolled in the Columbia University School of Journalism.

In 1923, Belk married Lucile Marie Bullard of Durham. Their only child, Marie Belk Lipton, was fatally injured in an automobile accident on 28 Feb. 1950.

In 1926, Belk became editor and managing editor of the *Goldsboro News*. When the *News* merged with the *Daily Argus* in 1929 to form the *Goldsboro News-Argus*, he was managing editor, a position he held until 1955. He was editor from 1949 until his appointment as editor emeritus in August 1968. After retirement he continued to write a daily editorial column for the *News-Argus* and a weekly editorial for the *Greensboro Daily News*.

Congenital cataracts on both eyes had prevented Belk's entering school until he was nine. Operations undergone while he was in college helped vision in his left eye, but the right eye remained in poor condition. After diagnosis of a detached retina in his left eye in 1952, Belk underwent a series of operations. Brief success was followed by a heart attack and a second detached retina. By 1955 he was totally blind. With his wife's aid, he continued his editorial duties.

A Democrat, Belk wrote mildly worded editorials demanding greater responsiveness from local and state government. He candidly advocated mutual respect in matters of race and religion and actively supported civic responsibility. Many of his later columns were well-honed essays based on folk customs and personal reminiscences.

Widely respected by his fellow journalists, Belk was a member of the American Society of Newspaper Editors and of the Associated Press Managing Editors. He was president of the Eastern North Carolina Press Association (1944), the North Carolina Press Association (1950–51), the Associated Press News Council (1953), and the North Carolina Associated Press (1950–51). Many young reporters who worked under him at the

News-Argus advanced to rather prominent positions in journalism.

In 1960, Belk was appointed to the President's Committee for Employment of the Physically Handicapped. He served as trustee of East Carolina University from 1947 until his death and as chairman of the board in 1963–64. He was president of the North Carolina Literary and Historical Association (1963–64) and served on the North Carolina Citizens Committee for Better Schools, the executive committee of the Carolina Tercentenary Committee, and the North Carolina Study Commission for Vocational Rehabilitation. He was a member of the Aycock Memorial Commission, and in 1959, following the opening of the restored Charles B. Aycock birthplace in Wayne County, he presented a paper at the annual meeting of the Literary and Historical Association; in keeping with Aycock's program as governor (1901–5), the theme of the meeting was education, and Belk's paper, "A Ten Year Plan for North Carolina," pleaded for greater public support of the public schools and the development of community and evening colleges. Belk was active in local affairs, president of the Goldsboro Rotary, and an honorary life member of the Jaycees. He was a deacon in the Madison Avenue Baptist Church, an influential layman in the Baptist State Convention, and a director of the *Biblical Recorder*, official newspaper of the convention.

Belk was the recipient of the Goldsboro Rotary Club's Honorary Citizenship Award in 1957, an award that had been presented only twice in forty years. In 1961 he received the Handicapped Man of the Year Award from the Governor's Committee on Employment of the Handicapped. In 1966 a dormitory at East Carolina University was named for him. He was honored at a testimonial dinner in October 1968 at the Sir Walter Hotel in Raleigh.

Belk died in a Goldsboro rest home, following a year of failing health, and was buried in Willow Dale Cemetery, Goldsboro.

SEE: Henry Belk, "A Ten Year Plan for North Carolina," *North Carolina Historical Review* 37 (1960); North Carolina Collection (University of North Carolina, Chapel Hill), for newspaper clippings; William S. Powell, ed., *North Carolina Lives* (1962); *Who's Who in America*, 1970–71; *Who's Who in the South and Southwest*, 1967–68.

GEORGE W. TROXLER

Belk, William Henry (2 June 1862–21 Feb. 1952), merchant, was born in Lancaster County, S.C., of English and Scottish ancestry. His father was Abel Nelson Washington Belk, a farmer, who was drowned by Sherman's raiders in 1865 for refusing to divulge the whereabouts of his father's gold mine. His mother was Sarah Narcissus Walkup.

Belk received his first education at home from his mother, who had been educated at Carolina Female Academy in Ansonville. Later he attended the local one-room schoolhouse. In 1873 the family moved to Monroe, and Belk attended school there and in nearby Mecklenburg County. He could not afford to attend college.

At the age of fourteen, Belk went to work in a dry goods store at a salary of five dollars a month. After eleven years he had become head man in the store. The next year, when he was twenty-six years old, he decided to establish his own business. With $750 he had saved, $500 borrowed at 10 percent interest, and $3,000 worth of merchandise for which he traded, Belk opened a store in Monroe on 29 May 1888. He called his store the "New

York Racket," liking the name because it "sounded big." A little more than six months later, with the slogan "Belk Sells It for Less," he had paid off the money he had borrowed, covered his expenses, and made a clear profit of $3,100. Three years later he persuaded his brother, John Montgomery, a practicing physician, to give up his profession and join in the mercantile venture. They worked as a team from that time until the death of Dr. Belk in 1928.

Several of Belk's policies were unique at the time. Merchandise was clearly marked and was sold at the price marked; there was no haggling at the counter. If a customer bought an article, took it home, and found that it was not what he wanted, he could return it and get his money back. In addition to these innovations, he introduced another merchandising idea that was far more radical: he sold for cash only. Therefore, he had no accounts to record, no notes to accept, no mortgages on farm crops and animals to foreclose, and no customers distressed and angry because he had dispossessed them of their property. The business continued to grow, not spectacularly, but steadily. There was no work about the store that he did not do, and he demanded more of himself than of any of those who worked for him.

In 1882, Belk opened a second store, this time in Chester, S.C. A year later he opened another in Union, S.C. On 25 Sept. 1895, the Belks opened a store in Charlotte and called it Belk Brothers Company. As the years went on, new Belk stores began to appear throughout the Southeast. Belk watched constantly for promising young men who were honest, willing to work, and striving for a chance. By linking his name and his support to each business, he helped it to become successful in its home community. The training of so large a number of good solid businessmen in many communities was one of the great services Belk rendered. Today, there are some four hundred Belk and Belk-related stores in seventeen southeastern states and Puerto Rico.

One of Belk's finest innovative achievements was the development of a centralized buying service. Such a service enabled each store to have the benefit of the advice of purchasing specialists in every merchandising area. This technique has been extended to other aspects of retailing and now all Belk stores have direct access to specialists not only in merchandising, but also in personnel recruitment and management, accounting and auditing, real estate planning, construction and financing, architectural and interior planning and design, traffic management, labeling and packaging, printing and advertising, benefits and compensation, and legal matters and financial planning. Belk Stores Services, Inc., with offices in Charlotte and New York City, employs nearly a thousand such specialists and is the end result of one aspect of Belk's merchandising genius.

Belk was not socially active and certainly not politically oriented. Although he voted the Democratic ticket, he had serious doubts about New Deal legislation and looked with horror upon any political system resembling a welfare state. He was a member of the Scottish and York Rite Masons and the Order of the Mystic Shrine.

Belk was a devout member of the Presbyterian church. He was greatly interested in Presbyterian Junior College in Maxton, and he contributed heavily to its work. Other special interests included Presbyterian Hospital in Charlotte and the Presbyterian Orphans' Home at Barium Springs. He and his brother John established a hospital in Tai-Chow, China, known as the "Sarah Walkup Belk Memorial Hospital" in honor of their mother. Through the John M. Belk Memorial Fund, he assisted some 335 churches and manses in their building programs. Portions of the store profits and of his personal income were used for these and other philanthropic purposes.

On 9 June 1915, Belk married Mary Lenora Irwin, and to them were born six children: William Henry, Jr., Sarah, John Montgomery, Irwin, Henderson, and Thomas Milburn.

Belk died in Charlotte and was buried in Elmwood Cemetery there. Several fine portraits exist, which are displayed in Charlotte at the offices of Belk Stores Services, Inc.

SEE: LeGette Blythe, *William Henry Belk* (1950).

PAUL B. WYCHE, JR.

Bell, Henry Haywood (*13 Apr. 1808–11 Jan. 1868*), U.S. naval officer, was the son of Mary Haywood and Robert Bell and was probably born in Franklin County, where his parents lived. He was appointed midshipman in the U.S. Navy 4 Aug. 1823 and was promoted to lieutenant 3 Mar. 1831, commander 12 Aug. 1854, commodore 21 Aug. 1862, and rear admiral 25 July 1866.

Upon his appointment as a midshipman, he served aboard the *Grampus*, where in 1828–29 he aided in clearing the Cuban coast of pirates. He next served with the East Indian Squadron for a number of years and in 1856 commanded the flagship of the squadron, *San Jacinto*. Revenging an insult upon the American flag, he took a prominent part in the capture and destruction of the barrier forts near Canton, China. He was in command of one wing of a landing party from the fleet that stormed the first fort and held it until the following day, when the remainder of the fleet shelled the other forts into submission. When he returned to the United States, he had secured a reputation as a brave and high-spirited officer; he held the rank of captain and was on a quiet shore leave when the storm of Civil War burst upon the country.

At the outbreak of the Civil War, Bell was compelled to make the decision between devotion to his native state and loyalty to the flag under which he had served long and honorably. Many factors claimed his allegiance to the southern Confederacy. He was a native North Carolinian and had a large and influential family there, to whom he was most affectionately attached. His wife's family, of Virginia, contained several distinguished southern politicians and was connected with the secession leadership in that state. However, Bell's strong and disciplined sense of duty, forever in turmoil with other considerations, overpowered the devotion he felt for his native state. His friend Edward A. Pollard wrote that an attempted conversation on the subject was cut short by Bell's emphatic and decisive declaration, "I have made up my mind; I shall stand by the flag."

At the beginning of the Civil War he was appointed fleet captain of the West Gulf Squadron under Admiral D. G. Farragut. His first important assignment of the war was given at New Orleans: upon its capture, Farragut chose Bell to confront the riotous mobs in the city and raise the American flag above the Custom House.

After the events in New Orleans, Bell took part in the operations on the Mississippi River, including the siege of Vicksburg. In 1863 he was, for a time, in command of the West Gulf Squadron, Admiral Farragut having been relieved and Admiral Porter having command of the western waters above New Orleans. Bell's blockading fleet stretched from Mobile to Galveston. In 1865, his health failing, he was placed in command of the

Brooklyn Navy Yard. He was ordered to command the East India Squadron later that year and was active in subduing pirates infesting the China seas. On 25 July 1866 he was appointed rear admiral. In 1867, at his own request, he was placed on the retirement list. While awaiting his relief, he was drowned when his barge, the U.S. steamer *Hartford*, capsized on a bar as he was attempting to enter the Yodo River. He was buried at Hiogo, Japan, with American and British squadrons taking part in the funeral ceremonies.

Before the Civil War, Bell was an unwavering Democrat, and his sympathies were in entire opposition to the anti-slavery party. Records reveal that he was an active member in the Shanghai Episcopal Church of Our Savior in Japan. Letters from Bell to a son remain; however, the son's name is not mentioned, nor is any other person except for Mrs. Bell. The son was born 22 Apr. 1855. Bell's widow died in 1886.

SEE: *Appleton's Cyclopedia of American Biography*, vol. 1 (1887); *DAB*, vol. 1 (1928); *Nat. Cyc. Am. Biog.*, vol. 2 (1892); *New York Times*, 19 Feb. 1868, 5 May 1868; E. A. Pollard, ed., "The Story of a Hero," *Galaxy*, November 1868; *Who Was Who in America, 1607–1896*.

KEVIN OWEN EASLEY

Bell, Jesse Spencer (*1 Apr. 1906–19 Mar. 1967*), federal judge and state legislator, was a native of Charlotte, the son of James Ardrey and Jessie Mabel Spencer Bell. Having attended Charlotte public schools, he entered Duke University and received his A.B. degree in 1927. He then began studies at Duke Law School but switched to The University of North Carolina. After study at Harvard Law School during 1929, he was admitted to the bar that same year. He returned to The University of North Carolina, receiving his LL.B. in 1930.

Bell initially practiced law with his father, with state Senator H. N. Pharr, and with the latter's son, Neal Y. His career was interrupted by World War II; drafted in 1941, he served until 1946, when he was discharged with the rank of major. In 1943, Bell married Katherine Castellet. After the war he returned to Charlotte, where he later formed the firm of Bell, Bradley, Gebhardt and Delaney.

Bell served as president of the Mecklenburg Bar Association (1952–53) and of the North Carolina Bar Association (1953–54). In 1955 he was appointed chairman of the bar association committee on reorganization of the state courts. The committee recommended the establishment of a uniform system of district courts under the state supreme court; most of its suggestions were enacted in the early 1960s.

Locally, Bell was active in the Social Planning Council of the Charlotte-Mecklenburg United Community Services. He served as the first chairman of the city-county planning commission, strongly advocating perimeter zoning to control suburban growth. In 1957 he was appointed to the state senate, to which he successfully won reelection twice, serving until 1961. Here he followed his father: James Ardrey had served two terms as state senator from Mecklenburg. Both his appointment and his reelection in 1958 split the Democratic party in the county. In Raleigh, Bell pushed for legislation enabling cities to participate in federal urban renewal programs and for reapportionment of the General Assembly.

In 1961, President Kennedy appointed Bell to the U.S. Fourth Circuit Court of Appeals. In 1965, Bell participated in the decision requiring reapportionment of the state's legislature and its congressional districts.

When he died, he had just been named by Chief Justice Earl Warren to head a study committee of federal judges to prepare guidelines for courts, judges, and lawyers on the question of free press versus fair trial.

The *Charlotte News* named Bell the "Man of the Year" for 1955. In 1960, Catawba College bestowed on him an honorary LL.D. The North Carolina Bar Association presented him its John J. Parker Award for Conspicuous Service to Jurisprudence. He died of a massive heart attack just short of his sixty-first birthday and was buried at Elmwood Cemetery in Charlotte.

SEE: *Chapel Hill Weekly*, 29 Mar. 1967; *Charlotte Observer*, 20 Mar. 1967; *North Carolina Manual* (1961); Raleigh *News and Observer*, 2 Mar. 1958, 20 and 21 Mar. 1967; *Who's Who in America*, 1964–65.

WILLIAM T. MOYE

Bell, Lemuel Nelson (30 July 1894–2 Aug. 1973), doctor and Presbyterian layman, the youngest child of James H. and Ruth McCue Bell, both of Scotch-Irish descent, was born in the house of the superintendent of the Longdale Mining Company above Clifton Forge, Va. His father, then director of the mine's commissary, shortly thereafter moved with his family to the town of Waynesboro, Va., where Nelson attended public schools and was graduated in 1911.

For one year, 1911–12, he studied at Washington and Lee University in Lexington, first in the prelaw program and then, after deciding to be a foreign missionary, in the premedical program. From 1912 until he became a doctor of medicine in 1916, he studied at the Medical College of Virginia in Richmond (in 1913, as a member of the school's Medical Corps, he marched in the first inaugural parade of his distant cousin Woodrow Wilson). In 1915, after a successful minor league baseball summer career, he rejected an offer to become a professional pitcher for the Baltimore team of the Federal Baseball League in order to continue his studies.

Upon graduation, Bell served a brief internship at the Summerlee Coal Mines of the New River Company in West Virginia, and late in 1916 he and his bride of six months arrived in Tsingkiangpu, China, where at the age of twenty-two he became a surgeon at the largest Presbyterian hospital in China. He remained there, except for furloughs and one forced evacuation during disturbances in 1927–28, until the threat of war between the United States and the occupying Japanese forced him to bring his family home in 1941. During one furlough, in 1922, he studied on a Rockefeller Foundation Grant at the Mayo Clinic, the New York Post Graduate Hospital, and Massachusetts General Hospital.

In 1941, Bell settled in Montreat; from then until 1956 he practiced medicine in nearby Swannanoa and was surgeon on the staffs of all the hospitals in Asheville. He was a member of the American Medical Association and the North Carolina Medical Society and was a fellow of the American College of Surgeons.

In 1942, in response to what he considered the alarming growth of liberal theology in his church, Bell, though himself without formal theological training and without formal journalistic credentials, founded the *Southern Presbyterian Journal* to promote a return to evangelical, Bible-centered, Reform theology. From a monthly in 1942, the journal grew to be a semimonthly in 1945 and a weekly in 1950. In 1959, when its second editor was selected, its name was changed to the *Presbyterian Journal*. Bell, never the journal's editor but from the beginning its publisher, feature writer, and guiding light, left it in 1971 when its board officially supported a move to form a new, more conservative church, one that would withdraw from his church, the Presbyterian Church in the United States (Southern).

In 1948, Bell was elected to his church's Board of World Missions on which he served for seventeen years. In 1950 he led the opposition to the proposed merger of his church with the United Presbyterian Church in the United States (Northern). The Northern church, he argued, was no longer true to the Bible, and to join with it would be to sell out to liberalism. He made speeches and wrote articles branding the merger a potential tragedy for the Southern church, which was one-third the size of the Northern church and could not hold its own in theological debate. His cause prevailed, and the proposal was dropped.

In 1956, after his second severe heart attack in five years, Bell retired from active medical practice. The same year, with the aid of his son-in-law, the Reverend Billy Graham, and the president of the Sun Oil Company, J. Howard Pew, he founded another journal, *Christianity Today*, to offset on the interdenominational Protestant level the theological liberalism he had fought within his own church in the *Southern Presbyterian Journal*. He served as the new journal's unnamed publisher and as its first executive, and in later years he also wrote its most popular feature article, "The Layman and His Faith." *Christianity Today* proved a solid financial success. It surpassed in subscriptions after only six years the long-time voice of liberal Protestant thought, the influential *Christian Century*, the very journal Bell and Graham had hoped *Christianity Today* would counteract.

Despite a third and then a fourth heart attack during the 1960s, Bell continued to play an active part in his church's life, and in 1972 he was elected moderator of the 112th annual General Assembly of the Presbyterian Church in the United States. Though chosen as a man with conservative ties who yet favored denominational unity, it was under his administration that the dissident members of the church finally broke away to found the new National Presbyterian Church. Successful in preventing union with the Northern church, he was unable to avoid the split in the Southern church, a split he opposed but one that, ironically, grew in part from his own earlier opposition to liberal thought.

Bell died shortly after the end of his term as moderator and was buried in the cemetery of the Swannanoa Presbyterian Church in Swannanoa.

Bell's marriage, on 30 June 1916, to Virginia Myers Leftwich of Waynesboro, Va., produced five children: Rosa (Mrs. C. Donald Montgomery) of Los Alamos, N.M., born in 1918; Ruth (Mrs. Billy Graham) of Montreat, born in 1920; Lemuel Nelson, Jr., who was born and died in 1925; Virginia (Mrs. John N. Somerville), a missionary in Korea, born in 1927; and the Reverend Benjamin Clayton, a Presbyterian minister in Dallas, Tex., born in 1932.

In addition to his medical practice, his journalistic endeavors, and his church work, which included twice moderating the Asheville Presbytery and sitting as trustee for two of the denomination's colleges, Bell was a member of the board of directors of the Billy Graham Evangelistic Association, the Blue Ridge Broadcasting Corporation, the Christian Broadcasting Association of Honolulu, and the Mountain Retreat Development Corporation of Montreat. As a conservative who opposed liberal theology, social and racial legislation, and philosophical "humanism," though himself a man most liberal with his time and energy in service to all men, Bell was given seven awards by the Freedom Foundation of Valley Forge, Pa., including in 1957 the prize for best editorial of the year, "What of Tomorrow?" which first appeared in the *Southern Presbyterian Journal*.

SEE: Lemuel Nelson Bell, *Convictions to Live By* (1966), *While Men Slept* (1970), and editorials in *Christianity Today* (1956–73) and *Presbyterian Journal* (1942–71); John C. Pollock with Lemuel Nelson Bell, *A Foreign Devil in China* (1971); *Who's Who in America*, 1972–73.

JAMES THOMAS BAKER

Bell, Martha McFarlane McGee (*1735–9 Sept. 1820*), one of the heroines of the American Revolution, was born in Orange County. No positive record of her parents' names has been located, but her maiden name indicates that she was of Scotch-Irish ancestry. From her childhood she possessed a strong mind and will and manifested devotion to the country of her birth.

In the year 1759 she married Colonel John McGee, a widower with two children, Samuel and Elizabeth. McGee was a commissioned officer in the British army who had come to North Carolina with his parents as a permanent settler. In 1753 he had been granted a large tract of land in Orange County, and there he established a gristmill and ordinary at the headwaters of Sandy Creek along the trading path from settlements farther west to markets in Virginia. He soon became a large landowner. He was the originator of the "Presbyterian Society" located at the "Head of Sandy Creek," which was one of the earliest religious meetings of the area.

Five children were born to John and Martha McGee: John; Andrew; William, who married Anna King; Jane or Jean, who married John Welborn; and Susannah, who married Elisha Mendenhall.

The McGee Ordinary, homeplace, mill, and trading post was an exchange center for colonial news covering a large area. McGee's commission no doubt made him disliked by the "Regulators" who lived in this community, but from all accounts he remained as neutral as possible.

His untimely death in 1773 left Martha the richest widow in that frontier region. She was sought after by many widowers and bachelors; she was accustomed to a hardy life, however, and carried on by herself the business she had inherited. On 6 May 1779 she married William Bell, an ardent patriot who shared her own zeal for the cause of freedom from Great Britain. He operated a gristmill in the Deep River community, which became a part of the new Randolph County formed the same year. Bell was elected the first sheriff of the county 13 Dec. 1779 and later became clerk of court. His mill was a gathering place for Whigs.

Mattie Bell traveled many miles day and night, serving as nurse and midwife to people in the surrounding countryside. Her name became revered in every household for her assistance in time of need.

Her greatest fame is based on General Cornwallis's visit to Bell's Mill after the Battle of Guilford Court House on 15 Mar. 1781. Cornwallis moved southward to the mill in order to rest, regroup, and care for the wounded. He also needed provisions and wished to use the mill for grinding corn meal to feed the troops. Family annals state that she regarded Cornwallis as a perfect gentleman even though he was an unwanted guest. She extracted a promise from him that he would do no harm to the home or mill in exchange for her hospitality. Legends persist about the events of the two or three days Cornwallis stayed at the mill. Martha Bell's diary, which is quoted by the family, has disappeared from sight, but there can be no doubt of the courage and spirit she showed as she endured the presence of enemy troops in her own home.

As soon as Cornwallis left Bell's Mill, General Harry Lee arrived. Mattie Bell served as his guide to the next campground of the British general, and her knowledge of the countryside enabled Lee to stage a successful counterattack with his small cavalry force. Her services as a nurse kept her in touch with events, and she was often able to penetrate enemy lines and report on troop movements.

Before the cessation of hostilities she rode horseback with Mrs. Mary Dougan to Wilmington, N.C., in an unsuccessful attempt to see her son, Colonel Thomas Dougan, who was a prisoner aboard a British ship in the harbor.

Because the Bells were such active Whigs, Colonel David Fanning, leader of the Loyalist troops in the area, made many attempts to catch William Bell at home. This constant danger forced Bell to hide out or stay with patriot forces for months at a time. While he was away, Martha assumed responsibility for the home, children, mill, and farm. On one day in 1781 Fanning came to the mill intent on killing the Bells, but the family's display of strength caused the attacking party to leave without killing anyone or burning the house.

Martha Bell was instrumental in founding Old Union Methodist Church, where some of the first camp meetings in North Carolina were held. Two of her sons were ministers (John a Methodist and William a Presbyterian), and her other descendants have included educators, attorneys, and legislators.

Martha Bell died a year before her husband, whose death occurred on 22 Oct. 1821. They were buried in the Bell-Welborn graveyard near New Market School in Randolph County. A marker at the site of the Battle of Guilford Courthouse, placed there by the Alexander Martin Chapter of the DAR in 1929, honors her memory. The tribute reads, "Loyal Whig, Enthusiastic Patriot, Revolutionary Heroine."

SEE: Bell family papers and reminiscences (Randolph Public Library, Asheboro); E. W. Caruthers, *Revolutionary Incidents* (1854); J. Bryan Grimes, ed., *Abstract of North Carolina Wills* (1910); Mary Lazenby, *Herman Husband* (1940); *North Carolina Booklet*, vol. 16 (1916–17); Randolph Public Library (Asheboro), for clippings; William L. Saunders and Walter Clark, eds., *Colonial and State Records of North Carolina*, 30 vols. (1886–1914).

JOSEPH R. SUGGS

Bell, William (*28 Oct. 1783–17 Sept. 1867*), architect and builder of the U.S. Arsenal at Fayetteville, was born in Aberdour, Fifeshire, Scotland. The names of his parents and details of his early life are unknown; but he married Margaret Robinson, became the father of six children, and settled in Edinburgh to practice his profession. In about 1834, influenced by enthusiastic letters from friends who had moved to the United States, he decided to emigrate. He lived for a short time in Yonkers, N.Y., before moving to Washington, D.C., and becoming a member of a firm whose business was the construction of government buildings. In 1835 he was sent to Charleston, S.C., as assistant to Frederick Wesner, the architect for a U.S. Arsenal being built there.

A year later the federal government authorized the construction of another arsenal in Fayetteville, choosing that site because of its central location between Harper's Ferry and Savannah and because of its reputation as an inland port. Bell was commissioned to plan and supervise its construction and began the work in 1838. This arsenal, which played a prominent part in military history during the Civil War, has been described as "the

19th century counterpart of the modern Fort Bragg." The complex of buildings covered nearly 40 acres of a 104-acre tract and was the largest arsenal south of Washington. Intended as a major storage center for muskets in the southern states, it had already received twenty-five thousand muskets by 1840, although the majority of the buildings were far from completion. Planned also as a site for the manufacture of artillery carriage and the repair of arms, the arsenal was considered one of the most important military installations in the country by 1841.

Because of the outbreak of the Civil War, the arsenal was never really completed. On 22 Apr. 1861 it was seized by the State of North Carolina, and on 5 June it was turned over to the Confederacy. This was a highly important event of the war, since the South had no other supply of arms or machinery for manufacturing munitions.

Bell, who was sixty-eight at that time, stayed on as superintendent of the property; and he lived to see it, the most important work of his life, totally destroyed by General Sherman in March 1865. The shock was extreme, and he never recovered from it. He died a year and a half later and was buried in Old Cross Creek Cemetery, Fayetteville.

SEE: W. K. Boyd, *The Story of Durham* (1925); *Fayetteville Observer*, 12 July 1964, 8 Feb. 1970, 21 Oct. 1972, 23 Aug. 1974.

                                                                                                    MENA F. WEBB

Bellamy, John Dillard *(24 Mar. 1853–25 Sept. 1942)*, congressman, legislator, attorney, and manufacturer, was born in Wilmington, the son of Dr. John Dillard Bellamy and Eliza McIlhenny Harriss. He was educated under George W. Jewett at the Cape Fear Military Academy and was graduated from Davidson College in 1873. After receiving a degree in law from the University of Virginia in 1875, he began the practice of law in Wilmington, where he soon became the city attorney. He served in the North Carolina Senate in 1891–92 and in Congress from 1899 to 1903. He was counsel for the Atlantic Coast Line Railroad and afterwards for the Seaboard Air Line Railway. He established and was the principal owner of the Wilmington Street Railway for a number of years, until it was electrified. He was president of the North Carolina Terminal Company; president and owner with his son-in-law, J. Walter Williamson, of the Bellwill Cotton Mills; largest stockholder of the Delgado Cotton Mills; and the largest local owner of the capital stock of the Carolina Insurance Company.

An active Democrat, Bellamy was a delegate to the national conventions of 1892, 1908, and 1920. He was a delegate to the Washington Disarmament Conference in 1924 and in 1932 was the commissioner from North Carolina to celebrate the 200th anniversary of the birth of George Washington. In 1936 he was selected to cast the electoral vote of North Carolina for Franklin D. Roosevelt.

Bellamy was grand master of the State of North Carolina of the Independent Order of Odd Fellows in 1892 and representative to the sovereign grand lodge of that order for the two following years. He was the author of *Address on the Life and Services of General Alexander Lillington* (Washington, 1905), *Sketches of the Bar of the Lower Cape Fear* (Raleigh, 1925), *Memoirs of an Octogenarian* (Charlotte, 1942), and *Sketch of Maj. Gen. Robert Howe of the American Revolution* (Wilmington, 1882).

Bellamy was a Presbyterian. He married Emma Mary

Hargrove, daughter of Colonel John and Mary Grist Hargrove, in 1876. Their children were Mrs. James Walter Williamson, William McKoy, Emmett Hargrove, Mrs. J. Leeds Barroll, Jr., and Mrs. Nelson McRae.

Bellamy was buried in Oakdale Cemetery, Wilmington.

SEE: *Bio. Dir. Am. Cong.* (1961); *Cyclopedia of Eminent and Representative Men of the Carolinas in the Nineteenth Century* (1892); *History of North Carolina*, vol. 4 (1956); North Carolina Bar Association, *Proceedings* 27 (1925); 45 (1943); *North Carolina Biography*, vol. 4 (1919); Leonard Wilson, *Makers of America*, vol. 2 (1916).

                                                                                            WILLIAM S. POWELL

Bellamy, William *(24 Oct. 1770–5 Oct. 1846)*, pioneer Methodist minister of Edgecombe and Nash counties, was a leader in the founding of the Methodist Protestant church in Eastern Carolina. He was the son of William Bellamy, a man of considerable wealth in Edgecombe County, and his wife, Mary Clinch.

Bellamy was admitted into the Virginia Conference of the Methodist Episcopal Church in 1791 and was appointed to serve the Bladen Circuit in North Carolina. As "a rising young man of more than ordinary ability," he also served the Guilford, Contentney, Hanover (Va.), Roanoke, and Tar River circuits during the 1790s. He was made a deacon in 1793 and an elder in 1795. As president protem of the Roanoke District Conference of local ministers, Bellamy sent an "Address to the Bishops and Virginia Annual Conference of the Methodist Episcopal Church" on 7 Dec. 1821, in which he expressed opposition to the stand taken by the general conference in 1820 enacting special rule for the governing of local preachers without their consent.

On 6 Nov. 1824, Bellamy joined the Roanoke Union Society as a protest against the authority assumed by the leaders of the Methodist Episcopal church; he was at that time appointed to serve on the corresponding committee. At a meeting held on 30 April 1825, he was appointed to serve on an editorial committee authorized "to publish such pieces for this society as . . . will tend to promote a reformation in the Methodist Episcopal Church, or promulgate the wishes and views of this society for that purpose." On 14 Aug. 1828, Superintendent William Compton, who was newly appointed to the Roanoke Circuit and noted for his persecution of the "reformers" in the adjoining Granville Circuit, wrote to Bellamy, telling him to withdraw from the Roanoke Union Society and to cease to patronize the *Mutual Rights* (a reform paper published in Baltimore), or to prepare for trial. On 30 Aug., Bellamy and six other local ministers were summoned to appear before Compton; when they were not present on the designated date, they were suspended from the exercise of the duties of the ministry. On 25 Oct. 1828, Bellamy was brought to trial. Despite a firm and resolute defense, "the Rev. William Bellamy, one of the first itinerant preachers who had traveled in Carolina, who had served as yoke-fellow with Bishop (Enoch) George in those early days of Methodism, was found guilty—expelled [from] the church—the seal of official silence set upon his lips."

Bellamy was present on 19–20 Dec. 1828 at the organizational meeting of the North Carolina Annual Conference of the Methodist Protestant Church at Whitaker's Chapel, near Enfield in Halifax County. During the years following the establishment of this new branch of Methodism, Bellamy continued to serve as a minister on the Roanoke Circuit, which became one of the first circuits affiliated with the reform group. He collected material to write a history of Methodist reform in the "Old Roanoke District," but he died before the work was completed. He attended the General Conference of the Methodist Protestant Church in Cincinnati in May 1846.

Bellamy was named as a trustee of the Methodist church at Vaughan's Branch in Edgecombe County and was also a trustee of Battles' Meeting House at Battleboro. In 1842 he participated in a Fourth of July celebration held at Falls Church in Rocky Mount.

Bellamy's home, Oak Forest, in Nash County, near Battleboro, was built in 1826. In 1840 he owned thirty-four slaves. He was married to Mary Crowell of Halifax County (30 Mar. 1772–22 Sept. 1836). He "lived to a ripe old age, and died honored and respected by all who knew him." He was buried in the family cemetery at Oak Forest.

SEE: W. L. Grissom, *History of Methodists in North Carolina*, vol. 1 (1905); *Minutes of the Methodist Conferences* (1813); John Paris, *History of the Methodist Protestant Church* (1849).

RALPH HARDEE RIVES

Belo, Alfred Horatio (27 May 1839–19 Apr. 1901), journalist, was born in Salem of Moravian ancestry. His father was Edward Frederick Belo, a cabinetmaker, merchant, and would-be railroad builder. His mother, Caroline Amanda Fries, was also of Moravian descent. Brought up in comfort and plenty, Belo was educated at Salem Boys' School, the Masonic Institute at Germanton, and Wilson's Academy in Alamance County. Under his father's discipline, he worked diligently, during vacations and after school, in his father's store, at the mill, or on the farm. By 1860 his father sent him to New York and other large cities with a free hand to purchase merchandise for the general store.

Though against secession, Belo sided with the South and helped form a company in 1861. Commissioned a captain in the Forsyth Riflemen, he served in Virginia, then as adjutant of the camp of military instruction near Raleigh, and later in many campaigns in Virginia. He was with Longstreet in the attack on Suffolk, where he became involved in a well-known and violent dispute involving Colonel J. K. Connally, Colonel L. R. Terrell, and Captain John Cussons, over the questionable behavior of the Fifty-fifth North Carolina Regiment in protecting Stribling's Battery. In the first round of the duel, Cussons received a hole in his hat; in the second, Belo's neck was grazed, though he was ready for a third round when the dispute was settled by agreement among the officers involved. During extensive service in the Virginia campaigns, he received severe wounds at Gettysburg and Cold Harbor. His valor was honored for the rest of his life.

Immediately after the Civil War, either because of his health or in order to join General Kirby Smith, Belo set out on horseback for Texas. He served for a brief time as tutor to the children of a planter near Houston. In August 1865, in answer to an advertisement for a bookkeeper, he joined the *Galveston News*. The *News* was then controlled and edited by Willard Richardson, a transplanted South Carolinian and an extravagant admirer of John C. Calhoun. Belo was admitted to partnership in the company on 4 Mar. 1866. After Richardson's death in 1875, Belo purchased the paper, apparently with money from his wife's family. He established A. H. Belo and Company, installed improved machinery, and proceeded to make the *Galveston News*

into a strong paper with nearly state-wide circulation.

As the North Texas area grew, Belo found he was unable to get adequate railroad connections and postal facilities to all parts of Texas from his extreme eastern location. In 1885 he chose Dallas as a central and suitable location for better distribution of a newspaper, moved there, and undertook a new paper. His *Dallas Morning News* soon outgrew the *Galveston News*. For a time both papers were issued simultaneously every day in the year. Belo and his associates established special service to Ft. Worth, insuring connections with the west, southwest, and south of Texas. He also published weekly and semiweekly editions of both papers. In the first edition of the *Dallas Morning News*, 1 Oct. 1885, Belo laid down his editorial policy as commitment to "reform and progress but also to uncompromising conservatism in the fundamental point of law and order as absolutely indispensable to liberty and security." The new paper was greeted by the *Houston Age* as sure to be frequently on the wrong side of public policy and sure also to be "a splendid illustration of live, enterprising, talented, pushing, ambitious Southern journalism." This was something of a true prophecy: the *Dallas Morning News* became and remained a strong voice for conservative institutions, with a wide circulation and substantial influence on the political life of the state.

On 30 June 1868, Belo married Jeannette Ennis, the daughter of Cornelius Ennis, a wealthy merchant, cotton buyer, and railroad builder who came to Texas from New Jersey in 1839. They had two children, A. H., Jr., who died in 1906, and Jeannette, who married Charles Peabody. Belo never discarded his affection for his native state; he died there, in Asheville, and was buried in the Moravian Cemetery in Salem (his wife's religious affiliation prevented the choice of the Moravian Graveyard, which he would have preferred). Though always a Moravian at heart, Belo became an Episcopalian. He was nominally a Democrat, for local reasons, but in reality he preferred the Republican party, perhaps because of his Whig background. He professed to be a close friend of President Cleveland.

SEE: Sam Acheson, *35,000 Days in Texas* (1938); Samuel A. Ashe, ed., *Biographical History of North Carolina*, vol. 5 (1906); John Henry Brown, *Indian Wars and Pioneers of Texas* (n.d.); *Dallas Morning News*, 1 and 8 Oct. 1885, 20 Apr. 1901, 1 Oct. 1935; Douglas S. Freeman, *Lee's Lieutenants*, vol. 2 (1943); *Winston-Salem Journal-Sentinel*, 15 and 22 Dec. 1935; Winston *Union Republican*, 4 Oct. 1883, 13 Aug. 1896, 25 Apr. 1901.

NANNIE M. TILLEY

Belo, Frederick Edward (27 June 1811–2 Oct. 1883), an entrepreneur best known for his construction of the Belo House in Winston-Salem, was born in Salem. Edward was the second child of John Frederick and Maria Strupe Belo [Bölow].

Belo received his primary education in Salem at the Moravian Boys' School, entering in 1817. He then received training in cabinetmaking with a local joiner named Petersen. In 1827, Belo went to Bethlehem, Pa., for further training with a friend of the family. By 1832, he had settled in Philadelphia, but he soon returned to Salem and there married Amanda Fries in 1837. Their marriage produced four sons and three daughters.

As a businessman, Belo was unrivaled in productivity. In addition to his cabinetmaking trade, he ran a linseed oil mill and erected an iron foundry, casting railings, bars, and decorations. Prominent in his community, he was elected an elder in the Moravian church. However, a conflict between Belo's business interests and the ideas of the rest of the elders, exampled by a difference of opinion over Belo's wish to build a stable adjoining a street leading to the cemetery, led Belo increasingly to dissociate himself from the affairs of the church. He left the post of elder and concentrated on his business activities, building dams, mills, and a new dry goods store, the Belo House.

By 1849, Belo's general store was completed, two stories tall with 150 feet of frontage on Main Street. It was constructed of red brick and decorated with Corinthian columns (the models for which he carved) and with iron railings and grills made at his foundry. With the name "Belo" on the front in gold letters, the store was impressive. The first floor was used for business and the second as living quarters for the Belo family; a third story, added in 1860, housed clerks and assistants of the store.

When the Civil War broke out, Belo retired to farm. Later coming out of retirement, he presided over the company that built a railroad between Winston-Salem and Greensboro and was active in developing industry. Belo retired again, to indulge his interest in flowers, and built a greenhouse behind his home for that purpose. He died in Salem and was buried in the Salem Cemetery.

SEE: Adelaide L. Fries, *Forsyth: A County on the March* (1949); *History of North Carolina*, vol. 6 (1919); Minnie J. Smith and Kenneth G. Hamilton, eds., *Records of the Moravians in North Carolina*, vol. 9 (1964), vol. 10 (1966), vol. 11 (1969); *Winston-Salem Journal*, 2 Sept. 1961.

ROGER N. KIRKMAN

Benbow, De Witt Clinton (23 Feb. 1832–2 Sept. 1902), businessman and philanthropist, was born near Oak Ridge in Guilford County, the youngest of five children of Charles Benbow and Mary Saunders. His earliest ancestor in America emigrated from Wales in 1718 as a boy of fifteen, bound for his passage money to a Quaker who settled first in Pennsylvania and then in North Carolina. Quakers became numerous in Guilford County, and some, like the Benbows, prospered. After a basic education near home, De Witt Clinton was able to attend the Moses Brown Friends' School, Providence, R.I., and the Baltimore College of Dental Surgery. He received his professional degree in 1855, returned to his native state to practice at Fayetteville, and became secretary and youngest charter member of the North Carolina Dental Society. Benbow practiced dentistry for six years. Part of his work was itinerant: he would advertise locations and hours in the newspapers and then journey to Wilmington, Raleigh, Greensboro, and other places to perform his services. Increasingly during this period he ventured into business. He bought and operated the Cross Creek Cotton Factory, where he had once worked as a boy, and invested in valuable property, expecially large tracts of pine land. Fayetteville in 1861, however, was an uncomfortable spot for an able-bodied pacifist who appeared to be profiting while other young men were marching off to war. The hostility, felt most keenly by his wife, was such that Benbow hired a substitute to fight, sold both his dental practice and the cotton mill, and moved to Greensboro.

In that small county seat he found a fair field for his enterprise. He acquired property, erected buildings, and engaged in merchandising on South Elm Street, the town's main thoroughfare. Then, convinced that Greensboro's location at the junction of the North Carolina and Piedmont railroads was justification, he decided to build a hotel. When it was still only partly finished, about sixty newspaper editors from New York, Pennsylvania, and New Jersey visited Greensboro as part of a long-planned excursion into the upper South. Their welcome and entertainment by Benbow, other leading men, and the general populace stimulated widespread, favorable publicity. The hotel formally opened on 30 May 1871, with ex-governor Zebulon B. Vance, who made a speech to the northern editors, and was the first to sign the register. Completed the next year, the Benbow House astonished almost everyone with its four stories, seventy-four rooms, and cost of $40,000. The doctor's diagnosis was correct: a first-class hotel would attract commercial travelers and other patrons from scores of miles around. A dairy, a vegetable garden, and a vineyard were adjuncts of the establishment. But there was no bar; the proprietor used neither alcohol nor tobacco. Unquestionably, the Benbow provided major impetus toward transforming Greensboro from a little town to an important city.

Benbow's success in business continued for the next twenty years. Of greatest significance in his career between 1872 and 1892 was his role as civic leader and generous benefactor. As an alderman in the mid-1870s, he campaigned, against strong opposition, for graded schools both white and black and for a city market. When educators were struggling to establish the school that later became Bennett College for black women, he assisted with both money and leadership. Similarly, he rescued the white Greensboro Female College. During reconstruction of its fire-gutted main building, the work superintendent died in a fall, and a bank failure deprived the institution of most of its funds. Benbow immediately took charge of the work and paid all wages and bills.

Beginning in 1879, Benbow called for the establishment of a school to train young women as teachers in the public schools. Twelve years later a crusade led by Sidney M. Finger, Edwin A. Alderman, Charles D. McIver, and Benbow culminated in the establishment of the Normal and Industrial School for White Girls. In this instance and in that of the Agricultural and Mechanical College for Negroes, established the same year, 1891, Greensboro outbid other cities for the schools. Benbow was the acknowledged leader of both efforts. In launching his campaign, he made what his friends regarded as "the speech of his life." He rallied businessmen and other citizens to subscribe privately $30,000 for the Normal School and $8,000 for the A. & M. College, so that Greensboro would get these institutions even if the required bond issues failed to pass. This kind of support so pleased the people that their approval at the ballot box was almost unanimous.

From 1881, Benbow served as a trustee of the Quaker school that evolved into Guilford College, and in 1891 he was present at the establishment of the Greensboro Monthly Meeting of Friends. He was one of five incorporators of the Guilford Battleground Company. In politics he affiliated with the Republicans.

By 1892, Benbow's fortune was estimated at about half a million dollars. In addition to various other enterprises, he had invested in the North State Improvement Company, which undertook to build the Cape Fear and Yadkin Valley Railroad. Though the railroad did benefit Greensboro and the rest of its territory, the company was ruined by the financial panic of that time. The principal men, involved in a desperate move, decided to endorse notes individually, and this decision was their undoing. For ten years, Benbow defended himself against various lawsuits, most of which were eventually compromised, but the strain and his age took their toll. One consolation there was, nevertheless: he lived to supervise the building of a new Benbow House, to see his son operate it, and to reside there himself. It was altogether fitting that, when he died, the services were conducted at the new Benbow by two Friends ministers. Burial was at Greene Hill Cemetery.

Mary Elizabeth Scott, whom Benbow married on 30 Nov. 1857, had died five years earlier. Three of their children survived them: Charles D., who became closely associated with his father's business interests and who later played a part in the development of St. Petersburg, Fla.; Mrs. Mary B. Crawford; and Lily.

SEE: J. W. Albright, *Greensboro* (1904); E. S. Arnett, *Greensboro* (1955 [portrait]); Samuel A. Ashe, ed., *Biographical History of North Carolina*, vol. 1 (1905 [portrait]); Dr. Edward P. Benbow, Jr., Greensboro, personal information; B. D. Caldwell, *Founders and Builders of Greensboro* (1925 [portrait]); *Greensboro Patriot*, 3 and 10 Sept. 1902; Greensboro *Daily Record*, 2 and 3 Sept. 1902; Greensboro *Daily Workman*, 13 June 1891; N. H. Hotchkiss, *Pine and Palm* (1873); North Carolina Dental Society, *History* (1939).

STUART NOBLIN

Benbury, Thomas (*28 Nov. 1736–6 Feb. 1793*), revolutionary leader, was born in Chowan County of English ancestry. His father was John Benbury; his grandfather, William Benbury, came from England to settle near Edenton about 1701. A planter, Thomas Benbury entered political life at an early age. He became sheriff of Chowan County by 1769 and a member of the provincial legislature by 1773. As the Revolution approached, he became an ardent Whig and sat in the five provincial congresses, beginning with that at New Bern in August 1774. He served on various committees in the congresses and was also a member of the committee of safety in Chowan County. When the revolutionary military forces were organized, he entered as a major in the Chowan militia and rose to the rank of brigadier general. He served in the state legislature from 1776 to 1782 and was elected speaker of the house for the terms from 1778 to 1782. He was succeeded in the legislature as delegate from Chowan County by his son, Richard Benbury.

After the war, in 1784, Benbury was appointed collector of customs for the State of North Carolina at "Port Roanoke," which included all the Albemarle Sound area. After North Carolina ratified the Constitution in 1789, President George Washington appointed him federal collector of customs for the Port of Edenton.

In addition to his other duties, Benbury served most of his adult life as a justice of the peace and as a vestryman in the Anglican church in Edenton. He died in Edenton and was buried in the Episcopal churchyard there.

Thomas Benbury was twice married: first to Thamir Howcott, in 1761, and second to Elizabeth (maiden name unknown), in 1769. By his first wife he had two sons, Thomas and Richard, and by his second wife, a daughter, Mary. A great-grandson, Captain John Benbury of the First North Carolina Regiment in the Confederate Army, was killed at the battle of Malvern Hill, 1 July 1862.

SEE: Samuel A. Ashe, ed., *Biographical History of North Carolina*, vol. 1 (1905); Richard B. Creecy, Memoirs of the Creecy and Benbury Families (Library, University of North Carolina, Chapel Hill), clippings; *North Carolina Booklet*, vol. 18 (1919); William L. Saunders and Walter Clark, eds., *Colonial and State Records of North Carolina*, 30 vols. (1886–1914); Sons of the American

Revolution, North Carolina Society, *Lineage Book of Past and Present Members* (1951).

ELMER D. JOHNSON

Bennehan, Richard (*15 Apr. 1743–31 Dec. 1825*), merchant, planter, builder, and pioneer in the tobacco industry and in education, was born near Warsaw, North Farnham Parish, Richmond County, Va. The fifth of seven children, he was the son of Dudley and Rachel Bennehan. The Bennehans, who were of Irish extraction, appear in Virginia records first with Richard's grandfather Dominick, whose name occurs in Richmond County legal documents as early as 1694 and who died in 1716. Dominick and his wife Elizabeth had four children, Elizabeth, Alexander, Frances, and Dudley. Dudley Bennehan (1713–49) died when Richard was only six years old.

After serving an apprenticeship of several years in the mercantile business in Richmond County, Bennehan left for Petersburg, Va., in 1762. He carried a recommendation from his former employers declaring that he had always "discharged his trust with fidelity and to the approbation of his employers" and that he was a "sober, honest, and well-behaved person." At Petersburg he found employment with a firm of merchants, one of whom, Edward Stabler, became an intimate and helpful friend.

In the second half of the eighteenth century, ships put in at Petersburg from all over the world, and merchants and bankers in Petersburg kept in close touch with their counterparts in London, Glasgow, and other European cities. Over roads leading south and southwest from Petersburg, mail and news from Europe as well as trade commodities were able to reach people in the backwoods and on the cotton and tobacco plantations of southern Virginia and North Carolina. Bennehan's experience at Petersburg was of incalculable value to him, teaching him the ways of international banking and trade, on the one hand, and the ways of the large planter and the backwoodsman, on the other. On a road about half way between Petersburg and Salisbury and fifteen miles northeast of Hillsborough, a Scot by the name of William Johnston owned an extensive plantation called Snow Hill and maintained a large store with which customers from Orange and nearby counties did business. In 1768 he needed a manager for the store and offered the position, with a one-third share in the business, to Bennehan. Bennehan accepted and in December established himself at Snow Hill; henceforth North Carolina was to be his home.

The partnership with Johnston brought Bennehan in contact with a capable businessman who was closely associated with important people and activities throughout the colony. The partnership flourished, and a strong mutual respect was maintained until Johnston's death in 1785.

In 1776, Bennehan married Mary Amis, daughter of Thomas Amis of Halifax and sister of a younger Thomas Amis, who distinguished himself in the Revolution. In the same year, Bennehan made his first purchase of land—893 acres three miles northeast from Snow Hill on the west side of the Flat River—from Tyree Harris, who had been sheriff of Orange County during the Regulator movement. This was the beginning and nucleus of the Stagville-Fairntosh complex of plantations on the headwaters of the Neuse River, which before the end of the nineteenth century would amount to more than thirty thousand acres. In 1787, Bennehan purchased from Judith Stagg, widow of Thomas Stagg, 66 acres of land high on a ridge just west of the river-valley land bought from Tyree Harris some years earlier. Here in 1799 he built a house that he called Stagville, still standing in 1974. By 1800, Bennehan owned over 4,000 acres and 44 slaves; two children were born to the Bennehans: Rebecca (1778–1843), who in 1803 married Duncan Cameron; and Thomas Dudley (1782–1847), who never married. With the help of his enterprising son and of Duncan Cameron, a lawyer with an excellent head for business, Bennehan greatly increased the extent of his land holdings before his death in 1825.

One of Bennehan's best friends in the last decade of the eighteenth century was William Richardson Davie of Halifax, son-in-law of another close friend, General Allen Jones. Bennehan joined forces with Davie and Jones when they led the movement in the early 1790s to found the city of Raleigh as the capital for the state. Davie was instrumental in making Bennhan one of the five commissioners who bought the Joel Lane plantation of a thousand acres and there laid out the city of Raleigh. When lots of one acre each were offered for sale in 1793, Bennehan bought four, making up a square between what are now Bloodworth, Person, Hargett, and Morgan Streets, where Hugh Morson High School was later built. Bennehan Street was created when each of the commissioners had a street named for him.

Bennehan also joined Davie and Jones in encouraging the establishment of The University of North Carolina. Davie had great confidence in Bennehan's advice, corresponded with him frequently about various problems, and sought his practical assistance. In October 1793, Bennehan donated fifty bushels of shells for making mortar for the construction of Old East. These had to be brought by boat from Wilmington to Fayetteville and then hauled by wagon to the building site. Later he gave an air pump for scientific experiments and in 1796 thirty-two books for the library. In 1799 he became a member of the board of trustees and of the visiting committee, which was responsible for inspecting the institution from time to time and reporting back to the trustees. He was the first of eight Bennehans and Camerons who served as trustees of the university. His son, Thomas Dudley, was a student at the university, a member of the Dialectic Society, and from 1812 until his death in 1847 a trustee.

When William Johnston's only daughter, Amelia, moved to Kentucky, Bennehan bought Snow Hill Plantation and a large tract of land on the east side of Flat River joining the Stagville land. At the time of Rebecca's marriage to Duncan Cameron, he gave them three hundred acres, which became the nucleus of Fairntosh Plantation.

Bennehan was buried beside his wife, who had died in 1812, in the family plot near the Stagville house, where his son was later interred. Portraits are in the possession of his descendants Mrs. John W. Labouisse and Mrs. Eric van Lennep.

SEE: Samuel A. Ashe, ed., *Biographical History of North Carolina*, vol. 3 (1905), and *Cyclopedia of Eminent and Representative Men of the Carolinas of the Nineteenth Century* (1892); Kemp P. Battle, *History of the University of North Carolina*, vol. 1 (1907); Cameron Papers (Southern Historical Collection, University of North Carolina, Chapel Hill), for the ledger books and other records of the Snow Hill store; Elizabeth Cometti, "Some Early Best Sellers in Piedmont North Carolina," *Journal of Southern History* 16 (1950); R. D. W. Connor, L. R. Wilson, and H. T. Lefler, *A Documentary History of the University of North Carolina*, 2 vols. (1953); North Farnham Parish, Va.,

Vestry Book (courthouse, Richmond County, Warsaw, Va.); Orange County legal records (Hillsborough, N.C.); Richmond County, Va., legal records (Warsaw, Va.); Blackwell P. Robinson, *William R. Davie* (1957); William L. Saunders and Walter Clark, eds., *Colonial and State Records of North Carolina*, vols. 7, 10, 13 (1890, 1893, 1896); John H. Wheeler, *Reminiscences and Memoirs of North Carolina* (1883–84).

CHARLES RICHARD SANDERS

Bennett, Hugh Hammond (15 Apr. 1881–7 July 1960), soil conservationist, was born near Wadesboro to William Osborne and Rosa May Hammond. His father had farmed a plantation of about fifteen hundred acres from the time of the Civil War. Bennett graduated from the D. A. McGregor School in Wadesboro in 1896. After farming for one year, he entered The University of North Carolina and studied chemistry and geology. In the spring of 1899 he dropped out of the university for financial reasons and worked for two years as an apprentice in the Parsons and Hardison drug store in Wadesboro. Bennett then returned to Chapel Hill and in 1903 received a B.S. degree.

In the summer of 1903, Bennett accepted a $1,000-a-year job as a soil scientist with the Soil Survey Division of the Bureau of Soils in the U.S. Department of Agriculture. In 1909 he became inspector of soil surveys for the southern division of the bureau. Also in 1909 he was a member of an expedition to study the agricultural possibilities of the Panama Canal Zone. He traveled to make the first soil surveys of Alaska in 1914 and 1916. In 1919 he served on an international commission to settle the Nicaragua-Guatemala boundary dispute. During the winters from 1925 until 1932 he directed a soil survey of Cuba.

While making soil surveys, Bennett learned of the causes and effects of soil erosion, especially sheet erosion. Although the chief of the Bureau of Soils had written in 1909 that the "soil is the one indestructible, immutable asset that the nation possesses," Bennett became the chief advocate for measures to prevent the destruction of the soil by erosion. For years his warnings were ignored by most people. He supervised an investigation into soil erosion and moisture conservation for the Department of Agriculture's Bureau of Soils and Chemistry from 1928 to 1933. Bennett's major opportunity came in 1933, when he became director of the Soil Erosion Service in the Interior Department. A year and a half later he moved back to the Agriculture Department to head the newly created Soil Conservation Service.

Bennett wanted the Soil Conservation Service to supply the nation with scientific research, technical assistance, and leadership, but he expected the farmers to organize their own groups at the local level. He urged the states to adopt the Standard State Conservation Districts Law, which would let the farmers organize soil conservation districts at the local level, independent of the Soil Conservation Service. As director, he also worked to simplify and standardize the soil survey maps in the United States.

Known as both "the Chief" and "Big Hugh," Bennett worked continuously to spread his ideas on soil erosion and conservation. Although in many ways always a farmer from Wadesboro, Bennett had an impressive personality and an engaging speaking style that made him an effective evangelist before both farmers' groups and congressional committees. As director of the Soil Conservation Service from 1935 until his retirement in

1951, he developed the service from an idea to a government organization of thousands serving the nation's farmers. In 1953 he denounced the reorganization of the Soil Conservation Service by Secretary of Agriculture Ezra Taft Benson as a "political experiment."

Bennett received an LL.D. from The University of North Carolina in 1936, a D.Sc. from Clemson College in 1937, and a D.Sc. from Columbia University in 1952. In 1946 the governor of North Carolina declared 9 Sept. "Hugh Hammond Bennett Conservation Day in North Carolina"; on that day also the citizens of Wadesboro had a celebration in his honor. In 1947 the Department of Agriculture awarded him its first distinguished service award. The American Geographical Society presented him its Cullum gold medal in 1947. Bennett received the Izaac Walton League's highest award in 1951. Upon his retirement in 1951, the Raleigh *News and Observer* declared that "When history finally sets up the measure of the contribution of men in our times, it may very well be that so far as North Carolina is concerned Hugh Bennett of Wadesboro will be recognized as the most important North Carolinian of this generation."

An Episcopalian and a Democrat, Bennett also belonged to many professional organizations. He was a member of the Soil Conservation Society of America, the American Society of Agronomy, the American Geographic Society, the American Association for the Advancement of Science, the International Union for the Protection of Nature, the Association of American Geographers, the Washington Academy of Science, the Friends of the Land, the American Forestry Association, and Phi Delta Theta. He also belonged to the Cosmos Club and the Explorers.

Among Bennett's scores of articles and books are *Soil Conservation* (1939), *Elements of Soil Conservation* (1947), and *The Soils and Agriculture of the Southern States* (1921).

In 1907, Bennett married Sarah Edna McCue; they had a daughter, Sarah Edna. Mrs. Bennett died in 1909, and in 1921 Bennett married Betty Virginia Brown. They had one son, Hugh Hammond, Jr. For many years, while working in Washington, Bennett lived at Eight Oaks in Falls Church, Va. He died of cancer in Burlington and was buried in Arlington National Cemetery.

SEE: Wellington Brink, *Big Hugh: Father of Soil Conservation* (1951); *Greensboro Daily News*, 8 July 1960; Raleigh *News and Observer*, 10 Sept. 1946, 17 and 18 Jan. 1951.

CHARLES W. EAGLES

Bennett, Risden Tyler (18 June 1840–21 July 1913), Confederate colonel, congressman, and superior court judge, was born in Anson County, the son of Nevil and Catherine Harris Bennett. He attended Gouldsfork Academy near his home and was graduated from Anson Institute, Wadesboro. He enrolled briefly at The University of North Carolina but withdrew and went to the West, where he lived a varied life, including some time spent with Indians. He wanted to remain in the West, but his guardian, George Tittle, sent him fare and insisted that he return. He attended Davidson College in 1859 and afterward studied at Cumberland University and Lebanon Law School. His law study was completed under Judge Richmond M. Pearson, and he began practice in 1860. He was an ardent believer in states' rights and enrolled in the Anson Guards in 1861, attaining the rank of colonel of the Fourteenth Regiment, N.C. troops. He was wounded at Gettysburg.

After the war Bennett became a law partner of Judge Thomas S. Ashe. In 1872–74 he represented Anson

County in the General Assembly, and in 1875 he was a delegate to the constitutional convention. Appointed in 1880 to fill an unexpired term as superior court judge, he was afterward elected in his own right, serving until he resigned in 1882. He was a member of Congress from 1885 to 1887. He was interested in cultural and educational affairs and made available a collection of a thousand books to start a library in Wadesboro.

Bennett is said to have been reared a Primitive Baptist, but during the Civil War he was baptized by a Methodist chaplain. Later he joined the Episcopal church. While at home on leave recuperating from wounds, he was married to Kate Shepherd; they became the parents of Mary, who married Eugene Little; Effie Nevil, who married John D. Leak; and Kate. Twin sons died as infants. Bennett was a popular orator and writer and contributed to Charlotte and Wadesboro newspapers. He died in Wadesboro and was buried near his birthplace a few miles from town.

SEE: *Bio. Dir. Am. Cong.* (1961); Jerome Dowd, *Sketches of Prominent Living North Carolinians* (1888); *Greensboro Daily News*, 20 Apr. 1944, 28 Oct. 1962; John A. Livingston, *Risden Tyler Bennett* (1933?); Mary L. Medley, *History of Anson County, North Carolina* (1976); Raleigh *News and Observer*, 23 Nov. 1933; North Carolina Bar Association, *Proceedings* 22 (1920); 205 *N.C. Reports* (1933).

MARY L. MEDLEY

Benton, Angelo Ames (1837–29 Sept. 1912), Episcopal clergyman and scholar, was born at Canea on the island of Crete. His father, the Reverend George Benton, was serving at the time as an Episcopal missionary in Greece. In 1845 the elder Benton settled in North Carolina and, until he died in 1862, did missionary work at Rockfish in Cumberland County. A. A. Benton was educated at Trinity College, where he received a B.A. in 1856 and an M.A. in 1860. He was ordained deacon by Bishop Thomas Atkinson in 1860 and was assigned to Trinity Church, Scotland Neck, to assist Dr. Joseph Blount Cheshire. In Scotland Neck his specific charge was a chapel erected for the use of the Negroes living on the plantations of parish members on the Roanoke River.

Benton left Scotland Neck in 1861. Having been ordained to the priesthood by Bishop Atkinson in 1863, he ministered to his father's congregation at Rockfish for two years. In 1865 he became rector of St. Timothy's Church in the growing community of Wilson; he is said to have also officiated occasionally in Rocky Mount. From 1872 until 1878 he was rector of St. Paul's Church in Edenton. In the latter year, he returned to Rockfish, where he remained for five years.

In 1883, Benton accepted a post as professor of Greek and Latin at the College of Delaware. He later went to the University of the South at Sewanee, where he was professor of dogmatic theology. His alma mater awarded him a D.D. degree in 1888. Benton remained at Sewanee until 1894. Returning then to the ministerial field, he was rector first of St John's Church, Albion, and then of St. Paul's Church, Pekin, both in the Diocese of Springfield in Illinois. He retired in 1904 and lived at Crafton, Pa., until his death.

Benton was among the first to take an interest in the colonial antecedents of the Episcopal church in North Carolina. From legislative statutes he compiled a list of the old colonial parishes of the Church of England in the state and submitted his findings to the convention of the diocese in 1874. The result of his researches was printed in the convention journal of that year. Later Benton compiled *The Church Encyclopedia*, first published in New York in 1883. It was popular in its day, and successive editions were published in Philadelphia in 1884, 1885, and 1886. In 1890 he prepared an edition of the works of Virgil for use in schools.

SEE: M. De Lancey Haywood, *Lives of the Bishops of North Carolina* (1910); *Living Church Annual*, 1890–1913; *Lloyd's Clerical Directory*, 1895–1913; Stuart Hall Smith and Claiborne T. Smith, Jr., *The History of Trinity Parish* (1955).

CLAIBORNE T. SMITH, JR.

Benton, Lemuel (*1754–18 May 1818*), planter and congressman, was born on his father's plantation, Oxford, in Granville County, the son of Samuel Benton and his wife, Frances Kimbrough Benton. His father was prominent in the area and served as justice of the peace, sheriff of Granville County, registrar, clerk of court, chief military officer, and from 1760 to 1768 a member of the assembly in New Bern. Lemuel's nephew was Thomas Hart Benton.

Although most of his adult life was spent in South Carolina, before Benton emigrated he and his brother Jesse signed the "Redressor Papers" in protest of the Regulator movement in North Carolina and "in support of the Laws and Constitution of our country." Soon thereafter, however, he left North Carolina and settled in the section of Cheraw District that is now Darlington County, S.C. There he became a planter and acquired extensive landholdings. During the Revolution, he attained the rank of colonel and successfully served under General Francis Marion as commander of the Pedee forces, retaining his commission for several years after the war, until he resigned in 1794.

Benton also proved to be a dedicated civil servant. He was a member of the South Carolina legislature in 1781–84 and 1787; Darlington County court justice from 1785 to 1791; escheator of Cheraw District, 1789–91; and delegate to the state constitutional convention in 1790 and to the 1788 convention in Charleston that ratified the federal Constitution. His most hard-earned victory probably came when he was elected the first congressional representative from the Pedee District. His unequaled speaking ability gained him the position, and he served as a Democrat in the Third, Fourth and Fifth Congresses, 1793–99. He was then defeated for reelection because of his opposition to the administration of John Adams. He returned home and resumed his agricultural pursuits until his death. He was buried on his estate, Stony Hill.

Benton married his first cousin, Elizabeth Kimbrough; they had four daughters and four sons, but of the sons, only one reached manhood.

SEE: *Biog. Dir. Am. Cong.* (1961); *Darlingtonia* (1964); Alexander Gregg, *History of the Old Cheraws* (1867); Alma Cheek Redden, *A Chronicle of Two Pioneer Families: The Bentons and the Taylors of the North Carolina Back Country* (1969); William L. Saunders, *Colonial Records of North Carolina*, 10 vols. (1886–90); *Who Was Who in America, 1607–1896*.

LUCIUS MCGEHEE CHESHIRE, JR.

Benton, Samuel (*d. 1770*), colonial official, was a native of England (probably Worcester County); he owned land in the part of Craven County that became Johnston County in 1746 and also in the part of Edgecombe that became Granville County the same year. At that time he was living on Tar River in Granville County. He was appointed a justice of the Granville County court in 1746

by Governor Gabriel Johnston, reappointed in 1753 by Acting Governor Matthew Rowan, and reappointed in 1755, 1760, and 1764 by Governor Arthur Dobbs. He was sheriff in 1764 and a member of the House of Commons from 1760 to 1768. He was registrar of the county from 1761 until his death in 1770 and clerk of the court of common pleas and quarter sessions from 1764 to 1770. He was a lieutenant colonel of the militia under Governor William Tryon in 1768 during some of the Regulator troubles.

Benton introduced the bill in the assembly that divided Granville County in 1764, creating Bute County of the eastern portion. The act directed that the new county seat for Granville County be established at Oxford Plantation, part of a thousand acres of land owned by Benton. He gave land for the courthouse. Some time prior to 1763, Benton is said to have been responsible for the erection of St. George's Chapel in the area that remained Granville County.

Benton was probably buried in a family cemetery at his plantation. He was survived by two sons, Jesse and Samuel, Jr.; Jesse was the father of Thomas Hart Benton.

SEE: William Nisbet Chambers, *Old Bullion Benton* (1956); Elizabeth H. Hummel, *Hicks History of Granville County* (1965).

WILLIAM S. POWELL

Benton, Thomas Hart (*14 Mar. 1782–10 Apr. 1858*), senator and representative from Missouri, was born near Hillsborough, the third child and eldest son of Jesse and Ann Gooch Benton. His paternal grandfather, Samuel Benton, was a substantial landed proprietor in Granville County who served as a justice of the peace and a member of the colonial assembly prior to the Revolution. Jesse Benton moved from Granville to Orange County, became a prominent lawyer, and was a member of the assembly in 1781. Owner of a plantation on the banks of the Eno River, he also speculated heavily in Tennessee and Kentucky lands. His wife was the niece and ward of Thomas Hart, a wealthy Virginia landowner and merchant who became one of the leading settlers in early Kentucky. Thomas Hart Benton thus belonged to a family well established in Piedmont North Carolina.

Jesse Benton died during the winter of 1790–91, leaving his widow and seven children with an apparently large estate, though title to much of the land he claimed was never validated. Thomas Hart Benton attended school in Hillsborough and entered The University of North Carolina shortly after Christmas 1798. His stay at Chapel Hill was brief, for he left in disgrace less than three months later, following his expulsion from the Philanthropic Society after he confessed to stealing money from his roommates. Although this incident was known to many contemporaries, it was rarely used publicly by his opponents during his long and often stormy career in public life. Nevertheless, one modern biographer believes the realization that this youthful blot upon his record would probably be fully aired in a national campaign influenced Benton's inflexible refusal to seek the presidency or vice-presidency. Another biographer maintains that this episode "gave him an overreaching need to prove himself" and contributed to his "trigger-touchy sense of personal honor."

In 1801, Ann Gooch Benton moved with her children to a 2,560-acre tract near the present-day village of Leipers Fork, Tenn., about twenty-five miles southwest of Nashville. This land was all that Jesse Benton's heirs were able to obtain of the more than 20,000 acres he originally claimed in Tennessee. As the oldest son, Thomas Hart Benton assumed the role of *paterfamilias* in establishing a plantation on the "widow Benton's settlement." He later taught school while undertaking a course of readings to prepare himself for a legal career. He was admitted to practice at Franklin in 1806. He also took a keen interest in politics, as a supporter of the Thomas Jefferson administration and a proponent of state judicial reform. As a member of the Tennessee Senate in 1809, he secured the enactment of some of the court reforms he had earlier advocated. Although his law practice soon became quite flourishing, his health was for a time precarious; he ultimately recovered from an incipient attack of tuberculosis, a disease that took the lives of three of his sisters during the family's residence in Tennessee.

Benton actively supported entry into the War of 1812 and was elected colonel of the Second Regiment of Tennessee Volunteers. He also became an aide de camp to General Andrew Jackson, whose friendship he had earlier won. He accompanied Jackson on his expedition to Natchez in 1813 and on the return march to Tennessee after Jackson's refusal to obey the War Department's order to disband his troops in the Mississippi Territory. Benton shortly thereafter went to Washington, where he obtained the government's consent to honor Jackson's claim for the expenses incurred on the unauthorized march from Natchez to Nashville. Upon his return from Washington, an incident occurred that led to a decade-long rupture between Benton and Jackson. In Benton's absence, Jackson had served as William Carroll's second in a duel with Jesse Benton, Thomas's brother, who was wounded in the affray. Informed of Jackson's role in the affair, Thomas Hart Benton voiced his disapproval, and when Jackson sought to "horsewhip Tom Benton" for his alleged impudence, a brawl ensued at a Nashville tavern and one of the Benton brothers wounded Jackson in the shoulder so seriously that he nearly lost his left arm. Though Benton remained under Jackson's command, he was disappointed in not being assigned to action, and he was en route to Washington to seek a transfer to the Canadian front when his fellow Tennessee soldiers participated in the routing of the British army at New Orleans on 8 Jan. 1815.

Later that year, Benton moved to Missouri, which he had first seen on the trip down the Mississippi River to Natchez in 1813. Settling in St. Louis, he quickly became one of the leading lawyers of the city, developing a considerable practice in land claims and titles. His interest in politics, in which he sided with the city's older French faction, soon involved him in numerous controversies, including one with Charles Lucas, whom he killed in a duel on 27 Sept. 1817. Benton was widely criticized for provoking a second meeting between Lucas and himself and never consented thereafter to participate in an affair of honor.

On 20 Mar. 1821, Benton married Elizabeth McDowell, a member of a prominent Lexington, Va., family.

While continuing his law practice, he served as editor of the *St. Louis Enquirer* from 1818 to 1820, in which capacity he championed western interests and the statehood movement in Missouri. In the congressional controversy on the latter question, he took a militant position on the proslavery side, and upon the admission of the new state he was elected one of its U.S. senators. He was subsequently reelected four times and served until 3 Mar. 1851, the first senator to hold office for thirty consecutive years. As a freshman senator, Benton worked hard to broaden the base of his political support

in Missouri, proving himself adept at the representation of special interests. More significantly, in view of his later political career, he began to emerge as a spokesman for political democracy and a liberal national land policy.

In the presidential campaign of 1824, Benton supported Henry Clay, who had married his cousin, Letitia Hart, although Clay's American System was repugnant to Old Republicans, such as John Randolph of Roanoke and Nathaniel Macon, with whom Benton had become intimate friends. In the meantime, his strained relations with Jackson had been repaired during the latter's tenure as senator from Tennessee from 1823 to 1825. When Clay was eliminated from consideration for the presidency in the election by the House of Representatives in 1825, Benton supported Jackson over John Quincy Adams and William H. Crawford. During the political battles of the Jackson administration, Benton occasionally took an independent course, as evidenced by his support in May 1830 of the Maysville Road Bill, which Jackson vetoed.

Benton's greatest influence upon Jacksonian policy was in matters relating to banking and currency. An opponent of all banks and an advocate of an exclusively metallic currency, he earned for himself the cherished nickname "Old Bullion," and his influence upon the administration's policies in these matters has led some historians to view him as a member of Jackson's "Kitchen Cabinet." With Van Buren in the White House, Benton continued to champion hard-money principles, although he reluctantly supported the administration's Treasury Note legislation, passed in order to meet the financial exigencies caused by the Panic of 1837. More to his liking was the new president's Independent Treasury plan, whose enactment in July 1840 he approved as leading to a divorce of the federal government from all banking institutions and as a step toward ending the acceptance of bank notes by the treasury. Benton became one of the national leaders of the hard-money or Locofoco wing of the Democratic party in opposition to the pro-bank conservatives, many of whom joined the Whig party.

During the administrations of William Henry Harrison and John Tyler, Benton found himself once again in opposition. His die-hard determination to support Van Buren, who had been defeated by Harrison in 1840, in his bid for another term in 1844 led to a further weakening of Benton's political position in Missouri. Although he had denounced the Adams-Onis Treaty of 1819 for surrendering American claims to Texas and had advocated the purchase of Texas from Mexico during the Jackson administration, he vehemently denounced the Texas annexation treaty of 1844, which was generally popular in his state. Although he had supported Van Buren at the Democratic convention of May 1844, he endorsed the party presidential candiate, James K. Polk. Nevertheless, the Whigs widely distributed Benton's speeches on the Texas issue in an effort to weaken Polk's candidacy, and his opponents in Missouri cited them in an effort to defeat the senator's bid for a fifth term. In November 1844, the same month that Polk won a narrow victory over Clay in the presidential contest, the Missouri legislature reelected Benton, although by his smallest margin of victory in twenty-four years. On 28 Feb. 1845, Congress passed a joint resolution providing for the annexation of Texas.

With President Polk, Benton's relationship and influence varied from time to time. In the early stages of the Mexican War, Benton, then serving as chairman of the Senate Military Affairs Committee, was a major adviser to Polk. At one time the president was prepared to appoint him a lieutenant general in command of both the military and diplomatic efforts in Mexico, but Benton's enemies in Congress succeeded in blocking the legislation necessary to revive the rank held previously only by George Washington. The Senate later confirmed his appointment as major general, but he declined the commission because he was not given chief command of the army over the two Whig generals, Zachary Taylor and Winfield Scott. Benton took a keen interest in the Mexican War controversies involving the dashing Colonel John C. Frémont, who had married his daughter, Jessie Ann. He ultimately broke irrevocably with Polk in February 1848, when the president declined to disallow a court martial verdict finding his son-in-law guilty of insubordination.

In the controversy over slavery in the territories in the late 1840s, Benton took a stand that further alienated many of his constituents. Although he voiced disapproval of the Wilmot Proviso as dangerous to the preservation of the Union, he voted for the organization of the Oregon Territory with a rider prohibiting slavery. His opposition to Calhoun's Southern Address of January 1849, endorsed by a majority of the members of Congress from the slaveholding states, prompted the Missouri legislature to pass a resolution instructing the state's senators to "act in conformity" with the proslavery position. Declining to accept these instructions, he took the issue to the people in a vigorous stumping tour of the state in the summer and early fall of 1849. Yet despite his growing hostility to the southern extremists, he supported Lewis Cass, the regular Democratic candidate for the presidency in 1848, over his old friend Van Buren, the standard bearer of the newly created Free Soil party.

Benton opposed the Compromise of 1850 on the grounds that it was "a *capitulation* to those who threatened secession." The debates on that question involved him in the most acrimonious personal controversies of his senatorial career, culminating in a confrontation with proslavery Henry S. Foote of Mississippi, who brandished a revolver when he apparently thought that Benton intended violence. When the omnibus bill embodying the compromise was finally divided into separate pieces of legislation, Benton voted for most of the individual bills. The proslavery Missouri Democrats, led by Benton's senatorial colleague David R. Atchison, were determined to block his bid for a sixth term. In January 1851, a coalition of anti-Benton Democrats and Whigs in the legislature chose a proslavery Whig as his successor.

For Benton, defeat did not mean retirement. In 1852 he was elected to the U.S. House of Representatives from a southeastern Missouri district that included St. Louis. While awaiting the beginning of his congressional term, he began the writing of his *Thirty Years' View*, a massive history of the workings of the American government during his senatorial career. Published in 1854 by D. Appleton and Company, it sold more than fifty thousand copies. Although he supported Franklin Pierce for the presidency in 1852, he soon denounced the new president's policies, opposing the Kansas-Nebraska Bill and the administration's designs on Cuba. In 1854 he was defeated for reelection to the House in a campaign during which the ill health of his wife kept him in Washington. He also failed in a bid for Atchison's seat in the Senate in 1855; a bitter legislative battle led to a senatorial vacancy for two years, because no candidate could obtain a majority. In his last try for political office, a campaign for the governorship in 1856, he ran third in a race won by a proslavery Democrat. In the presidential campaign of that year, Benton supported the Democrat

James Buchanan, even though his son-in-law Frémont was the candidate of the new Republican party. He opposed the Republicans because he believed that such a sectional party might endanger the preservation of the Union.

Benton's last years were saddened by tragedies and setbacks, which nonetheless failed to conquer his spirit. After ten years of invalidism, his beloved wife died in September 1854; and the following February his residence in Washington was consumed by flames, destroying his papers and the partially completed second volume of the *Thirty Years' View*. The fire, while delaying publication, did not prevent him from completing the work. Volume two, covering the period from 1837 to 1851, appeared in May 1856, only six months later than originally planned. It was a spirited vindication of Benton's pro-Union course in the sectional controversies of his later senatorial career. In 1856 and 1857 he visited several northern states on an extended lecture tour, cut short because of painful injuries he received in a railroad accident at Pittsburgh in May 1857. Returning to Washington, he wrote a critical essay attacking the Dred Scott decision and defending the right of Congress to legislate on the subject of slavery in the territories. Despite rapidly failing health, he resumed work on a project begun earlier, the sixteen volumes of the *Abridgment of the Debates of Congress from 1789 to 1856* [1850], most of which were published posthumously. He completed work on the last volume on 9 Apr. 1858, only one day before his death from a disease diagnosed as cancer of the bowels.

By many of his contemporaries, Benton was considered equal if not superior to Clay, Calhoun, and Webster, with whom he often contended on the floor of the Senate. Though a household word in his day, he made less impression on later generations, partly because most nineteenth-century historians were Whiggish in their sympathies, and twentieth-century scholars have tended to view Jackson, not Benton, as the symbol of the political movement they both espoused. As an orator, Benton was never as popular as his senatorial rivals, because his speeches tended to be long, statistical, and bookish; his enemies accused him of playing "schoolmaster" to his colleagues by flaunting his self-acquired learning, of which he was inordinately proud. Because of his egotistical and overbearing nature and his strong, unyielding convictions, he acquired a host of enemies. Though pompous and austere in public, he was warm and tender enough in his familial relationships to attract the attention of such an inveterate foe as John Quincy Adams.

Benton's early senatorial career won him recognition for his advocacy of political democracy and a liberal public land policy, and he later achieved prominence as the champion of hard money. But it was his steadfast devotion to the Union, in the face of mounting sectional sentiment in Missouri, that won him a place among the eight congressional leaders whom John F. Kennedy believed best exemplified the quality of political courage. His concern for the survival of the Union caused him to reject both proslavery and antislavery extremists; thus, while opposed to the extension of slavery, he never espoused emancipation. Though the Civil War that he had fervently hoped to avert began only three years after his death, Missouri did not join the ranks of the Confederacy, thanks in part to his long crusade for the Union and the work of such men as Frank P. Blair, Jr., and B. Gratz Brown, former protégés whose political principles he had helped to mold.

SEE: William Nisbet Chambers, *Old Bullion Benton* (1956); Rudolph E. Forderhase, "Jacksonism in Missouri" (Ph.D. diss., University of Missouri—Columbia, 1968); William A. Hansen, "Thomas Hart Benton and the Oregon Question," *Missouri Historical Review* 63 (1969); John F. Kennedy, *Profiles in Courage* (1956); Perry G. McCandless, "The Political Philosophy and Political Personality of Thomas H. Benton," *Missouri Historical Review* 50 (1956), and "The Rise of Thomas H. Benton in Missouri Politics," ibid.; William M. Meigs, *Life of Thomas Hart Benton* (1904); John V. Mering, *The Whig Party in Missouri* (1967); Joseph M. Rogers, *Thomas H. Benton* (1905); Theodore Roosevelt, *Thomas Hart Benton* (1886); Stephen Sayles, "Thomas Hart Benton and the Santa Fe Trail," *Missouri Historical Review* 69 (1975); Robert E. Shalhope, "Thomas Hart Benton and Missouri State Politics," *Bulletin of the Missouri Historical Society* 25 (1968–69); Elbert B. Smith, *Magnificent Missourian* (1958).

EDWIN A. MILES

Benzien, Christian Ludwig (*19 July 1753–13 Nov. 1811*), Moravian minister, was born in Westminster, London, to Christian Thomas Benzien and Anna Maria Neisser. As an infant, he came with his parents to America, where they settled in Pennsylvania. He attended schools of the Moravian church in Nazareth and Bethlehem and entered church service as a bookkeeper in Bethlehem in 1769. On 26 Aug. 1781, answering a call to Wachovia, he arrived in Salem. From his first position as Single Brethren Choir Helper (Pfleger), he was ordained a deacon in December 1781; he became the head of the Choir of Single Brethren in 1786. Benzien traveled extensively in neighboring areas to preach and baptize; he also often accompanied Traugott Bagge and Fredrick Marshall to the assembly and on public business. He wrote many hymns that were read and sung in Home Church in Salem and also preached in both German and English to the congregation. On 27 Aug. 1788, Benzien was chosen as a delegate to the General Synod in Europe, which required him to leave Salem for almost two years. While attending the synod he married, and returned with his new wife, Anna Dorothea Böttger, in June 1790.

Because Benzien was assistant to the Reverend Fredrick Marshall in the management of all affairs in Wachovia concerning the Unity of Brethren (Moravians), when Marshall died in 1802, Benzien became the Proprietor of the American Estates of the Unity of the Brethren, as stipulated in Marshall's will. The new position put Benzien in authority over the lease, rental, and sale of all lands owned or controlled by the Unity. In addition, Marshall's death also left him the religious leader of Salem and Wachovia.

Benzien's first wife died in childbirth in 1801, and he married Dorothea Sophia Elisabeth Bötticher in 1802. His three children, Lydia Theodora, Wilhelm Ludwig, and Christian Thomas, were all born to his first wife. At his death in Salem, Benzien was listed as Administrator of the Unity in Wachovia and a member of the Helpers' Conference for the Whole; he and his wife were Choir Leaders of the Married People. The collection of Old Salem, Inc., includes a photograph of a silhouette of Benzien.

One of Benzien's sons, Ludwig, was also an important member of the Salem community. He was Vorsteher for the town and a musician and composer. While a teacher at the Boys' School, he taught music, concentrating on the violin and organ. He cared for the organ and was organist for Home Church in Salem for many years.

SEE: Christian Ludwig Benzien, personal memoir and letters (Moravian Archives, Winston-Salem); Moravian Church Archives (Winston-Salem), for Aufseher Collegium Minutes, Elders Conference Minutes, Helfer Conferenz furs Ganze Minutes, Salem Diary, and Wachovia Memorabilia; *Raleigh Register*, 22 Nov. 1811 (obit.); Raleigh *Star*, 29 Nov. 1811 (obit.).

JAN HIESTER

Bernard, William Henry (*1 Jan. 1837–19 Feb. 1918*), newspaper editor, was born in Petersburg, Va. His father was Peter Dudley Bernard, a printer and publisher, who owned and edited the *Southern Planter*, an agricultural magazine, in Richmond; his mother was Sarah Lloyd White. Bernard's paternal grandfather fought under George Washington in the American Revolution and died from wounds received at the Battle of Brandywine. His maternal grandfather was Thomas Willis White, founder and editor of the *Southern Literary Messenger*.

The family moved to Richmond soon after Bernard's birth. He was educated at the private schools of Pearman and Fox, the Rumford Military Academy in King William County, and Richmond College, where he was one of the editors of the *Star*, a publication of the Mu Sigma Rho Society.

Leaving college at the age of eighteen, before being graduated, Bernard went to Texas in 1855 to study law with William Stedman, a prominent attorney and a native of Chatham County. His interests were in journalism, however, and he soon abandoned the study of law to publish a weekly paper, the *Star Spangled Banner*. Yielding to an inclination for wit, he established *Young America*, a weekly publication of humor. He left Texas in 1858 and returned to Virginia. In 1859 he married Maggie Stedman of Fayetteville and went to live in Helena, Ark.

During this period, Bernard was a member of the Whig party, supporting the Union and disinclined to the extreme action favored by the Southern Democrats. But when the Civil War broke out, Bernard chose to support the Confederacy. He moved to Fayetteville in March 1861 and enlisted in Company H, First Regiment, North Carolina Volunteers. He fought at the Battle of Bethel, the first engagement of the war. When his regiment was later disbanded, he received an honorable discharge because of physical disability.

Following his discharge, Bernard returned to journalism, working for the *Presbyterian* and the *Daily Telegraph* in Fayetteville until 1865, when he left to found the Wilmington *Dispatch* with Colonel John D. Barry and others. He left this association in 1867 and established the Wilmington *Star*, later called the Wilmington *Morning Star*. For the next forty years, Bernard served as editor of this paper and wrote a daily column.

Bernard was an active Democrat and wielded great influence as the editor of one of the state's major newspapers. He never held an elective office but often served as manager of political campaigns. In 1870 there was a majority of Republican voters in New Hanover County. The Republicans believed that the Democrats would not submit a party ticket for the election and thus had several candidates for several offices. Bernard and other members of the Democrats' county executive committee, however, composed a ticket that was kept secret until the morning of the election, when it was distributed to all the polling places in the county. This tactic won for the Democrats a seat in both the state house and the state senate, as well as the election of some county officials. Bernard also helped to elect the Democrat Alfred N. Waddell to Congress in this same year and then managed his reelection in 1874. He served as chairman of the county executive committee for several years. In 1891 he managed John D. Bellamy's election to the legislature. During the next ten years, Bernard was a member of the state Democratic executive committee.

Bernard, an Episcopalian, was buried in Oakdale Cemetery, Wilmington. He was survived by two sons and three daughters: Mrs. R. A. Kingsbury, E. H., Maggie A., Mrs. Malcolm McKay, and William S.

SEE: C. A. Evans, ed., *Confederate Military History*, vol. 4 (1899); Perkins Library (Duke University, Durham), for a biographical MS; Wilmington *Morning Star*, 20 Feb. 1918.

SAMUEL M. GAINOR

Bernard, William Stanly (*15 Sept. 1867–7 May 1938*), professor of Greek in The University of North Carolina, was born in Greenville, the son of Dr. William Augustus Bernard, a surgeon captain in the Confederate Army, and Mary Smith, said to have been a direct descendant of Landgrave Thomas Smith of South Carolina. From 1893 to 1895 he was a student in the Episcopal Theological Seminary of Virginia. He next served as commandant and instructor in Trinity School at Chocowinity. He entered the university as a special student in 1897, was a member of the Philanthropic Literary Society, editor of the *North Carolina University Magazine* (1899–1900), an outstanding debater, and one of the first three docents licensed to coach unprepared students (in Greek and Psychology). In 1900 he was awarded the A.B. degree and in 1904 the A.M. degree. He served as university librarian in 1900–1901, when reclassification of the library holdings was begun according to the Dewey System.

Bernard taught English briefly (1902–4) in the university (his readings of "Enoch Arden" were later famous); but he had already been appointed instructor in Greek under Eben Alexander in 1901 and had begun a brilliant teaching career in the classics that was to establish him (with the affectionate nickname of "Bully" Bernard) as one of the most memorable teachers in the university. Thomas Wolfe, in *Look Homeward, Angel*, refers to him as "Buck" Benson and pays eloquent tribute to "the vast sea-surge of Homer" as he heard it first to Professor Bernard's "slowly pacing feet and hexametrical drawl." Over the next thirty-eight years many generations of Carolina students were to experience the magic of "Bully" Bernard. Professor Archibald Henderson referred to him as one of "the eloquent spellbinders" on the faculty.

In 1905, Bernard won an Early English Text Society Prize, and the following year he was promoted to the rank of associate professor of Greek. He studied at The University of Chicago in 1906 and at Columbia University in 1909, 1910, and 1911. In 1909, President Francis P. Venable appointed him chairman of a committee to plan the reorganization of the alumni association, and his committee's recommendations were basic to the association's future development. He was one of four advisers on the debate committee during a period when the literary societies were outstandingly successful in their debating contests.

Under President Harry Woodburn Chase, Bernard presided over the historic meeting of 2 Oct. 1920 at the boardinghouse known as "The Coop" that led to the great "Campaign for Higher Education in North Carolina" in 1920–21. During the next decade he spoke in behalf of the university at numerous alumni banquets and dinners throughout the state. In 1920 he was promoted to the rank of professor of Greek, and on 8 July of that year he married Mrs. Adeline Dewey Claypoole Mitchell (1878–1935) of New Bern, by whom he had one child, Mary Stanly.

In the summer of 1924, Bernard introduced what seems to have been the first course in art history in the university; later he added two other courses in the subject. Although he was an Episcopalian, he taught for many years a large Bible class for men in the Chapel Hill Methodist Church. He was a member of the Order of Gimghoul and of Phi Delta Theta Fraternity and was faculty adviser to the Order of the Grail, of which he was an honorary member. In the early twenties he drove a Twombley convertible motor car that was something of a sensation in Chapel Hill.

The evening before his death of a sudden heart attack, Bernard met with the Order of the Grail, which thereafter established a Bernard-Grail scholarship in his memory. He was buried with his wife and his sister, art teacher Mary Augusta Bernard (1864–1933), in the old Chapel Hill Cemetery.

SEE: Kemp P. Battle, *History of the University of North Carolina*, vol. 2 (1912 [photograph]); Chapel Hill *Daily Tar Heel*, 10 and 20 May 1938, 1 Dec. 1938; *Chapel Hill Weekly*, 13 May 1938; *Durham Morning Herald*, 9 May 1938; *Durham Sunday Herald-Sun*, 8 May 1938; *Greensboro Daily News*, 8 May 1938; Archibald Henderson, *The Campus of the First State University* (1949); Raleigh *News and Observer*, 10 May 1938; *University of North Carolina Catalogue*, 1920–21; Louis R. Wilson, *The University of North Carolina, 1900–1930* (1957 [photograph]).

ALFRED GARVIN ENGSTROM

Bernheim, Gotthardt Dellman (*8 Nov. 1827–24 Oct. 1916*), Lutheran pastor, educator, and author, was born in Iserlohn, Westphalia, East Prussia. His father was John Herman Bernheim, a Jewish convert to Christianity who, following his baptism, entered the Lutheran ministry and labored as a missionary to Jews under the direction of the London Missionary Society. His mother was Lizette Dellman. In 1832 the Bernheims emigrated to the United States and settled in western Pennsylvania, where Pastor Bernheim became a member of the Lutheran Ministerium. Here Gotthardt, the elder of two sons, received his early education and was confirmed into the Lutheran faith in Armstrong County. In 1846 he rode horseback to Lexington, S.C., to attend the South Carolina Synod's Classical Institute and Seminary, where he was graduated in 1849. Licensed in the same year and ordained in 1853, he was pastor of St. Andrew's Church, Charleston, from 1853 to 1858. Later his brother, Charles Herman, was educated for the Lutheran ministry and became a prominent pastor in southern churches.

In 1858, Bernheim affiliated with the North Carolina Synod and until 1860 served the historic St. John's Church in Cabarrus County and New Bethel Church in Stanley County. At the same time his interest in the educational mission of the church led him to accept a position as financial agent for the emerging North Carolina College, a Lutheran institution for men in Mt. Pleasant. Soon he was elected to its first board of trustees. In 1861 he removed to Charlotte to become pastor of St. Mark's Church which he had previously organized, and of St. Michael's, Troutman. He served both churches until 1865. Following his Charlotte pastorate, he worked actively in the North to secure funds for the purchase by the North Carolina Synod of the North Carolina Female Seminary, later Mont Amoena Seminary, at Mt. Pleasant. Successful in this venture, he was elected president of the seminary and occupied that position from 1868 to 1870. During these years he also organized and was first pastor of Ebenezer Church, Rowan County. Afterward, he was called to the pastorate of St. Paul's Church, Wilmington, where he remained from 1870 to 1882. While at St. Paul's, Bernheim established a parochial school and the St. Paul's Female Seminary. In 1877 he was the recipient of an honorary D.D. degree. Following his ministry in Wilmington, he was briefly president of North Carolina College. Then he left the state to serve Grace Church, Phillipsburg, N.J., from 1883 to 1892. He returned to North Carolina in the latter year to accept a call to St. Matthew's Church, Wilmington, where he remained until 1901. In that year he retired at Charlotte and was supply pastor of St. Luke-Morning Star Parish in Monroe from 1905 until 1907. At that time he again became interested in educational pursuits and joined the faculty of Elizabeth College, a Lutheran institution for women located in Charlotte, where he was dean of the faculty and professor of the English Bible and sacred literature.

Bernheim's influence was especially apparent in the work of the North Carolina Synod and Ministerium of the Evangelical Lutheran Church. In 1861 he was elected secretary of the synod and in 1863 and 1878 he was its president. During the Civil War he was influential in organizing the General Synod of the Evangelical Lutheran Church in the Confederate States of America and served as a delegate to its sessions. For many years he was an officer of the Missionary Society of the Evangelical Lutheran Synod of North Carolina.

Bernheim's literary contribution was considerable and widely recognized. He was associate editor of the southern general synod's the *Evangelical Lutheran* in 1866 and 1867 and edited a literary magazine, *At Home and Abroad*, from 1881 to 1883. His published works include *History of the German Settlements and of the Lutheran Church, in North and South Carolina* (1872); *The First Twenty Years of the History of St. Paul's Evangelical Lutheran Church, Wilmington, N.C.* (1879); and, in cooperation with G. H. Cox, *The History of the Evangelical Lutheran Synod and Ministerium of North Carolina* (1902).

Bernheim was married twice: on 25 Apr. 1854 to Elizabeth Crowe Clayton of Charleston, S.C. (eight children); and after her death to Amanda Ella Lease of Nokomis, Ill. on 22 Apr. 1897 (five children).

SEE: Hugh G. Anderson, *Lutheranism in the Southeastern States, 1860–1886* (1969); G. D. Bernheim, *The First Twenty Years of the History of St. Paul's Evangelical Lutheran Church* (1879), *The History of the Evangelical Lutheran Synod and Ministerium of North Carolina* (1902), *History of the German Settlements and of the Lutheran Church in North and South Carolina* (1872), and, ed., *At Home and Abroad: A Monthly Journal of General Literature and Information* (1881–83); *Charlotte Observer*, 25 Oct. 1916; *Life Sketches of Lutheran Ministers* (1966); *Lutheran Church Visitor*, 2 Nov. 1916; Paul McCullogh, ed., *A History of the Lutheran Church in South Carolina* (1971); *Minutes of the Evangelical Lutheran Synod and Ministerium of North Carolina*, 1857–83, 1892–1900; Jacob L. Morgan, ed., *History of the Lutheran Church in North Carolina* (1953); Abdel R. Wentz, *The Lutheran Church in American History* (1923); William T. Whitsett, "A Lutheran Romance," *Lutheran*, 10 Sept. 1931.

ROBERT W. DELP

Berry, Charles (*d. 29 Dec. 1765*) chief justice of the North Carolina Supreme Court by appointment of the secretary of state for the southern department on 27 Nov. 1758. A resident of London but not a barrister, Berry's nomination came to the board of trade from Horace Walpole. Berry did not come into the colony to assume his duties until 6 Dec. 1759. Prior to his arrival, he was asked by the board of trade to render an opinion on the validity of the North Carolina Supreme Court Act of 1754. Berry recommended disallowance, because the bill undercut the royal prerogative by placing the appointment of associate justices in control of the General Assembly, and the board agreed with his advice in its recommendation to the Privy Council. However in May 1760, after six months in North Carolina, Berry reversed himself and supported a similar legislative measure claiming that his previous stand was based on an unfamiliarity with the operation of the provincial court system.

In September 1759, before Berry arrived in the colony, Governor Arthur Dobbs nominated him to a seat on the royal council, even though the two men had never met. On 2 Jan. 1760, Dobbs persuaded the council to approve a temporary appointment for Berry to fill a council seat left vacant by the suspension of Francis Corbin. However, when Dobbs received a new set of royal instructions in March 1762, Berry was not listed as a councilor. In fact, he had not attended a meeting of that body since early in 1761. Still, the governor was anxious to have Berry in the upper house, and the board of trade assured him in May 1762 that Berry would succeed to the seat vacated by the death of John Swann. Two years later, on 19 Apr. 1764, Berry received his mandamus and was seated as a junior councilor.

During 1762, Berry became involved in a quarrel with the provincial secretary, Benjamin Heron, over who should control the appointment of superior court clerks. Berry contended that the prerogative for this lucrative privilege traditionally belonged to his office, but Heron replied that his commission authorized him to appoint all court clerks. Unable to obtain satisfaction from the governor, Berry appealed to the board of trade for a ruling in the matter, but the question was not settled during his lifetime.

On 21 Dec. 1765, Berry shot himself in the head with a pistol; he died eight days later. What drove him to suicide is not known, but in his history of North Carolina, F. X. Martin relates a rumor that Berry was upset by the coldness of Governor William Tryon after Berry released a man the governor wished to see sentenced for dueling. Whatever the cause, the coroner ruled the suicide "an act of lunacy." Berry, who had resided in New Hanover County, was survived by a wife but no children.

SEE: H. B. McKoy Collection (Southern Historical Collection, University of North Carolina, Chapel Hill); William L. Saunders, *Colonial Records of North Carolina*, vols. 5–7 (1887–90).

WILLIAM S. PRICE, JR.

Berry, Harriet Morehead (*22 July 1877–24 Mar. 1940*), leader in the good roads movement in North Carolina and a civic and political activist, was born in Hillsborough, the daughter of Dr. John and Mary Strayhorn Berry. Harriet Berry's grandfather, Captain John Berry, a state legislator, building contractor, and architect, designed and constructed one of the first buildings at Wake Forest College, Smith Building (later the Playmakers Theater) on the campus of The University of North Carolina, the courthouse at Hillsborough, and other notable buildings in the state. He served in the state legislature and was a member of the North Carolina Secession Convention of 1861 and of the convention that restored the state to the Union in 1865.

Educated first at home by her mother and at the Nash-Kollock school in Hillsborough, Miss Berry entered the State Normal and Industrial School (now The University of North Carolina at Greensboro) in 1892 and was graduated with honors in 1897. She then took a position as instructor at the Oxford Orphan Asylum in Oxford, but after two years of teaching returned to the State Normal and Industrial School to take the commercial course. Completing the two-year course in less than a year, she was recommended by her instructor for a job as stenographer to Dr. Joseph Hyde Pratt, mineralogist on the North Carolina Geological and Economic Survey at Chapel Hill.

Harriet Berry began her work with the Geological and Economic Survey in February 1901. Although she was hired as a stenographer, she quickly became involved with many phases of the survey's work. Under state geologist Joseph Austin Holmes, the North Carolina Geological and Economic Survey had taken the lead in movements to encourage conservation and, particularly, to promote the building of better roads. Working with Holmes as well as with Pratt, Harriet Berry assumed much of the responsibility for providing the staff work on which the survey's technical investigations and its reform activities rested. In 1904 she was made secretary to the survey.

In 1906, Joseph Hyde Pratt succeeded Joseph Holmes both as state geologist and as secretary of the North Carolina Good Roads Association. Working closely with Pratt, Miss Berry became increasingly involved in the organization of the good roads movement on the state level. When Pratt went into the army in 1917, she became acting head of the survey, kept up the technical work of the office, and continued the agitation for active participation by the state in road construction. In 1919 she led the North Carolina Good Roads Association in an attempt to secure passage of a law creating a highway commission with authority and funds to construct a state system of hard-surface roads. The General Assembly failed to enact what she considered an adequate law, and she set out to strengthen her organization in anticipation of the 1921 legislative session.

Between 1919 and 1921, Miss Berry spoke in eighty-nine of North Carolina's hundred counties and flooded the state with news releases, letters, petitions, and circulars. Through her strenuous efforts in those two years, she increased the membership of the North Carolina Good Roads Association from 272 to 5,500 and built its treasury from less than $2,000 to more than $12,000. Overcoming opposition from within her organization and from other good roads groups, she led a unified and enthusiastic good roads movement to the 1921 General Assembly and emerged with a road law that created a powerful state highway commission and committed North Carolina to the construction of a state system of modern highways. Generally recognized as the guiding spirit behind the road law of 1921, she was hailed by the Raleigh *News and Observer* as "the best woman politician in the state."

In 1921, Miss Berry left the Geological and Economic Survey, in part because of a change in administration and in part because of bitter feelings resulting from the fight for the road law of 1921. In 1922 she joined the staff of the

Greensboro Daily News as editor of the Department of Industries and Resources. Through her newspaper work, she campaigned for better schools and for the creation of an organization to advertise North Carolina's advantages for industry, tourists, and settlement and to promote the orderly development of the state's resources. In 1924 she became secretary of the North Carolina Credit Union Association, which encouraged farmers to form local cooperatives, pooling their financial resources to create a fund from which members could borrow at a cost substantially below bank interest rates. She joined the North Carolina Department of Agriculture in 1925, employed initially as editor of the department's *Market News* and then as director of publicity for credit unions. In 1927 she became state superintendent of savings and loan associations, continuing in that position until poor health forced her to retire in 1937.

Miss Berry then returned to her home in Chapel Hill, keeping up her old interests to the extent her declining health would allow and beginning both an autobiography and a history of the good roads movement in North Carolina. She died in Chapel Hill in 1940 of heart trouble and complications. An Episcopalian, she was buried after a graveside service in the Chapel Hill Cemetery.

Harriet Berry was a lifelong Democrat, serving her party on local, state, and national levels. She was a member of the state Democratic executive committee and a delegate at large to the Democratic National Convention of 1924. She was a member of the Legislative Council of Women in World War I and was a supporter of woman suffrage, serving as head of the Chapel Hill Equal Suffrage League and at one time as vice-president of the North Carolina Equal Suffrage League.

Harriet Berry's friends remembered her as a delicate woman of refined tastes, with a strong but quiet voice and the hands of an artist. She was also a person of inflexible will and a skilled political infighter. To one prominent politician, who crossed her in the campaign for the road law of 1921, she remained "that waspish woman." In Harriet Berry's personality, a love of poetry and music mixed somewhat incongruously with intense ambition and an amazing capacity for hard work. This personality, in turn, was guided by an intellectual and moral conviction prefigured in her honors address as a college senior, "The Jingle of the Guinea." In this essay, which was printed in several North Carolina newspapers and long remembered in the state, she argued that the health of a society lay in the well-being of all its members, not in the wealth of a minority. The conviction that she labored for the benefit of the people sometimes led Harriet Berry to blur the distinction between her cause and her ego and occasionally warped her judgment of those who sincerely opposed her. Her central role in the creation of North Carolina's highway system and her long years of public service, however, are eloquent testimony to her vision of a life dedicated to the service of her state.

SEE: Harriet Morehead Berry Papers (Southern Historical Collection, University of North Carolina, Chapel Hill); Cecil Kenneth Brown, *The State Highway System of North Carolina: Its Evolution and Present Status* (1931); North Carolina Geological Survey Papers (Southern Historical Collection, University of North Carolina, Chapel Hill); *Notable American Women, 1607–1950* (1971).

HARRY W. MCKOWN

Berry, John (*18 Aug. 1798–11 Jan. 1870*), self-taught builder-architect and Orange County politician, was born near Hillsborough, the son of John Berry, Sr., and Rhoda (Rosanna?) (Whitted?) Berry. According to family tradition, John Berry, Sr., was killed in the Battle of New Orleans.

On 15 June 1805, when her son was seven years old, Mrs. Berry purchased Lot 54 on West Queen Street in Hillsborough, where she afterward built the little Berry Brick House. A near neighbor, master brickmason Samuel Hancock, who may have built the house, gave Berry early training in the craft of bricklaying, but there is no preserved record of any formal apprenticeship. An early brick building, almost certainly built by Hancock and Berry, is the small (30 × 50 feet) Presbyterian church on West Tryon Street, begun in the autumn of 1815. The names of Samuel Hancock, Mrs. Rhoda Berry, and John Berry all appear in the 1816 pew rental list of the church. A preserved receipt of 28 Aug. 1819, signed "John Berry for Hancock & Berry," for work done on Frederick Nash's house, indicates that the two men may have been informal partners, at least in the first several years of their association. Hancock's inability to write prevented his keeping any ledgers or records of work done, and so far as is known, Berry himself kept no ledgers.

The two men are thought to have built the two-story Hillsborough Academy building in the "New Town" of 1821; the Masonic Hall, designed by state architect William Nichol, begun late in 1823 and finished in 1825; St. Matthew's Episcopal Church, 1825–26; and St. Luke's Episcopal Church in Salisbury, completed in 1828. These last several buildings directly and indirectly provided young Berry the contacts he needed with trained architects, and the Salisbury project also taught him the complicated logistics of erecting buildings at a considerable distance from home. Francis Lister Hawks, grandson of John Hawks, the English architect of Tryon Palace, was then briefly resident in Hillsborough and is thought to have introduced Berry to some of his grandfather's books on architecture. In any case, Berry became familiar with the carpenters' patternbooks of the day, on which he drew heavily for designs. His copy of Owen Biddle's *Young Carpenter's Assistant* (Philadelphia, 1805) has been preserved. He is said to have proved himself an accomplished draftsman, but none of the preliminary sketches that he customarily sent by letter to prospective employers has come to light.

Berry joined the Orange Guards, and the title "Captain," thereafter always given him, was apparently derived from that service. The *Hillsborough Recorder* chronicles Berry's growing concern with civic affairs in Hillsborough—he was repeatedly marshal of the day for Independence Day celebrations, senior warden and grand master of Eagle Lodge No. 19, A.F. & A.M., one of the managers of the Orange County Sunday schools, and a Town commissioner in 1842–47.

On 6 Mar. 1827, Berry married Elizabeth Ann ("Betsy") Vincent, daughter of Thomas and Elizabeth Cooksey Vincent of the Crossroads community. Their eight children were sons Cicero and John (later Dr. John Berry) and daughters Amanda, Josephine, Rosanna, Elizabeth Ann, Maria, and Caroline Victoria. Several of the Berry daughters displayed a marked ability in art and studied at the Pratt Institute in Philadelphia.

In the 1830s, Berry began a notable series of twelve buildings around the state: the Caswell County Courthouse in Yanceyville, 1831–33, a 60 × 40-foot structure with a 26-foot elevation, a cupola, and a dome; the two-story stone jail in Hillsborough, 1835; the Wake Forest College main building, a 65 × 132-foot brick over

stone structure with a central block three stories high and two wings four stories high, 1835–37; two impressive brick faculty houses on the Wake Forest College campus, 1838; the Orange County Courthouse in Hillsborough, with Doric portico and cupola—the structure generally regarded as Berry's masterpiece—1844–45; the Smith Building (Playmakers Theater) on The University of North Carolina campus, designed by Alexander Jackson Davis and contracted for by Berry and Henry Richards, Sr., 1851; St. John's College (the Oxford Orphanage) at Oxford, a 122 × 40-foot building four stories tall with a basement, 1855–57; the Methodist Episcopal church in Hillsborough, apparently designed by Berry, 1860–61; the Hillsborough Military Academy and the Commandant's House in West Hillsborough, both designed by Colonel Charles Courtney Tew after the Citadel and built by Berry and Richards, 1859–61; and the Hillsborough Baptist Church, designed by William Percival, begun by D. Kistler, and, after various difficulties, completed by Berry, ca. 1860–70.

From about 1850 onward, Henry Richards, Sr. (1813–90), Hillsborough builder, appears to have worked closely with Berry, although he was never a partner, according to the Berry family. In earlier years, John A. Faucett, a skilled carpenter, had also been associated with Berry. As a matter of policy, Berry trained slaves as skilled brickmasons, tinners, and carpenters and gave them their freedom when they reached master status. Among such trained and freed black craftsmen were "Ned my tinner valued at $2000" (later known as Ned Haughawort) and "Joe my carpenter" (later known as Joe Nichols).

Berry also either renovated entirely or did the brickwork on several dwelling-houses in the Hillsborough area, somehow fitting them into his busy building schedule. These included the Frederick Nash house (later the Nash and Kollock School), 1819; John Knox Witherspoon's Twin Chimneys, 1819; the Anne Call Cameron house, possibly built entirely by Berry and Hancock, ca. 1826; Burnside, with chimneys, a separate kitchen, and a magnificent octagonal brick ice-pit, built for Paul C. Cameron, 1835; the Peter Browne Ruffin house (earlier the Allen Jones Davie house), renovated in the late 1840s by Cadwallader Jones, Sr., including a new three-story brick kitchen; Sunny Side, Berry's enlargement and renovation of a St. Mary's Road farmhouse into a country home for himself, ca. 1846; the Burwell School, an enlargement and renovations, 1848; and Sans Souci, an enlargement of the William Cain town house, after 1856. In several renovations, such as the Burwell School and the Peter Browne Ruffin house, Berry created entirely new facades and completely reoriented houses.

Apparently Berry began as a young man to collect the sizeable library left at Sunny Side, his second and final home northeast of Hillsborough. A catalogue of the surviving segment of the library, chiefly law books, was compiled by Berry's late granddaughter, the lawyer Margaret Berry Street, who recalled the unbroken collection as having contained "a good representation of nearly all the classics."

In addition to his multiple building activities, Berry somehow found time for active involvement in local and state politics, which from the late 1840s onward amounted to an important second career. He served five terms as state senator in 1848, 1850, 1852, 1864, and 1866 and one term as state representative in 1862. He was also a member of the constitutional conventions of 1861 and 1863 and served as a presidential elector. He was also a trustee of Wake Forest College for twelve years from 1850 to 1862.

Although Berry seems always to have remained steadfast in his political views as a member of the Democratic party, he shifted his church affiliation from the Episcopalian (he had been a vestryman in 1842–43 at St. Matthew's Church) to the Baptist church. He may have joined the Presbyterian church in his youth.

Berry's final building venture, in the winter of 1869–70, was a two-story brick structure in downtown Hillsborough, a combined store and ballroom, to be known as the "Berry Building." He caught a severe cold from exposure to the December weather and died of pneumonia at Sunny Side at the age of seventy-two. He was buried in the Berry plot in Hillsborough's Old Town Cemetery, within feet of one of his first buildings, the Presbyterian church. His careful will bequeathed at least 1,238 acres, 42 slaves, a number of town lots, several houses besides Sunny Side and the Berry Brick House, his library, bank stocks and bonds, $11,000 in cash, livestock, and so on to his widow Elizabeth, and the eight Berry children.

Two portraits of Berry were commissioned by the Caswell County Commissioners shortly after his successful completion of the courthouse at Yanceyville in 1833, and one of these still survives as the property of a descendant. A later daguerreotype of Berry and his wife is also in existence. In 1964 a bronze plaque honoring Berry as "a contributor to the tradition of American architecture" was affixed to the Old Orange County Courthouse, a National Register structure; and a further memorial to him is the chancel in the Hillsborough Presbyterian Church, presented by members of the Berry family in 1948.

SEE: Berry Papers (Manuscript Department, Library, Duke University, Durham); *Durham Morning Herald*, 20 Feb. 1949; Mary Claire Engstrom, "Records of Hillsborough Historic District" (North Carolina State Archives, Raleigh), and "Records [Hillsborough] of Historic American Buildings Survey" (National Park Service, Dept. of the Interior, Washington, D.C.); Eva Ingersoll Gatling, "John Berry of Hillsboro," *Journal of the Society of Architectural Historians* 10 (1951); *Hillsborough Recorder*, 16 and 22 June 1825, 15 Sept. 1825, 14 Mar. 1844, 9 and 23 May 1844, 13 June 1844, 26 Jan. 1870 (obit.); Orange County Deed Books 13, 17, 33, 35, and Will Books E (for Thomas Vincent's will) and H (for John Berry's will) (Orange County courthouse, Hillsborough); G. W. Paschal, *History of Wake Forest College*, vol. 1 (1934); Pew Rental Lists, Hillsborough Presbyterian Church, 1816, 1817 ff.; Raleigh *Daily Sentinel*, 18 Jan. 1870 (obit.); Henry S. Stroupe, "John Berry—Builder of the First College Building," *Wake Forest Magazine*, February 1965; James Webb Papers (Southern Historical Collection, University of North Carolina, Chapel Hill).

MARY CLAIRE ENGSTROM

Bethea, Neil Graham (*11 Oct. 1872–24 Feb. 1957*), Methodist Protestant evangelist and minister, was born in Little River, near Fayetteville, the son of William Cameron and Mary Jane Morris Bethea. At an early age, he moved with his family to Burlington. He attended public schools and Catawba College, but because of poor eyesight he did not complete his college course. He joined the North Carolina Annual Conference of the Methodist Protestant Church in 1897 and served for forty-seven years as an active minister and for five additional years as a retired "supply" minister. He was ordained an elder in 1902.

Bethea was an accredited instructor in training classes in his denomination and was sought after for youth assemblies and community training schools. He was active among the leaders in founding High Point College, a school to which all his younger children went for their higher education. In appreciation and recognition of his successful ministry and dedication to the cause of Christian education, High Point College bestowed upon him the honorary D.D. degree in 1934.

Bethea served as conference evangelist for a number of years, traveling across the state holding ten-day revivals "wherever people would gather to listen." In his early ministry, he traveled on foot and by horseback. He said of his methods: "I didn't do anything fancy. I'd give my sermon, pray, and ask them to come to the altar, and they came." He preached over 20,000 sermons and recorded some 8,061 conversions. His first pastorate was in Ellenboro, after which he went to Bessemer City, where Bethea's Chapel was later built and named in his honor. He also served pastorates at Gibsonville, Yarborough, Granville Circuit, Halifax Circuit, Lexington, Asheville, Fletcher, Tryon, and Swannanoa. He served as the conference missionary secretary in 1915–16. In 1926 he made an extensive tour of Palestine.

Bethea attended seven general conferences of the Methodist Protestant church and was an alternate delegate at the uniting conference of the three branches of Methodism in 1939. He retired in 1949.

On 6 Dec. 1899, Bethea married Hattie C. Warlick, daughter of Samuel M. and M. Frances Wood Warlick of Pleasant Hill in Cleveland County. To this union were born five children. Bethea died in Greensboro and was buried there in the Guilford Memorial Park.

SEE: *Greensboro Daily News*, 1954; *Journal of the North Carolina Annual Conference of the Methodist Protestant Church*, scattered issues; *Journal of the Western North Carolina Methodist Conference*, 1957; *Who's Who in Methodism*, 1952; Mrs. A. G. Willcox, Sr. (Enfield, N.C.), personal contact.

RALPH HARDEE RIVES

Bethell, William (*1744–April 1804*), revolutionary soldier and legislator, was born in Virginia and settled in northern Guilford County before the American Revolution. During the war he was a captain in the Guilford County militia, which was commanded by Colonel James Martin. In the Moore's Creek Bridge campaign in 1776, Bethell took part with the militia in the occupation of Cross Creek. He was in service again in 1779 when the county militia was called to disperse a Tory force in the Yadkin River Valley. In the summer of 1781 he was in command of a troop of mounted infantry from Guilford County in General Griffith Rutherford's successful campaign to force the British evacuation of Wilmington. In this campaign, Bethell served under the command of Colonel Robert Smith in the skirmish at Moore's Plantation.

After the war, Bethell returned to his sizeable plantation on Lick Fork and Hogan's Creek. On 29 Dec. 1785, the new county of Rockingham was created from the northern part of Guilford County. Appointed as one of Rockingham's first justices of the peace, Bethell also was elected as one of the county's first members of the General Assembly. He served four terms in the House of Commons, from 1786 to 1789, and one term in the state senate in 1790. In this period the leading issue facing the General Assembly was the ratification of the federal Constitution. Bethell and the Rockingham County legislative delegation were solidly anti-Federalist, voting against the two constitutional conventions held in North

Carolina in 1788 and 1789. In the General Assembly of 1788, Bethell seconded a motion by Thomas Person of Granville County to reconsider a resolution for a second convention, but the motion was defeated. In this same session, Bethell served on a house Committee on Public Revenue. In the 1790 session of the state senate, he was on the Committee of Propositions and Grievances, a committee to consider the division of Caswell County, and a committee to examine the engrossed bills.

When the constitutional conventions of 1788 and 1789 were held to consider ratification of the U.S. Constitution, Rockingham County elected anti-Federalist delegates. Bethell was a delegate to both conventions. In the first, which met at Hillsborough 25 July–4 Aug. 1788, Bethell and the Rockingham delegation voted with the majority to offer a declaration of rights and twenty-six amendments. At Fayetteville, where the second convention met 16–22 Nov. 1789, he and his colleagues voted with the minority against ratification of the Constitution.

From 1790 until his death fourteen years later, Bethell was active in the county government. By 1792 he was clerk of court, and he retained that position until his death. He served on various special committees; in 1799 he was appointed a trustee responsible for promotion of the new town at the county seat, Wentworth. He continued to be a captain in the county militia for the remainder of his life. By 1800 he was the third largest slaveholder in the county with thirty slaves and had accumulated an estate of over eight thousand acres of land.

Bethell married Nancy Stubblefield (d. 1826). They had four daughters, Suky, Jeany, Nancy, and Sine; and four sons, William, John, Alfred, and Pinckney. The Bethells attended the Lick Fork Primitive Baptist Church, near their home. After the death of her husband, Nancy Bethell married George Roberts. The eldest son of William and Nancy Bethell, William, Jr. (1764–1834), was as active as his father in state politics. He became a brigadier general in the state militia (1818–29), served five terms in the House of Commons (1815–20), and served two terms in the state senate (1828–29).

SEE: Walter Clark, ed., *State Records of North Carolina*, 16 vols. (1895–1905); Marjorie Craig, *Family Records of Henrietta Alberta Ratcliffe and Jasper Newton Craig* (1955); E. W. Dixon, *Williamson, Bethel and Allied Families of North Carolina* (1956); Guilford County Deeds and Land Entries, 1779–95 (North Carolina State Archives, Raleigh); *North Carolina Manual* (1913); Revolutionary Army Accounts (North Carolina State Archives, Raleigh); Rockingham County Court Minutes, Deeds, and Wills (North Carolina State Archives, Raleigh); U.S. Census (1790, 1800).

LINDLEY S. BUTLER

Bethune, John (*1751–23 Sept. 1815*), Presbyterian minister, was born on the Isle of Skye, Scotland, and raised in the Parish of Sleat under the ministry of the Reverend John MacPherson. MacPherson impressed upon the young man the importance of learning and encouraged him to enter the ministry and continue his education at King's College, Aberdeen. Bethune returned home from his studies to find the people of Skye planning almost en masse to leave their homes and settle in North Carolina. He soon caught the emigration fever and came over as early as 1773 as a licentiate of the (Presbyterian) Church of Scotland. Here, on McLendon's Creek in what is now Moore County, he settled with his mother, Christian, and his maternal grandparents,

Donald and Katherine Campbell of Scalpay. In the few years before the outbreak of the American Revolution, Bethune ministered to the Highland Scots around him in their native Gaelic tongue. He organized the present-day Mt. Carmel Presbyterian Church near Ellerbe.

Early in 1776, North Carolina Highlanders loyal to the king set out for the coast to join Governor Josiah Martin, and Bethune went along as their chaplain. They were intercepted at Moore's Creek by Americans who got there first, set up a defensive position on the opposite side of the stream, removed the plank from the bridge, and greased the two log beams that remained. Bethune and other officers were taken prisoner and sent to Philadelphia for confinement. Their imprisonment was not of long duration. They were given their freedom sometime in November of that year on their promise not to take any further part in the war. Upon his release, Bethune made his way to Halifax, Nova Scotia, where he was made chaplain to the First Battalion of Royal Highland Emigrants. On 23 Nov. 1778, because he was "in some distress for want of money," he was appointed chaplain to the entire regiment by Captain Alexander MacDonald. While the regiment was stationed in New York State, he met Veronica Wadden, a native of Switzerland, whom he married 30 Sept. 1782.

After the peace, the Bethunes took up residence in Montreal, along with other United Empire Loyalists. Many of these looked upon him as their leader, and he drew them together to form the first Presbyterian congregation in the city, the St. Gabriel Street Church. Here he ministered from 12 Mar. 1786 until 6 May 1787, when he and his family moved to Upper Canada (now Ontario).

Basic to their decision to move was the lure of land, which was being granted to United Empire Loyalists in appreciation for their services during the war. As a chaplain, equivalent in rank to a captain, Bethune was entitled to three thousand acres. He settled at Williamstown, Glengarry County, and began his ministry there, thus becoming the pioneer Presbyterian minister in what is now the Province of Ontario. He soon organized churches at Williamstown, Martintown, Summerstown, Cornwall, and Lancaster and ministered to them until his death. He was buried beside his wife in the churchyard at Williamstown.

John Bethune was the first minister of any denomination to serve in what are now Moore, Montgomery, Richmond, and Anson counties, N.C., and the first Presbyterian minister to serve in the city of Montreal, Quebec, and the Province of Ontario.

SEE: Archives of Ontario (Toronto); Glengarry Historical Society (Williamstown, Ontario, Canada); *A History of the Scotch Presbyterian Church, St. Gabriel Street, Montreal* (1887); William L. Saunders and Walter Clark, eds., *Colonial and State Records of North Carolina*, vols. 10–11 (1890–95); Hew Scott, *Fasti Ecclesiae Scoticanae*, vol. 7 (1928).

JAMES MACKENZIE

Bethune, Lauchlin (*15 Apr. 1785–10 Oct. 1874*), congressman and planter, led the Democratic party in the upper Cape Fear region in the 1830s, the formative years of the second American party system. He was born in Cumberland County and lived there most of his life in the sandhills district of Quewhiffle. He was educated privately and at the Lumberton Male Academy. His political career began in 1817, when he was elected state senator from Cumberland. He served six more terms in the senate, in 1818, 1822–25, and 1827.

In 1831, Bethune sought the seat in Congress held by freshman Representative Edmund Deberry of Montgomery County. In that election, Bethune won the right to represent the Seventh District by the narrow margin of thirty-seven votes. Deberry was an opponent of Andrew Jackson and later became the standard-bearer of the local Whig party; Bethune ran against him as a supporter of Jackson.

Once in Washington, Bethune's career in the Twenty-second Congress was not outstanding. He served as a member of the Committee on Elections but never addressed the House during his term of office. His votes were cast consistently in support of Jackson's administration and the principles of limited government. Thus, in crucial roll calls, he voted against congressional attention to internal improvements, against expanding the jurisdiction of the U.S. Supreme Court, and against the rechartering of the Bank of the United States.

After serving one term, Bethune lost his seat in Congress to Deberry. The two politicians continued to contest the seat in 1835 and 1837, Deberry winning by increased majorities on both occasions. Bethune's major political service thus arose from his activities as party spokesman and organizer and not from his tenure in office. Throughout the 1830s and 1840s, he acted as chairman of Democratic meetings in Cumberland County and as a delegate to district and state conventions of the party. In his campaign circulars and addresses, he popularized opposition to the protective tariff, opposition to federal support of internal improvements, and support of states' rights and promoted the other standard doctrines of his party.

The only exception to his consistently Democratic views was his banking policy. Bethune's shifting positions on this subject indicate the growing power of party regularity on the opinions of local political figures in the Age of Jackson. In June 1832, Bethune expressed public disapproval of the rechartering of the Bank of the United States as a matter of policy. He did not regard the bank as unconstitutional, for he proposed remedying its monopoly features by the chartering of two or three national banks in its stead. But when Jackson vetoed the recharter a month later on constitutional grounds, Bethune reversed himself. In 1836 he introduced resolutions to a meeting of the Cumberland County Democratic party that denounced banks and all chartered corporations as dangerous instruments of "associated wealth," which had always been the "main key stones of monarchies and aristocracies." The resolutions passed unanimously, and extreme hostility to all banks was the principal feature of Bethune's congressional campaign circular of 1837.

After his defeat in that election, Bethune no longer sought public office but retired to his plantation. The next decades brought him more success from agriculture than he had ever enjoyed in politics. While he was still a state senator, he had been the owner of 11,500 acres in Cumberland County. By 1860 he was the master of thirty-eight slaves. His political hostility to "associated wealth" clearly did not interfere with his private ambitions, nor did his economic opinions arise from a life spent in poverty.

Bethune was buried in the Presbyterian Cemetery in Aberdeen.

SEE: Harry L. Watson, " 'Bitter combinations of the neighbourhood': The Second American Party System in Cumberland County, North Carolina" (Ph.D. diss., Northwestern University, 1976).

                                                                    HARRY L. WATSON

Betts, Alexander Davis (25 Aug. 1832–15 Dec. 1918), Methodist minister and Confederate chaplain, the son of Temperance Utley and William Betts, was born in Blockersville (now Stedman), Cumberland County. At the age of seventeen, when he was playfully trying to ride a young steer, he was thrown and sustained an injury that left him lame for life. At the nearby Summerville Academy he began a classical education, and he entered The University of North Carolina as a member of the class of 1855. He received the A.B. degree and a few years later the M.A.; in 1895 the university honored him with the degree of D.D. Betts remained a loyal friend to the university and attended University Day and commencement a number of times. In 1882 he wrote a hymn for University Day, and he was a trustee from 1879 until 1895. Shortly before graduation day in 1855, Betts married Mary E. Davis of Chapel Hill, adopting her maiden name as his own middle name in her honor.

In Chapel Hill, Betts was converted to Methodism in 1853, and there he was licensed to preach in 1855. For a brief time, however, he taught in a Pittsboro academy. Soon afterward he became "supply" minister to the Methodist church in Martinsville, Henry County, Va. In gratitude for his warm reception there, he named his newborn son Henry for the county.

Before the Civil War, Betts served churches in Sampson County, Smithville (now Southport), Elizabethtown, and Smithfield. After the war he served in many places, as Methodist ministers customarily do. Among his assignments were churches in the counties of Anson, Brunswick, Carteret, Craven, Duplin, Guilford, Harnett, Jones, Nash, and Wilson. In 1908 he was superannuated but continued his work by preaching upon invitation and working with schools and prisons in various parts of the state.

After the death of his first wife (5 Sept 1879), Betts in 1881 married Priscilla M. Debnam. Six of his eleven children were living at the time of his death: the Reverend W. A., J. R., Sallie, Dr. J. S., Mrs. L. P. Wokins, and Mrs. R. L. Davis.

On 25 Oct. 1861, Betts was commissioned chaplain of the Thirtieth North Carolina Regiment; he served throughout the Civil War. General Robert E. Lee is said to have spoken of Betts on one occasion as "that model chaplain." Betts kept a journal, published in 1904 as *Experiences of a Confederate Chaplain* (Piedmont, S.C.), in which he recorded detailed and moving accounts of his work.

SEE: *The Chaplain* 24 (Mar.–Apr. 1967); Daniel L. Grant, *Alumni History of The University of North Carolina* (1924); Thomas N. Ivey, ed., *Handbook of the Methodist Episcopal Church, South, in North Carolina* (1905); Thomas N. Ivey, ed., *Southern Methodist Handbook* (1913, 1919); Methodist Church, *Journal of the North Carolina Conference* (1919); James Paul Pegg, *Tar Heel Chaplain* (n.d.); *Trinity Alumni Register* 4 (Jan. 1919).

                                                                    LOUISE C. SMITH

Bickett, Thomas Walter (28 Feb. 1869–28 Dec. 1921), attorney general (1909–17) and governor (1917–21) of North Carolina, was born in Monroe, the eldest of four children of Thomas Winchester and Mary Covington Bickett. His father, a druggist, died when Thomas Walter was thirteen years old.

After being graduated from Wake Forest College in 1890, Bickett taught in the public schools for two years, first in Marion and later in Winston-Salem. He studied law at The University of North Carolina in the fall of 1892 and in February of the following year was admitted to the bar. He practiced briefly in Monroe and in Danbury before moving in 1895 to Louisburg, where he soon became the senior partner in the firm of Bickett, White, & Malone.

Bickett, a Democrat, first held public office in 1907 as a member of the state house of representatives, to which he was elected by the voters of Franklin County in the general election of 1906. Probably the most reform-minded General Assembly of the progressive era, the 1907 legislature enacted a substantial body of progressive legislation. A very humane man, Bickett was largely instrumental in securing passage of a bill to enlarge and improve the state's facilities for treatment of the mentally defective. He was also a staunch supporter of the bill to establish the East Carolina Teachers' Training School.

At the 1908 Democratic State Convention, Bickett won widespread recognition for a forceful speech nominating Ashley Horne for the governorship. Horne lost the nomination, but Bickett, in part at least because of his speech, was nominated for the post of attorney general. Bickett was twice elected attorney general, first in 1908 and again in 1912, and in that capacity ably defended the state's interests in cases appealed to the U.S. Supreme Court. In frequent demand as a public speaker, he emerged during his second term as a likely prospect for the gubernatorial nomination in 1916.

In the 1916 Democratic gubernatorial primary, the first such contest since enactment of the state-wide primary law in 1915, Bickett polled 63,121 votes to E. L. Daughtridge's 37,017; he subsequently defeated Frank A. Linney, the Republican candidate, in the general election. Inaugurated governor on 11 Jan. 1917, he was in office less than three months before the United States entered World War I.

As wartime governor, Bickett cooperated fully with the national authorities during the crisis of 1917–18. In various public statements, he defended America's entry into the war, explained the operation of the federal draft law, and encouraged North Carolinians to fulfill their patriotic duty by supporting the Liberty Loan drives. On one notable occasion in June 1918, he traveled to mountainous Ashe County and personally persuaded some army deserters and draft dodgers, who had banded together and absconded to the hills, to surrender themselves to the authorities. In so doing, he rejected the advice of the state's adjutant general, who had recommended the use of force to subdue the defiant mountaineers.

During his governorship, Bickett proved to be a modest reformer. Many of his achievements foreshadowed those of his immediate successors— Cameron Morrison (1921–25), Angus W. McLean (1925–29), and O. Max Gardner (1929–33)—during whose administrations North Carolina achieved a nation-wide reputation as the most progressive state in the South. In his messages to the General Assemblies of 1917 and 1919 and to the special session of 1920, Bickett made numerous legislative recommendations, most of which ultimately were enacted into law.

From the very outset of his administration, Bickett manifested a special desire to improve the quality of rural life in the state. At his behest, the General Assembly of 1917 enacted several measures with this purpose in mind, among them acts to encourage the teaching of agriculture and home economics in the rural schools and to limit the amount of interest landlords could charge for extending supplies or credit under the crop-lien system.

In response to Bickett's appeals, the legislature expanded the duties of both the state board of health and

the board of charities and public welfare, previously known as the board of public charities. In the area of public education, the General Assembly increased the minimum school term from four to six months, inaugurated a state-wide teacher-certification program, substantially increased teachers' salaries, and authorized a half-million dollar state bond issue to assist counties in the construction of new schoolhouses. Perhaps one of Bickett's most significant contributions to educational progress in the state was his selection in 1918 of the able Eugene Clyde Brooks as state superintendent of public instruction. Despite the state's traditional hostility to large bonded debts, the 1917 General Assembly approved, with Bickett's endorsement, a $3 million bond issue to finance a six-year expansion program at the state's institutions of higher learning and hospitals for the mentally and physically defective. According to Harry Woodburn Chase, president of The University of North Carolina in the 1920s, this authorization marked the "turning point" in the state's attitude toward institutional financing.

One of the most enduring legacies of the Bickett administration was in tax reform. As early as 1913, Bickett, then attorney general, had advocated revisions in the state's cumbersome revenue structure. The reforms adopted during his term as governor were incorporated in the Revaluation Act of 1919 and the Revenue Act of 1920, by the terms of which all property in the state, both real and personal, was reassessed under state supervision according to uniform standards of valuation. More significantly, however, the acts stipulated that thereafter the state government was to derive its revenue, other than that supporting the school fund, from income, inheritance, franchise, and license taxes and to relinquish to the counties the exclusive right to tax property. These and related tax reform measures modernized the state's revenue structure and provided for a more equitable distribution of the tax burden.

During the Bickett administration the good roads movement in the state reached its peak. By 1919 the good roads enthusiasts, organized into several state-wide associations, were demanding a multimillion dollar highway expansion program, to be financed through the sale of state bonds. Unlike his immediate successor, Cameron Morrison, who enthusiastically championed a costly highway program, Bickett was opposed to the issuance of large quantities of road bonds. No spectacular construction program was approved during his term as governor. But the state highway commission, until then largely an advisory body, was reorganized and its duties enlarged. Bickett's 1919 selection of Frank Page as chairman of the commission proved to be one of his wisest appointments.

Bickett's oft-expressed concern for the lot of the oppressed and disadvantaged among the state's population, the tenant farmers, blacks, and prison inmates, marked him as a man of humane disposition. Although some modest prison reform measures were adopted by the state at his instigation, prison conditions in North Carolina still were substandard at the end of his administration in 1921. Bickett's concern for the well-being of prison inmates, as well as his sense of justice, caused him to adopt what many citizens in the state regarded as an excessively lenient pardon policy. To his credit, he was probably the first governor in the state's history to confront a mob bent on lynching a prisoner held in a county court house and to persuade it to disperse.

While a traditionalist in his attitude toward race relations, Bickett nonetheless manifested a sympathy for the lot of the blacks uncommon among southern politicians of his time. He paroled or pardoned some four hundred black prisoners, supported increased spending for black education, and made recommendations to the General Assembly that resulted ultimately in the establishment of a sanatorium for black tuberculars and a reformatory for black delinquent boys. On at least one occasion he denounced as "sinful" the racist pronouncements of the Loyal Order of Klansmen. "The South needs good and brave governors such as . . . Bickett," declared the Norfolk (Va.) *Journal and Guide*, a black newspaper, in 1921.

Upon his retirement as governor in January 1921, Bickett purchased a home in Raleigh and formed a law partnership with Attorney General James S. Manning and Garland S. Ferguson, Jr. On 27 Dec. 1921, less than a year after leaving office, he suffered a stroke. He died the following day at the age of fifty-two and was buried in Louisburg.

Bickett married Fannie Yarborough, the daughter of Colonel William Yarborough, in Louisburg on 29 Nov. 1898. Of the three children born to the couple, only one, William Yarborough, survived infancy. Bickett was a member of the Masonic Order and of the Episcopal church.

SEE: *History of North Carolina*, vol. 4 (1919); Beth G. Crabtree, *North Carolina Governors, 1585–1958* (1958); *DAB*, vol. 2 (1929); Sue Sandra Horton, "The Political Career of Thomas Walter Bickett" (M.A. thesis, University of North Carolina, 1965); James S. Manning, "Thomas Walter Bickett," North Carolina Bar Association, *Proceedings* 25 (1922); Santford Martin, comp., and R. B. House, ed., *Public Letters and Papers of Thomas Walter Bickett* (1923); North Carolina State Archives (Raleigh), for Bickett's official papers and a collection of Fannie Yarborough Bickett's private papers; Raleigh *News and Observer*, 29 Dec. 1921; Gary Trawick and Paul Wyche, *One Hundred Years, One Hundred Men* (1971).

NATHANIEL F. MAGRUDER

Biddle, Mary Duke (16 Nov. 1887–14 June 1960), philanthropist, was born in Durham to Benjamin Newton and Sarah Pearson Angier Duke. Educated first in the public schools of Durham, she was graduated from Trinity College in 1907. She traveled extensively in Europe, was presented at the Court of St. James, and was frequently in New York even before her father acquired a Fifth Avenue home there soon after the turn of the century. A lover of opera, she became a serious student of vocal music and patron of the arts. In June 1915, shortly after her brother, Angier Buchanan Duke, married Cordelia Biddle of Philadelphia, Mary Duke married Anthony J. Drexel Biddle, Jr., Cordelia's brother. Anthony and Mary Biddle had two children, Mary Duke II (later Mrs. James H. Semans) and Nicholas Benjamin Duke; they were divorced in 1931. Until her death, Mrs. Biddle maintained homes in New York City, Durham, and Irvington-on-the-Hudson, N.Y.

Continuing a philanthropic tradition begun by her paternal grandfather, Washington Duke, and long sustained primarily by her father, she began making substantial benefactions to Trinity College in the 1920s. In 1931 she purchased the Washington Duke Homestead and gave it to Duke University, which transferred title to the State of North Carolina after the homestead was designated a National Historic Landmark in 1968. In 1938, Mrs. Biddle gave the Sarah P. Duke Gardens of Duke University as a memorial to her mother, and

shortly after World War II she met an especially critical need of Duke University with a gift of $1.5 million for expansion of the main library. Numerous other gifts went to North Carolina College in Durham, Lincoln Hospital in Durham, and various institutions elsewhere in North Carolina and in New York.

In 1956 she established the Mary Duke Biddle Foundation in order to continue to support, after her death, those institutions and activities in North Carolina and New York that had long been of interest to her; by her will she left her residuary estate to the foundation. She directed that at least half the income of the foundation should go to Duke University. Between 1956 and 1972, the foundation disbursed nearly $5.6 million for projects at Duke University, elsewhere in North Carolina, and in New York. Because of her love for art and music, the foundation has been especially, although not exclusively, interested in the arts.

A lifelong member of Duke Memorial Methodist Church in Durham, she was buried in the Duke family mausoleum in Maplewood Cemetery in Durham. There are portraits in the Rare Book Room of the W. R. Perkins Library and in the Mary Duke Biddle Music Building at Duke University.

SEE: Robert F. Durden, *The Dukes of Durham* (1975); *Durham Morning Herald, Durham Sun*, 15 June 1960; *New York Times*, 15 June 1960.

ROBERT F. DURDEN

Biggs, Asa (4 Feb. 1811–6 Mar. 1878), jurist and senator, was born in Williamston, Martin County, the son of Joseph Biggs, a merchant and Primitive Baptist preacher, and his third wife, Chloe Daniel. His grandfather, Joseph Biggs, had come from Virginia as the first of the family to settle in Martin County. Educated at Williamston Academy, a school established in 1820 in large part through the efforts of his father, Asa Biggs entered mercantile work as a clerk at the age of fifteen. Two years later he was engaged by Henry Williams to manage a mercantile firm in Williamston. After reading law, he was admitted to the bar in 1831 and opened a law office in Williamston.

Though not a candidate, Biggs was elected to the House of Commons in 1840. Reelected in 1842, he left the Whig party, which his ancestors had supported and became a leader of the Democratic faction in the assembly. He was elected to the state senate in 1844 and was nominated without his knowledge in 1845 to run for David Outlaw's seat in the House of Representatives. Although he won that election, he was defeated by Outlaw in 1847, in the only election he lost in his political career. In 1848 he was a presidential elector on the Cass-Butler ticket, and in 1854 he returned to the state senate to represent the district comprised of Martin and Washington counties. In the same year he was elected to the U.S. Senate by the legislature. Never happy in the Senate, he accepted an appointment offered by President Buchanan in 1858 as federal district judge. An ardent supporter of slavery and states' rights, he approved of secession and resigned his federal position in 1861 to take a seat in the Secession Convention. He served as a Confederate district judge from June 1861 until the end of the Civil War.

Biggs stressed economy and efficiency in government and opposed any measure that he thought interfered with individual liberty. Disagreeing with the Whig party's support for internal improvements, he joined the Democratic party and aligned himself with the faction opposing federal expenditures that could lead to governmental control over personal affairs. When a young man he had supported Andrew Jackson, but as a delegate to the state constitutional convention of 1835, he voted with the planter interests he represented in the eastern part of the state. Appointed to the Finance Committee and the Committee on Territories in the U.S. Senate, he was in a position to work for issues, such as economy in government and the right to own slaves, that he considered essential in protecting the individual from governmental interference. Feeling somewhat inadequately trained for political life in Washington, however, he was more comfortable in antebellum political and judicial circles in his state.

As a prominent lawyer in the eastern part of the state, Biggs was selected to represent the trustees of The University of North Carolina from 1839 to 1851 in cases involving the university's share in estates of citizens dying intestate. His increasing reputation as a lawyer, together with his reputation as a politician whose principles usually took precedence over political expediency, led to his appointment by Governor John W. Ellis to join Bartholomew F. Moore in codifying the laws of his state. The Moore and Biggs *Code*, adopted in 1854, formed the basic legal document of the state until Reconstruction. He was again called upon in 1858 to exercise his legal and organizational ability, when he was appointed a federal judge. Succeeding Henry Potter, who had been appointed by Jefferson in 1801, he found that the district court over which he was to preside had languished during the last years of Potter's tenure and that extensive reorganization was necessary if the court were to operate efficiently.

Though a politician himself, Biggs felt strongly that the courts should remain free from both political control and involvement in politics. In 1869, therefore, he joined a number of lawyers in the state in formally protesting what they considered improper interference in political matters by the judges of the state supreme court. The court responded during its June term by requiring these lawyers to show cause why they should not be held in contempt for publicly expressing their criticisms. The judges further stipulated that no lawyer who had signed the protest could practice in the court until he had apologized for his statements. Refusing to recant and responding to financial difficulties brought on by the war, Biggs moved to Norfolk, Va., where he, with his brother Kader, organized a mercantile house. He also entered into a law practice with W. N. H. Smith, who later became chief justice of the Supreme Court of North Carolina.

Biggs was married on 26 June 1832 to Martha Elizabeth Andrews, who bore him ten children, six of whom survived him. One of his three sons, Henry, was killed at Appomattox on 8 Apr. 1865. Another, William, also served in the Confederate Army and later became editor of the *Oxford* (N.C.) *Free Lance*. Biggs's other children included Asa Thomas, Lucy E., Patricia, and Cottie. Never wealthy, he often despaired of being able to provide for his large family. He moved to Dalkeith in 1863 to settle on land he had acquired there; after the war he practiced law in Tarboro until he moved to Norfolk. A devoutly religious man, he experienced a religious conversion and described it in an autobiography written for his children in 1865 (published in 1915 by the North Carolina Historical Commission). He died in Norfolk and was buried in Elmwood Cemetery there. A portrait was presented to the federal court in Raleigh.

SEE: *Autobiography of Asa Biggs*, ed. R. D. W. Connor (1915); Asa Biggs Papers (Library, Duke University, Durham, and North Carolina State Archives, Raleigh); *Biog. Dir. Am. Cong.* (1950); *Congressional Globe*, 1855–56; *History of North Carolina*, vol. 4 (1919); *DAB*, vol. 2 (1929); *Memorial Proceedings and Tributes of Respect to the Memory of the Late Asa Biggs* (1878); Raleigh *News and Observer*, 7 Mar. 1878; David Settle Reid MSS (North Carolina State Archives, Raleigh, and Southern Historical Collection, University of North Carolina, Chapel Hill); F. S. Spruill, *Presentation of Portrait of Honorable Asa Biggs to United States District Court* (1915).

PAUL I. CHESTNUT

Biggs, James Crawford *(29 Aug. 1872–30 Jan. 1960)*, jurist and U.S. solicitor general, was born in Oxford, the son of William Biggs and his wife, Elizabeth Arrington Cooper. William Biggs, a former captain in the Confederate Army, practiced law for a short time after the Civil War; later he turned to free lance, pro-Conservative journalism, editing the Tarboro *Southerner* and the *Oxford Free Lance* and eventually helping to organize the North Carolina Press Association. James Crawford Biggs's paternal grandfather was Asa Biggs, judge and senator; his maternal grandfather, James Crawford Cooper, a banker and merchant, was chairman of the Granville County Board of Commissioners.

Biggs was graduated from the Horner Military School in 1887 and then worked for two years before entering The University of North Carolina. He was graduated from the university *summa cum laude* in 1893 with the degree of Ph.B.; the valedictorian of his class, he had won the Greek medals for 1891 and 1892 and the Willie P. Mangum Medal for his senior oration, "The True American." He was elected to Phi Beta Kappa and joined Zeta Psi, the Philanthropic Literary Society, and the Order of the Gimghouls. He served as editor of both the *Tar Heel* and the yearbook, the *Hellenian*, and as an associate editor of the *University Magazine*. He was elected chief marshal of the commencement of 1892 and president of his senior class. A proficient baseball player, Biggs was also the star end on the university's celebrated football squad of 1892, which won the unofficial southern collegiate championship.

After graduation, Biggs taught school in Virginia and then returned to Chapel Hill in 1894 to study law; he was admitted to the bar that same year. Opening practice in Oxford, he almost immediately rose to distinction. In 1895 he associated with R. W. Winston and F. L. Fuller of Durham in the firm of Winston, Fuller, and Biggs. He was soon elected chairman of the Granville County Democratic Executive Committee and mayor of Oxford for two terms (1897–98).

In 1898, Biggs was appointed assistant professor of law at The University of North Carolina, to succeed Thomas D. Warren. His tenure was brief (1898–1900) but eventful. On the death of Dr. John Manning in February 1899, he was named acting dean of the law school. About the same time, he became involved in the campaign for the organization of a state-wide bar association. He saw the need for such an organization to oversee professional standards and practice, approached several prominent attorneys, drafted a proposed constitution and by-laws, and then, on 21 Jan. 1889, distributed a circular letter calling for a meeting in Raleigh on 10 Feb. of the same year. At that meeting, his constitution was adopted and he himself was elected secretary and treasurer of the new association, posts he held until his elevation to the bench; it is his "painstaking and enthusiastic work" that is given major credit for the association's survival and growth. Throughout his career, Biggs remained active in bar association affairs, strongly advocating stricter educational standards for lawyers. In 1914 he was elected president of the North Carolina Bar Association; in 1930 he was president of the Wake County bar; and in 1933 he was elected vice-president of the American Bar Association from the Fourth Federal Circuit.

Meanwhile, in 1900, Biggs reentered practice in Durham, first as an associate of R. B. Boone and V. S. Bryant in the firm of Boone, Bryant, and Biggs, and later as an associate of R. P. Reade in Biggs and Reade. Again he advanced rapidly and soon was attorney for Durham County. In 1902 he was chairman of the Durham County Democratic Executive Committee and in 1905 he was elected for one term to the state house of representatives. From 1905 to 1907 he acted as a supreme court reporter. At the age of only thirty-four, he was nominated on the first ballot over two other contenders at the Democratic convention for the Ninth Judicial District for a seat on the state superior court. He was elected and served as a justice until 1911, when he resigned to become a professor of law at Trinity College (1911–12).

A staunch Progressive and an anti-Simmons man, Biggs supported the abortive "Progressive Democratic Convention" in Raleigh in April 1914 and was a member of the committee, together with Josiah Bailey, Clarence Poe, Dr. H. Q. Alexander, Alfred M. Scales, and Augustus Graham, designated to present the convention's resolutions to the regular Democratic State Convention's platform committee. Perhaps as a result, his own political career was dormant until August 1917, when he was appointed special assistant to the U.S. attorney general for the prosecution of the Southern Pacific Railroad for land fraud. Biggs's successful prosecution earned him a national reputation in the field of land claims and further federal appointments. In 1919 he argued for the U.S. government before the Supreme Court in the celebrated "Elks' Hills" case; and in 1920 and 1921, he was again a special assistant, directing the condemnation proceedings against the land on which Fort Bragg was located.

In 1928, Biggs publicly supported Al Smith for president. In May 1929, Governor O. Max Gardner appointed him chairman of the state board of elections, a post he held until 1932. Then, in a surprise move in April 1933, President Franklin D. Roosevelt appointed him solicitor general of the United States.

Biggs's traditionalism (he required all his subordinate attorneys to appear in court in frock coats with long tails) and his deep reverence for the Supreme Court and the power of judicial review soon clashed, however, with the philosophy and style of the younger, more liberal New Deal officials. Gradually, as many important matters as possible were channeled around his office. Finally Biggs resigned in March 1935; perhaps Roosevelt's letter of regret, which was headed "Dear Clay" instead of "Dear Crawford," best illustrates Biggs's isolation from the White House.

Nevertheless, Biggs maintained connections with Roosevelt's administration. In May 1935, on the nomination of Jesse Jones of the Reconstruction Finance Corporation, he was elected to a one-year term as a neutral director of the Wheeling and Lake Erie Railroad, then a center of controversy (and occasional physical violence) between rival shareholding factions. Between 1935 and 1938 he was again a special assistant to the attorney general, for the prosecution of claims against the Northern Pacific Railway Company concerning nearly 2.8 million acres of public land.

The rest of Biggs's career, until his retirement in 1950, was given to private practice in Washington, D. C., and in Raleigh. He died at his home, Hardimont estate, outside Raleigh, and was buried in Oakwood Cemetery.

A trustee of the Methodist Orphanage in Raleigh and of The University of North Carolina from 1919 until his death, Biggs also served as adjutant of the Third Regiment, North Carolina State Guard (1894–98). A member of the American Law Institute, the North Carolina Commission for Improvement of the Laws, the Sons of the American Revolution, and the Society of Mayflower Descendants, he was elected to the executive committee of the North Carolina Literary and Historical Association in 1948. He belonged to the Edenton Street Methodist Church in Raleigh.

Biggs married Marjorie C. Jordan on 7 Feb. 1906; they had one daughter, Marjorie (b. 1911).

Biggs's published papers include "Federal Practice and Procedure," *North Carolina Law Review* 8 (1930); "The Power of the Judiciary over Legislation" (presidential address before the North Carolina Bar Association, 2 Aug. 1915; Washington, D.C.: U.S. Government Printing Office, 1916); and "Religious Belief as Qualification of a Witness," *North Carolina Law Review* 8 (1929). As secretary of the North Carolina Bar Association, he wrote its *Reports of the Annual Meeting* from 1899 to 1906.

A typewritten manuscript of Biggs's address "The Supreme Court of the United States," delivered to the annual meeting of the Maryland State Bar Association, 29 June 1934, is in the North Carolina Collection of the Library of The University of North Carolina.

SEE: Kemp P. Battle, *History of the University of North Carolina*, vol. 2 (1912); Fannie Memory Blackwelder, "Organization and Early Years of the North Carolina Bar Association," *North Carolina Historical Review* 34 (1957); R. D. W. Connor, *History of North Carolina*, vol. 5 (1919); "James Crawford Biggs," *North Carolina Law Journal*, October 1901; *New York Times*, 16 Apr. 1933, 24 Feb. 1935, 15 and 19 Mar. 1935; Raleigh *News and Observer*, 21 Aug. 1917, 15 Mar. 1935, 31 Jan. 1960; Joseph F. Steelman, "The Progressive Democratic Convention of 1914 in North Carolina," *North Carolina Historical Review* 46 (1969); "Why J. Crawford Quit His Job," *State* 2 (6 Apr. 1935); R. W. Winston, "James Crawford Biggs," *North Carolina Bar Association Report of 1906*.

BENNETT L. STEELMAN

Biggs, Timothy (d. ca. 11 Feb. 1684/85), colonial official, is said to have gone to Albemarle from South Carolina. If so, he evidently had residences in both colonies at the same time, living intermittently in each, for the periods of his association with the respective settlements overlap by several years. Possibly there were two men in Carolina bearing the name. It also is uncertain whether a Timothy Biggs who lived in Boston in 1665 was the one who later lived in Albemarle. A Timothy Biggs arrived in South Carolina in 1670 or 1671, apparently from Virginia. He was a merchant and was called Captain. In 1672 he owned a lot in Charles Town and was a member of the parliament. He was described as "one of the Freemen" of that colony as late as March 1677, and a survey warrant for three hundred acres of land was issued for him on 21 Apr. 1677.

Meanwhile, in the North Carolina colony, a Timothy Biggs took possession of a plantation in Perquimans Precinct formerly owned by George Catchmaid, whose widow, Mary, had married Biggs. Biggs assumed ownership of the plantation before 11 Mar. 1673/74, when he signed a commitment to provide George Durant, his neighbor, with papers needed to clear Durant's title to his own plantation, which had been improperly included in George Catchmaid's patent. By May 1676, Biggs had become prominent in the Albemarle political party led by Thomas Eastchurch and Thomas Miller. His later accounts of events in Albemarle indicate that Biggs had personal knowledge of affairs in the colony at least as early as 1675.

On 21 Nov. 1676 the Carolina proprietors appointed Biggs to the Albemarle council as deputy of the Earl of Craven. The appointment probably was made through the influence of Thomas Eastchurch and Thomas Miller, who had gone to London to seek offices for themselves and their supporters. Shortly before their trip to London, Miller had been tried and acquitted in Virginia by the governor, Sir William Berkeley, and the Virginia council on charges brought by his political opponents in Albemarle. Biggs had been with Miller in Virginia during the trial and afterward had carried a copy of the council's order to members of his party in Albemarle.

Biggs assumed office as council member in July 1677, when Miller returned from London and established himself as president of the council and acting governor. About the same time, Biggs took office as deputy collector of customs by appointment from Miller, who had been commissioned collector of customs.

Biggs remained in office only a few months, for Miller's government was overthrown in early December 1677, when the uprising called Culpeper's Rebellion occurred. Biggs was imprisoned during the revolt and charged with murder. Miller and other council members were likewise imprisoned under serious charges, but the trial of the accused officials was interrupted and never resumed. Biggs escaped from prison soon after the aborted trial and fled to Virginia.

From Virginia, Biggs went to England, arriving in about April 1678. After reporting to the proprietors on the Albemarle revolt, he undertook to carry the matter to Crown officials but desisted at the urging of the proprietors. In September 1678 he received a commission from customs officials appointing him comptroller and surveyor general of customs in Albemarle, an office not previously existing in the colony. He returned to Albemarle in February 1678/79 and undertook to administer his new office. He appears also to have undertaken to act as customs collector by virtue of his earlier appointment as deputy collector by Thomas Miller, who was still held prisoner.

Biggs's attempt to take over "the king's affairs" in Albemarle was met by opposition and threats from the colonists, particularly John Culpeper, who had been appointed customs collector by the rebel assembly. Biggs further antagonized the colonists by helping Thomas Miller escape from prison. Threats against him became so menacing that he again fled to Virginia.

Biggs went again to London in 1679, but his stay was short. By February 1679/80 he had returned to Albemarle and renewed his efforts to officiate as comptroller and surveyor general of customs. He was again opposed in those efforts, this time by Robert Holden, who had arrived from London some months earlier with a commission from customs officials appointing him customs collector. Holden, who also was secretary of the colony and held several other offices, obstructed Biggs's efforts by having his deputies arrested and thrown in prison on trumped-up charges. On 27 Mar. 1680 the general court suspended Biggs's commission, ruling that it had been superseded by

Holden's. In protest, Biggs withdrew from the council, on which he had resumed his seat as Lord Craven's deputy, and also persuaded another council member, James Hill, to withdraw.

Biggs's activities as customs official appear not to have been terminated by the court's action, although they may have been suspended temporarily. Records indicate that Biggs was handling customs matters as late as 1684. By that time, however, Robert Holden had left the colony. He had been arrested for several crimes, among them fraud in the handling of the customs, and apparently had been banished. Possibly Biggs's commission was reactivated upon Holden's departure.

Biggs continued to be involved in difficulties and controversies. In 1683 he went to London and complained to the proprietors of injuries done him by Seth Sothel, then governor of Albemarle. The nature of those injuries is not known, as the pertinent surviving records relate chiefly to Biggs's complaints about general conditions in the colony and the proprietors' policies. Biggs was particularly disturbed that leaders in the revolt against Thomas Miller now held high offices with the proprietors' sanction. He maintained that he could not get fair treatment in the courts because they were controlled by his former enemies. The proprietors attempted to alleviate Biggs's situation, although at times they indicated impatience with him. In 1683 and again in 1684 they appointed him to the office of surveyor general. Respecting his complaints against Sothel, they directed that Biggs set down his alleged injuries in writing, specifying them in "distinct articles," so that they could be investigated.

The proprietors complied with an unusual request Biggs had made for a special grant "confirming" to him and his wife the Catchmaid land, which consisted of 3,333 acres. Biggs requested "confirmation" of his claim to the Catchmaid property no doubt because his right to the land was challenged from two directions. A portion of the land had been bought from the Indians and seated by George Durant before George Catchmaid secured his patent and, by accident or design, had Durant's plantation included in his grant. Under pressure from Durant, both Catchmaid and Biggs had recognized Durant's right to that portion and had promised to procure the proper papers to secure it to him, but neither fulfilled the promise.

The second challenge to Biggs's claim was from Edward Catchmaid of London, nephew of George Catchmaid. Edward claimed the property on the ground that his uncle had had no children and had died intestate, which, under the common law, would give right to the property to Edward, as heir at law, not to Catchmaid's widow. Biggs apparently hoped to undercut Edward's claim, and perhaps Durant's also, by securing a grant directly from the proprietors.

Although the proprietors complied with Biggs's request and on 26 Mar. 1684 granted the land to Mary Biggs, their action was later invalidated. On complaint from Edward Catchmaid, the proprietors directed Governor Sothel to investigate the matter and settle it according to law; they had made the grant, they said, because Biggs told them that George Catchmaid bequeathed the property to his wife by will, and they had not intended to deprive Edward or anyone else of his lawful rights. As a result of Sothel's investigation, Edward Catchmaid's claim was upheld. Finally, in 1697, in a suit brought by Durant's sons against Edward Catchmaid, the Court of Chancery issued a decree sustaining the Durant claim.

Biggs's death probably occurred on 11 Feb. 1684/85,

although the year was set down in Perquimans records as 1683/84: records of the county court show that Biggs was alive and had a case in court in October 1684 but was dead by April 1685. Mary Biggs died on 29 Oct. 1685. There were no children.

Although some historians have thought that Biggs was a Quaker, that impression probably is erroneous. Records show that Biggs was not averse to taking oath nor to the use of armed force, and his aggressiveness and vindictiveness were likewise out of harmony with Quaker teachings. It is true that Biggs's name appears on a "Remonstrance" that Albemarle Quakers sent to the proprietors, but the document clearly shows that Biggs signed it as a public official, in effect, a notary before whom the signatures were affixed. Quakers in the colony generally shared Biggs's political views, but Biggs does not appear to have shared their religious beliefs.

Biggs was intelligent and well educated and also courageous, but he failed in his efforts to have Albemarle governed in what he considered the right way. Nevertheless, he made a significant contribution. The documents he prepared for the proprietors and Crown officials in his various controversies are among the most important surviving records of early Albemarle. His real service was that of unwitting recorder for future generations of significant aspects of the early history of the colony.

SEE: Agnes Leland Baldwin, comp., *First Settlers of South Carolina* (1969); Timothy Biggs, "A Narrative of The Transactions past In the Conty of Albemarle Sence Mr. Tho. Miller his Arrivall there" (Arents Tobacco Collection, New York Public Library, New York City; photocopy in North Carolina State Archives, Raleigh); Langdon Cheves, ed., "The Shaftesbury Papers and Other Records Relating to Carolina . . . Prior to 1676," *Collections of the South Carolina Historical Society* 5 (1897); J. R. B. Hathaway, ed., *North Carolina Historical and Genealogical Register*, 3 vols. (1900–1903); North Carolina State Archives (Raleigh), for Council Minutes, Wills, Inventories (1677–1701) and Perquimans Births, Marriages, Deaths and Flesh Marks (1659–1739); Mattie Erma Edwards Parker, ed., *North Carolina Higher-Court Records, 1670–1696* and *1697–1701* (1968, 1971); Perquimans County Deeds, Book A, 1681–1716 (Perquimans County Courthouse, Hertford; microfilm in North Carolina State Archives, Raleigh); Hugh F. Rankin, *Upheaval in Albemarle: The Story of Culpeper's Rebellion* (1962); Alexander Samuel Salley, Jr., ed., *Warrants for Lands in South Carolina, 1672–1711* (1973); William L. Saunders, ed., *Colonial Records of North Carolina*, vol. 1 (1886); Ellen Goode Winslow, *History of Perquimans County* (1931).

MATTIE ERMA E. PARKER

Bignall, Robert (*ca. 1730–87*), revolutionary patriot, first appears in the records of Edgecombe County in 1756, when he was witness to several deeds. His antecedents are unknown. He was one of the first settlers in the town of Tarboro when it was laid out in 1760, and he became a wealthy merchant. At the onset of the Revolution, Bignall was a member of the North Carolina Provincial Congress held at New Bern in 1775; he was later a member of the committee of safety. In 1779 he was president of the council and acting secretary of state. Later he advanced the state sixty thousand pounds for public expenditure.

His will, dated 5 June 1786 and probated in October court in 1787, devised a large amount of silver plate and other personal property. The lengthy inventory of his estate included an undated certificate of money of his own "lent to Governor Caswell for the use of North Carolina."

Bignall was married, prior to 1767, to Margaret Parish of Norfolk County, Va., who died before him. According to his will, he had sons Robert and Edward, underaged at the time of his death, and daughters Sarah, Peggy, and Ann, the wife of Joseph Speed of Mecklenburg County, Va. Of the sons, Robert married Elizabeth, the daughter of Blake Baker of Halifax, and Edward married Peggy Washington Haywood, the daughter of Egbert Haywood.

SEE: Deeds and Wills of the County of Edgecombe (North Carolina State Archives, Raleigh); William L. Saunders, ed., *Colonial Records of North Carolina*, 10 vols. (1886–90); Sons of the American Revolution, North Carolina Society, *Lineage Book of Past and Present Members* (1951); Joseph W. Watson, *Estate Records of Edgecombe County, 1730–1820* (1970).

CLAIBORNE T. SMITH, JR.

Binford, Helen Bills Titsworth (*28 Dec. 1885–4 Oct. 1952*), Quaker educator and leader, was born in Western Springs, Ill., of English ancestry. She was the daughter of Abraham Dunham Titsworth, Jr., and Mary E. Harrison Titsworth. Educated first in the schools of Richmond, Ind., and Whittier, Calif., she was graduated from Earlham College, Richmond, Ind., in 1907 with an A.B. degree. She remained at Earlham for a year of graduate study and studied modern languages and music in Europe in 1909–10. She taught languages for the next two years at Friends University, Wichita, Kans., and for the following year at Maryland College for Women. She married Raymond Binford in 1913 and spent the next thirty-eight years with him in a variety of leadership positions in Quakerism and in higher education, most of them at Guilford College, where he was president from 1918 to 1934.

In addition to her career as a language teacher (English, French, and German) at Guilford in 1925–27 and 1930–32 and as college hostess, Helen Binford was among the most active women in North Carolina public life from 1918 to 1952. Her interest in the local schools of Guilford County, in which she had four children, led her to become president of the North Carolina Congress of Parents and Teachers and national secretary of the PTA. She was among the early leaders of the North Carolina Council of Churches and served as director of the Carolina Institute of International Relations, under auspices of the American Friends Service Committee (AFSC), a forerunner of the Southeastern Regional office of the AFSC.

She was chairman of the Girls Aid Committee of Guilford College and was in great demand locally and nationally as an able and forthright speaker on the causes of world peace, race relations, and women's education. As a member of the Religious Society of Friends (Quakers), she was active in New Garden Monthly Meeting, North Carolina Yearly Meeting, and the national and international branch of Quakers known as the Five Years Meeting of Friends (now the Friends United Meeting). She also traveled widely on behalf of the Friends Fellowship Council and Friends World Committee for Consultation. She served as codirector of the Civilian Public Service Camps for conscientious objectors at Buck Creek, near Marion, and at Gatlinburg, Tenn., from 1940 to 1943, and of an international work camp under the AFSC in Mexico in 1945. She then returned to teaching for two final years at William Penn

College, Oskaloosa, Iowa, from 1948 to 1950. She was a member of the Democratic party.

Helen Binford was mother of four children: Anna Naomi Kirschner, Richard Titsworth, Frederick Harrison, and Mary Margaret Bailey. She died at Guilford College and was buried in New Garden Cemetery. Her portrait hangs in the Board Room of Guilford College.

SEE: Dorothy L. Gilbert, *Guilford: A Quaker College* (1937); Guilford College Archives (Greensboro), for a memorial to Helen Binford.

J. F. MOORE

Binford, Raymond *(15 July 1876–27 June 1951),* president of Guilford College, was born in Carthage, Ind., of English ancestry. His father was Josiah Binford, a Quaker farmer, and his mother was Margaret Hill Binford. He grew up in Carthage, Ind., and Wichita, Kans., and attended the Haviland (Friends) Academy. He received the B.S. degree at Earlham College, Richmond, Ind., in 1901; the M.S. degree at The University of Chicago in 1906; and the Ph.D. at Johns Hopkins University in 1912. He served as professor of biology and geology at Guilford College, near Greensboro, from 1901 to 1914 and from 1918 to 1934. From 1914 to 1918 he was professor of biology at Earlham College. He taught for shorter periods at North Carolina Agricultural and Technical College (Greensboro) and William Penn College (Oskaloosa, Iowa). He served as president of Guilford College from 1918 to 1934 and president emeritus from 1934 to 1951, devoting forty-six years of service to this one institution.

He was recorded a Friends minister in 1905 and spent the remainder of his life as a Quaker educator and minister in a variety of positions of leadership in the religious Society of Friends and in higher education in the United States. As a scientist-educator, he achieved distinction for his creation of a liberal arts curriculum combining his insights into the natural, social, and spiritual dimensions of life. In the period following World War I he concentrated upon the development of a well-trained faculty and an integrated curriculum expressing the Quaker concern for total development of human personality, while at the same time bringing Guilford College to accreditation in 1926 with sound financing and administration.

His Quaker leadership was expressed not only through New Garden Monthly Meeting and North Carolina Yearly Meeting of Friends, but also through the national and international branch of Quakerism known as the Five Years Meeting of Friends, which he served as a member of the executive committee and chairman of the board of education. From 1941 to 1943 he was director of the Civilian Public Service Camps for conscientious objectors to World War II, at Buck Creek, near Marion, and at Gatlinburg, Tenn. He also directed an international work camp in Mexico under the American Friends Service Committee in 1945. He served under the Friends Fellowship Council and Friends World Committee for Consultation as a Travelling Minister, visiting Friends on spiritual missions throughout North America. He was the first president of the North Carolina College Conference, in 1921.

Through all these years his leadership was expressed in partnership with his wife, Helen Titsworth Binford, who was either officially or unofficially codirector or coparticipant in all these activities. In a period between the two world wars and before racial integration in the South, he was an active leader of the movement for racial equality, world peace through nonviolence, and ecumenical cooperation of all religions. His main emphasis in these efforts was expressed through his work as a scientist and educator, based on his interpretation of the spiritual nature of the universe. He expressed his political convictions through membership in the Democratic party.

Binford's marriage to Helen Bills Titsworth took place on 20 June 1913 at Richmond, Ind.; they had four children: Anna Naomi Kirschner, Richard Titsworth, Frederick Harrison, and Mary Margaret Bailey. He died at Guilford College and was buried at New Garden Cemetery. His portrait hangs in the Library of Guilford College.

SEE: Alma T. Edwards et al., *A Tribute to Raymond A. Binford* (1961); Dorothy L. Gilbert, *Guilford: A Quaker College* (1937); Guilford College Archives (Greensboro), for a memorial to Raymond Binford.

J. F. MOORE

Bingham, Lemuel *(23 June 1795–13 Nov. 1885),* newspaper editor, was a native of Pittsfield, Mass. A printer by trade, he was brought to Salisbury in 1820 by Charles F. Fisher to found the *Western Carolinian,* first successful newspaper west of Hillsborough. It was not the very first paper for Salisbury—there is evidence of another one published there about 1814—but it was the first to draw more than a passing notice. Fisher, a backer of John C. Calhoun in politics, established the *Western Carolinian* as an instrument to forestall the election of William H. Crawford as president of the United States by supporting Calhoun for vice-president and either John Quincy Adams or Andrew Jackson for president. Publication of the *Western Carolinian* began 10 June 1820. Bingham remained with it until some time in eary 1823, when Fisher decided to back Jackson for president rather than Adams. Then Bingham turned the publication of the paper over to Philo White, a New York printer, who had joined him some six months after it had been founded.

White made the *Western Carolinian* an organ for Jackson; Bingham went to Fayetteville, where the *Fayetteville Observer* had just changed ownership. From there he worked for Adams's candidacy until the end of the 1824 campaign. Throughout his career as a newspaperman, Bingham was consistently pro-Adams and a supporter of his wing of the National Republican party, advocating manufacturing and a protective tariff and opposing nullification.

Soon after the 1824 campaign ended, Bingham went to the village of Charlotte, county seat of Mecklenburg County, and established the first newspaper there, the *Catawba Journal,* which he published some three or four years. In May 1828 he moved it to Salisbury and continued it as the *Yadkin and Catawba Journal* until early 1834, when it was discontinued for lack of patronage: another Whig newspaper, the *Carolina Watchman,* had been established there by Hamilton Jones and had become the effective opposition to the *Western Carolinian* and its pro-Calhoun policies. There was not then room for three newspapers in Salisbury.

Early in his stay in North Carolina, Bingham married Jane Miller of Rowan County, daughter of George Miller and granddaughter of Matthew Brandon. They had a family of twelve children. With the establishment of Davie County and Mocksville in the 1830s, they moved to Mocksville, where Bingham engaged in merchandising and established a tavern on Main Street catering to the students of the academy there. He was chosen clerk and master of equity of Davie County and held that position for many years.

In 1869, his wife dead, his property lost in a war to

which he was violently opposed, and his eyesight failing from cataracts, he moved to Statesville and made his home with his daughter, who was the wife of Judge David M. Furches, prominent Republican leader and candidate for governor in 1892. There he died and was buried in the Furches plot in Oakwood Cemetery.

SEE: Homer M. Keever, MS on the *Western Carolinian* (possession of the author); Statesville *Landmark*, 13 Nov. 1885 (obit.).

HOMER M. KEEVER

Bingham, Mary Lily Kenan Flagler (14 June 1867– 27 July 1917), philanthropist, was born in Kenansville at Liberty Hall, her grandfather's home. She was the daughter of William Rand Kenan and Mary Hargrave and the eldest of four children. Her brother and sisters were William R., Jr., Jessie Kenan Wise, and Sarah Graham. She was raised in Wilmington and later entered Peace College in Raleigh, where she majored in piano and voice.

On 24 Aug. 1901 she was married to Henry Morrison Flagler in Kenansville. Flagler was a cofounder of the Standard Oil Company, with John D. Rockefeller, and also became the prime developer of the Florida east coast. Mrs. Flagler took an active interest in her husband's vast business affairs. When he died in 1913, she assumed many of his charitable interests, such as hospitals, churches, and schools. She maintained homes in New York and Florida but spent considerable time in Raleigh, where she visited her aunt and uncle, Colonel and Mrs. Thomas S. Kenan.

In December 1916, Mrs. Flagler married Robert Worth Bingham of Louisville, Ky., but in July 1917 she died suddenly at her home in Louisville, leaving an estate of almost $100 million. One of the most important bequests was a trust fund known as the Kenan Professorship Fund, which annually supplements the salaries of the distinguished Kenan professors. Mrs. Bingham also set up a trust fund to protect and develop her Florida properties, including the Florida East Coast Railroad, Florida East Coast Hotel Company, Miami Power and Water Company, Model Land Company, and P. & O. Steamship Company. Her Palm Beach, Fla., estate, Whitehall, is now a museum open to the public.

A portrait of Mrs. Bingham hangs in the Henry Morrison Flagler Museum in Palm Beach, Fla., and another is in Kenan Dormitory at The University of North Carolina. Mrs. Bingham died childless and was buried in Oakdale Cemetery in Wilmington. She had attended the Presbyterian church.

SEE: Jacksonville *Florida Times-Union*, 28 July 1917; Kenan Family Records (in possession of the author); W. R. Kenan, ed., *Incidents by the Way* (1946); New York *News*, 28 July 1917; A.K. Register, ed., *The Kenan Family* (1967); *St. Augustine* (Fla.) *Record*, 28 July 1917.

T. S. KENAN III

Bingham, Robert (5 Sept. 1838–8 May 1927), headmaster of Bingham School and educational advocate, was born in Hillsborough, the fourth child of William James Bingham, then principal of Hillsborough Academy, and his wife, Elizabeth Alves Norwood. After studying at his father's school (1849–53), which by then had been moved to Oaks, he entered The University of North Carolina and was graduated in 1857, one of the four first honor men in his class.

In July 1857, Bingham was admitted as junior partner in his father's school, which assumed the firm name W. J.

Bingham and Sons. With his brother William, also a partner, he briefly toured Virginia to observe educational procedure at the University of Virginia and the more prominent secondary schools and then returned to Oaks to teach with the rest of the family. He received the M.A. degree from The University of North Carolina in 1860.

The Binghams were all firm Whigs who initially opposed secession. Nevertheless, Robert, who belonged to a company of Orange County militia, enlisted in state service with his compatriots on 8 Mar. 1862; on 25 Mar. he was elected captain of Company G, Forty-fourth North Carolina Infantry. On 26 June 1863 he was captured in the action at South Anna Bridge. He was interned at Johnson's Island and Fort Delaware until 27 Apr. 1864, when he was exchanged at Point Lookout, Md. He then rejoined his regiment and fought until the surrender at Appomattox Court House, 9 Apr. 1865, when he was paroled as a captain. Through most of his life, however, he was called by the honorific "Major"; later he was commissioned a colonel in the North Carolina National Guard.

After the war, Bingham resumed his post as instructor at the school, which had relocated in Mebane in 1864. On the death of his father in 1866, he became coprincipal with his brother, William. On William's death in 1873, he became headmaster and (after buying out the interest held by his cousin, William B. Lynch, in May 1879) sole proprietor. Under his administration, the Bingham School maintained and enhanced its nation-wide reputation. Enrollment gradually expanded to three hundred students. The military curriculum was reformed, and after 1882 commissioned officers were detached from the U.S. Army to serve as professors of military science and tactics. When Bingham moved the school to "Bingham Heights" near the French Broad River at Asheville in 1891, its facilities included the first gymnasium and swimming pool ever built specifically for secondary instruction in the South.

Bingham's most lasting influence lay in public education. Almost alone among private educators, he was convinced of the value of a public school system and lent it considerable support. As early as 1870 he was advocating free public schools for blacks, although he continued to believe in school segregation for the rest of his life. From 1877 to 1881 he lectured at the summer teachers' institutes at The University of North Carolina, and throughout the 1870s he delivered speeches at Wilmington, Raleigh, Goldsboro, and Charlotte as part of local campaigns to adopt county-option school tax referendums. On 15 Feb. 1884 he addressed the Superintendents' Department of the National Education Association, meeting in Washington, D.C., urging passage of the Blair Education Bill, which would have provided for an allocation from the federal surplus for the relief of impoverished southern school systems. So great was this speech's success that he was asked to repeat it at the NEA's general convention at Madison, Wisc., on 16 July that same year; reprinted in pamphlet form as *Educational Needs and Status of the New South*, it was widely distributed throughout the South and the nation. The campaign for passage of the Blair bill (and, in large part, Bingham's speech) helped to draw attention to the state of southern public education and generated further, more successful improvement campaigns.

On 2 Feb. 1873, Robert Bingham and his brother William were among a delegation of fifty-five dignitaries who met with the state senate in Raleigh to plead for a reopening of the university. On 9 July that same year, Bingham delivered a highly regarded speech on the same subject to a meeting of the state education association in

Raleigh. On 11 Nov. 1885 he was principal speaker at a mass meeting in Raleigh, organized by the Watauga Club, supporting the establishment of a state agricultural and mechanical college. Although originally opposed to women's education as a waste of funds, a tour of the Massachusetts school system, which in the elementary grades was staffed overwhelmingly by female teachers, converted him. At a meeting of the Black Mountain conference of the North Carolina Teachers' Assembly in 1884, he publicly advocated the recruitment of women as an answer to the state's teacher shortage. At the Black Mountain conference of 1886, he proposed a state institution for training women teachers. Contemporaries regarded these speeches as largely responsible for the organization of the state teachers' institutes, conducted once a year in every county of the state by Charles D. McIver and Edwin A. Alderman (1889–91), and, ultimately, for the establishment in 1891 of the State Normal and Industrial School for Women at Greensboro.

An active Mason, Bingham was senior grand warden of the Grand Lodge of North Carolina for 1880 and 1881 and grand master for 1882, 1883, and 1884. While in office, he was instrumental in reforming the administration of the Masonic Orphanage at Oxford, instituting supervision by a board of directors. A speech he delivered as grand master to a convention of the Grand Lodge in Raleigh, 13 Jan. 1885, led directly to a five thousand dollar appropriation by the General Assembly to establish an industrial training program at the orphanage, one of the first such programs in the South. An early believer in compulsory education, he was able, while a resident in Asheville, to steer a local-option compulsory attendance bill for the city through the legislature and then achieve its adoption through referendum by careful manipulation of the city's labor vote. This law, one of the first adopted in the South, was the forerunner of much later legislation.

A prolific writer and popular speaker, Bingham gained a wide audience through his articles on southern affairs. His writings included "An Ex-Slaveholder's View of the Race Question in the South," *Harper's Review* (international edition, July 1900) and "The Misunderstandings between the Sections of Our Common Country," *North American Review* (September 1904). A summary of Bingham's views on secession may be found in his 13 Oct. 1908 presidential address to the North Carolina Literary and Historical Association: "Secession in Theory, as the Framers of the Constitution Viewed It; Secession, as Practiced and as Sustained by the United States; Secession, as Attempted by the Confederate States."

Bingham, a Presbyterian elder and a life member of the National Education Association, also served as a director of the American National Bank and Wachovia Bank and Trust Company. In 1891, The University of North Carolina awarded him an honorary LL.D.; in 1929, Bingham Hall on the University campus was named in his honor; and on 12 Oct. 1939, a memorial tablet in his name was installed in the university's Memorial Hall.

An attack of influenza complicated by pneumonia finally forced Bingham to retire from the Bingham School in 1920. Since 1904 he had entrusted the future of the school to a board of trustees, but when he died in Asheville in 1927, it did not long survive him. In the autumn of 1928, the school closed, supposedly to carry out major new construction; it never reopened.

Bingham's first marriage, in 1861, was to Delphine Louise Worth (d. 1886) of Randolph County, the daughter of John Milton Worth (1811–1900), a state treasurer of North Carolina (1870–85) and a brother of Governor Jonathan Worth. The couple had five children, four of whom reached maturity: Mrs. Sol R. McKee of Asheville; Mrs. R. T. Grinnan of Raleigh; Robert Worth (1871–1937), newspaper publisher and U.S. ambassador to Great Britain (1933–37), who moved to Louisville, Ky.; and William (1873–91). Bingham's second marriage was to V. M. Woodward, the daughter of the Reverend B. F. Woodward of South Carolina.

Bingham was buried in Riverside Cemetery, Asheville.

SEE: Samuel A. Ashe, ed., *Biographical History of North Carolina*, vol. 6 (1907); "Colonel Bingham Dies in His Eighty-ninth Year," *Uplift* 15 (14 May 1927); Willard B. Gatewood, Jr., "North Carolina and Federal Aid to Education," *North Carolina Historical Review* 40 (1963); J. G. deRoulhac Hamilton, *Reconstruction in North Carolina* (1914); Hugh T. Lefler and Paul Wager, eds., *Orange County, 1752–1952* (1953); David Alexander Lockmiller, "The Establishment of the North Carolina College of Agricultural and Mechanic Arts," *North Carolina Historical Review* 16 (1939); M. C. S. Noble, "Col. Robert Bingham," *High School Journal* 3 (1920); "Past Grand Master Robert Bingham Dead," *Orphan's Friend*, 13 May 1927; Southern Historical Collection, Record Group 3731 (University of North Carolina, Chapel Hill) for some of Bingham's correspondence and records relating to his management of the school; Floyd C. Watkins, *Thomas Wolfe's Characters: Portraits from Life* (1956); Thomas Wolfe, *The Hills Beyond* (1941).

BENNETT L. STEELMAN

Bingham, Robert Worth (8 Nov. 1871–18 Dec. 1937), newspaper publisher and U.S. ambassador to Great Britain, was born in Mebane, the fourth child of Robert Bingham, headmaster of Bingham School, and his first wife, Delphine Louise Worth. His maternal grandfather, John Milton Worth (1811–1900), a brother of Governor Jonathan Worth, operated a general store in Asheboro, held considerable mining interests, and served as state treasurer of North Carolina (1870–85).

Bingham was graduated from the Bingham School in 1888 and attended The University of North Carolina from 1888 to 1891. There he won the Representative Medal in 1890 for his oration "Manifest Destiny and Manifest Duty." After two terms of graduate work at the University of Virginia, he taught at the family's school for two years, then reentered The University of North Carolina in 1896 to study law, finally receiving the LL.B. degree from the University of Louisville in 1897. Later, Bingham received honorary doctorates from Louisville and from the universities of London (1933), Cambridge (1935), and Oxford (1936). In 1899 he endowed The University of North Carolina's Robert Worth Bingham prize in debate.

After a year of postgraduate study at the University of Michigan, Bingham commenced practice in Louisville, Ky. In 1903 he was appointed to fill an unexpired term as county attorney for Jefferson County, Ky., and he was elected in his own right to a full four-year term the following year. In 1907 he was appointed interim mayor of Louisville for a few months, after both regular candidates were disqualified for election irregularities. In 1911 he was appointed to fill an unexpired term as chancellor of the Jefferson County circuit court, but he declined further nomination.

In August 1918, Bingham acquired a two-thirds interest in both the Louisville *Courier-Journal* and the afternoon *Louisville Times*, buying out the remaining third of each the following year. Under his management as publisher, the *Courier-Journal* retained the national prominence it had gained under Henry Watterson (Bingham himself went on to become a president of the Associated Press) but adopted a decidedly more liberal editorial stance, advocating prohibition and women's suffrage. Watterson, who had remained on the staff as "editor emeritus," resigned in 1920, when Bingham came out in support of ratification of the League of Nations Treaty.

When prices for burley tobacco dropped disastrously in 1920, Bingham, who had been impressed during a tour of California with the success of the citrus-growers' cooperatives, arranged a meeting between Aaron Sapiro, legal counsel for the co-ops, and representatives of burley interests. The result of this April 1920 conference was the organization of the Burley Tobacco Growers Cooperative Association, to which Bingham lent considerable editorial and financial support.

An independent Democrat, Bingham engaged in continual warfare with Kentucky's regular Democratic organization for nearly fifteen years. In 1932 he was among the earliest and most fervent supporters of Franklin D. Roosevelt, a long-time acquaintance, for the Democratic presidential nomination, reportedly donating fifty thousand dollars to his campaign. On 13 Mar. 1933, Bingham was appointed ambassador to the Court of St. James; the appointment was confirmed nine days later. Bingham's religion (unlike his Presbyterian forebears, he was a devout Episcopalian and a vestryman in his Louisville church); his love of fishing, hunting, and yachting; and his known respect for British culture (he had toured the Islands several times and had married his third wife in London) made him eminently acceptable to British officials. In fact, he was criticized by several congressmen as being too Anglophiliac, and his speech on arrival in Britain on 31 May 1933, prematurely pledging mutual tariff reductions, caused the administration considerable embarrassment.

Although Bingham lacked previous diplomatic experience, he proved a capable and fairly successful ambassador. He chaired several conferences in London in 1935 on world wheat control; played a major role in American response to the Italian invasion of Ethiopia, the outbreak of the Spanish Civil War, and the Japanese invasion of China; and conducted conversations on Anglo-American naval policy in the wake of the Japanese renunciation of the Naval Armaments Treaty of 1922. His primary mission, to negotiate an Anglo-American reciprocal trade agreement, proved a more difficult problem. He proposed tariff reductions and stabilization of the dollar and pound, policies bitterly opposed in Congress from fear that gains made by domestic price rises in the economy would be canceled. Primarily because of such fears, Bingham was passed over as American representative to the London Economic Conference (12 June–27 July 1933), and Roosevelt repudiated stabilization in his 3 July message to the conference. Nevertheless, by the time of Bingham's death, plans for opening intensive trade negotiations were already well underway.

A trustee of Berea and Centre colleges, and a president of the Kentucky Children's Home Society, Bingham remained deeply concerned throughout his life for the welfare of his adopted state. He was a director of the Louisville and Nashville Railroad and the American Creosoting Company and founded WHAS, Kentucky's first radio station. He was also a regent of the Smithsonian Institution, an active Mason (he was awarded the honorary title of past grand senior warden of the Lodge of Great Britain when George VI was made

past grand master), and an accomplished amateur organist and cellist.

On 20 May 1896, Bingham married Eleanor E. Miller of Louisville, who died in an automobile accident in 1913. The couple had three children, Robert Norwood, Henrietta Worth, and George Barry, who later became copublisher of the *Courier-Journal* and *Times* with his father. On 15 Nov. 1916, Bingham married Mary Lily Kenan Flagler (d. 28 July 1917), the sister of William Rand Kenan, Jr., and the widow of Henry M. Flagler. Her will, after being bitterly contested, left Bingham $5 million and endowed the Kenan professorships of The University of North Carolina. Several sources suggest that Bingham himself originally suggested the endowment. On 20 Aug. 1924, Bingham married Aileen Muldoon Hilliard of Louisville (d. 18 Mar. 1953).

Bingham died at Johns Hopkins University Hospital and was buried at Cave Hill Cemetery in Louisville.

SEE: James McGregor Burns, *Roosevelt: The Lion and the Fox* (1937); William E. Connelly and E. Merton Coulter, *History of Kentucky*, vols. 2 and 4 (1922); *DAB*, vol. 22, supp. 1 (1940); National Archives, Washington, D.C., Record Group 84, for MS material on Bingham; Julius W. Pratt, *Cordell Hull*, vols. 12 and 13 in *The American Secretaries of State and Their Diplomacy*, ed. Robert H. Ferrell and Samuel Flagg Bemis (1964); Raleigh *News and Observer*, 19 Dec. 1937, 6 July 1941; Joseph C. Robert, *The Story of Tobacco in America* (1949); Elliott Roosevelt and Joseph P. Lasch, eds., *FDR: His Personal Letters, 1928–1943* (1947–50); Franklin D. Roosevelt Library (Hyde Park, N.Y.), for MS material on Bingham.

BENNETT L. STEELMAN

Bingham, William (*2 Feb. 1754–5 Feb. 1826*), schoolmaster and professor at The University of North Carolina, was born in Kilmore Parish, County Down, Ireland, of a Protestant family that is reported to have emigrated from northern England in the seventeenth century.

Virtually nothing certain is known of Bingham's parents nor of his life prior to his arrival in Wilmington. According to his grandson, Robert Bingham, he entered the University of Glasgow in 1774 and "graduated with the highest distinction"; however, his name does not appear in the official *Roll of the Graduates of the University of Glasgow, 1727–1897*. After graduation, he was reportedly licensed to preach by the Presbytery of Glasgow and became a Presbyterian pastor in County Down. Robert Bingham states that his grandfather left Ireland to avoid arrest because of his membership in the United Irishmen, a Protestant organization dedicated to Irish independence. He also indicates that Bingham arrived in Wilmington early in 1789. Standard sources, however, date the United Irishmen's founding as 1791, so it appears that Bingham must have emigrated at a later date, or for other reasons. Once in Wilmington, he seems to have used Masonic connections to gain positions as a private tutor and, later, as headmaster of a local academy.

By 1794, Bingham had moved to Pittsboro, apparently for his health, and from this point onward his career is well documented. On 2 Jan. 1795 (not 1793, as Bingham family sources traditionally relate), he opened Chatham Academy, a private boarding school that quickly gained a wide reputation. By 22 June 1795, the *North Carolina Journal* listed it as one of four schools preparing students for admission to the upper classes at The University of North Carolina.

Bingham contributed twenty dollars to a state-wide

subscription fund in the early 1790s to finance the opening of the university. In 1801 he left Pittsboro to accept appointment as the university's professor of ancient languages, succeeding Archibald Debow Murphy. He remained there for four years, serving briefly as presiding professor, but resigned in 1805, partly because of dissatisfaction with the quality of the students and partly (according to contemporary rumor) because of the trustees' objections to his extreme Jeffersonian political opinions.

After leaving Chapel Hill, Bingham returned to Pittsboro and reopened his school. In 1808 he moved it to Hillsborough, where it remained, as Hillsborough Academy, until 1818. That year, desiring to raise his sons in a rural setting, he again relocated his school, in a log cabin on a farm he owned in the Mount Repose community, eleven miles northwest of Hillsborough. There he continued to teach until his death. A highly regarded teacher, Bingham founded a line of schoolmasters who remained influential in North Carolina for three generations. He was also among the first educators in the state to recognize the importance of women's education; in 1797, while still in Pittsboro, he erected a separate building for female students adjacent to his original academy and retained a woman assistant to aid in their instruction.

Bingham married Annie Jean Slingsby, the daughter of an officer in Cornwallis's army who had settled in the Cape Fear region. Two sons survived to adulthood: William James (6 Apr. 1802–19 Feb. 1866), who succeeded his father as headmaster at Mount Repose; and John Archibald, a Presbyterian preacher and tutor.

SEE: Samuel A. Ashe, ed., *Biographical History of North Carolina*, vol. 4 (1906); Kemp P. Battle, *History of the University of North Carolina*, vol. 1 (1907); Charles L. Coon, *North Carolina Schools and Academies, 1790–1840* (1915); Hugh T. Lefler and Paul Wager, eds., *Orange County, 1752–1952* (1953); Raleigh *News and Observer*, 6 July 1941; C. L. Raper, *The Church and Private Schools of North Carolina* (1898).

BENNETT L. STEELMAN

Bingham, William (*7 July 1835–18 Feb. 1873*), author and educator, was born in Hillsborough, the fourth child and eldest son of William James Bingham, headmaster of Hillsborough Academy, and his wife, Eliza Alves Norwood. Named for his paternal grandfather, who was a schoolmaster and professor at The University of North Carolina, he was also, on his mother's side, a great-grandson of James Hogg (1729–1805), a Hillsborough merchant.

At the age of ten, Bingham moved with his family to Oaks, a rural community twelve miles southwest of Hillsborough. Completing the course of study at his father's school at fourteen, he remained at home and worked at the family farm until 1853, when he entered The University of North Carolina. Graduating with first honors in 1856, he chose as the topic of his commencement address "The People and Their Common Schools." Soon afterward, his father employed him as a teacher. In January 1857 he was made a full partner in the school, under the firm name W. J. Bingham and Sons. Later that year, with his younger brother, Robert, he toured several private schools in Virginia to observe their teaching methods.

Bingham remained with the school for the rest of his life, initially concentrating upon the preparation of more advanced pupils for college. His father's failing health, and after 1861, his brother's absence with the Army of

Northern Virginia made him the dominant figure in the school's management. Late in 1863 he officially became headmaster. A year later, in December 1864, he succeeded in obtaining a special, thirty-year charter for the school from the General Assembly. Under its provisions, its pupils would be exempt from conscription until the age of eighteen but would receive military training, live under military discipline, and be liable for mobilization as a separate unit in case of local emergency. Bingham himself, as headmaster, became an ex officio colonel in the state militia, and his instructors were likewise granted militia commissions. By this charter, the school's curriculum was militarized for the first time, and, also for the first time, the school officially became "The Bingham School." That same month, Bingham moved the school from Oaks to Mebane, a railroad junction in eastern Alamance County, to give it better access to transport; and he reopened its boarding program, which his father, with a few exceptions, had allowed to lapse after leaving Hillsborough in 1845.

With the aid of his brother-in-law, Stuart White, and a cousin, William B. Lynch, whom he had accepted as partners in 1864, Bingham kept the school open throughout the Civil War, except for a brief period during Stoneman's Raid, when the student body was called to active duty. At the same time, by virtue of his militia rank, he exercised various military police functions for the state government throughout portions of Orange and Alamance counties. In 1865 he bought out White and Lynch's interests and resumed his position as headmaster and sole proprietor of the school.

Meanwhile, Bingham met with success in another quarter. During the war, he had written and published under Confederate imprint a Latin grammar (1863) and an edited translation of Caesar's *Commentaries* (1864). By the late 1870s, both were being used as textbooks in almost every state in the Union, and both remained in print for over twenty-five years. Bingham also produced an English grammar (1867) and a series of Latin readers; at the time of his death, he was preparing a textbook on Latin prose composition.

In early 1873, Bingham suffered an apparent physical collapse, attributed by contemporaries to strain and overwork. By 1 Feb. he was well enough to accompany his brother to Raleigh as a member of a delegation of fifty-five dignitaries petitioning the state senate to reopen the university. Three weeks later, however, he died in Gainesville, Fla., where he had traveled for his health, and was buried in the Mebane City Cemetery.

Bingham served as a Presbyterian elder for much of his adult life. Celebrated for an extraordinary speaking ability, he was also an accomplished pianist and organist and was highly regarded as an occasional poet. In December 1856 he married Owen White, the sister of a college friend. The couple had six children: William James (28 Nov. 1857–24 Jan. 1888), Ernest, Walter Lenoir (1863–86), Norwood, Herbert (1873–97), and Mary Stuart, who married Preston Lewis Grey, of Bristol, Va.

SEE: Samuel A. Ashe, ed., *Biographical History of North Carolina*, vol. 4 (1906); Kemp P. Battle, "Orange County," *Western North Carolina Historical and Biographical* (1890); William Bingham, *Caesar's Commentaries on the Gallic Wars* (1864), *A Grammar of the English Language* (1867), *A Grammar of the Latin Language* (1863), *A Latin Reader* (1869), *The Life and Writings of Hugh Miller* (1859), "The People and Their Common Schools" (North Carolina Collection, University of North Carolina, Chapel Hill), and "There Remaineth a Rest to the People of God," *The North Carolina Speaker*, ed. Eugene G. Harrell and John B.

Neathery (1887); Raleigh *State Chronicle*, 6 Dec. 1893; C. L. Raper, *The Church and Private Schools of North Carolina* (1898); Robert Hamlin Stone, *A History of Orange Presbytery, 1770–1970* (1970); Walter P. Williamson, "The Bingham School," *Our Living and Our Dead*, vol. 2 (1875).

BENNETT L. STEELMAN

Bingham, William James (*6 Apr. 1802*–19 Feb. 1866), popularly known as "the Napoleon of schoolmasters," was born in Chapel Hill, the oldest son of William Bingham, then professor of ancient languages at The University of North Carolina, and his wife, Annie Jean Slingsby. Most of his childhood was spent in Pittsboro and, after 1808, in Hillsborough, where the elder Bingham maintained two successive private boarding schools.

Educated by his father, Bingham taught school in Williamsboro for some time before entering The University of North Carolina in 1821. After taking a B.A. with first honors in 1825, he read law in the offices of Archibald D. Murphey. His father's death in February 1826 forced him to return home to complete the term's instruction at the family school in the Mount Repose community of Orange County. Shortly afterward, he decided to abandon law and to teach as a career. To prepare himself, he embarked on a lengthy tour of the better-known private schools of New England and Virginia in order to study their teaching methods.

In January 1827, Bingham returned the academy to Hillsborough, from which his father had moved it in 1818. There it rapidly gained a nation-wide reputation for academic excellence. By the 1840s, Bingham's school could boast of pupils from almost every state in the Union, and its tuition, $150 per year, was supposedly the highest charged by any preparatory school in the nation.

Meanwhile, Bingham participated actively in several major reform campaigns of the period. A long-time elder in Bethlehem Presbyterian Church, he spoke frequently in favor of temperance to public audiences. A slaveowner by inheritance, he was nevertheless a member of the American Colonization Society and possibly one other local manumission organization. For a brief period in 1827, he reportedly considered freeing his slaves and moving to Ohio, but he was dissuaded when he discovered the intolerable conditions under which many free blacks in the North lived. While normally shunning public office in any form, he served as corresponding secretary of the North Carolina Institute of Education (1831–32) and as a member of its executive board (1832–34). He was also among the founding members of The University of North Carolina Alumni Association.

In 1845, desiring to raise his sons in the country as his father had done, Bingham moved his school to the Oaks community, twelve miles southwest of Hillsborough. At the same time, he reduced his enrollment from over a hundred to thirty, in order to give his students closer personal attention. During this period, Bingham gratified an old ambition by conducting a model farm, experimenting extensively with new seed strains and new methods of cultivation. Agriculture was a lifelong concern of his: while still in Hillsborough, he had allowed two bondsmen to manage his farm without supervision, an exceptional step for the time.

Because of illness, Bingham was forced to suspend classes for some months in 1855. In January 1857, perhaps for this reason, he admitted his oldest son, William, as a partner in the school, under the name W. J. Bingham and Sons. The younger son, Robert, was admitted as a partner six months later, upon his

graduation. Soon enrollment increased to sixty, with Bingham taking charge of the younger pupils and leaving the advanced classes to his sons. He seems to have gradually retired from the school during this period, however, relinquishing complete control in late 1863.

A Clay Whig, Bingham opposed secession but accepted the Confederacy after Lincoln's call for troops. He moved with his family to Mebane in 1864; he died there and was buried in Mebane City Cemetery.

In 1827, Bingham married Eliza Alves Norwood, the daughter of Judge William Norwood of Hillsborough and a maternal granddaughter of James Hogg (1729–1805). The couple had seven children, five of whom survived to adulthood, including two sons: William (7 July 1835–18 Feb. 1873), who succeeded his father as headmaster of the school; and Robert (5 Sept. 1838–8 May 1927), who succeeded his brother.

SEE: *An Address by William James Bingham Delivered before the College Temperance Society at Chapel Hill* (1836); Samuel A. Ashe, ed., *Biographical History of North Carolina*, vol. 4 (1906); Kemp P. Battle, *History of the University of North Carolina*, vol. 1 (1907), and "Orange County," *Western North Carolina Historical and Biographical* (1890); Paul H. Bergerson, ed., "My Brother's Keeper," *North Carolina Historical Review* 44 (1967); J. G. deRoulhac Hamilton, ed., *The Papers of Thomas Ruffin*, vols. 1–2 (1918–20), and *The Papers of William Alexander Graham*, vol. 2 (1961); William Henry Hoyt, ed., *The Papers of Archibald D. Murphey*, vol. 1 (1914); Edd Winfield Parks, "Sawney Webb," *North Carolina Historical Review* 12 (1935); C. L. Raper, *The Church and Private Schools of North Carolina* (1898); H. T. Shanks, ed., *The Papers of Willie Person Mangum*, vol. 2 (1952); Southern Historical Collection (University of North Carolina, Chapel Hill), for letters of Bingham in various collections; Kenneth Stampp, *The Peculiar Institution* (1956); Robert Hamlin Stone, *A History of Orange Presbytery, 1770–1970* (1970); Walter P. Williamson, "The Bingham School," *Our Living and Our Dead*, vol. 2 (1875).

BENNETT L. STEELMAN

Bird, Valentine (*d. ca. 1679*), colonial official and a leader in Culpeper's Rebellion, settled in Albemarle before April 1672, at which time he was speaker of the assembly.

In 1675, Bird was appointed collector of the penny-per-pound tax that Parliament had recently imposed on tobacco shipped from one colony to another. Because of the hardship imposed by the tax, which threatened to destroy the tobacco trade of the colony, local officials agreed that Bird would collect only a small fraction of the amount specified by Parliament, and he is alleged to have permitted some tobacco to leave the colony tax-free.

Bird was one of the chief leaders in the 1677 uprising called Culpeper's Rebellion, in which the acting governor, Thomas Miller, was ousted from office. Bird helped plan the strategy for the revolt and headed the armed groups that seized and imprisoned Miller and several members of his government. He was a member of both the assembly and the council chosen by the rebels and was one of the judges appointed to try Miller for his alleged offenses.

Bird died soon after the revolt he had helped lead. He left a minor daughter, Sarah. His widow, Margaret, married John Culpeper in 1679 or 1680.

SEE: Timothy Biggs, "A Narrative of The Transactions past In the Conty of Albermarle Sence Mr. Tho. Miller his Arrivall there" (Arents Tobacco Collection, New York Public Library, New York City; photocopy in North Carolina State Archives, Raleigh); J. Bryan Grimes, ed., *North Carolina Wills and Inventories* (1912); North Carolina State Archives (Raleigh), for Albemarle Book of Warrants and Surveys (1681–1706), Council Minutes, Wills, Inventories (1677–1701), and Bond of Margaret Culpeper as Guardian for Sarah Bird (2 Feb. 1686); Mattie Erma Edwards Parker, ed., *North Carolina Higher-Court Records, 1670–1696* (1968); William S. Powell, ed., *Ye Countie of Albemarle in Carolina* (1958); Hugh F. Rankin, *Upheaval in Albemarle: The Story of Culpeper's Rebellion* (1962); William L. Saunders, ed., *Colonial Records of North Carolina*, vol. 1 (1886).

MATTIE ERMA E. PARKER

Bird, William Ernest (21 July 1890–22 Oct. 1975), educator, was the fifth of nine children born to Charles Asbury Bird and Sarah Ermina Terrell. Bird's paternal ancestors emigrated from England to Virginia, then to North Carolina. His grandfather, the Reverend John Williamson Bird, attained prominence as a Methodist circuit rider in southwestern North Carolina. Charles Bird earned a substantial reputation as a progressive farmer and a Democratic politician in Jackson County.

Born near Whittier, Bird studied in the Jackson County public schools and was graduated from Cullowhee Normal and Industrial School in 1911. His entire life was to revolve around the Cullowhee school, as it evolved into Western Carolina University.

Bird assumed his first administrative post in the fall of 1911 as principal of the public school at Addie. Seeking a college degree, he matriculated at Mars Hill College the following spring; soon he reentered Cullowhee, which was converting into a junior college. In 1915, Bird became one of Cullowhee's first three graduates to enroll directly in The University of North Carolina with advanced sophomore classification. He received his A.B. degree two years later. Between 1917 and 1920 he held a high school principalship at North Wilkesboro for two years and another at Sylva for one. He used his summers to earn his M.A. degree at George Peabody College for Teachers in Nashville, Tenn.

In 1920, President Robert Lee Madison of Cullowhee appointed Bird to teach English and to serve as his administrative assistant. For one year, Bird held the imposing title of vice-president; then his title was changed to dean. Except for a two-year interval as acting president, he served in the dual capacity of professor-administrator until 1956, prompting the *Asheville Citizen-Times* to label him "the sturdy oak" of Western Carolina College. He headed the English department from 1944 to 1947 and from 1949 to 1956. As dean, he played a key role in expanding the school's curriculum while preserving its original emphasis on training teachers.

On 9 Oct. 1947, President Hiram T. Hunter died, and Bird was designated acting president. He secured the state legislature's acceptance of a $2.05 million supplementary appropriation to facilitate a five-year building program inaugurated by Hunter. In addition, he articulated the college's formal educational philosophy, stressing the goals of integrating spiritual, intellectual, and practical development and of preparing students for life in a responsible, democratic society. At the end of his term, his professional colleagues selected him to preside over the North Carolina College Conference (1949–50).

In September 1949, Bird resumed his former dual post. However, in March 1956, on the verge of mandatory

retirement, he ascended to the full presidency. During his short term, Bird procured $975,000 from the state; he cooperated with the officials of other state universities to persuade the legislature to increase faculty members' base salaries and to augment the number of staff members; and he presided over the admission of Western Carolina's first black student. He resigned on 31 July 1957, but he remained connected with the school as president emeritus and college historian. In 1960, Western Carolina granted him an honorary doctorate and dedicated the Bird Administration Building.

An interest in local history stimulated Bird to help create the Western North Carolina Historical Association in 1951 and serve as its first president. His *History of Western Carolina College* was published in 1963. He also published two small volumes of precisely structured poetry, *Lyrics of a Layman* (1962) and *Level Paths: New Songs by the Layman* (1964). All Bird's writings reflected his self-discipline, joy in nature, pedantic conviviality, and devotion to spiritual values. A devout Methodist, he participated actively in local church work and sat on the Western North Carolina Methodist Conference's educational board. Early in life, he joined both the Masonic Lodge at East LaPorte and the Sylva Rotary Club, serving a stint as president of the latter.

Predictably, Bird met his wife at Cullowhee School. On 16 Aug. 1916, he married Myrtle Wells, the daughter of a Buncombe County farmer. The Birds had three children, all born between 1923 and 1926: Sarah Anne, Charles Wells, and Helen Gertrude.

Bird was buried in Thomas Cemetery, Qualla.

SEE: *Asheville Citizen-Times*, 22 Apr. 1956, 24 Oct. 1975; William E. Bird, *History of Western Carolina College* (1963 [photographs]); William E. Bird Papers (Archives, Western Carolina University, Cullowhee); *North Carolina: Rebuilding an Ancient Commonwealth*, vol. 4 (1929); *Who's Who in America*, 1964–65.

TIMOTHY J. WIEST

Birdsong, James Cook (15 Mar. 1843–18 June 1918), printer and state librarian, son of Miles and Dolly Graves Birdsong, was born in Southampton County, Va. In 1856 Birdsong entered the Petersburg printing establishment of Crutchfield and Campbell, publishers of the *Daily Express*. On 20 Apr. 1861, he enlisted as a private in Company B of the Twelfth Regiment of Virginia Infantry and remained at that rank until the end of the Civil War. He fought in the battles of Seven Pines and Second Manassas and on 2 May 1863, he was captured at Chancellorsville and taken to the Old Capitol Prison. He was released by exchange in September of that year. He was wounded through the right shoulder at Cold Harbor in May 1864 but continued to serve until the surrender at Appomattox Court House.

Birdsong moved to Raleigh in 1866 where he continued his career in printing. For many years he worked for Edwards and Broughton of Raleigh. Between 1876 and 1897 he held the position of examiner of state printing. A resolution of the North Carolina General Assembly on 6 Mar. 1893 directed him to prepare *Brief Sketches of the North Carolina State Troops in the War Between the States* (1894).

Upon the death of Randolph Abbott Shotwell, the Trustees of the Public Libraries appointed Birdsong state librarian. He assumed the duties in October 1885 and held the position until April 1893.

Birdsong married Ophelia Crocker, daughter of A.J. Crocker, in 1867. They had seven children, including Miles B., Mamie, John H., Edward G., Ludlow, and

Heber. For years Birdsong was clerk of the Raleigh Association of the Baptist Church and a member of the board of deacons of the Raleigh Baptist Tabernacle. He was a member of the Independent Order of Odd Fellows. Birdsong also held the positions of adjutant of the L. O'B. Branch Camp of Confederate Veterans and secretary of William G. Hill Masonic Lodge.

SEE: James Cook Birdsong death certificate 293 (N.C. State Board of Health, Raleigh); *Chas. Emerson & Co.'s Raleigh Directory, 1880–'81* (1879); Jerome Dowd, *Sketches of Prominent Living North Carolinians* (1888); D. H. Hill, *North Carolina*, vol. 4 in *Confederate Military History*, ed. Clement H. Evans (1899); Hill Directory Co., *Raleigh Directory, 1911–1912* (1911); Raleigh *News and Observer*, 19 June 1918; *Report of State Librarian* (Document No. 14, *Executive and Legislative Documents, 1887*); Charles A. Separk, *Directory of the City of Raleigh, 1896–'97* (n.d.).

MAURY YORK

Björkman, Edwin August *(19 Oct. 1866–16 Nov. 1951)*, journalist, literary critic, and translator, was born in Stockholm, Sweden, the son of Anders August and Johanna Elizabeth Anderson Björkman. He attended South-End Higher Latin School in Stockholm and worked as a clerk, journalist, and actor from 1881 to 1891. He was a founder of the Swedish Wholesale Clerk's Association and a member of the Lindberg Drama Company and Swedish Royal Theater Company in 1889–91.

In 1891, Björkman came to the United States and joined the Scandinavian colony in Minnesota, where he was editor of the bilingual *Minnesota Posten* of St. Paul (1892–94). He was a reporter and music critic for the *Minneapolis Times* from 1894 to 1897 and a reporter on the New York *Sun* and *New York Times* from 1897 to 1905, except for a tour of duty in 1898 with the Twenty-third Regiment of the New York Militia during the Spanish-American War. In 1906 he joined the editorial staff of the *New York Evening Post*, where he served until becoming department editor of the *World's Work* in 1909. From 1912 to 1915, Björkman was editor of the *Modern Drama Series*, where he quickly attained international eminence for his translations of plays by August Strindberg, Arthur Schnitzler, and other European dramatists. In 1914 he was awarded a scholarship by the American Scandinavian Foundation for critical studies in Europe.

During World War I, Björkman served in Sweden with the British Department of Information (1915–17) and as Director of the Scandinavian Bureau of the American Committee on Public Information (1918–19). In 1919 he was made a Knight of the Order of the Dannebrog by the Danish government in recognition of his wartime service. In 1920–21 he served as assistant director of the League of Nations News Bureau. For three years he was a lecturer in modern Scandinavian drama at Yale University.

Björkman settled in Waynesville, N.C., in 1925 and served as literary editor of the *Asheville Times* from 1926 to 1929. He subsequently worked for the U.S. Geological Bureau. From October 1935 to August 1941, he was director of the North Carolina Federal Writers Project of the WPA. Under his supervision, the group published *North Carolina: A Guide to the Old North State* in 1939. In 1947 he was president of the Asheville chapter of the Southern Conference for Human Welfare, and in 1948 he was a member of the executive committee of the Progressive party.

Björkman's novels, essays, poetry, and literary criticism reflect his concern with individual and collective freedom, civil rights, and the advancement of civilization. Among his major works are *Is There Anything New under the Sun?* (1911), *Gleams: A Fragmentary Interpretation of Man and His World* (1912), *Voices of Tomorrow* (1913), *Scandinavia and the War* (1914), *The Cry of the Ukraine* (1915), *The Soul of a Child* (1922), *Gates of Life* (1923), *The Search for Atlantis* (1927), *Ibsen as He Should Be Read*, and *The Wings of Azrael* (1934). He translated novels by Gustaf af Geijerstam, Frank Heller, Harry Soiberg, and Olav Duun. In 1926 he translated Georg Brandes's *Jesus: A Myth*. As editor of the *Modern Drama Series*, he translated four volumes of the plays of August Strindberg (1912–15), two volumes of plays by Bjornstjorne Bjornson (1913–14), plays by Hjalmar Bergstrom (1913), plays by Arthur Schnitzler (1915), and dramatic works by Gunnar Heiberg and Fritz von Unruh.

Björkman was married four times, first to Frances Maule, a suffragist, in 1906, and next to Virginia MacFadyen, an actress, in 1923. In 1930 he married Ellie May Platt, who died in Paris in 1932; and in 1934 he married Lucy Millender. Björkman died in Asheville and was buried there in Riverside Cemetery.

SEE: *Asheville Citizen*, 17 Nov. 1951 (portrait); Raleigh *News and Observer*, 18 Nov. 1951; *Who Was Who in America*, vol. 3 (1960).

MARCUS B. SIMPSON, JR.

Blackbeard the Pirate *(ca. 1680–22 Nov. 1718)*, picturesque colonial pirate, is usually said to have been born in Bristol, England. The circumstances of his early life are not known. Pirates rarely wrote about themselves or their families: each hoped to acquire a vast fortune and return to his former home without having tarnished his family name.

Because pirates tended to adopt one or more fictitious surnames while engaging in piracy, there is no absolute certainty of Blackbeard's real surname. In all the records made during the period in which he was committing his sea robberies, he was identified as either Blackbeard or Edward Teach. Numerous spellings of the latter name include Thatch, Thack, Thatche, and Theach, but Teach is the form most commonly encountered, and most historians have identified him by that name.

Captain Charles Johnson (recently thought to be a pseudonym for Daniel Defoe), a recognized authority on the pirates of the era, states emphatically in *A General History of the Robberies and Murders of the Most Notorious Pyrates*, originally published in 1724, that Edward Teach sailed for some time out of Jamaica on the ships of privateers during Queen Anne's War and that "he had often distinguished himself for his uncommon boldness and personal courage."

Sometime in 1716, Teach transferred the base of his operations from Jamaica to New Providence in the Bahama Islands. He served an apprenticeship under Captain Benjamin Hornigold, who was the fiercest and ablest of all pirates regularly operating out of the island of New Providence. Jointly they captured and looted a number of large merchant vessels. Having amassed a sizeable fortune and recognizing that the profitable days of piracy were nearing an end, Hornigold in early 1718 retired from piracy and took up the honest life of a planter on New Providence. He took full advantage of the king's pardon when Woodes Rogers arrived in Nassau on 27 July 1718 as the newly appointed governor of the Bahama Islands.

Teach converted a large French ship, *Concord*, which he and Captain Hornigold had captured, into a pirate ship of his own design. He renamed her the *Queen Anne's Revenge* and mounted upon her forty guns. The vessel was eventually manned by a crew of three hundred, some of whom had been members of her crew when she sailed under the French flag.

Most men of this period did not wear beards, but Teach discovered that he could grow a coarse, coal-black beard that covered the whole of his face. He allowed his monstrous mane to grow to an extravagant length, and he was accustomed to braiding it into little pigtails, tied with ribbons of various colors. As a finishing touch before a battle, he tucked under the brim of his hat fuses that would burn at the rate of a foot an hour, the curling wisps of smoke from which added to the frightfulness of his appearance. Across his shoulders he wore a sling with two or three pistols hanging in holsters, like a bandolier. In the broad belt strapped around his waist was an assortment of pistols and daggers and an oversized cutlass. Teach's deliberately awesome appearance in battle array had its effect. When ferociously attacked, the crews of many merchant ships surrendered without any pretense of a fight.

Near the end of May 1718, when Teach was at the high tide of his piratical career, he and his armed flotilla of five or six vessels appeared outside the entrance to the harbor of Charleston, S.C., and blockaded the busiest and most important port of the southern colonies. All vessels, inbound or outbound, were stopped and looted. Teach demanded and received from the governor of South Carolina and his council a chest of medicine. Without the firing of a single gun, the pirate king reduced to total submission the proud and militant people of South Carolina.

After the daring and bizarre blockade of Charleston, Teach and his small fleet sailed northward up the Atlantic into what is today commonly known as Beaufort Inlet, for a general disbanding of the crew of about four hundred men: Teach knew the "golden age of piracy" was nearing its end.

Sometime in June 1718, Blackbeard and at least twenty members of his crew passed through Ocracoke Inlet, N.C., entered Pamlico Sound, and headed for the town of Bath on the Pamlico River fifty-odd miles from the Atlantic Ocean. There they received from Governor Charles Eden a "gracious pardon" pursuant to proclamation from the king of England, intended to suppress piracy.

Teach acquired a home in Bath and, for a while, lived the life of a gentleman of leisure. He lost little time in selecting his fourteenth bride, a girl who was about sixteen years of age and the daughter of a Bath County planter. Governor Eden performed the marriage ceremony. But Teach had an unquieted passion for adventure. He was soon, once again, pirating on the high seas and bringing back to Bath his spoils.

Ocracoke Inlet was Blackbeard's favorite anchorage. All oceangoing vessels bound for or leaving settlements in northeastern North Carolina passed through this inlet, and he was usually to be found on the sound side of the southern tip of Ocracoke Island. His crew, however, was greatly reduced; his experienced officers and fighting men of former days were no longer with him, because there was no profit in associating with him unless he was actively engaged in looting vessels. It was here that Blackbeard's death occurred in a famous hand-to-hand battle with Lieutenant Robert Maynard, who had been sent by Governor Alexander Spotswood of Virginia to capture the pirate and his treasure.

Maynard ordered Blackbeard's head severed from his body and suspended from the bowsprit of one of Maynard's two armed vessels. The rest of Blackbeard's corpse was thrown overboard. The head of Blackbeard would be proof irrefutable that Maynard and his crew had slain the pirate chieftain, enabling them to collect the reward of one hundred pounds sterling offered by the Colony of Virginia.

SEE: Shirley Carter Hughson, *The Carolina Pirates and Colonial Commerce* (1894); Captain Charles Johnson, *A General History to the Robberies and Murders of the Most Notorious Pyrates*, ed. Arthur L. Hayward (1955); Robert E. Lee, *Blackbeard the Pirate* (1974); Hugh F. Rankin, *The Golden Age of Piracy* (1969).

ROBERT E. LEE

Blackburn, Edmond Spencer (*22 Sept 1868–12 Mar. 1912*), lawyer, legislator, congressman, and Republican party leader, was born on a small farm near the upper waters of Meat Camp Creek in Watauga County. He attended a public school in the area and later studied at Oak Hill Institute in Virginia. At the age of twenty he returned to Watauga County to teach at Cove Creek Academy. Here he earned a lasting reputation as a dynamic teacher and leader among the young men of his county. After some two years at Cove Creek Academy, Blackburn went to Statesville, where he studied law with Major H. Bingham. In 1890, Blackburn was admitted to the bar and commenced legal practice in Jefferson, Ashe County. In 1892 he was a candidate for elector-at-large for Benjamin Harrison. In the 1895 legislative session he was chosen reading clerk in the state senate. During the 1897 session of the legislature he represented Ashe County in the state house of representatives, and in 1898 he was appointed by President William McKinley to the position of assistant U.S. district attorney for the Western North Carolina District.

In 1900, Blackburn was the Republican party candidate for Congress from the Eighth District. He defeated his Democratic opponent, J. C. Buxton of Winston-Salem, and served in the Fifty-seventh Congress (4 Mar. 1901–3 Mar. 1903). In the 1902 congressional election he was defeated by Theodore F. Kluttz of Salisbury. The gerrymander of the Eighth District by the 1901 session of the North Carolina legislature was considered a major cause of Blackburn's defeat. In the 1904 election he defeated W. C. Newland, a Democrat, for the Eighth Congressional District seat in the Fifty-ninth Congress (4 Mar. 1905–3 Mar. 1907). During his second term in Congress, Blackburn married the socially prominent daughter of Colonel M. M. Parker of Washington, D.C. Blackburn's wife was the niece of Judge Alton B. Parker, Democratic presidential candidate in 1904.

Following his marriage, Blackburn moved his residence from Wilkesboro, where he practiced law, to Greensboro, apparently to avoid bringing his wife into what were described as the "wilds" of the Eighth Congressional District. After he relocated in Greensboro, Blackburn's role in Republican party politics in North Carolina steadily declined. During the 1906 congressional race, Democrat Richard N. Hackett of North Wilkesboro made much political capital from the charge that while Blackburn actually lived in Greensboro, in the Fifth Congressional District, he sought election to office in the Eighth. Hackett was elected to replace Blackburn in the district.

While residing in Greensboro, Blackburn sought to assert a larger role in the affairs of the Republican party. He was outspokenly critical of factional leaders who served as patronage brokers but who contributed little to the expansion of party strength at the state level or to the election of state Republican candidates to office. He challenged the Republican state organization, the party chairman, Thomas S. Rollins, and the mouthpiece of party leaders, the *Daily Industrial News* of Greensboro. Blackburn launched his own newspaper, the *Weekly Tar Heel* of Greensboro, to represent the views of a faction in the party strongly oriented toward the western and northwestern counties of North Carolina, the Republican party stronghold. He maintained that elected Republicans should have more control over the distribution of patronage among Tar Heels.

Blackburn challenged Spencer Bell Adams, the candidate of the Republican state organization, for chairmanship of the party executive committee in the state convention of 1906 in Greensboro. The impassioned speech Blackburn delivered from the balcony of Guilford Hotel to his followers from Western North Carolina was long remembered by party analysts. However, Blackburn was defeated by Adams in the contest for chairmanship. Subsequently, following his defeat by Richard N. Hackett in the congressional race, Blackburn's influence in state politics was eclipsed. A highlight of the Greensboro convention was the address by Secretary of War William Howard Taft, in which he charged that the Republican party in North Carolina would fare better if Democrats were given patronage appointments under a Republican administration. Taft's remarks were interpreted as a pointed indictment of Blackburn's role in the factional squabbling among Republicans, and Taft was thought to represent the views of President Theodore Roosevelt. In 1908 and 1910, Blackburn supported John Motley Morehead's campaign against factional rivals in the Republican party.

Subsequently, Blackburn resided briefly in Tulsa, Okla. Shortly thereafter he moved to Elizabethton, Tenn., and set up a law office. There he died of a heart attack, survived by his widow and two children. Blackburn was buried in Old Hopewell Cemetery, near Boone.

SEE: *Charlotte Observer*, 1900–1912; Greensboro *Daily Industrial News*, 1905–12; Greensboro *Weekly Tar Heel*, 1905–6; David C. Roller, "Republican Factionalism in North Carolina, 1904–1906," *North Carolina Historical Review* 41 (1964); Joseph F. Steelman, "The Progressive Era in North Carolina, 1884–1917" (Ph.D. diss., University of North Carolina, 1955), "Republicanism in North Carolina: John Motley Morehead's Campaign to Revive a Moribund Party," *North Carolina Historical Review* 42 (1965), and "The Trials of a Republican State Chairman," ibid. 43 (1966); Winston *Union Republican*, 1894–1912.

JOSEPH F. STEELMAN

Blackburn, William Maxwell (20 Apr. 1899–9 Dec. 1972), educator, son of Charles Stanley and Amy Malvina Waring Blackburn, Presbyterian missionaries, was born in Urumiah, Iran, and died in Durham. His paternal grandfather was a church historian and university president in the Dakota Territory; his mother's family in Columbia, S.C., could claim descent from John Howland of the *Mayflower*. When five years old, Blackburn came with his parents to South Carolina; the family moved from town to town, living off the meager rewards of the ministerial vocation. The memory of those hard times was to haunt Blackburn all his life, yet in a short, posthumously published memoir, he wrote with lively warmth of his boyhood in Seneca, S.C., and of the shaping influence on a poor preacher's son of his grandmother, Malvina Gist Waring, a novelist and "old reb" who had served the Confederacy. It was she who

encouraged his literary interests and in 1917 sent him to Furman University, where he was graduated in 1921 with an A.B. in English. There followed a University Scholarship in the graduate school at Yale and a year's teaching at Carnegie Institute of Technology, and then came recognition of his learning and strength of character: he was awarded a Rhodes Scholarship from South Carolina. The years at Hertford College, Oxford University, 1923–26, were among the happiest of his life, leading to B.A. and M.A. degrees and, perhaps of greater importance, confirming his sense of a mission as a humanist educator. At Oxford, too, it is not unreasonable to speculate, the passionate ethical idealism, the "sweet reasonableness" of Matthew Arnold, left their strong impression; certainly the immense learning that produced pioneering studies of *Literature and Dogma* (subject of Blackburn's Yale Ph.D. dissertation in 1943) was partly a debt paid to Arnold, a kindred spirit.

In 1926, Blackburn was drawn to Duke in that new university's massive effort to assemble a strong faculty for an "Oxford of the South." Here he was to teach English for forty-five years, with the exception of a period with University Training Command, Florence, Italy, in 1945. Throughout the Duke years, he remained professionally active in associations of college English teachers and of Rhodes Scholars. He became a full professor in 1953. In May 1966 he first served as an adviser to the National Endowment for the Arts.

As an author, Blackburn placed his own considerable literary talents, known to his friends and family through the terse, diffident, avuncular letters he wrote them, at the service of other writers, as their editor. After Arnold studies and a booklet, *The Architecture of Duke University* (1938), he edited three successive volumes of narrative and verse by Duke students, many his own and some, thus initially encouraged, on their way to literary fame. In 1969 appeared *Love, Boy*, poignant letters from one of those former students, Mac Hyman, revealing how tormented by self-doubt had been the humorist who wrote *No Time for Sergeants*. Earlier, in 1958, Blackburn's ingenious discovery and penetration of the materials published as *Joseph Conrad: Letters to William Blackwood and David S. Meldrum* had earned international critical acclaim, not least because, from their editing, the letters take on narrative form and show the heroism of Conrad's early struggle for recognition as an artist.

With imaginative power and a gift of sympathetic insight, Blackburn was able to grasp the essential design of a literary work as it surfaces from the creative process. This grasp of design was crucial to his success as a teacher of writers at Duke and, from 1969 until his death, at The University of North Carolina. When the London *Times Literary Supplement* editorialized in 1965 about the teaching of creative writing, Blackburn was hailed as the rare teacher possessing "the combination of critical acumen and charisma" feasible for the job. He himself, however, persistently refused to take credit for the successes of such former students as Pulitzer Prize winning novelist William Styron; even when featured on national television, Blackburn characteristically turned attention away from himself and onto his famous students. His modest claim was that he helped writers to become good readers. Yet no history of forces shaping modern letters in the South will be complete without notice of the influence of this quietly eloquent, plainly devoted teacher—a large man of noble bearing and mien, one whose unifying human qualities of courage, humor, and moral integrity helped to guide and inspire makers of literature.

His marriage on 28 Dec. 1926 to Elizabeth Cheney Bayne of South Manchester, Conn., ended in divorce in 1951; in July 1966 he married Roma Stewart Goodwin of Montreal. His children, both North Carolina-born, are Mary April (Mrs. Robert M. Hill) and Alexander Lambert.

Blackburn was buried in the Presbyterian churchyard, Marion Street, Columbia, S.C.

SEE: William M. Blackburn, "Sketches for a Memoir," *Duke Alumni Register* 58 (1973); "William Blackburn," *Furman Magazine* 19 (1972); *Durham Morning Herald*, 10 Jan. 1953, 27 Feb. 1954, 14 July 1954, 12 Aug. 1956, 28 Nov. 1958, 8 Mar. 1959, 7 Apr. 1960, 10 and 24 Dec. 1972.

A. L. BLACKBURN

Blackledge, William (*d. 19 Oct. 1828*), legislator, congressman, and businessman of Craven County, was the third of four sons and three daughters of Richard Blackledge and his wife, Ann. The elder Blackledge was extremely wealthy; upon his death in 1776, William inherited property including over a thousand acres of land, six slaves, a lot in New Bern, and mills at Beaver Dam.

Nothing is known of Blackledge's education or early life, except that in 1783 he was a student at Princeton. He became a friend of Willie Blount and of John Gray Blount, probably the most influential merchant in Eastern North Carolina at the turn of the century; and he entered politics in 1802, when he was elected to the state senate from Craven County to fill the unexpired term of Richard Dobbs Spaight, Sr., who was mortally wounded in a duel. He also served as a member of the House of Commons in 1809 and was elected a councilor of state by the General Assembly each year from 1814 through 1827.

He served four terms in the U.S. Congress from the Fourth District as a member of the Democratic-Republican party, from 1803 to 1809 and from 1811 to 1813. He was relatively quiet during his first term but gradually participated more and more. He supported the interests of merchants, since New Bern was a port city, opposing Jefferson's embargo as injurious to trade (1808) and favoring a large navy both in numbers and in size of vessels (1812). His opinion of the abilities of American seamen, in contrast to those of the British, was high. He favored a salt tax because it would encourage local manufacture of salt, a Federalist measure rather than a Jeffersonian. The Eighth Congress, of which he was a member, was active in impeaching Federalist judges; Blackledge was elected (2 Jan. 1804) by the House as one of the eleven floor managers to present to the Senate its case against Judge John Pickering.

Defeated for Congress in the election of 1808 by Federalist John Stanly, he returned as a War Hawk the following term. He voted yea on the declaration of war, saying, "Rather than submit to pretensions so degrading to our national honor, and which, if submitted to, must lead to consequences so destructive both to the agricultural and commercial interests of the nation, I do not hesitate to prefer war." United, he believed, the nation could defend her rights "against the combined powers of the earth." Because it was a war measure, he voted for the 1812 embargo; he supported fifteen of the sixteen war revenue acts (being absent for one vote) and bills for arming the militia and for building coastal defenses.

New Bern, however, was a wealthy port town containing many merchants and bankers who opposed war with Britain. Because of this opposition, and because of the fumbling ineptitude of the administration in prosecuting the war, Blackledge was defeated in the 1812 election by William Gaston of New Bern, a brilliant Federalist attorney who later had a distinguished career as a jurist. Blackledge never returned to Congress, devoting the remainder of his life to state service as an "elder statesman." He died at Spring Hill in Lenoir County; his wife, Winifred, died seven days later, 26 Oct. 1828. The *New Bern Spectator* lauded "his worth and public service," stating that his former opponents acknowledged "his uniform urbanity, kindness, and disposition to accommodate." He was said to have been an excellent husband, father, master, and citizen. His son, William Salter, also served in the U.S. Congress, 1820–23, and in the General Assembly of North Carolina.

SEE: *Annals of Congress*, 1803–13; *Biog. Dir. Am. Cong.* (1971); S. M. Lemmon, *Frustrated Patriots: North Carolina and the War of 1812* (1973); *New Bern Spectator*, 26 Oct. 1828, 1 Nov. 1828; *North Carolina Manual* (1913).

SARAH MCCULLOH LEMMON

Blackledge, William Salter (*1793–21 Mar. 1857*), congressman, was born in Pitt County, the son of William Blackledge, Sr. (d. 1828), who served several terms in Congress from the New Bern district during the Jefferson and Madison administrations. The family moved to Craven County not long after William Salter was born. He graduated from The University of North Carolina in 1812 and on 26 Apr. 1815 married Mary Hatch. He served one term in commons, 1820.

Blackledge was elected as a Republican to the Sixteenth Congress to fill the vacancy caused by the death of Jesse Slocumb in December of 1820. Reelected in 1821, he served in Congress until March 1823, when he chose not to run for reelection again. In the Seventeenth Congress he served as chairman of the Committee on Public Buildings. In his brief tenure in Congress he moved away from the strict constructionist ideas of his father and subscribed to the nationalistic policies of John C. Calhoun during the Monroe administration. As the election of 1824 approached, he supported John C. Calhoun's candidacy but opposed any alliance with Jackson.

After Blackledge left Congress, he became an enthusiastic supporter of John Quincy Adams and the National Republicans. He was an Adams elector in 1828. He remained active in the campaign for internal improvements, especially supporting the building of a railroad from New Bern through the central part of the state. In 1842 he served as commissioner to help determine the boundary between Jones and Craven counties. He died in New Bern and was buried in the New Bern Cemetery.

SEE: *Biog. Dir. Am. Cong.* (1971); D. L. Corbitt, *The Formation of North Carolina Counties* (1950).

DANIEL M. MCFARLAND

Blackmer, Sidney Alderman (*13 July 1895–5 Oct. 1973*), professional actor, was born in Salisbury, the son of Walter Steele and Clara De Roulhac Alderman Blackmer. He was graduated from Salisbury High School, Warrenton Academy, and in 1912, Mercersburg Academy in Pennsylvania. He planned to be a lawyer but was more attracted to football at The University of North Carolina, where he was a student between 1911 and 1915 and a star of the team. He went to Europe for a year before finishing college, tried in vain to enlist in the army, and returned to the university, where he stayed until 1915. He eventually did spend two years as a lieutenant in the field artillery in World War I.

Blackmer was a leader in his profession. He was a founder of the Actors' Equity Association and took a major role in the bitter actor-manager struggle of 1919. He was a member of the national executive board of the American Federation of Television and Radio Artists and was president of Theater Authority, the clearinghouse for benefit performances. He belonged to the Lambs and the Players, the two major clubs for actors in New York City.

Blackmer also served as national vice-president of the Muscular Dystrophy Association of America, raising millions of dollars to fight the crippling disease.

He was awarded the honorary Litt. D. degree from Catawba College in 1959 and the honorary L.H.D. degree from The University of North Carolina in 1964.

Blackmer's debut on the New York stage was in *The Morris Dance* in February 1917. He appeared with Pearl White in *The Perils of Pauline*, and from those early roles to his last major role as Ruth Gordon's husband in *Rosemary's Baby*—a span of fifty-five years—Blackmer always approached his parts with great seriousness.

For his first starring Broadway role, as an awkward young Virginia woodsman in the play *The Mountain Man*, Blackmer prepared by living, for the summer of 1921, unannounced and uninvited, with the isolated mountain people of northern Georgia, studying their dress, their speech, even the expressions in their eyes. Nearly thirty years later, when he was playing Doc, Shirley Booth's alcoholic husband in the William Inge drama *Come Back, Little Sheba*, Blackmer threw himself into the role in the character's drunken scenes with such relish that during the run of the play he suffered two broken ribs, a sprained ankle, a bloody nose, and severe bruises on his legs and chest. He won both the Donaldson Award and the Antoinette Perry (Tony) Award as best actor of the 1950 season for that role, the critical high point of his career.

Blackmer was probably better known to the general public for his characterization of Theodore Roosevelt, whom he played ten times in plays and movies, including *The Rough Rider*. With the right pair of glasses and a little makeup, Blackmer bore a startling resemblance to Roosevelt: "It *was* my father," Alice Roosevelt Longworth remarked after seeing one of Blackmer's performances.

In all, Blackmer appeared in more than forty Broadway plays, two hundred movies, and numerous television dramas. He played opposite nearly every leading lady of his era, from Shirley Temple (he was her adopted father in *Heidi*) to Helen Hayes, Eva LeGallienne, and Tallulah Bankhead.

Blackmer married Lenore Ulric, an actress, from whom he was divorced in 1939. Three years later he married Suzanne Kaaren, also an actress; they were parents of two sons, Brewster and Jonathon. Although Blackmer lived in New York, he retained his family home in Salisbury, where his children were reared and where he came to relax.

Sidney Blackmer died at the Sloan Kettering Institute for Cancer Research in New York City when he was seventy-eight. He was buried at the Chestnut Hill Cemetery in Salisbury.

SEE: *Charlotte Observer*, 13 Dec. 1931; Daniel L. Grant, *Alumni History of the University of North Carolina* (1924); *New York Times*, 7 Oct. 1973; *North Carolina Awards* (1972); Raleigh *News and Observer*, 8 June 1945, 23 Feb. 1964, 20 Sept. 1964, 1 Dec. 1971; Southern Pines *Pilot*, 16 Aug. 1972.

JO WHITE LINN

Blacknall, John *(ca. 1690–1749)*, Anglican missionary, came to North Carolina from London in the retinue of Sir Richard Everard, who arrived in Edenton in July 1725 as the governor newly appointed by the Lords Proprietors. The Parish Vestry Book for the period shows that Blacknall became "Received Minister Resident" at St. Paul's Church, Edenton, on 18 Aug. 1725, a month after Sir Richard was inaugurated as governor.

Blacknall brought with him from England his son, Charles Blacknall, who was about a year old. If his wife or other members of his family came, the scanty records make no mention of them. It is reasonable to suppose that his wife came also; but who she was, when and where they were married, who were her parents and who were his, where he was born, and the sources of his education—all these are questions for which answers remain to be found. Intensive research in appropriate American and British sources has produced little note of Blacknall before his coming to North Carolina. In a 25 Jan. 1726 letter from North Carolina written to the Bishop of London, Governor Everard wrote: "I'm greatly obliged to your Lordship for obliging me with my request and admitting the Rev. Mr. Blacknall to come with me to Carolina. He is a Gent*m* that's a very good Preacher, a Gent*m* perfectly sober, belov'd by all but Mr. Burrington's Party. He had made about 160 Christians since he has been here & I don't in the least doubt, but he'll double that number before he has been here a twelve month. . . . "

Governor Everard no sooner arrived in the colony than he began a bitter feud with former governor George Burrington, who was himself a bellicose character, fully as resourceful in the compounding of spite and meanness as Sir Richard. Each recruited his faction or, to use Everard's term, his "Party." Everard sought to involve and embroil Blacknall as his own partisan, no doubt surmising that the gentle rector's appreciation of past favors could be depended upon to draw him into Everard's squabbles with the Burrington faction. Indeed, the stratagem at first showed promise of success; for Blacknall, being inexperienced in the rough and tumble of politics, seemed unable to elude the tangled web of intrigue and counterintrigue, though he loathed it all. As Blacknall found his pressures from Everard increasingly distasteful and insufferable, extricating himself from the governor's toils became the supreme preoccupation of his mind.

The solution to his problem occurred to him while he was riding his circuit of chapels and congregations in the precincts of old Albemarle County to the eastward of Chowan. In the easternmost precinct, called Currituck, a white parishioner named Thomas Spencer presented himself with his bride-elect, a mulatto girl named Martha Paul. Blacknall well knew that it was unlawful in North Carolina for anyone to perform a marriage uniting a white person and a person known to be of Negro blood. He also knew that, with a large overbalance of white men in the Province of Carolina, "Winchester Weddings," sanctioned without racial scruple by the laws of biology however much forbidden by manmade law, were occurring with considerable frequency and were almost respectable in the eyes of many people. To officiate as minister at the wedding of the Spencers would, if he were indicted, cost him a fine of fifty pounds, half of which would be paid to the informer for tattling.

Blacknall conceived a plan to escape from the web of political intrigue by causing Everard and his party to *desire* him to leave the colony itself.

Spencer and Paul journeyed to Edenton, where Blacknall performed the marriage ceremony. Then, going straight to the chief justice of the province, Christopher Gale, Blacknall informed upon himself and registered his claim for that half of the fine which by law went to an informer. Blacknall was duly indicted but actually was never tried and fined. He was quietly advised to make an extended visit to Virginia and then decide to stay there. A mere misdemeanant would not be extraditable. He took the advice, waiting only long enough to collect his arrears in pay from the Vestry of St. Paul's before departing. The Vestry Book shows no note of his being dismissed nor of his having resigned. He simply went on the visit and was silently dropped. The account record shows Blacknall was paid a salary of fifty-four pounds, ten shillings, in 1726, a full year's pay. Since he departed before he had completed the year, this may be taken as evidence of goodwill or of good riddance. As for his indictment, the suit lingered in the general court of oyer and terminer and gaol delivery, being continued from term to term for some six months while the marshal repeatedly reported that the defendant was not to be found in the province. The attorney general tinkered with the idea of trying the newlyweds for the offense; but an indictment of them did not square with the statute. Blacknall never returned to the jurisdiction of North Carolina and so was never tried, convicted, or fined.

By July 1726, Blacknall was filling a temporary vacancy in Sittenburn Point Parish, King George County, Va., and appeared on the list of tithables as minister of that parish. Presumably, Sittenburn Point Parish became a part of Richmond County later that year: the 1726 list of tithables for Richmond County also shows Sittenburn Point Parish with Blacknall as minister.

By 1727 he had become permanently settled in Kingston Parish, Gloucester County, a location now in Mathews County, Va., across the river from the historic site of Yorktown. Here he spent the rest of his life as a beloved and successful minister, and here his son, Charles, grew to manhood. Letters in the Fulham Palace Papers, now in Lambeth Palace Library, London, show that Charles Blacknall was prepared to follow in his father's footsteps as rector; but the arrival of twins much too early after his marriage raised questions of "misbehavior." However, after a few months delay, he became rector-designate for Kingston Parish. Later he was made rector and served there until his own death in 1769.

SEE: Fulham Palace Papers, reels 4 and 5 (microfilm, Southern Historical Collection, University of North Carolina, Chapel Hill); Granville County Estate Papers (North Carolina State Archives, Raleigh); Laura Mac-Millan, *North Carolina Portrait Index* (1963 [portrait]); Emma R. Matheny and Helen K. Yates, *Kingston Parish Registers, Gloucester and Mathews Counties, Va., 1749–1827* (1963); *Middlesex County (Va.) Marriages, 1740–1852* and *Middlesex County (Va.) Deeds, 1740–1854* (1965); Records of the General Court of Oyer and Terminer and Gaol Delivery at Edenton, 26 July 1726, 3 Aug. 1726, 25 Oct. 1726 (North Carolina State Archives, Raleigh); Revolutionary War Pension Papers, Thomas Blacknall, no. S-46023 (National Archives, Washington, D.C.); St. Paul's Parish, Edenton, Vestry Book (transcript in North Carolina State Archives, Raleigh); *Virginia Gazette*, 13 Dec. 1770, 11 Apr. 1771, 12 Mar. 1772, 24 Jan. 1777, 27 Mar. 1778.

CHARLES R. HOLLOMAN

Blacknall, Oscar William (*6 Sept. 1852–6 July 1918*), business executive and author, was born on his father's farm near Kittrell. His father, Colonel Charles C. Blacknall, served the Confederacy in the Twenty-third North Carolina Regiment until he fell mortally wounded at the Battle of Winchester. The Blacknall family was seated in Buckinghamshire in England as early as the fourteenth century, on an estate known as Sulgrave Manor. The Reverend John Blacknall, a graduate of Magdalen College, Oxford, accompanied Sir Richard Everard, who had been appointed to succeed Governor George Burrington, to North Carolina in 1725. His grandson, Thomas Blacknall, enlisted as a revolutionary soldier at the age of sixteen. In 1795, Thomas Blacknall settled in Granville (presently Vance) County, where he married Polly Kittrell, a granddaughter of Jonathan Kittrell, one of the first settlers in the area, near the present town of Kittrell.

At the age of fourteen, having experienced poverty and a limited education, Oscar William Blacknall was employed as a clerk in a country store. Later he was employed by W. H. and R. S. Tucker and Company, a mercantile establishment in Raleigh. While in Raleigh, he studied law under R. H. Battle.

In 1871, because of poor health, he returned to Kittrell and there organized his own tobacco business, with Mazeppa his major brand of plug tobacco. After five years of hard work, this marginal business venture became successful enough to allow him time to pursue his literary interests. His first three articles were published in a North Carolina newspaper, and he was complimented and encouraged. Afterward he was successful in having his articles accepted for publication in *Atlantic Monthly, Oliver Twist, The Youth's Companion*, and *Kate Field's Washington*. He wrote articles dealing with life in the South during the Civil War, character sketches, and informative articles on fruit culture, many of which were syndicated in leading farm journals. He sometimes used the pseudonym David Dodge.

In 1888 he organized Continental Plant Company, a highly successful nursery business specializing in strawberry plants.

Blacknall married his double first cousin, Carrie Thomas Blacknall, on 27 July 1875. The first of seven children, Oscar ("Ossie") William, Jr., was born in 1880. The other children included Charles Harry, Shields Mallette, Gladys, Kate McClannahan, a child whose name is unknown, and Harcourt.

The family suffered a number of tragedies: the oldest son died of tuberculosis; two of the other children were suicide cases; and the sixth child died as an infant. On 6 July 1918, Blacknall shot his wife and his daughter Kate and then committed suicide. Newspaper accounts described it as a "triple tragedy" and expressed sorrow for the loss of the "head of the South's largest nursery" and members of his family.

In 1928, Blacknall's son Shields presented his father's collection of books to the Library of The University of North Carolina.

SEE: *Henderson Daily Dispatch*, 10 July 1918; Samuel Thomas Peace, *Zeb's Black Baby* (1955); Raleigh *News and Observer*, 7 July 1918; C. L. Van Noppen Papers (Manuscript Department, Library, Duke University, Durham); Weeks Scrapbook (North Carolina Collection, University of North Carolina, Chapel Hill) 3 (1893), 8 (1892).

B. W. C. ROBERTS

Blackwell, Robert Lester (*4 Oct. 1895–11 Oct. 1918*), Congressional Medal of Honor winner, was born in

Hurdle Mills in the Bushy Fork Community of Person County. He was the second son and youngest of six children of James B. Blackwell, a tenant farmer and Civil War veteran. Lester Blackwell attended Allen School of the Terrell system and, when he was drafted into the army on 19 Sept. 1917, was unmarried and a farmer in Person County. After basic training at Fort Jackson, S.C., he was assigned to Company K, 119th Infantry, Thirtieth Division, which arrived in France on 24 May 1918. The following October, Blackwell's bravery on the battlefield near St. Souplet, France, earned for him the only Congressional Medal of Honor awarded to a North Carolinian during the First World War. The citation reads: "When his platoon was almost surrounded by the enemy and his platoon commander asked for volunteers to carry a message calling for reinforcements, Private Blackwell volunteered for this mission, well knowing the extreme danger connected with it. In attempting to get through the heavy shell and machine gun fire this gallant soldier was killed." Blackwell also received the Cross of War from both the Italian and Portuguese governments. A monument was erected in his memory on the lawn of the Person County courthouse in Roxboro, and a North Carolina historical marker was placed along state Highway 49, near the site of his home.

SEE: *Durham Morning Herald*, 24 Oct. 1965; *Medal of Honor Recipients, 1863–1973* (1973); North Carolina State Archives (Raleigh), for the folder for Hist. Marker G-87; Raleigh *News and Observer*, 10 Nov. 1963; *Raleigh Times*, 24 Dec. 1966.

MARCIA TUTTLE

Blackwell, William Thomas (*12 Jan. 1839–12 Nov. 1903*), tobacco manufacturer and civic leader, was born near Woodsdale in northern Person County. His father was James Lipscomb Blackwell, his mother Eleanor Fox Buchanan. W. T., or "Buck," as he came to be called, was the eldest of their twelve children. He received a common school education and also taught briefly, but the necessity of helping his brothers and sisters turned him to trade. In 1859 he opened a store near Roxboro, the county seat. There he dealt in cotton, cotton yarn, pork, and general merchandise. Because of his family responsibilities he did not volunteer for military service during the Civil War; instead, he hired a substitute. In the sixties he began to speculate in plug (chewing) tobacco and to manufacture and sell smoking (pipe) tobacco. With James R. Day, he peddled his products through Eastern North Carolina by team and wagon and set up a jobbing house at Kinston. The most popular brand they handled was manufactured by John R. Green at the hamlet of Durham, twenty-six miles northwest of Raleigh. This brand was named "Best Flavored Spanish Smoking Tobacco," and the package at length bore the likeness of a bull. During the closing days of the war in North Carolina, both Confederate and Union forces reached Durham and many soldiers helped themselves to Green's tobacco. Rueful loss soon became golden opportunity for the owner, however, as orders for "Durham tobacco" arrived in surprising quantity from ex-soldiers in many states. Now in need of partners, Green persuaded Blackwell and Day to join him at Durham. When Green died in 1869, they purchased the business from his estate. The next year, Julian S. Carr bought a one-third interest in the firm. In 1871, Blackwell was thirty-two, Day thirty, and Carr twenty-six, and the assets of "W. T. Blackwell and Company" were approximately thirty thousand dollars.

The quality and popularity of the product labeled "Durham Smoking Tobacco," with a side view of a bull on the package, inspired clever and determined imitators. Two manufacturers in Virginia sold brands with "Durham" on the labels, and two in North Carolina used bull's head emblems. Litigation ensued. The stakes were high: Virginia tobacco interests had dominated in North Carolina for a long time and feared their new competition; the Blackwell Company was on the rise and knew that if its trademark were pirated the firm might well fail. The litigation extended over fifteen years before the proprietor of the trademark, W. T. Blackwell, won on all issues—but at a cost of about one hundred thousand dollars. Meanwhile "Bull Durham," as the product was popularly called, became a huge success, rewarding Blackwell several times over what he paid in legal fees. He and Day brought valuable experience in buying, selling, and judging leaf tobacco, while Carr proved to be an energetic and original advertiser. All three seemed to possess keen business sense. To help North Carolina farmers and manufacturers become independent of Virginia markets, Blackwell began the warehouse auctioning of loose-leaf tobacco on 18 May 1871. This was the first step toward breaking Virginia's monopoly and shifting the tobacco industry southward. In the beginning, Blackwell bought most of the leaf himself, but warehouses other than his own, and other buyers, quickly appeared. Spectacular and intriguing representations of the famous Durham bull on billboards, heavy advertising in newspapers, the offering of premiums, and the use of endorsements by well-known public figures made "Blackwell's Durham" familiar all over the United States and even abroad. By 1884 the company's annual manufacture amounted to more than five million pounds; the government revenue tax came to over six hundred thousand dollars. The village of three hundred people in 1869 had become a town of five thousand. The imposing "Bull factory," hard by the North Carolina Railroad, was one of the state's showpieces (National Register of Historic Places, 1974). Its powerful calliope, operated to imitate with amazing realism the bellowing of a bull, rent the air with its time signals and seemed to say daily to Durhamites that their town was one of push, progress, and prosperity and that tobacco was king. Over smoking tobacco, Blackwell reigned, so much so that his main rival in Durham, James B. Duke, decided to concentrate on cigarettes.

After Day became the first of the partners to sell his interest, Blackwell, in 1883, sold to M. E. M'Dowell and Company, a Philadelphia jobbing house with much capital and various branches. Carr too sold to M'Dowell but purchased stock in a separate new corporation and was made its president. Keenly aware of the name value, M'Dowell obtained a North Carolina charter for "Blackwell's Durham Tobacco Company." Capitalization was at five hundred thousand dollars.

The 1880s encompassed the heights and depths of Blackwell's career. As tobacco boomed in Durham, he financed the construction of several hundred workers' houses and other buildings. He actively supported the creation of Durham County from parts of Orange and Wake. He helped to promote the extension of railroads from Durham that would connect with lines to the north and south. Most vital in his own mind was the pledge he made after the state supreme court declared unconstitutional the act establishing the town's new graded school: the school committee, he asserted, could "draw on me for the balance that may be necessary to carry on the school as heretofore. . . . it should be sustained." The aid of Blackwell and others, together with legislation prohibiting racial discrimination, guaranteed educational progress. Hiram V. Paul in the 1880s dubbed him "the father of Durham"; William K. Boyd in the 1920s called him "Durham's preeminent pioneer citizen and philanthropist." A brother-in-law of Blackwell, however, stated in a private letter: " . . . he owned the Bull Durham brand exclusively . . . & he sold it for $100,000.00 when he could easily have gotten three to five hundred thousand for it." In 1884, Blackwell launched the state-chartered Bank of Durham, capitalizing it at fifty thousand dollars. This institution financed the operations of many local warehousemen and leaf dealers. Yet Blackwell's sympathy and generosity led him to authorize too many loans with insufficient security. Worse, he and the leading warehouseman, Edward J. Parrish, speculated heavily in leaf tobacco. Their efforts to "bull the market" miscarried, forced the bank to close in 1888, drove a number of businesses into bankruptcy, and brought about the failure of both men. Blackwell's straitened circumstances prevailed for the remainder of his life. A Democrat, he served as postmaster of Durham under Grover Cleveland's second administration, 1893–97.

On 27 Dec. 1877, Blackwell married Emma Exum, whose parents, the W. J. Exums of Hillsborough, were originally from Wayne County. The Blackwells became the parents of a daughter, Mary, who lived only five years, and a son, W. T., Jr., who in later years served as Durham's civil engineer. Blackwell's church membership was Baptist, and he was buried in Maplewood Cemetery. He was survived by his son, two brothers, six sisters, and his eighty-five-year old mother.

SEE: Blackwell Papers and C. L. Van Noppen Papers (Manuscript Department, Library, Duke University, Durham); W. K. Boyd, *The Story of Durham* (1925 [portrait]); Robert F. Durden, *The Dukes of Durham* (1975); Durham *Farmer and Mechanic*, 17 Nov. 1903; First National Bank of Durham, *Forty Years* (1927); Dr. Blackwell Markham (Durham), personal contact; H. V. Paul, *History of the Town of Durham* (1884); N. M. Tilley, *Bright-Tobacco Industry* (1948).

STUART NOBLIN

Blades, James Bishop (*14 Mar. 1856–23 Aug. 1918*), lumberman, industrialist, and financier, of English ancestry, was born at Bishopville, Md., the second son of Captain Peter Clowes Blades and Nancy Emeline West and a grandson of Greensbury Blades and William C. West, both of whom were successful farmers.

At the age of thirteen, left orphaned, he was sent to the home of an uncle, Ezekiel Williams Blades, in Barry, Pike County, Ill. After a few months he went back to his native town and began clerking in the country store of another uncle, James W. Evans. He attended public schools at Bishopville and Snow Hill, Md., and was graduated from Eastman Business College, Poughkeepsie, N.Y. For a year he taught school at Bishopville.

For several months in 1875 he and his older brother, William Benjamin, operated a mercantile establishment at Greenback, Va. Returning to Bishopville, they formed a merchandising partnership with their uncle under the name Evans & Blades. In 1877 they bought water-powered grist- and sawmills there.

This first milling venture was supplemented by purchases of timber tracts. After his attention was attracted to the virgin forests of the south, J. B. Blades in 1879 traveled on foot, muleback, and railroads through Florida and other southern states. Prospects appeared so bright that he and his brother decided to transfer their operations southward. Florida was considered too far from northern markets, so in 1883 they leased a mill site

and bought timberlands near Bath. The elder brother had charge of the sawmills and timber acquisitions, and the younger looked after the sales of the products. Realizing the importance of having a manufacturing plant near their mills, they selected Elizabeth City as their headquarters and moved there from Maryland in about 1888. Joining them were two younger brothers, Dr. L. S. and Carl G.

Previously, in 1886, the brothers had extended their transactions to Craven County, where timber and labor were plentiful and water transportation was convenient. In that year they leased a mill site on Trent River opposite the town of New Bern, and later they acquired much other real estate eastward. For them was established a post office, discontinued in 1935, which was named "Cherry Point," from the cherry trees growing on the "Point" on the south side of Neuse River east of Hancock Creek, now a part of the U.S. Marine Corps air station.

After traveling alone around the world in 1903, Blades decided to make his home at New Bern. There he and his oldest brother looked after their diversified local interests, while his son, Levin Carl, assumed management of the planning and sales divisions at Elizabeth City.

Surviving the 1893 panic, their business proved highly profitable. For twenty-four years in East Carolina they did much to start and develop modern methods of cutting trees and selling the output of their mills. Dry kilns were introduced, and marketing was expanded. Instead of selling logs outside the state, as other mill men were doing, they confined their operations entirely within North Carolina and thus substantially aided its economy. Most of their holdings, except the Elizabeth City branches, were sold in 1906 to the John L. Roper Lumber Company, owned and operated by the Norfolk and Southern Railroad Company. Although Blades objected, he finally consented to the sale when his brothers insisted that they wanted to retire from business.

At New Bern, Blades built on Broad Street a fine, new home with elaborate, carved mahogany interior woodwork. After being converted in 1939 to the Queen Anne Hotel and later razed, it became the site of the primary local branch of the First-Citizens Bank and Trust Company.

Blades assisted in organizing the Dixie Fire Insurance Company in 1906, then the largest firm of the kind in the South, and became its president. He was also president of the Dixie Insurance Company and vice-president of the North State Insurance Company and the North State Fire Insurance Company. To have closer contact with these corporations, he spent much time at Greensboro, and in 1910 he was instrumental in consolidating the companies. He was also vice-president of the First National Bank at Elizabeth City, and in 1906 he organized the New Bern Banking and Trust Company and became its president. He was president of the Blades Lumber Company and the J. B. Blades Lumber Company. Active in the New Bern Chamber of Commerce, he was the 1913 chairman of its railroad and water transportation committee. He was affiliated with, among other organizations, the Benevolent and Protective Order of Elks. A liberal donor to Methodist and other religious causes, he served as chairman of the board of trustees of the Greensboro College for Women.

During the summer of 1918, Blades went to Western Carolina for a vacation visit. While he was en route alone from Black Mountain toward Statesville, his car failed to make a curve near Marion, and he was killed in the accident. The funeral was at the Centenary Methodist

Church, of which he had long been a devout member. The body was taken for interment to the Odd Fellows cemetery at Bishopville, Md., where his parents were buried.

On 4 Feb. 1880, in Maryland, he had married Margaret Ann Warren of Whaleyville, Md., daughter of Joseph E. Warren and Milbourn Dale. To them were born five children, two of whom survived him: L. C. and James Vernon. After his wife's death, he was married on 4 Jan. 1904, at Clayton, to Pearl Tessie Robertson, daughter of Dr. James Battle Robertson and Julia Ann Ellington of Clayton. She also survived him.

SEE: James B. Blades (Manuscript Department, Library, Duke University, Durham); G. S. Carraway, *The Flying Marines* (1946); *History of North Carolina*, vol. 6 (1919); Family records and genealogies in the possession of descendants; New Bern *Sun-Journal*, 24 and 26 Aug. 1918; *Tarheel Banker* 19 (Apr. 1941).

GERTRUDE S. CARRAWAY

Blair, Hannah Millikan (1756–14 Jan. 1852), Quaker revolutionary patriot, was the daughter of William Millikan, first register of deeds of Randolph County, and his wife Jane Roan (or White?). She was born in Chester City, Pa., shortly before the family moved to Deep River in North Carolina. Married to Enos Blair, she became the mother of a new baby every year during the American Revolution yet managed to help soldiers with food, supplies, and other assistance that was in keeping with her Quaker religious beliefs. She was given certificates of appreciation and a small government pension for her service. She carried food and medicines regularly to patriots hiding in the woods from Tory raiders; she mended their clothes, carried messages for them, and occasionally held them in the house when Col. David Fanning and his raiders appeared.

She was credited with saving the lives of two men when she hid them in a corn crib and continued shucking corn while the Tories searched. On another occasion she ripped the corner of a feather bed tick and pushed a visiting patriot inside with the feathers. She threw the covers back so Fanning could see clearly under the bed, sat down, and began mending the torn ticking, saying "Thee may search as thee pleases." After a skirmish at Dixon's Mill in 1779 she learned that several soldiers were hiding in the countryside and took provisions to them. As she was returning, she was taken by Tories who demanded to know where the men were hiding. Insisting that she had only taken food to a sick neighbor ten or so miles away, she was released without revealing the hiding place. Tories, however, eventually burned the Blairs' house and barn and the family was forced to watch as all their possessions were consumed in the flames.

Between 1776 and 1800 the Blairs had thirteen children, twelve of whom lived to adulthood. Hannah is buried at Springfield Friends Meeting in High Point.

SEE: Judith Mower Goodman, "History of the Blair Family" (Blair genealogy file, Quaker Collection, Guilford College, Greensboro); Mrs. James Clifton Moore, ed., "North Carolina Heroines of the Revolution" (Greensboro Public Library rare book room); and Lynn Sherr and Jurate Kazickas, *The American Woman's Gazetteer* (1976).

PAULA S. JORDAN

Blair, William Allen (4 June 1859–2 Mar. 1948), chairman of the state welfare board in North Carolina, banker, and civic leader, was born in High Point to Solomon I. and Abigail Hunt Blair. His maternal grandfather had been a prominent Quaker minister and a founder of Guilford College. His father, a farmer and teacher, was a Moravian, and Blair continued the family interest in the Moravian church.

Blair exhibited early aspects of his later intellectual prowess. He was reading by age four. After education in the public schools and some work at Guilford, he left for Haverford College, from which he was graduated in 1881 as a member of Phi Beta Kappa. From there he went to Harvard for a second A.B. degree in 1882.

Blair returned to North Carolina as principal of the high school in High Point. For the next few years his career included several teaching or school administrative posts, as well as additional study. He was a teacher at the North Carolina State Normal School, principal of the high school in Winston-Salem (1885), and superintendent of the State Normal School (1887–89); he did graduate work at Johns Hopkins University and completed a master's degree at Trinity College (1889). While superintendent of the normal school, he became editor and owner of *School Teacher*, the largest educational magazine in the South. In 1889 he was North Carolina representative to the Paris Exhibition and delegate to the World Sunday School Convention in London.

In 1890 his career shifted from education to banking and business. He became president of the People's National Bank of Winston-Salem, a post he held until 1897, when the bank was reorganized and he took the position of vice-president. In this decade he also studied law and in 1894 was admitted to the North Carolina bar. His interest in banking led him to write a brief *History of Banking in North Carolina, from 1834 to 1898*.

In the 1890s, Blair also undertook the avocation in which he made his greatest contribution to North Carolina. In 1891, Governor Thomas M. Holt appointed him to the North Carolina Board of Charities and Public Welfare. By 1904 he was elected chairman of the board, a post he then held continuously until his death. When Blair first joined the board, its work was largely supervision of the few state institutions for the needy. In the Progressive Era, however, under the leadership of Blair and board member A. L. McAlister, the board reorganized and began systematically to encourage the creation of county welfare boards all over the state. The board also involved more professional social workers in its operation and pioneered the county unit welfare system, which was ideally suited to a predominantly rural state like North Carolina.

With the advent of the New Deal, the local welfare effort in the state was enormously expanded and partially subsumed in federal-state programs. Blair energetically involved himself in all these changes, often lobbying expertly with state and civic leaders to maintain the integrity of the state welfare system. In particular, he fought to keep that system out of politics, an accomplishment Governor Melville Broughton acknowledged when he said, upon the presentation of a certificate of appreciation to Blair in 1944: "I think it is significant that in the field of human welfare we have subordinated politics to a doctrine of genuine service in the State government. . . . The fact is significant that we have not let this agency of government be subjected to conditions and changes that ordinarily accompany political changes within the State government."

Aside from welfare leadership, the many accomplishments of Colonel Blair, as he was often affectionately called, included service as president of the North Carolina Bankers' Association (1898), as member of the U.S. Assay Commission (1905), as vice-president for North Carolina of the American Bankers' Association (1919), and as trustee of Peabody College for Teachers, Salem College, and Winston-Salem Teachers' College. He was the first president of the Winston-Salem YMCA. In addition to his continuing association with the People's Bank, he maintained business interests as editor and part-owner of the *High Point Enterprise* and as part-owner of the Pepsi-Cola and Orange Crush bottling companies of Winston-Salem and the Midas Mines and Gross Mines.

For most of his life, Blair made his home in Winston-Salem. He was married to Mary Eleanor Fries, the daughter of John W. Fries, part of a family of prominent Winston-Salem industrialists and bankers. The Blairs had three children, Mrs. R. A. McCuistion, Marian, and John Fries.

Even in his declining years of ill health, Blair continued to be interested in scholarship and public service; he wrote several articles on Moravian settlements and customs in North Carolina. He died at his home in Winston-Salem and was interred in the Moravian graveyard there.

SEE: Samuel A. Ashe, ed., *Biographical History of North Carolina*, vol. 4 (1906); Thomas S. Morgan, "A Step toward Altruism" (Ph.D. diss., University of North Carolina, 1969); North Carolina Association of County Superintendents of Public Welfare, *Leaders in North Carolina's Public Welfare Program* (1949); *North Carolina: Rebuilding an Ancient Commonwealth*, vol. 4 (1929); *North Carolina: The Old North State and the New*, vol. 3 (1941); *Prominent People of North Carolina* (1906); Raleigh *News and Observer*, 4 Mar. 1948; A. Davis Smith, *Western North Carolina* (1890).

THOMAS S. MORGAN

Blake, Lillie Devereux (12 Aug. 1835–30 Dec. 1913), author and suffragist, the daughter of George Pollock and Sarah Elizabeth Johnson Devereux, was born in Raleigh, a descendant of two famous churchmen of New England. Although she was named Sarah Johnson for her mother, her father called her Lily (Lillie) because of her unusual fairness, and she continued through life as Lillie. Her father, a descendant of colonial Governor Thomas Pollock, inherited Runiroi Plantation in Bertie County and lived there from 1827 to 1837. The plantation was in a "rich, low savanna lying on the Roanoke River not far from the Great Dismal Swamp." To escape the summer heat and threat of malaria, the family frequently traveled north in the spring, and George Pollock Devereux died en route in 1837. Lillie and her mother continued their journey to Connecticut; soon after arriving there a second daughter, Georgiana, was born. The Carolina plantation was sold and the Devereuxs made their home in New Haven.

Family connections in New England and many acquaintances of prominence led to an active social life; Mrs. Devereux had the dubious distinction of refusing to entertain Charles Dickens on his American tour because he had no letter of introduction. Lillie and her sister attended the Misses Agthorp's school, where they took the usual lessons in music, dancing, and drawing, followed by instruction in mathematics and philosophy and "other courses pursued by young men in the sophomore and junior classes at Yale," under the tutelage of a young theological student from the university. Lillie was introduced to society at seventeen.

According to her diary, she realized at sixteen "the position of my sex, feeling with indignation and humiliation . . . the role assigned to women." This conclusion remained with her, although she lived for several years a social life at watering places in Saratoga, Niagara, and West Point and visited New Orleans, Havana, and Philadelphia.

Lillie Devereux was twice married. Her first husband, Frank Geoffrey Quay Umstead, was the father of her two daughters, Elizabeth Johnson Devereux and Katherine Muhlenberg Johnson. He died, and she later married Grinfell Blake of Maine.

Suffering from ennui following confinement with her first daughter, Lillie began writing as a recreation. Thus began a literary career that became her chief means of support on the death of her first husband. Her spare time was spent in reading the classics and contemporary novels. She started writing a novel (*Rockford*) while publishing more lucrative short stories under various pseudonyms—Essex, Charity Floyd, Di Fairfax, Violet, and Tiger Lily. Her publications in *Harper's Weekly*, the *Saturday Evening Post*, the *New York Leader*, the *Sunday Times*, and many other periodicals earned a small monthly income and allowed an independence, fulfilling her resolution to "owe her position to her own exertions and not to any man's protection." In 1861 she moved to Washington, D.C., upon receiving commissions to print letters from the national capital to the *New York Evening Post*, the *New York World*, and the *Philadelphia Post*. Again she moved among such distinguished personalities as Dr. Verdi (nephew of the composer), Governor Andrew Curtin of Pennsylvania, and Anthony Trollope. She visited the White House, describing people and dress at the presidential levees. Her description of President Lincoln noted his "kindness and sadness of expression." The *War Press* commissioned several serials and short stories, demanding "themes of blood and love." On a second stay in Washington in 1864, she renewed her visits to the capitol, meeting another native North Carolinian, Andrew Johnson, and being received by General Ulysses Grant. Still reading voluminously, "not even scorning dime novels," she was delighted with Darwin, Spencer, and Huxley. She wrote "patiently and continuously" for more than thirty years in fifty different magazines. By 1882 she had written approximately five hundred stories, articles, speeches, and lectures and five full-length novels. She wrote and spoke in the high-flown speech admired in her day.

Lillie's second career began in 1869, when she joined the woman's suffrage movement. Descriptions of early suffragists are found in her diary. Her first glimpse of Susan B. Anthony was recorded with amazement at Miss Anthony's attire of a "bloomer costume of *printed dotted silk!*" The early suffragists offered their contemporaries the choice of "Hoops and Stays or Blouses and Freedom"; the latter represented convenience, health, or a gesture of freedom. Lillie herself was described as beautifully dressed, but at about the age of fifty she discarded the fashionable, heavily-boned, wasp-waisted corsets, in favor of the "more healthful dress for females" encouraged by Dr. Lewis, a popular health adviser.

After visiting the Woman Suffrage Headquarters and meeting Mrs. Elizabeth Cady Stanton and others prominent in the movement, Lillie decided, "They're ladies," and began to participate actively. Former society friends and relatives rejected her in her new-found field. Characteristically, she became completely involved. She studied and labored long and hard, "practicing gymnastics to expand my chest and strengthen my voice, exercising myself in elocution and studying politics, history and the laws, so I could deal with the questions of the day intelligently." A new social life evolved around an evening a week devoted to entertaining people important in literary and political life—Francis Brett Harte, Professor Goodyear, L. Bradford Prince (later governor of New Mexico), and Mrs. Frank Leslie, who made a financial success of her husband's publishing house.

Lillie played a prominent part in the National Woman's Suffrage Association and the American Woman's Suffrage Association. Her writing was channeled to the movement and included a contribution to the *Woman's Bible*, a publication based on Biblical criticism and ecclesiastical history, proving that there was "no explanation for the degraded status of women under all religious, and all so-called 'Holy Books.'" The book created a sensation when it was printed in 1895, with widespread coverage in New York papers. The clergy declared it the work of Satan.

Lillie—by then Mrs. Blake—was a natural organizer. She worked on the national level, but her chief success was in the state of New York. She championed the working people, particularly the women. *Fettered for Life, or Her Lord and Master*, published at her own expense, was an immediate success, selling thirteen hundred copies on the first day. An active lobbyist in the legislature, she pled for school suffrage, equality of property rights, women factory inspectors, women physicians in hospitals and insane institutions, and police matrons. A Committee on Legislative Advice was organized with her assistance, to help other suffragists; her leaflet of instructions was printed in the *Woman's Journal*. She succeeded in seeing the passage of legislation granting women the first vote in state elections and the right to become trustees of schools; with the support of Governor Theodore Roosevelt and over "the persistent opposition of the New York Police Department," a bill was passed providing for police matrons. Further legislation allowed women to retain citizenship following marriage to a foreigner, and her final accomplishment was the enactment of an equality of inheritance law by the New York assembly. Eventually the suffragist movement was accepted by "ladies of leisure," who were quickly recruited by Mrs. Blake. They met at the Plaza Hotel and made Sherry's their headquarters. Holidays and celebrations—Columbus Day and the World's Columbian Exposition in 1893—were used to further their goals. Pilgrim Mother's Day was celebrated, in imitation of the New England society for male descendants, by a dinner at the Plaza with important speakers, writers, lawyers, and authors.

At a 1907 testimonial dinner, Lillie Devereux Blake was recognized by a gift of one thousand dollars, which she spent on a trip to Europe. There she met with suffrage leaders in London. The following year she stopped writing and retired to a sanatorium, where she died. "Lillie Devereux Blake, Champion of Woman Kind," was memorialized the next spring in the Church of the Messiah.

SEE: Katherine Devereux Blake and Margaret Louise Wallace, *Champion of Women: The Life of Lillie Devereux Blake* (1943); *DAB*, vol. 3 (1929); *Eighty Years and More: Reminiscences of Elizabeth Cady Stanton* (1898).

BETH CRABTREE

Blakeley, Johnston (*October 1781–October 1814*), naval officer and hero of the War of 1812, was born near the village of Seaford in County Down, Ireland. His father, John Blakeley, emigrated with his wife and son to Wilmington when Johnston was two years old; John Blakeley's wife died on the voyage, and he and his son lived together for many years in Wilmington. Blakeley was educated at a school in Flatbush, Long Island, and from 1797–99 attended The University of North Carolina, where he was president of the Philanthropic Society. When his father died, Blakeley became the ward of Edward Jones of Rockrest, Chatham County. Left without funds by a disastrous fire that destroyed the Blakeley warehouses in Wilmington, Blakeley sought a career in the U.S. Navy and was appointed midshipman on 5 Feb. 1800. He served in the Mediterranean during the war with the Tripoli pirates, under Captain John Rodgers and Commodore Stephen Decatur; he was commissioned lieutenant 10 Feb. 1807 and on 4 Mar. 1811 assumed command of the schooner *Enterprise*. When war with England was declared in 1812, Blakeley was stationed at the Norfolk Navy Yard, and later he was sent to New Orleans. Becoming restless, he asked Edward Jones to intercede for a more active command for him. Through the influence of Congressman William Gaston and Senator James Turner, he was transferred to New Hampshire, where, on 19 Aug. 1813, the *Enterprise* captured the British privateer schooner *Fly* off Cape Porpoise, in Blakeley's first exploit.

Blakeley was promoted to command of the *Wasp*, under construction at Newburyport, described by one of its officers as "a beautiful ship, and the finest sea-boat, I believe, in the world." She carried twenty carronades and two long twelve-pounder guns, with a crew of 173. Blakeley was given sealed orders to sail to western Europe and create as much havoc as he could against British shipping, then to sail south to the Spanish coast, where the British were fighting Napoleon's armies, and finally to return to New Orleans.

The *Wasp* sailed 1 May 1814 with "a fine breeze at North West." Officers and crew were described by one of them as "young and ambitious—they fight with more cheerfulness than they do any other duty. Captain Blakeley is a brave and discreet officer—as cool and collected in action as at table." During the cruise to European waters, Blakeley spent long hours training his sailors and gunnery crews. When he reached his cruising station, the British vessels *Neptune*, *Reindeer*, and *Regulator* were quickly defeated and burned; the *William*, the *Orange Boven*, and the *Jenny* were captured and scuttled; the commandeered neutral vessel *Henrietta* carried the wounded from the *Reindeer* to port. Of these engagements, the one on 28 June with the *Reindeer*, a twenty-one-gun brig, was the most noted. The battle lasted nineteen minutes. Although the *Reindeer* twice approached close enough to board, both times the Americans beat her off. Blakeley praised his crew's "cool and patient conduct . . . while exposed to the fire of the shifting guns of the enemy" and the "animation and order exhibited when actually engaged." The *Reindeer* "was literally cut to pieces, in a line with her ports; her upper works, boats and spars were one complete wreck." The following day, Blakeley burned the remains of the *Reindeer* and limped into the friendly French port of L'Orient, with his foremast, rigging, and sails "a good deal injured." Five men were dead and fourteen wounded. Well received in France, Blakeley attended to his wounded and repaired his vessel. Finally, after sending home some of his wounded with their share of prize money, Blakeley set sail again 27 Aug. 1814, heading for the coast of Spain to intercept British supply ships.

Quickly the *Wasp* captured the brigs *Lettice* and *Bon*

Accord. Blakeley sighted a fleet of ten sail on 1 Sept., cut out and burned the brig *Mary*, laden with military stores, but was driven off by a seventy-four-gun frigate guarding the convoy. In the late evening of the same day he sighted four more sail and engaged the heavy brig *Avon* in a bitter fight lasting forty-seven minutes. The approach of three other brigs forced him to leave after receiving the surrender of the *Avon* but before his crew could board it. The *Wasp* drew off safely to repair her damage.

A lean three weeks followed, after which good fortune came again. Having seized the brigs *Three Brothers* and *Bacchus*, the *Wasp* captured the *Atalanta*, which was laden with wine, brandy, and silk. Since there was some doubt as to the nationality of the *Atalanta*, Blakeley did not follow his usual custom of burning her but instead put Midshipman David Geisinger and a prize crew aboard. On 22 Sept. 1814 the *Atalanta* set sail to Savannah, Ga., where she arrived safely in November. No further word was ever received from the *Wasp*.

Rumors flew to account for the mysterious disappearance of the valiant vessel. A privateer claimed to have seen the *Wasp* off the Canary Islands. The British frigate *Lacedemonian* was believed by some to have sunk her off Charleston, S.C. John C. Calhoun heard a report that she was operating in the Pacific Ocean. Blakeley was promoted to post captain, but he and his men never returned.

Blakeley was married in Boston to Jane Ann Hoope on an unknown date; they had one child, a daughter named Udney Maria, born in January 1815 after her father's disappearance. His widow remarried in 1820 and eventually moved to the island of St. Croix, where she had lived for a time as a child. Congress voted Blakeley a gold medal, and the North Carolina legislature in 1816 authorized a sword to be given to Mrs. Blakeley and offered to pay for the education of his daughter. Mrs. Blakeley suggested that a silver tea service would be more suitable for Udney Maria; accordingly, a suitably inscribed service was presented. The daughter attended school in Philadelphia, remaining there until 1829. She joined her mother in St. Croix, married Baron Joseph von Bretton in 1841, and died in childbirth together with her infant, 2 Mar. 1842.

Blakeley's portrait is at the Philanthropic Society Hall at The University of North Carolina in Chapel Hill. A poem written in 1854 may serve as a fitting epitaph:

No more shall Blakeley's thunder roar
Upon the stormy deep;
Far distant from Columbia's shore
His tombless ruins sleep;
But long Columbia's song shall tell
How Blakeley fought, how Blakeley fell.

SEE: *DAB*, vol. 3 (1929); William Johnson, "Biographical Sketch of Capt. Johnston Blakel(e)y," *University of North Carolina Magazine* 2nd ser. 3 (1854); S. M. Lemmon, *Frustrated Patriots: North Carolina and the War of 1812* (1973); National Archives, Record Group 45; A. R. Newsome, "Udney Maria Blakeley," *North Carolina Historical Review* 4 (1927); *North Carolina Booklet* 1 (1901).

SARAH MCCULLOH LEMMON

Blalock, Nelson Gales (17 Feb. 1836–14 Mar. 1913), physician, was born in rural Mitchell County. It is reported that his preparatory and subsequent college education were pursued in his home county, although the specific institutions are not listed.

He went to Jefferson Medical College, Philadelphia,

and was graduated with an M.D. degree in March 1861. He went immediately to Decatur, Ill., where he began a private practice. The demands of the Civil War challenged his professional skill, and he soon became a surgeon attached to the 115th Illinois Volunteers. He established an enviable record in the service. At the close of the war, he returned to Decatur and remained there until 1873.

Blalock left Decatur with a wagon train headed for the West Coast, finally settling in Walla Walla, Wash. There he continued his profitable practice until his death. He is said to have performed an average of one surgical operation a day, and delivered more than five thousand babies in his lifetime. His medical methods were very innovative; for example, he had early x-ray equipment in his office.

Blalock did not allow a busy practice to rule out his interest and participation in civic affairs. He served as mayor of Walla Walla for several terms and was a trustee of Whitman College there and also a member of the local school board. Among his state-wide activities, he is credited with inspiring a constitutional convention for Washington (1889) and helping to write the constitution himself.

Blalock had a variety of interests in agriculture and related projects: fluming lumber from nearby mountains, cultivating the growing of wheat in the uplands, and developing the still-famous Blalock Orchards, where he specialized in both fruit and vegetables.

He was married first to Panthea A. Durham, with whom he had one son, who succeeded to his father's practice in Walla Walla. Mrs. Blalock died in 1864. He later married Marie G. Greenfield, and they had two daughters.

He died in Walla Walla and was labeled at his death "the foremost citizen of the State of Washington."

SEE: *DAB*, vol. 2 (1929).

C. SYLVESTER GREEN

Blalock, Sarah Malinda Pritchard (ca. 1840–9 Mar. 1901), and **William McKesson ("Keith")** (ca. 1838–11 Aug. 1913), were Confederate soldiers. Malinda Blalock, North Carolina's only known female Civil War soldier, was the daughter of Alfred and Elizabeth Pritchard of Caldwell County and the wife of Keith Blalock, with whom she was living at or near Grandfather Mountain in Watauga County when the war began in 1861. On 20 Mar. 1862, Keith, although a convinced Unionist, enlisted in the Confederate Army (Company F, Twenty-sixth Regiment, North Carolina Troops), with the intention of deserting to Federal lines. Malinda cut her hair, donned men's clothing, assumed the name of "Sam," and enlisted with her husband. She was described as "a good looking boy aged 16[?], weight about 130 pounds, height five feet four inches." For the next four months she "did all the duties of a soldier" and was reportedly "very adept at learning the manual and drill." She tented with her "brother" Keith at the regimental camp near Kinston; opportunities to go swimming with other members of the company were declined.

After several weeks of duty at Kinston it became apparent to Keith that his plan to desert could not be realized immediately, and he decided to obtain a discharge. This was granted on 20 Apr. 1862, as a result of a severe rash that he contracted by rubbing his body with poison oak or poison sumac. Malinda thereupon disclosed the fact that she was a woman and was "immediately discharged." She and Keith, who was soon being sought as a fraudulently discharged deserter by Confederate authorities, then lived for a time in a hut on Grandfather Mountain, where they were joined by several other deserters. Following a fight with conscription officers and home guardsmen who attempted to apprehend the group, Keith fled with Malinda to Tennessee, where he became a recruiter for a Michigan regiment. Shortly thereafter the Blalocks joined the partisan unit of George W. Kirk and returned to North Carolina. Both Keith and Malinda played an active role in the guerrilla raids and personal vendettas that characterized the war in the mountains in 1864, and Keith served also as a guide for Confederate deserters and Unionists who sought to make their way through the mountain passes to Federal lines in Tennessee. Malinda was wounded in a skirmish during this period, and in another engagement Keith was wounded and blinded in one eye. In February 1865, Keith's stepfather, Austin Coffey, was murdered by Confederate sympathizers, and in February of the following year Keith shot and killed a man he believed had been involved in Coffey's death. Keith was apprehended shortly thereafter, but before he could be brought to trial he was pardoned by Republican Governor William W. Holden.

In later years the Blalocks farmed in Mitchell County and, for a time, "attempted merchandising." They resided in the Linville area, which became part of Avery County when the latter was formed in 1911. In 1874, Keith presented himself as a Mitchell County Republican candidate for the state legislature but was defeated. He and Malinda moved to Texas in 1892 or thereabouts; however, they subsequently returned to Mitchell County. Malinda died a natural death, but Keith was killed while operating a handcar on a mountain railroad. He was at the time a resident of Hickory. The Blalocks had at least four children: Columbus (b. ca. 1863), John (b. ca. 1869), Willie (b. ca. 1873), and Samuel (b. ca. 1877).

SEE: Nancy Alexander, *Here Will I Dwell: The Story of Caldwell County* (1956); John Preston Authur, *A History of Watauga County* (1915); Samuel A. Ashe, *History of North Carolina*, vol. 2 (1925); Bakersville *Mountain Voice*, 5 Nov. 1880; John G. Barrett, *The Civil War in North Carolina* (1963); Caldwell County Census (1850); Walter Clark, ed., *Histories of the Several Regiments and Battalions from North Carolina in the Great War, 1861–1865*, vol. 2 (1901); Shepherd M. Dugger, *The War Trails of the Blue Ridge* (1932); Mary Elizabeth Massey, *Bonnet Brigades* (1966); Mitchell County Census (1870, Linville Township); John W. Moore, *Roster of North Carolina Troops in the War Between the States*, vol. 2 (1882); National Archives, Record Group 109, War Department Collection of Compiled Military Service Records (Confederate), Records of the Twenty-sixth Regiment N.C. Troops; Raleigh *Weekly Era*, 13 Aug. 1874; W. W. Scott, *Annals of Caldwell County* (1924); Francis B. Simkins and James W. Patton, *The Women of the Confederacy* (1936); Watauga County Census (1860).

W. T. JORDAN, JR.

Blanchard, Andrew *(1728–87)*, printer, revolutionary official, and planter, was born in Elizabeth, N.J., the son of John and Mary Joline Blanchard, and after 1740 settled in New Providence, N.J., probably on land owned by his father. He married Mehitabel Arnett about 1758; they became the parents of Mary Ann; Jane, who married James Carney; Sarah, who married Dr. Edward Pasteur; Isaac; and Elizabeth. By the opening of the Revolution, the family was living in North Carolina, and Blanchard sent the children back to New Jersey to live with his brother, fearing that Tories in the state might harm them because of his own support of the Revolution. The children made the journey in charge of a trusted slave, Cromno or Quomono, who remained in New Jersey and was eventually freed.

Blanchard appears first in the records as part owner of the armed schooner *Johnston*, which was fitted out in New Bern as a privateer in June 1776. The following February he purchased a scythe blade and some old iron at the sale of property abandoned by the last royal governor, Josiah Martin, at the Palace in New Bern. In May 1777 he was paid £1,450 in connection with the manufacturing of guns for the state. The House of Commons in the spring of 1778 proposed that Blanchard be appointed first lieutenant for service at Fort Hancock, but the appointment went to someone else. In 1779 he was a justice of the Craven County court and apparently also a member of the New Bern Safety Committee. In the latter capacity he joined in signing a letter to Governor Richard Caswell discussing conditions in New Bern and relaying information about British activity in Suffolk, Va. The possibility of an invasion of North Carolina seemed real to the committee making the report. Blanchard also served during the same year on a court-appointed commission to examine the accounts of the estate of Lancelot Graves Berry. At some time during the Revolutionary War he was paid £1,215 as commissary to militia, and after the war the assembly of 1785 appointed him one of three commissioners in the New Bern District to pass upon pension applications from wounded and disabled soldiers.

In 1782, Blanchard acquired 123 acres on the Trent River in Jones County, but his primary place of residence probably was in New Bern or on his 450-acre plantation named Deep Gully, on Trent Road eight miles from New Bern.

It is as a partner in the printing firm of Hodge & Blanchard that Blanchard's name is most frequently encountered. In November 1785 the first issue of the newspaper *State Gazette of North Carolina* appeared; the earliest known surviving issue is dated 4 Oct. 1787, when Abraham Hodge, also a native of New Jersey, and Blanchard appear as publishers. It is likely that they established the paper, as contemporary sources note that it was being printed by them in August 1786. Between 1785 and 1787 the firm also printed both military and civil commissions, blank deeds, circular letters, and, when they held the state contract for printing, the laws of the state. Supplies for a printing establishment were difficult to obtain during a part of the time this firm existed, and in 1787 the partners were obliged to dispose of a warrant on the state treasury for one-half their annual allowance in order to get "some hard Money" to purchase materials needed to complete the public business. When a due bill was presented to the treasury it was refused, and the House of Commons ordered it paid. From this transaction it is revealed that the firm of Hodge and Blanchard did more work for the state than was required by their contract, and they were awarded the additional sum of £150. It was also noted that they had recently printed legislative journals and the treasurer's reports and furnished (but may not have printed) 150 copies of Baron Steuben's Military Instructions, 1,500 copies of the new federal Constitution, and 300 copies of a resolution calling for a constitutional convention.

The firm also engaged in printing for private persons and early in 1787 printed a sermon preached in Fayetteville on 27 Dec. 1786 by Dugald Crawford. Later that year they published an address by Archibald Maclaine that had been delivered on 30 Aug. 1787. With one exception their work bears a New Bern imprint; the thin volume of *Laws of North-Carolina* for 1786 bears the imprint: "Fayetteville: Printed by Hodge and Blanchard, Printers to the State." The legislature of that year met in Fayetteville, and the name used probably indicates that fact and not that the printing establishment was there.

Blanchard was dead by 14 Dec. 1787, when his administrators, Silas White Arnett and Isaac Blanchard, petitioned the assembly to delay a suit in which the estate was involved.

SEE: Clarence Brigham, *History and Bibliography of American Newspapers* (1947); Douglas McMurtrie, *Eighteenth Century North Carolina Imprints* (1938); Elizabeth Moore, *Records of Craven County, North Carolina* (1960); New Bern *North Carolina Gazette*, 26 Dec. 1795; *New York Genealogical and Biographical Record* 75 (1944); William L. Saunders and Walter Clark, eds., *Colonial and State Records of North Carolina*, 30 vols. (1886–1914).

WILLIAM S. POWELL

Bland, Edward (d. 1653), explorer, was the son of John Bland, a London merchant, and Susan Bland; John and Susan had four children, Susanna, John, Edward, and Theodoric. John, the oldest son, was a member of the old Virginia Company and sent Edward and Theodoric to manage his estate in Virginia.

When Edward Bland came to Virginia in 1647, he brought with him a nephew, George Proby, and twenty-four others. In a grant dated 10 Mar. 1647, he obtained thirteen hundred acres of land. He lived at Lownes Creek on the James River and at Kimages in Charles City County, establishing an eight-thousand-acre estate. He married Jane Gregory, daughter of his uncle, Gregory Bland; they had a son, Edward of Kimages.

Bland accompanied Abraham Woode, Sackford Brewster, and Elias Pennant as one of the leaders of an exploration expedition to upper Carolina in August and early September 1650. They traveled southwest from Fort Henry, now Petersburg, to Lake Gaston and the Clarksville, Va., area and from there to the Roanoke River and Albemarle in upper Carolina. Bland made a careful and apparently accurate note of distances, directions, and the streams crossed at every stage of the journey. He faithfully described the drainage, timber, and vegetation and named upper Carolina "New Brittaine."

After the expedition returned to Virginia, he petitioned the Virginia Assembly to allow him to explore and colonize the new territory. His petition was granted on 20 Oct. 1650, after he had sailed for England, on condition that he recruit one hundred able-bodied men for this purpose. His book *The Discovery of New Brittaine* was published in London in 1651 to assist him in recruiting the necessary pioneers to colonize Carolina, but he died on his Charles City County estate before he could carry out his plans.

He was buried on his estate. His widow Jane married John Holmwood of Surry County, died in 1664, and was buried at Westover.

SEE: Edward Bland, *The Discovery of New Brittaine* (1651); *Calendar of State Papers, Colonial Series, America and the West Indies*, vol. 5 (1893); Wesley Frank Craven, *The Southern Colonies in the Seventeenth Century* (1949); *Familiae Minorium Gentium*, vol. 2 (publication of the Harleian Society, vol. 38) (1895); F. B. Kegley, *Kegley's Virginia Frontier* (1938); Land Office (Richmond, Va.), for Grant Book No. 2; Charles McIntosh, "The Proby Family

of England and Hampton and Norfolk, Virginia," *Virginia Magazine of History and Biography* 22 (1914); Alexander S. Salley, Jr., *Narratives of Early Carolina* (1939); *Tyler's Quarterly Historical and Genealogical Magazine* 7 (1926).

JAMES H. BOYKIN

Blasingame, James Carter (9 June 1866–7 Oct. 1941), college president and businessman, was born in Zebulon, Ga., to Thomas J. and Cecelia Adams Blasingame. In 1892 he received the A.B. degree from the University of Georgia, being graduated with honors. Later he was a graduate student for several summers at the University of Chicago.

From 1892 until 1897, Blasingame was president of Jackson Institute in Georgia. During that time he brought the school from the verge of failure to a sound financial basis and greatly strengthened the curriculum. The enrollment increased from one hundred to three hundred. In 1897 he became the first president of Holbrook Normal College in Fountain City, Tenn. In 1899 he was elected to the presidency of another new institution, the Baptist Female University (now Meredith College) in Raleigh, a position he held only one year. His insistence on a largely elective course of study was decidedly out of harmony with the ideas of the founders and trustees of the school, and, though he had been active in the YMCA at the University of Georgia, neither as a student nor as an administrator had he had any experience in a denominational school. His letter of resignation and the minutes of the board of trustees accepting it show a clear and sympathetic understanding on both sides of the regrettable situation. During his one year he proved to be an able administrator, with initiative, enthusiasm, and vigor—all distinct assets to the new school.

From the Raleigh institution, Blasingame went to be superintendent of the North Carolina agents of the Mutual Life Insurance Company; subsequently, he accepted a similar position in Virginia with the New York Life Insurance Company. For a brief while he was president of the International Shoe Shining Company in Richmond, Va., a company organized to produce a newly patented machine for shining shoes automatically. World War I made the manufacture of the machine inadvisable, and he returned to the field of insurance.

He was married in 1896 to Virginia Lee McKie of Oxford, Miss. They had three daughters: Sara Cecelia (Mrs. Edgar R. Rowe), Eloise McKie (Mrs. Richard Florance), and Virginia Carter (Mrs. Roland R. Updegraff). From 1906 till his death, the family lived in Ashland, Va., where he took an active part in civic and religious affairs. A Democrat and a Mason, he served several terms between 1910 and 1918 on the Ashland Town Council; from 1920 to 1930 he was a member of the Ashland School Board. He was a deacon in Duncan Memorial Methodist Church, serving from 1928 to 1935 as treasurer. He was buried in the Woodland Cemetery in Ashland.

SEE: Alumni records of the University of Georgia (Athens); Mrs. James C. Blasingame and her daughters, correspondence; *First Annual Announcement of the Baptist Female University*; Mary Lynch Johnson, *A History of Meredith College* (1956); Minutes of the Board of Trustees of the Baptist Female University, 1899–1900, esp. 21 Apr. 1899 and 11 Apr. 1900; Raleigh *Biblical Recorder*, 3 May 1899, 26 July 1899, and scattered references; Raleigh *News and Observer*, 8 June 1900.

MARY LYNCH JOHNSON

Bledsoe, Moses Andrew *(27 June 1822–4 Nov. 1905)*, state representative and state senator, was born in Franklin County of English ancestry. His father was Aaron Bledsoe, farmer; his mother was Elizabeth Radford. Reared on land granted his ancestors by the king, he attended the local schools and finished his education at Herndon Academy at age seventeen. A year later he worked as a clerk in a store in Henderson, but soon he moved to Raleigh. There he studied law and was admitted to the bar in June 1844. In addition to practicing law, he formed a partnership with S. H. Young and became a merchant and also farmed near Raleigh.

Interested in local affairs, Bledsoe served gratuitously as county overseer of the public roads. He became chairman of the Democratic county committee and actively campaigned for the Democratic candidate in the presidential elections of the 1850s. He was elected to the state House of Commons in 1856. During the next years, Bledsoe advocated the ad valorem tax, which proposed that all property be taxed at its true value. This measure was designed to tax slaveholders on the value of slaves as property and was an alternative to the existing system by which slaveholders paid only a poll tax for each slave. In the party conventions prior to the 1860 election, the Whigs endorsed the ad valorem tax and the Democrats opposed it. Bledsoe chose to hold to his principles and ran as an independent for the state senate; he was elected after a hard campaign.

In 1856 the General Assembly appointed Bledsoe a director of the Insane Asylum; for six years he served as chairman of the board, managing the institution. In 1861, after North Carolina's secession from the Union, he was appointed by the governor as a director of the Cape Fear and Deep River Transportation Company, which position he held until 1865, when all state offices were declared vacant. During the Civil War, Bledsoe served first as quartermaster of the state and then as assistant adjutant general under General Lawrence Branch, General John F. Hoke, and General James Martin. In 1863 he relinquished this second position in order to work collecting taxes for the Confederate government.

Bledsoe was the Wake and Franklin County Democratic candidate for the state senate in 1868 but was defeated. The Democrats gained control of the General Assembly in 1870 and appointed Bledsoe a director of the North Carolina Penitentiary. He was elected chairman of the board and directed the construction of the buildings begun under the former Republican board. He ran for elective office only once more and was defeated for a seat in the U.S. Congress in a three-way race with Josiah Turner, Jr., and Joseph J. Davis. He continued to practice law in Raleigh until the last years of his life.

Bledsoe was married twice, to Martha C. Hunter of Wake County, and then to Donna Holt of Enfield, who survived him.

SEE: Moses A. Bledsoe, *Ad Valorem Taxation* (1859); John Nichols, *Directory of the General Assembly of the State of North Carolina for the Session Commencing Nov. 19, 1860* (ca. 1860); an unsigned biographical sketch of Bledsoe, ca. 1905 (Library, Duke University, Durham).

SAMUEL M. GAINOR

Bloodworth, Timothy *(1736–24 Aug. 1814)*, ardent patriot in the American Revolution, member of the Confederation Congress, vigorous anti-Federalist, U.S. congressman and senator, and collector of customs for the Port of Wilmington, was born in New Hanover County. He had two brothers, James and Thomas, who were active local politicians; their father was probably Timothy Bloodworth, who came to North Carolina from Nansemond County, Va., in the early years of the eighteenth century. A child of poverty, without formal education, young Timothy has been described as one of the most remarkable and versatile men of his era. His diligence and ambition more than made up for his lack of education as he pursued eight or ten different occupations—keeper of an ordinary and a ferry, preacher, doctor, blacksmith, wheelwright, watchmaker, farmer, and politician. He owned nine slaves and received grants for 4,266 acres of land. Most of all, he was a consistent and vigorous proponent of democracy before, during, and after the Revolution.

Elected to the legislative assembly in 1758 at the age of twenty-two, he was returned to that body frequently during the next thirty-five years. He also served in numerous other local political positions. Bloodworth, along with John Ashe, has been credited with the formation of the Wilmington Committee of Safety in 1775. As a member of this committee, as a legislator, and later as commissioner of confiscated property for the district of Wilmington, Bloodworth was known for his harsh treatment of suspected and known Loyalists. He was once accused of trying to depopulate New Hanover County.

In 1784, Bloodworth was elected to Congress; he resigned in August 1787 to return home to fight fiercely against the ratification of the Constitution, serving as a member of the Hillsborough and Fayetteville conventions. Emerging as one of several prominent radical leaders in North Carolina, he opposed virtually everything proposed by the Federalists. Defeated in his bid for a seat in the Senate in 1789, he was elected to the House of Representatives the following year. He replaced Benjamin Hawkins in the Senate in 1795, where he served until the inauguration of President Jefferson. Bloodworth was one of the first North Carolina Republicans to be rewarded by Jefferson. Soon after his resignation from the Senate, he was appointed collector of the Port of Wilmington. He served in this capacity until he resigned in 1807, apparently because of inefficiency in office: at the time of his death in 1814 he still owed the United States $22,500.

Bloodworth retired to his home near Burgaw, in present-day Pender County, and died while on a visit to Washington, N.C. Although he was survived by two daughters, Mary and Martha, he had been a widower since the death of his wife Priscilla in 1803.

SEE: Samuel A. Ashe, ed., *Biographical History of North Carolina*, vol. 3 (1905), and *Cyclopedia of Eminent and Representative Men of the Carolinas of the Nineteenth Century*, vol. 2 (1892); Walter Clark, ed., *State Records of North Carolina*, vols. 9, 12–13, 15–17, 19–22, 24 (1895–96, 1898–99, 1901–7, 1905); D. H. Gilpatrick, *Jeffersonian Democracy in North Carolina* (1931); *North Carolina Historical and Genealogical Register* 2 (1901); *North Carolina Historical Review* 1, 18–19, 23, 25, 43, 46 (1923, 1941–42, 1946, 1948, 1966, 1969); Malcolm Ross, *The Cape Fear* (1965); A. M. Waddell, *A History of New Hanover County and the Lower Cape Fear Region, 1723–1800*, vol. 1 (1909); A. M. Walker, comp. and ed., *New Hanover County Court Minutes, 1738–1800* (1958–62).

G. MELVIN HERNDON

Blount, Frederick *(1778–5 Sept. 1823)*, physician, the oldest son of James and Ann Hall Blount, was born at Mulberry Hill Plantation, Edenton. He is not to be confused with his uncle, Frederick Blount. His maternal grandfather was the noted colonial clergyman Clement Hall; his mother had been a participant in the Edenton Tea Party, 25 Oct. 1774. His aunt, Mary Blount, married the Reverend Charles Pettigrew, first bishop-elect of the Protestant Episcopal Diocese of North Carolina. He had one brother, Clement Hall (d. 1843), and one sister, Sarah Porter (d. 1837), who married James Fuller.

When Frederick indicated a desire to study medicine, his uncle Wilson Blount, by selling two horses, gave him financial assistance to attend medical lectures in Philadelphia. He returned to North Carolina and settled in Hillsborough but apparently failed to establish himself, for in 1806 he moved to New Bern to become the fifth physician to reside there. Here he lived a genteel life, practicing medicine, visiting relatives and friends, attending sporadically to a plantation, traveling to Edenton to see his relatives, and pursuing other leisurely occupations. Presumably reared as an Episcopalian, he became interested in Methodism later in his life. In 1812 he and his siblings were involved in court action in Edenton to settle the estate of their father, who had died intestate.

Blount married a widow, Rachel Whitfield Bryan, on 1 Oct. 1807. A son, Frederick, mentioned several times in correspondence with Ebenezer Pettigrew, appears to have died in early youth; a second son, Alexander Hall, and several unnamed daughters were mentioned in his will. Blount was buried in the family cemetery at Mulberry Hill; the date 5 Apr. on his tombstone appears to be an error.

SEE: Blount Cemetery (Mulberry Hill); Chowan County Records (North Carolina State Archives, Raleigh); S. M. Lemmon, ed., *The Pettigrew Papers*, vol. 1, *1685–1818* (1971); *Raleigh Register*, 26 Sept. 1823.

SARAH MCCULLOH LEMMON

Blount, Jacob (*1726–17 Aug. 1789*), planter, landholder, and revolutionary soldier, was born in Beaufort County, son of Thomas Blount and Ann Elizabeth Reading. His father was a landowner and planter. In 1748, Jacob Blount married Barbara Gray of Bertie County and for some years following resided near Windsor. He inherited land on Contentnea Creek, and between 1757 and 1783 he acquired an estate of approximately six thousand acres.

Blount was interested in political affairs and became very active in the colony before the Revolution. He represented Craven County in the General Assembly in 1766, 1768, 1769, and 1770–71. He took part in the Battle of Alamance against the Regulators, but later became active against royal authority. He was a member of the provincial congress at New Bern in April 1775, of the third provincial congress at Hillsborough, and of the fourth provincial congress at New Bern. He was a member of the committee of safety for Pitt County. During the Revolution, Blount was appointed paymaster for the Second Regiment, North Carolina Continental Line, and later he became paymaster for the whole province.

Blount was an active member of the Church of England and was a vestryman in Craven County. His home, Blount Hall, was located sixteen miles southwest of Greenville, first a part of Craven County but later included in Pitt.

Jacob and Barbara Gray Blount had seven children: William (b. 26 Mar. 1749), Ann (b. 3 Oct. 1750), John Gray (b. 21 Sept. 1752), Louisa (b. 17 Jan. 1755), Reading (b. 22 Feb. 1757), Thomas (b. 10 May 1759), and Jacob (b. 5 Nov. 1760). Barbara Gray Blount died on 8 Apr. 1763;

Jacob remarried, this time to Hannah Salter Baker, daughter of Colonel Edward Salter and widow of William Baker. Five children were born of this marriage, but only two lived to maturity: Willie (pronounced Wylie, b. 18 Apr. 1768), and Sharpe (b. 4 Apr. 1771). Jacob outlived his second wife also, and on 9 Aug. 1887 he married Mrs. Mary Adams. Two years after his third marriage, he died of "nervous fever" at Blount Hall.

SEE: A. B. Keith and W. H. Masterson, eds., *The John Gray Blount Papers*, vols. 1–3 (1952–65); S. M. Lemmon, ed., *The Pettigrew Papers*, vol. 1, *1685–1818* (1971); *N.C. Historical and Genealogical Register*, 1 (1900), 70, 449, 456, 523; 2 (1901), 468; 3 (1903), 386; William L. Saunders and Walter Clark, eds., *Colonial and State Records of North Carolina*, 30 vols. (1886–1914).

ARMISTEAD JONES MAUPIN

Blount (Blunt), James (*d. spring or summer 1686*), colonial official, and leader in Culpeper's Rebellion, moved to the Albemarle colony from Isle of Wight County, Va., between 1660, when the family was still in Virginia, and 1669, when Blount was a member of the Albemarle council. Presumably, the title captain, applied to him by his contemporaries, indicates his rank in either the Virginia or the Albemarle militia, or both.

By 21 Apr. 1669, Blount was a council member in the Albemarle colony. He was also on the council in 1672, 1677, 1679, 1681, 1684, and perhaps also in years not indicated in surviving records. In 1677, and apparently in other years, he was one of the burgesses representing Chowan Precinct and sat on the council by vote of the assembly, which then chose some of the council members.

Although Blount participated in the government over which the controversial Thomas Miller presided in the summer and fall of 1677, he was one of the leaders in the overthrow of Miller in December of that year. Not only did he help lead the upheaval, subsequently called Culpeper's Rebellion, but he became a member of the rebel parliament and the rebel council that governed the colony until 1679, when the proprietors reestablished government under their own authority.

After the restoration of *de jure* government, Blount served on the council at least in the years 1679, 1681, and 1684. He was a justice of the county court of Albemarle in 1682 and 1683.

Blount lived in Chowan Precinct, where he owned 300 acres of land in the 1670s. His holding was enlarged by a grant of 660 acres in 1684.

Blount was married twice. His first wife, whose name is not known, was the mother of at least five children: James, Thomas, John, Ann, and Elizabeth. Apparently James and Thomas, if not the other children, were born before their parents moved to Albemarle. They proved their headrights and were granted land in 1680, by which time both were married. Blount's first wife died between 27 Sept. 1670, when she was a witness in court, and 13 June 1683, by which time Blount's second marriage had taken place The second wife was Anna Riscoe, widow of Robert Riscoe of Albemarle and daughter of Belshassar Willix of Exeter, N.H. She and Blount probably were married shortly before 13 June 1683, when Blount obtained administration of Riscoe's estate "in right of his wife." If children were born of the second marriage, they apparently died in infancy.

Blount died between 10 Mar. 1686, when he made a codicil to his will, and 17 July, when the will was proved. By that time his two daughters were married and each had at least one child. They were referred to in the will as Elizabeth Hawkins, who had a son named John, and Ann Slocum, who had a daughter named Ann.

Blount's own son John was still a minor when his father died. John's brother Thomas became his guardian, but the guardianship lasted less than a decade, as John was married in 1695 to Elizabeth Davis, daughter of John and Mary Davis of Henrico County, Va. Thomas himself was married to his second wife, Mary Scott, about the time of his father's death, in the spring of 1686. James, Jr., gave his wife's name as Elizabeth in listing his headrights and also in his will.

Blount's widow, Anna, whom he called Ann in his will, married Seth Sothel, then governor of the colony and one of the proprietors of Carolina. After Sothel's death, she married John Lear, a prominent Virginian.

SEE: J. Bryan Grimes, *North Carolina Wills and Inventories* (1912); J. R. B. Hathaway, ed., *North Carolina Historical and Genealogical Register*, 3 vols. (1900–1903); North Carolina State Archives (Raleigh), for Albemarle Book of Warrants and Surveys (1681–1706), Albemarle County Papers (1678–1714), Council Minutes, Wills, Inventories (1677–1701), Guardian's Bond of Thomas Blount (1 Feb. 1686/87), and Will of James Blount; Mattie Erma Edwards Parker, ed., *North Carolina Higher-Court Records, 1670–1696* (1968); William S. Powell, ed., *Ye Countie of Albemarle in Carolina* (1958); Hugh F. Rankin, *Upheaval In Albemarle: The Story of Culpeper's Rebellion* (1962); William L. Saunders, ed., *Colonial Records of North Carolina*, vol. 1 (1886).

MATTIE ERMA E. PARKER

Blount, John (1671–1726), member of the council and justice of the general court, was the son of Captain James Blount of Chowan County and his first wife, whose name is not known. The elder Blount came to Chowan County in 1669 from Isle of Wight County, Va. John Blount inherited 640 acres on Albemarle Sound, Chowan County, from his father in 1686—a tract that came to be known as Mulberry Hill. He expanded his holdings in 1714 and 1717 to over 1600 acres. Blount was appointed vestryman at the organization of the first vestry of St. Paul's Parish, Chowan County, on 12 Dec. 1701 and served until 1709; he again served during the period 1713–15. He became a justice of the general court in 1703 and served at least into 1704; he was again a member from 1718 to 1722. He was also appointed a justice of the peace for Chowan County in 1716. In June 1722 he became a proprietary deputy with a seat on the council to represent Joseph Blake; he continued to serve until his death, which was announced at a meeting of the council in Edenton on 28 July 1726.

Blount was married to Elizabeth Davis, daughter of John and Mary Burton Davis of Henrico County, Va., by Captain John Fendall on 11 June 1695. Blount's will was drawn up on 27 Jan. 1726 and probated on 18 May. In it he named twelve children: John, who married Sarah E. Vail and inherited Mulberry Hill; Thomas, who married Elizabeth Whitmel, widow of George Pollock; Charles Worth, who married first Mary Clayton and second Martha Anne (family name unknown); James; Mary, who married Jonathan Jacocks; Martha, who married first Dr. Thomas West and second a man named Worseley; Hester, who married John Worley; Elizabeth, who married Dr. Samuel Padgett; Sarah, who married John Lovick; Ann, who married a Worley; Rachel; and Joseph, who married first Sarah Durant, second Elizabeth Hatch, widow of both William Reed and McRora Scarborough, and third Sarah Whedbee, widow of William Hoskins.

Elizabeth Davis Blount died probably during February 1733, as her will was made on the eighth of that month and probated in open court on 12 Mar. Both John and Elizabeth Blount were buried at Mulberry Hill, as was Captain James Blount and other members of the family.

SEE: Stuart Hall Hill Papers, vol. 2, sec. 1 (North Carolina State Library, Raleigh); George Holmes, *History of St. Paul's Episcopal Church, Edenton* (1964); *North Carolina Historical and Genealogical Register*, scattered issues; William L. Saunders and Walter Clark, eds., *Colonial and State Records of North Carolina*, vols. 1–4, 6, 24 (1886, 1888, 1905).

JOHN B. FLOWERS III
JAQUELIN DRANE NASH

Blount, John Gray (21 Sept. 1752–4 Jan. 1833), merchant and landowner, was born in Bertie County, the son of Jacob Blount and Barbara Gray. An important figure in the business and political life of North Carolina, he was a representative from Beaufort County in the House of Commons from 1782 to 1793, served in the senate three terms—1791, 1793, and 1795—and served on the council of state on several occasions. He was a member of the conventions at Hillsborough in 1788 and at Fayetteville in 1789 and played an important part in the ratification of the federal Constitution in 1789. He was a justice of the peace of Beaufort, commissioner of the Port of Bath, and postmaster at Washington from 1791 to 1815. He was a Federalist, but he took an active part in the election of Thomas Jefferson as president in 1800.

Blount was educated as a surveyor under the surveyor general to the Crown. He ran the Blounts' mercantile business in Washington and operated branches at Tarboro, Shell Island, and Prospect Mills. He and his brothers, Thomas and William, had large shipping interests, owning wharves, warehouses, flat boats, and sea vessels. They were among the greatest landowners in American history, with huge tracts from the Atlantic to the Mississippi. Blount and his brothers also owned sawmills, gristmills, tanneries, and cotton gins and engaged in agriculture and the slave trade.

Blount was a trustee of The University of North Carolina. He kept blooded horses and was a member of the Agricultural Board of North Carolina. He was an Episcopalian.

On 17 Sept. 1778, Blount married Mary Harvey, the daughter of Colonel Miles Harvey of Perquimans County. They had six children: Thomas, William Augustus, John Gray, Jr., Olivia, Polly, and Martha. Blount moved to the Forks of the Tar River, where he helped establish the town of Washington, and lived there the remainder of his life.

SEE: A. B. Keith and W. H. Masterson, eds., *The John Gray Blount Papers*, vols. 1–3 (1952–65); S. M. Lemmon, ed., *The Pettigrew Papers*, vol. 1, *1685–1818* (1971); William L. Saunders and Walter Clark, eds., *Colonial and State Records of North Carolina*, 30 vols. (1866–1914).

ARMISTEAD JONES MAUPIN

Blount, Mary ("Jackie") Sumner (1777–18 Dec. 1822), daughter and wife of revolutionary generals, by whose benefaction Christ Episcopal Church, Raleigh, was built, was born in Warren County at the home of her father, General Jethro Sumner. Her mother, before her marriage to General Sumner, had been the widow Heiss of New Bern. The Sumners were of English blood, Sumner's father, William, having emigrated from

England about 1690 to settle near Suffolk, Va. General and Mrs. Sumner had a son, Thomas Edward, who, like his sister, died without leaving a family.

In November 1796, Mary Sumner became the second wife of General Thomas Blount of Edgecombe County. Their large plantation adjoined the town of Tarboro, and their handsome house is still standing. Blount was North Carolina's representative in Congress at the time of their marriage and for sixteen years thereafter, until his death in office in Washington, where he was buried in the Congressional Cemetery.

Mrs. Blount's substantial fortune was distributed at her death to many relatives and friends. The most interesting bequest in her long and detailed will has as its object the "Building of a Protestant Episcopal Church in the City of Raleigh." The means was to be "a large sum of money now due to me by virtue of the will of my late husband," estimated to have been between ten and fifteen thousand dollars. Duncan Cameron, Esq., of Orange County and the Reverand William Hooper, "now of Fayetteville," were named agents to collect the money and carry out the intent of the will. "And whereas doubts have been entertained whether a bequest of this nature cannot be defeated by the interference of those on whom the law would cast the Estate in case of an intestacy, I do further will that the said Duncan Cameron and William Hooper...shall have the said legacy, stripped of any trust which can result to the benefit of my next of kin, and unfettered by any trust which can be enforced by any earthly tribunal: leaving the disposition of the said legacy to their consciences." Happily, the executors secured the money for the stated purpose, and in 1826 the present church lot was purchased and a frame building erected, the predecessor to the present handsome building.

Mrs. Blount's interest in building the Raleigh church was inspired by her rector in Tarboro, the Reverend John Phillips. As a missionary, he was credited with having revived the Tarboro church and with having started churches in Washington and Warrenton, in addition to the Raleigh church.

Mrs. Blount was buried in Calvary churchyard, Tarboro. A bolt of lightning, tradition says, destroyed her tombstone. It was replaced by a handsome stone, the gift of the congregation of Christ Church, Raleigh.

Mrs. Blount's portrait, painted in Washington, D.C., in 1820 by the Italian artist Pietro Bonanni, was bequeathed by her to her long-time friend, Moses Mordecai of Raleigh. It now hangs in the Mordecai House, a museum property of the city of Raleigh. The granddaughter of Moses Mordecai intended to give the portrait to Christ Church, and so stated in her will, but later revoked her intention.

Mrs. Blount died suddenly in Tarboro at the home of a friend.

SEE: Joseph Blount Cheshire, Jr., "Life of My Father" (MS, in the possession of J. B. Cheshire IV, of Raleigh); Edgecombe County Will Book E (North Carolina State Archives, Raleigh); Alice B. Keith, ed., *The John Gray Blount Papers, 1764–1795*, 2 vols. (1952–59); The Mordecai Papers (North Carolina State Archives, Raleigh); Nell Joslin Styron, *A History of Christ Church Parish* (1970); John H. Wheeler, *Historical Sketches of North Carolina* (1851).

JAQUELIN DRANE NASH

Blount, Nathaniel *(ca. 1748–1816)*, Anglican clergyman, was born in Beaufort County, the third of five sons of Reading Blount. Reared in a family of some means and influence in Eastern Carolina, Blount received sufficient education to study independently for Holy Orders. He was of an introspective and melancholy cast of mind, not a businessman, like many of his numerous Blount relatives, but devoted to religion. In 1773 he sailed to England, where he was ordained deacon on 19 Sept. and priest on 21 Sept. After he returned to America, one of his first acts was to erect a chapel on Chocowinity Creek in Beaufort County, near the present location of Washington. The structure was incorporated into present-day Trinity Church and moved a short distance in 1939 to a site on the Chocowinity-Greenville highway. During the Revolution, he preached frequently by request at patriotic political meetings. After his contract with the vestry of Pitt County was abrogated in the separation of church and state mandated by the state constitution of 1776, he lived almost entirely on the income from property left him by his father in 1776.

Following the winning of independence, Blount was contacted by the Reverend Charles Pettigrew of Edenton to meet in convention at Tarboro in an attempt to organize the Protestant Episcopal Diocese of North Carolina. Four conventions were held between 1790 and 1794, three of which he attended. At the fourth, he took active part in formulating the procedure for choosing a bishop and in debates on a constitution (which he signed) and served as an elected member of the standing committee. He greatly deplored the fact that Pettigrew, who was elected bishop, never attended a triennial convention to be consecrated. For this and other reasons, the Episcopal church in North Carolina declined steadily until 1817.

Blount was an energetic priest, riding great distances on horseback to preach, baptize, hold funerals, and perform marriages. He regularly attended two chapels near him, often visited three others in Beaufort County, and had three other counties on his busy schedule. Usually in poor health, he was nonetheless seldom prevented from trying to reach "poor perishing sinners" and lead them "by Faith, To The Throne of Grace." An advocate of infant baptism, he was bitter toward the Baptists; he disapproved of the Methodist separation from apostolic succession; and he likewise detested Thomas Paine and "his horrid principles."

Some time prior to 1779 he married Ann (maiden name unknown), who died in November 1798. They had at least five surviving children: Selina, Edward, Rebecca, Levi, and James. Blount died in 1816. The exact date and place of burial have, however, vanished from all but tradition.

His underlying strength and devotion to duty kept alive the Episcopal church in his area of the state. In the year of his death, no other Episcopal cleric was resident in North Carolina, and the church appeared dead. In the following year, however, a successful convention was held, which began a revival that Blount had helped to make possible.

SEE: Beaufort County Records (Washington); Sarah McCulloh Lemmon, "Nathaniel Blount," *North Carolina Historical Review* 50 (1973); S. M. Lemmon, ed., *The Pettigrew Papers*, vol. 1, *1685–1818* (1971).

SARAH MCCULLOH LEMMON

Blount, Reading *(22 Feb. 1757–13 Oct. 1807)*, major in the Continental Army during the American Revolution and an original member of the Society of the Cincinnati, was the third son of Jacob Blount and his wife, Barbara Gray. Jacob, son of the Thomas Blount to whom the Lords Proprietors had granted 266 acres of land in Carolina, became the father of a group of distinguished men.

William, one of the founders and first trustees of The University of North Carolina, a signer of the Constitution in Philadelphia, governor and U.S. senator from Tennessee, was the most famous of the Blount brothers. John Gray, who handled the vast Blount interests in shipping, merchandising, and land speculation, became a power in financial and political circles. While his brothers were acquiring great wealth, Reading distinguished himself in the Revolutionary War. Of the Blount brothers, it is said that William was the shrewdest and most ambitious, John Gray the smartest and most levelheaded, Thomas the most charming and lovable, and Reading the most daring and spirited. John Gray and Thomas were for many years trustees of The University of North Carolina, as was John Gray's son, General William Augustus.

Reading was born at Blount Hall, the home of his father, which was located near Contentnea Creek in the New Bern District (now Pitt County). His mother died when he was six, and Jacob was remarried two years later to Hannah Salter. Perhaps five children between the ages of six and fourteen were too overwhelming for a young stepmother; at any rate, Jacob's sons were educated under Thomas Thomlinson, who opened a school in New Bern in 1764.

After news came of Lexington and Concord in 1776, the North Carolina assembly met in Hillsborough and divided the state into military districts. Reading Blount, who was then nineteen and had as his only previous military experience drilling with the local militia, was commissioned a captain in the Third North Carolina Regiment on 16 Apr. 1776. This regiment, which was accepted by Congress on 7 May 1776, was commanded by Colonel Jethro Sumner, whose daughter Mary ("Jackie") married Blount's younger brother Thomas. Captain Blount became a major on 12 May 1778. In June of that year he was transferred to the Fifth North Carolina Continental Line. On 1 Jan. 1781, he was again transferred, this time to the First Continental Line. He served for nearly seven years.

At the Battle of Guilford Court House on 15 Mar. 1781, Blount was cited for bravery. Again at the Battle of Eutaw Springs, on 8 Sept. 1781, he was recognized by General Nathanael Greene for bravery beyond the call of duty. Legend says that through a misunderstanding of orders, a serious gap developed in the line of the Continental troops. Disaster seemed inevitable until the North Carolina battalion commanded by Ashe, Armstrong, and Blount came through with a brilliant maneuver averting catastrophe. General Greene went on record as saying, "I was at a loss which most to admire—the gallantry of the officers or the good conduct of their men."

At the conclusion of the war, Blount returned to Blount Hall and became involved in the mercantile, shipping, land dealing, and other business interests of John Gray and Thomas. He had a brief fling at politics, serving a term in the legislature from Pitt County. For two or three years, he joined Thomas in Tarboro, where a branch of the Blount business was in operation. There he entertained President Washington when he came to Tarboro on his southern tour. But he found that he was not interested in selling sugar and salt, rum and hardware, nor in scouting the area for tobacco, corn, and forest products to ship. He had apparently absorbed the routines of farm, mill, and shop as a boy at Blount Hall, and he wanted primarily to be a planter.

Blount was nearly thirty-seven when he married Lucy Harvey, younger daughter of Colonel Miles Harvey of Perquimans County and granddaughter of Governor Thomas Harvey. Mary, Lucy's older half-sister, was already the wife of John Gray Blount. The wedding of Lucy and Reading took place in the John Gray Blount home in Washington on 4 Feb. 1794. This house, built by John Gray Blount in 1778, was the sixth dwelling in the infant village at the Forks of the Tar and was occupied continuously by the Blount family until 1917. In 1923, "progress" demanded its demolition. John Gray Blount and his brother Bryan owned the Chocowinity Mills, opposite Washington on the Pamlico River, and he referred in deeds to this river location as his residence.

In 1796, Reading Blount bought three hundred acres of farm land on Tranter's Creek a few miles from Washington, on which there was a two-and-a-half-story house that he named "Bellefont." A feature of Bellefont, which is still standing after continuous occupancy for nearly two centuries, is a huge double-pent chimney, nineteen feet in width. This chimney has four fireplaces and four wardrobes constructed inside the chimney, each having an outside window.

This was Blount's home as, surrounded by a growing family, he raised flax and wheat, continued his buying and selling of land, and engaged in extensive operations in the lumber industry. He built another sawmill on Tranter's Creek in addition to the ones he already owned on Broad Creek and Pungo River.

In 1800, Blount was elected by the legislature to be major general of the First Division of Infantry of the state militia.

Blount died at the age of fifty at Bellefont. In Lucy Harvey Blount's Bible is written, "Major Reading Blount, the husband of Lucy and father of her children died October 13, 1807 at 2 o'clock in the morning." Interment was the following day. However, because there was no Episcopal priest in the area, the funeral was not held until two months later. On 8 Dec. 1807, family and friends met in the little burying ground on the south side of the house to read the burial service and give him "the full honors of war."

Seven months after Blount's death, Lucy gave birth to his ninth child, and in February 1818, she was buried beside him at Bellefont. Several of their children are buried in this family cemetery, which is maintained by the Blount Family Society.

SEE: *American Historical Magazine* 3 (1898); Samuel A. Ashe, ed., *Biographical History of North Carolina*, vol. 1 (1905); Blount Family Papers (North Carolina State Archives, Raleigh); Archibald Henderson, ed., *Washington's Southern Tour* (1923); Henry Knox, Secretary of War Report of Continental Army to Congress (in Frederick Anderson Berg, *Encyclopedia of Continental Army Units* [1972]); *The John Gray Blount Papers*, ed. Alice B. Keith and W. H. Masterson, 3 vols. (1952–65); W. H. Powell, comp., *List of Officers of the Army of the United States from 1779 to 1900* (1900); Proceedings of the First Meeting of the Society of the Cincinnati (The Society Museum, Washington, D.C.); Hugh F. Rankin, *The North Carolina Continentals* (1971); Papers of Lida T. Rodman (North Carolina State Archives, Raleigh); Phillips Russell, *North Carolina in the Revolutionary War* (1965); Marilu Smallwood, *Related Royal Families* (1966); Mrs. Louise Nutt Myers Weston (Washington, N.C.), memorabilia.

PAULINE WORTHY

Blount (Blunt), Thomas (*d. ca. Mar. 1706*), colonial official, was the son of Captain James Blount and his first wife, whose name is not known. The elder Blounts moved to Albemarle from Isle of Wight County, Va., between 1660 and 1669. Apparently Thomas and a brother, James, Jr., remained in Virginia for a time or returned there after their family's removal to Albemarle. Both Thomas and James, Jr., proved their own headrights and were granted land in Albemarle in 1680.

Like his father, Thomas Blount was called captain by his contemporaries, which presumably indicated rank in the militia of either Virginia or North Carolina, or both. Also like his father, he held civil office, including a seat on the council, in North Carolina. Blount's first known office was justice of Chowan Precinct court, of which he was the presiding judge in 1694. The almost total loss of the seventeenth-century records of that court renders it impossible to determine the length of his service.

In 1696, Blount was a member of the North Carolina council and was ex officio justice of the general court, then held by the council. From 1698 through 1701 he was justice of the general court by commission from the council but no longer a council member. In about 1696 and 1703 he was a member of the assembly, but the exact dates of his legislative service are not known. In 1699 he was member of a commission to investigate a charge of murder brought against a group of Indians, which was found to be false.

At some date subsequent to October 1701, the general court disqualified Blount for holding civil or military office in the colony during the remainder of his life. That action was taken because of the marriage of Blount's son James to Mary Tyler, sister of James's deceased wife, Katherine. Such a marriage, though admittedly outside the jurisdiction of the court, was prohibited by the Anglican church. As both Blount and Nicholas Tyler, the father of the bride, were alleged to have promoted the marriage, the court barred them from holding any office or trust in the colony. Although Blount's alleged offense was against the Anglican church, it seems not to have affected his standing in the church itself. He was on the vestry of St. Paul's Parish from the establishment of the parish, in 1701, until his death.

Blount lived in Chowan Precinct until about 1696, when he moved to Perquimans. Meetings of the assembly, council, general court, and court of chancery were held at his house in Perquimans in February 1696/97. He later resumed residence in Chowan and in September 1701 lived at the mouth of Kendrick's Creek in what is now Washington County. He made his home there for the remainder of his life.

Blount was married twice. His first wife probably was the Christian Blount named without identification among Blount's headrights in 1680, although possibly the "transport" was their daughter Christian. Five of the ten children who survived Blount appear to have been born of the first marriage. They were James, John, Sarah, Christian, and Ann. By the time Blount made his will, in 1701, the three daughters of the first wife were married and were noted in the will as Sarah Peirce, Christian Ludford, and Ann Wilson. Blount's second wife was Mary Scott, widow of Joshua Scott of Perquimans Precinct. That marriage took place in 1686, probably in April. The children born of it included sons Thomas, Benjamin, and Jacob and daughters Bithay (also called Billah) and Zilphia. Bithay married Kellem Tyler; Zilphia married John Edwards. In addition to his own children, Blount was responsible for at least two wards: his brother John, who was a minor when his father died, and Grace Scott, Blount's stepdaughter. It is not known whether he also was guardian for Grace's sister, Sarah.

Blount's will was proved 28 Mar. 1706. His widow became the wife of Captain Thomas Lee. Several of his children settled in the County of Bath, to the development of which they and their descendants made significant contributions. Among these was his son Thomas, who married Ann Reading, daughter of Lionel Reading, a prominent resident of the County of Bath.

Most writers on the Blount family have confused three individuals bearing the name Thomas Blount. The three are (1) the subject of this sketch, (2) his son Thomas, and (3) a putative uncle of the subject of this sketch, said to have been brother to the first James Blount and to have settled in North Carolina in the 1670s, but of whom this writer finds no trace in North Carolina records.

SEE: J. Bryan Grimes, ed., *Abstract of North Carolina Wills* (1910); J. R. B. Hathaway, ed., *North Carolina Historical and Genealogical Register*, 3 vols. (1900–1903); North Carolina State Archives (Raleigh), for Albemarle Book of Warrants and Surveys (1681–1706), Albemarle County Papers (1678–1714), Colonial Court Records (folder containing legislative papers in Box 192), Guardian's Bond of Thomas Blount (1 Feb. 1686/87), Perquimans Precinct Births, Marriages, Deaths and Flesh Marks (1659–1739), and Wills of James Blount, Thomas Blount, and Mary Lee; Mattie Erma Edwards Parker, ed., *North Carolina Higher-Court Records, 1670–1696* and *1697–1701* (1968, 1971); William S. Price, Jr., ed., *North Carolina Higher-Court Records, 1702–1708* (1974); William L. Saunders, ed., *Colonial Records of North Carolina*, vol. 1 (1886).

MATTIE ERMA E. PARKER

Blount, Thomas (*10 May 1759–1812*), landowner, merchant, congressman, and revolutionary soldier, was born in Craven County, the fourth son of Jacob Blount and Barbara Gray. His father was a prominent landowner, planter, and public officeholder in the colony.

Blount was closely associated with his two brothers, William and John Gray, in business and politics. It has been said that their financial interests were so closely interlocked that it is questionable whether any of the brothers ever knew exactly what was his. The Blount brothers' mercantile business became one of the largest in North Carolina, conducting stores, trading in land, and operating a fleet of ships engaged in European and coastal trade. The principal base of operations was at Washington, N.C., but other establishments were operated, and the one in Tarboro was under the charge of Thomas Blount.

Blount served in the Revolution as a lieutenant in the Fifth Regiment of the North Carolina Continental Line. During a portion of the war he was taken to England as a prisoner of war, and he later became a major general in the North Carolina Militia.

Blount was elected a trustee of The University of North Carolina on 3 Aug. 1792 and served until his death. He was one of the commissioners who laid out the city of Raleigh, and a principal street in that city bears his name. For a while he was a member of the U.S. Congress.

Blount was a member of the Episcopal church, and his wife, Mary Sumner, bequeathed money to Christ Church in Raleigh.

Blount was married first on 4 June 1782, to Martha Baker, daughter of Colonel Benjamin Baker. After his first wife's death, he married Mary ("Jackie") Sumner, in November 1796. She was the daughter of General Jethro Sumner, a distinguished Revolutionary War soldier and founder of the North Carolina Society of the Cincinnati. Both wives died without issue.

SEE: A. B. Keith and W. H. Masterson, eds., *The John Gray Blount Papers*, vols. 1–3 (1952–65); William L.

Saunders and Walter Clark, eds., *Colonial and State Records of North Carolina*, 30 vols. (1886–1914).

                                                      ARMISTEAD JONES MAUPIN

Blount, Tom, Tuscarora Indian chief. *See* Blunt, Tom.

Blount, William *(26 Mar. 1749–21 Mar. 1800)*, governor and senator, was born in Bertie County, the first son of Jacob and Barbara Gray Blount, one of the colony's earliest families. He obtained a good education in the private schools of the colony and served as paymaster of Continental troops during the Revolution. His four terms in the state's lower house, beginning in 1781, were followed by two terms in the senate. He also represented his state in the Continental Congress and in the convention of 1787 that drafted the Constitution of the United States. After North Carolina at first refused to join the new government, Blount won election to the second convention, in which he helped bring about the state's ratification of the federal Constitution. He also supported the cession of the state's western lands to the United States, and when that area was organized as the Territory of the United States South of the River Ohio, he was named governor and also superintendent of Indian affairs for the entire region south of the Ohio River. In the latter capacity, he negotiated the Treaty of the Holston of 1791 with the Cherokee Indians, by which they ceded to the United States a large amount of territory, much of which was already occupied by whites.

During the first stage of the territory's history, Blount had autocratic authority. He proclaimed laws, created new counties, and appointed civil officials. By 1794 the population was sufficient for the election of a territorial assembly, which in its first session chartered three colleges; one of these, the forerunner of the University of Tennessee, was named Blount College in honor of the governor. When a territorial census revealed a population adequate for statehood, Blount arranged for a constitutional convention, over which he presided as chairman, which drafted the state's first constitution. He was then elected as one of the state's first two members of the U.S. Senate.

His senatorial career was cut short by the so-called Blount Conspiracy, caused by a rumor that Spain was about to cede New Orleans and the Louisiana country to France, which action, it was expected, would deny the Americans the right to use the Mississippi River for the export of their surplus products. Blount therefore took over the leadership of a scheme, already being developed, to organize an expedition of frontiersmen and Indians to help the British, then at war with Spain and France, take New Orleans, Louisiana, and Florida away from Spain. Great Britain was bound by the treaty of peace of 1783 to permit free navigation of the Mississippi River by Canadians and Americans. Before the plan could be put in operation, a letter Blount had written about it fell into the hands of federal authorities, and as a result he was expelled from the Senate. He was also impeached by the House of Representatives but was acquitted in trial before the Senate, because of lack of jurisdiction. Blount remained popular in Tennessee, where he was elected to the state senate and its speakership. He did not run for reelection and was out of office at the time of his death.

On 12 Feb. 1778, Blount married Mary Molsey Grainger, the daughter of Caleb Grainger of the Cape Fear region of North Carolina. They had seven children: Cornelius, Ann, Mary Louisa, William Grainger, Richard Blackledge, Barbara, and Eliza. Blount was buried in the churchyard of the First Presbyterian Church, Knoxville, Tenn., where a marble slab marks his grave.

SEE: Samuel A. Ashe, ed., *Biographical History of North Carolina*, vol. 3 (1905); *Biog. Dir. Am. Cong.* (1928); *DAB*, vol. 2 (1929); W. H. Masterson, *William Blount* (1954 [portrait]); M. J. Wright, *Some Account of the Life and Services of William Blount* (1884).

                                                      STANLEY J. FOLMSBEE

Blount, William Augustus *(26 Oct. 1792–4 June 1867)*, landowner and soldier, was born in Washington, Beaufort County, the son of John Gray Blount and Mary Harvey. His father's possessions numbered hundreds of thousands of acres, a large portion of which were in Western North Carolina and what is now Tennessee. His grandfather was Captain Jacob Blount, paymaster of the North Carolina troops during the Revolution and an original member of the North Carolina Society of the Cincinnati.

When Blount was twenty years old, he volunteered to serve in the army at the outbreak of the War of 1812. He was commissioned a first lieutenant of the Eighteenth Infantry on 8 May 1812 and was promoted to captain on 4 Sept. 1813. During a part of his service he was stationed with the troops defending Charleston. Blount retired from the army at the close of the war on 15 June 1815. On 28 Nov. 1815, when he was only twenty-three years of age, he was elected major general of the Sixth Division, North Carolina Militia.

Blount was a large landowner and planter. His home was Meadowville Plantation, Chocowinty District, Beaufort County, and there he spent most of his life.

Blount represented Beaufort County in the 1825 state House of Commons and was reelected to serve in 1826 and 1827. He was elected a trustee of The University of North Carolina in 1826 and remained a trustee until his death more than forty years later.

Blount was devoted to the South. Age prevented his personal participation in the Civil War, but he spent his entire fortune in the furtherance of the southern cause. His only surviving son, Major William Augustus, Jr., was an aide-de-camp on the staff of General Lawrence O'Bryan Branch, C.S.A.; Branch married Blount's only daughter, Nancy Haywood.

Blount was twice married. His first wife was Nancy Haywood, the eldest daughter of Sherwood Haywood of Raleigh and a granddaughter of Colonel Philemon Hawkins of Warren County. The only children of this marriage were William Augustus and Nancy Haywood. After the death of his first wife, he married Anne Littlejohn, by whom he had no children. Blount was a member of the Episcopal Church.

The downfall of the Confederacy and the death of his son-in-law, General Branch, at the Battle of Antietam, were great blows to Blount; he did not long survive them. He died in the Branch house on Hillsborough Street in Raleigh and was buried in the Branch family plot of the old City Cemetery in Raleigh.

SEE: Samuel A. Ashe, ed., *Biographical History of North Carolina*, vol. 1 (1905); W. H. Masterson, ed., *The John Gray Blount Papers*, vol. 3 (1965); H. T. Shanks, ed., *The Papers of Willie Person Mangum*, vol. 2 (1952).

                                                      ARMISTEAD JONES MAUPIN

Blount, William Grainger *(1784–21 May 1827)*, congressman, was the oldest son of Southwest Territory Governor William Blount and his wife, Mary Grainger, the daughter of Colonel William Caleb Grainger of Wilmington. William Grainger ("Billy") Blount was born at Piney Grove on Great Contentnea Creek, Dobbs (now Pitt) County. Hugh Williamson addressed a letter to William Blount on 28 Nov. 1782 at "Piney Grove, near Washington"; though Piney Grove was near Washington, it was closer to New Bern in Craven County. Blount first studied at the New Bern Academy, of which his father was an original trustee.

In 1790, President Washington appointed William Blount, a former Continental officer and North Carolina signer of the federal Constitution at Philadelphia, the Governor of the Territory of the United States South of the Ohio River, better known as the Southwest Territory. He moved to Upper East Tennessee and established residence in the house of William Cobb. Two years later, Governor Blount moved with his wife and sons to elegant quarters in Knoxville. Billy was eight years old when he made this first trip to his new home in Knoxville. This house, known as the Blount Mansion in Tennessee, the oldest dwelling west of the Appalachian Mountains, was built in 1792 for William Blount, and it was here that Billy grew up and spent his formative years.

Blount studied French and music with a Mr. Faurnier in 1794, and in 1797 he was tutored in Latin by the Reverend Samuel Carrick, a Presbyterian minister. Later Carrick became president of Blount College (now the University of Tennessee); Billy's sister Barbara enrolled in the college and became one of America's first five co-eds.

When Governor Blount died on 21 Mar. 1800, the education of his children was taken over by his half brother, Willie Blount, who was also their legal guardian. Willie Blount, who served as the secretary to Governor William Blount, had been educated at Princeton University and was himself elected governor of Tennessee. He saw to Billy Grainger's legal training and had him admitted to the bar in 1805. Billy practiced law in Knoxville and also had avid agricultural pursuits. He was elected Tennessee secretary of state (1811–15) and subsequently was elected to the Fourteenth Congress to fill the Democratic seat left vacant by the death of John Sevier on 24 Sept. 1815. He took his seat on 8 Jan. 1816 and, reelected to the Fifteenth Congress, served until 3 Mar. 1819; he declined to run again, so that he could return to peaceful Tennessee and the practice of law and farming.

That Blount had a sense of pride and love of his family is attested by the two brick monuments with stone tops in the old First Presbyterian Church Cemetery at Knoxville, which he had placed at the grave of his father, Governor William Blount, and that of his beloved aunt, Ann Blount Harvey (Mrs. James Harvey), the sister of John Gray and William Blount. Blount moved to Paris, Tenn., in Henry County, some two hundred miles from Knoxville, where he set up a law practice and became the leading citizen. His new career was short lived, however: he died suddenly at age forty-three. His grave is located in the Paris, Tenn., City Cemetery.

SEE: *American Historical Magazine* 3 (1898); Samuel A. Ashe, ed., *Biographical History of North Carolina*, vol. 1 (1905); Blount Family Society Papers (in possession of the author); Archibald Henderson, ed., *Washington's Southern Tour* (1923); *The John Gray Blount Papers*, ed. Alice B. Keith and W. H. Masterson, 3 vols. (1952–65); Henry Knox, Secretary of War Report of Continental Army to Congress (Frederick Anderson Berg, *Encyclopedia of Continental Army Units* [1972]); Papers of Lida T.

Rodman (North Carolina State Archives, Raleigh); *Tennessee Historical Magazine* 9 (1926).

WILLIAM BLOUNT STEWART

Blount, Willie *(pronounced Wiley; 18 Apr. 1768–10 Sept. 1835)*, lawyer, judge, and governor of Tennessee, was born at Blount Hall, Craven County, the son of Jacob Blount and Hannah Salter Baker, widow of William Baker. He was educated at Princeton and Columbia and studied law in New Bern with Judge John Sitgreaves. His half brother William was appointed governor of the Territory South of the River Ohio in 1789, and Willie joined him there as his private secretary.

Willie Blount represented Montgomery County, Tenn., in the provincial assemblies of 1794 and 1795. When a portion of the territory became the State of Tennessee in 1796, he was elected by the legislature as a judge of superior court, but he soon resigned. He settled in Montgomery County in Tennessee, where he married Lucinda Baker, daughter of Major John and Ann Norfleet Baker, originally residents of Bertie County but residents of Tennessee at the time of the marriage. Willie and Lucinda Blount were the parents of two daughters, Eliza Ann and Lucinda.

In 1807, Blount was elected to the legislature; after one term he was elected governor of the state, in 1809. He served until 1815, the constitutional maximum of three consecutive terms. As governor he was instrumental in removing the Indian title to much of the land in the state and in improving transportation and communication facilities. His third term was devoted largely to warfare with the Indians and the British, as the War of 1812 was then in progress.

After the death of his first wife, Blount was married on 19 Feb. 1812 to Mary White, the widow of Hugh Lawson White, a native of Iredell County.

At the end of his third term as governor in 1815, Blount retired to his home, Bakerdon, in Montgomery County, Tenn., where he wrote a history of his adopted state (never published). He was a candidate for governor against Sam Houston in 1827 but was defeated. He was a Democrat, a strong supporter of Andrew Jackson, and an active member of the constitutional convention of 1834.

Blount was buried in Clarksville.

SEE: *DAB*, vol. 2 (1929); Elizabeth H. Peeler, "The Policies of Willie Blount as Governor of Tennessee," *Tennessee Historical Quarterly* 1 (1942).

STANLEY J. FOLMSBEE

Blue, Victor *(6 Dec. 1865–22 Jan. 1928)*, naval officer, was born in Richmond County of Scottish ancestry. His parents were John Gilchrist and Annie M. Evans Blue. Blue's father was a colonel in the Confederate Army; his grandfather, John Blue, was a colonel in the War of 1812; and two of his great-grandfathers served as captains: John Blue in the Continental Army and John Gilchrist in the British navy. Blue's father was a member of the North Carolina delegation considering the issue of secession from the Union and voted to secede, later raising a company and fighting with Robert E. Lee in the Army of Northern Virginia until the surrender at Appomattox.

Blue's family moved to Marion, S.C., when he was still a baby. His mother's family had long been prominent in South Carolina affairs, one member having served as governor of the state. Blue grew up in the area around Marion and was appointed to the U.S. Naval Academy on 6 Sept. 1883. He was graduated in 1887 and began a naval career spanning thirty-two years.

After graduating from the Naval Academy, Blue

distinguished himself at various assignments during the course of several wars, rising to the rank of rear admiral on 1 Apr. 1919. He served in Quinnebaug, 1887–89; on the *Pensacola*, 1889–91; in Charleston, 1892; at the Navy Yard, Norfolk, 1892–93; on the *Alliance*, 1892–94; on the *Charleston*, 1894; on the *Thetis*, 1894–95; on the *Bennington*, 1895–96; and at the Naval Academy, 1896–98.

With the outbreak of the Spanish-American War in 1898, Blue was assigned to the *Suwanee* of the Atlantic Fleet commanded by Admiral William Sampson. Blue twice led expeditions behind the enemy lines near Santiago, Cuba, first to communicate with the insurgent general-in-chief Maximo Gomez on mainland Cuba and next to obtain information concerning the number and position of the ships in the Spanish Fleet commanded by Admiral Pascual Cervera y Topate. During this second mission, Blue placed the first American flag on Cuban soil and then traveled seventy miles on muleback to obtain his information, which led to the American victory in the Battle of Santiago de Cuba on 3 July 1898. For his actions, Blue was awarded the Special Meritorious Medal and advanced five numbers in rank by the president.

Blue continued his naval service. He was commander of the *Yorktown*, Pacific Station, 1910, and chief of staff, Pacific Fleet, 1910–11; on 25 May 1911 he was made a member of the General Board of the Navy Department. In 1913, while still only a commander, Blue was assigned as chief of the Bureau of Navigation of the Navy Department. He held this position with the rank of rear admiral from 26 Mar. 1913 until 10 Aug. 1916. During World War I he commanded the battleship *Texas*, operating with the British Grand Fleet under Admiral David Beatty in the North Sea. He took part in receiving the surrender of the German Fleet on 21 Nov. 1918 and was reappointed chief of the Bureau of Navigation, 16 Dec. 1918. For his service in the war he received the U.S. Navy's Distinguished Service Medal with the citation, "For exceptionally meritorious service in a duty of great responsibility . . . ," and was decorated commander of the Order of Leopold by the king of Belgium.

Blue retired on 11 July 1919. He died at his home in Ft. George, Fla. In 1935, Destroyer No. 387 of the U.S. Navy was named the U.S.S. *Blue* in his honor.

Blue married Eleanor Foote Stuart on 17 Oct. 1899.

SEE: *Charlotte Observer*, 1898; Raleigh *News and Observer*, 5 July 1935; *Who Was Who in America*, vol. 1 (1943).

SAMUEL M. GAINOR

Blum, John Christian (*17 July 1784–18 Nov. 1854*), printer and editor, was born in the Moravian community of Bethabara to Jacob Blum and Maria Elisabeth Koch, originally of Pennsylvania. In 1787 the family moved to Salem, where Blum's father became the tavern-keeper for the Salem Moravian Congregation. Young Blum worked in the community store for Conrad Kreuser until Jacob Blum died in 1802, at which time he was appointed temporary landlord at the tavern. When a permanent tavern-keeper was found, Blum worked as a blue-dyer in the summer and a chair-maker or wheelwright for the Single Brothers Diacony. During his early adult years he also served as a member of the community council, as justice of the peace, and for a time as roadmaster. After his marriage in 1810 he resumed the position of tavern-keeper until, in 1815, his wife's poor health forced him to relinquish this post. At this time, Blum became the local agent for the Cape Fear Bank, a position he held until 1827.

Blum's most important career began in 1827 when he opened Salem's first print shop in his house on Main Street. His first intention was to print a weekly newspaper for the town, but this action was vetoed by the church. The Elders Conference and the Aufseher Collegium felt that a newspaper "might have various unpleasant results for local individuals, for the congregation town, and for the Unity itself." Blum was thus confined to job printing, including publication of *Blum's Farmer's and Planter's Almanac*, still published today in Winston-Salem. Early in 1829, Blum did expand his production to include a newspaper entitled the *Weekly Gleaner*, which aroused much public controversy. Blum promised, however, that his publication would not offend; he would print nothing of a personal nature, of party politics, or of religious controversy. "It will be our endeavor to pursue a course free from all bitter controversies, as they but excite the evil passion of our nature, without improving or benefiting society." But insufficient patronage and other difficulties caused him to discontinue the *Gleaner* after only one year. In the early 1830s, Blum started a new paper, *The Farmer's Reporter and Rural Repository*, which got him into trouble with the Aufseher Collegium, when he suggested in the paper that the town build a theater. He was forced to retract this statement in the next issue. Throughout his publishing career, Blum was in and out of trouble with the church over his editorial comments.

Issues of the *Gleaner* and later publications bore the imprint "printed by H. S. Noble, Salem, Stokes County North Carolina . . . John C. Blum, Proprietor." Noble was evidently working for Blum and continued to do so in a journeyman capacity for some time. Later, Blum's two sons, Levi and Edward, became printers with their father. By 1831, Blum had added the business of bookbinding, and in 1836 he also purchased a local paper mill. The paper mill, built in 1791, had belonged to Gottlieb Schober, who had sold an assortment of writing, printing, and wrapping papers, books printed in German and English on many subjects, and a large line of stationery items.

Though a layman, Blum was an active member of the Aufseher Collegium and also served as Fremdendiener (Curator of Strangers) for the community. Blum married Maria Elisabeth Transou in 1810. They had four children: Levi Vanniman, Maria Lavinia, Lucinda Paulina, and Edward Transou. There is a photograph of a nineteenth-century daguerreotype of Blum in the collection of Old Salem, Inc. His one-and-a-half story frame dwelling, built in 1815, still stands in Salem.

Blum was buried in God's Acre in Salem.

SEE: Moravian Church Archives (Winston-Salem), for Aufseher Collegium Minutes, Blum's personal memoir, Elders Conference Minutes, Salem Diary, and *Weekly Gleaner* (6 Jan. 1829–29 Dec. 1829).

JAN HIESTER

Blunt (or Blount), Tom (*ca. 1675–ca. 1739*), a head chief and king of the North Carolina Tuscarora Indians, of obscure parentage, lived in the Upper Towns. During his time these numbered seven and formed one of three confederacies of the Tuscarora nation; they were located in the upper coastal plains on the Tar and Roanoke rivers and their tributaries and were frequented by Virginia traders during Blunt's boyhood. In a matrilineal society, he rose to political power, as a member of the bear clan, through his mother and her people. Whether because of blood ties or admiration, his name is the same as that of two Englishmen, Thomas Blount of Chowan Precinct in

North Carolina and Tom Blunt, who from 1691 to 1703 served as Virginia's official interpreter to the Indians south of the James River. Blunt acquired a speaking knowledge of English.

The English of Carolina in particular were indebted to Tom Blunt for minimizing the Tuscarora War of 1711–13, by leading the Upper Towns on a neutral course, and for keeping the peace on the frontier for a quarter of a century afterward. By 1711 he was in high repute throughout the Tuscarora nation. The head men of the hostile towns consulted him as to what should be done with Christoph de Graffenried and John Lawson.

Virginia claimed much of the credit for keeping Blunt neutral during the war. His people had become dependent on Virginia traders: they had abandoned their bows, and control of their powder supply controled their take of game for food and skins. After Virginia invoked trade restrictions, Governor Thomas Pollock of North Carolina wrote Governor Alexander Spotswood of Virginia that Blunt was "very earnest for peace and to have trade as formerly." And de Graffenried, who credited Blunt with saving his life, said that this king and chief was "full of sense" and much inclined toward the English.

Near the end of the Tuscarora War, Blunt was persuaded to assist the English by bringing in King Hancock, ringleader of the 1711 massacre, for execution and by taking nearly thirty scalps of other leaders and enemies.

Immediately after the Indian hostilities had been crushed, the North Carolina council recognized Blunt for his faithfulness and good service and made him chief of all Indians to the south of the Pamlico River. About three thousand of the Tuscarora had survived the war. Of these, about one thousand subjected themselves to Blunt, and the remainder fled beyond the frontier and began migrating to the North. So reduced in strength, the Tuscaroras under Blunt found themselves exposed and open to attack by the Catawbas and other enemy Indians. In 1717, for greater safety, the North Carolina council permitted them to settle on their old Skanwaknee hunting grounds north of the Roanoke River in present Bertie County. Here they established two towns, one of which was Resootska, or "to our grandfather," named in honor of King Blunt.

The English treated Blunt as an absolute monarch. The few matters of misconduct of his Indians were taken directly to him, and he acted effectively to preserve the peace. In 1723 he informed the council that a group of northern Indians were expected that fall "to seduce the young men of the nation from him in order to Comit mischief." Following the Indian custom of hospitality, Blunt gave the unwanted visitors food and shelter, and they did no injury to the English of North Carolina.

Within a few years, Blunt, on the threshhold of old age, saw his nation weakening. Whites, hungry for land, began to encroach upon his reservation; by 1731 northern Indians had enticed away all but six hundred of his people; and an undetermined number had left to work for the whites.

Blunt was dead before 5 Mar. 1739. At this time the great men of the Tuscarora nation petitioned the North Carolina council to elect a new king.

Of the king's family, we know that his wife and two of his children and a sister's son were captured by the Meherrin Indians during the Tuscarora War and redeemed for him by the Carolina government.

SEE: Frederick Webb Hodge, ed., *Handbook of American Indians, North of Mexico*, vol. 2 (1907–10); F. Roy Johnson, *The Tuscaroras*, vol. 2 (1967); Herbert Paschal, Jr., "The Tuscarora Indians in North Carolina" (M.A. thesis, University of North Carolina, 1953); William L. Saunders, ed., *Colonial Records of North Carolina*, vols. 1–2 (1886).

F. ROY JOHNSON

Bodley, Joshua *(1705–3 Feb. 1775)*, attorney and land agent, may have been a native of Dublin, Ireland. He was living in the port city of Lorient, Britanny, France, on 3 Nov. 1755, when a marriage contract was drawn up with Jeane Henriette Damery or D'Amory, minor daughter of Jean and Helen Julienne Faret Damery. By this contract he settled on her forty thousand livres and guaranteed that her personal property, including jewels, would remain her own, free of any claim from him. These terms suggest that the fifty-year-old Bodley was comfortably fixed at that time.

On 1 Sept. 1756, Bodley was described as of the Parish of St. James's, Westminster, London, when he was appointed an agent in North Carolina for Earl Granville, who owned an interest in about half the land in the colony. Bodley was replacing Benjamin Wheatley, whose son was apparently brought up in Bodley's household. In September 1756, Bodley and Thomas Barker were appointed personal attorneys to Thomas Child, and in late May 1757, Bodley was named by the council to be one of the justices of Chowan County; he probably was then a resident of Edenton. In the same month, acting as Granville's agent, he commissioned John Haywood to collect and receive Lord Granville's quitrents in Edgecombe and Johnston counties. Conditions on Granville's lands were so unsettled and the question of quitrents and taxes so unstable that residents complained to the attorney general for relief. He advised a petition to the earl or an appeal to the assembly. A committee investigated the recent activity of Thomas Corbin and Joshua Bodley, both agents of Granville, and concluded that they had followed Granville's instructions concerning the manner of issuing land grants and taking fees. That their instructions had been changed from time to time, however, the people were unaware. Corbin, it was concluded, had been doing some questionable things, but the house was satisfied with Bodley's conduct. Nevertheless, in late January 1759, both men were seized by a band from Edgecombe County and taken by force to Enfield, the county seat. Those who took Bodley were drunk. They afterwards thrust a Bible into his hand and tried to make him take an oath "to something he would not attend to," but he was able to obtain his release. He was already trying to provide relief for the people who were complaining of Corbin's past actions. The charges against Bodley were certainly less serious than those against Corbin, and he was released first. As one witness later testified, Bodley "lukily got out of their hands." In April, Granville confirmed the appointment of both these men as his agents, and he also named Thomas Child, attorney general of the colony, to be his auditor.

At the same time Bodley was having trouble with the people of Edgecombe County, he also had trouble with a member of the assembly and temporarily with the governor. Bodley charged that assembly member Francis Brown had forsworn himself in legislative hearings into complaints against the proprietary agents. Brown assaulted Bodley and challenged him to a duel. A legislative committee investigated and found that the accusation against Brown was justified, and Brown was dismissed from the house. Bodley charged also that

Corbin had said, in his hearing, that Governor Arthur Dobbs had granted land the governor knew to be Granville land. An investigation made it clear that Corbin had lied, and after the governor had given him ample opportunity to support his statements, Corbin was dismissed from the council and from his position as an associate justice. To show that no disrespect was intended to Earl Granville, Dobbs sometime before 3 Aug. 1760 appointed Bodley to be associate justice in Corbin's place. In the same month, Auditor Thomas Child removed Bodley as Granville's agent because Bodley "hath under Colour of the Powers and Authorities so given to him by the said Earl as aforesaid behaved himself greatly to the prejudice and Hindrance of his Lordship's Interests and contrary to the general Trust and Confidence in him by the said . . . Commission." Child accused Bodley specifically of failing to submit a final account of receipts, disbursements, charges, and proceedings.

Maurice Moore, writing from the Cape Fear on 27 Jan. 1770 to Samuel Johnston, said that Bodley had spent several days with Bodley. Bodley was, said Moore, "a very respectable Gent and highly merits the friendly regard of every good man." Moore asked Johnston, "Does it not lie in your way to lend him an assisting hand in his Difficulties? If it does, to do so, would be to act a part worthy of yrself."

Bodley's home was Pembroke Plantation near Edenton, and at his death he was buried there. (The federal government later took over the plantation for a fish hatchery, and in about 1911 his body was removed to St. Paul's churchyard in Edenton.) Sir Nathaniel Duckenfield wrote to James Iredell on 26 Mar. 1775 from Manchester, England: "I received a letter a few days ago from Mr. Pearson in which he tells me that Mr. Bodley is dead. I think that compliments of congratulations are more proper than those of condolence to be presented to Mrs. Bodley on this occasion." Within two years the widow was married to Stephen Cabarrus, who was born only one year before she and Bodley had been married. Bodley was also survived by a sister in Waterford, Ireland.

SEE: Don Higginbotham, ed., *Papers of James Iredell*, vol. 1 (1976); *North Carolina Historical and Genealogical Register*, vol. 1 (Oct. 1900); notes in the possession of Miss Elizabeth V. Moore, Edenton; William L. Saunders and Walter Clark, eds., *Colonial and State Records of North Carolina*, 30 vols. (1886–1914).

WILLIAM S. POWELL

Boger, George *(15 Dec. 1782–19 June 1865)*, German Reformed minister, was born in Cabarrus County. His grandfather, Mathias, emigrated from the Palatinate in 1732 and settled in Lancaster County, Pa. His parents, Jacob Boger (12 Oct. 1745–25 Dec. 1831) and Barbara Loefler (Dec. 1750–15 Apr. 1819) of Berks County, Pa., moved to North Carolina and located on Buffalo Creek in the present Cabarrus County. Here Boger was baptized by the Reverend Samuel Suther, Swiss immigrant and pastor to early German Reformed congregations in North and South Carolina. He attended schools conducted by German masters until his fourteenth year, when he studied briefly with John Yeoman, who conducted an English school. In his sixteenth year, Boger was prepared for church membership by the Reverend Samuel Weyberg, pastor of Reformed churches in Cabarrus and Rowan counties. He was confirmed 12 May 1799 and soon began to study for the ministry under Reformed and Lutheran clergymen, while supplying

pulpits of various Reformed churches until his ordination on 6 Mar. 1803 at Mt. Zion (Savitz) Church in the present China Grove.

Among the churches served by Boger were Mt. Zion (Savitz), China Grove (1802–30); Bethany, Davidson County (1803–12); Bethel (Bear Creek), Stanly County (1806–30); Emmanuel, Davidson County (1812–27); Grace (Lower Stone), Rowan County (1803–30); New Gilead (Cold Water), Cabarrus County (1803–30). He also visited Reformed congregations in South Carolina. For a period after 1812 he was the only ordained minister of his denomination in North Carolina. The demand for worship services in the English language was later voiced in the churches, and Boger, who preached in German, relinquished his pastoral responsibilities to the Reverend Daniel B. Lerch in 1830. He continued, however, to play a significant role in the German Reformed church in North Carolina, and as a minister without charge he cared for the spiritual needs of Reformed congregations having no pastor. He was also active in the North Carolina Classis of the Reformed church and frequently delivered sermons in the German language at its annual meetings. He was elected treasurer of Classis in 1832 and was its representative at the meeting of the Evangelical Lutheran Synod of North Carolina in 1838. Moreover, he accepted appointments on committees of Classis to ordain ministers, examine candidates for ministerial standing, and report on the state of religion in the churches. Advancing years and declining health led him to retire from the ministry completely in 1847.

Because of his dedication to the church, "Father" Boger was revered as a loving, gentle, and patient servant of God. Upon the celebration of the tenth anniversary of the organization of the North Carolina Classis in 1841, the Reverend John Lantz's churches in Rowan and Cabarrus counties affirmed their determination to raise fifteen hundred dollars, to be called the "Boger Beneficiaryship" in honor of their former pastor. Many years later he was memorialized in the organization of Boger Reformed Church at Watts Cross Roads in Cabarrus County, on 29 Oct. 1905. The church edifice, dedicated 29 Apr. 1906, was constructed on land originally owned by Boger and donated by Mrs. Caroline Boger to commemorate him.

Boger was married three times: in 1806 to Elizabeth Hagler, who died in 1809, leaving no children; in 1810 to Elizabeth Barnhardt, who died in 1836, leaving ten children; in 1837 to Elizabeth File, who became the mother of two children. Following his death in Rowan County, Boger's funeral was conducted by the Reverend J. B. Anthony, and he was buried in the cemetery of historic Grace (Lower Stone) Church.

SEE: Frank K. Bostian, and others, *Dutch Buffalo Creek Meeting House* (1974); J. C. Clapp, *Historic Sketch of the Reformed Church in North Carolina* (1908); Carl Daye, *The Story of Boger Evangelical and Reformed Church, 1905–1955* (1955); Jacob C. Leonard, *History of the Southern Synod of the Evangelical and Reformed Church* (1940); Banks J. Peeler, *A Story of the Southern Synod of the Evangelical and Reformed Church* (1968); *Records of the North Carolina Classis of the German Reformed Church in the United States*, vols. 1–3 (1831–65); Jethro Rumple, *A History of Rowan County* (1881); William L. Saunders, ed., *Colonial Records of North Carolina*, vol. 8 (1890); Banks D. Shepherd, *New Gilead Church* (1966); George W. Welker, *A Historical Sketch of the Classis of North Carolina* (1895).

ROBERT W. DELP

Boggan, Patrick (*ca. 1725–1817*), Regulator and revolutionary patriot, was born at Castle Finn, County Donegal, Ireland, according to tradition. He was the son of Sir Walter Boggan. He was probably in his early twenties when he came to America with his two brothers, Benjamin and James, and a sister, Jane. They appear to have settled first in Maryland, later removing to Virginia, and all finally settling in Anson County. Jane Boggan married Thomas Wade, probably in 1743. Patrick Boggan is first recorded as living in North Carolina when he received a grant for 238 acres of land in Granville County from Lord Granville in 1752. In his deed he was described as "planter," and he signed the document himself.

Boggan married Mary Dobbs, an orphan of considerable wealth, and they had two sons and seven daughters: Benjamin, who married but died young without issue; Patrick, Jr., who married Martha Davidson; Jane, married to Pleasant May; Mary, married to John May; Fannie, married to Jimmy Cash; Peggy, who married Inigo Cash; Eleanor, who married William Hammond; Flora, married to James Pickett; and Lydia, married to Moses Coppedge.

By the time of his children's marriages, Boggan was a large landowner in Anson County, and he gave land and slaves to each of them. Much of his property is still owned by descendants. He also made generous gifts of land to his brother-in-law, Colonel Thomas Wade.

Boggan's name appears in 1768 on a petition to Governor William Tryon from residents of Anson County, complaining about their treatment at the hands of local officials. This affiliation clearly identifies him as a member of the group that came to be known as Regulators.

During the Revolution, Boggan was a captain of militia serving under his brother-in-law, Colonel Thomas Wade. He engaged in several raids against local Tories, sometimes in collaboration with partisan leaders from South Carolina.

The courthouse of Anson County had been located near the South Carolina line when the county was established in 1750, but after the creation of two new counties in the northern and eastern parts of Anson in 1779, agitation began for a more conveniently located county seat. In 1782, Boggan purchased seventy acres of land and donated it for a town to serve that purpose, which soon came to be called simply New Town. At the death of Colonel Wade in 1786, the name Wadesboro was adopted. In 1795, Boggan served the county as one of its justices.

Boggan's will is dated 1801, with a codicil added in 1803, but it was not probated until 1817, the presumed year of his death. At that time he owned more than a thousand acres of land. His last years, following the death of his wife, were spent with his daughter, Eleanor Hammond, in a house in Wadesboro that he had built for her at the time of her marriage. This house is still standing and is the oldest house in Wadesboro.

SEE: Anson County records (courthouse in Wadesboro and in N.C. State Archives, Raleigh); Kate Bennett, "Captain Paddy Boggan and His Times" (mimeographed, n.d., Wadesboro); Will Boggan, "A History of Anson County" (typescript, North Carolina Collection, University of North Carolina, Chapel Hill); Walter Clark, *State Records of North Carolina*, 24 (1905); William L. Saunders, *Colonial Records of North Carolina*, 7 (1890).

HARRIET H. ROBSON

Bogle, James (*Jan. 1817–11 Oct. 1873*), portrait and genre painter, was born in or near Fayetteville, or in Georgetown, S.C., a twin son of Dr. James and Sarah Auld Bogle. Dr. Bogle made his living both as a physician and as principal and teacher at various academies including the Franklin Academy in Louisburg and Fayetteville Academy. James may have attended the latter although of his early education nothing is known. In 1836 he went to New York City where he studied art under Samuel F. B. Morse. By 1838 he was traveling with his twin brother, Robert, through North Carolina and South Carolina, painting portraits and exhibiting genre paintings. By 1840 they had achieved such prominence as to be described by the *Charleston* (S.C.) *Courier* as the "Siamese Twins of the divine art." They worked in both Charleston and Baltimore during the years between 1841 and 1843. In Baltimore James apparently met Rebecca Riggs, daughter of a prominent businessman, and they were married in New York in January 1843. The young couple established their residence in New York. They became the parents of James, Jr., Rebecca Riggs, Elizabeth, Margaret Riggs, Virginia Waldron, and Aurelia Calhoun. By 1853 Bogle had set up his own school of painting and was widely known as a portraitist, having been elected an associate of the National Academy of Design in 1849. Among his works are portraits of John C. Calhoun, Daniel Webster, Henry Clay, and Millard Fillmore. His portrait of Judge William Gaston is owned by the Philanthropic Society of The University of North Carolina at Chapel Hill. The New York *Atlas* in 1852 commented that "Bogle, to our mind, is equal to any painter of the times . . . in every department of the art [he] is as nigh perfection as any man can be; and it is not extravagant to call him the Sir Thomas Lawrence of the United States." In 1861 he was elected to the status of Academician of the National Academy of Design. Bogle died in Brooklyn, N.Y., and was buried by his wife in Woodlawn Cemetery in New York.

SEE: Francis W. Bilodeau and Mrs. Thomas J. Tobias, *Art in South Carolina, 1670–1970* (1970); Bogle file, National Academy of Design Archives, New York; *Charleston Courier*, 14 Jan. 1840; Charleston *Mercury*, 7 Jan. 1842, 22 Mar. 1843; Charles L. Coon, *North Carolina Schools and Academies, 1790–1840* (1915); James H. Craig, *The Arts and Crafts in North Carolina, 1699–1840* (1966); Cumberland County Marriage Bonds (North Carolina State Archives, Raleigh); *Fayetteville Observer*, 23 Sept. 1852; Mantle Fielding, *Dictionary of American Painters, Sculptors & Engravers* (1960); George C. Groce and David H. Wallace, *Dictionary of Artists in America: 1564–1860* (1957); E. J. Hale Papers (North Carolina State Archives, Raleigh); Calvin Jones Papers (Southern Historical Collection, University of North Carolina, Chapel Hill); *National Academy of Design Exhibition Record, 1826–1860* (1943); New-York Historical Society, *Catalogue of American Portraits in the New-York Historical Society* (1974); Philanthropic Society Papers, 1851–52 (Southern Historical Collection, University of North Carolina, Chapel Hill); John B. Riggs, *The Riggs Family of Maryland* (1939); Anna Wells Rutledge, *Artists in the Life of Charleston* (1949); U.S. Census, 1820, Cumberland County (North Carolina State Archives, Raleigh).

ROGER N. KIRKMAN

Bogle, Robert (*Jan. 1817–after 1860*), portrait and genre painter, was probably born in or near Fayetteville, or in Georgetown, S.C., a twin son of Dr. James and Sarah Auld Bogle. Of his early education nothing is known, but he likely attended Fayetteville Academy, of which his father was principal from 1811 until his death before 1820. He probably followed his twin brother James to study under Samuel F. B. Morse in 1836, and by 1838 he traveled with James in North and South Carolina, painting portraits and genre paintings together. In 1843 Robert separated from his brother James and went to New Orleans in 1844, where he married Adelaide Bailey in 1845. His first daughter, Ada, was born in South Carolina ca. 1846, while a son, Robert, was born in Italy ca. 1848, and another, Harry, was born in Maryland ca. 1850. By 1859 he lived in Baltimore, but moved to Georgetown, D.C., in 1860, where he exhibited a portrait at the Washington Art Association. In November 1860 he appeared in Charleston; no trace has been found of his subsequent career.

SEE: Sources cited under James Bogle, *Catalog of the Works of Art Comprising the Fourth Annual Exhibition of the Washington Art Association* (1860).

ROGER N. KIRKMAN

Bond, William Robert (*20 Aug. 1839–20 June 1922*), Confederate soldier and author, was born in Halifax, the only child of Dr. Robert Cannon Bond and his wife, Martha Long. Dr. Bond was a native of Raleigh and, after attending The University of North Carolina, was graduated in medicine from the University of Pennsylvania. He settled in Halifax to practice and was the last representative from the borough in the House of Commons in 1835. William R. Bond received an A.B. degree from The University of North Carolina in 1861. He entered the Confederate Army and was assigned to Company F of the Forty-third North Carolina Regiment. He was later aide-de-camp to General Junius Daniel and eventually attained the rank of captain. Gravely wounded at the Battle of Gettysburg, he was captured on retreat and imprisoned for the remainder of the war.

In the decades following the war, the question whether the North Carolinian James Pettigrew or the Virginian George Pickett had advanced the furthest on Gettysburg became a subject of great interest and debate. Bond wrote a pamphlet supporting the North Carolinian, entitled *Pickett or Pettigrew*. It was published in 1888 and attracted considerable notice at the time. Bond also wrote an excellent, concise account of Halifax County for *In the Coal and Iron Counties of North Carolina*, edited by Peter M. Hale and printed in Raleigh in 1883.

In 1872, Bond married Eliza, the daughter of Dr. Stuart Hall of Scotland Neck; they had no children. They resided at Albin, a fine plantation house in Scotland Neck Bond had inherited from his aunt Eliza Bond, the widow of Colin M. Clark. Bond and his wife were buried in Trinity Cemetery in Scotland Neck.

SEE: Walter Clark, ed., *Histories of the Several Regiments and Battalions from North Carolina in the Great War, 1861–1865*, 5 vols. (1901); D. L. Grant, *Alumni History of the University of North Carolina* (1924); Stuart Hall Smith and Claiborne T. Smith, Jr., *The History of Trinity Parish* (1955).

CLAIBORNE T. SMITH, JR.

Boner, John Henry (*31 Jan. 1845–6 Mar. 1903*), a southern poet whose technique and themes are suggestive of the poetry of Edgar Allan Poe, was born in Salem during the same year in which Poe achieved international fame with the publication of "The Raven." He was the youngest of the three sons of Thomas Boner and his wife, Phoebe Nading. The family home on Salt Street was restored by Old Salem, Inc., in 1952 and is open to visitors. Baptized in infancy and confirmed in the Moravian church during his youth, Boner was educated in the Salem Boys' School. As a tall lad, with expressive gray eyes, he developed a predilection for reading and for dreaming. He became a leader in the Salem Literary Society and, socially, was especially popular with the girls at the Salem Female Academy. His love lyrics were frequently suggestive of Poe's poems of unrequited love, ending with the death of a beautiful girl during the flower of her youth. Walking along the Yadkin River, he would notice the flush upon his companion's cheek (the fatal sign of consumption), reflected by the roses surrounding the lovers. Although a romantic throughout his lifetime, he extended his themes beyond those of love to include reflections on the vicissitudes of "mirth and tears" in life, patriotism for the South (in particular, North Carolina and Salem), and the victory of immortality over death.

At thirteen, Boner completed his formal schooling and became an apprentice to L. V. and E. T. Blum, Printers, where he received training that was of value to him in his later literary endeavors. When the Blums' newspaper, the *People's Press*, failed, Boner established the *Salem Observer*, which survived for a year. A Republican in politics, he availed himself of every opportunity to advance his political opinions in both newspapers. He was later associated with the Asheville *Pioneer* as an editor. Leaving Salem—"A little town with grassy ways/And shady streets, where life hung low"—he went to Raleigh, where he served in 1868 as a reading clerk of the North Carolina Constitutional Convention and, in 1869–70, as the chief clerk of the house of representatives. During his last year of service with the state government, he married Charlotte A. ("Lottie") Smith of Raleigh.

He and his wife then left for Washington, D.C., where, as an adherent of the Republican party, he was awarded a position in the Government Printing Office. In 1878 he became the president of the Columbia Typographical Union. With the return of the Democratic party to power during the Cleveland administration, he was discharged from the Washington appointment, which he had held for sixteen years, because of "offensive partisanship."

About the time of this reversal in his fortunes, Boner published his first volume of poems, *Whispering Pines* (1883). Recognizing Boner's genius, the poet and critic Edmund C. Stedman, upon hearing of his dismissal, invited him and his wife to come to New York. Through Stedman's influence, he found employment on the editorial staff of the *Century Dictionary*, and later he assisted Stedman with his *Library of American Literature*. Boner's career in New York also included such responsible assignments as literary editor of the *World*, member of the editorial staff of the *Standard Dictionary*, and editor of the *Literary Digest*. In a manner typical of Poe, Boner rashly resigned from the editorship of the *Literary Digest* following a policy dispute with the publishers.

In 1893, Boner moved to a small house, Cricket Lodge, which he had built on Staten Island. It was here that he wrote one of his widely known poems, "Poe's Cottage at Fordham," and advocated the establishment of a Poe Association to preserve Poe's cottage. Boner's health and fortunes declined during his residence at Staten Island, as had Poe's at Fordham. By 1900, through the efforts of his friends in Washington as well as his associates in the Authors Club in New York, Boner was restored to his former position in the Government Printing Office. His fragile constitution compelled him to relinquish his duties, however; and after raising funds for the publication of a small booklet entitled *Some New Poems*, he went

> Back to the Old North State,
> Back to the place of his birth,
> Back through the pines' colonnaded gate
> To the dearest spot on earth.

When he viewed the dilapidated condition of his boyhood home, he was inspired to write the lines of his famous poem "Broken and Desolate,"

> There are some scenes that we should not
> Revisit, though most dear they be—
> Some things we nevermore should see—
> Some places that should be forgot.

His health partially restored, Boner returned to his duties in the Government Printing Office during January 1903. But paralysis in his writing hand, bronchitis, and tuberculosis had come to stalk him. Fortified in spirit with the Moravian belief in a glorious resurrection and with his personal conviction that "there is a hope of heaven in every human breast," he anticipated without regret his death, which occurred in Washington. He was buried in the Congressional Cemetery. In one of his early poems he had expressed the desire to lie in peace in his native Salem. To carry out the poet's wish, his friend Marcus Benjamin formed the Boner Memorial Association, and sufficient funds were raised so that his body could be reinterred.

On Sunday, 11 Dec. 1904, in Salem's Home Moravian Church, Bishop Edward Rondthaler officiated at the memorial service, which was attended by a large congregation and distinguished by the presence of Governor Robert B. Glenn. Among the many dignitaries was Marcus Benjamin, editor of the *National Museum*, who delivered a tribute. William A. Blair read from Boner's poetry.

Soon after his death, the finest of Boner's writings were collected and published in *Boner's Lyrics* (1903). Complimentary copies were sent to the contributors of the Boner Memorial Association, and the remainder of the edition was sold for the benefit of the poet's widow, who spent her last days in Salem.

SEE: Edwin Anderson Alderman, Joel Chandler Harris, and Charles William Kent, eds., *Library of Southern Literature* (ca. 1908); Marcus Benjamin, *A Memorial of John Henry Boner* (1905); *Charlotte Observer*, 7 Jan. 1906; Ernest McNeill Eller, Introduction to *Whispering Pines* (1954); *North Carolina Authors* (1952).

EDWARD L. STOCKTON, JR.

Bonitz, August Heinrich Christian Julius (*22 Dec. 1841–7 Feb. 1891*), editor and publisher, was born in Zellerfeld, Hanover, Germany, the fourth child of Johann Heinrich Wilhelm Bonitz and Dorothea Louise Schalitz. His father had been superintendent of a silver and copper mine, the "Dorothea," in the fabled Harz Mountains of northern Germany, a position held by his father and grandfather before him.

Before his seventeenth birthday, Julius emigrated with his family from Bremen to the United States, arriving in Baltimore aboard the barkentine *Vieland* on 22 June 1858.

The newcomers hardly had time to adjust to their new environment before the Civil War erupted. For some unrecorded reason, Bonitz had developed a loyalty to the Southern cause, and for three years and eight months he served in the ranks of the Confederacy.

After the war, Bonitz settled in Goldsboro, where he

established a mercantile business. His venture was fairly prosperous until he purchased a sizeable farm near Goldsboro, when the combined operations brought disastrous financial consequences. According to his own account, his capital was reduced to the sum of five dollars realized from the sale of his watch.

Bonitz's next undertaking was the recruiting of contract labor to work in the naval stores industry then centered in the pine forests of the Carolinas. As funds became available he started a brickyard, but once again his business collapsed, when a cold rain (and a lack of firewood, which he could not afford) ruined a large kiln of two hundred thousand brick. With considerable ingenuity, he was able to trade his mountain of partly cured brick for the tangible assets of a defunct newspaper, the Goldsboro *Star*. He moved the press and type to an old printing office building, and shortly thereafter the *Daily Rough Notes* made an unheralded appearance on the Goldsboro scene.

The old Whigs and the old Democrats united in 1868 to form the Conservative party, as the Whigs objected to being called Democrats. Bonitz's *Daily Rough Notes* was solidly aligned behind the Conservatives, and he vehemently opposed the military despotism and black rule of the radical Republicans. During the election period he was joined in his newspaper enterprise by Major William A. Hearne and Captain Swift Galloway, a pair of like-minded acquaintances. Despite their efforts, the scalawag, carpetbagger, and black elements that had combined to support a fellow editor, William W. Holden, were able to defeat Conservative Thomas Ashe in the race for governor.

Following the election the paper's name was changed from the *Rough Notes* to the *Messenger*. The triumvirate of associates did not endure for long: after a few weeks Hearne and Galloway withdrew, leaving Bonitz in sole control.

Keeping the *Messenger* viable was a struggle that demanded the utmost effort from Bonitz during the chaotic era of Reconstruction. He needed a twenty-four hour notice to produce even one dollar of his printer's overdue wages. And an even greater calamity lay ahead: on the night of 4 Sept. 1869, a fire raged through the business district of Goldsboro, leaving most of it in smoking ruins. The office and the equipment of the *Messenger* were destroyed completely. But Bonitz was far from defeated. Salvaging a handful of type and borrowing an amateur hand press, he brought out an "extra" two days after the fire in which the conflagration was described in all its spectacular detail. His "shop" was the open air beneath the boughs of an old sweet gum tree, with Bonitz setting the type and his foreman, W. H. Collins, operating the press. Readers gave him support by paying for their subscriptions in advance, and after a lapse of only four days, the *Messenger* resumed publication as a weekly, and occasionally semiweekly, paper.

Bonitz continued to publish his paper almost single-handedly, reporting, editing, soliciting advertising and doing other necessary chores. Gradually, as the *Messenger* prospered, he was able to lighten his labors by additions to his staff. Thus he was able to find the time to publish a sixty-eight-page booklet with a title almost as long: "The Murder of the Worley Family in Wayne County, N.C., and the Arrest, Trial and Execution of Noah Cherry, Robert Thompson and Harris Atkinson."

In June of 1887, with the encouragement of businessmen of Wilmington, he moved and became editor and publisher of the *Wilmington Messenger* in what was then the chief city of the state. Continuing his fervent support of the Democratic party in his editorial columns, he also advocated strongly the goal of wide public education, the achievement of which was yet some years in the future.

Bonitz's health had begun to fail before his move to Wilmington, and he died there. He was first buried in Wilmington, but his body was later moved to Willowdale Cemetery in Goldsboro, where it lies under an impressive and lengthily inscribed monument.

Bonitz was married on 22 Apr. 1873, in Lynchburg, Va., to Delia Alice Berndt, who was born 3 Jan. 1852 and died 23 Feb. 1931 in Oxford. They had four children.

SEE: John H. Bonitz, Jr., *Some Bonitz Families* (1973); Jerome Dowd, *Sketches of Prominent Living North Carolinians* (1888); Hugh T. Lefler, *History of North Carolina*, 4 vols. (1956); Weeks Scrapbook (North Carolina Collection, University of North Carolina, Chapel Hill).

WILLIAM UNDERWOOD

Bonn, Johann Jacob (5 Apr. 1733–31 Oct. 1781), physician, justice of the peace, sheriff, and clerk of court, was born in Skippack, Pa., to Mennonite parents. When Jacob was thirteen they each joined the Moravian church and moved to Bethlehem, Pa.

At first, Jacob was apprenticed to a tailor, but the confinement proved too much for his health. He then began to study medicine and surgery with Doctor John Matthew Otto and successfully completed an apprenticeship in 1758.

In November 1758 he visited Bethabara. Because the appointed congregational physician was away in Pennsylvania at that time, he assisted with the medical duties of the colony during his visit. In the spring of 1759 he returned to Bethlehem, but he visited the Bethabara colony again in June 1759, accompanying an official party. Shortly after his arrival, the crowded village was struck by a typhus fever epidemic, in which the congregational physician, Doctor Kalberlahn, lost his life. Bonn was appointed interim physician for the colony and functioned in this capacity until the permanent replacement, Doctor August Schubert, arrived to relieve him in September 1760. Bonn then returned to Bethlehem, Pa., and continued his association with Doctor Otto until July 1766. At that time he was called again to Bethabara as the congregational physician for Wachovia, a position he held commendably until his early death.

Bonn showed promise of executive ability, in addition to his medical talent. Shortly after his appointment, he was included in the welcoming party for the visit of Governor Tryon. The governing board selected him to be recommended for justice of the peace, and he received official appointment in Rowan County in April 1769. When Surry County was formed from Rowan in 1771, he became a justice in the new county; except for a brief period during the war, he was reappointed each year during his remaining years in Wachovia. The records indicate that this political office usurped at least 50 percent of his time. He was continually on the move visiting the six different villages in Wachovia: one day he would be found in one village collecting taxes, writing a will, performing a marriage ceremony, or acting as executor of an estate; and the next day he would be many miles away attending court in the county seat, which would detain him for several days. He appeared to be revered in his executive capacity and carried out his duties to the best of his convictions.

During the war years, the Moravian brethren, who did not believe in taking up arms, were in a precarious position. They were suspected by both the Tories and the Continental parties. Before the war, the deeds for the land in Wachovia were assigned to a church executive in England, and this was probably one reason for the frequent accusation of Toryism. When the brethren refused to bear arms in 1774 or to take the Oath of Allegiance to the state, there was a serious threat that they would lose their land and be forced to leave Wachovia. In 1775, Bonn was subjected to severe restrictions in the exercise of his legal office in the county, but he nonetheless continued to represent his people in legal matters, appeared at court, petitioned the assembly, and performed admirably in dealing with the problems of exorbitant penalty taxes for refusal of military service. In February 1778 he was appointed chairman of the county court but declined to serve: there were too many unsolved problems concerning military service and the Moravian brethren. Partly because of his patient persistence, the assembly rewrote the Oath of Allegiance in 1779. All the Moravian brethren took the revised affirmation to the state; their legal privileges were restored, the deeds for the land in Wachovia were assigned to the local administrator, and thereby both loss of land and expulsion from North Carolina were averted.

Bonn was described as a good man, and appears to have been successful in his medical practice. In 1760 a man came to Bethabara with an Indian arrow piercing his body through; Bonn removed the arrow and the patient recovered from this serious wound. If there were problems requiring help, he did not fail to avail himself of capable assistance. In April of 1781, for example, he had an elderly patient who needed a leg amputation. He called on a surgeon from Lord Cornwallis's army and assisted him in the operation. Bonn had a well-organized nursing service in the town of Salem, training midwives and apprentices to assist him with the problems of caring for the sick and disabled. He was quite astute in not taking sides and used good judgment when there were controversial problems. In 1780, when actual warfare was in the neighborhood, he had the responsibility of treating the wounded from both factions. He was never accused of bias and was shown gratitude for the care of the wounded and sick soldiers of both sides.

The years 1780 and 1781 were disastrous years of the war for Wachovia. Sick and wounded soldiers in several of the villages required many visits and much care. In January of 1781 a small hospital was set up in one of the houses in Salem, and the wounded were nursed there by the local people from January through April. In February, a Continental Army field hospital requested a building in which to set up temporary quarters. Two families were moved out, and a hospital occupied the vacated building for two days. Immediately afterward, Cornwallis's troops arrived and camped on both sides of Salem, one to the northwest in Bethania and the next to the southeast in Friedland. During this trying period, a smallpox epidemic was raging to the south in Friedberg. There was stealing and plunder in each village, and Bonn's much-needed horse was stolen. All this trouble came to a climax in October of 1781. Bonn arose on the morning of 31 Oct. with a severe headache. By 10:00 A.M. he had expired from what was described as apoplexy. He was buried 2 Nov. in God's Acre in Salem.

Bonn was married in November 1766 to Anna Maria Brendel. He taught her to be a successful midwife, and she practiced her art for many years in the villages of Wachovia. They had three children, two girls who died in early childhood, and a son, Johann Jacob, who followed in his father's footsteps to become a justice of the peace.

SEE: Adelaide L. Fries, ed., *Records of the Moravians in North Carolina*, vols. 1–3 (1922–26); Memoir of Johann Jacob Bond (MS, Moravian Archives, Winston-Salem); Wachovia Church Book (MS, Moravian Archives, Winston-Salem).

LAURA M. MOSLEY

Bonner, Herbert Covington (*16 May 1891–7 Nov. 1965*), congressman, was born in Washington, Beaufort County, the son of Hannah Selby Hare and Macon Herbert Bonner, both of families that had resided in the coastal area since colonial times. He attended Warrenton Academy from 1906 to 1909 and then traveled small towns as a snuff salesman. He served overseas in World War I as a sergeant in the 322nd Infantry, Eighty-first Division, and after the armistice attended officers' training school at Longres, France.

In 1921, Bonner went to Washington as an aide to his neighbor, newly elected Congressman Lindsay C. Warren. In 1940 he was elected as a Democrat to the congressional seat representing North Carolina's First District, when Warren was named comptroller-general of the United States. Bonner served for nearly twenty-five years, until his death from cancer. He was chairman of the House Marine and Fisheries Committee, where he earned the title of "father" of the first nuclear-powered merchant ship, the *Savannah*. His legislative interests were directed toward subjects of concern to his sprawling district—Coast Guard appropriations, roads, navigation projects, and farm subsidies. While not an innovator, he backed such projects as establishment of Cape Hatteras National Seashore and the social programs of the Roosevelt and Kennedy administrations. During World War II he headed a committee that investigated war profiteering; he was an original member of the House Un-American Activities Committee but voted against making the committee a permanent one. Bonner was popular with colleagues and constituents and seldom faced serious political opposition. His extensive congressional correspondence and other materials were given to the Southern Historical Collection at The University of North Carolina at Chapel Hill.

Bonner, an Episcopalian, was married to Eva Hassell Hackney of Washington, who survived him. He was buried in Oakdale Cemetery just a few hundred yards from his birthplace. A portrait of him by Mabel Pugh hangs in the committee room of the Merchant Marine and Fisheries Committee, Cannon House Office Building, Washington, D.C.

SEE: *Biog. Dir. Am. Cong.* (1971); *Congressional Record*, House of Representatives Proceedings, 10 Jan. 1966; *New York Times*, 8 Nov. 1965; Raleigh *News and Observer*, 8 Nov. 1965.

ROY PARKER, JR.

Bonnet, Stede (*hanged 10 Dec. 1718*), army officer, planter, and "Gentleman Pirate," was said to have come from a good English family. Of his early life little is known, but he was considered to be a "gentleman that has had the Advantage of a liberal Education" and was "generally esteemed a Man of Letters." He gained the rank of Major in either the British army or the militia.

He went to Barbados as a sugar planter, prospered, and enjoyed the company of the best society in Bridgetown. Without warning, this seemingly respectable citizen suddenly turned pirate, leading his neighbors to feel that he had suffered a mental derangement (although some thought his disaffection was the result of the nagging tongue of a shrewish wife).

In early 1717, Bonnet, unlike most pirates who stole their ships, purchased a fast sloop that he named the *Revenge*. He paid the members of his crew out of his own pocket. Capturing ships off the Virginia and New England coasts, he established a tradition of burning every vessel from Barbados, although he often released those of a different registry after stripping them of their cargo. Sailing to the southward to the Bay of Honduras, Bonnet met up with the noted Edward Teach, better known as Blackbeard. Teach made Bonnet a virtual prisoner aboard his ship, the *Queen Anne's Revenge*, while placing one of his own men in command of the *Revenge*.

After cruising the sea lanes between the Bahamas and the Carolinas, the pirate flotilla put into North Carolina's Topsail Inlet. Here Teach and Bonnet parted company, and Bonnet traveled to Bath to seek the king's mercy under the Royal Proclamation of 5 Jan. 1718. Governor Charles Eden granted him permission to sail to the Virgin Islands to secure a commission as a privateer. Returning to Topsail Inlet, Bonnet discovered that Teach had abandoned the *Revenge* and marooned twenty-five of the crew on a sand bar. After a futile pursuit of Teach, Bonnet returned to pirating, changing his name to "Captain Thomas" and that of his ship to the *Royal James*.

After capturing a number of vessels, the *Royal James* began to leak badly. The ship was run into a waterway off the Cape Fear River so that her hull might be scraped clean of barnacles. The crew of a captured vessel were allowed to go free, and they spread the word that a pirate ship was careened in the lower Cape Fear. Captain William Rhett, receiver-general of South Carolina, had led two sloops out from Charleston in search of the notorious pirate Charles Vane. Informed of the ship in the Cape Fear, Rhett steered there on the chance that it might be Vane. In the afternoon of 28 Sept., in sight of the pirate sloop, Rhett's vessels ran aground. The following morning the South Carolina sloops were afloat. After the ensuing six-hour fight, Bonnet surrendered, but only after Rhett promised to intercede with the authorities on his behalf.

On 25 Oct., three days before his scheduled trial, Bonnet escaped and hid on Sullivan's Island in Charleston harbor. He was recaptured by Rhett. On 25 Oct. 1718, the twenty-nine members of his crew were tried and convicted, and on 8 Nov. they were hanged and buried below the high water mark at the edge of the marsh.

Bonnet was brought to trial two days later, and on 12 Nov. Judge Nicholas Trott condemned him to hang. On 10 Dec. 1718 Bonnet was executed at White Point. He was buried at the edge of the swamp alongside the bodies of the men he had led to their doom. Although sometimes termed the "Gentleman Pirate," Bonnet had proved not very successful in either capacity.

SEE: Philip Gosse, *The History of Piracy*, 3rd ed. (1946); Captain Charles Johnson, *A General History of the Pyrates*, ed. Manuel Schonhorn (1972); Patrick Pringle, *Jolly Roger* (1933); Hugh F. Rankin, *The Golden Age of Piracy* (1969).

HUGH F. RANKIN

Boon, Ratliff (*18 Jan. 1781–20 Nov. 1844*), representative from Indiana, was born in Franklin County. Boon moved with his parents to Warren County, Ky., attended public schools, and then moved to Danville, Ky., where he learned the gunsmith's trade. He married Deliah Anderson and with his father-in-law went to Indiana in 1807 or 1809. He bought land about two miles west of what is now the city of Boonsville, which was named for him when it was made the seat of Warrick County, Ind., in 1818. Boon lived on a farm three miles west of Boonsville until 1836, rearing a family of five boys and five girls. In 1836 he moved to Boonsville.

Boon was appointed the first treasurer of Warrick County upon its organization in 1813. In 1816 he became his county's first representative, serving in the first and second assemblies. In the third assembly, in 1818, he was a senator. Before his term as senator expired, he was elected lieutenant governor of Indiana. Before his second term as lieutenant governor expired, he had been elected to the Nineteenth Congress as a Jacksonian Democrat. Upon the resignation of Governor Jonathan Jennings Boon became, for a brief term (12 Sept.–5 Dec. 1822), the second governor of Indiana. He was again elected lieutenant governor in August 1822 and served until 30 Jan. 1824, when he resigned to become a candidate for the Twentieth Congress.

In 1826, Boon ran for election as U.S. senator to the Twentieth Congress but was defeated by O. H. Smith. He was, however, elected to the Twenty-first Congress and to the four succeeding congresses (4 Mar. 1829–3 Mar. 1839). At the time of his defeat, he retired from Congress and moved from Indiana to Pike County, Mo. Here he became a vehement and unsuccessful opponent of Thomas H. Benton, a dominant figure in Missouri politics at the time. Boon died at his home in Louisiana, Mo., and interment followed in the Riverview Cemetery there.

Boon was a typical pioneer in the early days of Indiana. He had little education but was a man of strong common sense. He held a long list of political offices over twenty-six years. During his time in Indiana, he helped organize the Jacksonian Democratic party, and during his official career he was its outspoken champion. He stood stoutly for the rights of the common people, even in the face of the eloquence of Clay and Calhoun. Little can be said of Boon's career in politics; he was entirely outclassed in Congress. When not in political office, he worked on his farm and kept up his political contacts.

SEE: *Biog. Dir. Am. Cong.* (1971); George S. Cottman, *Indiana* (1925); Logan Esarey, ed., *Indiana Historical Collections*, vol. 12, *Messages and Papers of Jonathan Jennings, Ratliff Boon and William Hendricks* ([portrait], 1924); *Nat. Cyc. Am. Biog.*, vol. 13 (1906); *Who Was Who in America, 1607–1896.*

AMANDA B. BURTON

Boone, Daniel *(1734–16 Sept. 1820)*, hunter and trusted leader, was several times a member of the Virginia legislature and a syndic (commander) of the Spanish Femme Osage District, now part of Missouri. Boone lived more years in North Carolina than in any other territory or colony. He was born of Quaker parents in Oley Township, present Berks County, Pa. Squire Boone, his father, was a native of Bradninch in Devon, England. His mother, Sarah Morgan Boone, was of Welsh ancestry.

Brought up in frontier Pennsylvania, the boy Daniel learned to be an expert hunter. When his family migrated southward to Virginia with the stream of settlers in about 1750, Daniel had probably preceded them on hunting expeditions. Later Squire and Sarah Boone moved their family of eleven children to North Carolina, where Squire became a justice of the peace when Rowan County was created in 1753.

Daniel Boone, twenty-one years old, served as a wagoner in Edward Braddock's campaign against the French and Indians in 1755, after which he married Rebecca Bryan. During the ensuing years he served as a ranger defending frontier North Carolina against Indian attacks; later he hunted throughout Western North Carolina and what became Kentucky and Tennessee. Eight children were born to the Boones before the family left North Carolina for Kentucky. In 1775, Boone arranged a treaty between Richard Henderson and his Transylvania Company and the Cherokee Indians, whereby Henderson purchased most of Kentucky and Tennessee from the Cherokees. Boone and thirty ax-men cut a road along the Warriors' Path, called the Wilderness Road; led settlers; and helped establish the frontier station, which was called Boonesboro. During the American Revolution it was dramatically defended against Shawnee attack through the planning and leadership of Boone.

His versatility was evidenced in many ways after the Revolutionary War. Indian attacks against Kentucky did not cease with the peace treaty of 1783; Boone arranged for a cessation of hostilities and an exchange of prisoners in 1787. He was engaged throughout the 1780s as a surveyor, storekeeper, and member of the Virginia legislature from Kentucky. Because of his failure to record his land claims and those of his clients, most of their claims were disallowed. Boone became dissatisfied and removed his family first to Kanawha County, Va., in 1789, and then to Charleston, which district he represented in the Virginia legislature and as lieutenant colonel-in-chief of the militia.

At age sixty-five, Boone led other relatives and friends to the Spanish territory of Louisiana in a portion of the present Missouri. He was offered 9,350 acres of land for inducing one hundred families to settle in the Femme Osage District and was appointed syndic, or administrator, of the district, with jurisdiction over civil and military affairs. When the United States purchased Louisiana, the U.S. land commissioners deprived him of his land because he had not cleared the required number of acres. A special act of Congress in 1814 restored 850 acres to him, and he lived in this district until his death. His two sons, Nathan and Daniel Morgan, became prominent in territorial and state politics.

SEE: John Bakeless, *Daniel Boone* (1939); Draper MSS (State Historical Society of Wisconsin, Madison); Ella Hazel Atterbury Spraker, *The Boone Family* (1922); John J. Van Noppen and Ina W. Van Noppen, *Daniel Boone* (1966).

INA W. VAN NOPPEN

Boone, Squire *(6 Dec. 1696–2 Jan. 1765)*, pioneer settler in Western Piedmont North Carolina and father of Daniel Boone, was born in Devonshire, England. His father was George Boone III; his mother was Mary Milton Maugridge. The family were members of the Society of Friends. George and Sarah Boone immigrated to Pennsylvania in 1717; their son, Squire, and another son and daughter had probably preceded them.

In 1720, Squire Boone married Sarah Morgan and moved to Bucks County, Pa., where he worked as a weaver, blacksmith, and farmer. In 1730 he and his wife purchased 250 acres in Oley Township, in present Berks County, Pa. Nine of their eleven children were born there, including Daniel in 1734. Boone was a trustee and overseer of the Oley Meeting.

On 11 Apr. 1750, Squire and Sarah Boone sold their 158-acre farm, and on 1 May 1750, they set out for North Carolina. Several factors seem to have influenced the move. The oldest children, Sarah and Israel, "married out," that is, married non-Quakers, and Boone was reprimanded by the church for allowing the marriages. The Boones were acquainted with the Morgan Bryan family, and with the Willcocksons, Grants, and others who migrated to the Yadkin River. A son, Jonathan Boone, had married Mary Carter, daughter of James Carter, founder of Salisbury, and had settled in the fork of the Yadkin and South Yadkin rivers in southern Davie County. Too, there was fertile and cheap land and abundant game available in North Carolina. Although Sarah Boone brought a certificate "to Friends in Virginia, Carolina and elsewhere," there is no evidence that the Boones united with a Quaker meeting; several became Baptists.

The Boone family may have "stopped over" in Virginia for perhaps a year or more, a frequent practice of migrating families. Squire Boone probably reached the Yadkin River in late 1751 or early 1752 and may have lived first at the site of Boone's Cave in Davidson County. A cave is there today on a high bluff well above the Yadkin River, and a replica cabin has been built at the site. One tradition holds that the Boones used this cave for shelter while building their cabin; by another the cabin was a fishing and hunting cabin used by the family. There are no known deed records to prove ownership by Squire or Daniel Boone to any land in Davidson County.

On 13 Apr. 1753, Boone received from Lord Granville a grant of "640 acres on South side of Grants otherwise Licking Creek." Sixteen known deeds drawn between 1753 and 1832 designate tracts of land on the present Elisha (formerly Grants or Licking) Creek and Dutchman Creek, in Davie County, as adjoining the Squire Boone grant or containing parts of it. A map based on research of deeds and grants from Mocksville eastward locates the 640-acre Boone grant at the confluence of Elisha and Dutchman creeks. The tract was on the west side of Dutchman, and most of it was on the south side of Elisha—one small part is across the creek. This is the property that Squire and Sarah Boone conveyed to Squire, Jr., on 12 Oct. 1759 and that was sold by him to Henry Baker and John Felker in Sept. 1767.

On 29 Dec. 1753, Boone received another Granville grant of 640 acres on both sides of Bear Creek. The tract, designated as in the Parish of St. Luke's, Rowan County, is two miles west of Mocksville in Davie County. On 12 Oct. 1759, Squire and Sarah Boone conveyed this land to Daniel Boone. In a deed dated 21 Feb. 1764, Daniel and Rebecca Bryan Boone sold their 640 acres on "Bair Creek" to Aaron Van Cleve. Subsequent deeds unmistakably trace this land to the present owners.

One of the earliest settlers in the Forks of the Yadkin, Squire Boone was prominent in Rowan County, formed in 1753. He was related by marriage to the Bryans, Willcocksons, and James Carter and was acquainted with others from Pennsylvania, Maryland, and Virginia who had migrated to the Yadkin River area and claimed extensive and valuable landholdings. He served as a justice of the first Rowan County Court in June 1753. Court minutes show him to have been a very faithful and active member through the year 1757. He served as a juror and for at least one year secured a license to operate a "Publick House at his own Plantation."

Apparently the danger of Indian raids on the frontier settlements in the Forks of the Yadkin area and westward during the French and Indian War led the Boones to convey their lands to Squire, Jr., and Daniel and move to Maryland in 1759. The *Records of the Moravians* note that perhaps half the people left the area because the Indians kept the land in terror by robbing and murdering. Too, civil strife, later to become the Regulator movement, was

beginning, and resentment was bitter in the back country over the dominance by the east in the government. Extant records suggest the Boones (and Bryans) were not Regulators, but most of their neighbors were.

The fact that Squire and Sarah Boone disposed of their land before they moved to Maryland would strongly indicate that they did not plan to return. However, they did return in the spring of 1762, on horseback, it is said. It is thought that they lived at the Bear Creek site, the property of Daniel Boone. Whether Squire Boone was living there at the time of his death is not known. One record states that he died at his residence at the Buffalo Licks. Both maps and extant records refer to licks on Elisha, Cedar, Buffalo, and Dutchman creeks in the vicinity of the first Squire Boone grant; Daniel had sold the Bear Creek property in February 1764, but Squire, Jr., did not sell the Elisha Creek site until September 1767.

Boone was buried at Joppa Cemetery, then called Burying Ground Ridge, in Mocksville, now on Highway 601. The inscription on the soapstone grave marker reads: "Squire Boone departed this life they sixty ninth year of his age in thay year of our Lord 1765 Geneiary tha 2." Sarah Morgan Boone died twelve years later and was buried beside her husband.

SEE: L. C. Draper Collection (State Historical Society of Wisconsin, Madison); Adelaide L. Fries, ed., *Records of the Moravians in North Carolina*, 8 vols. (1922–54); Martin Collection (Davie County Library, Mocksville); McCubbins Papers (Rowan County Library, Salisbury); R. W. Ramsey, *Carolina Cradle* (1964); J. K. Rouse, *North Carolina Picadillo* (1966); Ella Hazel Atterbury Spraker, *The Boone Family* (1922); James W. Wall, *History of Davie County* (1969).

JAMES W. WALL

Borland, Solon (*11 Aug. 1811–31 Jan. 1864*), U.S. senator, diplomat, attorney, physician, Confederate general, and journalist, was born in Nansemond County, Va. In about 1818, his parents, Dr. Thomas Borland, a native of Scotland, and Harriet Godwin Borland, moved with their three sons to Murfreesboro, where Solon was to spend his next sixteen years. Solon was educated at Hertford Academy in Murfreesboro. He gained a brief notoriety in 1827 when, following an altercation with Murfreesboro merchant James Morgan, Solon and an older brother attacked Morgan with a knife and almost killed him.

In 1831, Borland was an officer in a Murfreesboro cavalry company that took part in the suppression of Nat Turner's Revolt in nearby Southampton County, Va. Again Borland's name was before the public when he and members of his detachment accused members of another detachment of robbing the bodies of slain Negroes in violation of the rights of the Negroes' owners. At a July fourth celebration near Murfreesboro in 1831, Borland, not yet twenty years of age, was one of several orators of the day.

In 1836, Borland went to Philadelphia for medical training; he practiced briefly after that in Virginia as a dentist and later practiced as a physician. A monograph he published in Arkansas in 1845, entitled *The Milk Sickness in Humans, or the Trimbles in Animals*, is thought to have been the first scientific work published in that state. Previously, however, he had become active in journalism. His first journalistic venture is said to have been the founding of a newspaper at Portsmouth, Va., probably in the early 1830s. In 1839 he became editor of the Memphis (Tenn.) *Western World* and subsequently held editorial positions in Kentucky and in Little Rock, Ark.

Borland was a presidential elector in Arkansas in 1845 and in the following year raised a cavalry company there for service in the Mexican War. Appointed to the U.S. Senate following the resignation of A. H. Sevier in 1848, Borland won election in his own right in 1849 and served until his own resignation in 1853. He was appointed in the same year minister to Central America and, during his term, was a principal in the circumstances leading to the destruction of Greytown in 1854 by the U.S.S. *Cyane*. Borland was offered the governorship of the Territory of New Mexico but declined in order to practice law in Little Rock.

In the spring of 1861, prior to the secession of Arkansas from the Union, Borland organized a body of troops and took possession of Fort Smith for the Confederacy. He afterward became colonel of the Third Arkansas Cavalry, a unit he personally recruited. He died while on service in Texas in 1864.

Borland was married three times: to Mrs. Huldah Wright of Suffolk, Va., by whom he had two sons; to a Mrs. Hunt of Tennessee; and to Mary J. Melbourne of Little Rock, by whom he had another son and two daughters.

SEE: *DAB*, vol. 2 (1929); *Memphis Arkansas and Ouachita Christian Advocate*, 9 June 1859; *Nat. Cyc. Am. Biog.*, vol. 4 (1899 [portrait]); William D. Valentine, Diary for 10 May 1848 (Southern Historical Collection, University of North Carolina, Chapel Hill).

THOMAS C. PARRAMORE

Bosley, Harold Augustus (19 Feb. 1907–20 Jan. 1975), clergyman, theological educator and author, was born in Burchard, Nebr., the son of Augustus Merrill and Effie Sinclair Bosley. Following his preparatory schooling in Burchard, he entered Nebraska Wesleyan University, Lincoln, in 1926 and was graduated with a B.A. degree in 1930. He then went to The University of Chicago, was graduated with a B.D. degree in 1932, and received the degree of Ph.D. in Christian Studies in 1933.

His first year out of Chicago, he was director of Religious Activities at Iowa State University, Ames; he went from there in 1934 to the University of Northern Iowa (then known as Teachers College), Cedar Falls. For the five years he was there, Bosley was in great demand as a preacher and lecturer, and he early confessed that preaching was a prime interest of his professional life. He was then called to the pastorate of the prestigious Mount Vernon Place Methodist Church, Baltimore, where he served for nine years (1938–47).

In addition to his ministry in Baltimore, Bosley was a regular preacher at many conferences of college students. He was stated lecturer at the Pacific School of Theology, Berkeley, Calif.(the Earl Foundation Lectures), in 1940; the Pastors' Institute, Chicago, in 1943; Rochester-Colgate Divinity School, Rochester, N.Y. (Ayer Foundation Lecturer), in 1944; the Pastors' School, Florida Southern College, Lakeland, in 1946; Westminster Theological Seminary, Westminster, Md. (visiting professor of Christian ethics), in summer 1945; and Crozer Theological Seminary, Chester, Pa. (visiting lecturer in the philosophy of religion), in 1947. His preaching and three published books in religious thought resulted in an invitation to Duke University in 1947 to become dean of the Divinity School. His three years there were busy ones for Bosley. Added to his administrative duties, he shared the title of Preacher to the University with two associates, Dr. Franklin Simpson Hickman and Dr. James T. Cleland; gave the Russell Foundation Lectures at Tufts University, Medford, Mass., in 1948; and produced another distinguished

volume that received wide praise and established him as a definitive scholar in Christian thinking.

In early 1950 he was invited to the pulpit and pastorate of the famous First Methodist Church, Evanston, Ill., to succeed Dr. Ernest Freemont Tittle. During his twelve years in Evanston, Bosley continued both his internal and external ministries. He visited Carnahan Seminaries and Schools in Latin America in 1951; lectured and preached on a special mission to Japan and Korea in 1955; gave the Mendenhall Lectures at DePauw University, Greencastle, Ind., in 1957; and gave the Willson Lectures at McMurray College, Abilene, Tex., in 1959.

Bosley published six more books before 1962, when he was called to be senior minister of Christ Church, Methodist, New York City, succeeding Dr. Ralph W. Sockman. Bosley spent twelve years in that important pulpit, retiring in June 1974. Several more books and numerous important lectureships and preaching missions occupied the final years of his expansive and influential ministry.

Along the way many recognitions were bestowed on Bosley, including several honorary degrees: D.D., from Nebraska Wesleyan University, Lincoln, in 1943, from Northwestern University, Evanston, Ill., in 1950, and from Manchester College, North Manchester, Ind., in 1964; Doctor of Sacred Theology, from Ripon College, Ripon, Wisc., in 1953; and Doctor of Humane Letters, from Cornell University, Ithaca, N.Y., in 1953.

Among Bosley's best known books are, *The Quest for Religious Certainty* (1939); *The Philosophical Heritage of the Christian Faith* (1944); *On Final Ground* (1946); *Main Issues Confronting Christendom* (1948, a choice of the Religious Book-of-the-Month Club); *A Firm Faith for Today* (1950, a selection of the Pulpit Book Club); *The Church Militant* (1952); *Preaching on Controversial Issues* (1953); *What Did the World Council Say to You?* (1955); *Sermons on the Psalms* (1956); *Sermons on Genesis* (1958); *Doing What is Christian* (1960); *He Spoke to Them in Parables* (1963); and *The Mind of Christ* (1966). He also wrote numerous articles and book reviews in such journals as *Christendom* ("The Church Examines Itself," 1938) and *Religion and Life* ("The Intellectuals' Crisis in Religion," 1940).

Bosley was a member of the Association of Methodist Theological Schools (president, 1949); Board of Trustees, Morgan State College, Baltimore; the Merchants Club of Baltimore; the American Philosophical Association; and the Fellowship of Reconciliation. In all his places of residence, he made himself an active member of the community and involved himself in numerous civic affairs. He was especially active during his three years at Duke.

Bosley was married 21 July 1928 to Margaret Marie Dahlston; they had five children: Paul Shailer, Sidney Stanton, Norman Keith, Diane Marie, and David Merrill. During his pastorate at Christ Church, the family lived in Bronxville, but upon his retirement they established residence at Beach Haven Terrace, N.J., where Bosley died.

SEE: Data Files (Office of Information Services, Duke University, Durham); *Who Was Who in America, 1607–1896*.

C. SYLVESTER GREEN

Bost, Annie Kizer (27 Oct. 1883–6 Sept. 1961), commissioner of the North Carolina State Board of Charities and Public Welfare and an active participant in women's clubs, civic work, and the Democratic party, was born in Enochville, the daughter of Robert Graham and Cora Belk Shipman Kizer. Her father was superintendent of the Rowan County public schools. Mrs. Bost attended Salisbury public schools and private schools before her entry into the Women's College of North Carolina, where she was graduated in 1903.

After graduation, she taught in the public schools of Salisbury until her marriage in 1909 to William Thomas Bost, a newspaper reporter from Salisbury. She and her husband settled in Raleigh in 1912, where he soon became and served as the Raleigh correspondent for the *Greensboro Daily News* for thirty-seven years. The Bosts had two sons, William Thomas, Jr., and John Shipman.

In Raleigh, Mrs. Bost became active in civic affairs and club work. She was a trustee of Olivia Raney Library beginning in 1920. She was president of the Raleigh Woman's Club, the largest in the state, from 1921 to 1923, and participated in the North Carolina Federation of Women's Clubs, holding the post of state executive secretary from 1927 to 1930.

In 1930, when Kate Burr Johnson resigned as commissioner of the State Board of Charities and Public Welfare, Governor O. Max Gardner, a close friend of W. T. Bost, appointed Mrs. Bost commissioner. She therefore presided over the welfare program in North Carolina during the years of New Deal transition into a major welfare establishment. In that critical period she fought successfully to have the new federal welfare programs incorporated into the existing welfare department. She continued in the post until 1944, gaining a national reputation as one of the few women state welfare directors in the United States.

Mrs. Bost became a charter member of the American Public Welfare Association when it was founded in 1930. An active member of the North Carolina Conference for Social Service, she served as president in 1937–38. She was vice-chairman of the National Council of State Public Welfare Administrators in 1941–42.

After her retirement from the welfare administration, she continued to serve in a public role. Governor Joseph M. Broughton, Jr., appointed her to the North Carolina Unemployment Compensation Commission (now the Employment Security Commission), where she served from 1944 to 1949. She edited the *North Carolina Clubwoman* from 1951 to 1954.

Among her other services and distinctions, Mrs. Bost was a delegate to the Democratic National Convention in 1944, a trustee of the Women's College, state chairman of Tuberculosis Seal sales in North Carolina in 1956, and a member of the executive board of the state legislative council. She received an LL.D. from Women's College in 1942. A building at the Hoffman School for Boys was named in her honor in 1955, and a scholarship in her name was established at The University of North Carolina.

Mrs. Bost was a charter member and active participant in the Holy Trinity Lutheran Church of Raleigh, where her funeral was held. She was interred in Oakwood Cemetery of Raleigh.

SEE: Carl Goerch, *Characters . . . Always Characters* (1945); Robert C. Lawrence, *Here in Carolina* (1939); Thomas S. Morgan, "A Step toward Altruism" (Ph.D. diss., University of North Carolina, 1969); North Carolina Association of County Superintendents of Public Welfare, *Leaders in North Carolina's Public Welfare Program* (1949); *North Carolina Manual* (1943); William S. Powell, ed., *North Carolina Lives* (1962); Raleigh *News and Observer*, 16 and 20 Feb. 1944, 7 Sept. 1961; Harriette

Hammer Walker, *Busy North Carolina Women* (1931).

THOMAS S. MORGAN

Bost, William Thomas ("Tom") (2 Jan. 1878–13 Sept. 1951), long-time columnist for the *Greensboro Daily News*, "Boswell to the state government," and one of the most widely known political reporters in the state's history, was born on a farm at South River, eight miles north of Salisbury. He was one of eleven children of a Confederate veteran who had ridden with Jeb Stuart. The South River community into which he was born had a public school term of only six weeks, but Bost and other community children attended a nine-month school term supported by the people of the local community, although Bost later recalled that the people of the community were "utterly moneyless." He passed entrance examinations (required because he did not have a high school diploma) and entered The University of North Carolina in 1898, but he remained at the university only two and a half years.

On 1 Jan. 1901, Bost began his life's work by becoming a reporter on the Salisbury *Truth-Index*, a morning daily, at a salary of six dollars a week. Thirteen weeks later the paper folded, however, and Bost returned to the family farm. He reentered journalism on a part-time basis in 1904, working for the *Salisbury Post*. In 1905 the *Charlotte Observer* placed Bost at the head of its Salisbury bureau, and three years later he moved to Durham as a reporter for the *Durham Herald*. In 1912 he moved to Raleigh as city editor of the *News and Observer*, but he found the desk job too confining and, on 1 Sept. 1914, became Raleigh correspondent for the *Greensboro Daily News*, a position he held for thirty-seven years.

As a political reporter, Bost had few peers. His daily column "Among Us Tar Heels," a wide-ranging commentary, attracted and held a large audience. For thirty years he was recognized as the dean of capitol reporters; and with each biennial General Assembly session, his stories on pending legislation and his characterizations of North Carolina politicians delighted many of his readers and rankled others. Possessed of a phenomenal memory and rich in the lore of North Caroliniana, Bost took few notes when he covered a story, yet he established a strong reputation for accuracy in his reporting.

A lifelong Democrat, Bost credited William Jennings Bryan and Charles B. Aycock with giving him his political values. In later years he described himself as an ardent New Dealer and Fair Dealer. A lifelong Episcopalian, too—he nearly entered the ministry in 1899—Bost was an active lay reader and wrote a Sunday editorial around a religious theme for the *Daily News*. A perennial opponent of capital punishment, he witnessed more than 250 executions, covering them, he said, as a "religious duty," hoping to inspire sentiment against the death penalty.

A devoted family man, Bost married Annie Kizer of Salisbury on 28 July 1908; they had two sons, W. T., Jr., and John Shipman. Mrs. Bost served for years as state commissioner of public welfare and was almost as widely known as her husband. Vigorous and active as a journalist into his seventy-third year, Bost died in Raleigh at Rex Hospital following a brief illness and was buried at Oakwood Cemetery. At his death, Tar Heel editorialists noted the end of an era in North Carolina journalism.

SEE: *Asheville Citizen*, 15 Sept. 1951; *Durham Morning*

Herald, 5 Jan. 1948; Carl Goerch, *Characters . . . Always Characters* (1945); *Greensboro Daily News*; Robert C. Lawrence, *Here in Carolina* (1939); Raleigh *News and Observer*, 3 Jan. 1948, 29 Apr. 1951, 15 Sept. 1951.

A. M. BURNS III

Bourne, Henry Clark (*1 Aug. 1893–19 Nov. 1972*), attorney, farmer, publisher, and churchman, was born on the farm White Oaks near Tarboro, Edgecombe County. He was the son of Maria Toole Clark (25 Dec. 1859–4 June 1907), whose father was Governor Henry Toole Clark, and Henry Clay Bourne. He was educated in a private elementary school in Tarboro operated by Frank Wilkinson, in the Tarboro public schools, and at The University of North Carolina. On the death of his father in 1911 he was forced to leave college; he returned to Tarboro and read law under his uncle, John L. Bridgers, Jr. While reading law, he served as editor and business manager of the local newspaper, the *Daily Southerner*. He passed the state bar examination and was admitted to the bar on 28 Aug. 1917.

At the outbreak of World War I., Bourne enlisted in the army. He rose to the rank of sergeant major in the 156th Depot Brigade and was commissioned second lieutenant before his discharge at Camp Gordon, Ga., in 1919.

After the war he returned to Tarboro, and on 30 Nov. 1920 he married Marion Frances Alston of Raleigh. They had three children: Henry C., Jr.; Laura June, who married Willie J. Long, Jr.; and Joel K. Bourne resumed the practice of law with John L. Bridgers, Jr., and continued his practice until his death. He became the owner and publisher of the *Daily Southerner* and the owner and operator of considerable farm land in Edgecombe County, including the Penelo plantation.

He was county attorney for Edgecombe and solicitor of the county recorders court during his early practice. Primarily interested in civil law and trial work, he had an extensive practice in Eastern North Carolina and argued many cases in the Supreme Court of North Carolina and in the federal courts. He was a long-time member of the North Carolina State Bar Council from the Seventh Judicial District and served on many committees of the state bar and the North Carolina Bar Association.

Bourne was an active Democrat and held many positions in the party organization. He was county campaign manager for Governor William B. Umstead and several times a delegate to the state and national conventions. Active in the American Legion, he was elected state commander in 1931 and was immediately faced with the problem of the Bonus March of 1932, in which he played a vital role. He was a lifetime member of Calvary Episcopal Church in Tarboro, serving as a lay reader, member of the vestry, and senior warden. He was a frequent delegate to the diocesan and national conventions of the Episcopal church, was chancellor of the Diocese of North Carolina from 1960 until 1972, and served on many diocesan boards and committees.

Marion Frances Alston and Henry Clark Bourne were both buried in the yard of Calvary Church in Tarboro.

SEE: Edgecombe County Court Records (North Carolina State Archives, Raleigh); Episcopal Church records (Tarboro and Diocesan House, Raleigh); D. L. Grant, *Alumni History of the University of North Carolina* (1924); *North Carolina Historical Review* 51 (1974); Tarboro *Southerner*, scattered issues.

H. C. BRIDGERS, JR.

Bourne, Henry Clay (*15 Mar. 1840–22 Feb. 1911*), soldier, farmer, merchant, and public official, was born near Portroyal, Tenn., the son of Catherine White Wimberley and Milton Bourne. His mother was a native of Robertson County, Tenn., but his father was born near Tarboro. From his birthplace, Henry Bourne moved to Brandon, Miss. During the Civil War he served in the Sixth Mississippi Regiment, attained the rank of colonel, and was wounded in the Battle of Shiloh. He moved to Edgecombe County to the home of his cousin, Robert Diggs Wimberley, to recuperate from his wound and then operated the Confederate Commissary on the railroad near Tarboro until the end of the war.

In 1863 he married Florence Dickens (1842–22 Mar. 1884), and after the war they returned to Brandon. They had several children. One son, Hugh Dudley (22 Sept. 1867–8 Mar. 1898), was buried in Calvary Episcopal churchyard, Tarboro. Another, Louis Milton, was an attorney in Asheville.

In the late 1880s, Bourne returned to Tarboro and acquired a farm known as White Oaks, where he lived the rest of his life. On 20 Nov. 1890, he married Maria Toole Clark (25 Dec. 1859–4 June 1907), the daughter of former Governor Henry Toole Clark. They had three children: Mary Parker, who married Edward Rugley, Henry Clark, who married Marion Frances Alston; and Katherine Wimberley, who went to Puerto Rico to do missionary work at St. John's School and died in San Juan on 14 Dec. 1922, as the result of an attack by a barracuda.

In Tarboro, in addition to farming, Bourne was a commission merchant for a few years and then became active in politics. He was justice of the peace, magistrate, and sheriff of Edgecombe County and was much in demand as the principal speaker on significant local occasions, such as the memorial services for President Jefferson Davis and the welcoming-home of Governor-elect Elias Carr.

Bourne and his wives were buried in Calvary churchyard in Tarboro.

SEE: Calvary Churchyard tombstones (Tarboro); Edgecombe County Court Records (North Carolina State Archives, Raleigh); Family records (Tarboro); Tarboro *Carolina Banner*, scattered issues; Tarboro *Southerner*, scattered issues.

H. C. BRIDGERS, JR.
MRS. WILLIE J. LONG, JR.

Bower, William Horton (*6 June 1850–11 May 1910*), lawyer, legislator and congressman, was born near Wilkesboro, the son of David E. and Rebecca Horton Bower. He attended several academies and Finley High School in Lenoir, completing his formal education by the time he was sixteen. He lived on a farm until 1869, when he began the private study of law in the office of Colonel G. N. Folk; he was admitted to the bar in 1870. He practiced in Lenoir until 1876, when he moved to California to teach school. He remained there until the summer of 1880 and then returned to Lenoir.

In 1882, Bower was elected to the general assembly from Caldwell County. There he served on the Judiciary, Internal Improvements, and Privileges and Elections committees and was chairman of the Committee on the Public Library. In 1884 he was elected to the state senate.

In 1885 he was appointed solicitor of the Tenth Judicial District by Governor A. M. Scales, and the next year he was elected without opposition to a four-year term as solicitor.

Bower was an unsuccessful candidate for the Democratic nomination to Congress from the Eighth District in 1890. On the 147th ballot, he was defeated by W. H. H. Cowles. In 1892, Bower was elected as a Democrat to represent the Eighth District in the Fifty-third Congress. During his term, which lasted from 4 Mar. 1893 to 3 Mar. 1895, he served on the Committee on Indian Affairs and the Committee on Railways and Canals. He was defeated for reelection to Congress in 1894 by R. Z. Linney.

After his defeat, Bower returned to Lenoir and resumed his law practice. There he died; he was survived by his wife, the former Annie Malthaner of Pennsylvania, and a son, David. Bower was buried in Elkville Cemetery in Caldwell County.

SEE: Nancy Alexander, *Here Will I Dwell: The Story of Caldwell County* (1956); *Biog. Dir. Am. Cong.* (1961); *Congressional Directory*, 2nd ed., (1889); North Carolina Bar Association, *Proceedings* (1920); J. S. Tomlinson, *Assembly Sketch Book* (1883, 1885); Wilkesboro *Chronicle*, 18 May 1910.

JANET L. BLAIR

Bowie, Thomas Contee (*27 July 1876–12 Nov. 1947*), frequent member of the General Assembly of North Carolina, was a vocal representative of the mountain counties, an occasional state-wide political aspirant, and a caustic conservative critic. A descendant of prominent families, "Tam" Bowie was born in Lake St. Joseph, Tensas Parish, La., to John Ruth and Carrie Calloway Bowie. His father was a wealthy planter and his mother a descendant of James Calloway, a physician and member of the North Carolina assembly. Bowie became an orphan at age six; he moved to North Carolina, where he attended schools in Moravian Falls and Traphill and Mars Hill Academy. Interspersed with the schooling were forays to West Virginia—the first when he was only twelve years old—where he worked in coal mines. In 1895 he entered The University of North Carolina, completing a Ph.B. degree in 1899. As an undergraduate he won several distinctions for the oratorical ability he carried with him into his law practice and public career: the declaimers' medal, the debaters' medal, and the Willie P. Mangum medal. From Chapel Hill he went to Yale University to study political science but returned to The University of North Carolina to study law; he was admitted to the state bar in 1901.

Bowie immediately entered politics as the 1902 Democratic nominee for the North Carolina Senate from the strongly Republican district around Ashe County. He lost that race by only seventy votes. In 1908 he successfully campaigned for the state house of representatives but then declined to run for reelection. In 1913 he returned to the General Assembly and in 1915 was unanimously elected speaker of the house. Defeated from his district in 1916, he returned to the General Assembly in 1921, 1923, and 1925. After a break he reappeared in Raleigh in 1933 and 1935.

In the assembly he was a strong advocate of the interests of the mountain counties and came to be called by some reporters "the Lion of the Mountains." He successfully promoted two important pieces of legislation: a 1921 act to initiate a $50 million road building program in North Carolina and a 1923 act to enable the state to build a $10 million railroad to connect the mountain counties with Wilmington and the coastal regions. The implementation of the highway act effectively negated the importance of the railroad act, and the line was never built.

In 1927, Governor Angus W. McLean appointed Bowie one of two emergency judges on the superior court. This was his only state-wide office, although he tried twice unsuccessfully to bid for state-wide elective office. In 1924 he sought to be elected lieutenant governor and in 1932 he ran against Bob Reynolds for the Democratic nomination for U.S. Senate. As a senatorial aspirant, he campaigned for downward revision of the tariff, reevaluation of land values to lower the tax on farmers, and a program of economy on all levels of government. Those goals explain some of his conservative opposition to much welfare legislation and to the North Carolina Emergency Relief Administration in the 1930s, while he was again serving in the general assembly.

Following his 1935 service in the assembly, Bowie tried at least once again to obtain a seat in the house of representatives from Ashe County. In 1940, explaining that he was upset by the increases in local taxes, he sought to gain the Democratic nomination from W. D. Austin, who had been chairman of the Ashe County Democratic party from 1919 to 1925. Austin defeated him by a vote of 162 to 63 in the county convention and won the seat.

The county elected a Republican representative to Raleigh in 1943 and 1945. Bowie meanwhile, had retired to the practice of law, to the supervision of his considerable landholdings in the county, and to oversight of his cattle breeding experiments. He was also president of the First National Bank of West Jefferson, which he had helped to found. He maintained his law offices in the town and had a reputation as a colorful trial attorney.

Bowie married the former Jean Davis of Charlotte in 1906. They had three children: Thomas Contee, Jr., who later joined his father's law practice; Elizabeth, who married Carter Redd of Birmingham, Ala.; and Jean, who died in infancy.

Bowie died in North Wilkesboro and the body was returned to his home in West Jefferson for burial in a prominent mausoleum in what is now the West Jefferson Cemetery. There the body rests, along with those of his wife, his daughter, Jean, his son, who died in 1969, and his cocker spaniel, Chubby, who was his constant companion.

SEE: Appalachian State Teacher's College Alumni Association, *Hall of Fame* (1962); Chapel Hill *Daily Tar Heel*, 1 Mar. 1932; *Charlotte Observer*, 6 and 14 July 1940; 13 Nov. 1947; *Greensboro Daily News*, 13, 14, and 16 Nov. 1947; Thomas S. Morgan, "A Step toward Altruism" (Ph.D. diss., University of North Carolina, 1969); *North Carolina: Rebuilding an Ancient Commonwealth*, vol. 3 (1929); Raleigh *News and Observer*, 5 Nov. 1935, 13 Nov. 1947.

THOMAS S. MORGAN

Bowman, Jacob Weaver (*31 July 1831–8 June 1905*), legislator and judge, was born in Relief, Burke (now Mitchell) County. His parents were Joseph Bowman, a farmer and justice of the peace, and Sarah Garland. Bowman spent his early years on his father's farm. He attended the high school of Scott County, Va., in 1848 and 1849; with the encouragement of Morganton lawyer Colonel Burgess S. Gaither, he later studied law with Judge Richmond M. Pearson and in 1868 was granted his law license.

While serving in the legislature of 1860, Bowman, a Whig, worked to establish Mitchell County. He was elected to the legislature of 1868 and supported passage of Reconstruction and homestead legislation. A representative in the 1872 legislature that struggled for three weeks to elect a U.S. senator from North Carolina, Bowman supported the Republican candidate, John Pool. Opposing Pool were former Gov. Zebulon B. Vance and Judge A. L. Merriman. After Bowman had satisfied the proprieties of party etiquette by his support of Pool, he backed Merriman, the eventual winner, whome he greatly admired. Popular with his constituents, Bowman was unanimously elected to represent Mitchell County in the constitutional convention of 1875. He served his last term in the General Assembly in 1882.

In 1898, Governor D. L. Russell appointed Bowman to the superior court bench to fill the vacancy created by the death of Judge Leander L. Greene. After serving the remaining two years of Greene's term, Bowman retired to Bakersville to resume his law practice. It was said of his skill, "He is not eloquent and does not assume to be; but he is an antagonist worthy of the most eloquent man's best effort in the forum."

Bowman was an Episcopalian. He and his wife, Mary Minerva Garland, had eleven children.

SEE: John Nichols, *Directory of the General Assembly of the State of North Carolina, for the Session Commencing November 19, 1860* (1860); and Van Noppen Papers (Manuscript Department, Library, Duke University, Durham).

EMILY K. HIGHTOWER

Boyd, Adam (*25 Nov. 1738–1803*), clergyman and newspaper editor, was born in Montour County, Pa. His father, also named Adam Boyd, was a native of Balleymoney, Ireland, and served as an Old Side Presbyterian minister from his arrival in America until his death in 1768. Boyd's mother was Jan Creaghead (Craighead), daughter of a Presbyterian clergyman. There were eleven children in the family: Andrew, Mary, Hannah, Elizabeth, Samuel, Margaret, Janet, Agnes, Thomas, John, and Adam.

Nothing is known of Boyd's youth except that he received a classical education and was licensed to preach by the Presbyterian church. As a young man, he lived for a while in Bermuda with his brother John, but he left the West Indies and settled in Wilmington at least as early as 1764. Boyd did not follow his clerical profession but engaged in business in the Carolina port city, where he was socially popular and acclaimed as a literary figure. In 1769 he purchased a printing press and three sets of aged type from the estate of Andrew Steuart for thirty-eight pounds; on 13 Oct. of that year, he launched the *Cape Fear Mercury*, which was successful from the start.

Fourteen regular issues and four literary supplements of the paper have survived, showing the early issues to have been embellished with the royal arms of Great Britain and a Latin motto that, translated freely, stated: "Since I am concerned with and inquire about the true and proper, I am in this wholeheartedly." The only other newspaper in the colony at the time was the *North Carolina Gazette*, published at New Bern. The news sheet varied in size from twenty-one inches wide and seventeen inches long, with three columns on a page, to ten inches wide and thirteen inches long, with two columns on each of four pages. The subscription price for the weekly was sixteen shillings per year, and the contents included news items, fiction, and advertisements.

As a publisher, Boyd did not hesitate to print articles critical of the royal government, although he maintained friendly relations with Governor Josiah Martin, who appointed him registrar for New Hanover County in 1775. The governor frequently referred to Boyd's paper in his correspondence with the Earl of Dartmouth, and when he issued his "Fiery Proclamation" in 1775, he mentioned several statements published in the *Mercury*.

Boyd encountered financial difficulties in 1774, but the Wilmington Committee of Safety assisted him in resuming publication. The colonial assembly gave him a share of the official printing, and he was able to continue editing the paper until about January 1776. The royal arms no longer graced the front page, however: Boyd had become a patriot, a member of the committee of safety in Wilmington, and a member of the committee of correspondence. In these activities, he was associated with Cornelius Harnett, William Hooper, Alexander Lillington, James Moore, Archibald Maclaine, Richard Caswell, and Joseph Hewes. Fired with patriotic enthusiasm and faced with the increasing difficulty of obtaining paper and supplies under wartime conditions, he suspended publication of the *Mercury* and on 4 Jan. 1776 enlisted as an ensign in the First North Carolina Battalion.

Boyd was promoted to second lieutenant in 1776. He was made chaplain to the Second North Carolina Battalion eighteen months later and then elevated to the rank of brigade chaplain. He served under colonels Thomas Clark and Edward Buncombe and, in addition to his regular duties, officiated as judge of a military court and endeavored to obtain supplies and useful information for the army. He also assisted General Jethro Sumner in organizing the North Carolina chapter of the Society of the Cincinnati, and he was elected the first secretary of the organization. At the close of the war, the State of North Carolina awarded Boyd 7,200 acres in Davidson County, Tenn., for his military service.

A portrait of Boyd, painted in 1776 and now in the collection of Benjamin D. Palmer of New Market, Md., shows him to have been an attractive man whose facial expression denoted determination and zeal. In 1774 he married Mary Ivy DeRosset, widow of the prominent Dr. Moses John DeRosset and mother of Mary Magdalene and Armand John DeRosset. Boyd never had children of his own but was an affectionate and dutiful stepfather.

Being financially unable to reenter the publishing business at the end of the war, Boyd decided to seek ordination as an Episcopal minister. The Anglican Church of St. James, in Wilmington, which was attended by both the Ivy and the DeRosset families, had no resident minister, and Boyd was frequently requested to hold services there. However, increasingly serious attacks of asthma, which had begun while he was in the army, required him to move to a different climate. Because of her declining health, Mrs. Boyd made her home with her daughter, then Mrs. Henry Toomer, and her husband moved to Augusta, Ga., to serve St. Paul's Parish. On 18 Aug. 1788, in New London, Conn., he was admitted to the Holy Order of Deacons of the Protestant Episcopal Church in the United States by the newly consecrated Bishop Samuel Seabury, and the following day he was ordained into the Holy Order of Priests.

Boyd labored valiantly to rebuild his parish, which had been impoverished by the war and which was able to pay him very little for his services. Afflicted by increasingly poor health and grieved by the death of his ailing wife in 1798, Boyd determined to journey to Tennessee while he was physically able in order to liquidate the lands he owned there. In 1799 he visited both Knoxville and Nashville, in each place preaching the first sermon ever delivered there by an Episcopal clergyman. In 1800 the Harmony Masonic Lodge of Nashville requested him to compose a sermon in memory of George Washington. He complied and, although he had broken a leg in his travels and had to be carried to the pulpit in a chair, delivered the memorial sermon to an enthusiastic audience. This address was printed and is his only surviving composition.

Later, Boyd traveled to Natchez, Miss., where he made new friends and busied himself writing booklets for children. He died there, but the site of his grave is unknown.

SEE: DeRosset Family Papers, Group I (Southern Historical Collection, University of North Carolina, Chapel Hill); Andrew Fowler, "Biographical Sketches of the Clergy of the Protestant Episcopal Church" (3-vol. MS, Protestant Episcopal Church Historical Society, Austin, Tex.); Catherine DeRosset Meares, *Annals of the DeRosset Family* (1906); Durward T. Stokes, "Adam Boyd," *North Carolina Historical Review* 49 (1972), and "Different Concepts of Government Expressed in the Sermons of Two Eighteenth Century Clergymen," *Historical Magazine of the Protestant Episcopal Church* 40 (1971); Richard Webster, *A History of the Presbyterian Church in America* (1858).

DURWARD T. STOKES

Boyd, Bernard Henry *(16 Nov. 1910–28 Sept. 1975),* educator and clergyman, was born the second of the four sons of Frank Thomas and Eunice Beaty Boyd in Mt. Pleasant, S.C. Frank Boyd was a successful general contractor, and much credit must be given to him and to his wife for the encouragement and education their sons received. Mrs. Boyd taught the boys from their earliest years to love poetry and good literature, and this love not only remained with Bernard but was very much a part of his life: in the classroom or pulpit he could with seeming ease quote at length from works of the major English and American poets and from the Bible. Robert F., Bernard's oldest brother, was to become a Presbyterian minister; Francis Thomas, Jr., was a businessman who died only a few months before Bernard; the youngest, William Beaty, became a university president.

Bernard Boyd was educated in the public schools of Mt. Pleasant and at Boys' High School in Charleston across the bay. In the fall of 1928 he entered Presbyterian College, receiving his B.A. in 1932; following graduation he entered Princeton University for graduate study in English. He also became a student in Princeton Theological Seminary; he received his M.A. degree from the university in 1934 and his bachelor of theology degree from the seminary in 1935. He continued his graduate study at Union Theological Seminary, Richmond, Va., and after World War II completed his course work and was awarded the doctor of theology degree in 1947.

Upon graduation from Princeton, Boyd returned to his alma mater, Presbyterian College, where he was professor of Bible until 1947. His teaching was interrupted by the coming of the war. Though essentially a man of peace, he had been commissioned a reserve officer in the U.S. Army upon graduation from college. By 1943, with his students being called into service, he no longer felt inclined to use his ministerial exemption and volunteered for naval duty as a chaplain, with the request that he be assigned to the Marine Corps. He was ordained to the Presbyterian ministry, which had not previously been necessary as he had never before been charged with the pastorate of a congregation; within a few weeks after his military training was completed, he was shipped to the Pacific area. There he saw heavy fighting and was severely wounded in the battle for Okinawa. The war made a deep impression upon him,

and in later years he rarely mentioned his experiences under fire.

As a young faculty member at Presbyterian College, Boyd quickly established himself as a superior teacher and lecturer. Upon separation from military service he spent two terms at Union Theological Seminary and then returned to teach at Presbyterian College for one year. In 1947 he became professor of Bible at Davidson College, where he taught until 1950, when he received the offer of an endowed chair from The University of North Carolina. It was with reservation and considerable reluctance that Boyd accepted the James A. Gray Professorship of Biblical Literature; he was happy at Davidson and felt that in a smaller, church-related institution he could do his best work. But the decision to move to Chapel Hill was made, and he filled this new position with distinction for the remaining twenty-five years of his life.

Boyd undoubtedly felt a measure of disappointment during his first year at the university; his classes were small, and he questioned his decision to leave Davidson. But his capabilities as a teacher, coupled with his almost magnetic personality, soon brought increasing numbers of students, until well above two hundred were regularly enrolled in each of his lecture courses. Although students did not find Boyd's courses easy, his ability as a teacher was attested on at least three occasions: he twice received the university's Tanner Award for "excellence in inspirational teaching of undergraduate students," and he was presented the Nicholas Salgo Distinguished Teacher Award for "excellence as evidenced by . . . classroom effectiveness and ability to motivate and inspire students."

People across the State of North Carolina came to know Boyd through educational television programs that were scheduled for several years: "Bernard Boyd and the Bible," "The Origin and Significance of the Bible," and "Introduction to the New Testament Literature" each gained a wide audience. On countless Sundays he occupied pulpits, usually but not always Presbyterian. He was also in demand as a speaker for large church conferences. He was a member of the Society of Biblical Literature, American Schools of Oriental Research, American Academy of Religion, and Archaeological Institute of America; he prepared papers presented at some of their sessions.

Following a trip to Israel in 1956, Boyd became interested in archaeology; from 1963 on he visited the Holy Land each summer and actively participated in the excavations. Though self-taught as an archaeologist, he was educational director for the Institute of Mediterranean Studies from 1965 through 1967 and was its archaeological director after 1968. From 1968 to 1971 he was institute lecturer for the Archaeological Institute of America, and from 1966 until his death he was codirector or director of expeditions to Israel.

In 1944, only a short time before he was shipped overseas, Boyd married Thelma Hicklin of Richburg, S.C. They had two children, Donald Beaty and Karen Elizabeth. Boyd died suddenly of a heart attack shortly after he had finished a sermon as guest minister at Tabernacle Associate Reformed Presbyterian Church in Charlotte. Funeral services were held in University Presbyterian Church in Chapel Hill, and interment was in the new Chapel Hill Cemetery.

SEE: *Asheville Citizen-Times*, 18 Aug. 1957; Boyd family (personal contact); Chapel Hill *Daily Tar Heel*, 29 and 30 Sept. 1975; *Chapel Hill Weekly*, 26 Dec. 1962; *Charlotte Observer*, 30 Sept. 1975, 3 Oct. 1975; *Durham Morning*

Herald, 22 June 1974; *Greensboro Daily News*, 22 Nov. 1970; *Who's Who in America*, 1974–75.

                                          J. ISAAC COPELAND

Boyd, George Dillard *(19 May 1797–16 Apr. 1886),* legislator, merchant, and plantation and mill owner, was born in Rockingham County. He was a son of Andrew Boyd, by whose will he inherited part interest in a gristmill and farm on Piney Creek, near Speedwell Presbyterian Church, in 1815. Boyd continued buying adjoining land until he owned a plantation of 838 acres. He had opened a store by 1837. In 1860 he owned twenty slaves and had in operation a mill that produced both flour and corn meal and was also equipped to card wool. A steam-powered sawmill was operated adjacent to the gristmill.

As early as 1828, Boyd was appointed constable in his district. In later life he served many years as a justice of the peace. He was first elected a member of the House of Commons in the legislature of 1840. In the legislature of 1842 he served as a state senator and was appointed to the Committee on Education and the Literary Fund. He continued to represent his district in the state senate during the sessions of 1844, 1846, and 1852. As an ardent Democrat, he ran for Congress against R. C. Puryear in 1853, but he was defeated by about three hundred votes because of an overwhelming Whig majority in the district. Returning to the state senate in 1854, he was appointed to the Propositions and Grievances Committee. He continued to serve as a state senator during the sessions of 1856 and 1858.

On 19 July 1827, Boyd married Minerva Hill, daughter of Samuel Hill of Rockingham County. Five sons were born to this marriage, the eldest dying in infancy. The second son, John Hill, entered the Confederate Army as captain of Company L, Twenty-first North Carolina Regiment, and died in Richmond, Va., 28 Aug. 1861, from exposure and disease. The third son, Samuel Hill, entered service as captain of Company E, Forty-fifth North Carolina Regiment, was later promoted to colonel, and was killed at Spottsylvania Court House on 19 May 1864. The fourth son, George Fulton, first enlisted in a Mississippi regiment but later transferred to the Forty-fifth North Carolina Regiment, became lieutenant of Company A, and was killed at Gettysburg 1 July 1863. The fifth son, Colonel Andrew Jackson Boyd (24 Feb. 1836–18 Aug. 1893), became a lawyer and businessman of Reidsville.

Minerva Hill Boyd (b. 1808) died on 2 Mar. 1844 and was buried in Rockingham County. On 29 Mar. 1859, Boyd married Eliza C. Webb, a native of Georgia. One daughter, Minerva, was born to this marriage; she married Joseph H. Blackwell of Reidsville in 1883.

When Boyd died in 1886, he was buried beside his three sons in the Methodist church cemetery in Wentworth. His second wife died 11 July 1903 and was buried in Reidsville.

SEE: Samuel A. Ashe, ed., *Biographical History of North Carolina*, vol. 7 (1908); Lindley S. Butler, *Our Proud Heritage: Rockingham County* (1971); *North Carolina House and Senate Journals*, 1842–43, 1854–55; Receipt from Boyd's store, 1837 (possession of Robert Wray Carter, Jr.); *Reidsville Times*, 18 Oct. 1883; Rockingham County Minute Docket of Pleas and Quarter Sessions, August Term, 1827; Rockingham County Will Books A and B (North Carolina State Archives, Raleigh); *Sketches of the County of Rockingham* (1884): U.S. Census (1860, 1880).

                                   ROBERT WRAY CARTER, JR.

Boyd, James *(2 July 1888–25 Feb. 1944),* novelist, was born in Harrisburg, Pa. He was the eldest son of Eleanor Gilmore Herr and John Yeomans Boyd, a prominent businessman, Presbyterian layman, and heir to a fortune based upon an iron and coal business in central Pennsylvania dating from the middle of the nineteenth century. Near the end of the century, Boyd's grandfather purchased a large tract of land near Southern Pines and established a residence that later became the novelist's permanent home.

Boyd attended the Hill School in Pottstown, Pa. (1901–6), received an undergraduate degree from Princeton University (1910), and spent two further years in study at Trinity College, Cambridge. He joined the faculty of Harrisburg Academy in 1912 as an English and French teacher. Recurrent illness forced his retirement from teaching after only two years and led to an extended period of convalescence in Southern Pines, where he had visited periodically with his parents since early childhood. Following brief employment on the editorial staff of *Country Life in America* during the fall of 1916 and a short period of volunteer work with the Red Cross, Boyd received a commission as second lieutenant in the U.S. Army Ambulance Service on 28 Aug. 1917. As commanding officer of Ambulance Service Section 520, he served briefly in Italy in June 1918 and subsequently in France, where he participated in the St. Mihiel campaign and the Meuse-Argonne offensives. He was discharged on 2 July 1919.

At the end of 1919, Boyd moved permanently to Southern Pines and began his career as a writer. He had written stories, poetry, and plays intermittently since his early teens but, during his employment on the staff of the Harrisburg *Patriot* in 1910 and *Country Life* in 1916, had published nothing except news stories, minor articles, and cartoons. His move to North Carolina was a crucial event in his career. The move dictated partly by his desire for a quiet place to work and a milder climate than that offered by central Pennsylvania, was motivated primarily by a strong personal attachment to the Sandhills region developed during earlier visits with his parents and grandparents. The region was to provide him with materials for much of his writing during the next twenty-five years.

By 1930, Boyd's articles and stories had begun to appear regularly in *Scribner's Magazine*, *Century Magazine*, *American Mercury*, and elsewhere. Stories with recognizable North Carolina settings include "Sound of a Voice" (1921), "Old Pines" (1921), "Verse on the Window" (1922), "Shif'less" (1922), and others. Boyd continued to publish stories and other short pieces for more than fifteen years, but by 1922 he had turned his attention primarily to the historical novels that were to consume most of his creative energy and upon which his literary reputation chiefly rests.

Three of Boyd's five historical novels are set wholly or partially in North Carolina, which he once called "the least romantic but most distinctive and solid of the Southern states." *Drums* (1925), acclaimed by many critics as the best novel ever written about the American Revolution, is set largely in Edenton. *Marching On* (1927), a novel of the Civil War, is set mostly in Wilmington and elsewhere in the coastal region. *Long Hunt* (1930), about the long hunters on the trans-Appalachian frontier during the late eighteenth century, has its opening scenes set in the western part of the state. Two additional novels were *Roll River* (1935), a partly autobiographical account of a Pennsylvania industrial family at the turn of the twentieth century, which reveals much about the background of Boyd's family in Pennsylvania before he established himself in North Carolina, and *Bitter Creek* (1939), Boyd's last novel, set in the Wyoming cattle country in the 1890s.

Boyd's work drew him into close relationships with many other North Carolina writers, as well as with those from outside the state who wrote about the South. Among them were Paul Green, Thomas Wolfe, Sherwood Anderson, William Faulkner, Struthers Burt, and John Galsworthy. During the year 1927–28, Boyd served as president of the North Carolina Literary and Historical Association. In 1938 he was awarded an honorary degree by The University of North Carolina, in recognition of his service to arts and letters in the state. In 1939 he was elected to the original board of the North Carolina Society for the Preservation of Antiquities. National recognition of his work included election to the National Institute of Arts and Letters in 1937 and to the Society of American Historians in 1939.

Boyd's novels, especially *Drums* and *Roll River*, were enthusiastically received by both critics and the reading public and have recently come to be recognized as representing major steps in the development of the historical novel as a genre, carrying it beyond the older historical romance through greater historical accuracy, psychological and sociological awareness, moral and aesthetic sensitivity, and formal control.

In 1940, Boyd organized and served as national chairman of the Free Company of Players, a group of American writers concerned about the antidemocratic attitudes beginning to manifest themselves in American life as a result of the war in Europe. The group, which included Orson Welles, Archibald MacLeish, Paul Green, William Saroyan, Stephen V. Benét, Sherwood Anderson, and others, produced and broadcast a series of original radio plays early in 1941. Their defense of constitutionally guaranteed freedoms during a period of national emergency incurred the wrath of conservative interests, who took the plays to be subversive or un-American. Right-wing opposition to the plays was led by the Hearst newspapers. William Randolph Hearst had been embroiled for several months in a controversy with Orson Welles, a member of the Free Company, whose movie *Citizen Kane*, widely assumed to be a portrait of Hearst, premiered in New York during the early Free Company broadcasts. Joined by the Veterans of Foreign Wars, the Hearst opposition proved formidable but did not succeed in stopping the Free Company series.

In 1941, Boyd bought and became editor of the Southern Pines *Pilot*, which he transformed from a conservative, nearly defunct country weekly to a progressive regional newspaper repeatedly honored for its excellence by the North Carolina Press Association.

Boyd was married on 15 Dec. 1917 to Katharine Lamont of Millbrook, N.Y., daughter of Daniel Scott Lamont, who was secretary and aide to President Grover Cleveland during Cleveland's first administration and secretary of war during his second. Their three children were James, Jr. (b. 1922), Daniel Lamont (b. 1924), and Nancy (b. 1927). In politics, Boyd was a liberal Democrat. He maintained no formal religious affiliation. Throughout his residence at Southern Pines, he was an avid fox-hunter; he was founder and master of the Moore County Hounds, one of the outstanding hunts in the United States.

Boyd suffered a fatal cerebral attack while attending a seminar on American customs with a group of British army officers at Princeton University. His ashes were returned to Southern Pines for burial on the family property. His *Eighteen Poems*, written toward the end of his life, appeared a few months later.

SEE: James Boyd, *Old Pines and Other Stories* (1952), and, ed., *The Free Company Presents* (1941); North Carolina Collection (University of North Carolina, Chapel Hill), Princeton University Library, and the files of Charles Scribner's Sons (New York), for Boyd's MSS and personal papers; *Encyclopedia of Pennsylvania Biography*, vols. 1 and 3 (1914); *Princeton University Library Chronicle* 6 (1945); David E. Whisnant, *James Boyd* (1972).

DAVID E. WHISNANT

Boyd, James Edmund (*14 Feb. 1845–21 Aug. 1935*), lawyer and judge, was born in that part of Orange County which is now Alamance County, the son of Archibald Hill and Mary Weatherly Boyd.

He attended Graham Academy and studied at Davidson College for two years (1862–64). At the age of sixteen, he enrolled in the Thirteenth North Carolina Infantry; later he joined the First North Carolina Cavalry and fought with Lee and Jackson in Virginia. He was a courier at Appomattox and carried a message from General Lee to General Grant requesting a meeting to arrange for the surrender.

The years of 1866 and 1867 were spent reading law under Judge Thomas L. Ruffin, and Boyd was admitted to the North Carolina bar in 1868. He began the practice of law in Graham and was elected a member of the General Assembly (1874–75). He was also a delegate to the convention of 1875. After removing his residence to Greensboro, he served as the U.S. attorney for the Western District of North Carolina from 1880 to 1885 under appointment of President Hayes. He was also elected mayor of Greensboro in 1894. The office of second assistant attorney general of the United States was given to him in 1897 by President McKinley. He was appointed judge of the federal district courts in the Western District of North Carolina in 1901 and served for twenty-three years with distinction. He was also a delegate to the 1904 Universal Congress of Lawyers and Jurists.

Boyd married Sallie Holt, member of a prominent and well-known family of Alamance County, on 12 Sept. 1868. One son, Thomas, died soon after he finished his law course. Sallie Boyd died in 1928, and Boyd died in Greensboro at the age of ninety.

SEE: R. D. W. Connor, *North Carolina: Rebuilding an Ancient Commonwealth*, vol. 2 (1929); Data Files, Alumni Office, Davidson College, Davidson; *Greensboro Daily News*, 22 Aug. 1935.

HORACE ALEXANDER HESTER

Boyd, Thomas (*died ca. 1715*), colonial officer, first appeared in the records of North Carolina in the summer of 1697. He frequently acted as an attorney before the general court in the early eighteenth century, and in 1702 he married the widow of John West of Pasquotank Precinct.

In March 1706, Boyd was appointed provost marshal, the chief enforcement officer of the higher courts. By July 1708 he was elevated to a justiceship of the general court, after having been speaker of the General Assembly during the previous November. An Anglican and a member of the Pasquotank vestry as early as 1710, Boyd opposed the dissenter forces of Thomas Cary in the Cary Rebellion. He served on the council of Governor Edward Hyde from June 1711 and appealed to Virginia for aid against the Cary rebels. During the Tuscarora War, Boyd was a colonel in the militia and once led two hundred troops into a skirmish with the Indians. In May 1714 he fed and sheltered the Hatteras Indian tribe at his own plantation in order to encourage them to fight the Tuscaroras.

Boyd served with regularity on the council through 6 Nov. 1714 but died soon after that date. Although he was named to the vestry of the southwest parish of Pasquotank Precinct in the Vestry Act of 1715, a petition filed with the council in November 1719 implies that Boyd had died five years earlier. He died intestate leaving four sons. two by his wife's former marriage. His son Thomas became attorney general of the colony in 1725, after previous service in the assembly, and is sometimes confused with his father.

SEE: Mattie Erma Edwards Parker, ed., *North Carolina Higher-Court Records, 1697–1701* (1971); William S. Price, Jr., ed., *North Carolina Higher-Court Records, 1702–1708* (1974); William L. Saunders, ed., *Colonial Records of North Carolina*, vols. 1–2 (1886).

WILLIAM S. PRICE, JR.

Boyd, William Kenneth *(January 1879–19 Jan. 1938)*, historian, was born at Curryville, Mo., the second son and the youngest of six children of the Reverend Harvey Marshall and Mary Elizabeth Black Boyd. His father, a native of Kentucky, was of Scottish descent; his mother came from a Virginia family with English ancestry. The Boyd family soon moved to Weaverville, where Harvey Boyd was a Presbyterian minister. William attended Weaver College and then in 1895 entered Trinity College, recently removed to Durham from Randolph County, as a junior. At Trinity his chief interests were history and English literature; he took an A.B. degree in 1897 and an M.A. in 1898. In the latter year he served as an assistant to John Spencer Bassett, who became an important influence on his career. For two years, Boyd was a master in history in Trinity Park School (a preparatory school for the college); after two more years as adjunct professor of history at Trinity, he entered Columbia University, where he received the Ph.D. degree in 1906. He interrupted his studies at Columbia to serve on the staff of the Encyclopedia Britannica in 1904–5 and as an instructor in history at Dartmouth College in 1905–6. In September 1906 he returned to Trinity College as professor of history, and there, except for brief intervals, he remained. During a period as visiting scholar at the University of Pennsylvania in 1921 he discovered in the Library of the American Philosophical Society the secret history, previously unused and practically unknown, of William Byrd; later he edited it as Byrd's *Histories of the Dividing Line betwixt Virginia and North Carolina* (1929).

Boyd went to Trinity just as his mentor, Bassett, was leaving after a famous controversy known as the "Bassett Affair." Like Bassett, Boyd was a trenchant critic of an antiquated society intent on using history to support a patriotic bias, but his methods were not controversial. Although he was personally rather shy and reticent, with no gift of small talk, his enthusiasm for good causes soon made him a leader on academic committees. For two summers he directed the summer school; when the Student Army Training Corps was approved for Trinity in 1918, he was chosen to direct its academic program. For ten years (1919–29) he was coeditor of the *South Atlantic Quarterly*, a literary and historical journal founded at Trinity in 1902. He contributed numerous essays to the *Historical Papers* of the Trinity College Historical Society and wrote articles for *The South in the Building of the Nation* and for the *Cambridge History of American Literature*. With Smith Burnham, he wrote *A History of the United States for Schools* (1921); with Robert P. Brooks, *A Selected Bibliography and Syllabus of the History of the South, 1584–1876* (1918); and with J. G. deRoulhac

Hamilton, *A Syllabus of North Carolina History, 1584–1876* (1913). He edited several volumes of source materials, of which the most important was *Some Eighteenth Century Tracts Concerning North Carolina* (1927). While he was president of the North Carolina State Literary and Historical Association (1921–22), the *North Carolina Historical Review* was planned. In 1935 he became a member of the North Carolina Historical Commission.

It was as a teacher, writer, and builder of the library that Boyd was primarily known. At Columbia his doctoral dissertation dealt with the Theodosian Code ("Ecclesiastical Edicts of the Theodosian Code," 1905), but at Trinity there was no opportunity for research in medieval history; Boyd, like Bassett before him, turned to local materials that both he and his students might find and use. He believed that local and regional studies were the best preparation for understanding the character and results of national policies; and he thought that for a society to begin to understand itself, it must go beyond the narrowly political and examine the social, economic, and institutional matrix. He stressed, for example, the historical study of organized religion. In 1919 he contributed a volume, *The Federal Period, 1783–1860*, to a three-volume history of North Carolina. It was notable for its emphasis on the broader aspects of history and was characterized by R. D. W. Connor as the "first adequate interpretation of the history of the period." Boyd had a stimulating effect upon his students: he urged them to collect local materials and to publish articles in the college publications; he was fertile with suggestions; and he had the knack of opening students' minds with unassuming but relevant questions. He was a prober and a thinker, by nature practical and direct rather than doctrinaire. *The Story of Durham, City of the New South* (1925), in which he was assisted by some of his students, revealed the new economic life and new social forces of a city of the modern South, and proved more prophetic than the Agrarian crusaders then beginning to be heard.

As Trinity became Duke, Boyd remained chairman of a growing department; he directed most of the dissertations in American history and increased his collecting activities. Through the generosity of the children of George Washington Flowers, and especially of W. W. Flowers (a Trinity graduate, a friend of the Dukes, and an official of the Liggett and Myers Tobacco Company), Boyd was able in the late twenties to devote time and money to the acquisition of southern Americana for the Duke University Library. His success was notable, and the Flowers Collection became a significant research source for Duke students, teachers, and visiting scholars. In 1930, Boyd became director of libraries at Duke; he relinquished that position in 1934 but continued to teach, direct graduate students, and manage the Flowers Collection. He probably did more than any other individual to turn Duke's small college library into a university research library.

Boyd's first wife was Pat LeGrand of Rockingham. They were married 22 Dec. 1908; she died 10 Sept. 1924, leaving one daughter, Mary Elizabeth. Boyd was married again, on 11 Aug. 1931, to Marion Colley. She was a former journalist and was said to have been the first woman delegate to the Democratic National Convention. After Boyd's death she returned to her native Washington, Ga., where she died in 1973 at the age of ninety-eight. Boyd's only child, Mary Elizabeth, was married on 27 May 1938 to William B. Hamilton (d. 17 July 1972), professor of history at Duke University; she died 5 Mar. 1954, leaving one child, Elizabeth Cavett (b. 5 Feb. 1940).

Boyd was a member of the American Historical Association and other professional organizations; the Methodist Episcopal Church, South; and Phi Beta Kappa. He was buried in the Maplewood Cemetery in Durham.

SEE: Joseph Penn Breedlove, *Duke University Library* (1955); *DAB*, vol. 22 (1958); *Durham Herald*, 29 Jan 1938; *In Memoriam: William Kenneth Boyd*, Trinity College Historical Society Historical Papers, ser. 22 (1938); Earl W. Porter, *Trinity and Duke, 1892–1924* (1964); Nannie M. Tilley, *The Trinity College Historical Society* (1941); *Who's Who in America*, 1936–37.

ROBERT H. WOODY

Boyden, Nathaniel (*16 Aug. 1796–20 Nov. 1873*), lawyer, congressman, and jurist, was born in Conway, Mass., to John and Eunice Hayden Boyden. Both parents were of English ancestry and were descended from settlers who arrived in the Massachusetts Bay Colony in the 1630s. John Boyden was a sturdy farmer and revolutionary soldier; Eunice Hayden Boyden was the daughter of a Conway physician. Nathaniel Boyden served in the War of 1812 (having enlisted at age fifteen) and was the recipient of a land warrant of 160 acres. He received a liberal education at Deerfield Academy prior to attending Williams College and Union College of Schenectady, N.Y., where he was graduated in 1821. While in college, he studied law under the tutelege of his uncle, Moses Hayden, a New York congressman (1823–27).

In 1822, Boyden came south to seek his fortune. He decided to settle first in Guilford County, which he believed to be very promising. He was destined to make the Old North State his home but would move several times before settling permanently in Rowan County. While reading North Carolina law, Boyden taught school at Kings Crossroads, a community in northwest Guilford, and in Rockingham County. He was admitted to the bar in December 1823 and settled in Stokes County near Germanton. In 1832 he removed to Surry County. There he remained for a decade, gaining success as a lawyer and entering active political life as a two-term member of the house of commons (1838–42). In 1842 he established his home in Salisbury, where he was to reside until his death; and by 1844 he was so well accepted that Rowan County voters sent him to the state senate.

Boyden was an able lawyer noted for his untiring industry, extraordinary memory, rational powers, moral courage, and integrity. He flourished on the intellectual give and take of legal debate. His practice was broad and at times included a twelve-county circuit and forty-eight courts each year. For thirty years he regularly attended the session of the state supreme court. In May 1871, as a capstone to his career, Boyden himself became an associate justice of North Carolina's highest court, through appointment by Republican Governor Tod R. Caldwell.

In politics, Boyden was successively a Madison Republican, a National Republican, a Whig, and after 1868, a Republican. Nevertheless, he contended that he had always followed conservative principles and described himself as a lifelong Whig. As a member of the Thirtieth Congress (4 Mar. 1847–3 Mar. 1849), Boyden was deeply disturbed by the Mexican War, popularly known among Whigs as "Mr. Polk's War." He denounced Polk with enthusiasm, characterizing the president's Mexican policy as tyrannical and aggressive, while lamenting Polk's excessive timidity in Oregon. He

attacked Polk's extravagance but supported payment for Mexican territory as preferable to outright seizure without compensation. While his position was typically Whig, Boyden's views were strongly held and clearly articulated. His firmness was a landmark of his political career, even when his views were unpopular and his role controversial. Despite his southern interests and family ties, Boyden was adamantly opposed to secession and warned that the consequences for the South could only be disastrous. He considered secession a grave political error and expected the ultimate defeat of the Confederacy. Nevertheless, he subscribed some Confederate loans, sold his Salisbury foundry to the government for the manufacture of weapons, and supplied a son, Archibald Henderson, to the Confederate Armies. He sympathized with the southern people in war and lamented the harsh penalties imposed on them in peace, but he believed that simple justice required some concessions to the freedmen. He counseled acceptance of defeat and, in time, of congressional Reconstruction, though he opposed the Reconstruction Acts.

Inevitably, Boyden's ideas and role in the Reconstruction period have been misunderstood. His stance was generally unpopular, and his reputation has suffered as a consequence. His position warrants careful consideration. Family tradition suggests that President Lincoln had decided to name Boyden provisional governor of North Carolina shortly before John Wilkes Booth intervened. Subsequently, Boyden served as a member of the constitutional convention of 1865, where he introduced the resolution to repeal the secession ordinance. He was a member of the 1866 commission that developed the "North Carolina Plan" to insure "impartial justice and universal amnesty," only to have it defeated by the legislature. Boyden served as a delegate to the National Conservative Convention in August 1866; and, in a special election, he was chosen as a Conservative to represent the Sixth District in the Fortieth Congress. He was seated by the House of Representatives on 13 July 1868 and served until 3 Mar. 1869. When Boyden stood for reelection in 1868, he ran as an Independent with Republican tendencies and support. He was especially disturbed that the Democratic party had nominated Frank P. Blair as its vice-presidential candidate. The party's endorsement appeared to signal acceptance of Blair's publicly stated view that the executive should order the army to overturn the existing southern state governments and thus restore constitutional rule. Boyden denounced the Blair position as a strange brand of conservatism and constitutionalism. He feared that a Democratic victory might foreshadow the resumption of civil war. He clearly considered Grant and Republicanism preferable. Defeated in a disputed election by Francis E. Shober in 1868, Boyden eventually became a Republican, maintaining that it was the Democrats who had abandoned conservative principles. He served as a defense counsel in the Holden impeachment trial and was appointed to the North Carolina Supreme Court by Governor Caldwell. In the eyes of his erstwhile political allies, Boyden had joined the hated scalawags. His reputation suffered accordingly.

Boyden was married first, in June 1825, to Ruth Martin, a great-niece of Governor Alexander Martin. She died in August 1844, leaving four children, Nathaniel, John Augustus, Sarah Ann, and Ruth. In November 1845, Boyden married Mrs. Jane Henderson Mitchell, a daughter of Archibald Henderson and a niece of Chief Justice Leonard Henderson. A son, Archibald Henderson, was born to this union. The *North Carolina Portrait Index* lists an oil painting of Boyden by William G. Brown, dated 15 July 1852; this canvas is owned by Boyden Brawley of Salisbury. Boyden was interred in the Lutheran Cemetery in Salisbury.

SEE: *Biog. Dir. Am. Cong.* (1961); Nathaniel Boyden, *To The People of the Sixth District of North Carolina* (1868); *Congressional Globe*, 1847–49, 1868–69; Walter Clark, *History of the Supreme Court Reports of North Carolina* (1918); J. G. deRoulhac Hamilton, *Reconstruction in North Carolina* (1914); *History of North Carolina*, vol. 4, *North Carolina Biography* (1919); John H. Wheeler, *Reminiscences and Memoirs of North Carolina* (1883–84).

MAX R. WILLIAMS

Boylan, William (*1 Sept. 1777–15 July 1861*), journalist, planter, and advocate of internal improvements, was born in Somerset County, N.J., the fourth son of fifteen children of John and Elizabeth Hodge Boylan. He moved to Fayetteville in 1796 to join his uncle, Abraham Hodge, who published the *North-Carolina Minerva, and Fayetteville Advertiser*. In 1799, Boylan moved to Raleigh, where he received the printing patronage of the Federalist party until political changes brought to power the Republican party and Joseph Gales's rival paper, the *Raleigh Register*. In the heat of political passions, Boylan engaged Gales in a street brawl for which he was fined a hundred pounds, but in later years the two men served amicably on many state-wide committees. From 1803 to 1820, Boylan's newspaper was known as the *Minerva*, although Boylan himself sold his interest in 1810 to devote his attention to other matters.

Boylan served one term as councilor of state (1806) and four terms as a Federalist representative to the General Assembly from Wake County (1813–16). He detested Thomas Paine and attacked Jefferson for entertaining the author of *Common Sense*, together with "other vagabonds," in the White House. He was a close friend of William Polk and John Steele and supported the Hamiltonian-Whig economic philosophy. During the War of 1812 he violently opposed President Madison and attempted to create a Peace party within the state to prevent a Madison victory in 1812. As a member of the General Assembly he opposed the right of the assembly to censure Senator David Stone, an opponent of Madison's war efforts.

In 1815 he was appointed to a house committee for studying means of improving inland navigation, an idea initiated by Archibald D. Murphey. Together with Murphey, Gales, and two others, Boylan surveyed the Tar, Neuse, and Yadkin rivers, contemplated a canal to link the Yadkin with the Cape Fear, and in 1818 surveyed the Cape Fear. His interest in internal improvements led him to support the building of railroads as well as canals. He served as president of the Raleigh and Gaston Railroad, chartered in 1835 and completed in 1840; and he lent his influence and speaking ability in 1849–50 to urge the public to subscribe to stock in the projected North Carolina Railroad. He reminded his listeners that the state had produced only tar, pitch, and turpentine in years past; he hoped to see better economic conditions before he died, he added, and he urged the construction of railroads as a means to that end.

Boylan supported the State Bank of North Carolina (1810–35), succeeding William Polk as its president; he was president from 1820 to 1828 and also president pro tem of the Second Bank in 1840. Interested in agriculture, he acquired three plantations in Wake County; invested in properties near Chapel Hill, in Johnston County, and

in Mississippi, and was perhaps the first cotton grower in Wake County. He served one term as treasurer of the North Carolina Agricultural Society (1818), and he was once requested to acquaint the New York editor of the *Farmer's Library* with southern agriculture. As did many wealthy planters of the region, he sought relaxation and escape from the summer heat by making annual pilgrimages to White Sulphur Springs, Va.

Boylan, as a public-spirited citizen, was a charter supporter of the Raleigh Academy in 1801. He was responsible for building the first county poorhouse in Wake, and in the "big snow of '57" sent loads of firewood from his estate to the Raleigh poor. When the state capitol was burned in 1831, he served on the commission to erect a new capitol.

Boylan married Elizabeth Stokes McCulloch (or McCullough) and made his home in the former residence of Joel Lane, which he purchased from Peter Brown. At one time he owned most of southwest Raleigh. One son, Alexander McCulloch, received the A.B. degree from The University of North Carolina in 1823; another, William Polk, did likewise in 1825; both became planters. A third son, William Montfort, gained a reputation as a gay blade; he built Montford Hall, which has been remodeled as a church in Boylan Heights, Raleigh. Following the death of his first wife, Boylan married Jane Elliott. He had a total of eleven children.

Upon his death in 1861, Boylan was interred in the Raleigh City Cemetery. His tombstone notes his patriotic, civic-minded contributions to his adopted state.

SEE: Moses N. Amis, *Historical Raleigh from Its Foundation in 1792* (1902); Samuel A. Ashe, ed., *Biographical History of North Carolina*, vol. 6 (1907); Hope S. Chamberlain, *History of Wake County* (1922); *History of North Carolina*, vol. 2, *The Federal Period*, by W. K. Boyd (1919); S. M. Lemmon, *Frustrated Patriots: North Carolina and the War of 1812* (1973); *North Carolina Manual* (1913).

SARAH MCCULLOH LEMMON

Boynton, Charles Lawrence (*7 Feb. 1864–16 Sept. 1943*), botanist and zoologist, was born in Vineland, N.J., of Scotch-Irish ancestry. His father, Charles A. Boynton, was a descendant of John Boynton, who arrived from England in 1638 and settled in the town of Rowley, Mass. His mother was Rebecca Campbell, a descendant of Alexander Campbell, who emigrated from Ireland to New Hampshire in 1728. Boynton attended public schools in New Jersey and moved with his family to Highlands in 1880.

Stimulated by the profusion of flora and fauna around Highlands, Boynton soon developed a keen interest in natural history. He traveled widely through the southern Blue Ridge Mountains, recording his observations and collecting a great variety of animal, plant, and insect specimens. In June 1885 he accompanied Dr. William Brewster, the Harvard ornithologist, during his survey of Western North Carolina bird life. Boynton corresponded with Brewster during the following years, sending valuable specimens and important notes, many of which were incorporated into Brewster's classic papers on southern Appalachian avifauna; other records were sent to H. H. Brimley for inclusion in *Birds of North Carolina*. In 1886, Charles and his brother Frank guided Dr. Charles Sargent, the Cornell botanist, on a field trip into the Keowee River gorge, where they rediscovered the rare endemic flower *Shortia galacifolia*.

Boynton was married in 1894 to Mary Ethel Anderson. In 1895 he moved to Biltmore. From 1896 to 1905 he served as director of the George Vanderbilt Herbarium, during the period when Dr. Carl Schenck was manager of Vanderbilt's Pisgah Forest Estate and director of the first school of American forestry. Boynton traveled widely throughout the United States, collecting large numbers of plant specimens for the herbarium, the collections of which were used in the training program of the Forestry School.

In 1905, Boynton purchased a farm in Lodi, Calif., where he engaged in ranching until his death. He was buried in Lodi. Although he never published his observations, many authors incorporated his data into their works, thus providing valuable information on the plant and animal life of the southern Blue Ridge Mountains during a period when much of the region was undisturbed by human activity.

SEE: W. Brewster, *The Auk*, vol. 3 (1886); T. G. Pearson et al., *Birds of North Carolina* (1919).

MARCUS B. SIMPSON, JR.

Bradford, Henry Bartlett (*4 Dec. 1761–14 Mar. 1833*), Methodist minister and church founder, was the son of Colonel John Bradford and his first wife, Patience Reed Bradford, of Halifax County. He was a direct descendant (great-great-great-grandson) of William Bradford, governor and deputy governor of the Plymouth Colony from 1621 until 1656. Henry's father was one of the first commissioners of the peace for Halifax County, a member of the assembly, a delegate to the fourth provincial congress in 1776, a revolutionary soldier, and a representative to the first General Assembly of North Carolina under the constitution of 1776. Colonel Bradford settled near Enfield, Halifax County, on land granted by Lord Granville; a portion of this land was given to Henry.

Henry Bradford married Sarah Crowell, daughter of Edward and Martha Rayburn Crowell, on 1 Jan. 1782. The ceremony was performed by a friend of the Bradford family, the Reverend Francis Asbury. Henry and Sally, as she was known to her friends and relatives, made their home near Enfield on the land given to Henry by his father. The union produced ten children and many descendants, most of whom now live outside North Carolina.

Bradford did not share his father's love for military life or politics, even though he had seen service as a private in the Revolutionary War. His leaning, for which the acquaintance with Francis Asbury was undoubtedly responsible, was toward the Methodist Episcopal church. Although he was never ordained by the church, Bradford frequently preached to the people in the area around Enfield, gaining for himself a reputation as a competent minister. Even Bishop Asbury, who visited the local church in 1802, complimented Bradford for his work in behalf of Methodism.

By the late eighteenth century, Bradford had a regular congregation attending his sermons, which, prior to the erection of the first house of worship, were camp meetings held on his land near Enfield. Temporary log huts in the arbor provided shelter from inclement weather. A building called Bradford's Meeting House was completed about 1790, and a few years later the congregation had grown large enough for incorporation into the Methodist Episcopal Church in America.

During the first quarter of the nineteenth century, concern for reform within the Methodist Episcopal church provoked internal quarrels and led to schisms within the church body. Bradford supported the movement for change and demonstrated his activism by joining the Roanoke Union Society, an organization formed for serious consideration of reform measures within the Methodist church. Bradford hosted three meetings of the society in 1824 and 1825, despite its censure as a subversive group by the church hierarchy. A few years later, Bradford was among a group of ministers called to appear before the board of bishops for activity in the Roanoke Union Society and for patronizing *Mutual Rights*, a publication advocating church reform. In December 1828, Bradford was a delegate to the assembly that created the Methodist Protestant Church in North Carolina. He immediately joined the annual conference and began riding the Roanoke Circuit from his home near Enfield.

Bradford continued his work for the Methodist Protestant church until his death. His widow left North Carolina to live with her son Richard in Florida, where she died five years later.

SEE: G. L. E. Carroll, ed., *Francis Asbury in North Carolina* (1964); J. E. Carroll, *History of the North Carolina Annual Conference of the Methodist Protestant Church* (1939); Halifax County Records (North Carolina State Archives, Raleigh); Halifax *Free Press*, 10 Dec. 1824; *Journal of the North Carolina Annual Conference of the Methodist Protestant Church* (1836); John Paris, *History of the Methodist Protestant Church in North Carolina* (1849); Tarboro *Free Press*, 23 March 1833.

JERRY L. CROSS

Bradham, Caleb Davis (*27 May 1867–19 Feb. 1934*), founder of Pepsi-Cola, pharmacist, and Shriner, was born at Chinquapin, Duplin County, the son of George Washington and Julia McCann Bradham. He was of English and Scotch-Irish descent, and his American background included a great-great-great grandfather, John McCann, who was an officer in George Washington's army. He attended several North Carolina academies before entering The University of North Carolina in 1886. After three years he left to study medicine at the University of Maryland. Before he finished his funds gave out, and he returned home to teach in the Vance Academy in New Bern, a private school run by Appleton and Augusta Oaksmith.

Bradham continued to be interested in medicine, and after two years he went back to Maryland and entered the College of Pharmacy. Upon completion of those studies, he purchased a New Bern drug store and established "Bradham's Pharmacy," where the Pepsi-Cola story began. It was his pleasure to concoct soft drinks for the friends always gathered around his soda fountain. With his medical background and his knowledge of compounding prescriptions, it was natural for him to experiment with new flavor combinations. In the late 1890s he produced a beverage of his own creation and began offering it at his fountain. It was successful immediately and his friends promptly named it "Brad's drink." In 1898, however, for reasons no one knows, young Bradham changed the name to "Pepsi-Cola."

In 1902, the year he married Sarah Charity Credle of New Bern, he turned his drug store over to an assistant in order that he might devote all his time to developing Pepsi-Cola into a full business. His application to register "Pepsi-Cola" as his trademark was filed 23 Sept. 1902 and is the earliest dated document in the history of the company. The U.S. Patent Office accepted the mark and registered it on 16 June 1903. In April of the same year the trademark was registered in the Office of the Secretary of State of North Carolina.

Bradham formed the first Pepsi-Cola Company in

December 1902, and it became a corporation under the laws of North Carolina. It began in the back room of the drug store and was an immediate local success. He mixed his syrup, packaged it, and went out to build sales. He was a popular man and a superb salesman, and it was not long before his drink became a nationally known product. He franchised other territories in rapid succession until, by the end of 1910, there were at least three hundred bottlers spread over twenty-four states. He continued to prosper until after World War I; then, despite a hard fight, the rise and fall of the sugar market caused his twenty-year-old company to fail. At this time, the technology of bottling had not been perfected, and Bradham knew little of advertising and marketing. It was said that "he had a modern business in the wrong decades; he was a third of a century ahead of his time."

Although Bradham found his business engrossing, it did not monopolize his life. He went far in the Shriners and was made recorder of the Sudan Temple. In 1930 he was retired as "Recorder Emeritus." He was a bank officer and honorary president of a state-owned railroad. He was one of the founders of the North Carolina Naval Militia, with headquarters in New Bern; later it became the Naval Reserve. When he retired, he did so with the rank of rear admiral.

Bradham was interested in and always supported the School of Pharmacy of The University of North Carolina. In 1901 he offered the Bradham Prize to the student making the highest average during the two (later three) years of study. He continued to give the prize until 1930, shortly before his death.

He enjoyed boating, hunting, and fishing and was considered a fine marksman. He was a member of the Presbyterian church and a lifelong Democrat.

Bradham had three children, Mary Bradham Tucker of Edenton, Caleb Darnell of New Bern, and George Washington of Greensboro.

SEE: *American Soft Drink Journal*, July 1973; F. A. Birmingham, "The Pepsi-Cola Story," *Saturday Evening Post* 246 (1974); Milward W. Martin, *Twelve Full Ounces* (1962); Alice Noble, *The School of Pharmacy of the University of North Carolina* (1961); Mary Bradham Tucker, personal interview (November 1974).

ELIZABETH H. COPELAND

Brady, John Everett (22 July 1860–20 Jan. 1941), educator and writer, was born in Alamance County, the son of Rufus Archibald Brady and his wife, Martha Jane Hart.

Brady attended The University of North Carolina, receiving the A.B. degree in 1881. Traveling to Europe, he studied also at the Sorbonne and at Heidelberg. In Heidelberg he received both the A.M. and the Ph.D. degrees from the German University in 1888.

Returning to America the same year, Brady became a professor at Smith College in Northampton, Mass., where he served as head of the English and Latin departments for forty years (1888–1928). He wrote several works, including *Sound Changes in Modern Greek* (in German), *Studies in Quintus Curtius Rufus*, and *Women in Roman Literature*. He was a member of the American Philological Association and the Classical Association of New England.

A Presbyterian, Brady spent most of his life at Northampton. He was married first on 20 Aug. 1889 to Mary Taylor Seelye. Following her death, he married Annie McGhee Joyner, a widow from Franklinton. Brady had no children of his own but left several stepchildren. He spent his last years at Franklinton and following his death there was buried in Fairview Cemetery.

SEE: D. L. Grant, *Alumni History of the University of North Carolina* (1924); Raleigh *News and Observer*, 21 Jan. 1941.

JAMES ELLIOTT MOORE

Bragg, Braxton (22 Mar. 1817–27 Sept. 1876), a professional soldier who served with distinction in the U.S. Army during the Mexican War and with less success as commanding general of the Army of Tennessee, Confederate States of America, during the Civil War, was born at Warrenton, one of six sons of Thomas and Margaret Crossland Bragg. His elder brothers, John and Thomas, both became successful lawyers, and both had distinguished political careers. Less notable were Alexander, a successful architect; Dunbar, a Texas merchant; and the youngest, William, who was killed in the Civil War.

Bragg's father moved to Warrenton in 1800 to practice the trade of carpentry and was so engaged when he married Margaret Crossland in 1803. Ambitious and intelligent, the carpenter became a contractor, eventually acquiring a two-story brick home in Warrenton and about twenty slaves. The family was considered respectable, but an indication of the degree of its acceptance by the cream of Warrenton society is given in a letter from Congressman David Outlaw to his wife, dated 1 Aug. 1848: Outlaw expressed the hope that the people of Warrenton would properly honor Braxton upon his return from the Mexican War, adding that Colonel Bragg "must in his heart despise those who were formerly disposed to sneer at his family . . . as plebians."

Bragg followed his elder brothers to Warrenton Academy, and with the help of Senator Willie P. Mangum secured an appointment to the U.S. Military Academy at West Point, where he was graduated near the top of his class in 1837.

As a lieutenant of artillery, he was posted to Florida and participated in the Seminole War, but his health failed and he was sent home to recover. Upon his return to active duty, he acquired a reputation as an intelligent and hard-working but quarrelsome officer. Ironically, during this period he formed close and lifelong friendships with two other young officers, George H. Thomas and William T. Sherman, both of whom would later be instruments of his defeat on Civil War battlefields.

He placed his career in jeopardy in 1844–45 with a series of articles in the *Southern Literary Messenger* in which he attacked the entire army administration, reserving his harshest criticisms for its commander, General Winfield Scott. Though his pleas for reform may have been sound, they led to his arrest and court-martial on charges of insolence and disobedience. He was found guilty of disrespect for superior officers and received official reprimands and suspension of rank and command for a period of two months. His appeal failed to get the sentence reversed, and though he had powerful friends in both the government and the army, his career appeared blighted. Then, in June of 1845, he and his company were ordered to join General Zachary Taylor's army, for the protection of Texas against Mexico.

His service during the Mexican War was exemplary; he was twice breveted and then promoted to the rank of captain of artillery. At Buena Vista, he personally directed his battery in a series of actions that broke a Mexican attack and led to an important American victory. He was breveted lieutenant colonel and returned to the United States a national hero, the man who, according to popular legends, had stopped the Mexicans with "a little more grape."

In 1849, while assigned to duty in New Orleans, he met and married Louisiana heiress Eliza Brooks Ellis. The couple spent the next six years at various military posts, but neither Bragg nor his wife was satisfied with the necessity of living on the frontier. On 31 Dec. 1855, Bragg resigned his commission after a dispute about assignments with Secretary of War Jefferson Davis; in February 1856 he bought a sugar plantation near Thibodaux, La. Successful as a planter, Bragg also became commissioner of public works, designing and constructing drainage and levee systems.

As the secession crisis approached, Bragg became reluctantly involved in preparations for war. He had not favored secession but in 1861 told his friend Sherman that sectional bitterness had become so strong that it might be better if the South departed in peace.

Bragg became a major general in the Louisiana militia and was commissioned a brigadier general in the Confederate Army, commanding coastal defenses in the region from Pensacola, Fla., to Mobile, Ala. In January of 1862 he was promoted to major general, and one month later he asked for the transfer of his command to the north, where he felt it would be needed. His request was granted, and he moved to Corinth, Miss., joining the army of General Albert Sidney Johnston. From Corinth, the army moved to Shiloh, with Bragg in the dual role of commander of the Second Corps and chief of staff. He displayed both courage and energy at the Battle of Shiloh, was rewarded with a promotion to general, and on 27 June relieved General Pierre Beauregard as commander of the Army of Tennessee.

From this point his fortunes went downhill, and with them the fortunes of the Confederacy. An excellent subordinate in combat, Bragg simply lacked the qualities essential for success in a field command. Often opening opportunities through bold and sometimes resourceful action, he almost invariably lacked the persistence to exploit advantages. He was never able to win the loyalty and trust of his own subordinates, and at one point, after the Stone River debacle, they openly called for his resignation. Still, Davis stood by him until the disaster at Chattanooga compelled his replacement in December 1863.

His career, rich in irony, might have provided not one of the Confederacy's most signal failures but its most spectacular success, if only he had been placed in his proper role. Both friends and foes agreed that Bragg would have been invaluable to the southern armies if Davis had made him inspector general early in the conflict, making use of his superb talents for organization and discipline. Instead of an outstanding inspector general, Davis opted for an inferior field commander.

Following his removal from command, Bragg was summoned by Davis to Richmond, nominally as commander in chief but actually as military adviser to the Confederate president. Bragg accompanied Davis on the flight south in 1865, was captured 9 May, and received a parole.

His postwar career involved work as a civil engineer in Alabama and Texas. He was a resident of Galveston at the time of his sudden death.

SEE: R. Ernest Dupuy and Trevor N. Dupuy, *Military Heritage of America* (1956); Grady McWhiney, *Braxton Bragg and Confederate Defeat*, vol. 1 (1969); D. C. Seitz, *Braxton Bragg* (1924).

C. E. PITTS

Bragg, John (14 Jan. 1806–10 Aug. 1878), lawyer and Democratic political figure prominent in both North Carolina and Alabama, was the eldest of six sons born to

Thomas and Margaret Crossland Bragg of Warrenton. Two brothers, Braxton and Thomas, also had distinguished careers. For a brief family history, see the biography of Braxton Bragg, above.

Bragg received his early education at Warrenton Academy and was graduated in 1824 from The University of North Carolina, in the same class with James Bryan, Thomas Dews, William A. Graham, and Matt E. Manley. Following graduation, he read law in the Warrenton office of Judge John Hall of the North Carolina Supreme Court and was admitted to the bar in 1830. He was also elected in that year to the North Carolina House of Representatives, where he served five terms. In 1835 he was appointed by President Andrew Jackson to the prestigious board of visitors for the U.S. Military Academy at West Point.

Though, by any objective standards, Bragg was becoming a successful young lawyer-politician, he became convinced that the "new lands" of the southwest offered far greater professional and political opportunity for an ambitious young man than did his native state. In the fall of 1835 he moved from Warrenton to Mobile, Ala., making the long overland trip in a small surrey that also carried all his personal belongings, accompanied only by a single Negro bodyservant on horseback.

Bragg established a successful law practice in Mobile and in 1836 temporarily took the editorship of the *Mobile Register* during the illness of its regular editor. The *Register* was a Democrat-oriented paper, and both the paper and its temporary editor supported Jackson's party during the 1836 presidential campaign. Bragg's affairs prospered, partly because in 1839 he became the attorney for the Branch Bank of Mobile, and in 1842 he was appointed to a vacancy as judge of the Tenth Judicial District Circuit Court of Alabama. He subsequently won election to the post and served for nine years as a circuit court judge.

Bragg was a states' rights Democrat, not inclined to compromise his principles, and in the wake of the furor over the Compromise of 1850 he was induced to accept his party's nomination for the U.S. House of Representatives. His chief rival was Unionist party candidate C. C. Langdon, editor of the *Mobile Advertiser*. Bragg opposed secession, declaring that it was not a viable course of action, and maintained that he was a better Unionist than Langdon. In fact, both men favored the antisecessionist "Georgia Platform," but Bragg was able to unite Langdon's opposition and so won handily. He served in Congress from 4 Mar. 1851 until 3 Mar. 1853 but was dissatisfied with the role of a congressman and emphatically refused to run for reelection to a second term. He returned to Mobile, where he practiced law and continued his interest in politics. In 1861 he served as a delegate from Mobile County to both the Alabama Secession Convention, where he voted for secession, and to the state's constitutional convention.

When war came, he was physically unable to perform military service, and he spent the war years as a planter in Lowndes County. In 1847 he had married Mary Frances Hall, daughter of Henry M. Hall, a planter and businessman of Lowndes County; the union ultimately produced six children. His plantation home was destroyed by Union forces in 1865, and according to contemporary accounts only the entreaties of his wife and children prevented his being hanged as the brother of Confederate General Braxton Bragg.

Following the war he returned to Mobile to the practice of law until his death.

SEE: C. P. Denman, *The Secessionist Movement in Alabama*

(1933); Thomas M. Owen, *History of Alabama and Dictionary of Alabama Biography* (1921).

C. E. PITTS

Bragg, Thomas *(9 Nov. 1810–21 Jan. 1872)*, lawyer, governor, U.S. senator, and Confederate cabinet member, was one of six sons of Thomas and Margaret Crossland Bragg of Warrenton. Two brothers, Braxton and John, had distinguished careers. For a brief family history, see the biography of Braxton Bragg, above.

Bragg attended Warrenton Academy for nine years and was for three years thereafter a student at Captain Alden Patridge's Military Academy at Middletown, Conn. As had his elder brother, John, he followed his formal education by studying law under the tutelage of Judge John Hall of the North Carolina Supreme Court; he was admitted to the North Carolina bar in 1832. He established a successful law practice in Jackson, Northampton County, and entered politics as a Democrat. Success did not come as quickly in politics as it did in law, however, partly because Northampton was a stronghold of Whiggery. Bragg persevered and was elected in 1842 to a single term in the North Carolina House of Representatives, where he served as chairman of the judiciary committee. He became one of his party's leaders, serving as a delegate to the Democratic conventions of 1844, 1848, and 1852, and in 1854 he won an uphill battle for the North Carolina governorship. He served two terms as governor, championing a wider franchise, internal improvements, and an improved banking system. As a states' rights Democrat, he expressed opposition to federal encroachment but counseled moderation in resistance to it.

In 1859 he was elected to the U.S. Senate, where he served until his withdrawal 6 Mar. 1861, before North Carolina's secession from the Union. He made few public comments on secession but revealed privately and in his diary that he considered it an impractical, unwise proceeding, no matter how justified.

Following his withdrawal from the Senate, he returned to his native state. There he was engaged in helping to prepare North Carolina's military forces for the looming conflict when he was asked by Confederate President Jefferson Davis to succeed Juda P. Benjamin as attorney general of the Confederacy, after Benjamin had been switched to another post. Bragg accepted, serving ably from 22 Nov. 1861 until 18 Mar. 1862, when he fell victim to internal political bickering. He resigned in order to allow Davis to appoint Thomas H. Watts of Alabama to the position, in response to a demand by former Union Whigs for a post in the Davis cabinet. As attorney general, Bragg drafted a plan for the organization of his department and was active in attempts to solve such problems as disloyalty to the Confederacy, the activities of Unionists within the South, the relations of the central government with the various Confederate states, treaties to be negotiated with the Indians, and the naturalization of aliens by the Confederacy.

Following his resignation from the cabinet, he moved to Petersburg, Va., the ancestral home of his wife, Isabelle Cuthbert Bragg, whom he had married in October of 1837. He lived there until 7 Nov. 1862, when he returned to North Carolina, working in Raleigh as both a personal representative of Davis and the chairman of a citizens' effort to keep the state committed to the Confederate cause. Despite his private belief that disaster was ultimately in store, he was effective in keeping North Carolina behind the Davis government.

After the conflict was over, he resumed the practice of law and again became involved in state politics, fighting for the realization of his ideals of good government. One of the last acts of his career, shortly before his death, was to serve as counsel for the impeachment of former friend and political ally Governor William W. Holden; he helped to secure convictions resulting in Holden's removal from office.

SEE: Samuel A. Ashe, *History of North Carolina*, vol. 1 (1908); Hugh T. Lefler and Albert R. Newsome, *North Carolina: The History of a Southern State* (1954); W. J. Peele, ed., *Lives of Distinguished North Carolinians* (1908); Southern Historical Collection (University of North Carolina, Chapel Hill), for Thomas Bragg's diary, on microfilm.

C. E. PITTS

Branch, Douglas McKinley *(8 Nov. 1908–1 Feb. 1963)*, Baptist minister and general secretary-treasurer of the North Carolina Baptist State Convention, was born in the Mount Moriah community of Wake County and was the son of Atlas M. and Nora Branch. His primary education was obtained at Mount Auburn and Garner schools. He entered Wake Forest College in the spring of 1934, and in the fall of 1935 his home church, Mount Moriah, Wake County, ordained him to the full gospel ministry. While a student at Wake Forest College, he served Youngsville, Bethlehem, and Bethel Baptist churches in Wake and Franklin counties. He was graduated from Wake Forest College *cum laude* in 1937.

Branch was pastor of Cary Baptist Church from 1939 until 1941. During this time he served a term as moderator of the Raleigh Baptist Association and attended Duke Divinity School. He was then appointed a general missionary for the Piedmont area of North Carolina. He served in this capacity from 1941 to 1943, working under the State Mission Board of the North Carolina Baptist State Convention. He then resigned to pursue further studies at the Southern Baptist Theological Seminary, Louisville, Ky., in 1943–45; he supplemented this study with summer attendance at the Presbyterian Seminary, Louisville, Ky.

Following the completion of three full years, Branch accepted the call to become pastor of the Scotland Neck Baptist Church and returned to North Carolina in 1945. From 1947 to 1953 he was pastor of the First Baptist Church, Kannapolis. In this position, within one of the most industrialized communities in North Carolina, he had the opportunity to become acquainted with the Piedmont area of the state. In 1953, after a successful pastorate in Kannapolis, during which time he served as moderator of the Cabarrus Baptist Association (1949–50), he was extended a call to become pastor of the First Baptist Church of Rocky Mount. While there he also served as moderator of the North Roanoke Baptist Association.

In 1949 Branch was appointed to and served on a committee to prepare a nine-year program of advance for North Carolina Baptists. The pastors of North Carolina called upon him in 1950 to serve as the president of their conference, and he was a member of the Committee on Committees of the Baptist State Convention for one year. In 1952 he was elected the first vice-president of the Baptist State Convention; and when the convention president, Archie Ellis, moved from North Carolina, it became Branch's responsibility to preside. Subsequently, he was elected and twice served as the president of the convention in his own right (1953–54). When North Carolina Baptists decided to make a thorough study of the total organized life of the convention, Branch was a member of the "Committee of 25." He served for five years on the executive committee of the Southern Baptist Convention.

In 1959, at a special session of the Baptist State Convention, Branch was nominated and elected general secretary-treasurer of the North Carolina Baptist State Convention. His installation service was held in the First Baptist Church, Raleigh on 30 June 1959. He succeeded Maloy Alton Huggins as the principal administrator and coordinator of the mutual but not always identical interests of 871,370 North Carolina Baptists and 3,310 self-governing and often vigorously self-sufficient Baptist churches.

From 1956 to 1959, Branch served as trustee of Wake Forest College and, from 1947 to 1958, as vice-chairman of the board. The college honored him with a D.D. degree in 1956. During 1950 he served on the board of trustees for Wingate College.

While Branch was returning from an engagement at Chowan College, Murfreesboro, his car struck a stalled truck near Ahoskie and he was fatally injured. His funeral services were conducted 3 Feb. 1963 in the Forest Hills Baptist Church, Raleigh, and interment was in Memorial Park, Raleigh.

Branch was married 2 June 1933 to Jessie Walker of Windsor. They had three children, Mrs. Ben Sutton, Jessica Diana, and Douglas, Jr.

SEE: Baptist Historical Collection (Wake Forest University, Winston-Salem), Biography File; Baptist State Convention Headquarters (Raleigh [photograph]); *Encyclopedia of Southern Baptists*, vol. 3 (1971); *North Carolina Baptist State Convention Annuals, 1952, 1953, 1954*; Raleigh *Biblical Recorder*, 9 Feb. 1963; Wake Forest University Alumni Office questionnaire.

JOHN R. WOODARD, JR.

Branch, John (4 Nov. 1782–4 Jan. 1863), governor of North Carolina, U.S. senator, secretary of the navy, and governor of Florida, was born in the town of Halifax. His father, John Branch, Sr., was a wealthy landowner and something of a local celebrity because of his success in ferreting out Tories in Halifax County during the Revolution. The older Branch fathered eight children by two wives. The first, and mother of John Branch, Jr., was Rebecca Bradford, daughter of Colonel John Bradford.

The younger Branch was born to wealth, and his tastes and inclinations were decidedly patrician. He attended The University of North Carolina and later studied law under Judge John Haywood, but he devoted his time to politics rather than to the practice of law. He was elected for seven terms to represent Halifax County in the senate of the state General Assembly. He was elected speaker of the senate in 1815 and held that office until his election as governor in 1817. He served three terms as governor.

It should be remembered that success in state politics was not necessarily evidence of great personal popularity. To be allowed to vote for a senator, one had to own a minimum of fifty acres of property; the property qualifications disenfranchised significant percentages of the electorate, often as much as 25 percent. In addition, the requirement that a senator had to own three hundred acres or more to hold office greatly reduced the number of citizens eligible to run for a senate seat. The governor was elected by the General Assembly. Branch's success in the legislature was based upon his wit and charm. He flattered members of the assembly profusely when he wished their support, and he was famous for his lavish dinners and parties. His ability to win support did not,

however, extend beyond the legislature. When he ran for governor in 1838, after the office had been made elective, he was defeated.

Politically, Branch was a Democrat, committed to the concept of state sovereignty. "The powers of the General Government are constantly increasing," he once noted, "and American liberty depends on the preservation of state rights and state powers." After a successful term in the U.S. Senate, Branch was appointed secretary of the navy by President Andrew Jackson, as a reward for North Carolina's support in the election of 1828. Branch was the first North Carolinian to hold a cabinet position.

Branch was an outspoken critic of banks and federal internal improvements. Although this opposition was a sound Jacksonian position, he was unfortunate enough to lose favor with the president over an embarrassing social incident known as the "Eaton Affair." Washington gossip made much of the marriage of John Henry Eaton, Jackson's secretary of war, to Margaret O'Neale Timberlake, the daughter of a Washington tavern-keeper. Mrs. Eaton's prior occupation as a barmaid, the fact of a previous marriage, and rumors of amorous affairs were enough to bar her access to Washington society. Although Jackson insisted that marriage had "restore[d] Peg's good name," the wives of the cabinet members, especially Mrs. Branch, were very pointed in their insults toward her.

Because of increasing bitterness within his official family, Jackson "reorganized" his cabinet. Branch resigned his post but contended that his resignation was the result of a "malign influence" upon the president. The "malign influence" of which he complained was that of the secretary of state, Martin Van Buren, who used the opportunity to befriend the Eatons and thus ingratiate himself with the president. In the 1832 presidential campaign, Branch tried unsuccessfully to drive Van Buren, Jackson's choice for the vice-presidency, off the Democratic ticket.

Branch served one term in the House of Representatives after his resignation from the cabinet, but his most important service was in the state constitutional covention of 1835. He spoke in favor of allowing free Negroes the right to vote and of removing all religious qualifications for officeholding. When the other delegates voted against him, Branch told the convention that he had not attended to "accommodate the ill-founded prejudices of the people."

In 1836, Branch began to acquire large estates in Florida. He and his family eventually moved there, where in 1843 he was appointed governor by President Tyler. During his term in office Florida became a state. He returned to North Carolina in 1851 and remained there until his death.

Although Branch was an opponent of federal participation in the lives of the people, he did support a variety of state schemes for public education and internal improvements. He was a former president of the North Carolina branch of the American Colonization Society.

Branch married twice. His first wife, the mother of his nine children, was Elizabeth Foort (d. 1851); his second wife, whom he married in 1853, was Mrs. Mary Eliza Jordan Bond.

SEE: Branch Papers (Southern Historical Collection, University of North Carolina, Chapel Hill); Governor Branch's Letter-Book (North Carolina State Archives, Raleigh); William S. Hoffmann, "John Branch and the Origins of the Whig Party in North Carolina," *North Carolina Historical Review* 35 (1958); *Niles' Weekly Register*, September 1831; *North Carolina Booklet*, vol. 15 (1915);

Raleigh Register, September 1831; Reports of the Secretary of the Navy, 1830–31.

HAROLD J. COUNIHAN

Branch, Lawrence O'Bryan *(28 Nov. 1820–17 Sept. 1862)*, lawyer, U.S. congressman, and Confederate soldier, was born in Enfield of a prominent and wealthy family. His parents were Joseph and Susan Simpson O'Bryan Branch. The family lived in Tennessee until Joseph's death in 1827 (Susan had died two years earlier); Lawrence was returned to North Carolina to become a member of the household of his distinguished uncle, John Branch. When his kinsman was appointed secretary of the navy by President Andrew Jackson, young Branch went with him to Washington, D.C. After studying under several tutors, one of whom was Salmon P. Chase, he attended Bingham Military Academy in North Carolina. Then followed a short stay at The University of North Carolina and graduation with distinction from Princeton in 1838.

While working as a newspaper editor in Nashville, Tenn., Branch studied law. He was not admitted to the bar until he moved to Tallahassee, Fla., however, and then, because he was not of age, it took a special act of the territorial legislature to gain him his license in 1840. During the Seminole War he served as an aide to General Robert R. Reid. In 1844 he married Nancy Haywood Blount, daughter of General W. A. Blount of Washington, N.C. Four years later he moved to Raleigh to continue the practice of law.

In 1852, Branch became president of the Raleigh and Gaston Railroad Company. At the same time he started an active political career, having been chosen as an elector on the Democratic ticket of Franklin Pierce and William R. D. King. Despite a reluctance to run, he was elected to the U.S. House of Representatives in 1854 and was to serve in that body continuously from 1855 to 1861. He was not a candidate for renomination in 1860. As a staunch Southern Democrat, he spoke forcefully in defense of his district, state, and section; yet he never hesitated to caution the South against extremism. His speeches were primarily those of a southern moderate. Although he had been a constant supporter of the president in the House, in December 1860 he refused the position of secretary of the treasury in Buchanan's cabinet (once before he had declined a cabinet post, that of postmaster general).

Opposed to the "coercion" of the southern states, he advocated secession. When North Carolina withdrew from the Union, he enlisted as a private in the Raleigh Rifles, but shortly thereafter the governor appointed him state quartermaster general. Desiring service in the field, Branch resigned to become colonel of the Thirty-third North Carolina Regiment. On 17 Jan. 1862 he was promoted to brigadier general in the provisional Confederate Army. March 1862 found him in command of the Southern troops defending New Bern against Burnside's Union forces. Even though the loss of New Bern was a great blow to North Carolina, Branch escaped the scathing criticism leveled against a number of his fellow officers. To most observers he did about as well as could be expected from a "political general."

After retiring to Kinston, he was ordered to Virginia. His brigade, which consisted of the Seventh, Eighteenth, Twenty-eighth, Thirty-third, and Thirty-seventh North Carolina regiments was attached to A. P. Hill's division, Stonewall Jackson's corps. Action soon followed at Hanover Court House, the Seven Days' battles around Richmond, and the Second Manassas and Antietam

campaigns. Branch was killed at Antietam. As a brigade commander in Hill's famous light division, he had led his troops on a rapid march from Harper's Ferry to Sharpsburg. He arrived on the field of battle in time to help stem the Union advance and save Lee's right flank from a crushing defeat. Soon afterward, as he stood talking with three fellow officers, he was hit by sharpshooter fire. He fell dying into the arms of a staff officer. General Hill wrote: "The Confederacy has to mourn the loss of a gallant soldier and accomplished gentleman. He was my senior brigadier, and one to whom I could have intrusted the command of the division, with all confidence." He left one son, W. A. B. Branch. Interment was in Old City Cemetery, Raleigh.

SEE: Samuel A. Ashe, ed., *Biographical History of North Carolina*, vol. 8 (1917); John G. Barrett, *The Civil War in North Carolina* (1963); *Biog. Dir. Am. Cong.* (1961); Walter Clark, ed., *Histories of the Several Regiments and Battalions from North Carolina in the Great War, 1861–1865*, vol. 4 (1901 [portrait]); *Congressional Globe*, 1855–61; C. A. Evans, ed., *Confederate Military History*, vol. 4 (1899 [portrait]); D. H. Hill, *Bethel to Sharpsburg*, vols. 1–2 (1920); John Hughes, *Lawrence O'Bryan Branch* (n.d.); Ezra Warner, *Generals in Gray* (1964[portrait]).

J. G. BARRETT

Branch, William Augustus Blount *(26 Feb. 1847–18 Nov. 1910)*, Confederate soldier, planter, and congressman, was born in Tallahassee, Fla., the son of General Lawrence O'Bryan Branch, C.S.A., and Nancy Haywood Blount. His father, a North Carolinian, was practicing law in Florida at the time. Branch was educated at Lovejoy's Academy in Raleigh, Bingham Military Academy near Mebane, The University of North Carolina, and Virginia Military Institute at Lexington.

Branch joined the Confederate Army as a courier on the staff of General R. F. Hoke, and surrendered with General Joseph E. Johnston's army in 1865. He studied law but never practiced. In 1867 he took charge of his landed estate in Beaufort County and engaged in agricultural pursuits for the rest of his life.

Branch was elected as a Democrat to the Fifty-second and Fifty-third Congresses and served from 4 Mar. 1891 to 3 Mar. 1895. He was a member of the North Carolina House of Representatives in 1896.

Branch married his cousin, Eliza Blount, daughter of William Augustus Blount, Jr., and Mary Washington. They had four children: Lawrence O'Bryan; William Augustus Blount; Eliza, who married Bayard Whitehurst; and Laura, who married John Stedman.

Branch died in Washington, N.C., and was buried there.

SEE: *Biog. Dir. Am. Cong.* (1961); Daniel L. Grant, *Alumni History of the University of North Carolina* (1924); Ursula F. Loy and Pauline M. Worthy, *Washington and the Pamlico* (1976).

ARMISTEAD JONES MAUPIN

Branson, Eli *(d. ca. 1818)*, a Regulator and Loyalist, was born in Virginia. The family moved to Chatham County, where Branson inherited land from his father and was active in the Regulator movement. In 1776 he led a Loyalist company at the Battle of Moore's Creek Bridge. After the defeat he hid for a while in North Carolina, and in 1777 he joined Sir William Howe's forces in Pennsylvania. After the British evacuated Philadelphia, Branson returned to North Carolina. There he corresponded with John Hamilton, a leader of North Carolina Loyalist forces in Georgia and South Carolina, and in 1781 he joined Cornwallis at Hillsborough as captain of a company of North Carolina Volunteers. Branson and several members of his company were captured at Yorktown. When released, they were attached to the New York Volunteers and went to New York. On the British evacuation in 1783, Branson went to New Brunswick and was given a lot at Parrtown (part of present-day St. John). He was in England for a while in the mid-1780s and considered settling in the Bahama Islands, but by 1788 he was living in Canada, probably Montreal.

During the postwar years Branson corresponded with his brother in Chatham County, and apparently Eli Branson returned to Chatham County in 1815 and died there in 1818. This man's widow, Mary, married Thomas Branson, and he had at least two sons, Benjamin and Henry M.

SEE: North Carolina State Archives (Raleigh), for an Eli Branson deed in Chatham County Deed Book T and for the Eli Branson Estate Papers in Chatham County Estates; P.R.O., A.O. 12, 13, 139; ibid., F.O. 4; ibid., T 64; ibid., W.O. 65; Public Archives of Canada (Ottawa) for Lawrence Collection, Chipman Papers, Muster Rolls of North Carolina Volunteers; William L. Saunders, ed., *Colonial Records of North Carolina*, vols. 7–8 (1890); Esther Clark Wright, *The Loyalists of New Brunswick* (1955).

CAROLE WATTERSON TROXLER

Branson, Eugene Cunningham (6 Aug. 1861–13 Mar. 1933), educator, author, and editor, was born in Morehead City, oldest of the seven children of the Reverend Levi and Edith Cunningham Branson. The Reverend Mr. Branson, an ordained Methodist minister, occupied various pulpits and traveled extensively in the United States and abroad; he established a book store and publishing firm in Raleigh, which he operated for many years.

Little is known of Branson's early education; his schooling was probably conducted in his home or in a small private school. He entered Trinity College (now Duke University) in 1877 and completed an M.A. degree in 1879. He also attended George Peabody Normal College in Nashville, Tenn., where he received another M.A. degree in 1883. Following graduation from Peabody, Branson worked fourteen years in secondary education as principal of a high school in Raleigh and as superintendent of public schools in Wilson, N.C., and Athens, Ga. (the first public school system in Georgia). Before leaving North Carolina he became the youngest member of the Watauga Club, an organization of leading cultural and political men in Raleigh who studied the state's social and economic resources and offered suggestions for their utilization. While in Georgia, Branson wrote three publications for public school use: *Methods of Teaching Arithmetic* (1896), *Methods of Reading and Spelling* (1896), and a chapter in *Page's Theory and Practice of Teaching* entitled "Fitness to Teach" (1899).

Branson left secondary education for higher education in 1897, when he accepted an appointment as professor of pedagogy at Georgia Normal and Industrial School in Milledgeville. He remained at the Milledgeville school until 1900, when he became the president of State Normal School of Georgia in Athens. While serving the Athens school he organized the Georgia Club in 1902, to familiarize future teachers of Georgia with their state, and established the state's first department of rural economics and sociology in 1912. He also found time to write *Branson's Common School Speller* published in 1903, and to edit an eight-page magazine called *Home and Farmstead* in 1912, which printed studies of rural conditions in Georgia made by the rural economics and sociology department.

Branson's work in Georgia prepared him for greater achievement in his native state, where he returned in 1914 to head The University of North Carolina's new department of rural social economics. For almost nineteen years, he ably administered the department's four-fold work: (1) offering formal textbook courses, (2) establishing a seminar library, (3) conducting regional studies on county government, and (4) answering calls for information and assistance from citizens of the state. The success of his work in North Carolina led to the establishment of similar departments of rural social economics in Virginia, Tennessee, and South Carolina.

The courses Branson taught were unique as well as popular. While using textbooks as a background for interpretation, he explored the problems of rural life in North Carolina and suggested constructive policies to meet them. The courses were strictly elective and open only to juniors, seniors, and graduates; Branson spoke the language the young men of the twentieth century were eager to hear, however, and his courses were taken by over four thousand students. Three of his students attained prominence in the field of rural social economics: Wilson Gee in Virginia, J. A. Dickey in Arkansas, and S. H. Hobbs, Jr., in North Carolina. In addition to teaching at The University of North Carolina, Branson held summer school seminars in California, Utah, Texas, Alabama, Tennessee, and Louisiana.

The rural social economics seminar library established by Branson was one of the first of its kind in the nation. More important than the books purchased by the library's meager annual fund were the newspaper clippings, learned journal articles, monographs, bulletins, and reports assembled daily by the department staff. This holding of material dealing with country life in the state, the nation, and many foreign countries became a clearinghouse of information for readers, scholars, and leaders of the state in matters concerning North Carolina.

With the aim of improving local government throughout North Carolina, Branson supervised field workers in the study of county government in sixty-one rural counties of the state. This work earned him an appointment to Governor Angus W. McLean's advisory commission on county government and influenced the introduction of various reform bills in the 1927 state legislature: the county fiscal control bill, the county finance act, the county management system act, and a tax-collecting act.

Perhaps the most far-reaching work of the rural social economics department was the answering of calls for information and assistance—two thousand a year, on the average—from the citizens of the state. It was not unusual for such requests to require days of research.

In addition to departmental duties, Branson worked as editor from 1914 until 1922 of the weekly university *News Letter*, a one-page, widely circulated paper (18,000 subscribers and 310 newspapers), discussing specific facts about county affairs as well as general social and economic problems of North Carolina. He also helped organize in 1914 the North Carolina Club, a group of faculty members, students, and townspeople interested in the study of problems facing the state. Papers delivered by members at club meetings were compiled into yearbooks, which were made available to interested citizens of North Carolina.

Branson was awarded a Litt.D. degree by the University of Georgia (Athens) in 1919 and the same year was appointed a Kenan professor at The University of North Carolina. He was given a leave of absence in 1923 to study agricultural conditions in various European countries, especially Denmark; as a result, he wrote a widely acclaimed book entitled *Farm Life Abroad* (1924). He delivered many addresses and wrote extensively on the subjects of farm tenancy, illiteracy, farm credit, and crop diversification; and he championed movements for farm land reclamation, better port facilities, and good roads for North Carolina.

Although a Presbyterian and a Democrat, Branson was respected by men of many religious and political backgrounds. His faith in humanity and infinite patience with his fellowmen were characteristics most admired by those who knew him. His marriage on 27 Sept. 1889 to Lottie Lanier of West Point, Ga., produced four children: Frank Lanier, Edith Lanier (Mrs. Young B. Smith), Phil Lanier, and Elizabeth Lanier. Branson died in Duke Hospital and was buried in Old Chapel Hill Cemetery.

SEE: Eugene Cunningham Branson Papers (Southern Historical Collection, University of North Carolina, Chapel Hill); Lanier Branson, *Eugene Cunningham Branson* (1967); *Durham Herald-Sun*, 19 Mar. 1933; *Greensboro Daily News*, 15 and 19 Mar. 1933; Almonte Charles Howell, *The Kenan Professorships* (1956); Raleigh *News and Observer*, 20 Nov. 1927, 14 Mar. 1933; Gary Trawick and Paul Wyche, *One Hundred Years, One Hundred Men*, (1971); *University of North Carolina News Letter*, 29 Mar. 1933; *Who Was Who in America*, vol. 1 (1943).

RICHARD A. SHRADER

Branson, Levi (*5 Feb. 1832–5 Dec. 1903*), educator, Methodist minister, writer, editor, and publisher, was born and reared on a farm in Randolph County about five miles south of Asheboro. He was the second of nine children born to William Branson (1804–79) and his first wife, Martha Nance (1810–64). His paternal grandfather and great-grandfather—both also named Levi—and his great-great-grandfather, Thomas Branson, were prominent farmers in the Randolph County area before the Revolution, when the area was part of older counties.

Young Levi Branson was schooled at home in the history and traditions of the Branson family. He received his formal education in the public schools and at Trinity College in Randolph County. After being graduated with the A.B. degree, Branson became a schoolteacher, at the same time taking graduate studies for the A.M. degree. Conspicuous energy and success in the teaching profession brought him to the attention of the Reverend W. H. Cunniggim of Hookerton, a Methodist minister and educator who in the early 1850s led a group of citizens in establishing Lenoir Male and Female Seminary at the place now called The Institute, located near the Lenoir and Greene County lines northeastward of LaGrange in Lenoir County.

Branson was employed as principal of Lenoir Male and Female Seminary in 1855. In 1856 the board of directors changed the school's name to Lenoir Collegiate Institute, expanded the curriculum tq add the first two years of a college liberal arts program, and elected Branson president. He immediately launched a major building program. Included were new residence halls, a new classroom building, and a Methodist church. In April 1857 newspaper advertisements announced the opening of the new facilities.

On 18 Nov. 1858, Branson married Edith Ann Sarah Cunniggim, daughter of W. H. Cunniggim (Cunning-

ham), at The Institute Methodist Church. To their marriage seven children were born, three of whom died in infancy. The four surviving children were Eugene Cunniggim (b. 6 Aug. 1861); Lillian Cunniggim (b. 2 Apr 1866), who married George T. Simmons, a Methodist minister; Edith Myrtle Cunniggim (b. 9 Nov. 1867), who married J. Quinton Adams, native of Lynchburg, Va., and settled in Atlanta, Ga.; and Daisy Cunniggim (b. 6 Nov. 1872), who was living with her parents in Raleigh in 1898.

As president of the institute, Branson was highly active in developing other educational and cultural interests in the Lenoir and Greene county area. He was a founder of the Lenoir County Educational and Literary Association, which is still in existence under a slightly altered name. He served several years as its secretary and was a strong friend of the first state superintendent of schools, Calvin Wiley. Through the influence of his educational and literary association membership, a number of lending libraries were opened in private homes and businesses. He aroused an interest in local and state history, leading to organization of a local historical association. His great admiration for his father-in-law led him to enter the Methodist ministry as an additional career of service.

The institute flourished until the Civil War forced the closing of the college program. The lower-level programs continued until the 1880s, but by 1862, Kinston and Lenoir County were being attacked by Federal forces based at New Bern. Branson moved his family to Raleigh, bought the inn on the site of the present Justice Building (the location of Casso's Tavern in 1796), and became editor and publisher of elementary school textbooks. The inn became for the next thirty years the Branson House. Operated by Mrs. Edith Branson, it was a popular boardinghouse. The Bransons sold it to the Reverend Isaac J. White in about 1896, but it was still operating as the Branson House in the early 1900s.

Branson's publishing business was sustained even during the Civil War. Parents wished to have children of the Confederacy educated from textbooks with a slight flavor of patriotism. Textbooks Branson published in 1863 included *Levi Branson's First Book in Composition, Especially Designed for the Use of Southern Schools; A Geographical Reader for Dixie Children*, written by his sister, Mrs. Marinda Branson Moore, who was a schoolteacher in Rockingham County; and York's *Grammar*, which, one may hope, gave due emphasis to southern accents.

Perhaps his best-known publication was Branson's *North Carolina Business Directory*, a major periodical of great interest and usefulness at that time and permanently valuable to researchers in North Carolina history of the last half of the nineteenth century. The *Business Directory* was published in Raleigh at irregular intervals from 1865 to 1896—eight issues in all. Branson personally edited all editions and published most editions. He never ceased to take a keen interest in educational, civic, and religious activities and developments in his town and in the state at large. In compiling editions of the *Business Directory*, he maintained for more than thirty years a continuing correspondence and acquaintance with hundreds of the best informed citizens in every county, town, and village; his files became a huge archive. In his later years, his daughters and his wife became able assistants in his editing and publishing work. His last venture in publishing was a first issue and prospectus for a new quarterly periodical proposed in 1898 and titled Branson's *Magazine of Genealogies*. It included, by way of illustration, some genealogical materials on the Branson family. Failing health and energies scuttled the enterprise but not the idea: his friend and admirer the Reverend J. R. B. Hathaway brought it to fruit in publishing the *North Carolina Historical and Genealogical Register* for a few years in the early 1900s.

By 1903, repeated illnesses led Branson and his wife to go to Atlanta to stay with their daughter and son-in-law, Edith and Quinton Adams. Branson died at their home in Atlanta. His body was returned by train to Raleigh for his funeral and was interred in Oakwood Cemetery on 6 Dec.

SEE: County Records of Randolph, Guilford, Orange, and Wake (North Carolina State Archives, Raleigh); Talmage C. Johnson and Charles R. Holloman, *The Story of Kinston and Lenoir County* (1954); Kinston *American Advocate*, 1855–62; Private collection of materials relating to Lenoir County (possession of Charles R. Holloman, Raleigh); Raleigh newspapers, 1862–1903.

CHARLES R. HOLLOMAN

Brantly, William Tomlinson [Theophilus] (23 Jan. 1787–28 Mar. 1845), Baptist clergyman, college president, and editor, was born in Chatham County, the son of William Brantley and the grandson of John Brantley, who settled on an 880-acre tract along Rocky River in 1749. At some unknown time he came to be called Theophilus and without actually changing his name legally, he dropped Tomlinson and substituted Theophilus. Born into a family of many children and moderate means, Brantly had little opportunity of receiving an adequate education or of escaping the small farm operated by his father. During the Second Great Awakening, however, he found a way to become a national success. Converted at a Baptist revival meeting in 1802, he began preaching throughout Chatham County. His sermons soon brought him under the notice of a wealthy neighbor who offered, on the condition that he prepare himself for the undertaking, to pay his expenses for a college education. When the doors of South Carolina College first opened in 1804, Brantly was among the initial entering class. Before he was graduated in 1808, he had found in the college's first president, Jonathan Maxcy, the man after whom he would style his life. After serving distinguished presidencies at Union College, N.Y., and at Brown University, Maxcy had come to influence a generation of southerners at South Carolina College.

Upon graduation, Brantly settled at Augusta, Ga., serving as rector of Richmond Academy. There he organized the First Baptist Church, making it within two years one of the largest in Georgia. At the same time he married Mrs. Anna McDonald Martin of Sparta, Ga., the sister of Georgia Governor Charles J. McDonald. His marriage and his apparent talents as a clergyman enabled him to become one of the most famous Baptist divines in America. In 1811 he moved to Beaufort, S.C., where he took over the important Baptist church of that town. He also created the short-lived Beaufort College. Although the college did not last beyond his departure in 1818, it numbered among its graduates Basil Manly, Sr., and Richard Fuller, two who took over the mantle of leadership among Southern Baptists after Brantly's death. After his stint in Beaufort and the death of his wife, Brantly returned to Augusta, where he served the church he had previously organized and resumed the rectorship of Richmond Academy.

In 1826 Brantly was invited to become pastor of perhaps the largest Baptist church in America, First Baptist in Philadelphia, recently left vacant by the death

of Henry Holcombe. In Philadelphia he made a national name for himself as a preacher and editor. Many of his sermons were published individually, and he published a large volume of *Sermons* in 1837. He took over the sagging *Columbian Star*, the national Baptist weekly; renaming it the *Christian Index*, he managed it successfully until 1832, when, as a result of his heated endorsement of South Carolina in the Nullification controversy, he lost the bulk of his northern readers. Although he gave up the newspaper in 1833, he remained in Philadelphia until 1837, apparently as popular as ever with his parishioners. When his health failed that year, he was offered the pastorate of First Baptist in Charleston, S.C. Not content with a full-time pastorate alone, he accepted first the editorship of the *Southern Watchman and General Intelligencer* and then the presidency of the College of Charleston in 1838. Relinquishing the paper, he served his dual functions as minister and college president quite well until July 1844, when he suffered an apparent stroke that left him totally paralyzed and senseless until his death in Augusta, Ga., eight months later.

Following the death of his first wife, Brantly married Mrs. Margaret Joyner of Augusta in 1819. To the first marriage was born William Theophilus (1816–82) and to the second John Joyner (1821–1902). Both men became widely known Baptist clergymen in their own rights.

SEE: William T. Brantly Papers (Maryland Historical Society Library, Baltimore); William Cathcart, *The Baptist Encyclopedia* (ca. 1880); *Encyclopedia of Southern Baptists*, 3 vols. (1958–71); Charles E. Taylor, *Brief Memoir of the Reverend William T. Brantly* (1846).

LARRY EDWARD TISE

Braswell, James Craig (17 Aug. 1868–17 Apr. 1951), banker and community leader, was born and reared near Battleboro, a son of Thomas Permenter Braswell and his wife, Emily Stallings. The founder of the line was the Reverend Robert Bracewell of Isle of Wight County, Va., and James Craig Braswell's branch has been substantially involved for over two hundred years in the life of Edgecombe County. After doing his preparatory work at Horner's Military Academy in Oxford, Braswell received his B.S. degree in 1890 from The University of North Carolina.

He worked for a while as a representative of Bradstreet & Company before forming the Braswell-Gravely Company, exporters of leaf tobacco, and beginning an active association with the development of the Rocky Mount tobacco market. He withdrew from this firm in 1918. In the same period he was involved in the Planters Cotton Oil and Fertilizer Company, while he and his two brothers pioneered in developing and promoting agriculture in Nash and Edgecombe counties. His own planting interests grew to several thousand acres in Nash County, and he also accumulated considerable property in Rocky Mount.

On 7 Feb. 1899 he became the first president of the Planters National Bank and Trust Company, in the organization of which he had recently assisted, and he remained in that office until he was elected chairman of the board of directors on 11 Jan. 1944. In 1911–12 he was president of the North Carolina Bankers Association. He served as vice-president of the Rocky Mount Savings & Trust Company and was long a Class A director of the Federal Reserve Bank of Richmond. He also held the positions of president of the Citizens Building & Loan Association; director of the Norfolk Trust Company; secretary of Williamson, Bulluck & Company (insurance); and treasurer of the Rocky Mount Hosiery Company, the Underwriters Fire Insurance Company of Rocky Mount, and the North State Fire Insurance Company.

Braswell was very active in Masonic affairs. He also belonged to the Rocky Mount Kiwanis Club, of which he was a charter member. He was grand master of Masons in the state in 1920. He was long a steward of the Methodist Episcopal church of Rocky Mount and was for more than forty years a member of the board of missions of the North Carolina Conference, serving as treasurer from 1921 until his death. He was very interested in the Methodist Orphanage at Raleigh and was for a time chairman of its board of directors. He was also for many years a member of the board of directors of the Rocky Mount YMCA.

Braswell was a founder (and frequent chairman) of the city school board, as well as a member of the board of the Eastern North Carolina Training School. He was a charter member and sometime president of the Rocky Mount Chamber of Commerce and for eighteen years a city alderman. During World War I he served on the Nash County Exemption Board. Modest, public-spirited, generous, and popular among all economic and social classes, he was for over a half century an active supporter of every major project associated with the advancement of the city where he lived and died.

On 12 July 1901 he married Lillian Grizelle Burton (19 Sept. 1880–14 Mar. 1947), daughter of Robert Carter Burton and his wife, Nannie Walker, of Durham. Mrs. Braswell held a B.A. degree from the Greensboro College for Women. Four children were born to this union: James Craig, Jr. (24 Apr. 1902–9 July 1923); Robert Russell (11 May 1905–29 Oct. 1973), who married Hazel Unalea Strickland; Lillian Duval, who married A. Bingham Owens of Atlanta; and Nancy Burton, who married H. Dail Holderness of Tarboro.

SEE: *North Carolina: Rebuilding an Ancient Commonwealth*, vol. 4 (1929); *North Carolina: The Old North State and the New*, vol. 4 (1941); Rocky Mount *Evening Telegram*, 18 Apr. 1951; *Who's Who in America*, 1928; *Wilson Daily Times*, 19 Jan. 1960.

HUGH B. JOHNSTON, JR.

Braun (or Brown), Michael (*ca. 1722–1807*), frontiersman, master builder, and entrepreneur, is said to have been born in Hesse-Darmstadt, Germany. He stepped upon American soil at the port of Philadelphia 26 Sept. 1737, alighting from the ship *St. Andrew Gally*, John Stedman, master, from Rotterdam but most recently from Cowes. At that time, Braun was a lad of about sixteen; along with 140 other immigrants from the Palatinate, he took the oath of allegiance to his newly adopted country that very day. For fifteen or twenty years he stayed in Pennsylvania, having learned the trades of wheelwright and printer, and then he headed with his family and a good bit of money to the rolling hills of North Carolina. There he moved to the focus of North Carolina's pioneer history, becoming one of America's legendary frontiersmen.

He bought his first land in Rowan County from John Dunn in 1758; he and Dunn were among the first settlers of this area and were friends and neighbors. Braun bought many lots in the town of Salisbury, built several houses there, and lived there before settling a few miles south of the town by the Granite Ridge, near what is now Granite Quarry. In 1766 he laid the cornerstone to the Old Stone House, the oldest house still standing in Western North Carolina. The house is built of native

stone with portholes in the gables. The lower floor contains five rooms, well finished with plaster, one of which is a kitchen with a chimney eight feet long and four feet deep. The stone over the front door is inscribed MICHAEL BRAUN MRICHREDA BRAUN IO PE ME BE MI CH DA M'1766. Tradition says the main part of the British army passed by the Stone House on the evening of 2 Feb. 1781 on the way to Alamance and that the deep gash in the old walnut facing of the door was made by a British sabre.

Braun was a rich and influential man for his time and place and a conscientious citizen. He was called esquire. In town he had a number of varied business interests: he kept an ordinary and had a tanyard, as well as renting his other houses. The year after he came to Rowan he was appointed magistrate in Captain Peter Faust's company. In 1761 the court minutes show that he was appointed constable, a position of some importance at that time. In 1765 he was overseer on the roads, and many times he served as a juror. He was appointed justice 6 Aug. 1777. The census of 1790 shows that he had fifteen slaves.

Braun and Frederick Fisher gave more than one hundred acres of land for the Dutch Pine Meeting House (now Union Evangelical Lutheran Church), and the original deed was made to them. It is safe to assume they were members of this early church.

Braun appears to have had at least three wives. From Pennsylvania he brought with him his wife Margareta, by whom he had six sons—David, Peter, Moses, James, and Jeremiah—and three daughters, who all died young. Margareta Braun died 20 July 1771, at the age of thirty-seven years, two months. She was buried in the Michael Braun Graveyard, once surrounded by a stone wall. In 1779 a wife named Rosanna signed a deed with Braun; and his wife at the time of his death was Eleanor Wakefield Reeves of Maryland, whose daughter Clementine, born after his death, later married Charles Verble.

Braun wrote his will 12 Oct. 1807 and died before 2 Feb. 1808, when it was proved in open court in Rowan County and ordered recorded in Rowan County Will Book D:17. In this will he left Eleanor the Stone House and named Montford Stokes guardian for his unborn child. His grave, presumably in the family graveyard, is unmarked, as are those of his other wives and his daughters.

SEE: Richard L. Brown, *A History of the Michael Brown Family* (1921); Roscoe Brown Fisher, *Michael Braun (Brown) of the Old Stone House, His Influence and Descendants* (1975); McCubbins Collection, Rowan Public Library (Salisbury); Rowan County wills, deeds, inferior court minutes (North Carolina State Archives, Raleigh); Jethro Rumple, *A History of Rowan County* (1881).

JO WHITE LINN

Brazier, Robert H. B. (*d. 5 Jan. 1837*), cartographer and civil engineer, was born of unknown parentage in Great Britain, where he received his professional training under John Rennie (1761–1821), the Scottish civil engineer chiefly remembered as the designer of Southwark, Waterloo, and London bridges, the London and East India docks, Plymouth breakwater, and so on. Brazier came to North Carolina in company with Hamilton Fulton in July 1819, at the instigation of Peter Browne, and entered into a contract with the commissioners as assistant to the principal engineer. His contract was not confirmed by the board of internal improvements until February 1820, though he had already entered upon his duties under Fulton, who had been appointed principal engineer. Browne's endorsement of Fulton and Brazier brought the two engineers under fire from Browne's political opponents, and efforts to manipulate the internal improvements programs to secure the major benefit for the eastern region of the state resulted in organized opposition by legislators from the Piedmont and Western regions. The continued existence of the board of internal improvements itself was precarious. Unexpectedly, the principal engineer of the State of Virginia died, and in 1822 Brazier applied to that state's board of public works for the post, in the hope of stabilizing his professional position and of finding more congenial working conditions. As his references he named William Ruffin, the celebrated teacher of law, William Nichols, architect of North Carolina, and Governor Gabriel Holmes. He was unsuccessful in his application and remained at his post in North Carolina.

Despite what can only have been a galling situation, marked by an ever deteriorating relationship with the board of internal improvements and reductions in salary during the years 1820 through 1823, Brazier completed surveys and drew maps, plans, profiles, and transverse sections of the principal North Carolina watercourses from Yadkin River east to Roanoke Inlet. After an altercation over his account of expenses, Brazier resigned his office as assistant engineer effective 19 Feb. 1824 and then wrote what the board of internal improvements chose to view as a "disrespectful" letter, in which he demanded settlement of the controversial account. Brazier's resulting lawsuit against the board was successfully concluded in Wake County Superior Court when he was awarded damages in 1825.

After a two year period in which he made patent drawings and undertook private surveying (including the survey of the Buncombe Turnpike), Brazier resumed a contractual relationship with the board of internal improvements. He commenced his survey of the state's swamp lands in the spring of 1827 and was considered by the board the assistant engineer to the state, this time under Alanson Nash, who had been hired from New York, on the recommendation of DeWitt Clinton, following Hamilton Fulton's departure from the state. After presenting his report on the swamp lands to the General Assembly late in 1827, and his expense accounts to the board of internal improvements early in 1828, Brazier's connection with internal improvements in North Carolina came to an end.

For the next few years, Brazier supported his family by private surveying and by delineating survey plats for landowners in Wake and surrounding counties. His map of the route from Raleigh to Cobb's Mill (1831), his survey plat of the 7,383-acre Jeffreys tract in Wake and Franklin counties (1832), and his plan of the Rolesville tract in Wake County (1833) are typical examples of his piecework. During this period the position of principal engineer to the State of Virginia became vacant once more, and in 1831 Brazier again applied for the office. Governor Montfort Stokes, jurist and U.S. senator James Iredell, Attorney General Romulus M. Saunders, and several other state officers and leading citizens of Raleigh testified to Brazier's skill as a practical surveyor, expressing to the Virginia board their opinion that "as a Draughtsman, it is believed that [Brazier] has no superior in the country." But the application failed of success. Brazier was, however, given brief employment by the Virginia Board of Public Works, and in 1831 he completed surveys and drawings of "A Plan of the Blackwater River from New South Quay to Rattlesnake Swamp" and "A

Survey of a Proposed Line of Canal from Blackwater River to Pagan Creek Near Smithfield."

Simultaneously with these smaller efforts, Brazier undertook his greatest work. He had, in 1821 and again in 1822, been one of the commissioners appointed by the General Assembly to lay out anew and map the streets of Fayetteville. At this time, presumably, he made the acquaintance of the legislator, newspaper publisher, and Fayetteville postmaster, John MacRae. By 1825, MacRae had conceived the notion of bringing out a new, authoritative map of the state. In 1826 he presented this idea to the General Assembly and won its approbation and support. Through the assistance of Governor John Owen, MacRae in 1829 secured the services of Lieutenant William Henry Harford of the U.S. Corps of Engineers for production of the projected map, but nothing came of their joint efforts. At this point, MacRae turned to Brazier, whose handsome plan of Fayetteville he had published in 1825. By July 1831, Brazier had completed most of the surveying required for the map, and his finished manuscript was ready for the engraver in 1832. The responsibility for engraving the map was entrusted to Henry Schenck Tanner of Philadelphia, and the finished prints were published jointly by MacRae in Fayetteville and Tanner in Philadelphia in 1833. Published under the title "A New Map of the State of North Carolina Constructed from Actual Surveys, Authentic Public Documents and Private Contributions," this carefully drawn and elegantly executed map was the first authoritative work of its kind to appear since Jonathan Price and John Strother completed their surveying of the state in 1798 and published their map in 1808. Brazier's map of North Carolina remained the standard authority for cartographers until 1857, when it was superseded by the compilation of William D. Cooke and Samuel Pearce. In addition to the acknowledged edition of 1833, updated editions of Brazier's map were brought out without attribution of authorship by Wellington Williams of Philadelphia in 1854 and 1856.

After this major achievement of mapping the state, Brazier's life entered a rapid decline. During the period between the end of his employment by the board of internal improvements and the beginning of his work with MacRae, he had suffered financial reverses from which he never recovered. In May 1830 the mortgage on his Raleigh property had been foreclosed, and both real and personal property had been lost. By 1833 it was necessary for the charitable fund of Christ Church, Raleigh, to come to the aid of his family. In an effort to regain financial solvency, Brazier joined eleven associates in a speculative venture involving some Campbellton lots in Fayetteville in 1834, but this speculation failed to recoup his fortunes. In 1836 his affairs and finances fell to a new low, and he was again obliged to seek assistance from Christ Church. Then, following a severe ice storm during the Christmas holidays of 1836, Brazier fell from a pair of high steps and died of the effects in Raleigh. He was survived by his wife, Rachel, and his young son, James Henderson, both of whom were members of the Episcopal church; Brazier appears to have been an Anglican.

Though the rector of Christ Church very harshly wrote that Brazier had come to his death "by his own folly and wickedness," he acknowledged that the cartographer was a most excellent draughtsman "with the talents of an angel." In elegance of execution, Brazier set a standard yet to be met by a North Carolina cartographer. His original manuscript maps and surveys are characterized by a sureness of hand and eye, beauty of line, and delicacy of color. Brazier's principal surviving maps and surveys not otherwise noticed above are "Plan of Croatan and Roanoke Sounds Shewing the Proposed Situations of the Embankments and Inlet" (1820); "Plan and Sections of a Line of Canal From the Tar River to the Tossnot Creek and a Survey of that Creek to its Junction with the Contentney" (1820); "Plan and Sections of Part of Crab Tree and Walnut Creeks" (1820); "Plan of the Tar River from Louisburg to the Little Falls Showing the Proposed Situation of the Locks and Dams" (1821); "Longitudinal Section of the Tar River from Louisburg to the Great Falls" (1821); "Transverse Sections of the Tar River Between Louisburg and the Great Falls" (1821); "Transverse Sections of the Cape Fear River Between Buckhorn Falls and Campbellton" (1821); "Plan of the Cape Fear River Between Haywood and Campbellton And of a Proposed Line of Canal Between Foxes Islands and Campbellton" (1822); "Survey of the Cape Fear River from the Upper to the Lower Flats" (1823); "Plan of the Catawba River from the Devils Shoals to Near Sherril's Ford" (1824); "Longitudinal Section of the Catawba River from the Devils Shoals to the Mouth of Little Catawba River" (1824); "Plan of that Part of the Big Swamp Lying Between Sullivan's Mills & Lumber River in the County of Robeson" (1827); "Survey of the Great Swamp, Columbus County" (1827); "Plan of that Part of Uhara Swamp Lying Between the Road Leading from Jackson to Bryan's Cross Roads and Pottocasy Creek in the County of Northampton" (1827); "Plan of Part of Holly Shelter Swamp" (1827); "Plan of the Swamp Lands Between Albemarle and Pamlico Sounds" (1828); "Plan of the State Road from Fayetteville, Raleigh, Louisburg, Warrenton and Robinson's Ferry to the Virginia Line" (from H. Fulton's survey; 1822); and "Plan of the Road from Salem to Fayetteville by Randolph and Moore Court Houses" (from H. Fulton's survey, 1823). Works of Brazier not known to have survived, or yet to be discovered, are a survey of the Roundabout in Neuse River, Wayne County (1820); a survey of Tar River from the Great Falls to the Small Falls below Battle's Mills (1820); and a survey of at least a portion of Yadkin River (1820).

SEE: W. H. Hoyt, *The Papers of Archibald DeBow Murphey*, vols. 1–2 (1914); North Carolina State Archives (Raleigh), for Cumberland County Deed Book 40, Governors' Letter Books (vols. 28, 30), Governor's Office Records (Internal Improvements), Legislative Papers (1819–27), Map Collection, Records of Christ Church (Raleigh), Wake County Deed Books 7 and 9; *Raleigh Register*, 10 Jan. 1837; Virginia State Archives (Richmond), for Records of the Board of Public Works (Papers of Road Engineers and Assistants, 1825–82).

GEORGE STEVENSON

Breedlove, Joseph Penn (*14 July 1874–24 May 1955*), college and university librarian, was born near Oxford, the son of John Henry and Susan Caroline Hunt Breedlove. His formal education was received at Horner's School in Oxford and Trinity College, from which he received a B.A. degree in 1898 and an M.A. in 1902. He was librarian of Trinity College and Duke University from the summer of 1898 to September 1939 and acting librarian from April 1943 through August 1946, thus serving his alma mater over a span of forty-eight years. He directed the library during the important years of the institution's transition from a college to a university. During the period from 1939 to 1943 he retained, as librarian emeritus, certain administrative duties; and between 1946 and his death he completed a history of the library, *Duke University*

Library, 1840–1940: A Brief Account with Reminiscences, published by the Friends of the Duke University Library in 1955.

Breedlove was the second full-time librarian of Trinity College (the first served for only one year, 1894–95). Most of his predecessors were students or professors in the college. He assumed control of a collection of about ten thousand volumes, many of which had been given to the college by the Columbian and Hesperian literary societies in 1887. Upon appointment, his most pressing responsibility, as the only full-time member of the staff, was to classify and catalog the book collection. In preparation for these responsibilities, he spent the summer of 1900 attending Amherst College, where classes in library technology were taught by William Isaac Fletcher, a distinguished pioneer in the field of librarianship. Before the cataloging and classification were completed, Breedlove became involved in the pleasant work of planning Trinity's first library building. Completed in 1903, it was a gift from James Buchanan Duke, who later created the Duke Endowment and made possible the founding of Duke University. Breedlove was to assist in the planning of two more library buildings for the college and the university: the present East Campus Library, occupied in 1926, and the first unit of the General Library, completed in 1930. When he retired in 1946, the library had grown to almost a million volumes, and the staff, which consisted of only a single person in 1898, included seventy full-time employees.

Breedlove was one of the founders of the North Carolina Library Association and was its president in 1911 and 1912. He was a Democrat and a Methodist and at the time of his death was an honorary member of the board of stewards of the Duke Memorial Methodist Church. He was a member of Kappa Alpha Fraternity, Phi Beta Kappa, the Faculty Club of Duke University, and Omicron Delta Kappa and "9019" honorary fraternities. He was twice married: in 1905 to Bessie Bassett, who died in 1912, and in 1917 to Lucille Aiken. By his first marriage he had one daughter and by his second a son and a daughter.

Funeral services were held in the Duke University Chapel, and burial was in the Maplewood Cemetery, Durham. His portrait hangs in the Joseph Penn Breedlove Room in the Perkins Library of Duke University.

SEE: Duke University *Library Notes*, November 1955; *Durham Morning Herald*, 25 May 1955; *Durham Sun*, 24 May 1955; *Who's Who in Library Service* (1933).

BENJAMIN E. POWELL

Brehon, James Gloster (*ca. 1740–8 Apr. 1819*), Revolutionary War surgeon, was born in Ireland and there received a liberal education. On arriving in America, he first settled in Maryland. In the records of Maryland's Committee of Safety is an order of October 1776 for Brehon to deliver up all the books on physic taken on board any of the captured vessels at St. George Island.

Brehon removed to Warrenton and began to practice. He soon entered the service, however, and was appointed a surgeon in the navy. After serving at different posts until the end of the war, he returned to Warrenton to practice. In July of 1783 he married Mildred, the daughter of John Willis and Mary Hayes Plummer of Warren County. Mrs. Brehon died without issue in June 1803.

Brehon died in Warrenton. According to his obituary in the *Raleigh Register*, he was a prominent physician, had accumulated a large estate, and was well known as a student of botany. The historian John H. Wheeler described him as distinguished for his skill as a surgeon and for his learned scientific researches, adding that his "colloquial powers" were unrivaled. Brehon's large estate was inherited by his nephew, who was the son of James Somerville and Catherine Vekes and who had been adopted by Brehon. The adopted son took the name James Gloster Brehon, also became a physician, and died relatively young in Warrenton, 2 Oct. 1839; he donated the land for the Warrenton Male Academy (the site later occupied by the Graham School and eventually by Warrenton High School), and Brehon Street in Warrenton was named for him.

Another prominent early Warrenton physician, Thomas Benn Gloster, may well have been a relative of Brehon. According to family Bible records, Gloster was born in Limerick, Ireland, in 1763, left Limerick 1 July 1785, and on 20 Feb. 1786 "arrived in Warrenton, North Carolina, one of the United States of America." The records imply that he left Ireland with Warrenton as his goal. Gloster married, in 1795, Mary Hayes Willis, the younger sister of Brehon's wife, Mildred Willis. Gloster died in Warrenton 12 Jan. 1819, leaving two children, Arthur Brehon and Elizabeth Willis, who married John Anderson, a native of Scotland.

SEE: Elizabeth Wilson Montgomery, *Sketches of Old Warrenton, North Carolina* (1924); Warrenton *Warren Record*, 11 Nov. 1955; John H. Wheeler, *Reminiscences and Memoirs of North Carolina* (1883–84).

CLAIBORNE T. SMITH, JR.

Brevard, Alexander (*April 1755–1 Nov. 1829*), Revolutionary War officer, planter, and iron entrepreneur, was a native of Iredell County but spent most of his adult life in Lincoln County. The first Brevard ancestor in America was a Huguenot refugee who fled France when Louis XIV revoked the Edict of Nantes in 1685. After a brief sojourn in Ireland, this young man settled in Maryland and fathered a large family, including a son, John Brevard. John Brevard remained in Maryland long enough to learn the blacksmith trade and to marry Jane McWhorter. Sometime in the decade after 1740 he established a home in Iredell County, near the head of Rocky Creek.

When the American Revolution began, the John Brevards had eight sons, including Alexander and Joseph, and four daughters. All the Brevards were Whigs. When the British under Cornwallis crossed the Catawba River, they passed near the Brevard home; according to family tradition, a British contingent, finding only Mrs. Jane Brevard at home, burned the house and all the surrounding outbuildings to the ground. The explanation offered was that the family had eight sons in the rebel army; clearly, the family took the country's cause seriously.

By 1775, Brevard had acquired the rudiments of education and was prepared to devote his energies to service against the king. Early in the war he participated in the Snow Camp expedition against South Carolina Tories. He returned home in March 1776 but was soon called to go to Cross Creek to quell a rising among Scottish Tories. Subsequently, he joined the Continental Line as ensign in the Fourth North Carolina Regiment; in December 1776 he was promoted to first lieutenant. He fought in several battles in the North, most notably at Brandywine and Germantown in the abortive defense of Philadelphia. He went into winter quarters at Valley Forge, but with his health so endangered by the rigors of

campaigning that he was ordered home by General Washington himself. In 1779, Brevard became a captain in the North Carolina Militia; he joined the southern army of Horatio Gates in the campaign of 1780. He acted as quartermaster at the Camden fiasco, where, anticipating defeat, he tried unsuccessfully to save the wagons and supplies in his charge. After a change in commanders in which Nathanael Greene replaced Gates, events in the Carolinas moved rapidly to a conclusion. Brevard served throughout the campaign, undergoing the fiercest fighting at the Battle of Eutaw Springs, S.C., where he commanded a beleaguered company that sustained heavy losses. He resigned his commission on 1 Jan. 1783.

After the war, Brevard married Rebecca Davidson (1762–1824), the daughter of Major John Davidson (1735–1832) of Mecklenburg County, a practical blacksmith, opponent of British authority, planter, and ironmonger. In about 1792, Davidson, Brevard, and Joseph Graham (1759–1836), another Revolutionary War hero and son-in-law of Davidson entered partnership with Peter Forney, a pioneer in the Lincoln County iron industry; they purchased a share in the "big ore bank," a few miles east of Lincolnton, and made plans to erect facilities to manufacture iron products. Brevard moved his family to Lincoln County and settled on Leeper's Creek, where he built Mt. Tirza Forge; on adjoining land, Graham built Vesuvius Furnace. In 1795, Forney sold his interest in the partnership, and the others continued to operate under the name Joseph Graham and Company, with Davidson leaving actual management to his sons-in-law. The business proved highly lucrative, and additional land was acquired. By 1804, when Davidson sold his interest to Brevard and Graham, the company assets included over five thousand acres; nine slaves; improvements, equipment, and stock valued conservatively at $5,000; and cash and notes receivable in the amount of $8,876. Brevard and Graham continued the partnership as Brevard and Company until 1814, when the business relationship was dissolved. Subsequently, Brevard built Rehoboth Furnace near Mt. Tirza Forge. He manufactured and sold iron until his death in 1829; and the business remained in the family, despite declining profits, until 1870.

Like neighboring ironmongers, Brevard also engaged in various agricultural pursuits, which proved to be complementary. He accumulated a great estate and owned many slaves. His success was due in part to imaginative marketing practices. Seeking ever broader markets, he began to send iron products by wagon down the Catawba River Valley into South Carolina to Camden and below, especially when dry weather prevented boats from ascending the water highways from Charleston. His brother Joseph (1766–1821), a prominent Camden lawyer and judge, acted as agent in the ensuing transactions, advising his brother of market conditions and storing and selling iron as necessary. This outlet was invaluable.

Brevard never sought political office but was content to conduct his business, enjoy his family, and play the role of good citizen. Despite a retiring disposition, his manner was frank and candid. Industrious and honest, he was a devout Presbyterian. His marriage with Rebecca Davidson produced ten children; seven—Ephraim, Franklin, Harriett, Robert, Joseph, Theodore, and Mary—survived their father. Brevard was interred at Machpelah, a small Presbyterian church near his home, which was the burying ground of the Brevards and Grahams.

SEE: Alexander Brevard Papers (North Carolina State Archives, Raleigh); Brevard-McDowell Papers (Southern Historical Collection, University of North Carolina, Chapel Hill), for "Autobiography" of 22 Jan. 1827; Lester J. Cappon, "Iron-Making—A Forgotten Industry of North Carolina," *North Carolina Historical Review* 9 (1932); W. L. Sherrill, *Annals of Lincoln County* (1937); John H. Wheeler, *Historical Sketches of North Carolina* (1851).

MAX WILLIAMS

Brevard, John, II (1716–15 Sept. 1790), colonial official and patriot, was the son of John Brevard, first of the Brevards in the colonies. According to his grandson, Alexander, the first John Brevard "is supposed to have come of the Huguenots that had fled from the persecution in France. He came into America with a William Wallace and family from Ireland an orphan and then but a boy. The family of Wallace settled near the Head of Elk Cycil County Maryland. My grandfather we expect must have conducted tolerably well, for he married in a McKnitt family [Katharine McKnitt] that were respected and settled near head of Elk where my father [John Brevard II] was born. My father learned the Blacksmith trade with a son of the said William Wallace and in the 30th year of his age married a Jane McWhorter [daughter of Hugh MacWhorter of New Castle County, Del.] and settled on land near where he was born [;] there their first child was born, Ephraim, after Doctor Brevard. He [John] then came on to Head of Rocky River, then Anson County, afterwards Rowan, now Iredell County. . . ."

John Brevard II lived six or seven miles east of the present Centre Church in Iredell County. His early prominence is attested by his appointment as both vestryman (for the Parish of St. George), though a Presbyterian, and justice of the peace when Anson County was organized in 1749. The former appointment gave him a voice in local matters of charity, education, and religion, and the latter in law and government; as a justice of the peace he was entitled to be addressed as "Squire." The minutes of the court of common pleas and quarter sessions speak eloquently of his activities. Like other magistrates, Brevard owned slaves at an early date and probably also white servants, as there is frequent mention in the court minutes of indentures being lengthened because of misdemeanors.

While manifestly not a gentleman of fashion, Brevard was not a rustic. During his membership in the provincial assembly from 1754 to 1760, he had occasion to reside in New Bern, which afforded North Carolina's best society. Trade must have taken him also both to Philadelphia and to Charlestown, S.C., the choicest capitals in the colonies. Yet despite these ameliorating influences, Brevard was a wages-of-sin Calvinist: when one of his slaves committed an unnamed crime, the black was hanged until dead and then decapitated, with the head set up in grim warning to others.

Brevard had ample reasons, political, economic, and religious, for opposition to British rule in America. At the call of the first provincial congress in New Bern, a public meeting was held in Salisbury on 23 Sept. 1774 to elect a committee of correspondence as the congress had requested. Among the twenty-five appointees were Brevard and his son-in-law William Lee Davidson. This committee made inquiries into the conduct of sundry citizens to determine whether they were friends or enemies of the American cause, and Brevard appears to have been an active member. When a committee of safety for the District of Salisbury (comprising the western

portion of the state) was appointed on 9 Sept. 1775, Brevard was a member. In 1776 he was a member of the provincial congress meeting at Halifax. He was too old for active service in the army, but it is claimed that all eight of his sons fought for independence, Ephraim, John, Alexander, and Joseph as officers in the Continental Line. Dr. Ephraim Brevard, graduate of the college at Princeton, was Mecklenburg County's most distinguished penman for liberty and a physician in the Continental Army; he died as a result of disease contracted during the war in Charlestown, S.C. After the defeat and death of General William Lee Davidson at Cowan's Ford, on 1 Feb. 1781, Banastre Tarleton's greencoats pillaged the helpless citizens, burning the Brevard homestead.

Brevard had retained his office as justice of the peace when Rowan County was cut off from Anson in 1753, and he was reappointed by the provincial congress in 1776. In his latter years he was the most venerated citizen of lower Rowan (by then Iredell) County. Eighteenth-century records for Centre Presbyterian Church (Iredell County) have not survived, but there is no reason to doubt that Brevard was a ruling elder. He and his wife (who died 25 Mar. 1800, age seventy-three) are buried in the churchyard there.

Tradition states that Brevard called his plantation Purgatory. He reared a family of twelve children, many of whom achieved local prominence. Mary married General William Lee Davidson; Ephraim married Margaret Polk; John married Hannah Thompson; Hugh married Jane Young; Adam married Mary Winslow; Alexander married Rebecca Davidson; Robert probably migrated to Missouri; Benjamin migrated to Tennessee; Nancy married John Davidson (she and her husband were killed by the Indians in 1781); Joseph married Rebecca Kershaw; Jane married General Ephraim Davidson; and Rebecca married John Jones.

SEE: Brevard-McDowell Papers (Southern Historical Collection, University of North Carolina, Chapel Hill), for Alexander Brevard "Autobiography" of 22 Jan. 1827; Chalmers G. Davidson, *Piedmont Partisan* (1951); Rowan Court Minutes, 1753–86 (3-vol. MS, Salisbury); William L. Saunders and Walter Clark, eds., *Colonial and State Records of North Carolina*, 30 vols. (1886–1914).

CHALMERS G. DAVIDSON

Brevard, Joseph (19 July 1766–11 Oct. 1821), Revolutionary War soldier, jurist, and congressman, was a native of Iredell County and a long-time resident of Camden, Kershaw County, S.C. A younger brother of Alexander Brevard, Joseph was of Huguenot and Scotch-Irish extraction. While little is known of his early education, he wrote a beautiful hand and quoted Latin with facility. He entered the Continental Army at age seventeen and became a lieutenant in the Tenth North Carolina Regiment before transferring to the Second as regimental quartermaster.

Joseph Brevard settled in Camden, S.C., at the end of hostilities and there soon gained a reputation for industry and integrity. He was sheriff of the Camden District (1789–91), and in 1791 was appointed commissioner in equity for the Northern District of South Carolina. In 1792 he was admitted to the bar and entered partnership with William Falconer, then the most eminent lawyer in the northern part of South Carolina. Brevard was elected circuit court judge in December 1801 and served ably until forced by poor health to resign in December 1815. A noted legal scholar whose opinions were characterized by industry, learning, and eloquence, Brevard compiled three volumes of reports and an admirable digest of the statute law to 1814. Upon his resignation as judge he resumed his legal practice in Camden. In 1818 he was elected a member of the Sixteenth Congress (4 Mar. 1819–3 Mar. 1821). He was a member of the House Judicial Committee; and, while he was not active in debate, he upheld the Constitution, opposed raising the tariff, and supported the admission of Missouri as a slave state. He was not a candidate for reelection in 1820 and was defeated in a special election in March 1821.

In March 1793, Brevard married Rebecca Kershaw, a daughter of Colonel Eli Kershaw, a revolutionary soldier who died a British captive. The Brevards had four children—Alfred, Edward, Eugene, and Sarah Aurora—before their union was ended by the death of Rebecca in 1802. Joseph Brevard was buried in Camden's Quaker Cemetery.

SEE: *Annals of Congress; Biog. Dir. Am. Cong.* (1961); Brevard-McDowell Papers (Southern Historical Collection, University of North Carolina, Chapel Hill); John Belton O'Neall, *Biographical Sketches of the Bench and Bar of South Carolina* (1859); John H. Wheeler, *Historical Sketches of North Carolina* (1851).

MAX WILLIAMS

Brewer, Charles Edward (*12 July 1866–1 May 1941*), chemist and college president, was born in Wake Forest, the son of John Marchant Brewer, farmer, of Nansemond County, Va., and Ann Eliza Wait Brewer. She was the daughter of Samuel Wait, one of the fourteen founders of the North Carolina Baptist State Convention and the first president of Wake Forest College. Charles Edward was the youngest of ten children; the oldest, John Bruce, was for fifteen years president of Chowan College in Murfreesboro. The younger Brewer, prepared for college in Vine Hill Academy in Scotland Neck, received a B.A. (1885) and an M.A. (1886) from Wake Forest. He did further graduate study at Johns Hopkins University and at Cornell University, where he was made a member of Sigma Xi and received a Ph.D. in 1900. LL.D. degrees were conferred upon him by both Wake Forest College and Baylor University.

From 1889 to 1915, Brewer was professor of chemistry at Wake Forest; during the last three years of that period he was also dean of the faculty. In 1915 he was elected president of Meredith College in Raleigh, a position he held until 1939. For the last two years of his life he was president emeritus and professor of chemistry there. The twenty-four years of Brewer's presidency were among the most difficult of Meredith's existence. That Brewer came through them successfully was due in large measure to his remarkable administrative ability and his wholehearted devotion to the school. In 1925 the college was moved from a crowded city plot of less than four acres to its present 182-acre site three miles west of the capitol. To finance the move, a bond issue of $750,000 supplemented the amount realized from the sale of the original site. The nation-wide depression made it increasingly difficult to meet the bonds as they matured or even to keep up the interest on them, and the college was in grave danger of having to close its doors. The depression also caused a sharp decline in enrollment. Notwithstanding these difficulties, Meredith continued not only to exist but to prosper. During Brewer's administration, current expenses were met each year; the endowment was increased from $127,000 to $531,162; and the college property increased in value from $284,950 to $1,430,568. Although Brewer's first ten years

at Meredith were spent on the old campus, where little or no growth was possible, and although the five years of the depression caused a sharp decline in enrollment, the student body grew from 383 to 583 and the faculty and staff from thirty to sixty-four. The president's warm interest in each student and faculty member helped keep up the morale of the college during those discouraging years.

Even more significant than the material advance was Meredith's remarkable academic progress during Brewer's presidency, progress evidenced by recognition from accrediting agencies as well as by the success of students who went on to graduate schools. In 1921 the school was admitted to membership in the Association of Colleges and Secondary Schools of the Southern States; in 1924 its A.B. graduates were admitted to the American Association of University Women; and in 1928 it was placed on the list of colleges approved by the American Association of Universities, a distinction at that time accorded to only three other institutions in North Carolina, none of them colleges for women. Brewer was a member of the North Carolina College Conference and in 1922 was elected president of the North Carolina Education Association.

Brewer's influence extended beyond educational circles; he was also active in the work of the Baptist denomination in North Carolina. The Glen Royall Baptist Church in Wake Forest had its origin in the Sunday school he organized and served as superintendent until he moved away. In the First Baptist Church of Raleigh he was a deacon, a member of the choir, and for more than twenty years teacher of a large Bible class for men. He was recording secretary of the Baptist State Convention from 1908 until 1915, when he became chairman of the Layman's Missionary Movement in North Carolina. His activities in the Junior Order of American Mechanics went beyond the state: from 1911 to 1935 he served as a trustee of the National Orphans' Homes of that organization in Lexington and in Tiffin, Ohio; and he was first a state councilor, then a national vice-councilor, then a national councilor for the Order.

On 28 Oct. 1891, Brewer married Love Estelle Bell of Shawboro, daughter of Joseph Etheridge Cartwright Bell and Ellen Dozier Bell. The Brewers had four children—Joseph Bell, Ellen Dozier, Ann Eliza, and Charles Edward. The daughters carried on the educational tradition of their great-grandfather, father, and uncle: the elder at Meredith for forty-six years, the younger at Brenau College in Gainesville, Ga., for thirty years. Brewer died in Raleigh and was buried in the Wake Forest Cemetery. A portrait painted by L. E. Gebhardt and presented to Meredith by the class of 1924 is in Livingston Johnson Administration Building; another is in the classroom of the Jones-Brewer Bible class in the First Baptist Church of Raleigh.

SEE: Brewer family (personal contact); *Charity and Children*, scattered issues; Mary Lynch Johnson, *A History of Meredith College* (1956); Meredith College, minutes of the board of trustees and of the faculty and college publications, 1915–41; Raleigh *Biblical Recorder*, scattered issues; *Who's Who in America*, 1910–41.

MARY LYNCH JOHNSON

Brewer, John Bruce (*26 Oct. 1846–20 June 1929*), pioneer in the field of higher education for women, was born in Wake Forest, the oldest of ten children born to John Marchant and Ann Eliza Wait Brewer. John Marchant Brewer, a merchant-planter whose home was originally in Nansemond County, Va., had settled in Wake Forest after attending Wake Forest College from 1838 to 1840. The Brewer ancestry has been traced to one Thomas Brewer of Somerset and London, England, whose son, John settled in Warwick County, Va., before 1629. Ann Eliza Brewer, daughter of Samuel Wait, first president of Wake Forest College, traced her ancestry through the Wait, Merriam, and Conant families of early New England.

Brewer probably received his earliest education under the tutelage of professors at Wake Forest College and under the care of his grandfather, Samuel Wait. He attended Bethel Hill Academy in Person County for at least one year and then served with the Second Regiment, North Carolina Junior Reserves, from May 1864 to May 1865, seeing action in the battles of Kinston and Bentonville. He entered Wake Forest College upon being mustered out of the military, subsequently receiving both the B.A. (1868) and M.A. (1871) degrees.

For the greater part of the next half century, following graduation from Wake Forest, Brewer's life was devoted to educational interests. He served as teacher in Maple Springs Academy, Franklin County, 1868–70; coprincipal of Wilson Collegiate Institute, 1870–75; principal, Wilson Collegiate Seminary for Young Ladies, 1875–81; principal, Chowan Baptist Female Institute, 1881–96; principal, Franklin Female Seminary, Franklin, Va., 1901–7; and president, Roanoke Institute (now Averett College), Danville, Va., 1907–14. His service to higher education was completed with his election to the presidency of Chowan College, where he remained from 1918 to 1920.

Following his brief teaching experience at the Maple Springs Academy, Brewer was associated with Sylvester Hassell in the operation of the Wilson Collegiate Institute, a coeducational school over which Hassell served as principal. This coeducational enterprise was abandoned in 1875, with Hassell continuing the operation of a school for boys and Brewer becoming principal of the Wilson Collegiate Seminary for Young Ladies. Thus began his career in the field of higher education for women.

Brewer's earlier tenure at Chowan Baptist Female Institute saw vast improvements in both the physical assets of the campus and the quality of its academic programs. In June 1886 he recommended the appointment of a "Standing Building Committee," with responsibility for the planning and constructing of additional buildings, repairs, and other improvements. . . ." In 1895 he initiated the process of securing a change of charter for the institute, whereby it could be approved and recognized for the granting of academic degrees. At the time of his departure in 1896, Chowan Baptist Female Institute was generally recognized as second to none in academic reputation among the collegiate institutes for young women in North Carolina.

Though he had been offered the presidencies of such schools as Baptist Female University (now Meredith College), Richmond Female Institute (now Westhampton College of the University of Richmond), and Stephens College, Columbia, Mo., Brewer chose to cast his lot with the Roanoke Institute in 1907. It was here that he did probably his most outstanding work as an educator and administrator. The academic program was upgraded significantly. Of equal significance for the future of the school was Brewer's success in relocating the entire campus on a more promising site within the city of Danville.

Returning to the presidency of Chowan College in 1918, Brewer found himself expected to deal with the financial aspects of the institution only, while the academic department was left entirely to the supervision of an academic dean. Ensuing difficulties between the two men led to the early resignation of the dean, while Brewer, at the behest of the trustees, agreed to continue in office until a suitable president could be employed.

Brewer was married to Anne Elizabeth Joyner of Franklinton on 2 July 1873. To their union were born nine children: Julia Henderson, who married George Francis Thomasson; Anne Bruce, married to Claude Gore; John Bruce, who died in infancy; Mary Alice, married to John Gore; Jessie Thomas; William Marchant; Louise, who died in infancy; Merriam Conant, who died in infancy; and Elizabeth Joyner, married to Ralph Armstrong.

A Democrat and a Baptist, Brewer took an active interest in the affairs of his church and denomination, especially in the work of educational institutions and in the Baptist Orphanage in Thomasville. His portrait was presented to Averett College in 1938.

Brewer died in Blowing Rock, where he had been vacationing with two of his daughters. His body was returned to Wake Forest for interment in the family burial plot in the town cemetery.

SEE: "Minutes of Board of Trustees, Chowan College," 1881–96, 1918–20; Whitaker Library (Chowan College, Murfreesboro), for Julia Brewer Thomasson's "John Bruce Brewer" and other Brewer memorabilia (originals in possession of Mrs. I. S. London, Franklinton); Who's Who in America, 1912–13.

R. HARGUS TAYLOR

Brickell, John, early eighteenth-century naturalist and physician, was a native of Ireland. Virtually nothing is known of him before his appearance in North Carolina in 1729. His *Natural History of North Carolina*, published in Dublin in 1737 following his return from America, indicates that he was familiar with the coastal towns of Bath, Beaufort, and Edenton. This work, heavily plagiarized from John Lawson's *A New Voyage to Carolina* (1709), can be used for biographical information on Brickell only with great circumspection. Brickell also drew heavily on letters from the Reverend John Clayton to the Royal Society of London, 1693–94.

North Carolina records show that Brickell practiced medicine at Edenton during the winter of 1730–31 and that he was, during that time, physician to the family of Governor Sir Richard Everard. His name does not appear in North Carolina sources after July 1731, about which time he presumably returned to Ireland.

Brickell's *Natural History* reveals the mind and workmanship of a man of grammar school education at best. He was evidently unfamiliar with such great medical authorities of the age as Sydenham and Boerhaave, as he settled most issues by reference to Pliny the Elder. Irish subscribers to the book included, among medical men, mostly apothecaries and chirurgeons (surgeons), an indication that his contacts were mostly with the lower stratum of the profession. His observations in the area of folk-practices and remedies are not without value, however, and serve as an interesting complement to the more nearly scientific gleanings of Lawson. Brickell showed no discrimination whatever in recording the Carolina medical folkways, a fact which, however much it may please the folklorist, was a disservice to the medical practice of his day: shrewd uses of local herbs by the colonists received no greater emphasis in Brickell's notebook than did the practice of applying the anus of a hen to a snakebite.

Brickell is known to have published another work in

London in 1739, entitled *Catalogue of American Tree and Plants which will Bear the Climate of England*. It appears that he may have gone from Ireland to England and that he took with him from America a collection of seeds and plants, some of which he grew successfully. Of his later life and career, nothing is presently known.

Something must be said of the tissue of misconceptions that has attached itself to Brickell's name in various historical writings. A legend that he received any part of his education at Edinburgh University, then the leading medical school in the world, is without foundation in the school's alumni records. Another legend—that he was a brother of a colonial Bertie County Anglican priest, Matthias Brickell—is substantiated by no known record in North Carolina or in Great Britain. Indeed, the existence of such a person as Matthias Brickell is itself much in doubt. Finally, it is purely speculative to associate Brickell's name with that of a late eighteenth-century Georgia physician also named John Brickell and sometimes alleged to have been the son of the author of the *Natural History of North Carolina*.

SEE: John Brickell, *Natural History of North Carolina* (1737); M. B. Gordon, *Aesculapius Comes to the Colonies* (1949); Archibald Henderson, *North Carolina: The Old North State and the New*, vol. 1 (1941); North Carolina General Court Records, July 1731 (North Carolina State Archives, Raleigh); Marcus Simpson (personal contact).

THOMAS C. PARRAMORE

Bridgers, Ann Preston (*1 May 1891–3 May 1967*), teacher and actress. was born in Raleigh. During most of her childhood she lived in Adrian, Ga., with her parents, Annie Preston Cain of Hillsborough and Robert Rufus Bridgers, Jr., of Wilmington. She attended Mary Baldwin Seminary in Staunton, Va., and then Smith College in Northampton, Mass., where she received a B.A. degree in 1915.

After being graduated from Smith, she studied with the Henry Jewett Players of Boston and played a few minor roles. Returning to Raleigh, she taught in the public schools and served with the Selective Service Bureau. She went overseas in 1919 with the Smith College Unit of the YMCA. On returning to Raleigh again, she opened a gift shop and became president of the Raleigh Community Players.

In 1923 she sold her gift shop, moved to New York, and enrolled in dramatic school; there, according to a *New York Times* article entitled "And Who is Ann Preston Bridgers?" "she trifled with fencing, costuming, designing, carpentering, diction, dancing and even acting, the latter a purely academic interest inspired by a desire to familiarize herself with the fundamentals of the theatre *per se*."

For several years after 1923 she enjoyed considerable success in the theater, beginning as understudy for Lynn Fontanne in *Dulcy*. Her first major role was that of Mrs. Bercovitch in *Fall Guy*, in which with great acclaim she also portrayed two offstage voices, one Irish and one Jewish. Her next role was as the original Katie, the cigarette girl, in *Broadway*. By this time she had begun writing a play, *Norma*, which when submitted to George Abbott impressed him so favorably that he agreed to collaborate with her. Together they produced the hit show *Coquette*, in which she played a supporting role to Helen Hayes, the star, both on Broadway and on the road. For *Coquette*, Ann Bridgers received the Theatre Club's award for "the most pleasing play of 1927–28."

Forsaking Broadway, she traveled extensively in Europe for a few years and in 1933 moved permanently to Raleigh, where she became active in the Civic Music Association. She was also a member of the board of the Literary and Historical Association, an editor of the Survey of Federal Records, an occasional contributor to the *Raleigh Times* and *News and Observer*, and an early moving spirit in the formation of the Raleigh Little Theater.

An ardent Christian Scientist, Miss Bridgers died in Raleigh after a long illness and was buried in Oakdale Cemetery, Wilmington.

SEE: *New York Times*, 13 Nov. 1927; *North Carolina Authors* (1952); Raleigh *News and Observer*, 4 May 1967; Smith College Alumnae Register (1935) and Class of 1915 Reunion Book (1940).

H. C. BRIDGERS, JR.

Bridgers, Henry Clark (*7 Jan. 1876–13 Oct. 1951*), athlete, attorney, railroad man, and entrepreneur, was born just west of Tarboro, at Hilma, the home of his parents, Laura Clark and John L. Bridgers, Jr. He attended school locally and as a youth was noted for his collection of several hundred varieties of birds' eggs. At age sixteen he entered the University of the South at Sewanee, Tenn., and from there went to The University of North Carolina. At Chapel Hill he was a member of Sigma Nu Fraternity and the German Club, but his chief fame lay in his ability in tennis, trap shooting, and golf. He helped represent the university in tennis and shooting, and he is credited with having introduced golf at Chapel Hill. He received his law degree in 1895 and returned home to join his father's law firm.

Within a few years he had converted the western portion of his father's homeplace into a combined pasture-golf course and had built a railroad. The golf course, now Hilma Country Club, was one of the first in the state and has been played continuously since 29 Apr. 1899. When he was only twenty-two, he was elected president of the East Carolina Railway, which eventually ran from Tarboro to Hookerton, in Greene County, and literally created the towns of Pinetops, Macclesfield, and Fountain. As an attorney, he became local counsel for the Southern Railway. He let none of these activities interfere with sports, managing over the next twenty years to gather a large number of trophies in shooting, golf, and tennis and to achieve a modest national reputation in all three.

Along with his railroad operation, he became active in banking; by 1913 he had been made president of the First National Bank in Tarboro and the banks of Conetoe, Pinetops, Macclesfield, Fountain, and Hookerton. He was also president of ten other companies. In addition, he had acquired substantial farm lands, which he operated successfully; but unlike his father and grandfather, he had no inborn love of the soil. Briefly he ventued into publishing, acquiring a short-lived control of the Tarboro *Southerner*. He had a keen mind, a driving energy, and diverse interests.

On 12 Jan. 1912, Bridgers married Mary Meade Bernard (10 Oct. 1887–14 May 1930), of Petersburg, Va., daughter of Lucia Beverly Morrison and Judge David Meade Bernard II. They had a son, Henry Clark, Jr., and a daughter, Lucia Beverly. In 1924 they completed a Georgian-colonial home in Tarboro called Merriemeade, for which the architect, Dwight James Baum of New York, received national recognition.

Both Mary Meade and Henry Clark Bridgers died at Merriemeade and were buried in the yard of Calvary Episcopal Church in Tarboro. A portrait of each is in the possession of their children.

SEE: Kemp P. Battle, *History of the University of North Carolina*, 2 vols. (1907–12); Henry C. Bridgers, Jr., *East Carolina Railway* (1973), and *The Story of Banking in Tarboro* (1969); D. L. Grant, *Alumni History of the University of North Carolina* (1924); Archibald Henderson, *The Campus of the First State University* (1949); *Southern Architecture Illustrated* (1931); Tarboro *Southerner* scattered issues, 1898–1935; Tombstones, Calvary Episcopal churchyard (Tarboro); Trophies and news clippings, (possession of H.C. Bridgers, Jr.).

H. C. BRIDGERS, JR.

Bridgers, John Luther (29 Nov. 1821–22 Jan. 1884), attorney, agriculturist, and soldier, was born on a farm on Town Creek in southwest Edgecombe County. His father, second generation of the Bridgers family in the area, was the son of Briton Bridgers, who as a youth was brought there from Northampton County by his stepfather, Joseph Pender, in about 1770. The Bridgers in Edgecombe are descendants of Colonel Joseph Bridger, prominent seventeenth-century colonist of Isle of Wight County, Va. The "s" was first added to the name in court records of Bertie County in 1725.

John Luther Bridgers's mother was Elizabeth Kettlewells Routh, who, following the death of her husband, John Bridgers, married Elder Mark Bennett; young John studied under Bennett at the Town Creek Academy. In 1843, Bridgers was graduated with honors from The University of North Carolina, delivering the required commencement speech in French.

He settled in Tarboro, joining his brother, Robert R., and Robert H. Pender in the practice of law and in the mercantile business. County records attest to his success and prominence as an attorney. Throughout their lives, Robert and John Bridgers were friendly rivals, especially in agriculture. During the 1850s, they owned together more than six thousand acres, which they farmed with scientific fervor. Two of John's plantations, Strabane and Middleplace, frequently set production records. He was an enthusiastic supporter of the State Agricultural Society and a welcomed principal speaker at the annual state fair.

Bridgers was a director of the Tarboro branch of the North Carolina State Bank. He was the first University of North Carolina escheator appointed in Greene County. He served as a member of the state legislature and from this body was elected a councilor of state. He was a major subscriber to the construction of Calvary Episcopal Church in Tarboro. For most of his adult life, he lived at the Grove, a house built by Thomas Blount in 1808. Still standing and well preserved today, it once enjoyed a sweeping, unbroken view of the common of the town of Tarboro.

As war threatened, Bridgers was one of three delegates sent by North Carolina to Montgomery, Ala., to try to effect an amicable solution. Failing in this attempt, he was unanimously chosen captain of the Edgecombe Guards, an organization that had the unfortunate distinction of suffering the first southern casualty, Private Henry L. Wyatt, at the Battle of Big Bethel. Captain Bridgers was cited for gallantry in this action and promoted to lieutenant colonel of Heavy Artillery (Tenth Regiment, North Carolina Troops). As such he commanded Fort Macon until ill health forced his resignation. He subsequently served on the staff of Lieutenant General D. H. Hill and also assisted his brother, Robert, in managing the vital High Shoals iron furnace in Gaston County.

On 20 Apr. 1847, Bridgers married Rebecca Louisa Dicken (25 Feb. 1829–30 Oct. 1865) of Halifax County.

She was a great-granddaughter of Benjamin Dicken, one of the commissioners who laid out the town of Tarboro. They lost a son, Charles, in infancy; surviving were another son, John Luther, Jr., and a daughter, Routh E., who married Algernon E. Hassard-Short, an Englishman. On 4 Apr. 1867, Bridgers married his second wife, Mary Elizabeth Battle (10 Jan. 1844–19 July 1918), daughter of Joseph Sumner Battle and his wife, Mary Ann Horn. Children of this marriage were Marcus Milton, Loulie, Whitney, and Mary Horn. The Misses Loulie and Mary Bridgers were beloved, lifetime grade school teachers in Tarboro, and one of the schools there is named for them.

Plagued throughout his life by poor health and suffering severe financial setbacks in his old age, Bridgers in 1881 sold the Grove and retired to his Strabane farm, now a fraction of its former size, where he died three years later. He and both his wives were buried in the yard of Calvary Episcopal Church. There is a portrait of Colonel Bridgers by R. N. Brooke in the White House of the Confederacy in Richmond and another in the possession of his great-grandson.

SEE: H. B. Battle et al., *The Battle Book* (1930); Kemp P. Battle, *History of the University of North Carolina*, vol. 1 (1907); John Bennett Boddie, *Seventeenth Century Isle of Wight County, Virginia* (1959); John Luther Bridgers, Jr., Papers (Southern Historical Collection, University of North Carolina, Chapel Hill); Walter Clark, ed., *Histories of the Several Regiments and Battalions from North Carolina in the Great War, 1861–1865*, vol. 1 (1901); Court records of Bertie, Northampton, and Edgecombe counties (North Carolina State Archives, Raleigh); C. A. Evans, ed., *Confederate Military History*, vol. 2 (1899); *History of North Carolina*, vol. 4 (1919); Items in possession of H. C. Bridgers, Jr.; Jaquelin Drane Nash, *A Goodly Heritage: The Story of Calvary Parish* (1960); *North Carolina Manual* (1913); *North Carolina: Rebuilding an Ancient Commonwealth*, 4 vols. (1929); *Raleigh Register*, 24 Oct. 1857; Tarboro *Southerner*, 11 Apr. 1867, 30 Oct. 1902, 29 Oct. 1960; Tombstones, Calvary Episcopal churchyard (Tarboro); J. Kelly Turner and J. L. Bridgers, Jr., *History of Edgecombe County* (1920).

H. C. BRIDGERS, JR.

Bridgers, John Luther, Jr. (5 May 1850–1 Apr. 1932), attorney, farmer, guardsman, and author, was born in Tarboro at the Grove, the home of his parents, Rebecca Louisa Dicken and Colonel John L. Bridgers. He went to school locally under Professor F. S. Wilkinson and then briefly attended the Groves School in Granville County before entering the Virginia Military Institute. He was graduated from Virginia Military Institute in 1870 and, despite his military and civil engineering training, elected to read law in the office of George Whitfield in Wilson.

He passed the bar examination before attaining his majority and was required to wait until 1871 before being admitted to the bar. For more than half a century he conducted a successful law practice in Tarboro, with clients including the Atlantic Coast Line Railroad, the town of Tarboro, and Edgecombe County. He was judge of Edgecombe's first inferior court and was a very active member of the American Bar Association. An inveterate convention goer, he was also much in demand as a speaker at local functions, especially Democratic rallies. He held various offices in many local concerns.

He did not desert his early military training completely. For eight years he was captain of the Edgecombe Guards, and later he commanded the

Edgecombe Home Guards for several years, eventually holding a colonelcy on the staff of Governor A. M. Scales. During World War I he was chairman of the Council of Defense for Edgecombe County.

His greatest contribution to posterity was his collaboration with J. Kelly Turner in writing the informative *History of Edgecombe County*. However, neither law, writing, nor soldiering were his true fortes. His favorite occupations were hunting and looking after the crops on the more that fourteen hundred acres of his farms Middleplace and Teleco and his homeplace Hilma. He inherited his father's love for agriculture and devoted much of his energy toward its improvement.

On 11 Dec. 1872, Bridgers married Laura Placidia Clark (9 Nov. 1850–1 Mar. 1933), daughter of former Governor Henry Toole Clark. Their children were: Elizabeth Haywood, who married Pierre B. Cox and then Benjamin F. Finney, later vice-chancellor of the University of the South at Sewanee; Henry Clark; Mary Irwin, who married Frank P. Williamson of the Philippines; Laura Placidia, who married the Reverend Robb White; and Rebecca Routh. Both parents died at Hilma, and they along with three of their children were buried in the yard of Calvary Episcopal Church.

SEE: Bridgers's diary (1886–1924), diplomas, and commissions (possession of H. C. Bridgers, Jr.); Court records of Edgecombe County (North Carolina State Archives, Raleigh); *History of North Carolina*, vol. 4 (1919); *North Carolina: Rebuilding an Ancient Commonwealth*, vol. 3 (1929); North Carolina State Archives (Raleigh [photograph]); *North Carolina Year Book* (1914); Raleigh *News and Observer*, 14 Dec. 1872; Tarboro *Farmers' Advocate*, 12 May 1892; Tarboro *Southerner*, 12 Oct. 1899; Tombstones, Calvary Episcopal churchyard (Tarboro).

H. C. BRIDGERS, JR.

Bridgers, Robert Rufus (*28 Nov. 1819–10 Dec. 1888*), Confederate congressman and railroad official, elder son of Elizabeth Kettlewells Routh and John Bridgers, was born on a farm in southwestern Edgecombe County. Failing to apply himself during early education under Elder Mark Bennett at Town Creek Academy, he was put to work on the farm at age thirteen. Two years later, having acquired an appreciation for education, he attended Stony Hill Academy in Nash County. He was graduated from The University of North Carolina in 1841 with distinction, delivering his commencement speech on the science of law. Throughout his life he remained a staunch friend and supporter of the university. When the alumni association was organized in 1843, he was a charter member. He was a frequent donor to the university and a university trustee from Edgecombe County from 1858 to 1868 and from New Hanover County from 1879 to 1888.

Bridgers began law practice in Tarboro and soon entered the mercantile business and politics. He served as representative from Edgecombe County in 1844 and again from 1856 to 1860. He was extremely interested in agriculture and acquired extensive landholdings in Edgecombe and Halifax counties and in Florida.

On 11 Dec. 1849, Bridgers married Margaret Elizabeth Johnston (26 Aug. 1832–29 Aug. 1907), daughter of Emily Norfleet and Henry Johnston of Tarboro. Their children were Emily, Robert R., Preston L., Mark, Luther, George J., Mary, and Frank W. Margaret and Robert Bridgers were Episcopalians, and both were substantial contributors to Calvary Church in Tarboro and St. James Church in Wilmington.

Bridgers was one of the organizers of the Tarboro

branch of the Bank of North Carolina and in 1859 became its president, a position he held until the bank was forced to close in 1865. He was also instrumental in the construction of the Tarboro branch of the Wilmington and Weldon Railroad, becoming its president in 1865.

He was often called colonel, but no record of his military service during the Civil War has been found. Indications are that poor health precluded such service. However, his contribution to the Confederacy was substantial. He was a member of the Confederate Congress from 1862 to 1865, serving on the Military Affairs and Special Finances committees. He also operated the High Shoals iron furnaces, considered the second most important in the South for production of nails and rolled material.

In about 1871, Bridgers moved to Wilmington, because he had become president of the Wilmington and Weldon and the Wilmington, Columbia and Augusta railroads. Meticulous attention to detail and a thorough knowledge of civil engineering served him well during his distinguished railroad career. It was under his leadership that an association of railroads called the Atlantic Coast Line was formed, although it was several years after his death that these railroads became a company by that name. He was also an ardent proponent of the standardization of time, serving as president of the Southern Railways Time Convention.

Bridgers suffered a fatal stroke while testifying on railroad matters before the South Carolina legislature. Both he and his wife were buried in Wilmington's Oakdale Cemetery. A portrait of Bridgers hangs in the Philanthropic Society in Chapel Hill and another, by R. N. Brooke, is held by the White House of the Confederacy in Richmond.

SEE: Samuel A. Ashe, ed., *Biographical History of North Carolina*, vol. 1 (1905); Kemp P. Battle, *History of the University of North Carolina*, vol. 2 (1912); Henry C. Bridgers, Jr., *The Story of Banking in Tarboro* (1969); John Luther Bridgers, Jr., Papers (Southern Historical Collection, University of North Carolina, Chapel Hill); Court records of Edgecombe, Halifax, and New Hanover counties (North Carolina State Archives, Raleigh); D. L. Grant, *Alumni History of the University of North Carolina* (1924); *History of North Carolina*, vol. 2, *The Federal Period*, by W. K. Boyd (1919); Jaquelin Drane Nash, *A Goodly Heritage: The Story of Calvary Parish* (1960); New Hanover County Will Books F 238, F 244, and I 321 (North Carolina State Archives, Raleigh); Richard E. Prince, *Atlantic Coast Line Railroad* (1966); Raleigh *News and Observer*, 7 Jan. 1883, 11 Dec. 1888; John F. Stover, *The Railroads of the South* (1955); Tarboro *Free Press*, 15 Dec. 1849; Tarboro *Southerner*, 30 Oct. 1902; Wilmington *Weekly Star*, 14 Dec. 1888.

H. C. BRIDGERS, JR.

Briggs, Thomas Henry (*9 Sept. 1847–7 May 1928*), merchant, banker, and religious leader, was born in Raleigh, the son of Thomas Henry and Evelina Norwood Briggs. He attended Lovejoy Academy and was graduated from Wake Forest College in 1870. In that year he and his brother joined as copartners the wholesale and retail hardware business that their father had established in 1865. The firm, Thomas H. Briggs & Sons, is still operated by the Briggs family in its original building on Fayetteville Street, Raleigh. Young Briggs became active in community development and was one of the organizers of the local YMCA. He also assisted in organizing and became secretary and treasurer of the Wake County Cattle Club. He was an organizer of the Commercial National Bank and president of the Wake

County Savings Bank, treasurer and trustee of Wake Forest College, a trustee of the Agricultural and Mechanical College, Greensboro, and a member of the Raleigh School Committee. He spent a great deal of time in religious work, particularly in organizing Sunday schools and in extension work with the Baptist church.

Briggs married Sarah Grandy on 21 Oct. 1874; they were the parents of Willis Grandy and Elizabeth Norwood. Briggs was buried in Oakwood Cemetery, Raleigh.

SEE: *History of North Carolina*, vol. 4 (1919); *North Carolina: The Old North State and the New*, vol. 3 (1941).

WILLIAM S. POWELL

Briggs, William Cyrus *(20 Dec. 1861–8 Mar. 1918),* inventor, the son of Cyrus and Lydia F. Loring Briggs, was born in Turner, Maine, and educated locally. He moved to Brooklyn, N.Y., where he was an engineer and machinist, and he may also have lived in New Jersey for a time. He afterwards moved to Fayetteville, where he designed one of the first successful automatic cigarette-making machines, and in 1892 he settled in Winston. There he set up his machine tools in a corner of the J. A. Vance Machine Shops, in a move that is regarded as the initial step in the history of the Briggs-Shoffner Company. Briggs's cigarette-making machine was sold, together with the patents for it, to the Murai Brothers, Kyoto, Japan, after Briggs visited Japan in 1898.

The United Cigarette Machine Company of Lynchburg, Va., of which Captain James W. Gerow was president, sued Briggs for patent infringement. The case was heard in Asheville, with Colonel Clement Manly of Winston successfully defending Briggs. Gerow then offered Briggs a position with his company, and Briggs accepted, leaving Winston-Salem in 1913, the very year that Winston and Salem were consolidated. At United in Lynchburg, Briggs designed a totally new machine capable of producing four-hundred thousand cigarettes a day.

At his death in 1918, Briggs was survived by his wife, the former Hope Elizabeth O'Brien; two daughters, Mabel Loring and Hope Elizabeth; and a son, W. C., Jr. Another daughter, Julia Cecil (Mrs. Robert Walker) of Winston-Salem, died in 1915 at the age of twenty-six. Briggs's remains were temporarily interred in a vault in Lynchburg but moved in June to Turner, Maine, for burial in the village cemetery.

In 1842, when a railroad was built through Berwick, Maine, one William C. Briggs opened a "restorator," forerunner of the lunch counter. A special cake made by his wife became noted as Berwick cake. What relationship connected these two men of the same name is not known.

SEE: Edwin A. Churchill of the Maine State Museum (Augusta) to William S. Powell, letter (28 Feb. 1977); Diuguid's Mortuary, Lynchburg, Va.; Lynchburg *News*, 9 Mar. 1918; Maine State Museum, Augusta, for a typescript genealogy of the Briggs family; N. M. Tilley, *The Bright-Tobacco Industry* (1948); Turner, Me., Vital Records.

WILLIAM S. POWELL

Briggs, Willis Grandy *(9 Oct. 1875–24 Feb. 1954),* lawyer, newspaperman, and political leader, was born in Raleigh, the son of Thomas Henry and Sarah Grandy Briggs. He was educated at a school conducted by Charles C. Holden, at the Raleigh Male Academy, and at

Wake Forest College, from which he was graduated *cum laude* in 1896. He became city editor of the *Raleigh Evening Times*.

President Theodore Roosevelt appointed Briggs, a Republican, postmaster in Raleigh, and he continued to serve during the administration of William Howard Taft, leaving the position in 1914 when he returned to Wake Forest to study law. Admitted to the bar in 1915, he was promptly chosen city court prosecutor and continued to serve through 1921. During 1918–19 he was a member and secretary of the Raleigh Exemption Board, operating under the Selective Service System. He was assistant U.S. attorney of the Eastern District from 1921 until 1930 but resigned to resume the private practice of law. In 1928 he was a delegate to the Republican National Convention. In 1934 he was the Republican nominee for associate justice, North Carolina Supreme Court, and four years later was his party's nominee for Congress from the Fourth District, but he was not elected in either race.

Briggs was deeply interested in the history of Raleigh and Wake County, as well as of the State of North Carolina, and devoted considerable time to research, writing, and speaking on historical subjects. Among his published works were a history of the First Baptist Church in Raleigh and a biography of Henry Potter (1766–1857).

On 16 Feb. 1910, Briggs was married to Beulah Sanderlin; they were the parents of two daughters, Sarah Wooten and Eliza Sanderlin. He was buried in Oakwood Cemetery, Raleigh.

SEE: Greensboro *Daily Industrial News*, 17 Aug. 1906; North Carolina State Bar Association, *Proceedings*, vol. 20 (1922); Raleigh *News and Observer*, 26 Feb. 1954.

WILLIAM S. POWELL

Bright, Simon *(ca. 1702–ca. 1777),* colonial planter, county official, Anglican church leader, and militia officer, was the son of John Bright (ca. 1670–ca. 1720) of Bath County and his wife, Elizabeth (ca. 1680–1744). John Bright settled in Bath County before 1704 and by 4 July 1704 was residing on a plantation on the west side of Matchapongo River.

Simon Bright married Mary Reel, daughter of Peter Reel, Sr., of Craven Precinct, in about 1730; they had at least two children, Simon, Jr., and James, both of whom attained local prominence. A William Bright who died in Dobbs County in 1782 was probably also a child of Simon and Mary, and there may have been others.

Bright first entered public service in 1731 as a justice of the court for Craven Precinct. He served in that office until Johnston County was formed from upper Craven in 1746. By 1734 he had settled on a plantation called The Briery, situated on Great Briery Swamp north of Atkins' Bank (present Kinston); his brother, William, had settled on an adjoining plantation. Simon Bright's residence fell into the new county of Johnston, and he served that county alternately as justice and as high sheriff until 1757, when he refused reappointment. He also served as an officer of the Johnston County militia regiment until 1759, when his area was separated from Johnston to form the new county of Dobbs.

Bright's most enduring contributions were made in religion and education. He supported the idea that organized religion and schoolmasters should spread inland with the frontier. He became a member of the original vestry of St. Patrick's Parish, organized in 1746 for Johnston County, and labored in the religious and educational interests of the parish the rest of his life. As early as 1 Mar. 1735, Bright and his brother induced a schoolmaster, John Vernon, to come and settle with them. Vernon supervised the operation of Simon Bright's gristmill and taught children of the community until 1741, when he moved to Onslow County and was replaced by Thomas Branton. In those days the Anglican church had responsibility for public education and for public relief of the poor, as well as for Anglican religious instruction and worship services. A local congregation was organized with the schoolmaster as reader. In 1747, soon after St. Patrick's Parish was formed, the Brights enlisted the aid of their neighbors and of William Heritage, absentee owner of a large nearby plantation at Atkins' Bank, to build a chapel accessible to the Neuse River landing on the Heritage plantation, in the hope that an Anglican missionary could be brought to the community. It was several years before this hope was fulfilled by the arrival of the Reverend William Miller, who previously had served St. Gabriel's Parish in Duplin County. Miller remained at the chapel until 1775, when he declared his Loyalist sympathies and left North Carolina.

During his long tenure on the parish vestry, Bright was influential in the organizing of other Anglican congregations in Johnston County and later in Dobbs. At least two other chapels were built in Johnston during his tenure: Lee's Chapel was built in 1756 on lands of Timothy Lee accessible to a waterway thereafter called the Chapel Branch, a prong of Sandy Run, near the present community of Ormondsville in Greene County; the following year the Middle Creek Chapel was built on lands of Lodowick Tanner on Little Middle Creek, a site now in the Panther Branch Township of Wake County, derived from Johnston County in 1771.

The exact date of Bright's death is unknown. He appears on a Dobbs County tax list for 1769 in a household with his son James. He is mentioned as a witness in 1775. Dobbs voter lists made at Kinston in March 1779 do not register his name, and it does not appear on lists of Dobbs landowners and lists of taxables for 1780. Family tradition holds that Bright was buried in the old Caswell Cemetery on The Hill plantation, adjoining his home plantation, the Briery.

SEE: Beaufort County Deed Book 1 and Old Will Book, 1720–1842 (North Carolina State Archives, Raleigh); *Sketches of Church History in North Carolina* (1892); Craven County Court Minutes and deeds (1734–46), Deed Book (Miscellaneous Deeds, 1728–1868), and Will and Estate Settlement (North Carolina State Archives, Raleigh); Edgecombe County Wills (North Carolina State Archives, Raleigh), for the Will of Richard Lee, 1756; Fulham Papers (Lambeth Palace Library, London); Grantee Index of Johnston-Dobbs-Lenoir (North Carolina State Archives, Raleigh), for Wardens of the Church entry from Timothy Lee and Dobbs County landgrants issued to Robert Hart (no. 26), Timothy Lee (no. 887), and Charles Markland (1787); Johnston County Deed Book 1 (North Carolina State Archives, Raleigh), for a 1757 deed; Book 85 (Land Grant Office, Office of the Secretary of State, Raleigh), for a Bath County landgrant to Lewis Conner in 1730; *New Bern Sentinel*, 13 June 1829; North Carolina Landgrant Office, Book 2 (Office of the Secretary of State, Raleigh); North Carolina Museum of History (Raleigh), for the Caswell family Bible, printed in 1737; North Carolina State Archives (Raleigh), for File CCR 187; Records of Superior Court for New Bern District (North Carolina State Archives, Raleigh), for 1775 docket; William L. Saunders and Walter Clark, eds.,

Colonial and State Records of North Carolina, vols. 5, 7, 9, 22, 23, 25 (1887–1905).

CHARLES R. HOLLOMAN

Bright, Simon, Jr. (*ca. 1734–December 1776*), Continental Army officer, colonial planter, legislator, county official, and member of revolutionary provincial congresses of North Carolina, was born about 1734 in Craven Precinct at his father's plantation, The Briery. Known throughout his life as Simon Bright, Jr., he was the son of Colonel Simon Bright and his wife, Mary Reel.

The grantee index of deeds (1746–1880) of old Johnston, old Dobbs, and early Lenoir counties indicates that in or about 1758 deeds from Simon Bright the elder were registered by his sons Simon and James. On 3 Mar. 1759 a Johnston County land grant for two hundred acres was issued to Captain Simon Bright, son of Colonel Simon Bright. The latter document is the conclusive proof of Captain Bright's parentage, and land grants have been used to estimate his year of birth.

On 21 Apr. 1759, Bright was named on the first list of justices commissioned for the new county of Dobbs. He was one of the original purchasers of lots in Kinston when the town was founded in 1762, and he was appointed to the town's original board of directors and trustees. In 1761 he left the office of justice to serve briefly as high sheriff of Dobbs; returning to the bench in February 1763, he continued as a justice until 1768. In 1769 he again became high sheriff of Dobbs, holding the office until 1773. In the latter year, he resumed the office of justice and was also elected to the North Carolina General Assembly. He and Richard Caswell represented Dobbs County in the assembly in 1773, 1774, and 1775, serving concurrently also as justices.

In the War of the Regulation in 1771, Bright commanded a company of Dobbs militia under regimental commander Colonel Richard Caswell in the expedition mounted by the royal governor, William Tryon, against the Regulators. Bright's company saw action at the Battle of Alamance.

Bright was one of the six Dobbs County residents elected to the first provincial congress of North Carolina that met in New Bern in August 1774. Bright was elected to represent Dobbs in each of five successive provincial congresses, serving in all but the second provincial congress, held 13 Apr. 1775 at Hillsborough. Organized opposition to the provincial congress appeared in Dobbs County in the form of a petition to the royal governor, circulated in February 1775. The pro-congress leadership was needed at home, and consequently, only delegate Richard Caswell attended the second congress, although Bright and others had been elected.

On 1 Sept. 1775, Bright accepted command of a company in the Second Battalion (later designated Regiment) of the North Carolina Continental Line. During the following six months, he was in the field working to develop the military preparedness of the state. While thus engaged, he suffered in November 1775 an illness so severe that he despaired of recovery and wrote his will. Soon afterward, however, he recovered sufficiently to resume his military duties. In the late winter he suffered a relapse and temporarily retired to his home to recuperate. While on this leave, he was elected a delegate to the fourth provincial congress, to be held at Halifax on 4 Apr. 1776. This congress adopted the famous Halifax Resolves concerning independence. Despite the delicate condition of his health, he attended the congress, but returned home in such a weakened condition that he became despondent and resigned his

Continental command, doubting that he would regain the health to serve it. During the following summer, his health improved, only to relapse again in late autumn after he had been elected to represent his county in the fifth provincial congress, to convene at Halifax on 12 Nov. 1776. Again he left his sick bed to serve his county and state.

The fifth provincial congress wrote the original constitution of North Carolina and elected civil and military officers to serve the state and its counties until a general election could be held pursuant to the new constitution. Richard Caswell presided over the convention and was elected governor of the state for the interim period. As the delegation rode back toward Dobbs County, Bright became very ill and died soon afterwards. According to family legend, he was buried near his father's grave in the old Caswell cemetery at Newington-on-the-Hill, the site now known as Vernon Hall in Kinston.

Bright was married in about 1756 to Mary Graves, daughter of Thomas Graves of the Contentnea Neck of Craven County. He was survived by his wife and seven children: Simon, Graves, James, Mary, Nancy, Sarah, and Elizabeth. All of Bright's sons attained prominence in the political, social and economic life of Lenoir County. Two of them, Simon and James, served in the state legislature.

SEE: Craven County court records to 1860 (North Carolina State Archives, Raleigh); J. Bryan Grimes, *Abstract of North Carolina Wills* (1910); T. C. Johnson and Charles R. Holloman, *The Story of Kinston and Lenoir County* (1954); New Bern District Court records, 1760–1808 (North Carolina State Archives, Raleigh); William L. Saunders and Walter Clark, eds., *Colonial and State Records of North Carolina* (1886–1914).

CHARLES R. HOLLOMAN

Bright, Simon (*ca. 1757–1802*), Revolutionary War soldier, planter, county official, member of the convention that ratified the U.S. Constitution in 1789, and state senator, was born in Johnston County in or about 1757. He was the first son of Simon Bright, Jr., and his wife, Mary Graves. He received his early education under the Reverend William Miller at St. Matthew's Chapel at Kingston (now Kinston). When his father died in December 1776, Simon was a minor; he attained his majority shortly thereafter, in time to become one of the executors of his father's will.

While still a minor, he enrolled in the Dobbs County militia and saw action several times during the Revolution. Late in the war, he volunteered for twelve months' service with the North Carolina state troops, the forces kept under arms in readiness for either state defense or for orders from the Continental establishment. After the war, he continued to serve in the militia of Dobbs County and later of Lenoir County. By 1789 he was held in such high respect by the people of his county that he was elected, with Richard Caswell, Benjamin Sheppard, and Nathan Lassiter, to represent Dobbs County in the convention of 1789. Like other delegates from Dobbs, Bright was an ardent Federalist, holding a viewpoint shared by only the barest majority of the electorate of his county.

In 1790, Bright was sent to the state senate post vacated by the death of Richard Caswell. Disheartened by the political contentions then racking his county he retired to private life. About 1795 he was appointed a justice in Lenoir County; he held the office until the summer of 1799, when he was appointed and served

briefly as clerk of the county court, following the death in office of Winston Caswell.

In about 1777, Bright married a woman named Nancy, whose maiden name is not known. To their marriage nine children were born. When Simon died in 1802 in Kinston, his wife and seven of the children survived him, as did a number of grandchildren.

Though a grandfather, Bright was only about forty-five years old when he died. The last two years of his life were burdened with embarrassment, disgrace, and remorse arising from a criminal act so inconceivably rash and so inconsistent with his previous conduct and character as to indicate strongly the onset of a disease affecting the brain and destroying that gentility, common sense and judgment for which he had so long been distinguished and honored. On 11 Sept. 1799, Bright was sitting in his parlor visiting with the brothers John and Slade Gatlin, two good friends and close neighbors. They had been chatting pleasantly for some time when Bright abruptly changed his whole demeanor. He angrily declared, according to depositions made by the Gatlin brothers, "that he had missed two of his Turkeys, and suspected that they were stolen by some Negro and that he would charge his gunn and shoote the first Negro he met with and continue shooting until he killed the right one. Mr. Bright then went off in order to get Powder and Shot to load his Gunn." Shorly thereafter, he waylaid and shot in the street Mary, a highly respected slave woman belonging to Captain Jesse Cobb, another justice and the town's leading merchant. The crime shocked the small, close-knit community. Bright was indicted on the criminal charge and prosecuted. During the course of the prosecution his mental condition and general health deteriorated rapidly, terminating in his death before the prosecution could be concluded in the superior court for the New Bern district, to which his conviction in the county court had been appealed.

Bright was buried at Kinston.

SEE: Manuscript records of the Superior Court for the New Bern District, 1760–1808: Simon Bright Estate Papers; Case Papers in *Jesse Cobb* v. *the Heirs of Simon Bright*; Case Papers in the *State* v. *Simon Bright*; Case Papers in *Simon Bright* v. *Robert White, Sheriff of Dobbs County* (North Carolina State Archives, Raleigh).

CHARLES R. HOLLOMAN

Brimley, Clement Samuel (*18 Dec. 1863–23 July 1946*), zoologist and entomologist, was born in Great Linford, Buckingham County, England, the son of Joseph and Harriet Brimley, who immigrated with his family to Raleigh in December 1880. He received formal education at the Bedford County School in Elstow, England.

Shortly after arriving in North Carolina, Brimley and his brother Herbert opened a taxidermy and biological supply company in Raleigh, where they quickly established an international reputation as the leading naturalists of their time in the South. While Herbert became increasingly occupied with the activities of the North Carolina State Museum, Clement continued the operation of their business and prepared numerous papers on the birds, mammals, reptiles, amphibians, and insects of the Southeast, these writings appearing in the *Ornithologist and Oologist, Auk, Chat, Journal of the Elisha Mitchell Scientific Society, Copeia, Proceedings of the Biological Society of Washington*, and *Carolina Tips*.

In 1919, Brimley joined the Entomology Division of the North Carolina Department of Agriculture, eventually becoming associate entomologist and director of the museum's insect collection. He collaborated with T. G.

Pearson and with his brother Herbert in writing *Birds of North Carolina* (1919 and 1942) and with H. T. Davis in *Poisonous Snakes of the Eastern United States*. His *Insects of North Carolina* (1938) and his papers "Amphibians and Reptiles of North Carolina" (1939–43) and "Mammals of North Carolina" (1905 and 1944–46) were definitive compilations in their field. He was a member of the American Ornithologists' Union, Wilson Ornithological Society, and American Society of Mammalologists. He was a founder, life member, and president of the North Carolina Academy of Science and founder and president of the North Carolina Bird Club. In June 1938 he was awarded an honorary LL.D. from The University of North Carolina in recognition for his contributions to science.

Brimley was married to Annie Roberts; they had two sons, Ralph and Edwin. His brother Herbert was director of the North Carolina State Museum. Clement Brimley was a member of the First Presbyterian Church of Raleigh and was buried in Oakwood Cemetery.

SEE: *Chat* 10 (1946 [portrait]).

MARCUS B. SIMPSON, JR.

Brimley, Herbert Hutchinson *(7 Mar. 1861–4 Apr. 1946)*, zoologist and director of the North Carolina State Museum, was born in Willington, Bedfordshire, England, the son of Joseph and Harriet Brimley, who immigrated with their family to Raleigh in December 1880. Brimley received his formal education at the Bedford County School in Elstow, England, where he excelled in mathematics and sports.

Following unsuccessful attempts at farming and teaching, he and his brother Clement opened a taxidermy and biological supply company in Raleigh, where they quickly gained an international reputation as the leading naturalists of their day in the South. In 1884 the North Carolina Department of Agriculture commissioned Brimley to prepare a display of waterfowl and fishes for the State Centennial Exposition, and in 1892–93 he supervised the North Carolina zoological exhibition at the Chicago World's Fair. In 1893 the Department of Agriculture designated two rooms in its office building as the North Carolina State Museum, for the permanent display of the exhibits assembled by Brimley. On 15 Apr. 1895, Brimley was appointed curator of the museum, a post he held until 1928, when his title was changed to director. He served as director until 30 June 1937, when he became curator of zoology for the museum, a position he retained until his death. During the fifty years of his leadership, the institution grew into one of the best-known state museums in the United States, containing an outstanding collection of animal, plant, and geological specimens from the southeastern United States.

During his years with the state museum, Brimley worked with the North Carolina exhibits at various international expositions and published numerous scientific papers on the natural history of the Southeast, these appearing chiefly in the *Ornithologist and Oologist*, *Auk*, and *Chat*. He collaborated with H. M. Smith in writing *Fishes of North Carolina* (1907) and with T. G. Pearson and C. S. Brimley on *Birds of North Carolina* (1919 and 1942); both were regarded as classics in their fields. He served as a member of the advisory committee of the World's Congress on Ornithology in 1894–95. He was a member of the American Association of Museums, the American Society of Mammalologists, and the Museum Association of Great Britain; a founder and life member

of the North Carolina Academy of Science; founder, president, and life member of the North Carolina Bird Club; and full member of the American Ornithologists' Union. Actively involved in civic affairs, he was an honorary life member of the Raleigh Rotary Club, serving as its president in 1921–22. In 1924 he was president of the Raleigh Festival Association, and for many years he was a leader in the Boy Scouts of America, serving as district council president and receiving the Scouts' highest award for distinguished contributions. In addition to his natural history writing, Brimley composed poetry, some included in *North Carolina Poems*, edited by E. C. Brooks in 1912.

Brimley was married twice, first in December 1895 to Edith Jane Taylor, who died in January 1911, and then to Bettie Moore Love in February 1913. He had two sons, Robert E. and Arthur H. He was an active member of Christ Episcopal Church in Raleigh. Copies of numerous portraits are found in E. P. Odum's edition of Brimley's writings.

SEE: *Biographies of Members of the American Ornithologists' Union* (1954); *Chat* 10 (1946); E. P. Odum, *A North Carolina Naturalist: H. H. Brimley* (1949).

MARCUS B. SIMPSON, JR.

Brinkley, John Romulus (afterward changed to Richard) *(8 July 1885–25 May 1942)*, medical maverick, was born in the community of Beta near Sylva, Jackson County, apparently the illegitimate son of Dr. John Richard Brinkley and his wife's niece, Sarah Candace Barnett. The mother died when the son was five, and he was raised by the Brinkleys. The elder Brinkley died about 1896 and the younger Brinkley worked as a telegraph operator and delivered mail until his foster mother died in 1907. During those years, he eagerly read home-treatment books and Bible stories. His photographic memory stored this information for use at a later time. A month after the death of Mrs. Brinkley he married a local girl, Sally Wike, and they remained in the county for about a year while he continued to work as a railroad telegraph operator at Bryson City and Sylva. He, his wife, and a few other people began to travel in the area producing a play of some kind, dancing, and singing to attract a crowd to which Brinkley sold tonics and herb medicines. In 1908 Brinkley, his wife, and a young daughter moved to Chicago where he entered Bennett Medical College, an "eclectic institution." He worked at night and attended school in the day, but after three years he dropped out because of debt and broken health. For several years he drifted about the country, and on one occasion traveled to New York. During his years of wandering with his family, Brinkley began to identify himself as a doctor and offered his services as a "men's specialist" in Knoxville and Chattanooga, Tenn. In the spring of 1913 the Brinkleys were divorced and Mrs. Brinkley and their three daughters (a son had died) returned to her mother's home in North Carolina. Brinkley went to Memphis where he met and married Minnie Telitha Jones, daughter of Dr. Tiberius Gracchus Jones. The couple moved to Greenville, S.C., where Brinkley practiced with James E. Crawford as "Electro Medic Doctors" until a large number of unpaid bills resulted in a jail sentence. Bailed out by his father-in-law, Brinkley and his wife moved to Judsonia, Ark., in the summer of 1914, where he opened a practice as a specialist in diseases of women and children and was soon highly regarded by many. In less than a year, however, he was enrolled at the Eclectic Medical University in Kansas City where, after a year and the payment of one hundred dollars, he received a diploma. Arkansas was one of eight states that recognized such a diploma, and he was licensed to practice eclectic medicine in that state. Under interstate reciprocity Kansas also recognized his license when he moved there in 1916. It was in Milford, Kan., that "Dr." Brinkley began his climb to fame and fortune. He developed and publicized his goat gland operation in which he claimed to transplant the sex glands of young buck goats to men, thereby restoring sexual vitality and fertility to impotent or "tired" men. He also advanced other claims for his skill as a surgeon and attracted a wide following. He prescribed medicine by mail and established a powerful radio station to publicize his medical work as well as to broadcast his fundamentalist theology. It was also about this time in 1918 that he purchased a medical diploma fraudulently issued and backdated to 1913 from the National University of Arts and Sciences, St. Louis, Mo.

Brinkley's surgery and his sale of prescriptions brought him millions of dollars before 1930, when the Federal Communications Commission succeeded in closing his radio station. In retaliation, Brinkley ran for governor of Kansas as an independent and came very close to winning although he was merely a write-in candidate. Many believed that if the ballots had been counted more faithfully, and if the ones marked simply "Doc" had been credited to him, he would have been elected. In 1932 he ran again and so split the Democratic vote that Alfred M. Landon, a Republican, won in a year when Democrats were widely victorious in other elections. He then left Kansas and moved to Del Rio, Tex., to be near his new radio station across the border in Mexico. About 1933 he ceased his goat gland operations but continued to stress his prostate operations and to promote his prescription service. Among his medicines was a package of crystals, "Crazy Water Crystals," that was widely advertised. In North Carolina a popular Charlotte radio station broadcast a noon program of "hillbilly music" to promote this product. A later analysis revealed this to be Glauber's salt, a horse physic. The cut-rate competition of another "surgeon" in Del Rio led to Brinkley's removal to Little Rock, Ark., where he established several hospitals specializing in prostate operations which he cited as a cure for high blood pressure, hardening of the arteries, impotency, epilepsy, locomotor ataxia, constipation, diseases of the stomach, bowels, and kidneys, dementia praecox, neurasthenia, and sterility caused by mumps.

In 1938 Dr. Morris Fishbein, editor of the *Journal of the American Medical Association*, published an article in another journal in which he referred to Brinkley as a medical charlatan. Brinkley sued Dr. Fishbein for libel, but a jury found in favor of Fishbein. This stimulated a great many suits against Brinkley which he lost, and he was obliged to pay large sums of money. Charges of income tax evasion and mail fraud were also brought against him, his wife, and several of his associates. By February 1941 he was forced into bankruptcy. That fall he was in a Kansas City hospital where his left leg was amputated because of complications from a blood clot. The following spring he died in his sleep in San Antonio, Tex., survived by his wife and a son, John Richard, Jr., or "Johnny Boy." He is buried in Memphis, Tenn., in a copper casket he purchased some years before, and his grave is marked by a large bronze statue of a winged victory that once stood at his Del Rio mansion. Brinkley's exploits brought him immense wealth. He owned a number of expensive automobiles, a yacht, and extensive property in various parts of the United States. At times during his career he returned to visit the scene of his

youth, and shortly before he was beset by financial troubles he turned over to his son the 6,500 acres he owned there.

SEE: *Asheville Citizen*, 16 May 1960; Asheville *Citizen-Times*, 25 Jan. 1969, 18 Dec. 1977; Gerald Carson, *The Rougish World of Doctor Brinkley* (1960); Memphis *Commercial Appeal*, 28 May 1942, 6 Mar. 1977; Albert J. Schneider, " 'That Troublesome Old Cocklebur': John R. Brinkley and the Medical Profession of Arkansas, 1937–1942," *Arkansas Historical Quarterly* 35 (1976).

WILLIAM S. POWELL

Brinson, Samuel Mitchell (*20 Mar. 1870–13 Apr. 1922*), educator and congressman, was a native of New Bern. His father was William George Brinson (4 Jan. 1840–8 May 1896), a sergeant in Company K, North Carolina Regiment, Confederate States of America; his mother was Kittie Elizabeth Chesnut (14 Oct. 1842–21 June 1908), a daughter of Owen and Kezia Chesnut.

After attending private and public schools in New Bern, Brinson was graduated in 1891 from Wake Forest College. For a year he taught school in New Bern. In 1895 he was graduated in law from The University of North Carolina. Admitted to the bar the next year, he began the practice of law in his native town.

From 1902 to 1919 he was superintendent of public instruction in Craven County; the Brinson Memorial School in the county was named for him. In 1918 he was president of the Atlantic and North Carolina Railroad Company, which had been organized in 1854 at New Bern to operate trains from Goldsboro to the coast. He was long a devoted member and educational leader of the First Baptist Church of New Bern.

As a Democrat, Brinson was elected and reelected to Congress, serving from 4 Mar. 1919 until his death. He was buried at Cedar Grove Cemetery in New Bern.

Brinson's wife, Ruth Morton Scales (8 Mar. 1879–19 Jan. 1919), was born at Knoxville, Tenn., daughter of N. E. Scales and Minnie Lord Scales, both natives of Salisbury. The Brinsons had one daughter, Mary Steele.

SEE: *Biog. Dir. Am. Cong.* (1971); Brinson Family Bibles (in the possession of Harvey Chesnut, Washington, D.C., and Miss Mary Steele Brinson, Salisbury); Craven County Records (North Carolina State Archives, Raleigh); Tombstones, Cedar Grove Cemetery (New Bern).

GERTRUDE S. CARRAWAY

Britt, James Jefferson (*4 Mar 1861–26 Dec. 1939*), educator, lawyer, and U.S. congressman, was born six miles from Johnson City in Carter County, Tenn. His father was James Jefferson Britt, a farmer and mechanic, who served in the Union army during the Civil War; his mother was Nancy J. Underwood. The family farm was raided by both armies during the war, leaving an austere environment for Britt, the youngest of ten children. He attended school for only ten months during his childhood; all further education he gained on his own. By the time he was eleven years old, he was working in a shoe shop and learning the trade. After diligent self-education, Britt qualified as a teacher in 1877, at the age of sixteen. He taught for the next ten years, moving to North Carolina in 1880, and in the course of his continued studies earned a B.A. degree. Subsequently, he was principal of the Burnsville Academy for nine years, principal of the Bowman Academy in Bakersville for three years, and superintendent of public schools in Mitchell County for four years. He was offered a teaching position in mathematics at the State Agricultural and Mechanic College of North Carolina but declined because of poor health.

Having become interested in law, Britt studied in private law offices in the area. In 1903 he entered The University of North Carolina to study law; he completed his studies and was admitted to the bar in 1905, returning to the mountains to practice in Asheville. Combining his legal training with government service, Britt was cashier of the Internal Revenue office in Asheville from 1906 to 1909; special attorney for the U.S. Department of Justice 1906–9; assistant attorney general for the United States for the prosecution of civil cases in the Post Office Department, 1910; and third assistant postmaster general, by appointment of President Taft, from December 1910 to March 1913. In 1913 he returned to Asheville to practice law as the senior member of the law firm Britt and Toms.

Taking an active interest in politics, Britt became a leader in the Republican party. He was a delegate to the Republican National Convention in 1904 as a supporter of Theodore Roosevelt. He was the Republican nominee for Congress in North Carolina's Tenth District in 1906 but was defeated. Offered the nomination for governor on the Republican ticket in 1908, he declined, but he ran for the state senate and was elected, serving as minority leader during the 1908–9 term. In 1914, Britt was elected to the U.S. Congress from the Tenth District of North Carolina to serve in the Sixty-fourth Congress. He sought reelection for the next term in a notable race against Zebulon Weaver, the man he defeated in 1914. Weaver was declared the winner and seated in Congress, but Britt contested the election and ultimately prevailed after a diligent fight. Britt was seated on 1 Mar. 1919 and served until 3 Mar., drawing his salary for the full term although he actually served only three days. After this episode he retired from active political life. He served as chief counsel of the Prohibition agency in Washington and in 1926 was an unsuccessful candidate for chief justice of the North Carolina Supreme Court. In 1933 he retired from his Washington activities and returned to Asheville. In 1937 he was named to the National Republican Policy Committee to draft plans for the 1940 presidential race.

Britt was a member of the National Economy League and the Academy of Political Science. He held fraternal memberships with the Masons, the Odd Fellows, the Knights of Pythias, the Kiwanis International Club, and the Pen and Plate Literary Club of Asheville. He belonged to the First Baptist Church of Asheville and was well known as a Bible teacher. On 4 Jan. 1880, Britt married Mary J. Mosley, daughter of Reuben B. Mosley of Carter County, Tenn. They had eight children.

Britt died at his home in Asheville, and funeral services were held there at the First Baptist Church.

SEE: *Carolina Magazine* 53 (October 1922); *Greensboro Daily News*, 27 Dec. 1939; *History of North Carolina*, vol. 6 (1919); *North Carolina Manual* (1909, 1915); Raleigh *News and Observer*, 27 Dec. 1939.

SAMUEL M. GAINOR

Broadhurst, Edwin Borden (16 Aug. 1915–4 Apr. 1965), Air Corps general, was born in Smithfield, the son of Jack Johnson and Mabel Borden Broadhurst. Among his forebears were early American patriots Richard Warren, signer of the Mayflower Compact of 1620; Richard Borden, treasurer of the Rhode Island colony in 1655; and Colonel Needham Bryan, member of first

provincial congress of North Carolina in 1776 and colonel of the Johnston County Field Officers of Minutemen. Broadhurst was graduated from Smithfield High School as an honor roll student and an Eagle Scout. He attended The Citadel in Charleston, S.C., one year before receiving an appointment to the U.S. Military Academy in 1933. Broadhurst's scholastic record at The Citadel entitled him to enter West Point without the usual entrance examination.

After graduation from the academy in 1937 with a commission as second lieutenant in the field artillery, Broadhurst was assigned to Fort Sill, Okla. The following year he transferred to the Army Air Force, training as a pilot at Kelly Field, Tex. He was a classmate of World War II hero Colin P. Kelly, Jr., and the two men were assigned to March Field, Calif., on receiving their pilot's wings in February 1939.

Broadhurst was assigned to the Nineteenth Bombardment Group in the Pacific in 1941. He was at Clark Field on 7 Dec. 1941 when the Japanese attacked, destroying on the ground practically all the planes of the bombardment group. With a shortage of men and planes, the pilots flew as many as six missions a day. Broadhurst received the Silver Star for gallantry at Davao, Philippines, in January 1942. His Flying Fortress scored a direct hit on a battleship in the harbor at Davao, returning to the air base in an equatorial storm. The following March he and nine other American pilots escaped from Java in the last B-17 Flying Fortresses leaving before the Japanese took over the island from the Dutch. As the planes left the field, the Dutch set off mines placed under the runways for such an eventuality. During the fiercest fighting of the early days of World War II, the Nineteenth Bombardment Group became the most decorated and most honored unit of the American Air Corps. In the first year of combat the group received three Distinguished Unit citations. The Nineteenth evacuated General Douglas MacArthur to Australia, where he set up headquarters; later Philippine President Manuel Quezon was evacuated by the group.

Broadhurst flew twenty combat missions in the Philippines, Java, Australia, and New Guinea. He served as plans officer at Allied Headquarters in the southwest Pacific and received the Legion of Merit for his work. When the battleworn Nineteenth Bombardment Group was returned to the United States late in 1942, as a replacement training unit, Broadhurst was assigned to the Second Air Force at Colorado Springs.

On promotion to full colonel in July 1943, Broadhurst was assigned to the office of the assistant secretary of war, U.S. Air Force, in Washington. From 1947 to 1950 he headed the U.S. Military Mission to Chile. The Chilean government awarded him posthumously the Medale Militaire. Returning to the United States in 1950, he was assigned as chief of plans to the Strategic Air Command at Omaha, Nebr., and he spent most of his peacetime service with SAC. In September 1953, a year after a transfer from commanding officer of the Fifth Reconnaissance Wing at Travis Air Force Base, Broadhurst was promoted to brigadier general. The next year he was assigned to Fairchild AFB in Washington State as commander of the Fifty-seventh Air Division. In September 1955 he returned to SAC headquarters as inspector general, and two years later he became chief of staff with promotion to major general in March 1958. Broadhurst was sent to England in August 1961 to command the Seventh Air Division stationed at High Wyecombe. A little over a year later he returned to Washington, D.C., as assistant deputy chief of staff for Operation Headquarters, USAF. Upon his promotion to lieutenant general in 1963, he was the youngest of his rank in the air force and the highest ranking North Carolinian on active duty. The last command he held was chief of staff, United Nations Command, with the U.S. forces in Korea. He died of a heart attack in Seoul, Korea. His body was returned with all military honors and interred at Riverside Cemetery in Smithfield.

Broadhurst was eulogized as a "modest and unassuming man of superior intellect and capacity." Described as "worldly and sophisticated," he was also recognized as "a man of great humility and kindness, and one who never lost the common touch." His awards included the Silver Star, the Legion of Merit with Oak Leaf Cluster, the Air Medal, the Distinguished Flying Cross, and the Purple Heart. The posthumous award citation of the Distinguished Service Medal stated: "His dynamic leadership, tireless devotion to duty and outstanding tact and diplomacy in working with the United States and foreign embassies, local United Nations agencies, United States Operation Mission in Korea, United States Information Service and high level officials of the Republic of Korea Government and its Armed Forces furthered to a marked degree the accomplishment of the objectives of the United Nations Command United States Forces in Korea."

General Broadhurst was married to Viola Seubert, daughter of Herman Joseph and Regina Seubert, in Washington, D.C., 11 Mar. 1944. They had three children, Edwin Borden, May Ann, and Barbara Ellen.

SEE: *San Antonio* (Tex.) *Express*, 1 Feb. 1939; *Smithfield Herald*, 6 Dec. 1957, 8 July 1961; "Tribute to Lt. General Edwin Borden Broadhurst, USAF, before the United States Senate, Tuesday, April 6, 1965, by Senator Sam Ervin, Jr."

BETH CRABTREE

Brock, Ignatius Wadsworth (*12 Nov. 1866–8 Nov. 1950*), photographer and painter, was born near Comfort in Jones County, the son of Isaac Brock, a planter, and Harriet Carolina Koonce Brock. He attended the William Rhodes School in Jones County and later Davis and Oak Ridge academies, before studying art at Cooper Union Institute in New York in the early 1890s.

Early ambitions for a career as a landscape artist were sidetracked when Brock turned to photography for what he termed "sketching notes" for future oil paintings. The camera proved a natural medium for his talents, and this ability, coupled with economic necessity, led him to become an apprentice at the Gerock Studio in New Bern, where he worked with the tedious old-fashioned glass plates and developed the darkroom techniques that brought later fame. A few early paintings appeared in art galleries or as reproductions for Victorian magazine covers, and one even went to pay for back rent, but the camera soon replaced the brush as his means of livelihood.

A free spirit with more than a touch of the bohemian, Brock grudgingly settled into the routine of the photographic studio after his marriage in 1897 to Ora Koonce of Jones County. The couple was still honeymooning in the mountains when he decided to settle in Asheville and open his first studio on Biltmore Avenue near the old Swannanoa-Berkely Hotel. Initially he signed his work "Ignatius Brock"; he shortened this designation to "Nace" and eventually settled for "N. Brock," the signature that was best known across the United States and in Europe.

In the first two decades of the twentieth century, Brock's copyrighted pictures of mountain scenery,

animals, and children, along with his character studies and an occasional nude, were in heavy demand. Magazines such as *Inland Printer* made widespread use of his camera work for covers and interior illustration, and he appeared frequently as a teacher and lecturer. He worked primarily with a platinum in tones of black and sepia, and his pictures were priced from one to three dollars.

In 1903 he won the award of the Photographer's Association of Virginia and the Carolinas for best landscape photographs. After three successive wins, ending in 1906, he permanently retired the Slater Trophy of the American Aristotype Company for portraits in nation-wide competition, and he was the winner of Eastman Kodak's Angelo award. He received the $500 first prize offered by the International Photography Association and was a gold medal winner in international competition at Boston, Mass., and Edinburgh, Scotland. Other prizes included the Asheville trophy for the best portrait of a woman and Virginia-Carolinas Association gold medals for best genre photography and best small-size portraits.

But the little man with the piercing eyes, the tired felt hat, the unruly cowlick, and the straggly mustache cared little for prizes and acclaim. He divided his time among the outdoors, the corner poolroom, and his studio, where he designed special lenses to improve further the quality of his work and experimented with such innovations as blue light. In a never-ending search for perfection, he patiently developed a specially tinted glass plate that provided his darkroom with the pure blue of daylight. The innovation was then taken to a leading light bulb manufacturer with a request for bulbs tinted the identical shade of blue. The company said it was impossible, but within a few years began marketing blue bulbs that were virtual duplicates of the blue light Brock had developed.

Brock the photographer kept abreast and often ahead of the latest developments in his field and added many innovations of his own, but Brock the man refused to bow to conformity. A contemporary recalled him in 1897 as a "dirty, unkempt, unshaven man whose work was his only interest," and more than fifty years later an Asheville newspaperman described him in almost the same terms. "He walked in the pouring rain as though it were sunshine," Doug Reed wrote. "He slept in his clothes and they were sloppy, baggy and greasy most of the time. He would make a bag of peaches a meal. He frequented bars and had a heavy yellow mustache that looked nicotine stained although he never smoked. He once left a socialite seething in his studio while he went across the street for a pool game; but he could set his own time, name his own fee, and make his own rules, and still the people of Asheville shouldered and shoved for nearly half a century for the coveted spot in front of his camera."

Brock operated studios in a variety of locations, all in Asheville, before turning to free-lance portrait painting and the reproduction of miniatures, and in the twilight of his career he worked for E. M. Ball's Plateau Studio. He died in an Asheville nursing home four days short of his eighty-fourth birthday and seven years after his wife, Ora Koonce Brock. The couple were the parents of two daughters, Ora and Carolina, and two sons, Ignatius Wadsworth, Jr., and Isaac.

SEE: *Asheville Citizen*, 9 Nov. 1950; Asheville *Citizen-Times*, 6 Feb. 1949, 22 Jan. 1956; Mrs. Ora Brock Burgin (Weaverville, personal contact); *Inland Printer*, December 1906.

DICK BROWN

Brock, William Emerson *(14 Mar. 1872–6 Aug. 1950)*, U.S. senator from Tennessee and businessman, was born on a small tobacco farm near Mocksville, Davie County, the son of Richard Emerson and Mary Ann Howell Brock. With his three younger brothers and sister, he obtained his only schooling at a one-room, one-teacher school near his father's farm. His father's death ended Brock's formal education, and at age sixteen he became the family's breadwinner. Six years later he was hired for thirty dollars a month by a store in Winston-Salem. In 1896, R. J. Reynolds hired him as the first salesman for his rapidly expanding tobacco company. Brock's fortunes flourished with the company's, and he was soon named southern sales manager, with headquarters in Chattanooga, Tenn. In 1909 he purchased a small candy manufacturing company in Chattanooga, which he eventually developed into one of the largest of its kind in the South. Three years later he was elected president of the Chattanooga Chamber of Commerce.

Brock's first experience in politics came in 1912, when he managed the successful campaign of a Democratic candidate for Congress. The two succeeding campaigns he headed for the same candidate were also successful. Later, he managed campaign activities in the Chattanooga area for Governor Austin Peay. In 1929, Governor Henry Horton named him to serve out the unexpired term of Senator Lawrence D. Tyson, and in 1930 he was elected for the short term from November to March 1931. He did not run again. While in the Senate, Brock played a significant role in the passage of the Rivers and Harbors Bill, which provided for nine dams on the Tennessee River for navigation and flood control. He strongly supported the Muscle Shoals Development in Alabama, the predecessor of the Tennessee Valley Authority.

In 1940, Brock resigned as president of the Brock Candy Company and became chairman of the board. His son succeeded him as president of the family business. In addition to his business activities, Brock was well known for his endeavors in behalf of religious and educational institutions. He was delegate to the general conference of the Methodist church for twenty-five years and served as president of the Holston Conference Board of Church Extension for fifteen years. In the latter capacity he helped raise funds for the building of twenty churches in the Chattanooga area. He served as a trustee at Emory University in Atlanta, Emory and Henry University in Emory, Va., Martha Washington College for Girls in Fredricksburg, Va., and the University of Chattanooga. At the latter institution, he was chairman of the executive committee and largely responsible for the school's postwar building program.

In 1903, Brock married Marian Acree of Clarksville, Tenn., the daughter of a Baptist minister. The couple had two sons, William Emerson, Jr., and Richard Acree.

SEE: *Biog. Dir. Am. Cong.* (1971); *Chattanooga Times*, 6 Aug. 1950; *New York Times*, 6 Aug. 1950; *Who's Who in the South and Southwest*, 1947, 1950; *Who Was Who in America*, vol. 3 (1960).

E. A. HATFIELD

Brockwell, Sherwood Battle *(12 Oct. 1885–3 June 1953)*, state fire marshall and deputy insurance commissioner, the son of Thomas F. and Katherine McLeod Feggan Brockwell, was born in Raleigh. He began fighting fires in 1898 when he hitched the mules, lighted the fire box, and shoveled the coal for the Raleigh steam fire engine. In 1902, while a student at North Carolina Agricultural and Mechanic College, he was a special member of the Raleigh Rescue Steam Fire Engine Company. By 1908, when he was old enough to become a regular member, Brockwell became the company foreman, and in 1909 he became assistant chief. In 1912 he joined the New York City Fire Department for training in firefighting and administration, and his heroic rescues during a metropolitan fire there earned him much publicity. During his training, Brockwell foresaw the advantages of motorized firefighting equipment, and he brought the first motor equipment to Raleigh. From 1912 to 1914 he was chief of the Raleigh Fire Department, when he was also the youngest paid fire chief in the nation. As a result of his pioneering work in school safety and fire prevention, in 1914 Colonel James R. Young, state insurance commissioner, named him deputy insurance commissioner and state fire marshall, an appointment he held until his death.

As state fire marshall, Brockwell argued that the key to fire prevention and protection lay in the correct training for fire personnel. He initiated fire colleges and drill schools in North Carolina, Maryland (under the auspices of the University of Maryland), Virginia, and South Carolina, and for the Federal Bureau of Investigation in Washington. During World War II he studied at the Chemical Warfare School, Edgewood Arsenal, Md., to learn how to fight a new kind of fire. Returning home he began to conduct new drill schools in modern techniques and soon expanded his training to various southeastern states. Toward the end of World War II he was consulted by the Twentieth Air Force about co-relating incendiary tests and weather factors before the bombing of Japan.

Always concerned about relevant legislation, Brockwell designed a program for safe school buildings and school fire drills that was drafted into law by the General Assembly in 1919; it was followed in 1923 by a law requiring theater exits and in 1925 by the requirement that all buildings erected by the state be of fire resistant construction. Finally, in 1941, the General Assembly enacted into law the state building code, which Brockwell had drawn up with W. G. Guile. For his work in building safety, Brockwell was made an honorary member of the American Institute of Architects.

The author of numerous articles and manuals on fire prevention and firefighting, Brockwell held many offices in state and national fire associations and was the president of the Fire Marshall's Association of North America in 1935. In 1942 he joined the part-time instructional staff of the Institute of Government in Chapel Hill.

In 1904, Brockwell was married to Mildred Bagwell; they were the parents of four children, Louise, Mary, Sherwood, and Kenlon. Brockwell was a member of Christ Episcopal Church, Raleigh, and was buried in Oakwood Cemetery in Raleigh.

SEE: Horatio Bond, ed., *Fire and the Air War* (1946); Siler City *Chatham News*, 6 Aug. 1935; *Popular Government*, Feb. 1942; Raleigh *News and Observer*, 3 June 1953.

MARY JOSLIN JENKINS

Brodnax, Edward Travis *(31 Mar. 1796–7 June 1874)*, physician and state legislator, was born in Brunswick County, Va., the son of William Edward Brodnax, a leading planter and horseman of Brunswick County, and Sally Jones Brodnax. In 1811, William Brodnax purchased a large plantation in Rockingham County. Subsequently, two of his sons, Robert and Edward Travis, moved to the county and established the Brodnax family as a dominant influence on the antebellum economy and society of the area.

During the War of 1812, Brodnax served as a private in the Brunswick County militia, which was ordered to aid in the defense of Norfolk. Following the war he attended the University of Pennsylvania, graduating with an M.D. degree in 1818. By 1820 he had settled in Rockingham County on Sauratown Plantation, south of the Dan River. Within several decades his vast fortune included over a thousand acres of land, a gristmill, and a partnership in a store in Leaksville; his slaves increased from 41 in 1820 to 174 by 1860, at which time he was the largest slaveholder in the county.

Although engaged in the management of his extensive plantation and in the practice of medicine, Brodnax pursued a public career that involved service in politics, in higher education, and in his church. An early advocate of state development of the transportation system, he was appointed to the standing committee on internal improvements in his two terms in the House of Commons, 1822–23. During his terms in the state senate, 1827–28, he was appointed to select committees on internal improvements, tariff alteration, the formation of Cherokee County, and the South Carolina Nullification proposal. Brodnax attended the Internal Improvements conventions in Raleigh in 1833 and 1836. After the formation of the Whig party, he became an influential Whig leader in his county.

Brodnax was one of only five delegates to attend both the 1835 and the 1861 state constitutional conventions. In the 1835 convention he served on the committee to draft the amendment that excluded free blacks from voting. To the 1861 convention he was elected as a moderate Unionist. Although not a proponent of secession, when he realized that the majority in his county favored secession, he voted for it. Dr. Brodnax was on the original board of trustees of Greensboro Female College, founded in 1838, and he remained on the board until 1851. In 1844 he was an organizer and one of the first vestrymen of the Church of the Epiphany in Leaksville, the first Episcopal church organized in the county.

Brodnax married Janet Hamilton Chalmers (19 May 1809–11 Nov. 1846). They had no surviving children, but they adopted Mrs. Brodnax's orphaned nephew, Chalmers Lanier Glenn. Glenn, an attorney, and his wife, Annie Dodge, the daughter of James R. Dodge, lived at Sauratown Plantation with their three sons, James Dodge, Robert Brodnax, and Edward Travis Brodnax. After Glenn was killed in the Civil War, Dr. Brodnax adopted and educated the Glenn children. Robert B. Glenn became governor of North Carolina (1905–9), and James D. Glenn served as adjutant general of the state.

Privately owned portraits of Dr. and Mrs. Brodnax are illustrated in the *North Carolina Portrait Index*.

SEE: Brodnax Family Cemetery (Sauratown); John Wilkins Brodnax Papers (Southern Historical Collection, University of North Carolina, Chapel Hill); Church of the Epiphany Records (Eden); J. G. deRoulhac Hamilton, ed., *The Papers of Thomas Ruffin*, vol. 1 (1918); J. G. McCormick, *Personnel of the Convention of 1861* (1900); L. MacMillan, *North Carolina Portrait Index* (1963); *North Carolina House Journal*, 1822–23; *North Carolina Senate Journal*, 1827–28; Rockingham County Deeds and Wills (North Carolina State Archives, Raleigh); S. B. Turrentine, *A Romance of Education* (1946).

LINDLEY S. BUTLER

Brodnax, John Grammar (*14 Apr. 1829–9 May 1907*), physician and Confederate surgeon, was born in

Dinwiddie County, Va. He was the son of Brigadier General William Henry Brodnax of Greensville County, Va., and Ann Elizabeth Withers. General Brodnax was a prominent Virginia legislator, active participant in the African Colonization Society, and commander of the militia during the Nat Turner insurrection (1831). After graduating from Virginia Military Institute in 1848, John G. Brodnax decided upon a medical career, and the following year he completed the course of study at the Medical College of the University of Virginia. He spent a year in postgraduate study at Jefferson College, Philadelphia, and finished his general preparation as the resident physician of the Baltimore Almshouse. Determined to procure the finest medical education that could be obtained, he sailed for Europe, continuing his studies for three years (1851–53) in Paris. He enrolled in the School of France as a student of surgery, medicine, and percussion under leading physicians of the hospitals of the Hotel Dieu, La Charitie, and St. Louis. For nearly a year he concentrated on furthering his knowledge of skin diseases and diseases of the eye.

He returned to Virginia in November 1853 and began a successful general practice of medicine in Petersburg. Soon he renewed his acquaintance with his first cousin, Mary W. Brodnax, daughter of Robert Brodnax of Cascade Plantation, Rockingham County. Upon the death of her father in 1854, Mary Brodnax and her brothers inherited in trust the extensive family acreage on the Dan River. When Mary and John G. Brodnax married on 1 Oct. 1856, they established residence at Cascade Plantation. In addition to continuing his medical practice, Brodnax managed the farm operation for his wife. By 1861, when Mary Brodnax died, they had had two daughters, Nancy Wilson (b. 1857) and Mary Withers (b. 1860).

With the coming of the Civil War, Brodnax entered the Confederate service as a surgeon. In 1862 he was appointed the director of the South Carolina Hospital; at that time he was supervising five general hospitals in Petersburg, Va. The next year he was named director of the North Carolina hospitals at Petersburg and served as president of the examining board for furloughing and discharging disabled Confederate soldiers. He directed the exchange of prisoners in 1864, and when the exchange was discontinued, he was assigned to oversee the general hospital at Wake Forest. At the end of the war he was in charge of two general hospitals in Greensboro.

After the war he returned to Rockingham County, where he reopened his medical practice and managed the family plantation for his two daughters. On 24 Apr. 1866, he married Ella Preston Burch; they had one son, John Grammar, Jr. (b. 31 Aug.1868). In 1887, Brodnax moved to Greensboro; he remained there until his death thirty years later. In Greensboro he conducted a large medical practice, examined for insurance companies, and for fifteen years served as a surgeon for the Southern Railway Company. He was appointed to a board for examination of disabled soldiers applying for government pensions in 1887, and he was a member of the State Medical Society, the International Association of Railway Surgeons, and the Association of Southern Railway Surgeons. In the antebellum period he was a Whig, and after the war he became a Democrat. He was an active member of the Episcopal church.

SEE: Samuel A. Ashe, ed., *Biographical History of North Carolina*, vol. 3 (1905 [photograph]); John Grammar Brodnax Papers and John Wilkins Brodnax Papers (Southern Historical Collection, University of North

Carolina, Chapel Hill); L. MacMillan, *North Carolina Portrait Index* (1963 [portrait of Mary Brodnax]); *Transactions of the Medical Society* (1907).

LINDLEY S. BUTLER

Brogden, Curtis Hooks (*6 Nov. 1816–5 Jan. 1901*), governor and member of Congress, born on a small farm in Wayne County, was the son of Pierce Brogden and Amy Bread Brogden. As with most North Carolina farm boys of the time, his opportunity for formal education was limited, but Brogden diligently supplemented what he learned in the common schools with personal reading.

In 1838, before Brogden was twenty-two years old, he announced himself a Democratic candidate for the state legislature from Wayne. The youngest member elected to that session of the state house of representatives, he was to hold political office almost continuously for the next forty-one years. After seven terms in the lower house of the General Assembly, he ran successfully for the state senate in 1852, 1854, and 1856. The legislature in 1857 elected him state comptroller, a post he held for ten years, continuing in office through the crises of secession, Civil War, and Emancipation.

A staunch Jacksonian before the war, Brogden cast his first non-Democratic vote in 1862, when he supported nonpartisan Zebulon B. Vance for governor. He moved into the Republican party after the war, and as a supporter of Reconstruction he was once again elected to the state senate in 1868. In the same year he served as Republican presidential elector. Reelected to the state senate in 1870, he voted for acquittal in the impeachment trial of Governor William W. Holden.

The state Republican convention nominated Brogden for lieutenant governor in 1872, and with his running mate, Governor Tod R. Caldwell, he was elected by a margin of two thousand votes. When Caldwell died 10 July 1874, Brogden became governor, only a few weeks before his party suffered severe losses in the state legislative elections.

During his two-and-a-half-year tenure as governor, Brogden faced a strongly Democratic legislature. Fewer than one-third of the members in either house were Republicans. This Republican weakness, combined with Brogden's genial, unassuming personality, produced an administration less aggressively partisan than Governor Caldwell's. As chief executive, Brogden supported the policy of consolidating the state's railroad holdings and approved efforts to adjust, but not repudiate, the state debt. He placed a high value on education, even arguing unsuccessfully for the establishment of a Negro college.

Instead of seeking to succeed himself as governor in 1876, Brogden campaigned for a seat in Congress from the Second Congressional District, a heavily Negro district that included Wayne County. He defeated several rivals for the Republican nomination, including the incumbent representative, black politician John A. Hyman. Since the district was a Republican stronghold, he was easily elected, while still governor, in the November general election.

Although he had a reputation as a facile, flowery orator in North Carolina, Brogden was a quiet representative in Washington. He worked to gain internal improvements for his state and reduced internal revenue taxes. He also advocated direct presidential elections and pensions for Mexican War veterans. His vote with the Democratic majority for the army reorganization bill was unpopular with his Republican constituents.

Brogden was not renominated in 1878, a year of intense rivalry among second district Republicans. Amid charges of fraud, Democrats narrowly elected their nominee, William H. Kitchin. Two years later Brogden tried to regain a place in Congress. After many Republicans disputed the outcome of the turbulent regular convention, he issued a broadside declaring himself an independent candidate against the convention nominee, a northern immigrant named Orlando Hubbs. Brogden called for reduction in the tariff and other taxes and accused Hubbs of not representing the interests of the South. But his efforts collapsed when Republicans closed ranks in response to the entry of a third, Democratic candidate into the race. Wayne County was transferred to the Third Congressional District before Brogden's next campaign for Congress. In 1884 he was nominated, only to be defeated in the general election by Wharton J. Green, a Democrat.

Brogden won his last victory in 1886, running, as in his first campaign nearly fifty years earlier, for the General Assembly. In a house controlled by Republicans and independents, he spoke in favor of changing the centralized, indirect system of county government the Democrats had instituted ten years before in order to "save" Eastern North Carolina from "Negro rule." The house passed a bill changing the system, but the senate rejected it. Brogden was not reelected in 1888.

A lifelong bachelor, Brogden was a temperate man who used no tobacco and seldom drank. His habits were simple, his affections local and provincial. He rarely traveled beyond the boundaries of his native state. Through frugality he became one of the largest landowners in Wayne County.

Brogden died at the age of eighty-four and was buried in Willowdale Cemetery, Goldsboro.

SEE: *Address of Hon. C. H. Brogden, to the Voters of the Second Congressional District of North Carolina* [1880]; Samuel A. Ashe, ed., *Biographical History of North Carolina*, vol. 6 (1907); *Biog. Dir. Am . Cong.* (1971); *Legislative Biographical Sketch Book, Session 1887*; Raleigh *Signal*, 10 May 1888; Raleigh *Southern Illustrated Age*, 14 Aug. 1875; *Speech of Hon. C. H. Brogden Delivered before the Wayne County Republican Convention at the Town Hall in Goldsboro, N.C., Saturday, May 29, 1880*.

ERIC D. ANDERSON

Brookes, Iveson Lewis (*1793–30 Mar. 1865*), Baptist clergyman, planter, and Southern sectionalist, was the eldest of five sons of Jonathan and Annie Lewis Brookes and was born in Rockingham County. His father was a veteran of the Revolution. His parents had only recently moved to North Carolina from Spotsylvania County, Va., where many of his relatives continued to live; soon after his birth his parents moved permanently to Caswell County. Educated in a local academy during his early years, in 1812 Brookes enlisted in the American army. After seeing only limited action during the War of 1812, he entered The University of North Carolina. He was graduated in 1819 after developing what proved to be a lifelong acquaintance with both James K. Polk and Thomas Hart Benton. In his commencement address, entitled "Is the State of the World Better in the Present Age Than at Any Former Period?" Brookes expressed an optimism and an enmity to slavery that were totally antithetical to his later positions. Undecided about his future, he spent a year as a teacher in Greensboro.

During his senior year at the university, Brookes became acquainted with Basil Manly, a Baptist clergyman who would be his closest friend. After months of correspondence with Manly, Brookes became convinced that his greatest opportunities for the future lay in the Baptist ministry and in a lucrative marriage. Licensed to preach on 4 Dec. 1819 in North Carolina and ordained a month later at Georgetown, S.C., Brookes spent a year traveling throughout South Carolina as a domestic missionary for the Itinerant Board of the South Carolina Baptist Convention.

A year later he settled in Eatonton, Ga., as the rector of the town's academy and as the local Baptist clergyman. He also found there the first of his three wives, Lucina Sarah Walker, and the wealth he desired. From the Walker family, Brookes got control of vast plantations and slaves in Putnam, Jasper, and Jones counties, Ga. From a second wife, Prudence E. Johnson, whom he married in 1828, he obtained more property in Georgia. Upon the death of his second wife in 1830, much of his property was placed in guardianship for his one son. Not content with the already vast estates he had built up in Georgia, Brookes married Mrs. Sarah J. Myers in 1831 and obtained thereby two plantations in Aiken and Edge-field counties, S.C. Soon after this marriage he settled on an estate at Woodville, near Hamburg, in Aiken County, S.C., where he spent most of the remainder of his life. From Woodville he operated a vast network of plantations and gangs of slaves until his death only ten days before Lee's surrender at Appomattox Courthouse. He spent about four years in the mid-1840s as head of an academy for women in Penfield, Ga., and he kept up his associations with Baptist clergymen and retained the pastorate of a small church most of his life, but he remained primarily a large-scale planter.

Although he had opposed slavery as a student at The University of North Carolina, Brookes became a staunch defender of slavery and a rabid southern sectionalist. During the Nullification controversy, he was made a minuteman by Governor James Hamilton of South Carolina. In 1861, at the age of sixty-eight, he offered himself for service in the Confederate Army. From the first appearance of abolitionism he feared for the future of southern society. From 1835 he wrote dozens of defenses of slavery, most of them in the form of letters to northern antislavery periodicals. His most famous defenses were two pamphlets written during the crisis of 1850: *A Defence of the South against the Reproaches and Incroachments of the North* (1850) and *A Defence of Southern Slavery against the Attacks of Henry Clay and Alexander Campbell* (1851), the latter written at the behest of Governor James Henry Hammond of South Carolina. The productions of an enraged slaveholder revealing little of the optimistic and balanced thinking of his youthful years, those two documents stood as the most characteristic statements of a die-hard southern sectionalist who had learned to love the life of a slaveholding planter.

From Brookes's marriage on 22 Sept. 1822 to Lucina Walker (d. 26 Dec. 1826) there were three children, among them his only son, Walker Iveson (b. 21 Oct. 1826). Brookes's marriage on 15 Jan. 1828 to Prudence Johnson (d. 13 July 1830) produced two daughters. He married Sarah J. Oliver Myers on 1 Sept. 1831; she died in 1859 with no issue.

Brookes was buried in Augusta, Ga.

SEE: *Biographical Sketches of Prominent Baptists* (n.d. [photograph]); Iveson Brookes Papers (the libraries of Duke University, Durham; University of Alabama, University; University of North Carolina, Chapel Hill; University of South Carolina, Columbia).

LARRY EDWARD TISE

Brooks, Aubrey Lee (*21 May 1871–10 Jan. 1958*), lawyer, politician, and author, was born at Bethel Hill near Roxboro, in Person County, of English and Ulster Scot ancestry. His father was Zachary Taylor Brooks, a physician, and his mother was Chestina Hall.

Growing up as what he termed "a Person County farm boy," he enjoyed what he considered "the last word in human happiness—a gun, a dog, and a negro boy chum." In the poverty-stricken Reconstruction days, he developed early a sort of rugged, homespun philosophy that carried him through life, a philosophy based on the premise that "Whatever a man sows, that shall he also reap."

Tutored until he was ten by his mother, he then attended the Bethel Hill Academy for six years. His first job, at the age of seventeen, was that of teacher in a one-room free school two miles from his home, at the salary of $35 a month. After teaching for two years, he had saved enough money to enter The University of North Carolina, but he was prevented from completing his courses by an attack of typhoid fever. After a business course at the University of Kentucky, he reentered The University of North Carolina and completed the law course in September 1893.

Brooks entered practice with colonel Charles B. Winstead in Roxboro. He soon attracted the attention of one who was greatly to influence his life and political thinking, William Walton Kitchin, then chairman of the Person County Democratic Executive committee and later to be U.S. congressman (1897–1909) and governor of North Carolina (1909–13). Brooks and Kitchin traveled by horse and buggy to fill speaking engagements in the election of 1894; Brooks furnished the horse and buggy and Kitchin the oratory.

In 1896, Kitchin asked Brooks to nominate him for Congress against the Republican incumbent, Thomas Settle. Kitchin was nominated by acclamation, and Brooks became nominee for presidential elector. Soon after Kitchin's victory, Brooks was offered a law partnership by Colonel James E. Boyd of Greensboro, who had just been appointed assistant to the attorney general of the United States and was later to be federal judge for Western North Carolina. In Greensboro, Brooks began a distinquished legal career in which he, an avowed Jeffersonian Democrat, was to be associated closely with certain "pet" Republicans, beginning with Colonel Winstead in Roxboro and Colonel Boyd in Greensboro. When Boyd was elevated to the federal bench, Brooks chose a Republican national committee-man, Johnson J. Hayes of Wilkesboro, as his successor; Hayes remained in Brooks's firm until he was elevated to the newly created federal middle district court of North Carolina. In Hayes's place, Brooks chose Kenneth M. Brim, another Republican who had been referee in bankruptcy under Judge Hayes.

In 1898, Brooks was elected solicitor of the Ninth Judicial District, one of the richest and most populous sections of the state. There followed ten years of fighting against the most powerful vested interests in the state, the tobacco trust and the railroads. Aligning himself with W. W. and Claude Kitchin, Josephus Daniels, and Walter Clark, he ran headlong into difficulties with the powerful Furnifold Simmons machine. Indeed, Brooks felt that his defeat as a candidate to succeed W. W. Kitchin in Congress in 1908 and his defeat in the 1920 primary fight to succeed Lee S. Overman in the U.S. Senate were attributable to Senator Simmons's political machine.

Between these two political defeats, Brooks's brilliant legal career led Chief Justice Walter Clark to call him "the foremost and most successful lawyer in North Carolina."

In a period of over fifty years he participated in some of the most important and sensational court trials in North Carolina: the famous Cole case, which provided material for the Broadway success *Coquette*; *North Carolina Public Service Company* v. *Duke Power Co.*; the Ann Cannon-Smith Reynolds-Libby Holman case (as a result of which Brooks and other outstanding lawyers won $10 million for Ann Cannon); and the political suit brought by the trustees of the First Presbyterian Church of Greensboro against the Richardsons and the Vick Chemical Company.

Brooks also served as chairman of the Greensboro Chamber of Commerce, president of the North Carolina Bar Association, and general counsel of a number of insurance companies, including the Jefferson Standard Life Insurance Company. His professional eminence was evidenced by the fact that presidents Woodrow Wilson, Herbert Hoover, and Franklin D. Roosevelt considered him for a seat on the U.S. Supreme Court.

At The University of North Carolina, Brooks set up the Brooks Scholarship Fund (in excess of $1 million) for worthy students from the old Fifth Congressional District; he also established a revolving trust fund for The University of North Carolina Press. He gave a new $50,000 chancel and choir loft to the First Presbyterian Church of Greensboro and presented a 482-acre site, including a hunting lodge and a lake, to the General Greene Council of Boy Scouts of America.

Brooks devoted his last years to intellectual pursuits. His first book, *Walter Clark, Fighting Judge*, published in 1944 by The University of North Carolina Press, was a sympathetic treatment of the controversial chief justice. Later, in 1948 and in 1950, the university press published the two-volume *Papers of Walter Clark*, which he coedited with Hugh T. Lefler. In 1950 the same press published his autobiographical *Southern Lawyer: Fifty Years at the Bar*, replete with courtroom anecdotes, political contests, sensational trials, fox hunts, foreign travels, and friendships with such national figures as William Jennings Bryan, John W. Davis, Oliver Wendell Holmes, and Eleanor and Franklin D. Roosevelt. Finally, in 1954, Brooks's *Selected Addresses of a Southern Lawyer* appeared. At the time of his death he was collaborating with this writer on a biography of Chief Justice Thomas Ruffin. He received an honorary degree from The University of North Carolina, served as president of the Historical Society of North Carolina, and was a member of the Society of American Scholars.

Brooks was first married in 1895 to Maude Harris of Roxboro, by whom he had one son, Robert. His second wife was Helen Thornton Higbie of New Jersey, whom he married in 1910 and with whom he had three sons, Aubrey Lee, Jr. (killed in an automobile accident), Thornton Higbie (a partner in his father's law firm), and James Taylor (a physician in Greensboro). Mrs. Brooks died in 1974.

Brooks was buried in Green Hill Cemetery in Greensboro. A portrait of him, by Goris Gordon, hangs in his home, now occupied by his son James Taylor.

SEE: Aubrey Lee Brooks, *Southern Lawyer* (1950); Clifford Frazier, Sr., "Lives of Lawyers" (MS, possession of Robert H. Frazier, Greensboro); Henry R. Mathis, *Along the Border* (1964); *North Carolina Bar Association Report*, 1958; Blackwell P. Robinson, "Southern Lawyer, Gentleman, and Writer" (Memorial address before the Historical Society of North Carolina, 14 Nov. 1958); Scrapbooks containing letters and news clippings (possession of J. Taylor Brooks, Greensboro); *Who's Who in America*, 1954–55.

BLACKWELL P. ROBINSON

Brooks, Eugene Clyde (3 Dec. 1871–18 Oct. 1947), educator and public servant, eldest son of Edward and Martha Brooks, was born in Greene County and grew up on a farm in Lenoir County. He attended private and public schools near Grifton. After his graduation from Trinity College in 1894, he embarked upon a career in journalism, first as an assistant to Josephus Daniels, the new owner of the Raleigh *News and Observer*, and later as editor of the *Mirror* in Wilson. In 1898 he left newspaper work to become principal of the Ormandsville High School in his native Greene County, and in the following year he assumed direction of the Kinston Graded School. Despite his brief tenure in these positions, Brooks won a reputation as a "progressive school man" and inspired considerable enthusiasm for education in each community. He accepted an invitation to become the first superintendent of the Monroe City Schools in June 1900 and within a short time established one of the model school systems in the state. His efficient administration and bold innovations in Monroe attracted considerable attention in educational circles and actually marked the beginning of his rise to state-wide prominence.

In 1902, Brooks joined Charles D. McIver, James Y. Joyner, and others in an educational campaign initiated by Governor Charles B. Aycock, largely for the purpose of fulfilling his promise to provide white school children with the literacy qualifications required by the state's new suffrage laws. The campaign sought to win popular support for public education that would result in greater local taxation and school consolidation. As the first secretary of the central campaign committee, Brooks arranged hundreds of public addresses of prominent citizens, prepared and distributed large quantities of publicity literature, and issued periodic statements on educational conditions. Impressed by his conduct of the campaign, state superintendent James Y. Joyner persuaded him to leave Monroe and accept a position in the North Carolina Department of Public Instruction. His work there concerned rural libraries, courses of study, and loans for school construction. In this capacity he gained experience in educational administration, widened his circle of influential friends, and acquired an intimate knowledge of school conditions. Above all, he won the enduring respect and admiration of James Y. Joyner.

In 1904, with Joyner's aid, Brooks was appointed superintendent of the Goldsboro schools. His three years in this post were marked by several notable improvements in the city's schools, especially in increased salaries for teachers, larger libraries, an expanded curriculum, and the establishment of a textbook rental system. While in Goldsboro, Brooks was appointed a member of the Committee of Eight on History in the Elementary Schools, a national group sponsored by the American Historical Association, whose recommendations had a profound impact upon the teaching of history in public schools. He also became an influential figure in the North Carolina Teachers' Assembly and various other state school associations. In 1906, when these organizations decided to publish a journal, Brooks was selected editor, and for the next seventeen years he waged a relentless crusade for better public schools through the columns of *North Carolina Education*. His most persistent editorial campaign was in behalf of the six-month school term, which was finally established in 1918 by a constitutional amendment.

In the meantime, Brooks had left Goldsboro in 1907 to establish a department of education at Trinity College. For the next twelve years he gave his alma mater a preeminence in teacher training in the state. This unorthodox professor of education inspired a generation of teachers not only in his regular college classes but also through his extension program, the first in North Carolina for teachers already in service. His extension courses became the model for similar efforts elsewhere and served as a basis for his correspondence course, known as the Teachers' Reading Circle. While at Trinity, he served the Association of College and Preparatory Schools of the Southern States in various capacities and found time for research and writing. Six of the seven books he published were designed for public school use.

In 1919, Brooks was appointed state superintendent of public instruction to fill Joyner's unexpired term. A year later, he was elected by a vote larger than that of the heads of the ticket. Under his leadership between 1919 and 1923, the state's public schools underwent an extraordinary transformation. Largely through his efforts, the state adopted a uniform certification plan and salary schedule, improved the qualifications of its teaching and administrative personnel, and introduced sweeping changes in the method of financing public education, changes that placed greater emphasis on state control. No less impressive were his accomplishments in expanding high schools, vocational training, and pupil transportation facilities. His particular concern for black schools led to the launching of "the golden period of Negro education in North Carolina." The rapid changes and expansion during his tenure prompted Brooks to initiate an overall administrative reorganization of the department of public instruction on a divisional basis in an effort to achieve greater efficiency. He rounded out his term of office by codifying the public school laws in 1923.

In that year he assumed the presidency of North Carolina State College in Raleigh in order to direct its reorganization. During his administration the college witnessed a spectacular physical transformation and rose from the status of a trade school to that of a technological and professional institution of recognized standing. Despite his misgivings about the movement to make the college a part of the consolidated University of North Carolina, he refused to become either an obstructionist or a rallying point for opponents of the plan. Always sensitive to the interests of State College, he played a key role in the consolidation process and remained head of the Raleigh institution for several years after it had become a unit within The University of North Carolina.

While president of the college, Brooks devoted much of his energy to county government reform, a subject that had first attracted his attention during his tenure as state superintendent of public instruction. He was in no small measure responsible for securing legislation in 1927 and 1931 that wrought a veritable revolution in the administration of county fiscal affairs. At the same time he served as secretary of the North Carolina Park Commission, a position that exemplified his persistent interest in conservation. Largely through the work of the commission and its counterpart in Tennessee, the Great Smoky Mountains National Park became a reality in 1930.

Brooks married Ida Myrtle Sapp of Kernersville. They had three children, two daughters and a son.

SEE: "Dr. E. C. Brooks," *State* 5 (19 June 1937); "Eugene Clyde Brooks: An Autobiographical Sketch" (typescript, North Carolina State University Library, Raleigh); Willard B. Gatewood, Jr., *Eugene Clyde Brooks* (1960), and "Eugene Clyde Brooks—School Champion," *North Carolina Education* 26 (1960).

WILLARD B. GATEWOOD

Brooks, George Washington (*16 Mar. 1821–6 Jan. 1882*), lawyer and U.S. district court judge, was born in Elizabeth City. His father, William C. Brooks, originally of Gates County, was a prominent merchant and farmer. His mother, Catherine B. Davis of Pasquotank County, was the widow of Captain Hugh Knox before her marriage to Brooks. George W. Brooks was a voracious reader in his youth. He attended Henry Riddick's School near Sunbury and Belvedere Academy, established by the Society of Friends in Perquimans County. Too poor to attend college, he read law first with Charles R. Kinney and later with John C. B. Ehringhaus in Elizabeth City and was admitted to practice there in 1844. Brooks entered his practice almost penniless, but through diligence and faithfulness to his clients' causes, he established a thriving practice and a growing reputation by 1860.

On 20 June 1850, Brooks married Margaret Ann Costen of Gates County. They had five children: William, George, Margaret, Sarah, and James, all bearing the middle name Costen.

Brooks was a member of the Methodist Episcopal church and a Master Mason. A Whig in politics, he agreed to run for the legislature in 1852 to avert a local party schism. He was elected and served that term but refused reelection. By 1861 he had become convinced of the evil of slavery and favored manumission. He was a slave owner himself but purchased slaves at their own request, to save them from other slave buyers. He opposed secession and remained an avowed but inactive Unionist, spending the Civil War years at his home as a noncombatant.

In August 1865, President Andrew Johnson appointed Brooks federal district court judge for the District of North Carolina; he was confirmed by the Senate in January 1866. During the interval he served as a member of the state constitutional convention, playing an influential role in its deliberations. As the sole district judge in the state during a period of unusual turmoil, he had varied and exceptionally arduous duties.

In 1870, Brooks received state-wide attention for his role in terminating the Kirk-Holden War. Many citizens of Alamance and Caswell counties had been arrested for violence connected with the Ku Klux Klan. When Governor W. W. Holden frustrated the writs of habeas corpus issued in their behalf by state Chief Justice Richmond M. Pearson, the defendants got ex-Confederate General Mathew W. Ransom to petition Brooks for their release under the new Fourteenth Amendment. Brooks ordered the prisoners brought before him at the federal court in Salisbury. Governor Holden telegraphed President U. S. Grant to rescind Brooks's order but to no avail. On 19 Aug. 1870, Colonel George W. Kirk of the state militia presented the prisoners as ordered, and Brooks dismissed them all when Kirk failed to present any evidence to substantiate their continued imprisonment. Upon his return to Elizabeth City, Brooks was welcomed with a public demonstration. He continued to serve as district court judge for the remainder of his life.

He died after a lingering illness and was buried in Elizabeth City.

SEE: Samuel A. Ashe, ed., *Biographical History of North Carolina*, vol. 2 (1905 [portrait]); Pulaski Cowper, "Judge George W. Brooks" (North Carolina Collection, Clipping File, University of North Carolina, Chapel Hill); *DAB*, vol. 3 (1929); J. G. deRoulhac Hamilton, *Reconstruction in North Carolina* (1914); Raleigh *News and Observer*, 12 Sept.

1915; Allen W. Trelease, *White Terror* (1971).

W. MICHAEL GOLNICK, JR.

Brooks, Robert Nathaniel *(8 May 1888–2 Aug. 1953),* Methodist clergyman and educator, was born in Hollis, Cleveland County, the son of John and Louvenia Schanck Brooks. He held degrees from Bennett College in Greensboro, Gammon Theological Seminary in Atlanta, and Garrett Biblical Institute in Evanston, Ill. He also studied at Union Theological Seminary in New York and in Oxford University in England. He was ordained a deacon by Bishop Wilbur P. Thirkield and an elder by Bishop E. Hughes.

Brooks's pastoral minstry was limited. He was secretary of the Board of Sunday Schools in 1918, and served as president successively of Haven College, Meridian, Miss.; Central Alabama College, Birmingham; and Huston-Tillotson College, Austin, Tex. For ten years he taught church history at Gammon Theological Seminary (formerly Methodist, now merged with other seminaries as the Interdenominational Theological Center). In 1936 he was chosen editor of the *Central Christian Advocate* in New Orleans, a position he held for eight years.

In 1944, Brooks was elected to the episcopacy. In addition to presiding over his annual conferences, he served in several other capacities: trustee of various institutions of higher learning, member of the Board of Missions of Church Extension and Board of Lay Activities, president of the Methodist Federation for Social Action, and president of the College of Bishops of the Central Jurisdiction (black). He received honorary degrees from four colleges and universities.

Brooks was married to M. Edith Crogman. He was buried at the Gulfside Assembly, Waveland, Miss.

SEE: E. S. Bucke, ed., *The History of American Methodism,* vol. 3 (1964); Elmer T. Clark, *Methodism in Western North Carolina* (1966); *Methodist History,* October 1968; W. W. Sweet, *Methodism in American History* (1933); W. W. Sweet and Umphrey Lee, *A Short History of American Methodism* (1956); *Who Was Who in America,* vol. 3 (1960).

GRADY L. E. CARROLL

Broughton, Carrie Longee *(16 Sept. 1879–29 Jan. 1957),* librarian, was born in Raleigh, the daughter of Caroline R. Longee and Needham B. Broughton and a first cousin of Governor and U.S. Senator J. Melville Broughton. She attended Peace Institute, Meredith College, and the State Normal College.

The first woman to be appointed head of a state department in North Carolina and the fourth state librarian of North Carolina, Miss Broughton served from 1918 to 1956. She became assistant state librarian in September 1902, succeeding Marshall DeLancey Haywood. The state librarian at that time, Captain Miles O. Sherrill, retired in 1917. A series of men were named acting state librarian, as the idea of naming a woman to the post was not considered by the three trustees, Governor T. W. Bickett, Secretary of State J. Bryan Grimes, and Superintendent of Public Instruction J. Y. Joyner. Meanwhile, Miss Broughton was endorsed for the position by many citizens and organizations, including the North Carolina Library Association; the North Carolina Library Commission; many librarians, including those of Meredith College, Wake Forest College, Trinity College, Davidson College, and the Woman's College; and the president of the state federation of women's clubs. No one disputed her

competence. Opponents to her appointment raised the question of constitutionality, but Chief Justice Walter Clark of the state supreme court cleared the matter in a letter to the trustees, writing: "It is true, as someone has said, she is guilty of 'the atrocious crime of being a woman,' but she is a taxpayer, a good citizen, experienced and thoroughly competent. I have found nothing in the constitution of this State which forbids a woman to be appointed to any office. . . ."

On 31 May 1918, Miss Broughton was appointed until the General Assembly could meet. In the interim, she had to divide the salary with her assistant and the janitor. Finally, on 13 Mar. 1919, she was officially appointed with full salary.

Miss Broughton proceeded to organize what had begun as a miscellaneous collection in the secretary of state's office into the nucleus of a research collection for North Carolina state government and for writers, scholars, and others with information needs. She was also responsible for starting the excellent genealogical collection, which is a popular service of the present Division of the State Library of the North Carolina Department of Cultural Resources. As state librarian, she received many inquiries from descendants regarding marriages and deaths of early North Carolinians. To answer these, she began compiling records and collecting books and pamphlets. The *Biennial Report of the State Librarian of North Carolina* for 1 July 1926–30 June 1928 contained a fifty-eight page bibliography, "Genealogical Materials in the North Carolina State Library," compiled by Carrie L. Broughton and Pauline Hill, who was chief library assistant at that time. Supplements were issued in subsequent biennial reports. Beginning in 1944, the reports also carried compilations of marriages and death notices from 1799 to 1825 from the *Raleigh Register.*

By the time she retired in 1956, Miss Broughton had established a fine collection of books, periodicals, and newspapers pertinent to North Carolina history, people, and literature. Six months after her retirement, she contracted a brief illness and died.

SEE: Contemporary newspapers and periodicals (North Carolina State Library, Raleigh; Library, Duke University, Durham; North Carolina Collection, University of North Carolina, Chapel Hill); *North Carolina Biography,* vol. 3 (1929); Harriette Hammer Walker, *Busy North Carolina Women* (1931); *Who's Who of American Women,* 1937–38.

ELAINE VON OESEN

Broughton, Joseph Melville *(17 Nov. 1888–6 Mar. 1949),* governor of North Carolina and U.S. senator, was a Raleigh native, the son of Joseph Melville, head of the real estate firm of J. M. Broughton and Company, and Sallie Harris Broughton. His uncle, Needham Bryant Broughton operated a printing business. Graduating from the Hugh Morson Academy in 1906, the young Broughton entered Wake Forest College, graduating and entering law school there in 1910. That same year he was admitted to the bar, but he chose not to begin practice immediately. From 1910 to 1912, he was principal of the Bunn High School. In 1912 he was a reporter for the *Winston-Salem Journal* for a few months. He attended Harvard Law School for the 1912–13 year and began practicing law in Raleigh in 1914.

Broughton rapidly became involved in political and civic affairs in his native city. He had campaigned for Wilson in 1912, while a student at Harvard. Back home, he served as chairman of the Democratic party executive committee for Wake County from 1914 until 1916. In 1918 he was appointed to the Wake Forest College Board of Trustees, a membership he was to hold until his death, except for one year. At the same time he became a member of the board of trustees for Shaw University and began service of many years as its general counsel. He was president of the Raleigh Chamber of Commerce in 1918. During the 1920s he served on the Raleigh School Board (1922–29) and was twice appointed city attorney (1921–24).

Broughton twice won election to the state senate, serving from 1926 to 1930. As a member of the General Assembly, he pressed for extension of the school term and for workmen's compensation legislation. He also introduced and sponsored the Australian Ballot Act (1929). As a lawyer, he built up a very extensive civil practice, shunning criminal cases. In 1933 he served as president of the Wake County Bar Association, and he headed the North Carolina Bar Association in 1936. Also in 1936 he delivered the keynote speech at the Democratic State Convention. An active churchman, Broughton served as the Protestant chairman of the North Carolina Conference of Christians and Jews.

In 1940, Broughton ran for governor, winning the primary against six opponents and avoiding a second primary when runner-up Wilkins P. Horton of Pittsboro declined the opportunity to call for one. Broughton campaigned strongly for Roosevelt and carried the largest gubernatorial vote in state history to that time, becoming the first Raleigh native to be elected. As wartime governor, his achievements covered a broad range: enactment of a teachers' and employees' retirement plan and a salary raise for teachers, extension of the school term to nine months and addition of the twelfth grade, state aid to public libraries, reorganization of and larger appropriations for state hospitals and correctional institutions, aid to agriculture, organization of the Civilian Defense program, establishment of the state Medical Care Commission, and removal of the sales tax on food for home consumption. As North Carolina's first "regional governor" in several years, Broughton was active in regional and national affairs. He served on the executive committee of the National Governors' Conference and participated in National Planning Association efforts for the postwar period. In 1944 he was nominated for vice-president when Roosevelt refused Wallace a second term.

Broughton maintained many interests. From 1941 on, he served on The University of North Carolina Board of Trustees. He was president of the North Carolina Engineering Foundation, which supported the School of Engineering at North Carolina State College. He served as president of the Roanoke Island Historical Association and was a member of the Raleigh Board of Directors of Wachovia Bank. He continued an extensive law practice and engaged in many business activities. He acted as general counsel for the Flue-Cured Tobacco Cooperative Stabilization Corporation and the North Carolina State Ports Authority, both of which he had helped establish.

In 1948, Broughton ran for the U.S. Senate and defeated William B. Umstead, who had been appointed to fill the unexpired term of Josiah Bailey. Broughton took the oath of office on 31 Dec. 1948 and served the few months until his death. Throughout his career, he represented those not connected with the monied interests and the so-called machine, and he never lost a political contest.

An ardent Baptist, Broughton served as Sunday school superintendent at Tabernacle Baptist Church in Raleigh and taught the Men's Bible Class there for twenty-five years. When he went to Washington, he organized the Broughton Bible Class at the First Baptist Church.

On 14 Dec. 1916, Broughton married Alice Harper Willson, daughter of William Willson, grand secretary of the Grand Lodge of Masons of North Carolina. She, like her husband, had been born, reared, and educated in Raleigh. They had four children, Alice Willson, Joseph Melville, Jr., Robert Bain, and Woodson Harris. Broughton died of a massive heart attack and was buried at Montlawn Memorial Park in Raleigh.

SEE: *Asheville Citizen*, 7 Mar. 1949; *Biog. Dir. Am. Cong.* (1961); Beth G. Crabtree, *North Carolina Governors, 1585–1958* (1958); Emery B. Denny, *Address* (1959), and "Joseph Melville Broughton," in *Public Addresses and Papers of Robert Gregg Cherry*, ed. David Leroy Corbitt (1951); *Durham Morning Herald*, 10 Nov. 1940, 7 Mar. 1949; Hugh T. Lefler and Albert R. Newsome, *North Carolina: The History of a Southern State*, rev. ed. (1963); *North Carolina Manual* (1949); Raleigh *News and Observer*, 8 Mar. 1949, 18 July 1951.

WILLIAM T. MOYE

Broughton, Needham Bryant (14 Feb. 1848–26 May 1914), Baptist church leader, businessman, and community leader in Raleigh, was born near Auburn, the youngest of four sons and the fifth child of Joseph and Mary Bagwell Broughton. In 1854, Broughton's father died, and two years later his mother moved with her children to Raleigh. He attended school there until he was thirteen, when he was apprenticed as a printer to John W. Syme, editor and proprietor of the *Raleigh Register*. In 1864 the paper was suspended and Broughton went to work under John L. Pennington, editor of the Raleigh *Daily Progress*, where he met C. B. Edwards, his future partner. He later worked for newspapers in Richmond, Washingon, D.C., and New York City, but in 1869 he returned to Raleigh and married Caroline R. Longee. In 1871 he and Edwards bought the printing firm of Major W. A. Smith. The firm of Edwards and Broughton soon became the largest printing concern in the state; between 1887 and 1894 it received most of the business of printing and binding state publications. For a number of years, Broughton was also one of the owners of the *Biblical Recorder*.

Broughton was an active and dedicated Baptist layman. In 1874 he helped organize the Tabernacle Baptist Church, and in 1876 he was appointed deacon and superintendent of the Sunday school, in which capacity he served until 1913. From the late 1890s to 1913 he was vice-president of the Sunday School Board of the Southern Baptist Convention and a member of the executive committee of the International Sunday School Association. His religious activities led him into the fight for prohibition of alcoholic beverages, and in 1902 he was made president of the North Carolina Anti-Saloon League. On 27 May 1908 his efforts were rewarded with the triumph of state-wide prohibition.

A strong supporter of public education, Broughton was instrumental in saving the Raleigh public schools from bankruptcy in 1888 by securing a property tax increase in their behalf. In appreciation of his efforts, one of the city's high schools was named for him. He was also involved in locating both Meredith College and the North Carolina Agricultural and Mechanic College (later North Carolina State University) in Raleigh. He served as a trustee of these institutions, as well as of Wake Forest College, the Oxford Orphan Asylum, and the State School for the Deaf, Dumb and the Blind.

In 1900, Broughton accepted the Democratic nomination to the North Carolina Senate from Wake County in order to prevent its going to a "wet" candidate. He was elected but did not seek a second term.

Broughton retired from active life because of illness in 1913 and died in a Philadelphia hospital the next year. He was survived by his wife and six children, Edgar E., Effie, Mary Nelson, Rosa C., Caroline (Carrie) L., and Needham B., Jr.

Broughton was buried in Oakwood Cemetery in Raleigh. A nephew, J. Melville Broughton, became governor of North Carolina.

SEE: Tabernacle Baptist Church, Raleigh, *Our Record*, November 1913; Josephus Daniels, *Editor in Politics* (1941), and *Tar Heel Editor* (1939); George Washington Paschal, *A History of Printing in North Carolina* (1946); Raleigh *Biblical Recorder*, 23 Sept. 1941; Raleigh *News and Observer*, 27 May 1914.

CHARLES A. NEWELL, JR.

Brower, John Morehead *(19 July 1845–5 Aug. 1913)*, congressman and state legislator, was born in Greensboro, the son of John W. Brower and his wife. His father was a businessman in Mt. Airy. Brower received his early education from private tutors and at the Mt. Airy Male Academy.

After reaching maturity, Brower devoted most of his energy to tobacco farming and to his mercantile business. But during Reconstruction, he also became actively involved in North Carolina politics as a member of the Republican party. He served as a leader of the local Union League, and in this capacity he organized significant numbers of black voters for his party. Brower was a delegate to every Republican State Convention held from 1872 to 1896.

After suffering narrow defeats in bids for the North Carolina Senate in 1872 and 1874 and for the North Carolina constitutional convention in 1875, Brower ran for the state senate as an independent in 1878 and defeated Richmond Pearson. That same year he ran for Congress as an independent but lost. When he served briefly in the North Carolin Senate in 1879, he had himself listed as a Republican. In 1886 he campaigned as a Republican and won a seat in the U.S. Congress. After winning reelection in 1888, Brower lost the next race and soon returned to Mt. Airy, where he resumed his agricultural and mercantile pursuits. He again served briefly in the General Assembly as a member of the house of representatives in 1897, before moving to Oklahoma, where he spent the remainder of his life engaged in stock raising, real estate promotions, and lumber production.

Brower married Nannie M. Paine of Rockingham County; they had three sons and three daughters. He died in Paris, Tex., and was buried in Mt. Airy.

SEE: *Biog. Dir. Am. Cong.* (1950); Brower Family Papers (Southern Historical Collection, University of North Carolina, Chapel Hill); Greensboro *Daily News*, 9 Aug. 1913; *North Carolina Manual* (1913); Raleigh *News and Observer*, 9 Aug. 1913; J. S. Tomlinson, *Assembly Sketch Book* (1879).

K. RODABAUGH

Brown, Albert Erskine *(6 Aug. 1863–30 May 1924)*, clergyman and educator, son of William Albert G. Brown and Margaret Pattison Brown, was born in Jefferson City, Tenn. Following schooling in local preparatory schools, he attended Carson-Newman College and later Judson College in Marion, Ala., but there is no record of his

graduation from either. Carson-Newman, years later, conferred on him an honorary D.D. degree.

For eight years, 1881–89, Brown was a teacher at Fairview Institute, near Asheville. He was ordained in the gospel ministry in 1889 and served as pastor of Beaverdam, Berea, Mt. Carmel, and Asheville West End Baptist churches, all in the Buncombe Association, of which he was for several terms moderator. He served as secretary of the Mission Board of the Western North Carolina Baptist Convention (later dissolved) and as its president; still later he was assistant corresponding secretary (executive head) of the North Carolina Baptist State Convention.

His early pastoral ministry has been reported as very evangelistic. He soon became deeply concerned "by the ignorance of mountain preachers" and conceived as his mission the building of mountain schools, approved and often supported by the denomination. He resigned his local pastorates in 1899 and devoted the rest of his life to organizing and directing Southern Baptist Mountain Missions—churches and schools—a work underwritten jointly by the North Carolina Baptist State Convention and the Home Mission Board of the Southern Baptist Convention. During those years more than forty schools were established, with an annual enrollment exceeding sixty-five hundred in a day before public schools were universal in the mountain areas of the state.

Historians not only credit Brown with an educationally improved leadership in Western North Carolina but also attribute the ultimate development of education at both the secondary and college level to the impetus he provided and the vision he inspired. This educational zeal was a family trait: his father was the first president of Mars Hill College, and A. E. Brown was one of five children, all of whom were teachers and three of whom were ordained ministers.

Brown was married, in 1885, to Lamanda Whitaker of Henderson County. They had five children: William H., Jessie (Mrs. D. A. Greene), Beatrice (Mrs. Carl Gossett), Mack, and Mary (Mrs. Ray C. Hamrick).

SEE: Asheville *Baptist Messenger*, June 1924; *Asheville Times*, 30 May 1924; *Encyclopedia of Southern Baptists*, vol. 1 (1958); Mars Hill College Library (Mars Hill), for a file of sermons and addresses by Brown; Raleigh *Biblical Recorder*, 25 June 1924.

C. SYLVESTER GREEN

Brown, Bedford *(6 June 1795–6 Dec. 1870)*, farmer, legislator, and U.S. senator, was born in what is now Locust Hill Township, Caswell County, the third of eight children of Jethro Brown and Lucy Williamson Brown. He attended The University of North Carolina for one year and then, when only twenty years old, was elected to the House of Commons; there he served from 1815 through 1818 and again in 1823. From 1824 to 1828 he operated his farm, Rose Hill, but upon the death of Bartlett Yancey in 1828, Brown was chosen in a special election to succeed him in the state senate, over which Yancey had presided for eleven terms. Following his reelection in 1829, Brown was chosen speaker of the senate. Then, shortly thereafter, he was elected by his colleagues to succeed John Branch as U.S. senator from North Carolina.

Brown's role in the Senate from 1829 until 1840 was characterized by President Martin Van Buren, who described him as "an old and constant friend of Genl. Jackson and my own, one on whom as much as any other man, we relied for support of our respective administrations in the Senate. . . ." On most issues of the day, Brown was a partisan Democrat: he opposed a high tariff, a national bank, and internal improvements at government expense; and he supported the Jackson and Van Buren administrations almost without exception. He could not bring himself to support the force bill, however, though he repudiated the doctrine of Nullification while arguing that the "high-toned doctrine of the Federal party produced it. . . . It is by an improper pressure of the Federal Government on the rights of the States, and by exercising doubtful powers, that the State of South Carolina has been thrown into this position." It was in this debate that Brown stated his opposition to sectional views: " . . . if I have any patriotism, it is not that narrow, contracted patriotism which is confined to geographical limits. I trust it is that patriotism which looks abroad over the Union, and embraces every portion of my fellow-citizens." Brown's criticism of South Carolina's action and his opposition to the force bill represented a position that became characteristic of the states' rights Unionist. His dedication to the Union led him first to caution and then to berate southern senators like John C. Calhoun, who, Brown felt, were alienating moderate northerners by exaggerating the dangers of a small group of abolitionists. Brown argued that abolitionist petitions should be received and tabled, thus ignoring them, rather than debating them upon a motion to refuse to receive. In 1850 he wrote, "That the Abolitionists of the North have been greatly strengthened by the imprudent and violent course of a certain class of violent *disunion politicians* of the South by the most improvident course, for fifteen years past, I am positively certain. It has been the course of that class to which I refer, to abuse the whole North in their speeches and addresses for the acts of what at one time were the acts of a few. I remember for many years, while I was in the Senate, and when the Northern Democrats were warmly voting with us, that this was the language with Mr. Calhoun and his party for much of the time till they have left us with few friends in the North. . . . This can mean nothing but *Disunion! Disunion! Slave question or no Slave question!*"

In an effort to show popular approbation of their support of the Democratic administration in Washington, Brown and his colleague Robert Strange resigned in 1840 and placed their political fate upon the general election. The Whigs, however, won control of the General Assembly; Brown was replaced in the U.S. Senate by Willie P. Mangum and Strange by William A. Graham. The latter's term expired in 1842, and, with the Democrats again in control of the General Assembly, Brown offered himself for the seat. The Calhoun wing of the Democratic party, however, was determined to prevent Brown's return to Washington. They therefore put into nomination the name of another resident of Caswell County, Romulus M. Saunders. With the two factions unable to agree, and neither candidate willing to yield to the other, both eventually withdrew and William H. Haywood was elected.

Hurt and disillusioned, Brown sold Rose Hill and moved his family to Howard County, Mo., where they lived until 1847. In the latter year they moved to Virginia, settling first in Albemarle County and later in Fauquier County, where they lived until 1855, except for the winters of 1849–50 in Baltimore and 1853–54 in Savannah. In 1855, Brown repurchased Rose Hill and moved back to Caswell County. Within a year he was again active in politics, serving as vice-president of the state's Democratic convention delegation in 1856 and again in 1860. He was elected to the state senate in 1858

and was reelected in 1860 and 1862. He also served in the wartime convention.

Though Brown remained a staunch Unionist until the beginning of the Civil War, he voted for secession on 20 May 1861. Following the war, he served in the convention of 1865 and advocated a speedy return to the Union. In the same year he was narrowly defeated for Congress. Two years later, Governor Jonathan Worth sent him to Washington as a commissioner to discuss readmission to the Union.

In 1868, Brown was again vice-president of the state's delegation to the Democratic National Convention, and in the fall he was elected again to the state senate. The Republican-controlled senate, however, refused to allow him to be seated. His place was taken by John Walter Stephens, who two years later was murdered by the Ku Klux Klan.

Brown married Mary Lumpkin Glenn on 13 July 1816, and they had seven children: William Livingston, Bedford, Jr., Wilson Glenn, Isabella Virginia, Laura, and Rosalie. Brown was buried on the grounds at Rose Hill.

SEE: Samuel A. Ashe, ed., *Biographical History of North Carolina*, vol. 1 (1905); Brown papers (Manuscript Department, Library, Duke University, Durham; Southern Historical Collection, University of North Carolina, Chapel Hill); Houston G. Jones, "Bedford Brown," *North Carolina Historical Review* 32 (1955); David Schenck, *Personal Sketches of Distinguished Delegates to the State Convention 1861–62* (1885).

H. G. JONES

Brown, Calvin Scott (*23 Mar. 1859–9 Sept. 1936*), educator, editor, minister, and advisor, was born in Salisbury of black and Scotch-Irish ancestry. His father was Henry Brown, a farmer, and his mother was Flora Brown. Brought up in poverty, he was educated at Freedman's Aid Society School, Salisbury, and Shaw University, Raleigh, where he earned A.B., A.M., and D.D. degrees. He worked his way through Shaw University with the aid of a northern white church. In 1885, at the insistence of Dr. H. M. Tupper, president of Shaw University, he went to Hertford County to assume the pastorate of Pleasant Plains Baptist Church. In that same year he founded the all-black Chowan Academy, which later became Waters Training School and today is Calvin S. Brown School in Winton. He remained principal of the school until his death in 1936. For approximately fifty years he served alternately as secretary and president of the Baptist State Convention (black). For many years he served as moderator of the West Roanoke Association, and from its organization to his death he was president of the Lott Carey Foreign Mission Convention. For a number of years he was editor of the *Chowan Pilot* and the *Baptist Quarterly*, published in Raleigh. He was grand master of the Odd Fellows for a number of years, grand secretary of the Grand Masonic Lodge of North Carolina for about thirty years, and for several years grand master of that lodge. He was moderately active in Democratic affairs in Winton.

Brown, who traveled extensively in this country and in Europe and Africa, was offered a number of high and coveted positions; he chose, instead, to remain with the rural people of Hertford County, where he devoted his life's work and influence to the advancement of Negro educational and spiritual life. He was a talented, self-taught musician who played the organ and piano and blew the cornet in a local band he organized. He served a three-year term on the Hertford County Board of Education and was appointed to the Liberty Bonds campaign during World War I.

To Chowan Academy, Brown gave his personal attention and supervision for fifty-two years as principal. His wife shared her family wealth and her personal interest in the building and operation of the school. In the school's early years, Brown journeyed north each year to secure operating funds from sympathetic white and black friends. Both Brown and his wife taught at the school for a number of years without compensation, and when he was afforded a salary, he would often return the entire amount to the operation and maintenance of the school. Through support obtained from his northern friends, the Baptist Home Mission Society, and the Chowan Sunday School Convention, he was able to enlarge his academy with additional buildings in 1893, 1909, and 1926. The 1926 building, known as Brown Hall, was a brick structure with six classrooms, principal's office, library, stage, dressing rooms, and auditorium. In 1924 the school facility was taken over by the State of North Carolina, which ensured its survival. Brown's activities were not entirely confined to the principalship of the school: his example offered a model of character building to blacks throughout the northeastern section of North Carolina.

Brown was married on 8 Dec. 1886 to Amaza Janet Drummond of Lexington, Va.; they had nine children. He died in Winton, and he and his wife were buried on the grounds of C. S. Brown School there. There is a portrait of Brown in Winton.

SEE: E. Franklin Frazier, *The Negro Family in the United States* (1939); *National Cyclopedia of the Colored Race* (1919); Joseph Roy Parker, *The Ahoskie Era of Hertford County* (1939); G. F. Richings, *Among Colored People* (1902); J. A. Whitted, *A History of the Negro Baptists of North Carolina* (1908).

E. FRANK STEPHENSON, JR.

Brown, Cecil Kenneth (*24 Oct. 1900–1 Jan. 1957*), economist and educator, was born in Salisbury, the son of Pleasant Marion and Carolina Amery Shelton Brown. After receiving his education in Cleveland County schools, he entered Davidson College in the fall of 1917. He was an active member of the Davidson College community throughout his life. As an undergraduate he was an honor roll student, a member of the intercollegiate debating team for two years, president and critic of the Philanthropic Literary Society, a member of the YMCA Board of Control, president of Le Cercle Français, and valedictorian of the class of 1921. He was also a member of Phi Beta Kappa, Phi Delta Theta, Omicron Delta Kappa, and Sigma Upsilon.

In the summer of 1921, Brown attended the University of Besançon, France, and received the Certificat d'Etudes Français. Returning to the United States, he worked in his family's lumber business for one year before entering The University of North Carolina in 1922. There he held the position of teaching fellow and received his M.A. degree in 1923. He was again at the university from 1925 until 1927, when he received a Ph.D. He studied at Columbia University in the summer of 1927 and at the University of Chicago in the summer of 1929.

Brown began his teaching career at Davidson in 1923. He was an assistant professor of mathematics for two years. When he returned to The University of North Carolina in 1925, he worked as a research assistant at the Institute for Research in Social Science. He was promoted to research associate in 1929. He also served as

visiting instructor in economics at the university in the 1928, 1929, 1937, and 1952 summer sessions.

Brown rejoined the Davidson faculty as assistant professor of economics in 1927. In 1929 he was promoted to full professorship. He began to urge the faculty to approve honors in education during the early 1930s, believing that an honors program was necessary at Davidson in order for the school to fulfill its obligation as a liberal arts college offering education to meet the needs of its students. He continued to push this program until it was set up in 1940. Brown became dean of the faculty in 1941 and held that position until 1953.

During his career, Brown attended many educational conferences and conventions, including the meetings of the Southern University Conference, the Presbyterian Educational Association of the South, and the Association of American Colleges. He was vice-president of the North Carolina College Conference during 1948–49 and secretary-treasurer of the Council of Church Related Colleges of North Carolina from 1945 until 1950. He was secretary-treasurer of the Conference of Academic Deans of the United States from 1947 until 1950, when he was elected chairman. He was also a member of the American Economic Association and the Historical Society of North Carolina.

Brown was quite active in the Presbyterian church and, as a member of Davidson Presbyterian Church, taught the Men's Bible Class there. He was an elder in his church and was named moderator of the Concord Presbytery in 1948.

Brown was the author of *A State Movement in Railroad Development*, published in 1928 by The University of North Carolina Press, and of *The State Highway System of North Carolina: Its Evolution and Present Status*, published by the same press in 1931. He was also the author of a textbook in economics published in 1941.

Brown married Catherine May Mathews on 26 Aug. 1925; she died on 30 Apr. 1927. His second marriage was to Evelyn Hill of Tallahassee, Fla., on 29 June 1932. They had four children.

After his death, Brown's friends and former students established the Dr. C. K. Brown Scholarship Fund. He was buried in the Davidson College Cemetery.

SEE: Mrs. C. K. Brown (interview); Davidson College Alumni Files, Davidson; D. L. Grant, *Alumni History of the University of North Carolina* (1924); *Who's Who in the South and Southwest*, 1956; *Who Was Who in America*, vol. 3 (1960).

JUANITA ANN SHEPPARD

Brown, Charlotte Hawkins (*11 June 1883–11 Jan. 1961*), a pioneer in education and race relations, was born on a farm near Henderson, the granddaughter of a slave. Her mother, Caroline Frances Hawkins, moved to Cambridge, Mass., when Charlotte was a small child; there she married Edmund Hawkins, a brick mason.

A precocious child, Charlotte Hawkins distinguished herself as a superior student and a gifted musician in the Cambridge public schools. She attended Allston Grammar School and the Cambridge English High School. As a high school senior she met a woman who was to have a profound influence on her life, and the chance meeting was a story she never tired of telling. Employed as a babysitter for a Cambridge family, she was one day rolling a baby carriage down the street with one hand while carrying a copy of Virgil in the other. The juxtaposition attracted the attention of a passerby—Alice Freeman Palmer, second president of Wellesley College—who took an immediate interest in young

Charlotte Hawkins. On learning that the girl planned to enter the State Normal School at Salem, Mass., following high school graduation, Mrs. Palmer insisted on assuming responsibility for her expenses.

A second chance meeting, in 1901, with the field secretary of the Women's Division of the American Missionary Association, led Miss Hawkins to her life's work. She was persuaded by the field secretary to return to her native North Carolina to serve the American Missionary Association in its effort to bring education to southern Negroes. After receiving permission to leave Salem Normal School prior to the graduation of her class, she returned south on 10 Oct. 1901, bound for what she thought was a well-established mission school at McLeansville, a whistle-stop eight miles east of Greensboro. Four and a half miles from McLeansville, at what would later be called Sedalia, Miss Hawkins found the school, a crude building that served as a combination church and school, peopled with fifty barefoot children.

From these meager beginnings made even more desperate by the American Missionary Association's decision to close the school in 1902, Charlotte Hawkins worked to establish a new kind of school in rural North Carolina. Remembering her own experiences in the Cambridge public schools, she endeavored to create at Sedalia a school that would emulate the New England ideal in combination with the best of industrial education. Drawing on her friendship with Alice Freeman Palmer, Harvard's Charles W. Eliot, and Charles D. McIver, she returned to Massachusetts to solicit funds for her school, raising just enough to give the school life for one more year. She then reorganized the school and named it Palmer Memorial Institute, in honor of Alice Freeman Palmer, who had died in 1902. The first class met in a remodeled blacksmith's shed, and with the strong support of the people in the community the school survived. Her persistence on the school's behalf gradually found for her the support of Boston philanthropists, and she was also successful in enlisting the assistance of influential southern whites in nearby Greensboro. By 1910 property valuation amounted to $10,000, and the school's growth was just beginning. Support continued to develop, both in Greensboro and in Boston, highlighted by the interest of Mr. and Mrs. Galen Stone of Boston, who gave the school funds well in excess of $100,000 during the 1920s. Such generosity, coupled with the founder's skill and perseverance in procuring funds—she raised $350,000 in 1925 alone—made possible an impressive expansion and moderniza- tion of the school's facilities, despite disastrous fires in 1917 and 1922. The period of the depression, however, was a trying time for the school, although by 1946 the school's physical plant was valued at more than $500,000.

As her school grew in size and reputation, Charlotte Hawkins achieved state and national recognition. She spent the academic year 1927–28 studying at Wellesley, and she lectured frequently at Smith, Wellesley, Mt. Holyoke, and Radcliffe colleges, and at Howard University, Hampton Institute, and Tuskegee Institute. She received six honorary degrees, among them honorary doctorates from Lincoln University, Pa., in 1937, Wilberforce University in 1939, and Howard University in 1944.

She was also actively involved in efforts to improve race relations in the South. She was a charter member of the Southern Commission for Interracial Cooperation, a charter member of the Southern Regional Council, a member of the executive board of the Southern Region of the Urban League, a member of the Negro Business League, and a member of the home nursing council of the American Red Cross. In 1940, Governor Clyde R. Hoey of North Carolina appointed her to the state Council of Defense, thereby breaking a southern precedent by naming a black to that prestigious committee. In 1945 she received the second annual Racial Understanding Award of the Council for Fair Play, a group of northern and southern people interested in promoting racial harmony. She was also the first black woman to be elected to the National Board of the YWCA and was elected to that post by white women in the South through membership in the South Atlantic Field Committee. As president of the Federation of Colored Women's Clubs in North Carolina, she led a successful drive for the establishment of a state-funded home for delinquent black girls.

Charlotte Hawkins married Edward S. Brown on 12 June 1911. She was a Congregationalist and, although a lifelong Republican, a strong supporter of the New Deal, largely through her association with Eleanor Roosevelt.

She resigned the presidency of Palmer Memorial Institute in 1952, to be succeeded by her associate and former student Wilhelmina M. Crosson; she continued to serve as director of finance until 1955. Poor health sharply curtailed her activities in her later years, although she retained her strong interest in the school she had founded until her death at L. Richardson Memorial Hospital in Greensboro.

SEE: Benjamin Brawley, *Negro Builders and Heroes* (1937); Fred L. Brownlee, "She Did It," *American Missionary*, July 1927; Sadie Iola Daniel, *Women Builders* (1931); *Greensboro Daily News*, 10 Apr. 1947, 12 Jan. 1961 (obit.); *Who's Who in the South and Southwest*, 1947.

A. M. BURNS III

Brown, Edwin Pierce (18 Oct. 1903–14 Apr. 1972), manufacturer and Quaker leader, was born in the community of George in Northampton County, the son of Walter Jay and Lula May Vaughan Brown. He attended Olney (Friends) School in Barnesville, Ohio, and was graduated from Westtown (Friends) Boarding School at Westtown, Pa. He received his A.B. degree from Guilford College in 1926.

He began his business career in 1926, working with his father in Murfreesboro in the manufacture of baskets; as president of Riverside Manufacturing Company, he developed and diversified the company until it served the East Coast. As an industrial leader he served as president of American Package Corporation, as a director of the National Association of Manufacturers, and as an appointee of Governor Luther Hodges to the North Carolina Banking Commission. He served as a director of Virginia Electric and Power Company, the Farmer's Bank of Woodland, and Wachovia Bank and Trust Co. and was chairman of the board of trustees of Roanoke-Chowan Hospital in Ahoskie. He was a trustee of Guilford College from 1941 to 1972, and as its chairman from 1969 to 1972, following his retirement, he devoted almost all of his time to the development program of the college.

Brown's deep interest in civic and religious affairs was expressed through his support of many organizations and institutions, including Chowan (Baptist) College in his home town of Murfreesboro and the Murfreesboro Historical Association, of which he was president. As an elder in Rich Square Monthly Meeting of Friends and as clerk of the representative body of the North Carolina yearly Meeting of Friends (Conservative) in Woodland, he was recognized as a national and international leader of his branch of Quakerism, representing it at the Third and Fourth World Conferences of Friends, at Oxford, England, in 1952 and at Guilford College in 1967. He was especially noted for his interest in and assistance to deserving students, among whom were many fine athletes. Because of this special interest, he was elected to the Guilford College Athletic Hall of Fame and was given the Distinguished Alumni Award. As an industrialist, he was noted in Eastern North Carolina for his progressive relations with his employees, both black and white.

In 1933 he married Dorothy Heath, to whom were born four children: Edwin Pierce, Jr., Hannah Heath, Dorothy May (Mrs. Robert McBrayer Shoffner), and Andrew Vaughan. Brown died in Norfolk, Va., and was buried in the Murfreesboro Cemetery. Portraits of him are located in the Northeastern Oil Company office and the family home in Murfreesboro and in Roanoke-Chowan Hospital in Ahoskie.

SEE: *Memorial: Edwin Pierce Brown* (1972); Quaker records (Rich Square Friends Meeting, Woodland; Guilford College Archives, Greensboro); Raleigh *News and Observer*, 12 Apr. 1953 (portrait).

J. FLOYD MOORE

Brown, Frank Clyde (16 Oct. 1870–3 June 1943), professor, departmental chairman, university administrator, and collector of folklore, was born in Harrisonburg, Va. His parents were John Michael and Emma Catherine Liskie Brown. His formal education included an A.B. degree from the University of Nashville in Tennessee in 1893 and M.A. and Ph.D. degrees from the University of Chicago in 1902 and 1908. In 1909 he began a distinguished career as professor of English at Trinity College. An indefatigable worker, in and out of the classroom, he was known to students and colleagues as "Bull" Brown because of both his self-confident charge toward objectives and the roar of disapproval he directed most often not at unprepared students but at those who did not care whether they were prepared or not. A specialist in English literature, he excelled as an interpreter of Shakespeare to generations of students who prized his course as an essential to their liberal arts educations and who often acknowledged his influence long after they departed his classroom.

At the urging of John A. Lomax, president of the American Folklore Society, Brown organized the North Carolina Folklore Society in 1913 and served as its secretary-treasurer, program chairman, and primary collector until his death in 1943. *The Frank Clyde Brown Collection of North Carolina Folklore*, published by Duke University Press in seven volumes between 1952 and 1964, under the editorial supervision of Newman I. White and Paul F. Baum, represents Brown's lifetime of collecting. These volumes contain approximately thirty-eight thousand items, primarily from North Carolina, illustrating the folk ballads, songs, games, rhymes, beliefs, customs, riddles, proverbs, tales, legends, superstitions, and speech of common folk of the Southeast. Clearly, Brown's definition of folklore was governed more by inclusion than by exclusion, and the volumes bearing his name have been characterized as "the most imposing monument ever erected in this country to the common memory of the people of any single state." Brown's Ford automobile, equipped with a gasoline-powered generator to provide electricity for his recording equipment, was a common sight in the isolated backwoods, where more than once the recording of a familiar voice convinced awed listeners that the fashionably attired professor was not a revenue agent in

disguise. Brown took particular pride in recording unwritten ballads and songs, often tracing their origins as far back as the tenth and eleventh centuries. Through his interest in folklore he became a member of the American Folk Lore Society, the Folk Lore Society of England, and the Folk Song Societies of England, Ireland, Wales, and Scotland.

Between 1924 and 1930, Brown was deeply absorbed in the expansion of Trinity College into Duke University, serving as a member of the building committee of the board of trustees and as the first comptroller of the university. The latter position, created in 1926, required his services as the liason for architects, contractors, suppliers, administrators, and faculty in the designing, construction, and equipping of the redesigned East Campus, which became the Woman's College, and the completely new West Campus. He expertly handled a myriad of details and is credited with contributing many original ideas to the building plans, foremost of which was the discovery of the nearby Hillsborough stone and the recommendation that this exceptional material be utilized in the construction of the Gothic West Campus. He also served as university marshal, planning all major formal celebrations and entertaining numerous distinguished visitors to the new university.

Brown's published works included *Elkanah Settle: His Life and Work* (1910) and *Ballad Literature in North Carolina* (1915). He had memberships in the Modern Language Association of America; Newcomen Society of England; Phi Beta Kappa; Omicron Delta Kappa, of which he was national president in 1931–32; Sigma Upsilon; and Phi Delta Theta. His religious affiliation was Methodist and his political affiliation Democratic. In 1893 he married Ola Marguerite Hollis, who died in 1928, and in 1932 he married Mrs. Mary Henkel Wadsworth; her son, Joseph A. C. Wadsworth, became Brown's stepson. Brown was buried in Maplewood Cemetery in Durham.

SEE: Frank Clyde Brown Papers (Archives, Duke University, Durham), for W. Amos Abrams's "I Knew Frank Clyde Brown," advertising material concerning the equipping of Duke University, Joseph D. Clark's "Fifty Years of the North Carolina Folklore Society," and pictures and correspondence; Frank Clyde Brown Papers (Manuscript Department, Library, Duke University, Durham), for material pertaining to the Frank Clyde Brown Collection of North Carolina Folklore; Theodore Barry Buermann, "A History of the North Carolina Folklore Society" (M.A. thesis, University of North Carolina, 1963); *Durham Morning Herald*, 19 Oct. 1941, 3 June 1943; Raleigh *News and Observer*, 27 Oct. 1929; *Who's Who in America*, 1942–43.

W. E. KING

Brown, George Hubbard (3 May 1850–16 Mar. 1926), superior court judge and associate justice of the North Carolina Supreme Court, was born in Washington, N.C. His parents were Sylvester T. and Elizabeth Bonner Brown. His paternal ancestors included the Revolutionary War soldiers General Thomas Holliday and Captain George Hubbard. A maternal ancestor, James Bonner, founded Washington. Brown lived in Washington until 1866, when he left for two years at Horner's School in Oxford. In 1868 his skill as a telegrapher secured him a position in New York City, where he worked at the desk next to Thomas Edison. He returned to live with his parents in 1870 and to study law in Wilson, where they lived. In 1871 he and his parents moved back to Washington, and he began to study law with his future brother-in-law, James E. Shepherd. After passing the bar examination in 1872, he opened a law office in Washington. His law partner was Fenner B. Satterthwaite until the latter's death in 1882.

Active in politics, Brown served several years as chairman of the Democratic party in Beaufort County. In 1880 he campaigned unsuccessfully for the Democratic nomination for Congress from the First Congressional District. As a presidential elector from the First Congressional District, he cast a vote for Grover Cleveland in 1888. After practicing law with John H. Small from 1885 to 1889, he was appointed by Governor A. M. Scales to a vacancy on the superior court in the First Judicial District in 1889. In 1902, Henry Groves Connor defeated him for the Democratic nomination for associate justice of the state supreme court. Two years later he was elected to an eight-year term as associate justice of the North Carolina Supreme Court, and in 1912 he was elected to a second full term. He declined renomination in 1920 because an attack of influenza in 1918 had left him greatly weakened.

Robert Watson Winston called Brown "our Dissenting Judge—he was unwilling to bend the law to meet difficult situations or to win popular favor." According to Winston, Brown was "the acknowledged exponent of the vested interests of the State. . . . On the bench he stood for property and property rights as much as for the rights of persons."

After retiring from the bench in 1921, Brown served occasionally as a special judge appointed by the governor. Throughout his life he was fond of horses and enjoyed hunting. He died in 1926 of bronchial pneumonia. A lifelong member of St. Peter's Episcopal Church in Washington, he was buried in Oakdale Cemetery in Washington. He was survived by his widow, Laura Ellison Lewis, whom he had married on 17 Dec. 1874. They had no children. There is a portrait of Brown in the Supreme Court Building in Raleigh.

SEE: *In Memoriam: George Hubbard Brown* (1927); *North Carolina Bar Association Report*, 1926; Raleigh *News and Observer*, 17 Mar. 1926.

C. W. EAGLES

Brown, George Thomas (20 Aug. 1869–27 Nov. 1913), tobacco manufacturer, was born in Mocksville, the son of Rufus D. and Sarah Gibbs Brown. Rufus Brown and his brother, Dr. William Brown, had a small tobacco factory in Mocksville, which they moved, along with their families, to Winston in about 1875. This firm, Brown Brothers, was thus among the pioneer tobacco businesses of Winston; it continued in operation for many years after the death of Rufus Brown in October 1893.

George Brown was educated in the schools of Winston and at Davidson College, which he attended in 1887–88. In 1893 he married Elsie Thompson, whose sister, Minnie, was the wife of Robert Lynn Williamson. The two brothers-in-law formed a partnership for the manufacture of chewing and smoking tobacco, even though the effects of the financial Panic of 1893 were in full force. They took over the factory and brands of T. F. Williamson Tobacco Company, another pioneer tobacco firm in Winston, and began operation as Brown and Williamson on 1 Feb. 1894, with capital of ten thousand dollars and thirty employees. George Brown had received this ten thousand dollars from his father; he bought with it one hundred thousand pounds of tobacco, and he took charge of the office and buying for the partners. His brother-in-law, with the technical knowledge and practical experience, took charge of the manufacturing operations. In 1906 the business was incorporated in North Carolina as Brown and Williamson Tobacco Company, with Brown president, which office he held until his death, and Williamson vice-president.

Brown was taken ill suddenly at his home in Winston in the early evening of 26 Nov. 1913 and died the next day. He was buried in Salem Cemetery beside his wife and their only child, Minnie, who died in infancy. Brown was a member of the board of trade and the tobacco board of trade. He belonged to the First Presbyterian Church of Winston and served on its board of deacons; he was a Mason, Shriner, and Knight Templar and a charter member of the Twin City Club.

SEE: *North Carolina Biography*, vol. 3 (1929 [photograph]).

ANNA WITHERS BAIR

Brown, George W. (16 Dec. 1871–16 Oct. 1950), physician, was born at Brower's Mill, Randolph County, the son of W. Duncan and Mary Elizabeth Guthrie Brown. He attended local public schools and was graduated from Shiloh Academy in 1892. For the following several years he worked on a Texas ranch owned by a physician. He spent his evenings reading medical books and was encouraged to attend medical school; he studied at the Kentucky School of Medicine, where he was graduated in 1898. He remained in Kentucky for six years, practicing in Covington, where he fought a typhoid epidemic.

Moving back to North Carolina in 1904, he settled in Raeford and was a leader there for almost half a century. He was instrumental in lobbying the legislature for the creation of Hoke County in 1911. He was a member of the Hoke County Board of Education for the period 1915–24 and was its chairman for the last four of these years, a time during which a number of new county schools were erected. He was mayor of Raeford from 1939 to 1942 and county coroner for many years. In 1943 and 1945 he represented Hoke County in the General Assembly as a Democrat.

Brown's interests also extended to business and farming. He opened a drug store out of necessity: he had to roll his own pills for his patients. He and two other men opened the Bank of Hoke, which was later sold to the Page Trust Company. The bank closed during the depression, and Brown lost a considerable sum of money. He also owned several farms and was particularly interested in growing cotton and tobacco. Although his political and business interests were wide, he devoted most of his time to medicine. He made house calls until he was seventy-seven and continued to see patients until his death.

Brown married Lola Kendall Crump on 5 June 1905, and they were the parents of George Clarence, Walter Duncan, Eleanor Guthrie, and Rosa Adrienne. He was buried in Raeford.

SEE: Minutes of Hoke County Board of Education, 1911–27 (Raeford); Minutes of Raeford Board of Commissioners, 1937–43 (Raeford); *News-Journal*, 19 Oct. 1950; *North Carolina Manual* (1943, 1945).

HUBERT K. WOOTEN

Brown, Hamilton (30 Sept. 1786–27 Mar. 1870), planter, stockraiser, and land speculator, a resident of Wilkesboro, was the son of Jane McDowell and John Brown, a Scotch-Irish immigrant. Brown served as a lieutenant, Eighteenth Regiment, U.S. Infantry, in the War of 1812 and afterward was colonel of the Wilkes

County militia. He served a number of years as county justice and was sheriff from 1816 to 1818. He also served as overseer of a program to clear the Yadkin River, in order to allow the passage of boats up the Yadkin to the mouth of Buffalo Creek.

Brown inherited land in Wilkes and adjoining counties, as well as in Virginia, and purchased additional land in North Carolina and in Tennessee. He had business dealings in South Carolina, Georgia, Mississippi, and Texas. He inherited some slaves in Virginia from his mother's brother but was unwilling to separate the men (two of whom were skilled blacksmiths) from their wives and, being prevented by Virginia law from freeing them, he arranged for them to continue their work there under the modest supervision of a local resident.

Brown married Mrs. Sarah Gwyn Gordon, widow of Major Nathaniel Gordon (who died in 1829); they were the parents of two sons, Hugh Thomas (1835–61), a graduate of The University of North Carolina who was killed in the Civil War, and Hamilton Allen (1837–1917), who also served in the Confederate Army. Brown's stepson, General James B. Gordon, was killed near Richmond in 1864. Brown and his wife were buried in the yard of St. Paul's Episcopal Church, Wilkesboro.

SEE: Hamilton Brown Papers (Southern Historical Collection, University of North Carolina, Chapel Hill).

SARAH E. HOLEMAN

Brown, Hamilton Allen (25 Sept. 1837–9 Apr. 1917), Confederate officer and planter, was born the son of Hamilton and Sarah Gwyn Gordon Brown at Oakland, the old Gordon homestead in Wilkes County. He attended the Naval Academy at Annapolis as a member of the class of 1858 but was not graduated. On 3 June 1861 he became first lieutenant of Company B, First North Carolina Regiment. Because of his military training, he was detailed by Governor John W. Ellis to drill recruits and fit them for service. In the summer of 1862, when Colonel M. S. Stokes and other officers of his regiment in line for promotion were killed at Mechanicsville, Brown was placed in command. He was promoted to colonel in December 1863 and soon afterward took command of his regiment, which was then attached to General Stonewall Jackson's division. He was placed in command of the division's sharpshooters and is given credit for much of the fame of Jackson's division. It was related that Brown never ordered a man into battle but instead always said, "Follow me." He was wounded thirteen times but always stayed close to his men and returned to duty as quickly as possible.

On one occasion, Brown was left on the battlefield when his injuries were believed to be fatal. The Reverend George Patterson, chaplain of the Third Regiment, asked if he wanted a burial service read while he was still alive, explaining that there would probably be no time for the service after his death. The offer was accepted, and the service from the Book of Common Prayer was read. Brown fortunately recovered from his wounds; many years later in Tennessee he again met Patterson, who expressed surprise to find living a person over whom he had read the burial service. Brown replied that hearing his own burial service had brought him back to life instead of laying him away.

Brown served in the battles of Gettysburg, Culp's Hill, Richmond, and Petersburg, as well as in the campaigns of the Wilderness, Spottsylvania, and the Valley. On 24 Mar. 1865, at Fort Stedman, he and a portion of his command were captured by General Napoleon McLaughlin. Shortly afterward, McLaughlin was captured by a Confederate force. Later, however, the Confederates were forced to surrender; Brown was taken to Washington and then to Johnson's Island and finally was confined at Fort Delaware until 24 June 1865, when he took the oath of allegiance.

Brown returned to Wilkes County and played a minor role in local events of the early Reconstruction period. In 1868 he married his cousin, Amelia Selina Gwyn of Green Hill. In about 1871 they, together with Brown's brothers and a sister, moved to Columbia, Tenn., where they owned land. Brown increased his holdings and became a planter of modest means. He and his wife were the parents of four sons: Hugh Thomas, Hamilton, Gordon, and John. Brown was buried in St. Paul's Episcopal Church Cemetery, Wilkesboro.

SEE: *Carolina and the Southern Cross* 1, no. 6 (1913); Lyman C. Draper, *Kings Mountain and Its Heroes* (1929); Johnson J. Hayes, *The Land of Wilkes* (1962); Thomas Felix Hickerson, *Happy Valley* (ca. 1940); Louis H. Manarin, comp., *North Carolina Troops, 1861–1865* (1966); William B. Turner, *History of Maury County, Tennessee* (1955).

SARAH E. HOLEMAN

Brown, Henry Alfred (20 Sept. 1846–25 Apr. 1929), Baptist minister, was born in a log house near Wentworth in Rockingham County. His father was Robert Brown, a schoolteacher and farmer; his mother was Sarah Troth Brown. His grandfather, Robert Brown, had moved to Rockingham County from Winchester, Va.

Young Henry attended grammar school during the winter months at his father's school in the Piney Grove district. In March 1864, despite his mother's protests, Brown joined the Fourth North Carolina Battalion, commanded by Major John M. Reese. His company was stationed at Camp Davis on Masonboro Sound below Wilmington, where the company guarded the state salt works and tried to prevent slaves from escaping to the Federal gunboats. There Brown was stricken with malaria and hospitalized. After the bombardment of Fort Fisher in December 1864, the battalion was rushed by rail to Belfield, Va., to repulse a raid on the Weldon, N.C., railroad bridge. After skirmishing near Tarboro, the battalion was returned to Goldsboro and organized into the Third Regiment, North Carolina Reserves. They fought at Kinston and surrendered after retreating to Randolph County.

After the war, Brown worked on his father's farm and taught at the district school. He attended two preparatory schools in Guilford County, one at Center and the other at Monticello, and then entered Wake Forest College in the fall of 1867, as a beneficiary of the Beulah Baptist Association. He was an orator, and served the Euzelian Literary Society as a critic, secretary, and president. At his graduation in 1871 he delivered the salutatorian address, "We Should Take Things as They Are."

Shortly after the Civil War, Brown was converted and baptized in Troublesome Creek, Randolph County, and joined Summerfield Baptist Church. In August 1871, after his college graduation, he was ordained at Yanceyville by a presbytery consisting of Dr. W. M. Wingate and the Reverends F. M. Jones, S. G. Mason, W. S. Fontaine, F. M. Jordan, and P. H. Fontaine.

Soon after his ordination, Brown was engaged by the state mission board of the Baptist State Convention as a missionary in Rockingham, Guilford, Stokes, and

Forsyth counties. In later years, Brown related some of his experiences to his biographer: "I had eight or nine appointments to reach each month. This required riding on horseback nearly one hundred and fifty miles per month. I had to ford Dan River four or five times a month. Often it was swollen and I came near having trouble and being in danger on several occasions. I rode a hard-trotting horse which gave me fine exercise."

During his work for the convention, Brown began several missions and churches and assisted other pastors with revivals. The preaching and singing exhausted him and brought on a throat condition that caused him to give up his work for several months. He taught school and, after recovering from his throat condition, accepted the pastorate of the First Baptist Church at Fayetteville. He preached his first sermon there on the second Sunday in September 1874. His reminiscences of this pastorate were published in the *North Carolina Baptist* in 1903.

During the summer of 1877, Brown's health began to fail, and his mind returned once more to the Piedmont section of the state. The Baptist church in Winston and Red Bank Baptist Church in the northern part of Forsyth County were both without a pastor. The two boards of deacons, without consulting each other, unanimously called Brown to preach at Winston three Sundays a month and at Red Bank one. Brown thus began his forty years of work at the Baptist church in Winston, now the First Baptist Church, Winston-Salem. There were only 50 Baptists in the two towns of Winston and Salem in 1877, but during Brown's pastorate a new house of worship was begun; membership reached 2,739 by the time of his retirement.

Brown was also a leader in the Pilot Mountain Baptist Association. He aided in planning fifty of the sixty-three churches founded during his ministry in the area. He served as chairman and treasurer of the executive committee of the association for nearly twenty-five years and was a regular correspondent and writer for the *North Carolina Baptist* (Fayetteville) and for the *Biblical Recorder* (Raleigh). After his retirement in 1917, he was elected pastor emeritus of all the Baptist churches in Winston-Salem. Brown Memorial Baptist Church was named in his honor.

Brown returned to Wake Forest College in 1891 to deliver the alumni address, "What Has a Christian College the Right to Expect of Her Sons?" during commencement. The college granted him the honorary D.D. degree in 1895. He also served as trustee of Wake Forest from 1885 to 1902.

During his pastorate in Fayetteville, Brown met Julia Ellen Cain; they were married on 14 Nov. 1878. They had one son, Henry Wingate, and two daughters, Addie Pauline (Mrs. W. O. McCorkle) and Julia Eloise (Mrs. Henry S. Stokes).

Brown was buried in the Salem Cemetery, Winston-Salem, in a Masonic graveside ceremony.

SEE: Biography File (Baptist Historical Collection, Wake Forest University, Winston-Salem); First Baptist Church (Winston-Salem [photograph]); *Funeral Service in Honor of Rev. H. A. Brown* (1929); G. W. Paschal, *History of Wake Forest College*, vol. 3 (1943); Gilbert T. Stephenson, *The Pastor Beloved* (1925 [photograph]).

JOHN R. WOODARD

Brown, John (1738–1812), Revolutionary War officer and state legislator, was born in County Derry, Ireland. He migrated to Lancaster County, Pa., and taught school there for a while. He married Jane McDowell (1750–1838), the sister of Gen. Joseph McDowell and Maj. Charles McDowell. In 1772 they moved to Quaker Meadows, Burke County, with the McDowells; and soon afterward they moved to a farm on the north side of the Yadkin River, about four miles west of Wilkesboro.

Brown served under Col. Benjamin Cleveland in the Revolutionary army at King's Mountain, probably holding the rank of captain. After the war he was among the first board of magistrates when Wilkes became a county in 1778. The first Wilkes County Court was held at Brown's place near the bend of the Yadkin River. He became Wilkes County register of deeds in 1778 and served on a jury designated to lay out roads in the county. He represented Wilkes County in the North Carolina House of Commons for three years and also at the constitutional convention in Hillsborough in 1788. He was a prominent Mason.

Brown had eleven children, eight sons and three daughters. Two of his sons resided in Wilkes County, although he and the remaining six moved to Maury County, Tenn., where he obtained large land grants in the Duck River Valley in payment for negotiating treaties with the Indians.

Brown died in Wilkes County.

SEE: Lyman C. Draper, *Kings Mountain and Its Heroes* (1929); Thomas Felix Hickerson, *Happy Valley* (1940).

SARAH E. HOLEMAN

Brown, John (12 Aug. 1772–12 Oct. 1845), congressman and land speculator, was born in Kishacoquilla Valley and later lived in Lewistown, Pa., where he attended local common schools. In 1800 in Lewistown he began grist and sawmill businesses. He served in the Pennsylvania House of Representatives from 1809 to 1813 and represented the state in Congress from 4 Mar. 1821 until 3 Mar. 1825. In 1827 he moved to the community of Limestone in south central Buncombe County, N.C. (near the present community of Skyland), to engage in agriculture and the real estate business. The Browns eventually owned about a million acres of land in Haywood, Buncombe, and Mitchell counties.

Brown died in Limestone and was buried in Riverside Cemetery, Asheville. His wife, Ann (1777–1848), of Lewiston, survived, as did a son, William John (1803–84), and a grandson, John Evans (1827–95). An obituary notice in the Asheville *Highland Messenger*, 17 Oct. 1845, said, "Having died in a strange land, he was buried amongst strangers." Nevertheless, Brown's son and a number of grandsons lived in North Carolina. One grandson, Samuel Smith Brown, served with a North Carolina regiment during the Civil War and died in camp; another, William Caleb Brown, was a law partner of Zebulon B. Vance, served under Vance early in the war, and like his brother, died in camp from disease.

SEE: *Biog. Dir. Am. Cong.* (1971); Frontis Johnston, ed., *The Papers of Zebulon Baird Vance*, vol. 1 (1963).

WILLIAM S. POWELL

Brown, John Evans (Feb. 1827–9 July 1895), land developer, was born in Lewiston, Pa., the son of William John Brown (1803–84). He attended school in Wilmington, Del., and afterward studied medicine and law until ill health led him out of doors to Ohio and to North Carolina, where he became a surveyor. He moved to Buncombe County with his father about 1843 but left in 1849 to join the gold rush to California. He returned to

Asheville for a brief time in the fifties, but in 1856 he sailed from San Francisco for Australia, where he became a gold miner, sheep rancher, and businessman. In 1864 he moved to Canterbury, New Zealand, where he later settled. He was a member of the New Zealand General Assembly representing a district called Swannanoa and also Minister of Education, a position in which he did much to establish a system of free, compulsory education. He was a strong advocate of provincial federation, and actively interested in railroads. In 1858 he married Theresa Australia Peacock, an Australian by birth but the daughter of an English merchant and shipper of Sydney. She died in 1880 and in 1883 he married Mrs. Jane Emily Martin of Wellington, New Zealand. In 1884 he returned to North Carolina and in 1889 built Zealandia, a miniature of Moro Castle at Havana, on the crest of Beaumont, a mountain east of Asheville, where he resided until his death. He owned thousands of acres of land in the mountains of western North Carolina and in Tennessee, and Zebulon B. Vance was his legal agent for the sale of about fifty thousand acres. Brown was buried in Riverside Cemetery, Asheville, survived by his widow and by five children of his first marriage: Maria, Vance, and Potter of Asheville, Katie E. Blood of Brooklyn, and Sidney Herbert of Boston. Two children had died in New Zealand.

SEE: *Asheville Citizen*, 17 Dec. 1884; *Asheville Daily Citizen*, 9 July 1895; *Asheville Spectator*, 3 Sept. 1858; W. Vance Brown Papers (North Carolina State Archives, Raleigh); Buncombe County Deeds (Courthouse, Asheville); J. N. Ingram, "New Zealand's Early Destiny Directed by North Carolinian," *Uncle Remus Magazine*, Dec. 1911; "Memoirs of an American Gold Seeker," *Journal of American History* 2 (1908), 129–54.

FRONTIS W. JOHNSTON

Brown, Michael. *See* Braun.

Brown, Peter Marshall (*12 Nov. 1859–5 May 1913*), banker, mayor of Charlotte, and trustee of Davidson College, was born in Charlotte, the son of Colonel John L. Brown and Nannie Kerr Brown. Brown grew up amidst wealth, in a good social position; he attended Macon High School and Davidson College, from which he was graduated in 1880. He then began working in his father's hardware business, Brown and Weddington Company, where he proved to be well suited for a business career. When his father died in 1893, Brown remained in the successful hardware business for two years before selling his interest in order to devote his time to another business and to community service. He acted as a pioneer organizer and eventual president of the Southern Loan and Savings Bank and served also as a president of the Southern Real Estate Loan and Trust Company and as a director of the First National Bank. In these positions he was able to aid significantly in building Charlotte's commercial future.

Between 1896 and 1900, Brown served ably as chairman of the Mecklenburg County Commissioners. He accepted this responsibility willingly and performed key service to his county, which was taking a lead in local improvements. Brown's interest in Charlotte and his diligent efforts as a commissioner stood him in good stead when he sought election as mayor of the city: he was elected in 1901 and reelected in 1903.

Brown had a particularly strong interest in education. His concern was demonstrated in his services as school commissioner of Charlotte and as an active member of the Davidson College Board of Trustees.

Despite Brown's many responsibilities, he still found time to work for the Presbyterian church. He served as a deacon of the First Presbyterian Church of Charlotte and as a treasurer for the Presbyterian Orphans' Home at Barium Springs.

He was married to Jennie Beecher Bass on 14 May 1884. By this first marriage there were four children: Mrs. Gaston Galloway, John Bass, Mrs. Dolph M. Young, and William. Brown's wife died in 1898, and he was married on 8 Nov. 1905 to Daisy Bell Pharr, the daughter of a Presbyterian minister from Mooresville. There were no children by this marriage.

Because of good investments, especially in real estate, Brown became a very wealthy man. His wealth grew along with Charlotte, until his estate reached an estimated one-half to one million dollars.

SEE: *Charlotte Observer*, 5 May 1913.

STEVEN EDWARD CAMPBELL

Brown, Roy Melton (*11 Dec. 1878–16 Oct. 1962*), social work educator and administrator, was born near Boone, the son of Joseph Bobbitt and Franky Ashley Brown. His ancestors on both sides were small, home-owning farmers. Brown was educated in the public schools of Watauga County and at Globe Academy, Sutherland Academy, and Watauga Academy. He attended The University of North Carolina, where he received an A.B. degree in 1906. Later, he returned to the university for the M.A. in 1921 and the Ph.D. in sociology in 1929.

Brown began his career as a teacher of English in public schools and in college. He taught at Reidsville High School in 1906–7, was principal of Wiley elementary school in Raleigh during 1907–8, and taught English at Appalachian Training School for Teachers from 1908 until 1918.

His career in social work education and administration began after he completed his master's degree. From 1921 to 1922 he was a field agent in the reorganized North Carolina State Board of Charities and Public Welfare. He then served as director of the Division of Institutions for that board from 1922 to 1925, where he collected impressions and evidence for his future writing on poor relief in North Carolina. In the later 1920s he was a research assistant in the Institute for Research in Social Science at The University of North Carolina. In 1930 and 1931 he was engaged in research for President Hoover's Committee on Social Trends.

With the onset of the depression, Brown became more closely associated with the North Carolina welfare agencies. He was a technical supervisor for the governor's Office of Relief (1932–33) and director of social services in the North Carolina Emergency Relief Administration (1933–34). In these roles he was a source of immense strength and technical knowledge for the fledgling agencies attempting to cope with relief problems. He strongly advocated the preservation of the county unit system of welfare and the continuation of the traditional welfare department in an important role. He often found himself in conflict with federal bureaucrats, an attitude reflected in the history of North Carolina welfare he wrote later and left in typescript.

He did staff research on welfare administration in Oklahoma for the Brookings Institution from 1934 to 1935. In 1936 he returned to North Carolina to become director of the Division of Public Welfare and Social Work (now the School of Social Work) at The University of North Carolina; this school had been a pioneer in developing training for public social work, at a time when social work through public charities was still emphasized elsewhere. He held the position until 1945 and was long a close associate of Howard W. Odum. Brown remained a faculty member, retiring as professor emeritus in 1948.

Brown's importance as a consultant and resource for social welfare programs in North Carolina is not adequately reflected in a listing of his official responsibilities. Continuously active in public affairs and the promotion of social responsibility and interracial cooperation, he was early in his life secretary of the "People of Watauga County" (1914–17), was for about thirty years a member of the executive committee of the North Carolina Commission on Interracial Cooperation, and was a member of the North Carolina Conference for Social Service (beginning in 1914 and serving as president in 1943–44) and of the executive committee of the American Association of Schools of Social Work. From 1914 to 1920 he served as a member of the Boone School Board, and in 1923–24 he was alderman of the town of Cary. He was also a member of the Board of Public Welfare of Orange County.

Brown's publications included *Public Poor Relief in North Carolina* (The University of North Carolina Press, 1928), *The North Carolina Chain Gang* (written with J.F. Steiner, The University of North Carolina Press, 1927), and numerous articles and book reviews, including "Education for Public Welfare and Social Work," *Social Forces*, October 1939. After his retirement he began a history of public welfare in North Carolina, never published; the North Carolina Collection of the Library of The University of North Carolina has a typescript. Brown's personal papers are in the Southern Historical Collection there.

Brown married Julia Cole of Chapel Hill in 1906. They had two sons, Thomas Wiley and Francis Battle.

Brown died in Chapel Hill and was buried in the old Chapel Hill Cemetery.

SEE: D. L. Grant, *Alumni History of the University of North Carolina* (1924); Thomas S. Morgan, "A Step toward Altruism" (Ph.D. diss., University of North Carolina, 1969); William S. Powell, ed., *North Carolina Lives* (1962); Raleigh *News and Observer*, 17 Oct. 1962.

THOMAS S. MORGAN

Brown, Thomas (17 Jan. 1744–24 Nov. 1811), Revolutionary War patriot and senator of the North Carolina General Assembly, was born in Bladen County, the son of John and Lucy Bright Brown. His father, the oldest of four sons, was one of the many native Scots who settled along the Cape Fear River.

As early as February 1766, Brown became involved with the movement that was later to produce the American Revolution. He was part of a group of men from Bladen County who attempted to secure a redress of grievances during the Stamp Act troubles. He joined General Hugh Waddell in his expedition against the Regulators, prior to the Battle of Alamance and the joining of Waddell's force with Governor William Tryon's army. In June 1774 a committee of safety was organized for Bladen County with Thomas Brown a member. A year later, after taking an oath of secrecy, he attended in Wilmington a general meeting of the committees of safety in the Wilmington district and signed a bill of association, stating: "We do unite ourselves under every tie of religion and honor, and associate as a band in her defense against every foe; hereby solemnly engaging that whenever our Continental or Provincial councils shall decree it necessary, we will go forth and be ready to sacrifice our lives and fortunes to secure her freedom and safety." As a result, Brown became one of the foremost men of the Cape Fear in pushing forward the Revolution.

In 1775, Brown married Sarah Bartram, whose father, William Bartram, was also a patriot. Fellow patriot Thomas Robeson became Brown's brother-in-law by this union. Sarah bore her husband one daughter, Elizabeth, who, although dying at the age of five, outlived her mother, who died 29 Apr. 1779.

Brown, as lieutenant colonel of the Bladen County militia, distinguished himself highly at the Battle of Moore's Creek Bridge on 23 Feb. 1776. In May of that year he was raised to the rank of colonel and given command of a force of fifteen hundred men recruited from the Wilmington and New Bern districts for the protection of the Cape Fear against the British. With the disappearance of the British fleet from the Cape Fear, Brown's force was disbanded in August, and he returned to Bladen County to help suppress the Tories there. He became a member of the provincial congress that met at Halifax in November 1776 and took part in the formation of the state constitution.

From 1777 to 1781, Brown occupied himself with the control of the Tories in the Bladen County area. After the fall of Charleston to the British and the defeat of General Horatio Gates at Camden, Tory strength increased drastically. With the occupation of Wilmington on 28 Jan. 1781, General Alexander Lillington called for the militia of his district to form a body for opposition to the British. Lillington's forces held the British in their lines until Cornwallis's march down the Cape Fear forced the militia to disband and return to the protection of their home counties. The Cape Fear counties were overrun, devastated, and conquered by the Loyalists. Brown and his Whig followers were driven out of Bladen County and forced to live in the swamps of South Carolina.

In September 1781, Brown and some 150 followers proposed a daring night raid out of South Carolina to attack the Tory force of about 400 men at Elizabethtown. This determined assault was met with considerable resistance by the Loyalist forces, who lost most of their commanding officers without the Whigs suffering a single casualty. This victory disheartened many of the Tories in Bladen and Duplin counties, but it was not until the appearance of Generals Griffith Rutherford and Thomas Butler in October that the Whigs were allowed to control the area.

Brown was wounded on several occasions. He was known for his vigor and enterprise; in his relentless pursuit of Tories, he was an officer who gave no quarter.

After the war, Brown became a major general of the state militia and served in the assembly as a senator in 1785, 1786, and 1788. He also remarried, this time to Lucy Bradley, daughter of Richard and Elizabeth Sharpless Bradley. Of the four children by this union, the youngest daughter, Lucy, later became the wife of Governor John Owen of North Carolina.

Brown died at his residence near Ashwood in Bladen County.

SEE: Samuel A. Ashe, ed., *Biographical History of North Carolina*, vol. 6 (1907); *North Carolina Historical Review* 27 (1950); William L. Saunders and Walter Clark, eds., *Colonial and State Records of North Carolina*, 30 vols.

(1886–1914); Frederick G. Speidel, *North Carolina Masons in the American Revolution* (1975); John H. Wheeler, *History of North Carolina* (1851).

CLAUDE H. SNOW, JR.

Brown, William Albert Gallatin *(23 May 1830–25 Aug. 1906)*, Baptist educator, was born in Blount County, Tenn. His father was Jonathan Brown and his mother Rebecca Bowers Brown. When he was twelve years old, his father moved to Sevier County, Tenn. No church being convenient to the area, meetings were held in the Brown home, and eventually the Sugar Loaf Baptist Church was organized. At the age of twelve, William converted and joined the Nails Creek Baptist Church.

In 1856 he was graduated from Mossy Creek Baptist College (now Carson-Newman College), Jefferson City, Tenn. Immediately after graduation he went to Mars Hill as the first president of the French Broad Baptist Institute, now Mars Hill College. In 1858 he left Mars Hill College and went to Hendersonville to become editor of the *Bapist Telescope*, serving in this position until 1860, when he returned to Mossy Creek Baptist College as a professor of mathematics. In 1861 he resigned from the college to enter the Confederate Army. He served through the Civil War, although wounded at the Battle of Chickamauga. After the war he returned to teaching and for nearly fourteen years, during the trying period of Reconstruction, devoted himself to building and reestablishing the schools in his native Tennessee. In East Tennessee he served, either as founder or as teacher, Mossy Creek Female Institute, Mary Sharp College, Pineville Institute, and Riceville Institute.

When Judson College, Hendersonville, opened on 27 Jan. 1879, Brown was chosen principal and chairman of the faculty. He remained with Judson intermittently until 1887. When, in that year, the citizens of Fairview in Buncombe County erected a modern building and opened Fairview Collegiate Institute, Brown became the first principal and served there two years. He was near the end of his teaching career, since a growing deafness was making teaching increasingly difficult for him, but he did teach a short time in Brevard and later assisted his son Fred in a school at Dewitt in Henderson County. He wrote a great deal of poetry during his later years.

Brown married Margaret Amanda Pattison soon after his graduation from Mossy Creek. They had seven children, five boys and two girls, two of whom died in infancy. Three of the sons, Alfred Erskine, H. Dudley, and Thomas Luther, became ministers; the other son, Frederick Adolphus, and the daughter, Mrs. Sallie Adaline Brown Walker, became teachers. Brown's wife died 31 Jan. 1888. He died at the home of his son T. Luther. His body was returned to Fairview and buried with his wife and son Dudley in the old Cane Creek Cemetery.

SEE: Biography File (Baptist Historical Collection, Wake Forest University, Winston-Salem); John A. McLeod, *From these Stones: Mars Hill College* (1968 [photograph]).

JOHN R. WOODARD

Brown, William Hill *(1765–26 Aug. 1793)*, novelist and poet, was born in Boston, Mass., the son of Gawen Brown, a noted clockmaker, and Elizabeth Hill Adams Brown. At the age of twenty-three, Brown published a novel entitled *The Power of Sympathy*, now generally recognized as the first American novel. Published anonymously, the book related in transparent disguise a sordid story of scandal involving a prominent Boston family. During the next several years he wrote another novel, essays, plays, and poems, some of which were published posthumously.

In the summer of 1792, with the apparent intention of studying law in a climate devoid of the recriminations he had evidently aroused in Boston, Brown moved to North Carolina. He was at Hillsborough by 1 Aug. 1792, on which date he received from merchant Thomas O'Neill a promissory note in the amount of £165.6.3, North Carolina currency. Brown's destination in North Carolina was the village of Murfreesboro, in Hertford County, where O'Neill had a store and where Brown's sister Elizabeth lived with her husband, Murfreesboro merchant John Hichborn, also a Bostonian. Arriving in Murfreesboro before the end of October, Brown soon afterward began reading law with General William R. Davie of Halifax, one of the most eminent lawyers in the state.

Brown seems to have divided his time thereafter between Halifax and Murfreesboro. He made small purchases at the latter town in September 1792 and January 1793. Murfreesboro at this time had a flourishing commerce with northern and West Indian ports and was the scene of much speculation by merchant mariners from Massachusetts and Connecticut. Among these were Joseph Vollentine of Boston, brother-in-law of Brown's sister, Ann, and, until his death in 1792, Eli Foote, grandfather of Harriet Beecher Stowe. In January 1793, Elizabeth Brown Hichborn died at her husband's plantation near Murfreesboro; she was memorialized soon afterward in a poem written by her brother and published in the Halifax *North-Carolina Journal*.

Abraham Hodge, editor of the *Journal*, was evidently one of Brown's closest North Carolina friends. During 1793 the *Journal* carried several poems by Brown and apparently one or more essays as well. The most notable of these pieces was a mock-heroic poem entitled "The Lion and the Tarapen," supposedly based on an actual fight once staged in Halifax between a native terrapin and a menagerie lion. The poem was widely reprinted later.

In August 1793 the seasonal fevers struck as usual in Eastern North Carolina, ravaging especially those not yet acclimated to life in the South. Brown died at Murfreesboro and was probably buried in or near that town; the graves of some of his Hichborn kin are still to be seen at Murfreesboro. He had apparently brought with him from Boston some copies of his first novel, withdrawn from sale in Boston after the uproar it caused; the title was listed among those offered for sale at Henry Wills's bookstore in Edenton in November 1794. Brown's estate was settled by his brother-in-law John Hichborn and by Ellis Gray Blake, another Bostonian who had taken up residence in Murfreesboro; a suit brought by them in Edenton District Superior Court in 1796 sought and obtained payment of debts to Brown incurred in 1792 by Thomas O'Neill and by Andrew Burke, another Hillsborough merchant.

SEE: Edenton *State Gazette of North-Carolina*, 21 Nov. 1794; Halifax *Free Press*, 1 July 1830; J. R. B. Hathaway, ed., *North Carolina Historical and Genealogical Register*, vol. 2 (1901); North Carolina State Archives (Raleigh), for Edenton District Superior Court Papers (Estate Papers) and Unidentified Account Book (Murfreesboro, 1792–96); R. Walser, "The North Carolina Sojourn of the First American Novelist," *North Carolina Historical Review* 28 (1951).

THOMAS C. PARRAMORE

Browne, Peter (*ca. 1766–26 Oct. 1833*), counselor at law, was a native of Knockadock in Aberdeenshire, Scotland. He came to America at an early age, destitute of friends and fortune. There seem to be no records pertaining to his early life or formal education. For more than forty years, he was a citizen and resident of North Carolina. The rare endowments of his mind and the method that entered into his arrangements enabled him speedily to rise to eminence in the legal profession and accumulate great wealth. He pursued the practice of law in North Carolina in Windsor and next at Halifax. He was one of two patrons to whom Jonathan Price and John Strother dedicated their map of North Carolina, which appeared in an undated issue and later in one dated 1808. He represented Halifax County in the House of Commons in the General Assembly.

By 1814, Browne had removed his permanent residence to Raleigh, where he bought Wakefield, the colonial residence of the recently deceased Colonel Joel Lane, who figured prominently in the early history of Wake County and in the founding of Raleigh as the state capital. Before Raleigh was established in 1792, Lane's residence was the most important house in the area then known as Bloomsbury or Wake Crossroads. The county seat of Wake was originally Bloomsbury, and the deed for the site of Raleigh was negotiated at Wake Courthouse on Lane's plantation. Although Browne owned the Lane home and grounds only a few years, it was during this time that he damaged his reputation by an unforgettable deed. Finding the Lane burying ground, where the Lanes and many other early citizens were interred, an unprofitable piece of property, he had it plowed up and planted in cabbages. The desecrater was later described by one historian as an able lawyer but a miser and a utilitarian, respecting nothing above its value in dollars and cents.

Browne was listed on the 1814 Wake County Tax Lists as owning 296 acres and three slaves. In 1818 he sold the Lane home and his well-selected library to William Boylan, Raleigh editor and businessman. With an ample fortune and high reputation, he retired from his professional pursuits in his fifties and returned to Scotland to spend his remaining years. After an absence of three years, he returned to the United States, relocated in Raleigh, and resumed his career. In 1821 he accepted the appointment of justice of the peace. He served several times as chairman of Wake County court and was known for deciding cases with unprecedented facility and dispatch: few and brief were the arguments in Wake County court in his day. His extended career in legal and professional capacities included leadership in advocacy of internal improvements and service as head of the bar.

For a number of years, Browne was one of the leading stockholders of the State Bank of North Carolina, which had its principal branch in Raleigh. After serving as director in 1830 and early 1831, he was unanimously elected president to succeed Duncan Cameron, who had resigned. Browne remained president until his death. He was unmarried and left no relatives in the United States to inherit his large fortune, but a nephew in Scotland inherited half a million dollars from the estate. In 1834 his stock was sold to the highest bidder at the door of the Bank of North Carolina by the administrator, William Boylan.

Although portions of Browne's life are unrecorded, and although he was called a desecrater, he was recognized in North Carolina as one of the great lawyers of his time, along with such men as Edmund Badger, Thomas Ruffin, and Duncan Cameron. He was buried in Raleigh's City Cemetery, where a stately monument was erected to him by his nephew, Robert Simpson of Scotland. The monument did not escape desecration: some years ago, a vandal with a knowledge of stonecutting added two figures to the inscription of his age, which now reads, "aged 6711 years." Still later, vandalism reduced the table-like monument to a slab on the ground.

Two portraits of Browne exist and hang in Hayes Plantation in Edenton. The artist of the original portrait and its history are unknown, but the second portrait was painted by Edward Caledon Bruce in 1859. Bruce evidently copied his portrait from the earlier one.

SEE: Kemp P. Battle, *A Centennial Address, Oct. 18, 1892*; Carrie L. Broughton, ed., *Marriage and Death Notices* (n.d.); Marshall D. Haywood, *Joel Lane* (1900); L. Macmillan, *North Carolina Portrait Index* (1963); *North Carolina Booklet*, vol. 13 (1913); *North Carolina Historical Review* 31 (January 1954); *North Carolina Manual* (1874); North Carolina State Archives (Raleigh), for City Cemetery Index (Raleigh) and Wake County Tax Lists; W. J. Peele, ed., *Lives of Distinguished North Carolinians* (1908); *Raleigh Register*, 10 Dec. 1829, 9 Dec. 1830, 24 Feb. 1831, 7 Dec. 1832, 29 Oct. 1833, 12 Nov. 1834; Southern Historical Collection (University of North Carolina, Chapel Hill); David Lowry Swain, *Early Times in Raleigh* (1867); Tombstone, City Cemetery (Raleigh); Mrs. John Gilliam Wood, personal correspondence.

ELIZABETH E. NORRIS

Browne (Brown), William Garl, Jr. (*Oct. 1823– 28 July 1894*), Victorian portrait painter, was born in England, the son of William G. Browne, Sr., English landscape and genre painter who worked in the United States from about 1837 to about 1861. The younger Browne exhibited a portrait at the National Academy in 1840, shortly after arriving in the United States with his father; he is believed to have lived in New York during this period. In 1846, "William G. Brown, of London" advertised a portrait-painting studio at 146 Main Street, Richmond, Va., in the *Richmond Whig*. Browne earned instant, national fame through the public exhibition of a collection of portraits of General Zachary Taylor and his staff, painted at U.S. Army headquarters in Mexico during the summer of 1847. The portraits were shown in Washington, New York, and Baltimore in the fall of 1847 and received critical acclaim in major newspapers for their lifelikeness. With a national reputation at the age of twenty-four, Browne chose to spend his career in the South. Several hundred portraits of southern subjects are known (see the *catalogue raisonné* at the North Carolina Museum of Art), and at his death it was estimated that he had painted over a thousand portraits during his sojourn in North Carolina alone; but the full extent of his oeuvre remains a mystery because of his itinerant career.

During the 1850s, Browne traveled throughout the South, apparently without a permanent home. He must have worked extensively in North Carolina, for a large number of signed and dated portraits of North Carolina subjects remain from this period. The Federal Writers' Project (1942), *Raleigh, Capital of North Carolina*, states that Browne opened a studio on New Bern Avenue in 1860, and according to the artist's obituary in the Richmond *Times*, he resided in North Carolina during the war. Numerous signed and dated portraits of North Carolinians are extant from the war period, also. Browne is said to have been the designer of the North Carolina state flag, created during the constitutional convention of 1861, and he must therefore have had access to Raleigh at that time. According to Grimes family tradition, Browne had a studio in the backyard of the William Grimes home in the 400 block of Halifax Street, Raleigh, in about 1865. There are only two documented references to a Browne residence in Raleigh: in 1872 he advertised in the *Daily Sentinel*, a Raleigh newspaper, "Life-size pictures painted from life, Photographs or Daguerotypes," executed in his studio at 15 Fayetteville Street; and the Raleigh city directory of 1875–76 listed his studio and home as 13 Fayetteville Street.

The artist seems to have added the final "e" to his name in later life, for references from 1846 and 1847 and the Raleigh references of 1872 and 1875–76 spell his name "Brown." Sources conflict concerning the number and identity of Browne's wives. His obituary states that he had two wives: the first a Lynchburg woman who died soon after their marriage and the second a Miss Seabrook. Other sources mention only one wife, Mary McFeely of Charleston, whom he supposedly married in 1876. All sources agree that he had four children.

Browne set up a studio on Franklin Street, Richmond, and painted there from the 1880s to 1894, when he died during a visit with his sister in Buffalo, New York. He was buried in Forest Lawn Cemetery in Buffalo.

Famous for his warm and richly executed portraits of social, military, and political personages of his era, Browne painted in a fluid, realistic style that contrasted sharply with the naive techniques of most of the American portraitists who were his contemporaries. Browne left portraits of North Carolinians signed and dated from the 1840s through the 1880s, which are now owned by private individuals, usually descendants of the subjects, throughout the state and by institutions including the North Carolina Supreme Court, the North Carolina Division of Archives and History, the North Carolina Museum of Art, the Chapel Hill and Greensboro branches of The University of North Carolina, Davidson College, and Wake Forest University. His subjects, men and women prominent in state affairs, include Governor and Mrs. John Motley Morehead, Willie Person Mangum, Mr. and Mrs. Edwin Michael Holt, David F. Caldwell, Governor and Mrs. William A. Graham, Governor James Iredell, Richmond Pearson, Bartholomew F. Moore, Robert Strange, and many others. The known extent of Browne's oeuvre is constantly being enlarged through research, and his position as one of North Carolina's best known and most significant nineteenth-century artists is firmly secured.

SEE: Advertising circular of 1847 announcing public exhibition of Browne's paintings (possession of Mr. and Mrs. William B. Lucas, Eden); *Chataigne's Raleigh City Directory, 1875–76*; W. R. Edmonds and D. L. Corbitt, *The North Carolina State Flag* (1966); Federal Writers' Project, *Raleigh, Capital of North Carolina* (1942); George C. Groce and David H. Wallace, *The New-York Historical Society's Dictionary of Artists in America, 1584–1860* (1957); Cuthbert Lee, *Portrait Register*, vol. 1 (1968); L. MacMillan, *North Carolina Portrait Index* (1963); National Portrait Gallery (Washington, D.C.) for the entry on Browne from the Catalogue of American Portraits; North Carolina Museum of Art (Raleigh), for the catalogue raisonné prepared by R. Little-Stokes; Raleigh *Daily Sentinel*, 18 Dec. 1872; Raleigh *News and Observer*, 23 Nov. 1969; Richmond *Times*, 31 July 1894 (obit.); *Richmond Whig*, 8 May–17 June 1846; Valentine Museum, *Richmond Portraits in an Exhibition of Makers of Richmond* (1949); A. W. Weddell, *Portraiture in the Virginia Historical*

Society (1945); Westmoreland Club, Richmond, Va., 1916 Yearbook.

R. LITTLE-STOKES

Bruner, James Dowden (*19 May 1864–6 Apr. 1945*), educator and college administrator, was born in Leitchfield, Ky., the son of Isaac Willis and Maggie Ellen Rogers Bruner. The recipient of an early classical education, he was awarded degrees by Franklin (Ind.) College (A.B., 1888) and by Johns Hopkins University (Ph.D., 1894). He pursued additional studies in linguistics in universities in Paris and Bologna in 1892–93, and was awarded the honorary Litt.D. by Georgetown (Ky.) College in 1917.

Bruner taught Latin at Georgetown College in 1885–86 and French and German at Franklin College from 1887 to 1889. He was principal of Cary's Boy's School, Baltimore, Md., prior to his appointment as assistant professor of romance languages at the University of Illinois in 1893. He left this latter position in 1895 to become assistant professor of romance languages and literature at the University of Chicago. There he advanced to the rank of associate professor and served two years as the acting head of his department.

In 1905, Bruner became associate professor of romance languages and chairman of the department at The University of North Carolina. After four years there, he was elected to succeed John C. Scarborough as president of Chowan Baptist Female Institute, Murfreesboro, in July 1909. Under his administrative leadership, the trustees of the institute approved the change of its name to Chowan College; the state legislature allowed charter changes that enabled the granting of the standard A.B. degree, with the first such degrees awarded in 1911. Bruner earned the plaudits of the institution's board of trustees for his success in securing pledges of financial aid to the debt-ridden college and for an ambitious plan aimed at securing a sizeable general endowment.

His report to the college's board of trustees in May 1913 noted a greatly expanded curriculum, including the addition of instruction in the German and French languages, and a record enrollment of 150 during the previous academic year. One year later, however, Bruner submitted his resignation in the wake of rumors attributing to him certain unspecified moral indiscretions. The college's board of trustees accepted his resignation, after refusing to prefer charges against him or to be a party to any investigation of his conduct.

Returning to his native Kentucky, Bruner was elected president of Daughter's College, Harrodsburg, holding that office from 1915 to 1917. He subsequently taught languages at Kentucky State Normal School, Richmond (1917–21), Shurtleff (Ill.) College (1921–22), Carson-Newman (Tenn.) College (1922–27), and Tennessee State Teacher's College (1927–33). His retirement years were spent in Virginia, California, and Tennessee.

Bruner was the author of *The Pistoiese Dialect* (1894), *Studies in Victor Hugo's Dramatic Characters* (1908), and numerous magazine articles on philological and literary subjects. He also prepared and published editions of Chateaubriand's *Les Aventures du Dernier Abencerage* (1903), Feuillet's *Le Jeune Homme Pauvre* (1904), Hugo's *Hernani* (1906), Corneille's *Le Cid* (1908), Racine's *Iphigenie, Andromaque and Phèdre* (1921), and *Esther and Athalie* (1929). A revision of his edition of *Hernani* appeared in 1932.

A Democrat and a Baptist, Bruner married Elizabeth Cutting Cooley (d. 9 Apr. 1931) on 19 Dec. 1894. To them were born three sons, James Willis, Arthur Cutting, and

Lee Moulton. In 1935, Bruner married Helen Cooley McNitt, a niece of the first Mrs. Bruner.

Bruner was buried in Highland Memorial Cemetery, Knoxville, Tenn.

SEE: Minutes of the Board of Trustees of Chowan College (Murfreesboro) 1909–14; *Who Was Who in America*, vol. 4 (1968).

R. HARGUS TAYLOR

Bruner, John Joseph (12 Mar. 1817–23 Mar. 1890), newspaper editor, was born on the Yadkin River near Salisbury in Rowan County. His father, Henry Bruner, a gunsmith by trade, died when John Joseph was two. His mother, a granddaughter of Colonel West Harris of the Continental Army, returned to her home in Montgomery County with her three children. When Bruner was eight years of age, he returned to Salisbury under the guardianship of his uncle, Charles Fisher, attended school for one year, and then, at age nine, became an apprentice at the printing office of the *Western Carolinian*. The *Carolina Watchman* was established in 1832 to support Andrew Jackson's anti-Nullification policies and Whigism in general; Bruner became an employee of the *Watchman* at age thirteen, a part owner at twenty-two, and the sole owner in 1850, at thirty-three. His association with the *Watchman* was not continuous, but as often as he sold it to seek other ventures, he just as often returned and repurchased it.

Bruner's business acumen enabled him to make a comfortable living as a newspaper publisher and job printer. With the coming of the Civil War he became an ardent Confederate and exhorted his readers to put forth a greater effort to win the war. Like other newspaper editors of his day, he did not consider derogatory news about Salisbury or the Confederacy worthy of printing. His goal was to advocate and support whatever he thought was in the best interest of the public, and service to the public may be said to have been his formula for success as a newspaper publisher, both before and after the Civil War. He was among the foremost progressive leaders in Western North Carolina during the mid-nineteenth century. Bruner's example of a self-made man spoke forcefully to the common man, who could understand and respect individual achievement. His forthright approach and appeal to the public's common sense accounted for his effectiveness. It was said that over fifty newspapers sprang up as competitors during his lifetime, but they never succeeded in harming the *Watchman*, whose circulation at one time seems to have extended to approximately fifty counties in North Carolina. In his later years, as the oldest editor of one of the oldest newspapers in North Carolina, he was often called "Father Bruner" by fellow editors.

Bruner was an elder in the Presbyterian church; the "Protestant work ethic" may have motivated his continual efforts to better himself and the community.

In 1843, Bruner married Mary Ann Kincaid, granddaughter of Revolutionary War Colonel James Brandon. To this union thirteen children were born, five of whom grew to maturity. Perhaps the most famous of these was Thomas K., who for many years was the state secretary of agriculture and mining.

SEE: Hope Summerell Chamberlain, *This Was Home* (1938); Jethro Rumple, *A History of Rowan County* (1881); Salisbury *Carolina Watchman* under Bruner's editorship; Scrapbook (possession of Mrs. T. H. Miller, Statesville).

LOUIS A. BROWN

Bruton, John Fletcher (29 May 1861–26 Mar. 1946), lawyer, educator, banker, civic leader, and churchman, was born at Wentworth in Rockingham County, a son of the Reverend David Rasberry Bruton and his wife, Margaret Nixon, both notable in private education. After graduation from the Bingham Academy, Bruton moved to Wilson in the autumn of 1881 as a teacher in the Wilson Graded School. Although elevated to the rank of superintendent in June 1883, he soon afterward entered The University of North Carolina Law School and then, in the latter part of 1884, secured his license.

Returning to Wilson, he practiced for nearly two years in partnership with John Exum Woodard before establishing an independent practice, which he maintained for the remainder of his long career. Although he was never a candidate for political office, many honors resulted from the public confidence in his dedication to principle. From 1894 to 1897 he served as mayor of Wilson. He became vice-president and attorney of the First National Bank in 1897 (serving as its president from 1904 to 1932), and in the same year he was one of the organizers of the North Carolina Bankers Association, of which he was later a president. Bruton was a director of the Federal Reserve Bank in Richmond for ten years and was subsequently a member of the Federal Advisory Council to the Federal Reserve Board. He was a director and attorney for the Wilson Home and Loan Association for forty-five years and for a considerable time the president of the Wilson Trust and Savings Bank. He was a director and vice-president of the North Carolina Home Insurance Company and also served on the board of directors of the Carolina Telephone and Telegraph Company. For three years he was chairman of the Wilson County Board of Education.

In 1889, Bruton organized and was elected captain of Company F, Second Regiment of the North Carolina State Guard. Three years later he was commissioned colonel of the regiment, but the pressure of business commitments forced his resignation in 1900. He expressed a continuing interest in education by taking an active part in the founding of the Kinsey Female Seminary in 1897 (known as Atlantic Christian College since 1902). In 1900 he was elected a trustee of Trinity College, becoming chairman of the board in 1912. He continued as chairman of the board of trustees of Duke University from 1927 until his death. For more than fifty years he served on the board of the Wilson Methodist Church and also taught the Bible class that still bears his name.

On 15 Nov. 1887, Bruton was united in marriage by his father to Hattie Tartt Barnes (12 June 1863–10 Nov. 1954), daughter of John Thomas Barnes and his wife, Elizabeth Obedience Tartt. Bruton and his wife died in Wilson and were buried in Maplewood Cemetery, survived by two sons: John Barnes (28 Oct. 1888–27 Jan. 1960), who married Gladys Smith; and Howard Barnes (1 Nov. 1893–11 July 1971), who married Almira Woodard.

There is a portrait of Bruton in the Wilson County Courthouse.

SEE: *Who's Who in America*, 1928; *Wilson Daily Times*, 4 Dec. 1950, 18 Dec. 1951.

HUGH B. JOHNSTON, JR.

Bryan, Charles Shepard (16 Nov. 1865–28 Mar. 1956), army officer and financier, was the son of James Augustus Bryan and Mary Spaight Shepard, grandson of Congressman Charles Biddle Shepard and Mary Spaight Donnell, great-grandson of Judge John Robert

Donnell and Margaret Elizabeth Spaight, great-great-grandson of Governor Richard Dobbs Spaight, Sr., and Mary Leech, and great-great-great-grandson of Colonel Joseph Leech and Mary Jones. He was born in New York City, where his parents lived for a brief time, and was christened at Calvary Church by the Reverend Dr. Francis L. Hawks. He grew up in New Bern and went to Princeton College, where he was graduated in 1887 with the A.B. degree. Much of his adult life was spent in New York City, where he was a member of a firm on the stock exchange. In 1908 he sold his membership on the exchange and engaged in the fertilizer business. In 1916 he was commissioned second lieutenant in the Ordnance Department, and early in World War I he served for sixteen months with the French army. For gallantry in the Battle of Verdun he won the Distinguished Service Cross, Croix de Guerre with palm, and Military Cross of the Legion d'Honneur. For the remainder of the war he served as a colonel in the ordnance branch of the U.S. Army. He was graduated from the Army War College in 1923 and retired from army service in 1931.

Following his retirement, he lived in Asheville. He continued to own the land on which the Cherry Point Marine Air Station is now located. He undertook family genealogical research and historical writing and restored the Spaight cemetery at the old Clermont plantation near New Bern, erecting a tablet with the names and birth and death years of the eleven Spaight and Leech family connections buried there.

Bryan was a Mason for sixty years and was a member of the Sulgrave Institute and the University Club of New York City.

On 6 Feb. 1889 he married Annie Adams MacWhorter (20 Oct. 1866–28 Dec. 1940) of Augusta, Ga. They were the parents of one son, Gray MacWhorter, and two daughters, Mary Spaight Shepard (Mrs. Harold Hartshore) and Margaret Donnell. After Bryan's death in Asheville, his cremated remains were interred with Masonic honors in his father's lot in Cedar Grove Cemetery, New Bern.

SEE: Bryan Family Records (in possession of Charles Hall Ashford, Jr., New Bern); Minutes of St. John's Lodge, No. 3, A.F. & A.M. (New Bern); Tombstones, Cedar Grove Cemetery (New Bern); Emma Morehead Whitfield, comp., and Theodore Marshall Whitfield, ed., *Whitfield, Bryan, Smith and Related Families*, bk. 2 (1950).

GERTRUDE S. CARRAWAY

Bryan, Henry H. (d. 7 May 1835), congressman, was born in Martin County and attended local schools before moving to Tennessee. He married Milly Taylor 13 June 1799; they were the parents of a son and a daughter, Henry H. and Mariana T., who married William Dortch. In Tennessee, Bryan held several local offices and on 21 May 1808 was commissioned captain of the Twenty-fourth Regiment, Tennessee Militia (Montgomery County). On 29 Dec. 1808 he was promoted to first major.

Bryan was elected to the U.S. House of Representatives from Montgomery County, Tenn., in 1818 and served in the Sixteenth Congress (1819–21). He was appointed to the Committee on Private Land Claims and is recorded as introducing three petitions: two from constituents seeking compensation and one for a post road in Montgomery County. There is no further record of any action taken by him in Congress. He was reelected to the following session but did not qualify.

Bryan died in Montgomery County, the owner of eleven slaves and extensive property. His sole heir was

his daughter, but at a sale of some of his possessions, five different persons named Bryan made purchases.

SEE: *Biog. Dir. Am. Cong.* (1971); Bryan's will (Clarksville, Tenn.); Mrs. John Trotwood Moore, comp., *Record of Commissions of Officers in the Tennessee Militia, 1796 to 1811*, vol. 1 (1947); *U.S. House of Representatives Journal*, 1819–21; *Who Was Who in America, 1607–1896*.

H. JAMES HUTCHESON

Bryan, Henry Ravenscroft (8 Mar. 1836–14 Feb. 1919), attorney and judge, was born in New Bern, the sixth son of John Heritage Bryan and his wife, Mary Williams Shepard. Bryan's paternal grandparents were James and Rachel Heritage Bryan; James West Bryan was his uncle. His maternal grandparents were William and Mary Blount Shepard. Shepard, uncle of Nicholas Biddle, chief officer of the Bank of the United States, was a principal owner of the privateer *Snap Dragon*, made famous by Captain Otway Burns during the War of 1812.

John Heritage Bryan moved his family from New Bern to Raleigh in 1838 so that the eight sons might be closer to Chapel Hill and the daughters could attend St. Mary's School. The father practiced law at Raleigh.

Henry Ravenscroft Bryan (the middle name honoring the late Right Reverend John Stark Ravenscroft [1772–1830], first bishop of the Episcopal Diocese of North Carolina) attended the Raleigh Classical, Mathematical and Military Academy and then in 1856 was graduated with first and second honors and an A.B. degree from The University of North Carolina, delivering the Latin salutatory. The next year he was licensed to practice law in the county courts.

Prevented by an incurable physical disability from active participation in the Civil War, although an ardent supporter of the Confederacy, Bryan refuged with his family upstate. He returned home after the conflict and during the Reconstruction era defended many leading citizens of Craven and Lenoir counties, on trial for alleged 1868 Ku Klux Klan offenses.

Among Bryan's offices were vestryman (for fifty years) and junior warden of Christ Episcopal Church, University of North Carolina trustee, federal court clerk, justice of the peace, attorney for the Atlantic and North Carolina Railroad Company and the Craven County board of commissioners, city attorney and mayor of New Bern, director on the board of the state penitentiary, presidential elector, and judge of the superior courts. When he retired in 1907, after sixteen years on the bench, he wrote: "I served the state during my term to the best of my ability, and endeavored to administer justice without fear, favor or affection. I have never in that high and responsible office done other than my duty as I understood it."

Following Bryan's death in New Bern and burial there in Cedar Grove Cemetery, the General Assembly adopted a resolution of respect praising his "patriotic interest in public affairs" during his judgeship and adding that he upheld "with dignity, ability and great learning the loftiest traditions and ideals of that court." Memorial Hall at Chapel Hill has a tablet honoring him. A memorial tablet and his portrait are in the courtroom of the Craven County courthouse.

Bryan married Mary Biddle Norcott (11 Mar. 1841–21 May 1925) at New Bern on 24 Nov. 1859. Surviving him and his wife were three sons and five daughters: Sarah Frances (Mrs. John B. Broadfoot); Frederick Charles; Mary Norcott (Mrs. H. A. London); Henry R., Jr.; Shepard; Kate (Mrs. F. S. Duffy); Margaret Shepard; and Isabel Constance (Mrs. Edwin H. Jordan).

SEE: Bryan Family Records (in possession of Charles H. Ashford, Jr., New Bern); *North Carolina Manual* (1913); Emma Morehead Whitfield, comp., and Theodore Marshall Whitfield, ed., *Whitfield, Bryan, Smith and Related Families*, bk. 2 (1950).

GERTRUDE S. CARRAWAY

Bryan, James Augustus *(13 Sept. 1839–30 Jan. 1923)*, soldier, planter, and banker, was born in New Bern to James West Bryan and Ann Mary Washington. A grandson of James Bryan and Rachel Heritage and of John Washington and Elizabeth Heritage Cobb, he was also a nephew of John Heritage Bryan and a brother of Washington Bryan.

During the Civil War, Bryan was a major in the Confederate Army. Returning to his native town after the war, he became an extensive landowner, especially in James City, a settlement across Trent River from New Bern (a native told a newcomer, "Everything there not always belonging to God is now owned by Jim Bryan"). For some time, Bryan was president of the state-controlled Atlantic and North Carolina Railroad Company. From 1880 until his death he was president of the National Bank of New Bern.

In 1884 he bought the historic John Wright Stanley house, which he renovated and enlarged as his residence on its original site; after his death it was moved to make way for a new post office and federal building.

As a Democrat, Bryan was elected to the 1899 state senate and was instrumental in helping relieve Craven County from Reconstruction policies. That assembly established the modern spelling of New Bern; the final "e," Bryan and his associates claimed, had been erroneously added by northern soldiers occupying the city in Civil War years.

Bryan's first wife was Mary Spaight Shepard (18 Mar. 1843–1 Jan. 1892), whom he married 2 Nov. 1864 at Raleigh. She was a daughter of Congressman Charles Biddle Shepard and Mary Spaight Donnell, a granddaughter of Judge John Robert Donnell and Margaret Elizabeth Spaight, and a great-granddaughter of Governor Richard Dobbs Spaight and Mary Leech. James A. and Mary S. Bryan were the parents of Charles Shepard. All three were buried in Cedar Grove Cemetery, New Bern.

Bryan's second wife was Julia Rush Olmstead (30 Aug. 1843–22 May 1915), a descendant of Richard Stockton, New Jersey lawyer and signer of the Declaration of Independence. His third and surviving wife was Alice Hilliard Brown Biddle (9 April 1856–30 Dec. 1938), widow of Sheriff James Williams Biddle of New Bern.

SEE: Bryan Family Records (in possession of Charles H. Ashford, Jr., New Bern); Craven County Records (North Carolina State Archives, Raleigh); Tombstones, Cedar Grove Cemetery (New Bern).

GERTRUDE S. CARRAWAY

Bryan, James West *(7 Nov. 1805–28 Sept. 1864)*, attorney and legislator, was born in New Bern to James Bryan (1769–1806) and Rachel Heritage Bryan (1782–1842), who after her first husband's death was married 1 Oct. 1807 to Dr. Frederick Blount. John Heritage Bryan, a brother, born 4 Nov. 1798 at New Bern, was also a lawyer and statesman. He moved in 1838 to Raleigh, where he died 19 May 1870, with interment in Oakwood Cemetery. This branch of Bryans is said to have come to Craven County from Nansemond County, Va., in 1747.

In 1824, James West Bryan was graduated from The University of North Carolina. A classmate was William Alexander Graham, who became speaker of the state House of Commons, U.S. senator, governor of North Carolina, and secretary of the navy. The two friends married sisters, daughters of John Washington and Elizabeth Heritage Cobb Washington, who had moved to New Bern from Kinston. Bryan married Ann Mary Washington (19 Jan. 1814–29 Sept. 1864) on 19 Jan. 1831 at Christ Episcopal Church in New Bern. The bride was a Baptist but in 1839 joined her husband's church. He served as a vestryman and secretary of the vestry. Twin stained-glass windows, with the Bryan coat-of-arms, memorialize them in the church.

A Whig in politics, Bryan represented Carteret County at the 1835 state constitutional convention and in the state senate in 1835 and 1836. From 1835 to 1856 he was trustee of The University of North Carolina.

For some time, Bryan's family resided in the brick mansion started in 1803 by his father, who had died before it was completed. During the Civil War, Bryan died at Baltimore, Md.; his wife died the next day. Both were buried in Cedar Grove Cemetery, New Bern. Their surviving children were James Augustus (1839–1923); Washington, who married Mary Winder; and Laura (1837–68), who married Dr. James Bettner Hughes.

SEE: Bryan Family Records (in possession of Charles H. Ashford, Jr., New Bern); Gertrude S. Carraway, *Crown of Life: History of Christ Church, New Bern* (1940); Christ Church Records (New Bern); Craven County Records (North Carolina State Archives, Raleigh); *North Carolina Manual* (1913); Tombstones, Cedar Grove Cemetery (New Bern); Max R. Williams and J. G. deRoulhac Hamilton, eds., *The Papers of William Alexander Graham*, vol. 5 (1973).

GERTRUDE S. CARRAWAY

Bryan, John Herritage (Heritage) *(4 Nov. 1798–19 May 1870)*, lawyer and congressman, was born in New Bern, the son of James (1776–1806) and Rachel Heritage Bryan. He attended New Bern Academy, received the bachelor's and master's degrees from The University of North Carolina (1815 and 1820), studied law, and was admitted to the bar in 1819. On 20 Dec. 1821 he married Mary Williams Shepard, daughter of a New Bern merchant. He served as a member of the state senate in 1823 and 1824. In the latter year he worked for the ticket of Jackson and Calhoun, against that of W. H. Crawford.

In 1825 he defeated Old Republican Richard Dobbs Spaight in the election to represent the New Bern District in Congress. He was reelected without opposition in 1827. While in Washington, he was a steady supporter of the policies of President John Quincy Adams. He served in the House on the committees on Elections, the District of Columbia, and Roads and Canals. After the election of Jackson in 1828, Bryan declined to run for Congress again. When he returned home, he was active in opposition to Jackson and in the organization of the Whig party in his area.

After a decade of strenuous professional practice in the tidewater section, Bryan's health began to fail, and during the winter of 1828 he moved to Raleigh. Here he gradually abandoned his law practice but continued a busy life. He played a role in the affairs of the Whig party before the Civil War and was opposed to secession in 1860. He was an active Episcopal layman and during the fifties was secretary of the state Agricultural Society. In 1847 he was a member of the committee that welcomed President Polk to Raleigh. He was interested in internal improvements. For forty-five years he was trustee of The University of North Carolina, and for many of these years he served on the executive committee.

Bryan and his wife had a family of fourteen children. Seven of the sons graduated at Chapel Hill. One son, George, a captain in the Confederate service, died defending Richmond in 1864.

The war did great harm to the family business interests, and Bryan's health declined rapidly after 1868. He died in Raleigh and was interred in Oakwood Cemetery.

SEE: *Biog. Dir. Am. Cong.* (1971); Henry E. Bryan, "John Herritage Bryan" (Manuscript Department, Library, Duke University, Durham); John Herritage Bryan Collection (North Carolina State Archives, Raleigh).

DANIEL M. MC FARLAND

Bryan, Joseph Hunter *(1782–January 1840)*, congressman and planter, was born in Windsor, Bertie County. He represented Bertie in the House of Commons in 1804, 1805, 1807, 1808, and 1809. He was a trustee of The University of North Carolina from 1809 to 1817. In 1810 he was defeated in an attempt to gain the Halifax District seat in Congress from the incumbent, Willis Alston; but after Alston decided to step down in 1814, Bryan again became a candidate and defeated Thomas Burgess, Federalist, by over two hundred votes.

Bryan served two terms in Congress, from March 1815 to March 1819. While in Washington, he formed close friendships with Philip P. Barbour and John Randolph of Virginia and joined them in opposition to all measures increasing the powers of the central government, such as the federal bank, tariffs, and internal improvements. One of his last votes in Congress was against the amendment to the Missouri Bill introduced by James Tallmadge of New York, which would have prohibited further introduction of slaves into Missouri. In 1819 he did not run for reelection and Hutchins G. Burton was elected to take his seat from the Halifax District.

Soon after he retired from Congress, Bryan moved to Granville County, where he had acquired property. He continued active in politics and was suggested as a candidate for governor in 1821, 1824 and 1832. He was frequently mentioned in the press of the time as a leader of the faction of Richard Dobbs Spaight, Romulus M. Saunders, and the Old Republicans. He was active in the Jackson campaigns of 1824 and 1828 and was a delegate to the 1832 Democratic convention in Baltimore that nominated Jackson and Van Buren.

The trustees of The University of North Carolina appointed Bryan and Archibald D. Murphey as their agents in a dispute over claims to escheated military bounty lands in Tennessee. An agreement was reached on 26 Aug. 1822, and both agents received grants of land as part payment for their services. Bryan must have moved to Tennessee in about 1835. He died there at La Grange, Fayette County.

SEE: *Biog. Dir. Am. Cong.* (1971); William Henry Hoyt, ed., *The Papers of Archibald D. Murphey,* vol. 1 (1914); *Raleigh Register,* 24 Jan. 1840.

DANIEL M. MC FARLAND

Bryan, Joseph Shepard *(24 Aug. 1894–3 Nov. 1974)*, educator and lawyer, was born in Wilmington, the only son of Robert Kedar Bryan, Jr., and Gertrude Foy Shepard Bryan. He had one sister, Gertrude, who married lawyer Edward M. Toon. His mother was the daughter of Wilmington physician J. C. Shepard; his father was a Pender County planter and lawyer who served for many years as chairman of the county board of education. His grandfather, Robert Kedar Bryan, Sr. (1827–98), was a newspaper editor.

J. Shepard Bryan received a liberal education from Horner Military Academy in Oxford and in 1915 was graduated from The University of North Carolina. For the next twenty-two years, he dedicated his efforts to the advancement of public education. His first employment (1915–16) was as principal of a junior high school in Greensboro, Fla. He returned to North Carolina and served from 1916 to 1920 as principal of Hemenway Grammar School in Wilmington. For a brief period in 1917, he trained at First Officers' Training Camp at Fort Oglethorpe, Ga., but after his discharge for physical disability, he contributed to the war effort as a speaker and as chairman of the Junior Red Cross Division in Wilmington.

From 1920 to 1926, Bryan was principal of Wilson High School. In 1923 the school moved into new facilities that provided modern equipment for science, home economics, athletics, and other subjects. The high school achieved state-wide recognition for its diverse curriculum, qualified teaching staff, and student scholarship. Bryan's educational philosophy and administrative techniques were greatly influenced during this period by his friend and mentor, Wilson Superintendent Charles L. Coon.

Bryan was appointed in 1926 as superintendent of Dunn city schools, and for eleven years he sought to improve the course of study, the caliber of teaching, and the level of scholarship. While he was Dunn superintendent, Bryan studied law at Wake Forest College and was admitted to the bar in 1933. In 1934 he became Dunn city attorney, and in 1937 he retired from school work to enter full-time law practice. He acted as solicitor of Dunn's recorder's court and as president of the Harnett County Bar Association.

Bryan was a noted leader in community affairs and an active lay leader in the Methodist Episcopal Church, South. He served on the board of directors of the North Carolina League of Municipalities and was a district chairman of the Morehead Scholarship Fund. He was elected in 1937 as governor of District 188 of Rotary International and, during that year, attended meetings of the organization held in Switzerland and France. He was a member of the Kiwanis Club, the Junior Order of United American Mechanics, and the Democratic party.

On 27 Dec. 1921, Bryan was married to Anna Cavanaugh, with whom he later had two sons, Joseph Shepard, Jr., and Robert Cavanaugh.

Bryan died in Dunn at age eighty of a heart ailment, and burial took place at Greenwood Cemetery.

SEE: Charles L. Coon Papers (Southern Historical Collection, University of North Carolina, Chapel Hill; State Superintendent of Public Instruction Papers, North Carolina State Archives, Raleigh); Dunn *Dispatch,* 5 Nov. 1974; *History of North Carolina,* 6 vols. (1919); *North Carolina: Rebuilding an Ancient Commonwealth* (1929); *North Carolina: The Old North State and the New* (1941); Raleigh *News and Observer,* 5 Nov. 1974.

GEORGE-ANNE WILLARD

Bryan, Morgan *(1671–3 Apr. 1763)*, founder of a pioneer clan on the Forks of the Yadkin, was born in

Denmark and came to America from Ireland in 1695 or somewhat later.

By the time of his 1719 marriage to Martha Strode, Bryan owned land in Birmingham Township, Chester County, Pa. Shortly after his marriage, he moved farther west in the county and may then have begun trading activities with the Indians who came to the Conestoga River to exchange furs for goods.

For a time, Bryan lived in what is now Lancaster County, Pa., where he was associated with his younger brother William and the Linville brothers in the Conestoga trade. In the three years prior to 1729, he lived on a 137-acre farm in Marlborough Township, Chester County, among prosperous Quaker farmers.

Although Bryan went to Pennsylvania from northern Ireland under Quaker auspices and was closely associated with prominent Friends during his residence in Pennsylvania and for many years thereafter, he apparently held membership in the society for only a brief period. His only recorded formal affiliation is his listing on the rolls of the New Garden Quaker Meeting of Chester County in 1719.

Bryan's reputed family background suggests conversion to Presbyterianism, a deduction sustained by the fact that his younger brother William—who came to Pennsylvania from northern Ireland in 1718—helped organize the Donegal Presbyterian Church in Lancaster County in 1721–22 and by the fact that Morgan himself invited a Presbyterian minister to hold services at his frontier home in the Shenandoah Valley many years later.

Contact with Indians and white traders from the western hinterlands doubtless stimulated Bryan's interest in the Shenandoah country. With his Quaker friend Alexander Ross he explored the northern gateway to this beautiful valley in 1729. The following year, the pair presented a proposal to the council of Virginia and the governor for a large-scale colonization project. They were granted a one-hundred-thousand-acre tract in the vicinity of the present Winchester. It was stipulated that land patents would be granted within two years to one hundred families and that Bryan and Ross would divide the land in any manner agreeable to the settlers.

Virginia's colonial government had long attempted to discourage western settlement for fear of antagonizing the Indians, but the policy had proved unenforceable; the council apparently decided it wiser to populate the area in an organized way with hard-working Quaker farmers than to try to keep squatters and renegades out. Once the farmers were established, undesirables could be dealt with far more effectively through their local governments than through attempts at control from Williamsburg. Moreover, the Bryan–Ross project would test the validity of Lord Fairfax's claim to the Northern Neck region, which the council disputed.

The settlement venture was eminently successful. Through the 1730s and 1740s, Bryan lived at two or three locations in the region, as the needs of his growing family and his land-trading activities dictated. Real estate speculation seems to have been an important source of his income. As a result, he built less permanently than some of his contemporaries, whose farmsteads have survived to this day. Extending his activities progressively farther south into the valley, Bryan became a man of considerable means and influence. The records of Virginia's original western counties contain many references to his services as justice, surveyor, juror, and road overseer, as well as to his real estate transactions.

As Bryan's older children began forming their own

families, he searched for sufficient unclaimed land to support the future needs of the growing clan. The Shenandoah Valley was rapidly filling with people, and his own success as a promoter contributed to the need to look elsewhere. His sons scouted far to the south, and at length Bryan decided to lead his family to Lord Granville's land south of the Virginia border. Thus, in 1747, he began winding up his business affairs in the valley; in that year he gave power of attorney to a business associate to dispose of his remaining property and collect monies owed him.

Morgan and Martha Bryan, together with all their children and grandchildren, set out on the long journey south in the fall of 1748. The eldest son, Joseph, and his young family may have been left behind temporarily to help tie up loose ends. Also left behind was the grave of the Bryans' second child, Mary, who had died in 1743, a year after the death of her young husband, Thomas Curtis. The Curtis's infant daughter, Mary, left in the care of grandmother Bryan, was among the several young children who endured the long trek to Carolina. The Bryan caravan undoubtedly stayed for a time with Morgan's brother William, who, with his sons, had been the first to settle the present site of Roanoke, Va., in 1745. William, from whom William Jennings Bryan traced his descent, died in 1789 at the age of 104.

The Bryan clan reached the Forks of the Yadkin in the spring of 1749. The patriarchal Morgan was then seventy-eight years of age. Within four or five years, he laid claim to fifteen or more choice tracts within the Granville Grant, totaling several thousand acres. Son-in-law William Linville acquired two thousand acres and Joseph, Samuel, and Morgan, Jr., also purchased substantial acreage. Originally in Anson County, all the Bryan property lay within Rowan County when the latter was formed in 1753.

By the time the Moravians arrived from Pennsylvania in 1752 and selected the 155-square-mile tract that was to become Wachovia, the neighboring area to the west was already known as "the Bryan settlements."

Bryan's extensive purchases reflected not only his desire to acquire a legacy for his unmarried sons but also his intention to continue his activities as a land speculator. His many subsequent land transactions confirm this intent, and Rowan County records suggest that several sons followed their father's example. The heart of the Bryan Settlements described an arc across the northern half of the present Davie County. On the east, the arc anchored on the Yadkin with the property of Samuel Bryan, just south of the "shallow ford" where the "great wagon road" between Wachovia and the new county seat of Salisbury crossed the river. Morgan Bryan's Mansion House was located on Deep Creek about four miles north of the shallow ford.

The Bryans were soon joined in the Forks region by the Carters, Hartfords, Davises, Hugheses, Linvilles, Forbeses, Boones, and others, many of whom they had known in Virginia and Pennsylvania. Along with the heads of some of these families, Bryan played an important part in Rowan County's early government. Staunch Quaker Squire Boone, whose numerous sons included Daniel, served as the county's first justice, and Bryan was a member of the first grand jury.

The population of the Forks region grew rapidly during the 1750s as new families arrived in increasing numbers from the northeast. The decade saw the remainder of the Bryan sons marry and strengthen the clan's influence in the area north of Salisbury. William Bryan, the sixth son, married Squire Boone's daughter Mary. Her brothers Daniel and Edward married Bryan sisters Rebecca and Martha, daughters of Morgan's eldest son, Joseph. A few years later, George, another of Squire Boone's sons, married another of Morgan's granddaughters, Nancy Linville, daughter of William and Eleanor Bryan Linville. These marriages marked the beginning of a remarkable bond between the Bryan and Boone families, which was to persist for nearly a century. Succeeding generations saw several more Boone-Bryan marriages, as well as simultaneous migrations to Kentucky and, later, to Missouri.

The aging Morgan and Martha Bryan lived to see their children firmly established in the growing frontier community. They also survived the terrifying Cherokee raids of 1758–61 and saw their sons take part in the military actions that ultimately quelled the depredations and secured the region. Morgan, Jr., was a militia captain and Thomas an ensign. Sons Samuel, John, William, and James also performed militia service during the short but vicious war, during which hundreds of families fled the region and hundreds more were killed. Bryan and his wife did not live, however, to see the profound influence their children and grandchildren exerted upon local affairs during the tumultuous period of the Revolutionary War, nor the prominent role they played in wresting Kentucky from British-led Indians with the founding of Boonesborough and Bryan's Station.

Eight of the Bryan children survived their parents.

Joseph, father-in-law of Daniel and "Neddy" Boone, participated in his brother William's Kentucky land venture during the Revolution but returned to remain in the Bryan Settlements in Rowan County until about 1798. He was a suspected Loyalist; some of his sons served with local Tory militia and others with rebel irregulars. Joseph died in Kentucky in 1804 or 1805.

Eleanor Bryan Linville, whose husband, William, and son John were killed by Indians while hunting in the Blue Ridge Mountains in 1766, did not remarry; she left the Yadkin area with her married children after the Revolution and died in Kentucky in 1792.

Samuel, who served with distinction as a Loyalist colonel during the war, was tried and sentenced to death but exchanged for a rebel officer. In spite of the bitterness that persisted long after the Revolution, Samuel's personal stature was such that he was allowed to retain most of his property in the Bryan Settlements. He continued to live on the Yadkin until his death in 1798. At least one of his Tory sons moved to upstate New York after the war.

Morgan, Jr., who died in Kentucky around 1800, also helped his brother William establish Bryan's Station. Some of his sons may have served in the Revolution as North Carolina Loyalists, although Morgan and one of his sons are credited with rebel militia service in Kentucky.

James, who also helped found Bryan's Station, became a widower in 1770. His six small children were raised by niece Rebecca Boone and her husband, Daniel. James died in Kentucky in 1807; most of his children went to Missouri in 1800 with their uncle Daniel and his party of Boones, Bryans, and other relatives.

John, who is believed to have lost two Tory sons during the Revolution, farmed his land in the Bryan Settlements throughout his life. He died there in the winter of 1799–1800.

William—the intrepid but tragic "Billy" Bryan whom the Moravians admired—declined the king's commission as lieutenant colonel and instead organized and led the establishment of Bryan's Station (1775–79) near the present Lexington, Ky. He was killed there by

Indians in May 1780. Only weeks before his death, he lost a son in a similar Shawnee ambush near the station. A few months earlier, he had learned that most of his Kentucky land claims were invalid. William and two of his sons—branded as Tories in Rowan County—were credited with rebel service for having participated in militia actions against Kentucky's Indians.

Thomas, youngest of the children, shared his brothers' interest in Kentucky and is believed to have fitted out one of Daniel Boone's early expeditions. He saw service in the Rowan County militia prior to the Revolution and is thought to have had strong Loyalist sentiments. Thomas inherited his father's Deep Creek property but sold it to his brother William and was living elsewhere in the Settlements at the time of his death in 1777. One of his sons seems to have been killed in the war as a Tory officer. His widow, Sarah Hunt Bryan, later married the Reverend John Gano and moved with him to Kentucky in 1789.

Morgan Bryan, patriarch of the families that helped open Western Carolina and Kentucky to settlement, died on Easter Sunday 1763, at the age of ninety-two. Martha Strode Bryan had died a few months earlier, in August 1762. Both Morgan and his wife are believed to have been buried on their Deep Creek property. Martha Bryan's tombstone was found during the construction of a highway in northeastern Davie County many years ago and is now in the Rowan Museum at Salisbury.

SEE: Lyman Chalkley, comp., *Chronicles of the Scotch-Irish Settlement . . . from the . . . Records of Augusta County, Va., 1745–1800* (1966); Robert O. DeMond, *The Loyalists in North Carolina* (1940); J. F. Dorman, *Abstracts, Orange County (Virginia) Will Book I* (1966); Draper MS Collection (Wisconsin State Historical Society, Madison); Adelaide L. Fries, ed., *Records of the Moravians in North Carolina*, 8 vols. (1922–54); Handwritten copy of deposition signed by Samuel and Mary Hunt Bryan in 1830 in connection with Revolutionary War pension application (North Carolina State Archives, Raleigh); Historical Society of Pennsylvania (Philadelphia), for Chester County Deed Book B-3 and Tax Lists of Chester County; H. R. McIlwaine, *Executive Journals of the Council of Colonial Virginia IV* (1925); New Garden Meeting records (Swarthmore College Library, Swarthmore, Pa.); R. W. Ramsey, *Carolina Cradle* (1964); Rowan County records (North Carolina State Archives, Raleigh); Jethro Rumple, *A History of Rowan County* (1881); W. W. Scott, *History of Orange County, Virginia* (1907); John Shane, ed., Bryan Family Papers (MS Collection, Presbyterian National Historical Society, Philadelphia, Pa.); Paul H. Smith, *Loyalists and Redcoats* (1964); Frederick A. Virkus, ed., *The Abridged Compendium of American Genealogy* (1925); James W. Wall, *History of Davie County* (1969).

JOHN K. BRYAN, JR.

Bryan, Nathan *(1748–4 June 1798)*, Revolutionary War leader and member of Congress, was born in Craven County. He was the son of Hardy Bryan, who died in 1760, and was raised and lived most of his life on a plantation on the Neuse River. During the Revolution he served as a colonel in the Jones County militia, resigning this post in June 1779. He was also a justice of the peace. Because he was a noted Whig leader, his home was ransacked and his slaves carried off by the British forces on their way through North Carolina in August 1781.

Bryan was elected to the legislature in 1787 and again in 1791, serving until 1794 as a representative of Jones County. In November 1789 he represented Jones County at the convention in Fayetteville, when North Carolina ratified the Constitution of the United States. In 1794 he was elected to the U.S. House of Representatives; he served from 1795 until his death in 1798. He died in Philadelphia and was buried in the Baptist Cemetery.

Little is known of Bryan's family, although according to the census of 1790 he may have had five sons and three daughters, as well as fifteen slaves. He was described by contemporaries as "wealthy and talented," with personal attributes of "piety and usefulness." He was baptized in 1767 and was active in the Baptist church throughout his life.

SEE: *Biog. Dir. Am. Cong.* (1971); William L. Saunders and Walter Clark, eds., *Colonial and State Records of North Carolina*, 30 vols. (1886–1914); John H. Wheeler, *Historical Sketches of North Carolina* (1851).

ELMER D. JOHNSON

Bryan, Samuel (*ca. 1726–98*), Yadkin River pioneer and Loyalist officer, was born in what is now Lancaster County, Pa., to Morgan Bryan and his wife, Martha Strode. In 1730, Samuel's father obtained a 156-square-mile grant in Virginia's Northern Neck, near the present Winchester; Samuel and his six brothers and two sisters grew up there in a frontier environment but in a comparatively prosperous home. As the older children formed their own families, their father began searching for sufficient unclaimed land to support the future needs of the growing clan. Thus, in the fall of 1748, the entire Bryan family set out for the Yadkin River in newly organized Anson County, N.C. Several thousand acres were purchased from Earl Granville in the next few years by the married children and their father, most of them by Morgan Bryan for his younger, unmarried sons.

Samuel and the other Bryan children may well have been raised in the Society of Friends, although their mother had come to America among Huguenot refugees and their father's heritage was probably Presbyterian. Formal Quaker meeting affiliation was not maintained in Virginia, and no discernible church affiliation prevailed on the Yadkin. Traveling Moravian preachers ministered to the Bryans' spiritual needs and officiated at many of their marriages, baptisms, and funerals; Moravian journals contain many references to their "good friends," the Bryans.

Samuel Bryan proved to be among the more able and enterprising of the brothers. Like his father, he bought and sold a number of tracts as new Scotch-Irish and German settlers arrived seeking land. In the process, he established a farm of some two thousand acres on the west bank of the Yadkin, just south of the "shallow ford" crossing of the "great wagon road" that linked Salisbury, seat of newly formed (1753) Rowan County, with the Wachovian villages and the east. On this property, he operated a mill and a ferry and established fisheries by damming shoals and tributaries along the Yadkin. He was also authorized to operate an ordinary—a natural consequence of his proximity to the well-traveled wagon road.

Bryan was listed on the rolls of the Rowan County militia for 1754-55, along with his brother, Captain Morgan Bryan, Jr. During the French and Indian War, he and most of his brothers served in the militia patrols that ultimately put an end to the devastating Cherokee raids. At the height of the Indian activity (1758–61), most of the Bryan wives and children "went to forting" at Bethabara, Fort Dobbs, and other stockaded strongholds nearby.

With the death of their parents in 1761 and 1763, Samuel and his brothers shared in the division of the large estate. All were married and some were actively engaged in real estate transactions to consolidate and expand their substantial holdings. When smaller landowners banded together as Regulators to resist the government's oppressive and unevenly administered taxation, the Bryans and other long-established families of the region declined to support the Regulator movement.

In 1769, some two hundred Rowan County residents proposed Samuel and Morgan Bryan, Jr., as temporary vestrymen, in petitioning the royal governor for the establishment of an Anglican parish. This nomination not only evidenced the esteem with which Samuel and his brother were regarded but may have reflected their political orientation as well.

Discontent with Crown policies, festering in Western Carolina since the War of the Regulation, grew as events throughout the colonies gradually fostered a general alienation. However, Rowan County's increasingly rebellious mood was due far more to its resentment of the political and economic domination of the eastern part of the colony than to any widespread disaffection for the king. Samuel Bryan was among the first of several prominent citizens hailed before Rowan County's committee of safety, on 1 Aug. 1775. His brother Morgan, Jr., a member of the committee, was to have his own loyalty challenged on later occasions. Most of the better-situated families in the Forks of the Yadkin decried the growing schism. Samuel Bryan was among the first openly to declare himself a loyal subject of the king and, with 194 other residents of Rowan and Surry counties, he sent an address of loyalty to Royal Governor Josiah Martin in the fall of 1775. A few months later, having retreated from New Bern to the safety of the British warship *Scorpion* on the lower Cape Fear River, Governor Martin dispatched orders commissioning local justices whom he believed loyal to raise troops for the king throughout North Carolina. In Rowan County, Samuel Bryan and his brother William, together with William Spurian and Matthias Sapenfield, were so charged. Samuel promptly raised a company of men, but William was busy with an ambitious Kentucky land venture and did not accept the commission. William and several of his brothers and neighbors had been resolved for some time to establish their families anew in Kentucky, along with their Boone relatives; one important motive was to avoid the increasingly acrimonious Whig-Tory confrontations in Rowan County.

According to tradition, Lieutenant Colonel Samuel Bryan's authority to take his militia company to the support of the governor was challenged by one of his officers. Young Lieutenant Richmond Pearson had the foresight to instruct some of his Whig friends to load their muskets just before Bryan ordered the troops to assemble. When the group was informed that they were to rendezvous with the British, Pearson refused to obey and offered his resignation. Bryan ordered him arrested, but the armed Whigs forced an impasse. At length it was decided to settle the matter with a fistfight between Bryan and Pearson. Bryan lost, whereupon the lieutenant and his supporters departed with impunity. This tale may be apocryphal, but Bryan did, indeed, march his Rowan County men to Cross Creek in February 1776 to join a gathering band of North Carolina Scots. The Tory force of fifteen hundred to two thousand headed for the coast to link up with British troops expected to land shortly. On 27 Feb., however, the Highlanders were routed at Moore's Creek Bridge by a rebel force under Colonels Richard Caswell and Alexander Lillington. This first Whig-Tory battle so discouraged North Carolina's Loyalists that the British were denied their overt military support for at least two years. All the officers under Bryan were captured, but he and his remaining men managed to make their way home.

The Whigs, now in control of local government, intensified their persecution of Loyalists throughout the upland region. Bryan was among those forced to take to the woods. "The Bryans is hiding out," noted a contemporary Moravian journal entry.

In 1777, Bryan went to New York City to describe the plight of frontier Loyalists and seek relief for them. Lord Howe and North Carolina's refugee Governor Martin armed Bryan with proclamations and messages of encouragement for his beleaguered associates. Lord Cornwallis, British commander in the southern theater, sent instructions to all Loyalists in the South, however, to stand fast until he called upon them to assist him.

Harassment of Bryan and allied families in the Forks increased. Neutrality was impossible. Refusal to take the state's prescribed Oath of Allegiance and Fidelity meant confiscation of property and eventual expulsion from the state. Ironically, a number of accused Loyalist sympathizers would gladly have departed the state for Kentucky under William Bryan's leadership were it not for British-inspired Indian depredations throughout that "dark and bloody ground." Bryan's Station, Ky., begun in 1775 a few miles from Boonesborough, was not deemed safe to occupy until the fall of 1779, when several hundred Rowan County men, women, and children made the long trek via Boone's Wilderness Road through the Cumberland Gap.

Committed to the military effort, Samuel Bryan did not join the exodus. He and some of his nephews may have been involved in the fight at Ramsour's Mill on the Yadkin, where a substantial Loyalist force was defeated by a smaller Whig group in June 1780. Soon afterward, apparently convinced that he and his adherents could no longer weather local Whig pressure, Bryan raised the royal standard in the Forks of the Yadkin. At least 500 men responded to the call, and in late June, Bryan took them eastward with General Griffith Rutherford's rebel militia in hot pursuit. Gathering Loyalists as he went, Bryan shook off Rutherford and reached the Grassy Islands ford of the Pee Dee River. There his growing command was augmented by a few British dragoons, but at Colson's Mill on the Pee Dee, the poorly armed Loyalists were caught and mauled by a small Whig cavalry force under Colonel William L. Davidson. Nevertheless, Bryan got his men to the British post at Anson Court House, where he turned over his command of 810 men to Major Archibald McArthur, the British commander. There, Samuel Bryan's commission as colonel of the Royal North Carolina Militia was confirmed.

Writing three years later of Bryan's zeal and loyalty, North Carolina's ousted royal governor said, ". . . he fully evinced his influence to be greater in the County where he lived than that of any Loyalist who appeared in the Course of the War by bringing followers to join the King's standard at so late a period as the year 1780, from a considerable distance within the Country possessed by the enemy, to the number of 800 upwards. Upon the whole I am warranted to declare that I believe no man took his part during the rebellion upon more honest principles or supported it better. . . ."

After a series of feinting maneuvers and counter-marches in Anson County, Bryan took his men to Thomson's Creek. Leaving Lieutenant Colonel John Hampton in charge, he went to General Cornwallis's

headquarters at Camden. With three companies of men, he was sent to reinforce a mixed command of British and provincial troops at Hanging Rock in the South Carolina Waxhaws. General Thomas Sumter, with Colonel Andrew Neel and Major William R. Davie, attacked the position on 31 July 1780. The battle developed when Davie struck Bryan's men, thinking them the main body of defenders. The Tories were decimated in the surprise assault, but the attack faltered when the rebels began plundering the commissary. Bryan rallied his remaining men, slipped through a swamp around Sumter's right flank, and renewed the action. Again Bryan's provincials were badly mauled, but when Tarleton's infantry and the main body of Loyalists entered the fight, Sumter withdrew.

Returning to Camden, Bryan commanded one wing of John Hamilton's Royal North Carolina Regiment when Cornwallis met and completely routed General Horatio Gates's main army of Continentals and Whig militia on 16 Aug. 1780. But later that year, American fortunes improved. The smashing victory of the "over mountain men" in October at Kings Mountain demoralized the Loyalist militia; Gates's replacement as American commander in the South by General Nathanael Greene cheered Continentals and Rebel militia alike; and Daniel Morgan's remarkable success at Cowpens in January 1781 drew Cornwallis out for his fateful and eventually disastrous foray into the interior Carolinas. Bryan's activities during that period are unknown. He may have led some of the Loyalist troops who accompanied Cornwallis during his frustrating pursuit of Greene in early 1781. However, the Moravians failed to mention their old friend and neighbor in listing the officers who were with Cornwallis when the British passed through Salem on 10 Feb. Bryan is not mentioned as a participant in any of the subsequent series of British reverses, which culminated at Yorktown in October 1781.

The date and circumstances of Bryan's capture, together with that of Lieutenant Colonel John Hampton and Captain Nicholas White, have not been ascertained. The three were tried in Salisbury during the March term of court, 1782. State Attorney General Alfred Moore conducted the prosecution, and the Loyalist officers were ably defended by Richard Henderson, John Penn, John Kitchen, and Bryan's adversary at Hanging Rock, William R. Davie. Bryan and Hampton were charac-terized as men of unimpeachable honor and integrity who had committed no atrocities or acts of violence other than the seizure of food for the sustenance of their troops. Nevertheless, all were found guilty of "treason and felony" and sentenced to be hanged. At the time of sentence, the Rowan County Court took note of the plight of the families of the trio and allowed their wives to retain sufficient property to support their children. Bryan's wife was allowed to keep "about 900 acres where the family now lives," and the slaves, livestock, and furniture she could retain were listed in detail. It was also noted that eight daughters were living at home, the youngest of whom was about fifteen months of age.

The executions were delayed, however, when the defense attorneys petitioned Governor Thomas Burke for clemency. In the petition, Bryan was described as an "esteemed man of indomitable courage, of Candor and Sincerity, remarkably honest in his dealings and very friendly in his disposition." Executing him, the attorneys insisted, would be a "reflection on our Government." Burke extended clemency to all three, and the General Assembly endorsed his decision. An exchange of prisoners was arranged with the British. The governor went so far as to provide extra protection for the trio against the threatened violence of Whig zealots in the Salisbury area. In Charleston, British Lieutenant General Alexander Leslie played a role in the prisoner exchange and his letters reflect his high regard for Bryan. Burke wanted Colonel Elijah Clark of the North Carolina Militia exchanged for Bryan, but General Greene's command mistook these intentions and the three Loyalists were exchanged for Virginia officers. Bryan, Hampton, and White were sent to Charleston.

When word came that the British planned to evacuate the southern colonies, Loyalist leaders in Charleston made a last effort to regain at least part of their American holdings before the withdrawal. Twenty-five of the most influential were chosen to draw up a petition to Sir Guy Carleton, commander in chief of Charleston, asking that the Loyalist troops be permitted to keep the town and its artillery so as to bargain with the Whigs. Bryan was among those selected and penned his signature to the document. The petition was denied.

On 8 July 1782, Bryan's command was officially disbanded. The following month, he submitted a claim for back pay and appointed an attorney to handle his petition for compensation. In the petition, he sought half pay for his four years of forced inactivity between 1776 and 1780: his officers captured in February 1776 had ultimately reached New York City and received their pay, but because he had escaped capture and was under orders to await recall, he had not been paid; moreover, his long period of hiding and the clandestine encouragement of his followers had run him into debt. Bryan's petition, endorsed by Governor Martin, Lord Cornwallis, and Sir Guy Carleton, was ultimately denied.

In September 1782, Bryan sailed with other Loyalists for St. Augustine, Fla., with the hope that his wife and children could join him there. Early in 1783, however, the Loyalists, now gathered in large numbers in East Florida, were informed that the British must also abandon that region. Most of the refugees went either to the West Indies or to Nova Scotia. Bryan and others, however, took a schooner to Wilmington. Arriving on 10 June 1783, they were detained as "obnoxious characters" by local authorities but were ultimately permitted to go their way.

Bryan had been named personally in the General Assembly act giving the State of North Carolina title to confiscated Loyalist property. In many cases, however, the state did not exercise its right to sell such property. There is no record of Bryan's holdings being sold by the state, and his petition to the Crown for compensation made no mention of any loss of personal property or real estate. It is uncertain whether Bryan was ever officially pardoned by the state. Apparently he managed to resume his life as a farmer on his Rowan County plantation. That he could do so for fifteen more years is further tribute to his character and reputation, in view of the enduring bitterness and discrimination against former Tories that prevailed. At least five of his nephews and one or more of his sons saw active Loyalist service. Two are known to have been killed, and three others were apparently treated at a British military hospital in Wilmington while on active duty.

Samuel's brothers William, James, and Morgan, Jr., together with some of his nephews, were credited with Rebel military service, primarily against Indians in Kentucky. While later generations largely ignored Samuel and his achievements, his Loyalist activities do not appear to have alienated his surviving brothers and other relatives. He corresponded with those who had moved to Kentucky and as late as 1797 visited them in the company of his older brother Joseph, Daniel Boone's father-in-law. However, at least one son relocated in upstate New York, presumably to shed his Loyalist identification and make a fresh start.

On 5 Aug. 1798, Bryan made his will; it was probated during the November term of Rowan County Court. In it he named as beneficiaries his wife, Elizabeth (née McMahon), and eleven children: Samuel, Jr., Morgan, Ann Enochs, Margaret Ellis, Elizabeth Hampton, Sarah Linville, Mary, Martha, Elinor, Kezia, and Susanna. In 1808, presumably after the death of his mother, Samuel, Jr., sold the remainder of his father's Yadkin plantation.

Bryan and his wife were probably buried on the property, but the grave site is unknown.

SEE: Robert O. DeMond, *The Loyalists in North Carolina* (1940); Lyman Draper MS Collection (Wisconsin State Historical Society, Madison); English Papers, Loyalist Claims (North Carolina State Archives, Raleigh); Adelaide L. Fries, ed., *Records of the Moravians in North Carolina*, 8 vols. (1922–54); Rowan County Deed Books, Will Books, and Minutes of the Court of Common Pleas and Quarter Sessions, 1752–1808 (Salisbury and Raleigh); John Shane, ed., Bryan Family Papers (MS Collection, Presbyterian National Historical Society, Philadelphia, Pa.); Paul H. Smith, *Loyalists and Redcoats* (1964).

JOHN K. BRYAN, JR.

Bryan, Washington (*14 Aug. 1853–3 May 1927*), attorney and financier, was born in New Bern, the younger surviving son of James West Bryan and Ann Mary Washington. His paternal grandparents were James Bryan and Rachel Heritage; his maternal grandparents were John Washington and Elizabeth Heritage Cobb.

After attending St. Clement's Hall, a preparatory school at Baltimore, Md., and the University of Virginia, Bryan was graduated from Trinity College, Conn., receiving a number of scholarship medals and honors. He was a member of Phi Beta Kappa and of Alpha Delta Phi Fraternity. Besides having mastery of Latin and Greek, he spoke four modern languages.

While residing in the New Bern home of his parents, Bryan practiced law; he gave up the practice to pay more attention to his duties as president of the state-controlled Atlantic and North Carolina Railroad Company. After the death of his wife, Mary Winder, on 12 Dec. 1886, at Raleigh, he moved to New York City and dealt in stocks and bonds until his retirement.

Foreign travel then became his avocation. Making a special study of the Jewish people, he spent much time in Palestine. He declined appointments to consular or diplomatic service, but he made personal visits to Queen Victoria at Windsor, to the Court of Spain, and to the Vatican.

Intensely interested in Masonic affairs, Bryan joined St. John's Lodge, New Bern, in 1875; he was its 1877 junior warden.

Because of his aid in the building of the Cathedral of St. John the Divine in New York, his body was taken to its Chapel of St. James, and a memorial service was held there 5 May 1927. The funeral was held in Christ Episcopal Church, New Bern, where he had been baptized and had long been a member. Interment was in his paternal grandfather's vault in Cedar Grove Cemetery at New Bern, under a willow tree he had transplanted from the Island of St. Helena.

SEE: Bryan Family Records (in possession of Charles H. Ashford, Jr., New Bern); Gertrude S. Carraway, *Years of*

Light: History of St. John's Lodge (1944); Christ Church Records (New Bern).

GERTRUDE S. CARRAWAY

Bryan, William *(ca. 1733–80)*, early Yadkin River settler and Kentucky pioneer, was born in the vicinity of Winchester, Va., the fifth son of Morgan and Martha Strode Bryan. His father had helped settle a large number of families in northwestern Virginia on a one-hundred-thousand-acre grant he and a Quaker business partner obtained in 1730 from Virginia's government. In subsequent years, Morgan Bryan moved his family deeper into the Shenandoah Valley, as his land-trading activities and the needs of his growing family dictated. By the late 1740s, some of William's older brothers and sisters had married. Since the Shenandoah was being settled rapidly, the entire clan set out, under Morgan Bryan's leadership, for a new frontier region where land would be cheaper and more abundant. The location selected was the area between the Forks of the Yadkin River in what was then Anson County, N.C.

William's family made the long journey to the south by way of the Staunton River Gap, where relatives had established themselves on the site of the present Roanoke, Va. They arrived on the Yadkin in the spring of 1749, and Morgan and his older sons began purchasing large tracts of choice land from Lord Granville, whose extensive Crown grant included most of the northwestern part of the colony. By 1753, when Rowan County was created from a part of Anson, the area in the Forks of the Yadkin in what is now Davie County had become known as the Bryan Settlements.

Within three years of the Bryans' arrival, the Moravians from Pennsylvania bought land from Granville for their Wachovia settlement a few miles east of the Bryan Settlements. Families from Virginia and Pennsylvania followed, including that of Squire and Sarah Boone, with their eight sons and four daughters. In 1755, William Bryan married nineteen-year-old Mary Boone, daughter of Squire and Sarah and sister of Daniel Boone.

According to tradition, Daniel Boone first encountered his future wife, Rebecca Bryan, at that wedding. Rebecca was William Bryan's niece, daughter of his older brother Joseph. Daniel and Rebecca were married in the Settlements the following year. Tradition has it that the ceremony was performed by old Squire Boone, then a Rowan County justice. In later years, two more of William Bryan's nieces became his sisters-in-law by marrying younger brothers of his wife: Martha Bryan, Rebecca's sister, married Edward Boone; and Ann Linville, daughter of William and Eleanor Bryan Linville, married George Boone.

Very likely, William and Mary Bryan established themselves in a newly constructed cabin on one of Morgan Bryan's tracts in the Settlements. Rowan County records contain very few references to land transactions involving William; it appears, therefore, that he was not involved in real estate speculation to the same extent as his father and other family members. Neither does it appear that William developed a large permanent farm, as did his brothers Samuel and John. William's close ties with the venturesome Boone brothers may have led him to spend more time hunting and trapping than clearing and planting.

Bryan and most of his brothers served in the local militia during the Cherokee uprising of 1758–61. After the death of his parents in 1762–63, he and his six brothers and their sister, Eleanor Linville, shared in the division of the estate. In 1764, Bryan purchased his father's Mansion plantation on Deep Creek from his younger brother Thomas, who had inherited it. The Bryans were apparently well liked by their Moravian neighbors, even though their casual Christianity sometimes scandalized the disciplined brethren. "Billy" Bryan was a particular favorite in Wachovia. Traveling Moravian preachers were often guests in his home, and in later years some of his Moravian friends invested in his Kentucky land venture.

Some time after Squire Boone's death in 1765, the widowed Sarah Boone came to live with her daughter Mary and son-in-law William. A Moravian minister mentioned having seen "old Mother Boone, a Quaker," in Bryan's home in 1772. He also noted that Bryan's cabin was on the south side of the Yadkin at the western curve of the bend; this would place it just south of the "shallow ford" crossing of the Salisbury-Wachovia road near Samuel Bryan's estate and four or five miles from Morgan Bryan's original Deep Creek property.

William and his younger brother Thomas were greatly interested in Daniel Boone's expeditions into Kentucky. William, his nephew John Bryan, Jr., and possibly Thomas were members of the Boone party that set out for Kentucky—then part of Fincastle County, Va.—in September 1773. The group turned back a few miles short of the Cumberland Gap when Boone's sixteen-year-old son was killed by Indians.

In its preoccupation with the growing rift with England, the colonial government in Williamsburg could not control the pressure of Carolina frontiersmen upon Kentucky. Settlement was discouraged, and Kentucky pioneers had no hope of military protection from Virginia. Nevertheless, the Boones, Bryans, and many other Rowan County relatives and friends continued their explorations of the "dark and bloody ground" in 1774. Shortly after James Harrod built his first permanent "station" in Kentucky, Daniel Boone established Boonesborough. William Bryan and his party used Boonesborough as a base of operations while exploring the Elkhorn River area to the north.

At about the same time, Colonel Richard Henderson of Rowan County formed the Transylvania Company and purchased all of Kentucky from the Cherokees, in spite of the tribe's dubious right to sell it. Trail cutters under Boone began building a crude road for the company from the Holston River through the Cumberland Gap in the spring of 1775 to facilitate the sale of Kentucky land to settlers. Virginia acted promptly to thwart Henderson's scheme. Abandoning its futile discouragement of settlers, Virginia declared the Transylvania purchase illegal and passed a law offering four hundred acres of Kentucky land free to anyone who raised a crop and made "improvements" on his claim before 1 Jan. 1778. The new law also allowed such settlers to preempt an adjoining thousand acres for forty shillings an acre. This action killed the Transylvania venture and opened what became Kentucky County, Va., to settlement.

Daniel Boone moved his family to Boonesborough in the fall of 1775. The following spring, Bryan led a party to start construction of Bryan's Station sixteen miles north of Boonesborough on the Elkhorn River, near the present Lexington, Ky. Bryan became ill before reaching the Cumberland Gap and had to turn back. His party reached the Elkhorn, however, where they cleared and planted sixty acres and built a few cabins. Two black men stayed to tend the corn crop, and the Bryan party returned to the Yadkin to prepare to bring their families to the station in the fall.

The concern of the Shawnees and other tribes north of the Ohio River grew as increasing numbers of whites pushed into the Indians' traditional hunting grounds from the south. They appealed to the British commander at Detroit, who at first tried to placate them. As the colonial rebellion grew, however, the British began encouraging the Indians to drive the settlers from Kentucky. This increasing Indian activity persuaded Bryan to delay his plans to establish his Bryan's Station outpost.

In early 1776, Bryan declined a proffered commission from North Carolina's royal governor to raise and lead a Loyalist militia company. His brother Samuel accepted a similar offer and marched his company from the Forks region eastward that spring to meet disaster at Moore's Creek at the hands of rebel militia. Loyalist-Rebel confrontations grew more acrimonious after the Declaration of Independence, and by the later part of 1776, the rebels were in control of Rowan County government. By then, the Forks region—particularly the Bryan Settlements—was regarded as a center of Loyalist sentiment. Many members of the Bryan, Hunt, Hampton, and other prominent area families may not have shared Samuel Bryan's keen sense of duty to the king, but they did react cautiously to cries for American independence. As propertied citizens, they had much to lose from the economic and political anarchy that seemed to lie ahead, and because anything less than wholehearted support of independence amounted to disloyalty to the new state government, many were branded Tories. This status undoubtedly gave William Bryan and his relatives additional incentive to forsake Rowan County for Kentucky.

Thomas Bryan, William's younger brother, died in early 1777. His widow later sold his Kentucky property to William, who had helped Thomas establish the land claim the previous summer. Later in that eventful year, William's oldest son, Samuel, together with George Boone and other Rowan County men, went to the relief of Boonesborough in response to Daniel Boone's urgent request for help in holding off an Indian assault. The year also saw the Bryans and their relatives excluded from the militarily oriented Rowan County government—several of them, like Tory Colonel Samuel Bryan, having shown themselves to be Loyalists.

During 1778, pressure from the radicals increased. Rowan County court records of August list William Bryan and his sons Samuel and Daniel as Tories, along with brothers John, James, and Samuel and six nephews. The records also show that brothers Morgan, Jr., and Joseph took the state's Oath of Allegiance. In addition, heads of some of the related Hunt, Hampton, Hinkle, Linville, Forbus, Boone, Howard, McMahan, and Wilcoxen families were listed as suspected Tories.

According to a contemporary Moravian account, William Bryan planned to return to Kentucky in the spring of 1778. He did not go, perhaps being dissuaded by the return from Boonesborough of Rebecca Bryan Boone and her children, following the capture of Daniel by the Shawnees under Blackfish. In the spring of 1779, however, William finally returned to Bryan's Station in the company of his brothers Joseph, Morgan, Jr., and James and several of their sons. They built more cabins and began a stockade to enclose an area about thirty yards square. William's eldest son, Samuel, and his brother-in-law, William Grant, brought their wives and children to the station that spring, and others of the Bryan-Boone clans arrived in Boonesborough. After planting crops, William and his brothers returned to the Yadkin to ready their families for the trip.

In the fall, Bryan led a caravan of several hundred people along Boone's Wilderness Road into Kentucky. A participant later described the scene as "like an army camping out," with wagons strung out over half a mile along the narrow trace. They were unable to draw together at night for protection and unable to build fires for fear of attracting Indians. It was the largest single migration into Kentucky at that time.

Upon arrival, the party dispersed to various stations. At Bryan's, the men continued to enlarge the stockade and add more cabins—many of them two-family houses facing the center of the enclosed area with their thick rear walls an integral part of the palisaded perimeter. The stockade did not completely enclose the houses within for nearly a year and the two-story corner blockhouses were not completed for some time. Bryan and his cofounders all had two-acre lots at the station.

In October 1779, four land commissioners arrived in Kentucky from Williamsburg and began making the rounds of the several stations and small forts to process land claims. They arrived at Bryan's Station in January 1780. To add to the discomfort of short rations and the snow and ice of an unusually severe winter, William and his brothers learned that most of the land they had claimed lay within a survey completed a year earlier on behalf of absentee Virginia land speculators.

When spring came, the Shawnees took the warpath in greater numbers than ever to avenge raids on their villages conducted the previous fall by nearly three hundred Kentucky militia (including some of the younger Bryans). Several settlers were killed in scattered Indian raids, including sixteen-year-old William Bryan, Jr. A few weeks after his son's death, the intrepid Billy Bryan was mortally wounded when his hunting party was ambushed. He died shortly after making a will dated 23 May 1780.

Leaderless and disheartened, the Bryans began the long trek back to the Forks of the Yadkin in early autumn, returning, as Daniel Bryan later put it, "from the troubles of Kentucky to the troubles of North Carolina." Daniel also recalled that his arrival in Rowan County with his widowed mother found the man who had bought their Yadkin farm but had not yet paid for it "anxious to give it up, that he might get rid of the difficulties of the British and Tories and return to Virginia. We traded to him the pack horses that we had returned to Carolina on for the truck and corn. . . ."

Mary Boone Bryan stayed on the old Bryan Settlements farm until the fall of 1785. With her son Daniel and his family, she moved back to Kentucky to occupy her brother Daniel's farm on Marble Creek, Fayette County. She died in Kentucky in 1819.

No Bryans were present at Bryan's Station at the time its garrison withstood the famous Tory-Indian siege of August 1782. Eventually, however, the surviving founders of the station returned to Kentucky and lived out their years there. None of William and Mary Boone Bryan's nine surviving children remained in North Carolina. Most, like Daniel Bryan, established themselves in eastern Kentucky. When the Indiana Territory was opened to settlement after the defeat of the Shawnees at Tippecanoe, Samuel Bryan moved to central Indiana from Kentucky with two of his sons.

Both Samuel and Daniel received pensions for Revolutionary War service in Kentucky. Daniel gained some measure of fame with a small book of poetry, *The Mountain Muse*, which idealized some of the adventures of his uncle and namesake, Daniel Boone (Boone characterized the book, published in 1813, as rubbish). Daniel Bryan also furnished later interviewers and correspondents with many firsthand memories of the settlement of Kentucky, material since drawn upon by many historians.

For several years, Daniel battled in the courts with the Trustees of Transylvania University and others in an effort to recover some of his father's land on the Elkhorn. The school, first college west of the Appalachians, had been founded in 1780 with a gift of land including acreage to which William Bryan had been denied title. Ultimately, Daniel won back some of the land for which his father had fought and died.

SEE: Lyman Draper MS Collection (Wisconsin State Historical Society, Madison); Adelaide L. Fries, ed., *Records of the Moravians in North Carolina*, 8 vols. (1922–54); F. B. Kegley, *Kegley's Virginia Frontier* (1938); Rowan County Records (North Carolina State Archives, Raleigh); John Shane, ed., Bryan Family Papers (MS Collection, Presbyterian National Historical Society, Philadelphia, Pa.).

JOHN K. BRYAN, JR.

Bryan, William Shepard *(20 Nov. 1827–11 Dec. 1906)*, judge, was born in New Bern, the son of John Heritage Bryan and Mary Shepard Bryan. The Bryan and Shepard families had lived in New Bern for generations and had been active in local, state, and national affairs. John Heritage Bryan served as a trustee of The University of North Carolina, sat in the state senate, and represented North Carolina as a Whig member of the U.S. House of Representatives from 1825 to 1829.

John H. Bryan moved his family and his law practice from New Bern to Raleigh in 1839, and William S. Bryan read law in Raleigh with his father after his graduation from The University of North Carolina in 1846. In 1850, Bryan received the M.A. degree from the university. In December of that year he moved to Baltimore, Md., where he was admitted to the bar in 1851. He married Elizabeth Hayward of Talbot County, Md., in 1857.

Bryan established a distinguished law practice in Baltimore and in 1883 was elected to the Baltimore city seat on the court of appeals, the highest state court in Maryland. During his tenure as judge, Bryan devoted himself to the work of the court, winning respect for both his mastery of the law and his command of the detailed work of judicial administration. Bryan left the court in November 1898 and lived in retirement with his son, William Shepard, Jr. He died in Baltimore.

SEE: *Baltimore Sun*, 18 Mar. 1892, 29 Nov. 1898; William Shepard Bryan Papers (Southern Historical Collection, University of North Carolina, Chapel Hill); Daniel L. Grant, *Alumni History of the University of North Carolina* (1924).

HARRY MCKOWN

Bryant, Henry Edward Cowan ("Red Buck") *(3 Jan. 1873–3 Nov. 1967)*, journalist and political commentator, was born in lower Providence Township, Mecklenburg County, of English and Scotch-Irish ancestry. His father was Henry Bryant, a farmer, and his mother was Julia Parks. Brought up in a family of seven boys and one girl, he quickly learned to love farm life and the delights of a rural childhood, delights that all too often distracted him from his studies. He entered Carolina Academy at age seven, where his scholastic record was at best indifferent, and in 1889 proceeded to Raleigh to North Carolina State (then A. and M.) College. His indifference to scholarship led college officials to urge him to abandon school after his first

semester. He returned to his father's farm, remaining there until he entered The University of North Carolina in 1891, where his older brother, Victor S., was a law student. Despite problems with Latin and English, he earned a B.S. degree in 1895.

Upon graduation, he returned to Mecklenburg County and called upon Joseph Pearson Caldwell, editor and co-owner of the *Charlotte Observer*, volunteering to work for the *Observer* without pay until he knew enough about the newspaper business to deserve a salary. After he had completed two months without compensation, Caldwell placed him on the payroll at $20 per month. Caldwell also gave Bryant his nickname after the young reporter, a Democrat, was forced to flee an angry Republican convention in Maxton: the red-haired, freckled-faced lad must have run, Caldwell assumed, like a deer.

By 1898, Red Buck Bryant had established his reputation as a skilled and insightful journalist through his coverage of Charles B. Aycock's campaign for governor and through his reports on the Eastern North Carolina counties still under black control. He became the Washington correspondent for the *Observer* in 1907, a position he held until the death of Caldwell in 1911. He then moved to Montana, where he accepted a position on the Missoula *Missoulian*, a paper owned by Senator Joseph M. Dixon, a North Carolina native. Bryant endured Montana for nine months before returning to Washington, this time as a correspondent of the *New York World*. He remained with the *World* until its morning edition folded in 1931 and then joined the Washington staff of the *Boston Herald*. By then he was a member of the Gridiron Club and one of the most highly regarded and colorful journalists in the capital. He had returned to the South during World War I to describe the exodus of blacks to the North, and later he visited various areas of the North to report on the plight of blacks. He also did major pieces on the failure of prohibition in the South, on the Ku Klux Klan, and on the various branches of government in Washington. He covered every Democratic National Convention, and some Republican ones also, from 1904 to 1928.

In December 1943, after his wife's death, Bryant decided he had had enough of Washington and journalism and retired to North Carolina. His retirement was short lived, however; he soon began a series of forty-six articles for R. F. Beasley's *Farm and Home Weekly* on state politics, the *Charlotte Observer*, and J. P. Caldwell. A decade before, in 1933, he had written a short life of Caldwell; these articles expanded that biography. Bryant also wrote several articles for the same journal on Aycock's white supremacy campaign of 1898. In 1954 he rejoined the staff of the *Observer*, producing a weekly column, "Red Buck's Reminiscences," for the Sunday edition. His last by-line appeared in the Sunday edition of the *Observer* of 6 Nov. 1967, three days after his death.

An active journalist for seventy-two of his ninety-four years, Red Buck avoided tobacco, hard liquor, and coffee while embracing early morning strolls, a careful diet, and long hours at his typewriter. He counted among his friends many of the most powerful men of his times and was a regular visitor at White House receptions from the administration of Theodore Roosevelt to that of Franklin D. Roosevelt.

Bryant married Eva Sumner of Lincolnton in February 1900. The couple had one daughter, Betty, later Mrs. H. W. Northcutt of Morganton, with whom Red Buck resided during his last years. He was buried at St. Luke's Episcopal Church in Lincolnton.

SEE: H. E. C. Bryant File (*Charlotte Observer* Library); H. E. C. Bryant Papers (North Carolina State Archives,

Raleigh); H. E. C. Bryant, *Joseph Pearson Caldwell* (1933), and *Tar Heel Tales* (1910); *Charlotte Observer*, esp. 25 Aug. 1961, 2 Jan. 1966, 4 Nov. 1967; George Tayloe Winston, *A Builder of the New South* (1920).

THOMAS J. FARNHAM

Bryson, Joseph Raleigh (18 Jan. 1893–10 Mar. 1953), South Carolina state senator and U.S. congressman, was born in Brevard and moved with his parents, Robert L. and Mattie Allison Bryson, to Greenville, S.C., in 1900. He received his early education in the Greenville public schools. By working in local textile mills he made his way through Furman University, from which he was graduated in 1917 with a B.A. degree.

Bryson served in the South Carolina National Guard in 1915 and 1916; he reenlisted in the Medical Reserves Corps in 1917 and was discharged in 1918, as a second lieutenant. In 1920 he received his LL.B. degree from the University of South Carolina, was admitted to the bar, and began to practice in Greenville. He was later to receive an honorary LL.D. degree from Bob Jones University in 1948. On 5 Aug. 1920 he was married to Ruth Rucker.

Bryson was elected to the South Carolina House of Representatives in 1920 and served for four years. From 1929 to 1932 he served as a South Carolina state senator. After the death of U.S. Representative John J. McSwain in 1936, Bryson made an unsuccessful bid for the seat. In 1938 he entered the race again, this time against the incumbent, G. Heyward Mahon. In the first Democratic primary, the official count showed Bryson ahead by only eight votes. As a result, the state Democratic committee called for a second primary, which was held two weeks later. This time Bryson was nominated by a substantial margin. He served from 1939 until his death in 1953 as a member of the Seventy-sixth through Eighty-second Congresses from South Carolina's Fourth District. He was elected to four of these seven terms unopposed.

As a member of Congress, Bryson championed uniform freight rates and favored lowering the eligibility age for old age and survivors' insurance to sixty-two. He introduced a succession of prohibition bills between 1948 and 1953, carrying his fight for prohibition outside Congress by speaking at a number of Women's Christian Temperance Union conventions. He considered himself "internally, externally and eternally" dry. He opposed the 1949 Displaced Persons' Bill, which would allow more immigrants to enter the United States. Feeling Communist infiltration a real threat to the United States, Bryson introduced an Anti-Spying Bill in 1949, which was later incorporated into the Internal Security Act of 1950.

Bryson was an active Baptist and a member of a number of clubs and fraternal organizations, including the Shriners, the American Legion, and the Red Men.

Bryson died at Bethesda Naval Hospital of a cerebral hemorrhage. He was survived by his wife and five children, Joseph R., William J., David F., Ruth B. Thackston, and Judy B. Nelson. Bryson was buried at Woodland Memorial Park, Greenville, S.C.

SEE: *Biog. Dir. Am. Cong.* (1971); Columbia (S.C.) *State*, 11 Mar. 1953; *Congressional Quarterly Almanac*, vols. 2–9 (1947–53); *Greenville* (S.C.) *News*, 11 Mar. 1953; *Greenville* (S.C.) *Piedmont*, 11 Mar. 1953; *Newsweek*, 23 Mar. 1953; *New York Times*, 11 Mar. 1953 (portrait); *Time*, 23 Mar. 1953; *Who's Who in the South*, 1927; *Who Was Who in America*, vol. 3 (1960).

MARY A. BAKER

Buchanan, Harry Eugene (3 Sept. 1898–21 Sept. 1974), mountain region leader and moving picture theater official, was born in Sylva, the son of Marcellus and Laura Belle Leatherwood Buchanan. He obtained his early schooling in Jackson County and then attended Preparatory School of Trinity College and, in 1914–15, The University of North Carolina.

Starting at age seventeen as an agent for the Southern Railway, Buchanan afterward went into timber operations and opened a motion picture theater in Sylva. In Hendersonville, to which he moved in 1932, he was manager of the Carolina Theater. He was for many years legislative representative of the North Carolina Theater Owners Association, of which he was a director and at one time president.

Before leaving Sylva, Buchanan organized and became first president of the Chamber of Commerce and the Rotary Club and also served as mayor. Another Jackson County interest was the institution that later became Western Carolina University, where a dormitory was named in his honor in 1958. He was an active Democrat and a member of the Methodist church. In Hendersonville he helped organize the Western North Carolina Fair and the Chamber of Commerce. He was Henderson representative in developing the Asheville and Hendersonville Airport at Fletcher, and at the time of his death he was president of the Carolina Motor Club. He served in the state senate during 1967–68 and on the state Highway Commission during Governor William Bradley Umstead's administration.

Of lasting benefit to the region and particularly to the Eastern Band of Cherokee Indians was his leadership in establishing the outdoor drama *Unto These Hills*. This project was launched by Western North Carolina Associated Communities, a regional development organization Buchanan had served as president. Chartered in 1948 as the nonprofit Cherokee Historical Association, this corporation raised sufficient funds through donations to build Mountainside Theater at Cherokee. As chairman, Buchanan went to Raleigh for legislative help and secured a matching amount. Opening in 1950, this outdoor drama played in its first quarter century to over three million people. An adjoining project opened later as Oconaluftee Living Indian Village, and its annual attendance soon approached the count at the theater. During these years, Buchanan, as chairman and active leader, won strong support from nearby communities, from tribal chiefs and councils, and from U.S. Indian Service officials. All agreed that his skill and faithful work were the chief reasons for the success of the venture.

Buchanan's marriage to Pearl Long of Sylva in 1923 produced four children: Sara (Mrs. Charles W. Porter of Hendersonville); Jean and Pearl of Nashville, Tenn.; and Harry E., Jr., of Atlanta, Ga. Buchanan was buried in Keener Cemetery at Sylva.

SEE: Asheville *Citizen-Times*, 22 Sept. 1974; Daniel L. Grant, *Alumni History of the University of North Carolina* (1924); *North Carolina Biography*, vol. 3 (1941); *North Carolina Biography*, vol. 4 (1928); William S. Powell, ed., *North Carolina Lives* (1962); *North Carolina Manual* (1967).

GEORGE MYERS STEPHENS

Bullitt, James Bell (18 Jan. 1874–7 Mar. 1964), physician and professor of pathology, was born in Louisville, Ky., of English ancestors who had been for generations prominent in Virginia and Kentucky. His father was Thomas Walker Bullitt and his mother Annie

Priscilla Logan. He was educated at the Rugby School in Louisville, Washington and Lee University (A.B. 1894, A.M., 1895), and the University of Virginia (M.D., 1897). He continued his study in a New York hospital and then established a private practice in Louisville.

Bullitt returned to the University of Virginia in 1899 as demonstrator of anatomy until 1903, when he accepted a position as professor of anatomy in the University of Mississippi Medical School. There he began to demonstrate his well-rounded knowledge and varied interests, teaching bacteriology and histology as well as anatomy. He remained a distinguished member of Mississippi's faculty until his appointment in 1913 as chairman of the department of pathology of The University of North Carolina Medical School, a position he filled with distinction until his retirement in 1947. Bullitt entered the U.S. Army as a major in the Medical Corps and served in France at Base Hospital 65 from August 1918 until July 1919. He advanced to the rank of lieutenant colonel and later to that of colonel in the U.S. Army Reserve Corps. In 1948 he was honored by his former students when his portrait was presented to the Medical School. On his sixty-third birthday, the Medical School History Club changed its name to the James Bell Bullitt Club.

At Washington and Lee University, Bullitt had been initiated into the Phi Beta Kappa Honor Society and Phi Gamma Delta social fraternity; he was also a member of Phi Chi and Alpha Omega Alpha, honorary medical fraternities. He remained active in these organizations throughout his life, especially Phi Gamma Delta, offering counsel and strength to many generations of students. Bullitt was a Fellow of the American Medical Association and a member of the American College of Physicians, American Microscopic Society, American Society of Clinical Pathologists, Southern Medical Association, Society of Military Surgeons, North Carolina Medical Society, North Carolina Academy of Science, the Prehistorical Society of America, and the American Anthropological Association.

Bullitt's memberships in anthropological societies indicate the wide range of his serious interests. For years he was an avid collector of Indian artifacts in America and those of the Stone Age in Europe. On one occasion he almost got into serious trouble with the customs officials in New York when, on a return voyage from Europe, his remarks about the "precious stones" in his luggage were misinterpreted. This valuable collection of archaeological samples is now in the laboratories of The University of North Carolina.

Bullitt was married on 30 May 1901 to Evelyn Bryan at the University of Virginia. They had three children: Thomas Walker II (1901–5); James Bell, Jr. (1906–57); and Margaret (b. 1905), who married Guy Cardwell, Jr. Bullitt was an Episcopalian, serving on the vestry of the Chapel of the Cross in Chapel Hill. In politics, he was a Democrat. He died in Lexington, Mass., and was buried in the old Chapel Hill Cemetery (his tombstone incorrectly says he died in Chapel Hill).

Few men connected with The University of North Carolina have had Bullitt's breadth and depth of interests. Throughout his long career he was a powerful influence with both faculty and students.

SEE: Bullitt Family Records (in possession of author); *Chapel Hill Weekly*, 14 June 1946; *Durham Morning Herald*, 16 Dec. 1946; Minutes of the Faculty of The University of North Carolina, vol. 18 (Library, University of North Carolina, Chapel Hill); William S. Powell, ed., *North Carolina Lives* (1962); Raleigh *News and Observer*, 19 Jan.

1938, 8 Mar. 1964; *Who's Who in the South and Southwest*, (1961).

STERLING STOUDEMIRE

Bullock, Robert (*8 Dec. 1828–27 July 1905*), lawyer, soldier, judge, state legislator, and congressman, was born in Greenville, Pitt County. His father, Richard Bullock, and his mother, whose maiden name was Pannell, were also North Carolinians. Moving to Florida in 1844, Bullock settled in Marion County at Fort King, near present day Ocala, and began teaching school. He became clerk of the circuit court in 1851 and held the position for six years. He was married in 1852 to Amanda L. Waterman of Ocala.

When Indian troubles erupted on the Florida frontier in 1856, Bullock was commissioned by the governor to organize an independent company of mounted volunteers. As captain, he remained in the field for some eighteen months. On his return to Ocala, he studied law in the office of St. George Rogers and was admitted to the bar in 1861. In March 1862 he organized a company of troops and was elected captain. When Company G became part of the Seventh Florida Infantry, he was named regimental lieutenant colonel. After a few weeks at New Smyrna protecting the coast against Federal gunboats, Bullock was ordered to Tennessee to join Bragg's army. He served in the Kentucky campaign under General Edmund Kirby Smith, fighting at the Battle of Richmond. Promoted to colonel, he participated in the Tullahoma campaign and the Battle of Chickamauga. At Missionary Ridge, 25 Nov. 1863, he was captured and taken as a prisoner to Johnson's Island, Lake Erie.

Released for service by exchange in March 1864, Bullock resumed command of his regiment, and at the Battle of Resaca, when General J. J. Finley was wounded, he became brigade commander. The senior colonels entered a vigorous protest against this distinction of a junior officer, but he was eventually confirmed in rank as brigadier general as of 29 Nov. 1864. He was in command of the brigades at Kennesaw Mountain, Dallas, Peachtree Creek, and Atlanta and was severely wounded at Utoy Creek. Rejoining his command after the fall of Atlanta, he led his men through the fighting along the railroad toward Chattanooga and the Battle of Franklin (Tennessee), where he was slightly wounded. While engaged with Nathan Bedford Forrest at Murfreesboro in December 1864, he was again severely wounded and was released from service.

Returning to Ocala, Bullock took up once more the practice of law and became involved in a number of business enterprises, including a mercantile firm, a plantation he had rented, a cedar-cutting operation, and a contract to haul logs for another cedar company. He also managed a large herd of cattle at Orlando. Appointed judge of the probate court, he also served as a Freedman's Bureau agent. It was noted that he executed these responsibilities with racial equality; he was described even by Union officials as "a fairminded man." Settling many legal disputes by compromise, he eliminated the costs of trials and the problems of prejudicial juries.

Bullock was a partisan conservative Democrat, and notwithstanding his good Freedman's Bureau record, it came as no surprise when he was removed as judge during the Reconstruction days of 1868. He was nominated for lieutenant governor by the party convention meeting in Jacksonville in 1872. It was a Republican year in Florida, however, and he was not successful. In 1875 he lost a bid to be elected U.S. senator, but in the following year he was a presidential elector in the Tilden campaign. In 1878, Bullock resisted efforts of his friends to put his name up for nomination for congressman. Serving in the state legislature from Marion County in 1879, he was aligned with the Bourbon Democrats. In 1880 he came within one vote of being nominated U.S. senator by the legislature. He was a candidate for the Democratic party gubernatorial nomination in 1888 but lost this bid, also.

In 1881 he had become clerk of the circuit court, and he held that position until his election in 1889 to Congress. He served two terms and then refused renomination in 1892 in order to take over management of the orange and lemon groves he had acquired at Lake Weir. The great freeze of February 1895 forced his return to Ocala, where he was appointed judge of the Fifth Judicial District. He was elected to a four-year term in 1903 and was serving in that capacity when he died.

SEE: *Biog. Dir. Am. Cong.* (1971); Board of State Institutions, *Soldiers of Florida in the Seminole Indian, Civil, and Spanish-American Wars* (1903); R. L. Carson, "William Dunnington Bloxham, Florida's Two Term Governor" (M.A. thesis, University of Florida, 1945); J. W. Covington, "An Episode in the Third Seminole War," *Florida Historical Quarterly* 45 (1966); H. G. Cutler, *History of Florida Past and Present*, vols. 1–2 (1923); J. J. Dickinson, *Confederate Military History of Florida* (1899); "General Bullock for Governor" (miscellaneous MSS, P. K. Yonge Library of Florida History, University of Florida, Gainesville); E. R. Ott, "Ocala prior to 1868," *Florida Historical Quarterly* 6 (1927); E. R. Ott and L. H. Chazal, *Ocali Country: A History of Marion County, Florida* (1966); R. R. Rerick, *Memoirs of Florida*, vol. 2 (1912); J. H. Shofner, *Nor Is It Over Yet: Florida in the Era of Reconstruction* (1974); J. Wallace, *Carpet-Bag Rule in Florida* (1888, 1964).

SAMUEL PROCTOR

Bulwinkle, Alfred Lee (*21 Apr. 1883–31 Aug. 1950*), congressman, was born in Charleston, S.C., to Herman and Frances McKean Bulwinkle. His father was a German immigrant who developed a successful career as a cotton factor and commission merchant. Alfred Lee Bulwinkle moved with his parents to Dallas, N.C., in 1891, where he was educated in the public schools. He studied law at The University of North Carolina in 1903–4 and was admitted to the bar in 1904. He first practiced law independently in Dallas and then moved to Gastonia, where in 1914 he established a law partnership with Robert Gregg Cherry, a future governor of North Carolina. From 1929 to 1931 he practiced alone; then in 1931 he began a professional association with Stephen B. Dudley that continued until Bulwinkle's death.

Bulwinkle gained the title "Major" from his involvement in World War I. He had been commissioned a captain in the National Guard in 1909. He served in 1916–17 on duty against Mexico. From 1917 to 1919 he was a major in the Field Artillery and had service overseas. After the war he resumed his law practice.

Bulwinkle's political career began before the war. He served as alderman in Dallas and then, from 1913 to 1916, as prosecuting attorney for the municipal court of Gastonia. After his military duty, he was elected to the House of Representatives in 1920 from what was then the Tenth Congressional District. He continued to be reelected from that district until he was defeated in 1928 by Republican Charles R. Jonas, Sr., from Mecklenburg County, in the Hoover sweep of that year.

After his defeat, Bulwinkle practiced law and helped prosecute and convict Fred E. Beal and a group of Communists for the murder of the police chief involved in the strike at Loray Mill in 1929. For this action, Bulwinkle won the continued opposition of the Communist *Daily Worker*.

He was again successful in his election in 1930 in the new Tenth Congressional District, which contained the same counties as the previous ninth. In 1940 the General Assembly redistricted the state and placed Gaston County in the eleventh district, removing Mecklenburg County from Bulwinkle's constituency. That county had provided his major opposition in the Democratic party in the form of Hamilton C. Jones, who was then elected to Congress from the newly created tenth district. Bulwinkle continued uninterrupted service in Congress from 1931 until his death in 1950.

In Congress, Bulwinkle was not a figure of major prominence. He sought to improve the benefits of veterans, and he was an important member of the House Committee on Interstate and Foreign Commerce. At the time of his death, he was the second ranking Democrat on that committee and chairman of its subcommittees on Transportation and on Communications. Bulwinkle helped organize the House Veterans Committee after World War I and helped draft the veterans' benefits act in the 1920s. Probably his most famous piece of legislation was the Reed-Bulwinkle Act of 1948, which exempted trucking companies and railroads from prosecution under the Sherman Anti-Trust Act. The legislation was vetoed by President Harry S. Truman but was passed over the veto by the Republican Eightieth Congress.

Bulwinkle had a generally conservative image as a congressman, but he supported liberal legislation in the early New Deal years and helped to write the first wage and hour law, as well as much public health legislation, including the Cancer Research Act, the Tuberculosis Control Act, and the Venereal Diseases Act. He was House floor leader for the first hospital construction act.

Because of his involvement in interstate and foreign commerce, Bulwinkle became quite knowledgeable about aviation; he was appointed U.S. delegate to the International Aviation Conference in Chicago in 1944 and U.S. adviser to the International Civil Aviation Organization at Montreal, Canada, and Geneva, Switzerland, in 1947.

Bulwinkle married Bessie Lewis, a daughter of James R. and Catherine Lineberger Lewis of Dallas, N.C., in 1911. They had two children: Frances McKean, who married E. Granger Williams of Little Rock, Ark.; and Alfred Lewis, who, after completing law school, joined his father's practice in Gastonia.

Bulwinkle became ill with multiple myeloma, a chronic bone disease, shortly after winning his election in 1948. While others were being sworn in in 1949, he was being treated in Bethesda Naval Hospital. He attended his last congressional session only for a few days and then in a wheel chair. He had returned to Gastonia to recuperate when he died in 1950. His body was interred in Oakwood Cemetery there.

SEE: *Asheville Citizen*, 1 Sept. 1950; *Biog. Dir. Am. Cong.* (1971); *Gastonia Gazette*, 1 Sept. 1950; *North Carolina: The Old North State and the New*, vol. 4 (1941); Douglas Milton Orr, Jr., *Congressional Redistricting: The North Carolina Experience* (1970); Raleigh *News and Observer*, 2 Sept. 1950; U.S. 82nd Congress, 1st Session, 1951, House, *Memorial Services . . . of Alfred Lee Bulwinkle*.

THOMAS S. MORGAN

Bumpass, Frances Webb (*26 Sept. 1819–8 May 1898*), newspaper publisher, teacher, and church worker, was born in Halifax, Va., to Henry and Harriet Dickens Webb. Educated by her parents and by private teachers in North Carolina, she also studied Greek and other advanced subjects with the Reverend D. C. Doak, a Presbyterian clergyman of Orange County, North Carolina. As she recorded in her journal, her parents early impressed upon her that "the duties of domestic life were not to occupy her time, but that . . . she should train the minds and instruct the souls of others." Frances Webb began teaching in Granville County soon after passing her own examinations. In 1842 she married the Reverend Sidney Bumpass, a scholarly Methodist clergyman, and for several years they moved from one rural congregation to another as his assignments dictated. Because he often was sent to "build up" small congregations, his stipend was low and Frances Bumpass taught to add to the family income.

In 1847 the Reverend Mr. Bumpass was appointed presiding elder of the Greensboro District and trustee of Greensboro Female College, a Methodist institution of which he had been an early advocate. After he built a home in Greensboro, Frances became a prominent participant in the college and church community. The couple had often talked of publishing a newspaper for the Methodists of North Carolina, and in May 1851 the *Weekly Message* first appeared as a special number of the *Greensboro Patriot*. Having acquired his own press, Bumpass began regular publication in October but shortly after contracted typhoid fever. He died in December, barely three months after beginning the newspaper. Other ministers and various friends advised Frances Bumpass to sell the press, but she announced promptly that she intended to continue publication at least until November 1852, when she expected the annual Methodist conference would discuss the possibility of adopting the *Weekly Message* as a church publication.

The public looked askance at a woman doing business, so she hired a manager in order to avoid the social stigma. He proved to be undependable, however, and the paper fell into financial difficulties that were so serious the conference declined to take it over. At this point Mrs. Bumpass took over publication herself in her own home and, with servants and boarding students from Greenboro College trained to run the press, kept the *Weekly Message* on a regular schedule for twenty years. In the turbulent years before the Civil War her editorials urged moderation and order. After North Carolina seceded she called for prudence and reason, unselfish work for God, and survival in the face of war. When the shortage of paper forced rationing in the state, pleas were sent to the governor to allow the *Message* to continue. He consented and only during the few months of the Federal occupation of Greensboro in 1865 did it cease publication. In 1872, when the Methodist Church began to publish the *North Carolina Advocate* Mrs. Bumpass finally closed the *Weekly Message*. She then opened a school in her home as a source of income and turned her organizational skills to building a recognized place in the church for women's activities. "Too long," she said, had women "hesitated, fearful, lest it be said they were stepping beyond their sphere." College educated women, she argued, should be sent as missionaries throughout the world. She was instrumental in the 1878 organization of the Women's Foreign Mission Society of the Methodist Church and traveled extensively for the society, helping to arouse the interest of women throughout the country, until failing

health immobilized her. She served as corresponding secretary, first of the North Carolina Conference division of the Society, then of the Western North Carolina Conference division, from 1878 until her death. She was buried in Greensboro.

The Reverend and Mrs. Bumpass were the parents of four children: Duella Bumpass Troy, Eugenia, the Reverend Robah Bumpass, and Terrelius, who died in childhood.

SEE: Eugenia H. Bumpass, *Frances Webb Bumpass, Autobiography and Journal* (1899); Nell Craig, "Mrs. Frances Bumpass Edited for Twenty Years the 'Weekly Message,'" *Greensboro Daily News*, 10 May 1925; Emily Hedrick, "Past is Alive and Well in Ante-Bellum Home," *Greensboro Daily News*, 21 July 1968; Ethel Troy, chapters from an unfinished biography of Frances Webb Bumpass, in the possession of Sue Vernon Williams, Greensboro; Ethel Troy, "Frances Webb Bumpass, Lady Editor, Ran Newspaper in Old Greensboro," *Greensboro Record*, 10 Mar. 1951.

PAULA S. JORDAN

Buncombe, Edward (*1742–May 1778*), planter and officer in the Continental Line in the Revolutionary War, was born on the West Indian island of St. Christopher, of English ancestry. His father, Thomas Buncombe, was a planter; he and his wife, Esther, had four children, of whom Edward was the second. Joseph Buncombe, brother of Thomas, owned land in North Carolina that he bequeathed to Edward. In about 1768, Edward left St. Christopher to make his permanent home in what was then Tyrrell County, on Albemarle Sound. Erecting a residence called Buncombe Hall at the present site of the community of Chesson, he became noted for his hospitality, as recorded, for instance, by Josiah Quincy in 1773 (the editor of Quincy's journal identifies the host erroneously as Richard Buncombe). The house was still standing as late as 1874. Buncombe eventually owned four square miles of land and at least one trading vessel, the *Buncombe*, which was registered at Port Roanoke.

Buncombe served the colony as a justice of the peace and as commander of the Tyrrell County militia regiment. He supported Governor William Tryon in 1771 against the Regulators but was not called into service. As the Revolution approached, Buncombe Hall was the scene of a conference held on 4 Apr. 1774 at which Buncombe, John Harvey, and Samuel Johnston discussed a decision to call an assembly in defiance of the royal governor. This assembly, the first such in the colonies, met at New Bern 25 Aug. 1774.

Buncombe was elected colonel of the Tyrrell County militia on 9 Sept. 1775 and transferred to the Fifth Regiment of North Carolina troops in the Continental Line on 17 Apr. 1776; there he was assigned to the brigade of General Francis Nash. His colonelcy was confirmed by the Continental Congress 7 May 1776. The brigade served at Charleston, S.C., until March 1777, when it marched north to join General George Washington. At Trenton, Buncombe served as president of a court martial on 22 Aug. 1777, and at Philadelphia he was named field officer for the day on 26 Aug. 1777. He also signed a petition, together with other North Carolina colonels, asking the state delegation to the Continental Congress to protest the appointment of a Dr. Hand of Pennsylvania to replace Carolinian Brigadier General James Moore, deceased.

Buncombe fought with his regiment at the battles of Brandywine and Germantown. He was severely wounded 4 Oct. at Germantown and left for dead. Recognized by a former schoolmate in the British army, he was removed to Philadelphia and paroled. Colonel Alex Martin hoped to exchange British prisoners for him, but the exchange was never accomplished. Without funds for proper medical attention (he had paid many military expenses out of his own pocket) and unable to return home, Buncombe failed to make a complete recovery; in May 1778, while sleepwalking, he fell down a flight of stairs, reopened his wound, and bled to death. He was interred in the graveyard of Christ Church parish, Philadelphia. The grave is not marked, and the parish register lists him as Cornelius Buncombe.

In 1791, Buncombe County was created in North Carolina and named for Edward Buncombe. Felix Walker, U.S. congressman (1817–23) from that county, was responsible for introducing into American usage the term "bunkum," later shortened to "bunk."

Buncombe was an Anglican by faith. He was married on the island of St. Christopher to Elizabeth Dawson Taylor on 10 Apr. 1766. They had three children: Elizabeth Taylor (b. 11 Mar. 1767), who married John Goelet of New York on 23 Oct. 1784 and eventually returned to live at Buncombe Hall; Thomas (b. 3 Feb. 1769), and Hester (mentioned only in Buncombe's will).

SEE: Marshall DeLancey Haywood, *Builders of the Old North State* (1968); *North Carolina Booklet*, vol. 2 (1902); William L. Saunders, ed., *Colonial Records of North Carolina*, 10 vols. (1886–90); Tyrrell County records (North Carolina State Archives, Raleigh); John H. Wheeler, *Reminiscences and Memoirs of North Carolina* (1883–84).

SARAH MCCULLOH LEMMON

Bundy, William (d. 27 Mar. 1692), colonial official, settled in Albemarle in 1663 or 1664. He was a member of the council of the Albemarle colony in 1684 and a justice of Perquimans Precinct Court, 1690–92. He lived in Perquimans Precinct, where he held at least 170 acres of land, granted him in 1669.

Bundy, a devout Quaker, was active in the Perquimans Monthly Meeting. In September 1679 he joined with other settlers of his faith in sending to London a signed "Remonstrance" regarding the current disorders in the colony. In June or July 1680 he and several other Quakers were fined and imprisoned for about six months for refusing to bear arms "in the musterfield."

Bundy was married twice. His first wife, Elizabeth, bore him four children: Mary, Caleb, Samuel, and William, Jr. She died on 4 Mar. 1676/77. Bundy's second wife was Mary Pearce, widow of John Pearce and daughter of Joseph Scott. Their marriage took place on 15 Dec. 1683 and a daughter, Sarah, was born to them.

Bundy's three sons settled in Pasquotank Precinct, where they held adjoining tracts of land. Caleb and Samuel were early members of the Quaker meeting in Pasquotank. Caleb married Jane Manners, daughter of Perigreen and Frances Manners, in 1690. Samuel married Tamer Symons, daughter of Jeremiah Symons, in 1696. No marriage record has been found for William, who died 28 July 1700. Bundy's older daughter, Mary, was married to Timothy Cleare, son of William Cleare, in 1685. She died in 1694, and Cleare subsequently married Hannah Snelling, a widow. Although Bundy's other children had married members of their own faith, his younger daughter, Sarah, married Francis Pettitt of Chowan in 1711; the Perquimans Monthly Meeting declared her "out of union," as her husband was not a Friend.

Bundy's executors were his son Caleb and Timothy Cleare.

SEE: Guilford College Library (Greensboro), for Quaker records; J. R. B. Hathaway, ed., *North Carolina Historical and Genealogical Register*, 3 vols. (1900–1903); William Wade Hinshaw, comp., *Encyclopedia of American Quaker Genealogy*, vol. 1 (1936); North Carolina State Archives (Raleigh), for Albemarle Book of Warrants and Surveys (1681–1706), Albemarle County Papers (1678–1714), Perquimans Births, Marriages, Deaths and Flesh Marks (1659–1739), Perquimans Precinct Court Minutes (1688–93); Mattie Erma Edwards Parker, ed., *North Carolina Higher-Court Records, 1670–1696* and *1697–1701* (1968 and 1971); William L. Saunders, ed., *Colonial Records of North Carolina*, vol. 1 (1886); Ellen Goode Winslow, *History of Perquimans County* (1931).

MATTIE ERMA E. PARKER

Bunker, Eng and Chang (May 1811–17 Jan. 1874), the first Siamese twins to receive world-wide attention, were born in the fishing village of Meklong, Siam, of obscure parentage. Their nationality became the name for the birth defect in which two persons are physically joined together. Eng and Chang, unlike some grotesquely deformed Siamese twins, were completely normal except for a thick but pliable band of flesh connecting them at the chest. During their childhood the band became stretched enough to allow them to stand side by side with relative freedom of movement. The condition initially caused alarm and consternation among the villagers, some of whom feared the extraordinary birth as a harbinger of doom. Because of a determined mother and their own adaptability, the two boys grew up as normally as possible, even raising ducks to help support their family, and were gradually accepted by the community.

The twins would probably have lived out their lives in obscurity had it not been for a Scottish trader, Robert Hunter, and a New England sea captain, Abel Coffin, who in April 1829 persuaded the twins to go abroad with them. They arrived in Boston in August of that year, having acquired a working knowledge of English on the voyage. During the following eight years, they toured the United States and Europe, first under the auspices of Hunter and Coffin and later with P. T. Barnum. They drew large crowds wherever they went, performing feats of strength and dexterity. They also caused considerable stir among the medical profession, whose members never tired of conducting tests on them and speculating on the cause of and solution to their malady.

Eng and Chang, in their mid-twenties, gave up their original plans of returning to Siam. They decided to become naturalized American citizens, to break with Barnum, and to conduct their own shows. Upon learning that a surname was one of the requirements for naturalization, they accepted the suggestion of a bystander, Fred Bunker, that they use his name.

Touring on their own, the twins acquired considerable wealth but grew weary of life on the road. At the suggestion of Dr. James C. Calloway of Wilkesboro, who met Eng and Chang in New York, they included Wilkesboro in their itinerary. They arrived there on 7 June 1837 and found the quiet little community and surrounding countryside much to their liking. Within two years they stopped touring and opened a general store in Traphill, a nearby community. They also bought some land and began raising corn and hogs.

Shortly after settling in Traphill, Eng and Chang struck up a friendship with two sisters, Adelaide and Sarah Yates. When it became apparent that a romantic relationship was developing among them, the community was outraged. Nevertheless, they were married 13 Apr. 1843, Eng to Sarah and Chang to Adelaide. The former couple eventually had ten children, the latter twelve. All were normal, with the exception of a boy and girl of Chang's, who were deaf mutes.

As their families grew, the twins found it necessary to establish separate residences. In 1846 they moved to nearby Surry County, where they built two houses about a mile apart on the same tract of land. The families of each of the twins stayed at their respective houses, while Eng and Chang took turns visiting every three days. They followed this pattern for the rest of their lives.

The prosperity they achieved as farmers was devastated by the Civil War. To recoup their fortune, they reluctantly decided to rejoin Barnum and tour once again. No longer having the exuberance of youth, they bolstered their spirits with the hope that while touring in Europe they could find a doctor who would separate them. Chang had become dissipated from drinking too much, and was losing his health; consequently, they were becoming irritable toward each other. Unfortunately, no doctor would touch them. They returned home in 1871, having accumulated money but having lost the last hope of separation, which had become the most important thing in their lives.

On the voyage across the Atlantic, Chang suffered a stroke and partial paralysis. He recovered partially, but from that time his health began to decline inexorably. It is remarkable that their families managed to endure the strain as well as they apparently did, considering the increasing severity and frequency of the twins' fights. On 12 Jan. 1874, Chang was stricken with severe bronchitis, accompanied by chest pains. The condition grew worse, and he died in his sleep in the early morning of 17 Jan. Although there was nothing organically wrong with Eng, he was horrified upon waking to find his twin dead, thinking that he would soon follow: they had always regarded themselves as one, signing their names "Chang Eng," rather than "Chang and Eng." A doctor was summoned to try to perform a desperate operation, but Eng died before he arrived. An autopsy conducted in Philadelphia led doctors to conclude that while Chang had died of a cerebral clot brought on by the previous stroke, complicated by pneumonia, Eng had actually died of fright. A partial examination of the connecting band, limited by the family's wish that it not be cut from the front, revealed that their lives were connected by a "quite distinct extra hepatic tract" and that an artery and some nerve connections ran between them; thus, Eng may have suffered from loss of blood from Chang's dying body.

They were buried in a common grave in the White Plains Baptist Church cemetery in Surry County. They were survived by their wives and all but one of their children.

SEE: *Asheville Citizen*, 5 Dec. 1962; Kay Hunter, *Duet for a Lifetime* (1964); *National Enquirer*, 6 Oct. 1971; North Wilkesboro *Journal-Patriot*, 12 Oct. 1967; Raleigh *News and Observer*, 1 Jan. 1961, 28 Oct. 1962, 30 May 1965; *Winston-Salem Journal*, 9 Apr. 1950; Winston-Salem *Twin City Sentinel*, 7 Jan. 1969.

DARRYL TRAYWICK

Bunn, Benjamin Hickman (*19 Oct. 1844–25 Aug. 1907*), congressman, was the son of Redmund Bunn of Nash County and his wife, Mary Hickman Bryan. The Bunn family had long been prominent in Nash County, and members were among the pioneer settlers around the Falls of the Tar River. Bunn was educated at the Rocky Mount Academy and was preparing to enter The University of North Carolina when the Civil War broke out. He enlisted in the Confederate Army at age seventeen and served throughout the war. Entering the army as a first lieutenant in the Thirtieth North Carolina Regiment, Bunn later served in the Forty-seventh North Carolina Regiment and, toward the end of the war, was captain of a company of sharpshooters. He was twice wounded, once at Gettysburg and again before Petersburg, in 1865. His two brothers, William Henry and Elias, who were also in the Confederate Army, died in service.

At the conclusion of the war, Bunn read law under his uncle, William T. Dortch, in Goldsboro; he received his license in June 1866 and his superior court license a year later. Gifted with a quick mind and good memory, he was a forceful advocate and appeared in almost every important case tried in Nash County during the next forty years. He served as county attorney for thirty years and was attorney for the Atlantic Coast Line Railroad for much of his professional career.

Largely at the instigation of Bunn, the Rocky Mount depot was incorporated as a town by the legislature in 1867, and he was elected the first mayor. He was elected a member of the constitutional convention of North Carolina in 1875 and rendered important service as secretary of the Committee on Privileges and Elections. Elected to the General Assembly in 1882, he was appointed chairman of the joint committee on the code.

Bunn was elected to represent his district in Congress in 1888 and served for three terms. He was given the chairmanship of the Committee on Claims and in this capacity performed competent legislative service, examining claims and drawing up reports for action by Congress. In his report on the bill for the relief of J. M. Lanston, he set forth the expenses of every contested election since the organization of Congress. Bunn's speech on the Federal Election Bill, setting forth the southern thought on sectionalism, was widely circulated, and parts of it were inserted in the Democratic handbook for the next campaign.

After retiring from Congress, Bunn was postmaster of Rocky Mount from 23 Apr. 1895 until 27 July 1897. He served for a time as president of the Rocky Mount Mills and was so acting when its management started the company on its modern era of development. He was also interested in progressive farming.

On 7 Nov. 1871, Bunn married Harriet, the daughter of Dr. James Jones Philips of Edgecombe County. The Bunns were the parents of nine children: James P.; Mary, the wife of Dr. George Wimberly; Benjamin, Jr.; Annie Lee, wife of Robert Davis; Laura-Maude, wife of Kemp Davis Battle; Catherine, who married William C. Woodard; Hattie; Bessie; and Redmund, who died young.

Bunn died at his country home, Benvenue, several miles northwest of Rocky Mount, and was buried in Pineview Cemetery.

SEE: Mrs. Kemp D. Battle, personal communication; *Biog. Dir. Am. Cong.* (1971); James P. Bunn, "Benvenue" (in the personal papers of Mrs. Kemp D. Battle).

CLAIBORNE T. SMITH, JR.

Bunn, Henry Gaston (*12 June 1838–17 July 1908*), Confederate colonel and chief justice, Arkansas Supreme Court, was born at Rocky Mount, Nash County, the son of David and Elizabeth Bunn. He removed with his parents to Fayette County, Tenn., in 1844, and thence to

Ouachita County, Ark., in 1846. He returned to North Carolina in January 1859 as a student at Davidson College, remaining there until the outbreak of the Civil War.

Returning to Arkansas, Bunn volunteered in the Confederate Army and became third lieutenant in Company A, Fourth Arkansas Regiment (McNair's). In November 1861 he was made adjutant of the regiment. At the battle of Pea Ridge he was wounded and taken prisoner but escaped. In April 1862 he was raised to the rank of lieutenant colonel. Fighting with the Army of Tennessee, he was wounded during the fighting around Atlanta in 1864 and did not see action again until early in 1865. At the Battle of Bentonville in the closing days of the war (19–20 Mar. 1865), he commanded a brigade, retaining that command at General Albert Johnston's surrender on 26 Apr. 1865. Bunn then marched his men back to Arkansas.

Settling in Camden after the war, Bunn was admitted to the bar in 1866. He served as state senator from Ouachita County in 1873 and as a member of the constitutional convention of 1874. He practiced law successfully, serving as a special judge on occasion, until Governor William Fishback appointed him in May 1893 to fill the vacancy on the bench caused by the resignation of Chief Justice Sterling R. Cockrill. In 1896, Bunn was nominated by the Democratic State Convention and confirmed at the polls in September for an eight-year term as chief justice. In this office he opposed Attorney General and Governor Jeff Davis in his efforts to drive all trusts from Arkansas. In 1904, with Davis at the height of his powers, Bunn was defeated in the Democratic primary by Joseph M. Hill. After his retirement from the court, he moved to El Dorado, practicing law until his death in 1908.

Bunn was married twice: in 1865 to Louise E. Holmes, who died in 1866; and then to Aralee Conally, by whom he had five children. His remains were removed to Camden for burial.

Bunn was a lifelong Democrat and a Presbyterian.

SEE: *Arkansas Reports*, 57–73; *Biographical and Historical Memoirs of Southern Arkansas* (1890); C. A. Evans, ed., *Confederate Military History*, vol. 10 (1899); Little Rock *Arkansas Democrat*, 18 July 1908; Little Rock *Arkansas Gazette*, 18 July 1908.

MICHAEL B. DOUGAN

Burges (Burgess), Dempsey (1751–13 Jan. 1800), Revolutionary War leader and member of Congress, was born near Shiloh in Pasquotank (later Camden) County. His father was John Burges, a farmer and Baptist minister, of English ancestry.

Entering politics at an early age, Burges became a member of the assembly in 1773. In 1775 and 1776 he served in the provincial congresses meeting at Hillsborough and Halifax, representing Pasquotank County. When Camden County was created in 1777, Burges was on the committee appointed to lay out the new courthouse and jail. In the provincial congresses he served on various committees, including Ways and Means and the Regulation of Internal Peace, the latter being concerned with the detection and punishment of Tories.

Burges was commissioned a major in the Pasquotank militia in September 1775 and promoted to lieutenant colonel in April 1776. After the war he lived on his farm near Shiloh and remained active in both politics and the affairs of the Baptist church. He was elected a member of the U.S. House of Representatives in 1795 and reelected in 1797.

Burges was buried in the Shiloh Baptist Church cemetery. His wife's maiden name was Sawyer. According to the census of 1790, he may have had as many as two sons and two daughters, and he owned thirty slaves.

SEE: *Biog. Dir. Am. Cong.* (1971); *North Carolina Baptist Historical Papers*, vol. 2 (1897); William L. Saunders and Walter Clark, eds., *Colonial and State Records of North Carolina*, 30 vols. (1886–1914); John H. Wheeler, *Historical Sketches of North Carolina* (1851).

ELMER D. JOHNSON

Burges, Thomas (1712–12 Nov. 1779), Church of England clergyman, was born in the parish of Standon, Staffordshire, England, where he was baptized 6 Sept. 1712. He was the fourth of the fourteen children of John Burges and his wife, Dorothy, the daughter of William Lovatt of Clayton Hall in Staffordshire. It is not known what school he attended or when he took orders.

Burges was sent to America by the Bishop of London in 1741 and announced his intention of locating in North Carolina. However, for twenty years he was rector of Nottoway Parish in Southampton County, Va. According to the Halifax Registry, Thomas Burges "of Southampton County" bought 640 acres in Halifax (then Edgecombe) County in 1750; as Thomas Burges, "clerk," he sold the tract the following year. This purchase may reflect an abortive attempt to settle in North Carolina some years before he actually did so. In October 1759 the wardens and vestry of Edgecombe Parish, Halifax County, made an agreement with Burges to pay him £100 per annum as salary and £120 extra per annum in lieu of a glebe. He appears to have moved to his new charge in 1759, as he preached the funeral sermon of a Mr. Thomas at his home on Roanoke River near Norfleet's ferry in that year. In 1760 he purchased a lot in the town of Tarboro, which had just been laid out. On 20 Apr. 1762, Alexander Campbell of "the island of Martinico," merchant, sold Burges lot number 118 in the town of Halifax.

In 1756, prior to Burges's removal to North Carolina, the assembly had divided Edgecombe Parish of Edgecombe County, and the southern portion was given the name St. Mary's. In 1759 the upper part of Edgecombe County, which contained Edgecombe Parish, was constituted Halifax County, while the area encompassed by St. Mary's retained the old name of Edgecombe. The confusing combination Edgecombe Parish-Halifax County was the result. When Burges took over his duties, there were, in addition to the parish church at Conoconara, a few miles southwest of the present town of Tillery, chapels at Kehukee in eastern Halifax and Quankey in the northwestern part of the county and a chapel in Halifax Town. Burges resided near the main church at Conoconara. On 15 Feb. 1764, Egbert Haywood conveyed to him 1,041 acres on Conoconara Creek. In 1774, Elizabeth Parish was cut off from the western part of Edgecombe Parish; Halifax Town was included in the new parish, which appears to have been named for Elizabeth, wife of the current royal governor, Josiah Martin. From Burges's will, it is certain that he served both parishes until his death. Little is known of his ministry in North Carolina, but Governor William Tryon in 1768 referred to him as a "clergyman of worth and much respected."

Burges was buried in the yard of his parish church at Conoconara. His will, dated 1777, was not probated until 1794. A bill was passed by the legislature in 1787 to enable the wardens of the poor, the successor of the old parish vestry, to levy a special tax on the inhabitants of the county of Halifax to discharge debts due Burges, "now deceased," for ministerial duties performed in the year 1776.

Burges was married first in 1742 at Indian Springs in Southampton County, Va., to Miriam, surname unknown. Indian Springs was the glebe for Nottoway Parish and had been given to the vestry by Francis Clements in 1721. Mrs. Burges died in 1758 at age forty-two, leaving a son and two daughters. In 1760, in North Carolina, Burges married Mary, the daughter of Colonel John Haywood and his wife, Mary Lovatt. Burges's mother was a Lovatt, and the families may have been related. Of the children by his first marriage, Anna Maria married General Laurence Baker of Gates County and Dorothy married Colonel John Bradford of Halifax. The son, Henry John, was ordained by the Bishop of London in 1768 and on his return to America served at St. Mary's Parish, Edgecombe County, for a year. In 1772 he became rector of Newport Parish, Isle of Wight County, Va. An active patriot, he was a member of the committee of safety of the county in 1775 and later was imprisoned by the British. Thomas's son, Albridgeton S. H., attended The University of North Carolina, 1805–9, and became a physician. He lived in Raleigh for a time and was one of the founders of Christ Church there.

Burges and his second wife had only one child, a son, Lovatt, who was clerk of the Halifax County Court for many years. Among Lovatt's children was Thomas H., a prominent attorney in Halifax, who represented the borough in the legislature in 1819, 1821, and 1822. He inherited the lot in Tarboro his grandfather had purchased in 1760. In 1834 he deeded this property to Calvary Church, Tarboro, and it forms part of the lot on which the present Calvary Church now stands. A prayer book, printed in London in 1749 and inscribed "The Rev. Thomas Burges, Edgecombe Parish, Halifax County," was inherited by Burges's great-granddaughter, Mrs. Melissa Long, and was exhibited at the Convention of the Diocese of North Carolina held at Tarboro in 1890.

SEE: J. B. Cheshire, ed., *Sketches of Church History in North Carolina* (1892); Deeds and Wills of the County of Halifax (North Carolina State Archives, Raleigh); *North Carolina Booklet*, vol. 23 (1926); Stuart Hall Smith and Claiborne T. Smith, Jr., *The History of Trinity Parish* (1955).

CLAIBORNE T. SMITH, JR.

Burgevin(e), Henry Andrea (1836–27 June 1865), adventurer and mercenary, was the son of Andrea Burgevin, a Napoleonic captain who migrated to the United States in 1815, and his wife, the former Juliet Guillet of New Bern. Henry was probably born in his maternal grandparents' home in New Bern; he joined three older children, Caroline; Edmund, who would be adjutant general of Arkansas during the Civil War; and Mary. Because of his father's early death (*ca.* 1836), he was raised by his mother. In 1844 he became a page in the U.S. House of Representatives. He served for a portion of 1844 and from January to March 1845, when he was transferred to the Senate. He remained there until 1853. In Washington he attended private and public schools.

In 1853, Burgevin visited Hawaii, Australia, India, and the Middle East. He enlisted in the French army in 1855 and fought in the Crimean War. At the war's end, he returned to Washington, D.C., and began reading law. He expended his savings before completing his studies and moved to New York, where he worked for a newspaper and later in the U.S. Post Office. In 1859 he sailed to China aboard the *Edwin Forrest*, arriving at Shanghai on 18 Oct. 1859.

In April 1860, Burgevin became an officer in Frederick Townsend Ward's mercenary force, organized to defend Shanghai and its environs from the Taiping rebels. After an initial failure, the force captured the Taiping stronghold of Sungkiang. In late 1861, Ward and Burgevin began to achieve notoriety after Ward, at Burgevin's suggestion, organized a Western-led Chinese force that became know as the Ever-Victorious Army (EVA).

In engagements in 1861–62, Burgevin received at least three wounds. At Hsiao-t'ang (1 Mar. 1862) he suffered a rifle wound from which he never fully recovered. In 1862 the emperor awarded Burgevin a fourth degree and later a second degree mandarinship for his accomplishments against the Taipings. Following Ward's death in September 1862, Burgevin assumed command of the EVA and directed several successful sorties against the Taipings. However, a rift between Burgevin and his employers overshadowed the victories. The Manchus wanted Burgevin to assist them in an assault on the Taiping capital of Nanking, but Burgevin refused to participate until the EVA received its back pay and acquired additional funds for equipment. By late December the pay was almost three months in arrears. On 2 Jan. 1863, Burgevin and the Chinese banker responsible for provisioning the EVA quarreled over the monetary arrangements. Burgevin punched the banker and removed from the banker's residence forty thousand silver dollars which the banker had previously stated were to be used to pay the EVA.

The governor Kiangsu province, Li Hung-chang, used the incident to remove Burgevin from his command. Contending that he was only temporarily off duty, Burgevin placed an English officer in charge of the EVA and went to Shanghai to regain clear title to the command. Western officials in Shanghai were unable to alter Li's decision, but they did convene a mixed court of arbitration that awarded Burgevin approximately $32,600 in back pay. The Chinese refused to honor the award.

Meanwhile, Burgevin had taken his case to Peking and presented it to the Tsungli Yamen (foreign office). The Tsungli Yamen approved his reinstatement and sent a dispatch to this effect by messenger to Li. Li, however, disregarded it. Burgevin, who had accompanied the messenger, returned to Peking a second time but discovered that the Tsungli Yamen had lost interest in his case. Infuriated, he left Peking determined to obtain revenge. On 2 Aug. 1863, he and some associates joined the Taipings, but his stay with them was brief. In October he began negotiating with the new commander of the EVA, Charles George ("Chinese") Gordon. Initially, Burgevin proposed that the two establish a new kingdom in China. When Gordon refused, Burgevin requested and received an amnesty for himself and his followers. He crossed to Gordon's lines on 18 Oct. 1863.

On 1 Dec. 1863 the American consul general in China deported Burgevin to Japan. Burgevin returned to Shanghai in 1864, whereupon he was jailed and given a choice of standing trial for insurrection or returning to Japan. Burgevin chose Japan. Upon his return there, he conceived the idea of organizing an army to help the tozama daimyo (outer lords) overthrow the ruling Tokugawa shogunate. He sailed aboard the *Feipang* from Yokohama to Shimonoseki to discuss the matter with the tozama daimyo and was asked to return for their answer in a month or two. He reboarded the *Feipang* in the belief the ship was sailing to Hong Kong and then returning to Shimonoseki. However, once the vessel was at sea, the captain set his course for Shanghai.

In March 1865, Burgevin became a fugitive in

Shanghai. He subsequently considered rejoining the Taipings and went to Amoy to contact them. Initially he was unsuccessful, but on 15 May 1865, a man known as Stanley led him into a trap under the guise of escorting him to a Taiping encampment. With Stanley's assistance, Burgevin was arrested. The Manchus sent him to Soochow for trial in one of their courts. En route, the boat carrying Burgevin purportedly overturned while shooting a rapids in Chekiang province, and Burgevin, who was in chains, drowned. Skeptical American officials investigated the incident but could not prove there had been foul play. Burgevin was interred in Shanghai's foreign cemetery.

Burgevin had married a Chinese courtesan in 1862. There is no record of offspring. In the 1860s journalists added a final *e* to Burgevin's name.

SEE: Gerald Brown, "The Last Months of the Taeping War," *Harper's Monthly Magazine* 32 (Apr. 1866 [portrait]); R. H. Detrick, "Henry Andrea Burgevine in China (Ph.D. diss., Indiana University, 1968); Edward Forester, "Personal Recollections of the Taiping Rebellion," *Cosmopolitan Magazine* 22 (Nov., Dec. 1896 [portrait]); E. A. Lyster, ed., *With Gordon In China* (1891); Daniel J. MacGowan, "Memoirs of Generals Ward and Burgevine," *Far East* 8 (1877); *North China Herald*, 1861–66; Andrew Wilson, *The Ever Victorious Army* (1868).

R. H. DETRICK

Burgin, William Olin *(28 July 1877–12 Apr. 1946)*, congressman, lawyer, and businessman, was born on a farm in McDowell County, one of five children of Merrett Burgin, farmer, merchant, and Confederate Army veteran, and his wife, Mary Elizabeth Smith. Prior to Merrett Burgin's death in 1893, the family moved to Rutherfordton, where William attended a school conducted by Captain W. T. R. Ball and later worked on the family farm. After his father's death he went to work to help support the family, beginning a business career as a clerk in a general store. He attended the Rutherfordton Military Institute in 1903 and 1904, after which he became a traveling salesman. While in this position he became favorably impressed with Thomasville and opened a small dry goods store there.

He apparently was well liked in Thomasville, for he was elected mayor in 1908; he served until January 1910 and again from August 1910 to June 1911. As mayor he attracted attention through liberal positions on public questions. While mayor, Burgin became interested in the practice of law and, under the direction of A. F. Sams, a young Thomasville lawyer, read law at night. He fulfilled bar requirements after attending The University of North Carolina School of Law in the winter of 1912 and the spring of 1913. He married Edith Lee Greer of Lexington, on 12 Dec. 1912.

Upon acquisition of his license to practice law in 1913, Burgin moved to Lexington, where he resided for the remainder of his life. He did not abandon his business enterprises, for in 1909 he was one of the founders and the president of the People's Savings and Loan of Thomasville. Once in Lexington, Burgin began his practice, primarily in civil law, but continued to stay interested in corporate business. He was a smart businessman; that he was well respected is evidenced by his inclusion on the board of directors of the Mutual Savings and Loan in Lexington in 1919; his presidency of the Carolina Panel Corporation, founded in 1927; and his directorship of the Industrial Savings and Loan

Association, which he helped found in 1928. Burgin also held the position of director of the Bank of Lexington.

When Burgin moved to Lexington in 1913, he joined the National Guard; as a captain of Company L, he saw service on the Mexican border in 1916.

During the twenties, Burgin prospered materially (all his business connections were profitable); yet he gained a good deal of experience working with and for the people, both as a private lawyer and, from 1922 until 1928, as the county lawyer for Davidson County. He continued his law practice, but, in order to become engaged in solving the problems that faced the state in the depression, he ran for the North Carolina House of Representatives in 1930. The 1931 term proved the beginning of a political career. He was elected to the state senate in 1932, where, in 1933, he sponsored unemployment compensation and social security legislation, withdrawing his support only when he became convinced that it could not be enacted. After his term in the state senate, Burgin returned to private life until his election to the U.S. House of Representatives on 8 Nov. 1938. His election came after an unprecedented campaign and primary election between Burgin and C. B. Deane. A question was raised about the absentee ballots; the results had originally certified Burgin the winner by a hundred votes, yet Deane and the state board of elections maintained that if the illegal absentee ballots were thrown out, Deane would win by twenty-three votes. Arbitrators for the election dispute were selected, and the court ruled Burgin the victor just a few hours after Deane withdrew.

In January of 1939, Dwight L. Pickard, judge of Davidson County, entered into a partnership with Burgin, for civil practice only, and maintained the office while Burgin was in Congress.

In Congress, Burgin was appointed to the Committee on Foreign Affairs, of which he remained a member for the rest of his life. As representative of North Carolina's Eighth District, he was known for his ability, for close attention to his congressional duties, and for many qualities that made him a useful member of the House. Despite his difficulties in his first election to Congress, Burgin worked diligently and created a good record for himself. He ran on this record, and the people of his district endorsed him by overwhelming majorities for the next three elections. In Congress he was a steadfast supporter of Roosevelt's foreign policies and war measures.

On 23 Feb. 1946, Burgin announced that he would not run for reelection, yet he remained intensely concerned with the nation's foreign policy and until his death worked on a proposal calling for an immediate halt to the manufacture of atomic bombs.

From 1942 through 1946, Burgin suffered three heart attacks; on 10 Apr. he contracted a "coronary heart disease" that proved fatal less than two days later. The body was interred in the Lexington Cemetery.

His obituary listed his memberships in the Masons, Junior Order of United American Mechanics, and Knights of Pythias and noted that he was a steward of the Methodist church.

SEE: *Biog. Dir. Am. Cong.* (1971); *Charlotte Observer*, 23 Feb. 1946; D. L. Grant, *Alumni History of the University of North Carolina* (1924); *North Carolina Manual* (1933–44); *North Carolina: The Old North State and the New*, 4 vols. (1941); M. Jewell Sink, *Wheels of Faith and Courage* (1952); University of North Carolina Alumni Office (Chapel Hill), for newspaper clippings and other information.

TYNDALL P. HARRIS, JR.

Burgwin, George William Bush (2 Sept. 1787–9 Feb. 1854), planter, was born at his father's plantation, the Hermitage, in New Hanover County, six weeks before the death of his mother, Eliza Bush Burgwin. She was the daughter of an English merchant, George Bush, of Bristol. George's father, John Burgwin, was a substantial planter and merchant in the Cape Fear region, who had emigrated to America from Wales before the Revolution. Following his mother's death, Burgwin was reared at the Hermitage and educated by private tutors. Later, he was sent to school in New Jersey.

Upon the death of his father in 1803, he inherited several plantations in Bladen and New Hanover counties. His older brother, John Fanning, having inherited the Hermitage, George settled in Wilmington after his marriage to Maria Nash. During this time, the family spent their summers at Hillsborough.

Because John Fanning Burgwin desired to relocate at New Bern and Maria Nash Burgwin owned a substantial amount of land there, a significant transfer of family properties occurred in 1811. John Burgwin exchanged the Hermitage and Castle Haynes plantations, with the slaves thereon, for Mrs. Burgwin's estates and slaves in the New Bern vicinity. According to the agreement, Castle Haynes was settled on Maria Nash Burgwin and her heirs, while the Hermitage became the property of her oldest son, John Henry King. George Burgwin moved his family to the Hermitage in 1812 and spent the rest of his life there. At the same time, they began living in Smithville (now Southport) during the summers.

For most of his life, Burgwin spent his time directing the cultivation of the great family plantations, including the Hermitage and Castle Haynes. The principal crops produced on his properties were cotton and rice. He was given to agricultural experimentation and described in 1821 a horse-drawn seed coverer he had constructed which he was using to plant his cotton. He pointed out that it was superior to the hoe and saved the labor of six or eight field hands.

An Episcopalian, Burgwin led his family in worship from the *Book of Common Prayer* on Sundays at the Hermitage. He was interested in higher education and contributed a hundred dollars toward the completion of The University of North Carolina's South Building between 1809 and 1811. Known as a charming and handsome man, Burgwin was noted for his hospitality and delighted in filling the Hermitage with guests. During his lifetime, it was the scene of numerous entertainments, including balls and fox hunts.

Burgwin's wife, Maria Nash of New Bern, whom he married 7 Apr. 1807, was the daughter of Governor Abner Nash. She died shortly after learning of the death of her oldest son, John, in the Mexican War in 1847. The Burgwins were the parents of an outstanding family that played a significant role in North Carolina's history. Their eleven children were Frances Eliza Bush, Mary Nash (died young), John Henry King, Margaret Ann, Caroline Athelia, George Clitherall (died young), Frederick Nash (died young), Hassell Witherspoon, Ann Maria, Sarah Priscilla, and Nathaniel Hill.

After contracting erysipelas of the leg, Burgwin died at the Hermitage in the room in which he had been born. Originally buried on the estate, his remains were later removed, with those of his wife and son John, to Oakdale Cemetery in Wilmington. A portrait of Burgwin is in the possession of a descendant, George Collinson Burgwin III of Pittsburgh, Pa.

SEE: Samuel A. Ashe, ed., *Biographical History of North Carolina*, vol. 8 (1917); Kemp P. Battle, *History of the*
University of North Carolina, vol. 1 (1907); Collinson P. E. Burgwyn, personal correspondence (20 Feb. 1975); James G. Burr, *The Hermitage* (1885); Cornelius Oliver Cathey, *Agricultural Developments in North Carolina* (1956); Eliza B. Clitherall, MSS (Southern Historical Collection, University of North Carolina, Chapel Hill); Walter Burgwyn Jones, *John Burgwin, Carolinian; John Jones, Virginian* (1913); *Raleigh Register*, 22 Feb. 1854.

JAMES ELLIOTT MOORE

Burgwin, John (25 Feb. 1731–21 May 1803), colonial official and merchant, was born at Hereford, England. His father, John Burgwin (1682–1751), whose name was originally spelled Ap Gwyn, left his entire estate in South Wales, England, to an elder son, James B., forcing the younger boy to seek his own fortune elsewhere. By early in 1750/51, Burgwin was employed as a merchant in Charleston, S.C., with the firm of Hooper, Alexander and Company. The firm did business at Wilmington, and Burgwin apparently moved to the Cape Fear River area of North Carolina shortly thereafter. On 15 Feb. 1753 he married Margaret Haynes, daughter of Captain Roger and Margaret Haynes of Castle Haynes Plantation near Wilmington. Mrs. Haynes was the daughter of the Reverend Richard Marsden, rector of St. James Parish in Wilmington.

Burgwin's career soon included activities of a political and public nature. He held the position of quartermaster for the New Hanover County militia during 1754–55. Between 1756 and 1759 he served as clerk of the Bladen County Court, and from 1758 to 1761 he practiced law as an attorney commissioned before the Cumberland County Court. In 1760 he became clerk of the governor's council, a position he held until 1772; and in 1762 he was serving as private secretary to Governor Arthur Dobbs. It appears that Burgwin claimed residency in both Bladen and New Hanover counties, as he was named justice of the peace for Bladen County in 1762 and for New Hanover County in 1764. In 1768 he was appointed clerk of the superior court for the District of Wilmington, and in 1769 Governor William Tryon commissioned him clerk of the high court of chancery for North Carolina. Other public positions Burgwin held included Wilmington town commissioner (1769–75) and member of the General Assembly from Bladen County (1773). During 1772–73, Burgwin and Governor Josiah Martin became involved in a bitter controversy concerning the terms of Burgwin's resignation as clerk of the governor's council. Despite protests from the governor, the upper house went on record as stating that Burgwin as clerk had always acted "with the strictest integrity and Honor, and hath discharged all the duties of that office with skill and ability."

There is little doubt that Burgwin was quite successful in mercantile operations in Wilmington and the Cape Fear region between 1764 and 1775, and New Hanover County records reflect his deep involvement in real estate activities during the same period. By 1771 he was living at Third and Market Street in Wilmington in what was to become one of that city's most famous buildings, today known as the Burgwin-Wright House or Cornwallis House. He also owned Castle Haynes Plantation and the adjoining Hermitage Plantation, both of which he had inherited from his wife, who died on 19 Oct. 1770. In Bladen County he also owned Marsh Castle at Lake Waccamaw.

As the revolutionary movement developed during the 1770s, Burgwin apparently attempted to tread the narrow path between Whig and Tory. On one occasion he ran afoul of the Wilmington Committee of Safety by failing to supply gunpowder as requested. During a party at the Hermitage on 8 Jan. 1775, Burgwin suffered a severe broken leg while playing "blind man's bluff." On the advice of his doctor, he left the colony to seek treatment abroad for the illset fracture. When, in 1777, North Carolina passed legislation calling for the confiscation and sale of property belonging to persons outside the colony, Burgwin returned by way of New York to Wilmington, where he applied for North Carolina citizenship. In 1781, as British forces under Major James Craig occupied Wilmington, Burgwin once more fled the state. He traveled in Belgium, Denmark, and elsewhere in Europe, in addition to visiting Great Britain. On 27 Apr. 1782 he married Elizabeth Bush of Bristol, England.

After the hostilities had ended, Burgwin and his new family, which by 1784 included a son and daughter, returned to Wilmington. Obviously, many North Carolinians did not consider Burgwin a Tory. Archibald Maclaine, writing in 1782, commented of him: "I am perfectly satisfied that he is not an enemy of the state. . . . The fears arising from the consequences of a War was his only inducement to leave the country." Burgwin was successful in reclaiming his property, which had been subject to confiscation, and he resumed mercantile operations in Wilmington, Charleston, and Fayetteville.

Burgwin died at the Hermitage. His three children, all by his second wife, were John Fanning, born at Gloucestershire, England (14 Mar. 1783–18 June 1864); Caroline Elizabeth Burgwin Clitherall, born at Charleston, S.C. (9 Apr. 1784–9 Oct. 1863); and George William Bush, born at the Hermitage (2 Sept. 1787–9 Feb. 1854).

SEE: Eliza Caroline Clitherall Books (Southern Historical Collection, University of North Carolina, Chapel Hill); Cumberland County Court Minutes (North Carolina State Archives, Raleigh); Walter Burgwyn Jones, *John Burgwin. Carolinian; John Jones, Virginian* (1913); New Hanover County Deeds (North Carolina State Archives, Raleigh); William L. Saunders and Walter Clark, eds., *Colonial and State Records of North Carolina*, 30 vols. (1886–1914).

DONALD R. LENNON

Burgwin, John Henry King *(1 July 1810–7 Feb. 1847)*, U.S. Army officer and hero of the Mexican War, was born at the Hermitage, the home of his father in New Hanover County. Descended from a prominent Cape Fear River family, Burgwin was the eldest son of George William Bush Burgwin, a substantial planter, and his wife, Maria Nash, daughter of Governor Abner Nash. The Burgwins had played a prominent role in the affairs of North Carolina since the arrival of the progenitor of the family before the Revolution.

In 1811, Mrs. George W. B. Burgwin exchanged her plantation and slaves near New Bern for the lands and servants of her brother-in-law, John Fanning Burgwyn, of New Hanover County. According to the terms of the agreement, one plantation was settled on Maria Nash Burgwin and her children. However, the Hermitage estate, the ancestral home built by the first John Burgwin in 1753, was given to John Henry King Burgwin, who was only one year old.

Following preparation at local private schools, Burgwin was accepted as a cadet at the U.S. Military Academy at West Point on 1 July 1826. He was graduated from the academy on 1 July 1830 and appointed second lieutenant of the First U.S. Dragoons. Stationed on the frontier, Burgwin saw duty at Fort Des Moines, Iowa, Fort Leavenworth, Kans., Fort Wayne, Indiana Territory, Fort Gibson, Indiana Territory, Fort Towson, Indiana Territory, and Fort Croghan, Iowa. In addition, he went on several Indian expeditions, including those against the Towe-e-ash Villages (1834) and the Pawnee Villages (1844). He was also in the recruiting service for a time and provided water transportation for the naturalist and artist John James Audubon during one of his western tours. Burgwin was promoted to first lieutenant on 1 June 1835 and to captain on 31 July 1837.

With the beginning of hostilities with Mexico in 1847, Burgwin's regiment was ordered to present-day New Mexico. Shortly after their arrival, Colonel Sterling Price sent Burgwin and his command to dislodge a band of Mexicans holding a gorge leading to Emdubo. He found six hundred men posted on the steep sides of mountains above a pass that would admit only three men abreast. In the face of such overwhelming odds, he led a brilliant assault on 29 Jan. The Mexicans were repulsed with twenty of their men killed and sixty wounded, while Burgwin lost only one man. Marching through the pass, he occupied Emdubo and moved to Trampas, where he rendezvoused with Colonel Price. From there the U.S. forces marched to Pueblo de Taos, N.M., breaking a road through the snow covering it to allow the transport of artillery.

Reaching Pueblo de Taos, Price found that it had been heavily fortified. The stronghold was "surrounded by adobe walls and strong pickets, every part of which was flanked by some projecting building." Price opened fire with his batteries on 3 Feb. but retired shortly afterward. The following day the fire was resumed at nine o'clock in the morning. However, it was found impossible to breach the walls with the U.S. howitzers. Thereupon, Price decided to storm the church, which was situated in the northwestern corner of Pueblo de Taos.

Burgwin was given the task of leading the assault at eleven o'clock. While his men positioned themselves under the western walls of the church and attempted to make an opening with axes, the roof was fired, using a temporary ladder. Leaving the shelter provided by the wall of the church, Burgwin broke into the corral and attempted to force the main door. While doing so, he was fatally wounded when a rifle ball lodged in his chest. Shortly afterward Price rode up and told the wounded officer that whether he recovered or not, Price would testify to his gallantry. To this Burgwin replied, "I hope, Colonel, you will also bear witness that my company did its duty." He lingered for three days dying at Pueblo de Taos.

Initially buried at Fort Leavenworth, Kans., Burgwin's body was exhumed in 1848 and brought to North Carolina. During a public funeral in Wilmington, attended by thousands, prominent attorney Joshua G. Wright delivered an address. Afterward, Burgwin was buried at the Hermitage, the family plantation. In later years, Burgwin's and his parents' remains were reinterred at Oakdale Cemetery in Wilmington.

Burgwin was later distinguished by having two military installations named in his honor. During the Civil War, Camp Burgwin was established in Wilmington to train Confederate soldiers. Later, Camp Burgwin or Cantonment Burgwin was established near Taos, N.M.; it is now used as a research center.

An Episcopalian, Burgwin was unmarried at the time of his death. He was engaged, however, to a "lady of great accomplishments," then living at Fort Leavenworth, Kans.

SEE: James G. Burr, *The Hermitage* (1855); George W. Cullum, *Biographical Register of the Officers and Graduates of the U.S. Military Academy* (1891); *Raleigh Register*, 7 May 1847; Alice Read, *The Reads and Their Relatives* (1930); *Register of Graduates and Former Cadets (1802–1866) of the United States Military Academy*, Thayer Memorial Edition (1964).

JAMES ELLIOTT MOORE

Burgwin, Nathaniel Hill (*21 Feb. 1825–13 Aug. 1898*), corporation lawyer, civic leader, and Episcopal layman, was born at the Hermitage, the ancestral home of the Burgwin family in New Hanover County. He was the son of George William Bush Burgwin, Cape Fear planter, and his wife, Maria Nash, daughter of Governor Abner Nash. He is believed to have been named after Dr. Nathaniel Hill, who lived on the adjoining plantation, Cricket Hill.

Gifted with a brilliant mind, he began to prepare for college at the age of eight when he was enrolled in the noted school of William J. Bingham at Hillsborough. Within five years he was ready to enter The University of North Carolina, but his extreme youth prevented his enrollment until 1840. At that time he was admitted as a member of the sophomore class. Burgwin earned the highest honors in his class but was unable to complete his studies because of poor health. In 1842, at the age of seventeen, he began reading law under his brother-in-law, Judge Thomas S. Ashe. Later, he did further study with his uncle, Frederick Nash, who was appointed chief justice of the state supreme court. Long before reaching the age of twenty-one, Burgwin had passed his bar examinations; he was not allowed to practice, however, until attaining his majority. Admitted to the bar in 1847, he opened an office in Elizabeth City and began his practice.

Moving to Pittsburgh, Pa., in 1851, Burgwin continued to practice law until his retirement in 1890. He enjoyed a highly profitable and successful practice there. His career was filled with cases of paramount importance. In the *County of Allegheny* v. *Pittsburgh and Connelsville Railroad Company*, he represented the defendant with success; this was a test case involving one hundred thousand dollars and determined liabilities in excess of one million dollars for the defendant. On another occasion, Burgwin was involved in *Linton and wife* v. *J. B. Neal et al.* Burgwin brought this suit in equity into the U.S. Circuit Court when its jurisdiction was sustained against the Orphan's Court of the State of Pennsylvania. This case dealt with the settlement of the accounts of the various executors, guardians, and trustees appointed by the will of James Brown of Kittaning. Afterward, the substantial estate, consisting of property in several states, was divided among the heirs.

Burgwin represented Mechanics National Bank of Pittsburgh and the Pittsburgh Marine Bank. He was solicitor for the Dollar Savings Bank, in addition to being its oldest vice-president and oldest member of its board of trustees. He was also director of the Pittsburgh and Connelsville Railroad Company.

Active in politics, Burgwin adopted the Whig viewpoint in his youth. Following the actions of Henry Clay, however, he assumed an independent position. In Pittsburgh, he ran on the Citizen's ticket and was elected to represent Ward Twenty-three on the select council from 1869 until 1875. During this time he was chairman of the committee appointed to select a location for a city park. Under his leadership, the land now comprising Schenley Park was chosen.

A devout Episcopalian, Burgwin was extremely active in the affairs of his church. He spearheaded the effort that led to the division of the diocese of Pennsylvania to form the diocese of Pittsburgh in 1865. From 1871 until the time of his death, he represented his diocese in the general convention. He was a member of the committee on canons after 1871. In addition, he served on the committee to revise the constitution of the general convention and on the 1880 joint committee of twenty-one bishops, priests, and laymen that revised the *Book of Common Prayer*. An authority on canon law, Burgwin was frequently consulted by both clergymen and laymen. He was chancellor of the diocese of Pittsburgh for many years.

Burgwin was married on 29 Nov. 1849 to Mary Phillips. They were the parents of George Collinson, Henry Phillips, John Henry King, Sarah Ormsby, Augustus Phillips, and Mary. Following the death of his first wife in 1882, Burgwin was married on 1 Oct. 1888 to Susan Read, daughter of Henry K. Nash of Hillsborough. They had one son, Kenneth Ogden.

Burgwin died at Hassell Hill, his home in Pittsburgh. A portrait of him is now in the possession of George Collinson Burgwin of Pittsburgh.

SEE: Samuel A. Ashe, ed., *Biographical History of North Carolina*, vol. 8 (1917); Collinson P. E. Burgwin, personal correspondence (1975); James G. Burr, *The Hermitage* (1885); Walter Burgwyn Jones, *John Burgwin, Carolinian; John Jones, Virginian* (1913); Alice Read, *The Reads and Their Relatives* (1930).

JAMES ELLIOTT MOORE

Burgwyn, Henry ("Harry") King, Jr. (*3 Oct. 1841–1 July 1863*), one of the youngest colonels of the Civil War, was born at Jamaica Plains, Mass., in the ancestral home of his mother, née Anna Greenough. He was the first son of Henry King Burgwyn, planter of Thornbury, Northampton County, and a descendant of John Burgwin. A younger son of Henry King, Sr., was William H. S. Burgwyn. Harry received his early education from private tutors at his father's plantation and at academies in the North. When he was fifteen, he was sent to West Point to study privately, apparently in preparation for entering the military cademy, although he never did so. His tutor at West Point was Captain John Gray Foster, who later, as a Union major general, commanded the Federal forces in Eastern North Carolina. Burgwyn was graduated from The University of North Carolina in 1857, after which he enrolled at the Virginia Military Institute. There he was one of the cadets detailed to guard John Brown prior to execution. Graduating in April 1861, he left the institute with a letter of recommendation from Professor T. J. Jackson, soon to be famous as "Stonewall."

A few weeks after the secession of North Carolina, Burgwyn found himself with a major's commission. After a recruiting trip to Western North Carolina, he was assigned to command a "camp of instruction" near Raleigh, where Confederate volunteers were gathering to be formed into fighting units. At nineteen he was elected lieutenant colonel of the Twenty-sixth North Carolina Regiment, with a commission dated 27 Aug. 1861. The colonel of the Twenty-sixth was Zebulon B. Vance. Vance supplied the esprit for the regiment, Burgwyn the military discipline and skill. Until February 1862, the regiment was on Bogue Island as part of the defenses of Fort Macon. After the fall of Roanoke Island, the Twenty-sixth was ordered to New Bern. It took a conspicuous part in the Battle of New Bern, 14 Mar. 1862, being heavily engaged for three hours and retreating, according to enemy reports, only when its ammunition was exhausted. Burgwyn was praised by Vance for "great coolness and efficiency" during the Confederate retreat and was said to have been the last man to cross Brice's Creek to safety. Prior to this first action, Burgwyn had been unpopular because of his military rigor; thereafter he enjoyed the respect and confidence of the citizen soldiers.

In June 1862 the Twenty-sixth was ordered to Virginia, where it took part, although not a conspicuous part, in the Seven Days' battles outside Richmond, attached to General Robert Ransom's brigade. In the late summer of 1862, Vance resigned to become governor. Ransom objected to Burgwyn's promotion, declaring that he wanted no "boy colonels" in his brigade. However, the regiment twice voted its confidence in Burgwyn, and General D. H. Hill sustained the appointment. Thus Burgwyn became colonel at the age of twenty; while it is impossible to determine with certainty who was the youngest colonel in the war, he was one of the youngest regimental commanders on either side, especially at that early point in the hostilities. Following his promotion, the Twenty-sixth was transferred from Ransom's brigade to that of James Johnston Pettigrew. Pettigrew and Burgwyn were both modest, intellectual, ascetic, and completely dedicated to their duties. "Imitating each other," according to one veteran, "they reached the highest excellence possible of attainment" in soldierly traits. From August 1862 to May 1863 the brigade was engaged in a number of actions against Federal troops in Eastern North Carolina, most notably at Rawle's Mill in Martin County in November, at the Second Battle of New Bern in February, and at Blount's Creek in Beaufort County in April. In all these actions the Twenty-sixth performed with distinction, usually against larger Federal forces.

In May, Pettigrew's brigade was incorporated into the Army of Northern Virginia in time for the campaign into Pennsylvania. The stout yeomen of the Twenty-sixth Regiment, under the leadership of Burgwyn and Pettigrew, had reached a peak of morale that made them, as subsequent events were to show, the most distinguished unit of North Carolinians in the war. Henry Heth's division, of which Pettigrew's brigade was a part, became heavily engaged on the first day of Gettysburg, 1 July. During the morning, the Twenty-sixth lay under fire with an excellent view of the position it was to assault in the afternoon. At two o'clock, Pettigrew's brigade was ordered forward. Bearing the brunt of the assault, Burgwyn's men charged across a creek (Willoughby Run) and up the wooded slope of McPherson's Ridge, overrunning and driving off three lines of Federal artillery and infantry, including the famous "Iron Brigade." This twenty-minute action was one of the most heroic and bloody charges of the war. Out of 800 men, the Twenty-sixth reported 588 killed and wounded, which has been judged the heaviest loss in a single regiment on either side during a single day of the war.

As the Twenty-sixth engaged the second Federal line, the eleventh man carrying the regimental colors was shot down. Burgwyn grabbed the flag and within seconds received a rifle ball in the side, which passed through his lungs. He died within two hours, aged twenty-one. "His loss is great, for he had but few equals of his age," wrote an officer who reported Gettysburg to Governor Vance. Burgwyn was buried under a walnut tree near Gettysburg with a guncase for a coffin. After the war the remains were retrieved and reinterred in Oakwood

Cemetery, Raleigh. A Marine Corps camp in Alabama was later named for him.

An Episcopalian, Burgwyn died unmarried. He was described as slender and handsome, with brown hair and moustache, quick of movement, and with an authority unusual for his age.

Burgwyn was a conspicuous example of the young men of the antebellum planter class, who were nourished on southern patriotism and the military virtues and who, in the words of Eugene Genovese, "selflessly fulfilled their duties and did what their class and society required of them."

SEE: Samuel A. Ashe, ed., *Biographical History of North Carolina*, vol. 6 (1907 [portrait]); Burgwyn Family Papers (Southern Historical Collection, University of North Carolina, Chapel Hill); Walter Clark, ed., *Histories of the Several Regiments and Battalions from North Carolina in the Great War, 1861–1865*, vols 1–2 (1901); Williams F. Fox, *Regimental Losses in the American Civil War*, 4th ed. (1898); *Raleigh Register*, 22 July 1863.

                                                                                    CLYDE WILSON

Burgwyn, John Fanning (14 Mar. 1783–18 June 1864), planter and merchant, was born at Thornbury, Gloucestershire, England. He was the oldest child of Cape Fear merchant and planter John Burgwin, who had emigrated from Wales to the American colonies, locating near Wilmington in 1753. His mother, Eliza Bush, was the youngest daughter of Bristol merchant George Bush. His godfather was Edmund Fanning, governor of Nova Scotia. Following a prolonged absence abroad, John Burgwin brought his family to America in 1784 and settled them at his plantation home, the Hermitage, eight miles from Wilmington. After the death of Eliza Burgwin in October 1787, John Fanning was sent with his sister Eliza to be reared by relatives in England. Burgwin lived with a Quaker kinsman in Plymouth and attended private schools in that town. Later, he was further educated at Loughborough House, an academy near London. He returned to North Carolina with his sister in 1801 and took up his father's import-export business.

Upon the death of his father in 1803, Burgwyn inherited two plantations, the Hermitage and Castle Haynes, and settled at the former with his family. He furthered his father's mercantile interests and acquired several ships. Carrying on extensive trade with European ports, he traveled widely and maintained residences at a number of locations. He was in New York City in 1812 but returned to Wilmington five years later. For varying lengths of time, he resided in New Bern, Boston, and Philadelphia; the English cities of Bath, Bristol, Plymouth, and London; and Florence, Italy. Accumulating great wealth, he was alarmed when he found that drafts were being forged on his accounts in foreign banks. Consequently, he altered the spelling of his name from "Burgwin" to "Burgwyn," establishing a change that has been maintained by his descendants.

After his marriage to Sarah Pierrepoint Hunt of New Bern in 1806, Burgwyn gained access to substantial tracts of land in Jones and Craven counties, including the plantations Ravenswood and Alveston Hall. Deciding to move to New Bern in 1811, he exchanged his land and slaves at Castle Haynes and the Hermitage for those of his sister-in-law, Mrs. George W. B. Burgwin, in the Craven County area.

The death of Sarah Hunt Burgwyn's half-brother George Pollock, after a fall from his horse in 1840, brought additional property into the family's hands. Pollock's estate included plantations in Bertie, Chowan, Northampton, and Halifax counties. After extensive litigation with the rival Devereux family, Mrs. Burgwyn's heirs secured title to the Northampton properties, which were divided into numerous plantations, including Alveston, Hillside, Thornbury, Bull Hill, Cypress, Ochoneechee, and the Levels. Burgwyn managed these estates for his children and lived in Northampton County for a time, after disposing of his Jones and Craven properties, including his home at New Bern.

An Episcopalian, Burgwyn was a leader at Christ Church, New Bern, when it was reconstructed in 1824. In addition, he appears to have been interested in higher education: he contributed a hundred dollars toward the completion of South Building at The University of North Carolina during 1809–11.

Burgwyn was married twice. His first wife, Sarah Pierrepoint Hunt, was the daughter of Robert Hunt of New Jersey and his wife, Eunice Edwards. She died in 1823, and Burgwyn married Ellen Barber of Bath, England. All his children were by his first marriage: Julia Theodosia, George Pollock Alveston, Henry King, Thomas Pollock, John Collinson (died young), Edward Devereux (died young), William Devereux (died young), and Sarah Emily.

Continuing his travels to the end, Burgwyn died in Raleigh at the home of his son Henry K. and was buried in Oakwood Cemetery. A portrait is in the possession of Dr. Collinson P. E. Burgwyn of Newport News, Va.

SEE: Samuel A. Ashe, ed., *Biographical History of North Carolina*, vol. 8 (1917); Kemp P. Battle, *History of the University of North Carolina*, vol. 1 (1907); Collinson P. E. Burgwyn, personal correspondence (20 Feb. 1975); James G. Burr, *The Hermitage* (1885); Eliza B. Clitherall MSS (Southern Historical Collection, University of North Carolina, Chapel Hill); Walter Burgwyn Jones, *John Burgwin, Carolinian; John Jones, Virginian* (1913).

JAMES ELLIOTT MOORE

Burgwyn, William Hyslop Sumner (23 July 1845– 3 Jan. 1913), lawyer, soldier, and banker, has been described as the most versatile person ever to have lived in Vance County. The son of Anna Greenough of Boston and Henry King Burgwyn, a wealthy planter, he was born at Jamaica Plains, a part of Boston, and spent his childhood at Thornbury Plantation on the Roanoke River, Northampton County.

Every educational facility was afforded him. He was taught by private tutors until 1854, when, at age nine, he became a pupil at Chestnut Hill School near Baltimore, Md. In 1857 he became a student at Horner's School in Oxford. He entered The University of North Carolina in 1860 as a freshman but left school in 1861 because of illness. Later that year he entered Hillsborough Military Academy as a cadet. Burgwyn was an excellent soldier, and by the fall of 1861 he was appointed drill master of the camp of instruction near Raleigh. His strict attention to every phase of military duty impressed his superior officers, and he was elected lieutenant of Company H, Thirty-fifth North Carolina Regiment. He participated in all the battles in which the Thirty-fifth North Carolina engaged and became captain of the company in 1863.

Burgwyn was assigned to duty as assistant adjutant general of Thomas L. Clingman's brigade in January 1864. He was severely wounded at the Battle of Cold Harbor on 1 June 1864. As soon as his wounds healed, he

returned to duty, reaching his brigade in front of Richmond about the middle of September. He was wounded again on 30 Sept. 1864 in an assault on Fort Harrison. This time he was captured and taken to Fort Delaware, where he was kept a prisoner until March 1865. Through the intercession of Colonel William Norris of Baltimore, the Confederate States commissioner of exchange, Burgwyn was paroled, but he was not exchanged.

After the Civil War, Burgwyn returned to civilian life, but his military career was not at an end. While he was a lawyer in Baltimore, he offered his services to the governor of Maryland during the Baltimore and Ohio Railroad riot of July 1877. He was appointed lieutenant colonel of the Eighth Regiment. His excellent service caused him to be elected colonel of the Fifth Maryland Regiment, a celebrated military organization. Burgwyn also participated in the Spanish-American War. He was appointed colonel of the Second Regiment, North Carolina Volunteer Troops, in May 1898; the war was over, however, before he engaged in any fighting.

After the Civil War, Burgwyn entered The University of North Carolina as a sophomore and was graduated in June 1868 with first honors; he delivered the Latin salutatory address. He was a member of the Philanthropic Society of the university and a member of Zeta Psi Fraternity. He entered Harvard Law School in 1869 and was graduated in 1870. He then moved to Baltimore and was admitted to the Maryland bar. To broaden his education, he entered Washington Medical University of Baltimore in 1874. He received his diploma as a doctor of medicine in 1876 but never applied for a license to practice medicine.

Burgwyn returned to North Carolina in 1882 and located in Henderson. There he established the banking house of W. H. S. Burgwyn and Co., the first bank in Vance County. As a private bank, it was without any government permit or regulation other than an annual sworn statement of its assets to the tax lister. The Burgwyn Bank became a state bank, the Bank of Henderson, in 1884, and Burgwyn was its first president.

Burgwyn was generally connected with every noteworthy enterprise in Vance County and did everything in his power to promote the best interests of all in North Carolina. He established not only the bank in Henderson but also an electric light system, water works, and a tobacco factory. He served as president of the Henderson Female College from 1886 to 1891. He was appointed trustee of The University of North Carolina in 1883. In 1887 he was asked to represent North Carolina in the Southern Interstate Convention in Atlanta; he served again in the 1888 convention held at Montgomery, Ala., and he was chairman of the North Carolina delegation when this same convention met in Asheville in 1889. Burgwyn was one of the original callers of a convention of North Carolina farmers to petition the state legislature for the creation of an agricultural and mechanical college.

Burgwyn sold his banking interests in 1893, when he became national bank examiner for the southern states. He held this position for nine years, until he resigned in 1901 and moved to Weldon. In Weldon he established the First National Bank of Weldon and became its president. He also established a number of small town banks in the surrounding counties, including the Bank of Rich Square and the Bank of Ayden, both established in 1903, and the First National Bank of Rocky Mount and the Bank of Northampton at Jackson, both established in 1904. He became president of each of these banks. Other banks he established were the First National Bank of Roanoke Rapids, the Bank of Halifax, and a bank in Florida.

Aside from his business achievements and military distinctions, Burgwyn was an excellent orator and an author. He delivered many speeches all over the state on a variety of topics. In 1890 he addressed two literary societies of The University of North Carolina in an effort to establish a chair of history there. His address on the life and times of General Thomas L. Clingman in 1898 was a valuable contribution to the war literature of the South. In 1899 he addressed the State Bankers Association on the resources of North Carolina. While in Baltimore, Burgwyn published a *Digest of the Reports of the Court of Appeals of Maryland*. He was also the author of a number of valuable articles published by the industrial and political press. He wrote a sketch on Governor Z. B. Vance that was printed in the *Library of Southern Literature* and prepared sketches for Chief Justice Walter Clark on the "Regimental Histories of the 35th N.C. and Clingman's Brigade."

As an active member of the Episcopal church, Burgwyn was frequently a delegate to the diocesan convention. In 1886 and 1889 he was elected one of the lay delegates to represent his diocese to the general convention of the church.

Burgwyn married Margaret Carlisle Dunlop, daughter of James and Ann Dent Dunlop of Richmond, Va., on 21 Nov. 1876. They had no children.

Burgwyn died at the home of a nephew in Richmond. His body was moved to Raleigh, and he was buried in the Confederate section of the Raleigh Cemetery next to his brother, Colonel Henry Burgwyn, who was killed at Gettysburg.

SEE: Samuel A. Ashe, ed., *Biographical History of North Carolina*, vol. 8 (1917); Kemp P. Battle, *History of the University of North Carolina*, vol. 2 (1912); Burgwyn Family Papers (Southern Historical Collection, University of North Carolina, Chapel Hill); Walter Clark, ed., *Histories of the Several Regiments and Battalions from North Carolina in the Great War, 1861–1865*, 5 vols. (1901); Walter Burgwyn Jones, *John Burgwin, Carolinian; John Jones, Virginian* (1913); Samuel Thomas Peace, *Zeb's Black Baby: Vance County* (1955); Stephen B. Weeks, Scrapbook 1887–94 (North Carolina Collection, University of North Carolina, Chapel Hill).

JUANITA ANN SHEPPARD

Burgwyn, William Hyslop Sumner *(22 Jan. 1886–24 Jan. 1977)*, lawyer, judge, and bank president, was born in Jackson, the son of George Pollock and Emma Ridley Burgwyn. He attended John Graham's School in Warrenton, Episcopal High School in Virginia, and Georgetown College in Washington, D.C., and was graduated from The University of North Carolina Law School in 1908. He began the practice of law that year and in 1911 moved to Woodland. He represented Northampton, Bertie, and Hertford counties in the North Carolina Senate from 1917 until 1921 and again in 1925, and in 1923 he represented Northampton in the house. In 1925 he was president pro tem of the senate and in 1928 an unsuccessful candidate for lieutenant governor in the Democratic primary. From 1915 until 1932 he was a member of the board of trustees of The University of North Carolina. In 1918 he became a director of the Farmers Bank of Woodland, and in 1934 he became its president. From 1932 until 1937 he was solicitor of the Third Judicial District. Appointed a special superior court judge in 1937, he held the position until 1953. During his

long career on the bench, Burgwyn held court in eighty-eight of the state's hundred counties.

Burgwyn served as vice-chairman of the Roanoke River Basin Authority and was chairman of the Roanoke Valley Flood Control Committee, which played a major role in the construction of Buggs Island Dam in the late 1940s. He was a popular speaker; several of his addresses were published in pamphlet form, among them one on the military and civil services of General Matthew W. Ransom and one on the necessity of preserving memorials of North Carolina's past.

In 1911 he was married to Josephine Griffin of Woodland; they became the parents of John Griffin, W. H. S., Jr., Margaret E., and Henry K.

Burgwyn was buried in the family cemetery at Woodland.

SEE: *Durham Morning Herald*, 14 Sept. 1968; Raleigh *News and Observer*, 17 June 1953, 17 Dec. 1967; Samuel T. Peace, *"Zeb's Black Baby": Vance County* (1955).

WILLIAM S. POWELL

Burke, Mary ("Polly") Williams *(1 Feb. 1782–31 Jan. 1869)*, educator, was the only child of North Carolina's third governor, Dr. Thomas Burke (1747–2 Dec. 1783) of Hillsborough, and Mary ("Polly") Freeman (1752–23 Mar. 1836) of Norfolk, Va., a pioneer Presbyterian educator in North Carolina and Alabama in her own right. Mary Williams Burke was born in Warren County, the granddaughter of Ulick Burke and Letitia Ould (sister of Sir Fielding Ould) of County Galway, Ireland, and of the eccentric Englishman William Freeman and Tabitha Wilson of Norfolk. Miss Burke is thought to have been named for her father's friend, Colonel John Williams, in whose household Mrs. Burke had taken refuge for some time before the birth of her daughter.

Nothing is known specifically about Mary W. Burke's childhood years in Hillsborough. It seems likely that she lived but a short time, if ever, at her father's plantation Tyaquin, northeast of Hillsborough. By the terms of Governor Burke's will, her education was to have been supervised by his executors, Willie Jones (who did not serve) and James Hogg, but no record touching the matter has survived. Her girlhood was apparently spent at her mother's home on Churton Street in company with her two half-sisters, Frances Wilson Doherty (later Mrs. William H. Bond) and Helen Mason Doherty (later Mrs. David Yarbrough), children of her mother's second marriage, which took place on 25 Apr. 1785, to Major George Doherty (d. 1792). Her mother's older sister, Mrs. Frances Freeman McKerall Child, widow first of Captain John McKerall and second of Comptroller Francis Child, had lived in Hillsborough since 1769 and was almost certainly the reason the Thomas Burkes had settled in Orange County. The large McKerall-Child connection, together with her Doherty half-sisters, then and in later years constituted Mary W. Burke's family.

On 5 June 1810, Miss Burke, then twenty-eight years old and in command of virtually all of her father's estate, purchased for four hundred dollars her own modest home (now enlarged and known as Heartsease) on East Queen Street, Hillsborough. No earlier record associates the house with Governor Burke. On 6 Nov. 1817 her friend and neighbor Dr. James Webb deeded to her, for twenty-five dollars, a twenty-five-foot wide strip of land from the western side of his adjoining Lot 63. Here a log schoolhouse was built, in which Miss Burke was to teach the Webb children. It has been suggested, and seems likely, that she may have been teaching the young Webbs in her own home as early as 1812. In any case, the new schoolhouse, known as "Miss Polly Burke's School" from about 1818 to 1834, was opened to neighborhood children. No formal records remain of the little grammar school, usually cited in Presbyterian records as a significant forerunner of Mrs. Burwell's Female School (1837–57) and the Nash and Kollock Select Boarding and Day School for Young Ladies (1859–90).

An unpublished volume of reminiscences by Margaret Isabella Walker Weber, a former Burke student, noted that little five-year-old girls in bibs and pinafores were set to hemming sheets and towels before they could read, and that one of her own public appearances as a small child involved the difficult reading of Beattie's *Hermit*, printed with the old-fashioned long s's. Local tradition still has it that discipline within the school was severe. Students included Strudwicks, Nashes, Phillipses, Kirklands, the Carleton Walker children, and various daughters of Presbyterian families. The log schoolhouse still stands as part of the John Graham Webb house.

In September 1816, Miss Burke joined with eight other persons and the Reverend John Knox Witherspoon, pastor, to organize the Hillsborough Presbyterian Church. The first pew rental list of 1816 shows that she rented Pew 13 on the north side of the new brick church, and preserved sessions books and other church records disclose that she was a steadfast supporter of church activities for the next eighteen years.

In August 1834, Miss Burke sold most of her household goods and joined the considerable exodus of Hillsborough citizens to Alabama, a curious migration still not fully explained, but animated in part by a desire to escape the mounting local controversy over slavery. Mary W. Burke accompanied her niece, Eliza Mary Bond Johnston, Eliza's husband, George Mulholland Johnston, and their two-year-old son, George Doherty, to Greensboro, Ala., where she apparently planned to make her permanent home with the Johnstons. George Mulholland Johnston died on 5 Sept. 1834, however, after only two weeks in his new Greensboro home. Miss Burke, together with her niece and grandnephew, thereupon removed to nearby Marion, where her half-sister, Helen Mason Doherty Yarbrough, and her brother-in-law, David Yarbrough, were already established. Various Strudwicks, Webbs, and Youngs also lived in the area. The Perry County Court appointed Miss Burke guardian of little George Doherty Johnston, and she took complete responsibility for the boy's education and inheritance as well as temporary charge of Eliza Johnston's affairs.

On 4 May 1837 she sent her "unconditional" power of attorney to Dr. James Webb to dispose of her remaining Hillsborough property, excepting only her father's mahogany bookcase and a few oddments. In the 1840s she further directed Dr. Webb to present Governor Burke's papers to the North Carolina Historical Society; these became the Burke collections now in the North Carolina Division of Archives and History, Raleigh, and in The University of North Carolina Library, Chapel Hill. A small group of illuminating letters from Miss Burke to Dr. Webb has been preserved, demonstrating her own very considerable business ability and her constant reliance on Dr. Webb's judgment and advice.

Miss Burke began immediately to teach again, purchasing a schoolhouse of her own, where she welcomed the children and grandchildren of her relatives and old friends. Somehow, also, she managed to teach black children, especially the descendants of the remarkable Freeman servants. General George Doherty

Johnston, her ward and himself a testament to the efficacy of her teaching, wrote after her death that she had taught "many hundreds of students" and four generations in one family (probably his own). He noted, too, that she had virtually educated herself out of her own hunger for knowing, and that her remarkably retentive memory had stood both herself and her pupils in good stead. Her lengthy teaching career, over half a century, extended almost to her last days and encompassed the teaching of both females and blacks in an era when neither was usual.

When Miss Burke was seventy-nine, she suffered a fall resulting in a serious hip injury that confined her to her bed and an "armed chair" for the last eight years of her life. Even so, and in spite of exhausting bouts with asthma, she persisted in giving Latin lessons to a neighboring boy. She died at the home of her niece Eliza (then Mrs. Leonard A. Weissinger) and was buried in the Marion Cemetery in the Johnston lot. A photograph of a crayon portrait of Miss Burke in her later years is in the possession of the North Carolina Division of Archives and History, Raleigh.

SEE: Hillsborough Presbyterian Church, for Sessions Book I and Pew Rental Lists (1816–18, 1824); *Hillsborough Recorder*, 18 Dec. 1836; Henry Poellnitz Johnston, *The Gentle Johnstons and Their Kin* (1966); Ann Strudwick Nash, *Ladies in the Making* (1964); North Carolina State Archives (Raleigh), for Thomas Burke Papers and photograph of Mary W. Burke; Orange County Deed Books 13, 16, 25–27 (Orange County Courthouse, Hillsborough); Southern Historical Collection (University of North Carolina, Chapel Hill), for Thomas Burke Papers, Heartt-Wilson Papers (William Huntington to Caroline E. Heartt, letter, 1 Feb. 1869), Peter Mallett Papers ("Reminiscences of Margaret Isabella Weber"), and James Webb Papers (Mary W. Burke to Dr. James Webb, letters, 1836–45, and related records).

MARY CLAIRE ENGSTROM

Burke, Thomas (ca. 1744–2 Dec. 1783), governor and poet, was born in Ireland and grew up in Dublin, probably in a Protestant household. He migrated to the colonies following family quarrels in 1759 or 1760 and settled in Northampton County on the Eastern Shore of Virginia. He first practiced medicine but switched to law, which appeared more lucrative. While in Virginia he began to write poetry, and one of his early poems celebrated the repeal of the Stamp Act. A number of his poems and essays were published in the Virginia newspapers between 1766 and 1768 (they have been more recently collected by Richard Walser and published as *The Poems of Governor Thomas Burke of North Carolina* [Raleigh: State Department of Archives and History, 1961]). Burke moved to Norfolk in 1769 and in March of the following year married Mary ("Polly") Freeman. As a lawyer he was chiefly engaged in collecting debts for merchants, but his legal activities did include a correspondence with Thomas Jefferson.

In 1772, Burke moved to North Carolina, settling on a farm near Hillsborough. In 1775 he began his political career as a delegate to the second provincial congress. He was reelected to succeeding congresses and chaired the committee to draft a constitution in April 1776. As a result of his obvious talents, he was elected to the Continental Congress, where he served from 1777 until 1781. Almost alone among the members of Congress, he perceived the conflict between the continental establishment and the sovereignty of his state, which he vigorously asserted. In the debate over the Articles of

Confederation in 1777, Burke introduced a resolution guaranteeing those powers to the states that were not explicitly granted to the Confederation. This safeguard was incorporated into the Articles and later was the basis for the Tenth Amendment to the federal Constitution. With the British invasion of the South, however, Burke became increasingly nationalistic and participated in the campaign to establish import duties in 1780 and 1781.

In June of 1781, Burke was elected governor of war-ravaged North Carolina, and in October he was captured at Hillsborough by the Tory raider David Fanning. After he was paroled by the enemy to James Island near Charles Town, his life was threatened by Tory refugees and he was forced to flee. After his return to North Carolina, he resumed his duties as governor, setting off an undercurrent of criticism, especially among officers of the military who felt that his parole violation was an inexcusable breach of honor.

Burke left office in April of 1782, disillusioned with the revolutionary experiment in republicanism and favoring a more aristocratic system. Burdened with debts from his public service and weakened by his ordeal as a captive, he died and was buried on his farm near Hillsborough. He was survived by an infant daughter, Mary Williams Burke.

SEE: Sister Mary Carmelita Barrett, "Thomas Burke, Governor of North Carolina" (M.A. thesis, Catholic University, 1946); Elisha Douglass, "Thomas Burke: Disillusioned Democrat," *North Carolina Historical Review* 26 (1949); *North Carolina Booklet*, vol. 6 (October 1906); Jennings Sanders, "Thomas Burke in the Continental Congress," *North Carolina Historical Review* 9 (1932); Ruth Franklin Sutton, "Thomas Burke" (M.A. thesis, University of North Carolina, 1949); John S. Watterson III, "The Ordeal of Governor Burke," *North Carolina Historical Review* 48 (1971), and "Thomas Burke: A Revolutionary Career" (Ph.D. diss., Northwestern University, 1970).

JOHN WATTERSON

Burkitt, Lemuel (*26 Apr. 1750–5 Nov. 1807*), Baptist clergyman, member of the Hillsborough convention of 1788, and author of religious and other works, was born in the neighborhood of Yeopim Baptist Church, a few miles east of Edenton in Chowan County. His parents, Thomas Burkitt and his wife, Mary Evans, were among the charter members of the church. After receiving the best local education, he considered the study of law but not long afterward resolved to devote his life to the ministry. In July of 1771 he was baptized in the Pasquotank River by the Reverend Henry Abbot, and in the following September he was ordained a minister.

Burkitt spent much of the remainder of his life in evangelical work, preaching in Eastern North Carolina and southeastern Virginia. In 1801 he made a four-month tour with almost nightly preaching among the Baptist churches of Kentucky and Tennessee, bringing back with him the spirit of the Great Revival, which then swept through the churches of the Kehukee Baptist Association in North Carolina. His lifetime pastorate was the Sandy Run Baptist Church in Bertie County, where he was installed by Elders Jonathan Thomas and John Meglamre in November 1773. He became a frequent participant in the founding of churches and the installation of pastors and is known to have delivered the funeral sermons of Elders James Bell and Henry Abbot and that of Elisha Battle, Sr.

Burkitt began his long and immensely fruitful relationship with the Kehukee Baptist Association as a messenger from the Pasquotank church on 31 July 1773, when he was elected clerk for the first of some twenty-nine times. In 1775 he was a leader of the small group of "separate" churches when the first split occurred among the Baptists of North Carolina and the minutes were "Loste." On 9 Aug. 1777, when the Separates held their own association at Sappony Meeting House in Virginia, "being the first after the division took place at the Falls of Tar River," Burkitt resumed the office of clerk; he retained it through 1805, excepting the war years, 1779–81, when the Association did not meet, 1797 and 1802.

In addition to his part in the Great Split of 1775, Burkitt was a leader in three other important actions taken by the Kehukee Baptist Association: on 10 Oct. 1789, the Separates and Regulars were reunited as the United Baptist Association, with Burkitt as both clerk and treasurer; on 9 Oct. 1790, the Virginia members were allowed to withdraw in order to form the Virginia Portsmouth Association; and on 12 Oct. 1793, the remaining members whose churches lay south of Tar River were dismissed to form the Neuse Association. On 14 June 1805, Burkitt was a member of the joint committee from the three associations that evolved a practical foundation for "the first organized missionary work among the North Carolina Baptists."

Because Burkitt resided until about 1790 in Hertford County, where the early records were burned, we have little knowledge of his public life there. The 1779 tax list indicates that he already owned 100 acres, 3 slaves, 4 horses, and 7 cattle, worth in all £2,270, plus a tidy £84.12.4 in cash. Representing Hertford County at the celebrated constitutional convention held at Hillsborough in 1788, he took his seat on 25 July and was an outspoken anti-Federalist who demanded the maximum preservation of state rights and personal liberties. At the time of his death in Northampton County, his estate consisted of considerable real and personal property, including £41.6.9 in money, a brandy still, 11 slaves, 935 acres in four plantations, 5 horses, and over 50 hogs, sheep, and cattle. The surviving inventory and account of the sale of his household furnishings complete the picture of a very prosperous planter.

Burkitt was the author of several religious works, one of which (a collection of hymns) had unusual popularity. Few of his writings have survived the passage of time, but another publication was *An Abridgement of English Grammar, Partly Extracted from Eminent and Approved Authors with Observations Entirely New* (Halifax, 1793). Beginning in 1789, he was responsible for compiling and having printed the Minutes of Kehukee Baptist Association. For a dozen years following 1791 he was a contributor to John Rippon's London *Baptist Annual Register*. However, his chief claim to literary fame rests upon *A Concise History of the Kehukee Baptist Association, from its original rise to the present time* (Halifax, 1803), in which he was assisted by Elder Jesse Read, pastor of the Rocky Swamp Baptist Church in Halifax County.

In about 1778, Burkitt married Hannah Bell (2 June 1758–ca. 1806), daughter of Elder James Bell and his wife, Mildred Robinson, of Sussex County, Va. The Burkitts had seven children known to have survived childhood: Mary married John Halsey and later John Nixon; Nancy married Abednego Rutland; Thomas died unmarried; Lemuel married Mary Smith; Burges married Mary Hardin; William married Nancy Gordon; and Sarah married Nathaniel Thatch, William Long, and then Henry A. Long. In about 1807, Burkitt married as his second wife Prudence Watson of Virginia; she died in 1808, leaving an infant who briefly survived her.

SEE: Lemuel Burkitt and Jesse Read, *A Concise History of the Kehukee Baptist Association*, rev. ed. (1850); George Washington Paschal, *History of North Carolina Baptists*, vol. 1 (1930).

HUGH B. JOHNSTON, JR.

Burleson, Edward (15 Dec. 1793–26 Dec. 1851), Texas politician and Indian fighter, was born in Buncombe County. After moves to Tennessee and Alabama in 1814, he went to Missouri, where he commanded a company of Howard County militia and later was a colonel in the Saline County militia. By 1823, in Tennessee, he served as lieutenant colonel and later colonel in the Hardeman County militia.

After arriving in Texas in 1830, Burleson acquired title on 4 Apr. 1831 to a league of land in present Bastrop County, Stephen F. Austin's second colony. He served as delegate to the convention of 1833 at San Felipe from Mina Municipality. On 10 Oct. 1835, at Gonzales, Burleson was elected colonel of the only regiment organized under Austin. When Austin became commissioner of the provisional government of the United States, Burleson became first in command. Near Bexar, on 12 Mar. 1836, Burleson was elected colonel of the First Regiment of Texas Volunteers, which he commanded at the Battle of San Jacinto. A year later he became a brigadier general of the militia, and by 1838 he was a colonel of the first regiment of infantry in the regular army.

Burleson was politically active as a member of the Texas House of Representatives from Bastrop County in the second congress, 1837–38, and as a member of the Texas Senate in the third congress, 1838–39. After establishing the town of Waterloo in 1839, Burleson spent the following year fighting Indians, commanding regulars in the Cherokee War, but he did not participate in the Plum Creek fight.

Elected vice-president of the Texas Republic on 6 Sept. 1841, Burleson was inaugurated on 10 Dec. Largely through Sam Houston's efforts, he lost in his presidential candidacy against Anson Jones in 1844. Burleson was on James Pinckney Henderson's staff during the War with Mexico.

In the first and second legislatures, 1846–49, he was the senator from the fifteenth district, and was elected president pro tem. In the third and fourth legislatures he represented the sixteenth district, having moved to Hays County, where he built a home near the headwaters of the San Marcos River. At the time of his death, he was still senate president pro tem. On 24 Mar. 1846, Burleson County, Tex., was named in his honor.

In 1831, Burleson married Sarah G. Owen of Madison County, Ala.; six of their children survived infancy.

SEE: *DAB*, vol. 3 (1929); *Handbook of Texas*, vol. 1 (1952).

DONALD K. PICKENS

Burns, Otway, Jr. (1775–25 Oct. 1850), privateer, ship builder, and legislator, was born on Queen's Creek, Onslow County, about two miles from the present town of Swansboro. Of Scottish descent, he was the son of Otway Burns, Sr., and his wife, Lisanah. His paternal grandfather was Francis Burns, Sr., who emigrated from Glasgow, Scotland, in 1734 and died on Queen's Creek toward the end of 1791. Francis, Sr., had lived on the Northeast Branch of New River at the time of his marriage to Mary Otway in 1744. By her he became the father of Otway, Sr., and at some later time he moved to

Queen's Creek. His second wife was named Elizabeth, and she survived him by about five years. Otway, Sr., appears to have died intestate prior to July 1797, when a new overseer of the roads in the Queen's Creek area was appointed "in the room of Otway Burns, deceased." He evidently left his widow and six orphans: sons Francis II and Otway, Jr., and daughters Susannah, Mary, Elizabeth, and Experience. Otway Burns, Jr., appears to have had little formal education and to have taken to the sea quite early. His skill as a mariner soon became established, and in 1806 the Onslow County Court bound an orphan lad to him to learn navigation. In 1808, Burns deeded to his brother, Francis, all his interest in the land willed to the two of them by their grandfather, Francis, Sr.; in slightly less than ten years from that time, Francis II died.

Prior to the War of 1812, Burns had been a sailing master; immediately before the war he was in command of a merchantman plying between New Bern and Portland, Me. When the war broke out, Burns and others became interested in privateering. He purchased in New York the schooner *Zephyr*, built in 1808 on West River, Md., and shares were sold in New Bern and Tarboro to outfit the vessel. Among the chief stockholders were Colonel Edward Pasteur and William Shepard of New Bern. Armed with six guns and manned by a crew of eighty, the vessel, renamed the *Snap Dragon*, made three highly successful cruises, two to the West Indies and one to Nova Scotia, and was captured on a fourth voyage near Nova Scotia. Newspapers and court records are filled with reports of prizes to the *Snap Dragon* arriving in Beaufort or New Bern. Burns commanded during the three successful cruises. So many legends have been handed down concerning his prowess both in handling men and in handling ships that it is difficult to separate truth from fiction.

On the first cruise, a six months' voyage to the Spanish Main in 1812–13, the *Snap Dragon* captured eight vessels: three of these were unloaded and then burned; three were filled with prisoners to be released; one fine copper-bottomed sloop was turned into a tender and storehouse; and one prize, the *Fillis*, was sent to New Bern laden with three thousand goat skins, hides, mats, and yams. Eighteen valuable male Negro slaves were taken from another of the vessels. Following this exciting voyage, the *Snap Dragon* returned to Beaufort for a brief rest and then on 3 June 1813 headed for Nova Scotia and Newfoundland to intercept British ships en route to Canada. This was the most rewarding voyage of all, since Burns captured some half million dollars' worth of cargo, besides one prize that was retaken by the British. Upon her return, the *Snap Dragon* was so loaded that the crew was sleeping on deck. Auctioned at William Shepard's warehouse after wide advertising, the goods were sold for more than four hundred thousand dollars in addition to the price brought for a brig. Each crew member received three thousand dollars and the investors divided the remainder. A third voyage in early 1814, again to the Spanish Main, resulted in only one known capture and an inconclusive battle with an eighteen-gun British privateer. When the *Snap Dragon* left on 26 May 1814 for her final cruise, under the command of Captain W. R. Graham, Burns remained home, reportedly because incapacitated with rheumatism. The *Snap Dragon* met her fate 30 June 1814, when she was captured by the British sloop of war *Martin* (not, as legend has it, by the fifty-four-gun frigate *Leopard*, disguised as a merchantman). An original watercolor painting depicting the capture of the *Snap*

Dragon by the *Martin* is in the files of the Mariners' Museum, Newport News, Va.

Having entered the War of 1812 as a mariner and shipbuilder with connections in Swansboro, Beaufort, and New Bern, Burns emerged from the war as North Carolina's greatest privateer hero. After the war's close, he returned to shipbuilding. In 1818 he built the steamer *Prometheus* at Swansboro. The first steamboat built in the state, the *Prometheus* operated on the Cape Fear River. Other vessels built by him in Carteret County include the *Warrior* in 1823 and the brig *Henry* in 1831.

In addition to shipbuilding, Burns engaged in a variety of other ventures. In 1820 he bought a ten-acre tract on Taylor's Creek near Beaufort, where he and Asa King (co-owner) erected a salt works in which Burns retained an interest until at least 1826 (when it was mortgaged) and possibly later. As early as 1819, and as late as 1829, there are mentions of a store that Burns owned on leased ground adjoining his home on Front Street, Beaufort. His mortgage deeds indicate the possession of farm lands, equipment, and livestock; varying numbers of slaves; and nets and an assortment of boats (schooners, flats, seine boats, sailboats, and canoes), indicating his operation of both merchant and fishing vessels. By act of assembly in 1822, Burns was named one of the commissioners of the Clubfoot and Harlows Creek Canal Company, in which he owned five shares of capital stock. In 1829 he and Dr. James Manney of Beaufort were operating brick kilns to manufacture bricks for the construction of Fort Macon.

Burns's political career began in 1821 with his election to represent Carteret County in the North Carolina House of Commons; he served in the house during the assemblies of 1821–22, 1822, 1824–25, 1825–26, 1826–27, 1827–28, and 1832–33. As a member of the senate from Carteret County, Burns served in the assemblies of 1828–29, 1829–30, 1833–34, and 1834–35. His political career paralleled a time of heavy indebtedness in his private enterprises, there having been at least nine mortgage deeds executed by him in Carteret County between 1821 and 1834, with indications that the debts were increasing in size. His personal fortunes were doubtless worsened by his political fate in 1835. His last act before the adjournment of the General Assembly in early 1835 had been to vote in favor of a state constitutional convention to consider increasing western representation and electing the governor by popular vote. The bill passed the senate by a vote of thirty-one to thirty, and the convention was called. For his vote, Burns was repudiated by his eastern constituency, but Burnsville—seat of Yancey County—was named for him by grateful westerners. A second North Carolina town, Otway in Carteret County, was also named for him.

A Democrat in straitened circumstances, he was appointed by President Andrew Jackson as keeper of the Brant Shoals Light-House at Portsmouth in 1836. After his second wife's death in 1839, Burns mortgaged his home at Portsmouth and appears eventually to have lost it to his son Owen, to whom he mortgaged it for seven hundred dollars in July 1840, and who subsequently mortgaged it himself in February 1849. Settling in the Outer Banks village of Portsmouth, Burns settled into his old age; he enjoyed wearing his naval uniform, drinking good whiskey, and quarreling.

Burns was married three times. In youth he had been a neighbor of the Grant family on Queen's Creek, and on 6 July 1809 he was married to Joanna Grant, his third cousin by popular reckoning and a daughter of Colonel Reuben Grant. Early in 1810, Burns bought a lot in Swansboro, and that same year he and Joanna became

the parents of Owen, Burns's only child. Burns and his family apparently continued living in the Swansboro area throughout the period of his involvement in the War of 1812 until about the time of his separation from Joanna, when, in January 1814, he gave public notice that he would no longer be responsible for her debts. At about this time, Joanna Burns removed to Jones County, where her next of kin lived; there she died on 6 Sept. 1814, apparently leaving Owen in the care of her relatives for the next few years. The guardianship bond that Otway Burns was required to execute for Owen on 18 June 1819 may indicate the time when Burns first received custody of his son.

Following the death of his first wife, Burns was married to Jane Hall, daughter of David and Naomi Hall of the Beaufort-North River area; born 22 Mar. 1794, she was just slightly over half the age of her husband. This marriage bond was dated 4 Dec. 1814; and five months later, Burns bought house and lot number 16 in Beaufort Old Town, where they took up residence. The second Mrs. Burns died at Portsmouth on 24 Oct. 1839 and was buried in the Anne Street Cemetery, Beaufort.

The third Mrs. Burns was Jane Smith of Smyrna. This marriage bond was dated 22 Feb. 1842; she evidently predeceased her husband, since she was not enumerated in the 1850 census, which listed the solitary Captain Otway Burns as a mariner "in his dotage" living in the home of John S. Hunter of Portsmouth.

Burns's only child, Owen, served in the U.S. Navy from 1834 to 1840. In 1849 he married Martha Armstrong, daughter of Solomon Armstrong and granddaughter of General John Armstrong. Owen and Martha Burns were the parents of I. R., Eugene, Richard Jerome, Charles O., Walter Francis, Edwin Oscar, Owen, Jr., and Lillian.

Burns was buried without ceremony in the Anne Street Cemetery in Beaufort. On 4 July 1901 his grandchildren unveiled there a grave monument surmounted by a cannon, which was dedicated by then Chief Justice Walter Clark but which contained erroneous information about Burns's parentage. A statue of Burns was unveiled at Burnsville on 5 July 1909. An original portrait and photographs of the portrait and monument are in the possession of the Division of Archives and History, Raleigh.

SEE: Samuel A. Ashe, ed., *Biographical History of North Carolina*, vol. 1 (1905); Walter Francis Burns, *Captain Otway Burns* (1905); *DAB*, vol. 3 (1929); S. M. Lemmon, *Frustrated Patriots: North Carolina and the War of 1812* (1973).

SARAH MCCULLOH LEMMON
TUCKER REED LITTLETON

Burrington, George (*ca. 1682–22 Feb. 1759*), colonial governor, was born in Devonshire, England. His father was Gilbert Burrington, and his relatives were among the earliest supporters of William III in the Glorious Revolution of 1688. Included among the Burrington clan was one member of Parliament from Devon. This sort of family prominence was most advantageous to a young man in the eighteenth century, and Burrington was fortunate to have as his friend Thomas Pelham-Holles, Duke of Newcastle-upon-Tyne of the third creation. Newcastle was a master of patronage during the first half of the eighteenth century, and he helped Burrington procure an army commission in 1715. Later, when he was secretary of state for the Southern Department, Newcastle was to obtain the royal governorship of North Carolina for his friend.

Burrington has the unique distinction of having served as both proprietary and royal governor of the North Carolina colony. How he received his initial appointment as proprietary governor on 26 Feb. 1722/23 is unknown, but one suspects the influence of Newcastle again. The leading figure among the Lords Proprietors at the time was John Carteret, later Earl Granville, who was a close political associate of the duke. In any case, Burrington went to North Carolina and was sworn in as governor in Edenton on 15 Jan. 1723/24. A strong-willed, sometimes violent man, the new governor soon quarreled with some of the leading men of the colony. Although he did not have an immediate argument with his predecessor, president of the council William Reed, Reed did not attend council meetings between July 1724 and April 1725 because of disagreements with the governor.

According to testimony given in England by Chief Justice Christopher Gale in January 1725, Burrington made menacing statements about Gale from his first days in the colony. During the general court session of July 1724, Burrington openly insulted Gale before the court. On 23 Aug., Burrington attacked Gale's house in Edenton, attempted to break down the door, and when that attempt failed, threatened to demolish the place with gunpowder. Shortly after this incident, the chief justice went to London to request the proprietors to remove Burrington as governor. Gale carried with him a letter signed by seven councilors of the colony supporting his charges. Although details are not known, it appears that the governor's animosity toward Gale may have dated from Gale's days as customs collector for the Port of Beaufort: Gale gave advice to his counterpart at Roanoke, who was quarreling with Burrington over seizure of a trading vessel.

Regardless of his problems in Edenton, Burrington was highly successful in the Lower Cape Fear region. More than any other governor, he was responsible for the growth of the area that by the 1750s had become the colony's richest. He liberalized the land-grant procedure and encouraged settlement by several trips there. In 1730 he purchased a ten-thousand acre tract called Stag Park in present-day Pender County, and eventually he built a summer home there. When he became royal governor, Burrington explored much of the Lower Cape Fear region on horseback and charted some of its waters. He personally oversaw construction of several bridges in the area. Finally, he did preliminary clearing for and urged completion of a highway linking the Neuse River communities with those in the Lower Cape Fear, thus expediting settlement.

In the summer of 1725, Christopher Gale returned to Edenton with Burrington's dismissal as governor. Burrington was in the Lower Cape Fear at the time, and on 17 July 1725, Sir Richard Everard was sworn in as his successor. After his ouster, Burrington remained in North Carolina for almost a year. His resentment against Everard grew, and on the night of 2 Dec. 1725 he went to the governor's house in Edenton and attempted to goad his successor into a duel. After calling Everard "a Noodle and an ape" and other more violent terms, but failing to receive satisfaction, Burrington left the governor's dwelling seeking a fight. He physically attacked at least two other houses in the neighborhood and earned criminal charges for his actions at the March 1726 general court. Although he was represented by counsel, Burrington did not appear in court, and the case was continued until July. In April he served in the lower house of the General Assembly from Chowan Precinct, but he returned to England before July.

After the proprietary transfer of North Carolina to the Crown, Newcastle secured the first royal governorship of the colony for Burrington. His commission was issued on 15 Jan. 1729/30, and he was sworn at Edenton on 25 Feb. 1730/31. As might be expected in light of his previous administration, Burrington still had some powerful enemies in North Carolina. Within the first six months of his new administration, he had alienated some of his previous allies as well. The governor persisted in his former style of invective and violent behavior. He openly insulted councillors, assemblymen, and judges who opposed him. By May 1731, Chief Justice William Smith was so angry with Burrington's methods that he went to England to seek his dismissal.

Engaged in a battle with the council for resistance to his land policies, Burrington quarreled with the lower house of the assembly concerning fee schedules in the colony. By 1732 many legislators were unalterably opposed to him. Attempting to rule increasingly by executive decree, the governor began illegally suspending uncooperative councillors and replacing them with his own allies. On 12 Nov. 1734, however, Burrington was notified that his successor, Gabriel Johnston, had arrived in the province, and his rule ended.

Burrington returned to London and spent the rest of his life there, his income from his North Carolina holdings providing him with a comfortable retirement. In May 1736 he told the board of trade that three provincial officials had tried to assassinate him in his final months as governor, but no investigation was instituted. Two years later, Burrington fathered a son named George. This boy was to be his father's sole legatee of landholdings in North Carolina amounting to not less than 18,400 acres. The former governor lived to an advanced age, but his death was a hard one. While taking an evening stroll in St. James's Park, London, he was murdered by a robber. As befitted Burrington, there were signs of a violent struggle.

SEE: *DAB*, vol. 3 (1929); Marshall DeLancey Haywood, *Governor George Burrington* (1896); James A. Henretta, "Salutary Neglect": Colonial Administration under the Duke of Newcastle (1972); William S. Price, Jr., "A Strange Incident in George Burrington's Royal Governorship," *North Carolina Historical Review* 51 (1974); William L. Saunders, ed., *Colonial Records of North Carolina*, vols. 2–4, 6 (1886, 1888); Strudwick Family Papers (Southern Historical Collection, University of North Carolina, Chapel Hill).

WILLIAM S. PRICE, JR.

Burt, (Maxwell) Struthers (*18 Oct. 1881–28 Aug. 1954*), writer, was born in Baltimore of Irish and Welsh ancestry. His parents were from Philadelphia, where he grew up and attended private schools. For two years he was a reporter for the Philadelphia *Times*; then he entered Princeton University, being graduated in 1904. After attending the University of Munich and Oxford University, he taught English at Princeton.

Captivated by the West, Burt settled in Jackson Hole, Wyo., in 1908. On 8 Feb. 1913 he married a writer, later known as Katharine Newlin Burt, and began homesteading in Wyoming; two children were born to them there, Nathaniel, who also became a writer, and Julia Bleecker (Mrs. George C. Attebury). In 1918, Burt was a private in the Air Service of the U.S. Army. His literary life was successful from the beginning, and remarkably so after the 1924 publication of *The Diary of a Dude-Wrangler*, personal experiences at Jackson Hole.

The Burts, seeking a mild winter climate, first went to Southern Pines in 1919 at the suggestion of James Boyd, a Princeton student of Burt's. For a number of years they rented various houses in the town. Though they remained legal residents of Wyoming, in 1927 they purchased and remodeled Hibernia, a large house adjoining that of the Boyds, calling it their second home. During winters in North Carolina, Burt was active in local and state affairs and was a member of the Kiwanis Club and the Southern Pines Library Association. His many letters to the editors of North Carolina newspapers reflected his agitation concerning such matters as what he termed the "billboard blight." He was president of the State Literary and Historical Association in 1939–40 and was awarded an LL.D. by The University of North Carolina at Chapel Hill. He was also a member of the American Institute of Arts and Letters and an elector of the Hall of Fame. In 1952, feeling that Hibernia was too large for them, the Burts sold the house but promised to return often to Southern Pines. Following a long illness, Burt died in Jackson Hole and was buried there.

In the High Hills (1914), a book of poems, was the first of Burt's nineteen titles and was succeeded by John O'May and Other Stories (1918). Three more books of poetry and three more collections of short stories were published, in addition to five novels: The Interpreter's House (1924), The Delectable Mountains (1927), Festival (1931), Entertaining the Islanders (1933), and Along These Streets (1942). For the most part about Philadelphians, the novels are subject, according to Nathaniel Burt, to "a sort of unwillingness to either accept wholly or wholly reject the conventions of Romance. There is always a love story, there is always a certain strict plotting of acceptance, withdrawal, misunderstanding, and final clinch that leads to much amusing discussion of the difference between men and women, but which does not escape a sort of artificiality." Probably because of its conventions and subject matter, Burt's fiction was featured in such well-paying magazines as Red Book, McCall's, Colliers, and the Saturday Evening Post. Two collections of essays, one volume of political satire, Powder River (1938) in "The Rivers of America" series, and Philadelphia: Holy Experiment (1945) rounded out his book-length publications. Burt was an Episcopalian and a Democrat. A portrait by the Philadelphia artist Adolphe Borie is a family possession.

SEE: Nathaniel Burt, "Struthers Burt '04," Princeton University Library Chronicle, Spring-Summer 1958; Burt Papers (Princeton University Library, Princeton, N.J.); Stanley J. Kunitz and Howard Haycraft, eds., Twentieth Century Authors (1942); North Carolina Authors (1952); Raleigh News and Observer, 31 Mar. 1952, 31 Aug. 1954 (obit.); Who Was Who in America, vol. 3 (1960).

                                                                    RICHARD WALSER

Burton, Hutchins Gordon (1774 or 1782–21 Apr. 1836), lawyer, congressman, and governor, was the son of John and Mary Gordon Burton. There is disagreement about his birthdate and birthplace, but the weight of evidence seems to confirm that he was born in Mecklenburg County, Va., in 1774. His father died when he was about three years old, and he went to live with his uncle, Colonel Robert Burton, at Williamsboro in what is now Vance County. After attending an academy at Williamsboro he was enrolled at The University of North Carolina from 1795 to 1798. Later he read law under Judge Leonard Henderson and in 1806 was admitted to the bar in Charlotte.

Burton represented Mecklenburg County in the House of Commons in 1809 and 1810. In the latter year the assembly elected him attorney general of the state, a position he held until his resignation in November 1816. In 1812 he married Sarah Wales Jones, daughter of Willie Jones of Halifax, and moved to his wife's home. He represented Halifax in the House of Commons in 1817.

Joseph H. Bryan retired from the Halifax-Tar River congressional seat in 1819, and Burton was elected to succeed him. Arriving in Washington in December, he found lodging on Capitol Hill at the mess of Alfred R. Dowson. This was the headquarters of a group of Old Republicans from the Roanoke area of Virginia and North Carolina: John Randolph, Nathaniel Macon, Weldon Edwards, Thomas H. Hall, Romulus M. Saunders, John Branch, and Willie P. Mangum all roomed there during Burton's time. Burton received important committee assignments in Congress; during the first session he was on the Post Office and Post Roads Committee, during the second on Military Affairs, and later on the Judiciary and Roads and Canals committees. He was a strict constructionist, and his votes generally showed opposition to any extension of federal power. In 1824 he was active in the congressional caucus that supported the candidacy of William H. Crawford and Nathaniel Macon to head the nation. After Crawford's health failed, Burton worked to throw the Crawford support to John Q. Adams.

Governor Jesse Franklin declined reelection in 1820, and Burton was defeated by Gabriel Holmes as a candidate to follow him. Old Republicans again supported Burton for governor in 1824, and he was elected over Montfort Stokes and Alfred Moore. Burton won on the sixth ballot in the assembly, and on 23 Mar. 1824 he resigned his seat in Congress to move to Raleigh.

Burton served as chief executive of North Carolina from December 1824 to December 1827. As governor he supported both internal improvements and public education. The first real step toward free education in North Carolina was taken in 1826 with the passage of the Literary Fund Bill, creating a fund for the support of common schools and a board to administer the fund. A serious setback to the cause of education occurred, however, when state treasurer John Haywood died in 1827 and the state treasury was found to be practically empty. During his term, Burton denounced northern abolitionists for agitating the slave question and supported passage of a law to keep free blacks out of the state. As chief executive he was host to many interesting visitors to Raleigh, including General Lafayette in 1825 and New York Senator Martin Van Buren in 1827. In 1825 and 1826, Burton was also grand master of Masons in North Carolina.

President Adams nominated Burton to be territorial governor of Arkansas in 1826, but the nomination was never confirmed by the U.S. Senate. Burton's term as governor ended in 1827, when James Iredell, Jr., began his administration. Burton returned to Halifax. In 1830 he expressed an interest in appointment to the U.S. Senate, but by then North Carolina was dominated by the followers of Jackson, for whom Burton showed little enthusiasm.

In the 1830s, Burton bought land in Texas and made plans to move there. He started a trip to inspect his western interests in the spring of 1836 but died suddenly at Wayside Inn, between Salisbury and Lincolnton, and was buried in the Unity Church yard at Beatty's Ford in Lincoln County. His wife and several children survived him. His widow later married Colonel Andrew Joyner.

SEE: W. C. Allen, History of Halifax County (1918); Samuel A. Ashe, ed., Biographical History of North Carolina, vol. 4 (1906); Biog. Dir. Am. Cong. (1971); H. G. Burton Papers

(North Carolina State Archives, Raleigh); *Congressional Directory* (1973); *DAB*, vol. 1 (1928); *Nat. Cyc. Am. Biog.*, vol. 4 (1889).

DANIEL M. MCFARLAND

Burton, Robert (20 Oct. 1747–31 May 1825), member of the Continental Congress, Revolutionary War officer, and planter, was born in Mecklenburg County, Va., the son of Tabitha Minge and Hutchings Burton and perhaps the grandson of Noel Hunt Burton, barrister, of Kingsbridge, London. Burton moved to Granville County in about 1775, in which year he married Agatha Williams, daughter of Judge John Williams.

At the beginning of the Revolution, Burton became a lieutenant of Continental artillery; afterward he was quartermaster general of North Carolina with the rank of colonel. He served as a member of the council of state from 1783 to 1785, again during the period 1800–1807, and again in 1813–15. He was president of the council in 1807, 1813, and 1815. He was elected to the Continental Congress in 1785 but not seated until 1786; although he was elected again in 1787, to replace Timothy Bloodworth, there is no record to indicate that he attended. In 1789, Burton gave the state a bust of John Paul Jones, destroyed in 1831 when the capitol burned. Granville County records for 1790 indicate that he owned fourteen slaves and 2,405 acres of land there, as well as nearly 6,000 in what was to become Tennessee. In 1813 he was a member of the commission to establish the line between North Carolina, South Carolina, and Georgia.

Burton's wife died in 1807; at his own death, he was survived by nine children. Two of his sons, Alfred M. and Robert H., both of whom attended The University of North Carolina, moved to Lincoln County. Robert H. was the grandfather of Confederate general Robert F. Hoke. The elder Robert Burton was the uncle of Hutchins G. Burton, governor of North Carolina.

Burton was buried on his plantation, Montpelier, at Williamsboro.

SEE: *Appleton's Cyclopedia of American Biography*, vol. 1 (1887); Samuel A. Ashe, ed., *Biographical History of North Carolina*, vol. 3 (1905); John H. Wheeler, *Historical Sketches of North Carolina* (1851).

MRS. JOHN C. BERNHARDT

Burwell, Margaret Anna Robertson. *See* Burwell, Robert Armistead.

Burwell, Robert Armistead (12 July 1802–5 Mar. 1895), Presbyterian minister and educator, was born in Dinwiddie County, Va., the eldest son of Colonel Armistead Burwell (1777–1841) and Mary Cole Turnbull; he traced his descent from Major Lewis Burwell I (1621–53) of Carter's Creek, Gloucester County, Va., who had come to Virginia in 1640. Burwell was graduated from Hampden-Sydney College, Farmville, Va., in 1823 and in the same year entered Union Theological Seminary, Richmond, Va., as one of the three members of its first class. On 23 Oct. 1826 he was licensed to preach by West Hanover Presbytery at Lynchburg, Va. He served as home missionary in Franklin County, Va., 1827–28, and as stated supply to Salem Church, Lexington Presbytery, 1829–30. On 27 Nov. 1830 he was ordained by West Hanover Presbytery at Peak's Church. He served as home missionary in Bedford County, Va., 1830–31, and as pastor of Wood's Church in Chesterfield County, Va., a few miles from Petersburg, 1831–35.

On 22 Dec. 1831, Burwell married Margaret Anna

Robertson (3 Oct. 1810–21 June 1871), founder and coprincipal of Mr. and Mrs. Burwell's Female School in Hillsborough (1837–57). Born in Richmond, Va., she was the daughter of Scots merchant William Bruce Robertson of Petersburg and Margaret Ann Spotswood (1792–1869) and in direct descent the great-great-granddaughter of Virginia's colonial governor Alexander Spotswood (1676–1740) and Ann Butler Brayne of London. Margaret Anna Robertson was reared in Petersburg by her mother's remarkable sister, Mrs. Susan Catharine Spotswood Bott ("Aunt Bott"), whose life of Presbyterian good works was sketched by her pastor, Dr. A. B. Van Zandt, in *The Elect Lady* (Philadelphia, 1857). The Presbyterian education and discipline received in the Bott home were later to provide Margaret Anna with the exact pattern and basic groundwork for the famed Burwell School.

In the late autumn of 1835 the young Burwells, with two small children, arrived in Hillsborough. Ten other children were to be born to them during their Hillsborough years. Robert Burwell assumed the pastorate of the Hillsborough Presbyterian Church, lately vacated by the Reverend John Knox Witherspoon. The Burwell family settled into the recently purchased Presbyterian manse on North Churton Street; the house was to become widely known as the Burwell School and is now a National Register house, owned and restored by the Historic Hillsborough Commission.

During the Reverend Mr. Burwell's pastorate, the Presbyterian Church built a new Sessions House, razed after a hundred years, and the brick church structure itself was renovated extensively. Burwell also was a moving force in the establishment of a new Hillsborough Literary Society, which flourished vigorously for a time.

To augment her husband's uncertain four hundred dollar per year salary, Mrs. Burwell in 1837, at Dr. James Webb's suggestion, began to teach some of the neighborhood children at a day school in her own home. Tradition says that Webb's daughter, Mary, was her first pupil and that Mary's companions were Annabelle Norwood and Sarah J. Kollock. The little day school quickly developed into a boarding school offering both a solid grammar school curriculum and the equivalent of high school courses, in two sessions per year. Girls from eight to eighteen years of age came from distant North Carolina and Virginia plantations and towns as well as from neighboring states.

French, Latin, Spanish, and Italian were taught by imported language masters, an innovation in female education in the Carolina back country of the 1830s. The same masters taught most of the "ornamentals," that is, piano, guitar, voice, painting, and drawing. Signor Antonio di Martino, a courtly Sicilian cavalry officer, was the most notable of the Burwells' imported "professors" and lived in Hillsborough for many years. Mrs. Burwell herself, besides overseeing every detail of the operation of the house, kitchen, and garden, taught "divisions" (classes) in English grammar, utilizing her favorite *Paradise Lost*, and took charge of Sunday afternoon studies in the Shorter Catechism.

Girls were expected to show and to prove definite progress in all areas, and this program of compulsory, orderly self-improvement was one of the best features of the school. Special emphasis was placed on improvement in handwriting, English composition, social manners, and dress. End of the year public oral and written examinations in all subjects, as well as musical concerts and exhibitions of art, needlework, and copybooks, were annually anticipated contributions to the culture of the entire area. The motto of the school was widely advertised: "Not how much but how well."

In 1848 the Burwells embarked on a considerable program of expansion. The Reverend Mr. Burwell on 30 Mar. resigned the pastorate of the Presbyterian church to become the active coprincipal of the school; he purchased outright the manse and its two acres of grounds and contracted with Captain John Berry at a cost of over twenty-five hundred dollars to renovate and enlarge the house. At about this time, also, the Burwells published their only *Catalogue*, a slender booklet printed by Dennis Heartt and now extremely rare.

Although the *Catalogue* describes a modest establishment, the Burwell School exerted a far-reaching influence out of all proportion to its size. Schools stemming from it either directly or indirectly included the Nash and Kollock School in Hillsborough; Susan Webb's Almeda School at Oaks (in which her famous brothers "Sawney" and John Webb were taught); Miss Emma Scales's Reidsville Female Seminary; the Mitchell sisters' Simonton Female College, later Mitchell College, and still later Statesville Female College at Statesville; the Charlotte Female Institute, later Queens College; and Peace Institute, later Peace College, Raleigh.

In 1857 the Burwells closed the Hillsborough School and removed to Charlotte. There the Reverend Mr. Burwell had been offered the principalship of the Charlotte Female Institute, which had just completed a new building. He also served as pastor of the Paw Creek Church in Mecklenburg Presbytery from 1859 to 1863. Apparently the Burwells operated the institute in Charlotte in much the same way as the Hillsborough school. In 1859 they offered their eldest son, John Bott, a partnership in the operation of the institute, which he accepted. An 1859 circular of the institute is signed, "Rev. R. Burwell & Son." During the Civil War, in which five of the Burwells' eight sons served, Mrs. Burwell cared for refugees in the institute building.

After a perceptible decline in health, Mrs. Burwell died on 21 June 1871 in Raleigh, at the home of her daughter Nannie (Mrs. W. H. Crow). She was buried in Elmwood Cemetery, Charlotte. A legend in her own lifetime, Mrs. Burwell was widely hailed as a superior administrator, teacher, wife, mother, gardener, and conversationalist. Tall and imposing in appearance, highly gregarious, and endowed with great energy, she embodied many of the characteristics of the colonial Spotswood family.

After Mrs. Burwell's death, Robert A. and John Bott Burwell assumed in 1872 the joint principalship of Peace Institute in Raleigh. Although the Reverend Mr. Burwell actually retired from active teaching in 1875, he continued to serve the institute in various ways until 1892. In later years he also served as pastor of the church at Oakland in Johnston County. In 1882 he received a D.D. degree from The University of North Carolina. He died in Raleigh and was buried in Elmwood Cemetery, Charlotte. John Bott Burwell continued as principal of Peace until 1890.

Portraits of the Reverend Robert A. Burwell and of John Bott Burwell hang at Peace College. A portrait of Mrs. M. A. Burwell hangs at Queens College.

SEE: "Autobiography ('Narrative') of John Bott Burwell" (possession of Mrs. Colvin McAlister, Fayetteville; copies in the James Webb Papers and Edmund S. Burwell Papers, Library, University of North Carolina, Chapel Hill); *Catalogue of the Burwell School* (n.d.); E. Daniel, "Memorial of Rev. Robert Burwell," *Minutes of the Synod of North Carolina* (1895); Drawing of the Burwell School (possession of the estate of Mrs. Mattie Burwell Murphy, Davidson); [Mary Claire Engstrom], "Mr. and Mrs.

Burwell's Female School," *News Letter No. 25* (Hillsborough Historical Society), January 1966; Hillsborough Presbyterian Church, for Sessions Book II, 1837–57; *Hillsborough Recorder*, 1837–57; Orange County Deed Books 33, 34, 37 (Orange County, Hillsborough); Sallie C. White, "A Brief Sketch of the Life of Mrs. M. A. Burwell," *Voices of Peace* 1 (1889); reprinted in *North Carolina Booklet*, vol. 21 (1921–22); A. B. Van Zandt, *The Elect Lady* (1857).

MARY CLAIRE ENGSTROM

Busbee, Charles Manly (23 Oct. 1845–7 Aug. 1909), attorney, was born in Raleigh, the eldest of the four sons of Perrin Busbee (22 Oct. 1816–16 Sept. 1853) and Anne Eliza Gales Taylor (13 Oct. 1825–23 Jan. 1892); portraits of Perrin and Anne Busbee by Garl Browne hang in the North Carolina Museum of Art. Charles Busbee's children thought that he was named for the celebrated Whig leader Governor Charles Manly, who was a close friend of Perrin Busbee. In 1863, Charles Busbee left Hampden-Sydney College in Virginia, where he had completed the sophomore year, to enlist in the Fifth North Carolina Infantry. The following year he was captured by the Union forces during the Battle of Spotsylvania Court House. After several months of captivity in Union prisons, including that on Sullivan's Island, S.C., where he was exposed to Confederate fire in retaliation for similar action taken by the Confederate garrison at Charleston against Union prisoners, Busbee was released in a prisoner exchange. He rejoined his regiment in time to participate in the final hostilities in the defense of Petersburg. Paroled after the surrender at Appomattox Court House, Sergeant-Major Busbee returned on foot to Raleigh, where his mother had difficulty recognizing her son in his bedraggled condition.

Through the munificence of Miss Sue Devereux, a friend of his mother's, Busbee was enabled to spend a year and a half at The University of North Carolina as a law student. On 14 Jan. 1867 he was licensed to practice in the courts of pleas and quarter sessions. A year later he was admitted to the bar of the superior courts of law and equity. Upon the admittance of his younger brother, Fabius Haywood, to the practice of law, the two formed a partnership. Subsequently, the brothers joined Judge E. G. Reade of Raleigh in the formation of the law firm of Reade, Busbee and Busbee. In his later years, Charles Busbee became a law partner of ex-Chief Justice James E. Shepherd; at the time of his death, Busbee was in partnership with his son Perrin.

Busbee served briefly as Wake County register of deeds shortly after his return to Raleigh in 1865. He was not an ambitious politician, however, although he served a term in the state senate in 1874 and one in the state house of representatives in 1884. These tours seem to have been undertaken in response to the wishes of his friends and associates, who held Busbee in great esteem. When, during a long convalescence from a near-fatal illness, his ability to practice law actively was impaired, Busbee's friends obtained for him an appointment by President Grover Cleveland as postmaster of Raleigh. He served in this post from 21 Mar. 1894 to 21 May 1898. Busbee's influence in the political field also complemented the efforts of his brother Fabius in contributing to the successful reorganization of The University of North Carolina in 1875.

Busbee was a devoted and energetic member of the International Order of Odd Fellows. He became a member of Manteo Lodge, No. 8, in 1870 and retained membership until his death. His state-wide popularity and leadership ability were reflected in his rise in the organization's councils; he achieved the highest office in the society when he was elected grand sire of the sovereign Grand Lodge of the world for the 1890–92 term.

On 30 July 1868, Busbee married Lydia Lambe Littlejohn (b. 7 May 1846) of Oxford, daughter of James Thompson Littlejohn and Phoebe Dozier. Seven children were born of this union: James Littlejohn (b. 20 May 1869), who subsequently changed his name to Jacques; Perrin (10 Feb. 1872–9 Jan. 1935); Sara Kelleck (8 Oct. 1873–29 Jan. 1875); Louisa Taylor (24 Mar. 1876–18 June 1945); Sophia Dozier (19 July 1877–19 Apr. 1975), who adopted the name Sophie Daugé, the original French version of her grandmother's maiden name; Isabel Bronson (13 Mar. 1880–27 Aug. 1966); and Christiana (21 Apr. 1883– 24 Sept. 1949). The Busbee girls were *fin de siècle* belles, but despite their popularity, none of them married.

Lydia Littlejohn Busbee died 21 Apr. 1887. On 1 Jan. 1891, Busbee married Florence Elinor Cooper (12 Mar. 1869–17 Oct. 1955) of Louisville, Ky., a niece of Governor Zebulon Vance's second wife. Three children were born of this marriage: Charles Manly, Jr. (3 July 1893–19 Jan. 1970); Susannah Steele (b. 24 July 1895), who married Captain Charles M. Jones, U.S.M.C.; and Florence Cooper (b. 9 Sept. 1898), who married Major General Albert C. Stanford, U.S.A. Charles Manly, Jr., was graduated from West Point in 1915 and became a brigadier general in the army during World War II, and both daughters married career officers: Captain Jones was an Annapolis graduate and General Stanford a West Pointer. Moreover, four grandsons obtained commissions in the army, three of them graduating from West Point.

In the summer of 1891, Busbee suffered a massive stroke that paralyzed his left side and confined him to bed for many months. Although leading medical men at Johns Hopkins Hospital in Baltimore despaired of his life, Busbee eventually achieved nearly complete recovery, left with only a slight limp. His recovery was attributed to his boundless determination to live, the unremitting care of his wife, Florence, and the constant encouragement of his legion of friends. After several years of painful convalescence, Busbee was able to resume active law practice until his death eighteen years after his initial seizure.

A lifelong member of Christ Episcopal Church in Raleigh, Busbee was interred in Oakwood Cemetery there.

SEE: Samuel A. Ashe, ed., *Cyclopedia of Eminent and Representative Men of the Carolinas of the Nineteenth Century* (1892); *North Carolina Bar Association Report*, 1910; Stephen B. Weeks, Scrapbook, 1887–94 (North Carolina Collection, University of North Carolina, Chapel Hill); *Who Was Who in America*, vol. 1 (1943).

J. D. F. PHILLIPS

Busbee, Fabius Haywood (*4 Mar. 1848–28 Aug. 1908*), attorney, was born in Raleigh, the second son of Perrin Busbee (22 Oct. 1816–16 Sept. 1853) and Anne Eliza Gales Taylor (13 Oct. 1825–23 Jan. 1892). Fabius Busbee was fourteen and a student at The University of North Carolina when the Civil War erupted. Two years later he volunteered for service with Company B, Seventy-second Regiment, Third Junior Reserves, in which organization he was shortly elected second lieutenant, becoming thus one of the youngest commissioned

officers in the Confederate States. Busbee's unit was called to active duty with General Joseph E. Johnston's army during the winter of 1864–65. Following the surrender of the force to General William Sherman near Durham Station, 26 Apr. 1865, Busbee returned home. He was able to resume his studies at the university, from which he was graduated as class valedictorian with an A.B. degree in 1868. Eleven years later The University of North Carolina conferred an honorary A.M. degree upon him for his work in promoting the successful reorganization of the university in 1875. He became a trustee of the institution in 1883, a post which he held continuously until his death twenty-five years later. In 1871, Busbee received honorary A.M. degrees from Trinity College in Hartford, Conn., and from the College of New Jersey at Princeton.

During his last year as an undergraduate at the university, Busbee studied law; in January 1869 he was licensed to practice. He initially entered into partnership with his older brother, Charles Manly. Soon, however, both brothers joined with Judge E. G. Reade of Raleigh, one of his examiners, to establish the firm of Reade, Busbee and Busbee. At first, Fabius Busbee conducted a general law practice; with the development of corporate interests in North Carolina, however, he devoted his efforts increasingly to corporation law, in which he soon achieved an enviable state-wide reputation. At the time of his death, Busbee was attorney for the Southern Railway, a position he had held for many years.

A lifelong Democrat, Busbee was a North Carolina delegate to the Democratic National Conventions of 1872 and 1892. In the interim, he was designated an elector for the unsuccessful Democratic presidential candidates in 1876 and 1880. Following President Grover Cleveland's first inauguration in 1885, Busbee was appointed U.S. attorney for the Eastern District of North Carolina; he served in this capacity until 1889. These appointments comprise Busbee's formal political career, but they merely hint at the extent of his influence among the leaders of his party throughout the state. His frequent service on state commissions during his life is evidence of the esteem in which his views on many subjects were held.

Busbee was considered by his contemporaries an exceptionally fine, at times eloquent, speaker. He was said to be forceful in expression, though occasionally nervous. He was considered generous and public-spirited and was thought to have a special fondness for literature. In 1880 he published *Busbee's Criminal Digest*.

On 16 Nov. 1870, Busbee married Annie McKesson of Morganton (13 Feb. 1851–16 Oct. 1874). Two daughters were born of this marriage: Margaret Finley (b. 9 Nov. 1871), who was married to First Lieutenant William E. Shipp, U.S.A.; and Anne Taylor (27 Feb. 1879–1927); who married Robert L. Thompson of Raleigh. Three years after the death of his first wife, Busbee was married on 5 June 1877 to Sally Hall Smith (d. 19 May 1931) of Scotland Neck. This union produced three children: Richard Smith (18 Apr. 1878–13 Mar. 1948); Eliza Taylor (12 Mar. 1880–20 Dec. 1954), married to Lieutenant Colonel Arthur Sylbert Pendleton, U.S.A.; and Philip Hall (20 Dec. 1881–4 Feb. 1948).

Busbee's numerous fraternal and professional society memberships included the Chi Phi Fraternity, Confederate Veterans, American Bar Association, and the Masonic Order, of which he served as grand master for North Carolina in 1885–86.

Enroute to Seattle, Wash., in late August 1908, to attend a meeting of the American Bar Association, Busbee was taken ill in the Yellowstone National Park.

He continued his journey to its destination, where his worsened condition, diagnosed as Bright's disease, required hospitalization. A few days later Busbee succumbed in Minor Hospital in Seattle.

Following the return of his remains to Raleigh, Busbee was honored at Christ Episcopal Church in a memorial service attended by his relatives and his many friends, including Governor Robert B. Glenn, the council of state, Chief Justice Walter Clark, and other high officials. Burial took place at Oakwood Cemetery in Raleigh. A portrait painted by his nephew, Jacques Busbee, is in the possession of a great-grandson, Richard Busbee Phillips of Sloatsburg, N.Y.

SEE: Kemp P. Battle, *History of the University of North Carolina*, vol. 2 (1912); *North Carolina Bar Association Report*, 1909; Raleigh *News and Observer*, 30 Aug., 5 Sept., and 6 Oct. 1908; Stephen B. Weeks, Scrapbook, 1887–94 (North Carolina Collection, University of North Carolina); *Who Was Who in America*, vol. 1 (1943).

J. D. F. PHILLIPS

Busbee, Jacques (born James Littlejohn Busbee) *(20 May 1870–21 May 1947),* artist and reviver of Jugtown Pottery, was born in Raleigh, the son of Charles Manly and Lydia Littlejohn Busbee. Busbee prepared for a career as an artist. After graduation from Horner Military Academy in Oxford, he studied at the National Academy of Design, the Art Students' League, and the Chase School, all in New York, and for a time painted portraits and landscapes. Some of his work is owned by the North Carolina Museum of History.

On 3 Nov. 1910 he married Juliana Royster of Raleigh, who had studied photography in New York and would be his partner in the revival of Moore County pottery. In 1915 the Busbees were living in Raleigh, where Jacques supplemented his income as a portrait painter by writing and lecturing on topics related to North Carolina and art. In 1915 a long-standing interest in locating local potters was revived when Mrs. Busbee discovered an orange glaze pie plate while serving as a judge at the Davidson County Fair. The Busbees returned to New York in 1916; their collection of North Carolina pottery aroused the interest of art experts, who encouraged them to market the pottery. In May 1917 the Busbees went to the northwestern part of Moore County around Seagrove in search of local potters. They found the pottery industry languishing; prohibition had restricted the sale of their most marketable product, and only a few older potters continued the trade. The Busbees scanned the area, collecting old ware and information about early potters. They found that English Staffordshire potters had settled in the area about 1740, and they amassed a large collection of local pottery. Although the local potters were descendants of these Staffordshire potters, they had modified the traditional patterns and glazes.

The Busbees saw their task as twofold: to develop a market for the pottery and to encourage the potters to produce more marketable and traditional ware, rather than imitations of dime store ware. To develop a market, Mrs. Busbee opened a tea room, the Village Store, in Greenwich Village, where pottery and other handicrafts could be introduced to the New York market. The southern cooking and unique atmosphere insured the success of the restaurant, and by 1926 there was a sufficient market for North Carolina pottery for Mrs. Busbee to sell the Village Store and join her husband at Jugtown.

While his wife was in New York, Jacques Busbee spent most of his time in Moore County obtaining pottery for market. He gave the first orders to the established potters and supervised the shipment of their goods to New York. Busbee found it difficult to persuade the potters to return to the older styles. In 1921, in order to have a greater control over design, he built the potter's shop to be known as Jugtown, between Seagrove and Robbins. He hired young potters who would more easily accept his art training and his insistence on traditional shapes and glazes. Several of his potters later established their own potteries. Ben Owen, who came to Jugtown in 1923, remained until after Busbee's death in 1947. Jacques Busbee was not himself a potter; he saw his role as that of teaching art form to the skilled potters and assisting in developing formulas for the glazes.

Busbee recognized the market demand for greater variety in form. A serious student of ceramics, he considered the primitive and early periods of Chinese ceramics to be "the classic periods of the world's pottery." Accompanied by Ben Owen, he visited museums to study Chinese pottery. Busbee assisted Owen in reproducing the unfamiliar forms and developed a "Chinese Blue" glaze. The Jugtown "translations" of Oriental ceramics were among the most popular pieces. The Jugtown potters produced a wide variety of utilitarian and decorative pieces in a variety of glazes: orange, buff, a gray salt glaze stoneware with blue decoration, frogskin, and white.

The Busbees wrote articles for numerous magazines and gave lectures on Jugtown pottery to publicize their enterprise. They preserved the rustic setting at Jugtown, and the hospitality of their log cabin added to the atmosphere. Visitors dined on traditional fare cooked over an open fire and were expected to assist in drying the dishes when Mrs. Busbee brought the dishpan to the table.

Jacques Busbee died of a heart attack after a two-week illness, and his ashes were scattered in the Jugtown yard. By 1947, Jugtown pottery enjoyed international acclaim. Although the Jugtown operation remained small, the Busbees had publicized local pottery and revived and enhanced the craft. A collection of Jugtown Pottery is a part of the permanent collection of the State Art Society and is preserved in the North Carolina Museum of Art.

SEE: Jacques Busbee, "Jugtown Pottery," *Ceramic Age* 14 (1929); Juliana R. Busbee, "Jugtown Comes of Age," *State* 5 (19 June 1937), and "Jugtown Pottery—A New Way for Old Jugs," *Bulletin of the American Ceramic Society* 16 (1937); Jean Crawford, *Jugtown Pottery History and Design* (1964); Mildred Harrington, "Interesting People: The Master Potter of Jugtown," *American Magazine*, June 1927; North Carolina Collection (University of North Carolina, Chapel Hill), for newspaper file; A. T. Robertson, Jr., "Meet the Busbees, of Jugtown," *State* 1 (18 Nov. 1933); *Who's Who in America*, 1924–25.

GEORGE W. TROXLER

Busbee, Juliana Royster *(10 May 1876–2 Mar. 1962),* promoter of pottery, was the daughter of William Burt and Julia Tutt Royster of Raleigh. She attended St. Mary's Junior College for two sessions and studied photography under her uncle. In 1910 she married a professional artist and illustrator, Jacques Busbee of Raleigh. In 1915, as fine arts chairman of the North Carolina Federation of Women's Clubs, she traveled throughout the state promoting folkcrafts. With her husband, she established Jugtown Pottery. (See the sketch of Jacques Busbee, above, for an account of the enterprise.)

In addition to her work at Jugtown, Juliana Busbee

was active in civic affairs. In 1930, as a member of the school committee in her community, she organized a school lunch program. She was a charter member and vice-president of the State Art Society and an honorary life member of the North Carolina Literary and Historical Association. On 31 May 1959, Woman's College awarded her the honorary degree of L.H.D.

After the death of her husband in 1947, Juliana Busbee and the Jugtown potter, Ben Owen, continued to operate Jugtown. Aware of her deteriorating health and failing memory, Mrs. Busbee sought help from friends and state agencies to continue operating the pottery. In 1958–59, hampered by her loss of memory, she signed two deeds to the Jugtown property: one to a committee of fifteen friends, the second to John Mare of Southern Pines. Both the committee and Mare formed corporations for the continuation of Jugtown, and both intended to provide for Mrs. Busbee's welfare. In April 1959, Mare assumed management of the pottery; however, Ben Owen—for thirty-seven years the Jugtown potter—did not approve of Mare's proposed changes and left. Jugtown was temporarily closed. Litigation between Mare's corporation, Jacques and Juliana Busbee's Jugtown, and the committee's Jugtown Incorporated began in April 1959 and was settled in December when an injunction against Mare was dissolved. During the litigation, Juliana Busbee was found to be incompetent, and P. H. Wilson of Carthage was appointed her guardian. She continued to live in her log cabin at Jugtown until her death. Following memorial services at the Busbee cabin on 5 Mar., her ashes were scattered in the yard.

Jugtown resumed operations in April 1960 under Mare's management, but his death in August 1962 cut short his plans for expansion. His executors continued operating Jugtown until they sold it in 1968 to Country Roads Incorporated, a nonprofit corporation devoted to the preservation and development of American handicrafts.

SEE: The biography of Jacques Busbee, above, for sources.

GEORGE W. TROXLER

Butler, John (d. 1786), brigadier general of the state militia and legislator of the revolutionary period, settled before May 1763 on the Haw River in the western edge of the Hawfields community, Orange County. During the period when his brother William was a leader of the Regulator movement, John Butler was sheriff of Orange County (1770). Although Butler testified to the General Assembly that the Regulators had obstructed him in carrying out his duties, he was mentioned in a Regulator petition of October 1770 as one of only two public officials charging fair fees for their services. After the Battle of Alamance, Butler signed petitions for clemency for former Regulators and sought pardon for his brother, one of the few leaders outlawed.

When the Revolution began, Butler was appointed to the committee of safety for the Hillsborough District by the third provincial congress, and on 9 Sept. 1775 he was commissioned a lieutenant colonel of the minutemen from Orange County. He participated in the Moore's Creek Bridge campaign, when the Orange County militia aided in occupying Cross Creek. He was elected a delegate from Orange County to the fourth provincial congress, which met in April 1776 at Halifax. There he was appointed to a committee for the purchase of arms, and on 22 Apr. 1776 he became a colonel of the Orange County militia, commanding the southern regiment. He

was reelected a delegate to the fifth provincial congress in November 1776.

Active in military and civil affairs throughout the Revolution, Butler served four terms in the House of Commons: 1777, 1778, and two sessions in 1784. In 1781 he was elected to one term in the state senate. From 26 June 1781 until 3 May 1782 he was on the council of state. He was an active member of the General Assembly. In the April 1784 session he was chairman of two important committees, Propositions and Grievances and the Committee to Reply to the Governor's Message, and he served on the Committee on Privileges and Elections. Although a military officer, he sponsored in this same session a bill for relief of Quakers, many of whom were pacifists, and a bill to reduce the confiscation of Loyalist property.

The General Assembly elected John Butler to the rank of brigadier general of the Hillsborough District on 9 May 1777. For the next seven years he held this position and rendered capable service as a recruiter of militia, a field commander in regular army campaigns, and an adversary of the Tories in the partisan warfare.

His field service as a militia general under Continental command included the command of a contingent of seven hundred militia sent to reinforce General Benjamin Lincoln at Augusta, Ga., in May 1779. In the ensuing maneuvers near Charlestown, S.C., Butler's militia performed well in the unsuccessful assault on the British works at Stono Ferry, 20 June 1779. The following year, Butler commanded a brigade under General Horatio Gates at the disastrous Battle of Camden on 16 Aug. When Cornwallis invaded North Carolina, occupying Charlotte on 28 Sept. 1780, Butler had his brigade posted between Charlotte and Salisbury, occasionally skirmishing with the British. After the British occupation of Wilmington on 29 Jan. 1781, Butler was ordered to defend the Lower Cape Fear region. However, General Nathanael Greene requested that the militia join his troop concentration in Guilford County, and Butler rendezvoused with Greene at High Rock Ford in March. Commanding a brigade on the front line in the Battle of Guilford Courthouse, 15 Mar. 1781, Butler vainly attempted to stem the early rout of the militia.

After Greene invaded South Carolina in April 1781, Butler remained in his district recruiting and sending reinforcements to the south. Encouraged by the presence of Cornwallis, the Tories of North Carolina rose in force in 1781. Under the notorious but brilliant leadership of David Fanning, the Loyalist militia in the center of the state terrorized and controlled large areas until the spring of 1782. Fanning's daring raid on the capital at Hillsborough on 12 Sept. 1781 achieved the capture of Governor Thomas Burke and numerous civil and military officers. Informed of the raid, Butler, with some four hundred militia, ambushed Fanning's command of over nine hundred Tories on 13 Sept. at Lindley's Mill on Cane Creek. After four hours of close fighting, resulting in a total of more than two hundred and fifty casualties on both sides, the outnumbered and outflanked Butler was forced to retire. Still hoping to rescue the governor, Butler pursued the Tories as far as Hammond's Creek, south of Elizabethtown, where he was surprised and defeated by a British force from Wilmington. Butler was joined by General Griffith Rutherford in October, and the militia remained in the field near Wilmington until the British evacuation in November. As Tory strength receded, Butler handled the negotiations with Fanning, who finally left the state in May 1782.

Butler resigned his commission on 2 June 1784. Although elected to the House of Commons in 1786, he died that fall before the session opened. The sole heir to his Haw River plantation was his wife, Anne. Butler, who was described as a "plain and simple" democrat by an earlier biographer, demonstrated his strength of character by his loyal service to the state through the many adversities of the Revolution. A recent detailed study of the Battle of Lindley's Mill provides abundant evidence of his competence as a tactical commander. In this battle, clever use of the terrain and effective leadership nearly wrested a victory from the capable Fanning. There were few instances in the war where heavily outnumbered militia fought so well. At a crucial time in the history of his state, Butler gave his last years as a legislator, general, and peacemaker.

SEE: Samuel A. Ashe, ed., *Biographical History of North Carolina*, vol. 1 (1905); E. W. Caruthers, *Revolutionary Incidents* (1854); Hugh T. Lefler and Paul Wager, eds., *Orange County, 1752–1952* (1953); A. I. Newlin, *The Battle of Lindley's Mill* (1974); Orange County Deeds and Wills (North Carolina State Archives, Raleigh); William S. Powell, James K. Huhta, and Thomas J. Farnham, eds., *The Regulators in North Carolina* (1971); Hugh F. Rankin, *The North Carolina Continentals* (1971); William L. Saunders and Walter Clark, eds., *Colonial and State Records of North Carolina*, 30 vols. (1886–1914).

LINDLEY S. BUTLER

Butler, Marion *(20 May 1863–3 June 1938),* agrarian leader and U.S. senator, was born near Clinton in Sampson County. His grandfather, James Butler, fought in the Revolutionary War, and his father, Wiley Butler, served in the Confederate Army. Wiley Butler, a yeoman farmer, married Romelia Ferrell, and Marion was the oldest of their six children.

Despite the poverty that afflicted Tar Heel farmers in the years after the Civil War, Marion Butler managed to graduate from The University of North Carolina in 1885. His plans to study law at the university were cut short, however, when his father died; though still in his early twenties, he had to assume the responsibility of running the family farm.

In addition to farming, Butler conducted an academy for the schooling of his younger brothers and sisters, as well as for the children of neighbors. When the Farmers' Alliance movement, destined to become the most militant agrarian combination in American history, spread from the Southwest into North Carolina in the late 1880s, he immediately joined the organization, and it provided him a ladder of political opportunity that he climbed with impressive speed. Possessing the formal education and literate articulateness lacking in many of his fellow farmers, he became president of the Sampson County Farmers' Alliance; he purchased a weekly newspaper in the county seat of Clinton, the *Caucasian* (which he subsequently moved to Goldsboro and then to Raleigh); and in 1890, at the age of twenty-seven, he was sent by the voters to the state senate as an Alliance Democrat.

In the legislature, Butler quickly emerged as the leader of the dominant agrarian forces, and in 1891 he became president of the state Farmers' Alliance. After the death in 1892 of another important agrarian leader from North Carolina, Leonidas L. Polk, Butler was elected president of the National Farmers' Alliance in 1893.

Ardent advocates of free silver and other financial and economic reforms, Butler and his followers in the Alliance had little use for Grover Cleveland, whom the national Democratic party renominated for the presidency in 1892. When the leaders of the Tar Heel Democratic party ruled that no member could "split the ticket," that is, vote Democratic in the state and local elections but not in the presidential race, Butler led thousands of Alliancemen in a bolt from the Democratic party—the "white man's party" that had ruled the state since Reconstruction—to join the new People's or Populist party.

In North Carolina the Populists entered the campaign of 1892 too late to hope for much, yet they and the Republicans together polled a larger vote than the Democrats. Butler then emerged as the nemesis of North Carolina Democrats, who dubbed him "the sly fox of Sampson County"; in the state elections of 1894 he led the Populists into cooperation with the Republicans, a policy known as "fusion." The combined forces of the Populists and the Republicans swept the state to gain control of both houses of the legislature and to send Butler to the U.S. Senate in 1895 for a full six-year term. In Washington he proceeded to shock veteran senators by his vigorous advocacy of reform and to take his place alongside other agrarian champions of the silver cause.

Butler achieved his greatest national prominence in 1896 when, as national chairman of the Populist party, he led in effecting the compromise whereby the Populists at their convention in St. Louis, Mo., endorsed William Jennings Bryan, already the Democratic nominee for the presidency, on a ticket with the Populists' own vice-presidential nominee, Thomas E. Watson of Georgia. In the momentous campaign that followed, Butler worked closely with Bryan and other national Democratic leaders to effect a policy of Populist-Democratic cooperation or fusion on the tickets for presidential electors, even though in North Carolina, Populists and Republicans continued to cooperate in many of the state and local elections.

After Bryan was defeated, the Populist-Republican forces extended their control in North Carolina in 1896. When the Tar Heel Democrats returned to power with their massive "white supremacy" campaigns of 1898 and 1900, however, Butler lost his seat in the Senate. He continued to serve as Populist national chairman until 1904, when he became a Republican. Although not he but Governor Daniel L. Russell originated the famous interstate lawsuit wherein South Dakota successfully sued North Carolina on certain railroad bonds that the latter state had semi-repudiated, Butler did play a secondary role in the affair; and for many years, almost until his death in fact, Tar Heel Democrats fought the Republicans by variations on the theme of "Butler, Boodle, and Bonds."

As a U.S. senator, Butler played a key role in the establishment of free rural mail delivery. He was also instrumental in the beginning of postal savings banks. In North Carolina he and his fellow agrarian reformers were proud of their contributions to the establishment of a state college for women at Greensboro, to the establishment of a state railway commission, and to other reforms. A conspicuous friend of public education at all levels, Butler stood by The University of North Carolina at a critical time and served as a trustee and a member of the executive board from 1891 to 1899.

While still a senator, Butler resumed his study of law at The University of North Carolina, and after retiring from public life he engaged in practice in Washington, D.C. He had married Florence Faison of Sampson County on 31 Aug. 1893, and they had five children: Pocahontas, Marion, Edward F., Florence F., and Wiley. Butler died in Takoma Park, Md., and was buried from St. Paul's Episcopal Church, Clinton, to which he and his wife belonged, in the Clinton Cemetery.

SEE: Samuel A. Ashe, ed., *Biographical History of North Carolina*, vol. 8 (1917); *Biog. Dir. Am. Cong.* (1950); Butler papers (Southern Historical Collection, University of North Carolina, Chapel Hill); *DAB*, vol. 22 (1958); Robert F. Durden, *The Climax of Populism* (1965), and *Reconstruction Bonds and Twentieth Century Politics* (1962); Helen G. Edmonds, *The Negro and Fusion Politics in North Carolina* (1951); *New York Times*, 4 June 1938; *Who Was Who in America*, vol. 1 (1943).

ROBERT F. DURDEN

Butler, William (*fl. 1768–73*), farmer and insurgent, was probably born in Virginia before 1730 and was likely the son of William and Frances Watson Butler. He was one of at least seven children: brothers Aaron, General John of Revolutionary War rank, and Edmund; half-brother William Watson, Jr.; and two sisters. Sometime previous to 1760 he married a woman named Phebe, by whom he had four children, Thomas, William, Jr., Edmund, and "Sister McConnell." In 1768, while living near Sandy Creek in Orange County, he was appointed a county tax collector; in 1770 he was appointed a deputy sheriff in Orange County.

Butler, described as "an able man of but little property," emerged as a principal leader of the Regulators by the late 1760s. He was central in events at Hillsborough in 1768 and 1770 and at Alamance Creek in 1771. Butler, along with two others, was declared an outlaw by the governor of North Carolina in June 1771. After the events at Alamance Creek, Butler apparently fled North Carolina and, by May 1773, settled at the "headwaters of Walker's Creek" in Fincastle County, Va. In 1772, John Butler of Orange County sought unsuccessfully to obtain a pardon for his brother from Governor Josiah Martin and then warned William against planning to settle in North Carolina again. William's brother Aaron was then living in Cumberland County, while William Watson, Jr., was resident near Charlotte. Nothing is known of the further life of William Butler.

Following Butler's death, his wife, Phebe, left Virginia in 1805 and settled with her son Edmund in Simpson County, Ky., near her nephew, Aaron Butler, Jr., who owned land in Sumner and Madison counties, Tenn. Phebe was still alive in 1826. William Butler, Jr., served in the Revolutionary War, settled in Iredell County, and possibly acquired 311 acres of land in the Ninety Six District of South Carolina in 1788. William's son was Lucius Quintus Cincinnatus Butler.

SEE: William S. Powell, James K. Huhta, and Thomas J. Farnham, eds., *The Regulators in North Carolina* (1971); William L. Saunders, ed., *Colonial Records of North Carolina*, 10 vols. (1886–90); Southern Historical Collection (University of North Carolina, Chapel Hill), for William Butler Papers and Regulator Papers.

JAMES K. HUHTA

Butner, Henry Wolff (*6 Apr. 1875–13 Mar. 1937*), army officer, was born in Pinnacle, Stokes County, the son of Frank A. and Sarah Wolff Butner. He was a cadet at Davis Military Academy in Winston before receiving an appointment to West Point in 1894. He was graduated from the U.S. Military Academy in 1898, when he was commissioned second lieutenant in the field artillery. He attended the Staff College in 1906. Promoted through the grades, he was colonel in June 1918, when he sailed for France as commander of the Sixteenth Field Artillery that participated in the Aisne-Marne operations around

Chateau Thierry and Vesle. In August 1918, while still a colonel, he was transferred to the First Division as commander of the First Field Artillery brigade, and he directed the activities of the Fifth, Sixth, and Seventh regiments of field artillery at St. Mihiel in the Meuse-Argonne offensive and the march on and capture of Sedan. He was made brigadier general, temporary, in October and during the occupation of Germany he remained in command of his brigade until May 1919, when he was ordered back to the United States to attend the Army War College. He was awarded the distinguished service medal and the Croix de Guerre for valor and efficiency. His promotion to brigadier general became permanent in 1930, and he was promoted to major general in 1936. After World War I he served for a time as commander of the Thirteenth Field Artillery at Fort Bragg, as commandant at Fort Bragg, as president of the field artillery board, and as commanding general of the army's Panama department, his last post from which he returned to the United States because of a critical heart condition which soon proved fatal. General Butner never married. Camp Butner, fifteen miles north of Durham, established in January 1942, was named for him. The camp closed in March 1946, but Butner continues to be the name of the community that developed around the camp and the health care services that were afterwards opened there.

SEE: Raleigh *News and Observer*, 16 Mar. 1930, 14 Mar. 1937, 19 Feb. 1942; Winston-Salem *Journal-Sentinel*, 21 Apr. 1957; *Who Was Who in America*, vol. 1 (1943).

WILLIAM S. POWELL

Buxton, Jarvis (*20 Feb. 1820–11 Mar. 1902*), Episcopal clergyman and educator, was born near Washington, N.C., the son of the Reverend Jarvis Barry Buxton, also an Episcopal minister. A few years later his father became rector of St. John's Church, Fayetteville, and young Buxton was reared there. After primary education at home, he attended the school at Flushing, Long Island, run by Dr. William Augustus Muhlenberg. This institution had been proposed as a model by Bishop Levi Silliman Ives for the Episcopal School for Boys in Raleigh, established in 1833. The Reverend Mr. Buxton, Sr., was on the committee for the establishment of the Raleigh school at the convention of the diocese in 1832.

Jarvis Buxton, Jr., was graduated from The University of North Carolina in 1839; his commencement speeches during his college years reflect an interest in political science. Having decided to become a clergyman, he was graduated from the General Theological Seminary in 1842. In 1846 he was in charge of the school at the Valle Crucis Mission, established by Bishop Ives and opened in 1845. Here he was ordained deacon by Bishop Ives in the chapel of the institution at Valle Crucis, 1 Aug. 1847. He was ordained priest by the same bishop at St. John's Church, Rutherfordton, on 17 June 1849 and continued as rector there until 1851. In that year he went to Asheville and established Trinity Church.

In 1854 the convention of the diocese of North Carolina, not discouraged by the failure of the school in Raleigh, authorized the establishment of a school for boys in Pittsboro. Funds were raised, and Buxton was elected principal. He accepted with reluctance, but when his parishioners at Trinity Church promised to establish a school in Asheville, the diocese abandoned the plan for the Pittsboro School. Ravenscroft School in Asheville was opened in 1856 under Buxton's guidance and was successful for many years.

Buxton was one of the first missionaries west of the Blue Ridge and in addition to Trinity Church, Asheville, he established missions throughout the mountain country. In 1891, after a ministry of forty-five years, Buxton (by then holding a D.D. degree) resigned the rectorship of Trinity Church and moved to Lenoir. There he was rector of St. James Church until 1900. He died in Asheville.

In 1852, the year after the death of his father, Buxton published an edition of the elder Buxton's sermons. At the 1890 convention of the diocese of North Carolina, held in Tarboro to celebrate the centennial of the first attempt to establish the diocese, he read a paper entitled "Missionary and Educational Enterprises," which was incorporated in *Sketches of Church History*, by J. B. Cheshire, Jr.

On 6 Jan. 1848 in Fayetteville, Buxton married Anna Nash Cameron, the daughter of Judge John A. Cameron of North Carolina and Florida. Mrs. Buxton died 30 June 1896. Dr. and Mrs. Buxton had eight children, of whom five survived their parents.

SEE: Samuel A. Ashe, ed., *Biographical History of North Carolina*, vol. 5 (1906); Kemp P. Battle, *History of the University of North Carolina*, vol. 1 (1907); M. DeLancey Haywood, *Lives of the Bishops of North Carolina* (1910); Protestant Episcopal Church in the U.S.A., *Journal of the Eighth Annual Convention of the Missionary District of Asheville* (1902).

CLAIBORNE T. SMITH, JR.

Buxton, John Cameron (30 Sept. 1852–26 Apr. 1917), attorney and banker, was born in Asheville, the son of Jarvis and Anne Cameron Buxton. He obtained his preparatory education in the local schools and at St. Clements Hall, Ellicott City, Md., from which he was graduated in 1869. He then attended Trinity College, Hartford, Conn., for three years (1869–72) and spent one year (1872–73) teaching in Edenton. The following fall he entered Hobart College, Geneva, N.Y.; he was graduated with the B.A. degree in 1874 as salutatorian of his class.

Having been admitted to the North Carolina bar in January 1875, after reading law under Judge John L. Baily of Asheville, Buxton went to Winston, where he was first associated with John W. Alspaugh in the practice of law. He opened a private office shortly thereafter and practiced independently until 1884, when he formed the law firm of Watson and Buxton, through association with Cyrus B. Watson. The firm was further expanded in 1896 to include the son of the senior partner and became known as Watson, Buxton, and Watson. In later years, Buxton returned to independent practice. He was recognized as a capable trial lawyer, and at one time he or his firms represented several railroads and other prominent corporations and individuals in the Winston-Salem area.

Through his law work, Buxton became active in banking circles. He was president of the First National Bank from 1890 to 1893 and was instrumental in its merger with the People's Bank. He was president from 1908 to 1917 of what became the Winston-Salem Savings and Loan Association.

He entered local politics in 1883 when he was elected mayor of Winston. Without seeking the office, he was nominated and elected from the Thirty-second Senatorial District to the North Carolina Senate, where he served for one term in 1885. He had been a delegate to the 1884 Democratic convention in Chicago, where he was influential in the nomination of Grover Cleveland for president. He was chairman of the State Democratic

Convention in Raleigh in 1887 and was an unsuccessful candidate for the U.S. Congress in 1900.

Always active in civic projects, Buxton served for twenty-seven years as president of the local grade school commission and was credited with securing several new school buildings for the city. Another successful effort produced a Carnegie Library for Winston. In addition to memberships in bar associations—American, North Carolina, and Forsyth County—he was a member of four fraternal groups, Elks, Odd Fellows, Knights of Pythias, and Order of Eagles, and also a member of the Twin City Club.

Throughout the years he was an active member of St. Paul's Episcopal Church. As a delegate to the general convention of the church in San Francisco in 1901, he was responsible for the defeat of a resolution that would have changed the name of the church from its traditional Protestant Episcopal. He was also a delegate to the general convention three years later in Boston in 1904.

Buxton was married on 16 Oct. 1877 to Agnes Cornelia Belo, daughter of Edward Belo, a leading citizen of Salem. They had four children: Cameron Belo, Caro Fries (Mrs. Henry Lee Edwards), Anna Nash (Mrs. Curt Beck), and Jarvis (who died in childhood). Buxton died at his home in Winston-Salem and was buried in that city.

SEE: Samuel A. Ashe, ed., *Biographical History of North Carolina*, vol. 5 (1906); *Nat. Cyc. Am. Biog.*, vol. 48 (1965); *North Carolina State Bar Proceedings*, vol. 19 (1917); A. Davis Smith, *Western North Carolina* (1890).

C. SYLVESTER GREEN

Buxton, Ralph Potts (22 Sept. 1826–6 Nov. 1900), superior court judge, mayor, constitutional convention member, and gubernatorial candidate, was born in Washington, N.C., in 1826, the son of the Reverend Jarvis Buxton, Sr., and brother of the Reverend Jarvis Buxton, Jr. The family moved to Fayetteville in 1832, where Buxton was educated at private academies. In 1845 he was graduated with honors from The University of North Carolina; he taught for one year before moving to Raleigh to read law under John H. Bryan. By 1848 he was pleading cases, and in 1853 he established a law office in Fayetteville. Four years later he was elected mayor of Fayetteville as an Independent, although he favored the Whig philosophy. In 1861 he ran unsuccessfully for the state convention as an antisecessionist candidate. Soon after, however, he was elected solicitor of the Fayetteville Judicial District, a position he held until the end of the war.

At the close of the Civil War, Buxton was aligned with the Republican party through an appointment to the superior court bench by Provisional Governor W. W. Holden. In 1865 he was also elected to the constitutional convention. He was elected superior court judge over Bartholomew Fuller in 1868 and continued to serve in this capacity until 1880.

Throughout Reconstruction, Buxton took both Republican and Democratic views, depending on the issue at hand. As a Republican member of the 1865 constitutional convention, he sided with the Democrats in opposing the repudiation of the war debt. He took the Republican view, however, in his opposition to the Ku Klux Klan in North Carolina. He ran as an Independent for the superior court in 1868 and polled many Democratic votes. Later that same year, however, he was attacked by the Democrats for appointing a Republican carpetbagger of dubious honesty as superior court clerk. The Fayetteville *Eagle*, a Democratic newspaper, viewed this action as a blight on Buxton's character. Buxton responded with a successful libel suit against the *Eagle* and soon emerged as a Republican leader in the Upper Cape Fear Valley. Many of the state's Democrats, however, continued to hold him in high esteem.

Buxton was reelected to the superior court in 1874 and one year later was elected to the state convention from Cumberland County. In 1876 the Republican party urged him to accept a nomination to Congress. He refused, saying that he preferred his life as a judge to that of a true politician. This refusal, however, did not lower his status in the North Carolina Republican party. In 1879 he received the complimentary vote of the Republican legislators for the U.S. Senate, and in 1880 he was nominated as the Republican gubernatorial candidate.

Buxton's campaign for governor in 1880 was a strange affair. He accepted the nomination on the grounds of strengthening the state Republican ticket but was not a very enthusiastic campaigner. In his "joint discussions" with Governor Thomas J. Jarvis, the Democratic candidate, Buxton's speeches were virtually the same text, regardless of where he spoke. His Democratic opponents observed that he was a victim of his own party affiliation. Indeed, Buxton's speeches tended merely to echo the state Republican platform: anti-Democratic, pro-Western North Carolina Railroad extension, pro-education, and pro-Negro rights. The issue of Negro rights was the foundation of Buxton's Republicanism: as early as 1844, he had favored the rights of Negroes to be free. His politics after the war reflected this sentiment: he opposed Southern Bourbonism and Democratic Redemption in North Carolina.

Buxton's Democratic opponents disagreed with his views but admired him as a man of stature. Although he received some of this Democratic backing in the election, he lost to Governor Jarvis, 121,832 to 115,589. It was a much closer election than the Democrats had foreseen and a disappointing loss for the Republicans.

Buxton returned to private practice in Fayetteville, where he became something of a legal mentor. Although the Republican party placed his name in the 1886 election for chief justice of the North Carolina Supreme Court, Buxton did not campaign and lost to Chief Justice W. N. H. Smith. Buxton was named superior court reporter in 1897 and served in that capacity until the day of his death.

Buxton was called a "safe rather than a brilliant jurist," noted for his patience and caution. He was also regarded as a prudent investor. In addition, he was known for a clever but delicate sense of humor. He was associated with several North Carolina literary societies and, a lifelong Episcopalian, was a lay reader and vestryman in St. John's Episcopal Church in Fayetteville.

At his death at the age of seventy-four, he was the oldest member of the Fayetteville bar. He was survived by his wife, Rebecca Bledsoe of Raleigh, whom he had married in Raleigh's Christ Church in 1860. They had no children.

SEE: Samuel A. Ashe, ed., *Biographical History of North Carolina*, vol. 5 (1906); Jerome Dowd, *Sketches of Prominent Living North Carolinians* (1888); Daniel L. Grant, *Alumni History of the University of North Carolina* (1924); Raleigh *Farmer and Mechanic*, 8 Nov. 1900; John A. Oates, *The Story of Fayetteville and Cumberland County* (1950); Undated newspaper clipping (North Carolina Collection, University of North Carolina, Chapel Hill). The North Carolina Collection also has the manuscript of an essay he wrote as member of the junior class at the University.

DAVID P. PARKER

Bynum, Jesse Atherton (*23 May 1797–23 Sept. 1868*), lawyer, congressman, and planter, was born in Halifax County, attended Princeton in 1818–19, studied law, and practiced in Halifax. He represented Halifax borough in the House of Commons in 1823, 1824, 1827, and 1828 and represented Halifax County in 1829 and 1830. In 1823 he was leader in the assembly of the William H. Crawford forces in opposition to the Fisher Resolutions, which condemned the caucus nomination of Crawford by Congress. No member was elected from the Halifax borough to the House of Commons in 1825, because of fighting between supporters of Bynum and of Robert Potter.

While in the assembly, Bynum was a member of the Richard Dobbs Spaight strict constructionist faction. He championed the interests of the Roanoke section, opposed creation of new counties in the West, and denied the power of the federal government to support internal improvements or protective tariffs.

In 1831, Bynum announced that he would be a candidate for the Halifax-Tar River seat in Congress but withdrew in favor of John Branch, who had just been forced to resign from Jackson's cabinet. Branch was not a candidate in 1833, and Bynum easily won the position over Andrew Joyner. Bynum was elected to four congressional terms and served from March 1833 to March 1841. He served variously on the committees on Claims, Manufactures, the Judiciary, and Foreign Affairs.

Bynum gained the reputation of a spitfire Democrat and antiabolitionist in the House. He was especially violent against abolitionists, identifying them with Whigs. The violence of his remarks caused a duel with Daniel Jenifer of Maryland in June 1836, during the debates on the admission of Texas and Arkansas. On 24 Jan. 1840, John Quincy Adams recorded: "Bynum spoke nearly four hours, with all his characteristic venom and vehemence and his usual disregard of truth." In April 1840, Bynum's remarks sparked a fight with Representative Rice Garland, Whig of Louisiana, on the floor of the House.

Bynum did not seek reelection in 1841, and his place was filled by John Daniel. Shortly afterward he moved to Alexandria, Rapides Parish, La., where he lived through the trying fifties and Civil War period as a planter. He died during the depths of Reconstruction and was buried in Rapides Parish Cemetery, Pineville, La.

SEE: *Biog. Dir. Am. Cong.* (1971); L. Falkner, *The President Who Wouldn't Retire* (1967); *Memoirs of John Quincy Adams*, ed. Charles Francis Adams, vol. 10 (1970).

DANIEL M. MCFARLAND

Bynum, William Preston (*10 June 1820–30 Dec. 1909*), jurist, prosecutor, and lawyer, was born on the plantation of his father, Hampton Bynum, on Town Fork one mile south of Germanton, in Stokes County. Bynum's grandfather was Gray Bynum, a native of England who moved south of Germanton from Virginia, with his friends Anthony Hampton and Joseph Winston, in about 1760; all three built homes within sight of one another on Town Fork. Gray Bynum married Margaret Hampton, daughter of Anthony and Ann Preston Hampton, and from this union came William P. Bynum's father, Hampton. In 1772, Anthony Hampton sold his land at Germanton to Gray Bynum and moved to Spartanburg, S.C., to establish there the Hampton family that included three Wade Hamptons, the last of

Civil War fame. Hampton Bynum married Mary Coleman Martin, daughter of John and Nancy Shipp Martin, and they reared five boys and three girls: William Preston, John Gray, Wade Hampton, James, Benjamin Franklin, Margaret, Harriet, and Martha. William received a log-school education near Germanton before he entered Davidson College in 1837. Being graduated as valedictorian of his class on 4 Aug. 1842, Bynum next read law under Richmond M. Pearson and was admitted to the bar in Rutherfordton.

After practicing law in Rutherfordton, Bynum moved to Lincoln County, where he married Ann Eliza Shipp, a cousin, on 2 Dec. 1846. Ann Eliza was the granddaughter of Thomas Shipp (Bynum's great-grandfather), the daughter of Bartlett Shipp, and the sister of Judge William M. Shipp of the North Carolina Supreme Court. Bynum practiced law at Lincolnton until the Civil War erupted.

Although he came from a Federalist-Whig family of strong nationalist convictions and although he opposed secession, Bynum was elected a lieutenant of the Beatties Ford Rifles and later was commissioned lieutenant colonel of the Second North Carolina Regiment, effective 8 May 1861. Bynum saw military action with the Second Regiment at the Seven Days' Battle, Mechanicsville, Cold Harbor, Malvern Hill, and Sharpsburg, and the regiment was in reserve at Fredericksburg. When the First Regiment lost all regimental officers at Malvern Hill, Bynum temporarily commanded it. When the Second's commander, Colonel Charles Courtenay Tew, was killed at Sharpsburg, Bynum commanded the Second. Bynum's military career ended on 21 Mar. 1863, when he resigned after the legislature elected him solicitor of the Seventh Judicial District on 2 Dec. 1862.

Bynum's political career spanned the years 1863 to 1879. It required great physical and moral courage to prosecute the numerous and violent lawbreakers in the mountain counties from 1863 to 1873, but Bynum had these qualities in abundance. His statement during Reconstruction that he needed no help from federal authorities to enforce the law won public acclaim. In 1865 he was elected a delegate from Lincoln County to the North Carolina Constitutional Convention. He helped to draft important amendments to the North Carolina Constitution, some of which the voters rejected. In 1866 he was elected to one term in the state senate to represent Lincoln, Gaston, and Catawba counties. In 1868 both political parties nominated him for a second term as solicitor, and he was elected. In the election of 1868 he threw his support to General U. S. Grant and the Republican party.

On 20 Nov. 1873, Bynum resigned his solicitorship to accept appointment from Governor Tod R. Caldwell to the unexpired term of Associate Justice Nathaniel Boyden of the North Carolina Supreme Court. Although Bynum had changed his political affiliation to Republican before his appointment to the supreme court, the epithet "scalawag," in its demeaning sense, could not be applied to him. His peers ranked him in company with Ruffin, Henderson, and Pearson as one of the ablest jurists to sit on the North Carolina bench. Before his term expired on 6 Jan. 1879, Bynum wrote some 346 opinions, including dissents, which revealed his great common sense, native reasoning ability, and clarity of style. His dissent in *State v. Richmond and Danville Railroad Company* warned that corporations might undermine government by the people. In *Manning* v. *Manning* he refused to interpret the law as granting wives greater property rights if the broader interpretation would undermine the institution

of marriage. But in *Taylor* v. *Taylor*, he declared his loathing of the custom of wifebeating. In *Lewis* v. *Commissioners of Wake County*, Bynum expressed a willingness for grand juries to investigate broadly but not to the point of becoming inquisitory; his dissent in *Wittkowsky* v. *Wasson*, however, revealed his commitment to the broad jurisdiction of the trial jury as being the best guardian of the rights of a free people. *State* v. *Blalock* was a landmark decision, broadening the definition of justifiable homicide. Bynum's decisions give evidence that he was greatly concerned that the letter and the spirit of the laws be observed.

In 1878 the Republican party urged Bynum to run for another term on the supreme court, but he refused that and all future entreaties to return to politics. In 1879 he took up residence in Charlotte, where he remained and pursued his legal career until his death.

There were born to Bynum and his wife two children, Mary Preston (1849–75) and William Shipp (1848–98), a lawyer and Episcopal clergyman of Lincolnton. By William Shipp and his wife, Mary Louisa Curtis, daughter of Moses Ashley Curtis, Bynum had eight grandchildren. Bynum's wife died in June 1885. One granddaughter, Minna, married Archibald Henderson, a noted mathematics professor of The University of North Carolina.

Having achieved financial independence by 1879, Bynum was able to engage in philanthropy. On the death of his grandson, William Preston, at The University of North Carolina in 1891, Bynum built a gymnasium in his memory. He also constructed Episcopal chapels at the Thompson Episcopal Orphanage and in Greensboro.

There is a portrait of Bynum in the North Carolina Supreme Court Building.

SEE: William Preston Bynum Papers (Library, University of North Carolina, Chapel Hill); *Charlotte Observer*, 1 and 17 Jan. 1910; *Greensboro Daily News*, 31 Dec. 1909, 1 Jan. 1910; Archibald Henderson Papers (Library, University of North Carolina, Chapel Hill); 70–79 *N.C. Reports*; Raleigh *News and Observer*, 31 Dec. 1909; W. L. Sherrill, *Annals of Lincoln County* (1937).

JOHN L. BELL, JR.

Bynum, William Preston, II (*1 Aug. 1861–7 Jan. 1926*), jurist, prosecutor, and lawyer, was born in Mc-Dowell County but was reared in Stokes County. He was the son of Major Benjamin Franklin Bynum and Charity Henrietta Morris and was named for a paternal uncle. Among his ancestors were the Hamptons, Prestons, and Martins of Stokes County. Bynum received the benefit of good books in his home and was formally educated at Kernersville High School and Dalton Institute in Stokes County and at Trinity College, from which he was graduated in 1883, after receiving the Braxton Craven scholarship award in his junior year. After attending Dick and Dillard Law School in Greensboro, Bynum was admitted to the bar in Charlotte on 7 Feb. 1884.

Although Bynum's career in politics was undistinguished, he made a good reputation for himself. After running unsuccessfully for the state senate in 1890, he was selected a North Carolina presidential elector on the Republican ticket in 1892. In 1894, during the Populist upheaval in North Carolina politics, Fifth Judicial District voters elected him solicitor. In this position he became "not merely a prosecutor of the guilty but a protector of the innocent." His reputation for fairness and justice continued when he resigned the solicitorship in October 1898 to accept appointment as a superior court judge for two months. On 1 Jan. 1899 the McKinley administration appointed him a special assistant to the attorney general, in which position his most notable accomplishment was the successful prosecution of the Asheville Bank Cases. In 1903 he resigned the office of special assistant and returned to private practice. His last forays into politics were as candidate for Republican presidential elector in 1912 and as Republican candidate for chief justice of the North Carolina Supreme Court in 1918, neither of which ventures was successful.

Although Bynum was not especially successful as a politician, he had a distinguished legal career. He first practiced law with kinsmen, William Preston Bynum in Charlotte from 1884 to 1887 and first Bartlett Shipp and then Judge John Gray Bynum in Greensboro from 1887 to 1902. Thereafter, until 1919, Bynum practiced alone. He took in as associates Sidney S. Alderman in August 1919 and Frank P. Hobgood, Jr., in January 1923, thus forming the firm of Bynum, Hobgood, and Alderman. Bynum's first notable achievement as a lawyer was the successful defense of state Supreme Court Chief Justice David M. Furches and Associate Justice Robert M. Douglas, both Republicans, in their 1901 impeachment trial before the North Carolina Senate on charges, largely political, that they had violated the North Carolina Constitution. Bynum achieved a national reputation when he pleaded before the U.S. Supreme Court for the appellees in the cases of *Hammer* v. *Dagenhart* (1918) and *Bailey* v. *Drexel Furniture Company* (1922), which resulted in two national child-labor laws being declared unconstitutional. In 1921 the State of North Carolina retained Bynum to assist the attorney general in defending the constitutionality of a 1921 North Carolina law taxing the incomes of corporations against legal attacks by four railroads. Bynum pleaded for the state in the railroad cases (*Atlantic Coast Line Railroad Company and others* v. *Daughton*, 262 U.S. 413), and the United States Supreme Court upheld the North Carolina law. The conditions giving rise to these last three cases confirmed Bynum in his view that the great danger of the nineteenth century was the growth of state power at the expense of federal powers, while the great danger of the twentieth century was the eclipsing of state power by federal power. This view was central to Bynum's presidential address to the North Carolina Bar Association on 29 June 1920 in Asheville.

Bynum's distinction as a lawyer won him recognition and honor on many levels. In 1911 the U.S. Court of Appeals for the fourth district appointed him chairman of a committee to cooperate with a committee of the U.S. Supreme Court to revise the rules of practice for courts of equity. His work resulted in new federal equity rules. In 1915, Governor Locke Craig appointed him to a commission to revise the system of court procedure and to formulate a uniform system of inferior courts for North Carolina. In 1925, Governor Angus W. McLean appointed him to a judicial conference. The American Bar Association recognized his ability when it elected him president of the general council for four years, a member of the executive committee for three years, and committee member to report on the practices and procedures of the U.S. Courts Martial. Bynum was president of the North Carolina Bar Association from 1919 to 1920. In 1922, The University of North Carolina awarded him the honorary LL.D. degree for professional achievement and service to the state, which included many years of service as a trustee of the university. He was a member of numerous fraternal organizations and of St. Andrews Episcopal Church in Greensboro.

On 9 Mar. 1892, Bynum married Mary Fleming Walker of Charlotte; they made their home in a house on the southeast corner of Lee and Arlington streets in Greensboro. Their only child, a son, died in infancy. Bynum was buried with his wife and son in Green Hill Cemetery in Greensboro.

There is a portrait of Bynum in the Guilford County Courthouse.

SEE: American Historical Society, *North Carolina* (1927 [photograph]); Sidney S. Alderman, "Memorial and Resolutions on the Death of Judge William Preston Bynum," Minute Docket 24 (Guilford County Courthouse, Greensboro); Benjamin Franklin Bynum Papers (Library, Duke University, Durham); Clifford Frazier, Sr., "Lives of Lawyers" (MS, possession of Robert H. Frazier, Greensboro); *North Carolina State Bar Proceedings*, vol. 28 (1926); "Presentation of Portrait," Minute Docket 29 (Guilford County Courthouse, Greensboro); Raleigh *News and Observer*, 8 Jan. 1926 (photograph); *Trinity Alumni Register*, vol. 5 (1927 [photograph]).

JOHN L. BELL, JR.

Byrd, Samuel ("Sam") Armanie, Jr. *(18 Jan. 1908–14 Nov. 1955),* actor, producer, and playwright, was born in Mount Olive, Wayne County, the son of Samuel Armanie Byrd, a local attorney, and his wife, Frances Lambert. His father's family had settled in Lenoir County in the late eighteenth century and had produced local leaders. Byrd grew up under the care of his mother, his father having died when he was a year old. When he was fourteen, his mother married William A. Zachary, and the family returned to Zachary's home in Sanford, Fla. Though Sam spent his remaining childhood years in his stepfather's Sanford home, his closest ties were in Mount Olive, and his literary works and stage characterizations most often reflected his earlier childhood experiences. His first award came in 1923, when the Mount Olive chapter of the Junior Order, United American Mechanics, gave him a prize for his declamation "Spartacus to the Gladiators."

Byrd was graduated from Sanford High School in 1925 and entered the University of Florida that fall, where he remained three years. While at the university, he became closely identified with college athletics and the Masqueraders, the campus drama organization (an earlier ambition had been to enter the diplomatic service).

On a trip to New York in 1929, he secured a small role in Winnie Baldwin's *House of Mander*, followed by appearances in *Café* and *The Duke and the Novice*. His first good role was in Elmer Rice's famous production of *Street Scene*, when he toured with the original cast in 1931. He did summer stock and small parts until 1933, when he was cast as Dude Lester in the Jack Kirkland play based on Erskine Caldwell's novel *Tobacco Road*, which opened at the Masque Theatre in New York on 4 Dec. 1933. The show was an instant critical success, and Byrd's interpretation of Dude secured for him a place in American theater history. He played in *Tobacco Road* for 1,151 performances and was awarded the Literary Digest Award as the Best Young Actor on Broadway during the 1933–34 season. In the 1937–38 New York theater season, he had the featured role of Curley in John Steinbeck's *Of Mice and Men*, and during the same season, Byrd produced his first major play, *Journeyman*, based on the novel by Erskine Caldwell. It was not a box office success. In 1931, Byrd purchased the rights to Samson Raphaelson's *White Man* and produced it, with himself in the leading role. The play, based on a story of blacks who pass for white, failed. In 1940 he produced Roark Bradford's dramatization of the John Henry stories, which brought Paul Robeson, the controversial black actor, back to the United States from London to sing the title role. Byrd's understanding of and sensitivity toward black subjects was ahead of its time in the American theater, and in spite of the quality of his productions, they failed to achieve the financial success he desperately needed to continue. In 1941 he produced *Good Neighbor*. Always a humorist, he said after his failures at producing plays, "I know there's money in show business, because I put it there."

Small Town South was begun in 1941, finished in January 1942, and published by Houghton Mifflin Company the same year. The book, based on Byrd's life in Mount Olive and Sanford, received the Life in America prize in 1942.

During 1942, Byrd entered the U.S. Navy as an ensign. He received the Bronze Star medal for working thirty-six hours expediting the evacuation of casualties from the Normandy beachhead during the D-Day Invasion in June 1944. It was on his experiences in the navy that he based his novel *Hurry Home to My Heart*, published in 1945, which centered principally in Mount Olive and Seven Springs. Byrd was promoted to lieutenant and transferred to the Pacific Theater in 1945. He saw service in the Battle of Okinawa and, as beachmaster of a landing operation, received the surrender of Japanese forces at Sasebo.

In 1946, Byrd received a John Simon Guggenheim Memorial Foundation Fellowship in creative writing, which included a five-month study of postwar conditions in England. Also in 1946 he served as a lecturer for the American Information Service, American Embassy, London. In 1947 and 1948 he was a lecturer in sociology at the College of Charleston, Charleston, S.C., where he lived at Prospect Hill Plantation. Under a renewal of the Guggenheim Fellowship in 1948–49, he traveled in southern France, Portugal, Gibralter, Spain, and North Africa. In 1949 he wrote, produced, and acted in *The Duplin Story*, an outdoor drama celebrating that North Carolina county's bicentennial. The next year he wrote and produced *For Those Who Live in the Sun*, another bicentennial drama, celebrating the founding of the Charleston Jewish community.

During the Coronation year, 1953, Byrd and Jack Hylton produced *Stalag 17* at the Princess Theatre in London; afterward he returned to his native Eastern North Carolina to edit the *Weekly Gazette* at LaGrange.

He entered Duke University Medical Center in March 1955 after a leg injury, at which time leukemia was diagnosed. His funeral was held in Mount Olive at the home of his cousin, Walter T. Cherry, with whom he had spent about six months of each year since 1931. He was buried in Maplewood Cemetery in Mount Olive.

Byrd was married to Patricia Bolam, whom he had met in 1944 on a beach near Plymouth in her native England when she was ten years old. After the death of her mother in 1946, Byrd received permission to bring her to America as his ward. She attended school in South Carolina, and in 1951 they were married in Carlisle, Cumberland, England. When they returned to America, they made their home in Seven Springs.

At the time of his death, Byrd was working with Marjorie Barkentin, Jacques Wolf, and Albert Johnson on a stage adaptation of James Joyce's *Ulysses*. He was a member of the Players and Lambs clubs of New York.

SEE: North Carolina Collection (University of North Carolina, Chapel Hill), for Sam Byrd Collection and Clipping File; Bernadette Hoyle, *Tar Heel Writers I Know* (1956).

JOHN BAXTON FLOWERS III

Cabarrus, Stephen (*29 Aug. 1754–4 Aug. 1808*), speaker of the North Carolina House of Commons and Trustee of The University of North Carolina, was born in Bayonne, France, scion of a family of merchants and ship owners. His grandparents were Barthelemy and Marie Fourçade Cabarrus, and his parents were Etienne Pierre and Catherine Suzanne Lancereau Cabarrus. His first cousin was the banker François Cabarrus, whose son-in-law, Jean Lambert Tallien, was influential in bringing the downfall of Robespierre and Jacobin rule in the French Revolution.

As a young man, Cabarrus decided to seek his fortune in the New World; he landed at Edenton, N.C., in 1776. He married Jeanne Henriette Damery Bodley, the well-to-do widow of Joshua Bodley, becoming master of his wife's estate, Pembroke, near Edenton, as well as the owner of an adjacent farm, named Bayonne in honor of his birthplace. His fortunate marriage to a wife about seventeen years his senior was largely responsible for his accumulation by 1777 of 1,980 acres of land and 60 slaves. In the following year his property was valued at £15,296. He was joined in America by his brothers Dominique, Thomas, and Auguste, and upon the untimely deaths of Thomas and Dominique, he adopted the latter's two sons, Thomas and Augustus.

Cabarrus was soon recognized as a man thoroughly devoted to his adopted homeland. Governor Alexander Martin commended his politeness and his attachment to the public interest. Cabarrus's fellow North Carolinians were apparently also impressed with his character and public spirit, for the citizens of Edenton elected him borough representative to the House of Commons in 1784. He continued to represent the borough and later Chowan County until his retirement from the political scene in 1805. While in the commons he served on many important committees; he was elevated to speaker in 1789 and frequently reelected. A supporter of the federal Constitution, he was a delegate to the Hillsborough convention of 1788 that rejected the document and to the Fayetteville convention of 1789 that ratified it. He aspired to a seat in the Congress of the new national government and in 1790 and 1793 ran for the House of Representatives from the Edenton District. He was defeated on both occasions but served as a presidential elector in the election of 1792. Although initially embracing the Federalist cause, he soon became active in the Republican party.

Denied a place in the national government, Cabarrus continued to be a prominent figure in the legislature of North Carolina. Early in his legislative career he recognized the importance to the state of education, and in 1785 he was the sponsor of a bill empowering the commissioners of Edenton to make part of the town common available to the trustees of the proposed Smith's Academy. He also supported a measure to establish a state fund to maintain institutions of learning at Hillsborough and elsewhere in the state. Appropriately, Cabarrus was appointed to the first board of trustees of The University of North Carolina in 1789, while he was speaker of the House of Commons; he served until 1792.

During Cabarrus's tenure as speaker, the legislature agreed to locate a permanent seat of government at Raleigh, and the commissioners of the new capital city named a street in his honor. The legislature of North Carolina further recognized Cabarrus's contribution to the state when it gave his name to a new county created from Mecklenburg in 1792. When the inhabitants of this area disagreed over the location of a courthouse, Cabarrus, in an effort to heal the division, wrote a letter to the citizens urging them to put away their disagreements and expressing the wish that harmony and friendship would soon be restored to the county. Heeding his advice and following his practical suggestions, the factions compromised their differences, located their seat of government halfway between the contesting areas, and named their town Concord and their chief street Union.

In addition to serving in state government and higher education, Cabarrus was an energetic Mason. A member of Unanimity Lodge No. 7 in Edenton, he was a delegate to the Tarboro convention of December 1787 that resulted in the reorganization of the Grand Lodge of North Carolina, after the interruption of its activities by the American Revolution.

Cabarrus was married in 1777 to Mrs. Jeanne Henriette Damery Bodley (29 Aug. 1754–11 Nov. 1799), widow of Lord Granville's last agent. They were the parents of one daughter, Henriette (16 Dec. 1777–16 Oct. 1784). Cabarrus was originally buried at his country seat but in 1911 was reinterred in the cemetery of St. Paul's Episcopal Church, Edenton.

SEE: Samuel A. Ashe, ed., *Biographical History of North Carolina*, vol. 2 (1905); Stephen Cabarrus, Letter to the People of the Standing Committee of Cabarrus County (11 Jan. 1794, Cabarrus-Slade Papers, Southern Historical Collection, University of North Carolina, Chapel Hill); Jean Cavignac, "Les Cabarrus Negociants de Bordeaux," *Revue Historique de Bordeaux* (1970); Chowan County Tax Records, 1777–78 (State Archives, Raleigh); Walter Clark, ed., *State Records of North Carolina*, vols. 16–22 (1899–1907); R. D. W. Connor, comp., *A Documentary History of the University of North Carolina*, 2 vols. (1953); Frank Daugherty, *Notes on the Cabarrus Family* (1932); Early Minutes of the Grand Lodge of North Carolina (Grand Lodge Headquarters, Raleigh); Edenton *State Gazette of North-Carolina*, 14 Dec. 1793, 30 June 1796; *Fayetteville Gazette*, 27 Nov. 1792, 11 Dec. 1792; D. H. Gilpatrick, *Jeffersonian Democracy in North Carolina* (1931); Halifax *North-Carolina Journal*, 9 Jan. 1793, 6 Feb. 1793, 21 Aug. 1793; Alice B. Keith and W. H. Masterson, *The John Gray Blount Papers*, 3 vols. (1952–65); Mrs. John Lanston, MS memoir (1863, in possession of Mrs. Eugene Marshall, Dallas, Texas); James L. Moore and Thomas H. Wingate, *Cabarrus Reborn* (1940); William C. Pool, "An Economic Interpretation of the Ratification of the Federal Constitution in North Carolina," *North Carolina Historical Review* 27 (1950); Louise I. Trenholme, *The Ratification of the Federal Constitution in North Carolina* (1932); John H. Wheeler, *Historical Sketches of North Carolina* (1851).

ROBERT W. DELP

Cabe, John (1752–21 Apr. 1818), planter, miller, and politician, was probably born in Pennsylvania, the son of Barnaby and Elizabeth Perkins McCabe, later Cabe. The family moved into Orange County in the late 1750s. They seem to have been identified with the Presbyterians of the New Hope Church area, though their names do not appear in the surviving church records. However, four of Barnaby's children, including John, married into families who belonged to that congregation.

John was educated at home at the Piper-Cabe schoolhouse located on his father's land on the Eno River. Though his education must have been somewhat limited, it nevertheless seems to have been solid. Both John and his brother William were among the contributors who gave twenty pounds toward the establishment of The University of North Carolina when funds were being raised.

Though his father became prosperous as a wagoner (working on Governor William Tryon's side during the Regulator troubles and on the American side during the Revolution), John attained a real affluence before his death in 1818, when his estate included over three thousand acres of land and sixty slaves. His mill on the Eno River, built before 1779, was the source of his prosperity; he was also half owner of a second mill downstream from his own, which he had built for his son-in-law.

Cabe must have shown an unusual capability for leadership, for he was elected delegate to the last provincial congress, which met in 1776 in Halifax, when he was only twenty-four years old. The confusion and near-riots that attended that election resulted in a second election, in which Cabe was again victorious, the only one of the candidates to be elected both times. Delayed by these disturbances, the delegates nevertheless arrived in Halifax in time to participate in the adoption of both the Bill of Rights and the Constitution itself. Cabe was elected to represent Orange County in the General Assembly in 1796, 1797, 1798, and 1800. He was appointed justice of the peace in 1801 and continued to serve in that office until his death. He thereby officiated in the legislative, judicial, and administrative affairs of the county.

Cabe was married at least twice: in 1786 to Gilbert Strayhorn's daughter Mary, with whom he had nine daughters; and in 1802 to Nancy Moreland. His daughters were Elizabeth (b. 1787), who married Benjamin Rhodes; Ann (b. 1788), married first to John Latta and second to Major Robert Donnell; Sarah (b. 1789), married to Joseph Latta; Mary (b. 1791), who married Mann Patterson; Rachel (b. 1792), married first to Moses McCown and second to Herbert Sims; Catherine (b. 1795), who married Benjamin Rogers; Lydia (b. 1797), who married Charles W. Johnston; Margaret (b. 1799), married to John W. Caldwell; and Jane (b. 1802), married to William T. Shields. Cabe was buried in the family graveyard on his Eno River plantation.

SEE: Hugh Conway Browning, *The Descendants of Barnaby Cabe (McCabe)* (1967); Hugh T. Lefler and Paul Wager, eds., *Orange County, 1752–1952* (1953).

JEAN BRADLEY ANDERSON

Cain, William (14 May 1847–7 Dec. 1930), civil engineer, mathematician, university professor, and author, contributed for over half a century to the advance of engineering theory and practice in his state and country. Although his life began and ended in Orange County, Cain's career carried him to Western and Eastern North Carolina and into South Carolina, and his influence on civil engineering extended even further.

Cain was the fourth in a line of William Cains to reside in Orange County. His Irish great-grandfather, who lived from 1743 to 1834, settled in Orange County, married the widow of Sir Thomas Dudley, served in the state legislature, and was an early patron of the new state university. The fourth William Cain was born near Hillsborough, the son of Dr. William and Sarah Jane

Bailey Cain. His father, who died when Cain was almost eight, was a planter and physician. His mother, the daughter of Judge John L. Bailey, was noted for her musical interests.

Cain spent his youth in Orange County, where he attended a private school in Hillsborough. From 1859 to 1866 he continued his education at the Hillsborough Military Academy, recently established by Colonel C. C. Tew. Cain's education was interrupted by the Civil War, and as a cadet of fourteen he served briefly as a drillmaster for Confederate recruits at Asheville and Wilmington; in the last stages of the war, he and fellow cadets guarded Union prisoners. After the war, Cain studied law under his grandfather, Judge Bailey, and then returned to the military academy (renamed the North Carolina Military and Polytechnic Institute) to earn the M.A. degree.

From 1866 to 1868, Cain worked on the staff of the North Carolina state geologist, W. C. Kerr. For the next twenty years he was alternately employed as a railroad surveyor and as an instructor at military schools. He was an engineer and surveyor for numerous railroads in North and South Carolina from 1868 to 1874 and again from 1880 to 1882. From 1874 to 1880 he taught math and engineering at the Carolina Military Institute in Charlotte; he held a similar position from 1882 to 1888 at the Citadel in Charleston. In 1888 he was elected professor of mathematics and engineering at The University of North Carolina. There he served as head of the department until his retirement in 1920. In 1918 he was selected as one of the original five Kenan professors in recognition of his teaching success.

Throughout his career, Cain engaged in original work in both pure and applied mathematics. One of the South's most notable engineers, he formulated important theories concerning the strength of masonry dams, reinforced concrete arches, earth pressures, and retaining walls. He insisted, too, that engineering theory have practical application: his formulas were influential on the building of railroads, bridges, and dams throughout the country.

The results of Cain's research were published in widely used civil engineering text books and in a variety of scientific journals. In the 1870s and 1880s, he contributed studies to the Van Nostrand Science Series, including *A Practical Theory of Voussoir Arches* (1874), *Maximum Stresses in Framed Bridges* (1878), *Voussoir Arches, Applied to Stone Bridges, Tunnels, Domes and Groined Arches* (1879), *Theory of Solid and Braced Elastic Arches* (1879), and *Symbolic Algebra and Notes on Geometry* (1884). Other books were *Practical Designing of Retaining Walls* (1888), *A Brief Course in the Calculus* (1905), and *Earth Pressure, Retaining Walls and Bins* (1916). He published numerous articles in *Van Nostrand's Engineering Magazine*, *Engineering News*, *Journal of the Franklin Institute*, and *Journal of the Elisha Mitchell Scientific Society*. His first scientific publication, "Uniform Cross-Section and T Abutments," appeared in the November 1874 issue of *Van Nostrand's Engineering Magazine*. Subsequent articles in the same journal included "Retaining Walls" in April 1880, "Earth Pressure" in February 1882, and "Trusses with Superfluous Members" in October 1882. Two of his most influential papers were "Unit Stresses," published in *Engineering News* in 1887 and "Experiments on Retaining Walls and Pressures on Tunnels," in *Transactions of the American Society of Civil Engineers* (1911).

In 1926, still productive, Cain received the J. James R. Croes Medal from the American Society of Civil Engineers for a paper entitled "The Circular Arch under Normal Loads." Cain had become a member of the society in 1888 and had served as a director of the organization from 1912 to 1914. The student chapter of the society at The University of North Carolina was named the William Cain Civil Engineering Society in his honor. Cain also held memberships in the American Mathematical Society, the Elisha Mitchell Scientific Society, the North Carolina Academy of Science, and the American Association for the Advancement of Science. In addition to the Croes Medal, he was honored for his work with the LL.D. from the University of South Carolina in 1916 and the Sc.D. from The University of North Carolina in 1920.

Cain represented a combination of the practical, technical bent of the New South and the romantic values of the Old South. He was both the pragmatic scientist and the Civil War veteran affectionately known as "the major." A courtly and gracious gentleman, Cain never married, still preferring at age eighty to wait for the "years of discretion." Those who knew him described him as industrious, exact, affectionate, loyal, kind, witty, and genial. His life, said Archibald Henderson, was "one of earnest endeavor, guided by high ideals and a strict devotion to duty." He loved classical music and was an accomplished violinist. He was also an avid sportsman, still pursuing his hobby of fly-fishing in 1930. He was active in the Protestant Episcopal church and served on the vestry of the Chapel of the Cross. Though not actively involved in politics, he was a loyal Democrat.

In his later years, Cain suffered from deafness. He was struck by an automobile while crossing the street in front of his Chapel Hill home and died a few hours later. The funeral was held at the Chapel of the Cross and interment took place in Hillsborough.

A portrait by William Steen is displayed in Phillips Hall at The University of North Carolina at Chapel Hill.

SEE: *Alumni Review*, January 1931; Samuel A. Ashe, ed., *Biographical History of North Carolina*, vol. 6 (1907); *Chapel Hill Weekly*, 12 Dec. 1930; *DAB*, vol. 21 (1944); *Greensboro Daily News*, 24 Jan. 1923; Archibald Henderson, "William Cain," *Journal of the Elisha Mitchell Scientific Society*, April 1924; Thomas Felix Hickerson, in *Transactions of the American Society of Civil Engineers* 95 (1931); North Carolina Collection (University of North Carolina, Chapel Hill), for a 1926 bibliography of Cain's works; North Carolina State Archives (Raleigh), for Cain correspondence in the Theodore Fulton Davidson Papers; Raleigh *News and Observer*, 21 Jan. 1923, 8 and 9 Dec. 1930; Southern Historical Collection (University of North Carolina, Chapel Hill), for the John Lancaster Bailey Papers, William Cain Books (including a 1925 memoir on his Civil War experiences), Archibald Henderson Papers [picture], and John Steele Henderson Papers; *Who's Who in America*, 1920–21.

GEORGE-ANNE WILLARD

Cairns, John Simpson (10 Feb. 1862–10 June 1895), ornithologist, was born in Lawrence, Mass., the son of John and Agnes Simpson Cairns. In 1855 his parents moved from Scotland to the United States, where the elder John Cairns served as foreman of various textile mills in New England. In 1870 the family purchased Reems Creek Woolen Mills and moved to Weaverville, N.C., where Cairns attended public schools and Weaver College. He served as secretary and business manager of Reems Creek Mills from 1882 until his death.

From early childhood, Cairns was interested in natural

history, and by age eight he had begun exploring the unspoiled wilderness country of the Great Craggy and Black Mountains. Although earlier naturalists had visited these mountain ranges, Cairns was the first to conduct systematic, year-round ornithological research in the southern Appalachians. His observations provided the best available description of the avifauna of the North Carolina mountains before extensive disruption of the original forests by human activities. He added over a dozen bird species to the state list and corresponded with many of the world's eminent zoologists, providing them with documentary specimens and important data. Many of his four thousand bird and egg specimens were added to the zoological collections of Harvard and Duke universities, the North Carolina State Museum, and the Philadelphia Academy of Natural Sciences, while a large portion of his collection was purchased by Dr. F. A. Sondley and eventually acquired by the city of Asheville.

From 1890 to 1895, Cairns worked with Samuel B. Ladd of West Chester, Pa., in preparing a book on the birds of the southern Appalachians. Cairns's untimely death abruptly terminated the project, and consequently, many of his observations were never published. His extant material includes two annotated checklists of the birds of Buncombe County, published in 1887 and 1889 in the *Ornithologist and Oologist*, and a similar list published privately in 1891 and included by F. A. Sondley in his *History of Buncombe County, N. C.* in 1930. Cairns's study of *Dendroica caerulescens* appeared in *Papers Presented to the World's Congress on Ornithology* in 1896, but a manuscript on the birds of Western North Carolina remains unpublished. Many of his observations are contained in a series of letters written from 1885 to 1895 to William Brewster of Harvard, and Cairns's extensive migration data were sent to the U.S. Biological Survey.

In 1889, Cairns was elected an associate member of the American Ornithologists' Union, and in 1894–95 he served on the advisory council of the World's Congress on Ornithology. Cairns was a close friend of Zebulon Weaver, who later served as congressman from the Eleventh Congressional District in the U.S. House of Representatives; Cairns's early influence was crucial in Weaver's enthusiastic legislative support of and lobbying for the establishment of Great Smoky Mountains National Park. In 1897, Dr. Elliott Coues honored Cairns—the only North Carolina resident ever to receive this distinction—by naming in his memory the Cairns Warbler, *Dendroica caerulescens cairnsi*.

Cairns was married on 16 Oct. 1888 to Lena Creasman at Haw Creek Episcopal Church, of which he was an active member. At the age of thirty-three he was killed by his own gun in a hunting accident near Balsam Gap in the Black Mountains. He was buried in Weaverville Cemetery. There is a portrait in the William Brewster Collection at the Archives Library, Museum of Comparative Zoology, Harvard University.

SEE: Asheville *Citizen-Times*, 4 Oct. 1970; *Auk* 13 (1895); T. G. Pearson et al., *Birds of North Carolina* (1919); N. Pickens, *Dry Ridge* (1962).

MARCUS B. SIMPSON, JR.

Caldwell, Charles (*14 May 1772–9 July 1853*), physician and medical educator, was born in Caswell County, the son of Irish immigrants. His father, Lieutenant Charles Caldwell, a devout Presbyterian elder, wanted his son to become a minister and opposed his desire to enter the legal profession. After some elementary education in local schools and study under a private tutor, Caldwell began teaching at the age of

fifteen in a grammar school, Snow Creek Seminary. At eighteen he established a similar school near Salisbury, remaining there for two years. In late 1791 or early 1792 he began a preceptorship in medicine, probably under Dr. Charles Harris, who at that time was practicing and teaching medicine in Cabarrus County. In the fall of 1792, Caldwell started the formal study of medicine at the University of Pennsylvania; there he had a number of notable teachers, his favorite among them being Benjamin Rush. In 1793, during an epidemic of yellow fever, Caldwell volunteered his services at Bush Hill, one of the hopsitals, or "pest houses."

After receiving his medical degree in 1796, Caldwell practiced in Philadelphia. Failing to attain his ambition of becoming a professor in the medical department of the University of Pennsylvania, he went in 1819 to Lexington, Ky. There he was professor of the Institutes of Medicine and Clinical Practice and helped to develop a famous medical library. In 1837 he moved to Louisville, becoming the first professor at the Louisville Medical Institute, now the University of Louisville School of Medicine. In 1849, against his will, Caldwell was retired because of his age. He spent much of his remaining time in writing his autobiography, of which William Osler said "Pickled, as it is, in vinegar, the work is sure to survive."

Caldwell was married twice. In 1799 he married Eliza Leaming of Philadelphia; their son, Thomas Leaming, was also a physician, and they may have had a daughter as well: the Caldwell lot in Louisville's Cave Hill Cemetery has a marker to Mary Caldwell Hunter, 1808–80, but Dr. Emmett Horine could find no proof of the relationship. Caldwell's first marriage was unhappy; the couple separated, and Mrs. Caldwell died in Philadelphia in 1834. On 8 Mar. 1842, Caldwell married Mrs. Mary Warner Barton.

Caldwell was a man of unusual intelligence, an impressive orator, and apparently a most successful teacher. He was for years associated with the periodical *Port Folio*, becoming its editor in 1814. He translated several medical works and wrote many articles on medical and other subjects. However, his obvious egotism and his caustic criticisms of those with whom he disagreed marred much of his work. In spite of his belief in conservative classical medicine and his occasionally original ideas on medical and social subjects, he was an ardent advocate of both phrenology and mesmerism.

SEE: Charles Caldwell, *Autobiography*, ed. Harriott Warner (1855); *DAB*, vol. 3 (1929); E. F. Horine, *Biographical Sketch and Guide to the Writings of Charles Caldwell* (1960); *Richmond and Louisville Medical Journal*, 1853; *Who Was Who in America, 1607–1896*.

DOROTHY LONG

Caldwell, David (*22 Mar. 1725–25 Aug. 1824*), Presbyterian minister, educator, physician, and states- man, was born in Lancaster, Pa., of Ulster Scot ancestry. He was the oldest of four sons of Andrew and Martha Caldwell, who were respectable farmers. David served as an apprentice to a house carpenter for four years and then carpentered on his own for four more years until he was twenty-five.

Deeply intent on becoming a Presbyterian minister, he made a contract with his three younger brothers, whereby he relinquished all claims to the parental estate in exchange for their help in securing enough money to send him through college. Accordingly, at the age of twenty-five, he entered the College of New Jersey, now Princeton University, from which he was graduated in 1761 at the age of thirty-six. After teaching a year and serving a year as a tutor at his alma mater, while he studied theology, he was licensed as a clergyman in 1763 by the Presbytery of New Brunswick. He served the next two years as a supply minister in various places in his native colony. His first definite assignment came on 16 May 1765, when he was appointed "to labor at least one whole year as a missionary in North Carolina." Ordained in July 1765, at the age of forty, he became one of the earliest Presbyterian divines in the sparsely and recently settled North Carolina back country.

Caldwell's move to what is now Guilford County came through the invitation of members of the Nottingham Colony of Pennsylvania, an Ulster Scot Presbyterian group who had asked him, before they came to North Carolina in the 1750s, to become their pastor after his ordination. In present central Guilford County he became pastor of Buffalo and Alamance churches, established by the Nottingham Colony. He was married in 1766 to Rachel Craighead, the daughter of the Reverend Alexander Craighead of Mecklenburg County, generally recognized as the most prominent Presbyterian minister west of the Yadkin River. The couple settled on a tract of land about three miles west of the center of present-day Greensboro, and two years later, in 1768, Caldwell was officially installed as pastor of Alamance and Buffalo congregations, which he served for nearly sixty years.

Meanwhile, in 1767, he established what came to be known as Dr. David Caldwell's Log College, a theological and classical school for young men that was soon recognized as one of the most outstanding schools in the South. His biographer, the Reverend Eli Caruthers, who succeeded him as pastor of Buffalo Church, wrote that "five of his scholars became governors of different states; many more members of Congress, some of whom occupied high standing . . . and a much greater number became lawyers, judges, physicians, and ministers of the gospel." Training from fifty to sixty students each year, he was, in the words of one of his pupils, "probably more useful to the church than any other man in the United States."

Aware also of the physical needs of his pioneer flock in the absence of a physician, Caldwell secured medical books from Philadelphia and soon became a self-taught, practicing physician. Because his doctor's fees, if there were any, and his two hundred dollar per year ministerial salary fell far short of providing for the Caldwell family of eight sons and a daughter, he turned to the successful cultivation of his land, eventually amounting to 550 acres on which he ran a successful plantation-type business.

In addition to these varied pursuits, Caldwell championed the cause of freedom in the War of the Regulation, the American Revolution, and the War of 1812. In the Regulator movement, culminating in the nearby Battle of Alamance, 16 May 1771, he was present on the battlefield and tried valiantly but in vain to persuade Royal Governor William Tryon to settle the matter without bloodshed. With the coming of the Revolution, he represented Guilford County at the Halifax provincial congress that wrote and adopted the constitution of 1776 and also at the Hillsborough constitutional convention that refused to ratify the U.S. Constitution. Caldwell, along with a majority of the delegates, insisted on a Bill of Rights.

As an ardent patriot during the Revolution, he exhorted his congregations to take up the sword; his biographer stated that every adult male member of Buffalo and Alamance churches joined in the fight when Lord Cornwallis invaded the area in March 1781. News

of Caldwell's activities provoked the British general to offer a two-hundred-pound reward for his capture, and Caldwell was forced to hide out in the swamps before and during the Battle of Guilford Courthouse, 15 Mar. 1781. After Cornwallis's departure, Caldwell went to the battlefield and aided a British physician in caring for the sick and wounded and burying the dead. When he returned to his home nearby, he found that Cornwallis's army had camped on his property and had destroyed what could not be devoured. The family Bible, private papers, sermons, and library—all were maliciously burned by the British officers who used the Caldwell house for their headquarters. Mrs. Caldwell and her children were forced to retire to a smoke house, where they survived for two days and nights with no food other than a few dried peaches she had happened to have in her pockets. Caruthers reported that when the British army left, "every panel of fence on the premises was consumed or carried away; every living thing was destroyed except one old goose."

After the war, Caldwell returned to his school, his churches, his medical practice, and his farm. In 1794 he was offered the first presidency of The University of North Carolina, because "beyond a doubt he was recognized as the leading educator of the state." Declining this offer, he continued to teach at his Log College until old age compelled him to retire, though as late as 1816 he was instructing a number of private students, among whom were John Motley Morehead and Archibald Debow Murphey, and he continued his ministry until 1820, when he was ninety-five.

Caldwell performed his last service to his country at the age of eighty-eight. When the United States entered the War of 1812, a meeting was held at the Guilford County Courthouse to round up volunteers, but none rallied to the cause. In order to avoid a draft, Caldwell was invited to preach at the courthouse on the subject of volunteering. So feeble that he had to be helped up the steps to the judge's bench, he nonetheless displayed a patriotic fervor equal to the occasion, taking as his text: "He that hath no sword, let him sell his garment, and buy one." When he finished speaking, there were more volunteers than were needed.

Caldwell died in his hundredth year and was buried at Buffalo Church. Perhaps Stephen B. Weeks best summarized Caldwell's great contributions when he wrote that, in the early days, "none did a nobler or more enduring work toward the greatness of the state than the Rev. David Caldwell, D.D., preacher, teacher and physician, counsellor and guide for his friends and neighbors, servant of the people in many ways, state builder and protagonist of learning in the wilderness of North Carolina."

No portrait of Caldwell was painted from life, but Mrs. Lottie P. Leonard, former art teacher at Claude Kiser Junior High School, painted one from written descriptions. It hangs in the Buffalo Presbyterian Church, Greensboro.

Caldwell's house and Log College, which were located on present Hobbs Road, just off Friendly Road, have long since disappeared, though recent excavations by the North Carolina Department of Archives and History have revealed the exact sites. On 6 Jan. 1975, the City Council of Greensboro voted unanimously to appropriate about ninety thousand dollars to help the David Caldwell Log College Corporation purchase about ten acres of the original site of these two structures (including his dam site and three springs); the city manager was authorized to negotiate for the purchase of an additional eight and a half acres of adjacent property to form a David Caldwell Memorial Park. It is hoped that approximately thirty acres will eventually comprise this historical and ecological project.

SEE: Ethel Stephens Arnett, *For Whom Our Schools Were Named* (1973); E. W. Caruthers, *A Sketch of the Life and Character of the Rev. David Caldwell* (1842); John H. Wheeler, *Historical Sketches of North Carolina* (1851).

BLACKWELL P. ROBINSON

Caldwell, David Franklin *(1791–4 Apr. 1867)*, lawyer, legislator, and judge, was born of Scotch-Irish ancestry in the eastern section of Iredell County. He was the son of Andrew Caldwell, an early settler of this region who often represented his county in the legislature. His mother was Ruth, the second daughter of William Sharpe, a member of the Continental Congress and of the Rowan Committee of Safety. David's siblings included two widely known brothers: Joseph P., congressman, and Dr. Elam of Lincolnton.

Caldwell pursued the literary course at The University of North Carolina, studied law under Archibald Henderson of Salisbury, and entered public life as a member of the legislature from Iredell County in 1816–19 and in 1825.

After completing his last term in the legislature he moved to Salisbury to practice law and soon became an active participant in the public affairs of Salisbury and Rowan County. He presided at the Fourth of July celebration in 1828, became a director of the Rowan County Chapter of the American Colonizing Society, and in July 1828 was appointed president of the Salisbury branch of the state bank upon the resignation of John L. Henderson. In 1829 he represented Rowan in the senate of North Carolina; in December he was elected speaker in place of Bedford Brown, who was elected to the U.S. Senate.

At the end of his term in the senate, Caldwell returned to Salisbury. There he again took up the practice of law, while engaging in the political contests of the day as a Whig and strong Unionist. His stand on Unionism involved him in an aborted duel with Charles Fisher, a Democrat, in 1833. In 1830, Caldwell helped to mediate a peaceful settlement between Governor John Owen and Senator Willie P. Mangum.

In July 1844, Caldwell was nominated by Governor John M. Morehead to the superior court bench, to fill a vacancy occasioned by the appointment of Judge Frederick Nash to the state supreme court. As a judge he presided with rare dignity, grace, discrimination, and impartiality. On 18 Jan. 1860 he offered Governor John Ellis his resignation, saying: "I cannot discharge the duties of President of the branch Bank about to be located at this place and the office of judge. At my time of life I prefer the former." So Caldwell relinquished the bench for the bank and held his position there until the outbreak of the Civil War.

Caldwell was twice married. In 1810 he married Frances M. Alexander, the daughter of William Lee Alexander and niece of Archibald Henderson. By this union he had six children: William Lee; Archibald Henderson; Elizabeth Ruth, who married Colonel Charles Fisher; Richard Alexander; Dr. Julius Andrew; and Fanny McCay, who married Peter Hairston. In 1835, Caldwell's first wife died, and in 1839 he married Rebecca M. Troy, widow of Matthew Troy and daughter of William Nesbit. She died in 1855 and was buried beneath the Session House of the First Presbyterian Church in Salisbury. Caldwell was buried in an unmarked grave beside his first wife in the old Lutheran Cemetery in Salisbury.

SEE: James S. Brawley, *The Rowan Story* (1953); Jethro Rumple, *A History of Rowan County* (1881); Salisbury *Carolina Watchman*, 9 Aug. 1839, 13 July 1844, 4 Dec. 1855, 21 June 1859, 24 Jan. 1860, 8 and 15 Apr. 1867; Salisbury *Western Carolinian*, 5 and 15 July 1828, 17 Feb. 1829, 15 Dec. 1829, 22 Oct. 1832, 18 Apr. 1835; H. T. Shanks, ed., *The Papers of Willie Person Mangum*, vol. 1 (1950); Noble J. Tolbert, ed., *The Papers of John W. Ellis*, vol. 2 (1964).

JAMES S. BRAWLEY

Caldwell, David Franklin *(5 Nov. 1814–29 Dec. 1898)*, businessman, editor, and politician, was born in Guilford County, about one mile from Greensboro, the son of Thomas and Elizabeth Caldwell. He received the limited education then available in the schools of Greensboro. For several years he worked on his father's farm outside the city and then, from 1841 to 1848, he worked with his three brothers in their father's small mercantile business. Tom Caldwell and Son's Cheap Store, as it was called, dealt in cheap cash bargains and gave credit. Caldwell's flair for business became quite evident as the store prospered.

Caldwell's political career began in 1848, when he was elected as a Whig to the North Carolina House of Commons. He was very popular with the people of Guilford County and was their choice almost unanimously for five successive terms until he retired in 1861. He was a strong Unionist, as were most of the Guilford legislators, and a bitter opponent of secession. He began to read law in 1860 and was admitted to the bar in 1861. At the outbreak of the Civil War he was already engaged in a lucrative law partnership with James A. Long in Greensboro. When North Carolina seceded, he went along with the majority and applied for a commission in the Confederate Army. The governor of the state, doubting his loyalty to the Confederacy because of his fierce opposition to secession, refused him a commission. He therefore enlisted as a private and served for two years.

In 1864, Caldwell reentered the political arena and was elected county attorney. He remained in this office until he retired from the legal profession, disgusted with the new code, in 1868. Caldwell is the authority for a report that President Lincoln considered him as a possible choice for provisional governor of the state in 1865. However that may be, he was a delegate to the state constitutional convention in that year.

In 1867, Caldwell took control of the *Greensboro Patriot*, the city's leading newspaper. After a year as proprietor and editor, he sold the paper to James and Robert Albright. In 1868, having affiliated with the Democratic party, Caldwell was elected to the U.S. Congress but was disqualified from serving by the Fourteenth Amendment. In 1872 he was a delegate to the Democratic National Convention that nominated Horace Greeley for the presidency. In 1878, Caldwell was elected to the state senate, where he served for one term and was chosen a member of the committee to compromise the state debt. He was described as an able and talented legislator who took a prominent part in debate on nearly every bill during his term.

Throughout his career, Caldwell took an intense interest in business affairs. He was especially interested in the building and financing of the North Carolina Railroad, driving its last spike on 29 Jan. 1856. He was also a stockholder in various other railroads and cotton mills. In 1889 he organized the Bank of Guilford and was made its president.

Caldwell never married. In 1898 he was paralyzed by a

stroke; after nearly a year of feeble health he died from the effects of another stroke. He was buried in the cemetery of Buffalo Presbyterian Church, of which he had been a member. There are no known existing portraits.

SEE: James L. Albright, *Greensboro, 1808–1904* (1925); E. S. Arnett, *Greensboro* (1955); Samuel A. Ashe, ed., *Cyclopedia of Eminent and Representative Men of the Carolinas of the Nineteenth Century*, vol. 2 (1892); David Caldwell Papers (Southern Historical Collection, University of North Carolina, Chapel Hill); *Greensboro Telegram*, 31 Dec. 1898; J. G. deRoulhac Hamilton, *Reconstruction in North Carolina* (1914); North Carolina Tombstone Records, vol. 1 (North Carolina State Archives, Raleigh); Sallie W. Stockard, *History of Guilford County* (1902); J. S. Tomlinson, *Assembly Sketch Book* (1879).

RONALD HARRELSON

Caldwell, Greene Washington *(13 Apr. 1806–10 July 1864)*, physician, lawyer, and congressman, was born in Gaston County near Tuckasegee Ford on the Catawba River. He received his early education under John Dobson and took a medical degree from the University of Pennsylvania in 1831. After a short private practice, he served as an assistant surgeon in the U.S. Army for four months in 1832. Dissatisfied with medicine, Caldwell turned to the study of law, was admitted to the bar, and established a law practice in Charlotte.

His political experience began with his election to the state House of Commons in 1836. He was reelected three times and then elected to the U.S. House of Representatives in 1841. He declined reelection to Congress and returned to Charlotte, where he was appointed superintendent of the U.S. Mint in 1844. He was the unanimous choice of the Democrats for governor in 1846 but declined the nomination.

The outbreak of war with Mexico prompted Caldwell to volunteer for the infantry. He was made captain of the Third Dragoons in 1847, with lieutenants E. C. Davidson, J. K. Harrison, and A. A. Norman. The unit saw little action, and Caldwell was mustered out 24 July 1848.

Caldwell returned to political life with his election to the state senate in 1849; at the same time, two of his lieutenants, Davidson and Harrison, were elected to the House of Commons. Caldwell was unsuccessful in a bid for Congress in 1851 and resumed his medical practice in Charlotte. He died there and was buried in the Old Cemetery.

SEE: J. B. Alexander, *History of Mecklenburg County from 1740 to 1900* (1902); *Biog. Dir. Am .Cong.* (1961); J. G. deRoulhac Hamilton, ed., *The Papers of William Alexander Graham*, vol. 2 (1961); H. T. Shanks, ed., *The Papers of Willie Person Mangum*, 5 vols. (1950–56); John H. Wheeler, *Historical Sketches of North Carolina* (1851), and *Reminiscences and Memoirs of North Carolina* (1883–84); *Who Was Who in America, 1607–1896*.

VICTORIA C. HOLLOWELL

Caldwell, Joseph *(21 Apr. 1773–27 Jan. 1835)*, mathematician, Presbyterian minister, and first president of The University of North Carolina, was born at Lamington, N.J., in northeastern Hunterdon County, the youngest of three children of Joseph and Rachel Harker Caldwell.

His father died two days before Caldwell's birth, and the family moved several times during Caldwell's early life. At an English school in Bristol, Pa., Caldwell received his first schooling. When the family moved to Princeton, he entered a grammar school in 1784 under the supervision of Dr. John Witherspoon, long-time leader of the College of New Jersey (Princeton University). When the Caldwell family moved to Newark, Joseph Caldwell's studies continued for a while under the tutelage of Dr. Alexander MacWhorter, a trustee of the College of New Jersey. Caldwell's formal education ceased when the family removed shortly thereafter to Elizabethtown, N.J., but then a visit from Dr. Witherspoon resulted in Caldwell's reentering the school at Princeton in 1787. A few months later he entered the College of New Jersey, from which he was graduated as Latin salutatorian in 1791 at the age of eighteen.

For some months afterward, Caldwell taught languages to young boys; soon he took a position as assistant teacher in a classical academy in Elizabethtown. At this time he began study for the ministry, which was interrupted by his selection as a tutor at his alma mater in 1795. There he received a license to preach from the Presbytery of New Brunswick.

The following year, Charles Harris, presiding professor and professor of mathematics at the fledgling University of North Carolina, asked Caldwell to succeed him as professor of mathematics. Harris was acquainted with Caldwell from their student days at Princeton, and the knowledge that Caldwell was a tutor there prompted his request. Caldwell accepted and moved to Chapel Hill in October 1796; except for a few temporary absences, he remained in North Carolina until his death.

When Harris resigned as presiding professor in 1797, in the third year of the university's existence, Caldwell took the post. He performed his administrative and teaching duties in an able and dedicated manner. In 1804 he married Susan Rowan of Fayetteville. That same year, when the position of president of the university was created, he was unanimously elected by its trustees.

That Caldwell's abilities were becoming widely known in the state is evidenced by his selection in 1807 as the astronomical advisor for the running of the boundary between North and South Carolina and Georgia, which was completed six years later. As a result of this work he received more than one enticing offer of a higher salary elsewhere. An especially tempting proposal from the College of South Carolina came soon after his accession to the office of president. The University of North Carolina trustees, unable to match the offer, nevertheless urged Caldwell's remaining, and Caldwell declined South Carolina's offer and others, both because of his growing attachment to North Carolina and because he disliked the moving and change involved.

In 1807, Caldwell's wife and infant daughter died. He remarried in 1809, to Helen Hogg Hooper of Hillsborough, widow of the son of William Hooper, a signer of the Declaration of Independence. During this period, Caldwell worked for the completion of the as-yet-unfinished South building, for many years the main facility on campus. The North Carolina legislature had withdrawn support and the building was roofless. Caldwell sought private funds to complete the project and during his vacation in 1811 raised the requisite twelve thousand dollars from various contributors in the state, matching the largest single contribution with two hundred dollars of his own. With this boost, the university prospered and, feeling that he could afford to relinquish his office to return to his studies and devote more time to teaching, Caldwell resigned the presidency in 1812. He concentrated his energies on the completion of a text on geometry, finally published in 1822.

In recognition of his achievements, Caldwell was awarded the D.D. degree in 1816 from both The University of North Carolina and Princeton. Robert Chapman, who had succeeded Caldwell as president, left the office that year and, after some persuasion, Caldwell reluctantly resumed it in 1817.

Under his guidance the university continued to grow; as a result, Caldwell urged the addition of a second hall, a new chapel, and enlargement of the original building, Old East. The faculty opposed this plea on the grounds that the university should first purchase books and such philosophical apparatus as telescopes, transits, and so on. In 1824, therefore, Caldwell traveled to Europe at his own expense to purchase six thousand dollars worth of materials for the university, which were of considerable aid to the quality of education there. Fund-raising for and construction of the new buildings was then begun, and all three building projects were eventually completed.

The last part of Caldwell's career presented many difficulties. The financial panic of 1825 resulted in a decrease in enrollment, and the trustees borrowed forty thousand dollars, a debt that caused much anxiety, to enable the school to continue. At about age fifty-six, Caldwell contracted a chronic illness that hampered his activities, to the sometime detriment of the institution, and eventually caused his death. Nonetheless, he produced several works during this period, most importantly his text on geometry *A Compendious System of Elementary Geometry* (1822). In 1828 he wrote, under the pseudonym "Carlton," a series on the desperate need for improved transportation in North Carolina; the series was compiled as *Letters of Carlton* and was followed in 1832 by a series entitled *Letters on Popular Education Addressed to the People of North Carolina*, in which he championed public education, chastising the state for its inaction and proposing a detailed state system of primary, secondary, and higher education. His pragmatic and farsighted views earned him a wide reputation as a progressive force in the state.

Caldwell contributed personally to the construction of the university by building an observatory in 1830, at a personal cost of over four hundred dollars. This, the first astronomical observatory for educational purposes in the United States, was built in order to make the most effective use of the instruments bought on Caldwell's European trip.

As Caldwell's health declined, his duties were increasingly delegated to younger members of the faculty. In 1833, Caldwell relinquished his authority in maintaining student discipline, a task he had performed almost since the beginning of the university. By 1835 he was in nearly constant agony, and he finally succumbed in Chapel Hill.

Caldwell's administration was marked by his zealous protection of the institution, the endless energy he devoted to it, and his strict discipline both in his studies and toward his students. Shortly after his death, his friends erected a sandstone obelisk to his memory on the campus of the university. This marker was replaced by a marble one erected in 1858 (under which now lie the remains of Caldwell, his wife, and his stepson), commissioned in 1847 by his former students.

SEE: Walker Anderson, *Oration on the Life and Character of the Rev. Joseph Caldwell* (1835); Kemp P. Battle, *History of the University of North Carolina*, 2 vols. (1907, 1912); R. D. W. Connor, ed., *A Documentary History of the University of North Carolina*, 2 vols. (1953); "Joseph Caldwell, D.D.,

First President of the University of North Carolina," *University Record*, 5 (April 1903); *DAB*, Fifth supplement (1977); Francis P. Venable, "A College President of a Hundred Years Ago," *University Record*, 91 (April 1911); Henry A. White, *Southern Presbyterian Leaders* (1911).

ROGER N. KIRKMAN

Caldwell, Joseph Pearson *(5 Mar. 1808–30 June 1853)*, state legislator and member of Congress, was born in the northern part of Iredell County, the fifth son of Andrew Caldwell and Ruth Reese Sharpe Caldwell. His maternal grandfather was William Sharpe, member of the Second Continental Congress from North Carolina from 1779 until 1782. Joseph was related to David Caldwell, member of the House of Commons when Iredell County was formed, and David Franklin Caldwell, Joseph's oldest brother, was a judge of renown.

Caldwell was educated at Bethany Academy near Statesville and then read law with his brother, Judge Caldwell, afterward becoming an attorney in Statesville. In 1833 he was elected to the North Carolina Senate from Iredell, and from 1838 until 1844 he was member of the House of Commons. In 1849, when Nathaniel Boyden of Salisbury declined to run again for the U.S. House of Representatives, Caldwell allowed his name to be put forward by the Iredell County Whigs for the place and was elected without formal oppositon from either party as representative from the Second North Carolina District. In 1851 he was reelected, again without opposition. In 1853 he declined to stand for reelection to a third term; he died in Statesville some two months before his successor was chosen.

In 1842 he married Amanda McCulloch, daughter of John McCulloch of Rowan County and a descendant of Thomas Polk. One of their daughters married Theodore Kluttz, later member of Congress from Salisbury. Another daughter, Janie, became a well-known teacher in Statesville. Caldwell's son, who was named for him and who was two weeks old when his father died, became one of North Carolina's most distinguished newspaper editors.

SEE: *Biog. Dir. Am. Cong*. (1928); Salisbury *Carolina Watchman*, 1849–51; John H. Wheeler, *Historical Sketches of North Carolina* (1851).

HOMER M. KEEVER

Caldwell, Joseph Pearson *(16 June 1853–22 Nov. 1911)*, newspaper editor, was born in Statesville just two weeks before the death of his father, the elder Joseph Pearson Caldwell, former state legislator from Iredell County and member of the U.S. House of Representatives. His mother was the former Amanda McCulloch of Rowan County.

The younger Caldwell, known as J. P. rather than junior, was not a college man, his only degree being an honorary LL.D. from Erskine College in South Carolina. In his boyhood, during the Civil War period, his schooling was in the hands of his older sister Jennie; he did attend some night classes later, but most of his education was acquired in the various newspaper offices where he worked.

At the age of fourteen, Caldwell began work as a printer's devil in the office of the *Iredell Express*, Statesville's first newspaper, which was published by E. B. Drake. At the end of the Civil War, soon after Caldwell began working there, the paper was renamed the *Statesville American*. Drake, who had been Whig and then Conservative, turned Republican in 1872, and Charles R. Jones of Williamsburg in north Iredell County set up a rival newspaper, the Statesville *Intelligencer*, as the Democratic opposition. By raising Caldwell's salary from five to six dollars a week, Jones enticed him away from the *American*. It was for the *Intelligencer* that Caldwell began to try his hand at writing, beginning with local news. His next experience was acquired with Colonel Johnstone Jones of the old *Charlotte Observer*, at thirty dollars a month as city editor. Then Charles R. Jones bought the *Observer* and gave up the *Intelligencer*. Caldwell remained with him until 1880, with the exception of a year's interlude as city editor for the Raleigh *News*. During those years with the *Observer* he rose to the position of assistant editorial writer.

In January of 1880, Caldwell was able to buy the Statesville *Landmark* from J. Sherman Ramsey. The *Landmark*, successor to the *Intelligencer*, had been established in 1874 by J. B. Hussey and had passed into Ramsey's hands in 1876. Under the guidance of Caldwell, from January 1880 until February 1892, this paper, although only a weekly, was recognized as one of the strongest and ablest newspapers in the state. When Caldwell went home to Statesville, the town was a trading town with a back country of seventeen counties. Before he left in 1892, railroads had been pushed through to Lenoir, Taylorsville, and North Wilkesboro, and those towns had cut into Statesville's trading territory. It became evident to Caldwell and other leaders that the town must turn to manufacturing, and he became a strong advocate of manufacturing as a way of life for Piedmont North Carolina. When he went to Statesville, Caldwell was a conservative, defending the Bourbonism of the Democratic party and using his influence to defeat more than one election for the establishment of a graded school in Statesville. Before he left, he had been converted to the concept of public schools by Charles D. McIver, and Statesville had its graded school. In 1886 the board of aldermen appointed him mayor of Statesville to replace B. F. Long, who had resigned to become district solicitor. In 1887 he was elected to a full two-year term, and he would have had no opposition had he chosen to run in 1889.

The Statesville mayoralty was the only elective office Caldwell ever held. He did hold one appointive political post, that of director of the state hospital at Morganton; he remained in this position until his death and was for some years president of the board of directors. For twenty years he was prominent in the councils of the Democratic party; he was a member of the state Democratic committee and in 1892 was delegate-at-large to the national convention. He was urged unsuccessfully to represent Iredell in the General Assembly, and although there was a movement on foot at one time to name him lieutenant governor, he would not consent.

In January 1892, Caldwell and D. A. Tompkins, an industrialist of Charlotte, bought the *Charlotte Chronicle*, successor to the weekly *Observer*. It was not the first time that Caldwell had a chance to return to Charlotte: in 1882 when Charles R. Jones deserted the Democratic party and talked of running for Congress as an independent, an offer to establish Caldwell with an opposition paper in Charlotte had come, but a purse of a thousand dollars from Statesville citizens, which he invested in a new press, kept him with the *Landmark*. When he left Statesville to take over the *Chronicle*, he sold half interest in the *Landmark* to Rufus Reid Clark, who had been his printer, but he continued to contribute to the paper until he sold Clark the other half interest in 1906.

The *Chronicle* was soon renamed the *Observer*, and Caldwell, in active management, built it to its present dominant status. As editor, he continued to emphasize manufacturing, as he had begun to do during his latter days with the *Landmark*. His position brought him into conflict with the Democratic leadership over the question of free silver. In 1896 he grudgingly backed William Jennings Bryan for president while attacking the free silver plank in his platform. In 1900 he refused to back Bryan and made the *Observer* an independent newspaper, a new concept in the days when all newspapers were supposed to be intensely partisan. Opposition was strong and at times verbally violent, but Caldwell did not budge from his position. He braved the storm and won, giving the press a liberty it had not known.

In June 1877, while working on the old *Observer*, Caldwell married Maggie Spratt of Charlotte. Three of their five children grew to maturity, two daughters and a son, Frank Caldwell of Charlotte. Maggie Spratt Caldwell died in Statesville in 1893, soon after her husband had bought the *Charlotte Observer*. Later, Caldwell was married a second time, to Addie Williams of Charlotte; they had one daughter.

Caldwell edited the *Observer* until 8 Mar. 1909, when he suffered a stroke of paralysis. At his request he was transferred to the state hospital at Morganton. There he died, after two years as a guest of the institution he had served so long.

SEE: Samuel A. Ashe, ed., *Biographical History of North Carolina*, vol. 1 (1905); *Charlotte Observer*, scattered issues; Statesville *Landmark*, 24 Nov. 1911 and scattered issues.

HOMER M. KEVER

Caldwell, Tod Robinson (1818–11 July 1874), lieutenant governor and governor, was born in Morganton, the son of an Irish immigrant who became a prominent Burke County merchant. He obtained the rudiments of reading and writing at a local school and then went to Hillsborough, where he prepared for college by studying under William J. Bingham. Caldwell entered The University of North Carolina and was graduated with honors in 1840. While in college, in addition to pursuing the regular curriculum, he read law under President David L. Swain. In 1841 he began practicing law in Burke County, and in the same year he won the first of many elections to public office, that of county prosecuting attorney. He never lost an election. His success as a criminal lawyer brought him a measure of fame in the mountain counties, which contributed to his election at the age of twenty-four to the state House of Commons. "A Henry Clay Whig of the most enthusiastic stripe," Caldwell served several terms in the house and in the senate, to which he was first elected in 1850.

During the sectional crisis of the 1850s, Caldwell, like most North Carolina Whigs, resisted the movement to take the state out of the Union. But unlike most of his fellow Whigs, he retained his allegiance to the Union after secession, taking no part in the war, although his only son to survive infancy fought in Lee's army—and died at Gettysburg. After the war, Caldwell, along with the many Union Whigs who were anxious for an early restoration of the state to the Union, served in the constitutional convention of 1865 called under President Johnson's plan of Reconstruction. When Johnson's lenient policies toward Confederates failed to result in reunion and, in fact, alienated the Republican majority in Congress, Caldwell disassociated himself from the president and in 1867 served as one of the founders of the Republican party in North Carolina. Although no friend of black rights when he joined the Republican party, he warmed to the idea of supporting its platform of Negro suffrage and rights. Before reentering politics, he served in 1865–66 as president of the state-owned Western North Carolina Railroad.

In the new government required under the congressional plan of Reconstruction, Caldwell was elected lieutenant governor on the Republican ticket headed by William W. Holden. As the presiding officer of the senate, he served with considerable tact and fairness to all factions. On 20 Dec. 1870 he assumed the duties of governor, when Holden was suspended from office pending his impeachment trial before the senate. Upon Holden's removal on 22 Mar. 1871, Caldwell became governor.

As governor, he faced the difficult task of working with a General Assembly dominated by Conservatives hostile to the very existence of the Republican party in the state. Nevertheless, his sense of moderation and an obvious integrity in the performance of his duties went far not only to appease many of his political foes but also to win support for his much-abused party. Although his staff was reduced by the General Assembly to one secretary and his authority under the constitution challenged, he vigorously sought solutions to the more vexatious problems confronting the state during Reconstruction. He especially pressed the legislature for a systematic settlement of the state debt, which he claimed amounted to thirty-eight million dollars in 1873. He proposed that a compromise "be effected with the creditors, by which the whole debt could be reduced to an amount within the capacity of the State to pay." The General Assembly refused to cooperate with the scalawag governor in any plan for the settlement of the debt. When an arrangement with the state creditors was finally made in 1879, it followed Caldwell's general recommendations, although the conservative regime probably reduced the total amount of the debt far more than he would have desired.

With little success, Caldwell repeatedly urged the General Assembly to reinvigorate the languishing public school system that the Republicans had begun with considerable promise in 1868–69. He demonstrated no similar interest in the state university, which he believed "may be dispensed with until a new era of prosperity shall dawn upon us." As chairman of the board of trustees, he cautiously but unsuccessfully worked to place the university in the hands of "reliable Republicans" in anticipation of its reopening, after the closure of 1870.

He also futilely sought legislative action to restore law and order in the state and provide protection for the rights of black citizens, as called for by the Fourteenth and Fifteenth amendments. Caldwell's vigorous effort to prosecute the notorious Milton S. Littlefield and George W. Swepson, although ending in failure, demonstrated his determination to act scrupulously in enforcing the laws of the state against violators, despite possible close ties between the corruptionists and members of his party.

As a result of his successes, and in spite of the attempts of the Conservatives to discredit him, Caldwell in 1872 defeated Augustus S. Merrimon for governor by a margin of 1,898 votes. He did not live out the new term; he died suddenly at Hillsborough.

Caldwell was married in 1840 to Minerva Ruffin Cain of Hillsborough; he was the father of three daughters and two sons.

SEE: Annual Messages of Governor Tod R. Caldwell, 1871–73, in *Executive and Legislative Documents Laid before the General Assembly of North Carolina* (1871–72, 1872–73, 1873–74); Tod R. Caldwell Papers (Library, Duke University, Durham); J. G. deRoulhac Hamilton, *Reconstruction in North Carolina* (1914); *Harper's Weekly*, 7 Sept. 1872; *New York Times*, 12 July 1874; Otto H. Olsen, "Reconstruction and Redemption in North Carolina" (1974, in possession of the author, Northern Illinois University).

WILLIAM C. HARRIS

Caldwell, Wallace Everett (26 Apr. 1890–6 Oct. 1961), professor of ancient history at The University of North Carolina and grand master of Masons of North Carolina, was born in Brooklyn, N.Y. His father, Frank Eddy Caldwell, was a medical doctor in Brooklyn, and his mother, Ann Frances Horton Caldwell, was originally from Trumnsburg, N.Y. His ancestors included Colonel Joseph Caldwell of the American Revolution and John Winthrop and Richard Warren, who came to this country on the *Mayflower*. Wallace Caldwell was graduated from Boys' High School, Brooklyn, in 1906 and received the A.B. degree in 1910 from Cornell University, where he had been the holder of state and university scholarships and had earned membership in Phi Beta Kappa. He attended Columbia University from 1912 to 1915 and was a fellow there in the academic year 1914–15. He was awarded the doctorate in ancient history in 1919.

Caldwell's teaching experience included service as assistant master of the Bethlehem (Pa.) Preparatory School (1910–12), master of the Allen-Stephenson School in New York City (1912–14), instructor in Indiana University (1915–16), teacher in the High School of Commerce in New York City (1916–17), and instructor in Columbia University (1917–21). In 1921–22 he studied at the University of Ghent in Belgium on a C.R.B. Fellowship. In the fall of 1922 he went to The University of North Carolina as an associate professor of history; he was made a professor in 1928 and served as chairman of the department from 1951 to 1953. He taught in the summer of 1924 at Cornell University and in the summer of 1937 at the University of Michigan. At various times he gave courses at North Carolina College at Durham. In 1930–31 he spent the year in Europe on a Kenan Leave, and in 1954, on a Travel and Study Leave, he toured Europe and attended the meeting of the International Federation of Classical Societies at Copenhagen. He retired from full-time teaching in 1961.

Caldwell held membership and was active in a variety of professional organizations, including the American Historical Association, the American Philological Association, the Archaeological Institute of America (vice-president in 1951), the Archaeological Society of North Carolina (president from 1933 to 1936), and the Classical Association of the Middle West and South. He was on the board of editors of *Archaeology* in 1948. Caldwell published many articles and reviews in learned journals, Masonic publications, and several popular periodicals. His larger publications included his thesis, *Hellenic Conceptions of Peace*, and a translation of Jean Capart's *Thebes, The Glory of a Great Past. The Ancient World*, a college level text in ancient history, was published first in 1937 and revised in 1949; further revision was in process, with Dr. M. F. Gyles as coauthor at the time of Caldwell's death. He also wrote, with E. H. Merrill, a high school and popular text, *World History* (1949), which appeared in several editions. He collaborated wth Dr. W. C. McDermott in selecting and publishing *Readings in the History of the Ancient World* in 1951. *Laudatores Temporis*

Acti: Studies in Memory of Wallace Everett Caldwell, edited by Mary Frances Gyles and Eugene Wood Davis, was published in 1964 and *The Rock: Masonic Addresses by Wallace E. Caldwell*, with an introduction by Harold V. B. Voorhis, was published in 1966.

Caldwell was very active in Masonry: he received the Sublime Degree of Master Mason in Mistletoe Lodge No. 647 in Brooklyn in 1913 and became a member of University Lodge No. 408, Chapel Hill, in 1926, serving as master of this lodge in 1939. In 1950 he was installed as grand master of Masons in North Carolina. He was sovereign grand master of the Grand Council for Allied Masonic Degrees of the United States in 1954. He was a Royal Arch and Scottish Rite Mason and a member of the Shrine and the Order of Eastern Star. In 1952 he received the Joseph Montford Medal for meritorious service to Freemasonry, awarded by the Grand Lodge of North Carolina. He also was presented with the Pierpont Edwards Medal by the Grand Lodge of Connecticut and the Josiah Hayden Drummond Medal by Grand Lodge of Maine, both in 1954. He was awarded honorary membership in a number of North Carolina lodges and was greeted as an honorary grand master of the Grand Lodge of Greece in Athens on 5 Oct. 1954.

Caldwell's other activities included membership in the Sons of the Revolution and in the North Carolina Society of Mayflower Descendants, of which he served as governor from 1942 to 1945. Reared as a Con-gregationalist in the Plymouth Church of Brooklyn, he was active in the Presbyterian church in Chapel Hill until 1960, when he joined the Community Church. Politically, although he was proud of his support of Theodore Roosevelt in 1912, he maintained an interest in the Democratic party in North Carolina. He was an enthusiastic participant in and follower of sports; the program for the 1962 Atlantic Coast Conference Indoor Track Meet was dedicated to his memory.

On 8 June 1915, Caldwell married Harriet Wilmot of Brooklyn, N.Y. They had three children: Edward E., electronic engineer; Robert W., foreign service officer, Department of State; and Martha B., professor of art history at Madison College in Virginia.

Caldwell died in Chapel Hill and was interred at Greenwood Cemetery, Brooklyn. A sculpture head by Arnold Borden has been presented to The University of North Carolina and is in the North Carolina Collection. An oil portrait by Cuthbert Lee is owned by E. E. Caldwell.

SEE: Mary Frances Gyles and Eugene W. Davis, eds., *Laudatores Temporis Acti* (1964); Memorial tribute read at the General Faculty Meeting, University of North Carolina, Chapel Hill, 27 Oct. 1961; Southern Historical Collection (University of North Carolina, Chapel Hill), for most of Caldwell's papers; Harold V. B. Voorhis, introduction to *The Rock: Masonic Addresses by Wallace E. Caldwell* (1966); *Who's Who in America*, 1940–61.

MARTHA B. CALDWELL

Callis, John Benton (*3 Jan. 1828–24 Sept. 1898*), military leader and congressman, was born in Fayetteville. His parents moved to Tennessee when he was six years old and to Lancaster, Grant County, Wisc., six years later. Callis was schooled sporadically in the common schools in areas where he lived. He studied medicine for three years but abandoned the study before receiving a degree. He moved to Minnesota in 1849 and became one of the contractors building Fort Gaines (later known as Fort Riley).

In 1851, wanderlust took Callis to California, where he developed interests in mining and merchandising. In early 1853 he went to Central America, and six months later he returned to his former home, Lancaster, Wisc., spending seven years there in the mercantile business.

When the Civil War began in 1861, Callis joined the Wisconsin forces of the Union army as a lieutenant and soon became captain of the Seventh Regiment, Wisconsin Volunteer Infantry (the group often men-tioned in historical records as the "Iron Brigade"). Two years later he was promoted to major in the same unit. Then, following a wound at the Battle of Gettysburg, he was honorably discharged on 29 Nov. 1863.

The following year, President Lincoln appointed him military superintendent of the War Department, with headquarters in Washington, D.C., and there he served until December 1865. In the previous February he had been promoted to lieutenant colonel, and on 13 Mar. 1865 he was breveted colonel and brigadier general of the volunteers, being cited "for efficient and meritorious services." Subsequently, he was appointed captain in the Forty-fifth Regiment, U.S. Infantry. His military prowess at the Battle of Gettysburg resulted in his being again breveted as major, in 1867.

By 1865, Callis had settled in Huntsville, Ala., where he was named assistant commissioner of the Freedmen's Bureau. He held the post until 4 Feb. 1868, the same date he resigned his commission in the army.

After Alabama's readmission to the Union, Callis was a successful Republican candidate for the U.S. House of Representatives from the Fifth Alabama District. He served in the Fortieth Congress for less than a year (21 July 1868 to 3 Mar. 1869) and was not a candidate for reelection. During his short stay in Congress he was very vocal and exerted considerable leadership; he was the author of a resolution that served as a basis for the famous Ku Klux Klan Bill in the Forty-first Congress.

In mid-1869, Callis moved his family from Huntsville, Ala., to resettle in Lancaster, Wisc. He established a prosperous real estate business, to which he devoted his energies for the rest of his life.

In 1874, Callis made one further venture into public life, when he was elected to the Wisconsin General Assembly; he served for one year. He died in Lancaster and was buried in the Hillside Cemetery.

SEE: *Biog. Dir. Am. Cong.* (1971); *Nat. Cyc. Am. Biog.*, vol. 13 (1906).

C. SYLVESTER GREEN

Calloway, James (*23 July 1806–25 Dec. 1878*), physician and officeholder, was born on the South Fork of New River in Ashe County. He was a great-nephew of Daniel Boone and one of twelve children of Elijah and Mary Cuthbert Calloway, early settlers in the county.

Elijah Calloway, a prosperous planter, represented Ashe County in the state House of Commons for many years; James Calloway, educated locally, followed by representing the county for three terms—1828, 1830, and 1831. In 1838, Calloway was described as "now with the old fashioned [sic] Republicans, but not of the Presidents [Van Buren's] New fangled Democracy." William B. Mears, a representative from Wilmington, observed that Calloway "was a sensible, intelligent, liberal & clever fellow, as often on the right side, (as I thought) as any body. His whole course there [in the legislature], impressed me very favorably."

In the early 1830s, Calloway went to Philadelphia to study medicine at Jefferson Medical College; after graduation he settled in Wilkesboro and established a practice that took him into many surrounding counties.

On 25 June 1835 he married Mary L. Carmichael, daughter of Abner Carmichael, sheriff of Wilkes County. They had four children, Mary Virginia, Francis Caroline, Abner Sydenham, and Martha. By his marriage, Calloway became allied with one of the most powerful Whig families in northwestern North Carolina. Leander Bryan Carmichael, one of his brothers-in-law, was a colleague of Zebulon B. Vance in the 1854 General Assembly, and Calloway developed a friendship with Vance.

In 1838, Calloway, whose medical practice was flourishing, prevailed upon some of his political allies to secure for him appointment as surgeon of the Third Regiment of North Carolina Militia. As such he served under Lieutenant Colonel John Gray Bynum in the removal of the Cherokee Indians from southwestern North Carolina. Upon his return home, his medical practice expanded, and he also began to invest heavily in real estate in Wilkes and Ashe counties. In the 1850s he was believed to be the wealthiest Whig in Wilkes County.

Calloway's wife died in 1847, and he erected an elaborate marble tombstone over her grave in the Wilkesboro town cemetery. In 1852 he married Annie Perry Yeakle, daughter of William Yeakle of Hagerstown, Md., and Philadelphia. She had been a student at Edgeworth Seminary in Greensboro and had family connections in Wilkes County. They became the parents of Harriet Hoye, Elizabeth Charlotte, Annie Yeakle, Ruth Bowie, Jane Alice, and another daughter who died as an infant.

Although Calloway first opposed secession, after the firing on Fort Sumter he changed his position. He was elected a member of the North Carolina Secession Convention, at which, on 20 May 1861, he voted in favor of secession. The following year he was elected a member of the council of state.

The collapse of the Confederacy found Calloway's affairs "almost hopelessly embarrassed." His greatest property holdings in the postwar period lay west of the Mississippi River in Missouri and Kansas. Their management caused him to move to Kansas in 1870; his health failed while he was there, however, and he returned to Wilkesboro in 1872. He was a man of great religious principles and in 1849 helped to organize St. Paul's Episcopal Church in Wilkesboro. He then provided the funds to purchase an organ. He was buried in the churchyard.

Under the terms of his will, his property was left to his wife, their four surviving children and the two surviving children of his first marriage. Because of a number of small claims against the estate, his business affairs were not untangled until the mid-1880s, even though his executor, George H. Brown of Statesville, was an attorney of note.

SEE: Jerry C. Cashion, "Fort Butler and the Cherokee Indian Removal from North Carolina," unpublished research report (North Carolina State Archives, Raleigh); Governor Edward B. Dudley Papers (North Carolina State Archives, Raleigh); Joel T. Hubbard Papers (University Archives, Western Carolina University, Cullowhee); John G. McCormick, "Personnel of the Convention of 1861," *James Sprunt Historical Monographs*, No. 1 (1900); Wilkes County wills and estate papers (North Carolina State Archives, Raleigh); *Wilkesboro Witness*, 6 Feb. 1879.

RICHARD IOBST

Cambreleng, Churchill Caldom (24 Oct. 1786–30 Apr. 1862), congressman and diplomat, was born in Washington, Beaufort County. Little is known of his family except that one brother became an attorney in New York and another a naval officer. He attended school in New Bern and clerked in a store there before moving to New York City in 1802. He resided in or near New York City for the remainder of his life, except for a brief residence in Providence, R.I., in 1806, when he held a position as clerk in a financial institution there. Returning to New York, he became associated with John Jacob Astor in mercantile pursuits and traveled abroad extensively as one of Astor's representatives. He was also engaged in several other businesses and served as the principal officer of Cambreleng and Chrystie and of Cambreleng and Pearson. He was involved in railroad construction and, as the first president of the Saratoga and Schenectady Company when it was incorporated in 1831, was responsible for supervising the construction of this successful line in upstate New York. He was one of the first directors of the Farmers Fire Insurance and Loan Company.

Cambreleng was elected to Congress in 1820 as a Democrat and served until he was defeated in 1838. He soon became one of the major leaders of his faction and, with the election of Andrew Jackson, became one of the administration's principal spokesmen in the House of Representatives. The election of Martin Van Buren, a fellow New Yorker, further enhanced Cambreleng's influence. An effective politician and public speaker, he seldom revealed whether he spoke for himself or for the administration, and his speeches were often interpreted as representing the president's position. As chairman of the committees on Ways and Means, on Commerce, and on Finance, he was instrumental in formulating a large number of bills reaching the floor of Congress. He supported Jackson on the controversial U.S. Bank and in 1837 introduced legislation to abolish some tariff duties and greatly reduce others. Designed to dismantle Clay's American System, Cambreleng's proposed legislation was seen as indicative of the direction to be taken by Van Buren's new administration. His attitude was consistent with his own political past, however, for he had vigorously opposed the tariffs of 1824 and 1828. Though seldom considered an original thinker, he was admired for his common sense and clarity of expression, and several of his speeches and reports were published and widely circulated. His report as chairman of the Committee on Commerce and Navigation, published in 1830, was issued in several editions and reprinted in London for circulation abroad. After his defeat in 1838, he returned to private life until May 1840, when Van Buren wrote to ask him to go to Russia as minister. Cambreleng held this post until July 1841, when he was replaced by the new administration.

Though holding no other major office, he continued to be active in the affairs of his party on both state and national levels. He represented Suffolk County at the state constitutional convention of 1846 and, as chairman of the convention's Committee on Currency and Banking, prepared an important report on the need for a sound currency. In 1848 he attended the Democratic convention in Baltimore as a member of one of the two delegations sent from New York State. As a partisan of Van Buren, he was affiliated with the "Barnburners" of his state, opposing the rival faction in his party, known as "Hunkers." Upon the nomination of Lewis Cass, Van Buren's supporters returned to New York and at a meeting in Utica reaffirmed their support for their candidate. Cambreleng joined in the movement to nominate Van Buren and supported the Free-Soil party in the presidential campaign of 1848 when it selected Van Buren as its nominee. He returned to the Democratic fold in 1852, however, and supported the candidacies of Franklin Pierce for president and Horatio Seymour for governor.

Retired from active business pursuits, Cambreleng grew increasingly inactive after the campaign of 1852. His mercantile career had provided him with a comfortable income, and as he grew older he spent more time at his home in West Neck on Long Island. He was married to a former Miss Glover, but his later personal affairs, like his early life, are poorly documented. He had no children. He died at his home and was buried in Greenwood Cemetery in Brooklyn.

SEE: DeAlva Stanwood Alexander, *A Political History of the State of New York*, vol. 2 (1906); *Biog. Dir. Am. Cong.* (1950); Cambreleng letters in the Van Buren Papers (Library of Congress, Washington, D.C.) and in Benjamin F. Butler, *Private and Official Correspondence*, 5 vols. (1917); Cambreleng's published reports and pamphlets, for his political ideas; *DAB*, vol. 3 (1929); Alexander C. Flick, ed., *History of the State of New York*, vol. 6 (1934); Charles Lanman, *Biographical Annals of the Civil Government of the United States*, rev. ed. (1887); Ray B. Smith, ed., *History of the State of New York*, vol. 2 (1922); *Who Was Who in America, 1607–1896*.

PAUL I. CHESTNUT

Cameron, Alexander (d. 27 Dec. 1781), British Indian agent, was born in Scotland during the early eighteenth century and emigrated to the Southern colonies with a number of his countrymen in the 1730s and 1740s. It is not certain whether he engaged in planting or trading during his early years in the colonies, but his first recorded public service was as ensign in the British Independent Regulars. His unit was stationed at Fort Prince George, S.C., on the edge of the Lower Cherokee country, during 1762 and 1763, and he took advantage of the excellent opportunity to learn the Cherokee country and become acquainted with the natives. His acceptance by the Indians was no doubt enhanced by his marriage to a Cherokee girl. He came to be known among the Cherokees and the Creeks by the sobriquet of endearment "Scotchie."

After his demobilization, Cameron took up the two thousand acres of land to which he was entitled by his military service record. At about the same time he entered the service of the British Indian Department in the South. He received the appointment in part because of his frontier experience and in part because he was an acquaintance, if not a kinsman, of his countryman John Stuart, just appointed superintendent. Commissioned as principal agent for the Cherokees and then given a titular promotion to deputy superintendent in 1768, Cameron lived among or near his wife's people until 1776. He came to have great influence with the Cherokees, who deeded land to his sons, but he still could not stop wily whites from cheating the tribe of lands or prohibit illegal transactions like the Henderson Purchase of 1775.

When the rumblings of discontent arose between England and America in 1775, Cameron assured the Cherokees that they need not fear, for their lands and people were not threatened. Despite his pacific directions to the tribe, the pro-American frontiersmen viewed Cameron as an enemy; when revolutionary turmoil reached upcountry South Carolina, Cameron fled his plantation near the present Abbeville, S.C.,

moved deeper into the Indian country, and took up residence among the Overhill Cherokees.

From his new headquarters, Cameron strove to implement the superintendent's advice by urging the Cherokees to remain neutral. Such advice was hard to follow, however, since the tribe was faced with daily encroachment by white trespassers. In the spring of 1776, Cameron was joined in the Cherokee country by Henry Stuart, the superintendent's brother, who had come with instructions and ammunition. Shortly after Stuart's arrival, a band of Northern Indians reached the Cherokee country, intent on persuading the Cherokees to go to war. When the Cherokees heard of the insults to their brethren in the north, they would wait no longer; they determined to drive out the hated white settlers. Cameron tried to direct the attacks in such a way as to limit bloodshed, but it was largely impossible for him to do so.

In response to the Cherokee invasion came a series of punitive raids by the southern states, which leveled many of the towns and destroyed the supplies cached for the winter. Cameron was forced to flee into the Creek country to avoid capture by the Americans. For a time he lived with David Taitt, the British deputy for the Creek; then a band of pro-American Creeks plotted to assassinate the two whites, so they fled to the safety of Pensacola in the fall of 1777.

For the next eighteen months, Cameron attempted to carry out his duties from a distance. In addition to his normal responsibilities, he was assisting Superintendent Stuart, whose age and physical condition made him less and less effective. Then, in the spring of 1779, John Stuart died, leaving the post of superintendent vacant. Cameron and another of Stuart's deputies, Charles Stuart, assumed joint control pending the appointment of a successor.

To their great dismay, the decision made in London was to appoint not a successor but successors. That decision alone would have been disappointing, but far worse was the instruction that Cameron would superintend the western division of the department, which would give him jurisdiction over the Choctaws and Chickasaws, two tribes with whom he had had only incidental contact.

In truth, Cameron never recovered from the trauma produced by this situation. He tried to carry out his duties by sending messages from Pensacola to the tribes, but it proved an ineffective method. Both Governor Peter Chester of West Florida and General John Campbell of the Pensacola garrison believed that Cameron had no intention of taking up residence among the Choctaws and Chickasaws. The question became an academic one, however, for the Spanish capture of Mobile in 1780 and Pensacola in 1781 forced the British away from the Gulf Coast. Cameron traveled through the Indian country and reached the relative safety of Savannah, where he died.

SEE: John Richard Alden, *John Stuart and the Southern Colonial Frontier* (1944); John P. Brown, *Old Frontiers* (1938); David H. Corkran, *The Cherokee* (1962), and *The Creek Frontier* (1967); Robert L. Ganyard, "Threat from the West," *North Carolina Historical Review* 45 (1968); James H. O'Donnell III, *Southern Indians in the American Revolution* (1973).

JAMES H. O'DONNELL III

Cameron, Bennehan (9 Sept. 1854–1 June 1925), planter, railway executive, industrialist, and promoter of good roads, was born at Fairntosh in what was then Orange County, the son of Paul Carrington and Anne

Ruffin Cameron. At the death of his father in 1891, he received what was the heart of the Cameron land, the Stagville and Fairntosh plantations of 6,200 acres lying between the Little and Flat rivers. He also received the home his grandfather, Duncan Cameron, had built on Hillsborough Street in Raleigh; the four lots ("Bennehan Square") in Raleigh that his great-grandfather, Richard Bennehan, had bought when the city was first laid off in the last decade of the eighteenth century; and other holdings of land, stock, and personal property.

In him the pattern of life characteristic of his father, grandfather, and great-grandfather repeated itself once more, now for the last time in a male Cameron in direct line of succession. After preparatory school work under Samuel W. Hughes at Cedar Grove in Orange County and at Horner and Graves' Academy at Oxford, he attended Eastman's Business College at Poughkeepsie, N.Y., and then entered Virginia Military Institute. From there he was graduated with distinction in both scholarship and military proficiency in 1875. In later life he always took a great interest in military activities and was a keen student of military history. He studied law under his uncle, William Kirkland Ruffin, and was admitted to the bar in 1877. He practiced law for only a short time, however: like his father, he found that most of his time was needed for the management of his plantations and his other duties.

In him likewise appeared the same high respect for agriculture and interest in improving it that were conspicuous in his father. He was especially proud of his fine horses and his highly bred herd of Jersey cattle. He presented the famous stallion Choctaw to General Fitzhugh Lee, who rode him in Cuba throughout the Spanish-American War. Cameron was at various times a director and president of the state agricultural society, president of the National Farmers' Congress of America, a member of the Royal Agricultural Society of England, and president of the North Carolina State Fair Association.

At the same time, Cameron was greatly interested in finance and industry. He was a director of the Morehead Banking Company, and he helped to organize the First National Bank of Durham. He was director and president of the Rocky Mount Cotton Mills. Railroad building and consolidation were matters to which he also gave much attention. He was on the committee that built the Caraleigh Railway Branch and the Union Depot in Raleigh, and he was instrumental in helping to build and strengthen the Oxford and Clarksville Railroad, the Lynchburg and Durham Railroad, and the Durham and Northern Railroad. He was the leading figure in the building of the Oxford and Coast Line Railroad. A director of the North Carolina Railroad for more than thirty-five years, he had a large part in leasing it to the Southern Railroad. His greatest work in connection with railroads, however, was the bringing together of many small lines into the Seaboard Air Line system.

Far ahead of his day, Cameron vigorously supported all movements to build good roads, especially the great interstate highways. He was chairman of a committee that introduced a bill in the state legislature to issue fifty million dollars in bonds for the improvement of North Carolina roads. He was head of the Bankhead Highway Association, a movement to connect the southern states by excellent highways, and he was actively associated with the movement to build the Quebec to Miami Highway.

A friend to education like his ancestors, he was active in all movements to develop and strengthen The University of North Carolina, even though he had not

attended it, and he was a trustee of the institution for over thirty-four years. In politics he was a Democrat. His counsel was sought by many political and military leaders of the state, and he served in various capacities on the staffs of Governors Vance, Jarvis, Scales, Fowle, Holt, and Carr.

Cameron was treasurer of the North Carolina Society of the Cincinnati and through it was instrumental in having monuments commemorating General Francis Nash and General William Davidson erected on the battlefield of Guilford Courthouse. He was on the Stone Mountain Memorial Committee, which had huge figures of Confederate leaders carved on a granite monolith near Atlanta, and he once entertained Gutzon Borglum, one of the sculptors, in his home. A story that appeared in some of the newspapers, that parts of D. W. Griffith's famous film *The Birth of a Nation* were filmed at Fairntosh and the Duncan Cameron home in Raleigh, is untrue; but Cameron was a close friend of Thomas Dixon, who wrote *The Clansman*, the novel upon which the moving picture was based, and the principal family in the novel is given the name Cameron.

Cameron's devotion to his family traditions was constant. Even during the years when his children were growing up and he lived mainly in his Raleigh home, he spent several days out of every week on his plantations and maintained his legal residence at Stagville. Motivated by justifiable pride, he had a bronze tablet commemorating the Reverend John Cameron, his great-grandfather, placed in the Old Blandford Church at Petersburg, Va., on 25 Sept. 1908. He, his two little daughters, and his cousin, Governor William E. Cameron of Virginia, were present at the unveiling on 11 Oct.

Cameron had a vigorous constitution and enjoyed excellent health. Particular sources of delight for him were country sports, horses and horsemanship. He cherished the traditions handed down in the family concerning Sir Archie, the most famous race horse of the first quarter of the nineteenth century, which had belonged to an Amis relative of his great-grandmother Bennehan in Northampton County.

On the night of 27 Aug. 1891, Cameron became the hero of a train wreck near Statesville; he was almost the only one out of a hundred passengers not killed or seriously injured, and he saved many of his fellow passengers from death.

On 28 Oct. 1891, Cameron married Sallie Taliaferro Mayo, daughter of Peter H. Mayo of Richmond, Va., who had been on Robert E. Lee's staff. By this marriage there were four children: a son, Paul Carrington, who died in childhood; a daughter, Anne Ruffin, who died in infancy; and two other daughters who survived to maturity. Cameron died at Raleigh and was buried near his father at St. Matthews Episcopal Churchyard, Hillsborough. His two surviving daughters, Isabella Mayo (Mrs. Eric Norman van Lennep of Bridgewater, Conn.) and Sally Taliaferro (Mrs. John Witherspoon Labouisse) inherited respectively, with other property, the Stagville and Fairntosh plantations.

SEE: Samuel A. Ashe, ed., *Biographical History of North Carolina*, vol. 3 (1905 [portrait]); and *Cyclopedia of Eminent and Representative Men of the Carolinas of the Nineteenth Century*, vol. 2 (1892 [portrait]); Landon C. Bell, *Cumberland Parish, Lunenburg County, Virginia* (1930); Cameron Papers (Southern Historical Collection, University of North Carolina, Chapel Hill); *Charlotte Observer*, 1 Nov. 1931 (portrait); *Durham Morning Herald*, 30 Jan. 1927; Raleigh *News and Observer*, 2 June 1925,

1 June 1956, 15–17 June 1973; Manly Wade Wellman, *The Life and Times of Sir Archie* (1958); *William and Mary Quarterly* 18 (1910).

CHARLES RICHARD SANDERS

Cameron, Duncan *(15 Dec. 1777–6 Jan. 1853),* planter, judge, politician, and banker, was born in Mecklenburg County, Va. His father, the Reverend John Cameron (d. 1815), an Episcopal priest, was the son of Duncan and Margaret Bain Cameron of Ferintosh in the Highlands of Scotland and was descended from members of Clan Cameron of Lochiel. John Cameron, who received his M.A. from King's College, Aberdeen, in 1767, came with three of his brothers to Virginia in 1770. One of the brothers, Donald, later returned to Scotland; another, William, remained in Virginia; and the third, Ewen, married Frances Buford of Virginia in 1797 and later settled at Franklin, Tenn. In 1773, John Cameron married Anne Owen Nash (15 June 1755–25 Aug. 1825), daughter of Thomas and Mary Read Nash and niece of Governor Abner Nash of North Carolina and General Francis Nash. The Camerons' seven children were Mary Read, who married Daniel Anderson; Duncan; Jean, who married the Reverend Andrew Syme; John Adams, who married Eliza Adam and then a widow, Mrs. Catherine McQueen Halliday, settled in Fayetteville, and was drowned in the wreck of the ship *Pulaski*; Anne, who died young; William, who practiced law at Hillsborough, married Anna Call (daughter of Chief Justice John Marshall's brother-in-law Daniel Call), and was the grandfather of William Evelyn Cameron, governor of Virginia (1882–86); and Thomas, a physician of Fayetteville, who married Jane Wilder and later Isabella Wilkins. The Reverend John Cameron had numerous grandchildren; a great-grandson, Bennehan Cameron, provided a bronze tablet to commemorate him at Old Blandford Church, Petersburg.

Duncan Cameron studied law under Paul Carrington of Charlotte County, Va., and was admitted to the bar in North Carolina in 1798. A few years later he himself taught Willie P. Mangum. After practicing law briefly at Martinsville, then the seat of Guilford County, he established himself as a highly successful attorney at Hillsborough. A rivalry sprang up between him and another brilliant young Hillsborough lawyer, William Duffy, growing partly out of legal affairs and partly from the desire of both young men to win the hand of Rebecca Bennehan (28 Nov. 1778–6 Nov. 1843), only daughter of Richard Bennehan. Cameron succeeded with the young lady, whom he married at Stagville on 24 Feb. 1803. On 17 Apr. of the same year he fought a duel with Duffy at a place just above the Virginia line; Cameron received a minor wound in the left shoulder and Duffy was badly crippled by a bullet in the right hip. Duffy left Hillsborough but continued to practice law in Fayetteville.

Cameron became a trustee of The University of North Carolina in 1802, was judge of the superior court from 1814 to 1816, and at various times served as president of the State Bank of North Carolina, clerk of the North Carolina Supreme Court, and member of the board of internal improvements. Between 1802 and 1824 he served five terms in the house and three in the senate of the state. He was chairman of the committee to build the present state capitol of North Carolina and was a founder of Christ Episcopal Church in Raleigh and chairman of its building committee. When the old Episcopal School for Boys ceased to operate in 1833, he bought the property and established there St. Mary's School for Girls.

Cameron became one of the largest plantation owners and slaveholders in the South. A year after his marriage he built a mansion house, called Fairntosh, on an elevated site about a mile east of the Stagville house. Around this house he built many dependencies, including his law office, with nearby barns and other utility structures. He also built a chapel in a grove of trees about a quarter of a mile east of the new home and laid off the plot for the family cemetery nearby. By 1850 he owned many thousand acres of land—reported by some of his contemporaries as the largest plantation east of the Mississippi River—and over a thousand slaves. He established a way of life and an economy as well balanced and complete as that of a medieval lord. His correspondence and that of other members of his family, preserved in the Cameron Papers at The University of North Carolina, speaks frequently and characteristically of both the "white family" and the "black family" on the plantation, and the same doctors and preachers took care of the needs of both. There was never any question that economic needs would be met. In 1834, Cameron was elected president of the state's Colonization Society; the society offered some slaves their freedom and paid for their voyage to Liberia, from which some voluntarily returned to slavery. Promising Fairntosh slaves were given an education.

In about 1835, Cameron built a spacious home on ten acres of land directly across Hillsborough Street from St. Mary's School, and henceforth he and his family divided their time between this home and Fairntosh.

Duncan and Rebecca Cameron had two sons and six daughters. The older son died unmarried. Four of the daughters, Jean Syme, Mary Ann, Rebecca, and Anne Owen—all in the bloom of youth and all unmarried—died between 1837 and 1840. A fifth, Mildred, lived to old age but never married. The sixth, Margaret, married George W. Mordecai, who succeeded Cameron as president of the State Bank of North Carolina; but the Mordecais had no children. When Cameron died in 1853, practically the whole estate was handed down to the second son, Paul Carrington. Cameron, his wife, and most of his children were buried in the cemetery at Fairntosh. Many of the family letters reflect vividly the life of genteel people in North Carolina and Virginia in the late eighteenth century and throughout a great part of the nineteenth. One of Cameron's descendants, Mrs. John W. Labouisse, owns a handsome portrait of him.

SEE: Samuel A. Ashe, ed., *Biographical History of North Carolina*, vol. 3 (1905), and *Cyclopedia of Eminent and Representative Men of the Carolinas of the Nineteenth Century*, vol. 2 (1892); Landon C. Bell, *Cumberland Parish, Lunenburg County, Virginia* (1930); Cameron Papers (Southern Historical Collection, University of North Carolina, Chapel Hill); Hugh T. Lefler and Paul Wager, eds., *Orange County, 1752–1952* (1953); Benson J. Lossing, *Pictorial Field-Book of the Revolution*, vol. 2 (1850); Elizabeth Culbertson Waugh, *North Carolina's Capital, Raleigh* (1967); Stephen B. Weeks, "The Code in North Carolina," *Magazine of American History* 26 (1891).

CHARLES RICHARD SANDERS

Cameron, John Adams *(1788–14 or 15 June 1838),* lawyer, banker, editor, consul, and judge, was born in Mecklenburg County, Va., son of John Cameron (1744–1815), a native of Scotland and Presbyterian minister, and Anne Owen Nash (d. 1825), a niece of Abner Nash, governor of North Carolina in 1780–81. John Adams Cameron moved to North Carolina with his older brother, Duncan, when he was about ten. He received his bachelor's degree from The University of North Carolina in 1806 and his master's there in 1809. He then studied law and began to practice in Fayetteville, which he represented in the lower house of the General Assembly in 1810, 1811, 1812, and 1820. In 1820 and 1821 he was grand master of North Carolina Masons.

During the War of 1812, Cameron organized a troop in Fayetteville and held the rank of major. His military duties did not occupy him fully, however, because in 1812 he was the unsuccessful Federalist candidate for Congress against Republican John Culpepper. In 1815 he petitioned the assembly for the office of comptroller of the state, claiming that his capacity to practice law had been lost in the service of his country. He married Eliza Adam in January of 1815, but she did not live long; in October of 1818 the newspapers reported his marriage to Catherine Halliday, widow.

Federalists in 1817 obtained for Cameron the job of president of the Fayetteville branch of the U.S. Bank. Republicans in the assembly opposed the bank and placed a tax on it, which Cameron refused to pay when the U.S. Supreme Court denied the right of states to tax instrumentalities of the national government (*McCulloch v. Maryland*, 1819). In 1820, Cameron was again in the House of Commons from Fayetteville and active in the movement to revise the state constitution. In 1823 he was a delegate to the Internal Improvements Convention in Raleigh; by this time he was beginning to move away from his old Federalist ties.

In 1825 it was announced that Cameron would become the editor of the Fayetteville *North Carolina Journal*, which under his leadership became an abrasive champion of the cause of Andrew Jackson. In 1827 the editor was candidate, against his old opponent Culpepper, for the Fayetteville seat in Congress. Their political roles were reversed, but Culpepper was again successful. In 1829, Culpepper having retired, Cameron campaigned again as the Jackson candidate, this time against National Republican Edmund Deberry. Deberry, who accused Cameron of being overbearing and of having squandered two fortunes, won by slightly more than two hundred votes.

Defeated politically and in need financially, Cameron had to sell the *Journal* in 1830. Shortly thereafter, President Jackson gave him an appointment as consul to Vera Cruz, but the revolutionary state of Mexico and the low pay of State Department employees at that period soon reduced Cameron's financial circumstances even further. He again contacted his influential friends in Congress to find him a better job. This time he received an appointment as judge of the Western District Court of Florida, and in 1832 he moved to Pensacola. Six years later he boarded the new steamship *Pulaski* at Savannah for a trip north. Near midnight on 14 June 1838, the starboard boiler of the ship exploded. There were almost one hundred victims, and Cameron's body was never found.

SEE: Duncan Cameron Papers (University of North Carolina, Chapel Hill); Cumberland County Marriage Bonds, Series II (North Carolina State Archives, Raleigh); Fayetteville *North Carolina Journal*, 20 June 1838; S. M. Lemmon, *Frustrated Patriots: North Carolina and the War of 1812* (1973); *Raleigh Register*, 7 and 14 May 1813; H. T. Shanks, ed., *The Papers of Willie Person Mangum*, vols. 1–2 (1950–52).

DANIEL M. MCFARLAND

Cameron, Paul Carrington (25 Sept. 1808–6 Jan. 1891), planter, agricultural reformer, railway and road builder,

and friend of education, was born at Stagville, the home of his grandfather, Richard Bennehan. Son of Duncan and Rebecca Bennehan Cameron, he was named after his father's old law teacher. His own early teachers were Willie P. Mangum, John Rogers of Hillsborough, and a Dr. McPheeters of Raleigh. He also attended Captain Partridge's Military School at Middletown, Conn. After spending two years at The University of North Carolina, where he was noted for his pugnacious disposition and for his fiery red hair, which caused him to be given the nickname "Redbird," he transferred to Washington (now Trinity) College at Hartford, Conn., where he was a charter student. He was an excellent scholar; at the commencement exercises in August 1829 he received his degree and read a paper entitled "English Travellers in America," preserved in the Cameron Papers at The University of North Carolina.

For some time afterward, Cameron read law in his father's office in Raleigh, but he never practiced law or desired to be engaged in politics. Instead, he found his time occupied in managing the lands and business enterprises for which he became responsible. Agriculture was his chief interest and was the basis of his Jeffersonian philosophy. Samuel Ashe wrote of him: "He saw in agriculture the great mainspring of commerce, of prosperity and of social happiness, and the foundation upon which was laid the great superstructure of human advancement and enlightenment . . . ." It is not an overstatement to say that under him the plantation system in the southern United States achieved its highest point; the great estate that his grandfather, Richard Bennehan, his uncle, Thomas Dudley Bennehan, and his father, Duncan Cameron, had done much to bring into being came into full flower. By the time of the outbreak of the Civil War, Cameron, unquestionably the richest man in the state, had at least thirty thousand acres in not just one but a composite of large plantations—Snow Hill, Brick House, Stagville, and Fairntosh—with many adjoining small plantations and farms. His lands were spread over what are now three counties, Durham, Granville, and Wake, up and down the Neuse River and its headwaters, the Eno, Little, and Flat rivers, from Orange Factory and Lake Michie today in the northwest to Tilt Rock on the Neuse River below Fishdam Ford and the lower part of Oak Grove Township in Wake County in the southeast. The land had a great variety of soils, so that many kinds of crops could be profitably grown. There were not only central residences, with their auxiliary small houses and barns, for the four main plantations, but also many outlying groups of living quarters and utility houses for overseers and slaves.

Cameron's treatment of his slaves was firm but benign. "I had nineteen hundred of them once," he is quoted as saying many years after the Emancipation, "and I never was ashamed to look one of them in the face after they were freed." John H. Wheeler says that Cameron would tell with some zest how he had been prevailed upon by a friend to free a family of Negroes and to settle them in Liberia under the care of the American Colonization Society, with a gift of a thousand dollars and house and food for twelve months provided, and how at the end of the year they appeared at the door of his mansion and begged him to take them back. Years after the war, many of his former slaves would greet him with respect and affection, and many of them attended his funeral in 1891, at which eight of his old black servants, some of whom had been slaves, bore his coffin to the hearse.

The wealthiest man in the state at the beginning of the war, he was still the wealthiest, despite the loss of his slaves, at the end of it. By enterprise and sagacity he was soon able to reestablish the economy of his plantations and to extend and diversify his business activities on a secure and stable basis. Like his father and grandfather before him, he also continued to maintain a constant, lively, and helpful interest in education in the state. He took a particular interest in St. Mary's School in Raleigh, and through gifts of money and other practical assistance, such as repairs to buildings, he did much to enable The University of North Carolina to reopen its doors after the war. Of his relation to the university, it has been said, he was "a friend and counsellor under Swain and a father and guide under Battle." There was no activity he undertook with more zeal than that of strengthening and developing this institution. In gratitude for his interest and support, the university established ten Cameron scholarships, which his heirs still control.

Although Cameron seldom ran for office, he was very much interested in politics. In the days of Henry Clay he was a Whig, but as sectional strife became intensified and the Civil War approached he became a Democrat and remained one the rest of his life. In 1856 he was state senator from Orange County. He was chairman of the North Carolina delegation to the 1876 St. Louis Democratic convention that nominated Tilden for the presidency. He was conservative in his attitude toward social change but progressive in whatever had to do with improving the material accommodations of life—land, livestock, rivers, canals, railroads, forests, buildings, and industrial processes.

Cameron did much to give North Carolina an adequate railway system. He helped to promote the building of the North Carolina Railroad and was a director of the Raleigh and Gaston Railroad and Augusta Air Line in the days before these lines became parts of larger systems. He was also a banker and industrialist, owning considerable stock in two banks in Raleigh, the Citizens' and the Raleigh National, and in textile mills in Rockingham, Rocky Mount, and Augusta, Ga. At the time of his death his wealth was tremendous, and his holdings were extended in many directions throughout the state and elsewhere.

Cameron's wealth was large enough to be divided in very substantial shares among the members of his large family. In December 1832 he had married Anne Ruffin, daughter of Thomas Ruffin, chief justice of the state supreme court. She had borne him ten children, three of whom, Jean, Mary Amis, and Duncan, died in childhood. All seven of the other children, Rebecca, Anne Ruffin, Margaret, a second Duncan, Pauline Carrington, Bennehan, and Mildred Coles, married, and most had descendants. Rebecca married twice, first Walker Anderson and second Major John Washington Graham. Anne Ruffin married Major George Pumpelly Collins. Margaret was married to Judge Robert B. Peebles and Duncan to Mary Bagly Short. Pauline Carrington married William Blount Shepard; after her death, Mildred Coles became his second wife. Duncan died before his father's death in 1891, and hence Bennehan was the only surviving son. By the terms of the will he received Stagville, Fairntosh, the Duncan Cameron home in Raleigh, and much other property. Cameron's widow and three daughters were also provided for in the will; so were some friends, housemaids, and "Virgil, the carriage driver."

SEE: Samuel A. Ashe, ed., *Biographical History of North Carolina*, vol. 3 (1905 [portrait]), and *Cyclopedia of Eminent and Representative Men of the Carolinas of the Nineteenth Century*, vol. 2 (1892 [portrait]); Cameron Papers

(Southern Historical Collection, University of North Carolina, Chapel Hill); Raleigh *State Chronicle*, 15 Jan. 1891 (obit); John H. Wheeler, *Reminiscences and Memoirs of North Carolina* (1883–84).

CHARLES RICHARD SANDERS

Camp, Cordelia (22 May 1884–10 July 1973), teacher and writer, was born north of Rutherfordton, the daughter of Merritt Rickman and Letitia Morrow Camp. From her neighborhood one-room school she began teaching in McDowell County, and after further training at the Asheville Normal and Collegiate Institute she taught in Wake and Forsyth counties. She was graduated from The University of North Carolina with an A.B. degree in 1920 and five years later earned a master's degree from Columbia University. In 1956, Western Carolina Teachers College awarded her an honorary doctorate in education. In 1927 she joined the education faculty of Cullowhee State Normal School, now Western Carolina State University. After her retirement in 1950, a building on the campus was named in her honor, and her portrait hangs there. She also taught briefly at the Plonk School in Asheville.

Cordelia Camp was one of the state founders of Delta Kappa Gamma, teaching fraternity, and was chairman of its publication committee, which produced *Pioneer Women Teachers of North Carolina*. She was also the author of *The Influence of Geography on Early North Carolina*; *The Settlement of North Carolina* (with Eddie Wilson); *North Carolina Problems: A Handbook for Teachers*; *The Family of Merritt Rickman Camp*; *Governor Vance: A Life for Young People*; *David Lowry Swain: Governor and University President*; *A Thought at Midnight: The Story of the Asheville Normal School*; and *A History of Piney Knob Baptist Church*. For her writing she was awarded the Western North Carolina Historical Association's silver cup in 1964. She served as the association's secretary-treasurer for many years.

She was buried in Rutherford County at Piney Knob Baptist Church.

SEE: *Asheville Citizen*, 11 July 1973.

GEORGE MYERS STEPHENS

Campbell, Arthur Carlyle (28 Nov. 1894–27 July 1977), teacher and college president, was born in Buies Creek to James Archibald and Cornelia Frances Pearson Campbell. His preparatory education was at Buies Creek Academy and he received A.B. and M.A. degrees from Wake Forest College in 1911 and 1916, respectively. He also studied at Columbia University during the period 1920–23. The University of South Carolina awarded him the honorary LL.D. degree in 1929 and Wake Forest did the same in 1950. During the years 1911–17 and 1919–20 he was an instructor in English at Buies Creek Academy. In 1923 he joined the faculty of Coker College, Hartsville, S.C., as professor of English and head of the department and during the years 1925–36 he was president of Coker College. From 1937 until 1939 he was professor and head of the English department at North Carolina State College, and in 1939 he became president of Meredith College, a post he filled until his retirement in 1966. Campbell served a term as president of the North Carolina College Conference and of the Southern Association of Colleges and Secondary Schools. He was also a member of the State Education Commission, 1947–49, and an advisory member of the North Carolina Board of Higher Education, 1962–65.

In 1917–18 Campbell was the ranking band sergeant of the Field Artillery Band and in 1918 was commissioned second lieutenant in the field artillery. During the year 1946–47 he was president of the North Carolina Literary and Historical Association. He was a member of Phi Beta Kappa, a Democrat, and a Baptist. In 1925 he was married to Marion Lee Newman and they were the parents of Virginia Lee (Mrs. Randy Stanford) and Carlyle. He was buried in Buies Creek.

SEE: Raleigh *News and Observer*, 1 June 1958, 29 July 1977; *Who's Who in the South and Southwest* (1952).

WILLIAM S. POWELL

Campbell, Farquhard *(ca. 1730–1808)*, legislator and soldier, was born in Scotland. Facts concerning his parentage, place of origin, and the exact date of his emigration to North Carolina are not known and are further obscured by numerous romantic traditions that have circulated among his descendants for several generations. Cumberland County court minutes provide the first documentary evidence of his presence in the colony: his appointment in July 1756 as a justice of the peace for the county indicates that he was by that time already well established or well connected. The unfortunate destruction by fire of Bladen County records precludes the possibility of pinpointing more precisely his first appearance in the area; he was in the part of Bladen that became Cumberland in 1754.

In May 1761, Campbell was appointed surveyor for the county; he laid out the town of Campbellton, chartered the following year and presumably named for him, and later served as a commissioner of the town. In 1764 he was elected to the General Assembly as a representative from Cumberland, a post he held at every session until 1775. During the War of the Regulation he was appointed a captain by Governor William Tryon in 1771 and commissioned to raise a company of 150 men from Cumberland, Bladen, and Anson counties. Whether this company took an active part in the campaign is not shown in the records.

As events moved inexorably toward the Revolution, Campbell at first appeared to espouse the cause of liberty. As early as 1770 he was chosen by the Sons of Liberty as a member of a committee of thirty of the most prominent men of the Cape Fear, who were to consult upon such measures as would best evince their "patriotism and loyalty" to the common cause. On 20 July 1775 he was a member of the Wilmington District Committee of Safety, but by the fall of that year evidence of his equivocation had begun to surface and on 4 Sept. 1775, the provincial congress felt called upon to pass a resolution of confidence in his integrity. On 16 Oct. and 12 Nov. the royal governor, Josiah Martin, wrote Lord Dartmouth, the colonial secretary, lamenting "the inconsistency of Farquhard Campbell's conduct" but expressing confidence that he could reconcile their interests when able to meet with him.

From this correspondence and other records of the period, it is evident that Campbell was a man of superior consequence, both as a leader in the community and as a man of property. This latter condition no doubt inclined him to a conservative position on the question of revolution. That he, along with other Scottish immigrants, had lately arrived from the direct jurisdiction of the Crown, in contrast to the many colonists who were third or even fourth generation Americans, may be a further explanation of what can be characterized as his duplicity.

Whatever the explanation, his efforts at fence-straddling were unsuccessful. After the Battle of Moore's Creek on 27 Feb. 1776, he was taken prisoner, and the provincial congress on 20 Apr. 1776 found him guilty of assisting the enemy. Congress, fearing the personal and family influence of Campbell and other prisoners, removed them in the interests of public safety. They were accordingly sent to Philadelphia, later transferred to Baltimore, and thence sent to Fredericktown. On 3 Mar. 1777, Campbell wrote Governor Richard Caswell, requesting parole to North Carolina, and offering to mortgage his property as security for his good behavior. Parole was granted on 12 Apr. 1778.

Soon after the close of the Revolution, Campbell reestablished himself politically. He was a member of the state senate from 1785 to 1793. The senate on 11 Dec. 1790 passed a resolution to the effect that his wartime behavior was justifiable and that since he had subsequently comported himself as "a friend to the United States," he would be "entitled to all the privileges and immunities that all other good citizens of this State are entitled to."

Campbell was married three times: first to Isabella McAlester, sister of Colonel Alexander McAlester, by whom he had five daughters; second to Elizabeth Whitfield Smith, widow of Alexander Smith, by whom he had three sons; and third to Rachel whose maiden name is unknown, who survived him but had no issue. He was supposedly buried on his home plantation, across the Cape Fear River from Old Bluff Presbyterian Church, of which he was one of the founders in 1758. A monument to him and his son Robert was erected in the churchyard at a later date.

SEE: Cumberland County Minutes of the Court of Pleas and Quarter Sessions (North Carolina State Archives, Raleigh); William L. Saunders and Walter Clark, eds., *Colonial and State Records of North Carolina*, 30 vols. (1886–1914).

WILLIAM C. FIELDS

Campbell, James *(ca. 1700–1780)*, Presbyterian minister, was born at Campbelltown, Kintyre, Scotland, and emigrated to Pennsylvania in about 1730. He was licensed to preach by the Presbytery of New Castle in 1735 and transferred to the Presbytery of Philadelphia on 22 May 1739. In September of that year he became uncertain of his own personal salvation and ceased to preach. On 29 Nov. 1739, in this condition, he heard the famous English evangelist George Whitefield preach at Gilbert Tennent's Meeting House, New Brunswick, N.J., and sought an interview with him. Whitefield managed to remove his difficulties and encouraged him to resume his ministry.

In 1755, Campbell was visited by the Reverend Hugh McAden, who was on his way to North Carolina to ascertain the religious needs there and report back to the Synod of Philadelphia. Upon his return, McAden persuaded Campbell to settle among the Highland Scots in the Cape Fear Valley and minister to them in their native Gaelic tongue. Campbell did as suggested in 1756 or 1757, taking up land on the Cape Fear River near the present-day town of Linden. From there he served a vast area covering most of the present counties of Cumberland, Harnett, Hoke, and Lee, with occasional side visits to Raft Swamp in Robeson, Purity in South Carolina, and "other destitute settlements." He was the only minister to preach to the Scots in their Gaelic tongue until the coming of John Bethune and John

MacLeod in about 1773. He organized the present-day Barbecue Presbyterian Church near Broadway, Bluff Presbyterian Church near Wade, and Longstreet Presbyterian Church (now discontinued) at Fort Bragg.

The American Revolution divided the Highland Scots of North Carolina. For the most part, the older settlers were Patriots, the more recent ones Loyalists. One Sunday morning at Barbecue, Campbell forgot his congregation and prayed for the success of the American arms. After the service he was approached by an old Tory Scot, McAlpin Munn, who said, in effect, "If ever you pray again as you did this day, the bullet is molded and the powder is in my horn to blow it through your head." Campbell for the second time quit the ministry. A few weeks later, however, he happened to overhear an elderly woman cursing and was shocked. When he rebuked her, she replied, "Is it any wonder the devil can make the mouth of the woman to swear when he can stop the mouth of the minister?" Her words moved him to resume the ministry, but this time in Guilford County, a safe distance from McAlpin Munn and his bullet mold and powder horn.

In 1780, feeling his life fast drawing to a close, Campbell returned to his home on the Cape Fear. He was buried on his own land, on a bluff overlooking the river.

SEE: R. S. Arrowood, MS on James Campbell (Office, Synod of North Carolina, Presbyterian Church U.S., Raleigh); William Henry Foote, *Sketches of North Carolina, Historical and Biographical* (1846); Malcolm Fowler, *They Passed This Way* (1955); *George Whitefield's Journal* (1960).

JAMES MACKENZIE

Campbell, James Archibald (13 Jan. 1862–18 March 1934), educator and Baptist minister, was born in Harnett County, between the towns of Angier and Fuquay. He was the only surviving child of Archibald Neill Campbell and Huma Maniza Betts Campbell. The Campbells date their entrance into America from 1739, when a boat-load of Scots known as "The Legion of Restless Men" came to the Cape Fear Valley, in the general area of Fayetteville. The father of James Archibald Campbell, known as "Mr. Archie," was a part-time farmer, sometime blacksmith, and full-time Baptist preacher. He organized sixteen Baptist churches and baptized more than a thousand persons, the first of whom was his son James Archibald.

When young Campbell was six years old, he attended for a few months a one-room subscription school near his home. At the age of ten, he, along with his father, enrolled in a grammar school, also near his home. When he was seventeen, he attended for one year a boarding school in Apex. The following year he entered Oakdale Academy in Alamance County, near the town of Graham. He stayed there for two years and then was asked to assume the leadership of a newly organized school, Union Academy, in his home community. As principal of this school he was successful and was urged to continue, but he was eager for additional schooling himself. On his birthday in 1885 he became a student at Wake Forest College, where he remained for three school terms; in the spring of 1886, his financial situation made it necessary for him to return home, and his formal education ended for the time. In 1911 he and his two sons received the A.B. degree from Wake Forest College. In 1926 the college awarded him the honorary D.D. degree.

On 5 Jan. 1887, Campbell opened a private academy, under his ownership, at Buies Creek. He was to get no salary for his teaching, his only compensation coming

from the small tuition paid by his students. There were sixteen of these on the first morning: Buies Creek, a community of seven families, had been without a school for three years. The school took as its motto, "Ad Astra per Aspera"—To the Stars through Difficulty. The school grew until by 1900 it was one of the largest private academies in the state. Then on the night of 20 Dec. 1900 the school burned; arson was suspected. The only building left was a large floorless tabernacle used for commencement gatherings. This was equipped with rough benches, and the school reopened at the scheduled time in January 1901. Again it prospered.

In 1925, Campbell presented the school to the North Carolina Baptist State Convention. He had spent thirty-eight years in building it, and the property was valued at a half million dollars. Campbell received a little less than twenty-five thousand dollars, the figure he had suggested, but he continued to operate the school. In 1926 the institution was elevated to the status of a junior college, and the name was changed from Buies Creek Academy to Campbell Junior College.

Campbell was an active Christian minister as well as an educator and pastored Baptist churches during all the years he headed the school. There were times when he was pastor of five churches simultaneously. His school at Buies Creek was only four years old when he became pastor of the local Baptist church. In 1895 he resigned as pastor of the church, but in 1898 he accepted the position again and kept it until he died. During these years he was active in his denomination. He served as trustee of Wake Forest College for an unusually long time, long enough to vote for three presidents of the institution. He was also a member of the Democratic party.

On 18 Nov. 1890, Campbell married Cornelia Frances Pearson. Three children were born to them: Leslie Hartwell, who succeeded his father as president of Campbell College; Carlyle, president of Coker College in Hartsville, S.C., and Meredith College in Raleigh; and Mrs. Bessie Campbell Lynch, who taught music at Campbell for more than forty years, much of the time as head of the department.

Campbell's portrait hangs in the president's office at Campbell College. His body rests in the village cemetery near the school he founded. On 1 Apr. 1971, his name was entered into the North Carolina Education Hall of Fame.

SEE: Campbell College Archives, Carrie Rich Memorial Library (Buies Creek), for *Creek Pebbles* (college newspaper) and *Little River Record*, ed. J. A. Campbell; *North Carolina Baptist State Convention Annual*, 1912–34; J. Winston Pearce, *Campbell College* (1975); Raleigh *Biblical Recorder*, scattered issues.

J. WINSTON PEARCE

Campbell, John (ca. 1700–1781), legislator, political leader, and merchant, is believed to have been a native of northern Ireland, possibly from the town of Coleraine. He purchased land in Hertford (then Bertie) County in 1737 and by or before 1743 was settled as a merchant at Edenton. He seems to have been associated in these early years with Benjamin Hill of Bertie, whose daughter Mary he married before 1740. By 1747 he had moved to Lazy Hill Plantation on the Chowan River in Bertie, where he remained for the rest of his life.

Campbell became politically active in 1744 with his election to the House of Burgesses from Chowan County. Following in the political footsteps of his father-in-law, he succeeded Benjamin Hill as one of the leaders of the northern faction who opposed Governor Gabriel

Johnston's efforts to equalize the representation of southern and northern counties in the colonial legislature. He served as a commissioner for the Port of Roanoke in 1752 and in 1754 was elected to another term in the legislature. At this session, the factional issue came to a head in a struggle over the speakership between supporters of Campbell and Samuel Swann. Each received twenty-two votes in the balloting, but Swann at length yielded and Campbell became speaker, a position he held for two years before resigning because of ill health. He was only intermittently active in public affairs for some years after this, holding among other minor positions, those of assistant judge in 1756 and mail contractor in 1757.

After almost a decade of ill health and attention mainly to his private interests, Campbell served again in the legislature from 1767 to 1769 as a representative from Bertie; he served yet again in 1773 and closed his public career after his election to the provincial congress at Halifax in 1776.

The basis of Campbell's political influence was the considerable estate he accumulated in North Carolina and his success in mercantile pursuits. Governor Arthur Dobbs in 1760 referred to him as "the most eminent Trader in this Province"; and his landed properties included thousands of acres in Bertie, Chowan, Hertford, and other eastern counties, besides 12,500 acres in Anson County. A French visitor at Lazy Hill in 1765 described him as "a man generally Esteemed, and of the greatest property of any man in this part of the province. . . ." A portion of his success may have been linked to his relations with Joseph Montfort and Alexander McCulloch, two other men of considerable wealth and influence who were also sons-in-law of Benjamin Hill.

In spite of an integrity that seems to have been universally acknowledged, Campbell's private life was for many of his later years a source of scandal and turbulence. Having discovered evidence in 1759 that his wife was involved in an affair with the family physician, Dr. Robert Lenox, Campbell brought suit against the doctor for having seduced Mrs. Campbell. The plaintiff won a heavy assessment of damages against Lenox, procured an annulment or divorce from Mary Hill Campbell, and, before the case against Lenox was well begun, married Mrs. Priscilla Curle, a widow of Hampton, Va. In 1763, two years after Campbell's marriage to Mrs. Curle, Lenox brought suit against him for slander and was awarded half the damages assessed against him in the seduction suit. Campbell's second marriage had in the meantime turned sour, and he procured a divorce from Mrs. Curle, a daughter of Virginia merchant Andrew Meade. Before he wrote his will in 1777, Campbell had procured a third wife, who had the good fortune to be a principal beneficiary of his will.

Campbell left two sons, James and John, and a daughter, Sarah, who married Richard Brownrigg of Chowan. All were children of his first wife. Family tradition recalls the patriarch as a man of decided convictions, who, as a loyal Church of England man, "would not suffer a Baptist to come within his gates." His irascibility caused him to be known even among his intimates as "the bear." Near the end of his life he mourned to Joseph Hewes that far too many were attempting to profit from the war with England, that avarice "is now the ruling passion. High and low, rich and poor, have cast off humanity and conscience in dealing. . . . The people, ignorant of their danger, continue gaming, trading, forestalling, extortion, etc.,

etc. They will neither pump nor bail. . . . " He trusted, nevertheless, that Hewes and his colleagues would conduct the ship of state "well into Liberty Harbour, there to moor her safely and to remain forever."

SEE: W. H. Bailey, "Provincial Reminiscences," *North Carolina University Magazine*, n.s. 10 (1890–91); "Journal of a French Traveller in the Colonies, 1765," *American Historical Review* 26 (1920–21); T. C. Parramore, "The Saga of 'the Bear' and the 'Evil Geniis,'" *Bulletin of the History of Medicine* 42 (1968); William L. Saunders, ed., *Colonial Records of North Carolina*, vols. 5–6 (1887–88); University of North Carolina (Chapel Hill) Clipping File.

THOMAS C. PARRAMORE

Campbell, John Charles (*14 Sept. 1867–2 May 1919*), educator and social reformer, was born in La Porte, Ind., to Gavin and Anna Barbara Kipp Campbell. He spent his youth in Wisconsin, where he was graduated from Stevens Point High School. After graduating from Williams College in 1892 and Andover Theological Seminary in 1895, he taught three years in a mountain school at Joppa, Ala., before returning to Stevens Point to teach for one year. He subsequently served as principal of the Pleasant Hill Academy in Tennessee and as superintendent of secondary education, and dean and president of Piedmont College, in Demorest, Ga. (1901–7).

Campbell's interest in the Appalachian region, especially the western counties of North Carolina, began during his work in the mountains as a young employee of his father's railroad company. In May 1908 he attended the National Conference of Charities and Corrections in Richmond, at which he explained to Mrs. John Glenn, wife of a Russell Sage Foundation official, his plans for making a comprehensive survey of the region. Provided funds by the foundation, he and his wife, Olive Dame Campbell, traveled throughout the region until October 1912. Then the foundation created a Southern Highlands Division, of which Campbell became chief executive officer. Offices were established in March 1913 in Asheville, where the Campbells made their home until his death.

The aims of the division were to assemble and disseminate accurate information on economic, cultural, and social conditions in the region; to promote interagency cooperation; and to redirect philanthropic work toward the finding of viable alternatives for economic and social organization. In 1913, Campbell issued a call that resulted in the formation of the Conference of Southern Mountain Workers (now the Council on the Southern Mountains), of which he served as executive secretary until his death. The conference, an annual forum for discussion among teachers, preachers, social workers, and others in the mountains, in turn formed the Southern Highlands Handicraft Guild fifteen years later.

Throughout his years of work in the mountains, Campbell collected materials for a comprehensive survey of the Appalachian region. At his death, only the preface and one chapter of his projected book had been written; from his notes, his wife completed the writing. *The Southern Highlander and His Homeland*, published in 1921, immediately became and has remained after more than a half century one of the most comprehensive and durable studies of the region. In it the Campbells argued, as they did in many other contexts, that effective work for social change in the mountains should respect and seek to preserve the rich cultural heritage of the region and its people. Toward that end, Campbell studied intensively the Danish folk schools and other experiments in the use of traditional culture as a base for progressive social reconstruction. After his death, his wife established on the Danish model the John C. Campbell Folk School at Brasstown.

Campbell was married first to Grace H. Buckingham, who died in 1905. His second wife was Olive A. Dame of Medford, Mass., whom he married on 21 Mar. 1907 and by whom he had two children, Barbara and Jane, both of whom died in infancy. He was a member of the Congregational church.

SEE: John C. Campbell, *The Future of the Church and Independent Schools in Our Southern Mountains* (1917), "Mountain and Rural Fields of the South," *Annual Report of the Home Missions Council* (1916), *Piedmont College* (n.d.), "Social Betterment in the Southern Mountains," *Proceedings of the National Conference of Charities and Corrections* (1909), and *The Southern Highlander and His Homeland* (1921; rpt., 1969); John M. Glenn, *The Russell Sage Foundation* (1947); *Mountain Life and Work* 4 (memorial issue, April 1928 [photograph]); Henry D. Shapiro, Introduction to *The Southern Highlander and His Homeland*; Southern Historical Collection (University of North Carolina, Chapel Hill), for Campbell's personal papers; David E. Whisnant, "Controversy in God's Grand Division: The Transformation of the Council of the Southern Mountains," *Appalachian Journal* 2 (1974); *Who Was Who in America*, vol. 1 (1943).

DAVID E. WHISNANT

Campbell, Leslie Hartwell (3 Apr. 1892–25 Nov. 1970), educator, was born at Buies Creek. He was the oldest of the three children, two boys and one girl, of James Archibald Campbell, founder of Campbell College, and Cornelia Frances Pearson Campbell. His first Campbell ancestor in the New World was James Campbell, a Scotsman by blood, who came to North Carolina from the North of Ireland before the American Revolution. Leslie Campbell's paternal grandfather was the Reverend Archibald Neill Campbell, a long-time Baptist minister in the Harnett County area. Leslie's brother, Carlyle, served consecutively as president of Coker College, Hartsville, S.C., chairman of the Department of English, North Carolina State College, and president of Meredith College. His sister, Bessie Campbell Lynch, taught music at Campbell College and its predecessor institution, Buies Creek Academy.

Campbell received his elementary and secondary education at Buies Creek Academy, which was operated by his parents. In 1908 he entered Wake Forest College, where three years later he received the A.B. degree, *magna cum laude*, graduating in the same class with his father and his brother. The following autumn, he began teaching at Buies Creek Academy. He lived at home and, though he was given no salary, he received money from his father as needed. In 1916 he received the A.M. degree from Wake Forest College, and at about the same time he left teaching to operate a large general store in Buies Creek. In 1920 he returned to Buies Creek Academy, where he taught in the various grades. The academy then operated the public schools of its community and in fact continued to do so until 1946.

In 1925 the Baptist State Convention of North Carolina acquired Buies Creek Academy from J. A. Campbell for less than $25,000. The following year the academy became Buies Creek Junior College, adding the first two years of college work to the courses it continued to offer

at the elementary and secondary levels. Leslie Campbell was appointed the first dean of the new college. In 1926 the Baptist State Convention changed the school's name to Campbell College in honor of its founder, Leslie's father, who remained president until his death in 1934. Leslie Campbell succeeded his father as president of the college, which then had an enrollment of only 312 students and was facing serious financial problems brought on by the depression. During his first year as president, Campbell's salary was less than one thousand dollars.

From 1934, the first year of Campbell's presidency, to 1937, the Baptist State Convention was unable to give the college any financial support. Vegetables and other produce were frequently accepted in payment of tuition and fees. After 1937 the state convention resumed financial support, and in 1941 the school received full regional accreditation as a junior college.

Campbell College grew rapidly after World War II. Between 1954 and 1959 at least one major building a year was added to the campus, and by the later year enrollment had climbed to over nine hundred students. In 1961 the college became a senior institution, and sixty-nine-year-old Campbell embarked upon perhaps the busiest and most challenging eight years of his life. In November 1966 the college received full regional accreditation as a four-year liberal arts college, and on 1 June of the following year, Campbell retired as president. During the thirty-three years of his presidency, the school had grown from a struggling junior college of slightly over 300 students to a fully accredited four-year college with an enrollment of over 2,200 and a faculty of over 120, located on 570 acres, with total financial assets of over $7,000,000 and an annual operating budget of over $2,700,000.

A Democrat and a Baptist, Campbell was active in community and denominational as well as educational affairs. He served as trustee of both Pittman Hospital and Good Hope Hospital, president of the Harnett County Centennial Association (1955) and of the Harnett County Historical Society (1956), director of the Capital Area Development Association (1956), moderator of the Little River Baptist Association (1937–54), and first president of the Association of Eastern North Carolina Colleges (1966). In 1930 he was vice-president of the Baptist State Convention. He served for many years as a deacon of the Buies Creek First Baptist Church and was a principal founder of the Memorial Baptist Church, Buies Creek. In 1955 his alma mater, Wake Forest College, recognized his achievements as an educator and civic leader by bestowing upon him the honorary LL.D. degree.

In 1914, Campbell married Viola Haire of Cumberland County, who died in 1920. They had one son, Arthur Hartwell, state legislator and pioneer television executive. In 1925, Campbell married Ora Green, who survived him. With her he had four children: Catherine McLean Campbell King, Elizabeth Pearson Campbell Dail, Ora Green Campbell Elyson, and James Archibald, a physician in Charlotte. In the spring of 1970 Campbell suffered a severe heart attack from which he never recovered. He died of heart failure in Rex Hospital, Raleigh. Following funeral services in the Turner Chapel of Campbell College on 27 Nov., he was buried in the Buies Creek Cemetery. A portrait by William Fields hangs in the foyer of the president's office on the campus of Campbell College.

SEE: Campbell College Archives, Carrie Rich Memorial Library (Buies Creek), for files of college publications and other materials; *Durham Morning Herald*, 13 May 1962;

Fayetteville Observer, 30 Aug. 1959; *Harnett County News*, 20 July 1961; *North Carolina Baptist State Convention Annual*, 1934–70; Raleigh *Biblical Recorder*, scattered issues; Raleigh *News and Observer*, 12 Sept. 1954, 10 May 1961; *Raleigh Times*, 29 Aug. 1959.

W. CONARD GASS

Campbell, Olive Dame *(11 Mar. 1882–14 June 1954)*, founder of the John C. Campbell Folk School, was born to Lorin Low and Isabel Arnold Dame in Medford, Mass. She married John C. Campbell on 21 Mar. 1907 and moved to the mountains of north Georgia, where her husband was president of Piedmont College. From 1908 to 1912 she accompanied him through the mountains of Tennessee, Kentucky, Georgia, West Virginia, and North Carolina, surveying social and economic conditions. After 1913 she established residence in Asheville, where her husband was chief executive officer of the Southern Highlands Division of the Russell Sage Foundation. At his death in 1919, only the preface and first chapter of a projected study of the Appalachian region had been written; she completed the manuscript, which was published under her husband's name as *The Southern Highlander and His Homeland* in 1921.

During her early travels in the mountains, Mrs. Campbell began collecting traditional ballads and songs. She soon concluded, as she wrote in the *Survey* in 1915, that "the rich store still hidden away in the mountains has only been touched." Hearing in 1916 that the English collector Cecil J. Sharp was in the United States, she journeyed to Lincoln, Mass., to show him her collection. Their subsequent collaboration during a nine-week collecting trip produced major finds in such North Carolina locations as Hot Springs ("The False Knight upon the Road" and "Black Is the Color of My True Love's Hair"), White Rock ("Earl Brand"), Allanstand ("Lord Randall" and "Pretty Saro"), Big Laurel ("Cherry Tree Carol"), Allegheny ("The Wife of Usher's Well" and "The Wagoner's Lad"), Black Mountain ("The Maid Freed from the Gallows"), Spillcorn ("Hicks's Farewell"), and elsewhere. Of the 122 songs and ballads included in the collection published by Olive Dame Campbell and Cecil J. Sharp in 1917, *English Folk Songs from the Southern Appalachians*, thirty-nine had been collected by Mrs. Campbell before her expedition with Sharp.

After her husband's death, Mrs. Campbell became executive secretary of the Conference of Southern Mountain Workers, which he had founded; she held the position until 1928. In 1921 she joined the staff of the Russell Sage Foundation. Her lifelong interest in using traditional folk culture as a basis for social reconstruction led her in 1922 to accept a Scandinavian-American Foundation fellowship for an eighteen-month study of adult education in the Scandinavian folk schools.

In late 1925 she returned to North Carolina and established the John C. Campbell Folk School in Brasstown. In an adult education curriculum modeled upon the Scandinavian experience, the school offered courses in arts, crafts, music, dancing, agriculture, forestry, the organization and operation of cooperatives, and other subjects and skills judged necessary to improve the economic and social life of the community. In 1928, Mrs. Campbell published *The Danish Folkschool: Its Influence in the Life of Denmark and the North*. In 1928–29 she was instrumental in establishing the Southern Highlands Handicraft Guild, a marketing organization

for mountain craftsmen that maintains its headquarters in Asheville.

Mrs. Campbell's writings also include "Songs and Ballads of the Southern Mountains," *Survey* 33 (1915); "The Southern Highlands: A Selected Bibliography," *Bulletin of the Russell Sage Foundation*, 39 (February 1920); the compilation *Southern Highland Schools Maintained by Denominational and Independent Agencies* (New York: Russell Sage Foundation, 1921); *Adult Education in Scandinavia and America: Two Addresses Delivered at the Conference of Southern Mountain Workers, Knoxville, Tennessee, April 8–10, 1924* (New York: Conference of Southern Mountain Workers, 1924); "Flame of a New Future in the Highlands," *Mountain Life and Work* 1 (1925); "Adult Education as a Means of Vitalizing and Enriching American Life" and "Adjustment to Rural Change with Special Reference to Mountain Areas," in *Addresses and Proceedings of the National Education Association* (1929); "I Sing behind the Plow," *Journal of Adult Education* 2 (1930); *Singing Games Old and New* (Swannanoa, N.C.: Asheville Farm School, 1933); "Whittling: An American Folk Art," *School Arts* 45 (1946); "They Whittle While They Work," *American Magazine* 142 (1946); and *The Life and Work of John C. Campbell* (Madison, Wisc.: College Printing Co., 1968).

SEE: *Asheville Citizen-Times*, 16 June 1954 (obit.); Frederick L. Brownlee, *The John C. Campbell Folk School* (1952); John M. Glenn, *The Russell Sage Foundation*, vol. 1 (1947); Pat McNelley, *The First Forty Years: John C. Campbell Folk School* (1966); *Mountain Life and Work* 30 (1954); Southern Historical Collection (University of North Carolina, Chapel Hill), for Mrs. Campbell's diaries, MSS, and other personal papers (John C. Campbell Papers).

DAVID E. WHISNANT

Campbell, Robert Fishburne *(12 Dec. 1858–3 Apr. 1947)*, Presbyterian clergyman, was born the son of John Lyle and Harriet Hatch Bailey Campbell at Lexington, Va., where his father was a member of the faculty of Washington College (later Washington and Lee University). For five years during his early boyhood he was next-door neighbor to General Robert E. Lee. He attended Washington and Lee, graduating in 1878 with the B.A. degree, and after a year of further study he received the M.A. degree. Following a period of teaching in West Virginia and in his native state (1879–82), he entered Union Theological Seminary in Virginia; he was graduated in 1885.

Licensed on 30 Aug. 1884 and ordained to the gospel ministry on 18 May 1885 by Lexington Presbytery of the Presbyterian Church, U.S., he served as pastor of the Millboro and Windy Cove churches in Virginia from 1885 to 1889. After other pastorates at Davidson (1889–90) and Buena Vista, Va. (1890–92), he went to the First Presbyterian Church of Asheville in 1892. There he remained until his retirement in 1938, when he became pastor emeritus. The Campbell Memorial Chapel of the Asheville church bears testimony to the esteem in which he was held by the congregation. His denominational service included membership on a number of important committees of the general assembly and on the boards of several influential institutions. He was the moving spirit in the formation of the Synod of Appalachia in 1915 and the leader in organization of the interdenominational Good Samaritan Mission of Asheville in 1911.

Campbell was distinguished as a leader in the civic, as well as religious, life of Asheville, and for years was widely regarded as its first citizen. Davidson College conferred upon him the degree of D.D. in 1893. His denomination honored him with the highest elective office at its disposal when its general assembly chose him as moderator in 1927. In 1930 he delivered the Sprunt Lectures at Union Seminary in Virginia; these appeared in book form during the same year under the title *Freedom and Restraint*.

On 8 Oct. 1885, Campbell married Sarah Montgomery Ruffner of Lexington, Va., who died in 1917. They were the parents of one son, William Henry Ruffner, (b. 17 Dec. 1890). Campbell's second marriage was to Julia Berryman of Shelbyville, Ky., and took place on 18 June 1919. To this union, Robert Fishburne, Jr., was born on 10 Jan. 1921. Campbell died in Asheville and was buried in the city's Riverside Cemetery. His portrait is in the First Presbyterian Church of Asheville.

SEE: Ora Blackmun, *A Spire in the Mountains* (1970); C. Grier Davis, in Presbyterian Church in the U.S., *Minutes*, Synod of Appalachia (1947); Historical Foundation (Montreat), for the Campbell papers; E. C. Scott, comp., *Ministerial Directory of the Presbyterian Church, U.S.* (1942).

THOMAS H. SPENCE, JR.

Campbell, Samuel (*d. ca. 1790*), Loyalist militia colonel, was a native of North Carolina and a Wilmington merchant in partnership with Robert Hogg. In 1771 he embodied and led a company against the Regulators at Alamance. He raised a group of loyal militia from Wilmington for the Moore's Creek Bridge campaign and suffered some harassment from the committee of safety after their defeat. Campbell took the state oath of allegiance but avoided militia service by moving to the country and hiring a substitute. When the British forces reached Wilmington in 1781, he joined them as a militia captain and accompanied them on the evacuation to Charles Town. There he was colonel commandant of the North Carolina loyal militia and as such was the highest ranking refugee in the evacuation of the British forces from Charles Town to Nova Scotia. By May 1783 he was in Shelburne, Nova Scotia, with his family and several slaves. Campbell's wife, Alice, was Robert Hogg's widow; their son, Samuel, was born in Shelburne in 1788. Campbell received a warehouse lot and a wharf lot in Shelburne and fifty acres nearby, but he did not prosper. He received some money from Hogg's brother in Wilmington, who had managed to retain some of their property.

Apparently Campbell died in Shelburne, for his widow was living there in 1792, when she married Colin Campbell, a prominent lawyer who had gone from Scotland to New York at the beginning of the war. Samuel Campbell, Jr., became a justice of the peace and from 1820 through 1826 was a member of the Nova Scotia Legislative Assembly from Annapolis County.

SEE: Walter Clark, ed., *State Records of North Carolina*, vol. 24 (1905); Marion Gilroy, comp., *Loyalists and Land Settlement in Nova Scotia* (1937); Public Archives of Canada, British Headquarters Papers, No. 5951 (Ottawa); Public Archives of Nova Scotia, *A Directory of the Members of the Legislative Assembly of Nova Scotia* (1958); P.R.O., A.O. 13:138; ibid., T. 50:1 and 5.

CAROLE WATTERSON TROXLER

Cannon, Charles Albert (*29 Nov. 1892–2 Apr. 1971*), textile manufacturer, was born in Concord, one of ten children and the youngest of six sons born to James William Cannon, who founded Cannon Mills, and Mary Ella Bost Cannon.

At nineteen, Cannon quit school to enter the textile business, which held a lasting fascination for him. He became manager of the family-owned Barringer Manufacturing Company in Rockwell. He became Cannon Manufacturing Company's vice-president in 1916, and president of Cannon Mills in 1921, upon his father's death. Two years later he was named head of Cannon Mills, Inc., the company's New York selling agent.

Cannon was a textile marketing pioneer. His innovations included national consumer advertising, an individual trademark sewn on each towel and sheet, pastel colors, use of clear plastic wrappings for each product, matching towel ensembles, and trade style shows. Cannon Mills's product line was expanded to include sheets, hosiery, bedspreads, draperies, decorative fabrics, and blankets. Sales at the time of Cannon's death exceeded $305 million. His company dominated over 50 percent of the nation's towel business and over 20 percent of the sheet business. In these areas, Cannon Mills were "the professionals in the white goods business."

Cannon Mills were vertically integrated, all the way from raw cotton to the final product. Nearly all of the seventeen plants were located within a twenty-five-mile radius, and the company was totally dominated by Cannon. "Mr. Charlie," as he was affectionately called, was publicity shy but was nonetheless a vigorous business leader, a courtly competitor, a benevolent textile baron, and a community autocrat.

Kannapolis, which Cannon envisioned as a model mill town in the architectural image of Colonial Williamsburg, is the nation's largest unincorporated town (population over thirty-six thousand). Cannon politically dominated both "his" city and Cabarrus County. He served on the state highway and public works commissions and the state parks commission. In 1965, Duke University conferred a LL.D. on him. While he was a most inconspicuous man, he was generous to medical and educational causes, aiding Cabarrus Memorial Hospital, which he served as board chairman, and a memorial hospital at Banner Elk, named in honor of his son, Charles A., Jr., who died in World War II.

Cannon married Ruth Louise Coltrane, the daughter of a Concord banker, on 5 June 1912. She died in 1965 after a long illness. They had four children: Charles A., Jr., William C., Marian, and Mary Ruth. By the time of his death, Cannon had built a remarkably stable textile empire of nearly $250 million in equity without a single dollar of long-term debt.

SEE: *Forbes*, 15 July 1972; *Fortune*, February 1966; *Newsweek*, 12 Apr. 1971; *New York Times*, 3 Apr. 1971; *Time*, 12 Apr. 1971.

MARVIN KRIEGER

Cannon, James, III (*30 Nov. 1892–9 Mar. 1960*), clergyman and theological educator, was born the son of Bishop James, Jr., and Lois Virginia Bennett Cannon in Farmville, Va. His secondary education was completed at Webb School, Bell Buckle, Tenn., in 1910. He graduated from Trinity College (now Duke University) with a B.A. degree in 1914; from Princeton University, Princeton, N.J., with an M.A. in 1917; and from Princeton Theological Seminary with a Bachelor of Theology and Master of Theology in 1925. He studied at New College, Edinburgh, Scotland, in 1919 and at Garrett Biblical Institute, Evanston, Ill., between 1924 and 1927. He was awarded honorary degrees by Birmingham-Southern, Birmingham, Ala. (D.D., 1934), and by Kentucky Wesleyan College, Owensboro, Ky. (LL.D., 1936).

Cannon was editor of the *Richmond Virginian* and business manager of the *Christian Advocate* in 1914–15. Following his graduation from Princeton, he was an army YMCA worker in the United States, France, and Italy in 1917–18. He was ordained in the Methodist Episcopal Church, South, in 1917 and served as a chaplain, first lieutenant, AEF, in 1918–19. He received France's Croix de Guerre while senior chaplain, First Division.

Cannon returned to Trinity College in 1919 as assistant professor of biblical literature and Christian missions, becoming professor of the history of religion and missions in the School of Religion (now Divinity School) of Duke University in 1926. He was dean of the Duke University Divinity School from 1951 to 1958 and dean emeritus from 1958 to 1960. He was a member of Sigma Chi, Professors of Missions in Eastern Universities (president, 1941), and Phi Beta Kappa (chairman, South Atlantic District, in 1952; secretary of the Duke chapter from 1953 to 1960); and South Atlantic District senator from 1953 to 1960).

Cannon was the author of *History of Southern Methodist Missions* (1926) and (with H. E. Spence) *A Guide to the Study of the English Bible* (1926); he served as advisory editor of *The Muslim World* (1947–55). He was a scholarly and popular pulpiteer and lecturer, an astute teacher and counselor to college students, a respected and efficient theological education administrator, and a highly effective leader in the councils of his church.

He was married 22 Dec. 1920 to Margaret Wagner Few; they had two sons, James (deceased in his youth) and Walter Few. Cannon died in Durham, with interment in Maplewood Cemetery.

SEE: *Durham Morning Herald*, 10 Mar. 1960; Data Files (Office of Information Services, Duke University, Durham); *Who's Who in the Clergy*, vol. 1 (1936); *Who Was Who in America*, vol. 3 (1960).

C. SYLVESTER GREEN

Cannon, James William (*25 Apr. 1852–19 Dec. 1921*), textile manufacturer, was born near Sugaw Creek Church in Mecklenburg County. His father was Joseph Allison Cannon and his mother, Eliza Long. As a boy he worked on his father's farm and attended private school in the session house of the Sugaw Creek Presbyterian Church. At the age of thirteen he went to Charlotte and worked in a general store, where he was paid at first only room and board and later four dollars a month. In 1868 he moved to Concord and was employed as a clerk in the general store of Cannon, Fetzer, and Wadsworth, in which his brother, David Franklin, was a partner. Within three years, he was able to purchase an interest in the store, and he became active head of the business. During the next fifteen years, he developed this mercantile operation into one of Concord's leading firms. He became a leader of the community and took an interest in its business and social life.

Cannon's career as an industrialist was exemplary of the economic movement in the late nineteenth century that became known as the New South. As chief cotton purchaser for his store, he noted the weak economic structure in the Piedmont of North Carolina, whereby farmers sold cheap raw materials to northern manufacturers and in turn bought expensive finished goods. Like some of his more ambitious contemporaries,

he set out to develop the local industrial potential of his community as a means of escaping this ruinous business cycle. In 1887 he founded the Cannon Manufacturing Company. In this venture he himself was dependent upon outside capital to supplement his own investment. He borrowed seventy-five thousand dollars from northern banks and enlisted the technical assistance of the McGill and Wood Manufacturing Company of Philadelphia. Cannon's experience was in trading cotton, not processing it, and in this respect he was typical of many textile pioneers in the South. The testimony of a former employee, who went to work at the first Cannon plant in Concord at age eleven, recalled that Cannon was acutely aware of his lack of technical knowledge: "He would often come to the mill and look me up, a small boy, and ask me to show him how to operate the machinery. I remember very distinctly teaching him how to put up ends on the spinning frames and to dolph and many other things. At one time when we were cleaning and overhauling the spinning frames, Mr. Cannon donned blue overalls and came into the mill and worked by my side helping in this that he might get this experience. He asked many questions about the work and I tried in my boyish way to answer them."

This first mill, which operated at the site of the present Plant Number 2 in Concord, was completed in 1888. John M. Odell, then Concord's most prominent manufacturer, served as president of the company, and Cannon was secretary-treasurer as well as general manager and superintendent. The plant was small, only four thousand spindles and a few looms, but Cannon cloth rapidly achieved widespread popularity in the South, and by 1900 the company had expanded to Salisbury, Albemarle, Mt. Pleasant, and China Grove. Cannon's success was due in great measure to his marketing skill and his ability to develop a sophisticated sales organization. It was his marketing sense that led to the change in 1898 from Cannon cloth to Cannon towels, the first ever produced in the South. Cannon recognized that the era of home sewing was passing and that the cloth market was becoming more competitive. He also realized that middle- and lower-class southerners could not purchase towels cheaply.

Ultimately, Cannon decided to manufacture towels exclusively, a decision that led to the establishment of Kannapolis in 1906. This mill village was originally founded upon a six-hundred-acre tract of land seven miles from Concord on the border of Rowan and Cabarrus counties. As the Cannon empire grew— eventually plants were established in South Carolina, Georgia, and Alabama—Kannapolis became its capital, one of the world's largest unincorporated towns. Designed by E. S. Draper and Company, Kannapolis provided its inhabitants with religious, educational, and recreational facilities. Schools, parks, churches, dormitories, and the South's largest YMCA were built, owned, and operated by the company. The Cannon Manufacturing Company, which became the largest producer of towels in the world, and Kannapolis, sometimes known as City of Towels, stood as the capstones to Cannon's career.

Cannon was married on 24 Nov. 1875 to Mary Ella Bost of Concord. They had ten children: Joseph Franklin, Adelaide, Margaret, James William, Mary, Martin Luther, Eugene Thomas, James Ross, Charles Albert, and Laura. Cannon was a member of the Masonic Order, a political independent, and an active member of the First Presbyterian Church in Concord. He was buried in Oakwood Cemetery in Concord. A portrait is owned by the Cannon family.

SEE: James L. Moore and Thomas H. Wingate, *Cabarrus Reborn* (1940); James E. Smoot Collection (North Carolina State Archives, Raleigh); Gary Trawick and Paul Wyche, *One Hundred Years, One Hundred Men* (1971); Marjorie W. Young, *Textile Leaders of the South* (1963).

BRENT D. GLASS

Cannon, Joseph Gurney (*7 May 1836–12 Nov. 1926*), congressman and speaker of the U.S. House of Representatives, was born in New Garden, Guilford County, the son of Gulielma Hollingsworth and Dr. Horace Franklin Cannon, one of the founders of Guilford College. The family moved to Indiana when Cannon was six and afterward moved to Illinois. Cannon had a common school education and spent six months at the Cincinnati Law School; he was awarded an honorary LL.D. degree in 1903 by the University of Illinois. Admitted to the bar in 1858, he practiced first in Terre Haute, Ind., but within a few months moved to Tuscola, Ill. In that state he served as district attorney general from 1861 to 1868. He was elected as a Republican to Congress; during his service there (1873–91, 1893–1913, and 1915–23), he epitomized a certain style of congressional behavior, the man of pungent language, rough manners, decidedly illiberal views, and autocratic parliamentary authority. He was speaker of the House from 1903 to 1911 and received fifty-eight votes for the presidential nomination at the Republican National Convention in Chicago in 1908.

In Congress, Cannon served on the Committee on Post Offices and Post Roads; was a member of the Holman Commission, which investigated conditions on Indian reservations; and was active in the consideration of governmental reforms, in the currency and tariff debates, in the advocacy of a larger navy and reorganization of the army, and in the discussion of shipping and the Isthmian canal. He declined appointment to the peace commission after the War with Spain. As speaker he exemplified strong one-man rule, but he was finally defeated as speaker by a coalition of younger men from both parties; for many years afterward the House speakership was held by leaders of a different style. Nevertheless, Cannon, often known as "Uncle Joe," was popular personally. The first office building for congressmen in Washington was named for him—Cannon House Office Building—and there are four portraits and a bust of him on Capitol Hill.

Cannon married Mary P. Reed in January 1862; they were the parents of two daughters. He was a Quaker and remained proud of his North Carolina heritage, returning on occasion to visit the scene of his early childhood. He was buried in Spring Hill Cemetery, Danville, Ill.

SEE: *Biog. Dir. Am. Cong* (1971); *New York Times*, 13 Nov. 1926; W. H. Smith, *Speakers of the House of Representatives of the United States* (1928); *Who Was Who in America*, vol. 1 (1943).

ROY PARKER, JR.

Cannon, Newton (*22 May 1781–16 Sept. 1841*), military officer, congressman, and governor of Tennessee, was born in Guilford County, the son of Minos and Letitia Thompson Cannon. His father was a revolutionary soldier, and his grandfather, Richard Thompson, was said to have been the first man to fall at the Battle of Alamance in 1771. Cannon was educated in local schools and learned the saddler's trade. With his parents, brothers, and sisters, he moved to the frontier settlement in the Cumberland Valley of present Tennessee after the Revolution; the family returned to North Carolina until late in 1790 but then went back to Tennessee. In the Guilford County returns of the 1790 census, Minas [*sic*] Cannon's name appears.

Although Cannon's education was limited, he was a clerk, a merchant, a surveyor, and in time a wealthy planter of Williamson County, Tenn. He served briefly in the Creek War as colonel of a regiment of mounted volunteers. He served in the Tennessee Senate in 1811 and 1812 and again from 1829 to 1831. As a colonel of Tennessee Mounted Rifles during the War of 1812, he commanded the left column in the Battle of Tallushatchee on 3 Nov. 1813. He ran for Congress in 1810 but was overwhelmingly defeated by Felix Grundy; when Grundy resigned in 1814, Cannon was elected to succeed him. Except for one term, Cannon then served in Congress until 1823. He was a candidate for governor in 1827 but was defeated by Sam Houston. He served as an active member of the state constitutional convention in 1834 and in 1835 was elected the first Whig governor of Tennessee, serving until 1839, when he was defeated by James K. Polk. His administrations were characterized by considerable progress in state banking and internal improvements.

Cannon was married on 26 Aug. 1813 to Leah Pryor Perkins, who died three years later. On 27 Aug. 1818 he married Rachel Starnes Wellborn, eldest daughter of General James Wellborn of Wilkes County. Cannon was the father of eleven children. He was buried in the family cemetery on his estate near Allison, Williamson County, Tenn.

SEE: *DAB*, vol. 3 (1929); Family Bible and MSS (possessions of Mrs. Harry Evans, Nashville, Tenn.); Eugene Irving McCormac, *James K. Polk* (1922); *Nashville Whig*, 17 Sept. 1841; *Niles' Register*, 9 Oct. 1841; James Phelan, *History of Tennessee* (1885).

STANLEY FOLMSBEE

Cannon, Ruth Louise Coltrane (*15 Oct. 1891–22 Dec. 1965*), civic leader, preservationist, historian, and benefactor, was born in Cabarrus County, daughter of Mariam Winslow and Daniel Branson Coltrane. Her father was the founder of North Carolina's oldest national bank, Concord National Bank, and was a Civil War veteran. She was the wife of Charles A. Cannon, who was variously president and chairman of the board of Cannon Mills Company for fifty years. His father, James W. Cannon, founded the company in 1887.

Miss Coltrane was educated in the Concord public schools and was graduated *summa cum laude* from Greensboro College in 1911. An energetic and intelligent person, she never lost her love of learning. In 1965, Catawba College awarded her an honorary Litt.D. degree in recognition of her contributions to the cultural, educational, and religious life of the Concord-Kannapolis community and the state.

A history major in college, Mrs. Cannon kept this interest throughout her life. She was recognized as an authority on Cabarrus County history, especially the colonial and Confederate periods. She was chairman of the Cabarrus Committee of the National Society of the Colonial Dames of America and a member of the Daughters of the American Revolution, Daughters of the American Colonists, North Carolina Society of Descendents of the Pilgrims, Daughters of 1812, Daughters of Colonial Wars, and Colonial Dames Club of Washington, D.C. She served as chairman of the Confederate Museum in Memorial Hall in Concord. The Coltrane-

Harris chapter of the United Daughters of the Confederacy in Concord was named in honor of her father, and Mrs. Cannon was honorary president. She also served as president of the Dodson Ramseur chapter of the United Daughters of the Confederacy and was honorary president of the Ruth Coltrane Cannon chapter of the Children of Confederacy at Kannapolis. She played an active role for many years in the celebration of Confederate Memorial Day in Concord and especially enjoyed entertaining the hundreds of participating schoolchildren at her home, following ceremonies at the county's Confederate monument.

Mrs. Cannon worked throughout her life to bring an appreciation and better understanding of its heritage to North Carolina. She was the first woman to head the Roanoke Island Historical Association, which produces the *Lost Colony* historical drama. She also was interested in *Horn in the West*, an outdoor drama presented in Boone; an active supporter, she attended regularly. She took primary responsibility for the production of a volume listing all Cabarrus soldiers who participated in wars—*A History of Cabarrus County in the Wars*, privately published in memory of her father.

Active in restoration projects throughout the state, Mrs. Cannon collected data for a book, *Old Homes and Gardens of North Carolina*, which was published under her direction as chairman of the restoration committee of the North Carolina Garden Club. She also served on the steering committee of the North Carolina Society for the Preservation of Antiquities. She was president of this organization from its beginning and was named honorary life president. Annual teas honoring members and officers of this society were given by Mr. and Mrs. Cannon in their Blowing Rock home. She established, through this society, the Charles A. Cannon award, which has been given each year since 1948 for distinguished work in historical research, preservation, and restoration. An original member of the Tryon Palace Commission, Mrs. Cannon served the group for twenty years. She was also instrumental in such major restoration projects as Tryon Palace and Bath, as well as the creation of the Elizabethan garden at Manteo.

A skilled gardener, Mrs. Cannon promoted garden clubs and served for ten years as chairman of the life membership committee of the Garden Clubs of North Carolina. She was a member of the American Rose Society and the American Horticultural Society and organized the Concord Garden Club. Her love for gardens and restoration was exemplified in her work at her country home, For Pity's Sake, located on Lake Kannapolis. She devoted years to this home, which became famous for its antiques and gardens and attracted many visitors. Easter sunrise services for the community were a tradition in Kannapolis for many years.

Active in all phases of civic life, Mrs. Cannon helped start the Cabarrus Red Cross during World War II and served on the Concord School Board. She shared her husband's lifelong interest in Cabarrus Memorial Hospital. She helped organize the women's auxiliary there and compiled the group's cookbook. She and her husband also contributed to the Charles A. Cannon, Jr., Memorial Hospital at Banner Elk, named in memory of their son, who lost his life as an army pilot in World War II. The addition of the women's department of the Kannapolis YMCA in the 1930s was brought about by Mrs. Cannon. She contributed to the Church of God's Children's Home in Cabarrus County and the Grandfather Home for Children in Banner Elk. A dormitory at Wingate College was named in her honor to recognize her interest and contributions, and she also helped Lees-McRae College.

Mrs. Cannon inspired the rebuilding of Kannapolis's downtown business section. Harmonious colonial Williamsburg architecture was introduced in building programs of the early 1940s.

Music was an important part of Mrs. Cannon's life. She was instrumental in establishing the first music department in the Kannapolis schools, and the music building at A. L. Brown High School was dedicated to her memory in 1969. In the same year, the Cannon Music Camp was established at Appalachian State University, Boone, in her memory. There high school students receive four weeks of intensive training in music theory with individual lessons in their major instrument and group experience in ensemble, chorus, orchestra, and band. The university also named a residence hall in honor of Charles A. and Ruth Coltrane Cannon.

Mrs. Cannon was a member of the Central United Methodist Church until her marriage, when she joined the First Presbyterian Church in Concord. Mrs. and Mrs. Cannon gave a memorial organ to Central United Methodist Church in honor of her mother, Mrs. D. B. Coltrane. The Presbyterian church also benefited from their contributions, and Mrs. Cannon was active in several church departments.

Other organizations to which she belonged included the American War Mothers, Southern Historical Society, Mint Museum in Charlotte, Folklore Society, North Carolina Archaeology Society, North Carolina Symphony, and the study club affiliated with the North Carolina Federation of Women's Clubs. She was a director of the North Carolina State Art Society.

Ruth Coltrane was married 5 June 1912 to Charles A. Cannon. They were the parents of four children: William Coltrane of Concord; Mariam (Mrs. Robert) Hayes of Concord; Mary Ruth (Mrs. Richard) Spencer of Carmel, Calif.; and Charles A., Jr., who was killed in World War II.

Mrs. Cannon died at her home in Concord and was buried in Oakwood Cemetery there.

SEE: *Charlotte News*, 1 June 1965; Kannapolis *Daily Independent*, 23 Dec. 1965; *History of North Carolina*, vol. 3 (1956); Raleigh *News and Observer*, 30 Mar. 1958, 23 Dec. 1965; *Raleigh Times*, 2 Dec. 1965; personal papers in possession of the Cannon family, Concord; *Who's Who in the South and Southwest* (1961).

EDWARD L. RANKIN, JR.

Cantrell, John Roland (24 Apr. 1888–23 June 1968), minister, educator, and college president, was born in Spartanburg County, S.C., one of ten children of David L. and Elizabeth Cantrell. He attended the Baptist-supported Boiling Springs High School in North Carolina, completing his work there in 1919. Later he entered Wake Forest College, but not before facing a serious personal crisis: a call to the Christian ministry. Friends, well meaning, no doubt, urged him not to pull up stakes at the age of thirty-three, launch out on faith, and move his family to Wake Forest. But he obeyed the call, turning a deaf ear to those who tried to deter him. He sold his farm and horses and headed for Wake Forest, arriving there with about fifty dollars in his pocket. By working and borrowing, he obtained his degree from Wake Forest in 1924.

Even while a college student, he served as pastor of the Hillsborough Baptist Church. In 1928 he became an evangelist for the North Carolina Baptist State Convention. Some time thereafter he accepted a call to the Plymouth Baptist Church, serving there until 1931, when he resigned to become pastor at Newton. At the time of his arrival in Newton, the Sunday school enrolled about 200; when he left, enrollment averaged 367. Late in 1937 he felt called to accept the pastorate of the Calvary Baptist Church in Morganton, where he was to remain about two years, serving at the same time three small churches nearby.

In 1939, Cantrell left his pastoral duties in Morganton to become president of Boiling Springs Junior College, in which he had become interested while conducting a revival meeting at the Boiling Springs Baptist Church the previous summer. On 5 May the nominating committee of the board of trustees made official his election. His salary was set at two thousand dollars a year, plus an expense allowance, a home, and utilities.

Cantrell became interested in beautifying the college campus and set out trees and shrubbery, constructed walks, planted iris along the walks, built a lily pond, and added a porch to the boys' dormitory. To improve the appearance of the gymnasium—a storm-sheeted, weather-boarded, wooden frame building—Cantrell raised money, hired people to haul loads of rock to the campus from the fields of Cleveland County, and set rock masons to work on a project that ultimately cost seven thousand dollars. The result was a completely rock-veneered exterior.

During Cantrell's presidency, plans were carefully and quietly laid for the Greater Boiling Springs Junior College Campaign. On 21 Oct. 1941, the *Cleveland Times* broke the news in an extra edition: the campaign would seek to raise a hundred thousand dollars. Early the next year, former North Carolina Governor O. Max Gardner became interested in the college. Gardner is quoted as saying, "I've made all the money I want to make. Now I want a project." Boiling Springs Junior College seems to have been the project he wanted, and on 15 June 1942, the name of the college was changed to Gardner-Webb.

Gardner headed a blue ribbon committee of outstanding educators of North Carolina to survey the needs of the college. On 12 Nov. 1942 the committee reported and recommended that the college secure as president someone with a background more academic than Cantrell's. On 16 Apr. 1943, Cantrell submitted his resignation, to become effective 1 June.

But, at fifty-five years of age, Cantrell was not ready to be inactive. Immediately he reentered the Christian ministry full-time, accepting the pastorate of the Lattimore Baptist Church, from which he later retired as pastor emeritus. Gardner-Webb College eventually awarded him an honorary doctorate.

On 24 Nov. 1909, Cantrell married Lettie Henderson; to the union were born Letha Cantrell Cole, who died in a plane crash in 1949; Cletus H.; Dr. John W.; and Grace Cantrell Harmon. Cantrell was buried in the Cleveland Memorial Park in Boiling Springs.

SEE: *Biblical Recorder*, 17 Feb. 1968; Biography files, Baptist Historical Collection, Wake Forest University, Winston-Salem; Francis B. Dedmond, *Lengthened Shadows: A History of Gardner-Webb College, 1907–1957* (1957); North Carolina Baptist State Convention, *Minutes* (1967); *Wake Forest College Alumni Directory* (1961).

FRANCIS B. DEDMOND

Card, Wilbur Wade (9 Oct. 1873–3 Sept. 1948), director of physical education, was born in Franklinton, Franklin County, the son of Sabert Henry and Cecelia Bennett Fuller Card.

His preparatory schooling included attendance at the Franklinton Classical and Military Institute and at the Raleigh Male Academy. At both institutions his scholastic record showed superior grades, with an average consistently above 96; English, Latin, Greek, and mathematics were his major subjects. He entered Trinity College (now Duke University) in the fall of 1895, expecting to study to be a Methodist minister. His maternal grandfather and great-grandfather had been Christian ministers (Fuller Chapel near Kittrell was named for Jonathan Fuller, Card's great-grandfather). Later he changed his program and concentrated on athletics as a profession. That shift demanded an extra year of college, and he was graduated with the B.A. degree in 1900.

With the endorsement of three leading citizens of Durham—Benjamin N. Duke, Thomas J. Lambe, and J. H. Southgate, who became his bondsmen—Card was admitted to Harvard University, Cambridge, Mass., in the fall of 1900; there he took special courses in hygiene in 1900–1901. The following summer he was a student in the Sargent Normal School of Physical Education at Harvard, and he was graduated at the close of the 1902 summer session with a certificate indicating completion of the equivalent of four years of graduate work. He returned to Harvard every summer through 1913 and during two of those summers was an instructor in Hemenway Gymnasium, directed by the distinguished Dr. Dudley A. Sargent.

During his years as a student at Trinity College, Card was a member of the Columbian Society and competed on the track and baseball teams, the latter for all of his five years there; he was captain of the 1899 baseball team and from then on was known as "Cap." At Harvard he distinguished himself for his athletic prowess: he was ranked fifth among fifty strong men at Harvard and tenth among all collegians and was first in the backlift among all the college students participating in field trials at Harvard.

During the 1901–2 session, Card was director of physical education at the YMCA at Mobile, Ala. In the fall of 1902 he received an invitation from President J. C. Kilgo and returned to Trinity College, Durham, as director of physical education at the Angier Duke Gymnasium, a connection that continued for the rest of his life.

In the summer of 1914 Card worked in Baltimore, Md., in the city's recreation program; in 1915 he did similar work in Boston. During the First World War he was physical secretary at Camp Sevier, S.C., working for the National War Work Council of the YMCA. In appreciation of that work, he received a special certificate of commendation from the national office of the YMCA, signed by William Sloan, chairman, and J. R. Mott, general secretary. Beginning in 1923, he spent several summers as physical director of boys at Camp Etawah, Lake Junaluska, the Methodist Assembly Grounds.

Baseball was Card's favorite participatory sport. In addition to playing on the Trinity team, he played semipro baseball at Tarboro in the summer of 1898 and at Concord the following summer. The Boston National Baseball Team offered him a contract to play professional baseball in 1900, but he went to Harvard instead.

During the regular and summer sessions at Harvard, Card acquainted himself with all types of sports; he then brought back to Trinity for the student body there sports including gymnastics, association football, track, field hockey, bowling, swimming, fencing, volley ball, and basketball. He introduced basketball to North Carolina in 1905, and the first known collegiate game was played at

Trinity, 2 Mar. 1906, with the score Wake Forest, 8; Trinity, 6.

Card was widely recognized in his field. Beginning in 1921, he served as state chairman of the American Physical Education Association, and reports furnished by him were published in the *American Physical Education Review*. His staged gymnasium exhibitions were always popular attractions through the years. He was the marshal for the Collegiate Division of the First Annual Olympic Games held in Durham, 4–6 May 1922.

As his staff increased, and ultimately each sport had its special coaches, Card continued to find many things to keep him busy in the promotion of athletics at Trinity. He kept meticulous records, which, with a vast collection of clippings, are now preserved in special cases in the gymnasium at Duke. Those records served as the bases of a series of intriguing articles he wrote for the *State* magazine in the early 1940s. He told in fascinating style of the early athletes at Trinity, making multiple comparisons with more recent teams. He was proud of all of them and found it easy to write of superlatives: the best batter, the best fielder, the best pitcher, the best catcher, the best all-round player. He was also the author of *Health and Strength*, a packet of twenty-four illustrated positions for physical exercise, plus a list of sixteen health hints.

On 15 February 1953, the men's gymnasium on the Duke West Campus was designated the Wilbur Wade Card Gymnasium in memory of the one man who more than any other had framed the physical education and intercollegiate athletic program at Trinity/Duke, during forty-six years of service to that institution. That recognition capped a special ceremony held at the commencement luncheon on 29 May 1942, when a portrait of Card, painted by former student, Paul Whitener of Hickory, was presented to the university. It now hangs in the lobby of the new indoor stadium. In the presentation speech, Professor H. E. Spence of the Duke Divinity School, a member of the first basketball team at Trinity (1905–6), said, among other things: "'Cap's' greatest contribution . . . is in the realm of the intangible and the immeasurable. He has been a personal friend to thousands of discouraged young students. . . . No student was ever too insignificant to share his sympathetic attention. My most vivid recollection of him is his tireless attempt to teach a crippled boy the use of his helpless limbs. And many a man throughout the length and breadth of the world today owes his healthy body and fine frame of mind to the efforts of this man who cheered him on to success."

Card was married on 30 Dec. 1902 to Anna Luella Waldo, in Wyoming, Ohio. She was the daughter of Gersham Henry and Elizabeth Kendrick Waldo and was a prize-winning 1896 graduate of the Detroit Training School of Elocution and English Literature. She won considerable fame as a professional elocutionist, doing dramatic interpretations on many platforms. She continued her service to the community when she came to live in Durham, where she was a popular vocalist. The Cards had two children: Elizabeth Cecilia, born 17 July 1905 in Wyoming, Ohio, who married Wortham Clarence Lyon in Durham on 17 June 1925; and Helen Kendrick, born 1 Feb. 1911 in Durham, who married Oliver Wingate Upchurch on 24 Sept. 1938. Mrs. Card died 10 Feb. 1945. Both she and her husband were buried in the annex to Maplewood Cemetery, Durham.

Through all his years, Card was an active churchman. He was a member of the Edenton Street Methodist Episcopal Church, Raleigh, and of the Bible class taught there by Mrs. W. H. Bobbitt. In Durham he was a member for forty-six years of the Duke Memorial United Methodist Church, where he taught a Bible class in the Sunday school for thirty-five years and contributed to many other phases of the church's work.

SEE: Data Files (Office of Information Services, Duke University, Durham) and North Carolina Collection (University of North Carolina, Chapel Hill); *Duke Alumni Register*, scattered issues; Duke *Archives*, scattered issues; Duke *Chronicle*, scattered issues; *Durham Morning Herald*, 4 Sept. 1948 (obit.); personal memorabilia (possession of Mrs. O. W. Upchurch, Durham); *State*, scattered issues, 1942 ff.

C. SYLVESTER GREEN

Carlyle, Frank Ertel (7 Apr. 1897–2 Oct. 1960), congressman and lawyer, was the second son and third child of William Watts and Lillian Ottelia Vampill Carlyle. He was born in Lumberton and educated in local schools and at the Wilson Memorial Academy, Nyack, N.Y. He entered The University of North Carolina in 1916, but enlisted in the U.S. Navy in June 1918, serving the remainder of the year. He returned to the university and upon graduation was licensed to practice law in January 1921; he opened an office in his native town.

Carlyle was elected to the office of solicitor of the state's Ninth Judicial District in 1938, 1942, and 1946. He ran for Congress in 1948, was elected, and served three succeeding terms from 3 Jan. 1949 to 3 Jan. 1957. He was defeated in his bid for a fourth term in 1956 and resumed his law practice.

Carlyle was married to Lois Godwin Caldwell in 1927, and they were the parents of a daughter, Mrs. Doran Berry. At his death in 1960 he was buried in Meadowbrook Cemetery, Lumberton.

SEE: *Biog. Dir. Am. Cong.* (1961); Janie Carlyle Hargrave, personal interview (28 Jan. 1973); North Carolina Collection (University of North Carolina, Chapel Hill), for clippings.

MAUD THOMAS SMITH

Carlyle, Irving Edward (20 Sept. 1896–5 June 1971), lawyer, legislator, and civic leader, was born in Wake Forest, the son of John Bethune and Dora Dunn Carlyle. John Bethune Carlyle, a native of Robeson County and of Scottish ancestry, taught Latin at Wake Forest College from 1888 until 1911. Mrs. Carlyle was from Tennessee.

Irving Carlyle received the A.B. degree from Wake Forest College in 1917, *summa cum laude*. He had earned letters in baseball and basketball and was manager of the football team. French and German were his majors. During the school year 1917–18 he taught and coached at Rocky Mount High School. In September 1918 he entered the Field Artillery Officers' Training School in Louisville, Ky., receiving a commission as a second lieutenant in December. From that date until May 1919 he was director of physical education and coach of the basketball and baseball teams at Wake Forest College. The next school year he taught at Liberty Piedmont Institute, a Baptist academy at Wallburg.

With Professor Needham Y. Gulley's six-week quiz course at Wake Forest his only formal study of law, Carlyle passed the North Carolina bar examination in 1920. He spent the next two years as a student at the Law School of the University of Virginia but did not stay long enough to graduate. In September 1922 he opened a law office in Winston-Salem. The next year he became associated with the law firm of Manly, Hendren, and

Womble. The young lawyer later became a partner in the distinguished firm now named Womble, Carlyle, Sandridge, and Rice. In 1928 he was married to Mary Belo Moore of New Bern.

By 1930, Carlyle had begun to turn attention to the myriad other activities for which he became noted. In Winston-Salem he served as president of the Young Men's Christian Association, teacher of the Baraca Class of the First Baptist Church, and president of the Chamber of Commerce. He entered politics as Forsyth County manager of Cameron Morrison's 1932 primary campaign against Robert Reynolds for the U.S. Senate. Morrison lost in Forsyth but carried the state.

During the 1940s, Carlyle became known across the state. In 1941 he was a member of the house of representatives from Forsyth County, and in 1943, 1945, and 1951 he served in the General Assembly as the senator from Forsyth. In the senate he was chairman of the Committee on Education, the Finance Committee, and the Calendar Committee. He was a member of the state Advisory Budget Commission in 1945–46. He was a president of the North Carolina Bar Association and from 1936 to 1949 a member of the state board of law examiners. Beginning in 1948 he served fifteen years on the state board of public welfare. He gave another long period of service to the Educational Radio and Television Commission.

Always a liberal and a champion of minority groups, Carlyle often incurred the wrath of the more conservative elements in the state. Some influential persons were suspicious of a man who publicly proclaimed admiration for Franklin D. Roosevelt. Church leaders criticized him for not supporting a state-wide liquor referendum bill. Many objected to his support of Frank Porter Graham against Willis Smith in 1950. In 1952, Carlyle agreed to back William B. Umstead for governor, only to have Hubert Olive, an old friend and fellow Baptist, enter the campaign. Some Baptists never forgave Carlyle for not shifting his support to Olive. Although Carlyle was on the winning side with Umstead, he again found himself in the minority among Tar Heels when, as a member of the Democratic National Convention in 1952, he supported Adlai Stevenson.

The crisis in Carlyle's political career came in 1954. Clyde R. Hoey, North Carolina's senior U.S. senator, died that spring, leaving not only the vacancy as senator but that as keynote speaker for the 20 May North Carolina Democratic Convention in Raleigh as well. The belief was widely held that Carlyle would be appointed to the Senate, and Umstead encouraged the belief by asking Carlyle to make the keynote address. A routine anti-Republican, pro-Democrat speech was prepared. However, on 17 May the Supreme Court of the United States outlawed compulsory segregation of the races in the public schools. The next morning, Carlyle read in the newspapers Umstead's statement that he was "bitterly disappointed" with the decision. As related to Roy Thompson, Winston-Salem *Journal and Sentinel* reporter, Carlyle recalled, "I faced my conscience, and I knew that I had to say something meaningful to that convention." Fully aware of the consequences, Carlyle inserted an extra paragraph into his address: "The Supreme Court of the United States has spoken. As good citizens we have no other course except to obey the law as laid down by the court. To do otherwise would cost us our respect for law and order, and if we lose that in these critical times, we will have lost that quality which is the source of our strength as a state and as a nation." Although he received a big ovation, a friend remarked: "That's not approval of what you said. They're just admiring your

stinkin' courage." Governor Umstead and Lieutenant Governor Luther Hodges left without mentioning the speech, and Samuel J. Ervin, Jr., went to the Senate.

In 1955 and 1956, Carlyle made numerous speeches throughout the state in opposition to the Pearsall Plan, a legislative device for evading integration. In succeeding years he supported Terry Sanford for governor against his old friend and neighbor I. Beverly Lake; defended John F. Kennedy against the suggestion that he would be a puppet of the pope; spoke against capital punishment at the Baptist State Convention of North Carolina; and opposed the Speaker Ban Law. Perhaps the most important of his state-wide appointments came during this period, when he served as chairman of Governor Sanford's Commission on Education Beyond the High School, 1961–62. Out of the report of this group, commonly known as the Carlyle Commission, came the community college program and other significant developments in education.

First elected in 1946, Carlyle served sixteen years as a trustee of Wake Forest University, including five terms as chairman. He was chairman of the successful campaign in Winston-Salem to raise money for the removal there of Wake Forest. Earlier he helped The University of North Carolina get a four-year medical school in Chapel Hill. He was also a trustee of Goucher College and of East Carolina University.

Carlyle's honorary memberships included Phi Beta Kappa, Phi Delta Phi, Omicron Delta Kappa, and the Virginia Bar Association. Wake Forest conferred upon him the LL.D. degree in 1953 and in 1969 gave him its Medallion of Merit. The University of North Carolina awarded him the LL.D. in 1968. He was a member of the National Advisory Council on Neurological Diseases and Blindness, the American Judicature Society, and the North Carolina Rhodes Scholar Committee.

Carlyle died at his home adjacent to the Wake Forest campus and was buried in Salem Cemetery. There is a portrait in the home. Carlyle and his wife had two daughters, Elizabeth Moore (Mrs. Robert D. Byerly, Jr.) and Mary Irving (Mrs. Hugh B. Campbell, Jr.).

SEE: Irving Edward Carlyle Papers (Wake Forest University, Winston-Salem); Raleigh *News and Observer*, 21 May 1954; *Who's Who in America*, 1945–71; Winston-Salem *Journal and Sentinel*, 12 July 1970.

HENRY S. STROUPE

Carlyle, John Bethune (29 Mar. 1859–10 July 1911), college professor, was born at St. Pauls, Robeson County. The Carlyles lived in what is now Robeson County long before the county was established. Saunders Carlyle, a Scottish immigrant, settled there in the late eighteenth century and established his residence among the fertile fields bordering the quiet waters of Ten-Mile Swamp in Bladen (now Robeson) County. Among the children of Saunders Carlyle was Elias Carlyle (grandfather of John Bethune), who lived to the age of eighty-five, dying 24 Jan. 1881. He married Margaret Shank, who died 10 Mar. 1862. Irvin Carlyle, John Bethune's father, was born to Elias and Margaret Carlyle on 15 Feb. 1821. He married Annie Bethune, the daughter of John and Sarah McMillan Bethune. Irvin Carlyle served in Company D, Fifty-first Regiment of the North Carolina Infantry in the Confederate Army.

Immediately after the war, when young John Bethune Carlyle's school days began, the country was utterly impoverished and exhausted. The war left the Carlyles with little but their land, and under these conditions an education for the boys could not be considered. Besides, they were intended for the farm, to be tillers of the soil as their forebears had been. A common school education was considered sufficient to fill every requirement, and, hence, young Carlyle was sent first to Miss Celia Biggs, who taught a small subscription school in an old barn on Ten-Mile Swamp, and then to the common public schools of the neighborhood, his teachers being Margaret Evans and Calvin McIver. Then his education was deemed complete: he could both read and write.

Just here occurred one of those trivial events, small in themselves yet fraught with sufficient importance to change the entire current of an individual's life. The influence that caused Carlyle to secure an education and to enter upon his subsequent brilliant career was the running away of a mule. The mule became frightened and shied, overturning the cart and pinning young Carlyle under it. After this event the young boy was sickly, and his father, thinking that he might never again be fit for manual labor, considered the matter of a college education to prepare the youth as a teacher. At the age of fifteen he was sent to attend a boarding school for boys at Ashpole (now Fairmont) in Robeson County. Stimceon Ivey was principal of this school, and here Carylyle remained for three years, returning home and working on the farm during the summer months.

Borrowing the money, Carlyle entered Wake Forest College, from which he was graduated with an M.A. degree in 1887. He represented his literary society both as debater and as orator, taking the medals for oratory, for the best essay, for Greek, and for Latin. He was salutatorian of his class.

Leaving college, Carlyle taught for a year at Lumber Bridge and then was elected superintendent of public instruction of Robeson County; before he could take office he was elected assistant professor of languages at Wake Forest College. This chair he held from 1888 until 1891, when he was elected full professor of Latin. He remained at the college until his death, and from 1888 on, Wake Forest was the consuming passion of his life.

He was not only a capable and thoroughly efficient professor of Latin, but for many years he also served as fiscal agent for the college. From gifts given by hundreds of people in impoverished North Carolina, then suffering the aftereffects of the Cleveland panic, Carlyle secured money to build the Alumni Building and the College Hospital; a great deal of money was also gradually added to the college endowment. He widened the circle of the friends of the college and enlarged its material equipment, but he rendered his greatest and most lasting service as the encourager and inspirer of youth.

Despite multitudinous duties pressing upon him, Carlyle yet found time to serve as treasurer of the Student Aid Fund, president of the State Teachers Assembly, and president of the Baptist State Convention; he was also a lifelong Sunday school teacher and church deacon. He spoke frequently, in every county and in almost every town in North Carolina, on a variety of occasions: educational, patriotic, agricultural, fraternal and religious. He was also an excellent man of business. He helped organize the Bank of Wake, of which he was the first and only vice-president until his death, and he was a director in the Royall Cotton Mill.

While education was his vocation, politics was his avocation. Had he adopted a political career, all who knew him agreed that he would have been successful. He loved to lobby around the legislature, and few were quite as expert as he. He also thoroughly enjoyed addressing political conventions, and all evidence indicates that the people thoroughly enjoyed hearing him.

Carlyle married Dora Virginia Dunn of Leadville, Tenn. They had two sons, Irving Edward and John Bethune, Jr.

SEE: Robert C. Lawrence, *Here in Carolina* (1939); Lumberton *Robesonian*, 19 Oct. 1938; Raleigh *Biblical Recorder*, 9 July 1943; *Wake Forest Student* 31 (Feb. 1912 [photograph]).

L. W. FUQUA

Carlyle, John Bethune, Jr. *(8 Sept. 1901–1 Dec. 1951),* physician, was born in Wake Forest, the son of Professor John B. and Dora Virginia Dunn Carlyle. Young Carlyle was graduated from Wake Forest High School and received his A.B. and B.S. degrees from Wake Forest College. He then went to Jefferson Medical College in Philadelphia, where he received his degree in medicine. His internship was spent at Cooper Hospital, Camden, N.J., in preparation for a general practice to which he had been inspired at least partially by the untimely death of his father. It was at the suggestion of Dr. Thurman Kitchin, president of Wake Forest College, that the new doctor chose Burlington as the place to begin his medical career in the fall of 1928.

Recognized throughout the years as an outstanding general practitioner, Carlyle left his practice in Burlington shortly after the United States entered World War II and served with the Army Medical Corps for the next three and a half years. He was released with the rank of major and returned to Burlington to continue his medical practice.

Shortly after Carlyle returned home, he constructed his own clinic. His life as a physician might be said truly to have been that of the "family doctor" whose general practice was one of devotion to high ethical standards in the interest of public health and professional ministry to the ill and injured he was called to serve.

Carlyle's life as private citizen was dedicated to the ideals of civic and Christian citizenship applied to church, to education, to athletics, and to the social fraternity of brotherhood and fellowship. In all his activities he was modest and spread his influence quietly, seeking no public recognition or acclaim.

Carlyle married Grace Marie Elder in 1931; they had three daughters, Alice Dunn, Ann Marie, and Rebecca Elizabeth.

SEE: Burlington *Daily Times-News*, 1 and 4 Dec.1951; D. C. Johnson, *Men of Affairs* (1941); U.S. Army, *Historical and Pictorial Review of the Medical Department* (1942).

L. W. FUQUA

Carmichael, William Donald, Sr. *(10 Jan. 1873–25 July 1959),* tobacco company official, was born in Little Rock, S.C. His father was Captain William Donald Carmichael, a Confederate veteran who fought throughout the Civil War from Bull Run to Appomattox, except for a brief period when he was recovering from a battle wound. His mother was Agnes Caroline Harllee, also from Little Rock.

Carmichael studied at Oak Ridge Institute and entered The University of North Carolina in 1892. At Chapel Hill he intended to study law but turned to education because of his admiration for Dr. Edwin Alderman. Carmichael was interested in athletics at the university and served as manager of the baseball and football teams in 1896. He belonged to the Order of Gimghouls and the Kappa Alpha Fraternity. He was graduated from the university in 1897 with a Ph.B. degree.

Beginning in 1896, Carmichael was associated with the Durham city schools for fifteen years, including six years, from 1906 to 1912, as superintendent. In 1911 he was coauthor, with Dr. E. C. Brooks, of *The Geography of North Carolina*, published by Rand McNally.

In 1912 he became manager of the Durham branch of Liggett and Myers Tobacco Company. He was promoted to director in 1920 and to vice-president in charge of advertising in 1927. He moved to New York in 1927 and lived there until his retirement.

After his retirement to Chapel Hill in the early 1940s, Carmichael was active in Rotary, where he was made an honorary member, and in the local chapter of the American Red Cross, which he served as chairman in 1945–46. In recognition of his business leadership, he was made an honorary member of the Beta Gamma Sigma scholastic fraternity in The University of North Carolina School of Commerce in 1939. He maintained membership in the Metropolitan Club in New York.

Carmichael was very interested in the university and received an honorary LL.D. in 1946. He served as a trustee from 1925 to 1926 and as head of the Alumni Association in New York in 1932. He made contributions to the Emergency Student Loan Fund in 1932, when more than five hundred students were on the verge of departing the university because of lack of funds. He contributed to the building of Woollen Gymnasium and to the fund for the conversion of Person Hall into an art museum. Serving as the president of the class of 1897, he was a leader in the Alumni Annual Giving.

At Chapel Hill, Carmichael met Margaret McRobert McCaull of Salem, Va., a graduate of the Woman's College in Greensboro. They were married in Raleigh on 11 Oct. 1899 and had four sons: W. D., Jr., vice-president of The University of North Carolina; R. Cartwright, of Liggett and Myers Tobacco Company, Durham; Robert H., in the advertising business in New York; and H. Martin of Weston, Conn.

Carmichael was a Roman Catholic and a leader in the building of St. Thomas More Church in Chapel Hill. He was buried in the old Chapel Hill Cemetery.

SEE: *Chapel Hill Weekly*, 14 Jan. 1955; *Durham Morning Herald*, 16 Jan. 1955; Raleigh *News and Observer*, 26 July 1959.

MARTHA B. CALDWELL

Carmichael, William Donald, Jr. *(28 July 1900– 27 Jan. 1961)*, vice-president of The University of North Carolina, was born in Durham, one of four sons of William Donald and Margaret McCaull Carmichael. He was educated in the Durham public schools and served from 1918 to 1919 as a private in the U.S. Army Air Corps. He was graduated with a degree in commerce from The University of North Carolina in 1921. There he was an outstanding basketball player, playing on the team that won the Southern Intercollegiate Athletic Association Championship in 1921.

After a year of graduate work, he entered the advertising business in New York with the Newell Emmett Agency in 1922. From 1931 to 1936 he was an associate with Campbell Starling, a member of the New York Stock Exchange. In 1936 he took on a partnership in Carmichael and Carson, New York Stock Exchange.

In 1940 he returned to Chapel Hill to serve as finance officer for the consolidated University of North Carolina. His title changed several times, but whether as finance officer, comptroller, or vice-president, he raised millions of dollars for the university from the legislature, foundations and corporations, and individuals. He

served as acting president of the university in 1949–50, after Frank Graham resigned to accept an appointment as U.S. senator.

Carmichael's work reached to all areas of the consolidated university, and his influence was felt throughout the state. He brought to his work great charm and humor, delighting in a good story. Major achievements included his work with Kay Kyser in beginning the Good Health Campaign in the state and the establishment of the four-year teaching hospital at Chapel Hill. Without public funds he brought educational television to the three campuses at Raleigh, Chapel Hill, and Greensboro. When John Motley Morehead gave the university the Morehead Planetarium and established a scholarship program, Carmichael aided in administering this gift.

Carmichael was chairman of the governor's Advisory Commission on Atomic Energy in 1956. He was a member of the executive committee of the Boy Scouts, the Sons of the American Revolution, Kappa Sigma, and Sigma Upsilon. He served as chairman of the Roanoke Island Historical Association and was instrumental in the reopening of the production of *The Lost Colony* in 1946. He was also active in the construction of Reynolds Coliseum in Raleigh.

Carmichael married the former May Baldwin Waller on 16 Feb. 1924. The couple had two children, Margaret McCaull (Mrs. Robert) Lester and William D. III, both of Chapel Hill.

Carmichael, a Roman Catholic, was buried in the old Chapel Hill Cemetery. Memorials to him included buildings named after him on three campuses of the university: the television building in Greensboro, the gymnasium in Raleigh, and the auditorium at Chapel Hill. A portrait by C. J. Fox is in the office of the director of athletics in the auditorium at Chapel Hill.

SEE: *Durham Morning Herald*, 28 Jan. 1961; *Greensboro Daily News*, 1 Feb. 1961; Bucky Harward, "He Came Home Again," *Carolina Magazine* 70 (April 1941); "In Memoriam, William Donald Carmichael, Jr.," Minutes of the Board of Trustees of The University of North Carolina (Library, University of North Carolina, Chapel Hill); *Nat. Cyc. Am. Biog.*, vol. 49 (1966); *Who's Who in the South and Southwest* (1961); *Who Was Who in America*, vol. 4 (1968).

MARTHA B. CALDWELL

Carney, Stephen Wright *(1762–27 Dec. 1811)*, legislator, general of the state militia, and racehorse owner, was born in Norfolk County, Va., the son of Richard Carney, a well-to-do planter and vestryman of Portsmouth Parish. Carney's great-great-grandfather, William Carney, emigrated from England to Virginia in 1650 and died in Norfolk County in 1683. Richard Carney bought land in Halifax County, N.C., in 1777 but did not actually move the family there until about 1780. At this time the family consisted of Stephen; his brother, Richard, Jr.; sisters Nancy, who later married Roderick Cotten, and Elizabeth, who married Thomas Veale; and their mother, Mary. Another sister, Mary, had been married in 1770 to Slaughter Coffield of Nansemond County, Va., where she remained until after his death in 1785; at that time she moved to North Carolina as well. Richard Carney, Sr., prospered in Halifax County, becoming one of the largest land and slave owners, as well as justice, a post he resigned in 1789. His death on 18 Dec. 1792 was noted in an obituary in the 3 Jan. 1793 issue of the *North Carolina Journal*.

Stephen W. Carney in about 1790 married Priscilla Coffield West, widow of Israel West of Halifax County and daughter of West Coffield of Edgecombe County. Like his father, he prospered as a planter. At one point he owned several thousand acres of land and over thirty slaves. His home, shown on the Price-Strother map of 1808, was located near present Tillery in Halifax County and was frequently the scene of lavish entertainment and political discussion.

His political career officially began in 1791, when he was appointed representative to the House of Commons from Halifax County to complete the term of Thomas Tabb, who had died in office. Carney was elected to the house in his own right in 1793 and 1795. In 1796 he was elected state senator, a post to which he was reelected annually until 1803. Politically, he was a protégé of William R. Davie, whose post as major general of the Third Division of the state militia he was chosen to fill upon Davie's election as governor of North Carolina in December 1798. Starting as a major in the state militia in 1793, he rose to command the militia in five years and remained active in the organization until his death.

Horse-racing was the leading sport of the day among Eastern North Carolina planters, and Carney was one of its foremost figures. His imported thoroughbreds were widely sought after for breeding and were victorious on the leading tracks of North Carolina and Virginia. His most famous import was Citizen, purchased in England in 1803. Citizen had been one of the leading horses of his day in England and was brought to this country exclusively for breeding. Carney's Blank, a son of Centinel, raced Sir Archie in Scotland Neck in 1809, in the most celebrated race of its time. Blank lost, but it was the only time before or after that he did so.

After leaving the legislature, Carney, like his father, became a justice of Halifax County. He was active in the Masonic Lodge in Halifax and in 1811 was grand junior deacon of North Carolina Masons.

Priscilla Carney died 8 Feb. 1810, and on 6 Jan. 1811, Carney married Anne Northcott of Norfolk County, Va. Carney died at his home in Halifax, leaving no issue by either marriage, though he had a large number of nieces and nephews. His widow was married on 25 Aug. 1812 to Captain (later General) John Hodges of Norfolk County, Va., where she died 7 Mar. 1814.

SEE: Elizabeth Amis Cameron Blanchard and Manly Wade Wellman, *The Life and Times of Sir Archie* (1958); Court records of Edgecombe and Halifax counties (North Carolina State Archives, Raleigh) and of Norfolk County, Va. (Great Bridge, Va.); Walter Clark, ed., *State Records of North Carolina*, vol. 21 (1903); Coffield-Bellamy Papers (Southern Historical Collection, University of North Carolina, Chapel Hill); George Cabell Greer, *Early Virginia Immigrants* (1912); *North Carolina Journal*, scattered issues, 1793–1811; *North Carolina Manual* (1913); *Raleigh Register*, 17 Jan. 1812; Raleigh *Star*, 15 Feb. 1810; *Register of Officers, North Carolina Militia* (1800); Blackwell P. Robinson, *William R. Davie* (1957); *Virginia Magazine of History and Biography* 17 (1909–10).

J. WAYNE MODLIN

Carpenter, The Little. *See* Attakullakulla.

Carr, Elias (25 Feb. 1839–22 July 1900), planter, North Carolina State Farmers' Alliance Leader, and governor, was born at Bracebridge Hall, the family plantation in Edgecombe County near Old Sparta. Born into the planter aristocracy of Eastern North Carolina, he was the son of Jonas Johnston and Elizabeth Jane Hilliard Carr. Jonas J. Carr was the son of Elias and Celia Johnston

Carr, whose father was Colonel Jonas Johnston of Revolutionary War fame. Elizabeth Hilliard Carr was the daughter of James and Mourning Boddie Hilliard, who resided in Nash County. Both the Carrs and the Hilliards were among the earliest settlers of North Carolina and held their deeds of lands directly from the Lords Proprietors of the colonial period. Jonas J. Carr built Bracebridge Hall on the Tar River near his father's house, Aspen Hall. Constructed over a two-year period and completed in August 1832, the fine residence was surrounded by over two thousand acres of lush farmland.

Elias Carr was the third child born to his parents. An older sister, Mary, later married David Hinton and became the mistress of Midway Plantation near Raleigh; an older brother, William, ultimately settled in Warren County and died in 1871. A fourth child, James Hilliard, died in infancy. Elizabeth Hilliard Carr died in childbirth on 25 Dec. 1840, and Jonas J. Carr died on 16 May 1843. Left an orphan at an early age, Carr was reared by his aunt and uncle, Temperance Boddie and John Buxton Williams of Warren County.

Carr attended school in Warren County and also the famous William James Bingham School at the Oaks in Orange County. His higher education was acquired at The University of North Carolina (1855–57) and later at the University of Virginia.

On 24 May 1859, Carr married Eleanor Kearny, born on 1 Mar. 1840 at Shocco Springs in Warren County, the daughter of William Kinchin and Maria Alston Kearny. She was well educated and of distinguished lineage. Elias and Eleanor Kearny Carr had six children: William Kearny (b. 1860); John Buxton (b. 1862); Mary, who died in infancy; Elias, Jr. (b. 1866); Eleanor Kearny; and Annie Bruce.

Carr purchased his brother William's share of the family plantation and with his bride settled at Brace-bridge Hall. Hardly had he commenced his farming activities when the Civil War began. On 3 Sept. 1861 he enlisted as a private in Company G, Forty-first Regiment, Third Cavalry. A few months after his enlistment he was ordered to return home and operate his farm for the use of the Confederacy, but toward the war's end he saw active military service.

By the use of scientific methods, Carr gained widespread fame as a highly successful agriculturist who prospered even during periods of depression for most farmers. He realized early the merits of diversification and, in addition to growing cotton and later some tobacco, he produced corn, peas, fruits, and vegetables for home consumption and peanuts for market. A dairyman with a herd of purebred cattle, he sold milk and butter. He produced ensilage and educated farmers in the building of silos. He also marketed bricks and lumber. His meticulous habits led him to keep detailed records on such subjects as amount of rainfall, milk and butter production, and expenditures and returns; he knew the cost of cultivation and returns of each field and the milk production of each cow. A man of wealth, he owned several farms in Eastern North Carolina. Supplementing farming with some business activity, he was a stockholder in the Rocky Mount Mills and other enterprises. He lived the life of a country gentleman, and Bracebridge Hall epitomized southern hospitality.

Civic- and fraternal-minded, Carr was elected in 1869 to the school committee for Sparta Township. He also served for about fifteen years on the Edgecombe County Board of Commissioners. Proud of his ancestry, he was a charter member and first president of the North Carolina Society of the Sons of the Revolution, organized in 1893. Most of his public service revolved around agriculture.

He was first president of the Farmer's Institute of Edgecombe County, established for the purpose of instructing farmers in better methods. He was commissioned by the governor as a state delegate in 1886 to the National Farmer's Congress in St. Paul, Minn., and in 1893 to the World's Columbian Exposition in Chicago. From 1891 to 1893 he served as a member of the board of managers of the North Carolina Geological Survey.

Carr's first major service was as the first president of the North Carolina Farmer's Association, established in Raleigh in 1887. The primary purpose of the organization was to secure the establishment of an agricultural and mechanical college, an objective achieved in 1888. Carr became a member of the first board of trustees of the North Carolina Agricultural and Mechanic College.

The Farmers' Alliance movement catapulted Carr into the limelight. The Southern Alliance was established in North Carolina in 1887 and in January 1888 absorbed the Farmer's Association. An early leader in the movement, Carr was president of his sub-alliance, Sparta, No. 218, and of the Edgecombe County Alliance. He served on the first executive committee of the NCSFA until August 1889, when he was elected president of the organization. Reelected in 1890, he served the maximum term of two years. His leadership helped to secure the passage of an act to increase the school tax for improved schools. As an Allianceman he was instrumental in drafting the Ocala platform, adopted at the Ocala, Fla., convention in 1890. However, he opposed the 1892 St. Louis platform, which ignored the protective tariff (an issue important to Carr) and substituted government ownership and operation of railroads for government regulation and control. A staunch Democrat, he opposed the third-party movement that developed among Alliancemen and ultimately resulted in the formation of the Populist party.

In 1892 the Democratic party nominated Carr for governor. Politically unambitious, he accepted nonetheless, agreeing that he seemed the likely candidate to unify farmers behind the Democratic ticket. He received 135,519 votes; Republican candidate David M. Furches received 94,684; and Populist candidate Wyatt Exum, 47,840.

Lack of political experience did not lessen Carr's firmness and decisiveness in the gubernatorial office. His management of public affairs was as meticulous, efficient, and responsible as his handling of private affairs. His appointments generally were men of high caliber, and he periodically visited and inspected the state's educational, eleemosynary, and penal institutions. During the last years of his administration the penitentiary was self-supporting for the first time in its history. Some of his policies smacked of Bourbon democracy. He sought to publicize the resources of his state so as to attract both immigrants and capital. Accordingly, he published two articles: "North Carolina's Resources," in Southern States 1 (1893), and "Some Advantages Offered by the Southern States," in Harper's Weekly, 11 Nov. 1893. He encouraged the state's participation in such fairs as the Atlanta Exposition (1895) and the Baltimore Centennial Exposition (1897). He also supported the state geological survey, an Alliance achievement, and he regarded the money appropriated as the best investment made by the state for any single purpose.

The policies he advocated were enlightened, progressive, and humane. He attempted to improve the state's schools and roads. In his inaugural address he termed the roads "a disgrace to civilization." His main concern was the establishment of better rural schools,

and he advocated both increased taxation and compulsory education. His desire to expand public services was somewhat restrained by his reluctance to impose a heavier tax burden on the people, especially farmers, during a period of depression. The most controversial action of his administration was the lease in August 1895 of the North Carolina Railroad to the Southern Railway for ninety-nine years. He was often at odds with the Fusionist legislature of 1895, and when his term ended, the Fusionists had won control of all three branches of state government. But his message to the General Assembly of 1897, just prior to leaving office, was dignified and free of partisan rancor.

Carr retired to the farm life he loved at Bracebridge Hall, where he died. He was buried in the family cemetery there.

SEE: Samuel A. Ashe, ed., *Biographical History of North Carolina*, vol. 8 (1917); *Baltimore News*, 15 Jan. 1895; Elias Carr Papers and John Buxton Williams Papers (East Carolina University Manuscript Collection, Greenville); Clinton *Caucasian*, 2 June 1892, 14 and 21 July 1892, 1 Sept. 1892; Beth G. Crabtree, *North Carolina Governors, 1585–1958* (1958); *DAB*, vol. 3 (1929); Josephus Daniels, *Tar Heel Editor* (1939); *Fayetteville Observer*, 26 May 1892; *First Biennial Report of the State Geologist, 1891–1892*; *Goldsboro Argus*, 28 Nov. 1896; Governors' Papers and Letterbooks, 1893–97 (North Carolina State Archives, Raleigh); D. L. Grant, *Alumni History of the University of North Carolina* (1924); Marshall DeLancey Haywood, ed., *Membership and Ancestral Register, By-Laws and Charter of the North Carolina Society of the Sons of the Revolution* (1898); Louisburg *Franklin Times*, 10 June 1892; Lumberton *Robesonian*, 25 May 1892; John W. Moore, *Roster of North Carolina Troops in the War Between the States*, vol. 3 (1882); *Morganton Herald*, 19 May 1892; *North Carolina: The Old North State and the New*, vol. 3 (1941); *Progressive Farmer*, October 1889–December 1891; Raleigh *Christian Advocate*, 25 Jan. 1893, 24 Jan. 1894; Raleigh *Morning Post*, 31 July 1900, 30 Aug. 1900; Raleigh *News and Observer*, 24 Mar. 1888, 24 July 1900; Rocky Mount *Telegram*, 5 Aug. 1962; Tarboro *Southerner*, 9, 19, 20, and 22 Apr. 1896, 4 May 1896, 29 Oct. 1960; W. F. Tomlinson, *Biography of State Officers and the Members of the General Assembly of North Carolina* (1893); J. Kelly Turner and J. L. Bridgers, Jr., *History of Edgecombe County* (1920).

LALA CARR STEELMAN

Carr, James Ozborn (*6 Sept. 1869–7 Mar. 1949*), leader in law, politics, and education, was born on his father's farm south of Kenansville in Duplin County, the son of Joseph Hendley and Mary Susan Dickson Carr. He was descended from Joseph Carr, who is believed to have come to North Carolina in 1749 with a number of other Presbyterians from Ireland.

Carr worked on the family farm in the summers, attended the Samuel W. Clement School in Wallace and in 1895 was graduated from The University of North Carolina *cum laude*, with a membership in Phi Beta Kappa and a Ph.B. degree with honors in Latin. He was a speaker at the 1894 commencement and, in his senior year, was class orator and intersociety debater for the Philanthropic Society. After graduation he studied law at the university, though he never got a law degree. After teaching school in Mt. Olive, he passed the bar in 1896. He was always a supporter of the university, and his papers were given to its library after his death.

Active in Democratic politics from his university days, Carr ran for the General Assembly in 1896 but was defeated in the Populist and Fusion landslides. In 1898, as chairman of the county Democratic executive committee, he was nominated again for the house and won. During the 1899 term he met Representative George Rountree, a Democrat from New Hanover County, and the two men formed a law partnership in Wilmington; there Carr spent the rest of his life.

Carr's private law practice, with a number of different partners, continued to be his life's work; although he was repeatedly called to public service, he maintained a family tradition of personal independence. He was a lawyer's lawyer. Thoroughly knowledgeable in state and federal law, he made the bulk of his practice corporation law and enjoyed the intellectual give-and-take of courtroom work.

Although he could be forceful when he wished, Carr usually displayed an even temper, and his low-keyed sense of humor stood him in good stead with clients and judges alike. An avid bird and duck hunter, he did not participate in any other organized sport or recreation; but he read widely in North Carolina and American history and took in a bit of Mark Twain or Dickens on occasion.

Carr's law practice and devotion to the Democratic party made him well known throughout the state and beyond. In 1916, Woodrow Wilson appointed him U.S. attorney for the Eastern District of North Carolina, a post he retained until the end of World War I. Then he was named to the Mixed Claims Commission and spent several years prosecuting war claims against the German government, work that took him several times to England, France, and Germany. In 1923 he was appointed by the federal government to represent the receivers in the liquidation of several North and South Carolina national banks, work he continued to do for five years. He became U.S. attorney a second time from 1933 to 1945, but again resigned to devote full time to his private practice.

Carr also served state government, at the behest of several governors. Angus W. McLean appointed him in 1925 to both the North Carolina Judicial Conference, for four years, and the North Carolina Education Commission, which he chaired for the two years it took to make the first comprehensive study of the state's public school system. The 650-page report recommended, among other things, a minimum eight-month school term and financial help for poorer counties to maintain at least a six-month term. In 1930–31 he was on the state equalization board and in 1933–34 on the state school commission.

Carr served two terms as chairman of the New Hanover County Board of Education, from 1909 to 1916 and from 1927 to 1931. In those years, eight hundred thousand dollars were spent in a school building program for the county. For the new New Hanover High School, Carr donated the maple trees that still stand around the big building; the young trees came from a large maple in his own front yard at 1901 Market Street.

Carr's involvement with education went outside the state as well: in 1920 the U.S. secretary of the interior appointed him to a national advisory committee in connection with a survey of secondary education in the United States.

In 1931 and 1932, Governor O. Max Gardner appointed Carr to a commission to revise the state's constitution. That group's report called for broader legislative powers for the General Assembly combined with a strong executive (that is, a gubernatorial veto power), to make for greater centralization of government.

Carr was president of the Wilmington Star Company, newspaper publishers, from 1919 to 1927, and a founder and director of both the People's Savings Bank and Trust Company and the Carolina Savings and Loan Association. He was a member of the American, North Carolina, and New Hanover County bar associations, the American Society of International Law, the Association of the Bar of the City of New York, the Cape Fear Club, and the Cape Fear Country Club. For fifty years he was a deacon of St. Andrews Covenant Presbyterian Church. He was the author of *The Dickson Letters* (Raleigh, 1901) and *The Carr Family of Duplin County* (Wilmington, 1939).

Carr was married on 18 June 1907 to Susan LeRoy Parsley. They had three children: Katherine, now Mrs. Frederick Bolles Graham of Wilmington; Susan LeRoy, now Mrs. Horace Mann Emerson of Jacksonville, Fla.; and James Dickson Carr of Wilmington.

Carr died in Wilmington and was buried in Oakdale Cemetery there. There is a photograph but no other portrait.

SEE: Kemp P. Battle, *History of the University of North Carolina*, vol. 2 (1912); James Ozborn Carr, *The Carr Family of Duplin County* (1939); *Consolidated Report of the State Educational Commission on the Public School System of North Carolina* (1927); *Nat. Cyc. Am. Biog.*, vol. 37 (1951); *Report of the North Carolina Constitutional Commission* (1932); *University of North Carolina Catalogue*, 1895–96, 1896–97; *Who Was Who in America*, vol. 2 (1950).

EUGENIE W. CARR

Carr, Julian Shakespeare (13 Oct. 1845–29 Apr. 1924), industrialist and philanthropist, was born the son of John Wesley and Eliza Pannill Bullock Carr in Chapel Hill, where his father was a merchant. He attended The University of North Carolina from 1862 to 1864, when he enlisted and served as a private in the Third North Carolina Cavalry of the Confederate Army. He returned to the university for the year 1865–66 and then went to Little Rock, Ark., to engage in business with an uncle from 1868 until 1870.

When he returned to North Carolina, Carr joined the tobacco manufacturing firm of W. T. Blackwell and Company in Durham. Shortly afterward, his father gave him four thousand dollars to purchase a third interest in the company. Assuming financial management of the concern, he began a pioneering advertising campaign and used the Bull Durham trademark to publicize the tobacco manufactured by his firm. The name soon came to be known around the world, and the business flourished. Carr bought the interests of the other partners and in 1898 sold the business to the American Tobacco Company for almost three million dollars. He then engaged in extensive banking operations; organized and built a hosiery mill with plants in many towns in the state; was an organizer and builder of the Durham-Roxboro Railroad, which afterward became part of a larger line; and was active in electric and telephone companies. He also purchased a small weekly newspaper in Durham and converted it to a daily.

During his lifetime, Carr was said to have given away a fortune. His three great loves were the Methodist church, The University of North Carolina, and the Confederate veterans. To all of these he contributed generously. His concern with education was broad, and he also aided Davidson, Wake Forest, St. Mary's, Elon, and Greensboro colleges, among others. He contributed to orphanages and to homes for Confederate veterans and widows. As a trustee of Trinity College, then located in Randolph County, he led a campaign to raise funds to move the school to Durham, where it afterward became Duke University. He was also a benefactor of the Training

School for Colored People, Augusta, Ga., and American University, Washington, D.C. He was a member of the original committee that proposed the organization of the Methodist Assembly at Lake Junaluska and was on its first executive committee.

In 1881, Carr met a young Chinese boy, Charles J. Soong, who had arrived in the port of Wilmington aboard a trading ship. Carr learned that Soong had sought baptism at the local Methodist church and that he wanted to remain in America for an education. Carr aided him to attend Trinity College and then continue his education at Vanderbilt University. The two became lifelong friends, and Carr accepted Soong as a member of his own family. When he returned to China, Soong worked in the Methodist China Mission and established a business to print Bibles in Chinese. His youngest daughter was Madame Chiang Kai-shek.

As commander of the United Confederate Veterans in North Carolina, Carr held the honorary rank of major general and was thereafter known as General Carr. He was also an active Democrat, a generous contributor to the party, and a delegate to party conventions. In 1900, at the national party convention, North Carolina and Idaho cast their votes for Carr for vice-president. In 1897, Carr was one of the donors of a site for the Durham Public Library, which became the first publicly supported library in the state. He was a trustee of that library and of many schools and other institutions in the state, including The University of North Carolina and Greensboro and Trinity colleges.

Carr was married to Nannie Graham Parrish in 1873; they were the parents of Eliza Morehead, Lallah Rooke, Julian S., Jr., Albert Marvin, Claiborne McDowell, and Austin Heaton. Carr was buried in Maplewood Cemetery in Durham.

SEE: Samuel A. Ashe, ed., *Biographical History of North Carolina*, vol. 2 (1905); Nora C. Chaffin, *Trinity College*, (1950); Elmer T. Clark, *The Chiangs of China* (1943); C. Sylvester Green, ed., *General Julian S. Carr* (1946); *History of North Carolina*, vol. 6 (1919); *Who Was Who in America*, vol. 1 (1943).

LOUISE L. QUEEN

Carrick, John Lee (*27 July 1886–3 Feb. 1972*), clergyman and educator, was born in Davidson County, the son of Christopher Columbus and Nancy Elizabeth Thayer Carrick. His paternal ancestors appear to have migrated to North Carolina from northern Virginia during the early years of the nineteenth century.

Carrick received his elementary and high school training at Churchland School, Davidson County. He was awarded the B.A. degree from Wake Forest College in 1913 and, subsequently, the B.D. from Crozer Theological Seminary, Chester, Pa., and the M.A. from the University of Pennsylvania. Chowan College conferred an honorary D.D. upon him in 1935 in recognition of his services to the churches and to the college's board of trustees.

Carrick's early years, before his enrollment at Crozer Seminary, were spent in a succession of brief pastorates with Baptist churches in Rowan County (Trading Ford, 1908, 1910, 1912–14; Calvary, 1909; Enon, 1909, 1914; Rockwell, 1909) and in Chatham County (Sandy Branch, 1911–13; Rive's Chapel, 1912, 1913). Upon the conclusion of his studies in Pennsylvania, he served churches in the Virginia counties of Surry (Moore's Swamp, 1918, 1919); Isle of Wight (Mill Swamp, 1918, 1919); Northampton (Lower Northampton, 1920, 1921); and Southampton (Boykins, 1922, 1923; Branchville, 1922, 1923) and in the

City of Newport News (Orcutt Avenue, 1924–26). In 1927 he was called to the pastoral charge of the congregation of the Blackwell Memorial Baptist Church, Elizabeth City, where he served until 1935. In the latter year he was called to the pastorate of Jackson Memorial Baptist Church, Portsmouth, Va.

On 11 June 1937, Carrick was elected to succeed Roy R. McCollough as president of Chowan College. The trustees of the institution had voted in February 1937 to close the school at the end of the academic year because of annual operating deficits, which had been accumulating and absorbing part of the small endowment fund. However, at a special meeting of trustees and friends of the college on 16 April 1937, it had been decided to continue operation of the institutiton, but with the curriculum limited to a two-year, or junior college, program. It was to this situation that Carrick was invited, with instructions to secure a faculty and a student body. Faced with continuing financial crises and an enrollment of only seventy-seven students at the beginning of the fall term in 1940, Carrick submitted his resignation as president of the college on 11 Nov. 1940, the resignation to be effective with the conclusion of the current term.

Thereafter Carrick continued as pastor of Baptist churches in Hertford County (Mt. Tabor, 1938–41) and Gates County (Reynoldson, 1941–43; Roduco, 1941–43) in North Carolina and Nansemond County (Great Fork, 1944), Westmoreland County (Colonial Beach, 1945–49), and King George County (Round Hill, 1945–49) in Virginia. He concluded his active pastoral ministry with Rive's Chapel Baptist Church, Chatham County, which he had served previously while still a student at Wake Forest College. He lived in retirement in Siler City after 1953.

Carrick was a Mason and an independent in politics. He was married to Myrtle Burgwyn Teague on 12 June 1917. They had no children.

He was buried in a family plot in Oakwood Cemetery, Siler City.

SEE: Minutes of the Board of Trustees, Chowan College (Murfreesboro), 1937–41; *North Carolina Baptist State Convention Annuals*, 1908 ff.; Joseph Roy Parker, *The Ahoskie Era of Hertford County* (1939); *Virginia Baptist General Association Annuals*, 1908 ff.

R. HARGUS TAYLOR

Carrington, George Lunsford (*24 Jan. 1893–25 Jan. 1972*), pioneer surgeon, was born in Durham County, the son of Ursula Elizabeth Lunsford and Sterling R. Carrington, a prominent businessman in Durham. Carrington received his bachelor's degree and a master's degree in chemistry and zoology from Trinity College, now Duke University. He then entered The University of North Carolina Medical School, where he received his Certificate in Medicine. Then followed more training at Johns Hopkins Medical School in Baltimore, an internship there, and still further training at Yale Medical School and at New Haven, Conn., Hospital. Afterward he spent two years as chief resident surgeon at Bryn Mawr Hospital in Philadelphia.

After thirteen years of training, Carrington returned to Durham in 1924 to establish a private surgical practice and to spend one day weekly as a professor at The University of North Carolina Medical School. He was also involved in research projects at the university. He moved to Burlington in 1928 as a partner of Dr. Ralph E. Brooks at Rainey Hospital, which later became Alamance General Hospital and which was the forerunner of today's Memorial Hospital of Alamance.

Numerous honors came to Carrington during his lengthy career. The one he held closest, as he often said, was his selection in 1955 to receive from The University of North Carolina one of the first Distinguished Service Awards for his career and his contribution to medicine, as judged by the university faculty.

Carrington donated the land in Durham County on which Carrington Junior High School now stands. He was also generous in his contributions through the years to educational, medical, and religious interests. He was known in his profession for a long list of published research papers. Talented in writing, he had been editor of The University of North Carolina *Daily Tar Heel*. His interest in education also dated from his school years; upon graduation, he served as a principal in the Durham school system for a year before entering medical training at the university. At the university, he played varsity basketball for three years and achieved high scholastic rating, earning membership in Phi Beta Kappa. He also won honors during his medical training and practice, becoming a fellow in the American College of Surgeons and a member of the American Board of Surgery.

Carrington was married in 1921 to Maud Easter Black. His second wife was Elizabeth Scott whom he married in 1941.

SEE: Burlington *Daily Times-News*, 21 Sept. 1970, 2 and 29 May 1972; Daniel L. Grant, *Alumni History of the University of North Carolina* (1924); William S. Powell, ed., *North Carolina Lives* (1962).

L. W. FUQUA

Carroll, Dudley Dewitt *(28 July 1885–30 Nov. 1971)*, college professor and dean, was born in the Mizpah community of Stokes County, the son of Dewitt Valentine Carroll and Sallie Ann Lewis. He was educated at the Mountain View Institute, Guilford College (A.B., 1907), Haverford College (A.B., 1908), and Columbia University (A.M., 1916).

Dean Carroll, as he was known to almost everyone, was vitally involved in academic and public affairs for a span of almost half a century. He began his career as principal of Mountain View Institute (1908–9); then he was instructor in social sciences at Guilford College (1909–11), dean of Guilford College (1912–14), and assistant professor of economics at Hunter College (1915–18).

Carroll taught in the summer session at The University of North Carolina in 1917, and one of his students, Lenoir Chambers (later editor of the *Greensboro Daily News* and the Norfolk *Virginian-Pilot* and Pulitzer Prize winner), brought him to the attention of President Edward Kidder Graham. Graham offered Carroll a position, but because he was under contract to Hunter College for the following year, Carroll could not accept until the fall of 1918; then he was appointed professor of economics. The following year he became dean of the School of Commerce (later Business Administration), a position he held for thirty-one years. During his service in Chapel Hill, Carroll was at one time or another a member of almost every faculty committee, as well as the Chancellor's Advisory Committee. He was a member of Phi Beta Kappa and in 1955 was named Kenan Professor of Economics and elected chairman of the faculty, the highest honor his colleagues could bestow upon him. The trustees named the main building of the School of Business Administration Carroll Hall. Few persons have exerted stronger influence upon the faculty and students of The University of North Carolina than Carroll over his long tenure. His approach was always to obtain results

and to reduce to a minimum or avoid totally the red tape too often found in academic communities.

In 1938, when it was obvious that developments in Europe would lead to the greatest holocaust the world had known, Carroll, Dorothy Thompson, and Rabbi Stephen S. Wise advocated and got an open door policy for oppressed minorities who wished to seek refuge in the United States. When the Selective Service System was instituted, Carroll was named chairman of the Orange County Draft Board, even though he was a devout Quaker.

After the repeal of the Eighteenth Amendment to the Constitution, when Orange County voted wet, Carroll was named chairman of the Alcoholic Beverage Control Board of Orange County. It was the general feeling that this board was perhaps the best managed in the state and that Carroll, who never had a drink of whiskey, saw to it that alcohol would not be abused and that the profits from the system would be channeled without delay to the public schools.

Carroll's public service did not end with the control of alcohol and the management of conscription, both distasteful to his Quaker principles. An important figure in business affairs of Chapel Hill and the county, he was director of the Orange County Building and Loan Association from 1920 to 1950 and chairman of its board of directors from 1937 to 1950. He was active in the Society of Friends and was instrumental in developing a flourishing society in Chapel Hill; he acquired property for the society and directed the construction of the meeting house. He was a trustee of Guilford College from 1918 to 1946 and chairman of its board from 1933 to 1946. He retired from the university faculty in 1960.

Carroll, on 27 June 1918, married Eleanore Dixon Elliott. They had four children: Dudley DeWitt, Jr., Marshall Elliott, Eleanor Hillyard Carroll Roberts, and Donald Cary. A memorial service for Carroll was held in the Friends Meeting House, 11 Dec. 1971.

SEE: *Chapel Hill Weekly*, 27 Sept. 1940, 28 May 1953, 15 June 1969, 1 Dec. 1971; *Charlotte Observer*, 5 Feb. 1950; Minutes of the Faculty of The University of North Carolina, vol. 25 (Library, University of North Carolina, Chapel Hill); Raleigh *News and Observer*, 10 Aug. 1940, 25 Oct. 1944, 8 Dec. 1950; *University of North Carolina Alumni Review*, May 1940; *Who's Who in the South and Southwest* (1956).

STERLING STOUDEMIRE

Carson, Samuel Price *(22 Jan. 1798–2 Nov. 1838)*, congressman and secretary of state of Texas, was born at Pleasant Gardens, Burke County, the eldest son of John Carson and his second wife. His father represented Burke in the state legislature, as did three of his sons. Samuel Price was educated at home, engaged in agricultural pursuits as a young man, and served in the state senate from 1822 to 1824.

In August of 1825, Carson, as a Jackson-Calhoun supporter, won election to Congress over Robert Vance and James Graham in the Buncombe District. On Capitol Hill he formed lasting friendships with Samuel Houston, James K. Polk, and Warren R. Davis. He served first on the Indian Affairs and later on the Naval Affairs committees. He was a defender of states' rights and a strict constructionist and was opposed to national banks, internal improvements, and tariffs. He disapproved of John Quincy Adams and in time denounced Jackson as well. In 1832 he was a partisan of Philip Barbour. In 1827, Robert Vance tried to regain his old seat from Carson in a bitter campaign that resulted in a duel and the death of

Vance. In the next two elections, Carson suffered no real competition, but by 1833 his determined Nullification views brought both National Republican James Graham and Democrat David Newland into the contest against him. He lost to James Graham by 870 votes, after serving in Congress four terms. While in Congress he married Catherine Wilson of Tennessee; they became the parents of one daughter.

Back home, Carson was again a member of the state senate in 1834, but early the following year he made a trip to Mississippi and Texas to survey the possibilities of moving west. He and a brother were delegates in the North Carolina Constitutional Convention of 1835. He opposed restrictions on Catholics holding office, was against allowing free blacks the vote, and wanted popular elections for governor. At the end of the convention he let it be known that he was moving to Texas.

Texas declared its independence from Mexico a short time after Carson settled there, and he was elected to represent the Red River District in a constitutional convention. There his former friendship with Houston and his congressional experience gave him prestige. He missed election as *ad interim* president by just six votes and was made provisional secretary of state of the fledgling republic, serving from March to October 1836. During that summer he made a trip to Washington to solicit support for Texas from his old friends in Congress. In June and July, Congress voted to recognize the independence of Texas.

Already in ill health, Carson found his new exertions too strenuous. He eventually went to Hot Springs, Ark., in search of a cure. There he died and was buried in the government cemetery.

SEE: Sameul A. Ashe, ed., *Biographical History of North Carolina*, vol. 2 (1905); *Biog. Dir. Am. Cong.* (1971); W. S. Hoffmann, *Andrew Jackson and North Carolina Politics* (1971); R. N. Richardson, *Texas, the Lone Star State* (1943).

DANIEL M. MCFARLAND

Carter, David Miller *(12 Jan. 1830–7 Jan. 1879),* Confederate officer, legislator, and attorney, the son of David Carter and his wife Sarah Lindsay Spencer, was born in Fairfield, Hyde County. His father was a prosperous planter and landowner and sent his son to the Lovejoy Academy in Raleigh and to The University of North Carolina. Carter was graduated from the university in 1851 as an honor student and remained in Chapel Hill an additional year to continue study with the professor of law, William H. Battle. He began practice in Washington, Beaufort County, in 1852, as a partner first of Richard H. Donnell and later of Edward J. Warren. He quickly built a successful legal practice and in addition served as solicitor for the state in his judicial district.

In politics, Carter was a Unionist Whig, but in spite of his opposition to secession he entered the Confederate Army in May 1861, with a commission as captain of Company E, Fourth North Carolina Infantry. He was severely wounded in the right arm at the Battle of Seven Pines on 31 May 1862. Although he was promoted to lieutenant colonel of his regiment, to rank from 19 June, the slowness of his recovery prevented his serving and caused his resignation in December 1862. He was then appointed a judge of the military court, with the rank of colonel, and served first on the court of the Second (Jackson's, later Ewell's) Corps, and later as presiding judge of the Third (A. P. Hill's) Corps.

In the meantime, Carter had been elected to represent Beaufort County in the 1862–63 session of the lower house of the General Assembly of North Carolina. He was given leave of absence from the army during his legislative session; when he was reelected to the legislature in 1864, he resigned his army commission. He wrote in 1863 that peace could be made only by military decision, and as a soldier he supported the military aims of the Confederacy. As he viewed the developing situation from the perspective of a legislator, however, he began to support the idea of a negotiated peace. He urged concessions in the enforcement of conscription and tax laws for his neighbors in Beaufort and Hyde counties, who were frequently subjected to raids from the two armies, and he was a leader in opposing the suspension of the writ of habeas corpus. In January 1865 he was a member of a delegation chosen by the legislature for a secret mission to Richmond, in an effort to persuade the Confederate government to open negotiations for peace.

At the close of the war, Carter wrote that he was one of those "who served the Confederacy with fidelity, while it existed, and are now prepared" to yield to the United States "a loyal allegiance." He received an early pardon and was appointed solicitor by Provisional Governor William W. Holden. For more than a year he cooperated with Holden, his friends John Pool and William B. Rodman, and others who were seeking reconstruction of North Carolina under a leadership opposed to former secessionists. In September 1866 he attended the Unionist meeting in Raleigh that led to the formation of the Republican party in the state. Yet he was no bitter partisan; he was consulted by former Governor Zebulon B. Vance soon after the end of the war, and he maintained friendships with opponents of the Radical Republicans. He was alienated by congressional Reconstruction, and in November 1867, in a letter to John Pool that he gave to the newspapers, he opposed the call of the constitutional convention required by the First Reconstruction Act. In 1868 he was told that the Republican party of the state would request removal of his disabilities if assured of his support, but he refused to commit himself to the party and soon thereafter began to cooperate with the Conservatives. In 1872 he was nominated for election to Congress by the Democratic-Conservative party; he campaigned actively but unsuccessfully against the incumbent, Clinton L. Cobb.

Early in 1874, Carter moved his family to Raleigh. He continued to practice and to attend courts in his old circuit, where he had large holdings of farm and timber lands. He had a busy legal practice both in Raleigh and in his former circuit and was active in public affairs as a director of a bank and an insurance company, a member of the commission to build a new governor's mansion, and president of the board of directors of the state penitentiary. He was also a leader in the movement to reopen The University of North Carolina and cooperated with the new president, Kemp P. Battle, whose political course had been somewhat similar to his.

Carter died in Baltimore, apparently as a result of a heart condition that had afflicted him for about a year. He was a member of the Protestant Episcopal church, and his body was returned to Raleigh for a funeral service in Christ Church and burial in Oakwood Cemetery, which he had been a leader in founding.

Carter was married twice, the first time to Isabella Perry, daughter of David Bradley Perry of Rosedale, near Washington, N.C. She died in 1866, and in May 1869 he married Mrs. Harriet Armistead Ryan Benbury, widow of John A. Benbury of Albania, near Edenton. The daughter of John Jordan Ryan and Emily Turner and the stepdaughter of David Outlaw, she grew up in the Outlaw home in Windsor. Carter was survived by two children of his first wife, Sarah Lindsay and David M., Jr., and two of his second wife, Laura Lindsay and Frances Spencer. Although Carter always signed his name David M. or D. M., he was known familiarly as Miller.

SEE: Samuel A. Ashe, ed., *Cyclopedia of Eminent and Representative Men of the Carolinas of the Nineteenth Century*, vol. 2 (1892); Southern Historical Collection (University of North Carolina, Chapel Hill), for David Carter Papers, David Miller Carter Papers, Perry Family Papers, and a portrait by William Garl Browne.

CAROLYN A. WALLACE

Carter, Francis Graves (7 July 1912–16 June 1960), tobacco company official, was born in Dry Fork, Pittsylvania County, Va., the son of Claude Cameron and Erla Washington Ramsey Carter.

After graduation from high school, Carter worked in his father's stores; this experience in selling Reynolds tobacco products, coming in contact with the salesmen for the company, first kindled his desire to become a Reynolds salesman himself. He was employed by the R. J. Reynolds Tobacco Company as a trainee-salesman in 1934. After working territories in Winston-Salem, Virginia, and West Virginia, he was made division manager at Concord, heading a sales staff of five at the age of twenty-seven. He was appointed manager of the combined Concord and Winston-Salem divisions in 1942 and promoted to the post of assistant department manager of the Winston-Salem area in 1943; he then served as manager of a department that covered an area northward from the South Carolina line to Baltimore, Md., with headquarters in Richmond, Va. In 1949 he returned to Winston-Salem as a member of the executive sales staff. He was named assistant to the sales manager in 1952 and promoted to sales manager before the end of the year; elected a director and vice-president of the company in 1958, at the same time retaining his post as sales manager; and elected president of the company on 8 Oct. 1959, twenty-five years after having begun with the company as a "foot salesman." An associate described him as "a real developer of men—a challenger rather than a driver."

Not content to confine his talents to his career alone, Carter was a leader in church and community affairs as well. He was chairman of the Community Fund Campaign in Forsyth County in 1959, president of the Winston-Salem Sales Executive Club, and a director of the Winston-Salem Chamber of Commerce. He conducted workshops and seminars on sales management in New York and Atlanta, for the American Management Association and served as a member of that association's marketing council. He was a member of the American Society of Sales Executives, an organization made up of fifty of the nation's top sales executives; and he was a Shriner and a member of the Rotary, Old Town, and Twin City Clubs.

Carter attended the First Presbyterian Church, where he served as chairman of the board of deacons and was an elder. He helped to spearhead a movement in the Winston-Salem Presbytery to raise a minimum of $650,000 for the construction of four new churches. Politically, Carter was a Democrat. His hobbies were his home workshop and fishing. On 2 July 1935 he was married to Elizabeth Hamlet of Phoenix, Va. Their

children were Francis Cameron, Charlotte LeRoy, and Martin Hamlet.

SEE: Family records (in possession of the author); William S. Powell, ed., *North Carolina Lives* (1962); *Who's Who in the South and Southwest* (1961); *Who Was Who in America*, vol. 4 (1968); *Winston-Salem Journal-Sentinel*, clipping library.

ELIZABETH H. CARTER

Carter, John (1737–81), frontiersman, merchant, surveyor, land speculator, colonel of the militia, and legislator, was born in Cumberland County, Va. There is no known evidence that he was a relative of the famous Robert ("King") Carter. He married Elizabeth Taylor in 1758 and remained unknown until he, his wife, and their only child, Landon, emigrated to Western North Carolina (now Tennessee) in 1769 or 1770, settling in a valley, which came to bear his name, just west of the Holston River and a short distance below Long Island. In 1770 he formed a partnership with William Parker and opened a store to trade with the whites and Indians about a mile west of the present Church Hill community in Hawkins County.

When the Lochaber treaty line was completed in 1772, it was discovered that only one of the four settlements in present-day eastern Tennessee was within the area granted to England by the Cherokees (North-of-Holston). Instead of moving into the region opened by the Treaty of Lochaber, the settlers of Carter's Valley and Nolichucky hastened to the Watauga settlement. The Carters apparently moved to Watauga at this time also. Carter has been credited with the idea of forming an independent government for the community; he was one of the key figures in the 1772 formation of the Watauga Association, the first organized government west of the Alleghenies. He was a member of the five-man court created in 1772 and of the Committee of Thirteen established in 1775–76. He was also chairman of the group that petitioned the North Carolina legislature to annex the area in 1776. The district of Washington, which included the settlements along the Watauga, Holston, and Nolichucky rivers, was created in 1776. Carter was selected one of three delegates from the new district to serve in the North Carolina legislature, which in turn named him colonel of the militia and provided supplies to establish at his home a public magazine of military stores for defense of the area. When Washington County was created out of the Washington District in 1777, he was elected to the state senate. He was sent to the legislature a second time in 1781.

Carter was active throughout the Revolution defending the frontier against the Indians. In addition, he served as justice of the peace, surveyor and entry taker of lands. He was a partner of John Sevier and Richard Henderson in land speculation and at the time of his death was one of the largest landholders west of the Allegheny Mountains. He died as a colonel at the age of forty-four and was buried at his home just out of Elizabethton.

SEE: *American Historical Review* 3 (1898); O. Z. Bond, *The Family Chronicle and Kinship Book of Maclin . . . and . . . Related American Lineages* (ca. 1928); D. W. Carter, *Notable Southern Families: Carter of Tennessee including the Taylors* (1917); East Tennessee Historical Society *Publications* 2, 3, 7, 12, 14, 20, 21, 28, 34 (1930–62); J. G. M. Ramsey, *Annals of Tennessee* (1853); William L. Saunders and Walter Clark, eds., *Colonial and State Records of North Carolina*, vols. 10, 12, 14, 20, 23 (1890–1904).

G. MELVIN HERNDON

Carter, Landon (29 Jan. 1760–5 June 1800), political leader, was the only child of John and Elizabeth Taylor Carter. Born in Cumberland County, Va., Landon accompanied his parents to the raw frontier of the Holston River, a short distance below Long Island, when only ten years of age. The Carters moved to Watauga in 1772. His father was wealthy enough to send Landon to school at Liberty Hall in Mecklenburg County.

Toward the end of the Revolution, Carter was old enough to serve in the military. In 1780 he was named captain. He served with John Sevier's expedition against the Cherokee and participated in the Battle of Boyd's Creek, one of the best-fought engagements of the war on the frontier. During the course of that same year, he joined Charles Robertson's command in South Carolina. In 1781–82 he continued to fight in South Carolina under both John Sevier and Francis Marion. Several years later, in 1788, the North Carolina legislature appointed him major of horse, and in 1790, Governor William Blount named him commandant of the militia for the Washington District. He served as colonel in the Indian campaigns of 1792–93, and in 1796, Governor John Sevier commissioned him brigadier-general of the Hamilton District.

Although Carter's political career never extended beyond the state level, in less than two decades he held positions in three different states. In 1784 and again in 1789 he represented Washington County in the North Carolina legislature, and he was a member of the Fayetteville convention called to ratify the Constitution in 1789. In 1784 he was active in the movement for the establishment of the State of Franklin. He served as secretary of the Jonesboro convention, which forwarded the movement and was speaker of the first senate and a member of the first council of state. He served as secretary of the state and finally as entry taker for Franklin. When the Southwest Territory was organized in 1790, Carter was named treasurer of the Washington District, one of the three into which the territory was divided. In 1796 he represented Washington County at the convention that adopted the constitution for the new state of Tennessee. Shortly thereafter, the first legislature of the new state elected him treasurer for the districts of Washington and Hamilton. This same legislature created Carter County, named in his honor; Elizabethton (originally Elizabeth), the county seat, was named for his wife. Carter was trustee of Greenville College, founded in 1794 in Greene County, and a trustee and incorporator of Washington College at Salem in Washington County in 1795.

Carter inherited considerable acreage from his father and received ten thousand acres from the State of North Carolina as reimbursement for the expense incurred by his father in connection with Colonel Richard Henderson's purchase of Cherokee lands. Carter was also personally involved in land speculation.

Carter married Elizabeth Maclin on 26 Feb. 1784. She bore him seven children, four boys and three girls.

SEE: O. Z. Bond, *The Family Chronicle and Kinship Book of Maclin . . . and . . . Related American Lineages* (ca. 1928); D. W. Carter, *Notable Southern Families: Carter of Tennessee including the Taylors* (1917); East Tennessee Historical Society *Publications* 2, 12, 14, 16, 23, 27, 28, 30, 35 (1930–63); J. G. M. Ramsey, *Annals of Tennessee* (1853); Samuel Cole Williams, *History of the Lost State of Franklin*, rev. ed. (1933).

G. MELVIN HERNDON

Carteret (Cartrett, Cartwright), Peter (b. 1641), governor, secretary, and council member in North Carolina, was the son of Helier de Carteret and Rachel la Cloche Carteret of Saint Peter's Parish, Isle of Jersey. He was fourth cousin to Sir George Carteret, one of the original proprietors of Carolina.

On 3 Dec. 1664, the Carolina proprietors appointed Carteret secretary, council member, and assistant to the governor for the North Carolina colony, then called Albemarle. Carteret arrived in Albemarle on 23 Feb. 1664/65 to assume his offices. On 28 Oct. 1668, Governor Samuel Stephens appointed him lieutenant colonel of the Albemarle Militia. On 17 Jan. 1670, Sir George Carteret appointed him his deputy for Albemarle, validating under the recently adopted Fundamental Constitutions Carteret's earlier appointments, made under a different constitution. On 10 Mar. 1670, the Albemarle council appointed Carteret governor to fill the vacancy created by Stephens's death. The appointment was later confirmed by the proprietors, and Carteret continued as governor until his return to England in about June 1672.

In addition to his official duties, Carteret had responsibilities as agent for four of the proprietors, including his cousin, who had launched a joint business venture in Albermarle. The enterprise, located on Collington (then Colleton) Island and the nearby mainland, was a plantation on which a variety of activities were envisioned. In addition to the principal products of the colony, which were corn, tobacco, hogs, and cattle, the Collington Island plantation was intended to produce wine and whale oil in quantity for export to England and horses for export to Barbados.

On his arrival, Carteret found the Collington Island plantation hardly begun and its prospects far below the expectations of the investors. Needed laborers were lacking, and livestock and supplies, for which the investors had paid, had not been delivered. Carteret succeeded in producing some tobacco and whale oil for sale, but on the whole the venture failed. Frequent hurricanes destroyed buildings and fences; droughts, floods, and windstorms destroyed crops; disease and vermin killed livestock; and epidemics prevented the laborers from working for long periods. Moreover, the project was inadequately financed, and Carteret often found himself paying the running expenses from his own pocket. Two years after his return to England, he was still trying to get reimbursement for the £330 he had advanced.

As governor, Carteret faced yet more serious problems. The disasters that befell the Collington Island venture had likewise afflicted the colonists. Such calamities, combined with already existing handicaps, had reduced the settlers to poverty and near starvation. Dissatisfaction in the colony was increased upon receipt of the newly adopted Fundamental Constitutions, which imposed a form of government the colonists considered impracticable and land policies they deemed ruinous. Carteret, who sympathized with the settlers, was able to dispel the dissension that had previously rent the colony and to achieve a degree of unity, but he could do little to improve economic conditions without authority from the proprietors.

In the spring of 1672 the Albemarle council decided that Carteret should go to London as agent of "the People of Albemarle" to explain to the proprietors the problems of the colony and "treat with the Lords" for changes in policy. Although Carteret undertook the mission expecting to return, his departure in early summer marked the end of his association with Albemarle. On reaching London, he found that the proprietors had no interest in the colony. In fact, they then expected to dispose of Albemarle to Sir William Berkeley, who in return was expected to convey to them his interest in the remainder of Carolina. Although that expectation was never realized, it prevented the proprietors from taking any action respecting Albemarle for several years.

For a time, Carteret hoped to return to Albemarle, either as an official under Berkeley or in connection with the Collington Island property, which he proposed be turned over to him in lieu of the money owed him. He apparently had relinquished that hope by November 1676, when he gave power of attorney over his Albemarle affairs to William Crawford, who had assisted in managing the Collington Island plantation. Crawford appears to have liquidated Carteret's interests in Albemarle within the next few years.

SEE: *North Carolina Historical and Genealogical Register*, 3 vols. (1900–1903); North Carolina State Archives (Raleigh), for Albemarle Book of Warrants and Surveys (1681–1706) and Council Minutes, Wills, Inventories (1677–1701); Mattie Erma Edwards Parker, ed., *North Carolina Higher-Court Records, 1670–1696* (1968); William S. Powell, ed., *Ye Countie of Albemarle in Carolina* (1958); Hugh F. Rankin, *Upheaval in Albemarle: The Story of Culpeper's Rebellion* (1962); William L. Saunders, ed., *Colonial Records of North Carolina*, vol. 1 (1886).

MATTIE ERMA E. PARKER

Cartwright, Andrew J. *(1835–1903)*, minister and agent of the American Colonization Society, was born in Elizabeth City under circumstances as yet unknown: some contend that he was the son of slave parents and others that he was freeborn. Nothing is known about his early life except that he learned to read and write despite the lack of any formal education. If he did begin life as a slave, he left bondage through manumission or escape as a young man. Several years before the Civil War enforced emancipation, Cartwright was residing in New England and preparing himself for the ministry. By 1860 he was an ordained minister in the African Methodist Episcopal church and served as a regular circuit minister to the New England conference. He married a local woman on one of his circuits and eventually fathered four children, but knowledge of his family is limited to the fact that they could all read and write.

During the Federal occupation of Eastern North Carolina, Cartwright returned to his native state, preaching to the freedmen in the area around Albemarle Sound. He settled in Manteo, where in 1865 he established the first AME Zion church in northeastern North Carolina, the first in North Carolina having been established in New Bern the year before. Cartwright rode the circuit in the Albemarle section, founding numerous churches in Pasquotank, Perquimans, Currituck, Camden, and Hertford counties. For his contributions to the AME Zion church, he received appointment as presiding elder for the northeastern district of North Carolina. The position granted him the status of assistant bishop, with supervisory power over the resident ministers in the district counties.

Cartwright was an enthusiastic promoter of the camp meeting tradition, where sermons were fired with early nineteenth-century revivalism. His zeal for circuit riding and the popularity of his serivces made him a logical choice to represent the American Colonization Society in

North Carolina. For ten years he preached a mixture of spiritual salvation and fulfillment of Negro destiny through transport to Liberia. Most of the blacks who accepted the challenge were from counties where he regularly spoke. He himself eventually succumbed to his own enthusiasm for the venture. In January 1875 he requested and received funds from the American Colonization Society to journey to Liberia as a minister for the emigrants. Cartwright and some of his family sailed for West Africa, arriving there in June 1876; he thereby became the first missionary to Liberia.

Cartwright quickly discovered rampant immorality and religious indifference among both native Liberians and those recently arrived from America. The spirit of the evangelist rose to the challenge, prompting plans for a series of revivals in the towns and villages. His campaign opened at Brewerville on 4 July with less than stirring success. Undaunted, he persisted in his efforts and slowly but surely won converts to the AME Zion church. Even the lack of a house of worship (until 1892) did not deter the formation of a congregation, which numbered forty-nine by 1878.

The General Conference of the AME Zion Church in America, holding its 1880 meeting in Montgomery, Ala., officially accepted the establishment of the church in Liberia. Cartwright was named the official representative of Zion in Liberia and appointed presiding elder by Bishop Alexander Walters of the Seventh Episcopal District. The honor was granted partially in response to Cartwright's work but mostly because he was already settled in Liberia, where he had attained social and political status in the society. Even so, his appointment was not popular among a number of churchmen, including some of his own congregation. Laymen from Brewerville, unhappy with the slow progress of the church under Cartwright's supervision, petitioned the general conference to appoint Bishop James Walker Hood as resident head of the African mission. Bishop Hood had far too many other commitments to accept a new position, but he made clear his doubts that Cartwright could handle the job.

Time bore out Hood's prophetic skepticism. The work of supervising the growing missionary movement in West Africa was too much for Cartwright. No longer a young man, he was unequal to the task. Whether the parent church expected too much or Cartwright achieved too little, or perhaps both, the general conference of 1896 raised serious questions about his status as presiding elder in Liberia. The argument was extended to contest his role as an active minister in the AME Zion church, but his earlier success and lengthy service (over thirty years) had earned the respect and support of a large following. Debate over Cartwright's future was interrupted by the appearance of the man himself, there to make a progress report to the conference. The matter was dropped.

Cartwright returned to Liberia still the presiding elder of the West African District, but without the full support of the church. A disillusioned man, his last seven years were uninspired and uneventful. He died in Brewerville in 1903 at the age of sixty-eight.

Failure in later life has clouded his real contributions to the church and to religious history in general. He had neither the capacity nor the temperament to be the leader of a large sophisticated church body; he was first and foremost an evangelist, an organizer, a mover of people. His forte was establishing churches, preaching to the unenlightened, and recruiting for the American Colonization Society. Taken out of that element, he was doomed to failure and general obscurity.

SEE: David H. Bradley, Sr., *The History of the A.M.E. Zion Church* (1956); Cartwright Letters (National Archives, Washington, D.C.); E. E. Hale, "Some Notes on Roanoke Island and James River," *Proceedings of the American Antiquarian Society*, 21 Oct. 1864; Benjamin Quarles, *The Negro in the Civil War* (1953); *The Star of Zion* (1962); Walter L. Yates, "The History of the African Methodist Episcopal Zion Church in West Africa, Liberia, and the Gold Coast, 1880–1890" (B.D. thesis, Hartford Seminary, Hartford, Conn., 1963).

JERRY L. CROSS

Caruthers, Eli Washington (26 Dec. 1793–14 Nov. 1865), Presbyterian minister, educator, and historian, was born in Rowan County, near Salisbury. His parents were James and Elizabeth Lawrence Caruthers. The second of seven children, he received his early education from a tutor employed on his father's farm. He next attended a school taught by the Reverend Joseph Kirkpatrick, a Presbyterian minister. In 1812 he entered Hampden-Sydney College, where he paid his tuition by tutoring students. His college career was interrupted by a brief service in the War of 1812, after which he completed his baccalaureate degree at the College of New Jersey (now Princeton University). Following his graduation in 1817, he entered Princeton Theological Seminary to prepare for the ministry and was licensed to preach by New Brunswick Presbytery in April 1820. In 1821 he was called as minister of the Buffalo, Alamance, and Bethel Presbyterian churches of Guilford County; he was installed by Orange Presbytery in November of that year. He resigned the pastorate of Bethel Church after a year and gave up the Buffalo congregation in 1846. He remained as pastor at Alamance until 1861.

Like his predecessor in the pastorate at Buffalo and Alamance, David Caldwell, Caruthers was an advocate of the camp meeting and stressed the need for evangelism. Caruthers was known as an able minister, and over two hundred of his sermons in the collection of his papers in the Duke University Library demonstrate the high order of his homiletical ability. His sermons were usually didactic and were often elucidated by beautiful illustrations drawn from nature. Occasionally he abandoned this usual method to make earnest appeals to each class of his audience. He often exchanged pulpits with ministers of various denominations. Until 1846, when the congregation at Alamance required him to reside there, he lived in the little town of Greensboro.

Caruthers was much interested in education. He served as secretary of the Greensboro Academy and probably taught there in the 1820s. He was an active supporter of the Caldwell Institute, a Presbyterian preparatory school for boys, during the nine years (1836–45) it was located in Greensboro before its removal to Hillsborough. He served as teacher of Greek and for almost two years (1844–46) as president of the Greensboro High School, Greensboro's successor to the Caldwell Institute. In June 1847 he opened a classical school in the Alamance community. In 1850 he turned over the Alamance Classical School, as it was known by that time, to his assistant, Samuel Wiley, and began to devote his full energies to his ministerial duties and his historical research and writing.

It is as a historian of the American Revolution in North Carolina that Caruthers is best remembered. Recognizing the need to record facts concerning that period of the state's history before they should be lost to future generations, he wrote his first book, *A Sketch of the Life and Character of the Reverend David Caldwell, D.D.* (1842), which is less a biography than a repository of information about the Revolution and other aspects of state history. Caruthers's interest in the Revolution continued to grow, and he published two additional books concerning it: *Revolutionary Incidents and Sketches of Character Chiefly in the "Old North State"* (1854) and *Interesting Revolutionary Incidents and Sketches of Character Chiefly in the "Old North State," Second Series* (1856). Both volumes presented the Revolution as a civil war in North Carolina in keeping with Caruthers's belief, stated in the preface to the first volume, that "the horrors attending a 'civil' war should be held up as a warning against whatever might have any tendency to produce a similar state of things again." Much of the second series was a defense of the role played by the state militia in the war, especially at Guilford Courthouse. Caruthers received much help in gathering materials for these volumes from fellow historians President David L. Swain of The University of North Carolina and Griffith J. McRee of Wilmington. In turn, he supplied McRee with information useful in the preparation of his *Life and Correspondence of James Iredell* (2 vols., 1857–58) and tried, unsuccessfully, to secure subscribers for the work in Greensboro and the surrounding area. Caruthers regretted that his professional duties allowed him little time for historical study and that the smallness of his salary prohibited the purchase of more than a few books of history. In 1854, The University of North Carolina conferred upon him an honorary doctorate in recognition of his accomplishments as a historian and his contributions to the state as an educator and minister.

In addition to his published works, Caruthers left two book-length manuscripts of importance. The shorter of these is "Richard Hugg King and His Times," of which a typescript is to be found in the Richard Hugg King Papers, North Carolina Division of Archives and History, Raleigh. A biographical sketch of a leader in the Great Revival of the early nineteenth century in North Carolina, South Carolina, and Tennessee, it gives vivid descriptions of the revival as well as Caruthers's insight into the movement's emotional appeal. The longer manuscript, "American Slavery and the Immediate Duty of Southern Slaveholders," now located in the Manuscript Collection, Library, Duke University, was written at irregular intervals between 1840 and 1850 and includes several revisions and a second preface written in 1865. Described by John Spencer Bassett as "one of the strongest arraignments of slavery in the abstract that ever appeared," this work was undertaken at the request of a particular friend that Caruthers write down his views on the slavery question in order that they might be preserved for posterity. Unhappy with all previous publications on the slavery controversy, North and South, Caruthers "threw them every one aside and undertook to investigate the subject anew. . . ." He made the Bible his "main source of proof" and adopted as the basis of all his arguments "the fundamental principle that you can have no right to hold anything as property without an *express* grant from the Creator," which doctrine he declared he had never heard nor seen in any publication. Realizing that its publication or circulation would not be tolerated in any southern state at the time, Caruthers kept his manuscript secret from the public. The 1865 preface indicates, however, that he was by then contemplating publication, which was probably circumvented by his death shortly thereafter.

Caruthers's attitude toward slavery was nevertheless well known to his contemporaries. During the Civil War he had no sympathy for the southern cause, which he regarded as both unjust and ruinous for the South.

Nonetheless, the Alamance congregation contributed heavily to the war effort. Twenty-five members of the church enlisted in the Confederate armed forces, and of these twelve gave their lives. Tradition has it that Caruthers publicly prayed in 1861 that the young men who had gone into the army might be blessed of the Lord and returned home in safety although engaged in a bad cause. An apparently apocryphal story states that on the following day a congregational meeting at Alamance Church demanded his resignation (there is no mention of such a meeting in the "Minutes of Congregational Meetings" of the church). Caruthers's letter of resignation, dated 5 July 1861, gives poor health as the reason for his wish to retire from the active ministry, as does the historical sketch of Alamance Church published in 1880 by Calvin H. Wiley, to whom as clerk of session Caruthers's letter was addressed.

Caruthers, a lifelong bachelor, spent the remaining four and a quarter years of his life at the home of Fountain B. McLean near Greensboro. He died there and was buried in the graveyard of Alamance Church, where the congregation erected an appropriate marker over his resting place.

SEE: Alamance Presbyterian Church, for Minutes of Congregational Meetings (1820–65) and Minutes of Session (1820–65); J. S. Bassett, *Anti-Slavery Leaders of North Carolina* (1898); Kemp P. Battle, *History of the University of North Carolina*, 2 vols. (1907–12); C. R. Brockman, *Adams-Caruthers-Clancy-Neely and Townsend Descendants* (1950); Eli Washington Caruthers Papers (Manuscript Collection, Library, Duke University, Durham [photograph]); E. W. Caruthers, "Richard Hugg King and His Times" (Richard Hugg King Papers, North Carolina State Archives, Raleigh); S. N. Rankin, *History of Buffalo Presbyterian Church and Her People* (1934); C. L. Raper, *The Church and Private Schools of North Carolina* (1898); David Schenck, *A Short Sketch of the Life of Eli W. Caruthers* (1901); Southern Historical Collection (University of North Carolina, Chapel Hill), for Heartt Family Papers, Griffith John McRee Papers, and Wilson Family Papers; J. C. Wharton, "Rev. E. W. Caruthers," *College Message* 8 (1898); C. H. Wiley, *Alamance Church* (1880).

W. CONARD GASS

Cary, Thomas *(d. ca. 1720)*, deputy governor and council president, was born in England and related by marriage to the Quaker proprietor John Archdale. Cary apparently emigrated to South Carolina late in the seventeenth century. He established himself as a merchant and, by 1702, owned several sailing vessels. In June 1702 he was one of two men posting the two thousand pound bond required by the Lords Proprietors for Sir Nathaniel Johnson to become governor of Carolina. At the same time, Cary posted a similar bond for the new governor of the Bahamas. Clearly, he was a man of some wealth.

Despite his relationship to Archdale, Cary may have been Anglican. Sir Nathaniel Johnson, who made Cary his deputy governor in March 1705, was a "high Church" man himself, and it is hard to believe that he would have sent a dissenter into religiously troubled North Carolina, no matter what their personal relationship was. Upon his arrival in the Albemarle region in March, Cary allied himself with the powerful Anglican faction there. He enforced the statute requiring oaths of allegiance in order to hold public office and thereby excluded numerous Quakers from the November 1705 meeting of the assembly.

The dissenters retaliated by sending John Porter to England to seek Cary's removal by the proprietors. Armed with instructions suspending Johnson's authority over North Carolina and removing Cary from office, Porter returned and effected the election of William Glover as president of the council, and thereby new chief executive, in October 1707. Cary had been inspecting his holdings in South Carolina while this event transpired, and upon his return in November he began to seek ways to regain his office. By the summer of 1708, Glover had broken with the dissenters. Seeing his opportunity, Cary began courting the favor of Porter, the dissenters, and Bath County residents, who were dissatisfied with a political framework that favored the Albemarle region over any other.

At the assembly meeting in October 1708, two groups of councilors attended, one pledged to Glover and the other to Cary. Through the machinations of Porter and Edward Mosely, Cary's faction triumphed, and Glover fled to Virginia. The assembly then proceeded to nullify all test oaths. As council president, Cary replaced some local officials with dissenters, liberalized the land grant policy, and lowered the quitrent rate in Bath County.

Early in 1711, Cary was displaced by Edward Hyde as governor and withdrew to his home in Bath County. When Hyde called on the March assembly to enact new legislation against dissenters and urged the arrest of Cary and John Porter, Cary rallied his supporters, and the rebellion that took his name began. In addition to the Anglican-dissenter confrontation, there was a definite sectional aspect to the struggle. Of those Cary lieutenants who fought in the rebellion from start to finish, every one was a Bath County man.

On 27 May 1711, Hyde and a 150-man force marched on the Pamlico region to seize Cary. Armed with five artillery pieces and about forty men, Cary successfully withstood Hyde's assault; and on 1 June, Hyde returned northward. Heartened by this development, Cary outfitted a brigantine and sailed for Albemarle Sound in mid-June to overthrow the government. After a series of indecisive engagements, Governor Alexander Spotswood of Virginia sent a military force into North Carolina early in July to support Hyde. By 17 July, Cary's brigantine had been seized and he and his officers forced to flee into Virginia. There, in late July, Spotswood found Cary and his lieutenants hiding with the Kecoughtan Indians on the James River. He sent them to England to stand trial before the Lords Proprietors.

In September, Cary and four of his allies arrived in England. They appeared before the proprietors on 20 Nov. 1711. Hearings continued intermittently for nearly a year, after which the proprietors released the rebels. No representative of Hyde's government ever appeared in London to press charges, the colony being engulfed in the Tuscarora War. Cary returned to North Carolina in the spring of 1713, and as late as September some Albemarle leaders feared that he would lead another uprising. The proprietors had ordered that no local charges could be brought against him until Francis Nicholson had investigated the rebellion, and he never did so.

Cary apparently spent his few remaining years in Bath County in relative tranquility. He died between late 1716 and 1722: he was involved in a court action on the former date, and his son and heir, John, was in court on the latter.

SEE: British P.R.O. (London), for CO5/290; William S. Price, Jr., *North Carolina Higher-Court Records, 1702–1708* and *1709–1723* (1974 and forthcoming); William L . Saunders, ed., *Colonial Records of North Carolina*, vol. 1 (1886); Vincent H. Todd, ed., *Christoph Von Graffenried's Account of the Founding of New Bern* (1920).

WILLIAM S. PRICE, JR.

Cash, Wilbur Joseph (2 May 1900–1 July 1941), journalist and author, was born in Gaffney, S.C., of Ulster Scot and German ancestry, the oldest of three boys and one girl. His father, John William Cash, managed the company store of Limestone Mills; his mother, Nannie Lutitia Hamrick, had taught music in the public schools. First named Joseph Wilbur, Cash reversed the order of his names and commonly used only the initials. Schoolmates called him "Sleepy," and to newspaper friends he was "Jack." He attended the public schools of Gaffney until 1912, when his father moved to nearby Boiling Springs, N.C., to enter partnership in a general store with Wilbur's maternal grandfather, an upcountry Republican and first mayor of the town. Cash entered Boiling Springs High School (later Gardner-Webb College), a Baptist academy, where in April 1917 he gave the commencement address. During summers he worked on his grandfather's nearby farm.

During 1917–18, Cash worked at odd jobs in shipyards and cantonments from Maryland to Florida, mainly at Camp Wadsworth near Spartanburg, S.C., where his father organized a fleet of cars to transport soldiers. In 1918–19, at his father's urging, he attended Wofford College, but he disliked what seemed to him the narrow provincialism of the Methodist school (his reaction was in part a rebellion against a strict Baptist upbringing). In 1919 he went to Valparaiso University in northern Indiana, but dropped out at Christmastime. Early in 1920 he acceded to his father's wishes and entered Wake Forest College, despite misgivings about another "preacher college."

The college was supported by North Carolina Baptists but headed by Dr. William Louis Poteat, a biologist whose acceptance of Darwinian evolution made him the target of fundamentalist attacks. At Wake Forest, Cash awakened to new ideas, affected a bohemian style, and became a campus iconoclast. He read H. L. Mencken and copied his style in the student paper, the *Old Gold and Black*, which he served as associate editor in his senior year. He delighted in baiting the state Baptist organ, the *Biblical Recorder*, on such diverse issues as evolution and social dancing. During summers he helped out at a hosiery mill, of which his father had become superintendent. Graduated with an A.B. in 1922, he spent one year in the Wake Forest Law School but decided against legal practice; he taught English at Georgetown College in Kentucky for two years and at the Hendersonville School for Boys for one year and then decided to take up journalism.

Having worked as a student journalist and, in the summer of 1923, as reporter for the *Charlotte Observer*, he first took a job with the *Chicago Post* but soon returned to North Carolina as reporter for the *Charlotte News*. In the summer of 1927, threatened with a nervous collapse, he left for a bicycle tour through England, France, Italy, Switzerland, Germany, and Belgium. He returned to Boiling Springs for a stint as editor of the semiweekly *Cleveland Press* in nearby Shelby. During the campaign of 1928 his editorials attacked anti-Catholic prejudice against Al Smith. In 1929 he retired to Boiling Springs with the notion of making his way as a free-lance writer. His first magazine pieces appeared in Mencken's

American Mercury the same year: "Jehovah of the Tar Heels," a blast at Senator Furnifold M. Simmons, in July, and in October, "The Mind of the South," an idea that had incubated in his mind since, as an undergraduate, he had heard Professor C. C. Pearson discourse on "the Mind of Virginia" and "The Mind of North Carolina."

The second article caught the eye of Blanche Knopf, wife of New York publisher Alfred A. Knopf, who invited Cash to submit a plan or manuscript for a book. In March 1930, with the encouragement of Chapel Hill sociologist Howard W. Odum, Cash sent Mrs. Knopf the sketch of a book to be called *The Mind of the South*. Soon afterward, however, a physical collapse forced him to enter a Charlotte hospital for several months, after which doctors ordered him to quit writing and study and to get exercise in outdoor activity. For two years he did little serious writing, but in 1932 he went to work on the book in a back room of the Boiling Springs post office, where his aunt was postmistress. In that unheated room he continued to free-lance for various outlets and worked on his book with the agonized persistence of a perfectionist. He threw away more pages than he kept but persevered in the face of poor health, poverty, and monumental writing blocks.

In 1937, Cash's father's hosiery mill ran afoul of the business recession. John Cash got a job as a traveling shoe salesman, and W. J. returned to the *Charlotte News* as a full-time editorialist. He got the assignment to cover foreign affairs, a form of editorial "Afghanistanism" to keep him away from strictures on right thinking and the local powers. He had more latitude on the book page, where few but the local intelligentsia noticed his weekly column. In time snatched from his newspaper work, Cash brought his book to completion in July 1940. In February 1941, Knopf published *The Mind of the South*.

Cash and his fiancée, Mrs. Mary Ross Northrup, had agreed to postpone marriage until he finished the book. On Chrismas Day 1940 they were married by a justice of the peace in York, S.C. On 30 May 1941, with a Guggenheim Fellowship in hand, the Cashes left for Mexico City, where he planned to write the fictional saga of a southern industrial community. It was his cherished ambition to write a novel, and over the years he had made false starts on several. Along the way he stopped to give the commencement address at the University of Texas—his new fame had brought the invitation. In Mexico City, however, the combination of fatigue, altitude, and climate made him ill. On 30 June he suddenly became obsessed with delusions that Nazi agents were plotting to murder him in revenge for his editorials. The following day he fled alone and took a room at the Hotel Reforma, where he was found dead that night, hanged by his necktie from the bathroom door.

The cause of his death cannot be resolved with certainty. Evidence of Nazi agents is nonexistent, and an autopsy failed to reveal a brain tumor, reports of which were invented to spare mourners additional pain. Cash had a long personal history of neuroses, depression, fears of impotence, and endocrine disorders, but his biographer Joseph L. Morrison decided that these had at most a secondary importance. The most likely explanation was a suicidal fit resulting from an "acute brain syndrome," an affliction caused by unknown toxins in the system. Cash's remains were cremated, brought back by his widow for a funeral service at Shelby's First Baptist Church, and later interred in a vault in Sunset Cemetery.

Cash's reputation rests on his magnum opus, a brilliant masterpiece that transcended the limitations of his own and the historian's craft. The product of exhaustive reading, perceptive observation, and creative insight, *The Mind of the South* is by common consent a classic work of history and social criticism. Two major themes dominate the book: the uniformity of the southern mind and its continuity. Class conflict in Cash's view, was limited by the "proto-Dorian bond" by which the common white (like the Doric knight of Sparta) was elevated to the dominant class through the "vastly ego-warming and ego-expanding distinction between the white man and the black." While there were in truth many Souths, the "man at the center" was the back country yeoman farmer of the Old South and his descendants, the people from whom Cash himself sprang. The book challenged both the shopworn cavalier myth of the Old South and the legend of a progressive and modernized South. The region was like "a tree with many age rings, with its limbs and trunk bent and twisted by all the winds of the years, but with its tap root still in the Old South."

Cash explored many tenacious paradoxes—the juxtaposition of class unity and class exploitation, individualism and the "savage ideal" of conformity, fundamentalist morality and the "hell-of-a-fellow complex"—and the complicated interrelationship of these with race, romanticism, rhetoric, leisure, the cult of womanhood (the "lily-pure maid of Astolat"), the rape complex, violence, paternalism, demagoguery, and suspicion of outsiders.

The changing South of 1940 was the South still, at its best "Proud, brave, honorable by its lights, courteous, personally generous, loyal, swift to act, often too swift." But its special vices remained: "Violence, intolerance, aversion and suspicion toward new ideas, an incapacity for analysis . . . an exaggerated individualism and too narrow concept of social responsibility, attachment to fictions and false values, above all a too great attachment to racial values and a tendency to justify cruelty and injustice in the name of those values." The book ended on a note of pessimism. Soon the South would "have to prove its capacity for adjustment far beyond what has been true in the past." The "tragedy of the South as it stood in 1940" was the lack of "articulation between the new intellectual leaders and the body of the South."

The book was well received by reviewers, the only adverse notices being written by two of the Nashville Agrarian group whom Cash had severely criticized. Certain reservations, however, have been expressed in retrospect, most notably by C. Vann Woodward. The treatment of Reconstruction was untouched by the nascent revisionism of the time. The book was a study of "temperament" rather than "mind" and neglected southern intellectuals. It paid little attention to the mind of the black South or to many of the white dissenters—antislavery advocates, Unionists, Republicans, Readjusters, Populists, the peace advocates of World War I. And it was rooted in the Appalachian foothills with which Cash was most familiar, giving "an unbiased history of the South from the hillbilly point of view." Still, it would be difficult to challenge Joseph L. Morrison's judgment of *The Mind of the South*: "During this second half of the twentieth century, it has been accepted by virtually everyone that studies of the South—and by extension, of the Negro revolution—must begin where Cash left off."

SEE: R. B. Downs, *Books That Changed America* (1970); D. W. Grantham, Jr., "Mr. Cash Writes a Book," *Progressive* 25 (1961); Mary Cash Maury, "The Suicide of W. J. Cash," *Red Clay Reader* 4 (1967); J. L. Morrison, "A Biographical Detective Story," ibid., "Found: The Missing Editorship of W. J. Cash," *North Carolina Historical Review* 47 (1970), "A Good Afghanistanism: W. J. Cash as an Editorialist of the South," *Journalism Quarterly* 44 (1967), "The Obsessive 'Mind' of W. J. Cash," *Virginia Quarterly Review* 41 (1965), and *W. J. Cash: Southern Prophet* (1967); North Carolina Collection (University of North Carolina, Chapel Hill), for a recording of Cash's 1941 commencement address at the University of Texas; C. V. Woodward, "W. J. Cash Reconsidered," *New York Review of Books*, 4 Dec. 1969; E. M. Yoder, Jr., "W. J. Cash after a Quarter Century," *Harper's Magazine* 231 (1965).

GEORGE B. TINDALL

Caswell, Benjamin (*20 Apr. 1737–1791*), planter, revolutionary army officer, merchant, county official, and state legislator, was born at Joppa, Md., the fifth son of Richard Caswell the elder and Christian Dallam. He attended the parish school at St. John's (Anglican) Church at Joppa until his parents migrated to North Carolina. Thereafter, his education was provided by family members and local schoolmasters.

Caswell married Martha Singleton, daughter of Samuel and Hannah Singleton of Dobbs County and sister to Captain Spyers Singleton, who became noted as a Continental army officer and, after the Revolution, as a prominent businessman of Craven County. The marriage took place before December 1762, at which time the will of Samuel Singleton named Caswell as testator's son-in-law. Caswell and his wife settled on a plantation about four miles south of present Snow Hill, Greene County. The site is still identifiable by a small stream called Caswell's Branch and also by a site on nearby Great Contentnea Creek, which has been known as Ben Caswell's Landing since colonial times. The couple had several children. Although widespread destruction of local records leaves the report of these children incomplete, records of sons Samuel, Matthew, and Benjamin William and of a daughter, Sarah Rebecca, have been found.

Caswell's public services included periods as a justice of Dobbs County and several terms as sheriff of Dobbs (1774–77, 1780–84, and 1787–91). He served in the House of Commons in the General Assembly of 1781. He was active in the colonial militia of Johnston County and later was a lieutenant in the Dobbs militia; he was captain of a Dobbs militia company at the Battle of Alamance in 1771 and at the Battle of Moore's Creek Bridge in 1776. During the period 1777–79, he was captain of the light horse in the state regiment, a select force established by Governor Richard Caswell to guard the seat of state government, the governor's person, the General Assembly when in session, and the board of war. It also served as a recruiting and training unit for officers sent as replacements to the Continental regiments. In 1781, Caswell is shown on a list of disabled persons who volunteered for service when Kinston was under attack by British forces marching from Wilmington.

Caswell is occasionally noted as a merchant of Dobbs County, sometimes alone, sometimes associated with his brother-in-law, Spyers Singleton, and sometimes associated with Benjamin Sheppard, who resided at present Snow Hill.

Caswell died in November 1791, according to the last accounting returned for the sheriff of Dobbs County. His wife had died in 1790. Both were buried in the old cemetery close to the site of their former home, near present Snow Hill.

SEE: Caswell family record collection in the possession of Charles R. Holloman, Raleigh; Richard Caswell Papers (North Carolina State Archives, Raleigh); Family records, 1712–1790, Richard Caswell family Bible (North Carolina State Archives, Raleigh); Hillsborough District Superior Court Records (Case papers entitled The Governor vs. the Heirs of Richard Caswell) (North Carolina State Archives, Raleigh); Talmage C. Johnson and Charles R. Holloman, *The Story of Kinston and Lenoir County* (1954); New Bern District Superior Court Records (Several sets of case papers including those of Caswell family members and their heirs and estates, 1760–1808) (North Carolina State Archives, Raleigh); William L. Saunders and Walter Clark, eds., *Colonial and State Records of North Carolina*, vols. 8–25 (1890–1906).

CHARLES R. HOLLOMAN

Caswell, Martin *(15 Feb. 1733–ca. June 1789)*, colonial planter, county official, and colonel in the revolutionary militia of Dobbs County, was the third son of Richard Caswell the elder and his wife, Christian Dallam, and was a brother of Governor Richard Caswell. Martin was born at Joppa, Md., and received his early education in the parish school of St. John's (Anglican) Church there. When he was fourteen years old, his family migrated to New Bern and shortly thereafter settled near present-day Kinston. He received further education from his parents and older brothers and served an apprenticeship as assistant in the office of the clerk of the court of Johnston County.

At the age of twenty-one, Caswell became sheriff of Johnston County; he served from 1754 to 1756. He became a justice of the Johnston County Court in 1756 and continued to serve as a justice for Dobbs County when Dobbs was formed from eastern Johnston in 1759. In October 1763 he gave up the office of justice to become clerk of the court of Dobbs upon the death of Charles Young, former clerk of Johnston and first clerk of Dobbs. Caswell held this post for the next twenty-six years; accordingly, his tenure in the office covered almost the entire period of Dobbs County's existence. Until shortly before the Revolution, the clerk of the county court was also the register of deeds. The position was one of great influence in local government, inasmuch as the clerk was usually called upon to recommend persons to the royal governor for justices and other county offices.

Caswell held a considerable acreage but was not a wealthy man: his property was valued at £4,045 on a county-wide list of taxable property compiled in the year 1780.

Caswell became active in the colonial militia when he was sixteen years old. By 1761 he was captain of a company in the Dobbs militia, and he served at the Battle of Alamance in 1771. He was lieutenant colonel in 1776 at the Battle of Moore's Creek Bridge and became colonel in 1779.

In about 1754, Caswell married, probably in Johnston County (the public records of Johnston for that period have been burned). The maiden name of his wife has not been found, but a deed of record in Pitt County shows that her given name was Nancy. The couple had several children of whom knowledge is meager because Dobbs County records have also been burned. The names of six of their children have been proved from scattered record sources: Martin, Jr., James, Francis, William, Mary, and Nancy.

A note of Caswell's death during the summer of 1789 is of record. His name as clerk of the court of Dobbs disappears from Dobbs County Court transcripts sent to

the superior court for the New Bern District in June 1789. The place of his burial is not definitely known, but it is highly probable that he was buried in the Caswell family cemetery at The Hill, where his mother and father, according to their family Bible record, were buried. Nancy Caswell survived him for many years.

SEE: Sources cited under Benjamin Caswell.

CHARLES R. HOLLOMAN

Caswell, Richard *(1685–24 Apr. 1755)*, colonial merchant, planter, Maryland legislator, county court clerk, justice, and militia officer, was a native of London. His father's family was notable among the ranks of the English gentry: the lineage is traced to Henry Careswell (fl. 1440) of Staffordshire, whose son, Robert Careswell, became a prime officer in the household of Thomas, Lord Stanley, the first Earl of Derby. Robert's son, John Caswell of Wedon, shortened the surname, and this spelling was perpetuated among his descendants. Richard Slaney Caswell, father of the Richard who emigrated to America, used the Caswell spelling in registering his lineage and his ancestral coat of arms with the royal heralds during their Visitation of London in 1634.

The family name on Richard Caswell's maternal side was Smith. His mother's people were merchants engaged in overseas trade with the American colonies. Both parents died while Richard was still young, and his care was undertaken by his mother's brother, William Smith, a prosperous merchant who was married but without a child of his own. Smith and his wife gave their nephew parental affection and the advantages of education. As the youth grew into manhood, he entered naturally upon the career of a merchant in his uncle's business. In 1710, Mrs. Smith died. A few months thereafter, William Smith and his nephew decided to dispose of their London business and migrate to America to establish a mercantile business at Joppa, Md., where other relatives had previously settled. Joppa was at that time a flourishing colonial town and the most important port on the Chesapeake Bay.

In November 1711, Smith and his bachelor nephew departed London. They were to be the immigrant forefathers of a numerous clan of American revolutionary patriots that would include two state revolutionary wartime governors, three revolutionary generals, several colonels and captains, and Continental congressmen. The record of the arrival in Maryland on 2 Feb. 1712 appears in Richard Caswell's Bible. They soon established a residence and a mercantile business in Joppa.

Among their neighbors at Joppa were Richard Dallam and his wife, the former Elizabeth Martin (1685–1777), who had married at Joppa in 1702. They had a nine-year-old son, William Dallam, and an eight-year-old daughter, Christian Dallam. Smith, Caswell, and the Dallams became warm friends. In 1714, Richard Dallam died. A few months later, the two households were merged by the marriage of the widow Elizabeth Dallam and the widower William Smith. As the years passed, three children were born to the Smiths: two sons, Winstone and William, Jr., and one daughter, Elizabeth. All three grew to adulthood, married, and had children who were living during the Revolution. Samuel, a son of William, Jr., served his country as a general in the Revolutionary War and also in the War of 1812. He was in command of Fort McHenry, Md., when its spectacular bombardment by British warships during the War of 1812 inspired

Francis Scott Key to write "The Star Spangled Banner." The Smith daughter, Elizabeth, married John Paca; they became the parents of William Paca, signer of the Declaration of Independence, Revolutionary wartime governor of Maryland, lawyer, and judge.

On 12 Jan. 1723, Caswell married Christian Dallam. Following their marriage, they made their home at Mulberry Point on the Chesapeake Bay, near Joppa. Caswell continued in the mercantile business but branched out also into agriculture. On his farms near Joppa, called Caswell's Venture and Sterling Purchase, he produced tobacco, cattle, and other livestock for the coastal trade. The family were members of St. John's (Anglican) Church of Joppa, where Caswell served as a vestryman for many years. He was also a justice of the Baltimore County court, county coroner, and a captain in the county militia. From 1738 to 1743, he served in the legislature of Maryland.

During the early 1700s, commerce and politics shifted away from Joppa to Baltimore. By 1744, Caswell's mercantile business was ruined; his agricultural enterprises were too small and land prices had shot upward. His health also was failing. The future seemed darker as the town of Joppa, stagnating, approached abandonment. Finally, he decided to move his family to North Carolina, where he had friends at New Bern.

In the spring of 1745, Caswell sent his two oldest sons, William and Richard, both still minors, to North Carolina with letters of introduction and recommendation addressed to the royal governor and other friends at New Bern. The sons were to seek employment, obtain lands if possible, and otherwise prepare for the coming of the rest of the family. William Dallam, Caswell's brother-in-law, purchased Caswell's Joppa lands and other property in 1745, but Caswell's condition of health did not permit the journey to North Carolina until the following year.

With his wife and younger children, Caswell arrived in New Bern in the early weeks of 1746. At first they settled in New Bern, and Caswell went into business as operator of an ordinary. However, Richard, Jr., proved highly able and enterprising for a youth of eighteen years. Soon after arriving in North Carolina, William Caswell had found employment as deputy clerk of the county court of Johnston County, upon its being formed from Craven County in 1746; Richard, Jr., found employment even more quickly, as an assistant to the deputy surveyor general of the province, James Mackilwean. By 1747, young Richard had acquired by land grant a small plantation at a site now within the city of Kinston in Johnston (now Lenoir) County. He and William prepared a home there, to which the rest of the family moved in spring 1748. William then gave up his work with the county court to manage the plantation. The elder Richard Caswell was appointed to succeed William as deputy clerk; later he became clerk of the Johnston County court for a few years and thereafter served some months as a justice, until his death. He died and was buried at the family residence called The Hill (later renamed Newington-on-the-Hill and more recently Mount Vernon and Vernon Hall).

SEE: Sources cited under Benjamin Caswell; Maryland state, county, and parish records (Hall of Record, Annapolis, Md.); *The Visitation of London in 1634* (1916).

CHARLES R. HOLLOMAN

Caswell, Richard (3 Aug. 1729–10 Nov. 1789), militia officer and governor of North Carolina, was born at

Joppa, then a flourishing seaport and the county seat of Baltimore County, Md. His parents were Richard Caswell and Christian Dallam. Their plantation home, Mulberry Point, stood on a promontory north of the town, overlooking the Chesapeake Bay. He received his early education at the parish school taught by the Reverend William Cawthorn and the Reverend Joseph Hooper at St. John's (Anglican) Church in Joppa.

The elder Richard Caswell married late in life and had eleven children. By 1743 his health failed and, despite their youth, the two oldest sons, William and Richard, had to assume the major responsibilities of conducting their father's mercantile business and farming operations. This turn of events introduced Richard to business management and finance. However, the family fortunes went from bad to worse during Joppa's decline as a seaport, and in 1745 the family decided to follow family friends to North Carolina.

Baltimore County records show that the elder Richard Caswell sold his real estate at Joppa in 1745 to his brother-in-law, William Dallam. His health prevented early departure, however. It was finally decided that William and Richard, Jr., would go on to North Carolina to seek employment, obtain land if possible, and prepare a place to which the rest of the family could come.

Richard and William reached New Bern in late autumn of 1745 with a letter of recommendation from the governor of Maryland to North Carolina's royal governor, Gabriel Johnston. William was given employment in the secretary's office. Richard, then age sixteen, was made an apprentice to the surveyor general, James Mackilwean. For the next two years he lived with the Mackilwean family on their 850-acre plantation, Tower Hill, located at Stringer's Ferry on Neuse River, near present Kinston. During the rest of his life, Richard Caswell resided in that vicinity. By 1747 his training was completed, and he became deputy surveyor general upon reaching age eighteen. Also in 1747 he got his first land grant and built on it the home for his parents and their children. This home, then called The Hill, was renamed Newington-on-the-Hill by Caswell in February 1776; in about 1840 it was renamed Vernon Hall by a later owner, John Cobb Washington. After 1912 the house was rebuilt or greatly altered, but the present Vernon Hall and about six acres of ruined gardens and grounds still occupy the site. It was annexed to Kinston in the twentieth century.

While living with the Mackilwean family, Richard was introduced to North Carolina politics. James Mackilwean, besides being surveyor general, was long a member of the General Assembly, as was a neighbor, Dr. Francis Stringer. In his spare time, Caswell assisted Stringer in his business enterprises at Stringer's Ferry. The political interests and activities of Mackilwean and Stringer were educational for Caswell and offered him opportunities to become acquainted with other political leaders. When Johnston County was formed from upper Craven in 1746, the county seat was for several months at Stringer's Ferry. Richard's brother, William, and his father served as deputy clerk and clerk of the Johnston County court. Richard became an officer in the troop of horse of the Johnston County militia, and from 1749 to 1753 he also gained experience as deputy clerk. In 1753 he served a few weeks as the first clerk of Orange County court, when that county was formed from upper Johnston; he resigned upon being appointed high sheriff of Johnston.

On 21 Apr. 1752, Richard Caswell was married at Tower Hill to Mary Mackilwean (b. 1731), the daughter of James and Elinor Mackilwean. To this marriage three children were born. One daughter died at birth (15 Sept. 1753). A son, William (b. 24 Sept. 1754), grew to manhood and attained distinction during the Revolution. Another daughter (b. 4 Feb. 1757) apparently died in infancy. Mary Caswell died on 7 Feb. 1757, from complications of childbirth. During the marriage, the family lived at the Red House, a plantation home at the site of the present Richard Caswell Memorial Park in western Kinston. According to Caswell's will, his first wife and her son, Brigadier General William, are buried in the cemetery at the Red House plantation; their graves are unmarked, however.

On 20 June 1758, Caswell married Sarah Heritage (1740–94), a daughter of William Heritage and his first wife, Susannah Moore. To this marriage eight children were born: Richard, Jr. ("Dicky"; b. 15 Sept. 1759); Sarah (b. 26 Feb. 1762); Winston (b. 7 May 1764); Anna (b. 4 Dec. 1766); Dallam (b. 15 June 1769); John ("Jack"; b. 24 Jan. 1772); Susannah ("Susan"; b. 16 Feb. 1775); and Christian (7–9 Jan. 1779). Eight of the eleven children lived to adulthood.

Caswell's second father-in-law, William Heritage (ca. 1700–1769), also had a great influence upon Caswell's career. Heritage was a lawyer, planter, and political leader. From 1738 until his death in 1769, he served as clerk of the General Assembly, an influential post in the colonial government. He was a native of Bruton Parish, York County, Va., and had an excellent education. Caswell studied law under Heritage from 1758 to 1759 and was admitted to the bar on 1 Apr. 1759. At the same time he was commissioned deputy attorney general; he served in that post about four years.

From 1754 to 1776, Caswell was a member of the colonial assembly. In the period 1770–71 he was speaker of the house. As a legislative leader, he played a key role in the development and enactment of legislation relating to trade and industry, the court system, public defense, and humanitarian concerns. Most remarkable was his proposal for "erecting and establishing a free-school for every county," using as initial funding several thousand pounds granted to the province as reimbursement for aid rendered the Crown in the French and Indian War. The resulting "Address of the General Assembly," sent to the king in 1760, was cited to legislatures for many decades thereafter on behalf of free public schools. Caswell wrote the concept into the state's first constitution, as chairman of the drafting committee of the provincial congress of December 1776 that drew up the document.

The period from 1765 to 1775 was for North Carolina a decade of developing anti-British sentiment, protest activities, and public demonstrations. During this period, Caswell's private views were held in closest confidence, and to this day they are not certainly known. His public actions were ambivalent. Royal governors continued to trust him until April 1775; yet he held throughout the same period the highest confidence of the populace and their leaders in the assembly. In 1769 he was a leader in the "convention" into which the General Assembly at New Bern resolved itself immediately following Governor William Tryon's edict dissolving the assembly to prevent its resolving upon a public boycott of British goods. The congress defiantly adopted the boycott resolutions. Caswell was elected speaker of the next assembly, which expelled Harmon Husband, representative from Orange County and fiery advocate of the reforms demanded by thousands of back country Regulators. Governor Tryon immediately had Husband arrested, jailed, and charged with libel and sedition. Caswell was foreman of a grand jury that twice refused to indict Husband. Nevertheless, when the

Regulators threatened to march on New Bern, rescue Husband, and lay the town in ashes, Caswell, as colonel of the Dobbs militia, supported the royal governor's decision to fortify New Bern and organize an army to march against the Regulators. Caswell commanded the right wing of Tryon's army, which defeated a poorly equipped army of about 3,400 Regulators on 16 May 1771, at the Battle of Alamance.

A few months later, Caswell was appointed by the new royal governor, Josiah Martin, as one of three judges of the court of oyer and terminer and general gaol delivery. He was not reelected speaker by the next assembly, but on 8 Dec. 1773 he was appointed by Speaker John Harvey to serve with eight others as a standing committee of correspondence and inquiry. This committee supported cooperation of all the colonies in resisting the five Intolerable Acts of Parliament. Three of its members later served as state governor, two signed the Declaration of Independence, and three served as Revolutionary War generals. Caswell was a leader in all five of North Carolina's provincial congresses and also served in the First and Second Continental Congresses.

Royal Governor Josiah Martin reported that Caswell, after his return from the Second Continental Congress, became "the most active tool of sedition," a statement well justified by the facts. Caswell had conceived a daring plan to put all governmental powers at the disposal of the provincial congress. Alarmed by rumors of plans to take the governor and council prisoners, Martin fled the palace, calling upon the council members to join him aboard the British warship *Cruzier*. Caswell "had the insolence to reprehend the Committee of Safety for suffering me to remove from thence," Martin indicated later. The first step in Caswell's plan was thus frustrated, but not entirely: he prevailed upon council Secretary Samuel Strudwick to defect with the public records and hold them at the disposal of the provincial congress.

When the provincial congress met on 20 Aug. 1775, Caswell quietly arranged a further step: the seizure of the provincial treasury in order to deprive the royal government of tax support and to place all public revenues at the disposal of the provincial congress. This the congress did on 8 Sept. 1775, by electing its own treasurers of the province's two treasury districts. Caswell and Samuel Johnston were elected and bonded to receive all taxes and to emit bills of credit by authority of the provincial congress. Caswell immediately resigned as a delegate to the Continental Congress and accepted this more dangerous assignment. The plan was completed in the same provincial congress by providing for the military defense of its authority. It ordered under arms six battalions of five hundred minutemen each, and two additional battalions were ordered for a proposed Continental Army. Caswell was appointed commander of the minutemen for the New Bern District. Six months later he led this brigade to victory at the Battle of Moore's Creek Bridge on 27 Feb. 1776, against a force of Scottish Loyalists marching to Wilmington to unite with a royal fleet and army expected on the coast.

Caswell was elected governor of the state by the provincial congress in December 1776 and was reelected to annual terms under the constitution by the General Assemblies of 1777, 1778, and 1779. The constitution allowed only three successive terms. As governor he was incessantly raising and equipping troops. Besides providing for its own defense, the state sent more than eighteen thousand officers and men including Continentals to the aid of other states. Caswell was in poor health when he left office in April 1780, but he was immediately elected a major general by the General Assembly, placed in command of the state militia, and empowered to appoint staff officers.

Despite ill health, Caswell commanded the North Carolina Militia under General Horatio Gates at the disastrous Battle of Camden on 16 Aug. 1780, sharing the shame of the defeat. After taking steps to reorganize and to strengthen the militia for defensive actions in the west, he reported to the General Assembly at Hillsborough. The assembly took consideration of Caswell's illness and on 12 Sept. relieved him temporarily from command of the state militia, leaving him in the separate command of the North Carolina Partisan Rangers, guerrilla forces first established by Caswell in 1776 and kept under his command throughout the war. The militia was returned to his command a few weeks later.

From May 1782 until May 1785, Caswell served as state controller general and made headway in bringing order to the public accounts. In 1785 he was again elected governor and, by successive elections, served until 1788. When not serving in the governor's office, he had always been elected to represent Dobbs County in the General Assembly. His vigorous support of the proposed federal Constitution alienated his Dobbs constituency, however, and it denied him a seat in the constitutional convention held at Hillsborough in 1787. He was, however, reelected to the legislature.

The period from 1784 to 1789 was one of grief for Caswell. His two oldest sons, his oldest daughter, his mother, two brothers, and a sister all died. His throbbing headaches and giddiness came more often and stayed longer. These symptoms, of which he had complained at times since 1769, were evidently caused by high blood pressure. On 8 Nov. 1789, he suffered a fatal stroke of total paralysis while presiding over the state senate at Fayetteville. A state funeral was held at Fayetteville. His body was then taken to Kinston and buried in the cemetery at the Red House plantation. His widow, Sarah Heritage Caswell, died at Newington in 1794.

SEE: Clayton B. Alexander, "The Public Career of Richard Caswell" (Ph.D. diss., The University of North Carolina, 1930); Samuel A. Ashe, *Biographical History of North Carolina*, vol. 3 (1905); R. D. W. Connor, *Revolutionary Leaders of North Carolina* (1916); Francois X. Martin, *A Funeral Oration of the Most Worshipful and Honorable Major-General Richard Caswell* (1791); *Newbern Gazette*, 15 Dec. 1798; William L. Saunders and Walter Clark, eds., *Colonial and State Records of North Carolina* 8–22 (1890–1907); *University of North Carolina Magazine* 4 (March 1855); 7 (Aug. 1857); 7 (Nov. 1857).

CHARLES R. HOLLOMAN

Caswell, William (24 Sept. 1754–6 Jan. 1785), North Carolina adjutant general in the Revolution, Continental army captain, county official, state legislator, and planter, was the son of Governor Richard Caswell and his first wife, Mary Mackilwean. He was born at the Red House, a family plantation then in Johnston County. The home stood near the present site of the Governor Richard Caswell Memorial Park in Kinston, Lenoir County.

William received his early education from family members and from local schoolmasters. After he was ten years old, the school at the Herritage Chapel in Kinston, near the Caswell home, was taught by the Reverend William Miller, an Anglican clergyman. All Governor Caswell's sons received training by apprenticeship for

careers in the law. By 1774, William was serving as register of deeds of Dobbs County (formed from Johnston in 1759) under the tutelage of his uncle, Martin Caswell, long-time clerk of the Dobbs County Court. On 3 Sept. 1774, William went to Philadelphia with his father, on horseback, to attend the First Continental Congress. He kept a daily diary of his travels and a careful account of his expenses, now preserved in the state records of North Carolina and mistakenly attributed to Governor Caswell himself.

Upon his return to Kingston (renamed Kinston in 1784), William Caswell resumed his legal training and his work as register of deeds of Dobbs County. While his father was attending a later Continental Congress in May 1775, William received his first inkling of the hardships and dangers soon to be his lot as a soldier of the Revolution. A letter from his father, written from Philadelphia on 11 May 1775, described the growing spirit of Revolution and advised him to prepare to risk his life in the service of his country. He was commissioned an ensign in the Second Regiment of the North Carolina Continental Line 1 Sept. 1775. With other Continentals from the New Bern District, he was dispatched to join General Washington's forces in the North, where important campaigns against powerful British forces were impending. He served with valor in campaigns there for more than three years and suffered wounds at the Battle of Brandywine. He was with General Washington's army during the miserable winter at Valley Forge. Afterward, he was transferred to the Fifth Regiment of the North Carolina Continental Line, in which he was captain of Caswell's Company; in 1778 he was sent home in failing health.

Under the constitution of North Carolina adopted in December 1776, only members of the state legislature were elected by the people. All other state officers were elected by the General Assembly, which held two sessions in 1779. Thomas Gray and Captain Jesse Cobb represented Dobbs County in the first session, and William Caswell was elected to the House of Commons in the second session. He was also returned by the voters of Dobbs County in the general elections of 1780, 1781, 1782, and the second session in 1784.

Soon after Caswell's return home from the army in 1778, he was commissioned colonel of a large detachment of troops sent to the aid of South Carolina and Georgia. His commanding officer on this expedition, General John Ashe, urged upon the state board of war the need to commission a state adjutant general and recommended Caswell for the post. At a meeting of the board of war held in Tarboro on 4 Jan. 1779, Caswell was commissioned adjutant general with the rank of brigadier. He was one of the colonels under command of General Ashe at the Battle of Brier Creek near the Savannah River in Georgia in 1779; and later, as brigadier general, he led a command at the Battle of Camden, S.C., under General Horatio Gates, an engagement that resulted in a disastrous defeat. Caswell's forces supported General Nathanael Greene's operations against the British forces under General Cornwallis in 1780–81 and continued to carry out supporting operations against the British until Cornwallis's army surrendered.

After the war, Caswell lived at his plantation near Kinston, meantime serving as a state legislator and a justice of the county court. On 22 Dec. 1782 he was married in Dobbs County to Gathra Mackilwean, a daughter of his mother's brother, Francis Mackilwean, and his wife, Mary. William and Gathra had one child, Richard William, born on 17 May 1784 at Kinston.

Caswell died at Kinston and, according to his father's

will, was buried in the family cemetery there. His grave is unmarked. His wife, affectionately called Gatsey, died later that same year.

SEE: Sources cited under Benjamin Caswell; *North Carolina Gazette*, 26 Dec. 1777.

CHARLES R. HOLLOMAN

Catchmaid (Catchmaie, Catchmeyd, Ketchmaid), George (d. 1667),

burgess in the Virginia Assembly and later speaker of the North Carolina Assembly, came to America from Trelleck, Monmouthshire, England. He and his brother, Henry, of whom George was "Master," resided in Calvert County, Md., in 1652. In May 1653, George was accused of fathering a child by Mary Taylor, the wife of Robert Taylor of Virginia. Mary accused George of seducing her, and her husband insisted that George take the child; George, however, said that Mary had seduced him. Eventually, Taylor decided to keep the child if Catchmaid would give him ten thousand pounds of tobacco; he finally settled for two thousand pounds.

Catchmaid lived for a time in Nansemond County, Va., which he represented in the assembly held in 1659–60. A belief that he also served as clerk of court in Nansemond, expressed by a number of writers, appears to be erroneous. In about 1662, Catchmaid moved to the North Carolina area and seated a plantation on the peninsula now called Durants Neck, in Perquimans County. In 1666 he was speaker of the assembly of the colony, which at that time was known as Albemarle.

Catchmaid died in 1667 at his Albemarle plantation, Birkswear. His widow, Mary, married Timothy Biggs, who later became a member of the Albemarle council. George and Mary had no children.

Catchmaid left a will, dated 25 June 1664, which he had made in Virginia and placed in the custody of a Virginia friend, Thomas Ouldie. The will was probated in the County of Elizabeth City, Va., in February 1667/68, but it appears not to have been proved in Albemarle or otherwise to have become legally effective there. Although the existence of the Virginia will was known to some of Catchmaid's Albemarle friends, court testimony given in the 1690s indicates that in Albemarle he was deemed to have died intestate. Apparently, no official record of the will was entered in the North Carolina colony until 1731, when a certified copy was recorded in connection with transactions then being made respecting a portion of the Catchmaid land. Failure to prove the will in Albemarle, or loss of the record if such proof was made, probably accounts in part for at least one of several controversies that arose over the land.

In his will, Catchmaid named Colonel Edward Carter, a Virginian, his administrator. He bequeathed half his personal estate to his wife, Mary, and made bequests of personal possessions to Virginia friends; to the children of his two sisters, Elinor Wenslye and Jane Roper; and to the children of his deceased brother, Henry. He bequeathed his principal Albemarle plantation, Birkswear, to his only living brother, Thomas Catchmaid, who lived in England, and left another Albemarle plantation, consisting of fifteen hundred acres, to his nephew and godson, George Wenslye, who also lived in England.

One of the controversies over the Catchmaid land came to a head in the 1680s, after the death of Thomas Catchmaid. As heir-at-law, Edward Catchmaid of London, Thomas's only son, then claimed the Albemarle plantation called Birkswear, consisting of 3,333 acres. However, Timothy Biggs who had married Catchmaid's widow, also claimed the property, asserting that it had been inherited by his wife. Biggs had taken possession of the plantation in or before March 1673/74 and had lived on it, though intermittently, since that time. In his efforts to establish his alleged right, Biggs requested the Carolina proprietors to issue a patent "confirming" the land to himself or his wife. The proprietors, who had been told that George Catchmaid bequeathed the plantation to his wife by will, agreed to issue such a patent to Mary Biggs or, with Mary's consent, to Timothy Biggs. Presumably, Mary did not consent, for the patent was issued in her name.

Issuance of the patent to Mary Biggs was protested by Edward Catchmaid, who brought pressure from high officials in London to bear on the proprietors. Consequently, the proprietors rescinded their action and instructed the Albemarle governor, Seth Sothel, to investigate the matter and settle it according to law. In some way, however, the land fell into the hands of Governor Seth Sothel, apparently through a purported sale by one Timothy Burton of London. After Sothel's death there was litigation in the general court of Albemarle between Edward Catchmaid and those who claimed to have inherited the land through Sothel. The courts awarded the land to Catchmaid.

A second major controversy over Catchmaid's land began during Catchmaid's lifetime and involved George Durant, who owned an adjoining plantation. Durant had bought his own land from the Indians, had settled his family on it, and had cleared much of it before Catchmaid came to the colony. He had encouraged Catchmaid to move to Albemarle and had recommended that he settle on a tract next to his own, which Catchmaid did. By that time, however, new regulations concerning Albemarle land had been imposed, and it was then necessary for Durant to secure a patent from the Virginia governor, Sir William Berkeley, in order to have legal title to the land he had purchased. Ostensibly to save Durant a trip to Virginia, Catchmaid offered to secure a patent for Durant when he obtained his own, and Durant accepted the offer. Instead of securing a patent for Durant, however, Catchmaid had Durant's land included in his own patent, thus obtaining for himself legal title to the land. Although later, under pressure from Durant, he signed a paper recognizing Durant's right to the land at issue and agreeing to provide Durant with a proper patent for it, Catchmaid never fulfilled his agreement. When Timothy Biggs took possession of the Catchmaid land, Durant secured a similar acknowledgment and promise from Biggs, but Biggs, too, failed to perform his agreement. Durant's title to the land he held was not cleared during his lifetime. After his death, his sons, John and Thomas, took the matter to the Albemarle court of chancery, which in October 1697 issued a decree confirming their right to their land.

SEE: John Bennett Boddie, *Seventeenth Century Isle of Wight County, Virginia* (1938); William Waller Hening, ed., *Laws of Virginia*, vol. 1 (1823); Land Grant Office, North Carolina Secretary of State (Raleigh), for a certified copy of Catchmaid's will in Land Grants, vol. 19; Mattie Erma Edwards Parker, ed., *North Carolina High-Court Records, 1670–1696* and *1697–1701* (1968, 1971); Perquimans County Deeds, Book A (microfilm copy in North Carolina State Archives, Raleigh); William S. Powell, ed., *Ye Countie of Albemarle in Carolina* (1958); Hugh F. Rankin, *Upheaval in Albemarle: The Story of Culpeper's Rebellion* (1962); William L. Saunders, ed., *Colonial Records of North Carolina*, vol. 1 (1886); William G. Stanard and Mary Newton Stanard, comps., *The Colonial Virginia Register* (1902); Ellen Goode Winslow, *History of Perquimans County* (1931).

MATTIE ERMA EDWARDS PARKER

Cates, Charles Fletcher (15 Aug. 1872–3 Oct. 1947), businessman and agricultural leader, was born near the town of Swepsonville in Alamance County. His ancestors came to America from England and settled in Orange County in the late 1700s. His father, Henry Manly Cates, served with General Joseph E. Johnston at the Battle of Bentonville, and his mother, Elizabeth Bradshaw, was the daughter of a local planter. He had four brothers and a sister, Alonzo Edward, J. Sidney, H. Leo, Henry Roy, and Ione V. His father and sister and most of his brothers were Baptists; his mother was a Methodist.

Cates attended the local schools and also Scottsburg College in Scottsburg, Va. Following college he worked for a time as a traveling salesman with a wholesale grocery concern in Lynchburg, Va. He soon returned to the family farm near Swepsonville. In 1898 he established the Cates Pickle Manufacturing Company, carrying on a family tradition. Elizabeth Bradshaw Cates, an industrious woman, had earned the money for her children's education by preparing jams, jellies, pickles, and preserves, which were then sold by wagon throughout the Swepsonville community, a mill village on the Haw River.

In 1905, Cates bought a farm in the Woodlawn community near Mebane, also in Alamance County. From here, for the next several years, he continued to produce canned goods that were sold primarily to college cafeterias, including those of Salem, Trinity, and The University of North Carolina. Following World War I, food prices were controlled by the government, and the price of sugar was set at thirty cents a pound. Cates managed to obtain a supply of several freight car loads of this necessary ingredient, whereupon the price was reduced to ten cents a pound. The years 1919 and 1920 were critical ones, but the little company managed to survive.

Through various civic activities, Cates had made the friendship of John Sprunt Hill, an attorney in Durham who was a native of Faison in Duplin County. Hill had married into the wealthy Watts family of Durham and through attention to business had become a wealthy man. Desiring to do something for his native community of Faison, Hill persuaded Cates to move his pickle operation there, and the local farmers were soon persuaded to begin growing the variety of cucumber that was best for pickling.

After his move to Mebane in 1905, when his business prospered, Cates began to take an interest in the affairs of the community. He served as a committeeman for the Woodlawn School and also as a member of the Alamance County Board of Education from 1910 to 1914. He next served as a member of the Alamance County Board of Commissioners. He was defeated in a bid for election to the North Carolina Senate, probably because of his support of a bill passed in 1914, while he was a county commissioner, that allowed rural communities to incorporate. The Woodlawn community had incorporated in an effort to improve schools and roads, and taxes were, of necessity, raised. Cates continued to work for local improvements and, along with R. W. Scott, father of the late Governor W. Kerr Scott, was one of the prime movers in the school consolidation movement. The local school, Alexander Wilson High School, formed in 1922, was one of the earliest consolidated schools in North Carolina.

Cates was always interested in developments that would improve the life of his neighbors and fellow agriculturalists. He assisted in the organization of a number of farmers' cooperatives, the best known of which was the Guilford Dairy Cooperative. He later served as president of the North Carolina Milk Producers' Association. During the early 1900s he was active in the North Carolina Farmers' Alliance, serving as president and as a member of the executive committee that invited the Grange to organize in North Carolina. He served as a trustee of North Carolina State College in Raleigh and, following the establishment of the consolidated university system, was a member of the board of trustees of The University of North Carolina. He also served on the North Carolina State Board of Agriculture and was named a Master Farmer.

In 1900, Cates married Margaret ("Maggie") Pittard, the daughter of George Washington Pittard of the Grassy Creek community of Granville County. They had met while both were students at Scottsburg College. Three sons were born to them: Addis Pittard, long associated with Charles F. Cates and Sons and later president of A. P. Cates Pickle Sales Company; Chester Howard, a farmer and dairyman in Mebane; and George Henry, sales manager of Charles F. Cates and Sons Pickle Company.

Cates suffered a stroke of paralysis on 25 July 1947 during a business trip to Washington, D.C. He was a patient at Emergency Hospital in Washington and then returned home about one month before his death in Mebane. His funeral was held at Phillips Chapel Methodist Church, near Graham, and he was buried in the Bradshaw and Parrish section of the church cemetery.

SEE: Addis P. Cates of Faison, personal interview; *Greensboro Daily News*, scattered issues; North Carolina State Archives (Raleigh); Raleigh *News and Observer*, scattered issues.

CHARLES M. INGRAM

Catesby, Mark (3 Apr. 1683–23 Dec. 1749), naturalist, artist, and author of books on the flora and fauna of Carolina, was born probably in Castle Hedingham, Essex, England, the home of his maternal grandparents. He was the son of Elizabeth Jekyll and John Catesby and may have studied natural science in London. In 1712 he went to Virginia, where his sister and her husband lived; he remained seven years, sending seeds and plants to England. He was on friendly terms with William Byrd who permitted him to consult the manuscript history of the running of the dividing line between Virginia and North Carolina. Catesby traveled widely in Virginia, although the precise places are often in doubt. He went home to England in 1719 but returned to the colonies in 1722, arriving at Charles Town, S.C. He spent the next three years working from a base there. After having stayed for a time in the Bahamas, he returned to England in 1726 and devoted much of the remainder of his life to preparing drawings and the texts for *The Natural History of Carolina, Florida, and the Bahama Islands*, published in parts between 1731 and 1743, and *Hortus Britanno-Americanus; or, A Curious Collection of Trees and Shrubs*, published from 1763 to 1767, after his death. He died in London, survived by his wife, Elizabeth Rowland, and two children, Mark and Ann.

There is no evidence to suggest that he was ever in North Carolina, but he pictured and described plants, animals, reptiles, and insects found there. His account of the swallow-tail butterfly took note of Thomas Moffet's "Insectorum . . . Theatrum," for which John White provided a specimen from Roanoke, and Sir Walter Raleigh was mentioned in this connection.

Caudle

SEE: *DAB*, vol. 3 (1929); *DNB*, vol. 3 (1917); George Frederick Frick, "Mark Catesby," *Papers of the Bibliographical Society of America* 54 (1960); and Raymond Stearns, *Mark Catesby: The Colonial Audubon* (1961).

WILLIAM S. POWELL

Cathcart, William (ca. 1710–27 Feb. 1773), physician,

was a native of Genoch, Scotland. He was apprenticed in 1726 to a surgeon at Edinburgh, and there is evidence that he also pursued some studies at the University of Edinburgh. He reached Bertie County in 1737 and, with his brother John, entered into mercantile business there. Within two years, however, he had taken the title "practitioner of physick." In 1742 he married Penelope Maule, daughter of former surveyor general William Maule, and by this union came into the possession of his wife's large landed estate. The couple settled at one of their plantations on the upper Roanoke River in Northampton County. Penelope died early, but Cathcart again married well, this time to Prudence West, granddaughter of former governor Thomas Pollock.

Cathcart's wealth and social eminence thrust him into numerous offices of local leadership, including terms as sheriff, justice of the peace, and Anglican vestryman. He did not, however, seek major office, preferring his medical practice, the management of his estate, and the company of his books and a wide circle of acquaintants. He was on intimate terms with Governor Gabriel Johnston and named his only son after the governor, who was his first wife's stepfather.

On his son and his daughters, Peggy and Frances, Cathcart lavished his wealth, procuring for them the best education afforded by the times. It was Cathcart who brought to North Carolina, in the character of a tutor to his children, the Reverend Daniel Earle, later the most eminent Anglican churchman in the province. Gabriel Johnston Cathcart was sent to the University of Glasgow in 1759 but died soon after returning home at the completion of his course of studies. Peggy was married to the Reverend William McKenzie of the Church of England and Frances to Governor Samuel Johnston.

Testimony to the cultural and literary sophistication of the Cathcart family comes from the diary of Waightstill Avery, who visited with them on his way to a new home in Western North Carolina in 1767. Avery commented that he had been "Improved by his [Dr. Cathcart's] Company and diverted and pleased with his Daughters." Cathcart proved to be "a gentn. of extraordinary fine sense and great reading," while the girls were blessed with "the three greatest motives to be courted: Beauty, Wit and Prudence, and Money; . . . [they were] toasted in most parts of the Province." Some of Cathcart's library, bequeathed by him to Governor Samuel Johnston, now forms part of the library at Hayes Plantation, Edenton.

The Roanoke River farm was a preoccupation of Cathcart's, absorbing his interest and energies for many years. In a letter written in 1763 by his son, Gabriel, to John Cathcart in Scotland, Dr. Cathcart was described as "quite the farmer tho' on a different plan from what you pursue at Home—he raises little more wheat than to supply his Family, and some Oats for corn and fodder to his horses—his principal object is Indian Corn part of which he sends immediately to Mercate [Market] with the rest he fattens hogs and stall feeds Beef . . . ; his Overseers at the other Plantations go chiefly on Tobacco which he does not trouble himself with. . . . "

Cathcart died ten years after the death of his second wife.

SEE: "Biographical Sketch of Waightstill Avery with Illustrative Manuscripts," *North Carolina University Magazine* 4 (1885); Walter Clark, ed., *State Records of North Carolina*, vols. 22–23 (1907, 1904); North Carolina State Archives (Raleigh), for the Cathcart Family Papers and a deposition of John Dawson in the Bertie County Civil Papers.

THOMAS C. PARRAMORE

Cathey, George Leonidas (27 Nov. 1822–18 Jan. 1923),

school teacher and soldier, was born in Danville, Va., the son of William A. and Jennie Lessly Cathey, who took him at an early age to Iredell County, North Carolina, where George began teaching before the state had established its public school system. He later moved to Georgia, teaching there until he entered service. He was captain of Company C, Georgia Legion, Lisk's Brigade, during the Civil War.

He resumed his teaching career in Georgia following the war, but then moved back to North Carolina, teaching in Swain, Graham, and Macon counties. He retired at the age of 96, and a few years later took up residence in the Confederate Soldiers' Home in Raleigh. On 29 Nov. 1922, two days after his 100th birthday, the North Carolina Teachers Assembly awarded him a certificate of honor and merit in recognition of his record of more than three quarters of a century as a school teacher. He was buried in the Confederate Cemetery in Raleigh.

SEE: *North Carolina Education*, Dec. 1922; *Tenth Annual Report of the North Carolina Historical Commission, 1922–1924*; Raleigh *News and Observer*, 27 Nov. 1920, 19, 20 Jan. 1923; Death Certificate, George L. Cathey, 18 Jan. 1923, in State Board of Health, Raleigh.

H. G. JONES

Caudle, Theron Lamar (22 June 1904–1 Apr. 1969),

lawyer and assistant attorney general of the United States, was born in Wadesboro, the son of Theron Lamar Caudle, also a lawyer, and Susie Gooch Caudle. He attended Wake Forest College, where he was president of the student body and in 1926 received the LL.B. degree. Following graduation and admission to the North Carolina bar, he began the practice of law with his father's firm in Wadesboro.

From 1931 until 1939, Caudle served as prosecuting attorney for Anson County. In 1940, President Franklin D. Roosevelt appointed him U.S. attorney for the Western District of North Carolina. An editorial in the *Charlotte Observer* (6 Apr. 1969) declared that Caudle "raised the district's rating from about the lowest point to the highest in the entire federal court system in five years' time." As a result of this record, President Harry S. Truman in 1945 appointed him assistant attorney general in charge of the Criminal Division of the Department of Justice. In this position he was responsible for directing all criminal prosecution in the federal courts. Two years later he became assistant attorney general at the head of the Tax Division of the Department of Justice.

In 1951 a subcommittee of the House Ways and Means Committee began to look into the administration of the internal revenue laws, calling upon Caudle and others to testify. On 16 Nov. 1951, amidst widely publicized charges and countercharges involving automobiles, airplanes, fur coats, missing ballots, foreign travel, and tax evasion, Truman asked for Caudle's resignation. Between 19 Oct. 1951, when Truman had written Caudle a letter of appreciation, and 16 Nov., the president, according to *Newsweek* (26 Nov. 1951), became "worried about the effects of scandal on the voters next year and [determined] on a house cleaning which will sweep out all government officials whose outside activities—even though legal—might be open to criticism." Caudle resumed his law practice in Wadesboro, leaving frequently, however, to testify before investigative bodies in Washington and elsewhere.

In December 1955, nearly three years after the beginning of the Eisenhower administration, Matthew J. Connelly (Truman's appointment secretary), Caudle, and Kansas City lawyer Harry I. Schwimmer were indicted for conspiracy to defraud the federal government of income tax money. They were "accused of having worked together to violate bribery statutes, the Internal Revenue laws, and to obstruct the work of grand juries by giving evasive and fictitious testimony" (*Newsweek*, 12 Dec. 1955). During the trial, Schwimmer suffered a heart attack and was dropped as a defendant. At the end of a six months' trial, Caudle and Connelly were convicted of accepting oil royalties in exchange for interceding on behalf of Irving Sachs, a St. Louis shoe manufacturer charged in a 1947 case with attempting to evade $128,721 in taxes.

After the conviction but before the sentencing, the presiding judge was found fatally shot, an apparent suicide. His successor sentenced each defendant to two years in prison plus a $2,500 fine. Drew Pearson, among others, declared that the trial judge had been unstable and that there ought to be a new trial. On 20 June 1958, the Eighth Circuit Court of Appeals granted a stay of sentence pending a motion for a new trial. The case ultimately reached the Supreme Court of the United States, which declined to grant a new trial. Two additional appeals to the Supreme Court were likewise denied. In May 1960, Caudle entered the Federal Correctional Institution at Tallahassee, Fla. Five months later, after winning a "meritorious service" award from the prison, he was paroled. President John F. Kennedy pardoned Connelly in November 1962 but did not pardon Caudle. In August 1965, President Lyndon B. Johnson granted Caudle full pardon, restoring his rights to practice in federal courts and to vote in all elections. This pardon also enabled Caudle to attempt a political comeback. He entered the May 1966 Democratic primary in the Eighth Congressional District, losing to John G. Plumides by a vote of 26,766 to 17,321.

Published opinions of Caudle's role in the Truman presidency ranged from a comment on his career as an "accurate reflection of decay within the department" to a description of his "ordeal as the Dreyfus Case of the Eisenhower Administration." An editorial in the *Charlotte Observer* (6 Apr. 1969) concluded: "Our own view through the years was that Caudle on occasion acted indiscreetly, unwisely and naively in the high . . . political circles . . . to which he ascended. . . . But Lamar Caudle never gave the impression of being a venal or scheming man."

Caudle received LL.D. degrees from Duquesne University (1949) and Catawba College (1951). He was a member of the American and North Carolina bar associations and was president of the Federal Bar Association in 1946–47. He belonged to the Kappa Alpha Fraternity and the Omicron Delta Kappa society. In 1951 the government of Italy awarded him the Star of Solidarity. He was a Baptist and a Democrat. Caudle was married twice: in 1928 to Fairfid Monsalvatge, who died in 1961; and in 1963 to Mrs. Ellen Hildreth Koogler, who survived him. To Caudle and his first wife were born four

children, all of whom survived him: Theron Lamar III of Dallas, Tex.; Rose Antoinette (Mrs. Brevard Kendall, Jr.) of Florence, S.C.; Thomas Alfred of Atlanta, Ga.; and Fairfid Monsalvatge of New York, N.Y. Caudle died at his home in Wadesboro of a heart attack and was buried there in East View Cemetery. There is a portrait in the possession of Mrs. Kendall.

SEE: Theron Lamar Caudle Papers (Wake Forest University, Winston-Salem); *Charlotte Observer*, 2–6 Apr. 1969; *Greensboro Daily News*, 2 Apr. 1969; *Newsweek*, 26 Nov. 1951, 10 Dec. 1951, 18 Feb. 1952, 29 Sept. 1952, 25 June 1956, 18 Mar. 1957; *New York Times*, 2 Apr. 1969; Raleigh *News and Observer*, 3 Sept. 1952, 3 Apr. 1969; *Who's Who in America*, 1956–57; Winston-Salem *Journal and Sentinel*, 3 July 1958.

HENRY S. STROUPE

Chadbourn, James Harmon (23 Aug. 1853–2 Sept. 1913), manufacturer, was born in Wilmington, the son of George Chadbourn, who came from Maine to North Carolina in 1847. Chadbourn attended private schools in Wilmington and was graduated from Williston Seminary, Easthampton, Mass., in 1871. Returning to Wilmington, he entered the family lumber business there. In 1882 the Chadbourn Mill and Railway Company was formed to carry the timber enterprise into Columbus County. Chadbourn was placed in charge of this business, and under his direction the company purchased vast tracts of timberland and constructed a sawmill on the site of the present town of Chadbourn. A railroad was built to transport the great quantities of timber to the mill. The road was eventually extended to Conway, S.C., and to Boardman, N.C.; the short line, later purchased by the Atlantic Coast Line, became an important feeder line. After the sale of the railroad, Chadbourn returned to Wilmington and became president of the Chadbourn Lumber Company.

In addition to his connection with the family lumber business, Chadbourn was president of the Wilmington Chamber of Commerce, Inland Waterway Association, and Delgado Cotton Mills and a director of the Atlantic National Bank, Carolina Savings and Trust Company, Citizens' Building and Loan Association, and Consolidated Railway, Light and Power Company. He was also active in the Wilmington First Presbyterian Church and for many years was an elder.

Chadbourn was married to Blanche H. King, with whom he had seven children. He died at Witchwood, the family summer home in Asheville, and was buried in Oakwood Cemetery, Wilmington.

SEE: Samuel A. Ashe, ed., *Biographical History of North Carolina*, vol. 6 (1907); Wilmington *Morning Star*, 5 Sept. 1913.

DAVID H. ARMSTRONG III

Chaloner, John Armstrong (11 Oct. 1862–1 June 1935), author, industrialist, and philanthropist, was born in New York City in the home of his maternal ancestors, the prominent Astor family. The family name, originally spelled Chaloner, was first brought to America by the Reverend Isaac Chanler, a Baptist clergyman who migrated to Charleston, S.C., from Bristol, England, in 1710. Chanler's grandson, the Reverend John White Chanler, who was ordained in the Episcopal church, married Elizabeth Winthrop, the daughter of Benjamin and Judith Stuyvesant Winthrop, descended respectively from the first colonial governors of Massachusetts and New Amsterdam. His son, John Winthrop Chanler, married in 1861 Margaret Astor Ward, the only child of Emily Astor and Samuel Ward, the original "Uncle Sam" of American folklore. After the death of her mother, Margaret Astor Ward was reared by her grandfather, William Backhouse Astor, who declined to entrust his infant granddaughter to a son-in-law whom he considered unworthy of managing an Astor and, more especially, an Astor's fortune. The Astor family approved of her marriage to Chanler, a promising young New York lawyer. Although his family lacked the huge fortune of the Astors, by birth, education, social position, and personality he was an acceptable match for an Astor heiress. Elected as a Democrat to Congress in 1862, he served for three terms until his opposition to Boss Tweed of Tammany Hall cost him the support of his party in 1868. He never again sought public office, but he did remain active in party affairs and participated in the rehabilitation of the Democratic organization following the overthrow of its corrupt leadership.

John Armstrong, known among his family as Archie or Brog, was the eldest of eleven children, ten of whom survived, born to Margaret and John Chanler. He was sent to Rugby following the death of his mother. His reports while a student there indicated that, though mentally quick, he was too undisciplined for sustained effort. After receiving his bachelor's and master's degrees at Columbia University, he attended the Collège de France and the Ecole des Sciences Politiques. He was admitted to the bar of New York in 1885. After the death of their mother in 1875 and their father in 1877, the Chanler children were reared at an Astor estate, Rokeby, by a staff appointed by the children's guardians. Upon reaching his maturity, Chaloner (who was the only member of the family to revert to the original spelling of the name) received his portion of the inheritance and entered the social world to which he was entitled by birth and fortune. He formed a law partnership with W. G. Maxwell and Henry Van Ness Philip, but his interests soon turned to the promotion of newly patented inventions, such as the self-threading needle for sewing machines. He and his brother Winthrop formed a company that purchased a tract of land near Weldon, N.C., and established the Roanoke Rapids Power Company. The cotton mill and housing for the mill workers built in 1893 by this company formed the nucleus of the town of Roanoke Rapids. The mill was designed by Stanford White, the noted architect, a close friend of the Chanlers and a minor partner in the new company. Designed more for esthetic appeal than for practical use, the mill had to be remodeled before production could begin.

During the course of his frequent trips abroad and his many business ventures, Chaloner became increasingly interested in the occult and eventually devoted much of his time and money to the study and practice of spiritualism. Convinced that he was possessed of an "X-faculty," he boasted of having an inner voice instructing him in ways in which he could exercise his power of mind over matter. He went into self-induced trances and claimed that he had changed the color of his eyes. His family had him committed in 1897 to Bloomingdale, an asylum for the insane in New York. During his commitment, he wrote poetry and was allowed to study the insanity laws under which he had been incarcerated. Consistently proclaiming his sanity, he escaped in November 1900 and was concealed for six months by Dr. J. Madison Taylor, a prominent physician in Philadelphia. Several leading psychologists, including William James, examined him and agreed unanimously that he was sane. Moving to Lynchburg, Va., under the

assumed name of John Childe, Chaloner went to court to have his sanity legally restored. Successful in Virginia, where James testified in his behalf, he turned to the North Carolina courts, so that he could regain control of his business interests there. Though the courts of North Carolina agreed he was sane, he was still considered legally mad in New York and his fortune was controlled by his "former brothers and sisters," as he referred to his family. He fought for eighteen years to have the lunacy laws changed and his own sanity recognized.

Restricted to residence and travel only in Virginia and North Carolina, he wrote extensively, publishing his work through the Palmetto Press of Roanoke Rapids. *Four Years behind the Bars of Bloomingdale* appeared in 1906 and *Robbery under the Law* in 1914; he published collections of his poetry as well as several plays. Meanwhile, he continued his legal battles, winning several cases in which he charged libel of his name and reputation. Finally, in July 1919, he was declared sane in the state of New York and won full control of his fortune.

He used his money, estimated to be in excess of one and a half million dollars, to promote his pet projects, chief among which remained spiritualism. He lectured frequently and purchased a theater in New York City to assure himself of a platform from which he could bring messages from such dead luminaries as his great aunt, Julia Ward Howe, and Shakespeare. He turned his estate in Virginia into a rural community center, including a swimming pool, dance hall, and cinema, and at times had as many as 250 people on his payroll. He had created the Paris Art Fund in 1893, giving handsomely from his own funds to enable American artists to study in Paris, and later he established the Chaloner Prize for excellence in historical studies at Columbia University and a research fellowship at the Mackay School of Mines. He gave anonymously to numerous other institutions. He became especially interested in visual educational methods for rural areas and made two cross-county trips campaigning for such innovative techniques, leaving generous contributions to fund new projects at many stops along the way. His fortune was depleted by these varied philanthropies, and though his will included bequests to the universities of Virginia and North Carolina to endow scholarships in honor of Sir Walter Raleigh, no records at these two institutions indicate that funds were ever received from his estate.

Chaloner's last years were spent in Virginia in relative quiet and poverty. He was forced to abandon a scheme to import Chinese to replace black laborers leaving the rural South. His estate was ultimately mortgaged to pay living expenses. He had consistently nurtured his physical resemblance to Napoleon, and he spent his confinement, ill with cancer, among the many statues and relics of his idol he had collected; efforts to change his hair from gray to brown proved unsuccessful. In the spring of 1935 he entered the hospital at the University of Virginia, where his estranged sisters recanted and came to nurse him until his death. His expressed wish was to be buried between the men's and women's bathhouses beside the swimming pool on his estate, but his family's sense of propriety saw fit to have him placed in the burial ground of Christ Episcopal Church near the estate.

Chaloner was married in 1885 to Amélie Rives, daughter of Colonel Alfred Landon Rives of Castle Hill near Cobham, Va. Originally arranged for October, the wedding took place in June because of the furor aroused by the first of Amélie Rives's many novels, *The Quick or the Dead?* which included amorous passages that scandalized many of her readers. The Chanlers were particularly outraged by the resemblance of the principal male character in the novel to their brother and urged that the betrothal be terminated. In defiance, Chaloner advanced the date of his wedding and changed his will to exclude his brothers and sisters. The marriage was an unhappy one almost from its beginning. Amélie's chronic illness and possible addiction to morphine and his own temperamental outbursts led to frequent separations. In 1895 she went to South Dakota to procure a divorce under the less restrictive laws of that state and without the public scrutiny of the eastern newspapers, which referred to her often in their social and literary columns. She soon married Prince Pierre Troubetzkoy, a Russian to whom she had been introduced by Oscar Wilde during her travels apart from Chaloner. Chaloner had no children and never remarried, but he purchased the Merry Mills, an estate near Castle Hill, and enjoyed the company of the Troubetzkoys, who became his close friends as well as his neighbors.

SEE: J. Bryan III, ''Johnny Jackanapes, The Merry-Andrew of the Merry Mills'' *Virginia Magazine of History and Biography* 73 (1965); Margaret Terry Chanler, *Winthrop Chanler's Letters* (1951); Raleigh *News and Observer*, 27 Nov. 1935; Welford Dunaway Taylor, *Amélie Rives (Princess Troubetzkoy)* (1973); Lately Thomas, *A Pride of Lions: The Chanler Chronicle* (1971).

PAUL I. CHESTNUT

Chamberlain, G. Hope Summerell (*21 June 1870– 23 May 1960*), author, artist, clubwoman, house counselor at Duke University, and civic worker, was born in Salisbury. Although Mrs. Chamberlain did not use her first name, the first initial ''G'' is found on her early report cards from Augusta Female Seminary at Staunton, Va. She was the granddaughter of Elisha Mitchell, the geologist and botanist for whom Mount Mitchell was named. Her mother, Ellen H. Mitchell Summerell, came from an old New England line dating back to John Eliot, missionary to the Indians of Massachusetts. Dr. J. J. Summerell, Hope Summerell's father, who was of southeastern Virginia farming stock, became a physician in Rowan County. The Summerells had seven children, Hope being the youngest child and third daughter. Mrs. Summerell was responsible for her daughter's early education, but at the age of fourteen, Hope was sent to the academy in Hillsborough commonly known as Nash and Kollock's school. Continuing her formal training at the Augusta Female Seminary, she further pursued her primary interests in literature and languages. She then prepared to take the examinations for entrance to Wellesley College, but the illness and subsequent death of her mother required her to remain at home for four years to keep house for her father.

In 1891, Hope Summerell married Joseph Redington Chamberlain, the first professor of agriculture at the North Carolina State College of Agriculture and Mechanic Arts in Raleigh. A native of Kanona, N.Y., he graduated in the initial class in agricultural chemistry at Cornell. Teaching was not to be his life's work; he entered the fertilizer manufacturing business a year after his marriage. The Chamberlains' children were Mary Mitchell Chamberlain Moore, Jesse Mark, John Summerell, and Joseph Redington, Jr. In addition, they provided a home for two nephews and a niece.

During this time, Mrs. Chamberlain continued to cultivate her intellectual interests by studying and reading in German, French, and Italian. She served as food administrator of Wake County and as chairman of the Woman's Committee of the Wake County Council of

Defense in World War I. Mr. Chamberlain died in 1926, and the depression took away his widow's financial security; therefore, in 1931, she became the adviser to students in Pegram Hall at Duke University, remaining there for seven years. After a year and a half in California, she retired in Chapel Hill.

When she was over fifty years old, Mrs. Chamberlain began her writing career. At least three of her books have been published: *History of Wake County, North Carolina* (1922); *Old Days in Chapel Hill* (1926), a life of Cornelia Phillips Spencer; and *This Was Home* (1938), reminiscences about southern home life in Salisbury during the nineteenth century. Each volume portrays some aspect of local North Carolina history, giving anecdotes concerning the area. *This Was Home* was originally planned as the first part of a trilogy; the second portion was to concern state politics in Raleigh, and the final segment would bring the chronicle up to date. The last two parts, ''What's Done and Past'' and ''Oh Call Back Yesterday,'' were written but evidently never published. She left other manuscripts, ''Life Story of Elisha Mitchell, D.D.'' and ''Among Those Present: Fifty Years in the Old Home Town.'' She drew her own illustrations for her books.

Mrs. Chamberlain's other accomplishments included active participation in civic and social work. She served as president of the Raleigh Woman's Club in 1918 and 1919 and chaired various departments in the organization. For many years she also gave a series of lectures for the club, which spanned the winter months and dealt primarily with literature. She worked as chairman of the legislative committee of the North Carolina Federation of Women's Clubs; one result of her lobbying was the establishment of the state Home and Industrial School for Girls in Samarcand, an institution for which she was appointed a member of the board of managers in 1918. Other associations in which she held membership were the North Carolina Society of the Colonial Dames of America, the Fortnightly Review Club in Raleigh, and the North Carolina Literary and Historical Association, of which she was a vice-president. Continuing the dedication to relief work she began during the First World War, Mrs. Chamberlain sewed for the Red Cross during World War II. In addition to her other interests, she enjoyed drawing, oil painting, hooking rugs, process-etching, and the study of folkways.

She received several honors, including a Litt.D. degree from The University of North Carolina in 1932, the North Carolina Distinguished Service Award for Women in 1952, and, in 1955, the Algernon Sidney Sullivan Award of the Southern Society, as an outstanding alumna of Mary Baldwin College (Augusta Female Seminary).

There does not seem to be a formal portrait of Mrs. Chamberlain. She died in Chapel Hill and was buried in Oakwood Cemetery in Raleigh.

SEE: Hope S. Chamberlain Papers (Manuscript Department, Library, Duke University, Durham); North Carolina State Archives, Raleigh; and Southern Historical Collection (University of North Carolina, Chapel Hill); *North Carolina Authors* (1952).

SHARON E. KNAPP

Chamberlain, Joseph Redington (*22 Sept. 1861– 26 Apr. 1926*), industrialist, was born in Steuben County, N.Y., the eldest son of Jesse M. and Ervilla Ingham Chamberlain. His grandfather and namesake, Joseph Chamberlain, migrated from Vermont to upstate New York early in the nineteenth century. His father, Jesse, lured by the prospect of adventure and riches, joined the rush to the California gold fields in 1849. In spite of his success there, he became homesick and returned to Steuben County to purchase his brothers' interest in the family farm. Young Joseph attended the district school and the Hareveling Free Academy at Bath, N.Y. He won a scholarship to Cornell and enrolled there in 1884 to pursue studies in science and agriculture.

Soon after receiving his B.S. degree in June 1888, Chamberlain accepted a position as agriculturist with the North Carolina Agricultural Experiment Station in Raleigh. In June 1889 he was the first faculty member appointed by the trustees of the North Carolina College of Agriculture and Mechanic Arts. He served as professor of agriculture, live stock, and dairying at the college until 1892, when he resigned to take a position with the Caraleigh Phosphate and Fertilizer Works in Raleigh. He rose rapidly in the company and by 1896 had become president.

Chamberlain was an officer and principal stockholder in a number of other companies. He was president of the Farmers' Cotton Oil Company of Wilson, the Farmers' Guano Company of Norfolk, Va., and the Caraleigh Cotton Mills. He was vice-president of the Raleigh Cotton Mills, vice-president and one of the founders of the Capudine Chemical Company, founder of the Wake Seed Company, and a director of the Raleigh Banking and Trust Company.

Chamberlain was married in 1891 to Hope Summerell of Salisbury, daughter of Dr. J. T. Summerell and the granddaughter of Professor Elisha Mitchell, for whom Mount Mitchell was named. Chamberlain died suddenly and was buried in the Oakwood Cemetery in Raleigh. He was survived by his widow and four children: Mary M. Chamberlain Moore, Joseph R., Jr., Jesse M., and John S.

SEE: Samuel A. Ashe, ed., *Cyclopedia of Eminent and Representative Men of the Carolinas of the Nineteenth Century*, vol. 2 (1892); A. M. Fountain, *Place-Names on State College Campus* (1956); A. O. Goodwin, *Who's Who in Raleigh*, 1916; Raleigh *News and Observer*, 27 and 28 Apr. 1926; C. L. Van Noppen Papers (Manuscript Department, Library, Duke University, Durham), for MS sketch of Chamberlain by Samuel A. Ashe.

MAURICE S. TOLER

Chambers, Lenoir *(26 Dec. 1891–10 Jan. 1970)*, newspaper editor and biographer of Stonewall Jackson, was born in Charlotte, son of industrialist Joseph Lenoir and Grace Singleton Dewey Chambers. He was graduated from Woodberry Forest, Va., in 1910; received an A.B. degree from The University of North Carolina in 1914; and studied at the Columbia School of Journalism, N.Y., in 1916–17. After working on the Washington staff of the *New Republic*, he served overseas during World War I as a first lieutenant of infantry with the Fifty-second Infantry, Sixth Division, and later with division headquarters.

After the war, Chambers directed The University of North Carolina's news bureau until 1921, when he joined the *Greensboro Daily News*; there he was successively reporter, city editor, and associate editor. On the *News* he was associated with Gerald W. Johnson, also a distinguished North Carolina journalist and historian. In 1929, Chambers became associate editor of the *Virginian-Pilot* of Norfolk, Va., under Editor Louis I. Jaffe, who that year won a Pulitzer Prize for distinguished editorial writing. Chambers became editor of the *Norfolk Ledger-Dispatch* in 1944 and editor of the *Virginian-Pilot* in 1950, after Jaffe's death.

During the 1950s, Chambers's work on the biography of Stonewall Jackson was carried on simultaneously with an intense program of editorial writing during the decade of Virginia's massive resistance to the Supreme Court decision requiring desegregation of the public schools. His associates were awed that he could research and write history at night and during the day direct a forceful editorial page. Irate segregationists were astonished that the advocate of compliance with the Supreme Court decision was also a native North Carolinian and a biographer of a Confederate general. This was a key to Chambers's philosophy: a southerner by birth and by choice, he called upon the South to follow its best traditions, not its worst. The "best in the South" was not an acceptable phrase to him.

The year 1959 seemed to bring a peak to Chambers's career. In that year his two-volume biography of Jackson won critical acclaim, and his 1959 editorials won him the 1960 Pulitzer Prize. The *Virginian-Pilot* commented editorially after his death, "Mr. Chambers in the school issue defended law and justice and enlightenment and dignity and these were things he insisted upon year in and year out, consistently."

After retirement in 1960, Chambers wrote *Salt Water and Printers Ink*, a history of the Norfolk newspapers and their relationship with Tidewater Virginia, and *Notes on Occupied Norfolk*, a historical monograph. In 1960 he received the LL.D. from The University of North Carolina.

Chambers was a trustee of Woodberry Forest, Norfolk Academy, and the Norfolk Public Library, Va. He was president of the Norfolk Forum and a member of the American Society of Newspaper Editors, the Virginia Historical Society, the National Conference of Editorial Writers, Phi Beta Kappa, Sigma Alpha Episilon, and the Virginia and Norfolk Yacht and Country Clubs.

Chambers was married in 1928 to Roberta Burwell Strudwick. They had a daughter, Elizabeth Lacy (Mrs. Charles O. Burgess), and Mrs. Chambers had a son by a first marriage, Robert Strudwick Glenn.

SEE: Chambers Papers (Sargent Memorial Room, Public Library, Norfolk, Va., and Southern Historical Collection, University of North Carolina, Chapel Hill); Norfolk (Va.) *Virginian-Pilot* and *Ledger-Star* libraries; Virginia Historical Society (Richmond).

HAROLD SUGG

Chambers, Maxwell *(1780–7 Feb. 1855)*, planter and manufacturer, was born in Salisbury, the son of Joseph and Mary Campbell Chambers. His father died in 1784, and Maxwell was placed by the court under the protection of kinsmen Maxwell Chambers the elder and William Nesbit. He received his education in Salisbury and while yet a young man went to Charleston, S.C., in company with an uncle, Hugh Campbell. There he is supposed to have laid the basis of his fortune, which by the time of his death amounted to a half million dollars, a considerable amount for anyone living in Piedmont North Carolina between 1820 and 1850.

Following his return to Salisbury in about 1820, Chambers lived with his widowed half sister, Rebecca Nesbit Troy, in the former Salisbury Academy building (now the Josephus Hall House) on the corner of Bank and Jackson Streets, which she had acquired in 1825 when the academy closed. He never entered into regular business again, but set himself up as a one-man loan company. The many mortgages and deeds he executed show that he loaned money to prominent citizens in the county, often acquiring their homes or plantations when they failed to pay off their loans. It was said that he "never mixed business and charity together"; he "would give and take the last cent due in a trade, and when he chose to give, he gave liberally."

Three of his many homes he placed at the disposal of the Reverend Archibald Baker, pastor of the Presbyterian church in Salisbury. One of these homes, now the Rowan Museum, was called for years the Maxwell Chambers House. It was through Baker that Chambers was drawn to the support of Davidson College, to which institution he left a legacy of about $250,000, making it for a short time the wealthiest private college in the South. Owing to the limitations of the school's charter, however, the college could not receive the whole amount, and a considerable sum went to the Chambers heirs. With what funds the college did receive, Chambers Hall was erected, dwarfing in size and magnificence anything even at Princeton itself. It burned in 1921, and another Chambers Hall was erected on the site in 1929.

Chambers, whose name is closely identified with Salisbury, never actively sought public life either at the polls or in civic endeavors. He was, however, called upon by his fellow citizens to serve as a director in the Salisbury branch of the state bank in 1824, as one of the town's assessors in 1830, as a member of the building committee for Davidson College in 1835, and as a member of the town board in 1849.

In 1848, Chambers purchased for thirty thousand dollars the Salisbury Cotton Factory, which had come upon hard times since its opening in 1842. He renamed it the Rowan Factory but was no more successful in operating Salisbury's first textile mill than his predecessors had been; he sold it to his kinsmen, J. S. and P. B. Chambers. The mill later passed into the hands of Davidson College and in 1861 was sold to the Confederate government for use as a prison for Confederate felons and Federal prisoners of war.

The tradition that Chambers made his fortune in Charleston is seriously questioned. A thorough search of the Charleston census records, tax lists, city directories, and newspapers from 1800 to 1820 fails to reveal his name. If he did, indeed, operate a business there, he must have done so under an assumed name.

There is some indication that Chambers actually made his money by dealing in slaves. A kinsman was a slave dealer, and Chambers's great-nephew states that Maxwell Chambers used his brother Joseph as a front man in the slave trade in Alexandria, Va., and by so doing kept himself well in the background. In light of this information, it is significant that J. J. Bruner, editor of the local newspaper and elder in the Presbyterian church, failed to carry Chambers's obituary, as he customarily did when a prominent citizen died. His only remarks were confined to a notice of Chambers's death and of the fact that he had left a large legacy (consisting of two city blocks and other sources of income) to the Presbyterian church in Salisbury and a large amount to Davidson College. "He himself was not a member of any church," Bruner wrote, "but he has, however, left a name which will long be remembered by the church here."

If, indeed, Chambers was a slaver, his interest in blacks was ambivalent. Their welfare occupied him until he made his final will. In 1842 he was in correspondence with a free black in Fayetteville who had just returned from Liberia, Africa. This freedman was interested in removing other freed slaves to Ohio and asked Chambers's help. The tone of the letter indicates both

previous correspondence on the subject and Chambers's interest in the black man's welfare. A year before he died, Chambers manumitted eighteen or twenty of his slaves, giving them transportation to Oberlin, Ohio, and funds with which to begin life anew. At his death he freed forty-eight slaves with the same provisions for their safe journey to Ohio under his overseer, Moses Rimer.

Chambers was married to Catherine B. Troy, daughter of Matthew Troy the elder and the sister of Matthew Troy the younger. Although an attachment had long existed between the two, they were not married until 1836, when both were somewhat advanced in life; they had no issue. They moved into the Nesbit home on Innes Street, on the site of the present Salisbury Post building, and there they ended their days. "Aunt Kitty," as Mrs. Chambers was affectionately called, died at the age of sixty-five in 1852. Both were buried beneath the Lecture Room of the Presbyterian church in Salisbury, with earlier members of their families. By his will, Chambers provided funds and materials for the erection of the brick building over the graves.

SEE: Chambers Papers (Southern Historical Collection, University of North Carolina, Chapel Hill); Henry A. Chambers, "A History of the Chambers Family of Iredell County" (typescript, 1912, Davidson College Library, Davidson); Maxwell Chambers, correspondence (4 Feb. 1974); Chalmers Davidson, "Maxwell Chambers," *Davidson College Bulletin*, June 1969; John E. Patterson to Maxwell Chambers, letter (31 July 1842, possession of James F. Marsh, Salisbury); Rowan County records (Salisbury), for Deed Books in the Register of Deeds Office and Will Book K in the Clerk's Office; Jethro Rumple, *A History of Rowan County* (1881); Salisbury *Carolina Watchman*, 3 Feb. 1848, 8 Feb. 1849, 2 Dec. 1852, 3 Feb. 1853, 15 Feb., 8 Mar., 13 Nov. 1855; Salisbury *Western Carolinian*, 1 Dec. 1824, 16 Feb. 1830; H. M. Wagstaff, ed., *The Papers of John Steele*, vol. 2 (1924).

JAMES S. BRAWLEY

Chance, William Claudius, Sr. *(23 Nov. 1880–7 May 1970)*, educator and humanitarian, was born in Parmele. His parents were W. V. and Alice Chance; his grandparents, who reared him, were Bryant and Penethia Chance; all were former slaves. Brought up on a small farm in poverty-stricken Martin County, Chance set out at an early age to improve his living conditions. After struggling through high school, while working on the farm, he entered North Carolina Agricultural and Technical College in Greensboro. Four years later he was graduated with honors with an A.B. degree in agriculture. He received additional education from Howard University in Washington, D.C., spending four years there, of which the last year was devoted to the study of law. He earned other credits, intermittently, from Hampton Institute in Hampton, Va., North Carolina College at Durham, and La Salle University in Chicago, Ill.

It was after attending Howard's law school that Chance became impressed with the idea of building a school to improve the plight of blacks in Martin County. Upon returning to Parmele in 1909 he witnessed, among other deficiencies, the dreadful condition of the only local school for blacks. This school had one room, sixty pupils, one teacher, and a $160 annual appropriation from the state for its operation. To help remedy this situation, he founded a private school, using his home and a community church as the facilities. Serving as principal and one of the three teachers, he initially attracted about thirty students. For two years the teachers, mostly without salaries, provided a practical education, emphasizing agriculture, industrial and mechanical arts, and domestic science.

Chance's school was the first in Martin County to initiate a longer school term, eight months yearly. Later, in 1911, the black public school and his private school merged to become Parmele Industrial Institute, a public school, of which Chance was chosen principal. With the aid of such distinguished people as U.S. Representative John H. Small and Dr. Anson Phelps Stokes, secretary of Yale University, he was able to attract enough funds to erect the first brick school building in Martin County in 1914. Expanding from year to year, Parmele Industrial Institute had by 1948 experienced substantial growth. In that year the school had 460 students, 12 teachers, 78 veterans enrolled in the veteran trade school, and 4 buildings. Five years later the enrollment had increased to 600 students, 200 veterans, 15 regular teachers, and 5 additional teachers for the veterans. Because of Chance's devotion to his school throughout the years, the community changed the name of the school to W. C. Chance High School. Under his leadership, the school in 1948 had the highest percentage of graduating seniors entering college (70 percent) of any school in Martin County (the average was 50 percent). Many of his former students rose to become attorneys, doctors, college presidents, college deans, businessmen, ministers, school principals, and teachers.

Having achieved many of his goals, Chance retired in 1951. Four years later a fire destroyed most of the school complex, although classes continued to be held in the elementary school building until 1969.

Although he was going into retirement, Chance by no means was destined for inactivity. Realizing the inequities in the white and black schools in Martin County, he was instrumental in organizing black parents behind Attorney Herman L. Taylor of Raleigh, who filed a petition with the board of education in 1951. This petition demanded either equality in the distribution of appropriations to the school system or integration. It was alleged in the petition that more money, teachers, and buses were given to the white than the black schools, although 53 percent of the students in the county were black. Although no immediate remedies for the problems resulted, the petition did serve notice that Chance and other blacks were ready for some drastic social changes.

Chance became perhaps more widely known for his successful challenge of the Jim Crow policy on the Atlantic Coast Line Railroad. He filed suit to recover damages from the railroad on the grounds that because of his race, he was wrongfully ejected from a railroad car on 25 June 1948 in Emporia, Va., and subsequently subjected to unlawful arrest and imprisonment in connection with this ejection. At the time of the incident he was returning from a business trip in Philadelphia, Pa. Between July 1948 and November 1952, four court actions were heard in the U.S. Court of Appeals for the Fourth Circuit, which ruled in favor of Chance and outlawed the Jim Crow policy in interstate travel.

Having won such a significant victory at the age of seventy-two, Chance still remained active in community affairs. He was a Presbyterian and a member of the NAACP and the Republican party.

Chance was married twice: in 1917 to Evelyn Payton, who died in 1927; and in 1929 to Julia Johnson, who died on 8 Mar. 1972. He had seven children; William C., Jr., attorney in New York City; Warren C., teacher in New York City; Anson G., of the Seaboard Coastline Railway;

Harold P., former teacher in New York, now deceased; Mrs. Anice C. Wilson, executive director of Hopkins House Association in Alexandria, Va.; Wilbur J., former school principal in Caroline County, Va., now deceased; and Edward A., psychiatric social worker and director of social services at Spring Grove State Hospital in Baltimore, Md.

Chance died in Lynchburg, Va., while visiting his daughter and ailing wife, a patient in Guggenheimer Hospital. His body was returned to Bethel for burial about four miles from his birthplace in Parmele.

SEE: *Atlantic Coast Line Railroad Company* v. *Chance*, 198 F.2d. 549 (1952); *Atlantic Coast Line Railroad Company, Petitioner* v. *William C. Chance*, 341 U.S. 941 (1951); *Atlantic Coast Line Railroad Company, Petitioner* v. *William C. Chance*, 344 U.S. 877 (1952); *Chance* v. *Lambeth*, 186 F.2d. 879 (1951); Durham *Carolina Times*, 7 Sept. 1963; Norfolk (Va.) *Journal and Guide*, 7 Mar. 1953; Personal correspondence of Chance (possession of John T. Caldwell); Raleigh *Carolinian*, 8 Sept. 1951, 31 Aug. 1963; Raleigh *News and Observer*, 4 Apr. 1948; Williamston *Enterprise*, 7 Aug. 1951.

JOHN T. CALDWELL

Chancy (Chancey, Chansy), Edmund (Edmond) *(d. ca. 1677)*, council member in North Carolina, came to the colony before September 1670 and settled in Pasquotank Precinct. He was a member of the council in 1672 and died in or before 1677. Little more is known about his life.

In his will, Chancy named Valentine Bird trustee of his estate and custodian of his children; Bird died soon after Chancy's death, and his widow, Margaret Bird, settled the Chancy estate which was appraised at about £226. The estate was later placed in the custody of Matthias Towler, who was appointed guardian for Chancy's orphans.

Chancy left three or perhaps four children, apparently already motherless. Hannah, who seems to have been the eldest, married Thomas Burnsby (Bonsby, Burnby) in 1684. Edmund, Jr. (called Edward in some records), was about fourteen at the time of Hannah's marriage. He requested that his new brother-in-law be made his guardian, and the court complied. Edmund himself was married by September 1703 to a woman named Sarah. A third Chancy orphan was William, who married Deborah Simons, daughter of Jeremiah Simons, in February 1700/1701. An Elizabeth Chancy, who married Samuel Nicholson in about 1688, probably was a daughter of Edmund Chancy, Sr., but has not been positively identified as such. Edmund, Jr., William, and Elizabeth were Quakers; Hannah appears not to have belonged to that faith.

SEE: *North Carolina Historical and Genealogical Register*, 3 vols. (1900–1903); William Wade Hinshaw, comp., *Encyclopedia of American Quaker Genealogy*, vol. 1 (1936); Mary Weeks Lambeth, *Memories and Records of Eastern North Carolina* (1957); North Carolina State Archives (Raleigh), for Albemarle Book of Warrants and Surveys (1681–1706), application of Thomas Burnsby and Hannah Chancy for marriage license in 1684 (in Albemarle County Papers, 1678–1714), Council Minutes, Wills, Inventories (1677–1701), Guardians' bonds of Thomas Burnsby and Matthias Towler (in Administrators' Bonds), Perquimans Births, Marriages, Deaths, and Flesh Marks (1701–1820), Wills of Thomas Burnby [sic] and Jeremiah Simons (in North Carolina Wills); Mattie Erma Edwards Parker, ed., *North Carolina Higher-Court*

Records, 1670–1696 (1968); William S. Powell, ed., *Ye Countie of Albemarle in Carolina* (1958); Quaker Collection (Guilford College Library, Greensboro), for records of Pasquotank and Perquimans Monthly Meetings.

MATTIE ERMA E. PARKER

Chapman, Robert Hett *(5 Mar. 1771–18 June 1833),* Presbyterian minister and missionary and second president of The University of North Carolina, was born in Orangedale, N.J., the second of the three children of the Reverend Jedediah Chapman (27 Sept. 1741–22 May 1813) of East Haddam, Conn., and his first wife, Blanche Smith (d. Nov. 1773). The elder Chapman, a "warm" Whig during the Revolution, lived very close to the contested New Jersey battleground area and served occasionally as army chaplain. Robert Hett attended Nassau Hall (Princeton) as a pupil of Dr. John Witherspoon and in 1789 was graduated with a B.A.

After a year spent in "judicious reading," Chapman found himself deeply impressed with religion. "His convictions of sin were deep and pungent; his sense of hardness of heart and deep defilement, acute," his son wrote many years later. After some three years spent in a theological course, Chapman served briefly as instructor at Queen's College, New Brunswick, N.J. He was licensed to preach the Gospel on 2 Oct. 1793 and was installed as pastor of the Presbyterian church of Rahway, N.J., on 5 Jan. 1794. Three years later, on 14 Feb. 1797, he married Hannah Arnett, daughter of Isaac Arnett of Elizabethtown and the formidable revolutionary heroine Hannah Arnett. About 1805 the Chapmans removed to Cambridge, N.Y., where Robert Hett served the Presbyterian church until sometime in 1812.

Early in 1812 the trustees of The University of North Carolina, through their Committee on Appointments, offered Chapman the presidency of the university at a salary of twelve hundred dollars. Chapman's name had almost certainly been put forward by the university's first president, Dr. Joseph Caldwell, himself a Princeton graduate and a Witherspoon man. Caldwell had wished to be relieved of the presidency to become professor of mathematics and return to his prime interests, geometry and astronomy. Chapman's letter of acceptance, dated 12 Feb. 1812, emphasized his reluctance to abandon the ministry but stated frankly that his current pastor's salary was "utterly inadequate to the expense of a growing family." Another factor influencing his acceptance must have been the presence in nearby Hillsborough of a sizeable colony of Arnetts and Kollocks, including various Princeton graduates, all centered about the home of Frederick Nash and his wife, Mary Goddard Kollock, who was Hannah Chapman's niece. For the next several years, the entire Chapman family was to find a second congenial home in Hillsborough.

The brief Chapman administration has very generally been regarded as a failure, even a near-disaster, in university annals, but the Reverend Robert Hett Chapman, Jr., in his sketch of his father entitled "Life of Rev. Robert Hett Chapman Written by His Son . . . Talladega, Alabama" (ca. 1853–54), pictures it as a glowing missionary success with no hint of student turbulence or dissatisfaction. The younger Chapman states that his father, on arriving in Chapel Hill, found "the state of literature low and the pulse of piety lower still. In fact, the seat of the University itself was a moral desolation . . . little even of the form of religion was seen in all that region."

Kemp P. Battle stated in his *History of the University of North Carolina* that some of Chapman's troubles

stemmed from the extremely hot, partisan spirit engendered by the War of 1812. It was "a fatal obstacle," says Battle, that "he was a Peace Federalist and his students were in favor of the war. . . . To the minds of most Americans the word Federalist became synonymous with traitor. . . . Dr. Chapman was too honest to conceal or tone down his views." In January 1814 there occurred various nighttime depredations at the president's home—a gate taken down, a cart carried away, a small house knocked over. Later a student publicly defied Chapman in delivering the whole of a censored oration. Both he and his prompter refused to halt or sit down—and were cheered. Chapman's gatepost was tarred and feathered, a charge of gunpowder was placed in the doorknob of a tutor's door, dirks and pistols made their appearance, and the Grove (the campus of great oaks) was seriously damaged by lawless rowdyism. Various students were suspended, and the university's academic routine was shattered. Public opinion, including that of some of the more weighty trustees, adjudged Chapman a poor disciplinarian who had lost control.

The Chapmans themselves had suffered a series of family losses during their months in Chapel Hill. Last and most tragic was the death on 25 Nov. 1814 of their eldest surviving child, a fifteen-year-old daughter, Margaretta Blanche (b. 26 Oct. 1799), named for both Chapman's mother and his stepmother, Margaretta Le Conte. She was buried in the oldest section of the old Chapel Hill Cemetery.

On 23 Nov. 1816, Chapman "in solemn form" submitted his letter of resignation to the university trustees to take effect at the end of 1817. The trustees, however, accepted it to take effect immediately, paid Chapman a half year's salary, and allowed him the use of his house until the end of the next session. On 26 Dec. 1816, they reelected Joseph Caldwell president.

Battle's opinion that Chapman's defects "have been somewhat exaggerated" would seem to suggest simply that his interests and training did not fit him to be a university administrator. As a Presbyterian minister, he accomplished an impressive amount of solid, lasting mission work in the area. His zealous preaching in Hillsborough sparked an enthusiastic religious awakening that resulted in the building of the brick Presbyterian church (1815–16), the first church to be erected there since before the Revolution. "He was more highly gifted with power on his knees than any man I know," said Frederick Nash. "His public prayers warmed the hearts of all who heard them." Chapman organized a Presbyterian church in Chapel Hill; converted various students, notably John Knox Witherspoon; installed the Bible in the university and the catechism in the University Grammar School as textbooks; organized a chapter of the American Bible Society at Raleigh, as well as the Presbyterian Missionary Society of North Carolina; and generally proved himself a recognized leader in North Carolina Presbyterian circles. In 1815, Williams College, Williamstown, Mass., conferred on him the D.D.

On leaving Chapel Hill, Chapman went as pastor to the Presbyterian church in Leesburg, Loudon County, Va., and then to the pulpit of the Presbyterian church at Winchester, Va. After a decade in the Shenandoah Valley, he decided to emigrate West, spent a year or so in the North Carolina hill country in preparation, and finally in 1829 migrated entirely across Tennessee to Covington in Tipton County, a frontier presbytery.

In the spring of 1833 he journeyed by horseback to attend the General Assembly of the Presbyterian Church in Philadelphia. On his return, he stopped at Winchester at the home of his son-in-law, Thomas Allen Tidball, Esq., where he died unexpectedly of an intestinal ailment. He was buried in Winchester. Besides his wife, Hannah, he left seven surviving children (five had died earlier). Mrs. Chapman died in St. Louis, Mo., on 7 July 1845, at the home of her third son, Edward H. There is a framed silhouette of Chapman in the North Carolina Collection, University of North Carolina, Chapel Hill.

SEE: Kemp P. Battle, *History of the University of North Carolina*, vol. 1 (1907); Archibald Henderson, *The Campus of the First State University* (1949); "Life of Rev. Robert Hett Chapman . . . by His Son, Rev. Robert H. Chapman, Talladega, Alabama," in F. W. Chapman, *The Chapman Family* (1854; microfilm of the Chapman life in the North Carolina Collection, University of North Carolina, Chapel Hill); Frederick Nash, "Rev. John Wither-spoon," *University of North Carolina Magazine*, o.s. 20, n.s. 7 (1888); Raleigh *Star*, 26 July 1816, 9 Aug. 1816; James Webb Papers (Southern Historical Collection, University of North Carolina, Chapel Hill), for folders 24–120.

MARY CLAIRE ENGSTROM

Charles, Lucile Marie Hoerr (31 Aug. 1903–7 Mar. 1965), lecturer, scholar, and first director of dramatic arts at East Carolina University in Greenville, was a native of Chicago, the daughter of Charles Ferdinand Hoerr and Lillie Anna Sophia Oberman Hoerr. She received the Ph.B. degree in 1930 from the University of Chicago. In 1941 she received the M.A. degree from Columbia University and in the following year a master's degree from Yale University. She acquired a Ph.D. degree in educational psychology from Yale in 1943. She adopted her father's given name as her professional surname.

Dr. Charles served as the drama director at the Lenox Hill Neighborhood House in New York from 1930 until 1934 and was associated with the American People's School from 1934 to 1936. She conducted a series of radio programs under the auspices of the Columbia Broadcasting Company during the mid-1930s and was associated with the drama and speech department at Teacher's College, Columbia University, from 1937 until 1939. She was assistant professor of dramatic arts at Mary Washington College of the University of Virginia from 1943 until she went to East Carolina University in 1946 as associate professor of English and the first director of dramatic arts. She was the recipient in 1955 of a Bollingen Foundation Fellowship, which was renewed for a second year, to study at the famous C. G. Jung Institute in Zurich, Switzerland. After work at the Jung Institute, she returned to East Carolina University in 1957 and taught courses in English, speech, and drama until her death. In 1959 she was promoted to the rank of professor.

As the director of the dramatic arts program at East Carolina, Dr. Charles brought record progress between 1946 and 1953. Liveliness, color, and student development and growth were obvious under her capable leadership. Her dramatic activities included the production of three major plays each academic term, weekly workshop productions of one-act plays, and the broadcasting of several hundred radio shows. In addition, she founded the Eastern Regional Play Festival of the North Carolina Dramatic Association, which for a number of years in the 1950s was held annually on the campus of East Carolina University and in which drama groups from throughout Eastern Carolina—college, high school, and little theater groups—participated. She provided for her student actors numerous trooping experiences to schools, towns, and military bases in Eastern Carolina. Her selection of plays reflected her desire to present productions of literary as well as dramatic value, and she sought to have a balanced program with one modern comedy or drama, one classical play, and an annual play for children. As her drama program developed, Dr. Charles created and organized classes in acting and interpretation and play production, and in 1952 she started a special course, a dramatic arts workshop, which coordinated lectures from several university departments.

Dr. Charles was a member of the American Folklore Society and contributed to the *Journal of American Folklore*, the *New York Times*, *Theatre Magazine*, *Players Magazine*, *Journal of Adult Education*, *Theatre and School*, *North Carolina English Teacher*, and other publications. She conducted extensive research and investigation into primitive drama and in 1959 published *The Story of the Baby Spinx and Other Fables*. Following an extended illness with Guillain-Barre disease, she wrote of her psychological experiences during recovery; these writings were published in several popular and professional periodicals and in *Psychosomatic Medicine*. She was buried in Rosehill Cemetery, Chicago.

SEE: Lucile Marie Hoerr Charles Papers (East Carolina University Manuscript Collection, Greenville); *Directory of American Scholars*, vol. 2 (1964); *East Carolinian*, 11 Mar. 1965; Raleigh *News and Observer*, 9 Mar. 1965.

RALPH HARDEE RIVES

Chase, Harry Woodburn (11 Apr. 1883–20 Apr. 1955), university president, was born in Groveland, Mass., the son of Charles Merrill and Agnes Woodburn Chase. In 1900 he entered Dartmouth College, from which he received the A.B. degree, *magna cum laude*, in 1904. A Rufus Choate Scholar during his junior and senior years, he received special honors in French and philosophy and was ranked fourth in his class. He was admitted to Phi Beta Kappa and was a commencement speaker at his graduation.

Chase began his professional career in education in 1904 as a high school teacher. In 1908 he received his master's degree from Dartmouth, with a thesis entitled "Plato's Theory of Education." Not content with this preparation, he relinquished his position that year and entered the new, nationally acclaimed Clark University at Worcester, to study under Dr. G. Stanley Hall. He held a fellowship in psychology and served as the director of the clinic for subnormal children in 1909–10. He later translated and published the series of lectures delivered at Clark by Sigmund Freud, which influenced the development of psychoanalysis in the United States. Chase received the Ph.D. degree from Clark in 1910.

In September 1910, Chase became a member of the faculty of the department of education at The University of North Carolina. In 1914 he became professor of psychology and began to introduce laboratory courses and scientific methods in this new and expanding field. At the university, he served on various faculty committees and was chairman of the Committee on Intellectual Life. He was also appointed acting dean of the College of Liberal Arts, following the death of E. K. Graham in October 1918, and chairman of the faculty after the death of Marvin H. Stacy in January the following year. In June 1919 he was elected president of the university.

In December 1910, Chase married Lucetta Crum, a native of Indiana and a graduate of Coe College. She had been a graduate student at Clark University and had received the M.A. degree in 1910.

Although Chase was a native New Englander, he quickly adapted himself to the environment of North Carolina and identified himself completely with the interests of the university. During the eleven years of his presidency, he devoted his attention to objectives including the establishment of the office of dean of students and the transfer of the responsibility of supervising student discipline under the honor system from the office of the dean of the College of Liberal Arts to a committee of the faculty and the student council. The entire administrative structure of the university was entirely reorganized through the provision of administrative boards to formulate policies and advise the deans and officers of the principal units. William M. Kendal of the New York firm of McKim, Mead and White was appointed consulting architect to develop plans for the expansion of the physical plant by the addition of twenty-one new buildings and very extensive modification of three others, to accommodate a student body of 3,000. The faculty was increased from 78 to 115 members, and the annual support of the university from $270,097 in 1918–19 to $1,342,974 in 1928–29. There was a new emphasis on staffing the professional schools with faculty trained and experienced in professional education and administration instead of professional practice and on adopting national, to replace state and regional, standards of scholarship and attainment. The Graduate School was thoroughly reorganized for training teachers and professional experts, and a strong central library was built up for the support of research. The university defended academic freedom and the right to teach science against the nationwide fundamentalist crusade to outlaw the teaching of evolution; established new departments of dramatic art, music, journalism, psychology, and sociology and new schools of business administration, public welfare, and library science; and strengthened and enriched both the widely known Institute for Research in Social Science and The University of North Carolina Press.

Chase's decision to appoint a dean of students grew out of the confusion that resulted from the control of the students during World War I by military officers. Student morale greatly declined, and Chase found it necessary to place policy-making, curriculum management, and student conduct control under two full-time officers.

Another matter that severely challenged his leadership was that of establishing the principle of staffing professional schools with faculty members not only professionally trained but also experienced in professional teaching and administration. The test came in 1923 in the appointment of a dean at the Law School. The majority of the trustees were lawyers who thought the position should be filled by a distinguished attorney. Chase contended that the point of view held by the trustees was outmoded and insisted that training in law school administration was fundamental to the successful development of the best type of legal education. Merely practicing law did not provide the experience required in order to give legal training. Chase succeeded in establishing this principle throughout the university.

The establishment of the department of sociology and the encouragement of the Institute for Research in Social Science likewise called for long and diplomatic handling. Sociology was generally suspect in the South, not so much by churchmen as by industrialists and politicians, who saw sociology and socialism as related and horrendous subjects. Having secured the acceptance of a sociology department in principle, Chase appointed H. W. Odum, a native southerner who had trained with Chase at Clark and who was then serving as dean of the

College of Liberal Arts at the University of Georgia.

The most difficult of Chase's objectives was freedom to teach and publish, the fight for which lasted through several years and two 1920s assemblies of the legislature and of the Synod of the North Carolina Presbyterian Church. In defeating those who opposed the teaching of evolution in the university, Chase added to skill in presenting convincing arguments the support of several strong leaders of other churches and colleges in the state and of alumni and students. The margin of victory in both legislative contests was reasonably large and very gratifying.

During his stay in North Carolina, Chase held posts in the North Carolina College Conference, the Southern Association of Colleges and Secondary Schools, the National Association of State Universities, the National Education Association, and the American Association of Adult Education. He also served as a member of the boards of several educational foundations, including the General Education Board and the Julius Rosenwald Fund.

Chase left Chapel Hill in 1930 and became president of the University of Illinois in July of that year. He reorganized Illinois's administrative structure in very much the same manner as North Carolina's, establishing a number of new departments and schools. In 1933 he accepted appointment as chancellor of New York University and once again began a program of administrative reorganization and expansion.

Following his retirement in 1951 Chancellor and Mrs. Chase spent summers at their cottage at North Port, Long Island, and winters at Sarasota, Fla. He was at his Florida home when he died. He was survived by his wife; a daughter, Mrs. Marvin Stone; an adopted son, Carl; and a grandson, Harry Stone. Chase was an Episcopalian and a Democrat. The University of North Carolina has two portraits of him.

SEE: *American Mercury* 17 (June 1929); *Chapel Hill Weekly*, 15 Sept. 1968; *DAB*, Fifth Supplement (1977); *New York Times*, 21 April 1955; *The State University and the New South* (1920); University of North Carolina, *Alumni Review* 18 (March 1930); Henry M. Wagstaff, unpublished sketches of university administrators (1957), typescript, North Carolina Collection, University of North Carolina, Chapel Hill; L. R. Wilson, *Harry Woodburn Chase* (1960).

LOUIS R. WILSON

Chatham, Alexander (20 Jan. 1834–21 Jan. 1920), merchant, farmer, and industrialist, was born near Wilkesboro of English ancestry. His father, Martin Chatham, had come from Augusta County, Va., and located in Wilkes County in 1828. A machinist and farmer, Martin Chatham operated a foundry and a repair shop in Wilkesboro. Alexander's mother was Mary Elizabeth Cass Chatham.

Chatham served an apprenticeship in his father's shop where, in line with natural interest and proficiency, he developed a high degree of skill in mechanics. At the age of twenty-five he moved to Elkin and secured a position with Richard Gwyn, who operated a mercantile business, a large farm, and a cotton mill known as the Elkin Manufacturing Company. Chatham had been there about three years when he married his employer's daughter, Mary Elizabeth Gwyn, on 28 Sept. 1862. He served as a lieutenant in the Confederate Army during the Civil War and after the war became a merchant and a farmer.

In 1878, Chatham and his brother-in-law, Thomas L.

Gwyn, formed a partnership and built a small woolen mill, first known as Gwyn and Chatham, on Big Elkin Creek. This was the beginning of the Chatham Manufacturing Company, maker of world-famous Chatham blankets. In 1890, Gwyn sold his interest in the mill to Chatham's sons, and the name of the business was changed to Chatham Manufacturing Company.

Chatham operated a farm on the Yadkin River and organized and was first president of Elkin's first bank, the Elkin National Bank. His most vigorous years fell in the period of Reconstruction, and he became one of the founders of the New South. His enterprise gave the farmers of southwestern Virginia and northwestern North Carolina a market for their wool, as well as providing labor for the local people.

Chatham was married twice. Of his marriage to Elizabeth Gwyn, three sons were born, Hugh Gwyn (b. 1864), Richard Martin, and Paul. Elizabeth Chatham died 23 Dec. 1875. On 12 Jan. 1878, Chatham married Alice Hickerson of Wilkes County. The children of this marriage were Myrtle Elizabeth, James Alexander, Raymond Hunt, and Thomas Daniel.

Chatham was a Methodist. His death occurred in Elkin, and he was buried there.

SEE: Thomas Felix Hickerson, *Happy Valley* (1940); *North Carolina: Rebuilding an Ancient Commonwealth*, vol. 3 (1929).

GARLAND R. STAFFORD

Chatham, Hugh Gwyn (9 June 1864–10 Oct. 1929), industrialist, public servant, philanthropist, and promoter of various enterprises, was born in Elkin of English and Welsh ancestry. He was the eldest son of Alexander and Mary Elizabeth Gwyn Chatham, who later had two other sons, Richard Martin and Paul. Hugh's forebears were large landholders and active participants in public affairs. His grandfather, Martin Chatham, had a farm near Wilkesboro and operated a foundry and machine shop in the town; he served as a trustee of the Wilkesborough Seminary in the 1830s. His great-grandfather, James Gwyn, married Martha Lenoir, who figured with her father, Thomas Lenoir, in the revolutionary annals of the Carolinas; their son, Richard, who was born at the Green Hill Plantation near Ronda, was at one time a member of the state legislature and was active in county affairs. Alexander Chatham came to Elkin as a young man and was employed by Richard Gwyn, who operated a large farm, a mercantile business, and a cotton mill known as the Elkin Manufacturing Company; Chatham married the daughter of Richard Gwyn in 1862.

Hugh Gwyn Chatham was born on a plantation on the present site of Elkin. He attended public school there, was graduated from Jonesville High School, across the river from Elkin, and spent two years in Vanderbilt University. He then returned to Elkin and became his father's assistant in the blanket factory that Alexander Chatham and Thomas L. Gwyn had opened in 1878, where he had played and worked as a boy. This firm, Gwyn and Chatham until Gwyn sold his interest in 1890, was purchased by Hugh and his brothers. The name of the business was changed to Chatham Manufacturing Company; Hugh became an executive and when his father retired as president, succeeded him. The mill in its original location was operated by water power and was at a remote distance from the railroad. Early in Hugh Gwyn Chatham's presidency, a site accessible to the railroad was chosen. In 1906 another mill was built in Winston-Salem, where it was a factor contributing to the

city's growth as a manufacturing center. Chatham moved his residence to Winston-Salem and lived there many years.

During World War I, Chatham was a member of the Council of National Defense, and his duties took him to Washington frequently. Both plants of the Chatham Manufacturing Company were commandeered by the government, with Chatham as superintendent, and great quantities of blankets were produced for the armed services.

Chatham served on the executive committee of the board of directors of the Wachovia Bank and Trust Company. He was president of the North Carolina Railroad Company under Governors Charles B. Aycock and Robert Glenn and also president of the Elkin and Allegheny Railroad Company. In 1914 he was elected a member of the state senate. Largely through his efforts, Roaring Gap became beautifully established as a summer colony.

Chatham was married in 1894 to Martha Lenoir Thurmond of Ripley, Miss. They had two children, a son, Richard Thurmond, and a daughter, DeWitt. Richard Thurmond succeeded his father as president and chairman of the board of Chatham Manufacturing Company and served his district in Congress for two terms. DeWitt married Ralph P. Hanes, a prominent businessman of Winston-Salem.

Chatham was a Methodist, a Democrat, a Mason, and a member of the Knights of Pythias and of the Junior Order of United American Mechanics. He was buried at Elkin. When the first hospital was opened in Elkin in 1931, it was named the Hugh Chatham Memorial Hospital; a portrait of him hangs there. The Hugh Chatham Memorial Bridge across the Yadkin River was opened in 1933.

SEE: Thomas Felix Hickerson, *Happy Valley* (1940); *North Carolina: Rebuilding an Ancient Commonwealth*, vol. 3 (1929).

GARLAND R. STAFFORD

Chatham, Richard Thurmond (16 Aug. 1896–5 Feb. 1957), U.S. congressman, industrialist, and philanthropist, was born in Elkin, Surry County, the only son of Hugh Gwyn and Martha Lenoir Chatham. His grandfather was Alexander Chatham, founder of Chatham Manufacturing Company. Chatham was educated in the public schools, at Woodberry Forest School in Orange, Va., at The University of North Carolina (1915–16), and at Yale University (1916–17). He left college in 1917 to enter the U.S. Navy as a seaman, serving during World War I until discharged as an ensign in June 1919.

In July 1919, Chatham began work with his father's textile mill, Chatham Manufacturing Company, the world's largest manufacturer of blankets, in Winston-Salem. After serving as treasurer of the company, he became president in 1929 and chairman of the board of directors in 1945. His term as president was characterized by rapid expansion in capacity, variety of products, and profits. He served as a member of the North Carolina Board of Conservation and Development in 1938 and was president of the North Carolina Dairymen's Association.

During World War II, Chatham served in the U.S. Navy (10 Feb. 1942–25 Nov. 1945). He worked with the Bureau of Ordnance and the office of the secretary of the navy and then was assigned to combat duty in Europe and the Pacific theater. He attained the rank of commander in the U.S. Naval Reserve and was awarded the Bronze Star Medal, the secretary of the navy's Commendation Medal, the Royal Order of Nassau with Swords (from the Dutch government), and numerous battle stars and theater ribbons. After the war he founded a magazine called the *Navy Bulletin* (later *Armed Forces*) and operated it at a loss for five years.

With his only previous political experience being service as a county commissioner in Forsyth County, Chatham was unsuccessful in a 1946 attempt to win the Democratic nomination to the Eightieth Congress from the Fifth Congressional District. As a member of the Democratic party's National Committee on Finance during the election of 1948, he was an active supporter of President Truman and a substantial contributor to the party. He was elected to the Eighty-first Congress in 1948 and to the three succeeding Congresses (3 Jan. 1949–3 Jan. 1957). While in Congress, he was a member of the House Foreign Affairs Committee and was an advocate of a vigorous internationalist policy. He favored U.S. recognition of Red China and supported the Marshall Plan. He lost his seat in Congress in 1956 to Ralph J. Scott, primarily because he refused to sign the "Southern Manifesto," a document that pledged opposition "by all legal means" to the U.S. Supreme Court's 1954 decision outlawing segregation in public schools. Most of Chatham's southern colleagues in Congress signed the manifesto, and in North Carolina, Harold D. Cooley was the only non-signer to win renomination.

Chatham was a trustee of The University of North Carolina and of Woodberry Forest School; a member of the National Association of Manufacturers, until he resigned through unwillingness to accept its reactionary policies; president of the Winston-Salem Chamber of Commerce; and a member of the National Association of Wool Manufacturers, the American Legion, and the Veterans of Foreign Wars. His clubs included the Metropolitan Club and the Army and Navy Club in Washington, D.C., and the Racquet and Tennis Club in New York City. He was awarded an honorary Doctor of Textile Science degree from North Carolina State University in 1948. His religious preference was the Methodist church, and he belonged to Delta Kappa Epsilon Fraternity.

On 28 Oct. 1919, Chatham married Lucy Hodgin Hanes. Two sons were born to this marriage, Hugh Gwyn II and Richard Thurmond, Jr. After his first wife's death, Chatham married Mrs. Patricia Firestone Coyner, on 16 Nov. 1950. One son, Walter Firestone, was born to them. Chatham died in Durham and was buried in Salem Cemetery in Winston-Salem. In his final will, his estate was valued at almost $2,000,000. He left $250,000 to a charitable trust, the Chatham Foundation, set up for the education of worthy young people.

SEE: *Asheville Citizen*, 6 Feb. 1947; *Biog. Dir. Am. Cong.* (1961); *Chatham Blanketeer*, 11 Feb. 1957; *Durham Morning Herald*, 10 Feb. 1957; Raleigh *News and Observer*, 24 May 1948, 2 Feb. 1949, 14 Jan. 1951, 18 July 1956, 19 Feb. 1957; Gary Trawick and Paul Wyche, *One Hundred Years, One Hundred Men* (1971).

JULIAN M. PLEASANTS

Chavis, John (*ca. 1763–15 June 1838*), preacher and teacher, was probably the "indentured servant named John Chavis" mentioned in the inventory of the estate of Halifax attorney James Milner in 1773, though little is definitely known of Chavis's early years. Milner, whose private library was one of the best and largest in North Carolina, was closely connected with the Mangum,

Willie, and Jones families of Sussex County, Va., where he appears to have lived before coming to Halifax in about 1766. The Reverend William Willie of Sussex, whose surname was preserved in the branches of the Mangum and Jones families who moved to North Carolina, was beneficiary of the Greek and Latin volumes in Milner's estate and may have played a role in Chavis's training and education after Milner's death.

Chavis enlisted in December 1778 in the Fifth Virginia Regiment and served for three years in the Revolutionary War. Captain Mayo Carington, in a bounty warrant written in March 1783, certified that Chavis had "faithfully fulfilled [his duties] and is thereby entitled to all immunities granted to three year soldiers." In a 1789 tax list of Mecklenburg County, Va., Chavis was shown as a free black whose property consisted of a single horse. In the same year he was employed by Robert Greenwood's estate as tutor to Greenwood's orphans.

It is generally accepted that Chavis attended the Presbyterian Washington Academy, now Washington and Lee University. A certificate made out in Rockbridge County, Va., on 6 Apr. 1802 attests that John Chavis was known to the court and considered a free man and "also that he has been a student at Washington Academy where he went through a regular course of Academical studies." A certificate of 8 Nov. 1802 acknowledged that Chavis was a free black, forty years of age (indicating that his birth was in 1762 or 1763).

Charles Lee Smith and John Spencer Bassett, in 1888 and 1889, respectively, reported the tradition that Chavis studied at Princeton as a private student of Dr. John Witherspoon, then president of the college. No official records exist to prove the report, but recorded in the minutes of the trustees of Princeton University is the 26 Sept. 1792 recommendation of the Reverend John Blair Smith that "Mr. John Todd Henry of Virginia and John Chavis, a free black man of that state . . . be received" on the Leslie Fund. Besides his formal duties with the college, Dr. Witherspoon is known to have conducted private classes for graduates and others studying for the ministry; Chavis probably attended these classes. He may, in addition, have attended some classes at the college itself, but his name does not appear among either the graduates or the former students there. That his education was exceptional for the age is apparent from his later writings, especially his correspondence with Willie P. Mangum, as well as from his professional activities. He was almost certainly the most learned black of his time in the South, and perhaps in the United States.

On 19 Oct. 1799, Chavis requested from the Presbytery of Lexington in Virginia a license as a preacher, which was granted on 19 Nov. 1800. The record shows that "The said Jon Chavis [was voted a license] to preach the Gospel of Christ as a probationer for the holy ministry within the bounds of this Presbytery, or wherever he shall be orderly called, hoping as he is a man of colour, he may be peculiarly useful to those of his own complexion." Six months later, at his own request, he was transferred to the Hanover Presbytery, recommended by the Lexington Presbytery "as a man of exemplary piety, and possessed of many qualifications which merit their respectful attention."

From 1801 to 1807, Chavis served the General Assembly of the Presbyterian Church as a missionary to slaves in Maryland, Virginia, and North Carolina. He was provided a horse and funds for lodging. Dr. Archibald Alexander, a Princeton trustee and one of the founders of the Princeton Theological Seminary, was one of a committee of four to help Chavis in the discharge of his duties. Many of Chavis's reports of the religious conditions in places he visited, indicating the number of people in attendance at meetings he held, appear in the *Minutes of the General Assembly of the Presbyterian Church* and *The Associations Missionary Magazine or Evangelical Intelligencer*.

Chavis was a preacher both to blacks and to whites; he preached to and moved freely among white Presbyterians. In January 1802, Ann Smith, daughter of Samuel Smith in Granville County, wrote that she had heard of the Great Revival at Hawfields from Mr. Chavis and from William Webb, her uncle. Moses Hoge, later to become president of Hampden-Sydney College, wrote in 1802 about receiving reports of congregational activity from Mr. J. Chavis.

Chavis located in Raleigh in 1807 or 1808, where the Orange Presbytery, which included Raleigh, accepted him as a licentiate in 1809. Although never ordained or assigned a regular pastorate, Chavis preached until 1832. After the Nat Turner rebellion of 1831, blacks were restricted by law from preaching. Samuel Smith Downey and William McPheeters, a minister in Raleigh, were among the members of a committee appointed by the Orange Presbytery to assume responsibility for the care of Chavis and his wife. The presbytery decided to give him fifty dollars a year beginning in 1834 and apparently did so until his death in 1838. His wife was aided until April 1842, when it was reported that she was residing with friends. Her name is thought to have been Fanny or Frances: the 1840 Granville County census shows the name "Fanny Chavis, female, free colored, aged 36-55"; the editor of the papers of Willie P. Mangum gives her name as Frances Chavis. No children are known to have been born to Chavis and his wife.

In North Carolina, Chavis is better known for his teaching, which began in Raleigh as early as 1808. Through ads in the *Raleigh Register* on 25 Aug. and 1 Sept. of that year, he announced the opening of his school with a dual plan of organization: white students attended during the day and black students in the evening until ten o'clock. For a quarter century, Chavis taught in several counties, including Wake, Granville, and Chatham. It was known that he was a "good Latin and a fair Greek scholar." Willie P. Mangum was invited to attend his school examination in 1828. The editor of the *Raleigh Register* reported on 22 Apr. 1830 his attendance at the examination "of free children of color, attached to the school conducted by John Chavis. . . ."

Chavis was received as an equal in the homes of whites, and no letters written by him to whites reveal any evidence of social inequality. Prominent white families believed to have sent children to study under Chavis include the Mangums, Manlys, Harrises, Hendersons, Horners, Edwardses, Enlows, and Hargroves. Often named as his pupils are Priestly H. Mangum, brother of Willie P. Mangum; Charles Manly, a North Carolina governor; J. M. Horner; Archibald E. and John L. Henderson, sons of Chief Justice Henderson; and Abram Rencher. Some white students, including J. M. Horner, appear to have boarded in the Chavis home in order to attend the school session.

That Willie P. Mangum, U.S. senator, studied under Chavis is disputed by some. Their friendship bespeaks a teacher-pupil relationship, however. Chavis wrote long and intimate letters to Mangum for more than a decade, often criticizing the senator's political positions. He was critical of Mangum's support of Andrew Jackson, for whom he felt a great distaste. His political beliefs clearly label him a Federalist. He was opposed to the abolition of slavery, saying, "That Slavery is a national evil no one

doubts, but what is to be done? . . . make the best of a bad bargain." Having already lost the right to preach, he was denied the franchise in 1835. In September 1833, in an effort to earn money, he sent the presbytery "An Essay on the Atonement" and asked for help in publishing it. With or without the presbytery's assistance, the essay was published under the title *Chavis' Letter upon the Doctrine of the Atonement of Christ* (Raleigh, 1837).

The Oxford *Torchlight* of 28 Sept. 1880 reported that Chavis had died "at his residence between Oxford and Williamsboro, leaving descendants who are yet in the county. The writer remembers to have seen him when a short time before his death several of his white pupils, prominent gentlemen, called to see him. Chavis was then advanced in years, his white hair forming a strange contrast to his ebony face for he was of unmixed African descent. His manners were dignified yet respectful and entirely unassuming and his conversation sprightly and interesting." A Richmond Presbyterian paper reported his death in Orange County in the only other known obituary. Chavis Park in Raleigh, named in his honor, is located near the site of his school.

SEE: Daniel L. Boyd, "Free-born Negro: The Life of John Chavis" (B.A. thesis, Princeton University, 1947); Margaret Burr DesChamps, "John Chavis as a Preacher to Whites," *North Carolina Historical Review* 32 (1955); Edgar W. Knight, "Notes on John Chavis," ibid. 7 (1930); Annie G. Randall, "John Chavis," *Coraddi–State Normal Magazine* 10 (1905); G. C. Shaw, *John Chavis* (1931); Charles Lee Smith, *The History of Education in North Carolina* (1888); Stephen B. Weeks, "John Chavis," *Southern Workman*, Feb. 1914.

BARBARA M. PARRAMORE

Cheatham, Henry Plummer *(27 Dec. 1857–29 Nov. 1935)*, politician, educator, and racial spokesman, was born to a house slave on a plantation near Henderson. Treated with favor by his white father, a prominent planter, Cheatham experienced few of the physical hardships of slavery. After the death of his father, another white man, Robert A. Jenkins, took an interest in him and was largely responsible for providing him the opportunity to attend Shaw University. Although Cheatham studied law, he never became a practicing attorney. After graduating from Shaw in 1883, he served briefly as principal of the black normal school in Plymouth. Both his alma mater and Howard University later conferred honorary degrees upon him.

A dedicated Republican, Cheatham first entered politics in 1884, when he was elected register of deeds in his native Vance County. During his four years in this office, he broadened the circle of friends, both black and white, who later figured prominently in the realization of his political ambitions. He rose rapidly in Republican councils and was elected a delegate to district, state, and national conventions. Chosen as the party's nominee for Congress from the Second Congressional District, the so-called black second, in 1888, he waged a successful campaign against the white Democratic incumbent, Furnifold M. Simmons. At the expiration of his first term in Congress, Cheatham confronted a disorganized Democratic opposition and won reelection with a larger majority than in 1888. But his attempt two years later to retain his seat proved unsuccessful. The emergence of the Populist party and dissension among black voters caused by the question of fusion between Republicans and Populists contributed to his defeat. His 1894 and 1896 efforts to return to Congress as the representative of the black second also failed. As his political star waned, that of his rival and brother-in-law, George H. White, became ascendant.

In the House of Representatives (1889–93), Cheatham was cast as a racial spokesman, especially in the Fifty-second Congress, in which he was the sole black member. Though he championed the cause of black people, he remained aware that his constituency also included white voters. Throughout his two terms he strived to protect the interests of small farmers and home industry—to perform in a manner that would "be best not for one race or the other but for both equally." He sponsored a federal aid-to-education bill, opposed a tax on lard made from cottonseed oil, supported trust regulation and the silver purchase act, and attempted to get the federal government to compensate the depositors of the defunct Freedman's Bank. None of the measures he sponsored were enacted into law, not even his bill for an appropriation to finance a black exhibition at the Columbian Exposition in Chicago. The latter proposal became embroiled in the struggle over the federal election (force) bill, which he reluctantly endorsed. Even though he failed to win congressional approval of his legislation, he was remarkably successful in obtaining federal appointments for his constituents.

While a congressman, Cheatham not only expanded his land holdings in Vance and Warren counties but also purchased considerable property in Washington in the vicinity of Du Pont circle.

Although Cheatham held no other elective office after his departure from Congress, President William McKinley recognized his services to the party in 1897 by appointing him recorder of deeds, one of the highest offices bestowed upon black men at the time, for the District of Columbia. During his tenure as recorder (1897–1901), he continued to labor in behalf of black people and sought to use his influence with McKinley to protect their interests. A polished orator and loyal supporter of the president, he championed the cause of McKinley Republicanism in speeches throughout the United States during the political campaigns of 1898 and 1900. The rising tide of racial repression in these years prompted black citizens to demand federal action, and when the president failed to take a vigorous stand against lynching and other atrocities, his popularity among blacks declined dramatically. Not only McKinley but also such black appointees as Cheatham became the targets of bitter criticism from the black community. In fact, "Cheatham and Co." was described as a coterie of "white man made" black leaders whose advice to the president had been responsible for his "misguided southern policy." But Cheatham was not without his defenders. James E. Shepard, for example, who served for a time as his secretary and who later became a prominent educator, placed Cheatham in the vanguard of those black men responsible for the progress of the race.

Cheatham belonged to the conservative faction in the black community, and his tactics were similar to those of his friend Booker T. Washington. A man of "moderation, conservatism and well-tempered action," he was diplomatic and circumspect toward whites and was always popular with the old landed people. In dealing with blacks, Cheatham urged them to follow his example, "to be patient, persevering, philosophical, thrifty, self-respecting and far-seeing." The acquisition of property, character, and culture, he consistently maintained, would ultimately "win their place in the equation of civic virtue" and bring about "the triumph of the forces of right." Black critics of Cheatham might

quarrel with his penchant for social pacifism and his deferential behavior toward whites, but few disagreed with his ultimate goal—the elimination of racial prejudice and the achievement of first-class citizenship by the nation's black population.

By the time of Cheatham's retirement as recorder of deeds in 1901, the political fate of blacks in North Carolina had been sealed by a succession of legal and extralegal contrivances that virtually nullified the Fourteenth and Fifteenth Amendments. Unlike George H. White and certain other black political figures who sought to escape the heavy hand of Jim Crowism by settling in the North, Cheatham returned to North Carolina and put into practice his philosophy of racial uplift by assuming the direction of the Colored Orphan Asylum at Oxford, an institution he had helped to establish in the 1880s. When he took over the management of the orphanage in 1907, it was little more than a cluster of shacks. For the remainder of his life he labored in behalf of the institution, expanding and improving its housing and school facilities, brickyard, sawmill, and farm lands. He devoted a substantial portion of his own income to the orphanage and utilized his considerable powers of persuasion in perennial fund-raising campaigns. He not only prevailed upon the state legislature to increase its appropriation but also won for the institution the financial support of the Duke family, especially Benjamin N. Duke. By the end of his twenty-eight-year tenure as superintendent of the orphanage, Cheatham had transformed it from three or four ramshackle wooden structures located on a small farm into an impressive collection of brick buildings surrounded by several hundred acres of prime farm land. Like the Tuskegee Institute in Alabama, the Colored Orphan Asylum in North Carolina was a monument to the resourcefulness and tenacity of a single individual.

Cheatham was married twice: first to Louise Cherry, the daughter of Henry C. Cherry, a state legislator and influential Republican; and then, following her death in 1899, to Laura Joyner of Branchville, Va. There were three children by the first marriage and two by the second. Less than a month before his seventy-eighth birthday, Cheatham died suddenly at the orphanage.

SEE: Florence Beatty-Brown, "Henry Plummer Cheatham," *Negro History Bulletin* 5 (1942); *Biog. Dir. Am. Cong.* (1961); Maurine Christopher, *America's Black Congressmen* (1971); "Henry Plummer Cheatham," *Journal of Negro History* 21 (1936); Indianapolis *Freeman*, 29 May 1897.

WILLARD B. GATEWOOD, JR.

Cherry, Annie Moore (21 Sept. 1891–1 Feb. 1976), educator, daughter of William Rodney and Elizabeth Eleanor Moore Cherry, was born in Martin County but spent most of her early life in Hobgood and Scotland Neck, Halifax County, where she received her earliest education. She was graduated from the State Normal and Industrial School, now The University of North Carolina at Greensboro, in 1912 and in 1927 received the master of arts degree in education from Columbia University; afterwards she did further graduate work at Columbia, The University of North Carolina at Chapel Hill, and Duke University.

Miss Cherry's first teaching position was in Dunn, where she remained for four years. After brief service as rural elementary school supervisor for Harnett County, she became the first full-time rural elementary school supervisor in Halifax County in 1918 where she remained until 1933. During that time she worked with local home demonstration agents to develop hot lunch programs for rural schools and with educational personnel to introduce progressive teaching techniques. In 1921 she and Alonzo E. Akers, county school superintendent, wrote the script and directed teachers and pupils of the county in the presentation in Weldon of a pageant, *The Spirit of the Roanoke, A Pageant of Halifax County History*. Elizabeth Lay (Mrs. Paul) Green, who assisted in the production, termed the pageant "a worthy pioneer in North Carolina in Rural Community Drama by co-operative authorship."

Miss Cherry, after several years during which she was engaged in research with the North Carolina Department of Public Instruction, joined the faculty of Flora MacDonald College in Red Springs as professor of education and supervisor of student teachers in the elementary grades. She also taught in summer school at Western Carolina University, The University of North Carolina at Chapel Hill, Duke University, and The University of North Carolina at Greensboro. She frequently spoke before state and national educational organizations and was the author of a number of bulletins on school supervision. She was the third woman to serve as president of the North Carolina Education Association. She was both a trustee and president of the alumnae association of The University of North Carolina at Greensboro as well as a trustee of the Consolidated University of North Carolina. She was a member of Delta Kappa Gamma, honorary sorority for women educators.

Although she was a member of Enfield United Methodist Church she was buried in Trinity Episcopal Church Cemetery, Scotland Neck.

SEE: *Enfield Progress*, 5 Feb. 1976; *Roanoke Rapids Herald*, 2 Feb. 1976; A. E. Akers and Annie M. Cherry, *The Spirit of the Roanoke* (1921).

RALPH HARDEE RIVES

Cherry, Joseph Blount (*ca. 1816–18 Oct. 1882*), planter, lawyer, and public official, was born in Bertie County, the son of Solomon Cherry and brother of William Walton Cherry. Cherry was a student at The University of North Carolina in 1836–37 but did not graduate. He served in the North Carolina House of Commons in 1848, 1850, and 1852 and in the state senate from 1856 until 1860. As chairman of the Committee on Education in 1852, he introduced a bill, passed that year, to create the office of superintendent of public schools. Calvin H. Wiley was the first person to hold the position; he and Cherry, who became chairman of the school committee in Bertie County, became lifelong friends and frequent correspondents. As a member of the legislature, Cherry also introduced a bill to provide for the education of public school teachers by establishing scholarships for that purpose in private colleges.

In about 1860, the unfortunate purchases in the cotton market of a relative whom he had set up in business brought Cherry to financial ruin. The Oaks, the plantation home he had purchased from the widow of his brother, W. W., in 1850, was put up for sale by the sheriff. In a letter written at that time, Cherry remarked, "I find myself reduced to penury and misery." It appeared to him that his friends had deserted him; those "who in former days have clung to me to gratify their ambition when I could carry them along, now that I am fallen 'know me not.' In my difficulty my thoughts are turned to God and His mercy."

As issues leading to the Civil War came to a head,

Cherry stood firm for the preservation of the Union. He petitioned the governor to let the voters have a say in whether North Carolina should uphold the Union. His was an unpopular attitude in that part of the state and served to increase his feeling of isolation. When the war began he wrote to Wiley: "To my other misfortunes and miseries in this troubled world, war, dreadful cruel war is calling to the gory battlefield all my kindred. Brothers, nephews and children are, some gone and others preparing to go to the field, I fear, of carnage and death to fight in a fratricidal war . . . that we have done all we could to avert"; he added that "in a certain contingency," he was preparing to leave for the battlefield himself. He had supported the Union, but when the war began, loyalty to North Carolina led him to cast his lot with the Confederacy.

Cherry must have regained his property not long after it was advertised for sale, for by mid-1861 his address was once again the Oaks. After the war he resumed his law practice in Windsor, about three miles from his home, continuing it until his death. He was an active leader in the Democratic party and in 1879 was appointed by Governor Thomas J. Jarvis to represent North Carolina at board meetings and vote its stock in the organization that operated the Albemarle and Chesapeake Canal. Cherry was also interested in promoting the construction of additional canals in the East, since those already in operation had served the state well in the years following the Civil War.

Cherry married Sarah Outlaw, and they had several children. One of his sons, George Outlaw, a Confederate veteran, was secretary to Governor Zebulon B. Vance. A portrait of Cherry is owned by his great-grandson of the same name in Windsor.

SEE: Daniel L. Grant, *Alumni History of the University of North Carolina* (1924); M. C. S. Noble, *History of the Public Schools of North Carolina* (1930); Calvin H. Wiley Papers (Southern Historical Collection, University of North Carolina, Chapel Hill).

FRANCIS SPEIGHT

Cherry, Robert Gregg (*17 Oct. 1891–25 June 1957*), post-World War II governor of North Carolina and speaker and long-time member of the North Carolina House of Representatives, was born at Catawba Junction, near York, S.C., to Chancellor Lafayette and Hattie Davis Cherry. His mother died when Cherry was one year old and his father, a farmer and Confederate veteran, six years later. Cherry was sent to Gastonia, just across the state line, to live with his maternal grandfather, pioneer Gastonian Isaac N. Davis, and his uncle, Henry M. Lineberger.

Cherry attended the public schools of Gastonia and then was graduated from Trinity College in 1912. He completed a law degree at Trinity College in 1914, winning the Judge Walter Clark prize as the highest ranking student in the graduating class. Returning to Gastonia, he established a law practice with Alfred Lee Bulwinkle, long-time friend and future congressman from the area.

When the United States entered World War I in 1917, Cherry delighted in organizing among men in the Gastonia area a machine gun troop of the First North Carolina Cavalry, which he trained and commanded during service overseas. He always took great pride in having developed a group of local men into a fighting cadre. His interest in the military continued after the war, and he maintained membership in the National Guard until 1924.

Cherry returned from the service in April 1919 to find that his friends had nominated him for mayor of Gastonia. He entered the race, won it in May of that year, and was reelected in 1921.

In 1931, Willis Smith, in an effort to gain a network of supporters for his own bid for speaker of the North Carolina house, persuaded Cherry to run for the house from Gaston County. Cherry won the election and continued to win the races biennially through 1939. In 1941 and 1943 he switched to the state senate, where he continued to represent his Gaston County constituency. His service in the house of representatives led to his own election as speaker in 1937. His resolute handling of the house in that crucial year of significant legislation under Governor Clyde R. Hoey won him the title "The Iron Major," a reference also to his military career. Cherry dispatched important social legislation with ease and took a personal interest in the social welfare programs, serving on the state board of public welfare.

By the end of the 1930s, he was being mentioned as a likely candidate for governor. Fulfilling a youthful ambition, he won the office in 1944 on a platform stressing improved health care and education, without a burdensome increase in taxes.

Cherry became the first governor from Gaston County and served during the difficult period of postwar readjustment for the nation and the state. He found the state with a budget surplus, which he sought to spend wisely for capital improvements while making plans for retiring the bonded indebtedness. Probably his two greatest accomplishments were in the areas of health care and education. He worked especially to improve facilities for mental health, spending in four years almost $12 million in state and federal funds combined (in all the years previously, only about $11 million had been spent in North Carolina for mental health). He also promoted an increase of 83 percent in public schoolteacher salaries and simultaneously reduced the average pupil-teacher ratio in the schools. While he did not achieve the level of road construction for which he had hoped, he set the stage for the road-building program of his successor, Kerr Scott, by laying plans and obtaining the supplies for future highway construction.

Cherry did not achieve a state-wide liquor referendum or a department of police and public safety, goals he had noted in his inaugural address. He maintained a moderate political image for his state when he refused to join the Dixiecrat revolt from the Democratic party. His moderate image in race relations was enhanced by his commutation to life imprisonment of the death sentence of a black man convicted of raping a pregnant white woman.

A man of keen wit, he reacted philosophically and humorously to public response to his controversial actions. He delighted in bringing a common touch to the governor's office. He preferred simple foods to the usual executive fare and usually walked to work, rather than riding in the executive limousine. He often surprised salespeople and state officials by doing his personal shopping and making his own telephone calls.

After he left the governor's office in 1949, Cherry returned to his law practice in Gastonia. There he lived with his wife, Mildred Stafford Cherry, daughter of a mayor of Greensboro, whom he had married in 1921. The Cherrys had no children.

Cherry died in 1957 after several weeks of hospitalization for toxic poisoning. He was buried in the Gaston Memorial Park. Under the terms of his will, his wife placed his personal papers in the North Carolina Department of Archives where they, along with his official gubernatorial papers, are available to researchers.

SEE: David Leroy Corbitt, ed., *Public Addresses and Papers of Robert Gregg Cherry* (1951); *Durham Herald*, 25 June 1957; *Gastonia Gazette*, 25 June 1957; Thomas S. Morgan, "A Step toward Altruism" (Ph.D. diss., University of North Carolina, 1969); *North Carolina: Rebuilding an Ancient Commonwealth*, vol. 4 (1929); *North Carolina: The Old North State and the New*, vol. 4 (1941); Raleigh *News and Observer*, 26 and 28 June 1957, 4 Aug. 1957.

THOMAS S. MORGAN

Cherry, William Walton (1806–45), legislator, was born near Windsor in Bertie County. His father, Solomon Cherry, was at one time or another sheriff, clerk of the court, and member of the General Assembly. His uncle, William Cherry, was graduated from The University of North Carolina in a class of three in 1800, was a trustee of the university from 1804 to 1809, and had a brilliant career as an attorney until his untimely death, hastened by intemperance, at the age of twenty-seven.

Cherry studied at The University of North Carolina but did not graduate. He taught school for two or three years, married Mary Etheridge of Colerain, and was in the mercantile business for about two years. Afterward, he began the study of law with James H. Jones, a well-known lawyer of the day, and in due course was admitted to the bar. He became interested in politics and in 1838, after two unsuccessful attempts, defeated the wealthy and politically powerful Dr. Alexander Mebane for the state senate.

In the senate he was made chairman of the Committee on Education and in that capacity worked with those who had for several years been trying to establish free public education. His influence enabled a bill for that purpose to be reported favorably. Called the Cherry Bill, it passed the senate, and a similar measure was passed in the house. Cherry is thus associated with the establishing of free public education in North Carolina.

In 1840, Cherry was a delegate to the national convention of the Whig party in Harrisburg, Pa. He went as a supporter of Henry Clay for president, but after the nomination went to Harrison, Cherry worked diligently to help elect him.

In 1844, Cherry was again in the North Carolina legislature, this time in the House of Commons representing Bertie County. In 1845 he was unanimously chosen as the Whig candidate for the U.S. House of Representatives from the first district, but he died the following week. Having gone to Jackson to attend the Northampton County Court, he became very uncomfortable and unresponsive to friends' salutations in the court room on Monday morning. That night he went to bed with a severe chill, and his death occurred Friday morning, bringing to a close, when he was just thirty-nine, his brilliant and promising career.

SEE: Samuel A. Ashe, *History of North Carolina*, vol. 2 (1925); Richard Benbury Creecy, *Grandfather's Tales of North Carolina History* (1901); J. G. de R. Hamilton, ed., *The Papers of William A. Graham*, vols. 1 and 2 (1957; 1959); John Wheeler Moore, *History of North Carolina* (1885); William H. Valentine diary (Southern Historical Collection, University of North Carolina Library, Chapel Hill); Windsor *Ledger-Advance*, 18 Oct. 1956.

FRANCIS SPEIGHT

Cheshire, Joseph Blount (29 Dec. 1814–9 Sept. 1899), Episcopal clergyman and botanist, was born in Edenton, the second of nine children, of whom only he and two sisters grew to maturity. His father was John Cheshire, a successful merchant, shipowner, and proprietor of a shipyard and ropewalk. His mother, born Elizabeth Ann Blount, was great-great-granddaughter of James Blount of Chowan County, the first of the name to come to North Carolina.

Cheshire was educated at the Edenton Academy and at the Episcopal School for Boys at Raleigh, now St. Mary's College. The illness and death of his father caused a reverse in the family fortunes and brought his formal schooling to an end in his sixteenth year. He was befriended by James Cathcart Johnston of Edenton, a prominent lawyer, who recommended him as a student in the law offices of Thomas P. Devereux of Raleigh. He received his license in 1836, returning to Edenton to begin the practice of law. In 1837 he was licensed for the superior and supreme courts. Johnston gave him a valuable law library and a horse and buggy and desired that the young man should come and live with him at his plantation, Hayes. Cheshire declined the offer, feeling that he should remain with his mother and young sisters.

While in Raleigh, Cheshire was confirmed in the Episcopal church and became an active and devout churchman. After two years of law practice in Edenton, he realized that his true calling was to the church. With the funds realized from the sale of Johnston's gifts (his benefactor being unwilling to take them back), he returned to Raleigh to study theology under the personal supervision of Bishop Levi Silliman Ives. A fellow student who became a lifelong friend was Moses Ashely Curtis, later an eminent botanist. Cheshire's natural bent for horticulture, which later was to come to rich fruition, had its beginning at this time.

By Bishop Ives, Cheshire was ordained deacon in Christ Church, Raleigh, February 1840, and priest in St. James's Church, Wilmington, 9 May 1841. He was sent by the bishop to Windsor and Halifax but soon was invited to come and hold services at Scotland Neck. Here he established Trinity Church, remaining its rector for thirty-five years. In 1855 the brick church, the second in the community to bear the name of Trinity, was built under his direction.

Tarboro was without an active minister in the early 1840s, and its congregation was dwindling. Cheshire was asked to come there to preach, and so successful was this visit that he received a call to become rector of Tarboro in October 1842. For a time he divided his time among his four churches, but in 1848 the churches in Halifax and Windsor passed into other hands. For the next twenty years he was rector at both Trinity Church, Scotland Neck, and Calvary Church, Tarboro.

Cheshire was married on 8 Feb. 1843 to Elizabeth Toole Parker (1820–95), the daughter of his senior warden at Calvary Church, Theophilus Parker. Their children were the Right Reverend Joseph Blount, Jr. (1850–1932), fifth bishop of North Carolina, who married first Annie Huske Webb and second Elizabeth Landsdale Mitchell; Theophilus Parker (1852–93), who married Ida Staton; Annie Gray (1859–1951), who married Samuel Simpson Nash, and Katherine Drane (1862–1935). Several infants died early.

In 1869, Cheshire resigned his charge at Scotland Neck, ill health making the twenty-five-mile trip between the two parishes infeasible. His tenure at Tarboro continued until his retirement in 1892, covering a half century of service.

At every church he served, Cheshire beautified the surrounding grounds, sending near and far for cuttings, seeds, and plants of native and exotic varieties. The resulting churchyard gardens in these four Eastern North Carolina towns, particularly in Tarboro, are well known to students of horticulture and garden lovers alike.

Calvary's small wooden church soon becoming inadequate for the Tarboro congregation, a larger brick edifice was begun in 1859. The new church was planned to seat five hundred people, although the congregation then boasted but thirty-five families. Not a cent of debt was at any time incurred. The Civil War interrupted the work, and the church was boarded up; but in 1866 a good cotton crop enabled the congregation to resume construction. The handsome church was consecrated 10 May 1868 by Bishop Thomas A. Atkinson.

During the war, Dr. Cheshire (who had been presented a D.D. by Madison College, Sharon, Miss., in 1861) was one of those involved in the printing of the only edition ever issued of the *Prayer Book of the Confederate States*. Five bales of cotton were sent to England by blockade-runners, and their sale, at $196.20 each, financed the publication. The only difference between the Episcopal Book of Common Prayer and the new Confederate Prayer Book was the substitution of the word "Confederate" for the word "United," and an oversight left in one prayer the offending "United."

Shortly after the end of the war, Cheshire, with Bishop Atkinson and a few southern clergymen, attended the general convention of the church in Philadelphia in October 1865. Antisouthern feeling had been at its most intense in Philadelphia, and fears were voiced for the safety of the delegates. They were received with great kindness by their hosts, however, and their courage in this venture brought about a healing of the division between the factions and the eventual restoration of the church to its prewar unity.

For thirty-seven years without a break, Cheshire attended his own diocesan convention. A faithful country parson of the old school and a strong and moving preacher, he reached out to rich and poor, white and black. He conducted regular Sunday afternoon services for his black parishioners; they attended with the white congregation for communion and for confirmation. In 1873, Cheshire founded St. Luke's, consisting of eighteen black communicants, as the first black parish in the Diocese of North Carolina.

Cheshire's health failed, and he resigned as rector, becoming rector emeritus in 1889. The last public service he conducted as a minister of the church was the funeral of his wife in 1893. He was buried in Calvary churchyard.

A portrait in charcoal by his daughter, Kate, hangs in the sacristy of Calvary Church.

SEE: Joseph Blount Cheshire, *The Church in the Confederate States* (1912), and "Life of My Father" (MS, Southern Historical Collection, University of North Carolina, Chapel Hill); Jaquelin Drane Nash, *A Goodly Heritage: The Story of Calvary Parish* (1960); Stuart Hall Smith and Claiborne T. Smith, Jr., *The History of Trinity Parish* (1955).

JAQUELIN DRANE NASH

Cheshire, Joseph Blount, Jr. *(27 Mar. 1850–27 Dec. 1932)*, priest and bishop, the son of the Reverend Joseph Blount Cheshire, rector of Calvary Church, Tarboro, and Mary Toole Parker, daughter of Theophilus Parker and Mary Toole, was born in Tarboro in a house built by his grandfather Parker. His siblings were Theophilus, John, Elizabeth, Katherine Drane, and Annie Gray.

Cheshire received his earliest education at home from

his mother. At the age of nine he went to a school taught by the Reverend and Mrs. Thomas R. Owen. Two years later he entered the Tarboro Male Academy, where he was prepared for college by Frank S. Wilkinson. In February 1866 he was able to enter the freshman class at Trinity College, Hartford, Conn.; his father chose this school because it was under the control of the Episcopal church and because its president, Dr. John B. Kerfoot, was a personal friend. While at Trinity, Cheshire was a member of the Alpha Delta Phi Fraternity and in his senior year was president of his class. After three and a half years there, he was graduated in June 1869 with the degree of B.A.

From 1869 to 1871, Cheshire taught Greek and Latin at St. Clement's Hall, Ellicott City, Md. Then he began the study of law under the direction of William K. Ruffin of Hillsborough, son of Chief Justice Thomas Ruffin. Following several months' study with Ruffin and three months' work in the law office of Judge George Howard of Tarboro, he received his license to practice law in January 1872. He commenced his law practice in Baltimore in partnership with George Hooper, a Trinity College friend. This connection continued for fifteen months, until Cheshire returned to Tarboro to join the law firm of Colonel John L. Bridgers and his son, John L., Jr. Together they made up the firm of Bridgers, Cheshire and Bridgers. In addition to his law practice, Cheshire became secretary and treasurer of the Pamlico Banking and Insurance Company, a position requiring only a few hours of work each day.

As early as 1876, Cheshire decided that he would offer himself as a candidate for holy orders. He had been contemplating making this important step for several years but did not want to do so until he had made a success in his law practice. He began the systematic study of theology under the direction of his father. On 21 Apr. 1878 he was ordered deacon by Bishop Thomas A. Atkinson in Calvary Church, Tarboro. Following his ordination, Bishop Atkinson, upon the request of Kemp P. Battle, president of The University of North Carolina, assigned him to the Chapel of the Cross, Chapel Hill, where he was to serve his diaconate under the direction of Dr. Robert Sutton, rector of St. Bartholomew's parish, Pittsboro. On 30 May 1880, two years after going to Chapel Hill, Cheshire was ordained priest. In addition to his work at the Chapel of the Cross, he organized a mission and built a church in Durham, which he named for St. Philip, the Deacon.

In the spring of 1881, Cheshire accepted a call to become the rector of St. Peter's Church in Charlotte, one of the largest parishes in the Diocese of North Carolina. His ministry at St. Peter's was characterized by his activities in extending the missionary work of the Episcopal church not only in Charlotte but also in Mecklenburg and Union counties. During his twelve years as rector of St. Peter's, he increased its membership from 137 to 263. He organized and established St. Martin's parish, St. Michael and All Angels' mission for blacks, St. Mark's mission at Mecklenburg, and St. Paul's mission at Monroe. He sponsored the building of St. Peter's and the Good Samaritan hospitals, and assisted the Reverend E. A. Osborne in establishing the Thompson Orphanage. An important accomplishment of his ministry in Charlotte was an improved relation between the Episcopal church and the other local denominations.

In addition to his parochial and missionary work, Cheshire took an active part in the affairs of the diocese. He was chairman of the Committee on Canons for several years and, while holding this position, compiled an important revision of the diocesan canons. He also

served as a clerical deputy in the general conventions of 1886, 1889, and 1892. From 1885 to 1893 he was a member of the board of trustees of the University of the South.

Upon the request of Bishop Theodore Benedict Lyman for assistance in his office, a special convention of the Diocese of North Carolina met in Raleigh on 27 June 1893 for the purpose of electing an assistant bishop. Among the seven priests nominated, the Reverend Francis J. Murdock, rector of St. Luke's Church, Salisbury, and Cheshire were the leading candidates. After thirty-nine ballots, Cheshire was elected assistant bishop of the Diocese of North Carolina. His consecration took place on 15 Oct. 1893 in Calvary Church, Tarboro. Just two months later he became diocesan upon the death of Bishop Lyman. Cheshire was the first native clergyman of the state to be elected to the episcopate of North Carolina.

One of the first acts of his episcopate was the initiation of a vigorous missionary program in the mountain counties of the state. He soon realized that the work required more time than he could devote to it, and at the general convention of 1895 he proposed the creation of a missionary district composed of the western counties in his diocese. The proposal was adopted and the district was placed under his charge until a missionary bishop was elected. Three years later the Reverend Junius Moore Horner became missionary bishop of the Jurisdiction of Asheville.

At the annual convention of 1897, Cheshire proposed that St. Mary's School in Raleigh should be taken over as a diocesan institution. This school had been established in 1842 by Dr. Aldert Smedes, an Episcopal clergyman; it functioned as a private school under his direction and later under that of his son, the Reverend Bennet Smedes. When Smedes decided to discontinue operating the school, Cheshire saw the opportunity of making it an important educational institution for the diocese. His plan was adopted by the diocesan convention, and he raised the funds for the purchase of the property and for an endowment. Shortly afterward, Cheshire was able to make St. Mary's School an institution of all the dioceses of North Carolina and South Carolina, an acquisition he considered one of the most important accomplishments of his episcopate.

In his relations with his black clergy and laity, Cheshire was remarkably successful. When the separation of the races within the church was proposed, he was opposed to the move, but when he became convinced that the change was strongly desired by black churchmen, he supported the movement in the general convention. In 1918 the diocesan convention elected the Reverend Henry B. Delany suffragan bishop in charge of work among blacks. Delany had been archdeacon of the Convocation for Colored Work in the diocese for the past ten years.

Throughout his life, Cheshire had an abiding interest in history, particularly that of his church and state. In 1884 he was elected historiographer of the Diocese of North Carolina, an office he held until he became bishop. One of his earliest publications was a monograph, *The First Settlers of North Carolina Not Religious Refugees*, in which he maintained that the early settlers came not seeking religious freedom but for economic reasons. In 1892 he edited a volume of historical papers entitled *Sketches of Church History in North Carolina*, three of which were written by himself. The papers had been prepared for the one-hundredth anniversary of the first attempt to organize the Episcopal church in North Carolina following the Revolution. Cheshire's most ambitious and significant historical work was *The Church in the*

Confederate States, published in 1912. In this volume he described the organization of the Episcopal church in the Confederate States, its work among the soldiers, its attitude toward blacks, its publications, and finally the reunion of the church in 1865. Among other historical productions were *Milnor Jones, Deacon and Missionary* (1920); his reminiscences of North Carolina personalities and incidents, published in 1930 under the title *Nonnulla*; and several parish histories. Cheshire's work as a historian was recognized when in 1930 he was elected president of the State Literary and Historical Association. Other honors included the D.D. degree from The University of North Carolina (1890), the University of the South (1894), and his alma mater, Trinity College (1916).

Cheshire attended every meeting of the general convention of the church while he was bishop. He also attended the Lambeth Conferences of 1897, 1908, and 1920.

In 1922, after twenty-nine years in the episcopate, Cheshire gave his consent to the election of a bishop coadjutor to assist in the ever-growing work in his diocese. The Reverend Edwin Anderson Penick, then rector of St. Peter's Church, Charlotte, was elected to that office and consecrated on 15 Oct. 1922. From that time on, Cheshire gradually turned over the work of the diocese to his coadjutor.

In addition to his accomplishments as a clergyman, prelate, and scholar, Cheshire attained considerable skill and reputation as a sportsman. Fishing and hunting were the sports he enjoyed most. He once remarked that he had been fond of fishing from his boyhood but that his liking for it increased with age. His prowess as a hunter of wild turkeys was legendary in his diocese. He also had an enviable reputation as a raconteur of rare charm, and many of his stories were derived from his fishing and hunting experiences.

Cheshire was sometimes found unintentionally blunt and even brusque in his manner, as a result of his forthright and completely honest disposition. Bishop Penick described his counsel as "penetrating and true and bracing like fresh air in a stuffy room." In churchmanship, Cheshire was not a ritualist, but throughout his episcopate he emphasized the catholic character of the church and insisted upon a strict adherence to the rubrics of the *Book of Common Prayer* and the canons of the church.

In 1874, Cheshire married Annie Huske Webb of Hillsborough. They had six children, Elizabeth Toole, Sarah, Joseph Blount, Annie, James Webb, and Godfrey. Mrs. Cheshire died in 1897, and two years later, Cheshire married Elizabeth Lansdale Mitchell of Beltsville, Md. Portraits of Cheshire are owned by St. Augustine's College and St. Mary's College in Raleigh.

SEE: *Carolina Churchman*, 1909–35; Joseph Blount Cheshire, *Fifty Years of Church Life in North Carolina* (1926), and "Some Account of My Life for My Children," *Carolina Churchman*, January 1934–May 1935; Joseph Blount Cheshire Papers (North Carolina State Archives, Raleigh; Southern Historical Collection, University of North Carolina, Chapel Hill); *Journal of the Convention of the Diocese of North Carolina*, 1878–1933; Lawrence F. London, *Bishop Joseph Blount Cheshire* (1941).

LAWRENCE F. LONDON

Chesnutt, Charles Waddell (20 June 1858–15 Nov. 1932), writer, was born in Cleveland, Ohio, the first child of Andrew Jackson Chesnutt and his wife, Ann Maria Sampson, both of whom were born in freedom in North Carolina. During the Civil War, Andrew Jackson

Chesnutt served as a teamster in the Union Army, but when the fighting ended he returned to his home in Fayetteville to become a grocer. Charles and his mother followed in 1866. Charles spent the next seven years in Fayetteville working part-time in his father's store and studying diligently in the Howard School, an institution established by the Freedman's Bureau.

At the age of fifteen, Chesnutt went to Charlotte, where he became assistant to the principal of a school. His formal education curtailed, he embarked on a program of private instruction and extensive reading in ancient and modern languages, mathematics, music, and English literature. Leaving Charlotte in 1877, he returned to Fayetteville as first assistant to the principal of the recently opened State Colored Normal School. At the age of twenty-two he was appointed principal of the school, a post he held for three years.

In 1883, he left the South for New York, having taught himself stenography as preparation for a new career in the North. For six months he worked as a Wall Street reporter, contributing a daily column of stock market gossip to the New York *Mail and Express*. Later that year he moved to Cleveland, Ohio, where he secured a position in the accounting department of the Nickel Plate Railroad Company. Here he began studying law and writing his first stories and sketches. After passing the Ohio state bar in March 1887, he launched a successful business career in Cleveland as a court reporter, stenographer, and attorney.

With his wife, Susan Perry Chesnutt, a Fayetteville native, he raised four children, all of whom were college graduates: Ethel and Helen (Smith College), Edwin (Harvard University), and Dorothy (Western Reserve University). Although he traveled widely in the South and Northeast and made two trips to Europe, Chesnutt never again moved his residence from the city of his birth. He died and was buried in Cleveland.

As early as 1880, Chesnutt began to think seriously in his private journal about writing a book that would combat what he called "the unjust spirit of caste" in the United States. However, his literary career began with the publication of short stories, the first of which appeared in April 1885 in the S. S. McClure newspaper syndicate. Drawing upon his experiences in New York and his memories of life in the Sandhills region of North Carolina, Chesnutt wrote a number of humorous and pathetic sketches between 1885 and 1889. But his unusual treatment of slave superstitions in a story called "The Goophered Grapevine" caught the attention of the editors of the *Atlantic Monthly*. When they published the story in August 1887, it became the first work by an Afro-American to appear in that prestigious literary magazine. Subsequent "conjure stories" were accepted by the *Atlantic* and *Overland* monthlies. At the urging of Walter Hines Page, editor of the *Atlantic*, Chesnutt submitted to Houghton, Mifflin and Company a collection of these stories that was published in March 1899 as *The Conjure Woman*. These dialect tales, which focus on the life of the ordinary slave in central North Carolina, show Chesnutt's familiarity with the "plantation school" of southern writing and his skill as a transcriber of southern local color.

During the 1890s, Chesnutt was praised by a number of famous writers and critics, among them George W. Cable, James Lane Allen, and William Dean Howells, for his achievements as a short story writer. His second collection of short fiction, *The Wife of His Youth and Other Stories of the Color Line* (1899), ranged over subjects and themes no previous literary delineator of black American life had attempted to portray. The note of protest against racial discrimination was present in several of the stories, but Howells was impressed with the artist's control over his materials and tone throughout the volume. The book was popular enough to convince Houghton, Mifflin to publish Chesnutt's first novel, *The House behind the Cedars*, in 1900. A story of the attempts of two young Afro-Americans to pass for white in the postwar South, the novel was Chesnutt's most carefully wrought and evenly balanced long story. Like all three of his novels, it was set in the Cape Fear region of North Carolina. Chesnutt's second novel, *The Marrow of Tradition* (1901), drew upon an incident of North Carolina history, the Wilmington Race Riot of 1898, for its main action and central theme. The fiercely partisan tone of the novel convinced many reviewers that the book was an unreliable or even anti-white account of contemporary southern affairs. The book's failure to sell widely forced Chesnutt to give up his two-year-long effort to support his family on the emoluments of professional authorship. In 1905, his business affairs claiming most of his time once again, Chesnutt published his last novel, *The Colonel's Dream*, a story of an idealist's endeavor to revive a depressed southern town through the methods and influence of benevolent capitalism. The book received little critical notice.

Except for an infrequent short story, Chesnutt confined his literary labors after 1905 to articles, essays, and speeches, most of which dealt with the race problem in America. A friend of and correspondent with Booker T. Washington, Chesnutt nevertheless chided the Tuskegeean for his failure to argue vigorously enough for black political rights throughout the United States. Engaged in this cause as much as his time and health would permit, Chesnutt saw his literary reputation wane as the writers of the Harlem Renaissance, espousing new subjects and new standards for Afro-American fiction, gained pre-eminence in the 1920s. In 1928, however, the National Association for the Advancement of Colored People acknowledged his "pioneer work as a literary artist depicting the life and struggles of Americans of Negro descent" by awarding him the Spingarn Medal. Since his death, literary critics have assigned him the first rank among all black fiction writers of his day and an honored place in the history of southern literature. Of his six books, only the biography *Frederick Douglass* (Boston, 1899) has not been reprinted in a modern paperback edition.

SEE: Helen M. Chesnutt, *Charles Waddell Chesnutt* (1952 [photograph]); Chesnutt papers (Fisk University Library, Nashville, Tenn.).

WILLIAM L. ANDREWS

Chevin, Nathaniel (*d. ca. 1720*), justice and council member, first appears in the records of North Carolina late in 1695. By February of the following year, he was clerk of the Chowan Precinct Court, and throughout his life in the colony, his career was closely tied to the courts. Chevin was named to succeed William Glover temporarily as clerk of the general court in July 1697. Exactly three years later he assumed the position on a full-time basis, serving until October 1703, when Thomas Snoden succeeded him.

A staunch Anglican, Chevin served on the first vestry formed in Chowan Precinct late in 1701. A vestryman six and a half years, he served at various times as churchwarden and clerk. When he moved to Pasquotank Precinct in April 1708, he resigned from St. Paul's Parish vestry; in the Vestry Act of 1715, he was named first member of the Southwest Parish vestry of Pasquotank Precinct.

In July 1708, Chevin became a justice of the general court; he held that position through March 1712. Aided by his association with Thomas Pollock and others opposed to Thomas Cary, he became a council member as early as July 1711, under Governor Edward Hyde. An extremely active upper house member, Chevin served on the council through 1 Aug. 1717. Shortly after that time, he appears to have had a confrontation with Governor Charles Eden, which brought about his fall from favor. By March 1720, Chevin was dead.

SEE: Mattie Erma Edwards Parker, ed., *North Carolina Higher-Court Records, 1670–1696* and *1697–1701* (1968, 1971); William S. Price, Jr., ed., *North Carolina Higher-Court Records, 1702–1708* (1974); William L. Saunders, ed., *Colonial Records of North Carolina*, vols. 1–2 (1886).

WILLIAM S. PRICE, JR.

Child, Francis (*d. 7 Aug. 1792*), Revolutionary War officer, was apparently living in New Bern in 1768, when he was witness to a will there. He entered McRee's company of the Sixth North Carolina Regiment of the Continental Army as a lieutenant on 16 Apr. 1776 and was promoted to captain on 26 Jan. 1777. On 1 June 1778 he was transferred to the Third North Carolina Regiment. He was among the North Carolinians who arrived in Charleston, S.C., on 13 Mar. 1780 to reinforce the army of General Benjamin Lincoln. On 12 May 1780, following Lincoln's surrender, he was taken prisoner in Charleston. Child retired from military service at half pay in January 1781.

On 20 Nov. 1784, Child was elected comptroller of the public accounts of the State of North Carolina by the General Assembly, succeeding Richard Caswell. Prior to his appointment, Child had served as a clerk under Caswell. As comptroller, Child lived in Kinston and conducted the business of his office there until 1788, when he moved to Hillsborough.

Child was largely responsible for negotiating North Carolina's claims for reimbursement of war expenses with commissioners appointed by the Confederation Congress. After initial delays caused by the lack of a permanent state capital, he worked toward a settlement of these accounts between 19 Feb. 1788 and the time of his death.

Child was friend and associate of Richard Caswell, serving as a trustee for the estate of Richard Caswell, Jr. He held property in Kinston and in Orange County. His survivors included his wife, Frances, and three sons, Samuel, Wilson, and Francis. He died in Hillsborough after a lingering illness.

SEE: C. L. Davis, *A Brief History of the North Carolina Troops . . . in the War of the Revolution* (1896); *North Carolina Journal*, 22 Aug. 1792; Orange County Record of Wills, 1752–95 (North Carolina State Archives, Raleigh); William L. Saunders and Walter Clark, eds., *Colonial and State Records of North Carolina*, vols. 10, 13–21 (1890, 1896–1903).

DONALD E. BECKER

Child, Thomas (*fl. 1745–67*), attorney general, legislator, and agent and attorney to John Carteret, Earl Granville (proprietor of the northern counties of North Carolina), was born in 1720 or 1721 in the vicinity of Sudbury, Suffolk County, England, the youngest of the three sons of Richard Child, an eminent physician of that county. It is assumed that Child, like his older brothers Richard and John, was educated in the Yorkshire school of Dr. Kinsman at Bury. Unlike his brothers, however, he did not go on to Caius College, Cambridge, but was in the early 1740s put to reading law in the Middle Temple. Child was admitted a member of the Middle Temple on 22 Apr. 1746 and called to the degree of utter bar five weeks later on 30 May.

Late in 1745, Dr. Child learned through a friend's colonial correspondence of a vacancy in North Carolina's attorney generalship; he encouraged his son to apply for appointment to the vacant office. This Child did in December 1745, and after he interested Thomas Fonnreau, a minor member of Newcastle's administration, in his application, the appointment was granted on 8 Feb. 1746. Child left for North Carolina soon thereafter.

Child's initial appearance in North Carolina was in June 1746, when he assumed the duties of attorney general in the colony's general court. Within a few months, however, he had returned to London with the consent of Governor Gabriel Johnston. To Johnston, Child explained that affairs at home necessitated his return; in London, however, he reported to the secretary of state for the southern provinces that he had been compelled to leave North Carolina because of the unrest and confusion in the colony. In late 1748 and early 1749, Child joined an anti-Johnstonian party that sought the governor's removal by denouncing him to the board of trade. This party included Francis Corbin, who was one of Earl Granville's protégés, associates of the land speculator Henry McCulloh, McCulloh himself, and some merchants trading with North Carolina ports. Child's accusations against Johnston (maladministration in the court of chancery and the court of ordinary, imposition of inflationary economic policies, the granting of commissions to unfit and disloyal persons, and attempts to intermeddle arbitrarily in legislative representation) were outside the scope of his office as attorney general, and the sincerity of the charges may be open to question. In any event, the board of trade was not sufficiently moved by the testimony presented to it to recommend Johnston's dismissal from office.

While in London, in addition to agitating for Johnston's removal, Child sought appointment as proprietary agent to Earl Granville. The earl's deceased cousin, Lord Granville of Potheridoe, had married Rebecca, daughter of Sir Josiah Child, and it is not unlikely that the Childs of Suffolk were connected with the family of the London merchant. If so, Thomas Child probably made use of this connection in his application for the agency. Certainly he was found acceptable to Granville, and Child shared with Francis Corbin the duties of agent to the earl by a commission and a power of attorney drawn up in London on 18 Oct. 1749. Both agents returned to the colony, but after they had opened the proprietary land office in Edenton in October 1750, Child returned to London and stayed for nearly a decade. During this period he remained active in proprietary affairs and gradually assumed an ascendancy over Corbin in them.

By 1752, Granville warned the agents in the colony to be certain to remit all monies owing to Child, "as I shall particularly interest myself in his concerns." Child was entrusted with a role in the negotiations with the Moravians in London for sale of tracts totaling nearly one hundred thousand acres within the proprietary, and the deeds transferring title to these tracts were drawn up by him. Similarly, he negotiated contracts between Henry McCulloh and Granville involving nearly three hundred thousand acres in the proprietary, guided the earl clear of difficulty when Corbin's grants of land from these tracts resulted in legal action, and obliged McCulloh to renegotiate or forfeit upon expiration of the original

contract. When Corbin, because of mismanagement of the land office, became the object of a riotous attack in January 1759, Child persuaded Granville to remove Corbin and his coagent, Joshua Bodley; in April of that year, new and fuller powers as exclusive agent were granted to Child by the earl.

In July, the Privy Council reaffirmed Child's commission of 1746 as attorney general of North Carolina, and by September 1759 he was back in the colony. His first action in the proprietary land office was to turn out all the Corbin appointees. He then forwarded to the courts of the proprietary counties his new plan of business for the land office, assuring the earl's tenants through the county justices that Earl Granville "will do any Thing on his part that may be yet wanting to the Establishment of People's Rights"; Child further assured the tenants that in future dealings with his office, fairness and equity could be expected. In October he commissioned new entry takers, surveyors, and receivers of quitrents. By July 1760, most of the enormous backlog of delayed land grants, some of them pending completion for twelve years, was cleared up to the satisfaction of the Granville tenants, and the land office was restored to sound order.

While undertaking these reforms, Child became a decided supporter of the political and economic interests of the northern (proprietary) counties. With the former agent, Corbin, Robert Jones, proprietary collector of quitrents, and Thomas Barker, former proprietary collector, Child was active in the General Assembly in behalf of those interests during 1760 and 1761, when he represented Chowan County. Governor Arthur Dobbs labeled the group "the northern Junto," denounced Child as an opponent of the royal prerogative, and called for his dismissal as attorney general. But Dobbs's antagonism toward Child may in part be accounted for by the fact that the governor had run afoul of the ministry at home in 1759, when he followed Child's advice and gave his assent to acts of the assembly contrary to his own ministerial instructions.

Child, however, had no intention of remaining in the colony nor of retaining his offices. Selecting Robert Jones as his successor, he resigned the attorney generalship in his favor early in 1761; the warrant to commission Jones in the office was passed by the Privy Council on 14 Apr. of that year, and on 25 July 1761, Jones received his commission from Dobbs. In proprietary affairs, too, Child secured the transferral of part of his power to Jones. In about August 1761, Child left active management of proprietary affairs in the hands of Jones and removed to Suffolk, Va., where he took up residence. From there he maintained an oversight of the proprietary affairs until April 1763, when the death of John, Earl Granville, closed the land office. Upon receipt of the news of the proprietor's death, Child settled his American affairs and returned to London. There he attempted to persuade the new proprietor, Robert, Earl Granville, to sell him the proprietary lands in North Carolina. Though he was unsuccessful in the attempt, Child was able to buy from the second earl the quitrents from the nearly one hundred thousand acres owned by the Moravians. These he held until 1767, when he sold them to the Moravians; the sums involved are not known, but the fact that the Moravians were still paying for the purchase of the quitrents from Child as late as 1789 suggests that he found it a profitable venture. With this sale, Child dropped out of North Carolina affairs altogether; he was not involved with the plans of Robert, Earl Granville, during the years 1773 to 1776, to reopen the proprietary office in North Carolina. It is presumed that Child died in London in the early 1790s. A heavy charge against Child, that he conspired to defraud John, Earl Granville, continues to haunt his reputation. The basis for this charge was the oral report of a statement said to have been made during verbal testimony in the course of a trial in Edenton District Superior Court. Joshua Bodley, last of Corbin's coagents in the proprietary office, was with Corbin an object of the riotous attack on the agents in January 1759; with Corbin, he had been dismissed by Granville in April of that year. It appears that Child allowed Bodley to buy the office of proprietary collector of quitrents sometime later, but in August 1760, Child removed him from the exercise of any proprietary office. Bodley promptly sued, and the action dragged on in the civil courts and in chancery for a decade. While the suit was in progress, Bodley is said to have told the jury, presumably in November 1766, that he and Child had deliberately concocted a plan to deceive the earl in order to share profits from the proprietary quitrents, that as a result of this agreement he had bought the office of receiver from Child, and that Child, after accepting the price for the office, had defrauded him by revoking the appointment. Whatever the truth of this report, which is not reflected in the surviving records of the suit, Bodley was awarded damages of more than three thousand pounds. On the other hand, execution of the award was prevented by an injunction in chancery. The dispersal and partial disappearance after 1785 of the records of the colonial court of chancery prevent full exploration of this charge against Child. One wonders, however, whether a court of law would have awarded damages for a broken contract itself based upon fraud.

Child, an Anglican, was first married at the age of twenty-eight to the heiress Jane Arthington of Arthington, Yorkshire, at St. Dunstan in the West, London, on 12 June 1749. After her death, he married Ann Faver of Stafford, Staffordshire, at St. James, Westminster, on 18 Mar. 1756. He is not known to have had children by either marriage.

SEE: Allegations for Marriage Licenses, Surrogate, Bishop of London (Guildhall Library, London); Adelaide L. Fries, ed., *Records of the Moravians in North Carolina*, vols. 1–2 (1922); Granville Proprietary Records (Longleat, Wiltshire, England); Newcastle Papers (British Museum); North Carolina State Archives (Raleigh), for Chowan County Deed Books H, M, and N; Colonial Court Records, Edenton District Superior Court Records (1760–71), Governor's Office Records, Granville Papers, and Secretary of State Records; H. A. C. Sturgess, comp., *Register of Admissions . . . Middle Temple* (1949).

GEORGE STEVENSON

Chipman, Luzene Stanley (2 Sept. 1798–22 Nov. 1886), religious writer and Methodist preacher, was born near the New Garden Meeting House in Guilford County of Quaker parentage. Her father probably was Strangeman Stanley; her mother died when Luzene was ten.

On 1 June 1820, Luzene Stanley married Joel Chipman; he was not a Quaker and on 30 June she was disowned by the Society of Friends. Mrs. Chipman was influenced by the religious revivals that swept the state before the Civil War and began attending Methodist services. On 25 June 1832, the Moravian diarist at Friedland recorded that "curiosity took almost all our members to Waughtown today to hear a certain Mrs. Chipman of the Reformed Methodist denomination preach." Her early Quaker training, however, caused her great anguish in her new church, as she thought "singing could not be acceptable worship in the Divine sight."

"On one occasion, going to church all alone and meditating," she later wrote, "these words came into my mind, with such weight and distinctness, that at the first impulse, I thought some one had spoken to me: 'Cry aloud, spare not, lift up thy voice like a trumpet, and show my people their transgressions, and the house of Jacob their sins.' I stopped my horse instantly, and the most solemn feeling came over me . . . and I reasoned with myself whether I should go to church or turn back home again. I feared I should feel this awful weight at church, and I should become a reproach to the cause of truth. At length my mind became calm and I went on to the meeting; but my mind became covered in darkness, and O the many trials I underwent . . . I resolved through his grace, that if ever I felt the moving of the blessed spirit, in any requirement whatever, whatever might be the result, I would submit, let the world say what it might of me."

It apparently was soon after this event that Mrs. Chipman began writing her first book, although it did not appear in print for a number of years. Funds for its publication eventually came from the quarterly conference of the Methodist church, and *Earnest Entreaties and Appeals to the Unconverted with Persuasions to Religious Duties* (192 pp.) was published in Raleigh in 1852. Its eighteen chapters, each in reality a cleverly written sermon, bear such titles as "Reflections on Christian Experience," "Religious Education of Children," and "Think Not to Escape the Justice of God," suggesting that although outwardly a Methodist, inwardly she remained a Quaker. Mrs. Chipman's purpose, she recorded in the preface, was "to urge the blessed principles of Truth on the minds of those who may read its pages. . . . There is no beauty nor elegance of language to the ear; there is no new subject brought to light; it is no other than the principles of true Godliness as revealed by the Gospel of the Son of God. . . ."

"Dear Reader," she confided, "to have this little book brought before the public eye has been a matter of deep and humbling reflection, knowing my limited education and inability to write in a style that would meet the approbation of the community at large; and of course must undergo the contempt of the critic's eye, and the ridicule of the vain, therefore, I have for years kept it concealed; I have been in doubt, and distress has covered my mind. I strove to excuse myself, because my services were called for by the public in another way, and the care of a family occupied all my time; but this I found to be of little avail, this concern still followed me, and caused me many sleepless nights; I must encourage believers in their Christian duties, and tell sinners their career must lead to death."

On 7 July 1870, at the age of seventy-two, Mrs. Chipman was accepted, at her own request, as a member of the Deep River Monthly Quaker Meeting. This return to the faith of her childhood must have been a great comfort to her in her last years. In 1877, a quarter of a century after the appearance of her first book, she published a second one, *A Wonderful Revelation of Heaven by an Angel Sent from God to Luzene Chipman*. This little book, just twenty-three pages, was an account of a revelation that came to her in April 1874, while she was ill and unconscious; it also contained what appears to be a sermon, with the title "Christ Comforteth His Disciples."

Joel Chipman died on 11 July 1886 at the age of ninety-three, and Luzene Chipman died four months later at the age of eighty. Both were buried in the churchyard of the Deep River Friends Meeting in

Guilford County. They were survived by three children, one of whom, James Romulus Saunders, an honor graduate of Oak Ridge in 1852 who attended Trinity College before beginning the study of medicine, was convicted in 1856 of the murder of Martha Pennix, a servant girl in the Chipman home. He was sentenced to death but, while an appeal was pending, escaped and fled to Mexico. In 1877 a cousin, Paris C. Stewart, confessed to the murder, and Governor Zebulon B. Vance pardoned Chipman. In the meantime, he had married in Mexico and become wealthy. His sons were sent to the University of Virginia and his daughter to Sweet Briar, but he did not return to North Carolina.

There is a drawing of Mrs. Chipman in each of her books.

SEE: Each of Mrs. Chipman's books which contain much material of an autobiographical nature; *Greensboro Daily News*, 30 Nov. 1952; Raleigh *News and Observer*, 1 Nov. 1953.

WILLIAM S. POWELL

Christmas, William (1753/54–16 Dec. 1811), surveyor, cartographer, legislator, and militia and civil officer during and after the Revolution, was a son of John and Mary Graves Christmas. Despite a statement in his obituary describing him as a native of North Carolina, there is evidence to indicate that he was born in Hanover County, Va. His parents moved in 1757 to North Carolina (present-day Warren County), where John was a large landowner and captain of the Granville County militia in 1763. John acquired about ten thousand acres of land in Orange County, moved there in 1777, and died there six years later, having lived to see his five oldest sons serve as officers during the Revolutionary War.

It is presently not known where William Christmas was educated, but he may have acquired his skill as surveyor from his early associations with General Thomas Person, a Granville District surveyor, and with his own cousin, Richard Henderson, of Transylvania fame. General Person's estate records show that he had given Christmas his surveying instruments prior to his death in 1800, and Christmas's obituary credits him with helping Henderson to lay out Boonesboro in 1774. Besides his outstanding accomplishments as a surveyor in several North Carolina and Tennessee counties, Christmas is credited in his obituary with the laying out of towns in Kentucky, South Carolina, and Georgia. Having been appointed as surveyor for Bute County in 1778, he was one of the three surveyors named in the Bute County land grants and was responsible for running the line to divide Bute County into Warren and Franklin counties. He gave bond as county surveyor at the first Warren County court, May 1779, and it may have been after he resigned this office a year later that he laid out the towns of Warrenton and Louisburg, county seats of the two new counties. As deputy sheriff of Warren County, he returned the sheriff's account for the preceding year at the May court in 1780.

Christmas was commissioned ensign in the Bute County militia in 1777 and, from 1780 until the end of the Revolutionary War, served as staff officer of the Halifax Military District, Quartermaster Division, as Warren County commissioner for "collecting provisions tax and securing supplies and provisions for support of the Army and Navy of this and the United States in the Southern Department." On 12 Oct. 1780 the board of war, meeting at Hillsborough, commended him for his zeal and integrity in the service of his country not only as commissioner for collecting provisions but also as issuing

commissary to the troops. Brigadier General Jethro Sumner wrote Colonel Philemon Hawkins on 28 Jan. 1782, requesting that William Christmas, Esq., as "the most judicious person," impress two men with horses to act as courier for him. Christmas commanded the independent rifle corps under General Nathanael Greene at the battle of Guilford Court House.

Before the close of the war, Christmas had married Abigail, daughter of Atkins and Sarah Jones McLemore. Her father had been a member of the Granville County militia in 1754, represented Bute County in the House of Commons in 1778–79, and was one of the commissioners and trustees for establishing the town of Warrenton in 1779. When the North Carolina Provincial Congress held at Halifax in April 1776 appointed two men from each county to obtain firearms for the use of the troops, Atkins McLemore was one of the men from Bute County. In 1778, McLemore was appointed one of the commissioners for selling the remnants of the public gun factory in Bute County.

Christmas was appointed second major in the Franklin County militia in 1787, the year he moved to that county. He was promoted to first major in 1791 and lieutenant colonel commandant in 1795, serving in this last capacity until his successor was appointed by the council of state in 1800, on the eve of his departure for Tennessee. The Franklin County court minutes show that he served there as road juror, Halifax District court juror, tax collector, bridge commissioner, and county surveyor before he was elected to the state senate in 1792; previously, he had served as a representative from Franklin County in the constitutional convention of 1789 at Fayetteville, where he voted in favor of ratifying the U.S. Constitution.

In 1792, while Christmas was serving as senator from Franklin County court minutes show that he served there as road juror, Halifax District court juror, tax collector, bridge commissioner, and county surveyor sale of the lots was held, the commission named him its clerk. The plat (presumably in Christmas's hand) of the thousand-acre purchase of land and the original boundaries and streets of Raleigh is preserved in the State Archives.

Christmas was one of the surveyors whose work underlay the famous Price and Strother Map (1792), the first map of North Carolina from actual survey. His brother, Nathaniel, collaborated with Jonathan Price in planning and financing this map.

At the General Assembly of November 1799, Christmas was chosen as entry taker and surveyor general of North Carolina's reserved lands in the territory that had become the State of Tennessee. On his journey to Tennessee, he stopped on 5 Mar. 1800 in Orange County, where his mother was still living. He arrived in Nashville by 1 Apr., set up the entry office, and began surveying, having determined to move his nearest relatives and friends to Tennessee by the fall and to share the destinies of the state for life. In addition to the duties for which he had come, he was appointed by the Tennessee General Assembly as principal surveyor for the First District.

Christmas died in Williamson County, Tenn., survived by his wife and three of his four daughters. In Williamson County (where he owned much land), in the old Steele graveyard off the Lewisburg Pike, on Flat Creek between the Marshall County line and the Maury County line, there is a broken stone that probably marks his grave, though "William Chri——" is all that is legible.

SEE: Kemp P. Battle, *History of the University of North Carolina*, vol. 1 (1907); Governors Office Records and

Legislative Papers, 1792 (North Carolina State Archives, Raleigh); *North Carolina Minerva and Raleigh Advertiser*, 13 May 1800; *Raleigh Register and North Carolina State Gazette*, 7 Feb. 1812; *Raleigh Register and North-Carolina Weekly Advertiser*, 25 Mar. 1800; Records of Granville, Bute, Warren, Franklin, and Orange counties (North Carolina State Archives, Raleigh); Records of Williamson County, Tenn. (Tennessee State Library and Archives, Nashville); Report of Commission Establishing Capital (North Carolina State Archives, Raleigh); Blackwell P. Robinson, ed., *The North Carolina Guide* (1955); William L. Saunders and Walter Clark, eds., *Colonial and State Records of North Carolina*, vols. 10, 12–20, 22, 24 (1890–1907); Tennessee Legislative Petitions, 1807 (Tennessee State Library and Archives, Nashville); Mary L. Thornton, "The Price and Strother *First Actual Survey of the State of North Carolina*," *North Carolina Historical Review* 41 (1964).

M. H. D. KERR

Chronicle, William *(1755–7 Oct. 1780)*, a Lincoln County citizen-soldier of the Revolution, one of the heroes slain in the Battle of Kings Mountain, was the only son of William Chronicle, Sr. (ca. 1722–86), of Lincoln County and his wife, Dinah McKee Chronicle (ca. 1727–86), farmers of Pennsylvania Dutch origin. William Chronicle, Jr., was born in Rowan County. He received only the elementary education made available to youth in those days by the tutorship of family kindred, or a clergyman, or such a local schoolmaster as Frederic Baldstaff, who before the Revolution taught school in the neighborhood where the Chronicle family lived. Chronicle was appointed an officer in the county militia before he was twenty years old and, though he continued to retain his militia rank and responsibilities, was commissioned a captain in the guerilla organization known as the North Carolina Partisan Rangers.

From 1768 to 1779 the Chronicle family resided in Tryon County, created in 1768 from Mecklenburg County in honor of royal Governor William Tryon. Many leading people of the county, including the elder William Chronicle, did not like Tryon and favored the Regulator rebellion, which was crushed at the Battle of Alamance in 1771. Tryon County was abolished at the request of its own people, in order to curry support from its ex-Regulators at a crucial phase of the Revolution. Lincoln, one of two new counties formed in 1779 when Tryon was abolished, was named for a Continental Army officer from Massachusetts, General Benjamin Lincoln. When the Lincoln County militia regiment was organized in 1780, with William Graham as colonel and Fredrick Hambright as lieutenant colonel, William Chronicle the younger was elected major. Graham did not accompany the regiment to Kings Mountain because of illness in his family, and Chronicle led the charge of his regiment up the mountain slope. He was killed in action; his sword and spurs were brought home by his comrades and were given by his father to Chronicle's half brother, James McKee. Chronicle was never married. He had a sister, Sarah (ca. 1757–86), who married Abraham Scott and by 1785 had daughters (unnamed in the records) and sons named William and John. Chronicle's mother, whose maiden name has not been found, had been first married in Pennsylvania to a McKee who died in about 1753, during or soon after migration with his family to North Carolina. He left his widow with an infant son, James. The widow married William Chronicle, Sr., in 1754.

James McKee, in December 1801, while a resident of Lincoln County, petitioned the General Assembly to be allowed to inherit military lands and other benefits accruing to the estate of his deceased half-brother, "who was killed at the Battle of King's Mountain and died intestate leaving behind him no legal heirs." Petitioner McKee stated that "if the law of descent had been the same as it is at the time of this petition, then petitioner would be entitled to inherit this officer's estate." The General Assembly passed a special act in his favor. The statement that Chronicle left behind him no legal heirs at the time of his death was quite contrary to fact, however, inasmuch as his father, mother, sister, nieces, and nephews were still alive five years after the Battle of Kings Mountain, when Chronicle's father wrote his will. The will was duly probated and executed in Lincoln County in 1786. It is possible that all these legal heirs had died without descendants by 1801, but the failure to account for them is itself remarkable. McKee attained prominence in Lincoln County. Among his descendants was a grandson, William Henry, M.D. (7 Sept. 1814–Apr. 1875), of Raleigh, who was the father of James, M.D. (5 Jan. 1844–5 Jan. 1912), also of Raleigh.

Chronicle's place of burial is unknown, but presumably he was buried near where he fell at Kings Mountain battleground in South Carolina.

SEE: H. B. Battle et al., *The Battle Book* (1930); F. B. Heitman, *Roster of the Officers of the Continental Army* (1893); Cyrus Lee Hunter, *Sketches of Western North Carolina* (1877); North Carolina Military Papers of the Revolution (North Carolina State Archives, Raleigh), for no. 396; North Carolina State Archives (Raleigh), for the petition of James McKee (no. 184, Legislative Papers) and the will of William Chronicle, Sr. (C.R. 060.801.7); W. L. Sherrill, *Annals of Lincoln County* (1937).

CHARLES R. HOLLOMAN

Churton, William *(fl. 1749–December 1767)*, pioneer surveyor and cartographer for the Granville District, colonial official of Childsburgh (Hillsborough) and Orange County, and member for Orange in the colonial legislature, came from England to America in the 1740s as a surveyor attached to the Granville Land Office in Edenton. His English background is unknown, but it seems probable that he was a Londoner with family roots in Gloucestershire.

In October 1749, North Carolina's two appointed commissioners, William Churton and Crown lawyer Daniel Weldon, together with Virginia commissioners Joshua Fry and Peter Jefferson, extended the existing Virginia–North Carolina boundary line ninety miles westward beyond the Blue Ridge Mountains to Steep Rock Creek. At about this time, Churton evidently supplied the two Virginia surveyors with the topographical information concerning the Granville District that appeared on the 1751 Fry-Jefferson Map. The second (1755) edition of the map showed further significant increases in detail, especially in the vast area that Churton had just surveyed for the Moravians. No mention of indebtedness to Churton, however, appears on either edition.

Churton undertook a second arduous survey of mountainous western lands between August 1752 and January 1753, when he accompanied Bishop August Gottlieb Spangenburg and a party of Moravians to the "Blue Mountains" to survey tracts totaling 98,925 acres. The Spangenburg Diary and later Moravian records provide numerous brief personal glimpses of Churton, whom Spangenburg characterized as "certainly a reasonable man" and "excessively scrupulous" in his surveying practices. For the next fifteen years, until his death, the Moravians maintained a warm friendship with their "Good Companion . . . the Surveyor Mr. Churton."

It was Churton's custom to defer the actual drawing of plots and writing of descriptions (deed certificates) until he returned to Edenton. Only a few of his delicate plats of individual grants survive today, on tiny slips of paper, in the North Carolina Land Grant Office, Raleigh. Long delays in delivering the deed certificates were inevitable; and in various cases, notably that of the Quaker William Wiley, Churton assisted waiting grantees by paying accumulated quitrents for them and otherwise standing between them and the far-off Granville agent in Edenton.

In 1753, 635 acres were granted to Churton and Richard Vigers to hold in trust for the establishment of Salisbury (incorporated in 1755). Similarly, on 7 June 1754, 663 acres (also recorded as 653 acres) were granted to Churton to hold in trust for Francis Corbin to establish a town successively named Orange, Corbinton, Childsburgh, and Hillsborough, on the north bank of Eno River. Approximately 120 one-acre lots of the new town were staked out by Churton and his assistant surveyor, Enoch Lewis, in the late summer of 1754. It is also probable that Quaker surveyor James Taylor worked with Churton in Orange County in the early 1750s.

Although Churton had been appointed first public register of Orange County in 1752, he did not actually qualify until the 12 June 1753 court, because of his enforced absences on surveying expeditions. For the next full decade, until 1763, he occupied the post of register, but a deputy register, William Reed, of necessity served in his place. Churton served as member from Orange in the colonial legislature for approximately eight years, from 1754 to 1762, and as town commissioner of Childsburgh from its incorporation as a town in 1759 until his death. He was also officially appointed public surveyor of Orange County in 1757 and served as justice of the peace after 1757.

On the evidence of court minutes alone, Churton appears to have been a valued permanent resident of Childsburgh from 1757 onward. In 1759 he received by legislative grant four one-acre lots, F, G, H, and [K], in the low-lying southeastern quadrant of the town, "in Consideration of the many Services he hath performed for the Inhabitants of the said Town, and his Labour, Expence, and Pains in laying out the said Town." This gift of lots was reaffirmed in the 1766 legislative bill renaming the town Hillsborough. The lower portion of the street running north and south near Churton's lots had apparently been named Churton Street even before 1759.

The Spangenburg Diary had noted in September 1752 the great need for a "general surveyor's map of the Granville District," and from 1757, Churton appears to have been actively at work on the preparation of a topographical map of the Province of North Carolina. He himself, however, did not survey the southern and coastal areas, and for this data he had to rely on "information and old maps." In November 1766, Governor William Tryon laid the finished Churton Map before the General Assembly, which allowed Churton the "handsome gratuity" of £155. Governor Tryon further assured Churton that if he would endeavor "to complete and make perfect the southern and maritime parts of the province," he should with Tryon's approval take the map to England and present it to the board of trade.

When Churton in 1767 began actually to survey the coastal areas, he discovered the lower section of his map to be so defective that he "condemned and cut off that portion." He had already bequeathed the map to Tryon in case of accident, and when Churton unexpectedly died in December 1767, Tryon promptly arranged for the Swiss cartographer Claude Joseph Sauthier to execute the maritime section "from different surveys which several Gentlemen in the Province have obliged him with." The final draft of the third section of the map, delineating Mecklenburg County and the Cherokee dividing line (originally surveyed by Churton in 1756), was probably done by Captain John Abraham Collet, another Swiss cartographer and engineer, who was commissioned by Tryon to assemble and copy the entire map in final form and transport it to England. It was published in London on 1 May 1770 in a large format (43½" x 28⅝"), handsomely engraved by I. Bayley, under the title "A Compleat Map of North Carolina from an Actual Survey. By Cptn. Collet, Governor of Fort Johnston." It has remained a landmark in early North Carolina cartography.

Churton's will, probated 5 Jan. 1768 (but not registered or preserved in Orange County), left six of his Hillsborough town lots, nos. 5, F, G, H, I, and K, as well as a tract of land, to four London heirs, probably relatives: James and Dorothy Thompson and William and Sarah Bodington. All the rest of his estate, including his valuable papers, was left to Edmund Fanning.

The entire length of Hillsborough's north-south street, now its main street, was eventually renamed Churton Street, apparently the only memorial in North Carolina to the Granville surveyor whose early cartographic contributions have gone unacknowledged on any published map.

SEE: *A Complete Revisal of All the Acts of Assembly of the Province of North-Carolina* (1773); Walter Alves Papers (Southern Historical Collection, University of North Carolina, Chapel Hill); John Collet, *A Compleat Map of North Carolina from an Actual Survey* (1770); William P. Cumming, *The Southeast in Early Maps* (1958, 1962); Adelaide L. Fries, ed., *Records of the Moravians in North Carolina*, vols. 1–2 (1922); Minutes of the Orange County Inferior Court of Common Pleas and Quarter Sessions, September 1752– August 1763 (North Carolina State Archives, Raleigh); North Carolina Land Grant Records, Orange and Rowan County Files (Secretary of State's Office, Raleigh); Orange County Deed Books 1–3 (Orange County Courthouse, Hillsborough); William L. Saunders and Walter Clark, eds., *Colonial and State Records of North Carolina*, vols. 5–8, 23, 25 (1887–1905).

MARY CLAIRE ENGSTROM

Clark, Charles Cauthen (8 Dec. 1829–30 Oct. 1911), lawyer and politician, was born in New Bern, the eldest child of William Willis and Martha Stevenson Clark. He was the descendant of a wealthy and prominent New Bern family. Elijah Clark, his grandfather, had been sheriff of Craven County, one of the three organizers of the First Baptist Church of New Bern, and a successful merchant. His father was cashier of the Merchant's Bank of New Bern and by 1860 had accumulated $22,000 in real and personal property and seventeen slaves. Charles Clark received his preparatory education at the New Bern Academy and then attended Wake Forest College and Princeton University, obtaining the Bachelor of Arts and Master of Arts degrees from the latter institution in 1849 and 1852 respectively. After reading law with William H. Washington of New Bern, he was admitted to the bar and began an eminent legal career which spanned more than half a century. On 11 Jan. 1854 he married Fannie (Frances) Lawrence Howard, the daughter of a distiller who, like William Clark, was among the largest slaveholders in New Bern. Charles and Fannie Clark had four sons (William, Charles, Jr., George, and Edward) and four daughters (Mrs. Frances Walters, Mrs. Martha Burroughs, Mrs. Susan Heptinstall, and Mrs. Clarita Waters) who lived to adulthood.

By the eve of the Civil War, he had already established himself as one of the social and political leaders of New Bern. During the 1850s he had edited a newspaper for several years, started his law practice, and become a notable figure in the revitalized Whig party in Eastern North Carolina. He was also an active leader in the First Baptist Church (where he often took the pulpit in the minister's absence) and the Worshipful Master of the Saint John's (Masonic) Lodge from 1858 to 1860, a position which he held five times after the Civil War as well.

In 1860, his efforts as a Whig party organizer were rewarded when he was chosen as a presidential elector on the Constitutional Union party ticket and elected to the lower house of the state legislature. In February 1861, he was elected as a Unionist candidate to the convention that was to determine whether North Carolina would leave the Union. The convention proposal itself, however, was narrowly defeated, and the convention did not meet until after Abraham Lincoln had called for 75,000 volunteers after the firing on Fort Sumter. By that time Clark, like most other Whig Unionist leaders, had become resigned to the inevitability of disunion, and he signed the ordinance of secession in May 1861.

He and his family fled New Bern when it was occupied by Union troops in March 1862. Moving to Goldsboro, he soon joined the Thirty-first North Carolina Infantry Regiment, was named commissary sergeant on 22 Sept. 1862, and commissioned captain on 14 Oct. The following month he was elected solicitor of the Second Judicial District by the state legislature, and he resigned his army commission on 8 Dec. 1862. He continued to hold the office of solicitor for the remainder of the war.

After the war, he became one of the recognized leaders of the "Conservative" party, which had arisen as the state's predominant political force during the war years. Along with William Alexander Graham and Josiah Turner, Jr., he was instrumental in persuading Jonathan Worth to oppose Provisional Governor William Woods Holden in the crucial gubernatorial contest held in the fall of 1865. He ran for and won a seat in the state constitutional convention of 1865–66 claiming, like Worth and many other Conservative party candidates, that his antebellum opposition to secession was sufficient proof of his loyalty to the restored Union. In November 1865, he was elected as representative to the Thirty-ninth Congress from the Second Congressional District despite the fact that he could not take the "ironclad oath" of undeviating past loyalty to the Union. Although both of Clark's opponents in the congressional contest could swear to the oath, they received less than ten percent of the district's vote, giving Clark the largest margin of victory of any congressional candidate in 1865. However, due to the inability of six of the state's seven representatives to take the oath and to the growing rift between Andrew Johnson and the moderate and radical Republicans in Congress, North Carolina was denied representation in the Thirty-ninth Congress and Clark never took his seat.

During Jonathan Worth's tenure in office, he was the governor's close personal friend and adviser and in 1866 was appointed a director of the Atlantic and North Carolina Railroad. Though the Conservative party's fortunes temporarily faded with the advent of military reconstruction in the state, he remained an influential figure in the Conservative party and later in the Democratic party. He also managed to increase his personal fortune, despite the fact that much of the inheritance which he had stood to receive from his father and his in-laws had been decimated by the abolition of slavery. He also retained his position of social prominence, serving as Grand Master of Masonry in North Carolina from 1870 to 1872, trustee of Wake Forest College from 1871 to 1873, and trustee of the New Bern Academy.

In 1886 he again ran for office, winning a disputed election to the North Carolina Senate. In February 1887, however, the Senate upheld the challenge of George Green, Jr., of Carteret County, and Clark was removed from office. He returned to the New Bern law partnership which he had formed with his eldest son, William Willis Clark, II, who became a noted lawyer in his own right. The younger Clark was appointed U.S. Judge of the Eastern District of North Carolina in the latter days of the second Cleveland administration, but the appointment was not confirmed by the U.S. Senate. Another son, Edward, served as mayor of New Bern in the 1920s.

Charles Clark remained active in his law practice until the last years of his life. Shaken by the premature death of his son William in 1910, his health declined rapidly, and he died the next year. He was buried with Masonic honors in the Cedar Grove Cemetery, New Bern.

SEE: Census of 1850, 1860, and 1870; John L. Cheney, Jr., comp., *North Carolina Government, 1585–1974: A Narrative and Statistical History* (1975); "Collected Election Returns" (North Carolina State Archives, Raleigh) North Carolina; Frontis Johnson, ed., *The Papers of Zebulon Baird Vance* (1963); James L. Lancaster, *The Scalawags of North Carolina, 1850–1868* (1976); Raleigh *News and Observer*, 2 Nov. 1911; John Nichols, comp., *Directory of the General Assembly of the State of North Carolina, for the Session Commencing November 19, 1860* (1860); *North Carolina Booklet* 22 (1923); Herbert D. Pegg, *The Whig Party in North Carolina* (1968); North Carolina *Standard*, 27 Feb. 1861; New Bern *Times*, 20 Sept. 1865.

EDWARD R. MORAWETZ, JR.

Clark, David (*15 May 1877–15 Nov. 1955*), founder and publisher of *The Textile Bulletin*, was born in Raleigh to Susan Washington Graham and Walter Clark, chief justice of the state supreme court. After attending the Raleigh Male Academy, Clark enrolled in North Carolina State College. At eighteen he received a bachelor of engineering degree. During the period 1895–97 he taught mechanical drawing and took additional courses. He was graduated in 1896 with a degree in mechanical engineering and in 1897 with a degree in civil engineering. While a student he played on the college football and baseball teams for three years. In 1897 Clark enrolled at Cornell University to continue his engineering studies. Though he left Cornell in the spring of 1898 to serve in the Spanish-American War, he was awarded a mechanical engineering degree in absentia. Clark entered the military as an adjutant but afterward became captain of Company M, Second North Carolina Voluntary Infantry.

After returning to North Carolina from the service, Clark entered the cotton textile industry as a sweeper for fifty cents a day in the Ada Cotton Mill of Charlotte. He then worked for D. A. Tomkins Company of Charlotte as a mill engineer for about a year before starting his own cotton mill. His business failed in the panic of 1907, and Clark turned to journalism for employment. He became editor of the *Textile Manufacturer*, published by W. C. Dowd of the *Charlotte News*. In 1910 Clark quit working for the *Textile Manufacturer*, turned down an engineering job in Brazil, and decided to start his own journal. After a trial issue in January, the first issue of *The Southern Textile Bulletin* appeared on 2 Mar. 1911. In 1937 his flourishing company, Clark Publishing, started another publication, *The Knitter*, for the knitgoods trade. In later years Clark-Smith Publishing Company began *Southern Hospitals*, *Municipal South*, and *Southern Optometrist*. Clark worked as president of Clark Publishing, of Clark-Smith Publishing, and of Washburn Printing, a commercial printing house. Clark helped organize the Southern Textile Association in 1908 and served as its treasurer from 1908 to 1913. He also played a major role in establishing the Southern Textile Exposition in Greenville, S.C., in 1917. He joined his brother John Washington Clark in 1923 to establish Randolph Mills and was a member of its board of directors.

Two of Clark's major interests were Rotary International and North Carolina State College. He was the first member of the reorganized Charlotte Rotary Club and served as its president in 1917–18. He was elected governor of the Fifty-Eighth Rotary District in 1927 and organized fifteen new clubs in the district. The next year he became vice-chairman of Rotary International's extension committee, and in 1927 he was elected to the board of directors of Rotary International.

Clark served for many years on the athletic council of North Carolina State College and enthusiastically supported the college's teams. He helped raise money to build Reynolds Coliseum in Raleigh, and was instrumental in establishing the Textile Foundation at State College. In 1963 Mangum Hall on the State College campus became the David Clark Laboratories which housed the textile chemistry department and research facilities for the School of Textiles. Clark served for many years on the Board of Trustees of the Consolidated University of North Carolina but was frequently accused of attacking President Frank Graham and The University of North Carolina at Chapel Hill. Clark claimed in 1940 to be a friend of the university and only to oppose "a small group of radicals whom I regard as a cancer upon the institution." In particular he criticized professors he thought were communists, socialists, or atheists.

The *Charlotte Observer* described Clark as "a volunteer spokesman for an ultra-conservative philosophy in business and educational matters" and "a stirrer-upper of no mean proportions." He opposed child labor laws, shorter hours for women workers, and all attempts by unions to organize workers. The unofficial spokesman for the textile industry, Clark favored a North-South wage differential, which kept the wages of Southern workers lower than the wages paid workers in the North. In 1948 Clark was co-chairman of the States' Rights Party in North Carolina and campaigned for Strom Thurmond.

Clark belonged to the Democratic party and was a charter member of the Myers Park Methodist Church where he served as a steward. He was also a member of the Charlotte Country Club, the Charlotte Chamber of Commerce, the Masons, the City Club, and the Charlotte Textile Club. He married Aileen Butt on 8 Apr. 1916. He died in a Charlotte hospital after a heart attack and was buried in Raleigh's Oakwood Cemetery.

SEE: Paul Blanshard, *Labor in Southern Cotton Mills* (1927); Aubrey Lee Brooks and Hugh T. Lefler, eds., *The Papers of*

Walter Clark, 2 vols. (1948, 1950); *Charlotte Observer*, 16 Nov. 1955; David Clark, *Communism and Socialism at Chapel Hill* (1940); David Clark, *How College Radicalism Is Fostered* (1935); *David Clark Answers Pridgin* (1940?); Raleigh *News and Observer*, 19 May 1935, 16 Nov. 1955; *Textile Bulletin*, Nov. 1955.

DAVID CLARK
CHARLES W. EAGLES

Clark, Elijah. See Elijah Clarke.

Clark, Elmer Talmage (9 Sept. 1886–29 Aug. 1966), world Methodist leader, author, historian, and publicist, was born in Randolph County, Ark. He attended West Plains College, Mo.; Hendrix College, Ark.; and Vanderbilt University, Tenn. He earned the B.A. degree at Birmingham Southern College in 1926 and the M.A. degree at George Peabody College for Teachers in 1927. He received a B.D. degree from Temple School of Theology, Philadelphia, and an S.T.D. degree from the same school in 1925.

Clark served as a pastor in St. Louis, Mo. (1911–17), and then was correspondent of the *St. Louis Republic* and the *New York Tribune* from England, France, and Italy, and covering the American armies in the field, from 1917 to 1918. He was special publicity secretary of the American YMCA in England, Scotland, Ireland, and France in 1918. From 1919 to 1920, he was the national publicity director of the Centenary Commission of the Methodist Episcopal Church, South, raising a $53 million fund; he served in the same capacity for the Christian Education Commission of the Methodist Episcopal Church, South, raising a $33 million fund. He was editorial secretary of the Board of Education of the Methodist Episcopal Church, South, from 1923 to 1926 and assistant secretary of the Board of Missions from 1926 to 1938. He was editor of *World Outlook* (1938–52) and, after 1940, also editorial secretary of the Board of Missions and Church Extension of the Methodist Church. He was the guiding light of the World Methodist Council, the American Association of Methodist Historical Societies, and *Methodist History* (1962). In 1956 he scheduled the World Methodist Conference at Lake Junaluska.

Clark was a prolific writer. His mission study books include *Healing Ourselves*, *The Task Ahead*, *Thy Kingdom Come*, and *The Church and the World Parish*. Other books and booklets (interpretive and promotional) include *The New Evangelism*, *The Church Efficiency Movement*, *The Centenary Book of Facts*, *Talking Points on Christian Education*, *The Book of Home Mission Specials*, *The Rural Church in the South*, *The Negro and His Religion*, *The Latin Immigrant in the South*, *The Rebirth of Protestantism in Europe*, *What's the Matter in China? Methodism Marches On: The Story of Methodism Around the World*, *Latin America* (with Harry C. Spencer), *The Chiangs of China*, *The World Methodist Movement* (with Ivan L. Holt), *The Methodist Evangel*. He also wrote *Social Studies of the War*; *The Psychology of Religious Awakening*; *The Small Sects in America*; pamphlets on Francis Asbury, Charles Wesley, Isaac Watts, and the Wesley family; and a 200-page history, *Methodism in Western North Carolina*.

At Lake Junaluska, Clark assembled the world's largest Methodist print collection, the largest and finest collection of Wesley art objects, several Salisbury paintings, numerous Wesley manuscripts and several thousand old and rare volumes (estimated at one hundred thousand dollars in 1952). He helped restore Epworth, birthplace of John Wesley, and the home of Francis Asbury near Birmingham in England. He traveled to Europe twelve times. He compiled *An Album of Methodist History*, one of his best-known works, and with others edited *The Journal and Letters of Francis Asbury* in three volumes. Birmingham Southern College conferred on him the degree of Litt.D. and Southwestern University that of Doctor of Literature.

Clark was married to Mary Alva Yarbrough in 1923. He lived in Nashville and New York until his home, Amen Corner, was built at Lake Junaluska in 1941. At the time of his death, while in semiretirement, he was working on the *Encyclopedia of World Methodism*. He died in Birmingham, Ala., and was buried in Woodlawn Memorial Park in Nashville, Tenn. His career was chronicled in *Elmer T. Clark Memorial Edition (Methodist History)* in 1971; the World Methodist Building at Lake Junaluska has a painting of him by Salisbury.

SEE: Elmer T. Clark, *Junaluska Jubilee* (1963), and *Methodism in Western North Carolina* (1966); Elmer T. Clark, Jacob S. Payton, and J. Manning Potts, *The Journal and Letters of Francis Asbury*, 3 vols. (1958); Walter N. Vernon, *Elmer T. Clark Memorial Edition* (1971).

GRADY L. E. CARROLL

Clark, Henry Selby (9 Sept. 1809–8 June 1869), congressman, legislator, and lawyer, was born at the family home near Leechville, Beaufort County, the son of Henry Clark and his wife, whose family name was Selby. The Clark family had owned land there for at least two generations.

Clark was graduated from The University of North Carolina in 1828 and returned to his native county to practice law in Washington. At twenty-five he was elected as a Democrat to the House of Commons, where he served three terms, 1834–36. He was solicitor for the district in 1842. In the fiercely contested two-party politics of the day, he was a frequent campaigner and orator. When Democrats gerrymandered congressional districts in 1842, he was chosen as a Democratic candidate for a sharply divided district. During the course of his campaign, he challenged Henry Dimock, editor of the *North State Whig*, to a duel, claiming that untruths had been printed about him. The affair was held outside Beaufort County, as duels were illegal there. Shots were fired, but neither man was wounded. Clark was elected and served a single term in the Twenty-ninth Congress, 1845–47. As a member of Congress he supported U.S. claims to Oregon, and his speeches, several of which were published in pamphlet form, were widely acclaimed. He was defeated for reelection by the Whig candidate, Richard S. Donnell, whose measure he had taken in 1844.

The political ardor of "the chivalric Mr. Clark" cooled, and he moved to Greenville to practice law, taking little part in political affairs from that time on. During the early years of the Civil War he served as a member of a disbursing and safety committee of Pitt County. He owned extensive land at Gourdin's Depot in South Carolina and was there in 1861 and 1864, supervising farming operations by slaves.

Clark was married in 1835 to Alvaney M. Staton of Pitt County; they had no children. He was buried in the family cemetery near Leechville.

SEE: *Biog. Dir. Am. Cong.* (1971); Henry S. Clark letters (Southern Historical Collection, University of North Carolina, Chapel Hill); Raleigh *Daily Sentinel*, 23 June 1869; *Raleigh Register*, 2 June 1835; H. T. Shanks, ed., *The Papers of Willie Person Mangum*, 5 vols. (1950–56).

ROY PARKER, JR.

Clark, Henry Toole (7 Feb. 1808–14 Apr. 1874), lawyer, politician, and governor of North Carolina, was born on his father's plantation on Walnut Creek near Tarboro. His father, James West Clark, son of Christopher and Hannah Turner Clark, was a Princeton graduate (1796). He represented Bertie County in the North Carolina House of Commons in 1802–3 and in 1810–11 represented Edgecombe in the house, while his brother-in-law, Henry Irwin Toole, Jr., was state senator from the same county. From 1812 to 1815, James W. Clark represented Edgecombe in the state senate; then he served a single term in Congress (1815–17). He later served as chief clerk in the Navy Department (1829–31) under Secretary of the Navy John Branch, a close friend. James Clark's wife, Arabella Toole Clark, was a daughter of Henry Irwin and Elizabeth Haywood Toole, prominent Edgecombe citizens.

Henry T. Clark began his education at George Phillips's school in Tarboro and later entered a school in Louisburg. In 1822 he enrolled in The University of North Carolina, being graduated with the class of 1826. He studied law under a relative, William Henry Haywood, Jr., who later (1843–46) served in the U.S. Senate. Although his father joined the Whig party after Branch's resignation from President Andrew Jackson's cabinet, young Henry, influenced by his Haywood cousins, temporarily remained a Democrat. He, too, soon joined the Whigs, because of Jackson's efforts to destroy the Second Bank of the United States.

Clark engaged in law practice only rarely. After 1830 he took over the management of his father's plantation and business affairs. In 1835 he hired out a number of slaves to planters in Alabama, using James Hair as his agent. During the 1830s and 1840s, Clark continued to develop his extensive business interests in Tennessee and Alabama, undertaking long journeys on horseback to attend to his affairs.

Clark was married in 1850 to his cousin, the widow Mrs. Mary Weeks Hargrave, daughter of Theophilus Parker of Tarboro. They had two sons and three daughters: Haywood, Henry Irwin, Laura P. (later Mrs. John L. Bridgers), Maria Toole (later Mrs. Henry C. Bourne), and Arabella (later Mrs. Walter J. Smith). The family attended Calvary Episcopal Church of Tarboro.

In 1850, Clark was appointed colonel of the Twenty-first Regiment of North Carolina Militia by Whig Governor Charles Manly. In this capacity, as his later correspondence with Governor David Settle Reid reveals, he had the usual difficulties in equipping and arming his men. Also in 1850 he was elected to the state senate from Edgecombe; his easy victory may be attributed to the overwhelming strength of the Whig party in Edgecombe at this time. He remained a member of the senate until 1861 and was elected speaker in 1860, coming into the direct line of succession to the governorship, since there was no lieutenant governor in North Carolina until 1868. On 7 July 1861, Governor John Willis Ellis died of tuberculosis at the Red Sulphur Springs in Virginia. Clark was suddenly elevated to the governorship during the most serious crisis in North Carolina's history. Fortunately, even William W. Holden's *North Carolina Standard*, an opposition paper, supported the new governor.

On 16 Aug. 1861, Clark presented his official governor's message to the General Assembly. He began with words of praise for the assembly and a note of sadness for the late Governor Ellis: Ellis's "public and private virtues," he said, "have but recently been canvassed through the State, and their thorough endorsement by the people constitute his highest reward while living, and a rich legacy to survive him." Clark added that the cause of the Confederacy was just and that the Lincoln administration had forced North Carolina to go to war. He praised the army of volunteers, "who have come forward with brave hearts, and willing to enlist in the cause of their country." Then, after discussing the activities of the constitutional convention in preparing the defense of the state, he mentioned military needs, including the raising and supply of an army and the defense of North Carolina's long coastline. He described the threatened northern blockade and the former dependence of North Carolina on northern manufactured goods, concluding his able message with a statement on trade.

The history of the Clark administration is the history of the state at war: raising troops, improvising supplies and equipment, trying, unsuccessfully, to defend the vulnerable coastline, making political appointments, adjusting and regulating state-Confederacy relations, and fighting and dying for a cause that was irretrievably doomed, almost from the beginning. Clark's correspondence as governor concerns applications for commissions; camp life; the raising of companies and regiments; purchasing supplies in Europe; raising money; the activities of North Carolina and Confederate military and naval forces; the loss of such important positions as Hatteras Inlet, Roanoke Island, Albemarle Sound, New Bern, and Fort Macon; manufacturing military supplies and arms; and many other topics, mostly connected to military and naval affairs.

As northern troops gradually occupied much of Eastern North Carolina, a wave of defeatism swept over the people. Clark was unable to combat this feeling; though he was a capable man, his personality did not rouse the people to a fever pitch of patriotism. It remained for the more popular and dynamic Zebulon Baird Vance, who became governor on 8 Sept. 1862, to rally North Carolinians to the Confederacy.

Clark left the governorship to retire in his beloved Edgecombe County. He served as chairman of the county court of common pleas and quarter sessions and for one year, 1866, as state senator from Edgecombe. He spent a large portion of his last years studying North Carolina history and corresponded with such leading figures as Governor Jonathan Worth and Cornelia Phillips Spencer on this and other subjects. He was buried in the yard of Calvary Episcopal Church in Tarboro; his wife was buried beside him.

SEE: Charlotte *Western Democrat*, 16 July 1861; Henry T. Clark to Willie P. Mangum, letters (12 Mar. 1834, 8 Apr. 1834), in H. T. Shanks, ed., *The Papers of Willie Person Mangum*, vol. 2 (1952); *Hillsborough Recorder*, 17 July 1861; North Carolina State Archives (Raleigh), for Henry T. Clark Letter Book (1861–62), including Governor's Message, 16 Aug. 1861; Henry T. Clark to Cornelia Phillips Spencer, letter (11 May 1872, in Cornelia Phillips Spencer Papers, vol. 1, 1859–75), Henry T. Clark to Jonathan Worth, letter (20 Aug. 1867, in Jonathan Worth Papers, 1831–89), Governor's Papers (Henry T. Clark, 1861–62; David S. Reid, 1851, 1853, for letters of Henry T. Clark to General Haywood, 30 May 1853, 22 June 1853, 22 Dec. 1853, and to David S. Reid, 6 June 1851), portrait of Henry T. Clark, and will of Henry T. Clark (Edgecombe County Wills, 1831–1945); Library, Duke University (Durham), for Joseph Blount Cheshire, "Henry Toole Clark" (C. L. Van Noppen Papers), and sketch of Henry T. Clark in card index; Raleigh *North Carolina Standard*, 13 July 1861; Raleigh *State Journal*, 17 and 20 July 1861, 10 and 21 Aug. 1861; Salisbury *Carolina Watchman*, 15 July 1861; Southern Historical Collection (University of North Carolina, Chapel Hill), for entry of

22 July 1861 in David Schenck Journal, 1861, David Schenck Diary and Books, 1854–63; Tarboro *Daily Southerner*, 20 Feb. 1908.

RICHARD W. IOBST

Clark, James West (15 Oct. 1779–20 Dec. 1843), congressman, legislator, and chief clerk of the U.S. Navy Department, was born in Bertie County, the son of Christopher Clark of Elmwood on Salmon Creek, "a merchant of North England & Edenton," and his second wife, Hannah Turner. He was graduated from Princeton College at the age of eighteen in 1797 and in 1802 and 1803 represented Bertie County in the General Assembly. In 1802 he married Arabella, daughter of Colonel Henry Irwin Toole, a prominent planter of Edgecombe County. The couple lived first on Walnut Creek, eight or ten miles from Tarboro, but in 1830 built a house that still stands in Tarboro. Clark represented Edgecombe County in the General Assembly in 1810 and 1811 and in the senate in 1812, 1813, and 1814. He was a Madison elector in 1812. He was elected to Congress, served during 1816–17, but declined to run for a second term. In Congress he served on the Committee on Private Land Claims.

Remaining active in local politics, Clark was clerk of the North Carolina Senate for two sessions, 1827–28 and 1828–29. He became a strong Jacksonian and during the period 1829–31 served as chief clerk of the Navy Department under his friend, Secretary of the Navy John Branch, leaving when Branch resigned as a result of the Peggy Eaton affair, which sundered the Jackson cabinet. In 1837, Clark was appointed a member of the council of state to replace someone who declined to serve, but the constitutionality of his appointment was questioned and his name was withdrawn.

Clark and his wife were the parents of one son, Henry Toole, who became governor of the state, and three daughters, Laura (Mrs. J. W. Cotten), Maria (Mrs. Matthew Weddell), and Mary Sumner (Mrs. William George Thomas). Clark was buried in Calvary church cemetery, Tarboro. In 1844, perhaps as a posthumous honor, he was awarded an honorary M.A. degree by Princeton.

SEE: *Biog. Dir. Am. Cong.* (1971); Joseph B. Cheshire, *Nonnulla* (1930); Family letters (possession of Jaquelin Drane Nash, Tarboro); John H. Wheeler, *Historical Sketches of North Carolina* (1851).

ROY PARKER, JR.

Clark, Jerome Bayard (5 Apr. 1882–26 Aug. 1959), congressman, was born on Phoebus Plantation near Elizabethtown, Bladen County, son of John Washington and Catherine Amelia Blue Clark. He was educated in the Clarkton schools, at Davidson College, and at The University of North Carolina. He was admitted to the bar in 1906 and began practice in Elizabethtown. In 1915 he represented Bladen County in the state house of representatives, and he served as presidential elector for the Sixth Congressional District in 1916 on the Wilson-Marshall ticket. In 1920 he moved to Fayetteville, where he continued the practice of law. He was a member of the state Democratic committee from 1909 to 1919 and a member of the judicial conference from 1924 to 1928.

Clark was elected as a Democrat to the Seventy-first and to the nine succeeding Congresses (5 Mar. 1929–3 Jan. 1949), with opposition in his own party only twice and without opposition from any source in his election to the Seventy-eighth Congress. At the beginning of his second term in Congress, he was elected chairman of one of the election committees of the House, from which he was promoted to the Rules Committee. He was appointed a member of the special committee that investigated the seizure of Montgomery Ward by the government during World War II and wrote the report for the committee. He also served on the joint House and Senate committee that investigated the attack on Pearl Harbor and was a member of the subcommittee that prepared its report. Not a candidate for reelection in 1948, he resumed his law practice in Fayetteville.

Clark was a member and officer of Highland Presbyterian Church, the Masons, the Knights of Pythias, and O.D.K. On 2 June 1908 he married Helen Purdie Robinson, daughter of Dr. Heman Robinson of Elizabethtown. They had four children, Mrs. Julian B. Hutaff, Jerome B., Jr., Heman Robinson, and Mrs. George D. Jackson. Clark died in Fayetteville and was buried in Cross Creek Cemetery No. 3.

SEE: *Biog. Dir. Am. Cong.* (1961); Family Papers of the Reverend Byron Currie Clark (in the possession of the author); *North Carolina Manual* (1913); John Alexander Oates, *The Story of Fayetteville* (1950).

EDITH MONTCALM CLARK

Clark, John (*28 Feb. 1766–12 Oct. 1832*), governor of Georgia, was born in Edgecombe County. His father, General Elijah Clark, moved with his family from North Carolina to Wilkes, Ga., in 1773, but because there were no schools in Wilkes County, Clark was sent back to North Carolina for schooling in Wake County. He attended school until age fourteen, when he joined the army.

Clark served under his father in the Revolutionary War. He was made lieutenant at age fifteen and was a captain at age sixteen. Although just a boy, he did the service of the best soldier in the company's campaigns; after the Revolution he received eight hundred acres of land as his reward for "devotion to the cause of liberty." His military career did not end with the Revolutionary War. He was eager for military preferment. At age twenty-one he was a major in the state militia and fought in the Battle of Jack's Creek, named in his honor, against the Creek Indians. Years later, in the War of 1812, he was given command of the forces assigned to protect the seacoast and the southern boundary of Georgia.

For many years, Georgia politics revolved around the names of John Clark and George M. Troup. Between the two and their parties there was long and bitter strife. Partisan politics ran very high in Georgia, and political parties divided mainly on social lines. The Troup party was made up of slave owners and such well-to-do men as William H. Crawford, James Jackson, and Judge Charles Tait, and the democratic, small farmer, frontier element of the population constituted Clark's party. The Clark family had been prominent from the first in the North Carolina settlement in Georgia. General Elijah Clarke—the son dropped the final "e"—was more or less implicated in the Yazoo frauds, and James Jackson's arraignment of all Yazooites drove them into a defensive organization under John Clark. As leader of the faction, it was his agreeable duty to oppose the Virginians to the full extent of his power.

Clark had the art of surrounding himself with friends who supplied in culture what he lacked and whose devotion to him was beyond question. In 1787, when he married Nancy Williamson, the daughter of Micajah Williamson, he became allied with some of the leading families of the state. As a result, important civil offices became available to him. He ran for Congress in 1810 but lost the election to William Wyatt Bibb. In 1816 he was chosen as elector of president and vice-president.

There is no question that Clark had very bitter enemies, who were determined to prevent his ambitions from being realized and willing to use very questionable means to overthrow him as leader of the party. He was therefore very suspicious of those he considered his enemies and unrelenting in his hatred for them. A man from North Carolina, who knew of the hostility between the Georgia political parties, concocted a scandalous fraud to ruin Clark. Judge Charles Tait innocently fell into a trap set by this schemer, and Clark, putting together the circumstances, decided that Tait and William Crawford had entered into a conspiracy to defame him. To get revenge, Clark took a horsewhip and attacked Tait, who was lame, while the judge was quietly riding down a street in Milledgeville, Ga. Clark was prosecuted and fined two thousand dollars for the assault, but the fine was remitted.

Duels were a convenient way to get rid of political opponents and party leaders. Crawford challenged Clark to a duel on 6 Dec. 1804, but it was called off after the governor intervened. Bitterness between the two again reached a breaking point in 1806, and Clark challenged Crawford. They met on 16 Dec. at High Shoals, in Indian Territory. Clark harassed Crawford until he was angry and off his guard, and his disengaged wrist (which should have been behind him) was struck by Clark's shot. Instead of being appeased by his accidental success, Clark was furious that he had not killed Crawford. He renewed his challenge for a duel but, since they had no new quarrel, Crawford could decline without loss of honor. Therefore, Clark tried to obstruct Crawford's political advancement in any way possible. The more brilliant the achievements of Crawford, the more unrelenting was the hostility of Clark.

While Clark was becoming popular in state circles, Crawford was becoming prominent in national politics. The place Crawford left vacant in Georgia was filled by George M. Troup. The Clark and Troup parties contested in every election after 1807 with varying success. Their political battle did not become violent until after 1818, when the declining price of cotton sharply divided the prosperous from the less prosperous class.

Clark, a politician of the extreme Andrew Jackson type, won the governor's seat in 1819 by a majority of thirteen votes in the legislature; two years later he was reelected by a majority of only two votes. He was not a very able governor: Wilson Lumpkin, his strongest political colleague, has written that he supported Clark more from sympathy than from any appreciation of his ability. Clark did not accept partial support, however, and most of his associates yielded without question to his demands. Matthew Talbot, a Clark man, lost the 1823 election for governor to Troup by four votes. In 1825, Clark ran against Troup for the governorship. In the meantime, a constitutional amendment had transferred the election from the legislature to the people, with the Clark faction claiming credit for this democratic change. Troup won the election by a majority of 683 votes. Oddly enough, the newly elected legislature contained a majority of Clark men, indicating that Clark would have triumphed if the system had not been changed. At this point, Clark retired from politics. After his retirement, his party merged with the Democratic party under Jackson. The Troup faction became allied with the Whig party.

After accepting an appointment by President Jackson as Indian agent in 1827, Clark and his wife moved to Florida. They both died of yellow fever there and were buried in St. Andrews, Fla.

SEE: John H. Brown, ed., *The Cyclopedia of American Biography* (1900); Allen D. Candler and Clement A. Evans, *Georgia* (1906); Ellis Merton Coulter, *Georgia* (1960), and *Old Petersburg and the Broad River Valley of Georgia* (1965); Lawton B. Evans, *A History of Georgia* (1898); George R. Gilmer, *Sketches of Some of the First Settlers of Upper Georgia* (1926); Spencer B. King, *Georgia Voices* (1966); William J. Northen, *Men of Mark in Georgia*, 6 vols. (1906–9); Ulrich B. Phillips, *Georgia and State Rights* (1968); George Gilman Smith, *The Story of Georgia and the Georgia People* (1900); George White, *Historical Collections of Georgia* (1854).

JUANITA ANN SHEPPARD

Clark, John Washington

Clark, John Washington (5 Oct. 1887–18 Apr. 1969), textile manufacturer, businessman, and civic leader, was born in Raleigh to Susan Washington Graham and Walter Clark, chief justice of the state supreme court. At age fourteen Clark enrolled in North Carolina State College and was graduated in 1906 with a degree in textiles. In 1908 the Philadelphia Textile School (later Institute) awarded him a degree in cotton manufacturing. After graduation Clark returned to North Carolina and became manager for Erwin Cotton Mills.

In 1923 Clark and his brother, David, bought a cotton mill and a gristmill in Franklinville and established Randolph Mills. In 1939 Clark acquired Locke Cotton Mills of Concord and merged them with Randolph Mills. Clark served as president of the Southern Textile Association. His other business interests included a printing operation next to the Franklinville Mill, a flour and feed mill in Franklinville, a hatchery and broiler business, and a chicken processing plant. He also managed the 4,000-acre Ventosa Plantation in Scotland Neck.

Active in local and state affairs, Clark in 1924 founded and gave the first books to the Franklinville Library, the first in Randolph County. He also established a thirty-acre park for the town. He was an early advocate of flood control on the Roanoke River, which led to the building of the John H. Kerr Dam on Buggs Island. Clark served on the board of directors of the *Greensboro Daily News* and was active in the Rotary Club, the Methodist church, and the Democratic party.

He served on the Board of Trustees of the Consolidated University of North Carolina for thirty years, and in 1961 the General Assembly made him an honorary lifetime trustee. He was also on the Board of Trustees of North Carolina State College, and he presided over the college's General Alumni Association in 1945–46. At North Carolina State College, Clark was a founder and director of the Textile Foundation and a director of the Agricultural Foundation, the Engineering Foundation, and the Hofmann Forest. Called an "outspoken advocate of segregation" by the Associated Press, Clark in the 1950s fought integration of North Carolina State College.

Clark married Nannie Elizabeth Wright of Durham, and they had five children. He died of a heart attack in Asheboro and was buried in the Methodist Cemetery in Franklinville.

SEE: Aubrey Lee Brooks and Hugh T. Lefler, eds., *The Papers of Walter Clark*, 2 vols. (1948, 1950); John Washington Clark, *Letters of John Washington Clark* (1952); *Greensboro Daily News*, 19 Apr. 1969; Raleigh *News and Observer*, 13 June 1945, 16, 23 Feb. 1952, 19 Apr. 1969; *Who's Who in the South* (1927); James R. Young, *Textile Leaders in the South* (1969).

DAVID CLARK
CHARLES W. EAGLES

Clark, Thomas (August 1741–25 Dec. 1792), planter and Revolutionary War officer, was born in Wilmington, the son of Thomas Clark, merchant, and his wife, Barbara Murray, sister of Loyalist James Murray. Clark's sister, Ann, married William Hooper, a signer of the Declaration of Independence. Clark was sent to England to be educated and there learned the watchmaker's trade. He practiced this trade for a time in Boston, but in 1769 he returned to the Cape Fear to take charge of the estate of his uncle, James Murray. He participated in the Regulator campaign in 1771, listed first as "Provost Marshall General" and, several weeks later, as aide-de-camp to Governor William Tryon. He was wounded during the Battle of Alamance and received a legislative pension of ten pounds a year for the duration of his disablement.

In 1772, Clark was acting clerk of superior court for the Hillsborough District. His home, however, was at Point Repose Plantation, which had been bought by James Murray in 1739. Point Repose was purchased by Clark in 1783 after it had been confiscated by the state and sold as Loyalist property.

At the outbreak of the Revolution, the North Carolina Provincial Congress, acting on a resolution of the Continental Congress, created two Continental regiments of five hundred men each. The First Regiment was commanded by Colonel James Moore, with Francis Nash as lieutenant colonel and Thomas Clark as major. In this role, Clark participated in the Moore's Creek Bridge campaign, although neither he nor the regiment was engaged in the actual battle. On 10 Apr. 1776, when Moore was made a brigadier general, Nash was promoted to colonel and Clark to lieutenant colonel. At the siege of Charleston in 1776, Clark was in command of the 750 men of the First Regiment, 200 of whom he commanded in guarding the rear approach to the fort on Sullivan's Island.

After the repulse of the British at Charleston, the regiment was ordered north to join General Washington. Nash was promoted to brigadier general and Clark to colonel of the First Regiment on 5 Feb. 1777. At the Battle of Brandywine, Clark's regiment covered the retreat of the American army. At the Battle of Germantown the regiment was held in reserve, and Clark missed an opportunity to distinguish himself, a fact later used against him when he was considered for promotion. The North Carolina Continentals spent that winter at Valley Forge.

After General Nash was killed at Germantown, Clark and Jethro Sumner were both recommended for promotion to brigadier general by the North Carolina legislature. But Thomas Burke, delegate to the Continental Congress, worked against the elevation of Clark, and as a result, Sumner and James Hogun were made brigadiers on 9 Jan. 1779.

On 15 May 1778, Clark was given command of the North Carolina brigade without a promotion. On 29 May the Continental Congress consolidated the Fourth North Carolina Regiment into the First, with Clark designated as commanding colonel. The brigade was involved in the near-battle at Barren Hill and in the Battle of Monmouth fought on the right of the American line, although its only two casualties were a result of heat and fatigue. Clark was appointed a member of the court-martial board that tried and convicted Major General Charles Lee for misbehavior on the battlefield and disrespect to the commanding general at Monmouth.

Assigned to Baron von Steuben's division, Clark and his men were stationed at White Plains. Later the brigade was assigned to the division of Alexander MacDougall and stationed at Smith's Clove, but on 11 Dec. it was shifted to Paramus to block communications with the British in New York. It was pulled back to Smith's Clove and then recalled to Paramus. On 16 May 1779 the First and Second regiments, under Clark, were stationed near West Point to protect it and there bore the brunt of the British spring thrust. The enemy was turned back with the aid of the local militia.

In late 1779, Clark's First Regiment marched south with the North Carolina Brigade under James Hogun to aid in the defense of Charleston. On 12 May 1780, when the defenders of Charleston surrendered, Clark and 287 of his men became prisoners of war. Confined on Haddrell's Point, Clark became the acknowledged leader of the North Carolina prisoners after Hogun's death. When the North Carolina Line was reorganized, Clark, although still a prisoner of war, was given the command of the First Regiment. When finally exchanged, Clark was so ill that he was confined to his bed for some time. He was separated from the service on 1 Jan. 1783, and on 30 Sept. of that same year the legislature breveted him a brigadier general of the military district of Wilmington.

Clark was married to Sarah Moore Nash, the widow of General Francis Nash, in 1782; she died 6 Apr. 1783. There were no children. He afterward lived for a time in Hillsborough in the home of his sister, Ann Hooper. On 23 Oct. 1783, in Hillsborough, the North Carolina Society of the Cincinnati was organized with Brigadier General Jethro Sumner as president, Clark as vice-president, and Chaplain Adam Boyd as secretary.

While in Hillsborough, Clark became ill and remained so for a long time. He woke one morning suddenly blind and for much of the remainder of his life was cared for by servants. At his death, Point Repose was left to his nephew, William Hooper, Jr.

SEE: Walter Clark, ed., *State Records of North Carolina*, 20 vols. (1895–1914); Donald R. Lennon and Ida Brooks Kellam, *The Wilmington Town Book* (1973); Hugh F. Rankin, *The North Carolina Continentals* (1971); Nina Moore Tiffany, ed., *Letters of James Murray, Loyalist* (1901).

HUGH F. RANKIN
IDA BROOKS KELLAM

Clark, Thorne McKenzie *(21 Dec. 1889–11 Apr. 1971),* textile executive, banker, and community leader, was born in Raleigh to Chief Justice Walter Clark of the state supreme court and Susan Washington Graham. Clark was graduated from North Carolina State College in 1909 with a degree in engineering. After his graduation he attended business school in Poughkeepsie, N. Y., for one year. From 1911 to 1913 he worked as a civil engineer for a new railroad in Mexico and for the Piedmont and Northern Railroad in North Carolina and South Carolina.

In 1913 Clark became cashier of the Fourth National Bank in Fayetteville and later was employed as an executive with the Commercial National Bank in Raleigh. From 1917 to 1922 he worked as a national bank examiner, and in 1922 entered textile manufacturing. In Lincolnton Clark worked as manager and an executive officer of Anderson Mills, later Massapoag Mill, until retiring in 1957. He also served as president of the First National Bank of Lincolnton from 1949 to 1967 when he became chairman of the board. In 1970 when the bank became part of Carolina First National Bank, he was made chairman of the new bank's executive committee.

Clark was elected to a two-year term as mayor of Lincolnton in 1931 and represented Lincoln County in the General Assembly in 1937. He was chairman of the Lincoln County board of commissioners in 1940 and in

the 1960s helped organize Lincoln Industries, a local development corporation that attracted new industry to Lincolnton.

Clark was a Baptist, a Democrat, and a Mason. On 2 Oct. 1913 he married Mabel Gossett, the daughter of James P. Gossett, a textile manufacturer. They had four children: Thorne McKenzie, Jr., Sallie Brown, Walter, and David. Clark was buried in Hollybrook Cemetery in Lincolnton.

SEE: Aubrey Lee Brooks and Hugh T. Lefler, eds., *The Papers of Walter Clark*, 2 vols. (1948, 1950); *Charlotte Observer*, 12 Apr. 1971; *North Carolina Biography*, vol. 4 (1929); *North Carolina Manual* (1937).

DAVID CLARK
CHARLES W. EAGLES

Clark, Walter McKenzie *(19 Aug. 1846–20 May 1924),* chief justice of the supreme court, was born at Prospect Hill plantation in Halifax County. His father was David Clark II, a wealthy planter and a brigadier general in the North Carolina militia during the Civil War. His mother was Anna Maria Thorne of Halifax County. Walter Clark spent most of his byhod at Ventosa, his father's plantation on the Roanoke River. At eight years of age Clark went to Vine Hill Academy near Clarksville. In 1857 he attended Ridgeway School under the supervision of Professor William K. Bass, and in 1859 he studied with Professor Ralph H. Graves at Belmont School in Granville County. Clark entered Colonel C. C. Tew's Military Academy in Hillsborough in August 1860.

In May of 1861 Clark was selected to drill the state's first group of recruits for the Civil War. He went with the Twenty-second North Carolina Regiment when it was sent to Virginia later that year. He joined Colonel Matt W. Ransom's Thirty-fifth North Carolina Regiment in August 1862 and served as adjutant and first lieutenant. Clark witnessed the Second Battle of Manassas and participated in the capture of Harper's Ferry and the battles of Sharpsburg and Fredericksburg. When his regiment returned to North Carolina in February 1863, Clark resigned his commission and continued his education at The University of North Carolina. He studied with President David L. Swain and Professor William H. Battle and graduated first in his class in June 1864. The day after commencement Clark was elected major of the Sixth Battalion, North Carolina Junior Reserves; he fought the next year within the state and became lieutenant colonel of the Seventieth Regiment.

After the war Clark managed the family's plantation because his father was in poor health and he also supervised the Riverside plantation near New Bern, which his father had given him. In the late 1860s Clark supported industrialization for the South, advocated the importation of free white labor, and urged Southerners to get to work and forget the Lost Cause. He studied law on Wall Street in New York and at Columbian Law School in Washington, D.C., in 1866. In 1867 he received his license to practice law in Halifax County and opened his law office in Scotland Neck. The next year he was licensed to practice law before the supreme court. The University of North Carolina awarded the increasingly prosperous and prominent lawyer a M.A. in 1867. During the summer of 1871 Clark travelled widely in the American West. He lived briefly in Halifax in 1872 before moving to Raleigh in 1873. In the capital Clark practiced law, managed the Raleigh *News*, and served as a director and general counsel for the Raleigh and Gaston and the Raleigh and Augusta railroads.

When he moved to Raleigh, Clark joined the Methodist church. His father and most of the Clark family were Episcopalians, but his mother had joined the Methodist church shortly before her marriage. As an active Methodist, Clark wrote about the church's history, spoke at Trinity College in 1880 on the philosophy of religion, and attended many church meetings. In 1881 he represented the Southern Methodist Episcopal Church at the Ecumenical Conference of Methodism at London. At that time he travelled extensively in Europe. He was a delegate to the church's General Conference at St. Louis in 1890 and at Memphis in 1894.

Clark had a deep interest in North Carolina's history and laws. In 1882 he published *Everybody's Book, Some Points in Law of Interest and Use to North Carolina Farmers, Merchants, and Business Men Generally*. He compiled an annotated *Code of Civil Procedure of North Carolina*, which appeared in 1884 and became known as *Clark's Code*. He compiled and edited the *State Records of North Carolina* (16 vols., 1886–97). Clark also edited the *Histories of the Several Regiments and Battalions from North Carolina, in the Great War 1861–1865* (5 vols., 1901). He annotated over one hundred volumes of *North Carolina Reports* of the state supreme court.

In April 1885, Governor Alfred M. Scales appointed Clark a judge of the superior courts; he was elected to the post in November 1886. Three years later Governor Daniel G. Fowle named Clark an associate justice of the supreme court. The following year Clark won election to the unexpired term. In 1894 he was nominated by the Democratic party and endorsed by both the Populist and Republican parties for a full term on the supreme court. He won unanimously. In 1896 he refused the Democratic nomination for governor and chose to remain on the bench. In the same year, Clark, a supporter of free silver, received fifty votes for vice-president at the Democratic national convention.

For several years around the turn of the century, Clark was embroiled in many controversies. He attacked the American Tobacco Company for violating the Sherman antitrust law and argued that it unfairly destroyed competitors and mistreated farmers. He exposed the evils of the state's powerful railroads, the Southern, the Atlantic Coast Line, and the Seaboard. Clark charged that they issued illegal passes, set exorbitant rates, received unfair tax valuations, lobbied in the legislature, and interfered in state politics. In dissenting opinions, speeches, articles, and letters, Clark criticized the control over government exercised by banks, trusts, and railroads. In addition, he advocated many social reforms: postal savings banks, one-cent letter postage, popular election of senators, election of postmasters, an income tax, and woman suffrage. A. L. Brooks and Hugh T. Lefler called Clark "probably the most outspoken man in North Carolina or the South in advocating economic and social reforms." Clark also enthusiastically supported the Spanish-American war.

In 1897–98 Clark, a member of Trinity College's board of trustees since 1889, clashed with President John C. Kilgo of Trinity. Part of the controversy resulted from Clark's opposition to Kilgo's proposal to elect faculty members for four-year terms. A larger issue involved Kilgo's close relationship with the Dukes and the tobacco trust, which Clark strongly opposed. The two men also differed regarding state aid to higher education, because Kilgo joined the forces opposing state aid to The University of North Carolina while Clark supported The University of North Carolina. In the end Kilgo won the battle and Clark resigned from the board of trustees.

In 1902 Walter Clark sought the Democratic nomination for chief justice of the supreme court. The railroads, the American Tobacco Company, and most of the state's newspapers opposed Clark's candidacy. His strongest supporter was Josephus Daniels and the Raleigh *News and Observer*. After a bitter fight and a stirring nominating speech by Claude Kitchin, Clark won the Democratic convention's nomination. He was elected and later reelected to two additional terms. Clark served on the supreme court for thirty-five years and wrote 3,235 opinions. He made the court work efficiently, orderly, and promptly and was prominent in advocating the construction of a new building for the court.

In 1912 Clark fought three of the state's most powerful figures for the Democratic nomination for the U.S. Senate: Governor W. W. Kitchin, former governor Charles B. Aycock, and incumbent Senator Furnifold M. Simmons. Candidate Clark advocated destruction of the trusts, popular election of senators and federal judges, a tariff for revenue only, initiative, referendum, recall (except for judges), child labor laws, more public schools, extension of good roads, and the operation of telephone and telegraph by the post office department. After the death of Aycock, Simmons aimed his campaign against Clark because Kitchin posed little threat. Simmons won easily and Clark received only about ten percent of the vote.

After his defeat Clark continued to battle for "socialized democracy" in his many opinions, articles, addresses, and letters. He was a forceful supporter of woman's suffrage and served as legal adviser to the North Carolina League of Women Voters. He defended labor's right to organize and favored workmen's compensation laws and the eight hour day. He called for the abolition of the poll tax and an end to lynchings. Clark approved municipal ownership of utilities and advocated nationalization of coal mines, oil reserves, and water power sites.

Appointed by President Wilson, Clark served as an umpire for the National War Labor Board in 1917–18. Clark was president of the North Carolina State Literary and Historical Association in 1902. For many years he was chairman of the judiciary committee of the North Carolina Grand Lodge of Masons. Clark led the efforts to have the two dates, 20 May 1775 and 12 Apr. 1776, placed on the state flag and to have the state adopt as its motto, *Esse Quam Videri*.

Clark was married on 27 Jan. 1875 to Susan Washington Graham, daughter of William A. Graham, governor of North Carolina, U.S. Senator, and secretary of the navy. Their children were Susan, David, John Washington, Graham McKenzie, Walter, Thorne McKenzie, and Eugenia. Clark was buried in Raleigh. His portrait hangs in the Supreme Court Building and his papers are in the state archives.

SEE: Aubrey Lee Brooks, *Walter Clark, Fighting Judge* (1944); Aubrey Lee Brooks and Hugh T. Lefler, eds., *The Papers of Walter Clark*, 2 vols. (1948, 1950).

DAVID CLARK
CHARLES W. EAGLES

Clarke, Elijah (*1733–15 Jan. 1799*), Revolutionary War hero, Indian fighter, and land speculator, was born near Tarboro in Edgecombe County, the son of Scotch-Irish parents. He acquired no formal education. As a young man he moved to Anson County, where he built a home for himself and his family on the edge of the wilderness. Disturbed by many of the grievances that motivated the Regulators, he determined to leave North Carolina and in 1771 moved to a grant on the Pacolet River in

Spartanburg County, S.C. He found South Carolina unsatisfactory for farming, so in 1773 he pushed on to Wilkes County, Ga. Here he quickly gained prominence as a captain of the militia and a strong advocate of independence. His reknown grew even more rapidly once the Revolution began; he became a leading partisan commander in Georgia. He was wounded at Alligator Creek in 1778, was largely responsible for the patriots' victory at Kettle Creek in 1779, and was promoted to colonel by General Andrew Pickens. By 1780 he was leading troops in South Carolina, fighting there at Thicketty Fort, Cedar Springs, Camden, and Musgrove Mill, where he was seriously wounded. He also participated in the battles of Fish Dam Ford and Blackstocks, was wounded again at Long Cane, and defeated Major Dunlap—the man who had burned Pickens's home—at Beattie's Mill. In 1781 he returned to Georgia and, with Pickens and Colonel Richard Henry Lee, recaptured Augusta from the British. For his services in the war, North Carolina presented him with a gratuity of thirty thousand dollars and Georgia granted him the plantation of Thomas Waters, a Loyalist.

After the war, Clarke served in the Georgia House of Assembly, fought the Cherokees, negotiated a series of Indian treaties, and was promoted to brigadier general of the militia. At the same time he accumulated vast tracts of land through grants from Georgia and through various land speculating schemes. In 1793, frustrated by Spanish intrigues in Georgia, he joined a venture sponsored by Citizen Genet, the French minister to the United States, to drive the Spanish out of Florida. Clarke resigned his commission in the Georgia Militia to become a major general in the French army at a salary of ten thousand dollars a year. But Genet's recall was soon demanded by the Washington administration, and the plot came to nothing. The following year, Clarke became involved in another scheme to relieve Georgia of an oppressor, this time the Creeks. In the process he hoped to acquire additional lands for himself. He led a body of troops across the Oconee River into Creek territory and even went so far as to draft a constitution and erect a chain of forts in his "Trans-Oconee State" before Governor George Mathews of Georgia, at the request of the federal government, forced the abandonment of Clarke's republic. Clarke returned home without any charges being pressed against him: his popularity in Georgia defeated attempts by some citizens to have him arrested. In 1795, Clarke joined another expedition whose object was the expulsion of Spain from Florida. He organized an army of three hundred men, known as the Sans Culottes, and actually invaded Spanish territory before the scheme was again frustrated by Mathews. He continued to be involved in land speculations until his death at his Wilkes County home. He was buried at Woodburn in Lincoln County, Ga.

Married to Hannah Harrington, Clarke fathered eight children, including John Clark, *above*. There is a portrait at the Georgia Department of Archives and History.

SEE: Elijah Clarke Letters (Georgia State Archives, Atlanta); E. M. Coulter, "Elijah Clarke's Foreign Intrigues and the 'Trans-Oconee Republic,'" *Proceedings of the Mississippi Valley Historical Association* 10 (1920); *DAB*, vol. 5 (1930); L. F. Hays, *Hero of Hornet's Nest* (1946); R. K. Murdoch, *The Georgia-Florida Frontier* (1951); William J. Northen, ed., *Men of Mark in Georgia*, vol. 1 (1906).

THOMAS J. FARNHAM

Clarke, Francis Devereux (*31 Jan. 1849–7 Sept. 1913*), teacher of the deaf, was born in Raleigh. His father,

William John Clarke, was a lawyer, a major in the Mexican War and a colonel in the Civil War, and president of the San Antonio and Mexican Gulf Railroad. His mother, Mary Ann Bayard Clarke, was a writer. At the age of seven, Clarke moved with his parents to San Antonio, Tex., where he studied with Oliver D. Cooke, a former teacher at the American School for the Deaf. He also studied at the Raleigh Academy and, from 1861 to 1863, at Davidson College. During the Civil War he served in the Confederate Navy on the *Patrick Henry*, the *Tennessee*, the *Chicora*, the *Raleigh*, the *Richmond*, and *Torpedo Boat No. 3*. Engaged in the battles of Mobile Bay and City Point, he rose to the rank of lieutenant.

From 1865 to 1867 he worked with his brother in lumber and grocery businesses in Raleigh and Johnston County. In 1867 he went to New York City, intending to go to China in the merchant marine. In New York, however, he met his former teacher, Oliver D. Cooke, who persuaded Clarke to join him at the New York Institution for the Deaf. He worked at the school from 1868 to 1872 and again from 1878 to 1885. Between stints at the school he earned an M.A. degree in 1873 and a degree in civil engineering in 1875 from Columbia University and worked as a civil engineer in New York and in North Carolina.

In 1885, Clarke became superintendent of the Arkansas Institute for the Deaf in Little Rock. After seven years he left Arkansas to direct the state School for the Deaf in Flint, Mich. His *Methods Used in the Michigan School for the Deaf* was published in 1908. He served for three years as chairman of the Conference of Principals and Superintendents of Schools for the Deaf and was president for three years of the Convention of Teachers of the Deaf. He was also a member of the American Academy of Science. After moving to Michigan, Clarke joined the Masons. At the time of his death he was serving as grand master of the Michigan Grand Lodge. He also belonged to the Sons of the American Revolution.

In Middletown, Conn., Clarke married Cecelia Laura Ransom on 24 Sept. 1873. She was a native of Michigan and a niece of former Michigan Governor Epaphroditus Ransom. They had no children. Clarke died in Flint and was buried in the Glenwood Cemetery mausoleum.

SEE: *DAB*, vol. 4 (1930); *Flint* (Mich.) *Daily Journal*, 8 Sept. 1913; *Nat. Cyc. Am. Biog.*, vol. 22 (1932).

CHARLES W. EAGLES

Clarke, Mary Bayard Devereux (*13 May 1827– 30 Mar. 1886*), author and editor, was born in Raleigh, the daughter of Thomas Pollock and Catherine Anne Johnson Devereux. Her illustrious ancestors included the New England divines Jonathan Edwards and Samuel Johnson. The Pollocks (Polloks) were prominent in North Carolina history; the first came to Carolina from Scotland as a deputy of the Lords Proprietors Carteret and Beaufort, serving as their agent for fifty years. On the death of Governor Edward Hyde, Thomas Pollock, as president of the colonial council, was governor until the arrival of Charles Eden, Hyde's successor. When Eden died in 1722, Pollock again served as governor. The extensive land tracts he acquired remained in the family as plantations on the Roanoke, Chowan, and Trent rivers.

In a background of inherited wealth and emphasis on education, Mary Bayard's parents provided English governesses to superintend the education of their daughters. The only son, John, attended Yale, and the training of the daughters was described as equivalent to his course of instruction at the university. Mary Bayard inherited a family tendency toward consumption and lived for some time in the West Indies and later in Texas. Following her marriage to William J. Clarke, a native of New Bern and a Mexican War veteran, she lived on a sugar plantation in Louisiana. Just before the Civil War, the Clarkes returned to North Carolina and lived in New Bern and Raleigh.

Mrs. Clarke's first writing was recreative, succeeded by years of career writing to supplement her husband's dwindling income. Patriotic verses appearing in newspapers became household words in many southern hearts. These and other writings were published in *Mosses from a Rolling Stone, or Idle Moments of a Busy Woman*, sold for the benefit of the Stonewall Cemetery in Winchester, Va. In 1865 she edited *Southern Field and Fireside*, advertised as "entirely devoted to Polite Literature, [a] gem for the fireside, an ornament for the parlor, and an indispensable companion to the housewife and agriculturist." She wrote book reviews for the publishers Harper, Appleton, and Scribner and composed hymns (at five dollars apiece), an operatic libretto titled *Miskodeed*, and an opera intended for publication. Her translation of Victor Hugo's poems, republished in England, "attracted attention by the beauty and rhythm into which they are so truthfully rendered," and drew comment in France as "particularly happy." She contributed to the *Old Guard* (New York) and Demorest's *Monthly*, wrote novelettes published in *Peterson's Magazine*, and produced reminiscences of prominent North Carolinians for *The Land We Love*. She edited the *Literary Pastime*, a weekly journal published in Richmond. She was also recognized for collecting and preserving the writing of other North Carolina women. A most unusual contribution appeared in the records of the Supreme Court of North Carolina: in July 1868, Edmund Freeman, "venerable and beloved" clerk of the court, died at the stroke of noon on the day, hour, and minute when the term of the justices expired; Mrs. Clarke's poem commemorating the event was read by Daniel G. Fowle (later governor of the state), and on his motion the justices ordered it "spread upon and made a part of the minutes of the court."

Critics of Mrs. Clarke's work declared it romantic and imitative, although its references to North Carolina evidenced a "wholesome clarity of outlook." Her prose and poetry, according to other critics, were characterized by "simplicity, power and naturalness"; "her poetry in the parlor was what Daniel Webster's speeches were in the Senate." Editor William Seaton of the *National Intelligencer* predicted that she would make a name for herself among the nation's poets; she might not live "to see the noontide of her success but I already discern its dawn." *The Land We Love* received favorable criticism for an ability to present poetic beauty in the common things of everyday life with remarkable strength and richness of imagery. The *Southern Literary Messenger* described her as an elegant prose writer.

The Clarkes had two sons and a daughter. The eldest son, Francis Devereux, became a nationally recognized educator of the deaf.

Failing health in later years and periods of despondency led Mrs. Clarke to a temporary attachment to the Roman Catholic church and the Ethical Culture Society, but she ended life as a "faithful Protestant." She had a fatal stroke in 1886. The Raleigh *News and Observer* commented on the loss as that of "one of its most gifted daughters, whose facile pen wrought melodious verse, and whose writing attracted deserved attention and

admiration. She was a devoted daughter of the state and did more than any other woman to collect and preserve the literary work of others of her sex, who were its natives." She was buried in Cedar Grove Cemetery, New Bern.

SEE: Edwin Anderson Alderman, Joel Chandler Harris, and Charles William Kent, eds., *Library of Southern Literature*, vol. 2 (ca. 1908); *At Home and Abroad* 1, no. 4 (1881); William J. Clarke Papers (Southern Historical Collection, University of North Carolina, Chapel Hill); *DAB*, vol. 4 (1930); James W. Davidson, "Living Writers of the South," *North Carolina Poetry Review* (1934); W. Hall, *Poems* (1905); *Nat. Cyc. Am. Biog.*, vol. 8 (1898); New Bern *Our Living and Our Dead*, 12 Nov. 1883; Raleigh *News and Observer*, 1 Apr. 1886; E. G. Reade, *Southland Writers* (1870).

BETH CRABTREE

Clarke, William John (2 Aug. 1819–23 Jan. 1886), soldier, state official, and poet, was born in Raleigh, the only child of Ann Maria Robadeau and William F. Clarke. After his wife's death in 1822 the elder Clarke married Catherine B. Halander and they were the parents of a son, Charles, killed in 1861 in the Civil War, and two daughters. William John was graduated with honors from The University of North Carolina in 1841, was one of the organizing members of an alumni society in 1843, and received the M.A. degree in 1844. He also read law. On 9 Apr. 1847 he was commissioned captain, Company I which he raised in the Twelfth U.S. Infantry, and served in Mexico during the war with Mexico. At the Battle of the National Bridge he was severely wounded and was promoted to major for his gallantry in battle. His unit was disbanded 25 July 1848. At La Flurche, La., on 6 Apr. 1848, he married Mary Bayard Devereux of Raleigh who was living on a sugar plantation for the benefit of her health. The wedding was performed by her uncle, the Right Reverend Leonidas Polk, Episcopal bishop of Louisiana. They became the parents of two sons and a daughter.

Clarke began the practice of law in Raleigh and in 1849 was a candidate for a seat in Congress from the Sixth District. In a printed circular he described himself as a Democrat who favored strict construction of the Constitution and who believed that Congress could not pass laws restricting or prohibiting slavery. His opponent, John R. J. Daniel, the incumbent who was also a Democrat, was reelected. From 1850 until 1855 Clarke was state comptroller but was not a candidate for reelection in 1854. With his family, he moved to San Antonio, Tex., in 1857 because of the health of his wife. There he became president of the San Antonio and Mexican Gulf Railroad. At the beginning of the Civil War, Clarke was made a captain in the regular Confederate Army; but when he returned to North Carolina, he was commissioned colonel of the Fourteenth North Carolina Regiment (later redesignated the Twenty-fourth) and served in that rank throughout the war. At one time he commanded the brigade of which his regiment was a part, and he was highly recommended for promotion to brigadier general. His own commanding officer, M. W. Ransom, recommended him as did many others, and a petitition to this effect bearing many names was submitted to President Jefferson Davis. The appointment was never made, however, and Clarke is said to have been bitterly disappointed. On 15 May 1864, during the battle below Drewry's Bluff in Virginia, Col. Clarke's shoulder was shattered by a shell fragment and he never returned to his regiment. He was sent home to recuperate but on his way back to Virginia was ambushed, captured, and confined by the enemy in the prison at Fort Delaware, Del., from January to July 1865.

For a time after the war the Clarke family lived at Boon Hill (now Princeton) in Johnston County and he managed his interests in a lumber mill, in the Selma Iron Works, and in a mine near Greensboro. He was often in New Bern on business, occasionally for long periods of time, and after a few years moved there. In the fall of 1868 he became a trustee of New Bern Academy, and in 1869 became principal as well, serving until 1870. His wife and son were also teachers during the term 1869–70.

In his new home Clark declared himself to be a Republican and began at once to support candidates of that party for public office. In 1868 he campaigned for U.S. Grant and Schuyler Colfax as candidates for president and vice president and made speeches for Republican candidates generally.

During this period of great political unrest and Ku Klux Klan activity, Governor William W. Holden actively supported and tried to strengthen the Republican party in the state. He was also concerned about his own personal safety and wanted protection. On 7 June 1870 Clarke and others attended a meeting in the office of the governor where plans were made to organize a force of two regiments to arrest various persons in the state. Clark was tapped to command one of the regiments and he was sent to Washington to "secure an outfit for the force." On 18 June Clarke wrote Holden that President Grant had honored the request. By 19 July Clarke was in Raleigh with two companies of black troops from Wilmington and encamped in the city. Initially he had overall command of Holden's military force but later it was transferred to Colonel George W. Kirk of Jonesboro, Tenn., and the Kirk-Holden War followed.

Clarke was elected to the state senate from Craven County but resigned without having taken his seat on 22 Sept. 1870, a few days before Governor Holden appointed him judge of the superior court to fill a vacancy caused by a resignation. Clarke later said that he did not seek this appointment which apparently came because of a friendship formed thirty years previously when he and Holden had studied law together under Henry Watkins Miller of Raleigh. The Republican convention in 1874 declined to support Clarke for reelection and instead nominated a carpetbagger. Clarke campaigned as an independent urging North Carolina-born Republicans to support him and to take control of the new party from "a clique of Northern men, who assume to lead the party, and who have been guilty of acts, which, if persisted in, will be of the most ruinous tendency to the party." Clarke, nevertheless, was defeated and his opponent held the position for eight years until he resigned in 1882.

Clarke's efforts to mold a native Republican party continued and in Raleigh on 24 Dec. 1879 he began publication of a weekly newspaper, The Signal, to support that party's candidates. Mrs. Clarke contributed material of interest to women as well as some of her own poetry. The paper was remarkably unbiased and the editor frequently explained that he had no personal animosity toward Democrats. Clarke's last issue was dated 7 July 1880 and after a lapse of a little more than two weeks publication was resumed under the sponsorship of the Republican State Committee of North Carolina, Clarke's name no longer appearing in the masthead. Apparently forsaking politics, he afterward

devoted himself to the practice of law with his son in New Bern.

Clarke's literary talent was reflected in his contributions to The Signal but had made an earlier appearance in a lengthy poem written in 1840 while he was a student at The University of North Carolina. In 1846 this poem was printed in Raleigh by W. W. Holden as an eight-page pamphlet. Entitled The Harp of the South, A Poem. By A Soph of the University of North Carolina, it lamented the "paucity of poetic productions in the South" and was a plea for a Southern literary renaissance. Four of his poems were included in the two-volume anthology, Wood-Notes; or, Carolina Carols, edited by Mrs. Clarke and published in Raleigh in 1853.

Clarke, an Episcopalian, died in New Bern and was buried there in Cedar Grove Cemetery.

SEE: Samuel A. Ashe, History of North Carolina, vol. 2 (1925); Kemp P. Battle, History of The University of North Carolina, vol. 1 (1907); John L. Cheney, ed., North Carolina Government (1975); Walter Clark, Histories of the Several Regiments . . . (1901); [William J. Clarke], The Harp of the South (1846); William John Clarke Papers (Southern Historical Collection, University of North Carolina, Chapel Hill); [Mary Bayard Clarke], Wood-Notes, 2 vols. (1853); Daniel L. Grant, Alumni History of the University of North Carolina (1924); J. G. de R. Hamilton, Reconstruction in North Carolina (1914); New Bern, Daily Journal, 26 Jan. 1886; Raleigh, The Signal, 1879–80; Allen W. Trelease, White Terror, The Ku Klux Klan Conspiracy and Southern Reconstruction (1971); John H. Wheeler, Historical Sketches of North Carolina (1851).

WILLIAM S. POWELL

Clarkson, [Robert] Heriot (21 Aug. 1863–27 Jan.1942), civic leader and associate justice of the North Carolina Supreme Court, was born in Kingville, Richland County, S.C. His father, William Clarkson, was an officer in the Confederate Army and, after the war, a conductor for many years with the Southern Railway. His mother, Margaret Susan Simons Clarkson of Charleston, S.C., was of Huguenot descent. William and Margaret Clarkson had eleven children, nine of whom survived childhood.

William Clarkson and his family lived in Eastover, S.C., for several years during the Civil War and Reconstruction and moved from there to Charlotte in 1873. Young Heriot attended the Carolina Military Institute in Charlotte from 1873 until 1880, at which time he became a clerk with the legal firm of Jones and Johnston. He studied law at The University of North Carolina for nine months in 1884 and in October of that year was licensed by the state supreme court. He subsequently returned to Charlotte, where between 1888 and 1913 he practiced law in partnership with Charles H. Duls. In 1904, Governor Charles B. Aycock appointed Clarkson solicitor for the twelfth district, a position he retained until 1910. When Duls was selected for a superior court judgeship in 1913, Clarkson formed a partnership with Carol D. Taliaferro. In 1918, Clarkson's son, Francis Osborne, joined the firm.

Active throughout his adult life in political and civic affairs, Clarkson, a Democrat, first held public office in 1887–89 as alderman and vice-mayor of Charlotte, positions he again held in 1891–93. In 1896 he helped to organize a local white supremacy club, one of the many such organizations to appear in the state in the late 1890s. Defeated in 1896 by the Fusion candidate for a seat in the state house of representatives, he ran again in 1898 and was elected. As a member of the house he favored the proposed constitutional amendment disfranchising the blacks of the state; in 1900 he was active on the local level in behalf of the Democratic party's white supremacy campaign.

A dedicated and lifelong prohibitionist, Clarkson was one of the leaders of the movement to ban the manufacture and sale of intoxicating beverages in North Carolina. He was chairman of the local anti-saloon organization when Charlotte, following a referendum campaign, voted in 1904 to prohibit the sale of liquor. As president of the North Carolina Anti-Saloon League, Clarkson played a vital role in the enactment and subsequent approval in a state-wide referendum of the 1908 act banning the manufacture and sale of liquor. North Carolina, wrote the historian of the prohibition movement in the state, thus became "the first state to adopt prohibition by direct vote of the people." In 1923, Clarkson wrote the Turlington Act revising the state statutes to make them conform to the national prohibition law. Although a spokesman of the dry forces in the state, Clarkson, by this time an associate justice of the state supreme court, supported in 1928 the presidential candidacy of Alfred E. Smith, a critic of prohibition. In 1933 he was among those instrumental in organizing the dry forces in North Carolina to fight repeal of the Eighteenth Amendment.

Although a less significant figure in the good roads movement than in the prohibition crusade, Clarkson nonetheless made important contributions to highway development in the state. He was legal adviser to the Wilmington-Charlotte-Asheville Highway Association, established in 1918, and was active in the Citizens Highway Association, a more or less ad hoc group organized in 1920 to press for immediate enactment of a comprehensive state road law. As chairman of a legislative committee representing the various good roads organizations in North Carolina, he was largely responsible for drafting a proposed bill that, as modified by the General Assembly, became the Highway Act of 1921. This historic measure provided for a $50 million highway expansion program, to be financed through the sale of state bonds.

Having served in 1920 as manager of Cameron Morrison's successful campaign for the governorship, Clarkson in 1923 was rewarded by the governor, a close personal friend, with an interim appointment as associate justice of the supreme court. In 1924 he was elected to serve out the remaining two years of his predecessor's original term. He was reelected in 1926 and 1934 for full terms and by the time of his death was the senior associate justice of the court. As a supreme court justice, he rendered decisions upholding the state liquor laws, the "separate but equal" doctrine, and the right of laboring men to join unions. Forty-seven of his opinions appeared in *American Law Reports*.

An extraordinarily civic-minded person, Clarkson devoted much of his time during his long and useful life to worthy causes. He helped to found both the Crittenton Home in Charlotte and the Mecklenburg County Industrial Home. Over a period of years he sought unsuccessfully to persuade the General Assembly to establish a state-supported reformatory for black boys. Throughout his adulthood, he was active in the Episcopal church and the YMCA, serving from 1935 until his death as president of the Interstate YMCA of the Carolinas. For nearly twenty years (1923–42) he was a member of the North Carolina Historical Commission.

Clarkson was married on 10 Dec. 1889 to Mary Lloyd Osborne, the daughter of the Reverend Edwin A.

Osborne. The couple had nine children, five of whom survived childhood: Heriot, Jr., Francis Osborne, Edwin Osborne, Thomas Simons, and Margaret Fullarton (Mrs. John Garland Pollard, Jr.). Clarkson died in Charlotte and was buried in Elmwood Cemetery.

SEE: Johnnie Virginia Anderson, "Heriot Clarkson: A Social Engineer of North Carolina" (M.A. thesis, Wake Forest University, 1972); Samuel A. Ashe, ed., *Biographical History of North Carolina*, vol. 7 (1908); *Charlotte Observer*, 28 Jan. 1942; Clarkson papers (North Carolina State Archives, Raleigh; Southern Historical Collection, University of North Carolina, Chapel Hill); 185–220 N.C. *Reports; North Carolina: The Old North State and the New*, vol. 4 (1941); Carol D. Taliaferro, "Heriot Clarkson," *North Carolina State Bar Proceedings*, 1942; Daniel Jay Whitener, *Prohibition in North Carolina* (1945).

NATHANIEL F. MAGRUDER

Clary, John (d. Nov. 1825), enters history because of his political success following his conviction for fornication with his stepdaughter. Little is definitely known of his background, though existing records suggest that he was born between 1755 and 1765, the son of Barns and Mary Jordan Clary of Surry County, Va., and that he moved to Perquimans County in 1776. A Quaker at least for a time, Clary was married successively to Miriam Jordan, Peninah Anderson Copeland Newby Toms, and Jane Pointer Copeland. Of his known children, there were William and John by his second marriage and Susanna by the third. His family connections extended through the upper levels of Perquimans society and included holders of various offices.

In 1798, Clary built a toll float bridge across the Perquimans River at Hertford. He was its proprietor until his death, and its importance undoubtedly influenced local opinion of him. His holdings included several tracts of land in the county, about a dozen lots in the town of Hertford, a wharf, and a seine-fishing operation.

Clary's second marriage brought under his roof young Leah Toms, daughter of the thrice-widowed Peninah. In 1808, Clary was charged with adultery with his stepdaughter, and the following year he was convicted of fornication and fined. In August 1809, nonetheless, Clary's neighbors in Perquimans County elected him to the House of Commons. His reception in the legislature was cool, and following the introduction of a resolution proposing that the house "free itself from the contamination of grossly impure and unworthy characters," Clary resigned and went home to vindicate himself. On 15 Dec. 1809, his county, whose voters had proved themselves independent in the past, reelected him by an even larger margin than previously. Five days later, Clary returned triumphantly to the state house. The majority of the legislators were still in no mood to admit him to their company, and on 20 Dec., by a vote of sixty-eight to twenty-eight, the house voted to expel him as "guilty of a crime so enormous as renders it unfit that he should be permitted to continue a member."

Clary was involved in another suit related to his seduction of Leah. Six men, including a stepson, forcibly removed him from his home one night and covered him with tar and feathers. Thereupon, Clary brought charges against all six; the judge, while condemning Clary's attack upon his stepdaughter, ruled that "his crime, great as it is, cannot rightfully be punished by any man, except in the manner prescribed by law." All six men were convicted and fined, but Governor David Stone later remitted the fines.

The Perquimans County Court, of which Clary was a justice, continued to appoint him to positions of trust, including membership in 1822 on the committee overseeing construction of the county's courthouse.

Clary's contribution to history probably lies in the light that his conviction and subsequent prestige among his neighbors sheds upon the moral tone of his county, a tone perhaps not unlike that of the state in general in 1809.

SEE: North Carolina Collection (University of North Carolina, Chapel Hill), for a pamphlet on Clary; *North Carolina House Journal*, 1809; Perquimans County Records (North Carolina State Archives, Raleigh); *The Trial and Conviction of John Clary of Perquimans* (1810).

H. G. JONES
RAYMOND A. WINSLOW, JR.

Claxton, Philander Priestley (28 Sept. 1862– 12 Jan. 1957), educator, was born in Bedford County, near Shelbyville, Tenn., the son of Joshua Calvin and Anne Elizabeth Jones Claxton. He traced his lineage to nineteenth-century settlers who immigrated from England, first to North Carolina and subsequently to Tennessee.

Claxton's early education was given in the public schools of Bedford County. He was graduated from the Turrentine Academy near his home in 1878 and that fall entered the University of Tennessee, Knoxville, from which he was graduated in 1882 with a B.A. degree. Five years later he earned his M.A. degree from the same university. He was a member of Phi Beta Kappa and Phi Delta Kappa.

A number of institutions later conferred upon him honorary degrees: Bates College, Lewiston, Me. (1906), Litt.D.; Western Reserve University (1912), The University of North Carolina (1914), Allegheny College, Meadville, Pa. (1915), and University of Maryland, College Park (1921), LL.D.

Few men of the last hundred years in America have been as completely dedicated to educational expansion and progress as was Claxton. Upon graduation from the University of Tennessee, he went to North Carolina to teach in the public schools of Goldsboro (1882–83); in the following year he was superintendent of schools in Kinston. Then he went to Johns Hopkins University, Baltimore, Md. (1884–85), for special graduate study in educational methods and practices. He spent the following year traveling through Germany, analyzing the school systems and absorbing the cultural philosophy of the country's educational leadership. He visited England, Switzerland, Sweden, Denmark, and again Germany in 1896 and returned to Denmark for further observation in 1930.

Following his first visit abroad, Claxton served as superintendent of schools in Wilson (1886–87) and then went to a similar position in Asheville for six years (1887–93). After these eleven years of public school work in North Carolina, he became in 1893 instructor of pedagogy and German at North Carolina State Normal and Industrial School (now The University of North Carolina at Greensboro), an institution established two years previously. He was promoted in 1896 to professor of pedagogy and director of the Practice and Observation School and continued in that work until 1902.

In 1902, Claxton left North Carolina—and left it, because of his work toward better schools and more intelligent emphasis on teacher training a much more education-conscious state—to become professor of education at the University of Tennessee, Knoxville.

Four years later he was named professor of secondary education and inspector of high schools there.

This expansive experience in modern educational programs made Claxton a logical choice for the post of U.S. Commissioner of Education, which he filled with great credit to himself and great value to the nation for ten years (1911–21). When he resigned as commissioner, he became provost of the University of Alabama at University (1921–23) and then returned to his first concern as superintendent of schools, Tulsa, Okla. (1923–29). His final professional position was the presidency of Austin Peay Normal School, Tenn. (1930–46), which he undertook at the age of sixty-eight, when most men retire. He was elected president emeritus of Austin Peay upon his retirement and retained that title until his death eleven years later.

Throughout his career, Claxton received some chiding for changing jobs so frequently; his studied reply was first an admission of a constantly "shifting base," with the explanation that his whole field was so new that many areas and institutions sought his innovative educational leadership.

He was editor of the *North Carolina Journal of Education* (1897–1901) and the *Atlantic Educational Journal* (1901–3). His professional affiliations were many and varied: he was a long-time member of the Southern Educational Board and for one year chief of the board's Bureau of Investigation and Information (1903); superintendent of the summer school at the University of the South, Sewanee, Tenn. (1902, 1911); director of the Playground Association of America and the Moral Education Board; chairman of the executive committee of the National Storytellers' League; vice-president of the American School Peace League and the School Citizenship League; member of the executive council of the National Education Association; member of the board of awards of American University, Washington, D.C. (1915–21); director and member of the executive committee of the Boy Scouts of America; chairman of the Committee on State Educational Bill, Tenn. (1907–9); delegate to the World Federation Education Associations; and member of the American Association of Administrative Superintendents; the National Student Forum on Paris Pact (1929–38); the Federal Board on Vocational Education (1911–21); the National Committee on Highway Engineering and Highway Transportation (1920–21); the National Society for the Scientific Study of Education; the American Association for the Advancement of Science; the Rockefeller Sanitary Commission; the Committee on Codification of State (Tennessee) School Laws (1909–11); the Committee on Revision of State (Oklahoma) School Laws (1927–29); and the American Geographical Society.

Claxton was the author of *From the Land of Stories*; joint author, with M. W. G. Haliburton, of an edition of *Grimm's Fairy Tales*; and joint author, with James McGinnis, of *Effective English* (1917) and *Effective English, Junior* (1921). In addition, he wrote a large number of pamphlets, periodical articles, and speeches on a wide range of educational topics.

Claxton was married first (December 1885) to Varina S. Moore of Goldsboro (d. 1891); they had one daughter, Claire. His second marriage (September 1894) was to Anne Elizabeth Porter of Tarboro (d. 1905); they had four children, Henel Elizabeth, Calvin Porter, Anne Elizabeth, and Robert Edward. On 23 Apr. 1912, Claxton married Mary Hannah Johnson of Nashville, Tenn.; their two children were Philander Priestley, Jr., and Mary Payne.

After retirement, Claxton continued to make his home in Clarksville; he died there at the age of ninety-five.

Memorial services were held in Clarksville, and interment followed in Knoxville, Tenn.

Claxton was a pioneer in modern education. He was interested in educational administration only as it gave opportunity for improved teaching methods. Although he believed in methods, he stressed the content of instruction. He is credited with inaugurating and promoting the now familiar six-three-three plan: six years in elementary grades, three years in junior high school, and three years in senior high school, as preparation for college admission. He consistently stressed the responsibility of the federal government in education.

SEE: J. McKeen Cattell, ed., *Leaders in Education* (1932); *Nat. Cyc. Am. Biog.*, vol. 15 (1914); *Who Was Who in America*, vol. 3 (1960).

C. SYLVESTER GREEN

Cleveland, Benjamin *(26 May 1738–Oct. 1806)*, frontiersman, was born in Virginia on the now-famous Bull Run. He was the son of John Cleveland and the grandson of Alexander Cleveland, who came from England and settled in Virginia.

Benjamin Cleveland grew to be a very big man, often good-natured, but reckless, hot-tempered, and determined. He loved hunting and spent much of his time from early youth roaming the wilderness securing furs and skins. As a young man, he acquired the frontier lifestyle, which included gambling, horse-racing, carousing, drinking, and fighting. An early marriage to Mary Graves of Orange County helped to reform his wild life, and he made a reluctant attempt at farming.

At age thirty-one, Cleveland emigrated with his extended family to the North Carolina back country, settling near Mulberry Fields, Wilkes County. From his neighbor, Daniel Boone, Cleveland learned of the Kentucky country. In the summer of 1772, accompanied by four "long hunters," he set out to hunt and to explore the Kentucky wilderness. The party was seized and robbed by a band of Cherokees. The Indians took everything, leaving the tattered band to find its way back through miles of wilderness. Cleveland was a fighter and a man of action. Delaying only long enough to regain his strength and to select a party of riflemen, he boldly returned to the Cherokee country, retrieved his horses, and returned in triumph to the Upper Yadkin, his reputation as an Indian fighter solidly established.

When the American Revolution came, Cleveland lived in Surry County, within the Salisbury Military District, one of the six military districts of North Carolina. In September 1775 the provincial congress appointed him ensign in the Second Regiment of the North Carolina Continental forces. He did not accept the appointment, however, preferring to serve in the Surry militia, where he judged his "presence and efforts would be more useful." In the summer of 1776, when the Cherokee uprising began, Cleveland served a tour of duty as ranger on the headwaters of the Yadkin; in August he joined as captain a contingent of Surry militia in the expedition against the Cherokees. During the course of the campaign, the North Carolina and South Carolina forces completely destroyed thirty-six Cherokee towns. Prior to the negotiations at Long Island, Cleveland was stationed at Carter's Fort, from which his company of light horse patrolled the frontier. During the treaty negotiations, his company was ordered to Long Island to protect the negotiating commission.

The exact date on which Cleveland was appointed to the Surry County court is not known, but he sat as a justice for the November term in 1774; in December of the same year, he was appointed by the justices to serve as a juror at the superior court in Salisbury; and at the February term in 1775 he was chairman of the court. On 17 May 1775 news of the Battle of Lexington reached the Surry court. The transition from county court to safety committee was swift and decisive, and Cleveland was elected chairman. The safety committee virtually took over the local military establishment by the process of selecting representatives from each militia company to serve on the committee.

On the Upper Yadkin, the American Revolution was not primarily a conflict of colonists against Redcoats, but one of Americans against their neighbors. Cleveland's suppression of Tories was legitimized in two ways: by punitive legislation and by his authority as chairman of the safety committee, county court justice, and officer of militia. When the new county of Wilkes was formed from Surry in 1778, Cleveland was placed at the head of the commission of justices and was named colonel of the militia.

In 1776 the royal governor of North Carolina initiated a plan to conquer the state, and back country Tories were formed into militia companies. Cleveland took his company of riflemen to join the Surry militia, which summarily dispersed the Tory rising in Surry County. They then proceeded south to march against the Tories on the Cape Fear. "Tory risings" and "Patriot retaliations" were the most significant feature of the civil war on the Upper Yadkin. When Tory prisoners were taken, Cleveland administered punishment with his own sense of rigid justice. Reconstructed Tories were allowed to take an oath of loyalty to the state and were set free; unregenerate Tories were hanged. Cleveland's vigorous methods did not always find support. In the fall of 1779 two Tories were hanged by Cleveland scouts, and for this act he was indicted for murder in the superior court of Salisbury; he was ultimately pardoned by the governor. Cleveland himself was once captured by the frontier Tories, but the quick action of his brother, Robert, brought about his rescue.

In 1780, Lord Cornwallis began an invasion of North Carolina, basing his strategy on the assumption of large-scale Tory aid. Major Patrick Ferguson was instructed to serve as the British left wing on its northward thrust. His task was to arouse and enlist Loyalists in the upland on the western flank nearest the frontier. The over-mountain men accepted the challenge, assembled volunteers, and sent an express to Cleveland requesting him to join them.

On 6 Oct. Ferguson had reached a point near Kings Mountain, an outlying spur of the Blue Ridge near the North Carolina–South Carolina border. The Whigs reached the mountain about noon on 7 Oct., surrounded it, and began action on all sides. Three times Ferguson's men drove them back with bayonet charges, but the mountain men united and pushed him to one end of the ridge. Cleveland's column pressed forward, and as Ferguson attempted to cut through his lines, he was knocked from his horse by rifle fire. When Ferguson fell, the resistance of the Tories crumbled and they surrendered. This battle at Kings Mountain was the climax of the frontier civil war and the turning point of the war in the South.

When the Revolution finally closed, Cleveland was forced to surrender his land. He then migrated into the back country of South Carolina. In 1784 he became one of the early squatters in the Tugaloo River Valley. In South Carolina, Cleveland joined on the bench the old partisan leader General Andrew Pickens, serving as an associate judge of the court of Pendleton County for many years.

Before his death, he became so unwieldy in size that he could not mount his horse, gradually attaining the enormous weight of 450 pounds. He died quietly while sitting at his breakfast table, survived by two sons and a daughter. A nephew, Jesse Franklin, became governor of North Carolina.

SEE: Anthony Allaire, "Diary," in Lyman G. Draper, *Kings Mountain and Its Heroes* (1881); Lyman Draper Collection (State Historical Society of Wisconsin, Madison); Adelaide L. Fries, ed., *Records of the Moravians in North Carolina*, 8 vols. (1922–54); Robert L. Ganyard, "North Carolina during the American Revolution: The First Phase" (Ph.D. diss., Duke University, 1962); Land Entry Book 1778–81 (Wilkes County Courthouse; Wilkesboro); Lenoir Family Papers (Southern Historical Collection, University of North Carolina, Chapel Hill); Minute Book, Surry County Court of Pleas and Quarter Sessions, 1774–78 (Dobson); North Carolina State Archives (Raleigh), for Legislative Papers (1774–81), Surry County Records (1771–85), and Wilkes County Records (1778–85); William L. Saunders and Walter Clark, eds., *Colonial and State Records of North Carolina*, 30 vols. (1890–1914).

BETTY LINNEY WAUGH

Clewell, John Henry (19 Sept. 1855–21 Feb. 1922), Moravian minister and college president, was born in the Moravian community of Salem, the son of John David Clewell, a bookbinder and shoemaker, and Dorothea Matilda Shultz. He was educated at the Theological Seminary in Bethlehem, Pa., returning to Salem in July 1877 to assume the position of assistant teacher at the Boys' School. That year he organized a large and successful Bible class for young men. The next year he left Salem to further his studies at Union Theological Seminary in New York City. By 1882 he was pastor at Uhrichsville, Ohio, where he was praised for his energetic work in establishing a church in nearby Port Washington.

On 1 June 1884, Clewell was recalled to Salem as assistant principal of the Salem Female Academy, under Edward Rondthaler. Four years later, in May 1888, Clewell became principal. Under his direction the school prospered, and by 1892 there were over three hundred girls in attendance. During his principalship, electricity and modern plumbing were installed, and the new industrial department (forerunner of home economics) and department of natural science were introduced, in 1889 and 1902, respectively. In 1907 the Salem Female Academy became Salem Academy and College.

In addition to his duties as principal, Clewell was also very active in church and community affairs. In 1889 he served as pastor for Salem in the temporary absence of the pastor. He traveled extensively in this country and Europe. In 1898 he was elected by the district as an alternate to the General Synod of the *Unitas Fratrum*; he was thus in Europe from May until the end of June 1899. Clewell was given the degree of Ph.D. by the Moravian College in Bethlehem in 1900. In 1901 he served as curator for the Wachovia Historical and Archival Memorabilia, putting the material into easily accessible order and taking action toward the preservation of these historical records.

Clewell wrote articles for a number of publications and in 1902 published *The History of Wachovia in North Carolina*. From 1904 to 1908 he was editor of the monthly *Wachovia Moravian*, a paper in operation from 1893 to 1930. In 1906 he was appointed temporary president of the board of elders in the pastor's absence.

After twenty-two years as president of the Salem Academy and College, Clewell resigned on 7 May 1909 to take a similar position in Bethlehem, Pa., at the Moravian Seminary for Young Ladies. Under his leadership that school was greatly enlarged and improved. A new gymnasium was built in 1912, and college level courses were added to the curriculum. A charter amendment in 1913 changed the name to Moravian Seminary and College for Women at Bethlehem.

Clewell was married to Alice Wolle, and they had four sons. He died in Bethlehem.

SEE: John Henry Clewell, *The History of Wachovia in North Carolina* (1902); J. Taylor Hamilton and Kenneth G. Hamilton, *History of the Moravian Church: The Renewed Unitas Fratrum, 1722–1957* (1967); *Wachovia Moravian* 31 (Feb. 1922); E. Rondthaler, *The Memorabilia of Fifty Years, 1877 to 1927* (1928).

JAN HIESTER

Clinch, Duncan Lamont (6 Apr. 1787–27 Nov. 1849), officer in the U.S. Army for more than twenty-eight years, congressman from Georgia, and leader of the Whig party, was born at Ard-Lamont, the Edgecombe County home of his parents, Colonel Joseph John Clinch and Mary Lamont Clinch. He was appointed first lieutenant in the newly organized Third Infantry, U.S.A., in 1808 and served with his company in New Orleans in 1809–10 and in Baton Rouge in 1811–13. In 1814 he was transferred to the Tenth Infantry and commanded six companies of his regiment at Champlain on the northern frontier. He also served at Camp Lake Erie near Buffalo, N.Y. In 1815 he was transferred to the Fourth Infantry and served in North Carolina and Georgia; he commanded the eastern section of the Seventh Military Department, Division of the South, at Fernandina, Fla., and later at St. Mary's, Ga. He served on court-martial duty at Baton Rouge and at Jefferson Barracks in Missouri and commanded the regiment and post at Baton Rouge and Mobile Point, Ala. He was active in both the First and Second (or "Seven Years' ") Seminole wars in Florida; at the Battle of Ouithlacoochee, Fla., on 31 Dec. 1835, with only 200 regulars and 460 volunteers, he routed the enemy after an action lasting an hour, losing 4 killed and 59 wounded. In 1829 he was given the rank of brigadier general.

In 1836, after some twenty years in charge of military affairs in Florida, Clinch resigned from the army and settled into the life of a planter near St. Mary's, Ga. In 1843 he was elected to complete the vacancy in the House of Representatives left by the death of John Millen of Savannah. His major concern as a congressman was Georgia's claim for federal compensation for the state's expenditures for volunteers sent to fight the Seminoles. Clinch became a leader of the Whig party in Georgia and lost the governorship of that state in 1847 by less than thirteen hundred votes.

Clinch was married three times: first to Eliza Baynard Mackintosh, by whom he had eight children; then, following Eliza Clinch's death in 1835, to her cousin, Elizabeth Houston; and then to Sophia Hermes Gibbs Couper. One grandson, Duncan Clinch Heyward, later served as the governor of South Carolina. Clinch's daughter Eliza Baynard married General Robert Anderson of the U.S. Army, who is remembered for his role in Charleston in 1861 during the bombardment of Fort Sumter.

Clinch served as the president of the St. Mary's Bank, was the head of a transportation company, and, at his death, left an estate worth more than $2 million, including more than two hundred slaves. Clinch County, Ga., was named for him in 1851, and the former Fort Clinch on Amelia Island, Fla., is today a state park bearing his name.

Clinch died in Macon, Ga., and was buried in the Bonaventure Cemetery in Savannah.

SEE: *Nat. Cyc. Am. Biog.*, vol. 12 (1904); Rembert W. Patrick, *Aristocrat in Uniform–General Duncan L. Clinch* (1963).

RALPH HARDEE RIVES

Clinch, Joseph John, Jr. *(1754–95)*, Revolutionary War officer and political leader in Edgecombe and Nash counties, was the son of Elizabeth Goodrich and Joseph John Clinch of Surry County, Va. He went to Edgecombe County as a young child with his parents, settling near Tarboro and present-day Rocky Mount. He eventually owned some eleven hundred acres of land and sixteen slaves.

On 1 Sept. 1775, Clinch was appointed an ensign in the Second North Carolina Regiment; on 16 Apr. of the following year he was appointed by the North Carolina congress first lieutenant from the Halifax District. In April 1777 he became first lieutenant in the Third Regiment of North Carolina Continentals, and he was later promoted to lieutenant colonel. According to family records, he served for a brief period as an aide to General George Washington. Known as "The Terror of the Tories," Clinch raised and equipped a regiment for local service against the Tory faction of his area. His home, Ard-Lamont, was plundered by the Tories, and his favorite horse, Red Buck, was stolen, although later returned by a patriot.

Following the Revolution, Clinch continued to serve in the militia, was a justice of the peace, and was a representative from Nash County at the meeting of the North Carolina House of Commons in November 1786. In 1777 he was one of five commissioners appointed to run the dividing line between Edgecombe and Nash counties.

Though Anglican before the Revolution, Clinch and his wife, Mary Lamont Clinch, became active members of the Methodist Episcopal church in the years following the war. Clinch was the father of five children, including Duncan Lamont, who became a prominent soldier and Whig leader in the nineteenth century.

SEE: Rembert W. Patrick, *Aristocrat in Uniform—General Duncan L. Clinch* (1963); William L. Saunders and Walter Clark, eds., *Colonial and State Records of North Carolina*, vols. 10–13, 20, 24 (1890–1905).

RALPH HARDEE RIVES

Clingman, Thomas Lanier *(27 July 1812–3 Nov. 1897)*, antebellum political leader, Civil War general, and propagandist for Western North Carolina development, was born at Huntsville in Surry (now Yadkin) County. His grandfather, Alexander Clingman, had immigrated to Pennsylvania from Germany in the mid-eighteenth century and had come shortly thereafter to the western part of North Carolina. Thomas's father, Jacob Clingman, established himself as a merchant at Huntsville and married Jane Poindexter, whose ancestry included French and Scottish blood and a great-grandfather who was a Cherokee chieftain. Jacob Clingman died when his son was four years old, leaving Thomas to be reared and educated by his mother and an uncle, Francis Alexander Poindexter. In 1829, Thomas

Clingman entered The University of North Carolina as a sophomore, graduating in 1832 at the head of his class. Despite an illness that threatened his sight, he read law at Hillsborough under William Alexander Graham, at that time one of the leading lawyers in the state.

The year 1835 marked Clingman's entry into politics. Shortly after being admitted to the bar, he was elected from Surry County to the lower house of the North Carolina legislature. There he quickly allied himself with the newly formed Whig party, which was pushing for a revision of the North Carolina Constitution in the interest of more equitable representation for the western part of the state. His bid for reelection in 1836 was unsuccessful. Lured by the prospects of future development of the North Carolina mountain region, he soon moved to the vicinity of Asheville in Buncombe County, the area with which he identified himself for the remainder of his life.

In 1840, after practicing law for four years, Clingman was elected to the state senate, where he served only one term. In 1843 he sought and gained election to the U.S. House of Representatives; with the exception of the 1845–47 term, he remained in Congress as representative or senator until the beginning of the Civil War. He served in the House until 1858, when he was appointed senator to fill the unexpired term of Asa Biggs. In 1860 he was elected to the Senate for a term in his own right, and he was the last southern senator to leave the Congress in 1861.

Clingman entered the Congress in 1843 as a rabid Whig partisan. His adherence to national Whig policies in opposing the annexation of Texas and the Gag Rule, directed against abolitionist petitions, was, in fact, to cost him his seat in 1845. During his first term in Congress his denunciations of Democrats and Democratic policies were so vehement that they led to a duel with Democrat William L. Yancey of Alabama. The conflict was resolved with apologies after both combatants had fired and missed.

Increased agitation over the slavery issue and the question of southern rights, precipitated by the Mexican War, led Clingman to break with the Northern-dominated Whig party after his reelection to Congress in 1847. Though nominally a Whig until 1852, he drifted gradually toward the Democratic party and its representation of southern interests. Preferring to chart his own course, however, he never became an adherent of John C. Calhoun's effort to form a sectional party in Congress. Clingman opposed the Compromise of 1850, voting only for the Fugitive Slave Law. In 1852, along with thirteen fellow southern Whigs, he withdrew from the Whig Caucus when it refused to support the addition to the Whig Platform of a southern endorsement accepting as final the compromise measures and the Fugitive Slave Law. By 1854, when he backed the passage of the Kansas-Nebraska Act, Clingman had moved definitely into the Democratic fold. He continued to represent what he regarded as the interests and constitutional rights of the South until his withdrawal from the Senate at the onset of the Civil War.

In the Confederacy, Clingman served briefly as a commissioner to the provisional government at Montgomery. Though he had no military experience, he was commissioned in September 1861 as colonel and head of the Twenty-fifth North Carolina Regiment; in August 1862 he was made a brigadier general. He served without special distinction in Eastern North Carolina and Virginia, taking part in the Battle of Cold Harbor in Virginia near the end of the war.

After the war, Clingman was prohibited from

returning to politics by the amnesty provisions. Consequently, he turned to a career as a propagandist for Western North Carolina development. He lectured and wrote extensively about the mountain region and continued scientific studies of the area begun before the war. In the 1850s he had engaged in a running dispute with Dr. Elisha Mitchell of The University of North Carolina about the location of the highest peak in the Black Mountain range. Ultimately, Mitchell's name was given to the highest mountain in the range and Clingman's was given to another peak on the same ridge. The highest peak in the Great Smoky Mountains was also named for him (Clingman's Dome). After the war his studies focused on the geology of Western North Carolina and on experiments dealing with meteors and the height of the atmosphere. His only roles in postwar politics were services as delegate to the constitutional convention of 1875 and to the Democratic National Convention in St. Louis in 1876. He continued to lecture widely until his health failed him in his last years.

Clingman, who never married, died at Morganton; he was buried in the Riverside Cemetery in Asheville.

SEE: John Spencer Bassett, *The Congressional Career of T. L. Clingman*, Trinity College Historical Society Papers, ser. 4 (1900); Thomas Lanier Clingman Papers (Manuscript Department, Library, Duke University, Durham); Clingman-Puryear Papers (Southern Historical Collection, University of North Carolina, Chapel Hill); Clarence Newell Gilbert, "The Public Career of Thomas L. Clingman" (M.A. thesis, University of North Carolina, 1947); Marlene Deanna Siegmann, "Thomas Lanier Clingman, Political Pilgrim" (M.A. thesis, Wake Forest University, 1964); *Selections from the Speeches and Writings of Thomas L. Clingman* (1877).

H. THOMAS KEARNEY, JR.

Clinton, Richard *(1721–96)*, county and early state official, is believed to have been a natural son of John Sampson and a nephew of Colonel Charles Clinton, the father of Governor George Clinton and of General James Clinton of New York. The Clintons came from Ireland with Colonel John Sampson in about 1736 and were among the first to settle in the wilderness on the headwaters of the Northeast branch of the Cape Fear.

In 1775, Clinton represented Duplin County in the provincial congress held at Hillsborough. In February 1776 he organized a company of militia minutemen from upper Duplin and as captain of the company took part in the defense of Wilmington against the British. He was appointed colonel of cavalry in 1787 and later brigadier general of the Fayetteville District. When the state government of North Carolina was established by the adoption of the constitution at Halifax in 1776, Clinton became one of the first members elected to the House of Commons from Duplin; he continued as a representative from Duplin in each succeeding annual session until the creation of Sampson County at the April session of 1784. He was elected Sampson's first senator for the fall session of 1784 and was reelected as senator for eight of the following annual sessions. He also represented Sampson in the conventions held at Hillsborough in 1788 and at Fayetteville in 1789. He was one of the first justices of Sampson County and served as its first registrar of deeds. The seat of Sampson County was named Clinton in his honor.

In 1763, Clinton married Penelope Kenan (d. 1814), daughter of Thomas Kenan and his wife, Elizabeth Johnston Kenan. The Clintons had nine children:

William Sampson, who married first Sarah Seawell and second Patience Cook; Richard, married to Ferebee Hicks; Nancy Ann, married to Owen Holmes (1762–1814); Mary Eliza (1784–1858), who married Alfred Rowland (1777–1829); Rachel, who married Jacob Rhodes (ca. 1758–1824); Arabella, married to Isaac Lanier; Elizabeth, married to David Bunting; Owen; and Thomas.

SEE: Samuel A. Ashe, ed., *Biographical History of North Carolina*, vol. 5 (1906); Cora Bass, "Duplin County Marriage Bonds," *Sampson County Yearbook* (1957); Daughters of the American Revolution, Richard Clinton Chapter, "North Carolina Gravestone and Bible Records" (North Carolina Collection, University of North Carolina, Chapel Hill); Ida Kellam, "Gravestone Records, Oakdale Cemetery, Wilmington" (in possession of Mrs. Kellam, Wilmington); *Raleigh Register*, 13 Sept. 1811, 11 Nov. 1825, 27 May 1830, 25 June 1847, 4 Oct. 1848; Alvaretta Kenan Register, *The Kenan Family* (1967); Robeson County Will Book 1 (North Carolina State Archives, Raleigh); Sampson County Will Book 1 (North Carolina State Archives, Raleigh).

ALVARETTA K. REGISTER

Clitherall, James *(ca. 1740–ca. 1804)*, physician and Loyalist, was the son of John and Magdalen Clitherall of New Bern. Sent by his father in 1760 to study medicine at the University of Edinburgh, he became one of the few natives of North Carolina to receive a European university education during the colonial period. During 1760 and 1761, Clitherall was a student of Dr. William Cullen, then one of the leading medical teachers in the world. Clitherall did not receive a degree from Edinburgh but remained for seven years in Scotland and England in the capacity of a medical apprentice. In 1767 he returned to America, settling at Charleston, S.C., and soon establishing himself as a physician of prominence there. He inherited large tracts of land from his father and amassed a fortune in his own right by virtue of a successful practice.

Clitherall was a confirmed royalist and experienced difficulties with South Carolina authorities following the outbreak of the American Revolution. He remained at Charleston but served as a physician to a regiment of South Carolina Tories and signed a letter of congratulations to Cornwallis following the British victory at Camden. For the latter act he was banished to Florida. He returned to Charleston after the war, finding part of his property confiscated and his medical practice beyond rebuilding. He retired to a plantation near Charleston, called Preston, and remained there for the rest of his life as a gentleman farmer. He is said to have died in virtual impoverishment, the victim of a corrupt overseer. His first wife, Elizabeth [Inglis?], died in 1769, and Clitherall was married a second time, in 1775, to Mrs. Elizabeth Smith, widow of Thomas Loughton Smith. Clitherall had four children, one of whom, Dr. George Campbell, became a distinguished physician.

SEE: Eliza Clitherall, Autobiography and Diary, vol. 4 (Southern Historical Collection, University of North Carolina, Chapel Hill); *Hall's Wilmington Gazette*, 22 Feb. 1798; Joseph Ioor Waring, *A History of Medicine in South Carolina* (1964).

TOM PARRAMORE

Clodfelter (Gladfelder), Jesse *(b. 12 July 1804)*, cabinetmaker, was the first child of Maria Magdalena

Walk and John Gladfelder (the spelling was changed later) of the Friedberg community, now a part of Forsyth County. John worked there as a hatter, and so it is assumed that Jesse was born in the community. Little is known of Jesse Clodfelter's life, but it is recorded in the Davidson County court minutes for the May term in 1831 that he took Levi Roads "apprentice to the cabinetmaker's trade." There are several pieces of furniture—one corner cupboard and three chests of drawers—signed and dated by Clodfelter between the years 1834(6) and 1844. The chests of drawers relate in both visual comparison and construction details to the work of John Swisegood of Davidson County, and it is probable that Clodfelter was at one time apprenticed to Swisegood.

Deed transactions in 1830 for 81 3/4 acres "on waters of Frys Creek" and in 1839 for 87 or more acres "lying on Walk's Creek" are on record in Davidson County. In an estate voucher of 13 Jan. 1844, Clodfelter was paid for two coffins for Jack Mock (coffins were frequently furnished in the eighteenth and nineteenth centuries by cabinetmakers). From the amount of land owned by Clodfelter, it seems that he probably supplemented his cabinetwork with farming. However, on 10 May 1848, he sold both tracts of land to Adam Nifong.

Clodfelter was married three times. His first wife was Magdalena Hege and his second Anna Rosina Fischell. If there were children by these marriages, they are not known. The third marriage, to Maria Hartman, occurred on 30 July 1830, and seven children were born to this union. Maria died 17 Apr. 1845. As the marriage and birth records are from the Friedberg Church Book, it seems safe to assume that the family was Moravian. Clodfelter's death date and burial place are unknown.

SEE: Museum of Early Southern Decorative Arts (Winston-Salem), for references from research files; *The Swisegood School of Cabinetmaking* (1973).

WHALEY W. BATSON

Clopton, Abner Wentworth (24 Mar. 1784–20 Mar. 1833), clergyman and educator, was born in Pittsylvania County, Va., the second child of Robert and Frances Anderson Clopton. His father, a planter, had migrated to Pittsylvania from New Kent County, Va., following the Revolutionary War.

Young Clopton obtained the basic rudiments of an education through attendance at various common schools in the neighborhood of his boyhood home. A desire for further study led him to enroll at the Banister Academy, Pittsylvania County (1804–5) and to place himself under the tutelage of John W. Caldwell at the Guilford Academy, Guilford County (1805–6). After teaching for one year at a private school in Williamsburg District, S.C., he entered The University of North Carolina in January 1808, earning the A.B. degree in 1809 and the M.A. in 1812. He matriculated in the Medical School of the University of Pennsylvania in 1810 but did not complete the course of studies.

Clopton returned to Chapel Hill in 1812 to take charge of the preparatory school then connected with the university. His biographer, J. B. Jeter, has noted that his pupils were "almost universally the best that entered the regular classes of the University." As a supplement to his meager income as a teacher, and as an expression of his own deep sense of compassion for the sick, Clopton also engaged in the practice of medicine, to the benefit of both the students and the local residents of the university community.

Religious sentiments led Clopton to unite with Shockoe Baptist Church, Pittsylvania County, in 1812. Early in his career at Chapel Hill he began to give serious consideration to preparing himself for the ministry. Accordingly, he placed himself under the care of the Orange Presbytery (Presbyterian Church)—an unheard-of practice for an early nineteenth-century Baptist. He was ordained in October 1816, probably at the Mt. Carmel Baptist Church, near Chapel Hill.

Clopton left Chapel Hill in the summer of 1819 to help establish and to superintend the Milton Female Academy, Milton, which was opened in January 1820. He remained with the academy, also serving as pastor of a Baptist church in the vicinity until his removal to Charlotte County, Va., in January 1823.

The last ten years of Clopton's life were spent in Charlotte County, where he was pastor of the Ash Camp, Chaney's Chapel, and Mossingford Baptist churches. Throughout the period he also traveled extensively as an agent of the Baptist General Tract Society and, later, of Columbian College, Washington, D.C. He led in the organization of the Virginia Society for the Promotion of Temperance in 1826, traveling throughout Virginia, the Carolinas, and Georgia on behalf of temperance reform.

Clopton produced a variety of pamphlets and articles in promotion of the causes he espoused. Together with Eli Ball, he edited and published a collection entitled *Wisdom's Voice to the Rising Generation, Being a Collection of the Best Addresses and Sermons on Intemperance*. His method and manner of championing the Baptist cause in his "Review of Campbellism," which appeared in the pages of the Virginia Baptist weekly *Religious Herald*, prompted his biographer to evaluate him as an unsuccessful controversialist: "He was frequently impelled, by an ardent temperament, to employ expressions, which, if just, were repulsive, and likely to defeat his purpose."

An ill-suited marriage to Sally B. Warwick in 1803 terminated in a divorce obtained in 1809–10. He remained unmarried for the rest of his life.

Clopton was interred in the family cemetery in Pittsylvania County. His portrait is in the possession of the University of Richmond, Richmond, Va.

SEE: Woodford B. Hackley, *Faces on the Wall* (1972); Jeremiah B. Jeter, *A Memoir of Abner W. Clopton* (1837).

R. HARGUS TAYLOR

Cobb, Beatrice (13 Nov. 1888–11 Sept. 1959), newspaper editor and publisher and Democratic party leader, was born in Morganton, the eldest of six daughters of Theodore Gettys and Martha Kincaid Cobb. Educated first in the local schools, she enrolled at Asheville Normal School in 1907 and was graduated in 1909. She taught school in Hickory from 1909 to 1913, when she returned to Morganton to begin a newspaper career on the *News-Herald*, becoming owner and publisher at the time of her father's death in 1916. She also established the *Valdese News* in 1938.

One of the pioneer women leaders in the North Carolina Press Association, she served as its secretary-treasurer from 1922 until her death. From 1934 until 1952 she held the office of Democratic national committee-woman from North Carolina. She gained distinction in national Democratic circles and was the only southerner on the five-member committee to advise President Franklin D. Roosevelt in 1940 on a successor to James A. Farley, party chairman. Beginning in 1928, she was a

Cobb

390

delegate to several Democratic National Conventions.

The University of North Carolina awarded her an honorary LL.D. in 1949. She was a Methodist and an honorary member of the Morganton Kiwanis Club. Many of her writings dealt with her world travel experiences; after she became ill with acute leukemia she took a month's trip to Europe, from which she returned to enter Duke Hospital in Durham, where she died.

SEE: *Charlotte Observer*, 12 Sept. 1959; *History of the North Carolina Press Association* (1973); Morganton *News-Herald*, 11 Sept. 1959; Raleigh *News and Observer*, 12 Sept. 1959; *Who's Who of American Women*, vol. 1 (1958–59).

T. HARRY GATTON

Cobb, Clinton Levering (*5 Aug. 1842–30 Apr. 1879*), lawyer, merchant, and congressman, was born in Elizabeth City, the son of Thomas R. and Emily Harrington Cobb. A contemporary described him as having an average education. His father was a merchant, and as a youth, Cobb worked as a clerk in his dry goods store. In 1863 he participated in a public meeting in Elizabeth City at which resolutions were adopted that opposed blockade-running and sought the removal of a token state force, not strong enough to protect the area; in return for such action the town was to be free of any molestation by Federal troops then occupying Roanoke Island.

Cobb was admitted to the North Carolina bar in 1867 and began practicing law in his home town. At a Fourth of July celebration there in 1867, he was one of only two whites on the platform. He also engaged in mercantile business until 1868, when he ran as a Republican for Congress. He was successful and served in the Forty-first Congress (1869–71); reelected for two more terms, he continued to serve until 1875. Then, although he apparently had a better reputation than most Southern scalawags, he was defeated by Jesse J. Yeates, a Conservative from Hertford County. As a congressman, Cobb acted on behalf of President Grant in trying to get Randolph Abbott Shotwell, a North Carolina Conservative convicted upon false evidence, to implicate some leading Conservatives in Ku Klux Klan activity; in return for this information, Cobb promised Shotwell a pardon, but Shotwell refused and was imprisoned in Albany, N.Y. Cobb was also active in the establishment of the Life Saving Service along the coast.

After his defeat, Cobb returned home to resume his law practice. In 1872 he married Pattie Gaskins Pool, daughter of George D. Pool; the Cobbs were the parents of Paul and Clinton L. After an illness of several weeks, Cobb died in Elizabeth City at the age of thirty-seven and was buried in the Episcopal cemetery there.

SEE: *Biog. Dir. Am. Cong.* (1971); J. G. deRoulhac Hamilton, ed., *The Papers of Randolph Abbott Shotwell*, vol. 3 (1936); Records (possession of Mrs. William A. Peters, Jr., Elizabeth City); Stephen B. Weeks, Scrapbook (North Carolina Collection, University of North Carolina, Chapel Hill); *Who Was Who in America, 1607–1896*.

C. SYLVESTER GREEN

Cobb, Collier (*21 Mar. 1862–28 Nov. 1934*), college teacher and geologist, was born near Goldsboro at Mt. Ashburn plantation in Wayne County. His parents were Needham Bryan and Martha Louisa Cobb. Joseph Cobb, his first paternal ancestor, came to Jamestown, Va., in 1613 from Aberdeen, Scotland. A Baptist minister, Cobb's father held more than a dozen pastorates in his

career, from Moore's Creek to Lincolnton; when Collier was born, he was acting chaplain for the Second Regiment of the Army of Northern Virginia.

As a youth, Cobb, with his eleven brothers and sisters, was educated at home by his mother. A precocious child, he wrote, illustrated, and printed his own newspaper, the *Home Journal*, from 1871 to 1875. In 1872 he printed for private distribution a metrical version of Virgil's *Georgics*. At the age of twelve he helped take down in shorthand the Vance-Settle political debates. He began working in his teens on a map of North Carolina that was adopted by the state board of education in 1879 and went through six editions. After farming and teaching near Lilesville for a few years and working as a relief telegraph operator for the Central Carolina Railroad, he enrolled at Wake Forest College in 1878. In 1880 he left college and taught for a year at Locke Craig's Preparatory School in Chapel Hill. He also attended The University of North Carolina for one year. In 1881 he resumed teaching, first in Durham and the next year in Waynesville. From 1883 to 1886 he taught in Wilson, serving also as superintendent of schools during his last year. During the summer of 1885 he studied at the marine biological laboratory at Annisquan, Mass.

From 1886 to 1892, Cobb was an assistant on the U.S. Geological Survey. In 1888 he went to Harvard University, where he studied geology and assisted Nathaniel Southgate Shaler. At Harvard he was president of the Southern Club, secretary of the Natural History Society, and a member of the Free Wool Society. He paid for his tuition and expenses at Harvard by working as a correspondent for a syndicate of newspapers he established. After earning a bachelor's degree from Harvard in 1889, he was an instructor at the Massachusetts Institute of Technology and a lecturer at Boston University from 1890 to 1892.

In 1892, Cobb returned to Chapel Hill to become an assistant professor of geology and later the head of the geology department. In 1894 he received an M.A. degree from Harvard for work concentrating on the topographical features around Kings Mountain. The next year he studied briefly at the École Superieure des Mines in Paris. He was an officer with the Union Pacific expedition to the fossil fields of Wyoming in 1899. He continued to teach at The University of North Carolina for forty years and also taught at the Summer School of the South in Knoxville (1902, 1907), Biltmore Forest summer sessions (1905–12), and summer school at Cornell University (1928). In 1917, Wake Forest College awarded him an honorary Sc.D. degree.

Cobb was a member of the Elisha Mitchell Scientific Society, the Boston Club of Natural History, the Technology Club of Boston, the American Association for the Advancement of Science, the National Educational Association, the North Carolina Society of the Sons of the Revolution, the Southern History Association, and the Watauga Club in North Carolina. He was a fellow of the Geological Society of America. He was president in 1907 of the North Carolina Academy of Science and in 1908 of the Harvard Club of North Carolina. He served for many years as chairman of the Public School Committee in Chapel Hill. For twenty years he was superintendent of the Sunday school and a member of the board of deacons in the Chapel Hill Baptist Church.

In a memorial to Cobb, William F. Prouty, his successor as department chairman, wrote that Cobb's "interest in humanity was genuine and far reaching. . . . His striking personality, keen intellect, and remarkable memory, expressed in a wealth of rare anecdotes, made him the central figure in any group. . . . His teaching and personality so impressed his students that many of them went on to successful careers in geology." Many of Cobb's hobbies directly aided his work in the classroom. From his travels in Asia, Europe, Africa, and South America, he brought stories and jokes to stimulate his students, as well as the results of his geological researches. His skill as an artist and amateur photographer enabled him to illustrate his lectures, and a library of over ten thousand volumes assisted him in his teaching and research.

In his study of geology he concentrated on moving sands, coastlines, and soils. He published many books and articles, including "Where the Wind Does the Work" (*National Geographic Magazine*), "Notes on the Deflective Effect of the Earth's Rotation as Shown in Streams" (*Journal of the Elisha Mitchell Scientific Society*), "The North Carolina Coast: Its Perils and How They May Be Lessened" (*Proceedings of the Atlantic Deeper Waterways Association*), and "Dunes Sands and Eolian Soils in Relation to Present and Past Climatic Conditions of the Continent of North America" (*Compte-Rendu*). His *Pocket Dictionary of Common Rocks and Minerals* was widely used.

Cobb's interest in the land was not entirely academic. After seeing conservation exhibits at the Atlanta Exhibition in 1895, he acquired the gullied area in Chapel Hill known now as Cobb Terrace and began to develop it. After 1915 he successfully converted it into a residential park.

Cobb was married three times. On 27 Jan. 1891 he married Mary Lindsay Battle at Lilesville. They had three children, William Battle (1891), Collier, Jr. (1893), and Mary Louisa (1899). Mary Battle Cobb died in 1900, and four years later Cobb married Lucy Plummer Battle in Raleigh. They had one son, Richard Battle (1905). After Lucy Battle Cobb died, Cobb married Mary Knox Gatlin in Little Rock, Ark., on 27 Oct. 1910.

Early in the summer of 1933, Cobb suffered a slight stroke. Eighteen months later he died in Chapel Hill and was buried in the Chapel Hill Cemetery. A portrait hangs in the library of the geology department in Mitchell Hall at The University of North Carolina. In 1952 the university named Cobb Dormitory in his honor.

SEE: Samuel A. Ashe, ed., *Biographical History of North Carolina*, vol. 6 (1907); *Durham Herald-Sun*, 23 Mar. 1930; *Greensboro Daily News*, 22 Nov. 1932; *Journal of the Elisha Mitchell Scientific Society*, 1935; *Nat. Cyc. Am. Biog.*, vol. K (1967); Raleigh *News and Observer*, 22 Mar. 1931; *Report of Harvard College Class of 1889* (1909); *Who Was Who in America*, vol. 1 (1943).

CHARLES W. EAGLES

Cobb, Howell (*3 Aug. 1772–26 May 1818*), soldier and congressman, was born in Granville County, the son of John and Mildred Lewis Cobbs. He was given the name Howell for a maternal relative. The Cobbs family moved to Georgia in 1783 or 1784, and the family grew to prominence in that state. John and one of his sons, John A., served in the Georgia House of Representatives. The brothers both dropped the final *s* from their name.

Cobb joined the Second Sub Legion, U.S. Army, as an ensign on 23 Feb. 1793; he was promoted to lieutenant in due course. At the time of his resignation on 31 Jan. 1806, he was captain of artillery and engineers. In the meantime, he had established Cherry Hill Plantation near Louisville, Ga. Elected to Congress in 1806, he served from 1807 until 1812, when he resigned to serve as a captain in the War of 1812. At the end of the war he returned to his plantation, where he spent the remainder of his life and where he was buried. His nephew, Howell

Cobb (1815–68), was born at Cherry Hill and became a member of Congress, secretary of the treasury, and Confederate major general.

SEE: *Appleton's Cyclopedia of American Biography*, vol. 1 (1887); *Biog. Dir. Am. Cong.* (1971); Archibald A. Hicks, *History of Granville County* (1965).

A. C. MENIUS III

Cobb, John Blackwell (*5 Oct. 1857–9 Apr. 1923*), tobacconist and capitalist, was born in Caswell County, the son of Henry Wellington and Mary Howard Cobb. He was educated in private schools in his native county, and at the age of nineteen, with a borrowed five hundred dollars, he engaged in the leaf tobacco business as a pinhooker in Danville, Va. His initial profits were lost in the speculative sale of wrappers in St. Louis, but he eventually recovered and set out on a significant business career. In 1890 he joined the American Tobacco Company as a buyer of leaf tobacco. He moved to New York in 1894 and by 1896 was a vice-president of the firm, a position he held until his retirement in 1908. During the course of a busy life he also served as president and director of the American Cigar Company, the Cuban Land and Leaf Tobacco Company, the Havana American Company, and the Havana Commercial Company; as first vice-president and director of H. de Cabanas y Carbajal; as director of the American Snuff Company, American Stogie Company, Blackwell's Durham Company, the British American Tobacco Company, F. Garcia Brothers and Company, Havana Tobacco Company, the Industrial Company of Porto Rico, the International Cigar Machinery Company, Lurhman and Wilbern Tobacco Company, the Porto Rican American Tobacco Company, and the Louis K. Liggett Company; and as director and member of the executive committee of the United Drug Company.

Cobb owned nearly forty-four thousand acres of land between Greensboro and High Point and during the course of his life lived in Durham, St. Louis, Mo., and Stamford, Conn. He was married on 4 Jan. 1881 to Pricie Perkins Millner; they had two daughters, Mrs. Mary Howard Gilmour and Mrs. Lucy Langhorne Hill, both of whom lived in New York City at the time of his death. Cobb was in poor health for the last year of his life and was found dead in his stateroom aboard a train several hours out of Hot Springs, Ark. He was a Methodist and was generous to his childhood church in Caswell County. He provided funds for a private school in the county, now the John B. Cobb Memorial School, incorporated into the public school system, and he also left money to the University of Virginia and to members of his family. His estate was estimated at $50 million.

SEE: *Greensboro Daily News*, 10 Apr. 1923; *New York Times*, 10 and 26 Apr. 1923; *Tobacco*, 19 Apr. 1923, 25 Oct. 1923.

WILLIAM S. POWELL

Cobb, Lucy Maria (*24 Nov. 1877–6 July 1969*), folklore collector, teacher, and author, was born in Lilesville. She was a sister of Collier Cobb and a daughter of Martha Louisa Cobb and Needham Bryan Cobb, a Baptist preacher. Lucy Cobb attended St. Mary's School, the State Normal School in Greensboro, and Greensboro College for Women. She took a B.A. degree in 1921 at The University of North Carolina, completed an M.A. in English there in 1927, and studied further at Peabody College in Nashville and Columbia University in New York. She worked variously as Duplin County home demonstration agent, publicity agent for The University of North Carolina and for Campbell College, city editor of the *High Point Enterprise*, short-term teacher in both public schools and colleges, and feature writer for North Carolina newspapers.

In the 1920s she developed an interest in collecting folklore. She never did systematic or intensive field work, but her unpublished 106-page master's thesis, "Traditional Ballads and Songs of Eastern North Carolina," was the first sizeable collection of song texts made in the tidewater counties. During the thirties she collaborated with Mary Ann Hicks of Cary on a volume entitled *Animal Tales from the Old North State*, which contains forty-eight stories gathered from seven black informants in Johnston, Wake, Wilson, and Lenoir counties. The two women projected but did not complete another book of tales and one of children's traditional games. Miss Cobb later published several brief articles on folklore. None of these materials was assimilated into the *Frank C. Brown Collection of North Carolina Folklore*, though she also contributed a few items for its pages.

Lucy Cobb also participated in the Carolina folk-drama movement, on which she wrote one article. Her "Gaius and Gaius, Jr." was included in the second volume of *Carolina Folk Plays*. Two other unpublished plays—a comedy with the title "Some Women Are Like That" and another about Blackbeard, entitled "A Gift for Penelope"—received performances. She adapted the latter play as an operetta, "The Pirate and the Governor's Daughter," which was performed in 1956 in Raleigh, with piano score and lyrics by Dorothy Horne and orchestration by Patrick McCarty.

Miss Cobb's later writings concerned family history and genealogy.

Lucy Cobb was also active in the state's cultural organizations. She served as vice-president of the North Carolina Folklore Society and held membership and offices in the North Carolina Society for the Preservation of Antiquities, the North Carolina Art Society, the National Pen Women, the American Association of University Women, the Daughters of the American Revolution, and the Magna Charta Dames. In 1957 the North Carolina Society for the Preservation of Antiquities recognized her work by awarding her its Charles A. Cannon Cup.

SEE: *Chapel Hill Weekly*, 9 July 1969, 10 Sept. 1969; L. M. Cobb, *Cobb and Cobbs* (n.d.), "Drama in North Carolina," *Southern Literary Messenger* 2 (1940), "Gaius and Gaius, Jr.," in F. H. Koch, ed., *Carolina Folk-Plays*, 2nd ser. (1924), *The Preacher's Three: Stories of a North Carolina Childhood from Another Day* (1963), "Riddle," *North Carolina Folklore* 1 (1948), "Traditional Ballads and Songs of Eastern North Carolina" (M.A. thesis, University of North Carolina, 1927), and "Two Folktales," *North Carolina Folklore* 6 (1958); L. M. Cobb and Mary Ann Hicks, *Animal Tales from the Old North State* (1938), and "Proverbs," *North Carolina Folklore* 1 (1948); William S. Powell, ed., *North Carolina Lives* (1962).

DANIEL W. PATTERSON

Cobb, Needham Bryan *(1 Feb. 1836–31 May 1905)*, Baptist minister, educator, historian, and author was born in Jones County, the son of William Donnell Cobb and his wife, Ann Spicer Collier. He received his B.A. degree from The University of North Carolina in 1854 and received the first M.A. degree awarded by the university in 1856. He was given an honorary D.D. by Judson College, Hendersonville, in 1889. He studied law

under Judge William H. Battle while at Chapel Hill and continued his studies under Chief Justice Richmond Pearson, and then practiced law and taught school in Pitt, Wayne, and Greene counties for nearly three years.

In October 1859, Cobb left the Episcopal church in which he had been a vestryman and was baptized in Greenville by the Reverend Henry Petty. He was ordained a year later in Wilson by a presbytery of Baptist ministers consisting of Elders Levi Thorne, J. B. Solomon, Henry Petty, G. W. Keene, W. C. Lacy, and J. G. Barclay. In later years, Cobb remembered that his first baptismal service was conducted for some black slaves whom he baptised in the Nansemond River near Suffolk, Va.

Cobb volunteered and was commissioned 12 June 1861 as chaplain of the Fourth Regiment, North Carolina Volunteers (later the Fourteenth Regiment, North Carolina State Troops). After three months' service he resigned and served the remainder of the war as superintendent of colportage for North Carolina. During this period his many letters to the *Biblical Recorder* detailed his efforts to supply missionaries, tracts, and New Testaments for the soldiers.

After the Civil War, Cobb was associated with Dr. J. D. Huffham in editing the Raleigh *Daily Record* for six months. He also served as corresponding secretary of the Sunday School Board and later as a missionary of the State Mission Board within the bounds of the Eastern Baptist Association.

As a Baptist minister, Cobb served churches in Goldsboro, Elizabeth City, Shelby, Lincolnton, Lilesville, Rockingham, Fayetteville, Chapel Hill, Waynesville, Morganton, Hickory, Hillsborough, Cary, Sharon, and Wise, as well as a church in Portsmouth, Va. He served as president of the Baptist State Convention for three years, 1879–81, and as recording secretary of the convention for nine sessions. For four years he was secretary of the Board of Missions of the convention.

A "many sided man," as contemporaries described him, Cobb taught school while engaged in his pastoral work. He was president of the Wayne Institute and Normal College, professor of Latin and Greek at Goldsboro Female College, and principal of Lilesville High School.

From 1865 through 1893, Cobb was editor of the *North Carolina Almanac*. He was author of "Reply to Gray's Elegy," "Cold Water," and various other poems published in a volume entitled *Poetical Geography of North Carolina and Other Poems* (1887), which was used as a textbook in North Carolina schools.

While in Greenville in 1858–59, Cobb, then practicing law, began the study of Ben Pitman's system of phonography. Whether he was the first North Carolinian to study shorthand will probably never be known, but he was the first who acquired such proficiency in the art as to be recognized by the public as a shorthand reporter. His earliest pieces copied in his commonplace book are dated "Greenville, September, 1858." He copied much of the Bible and prepared his sermon notes in shorthand. He also prepared a shorthand primer for the instruction of his oldest son, Collier, then five years old. His first stenographic work was for the Raleigh *Daily Sentinel*, reporting the court-martial of Major John H. Gee for alleged cruelty to Union prisoners at the Salisbury Military Prison. After the trial, Cobb taught private classes in stenography in Raleigh and at Wake Forest College. Later he reported the 1870–71 campaign speeches of former Governor Zebulon B. Vance and of A. S. Merrimon. In 1880, while pastor in Chapel Hill, he lectured on stenography at The University of North Carolina.

Cobb was twice married. His first wife was Martha Louisa Cobb of Pitt County, whom he marred 27 Dec. 1859. To them were born twelve children. One son, Collier, became a distinguished member of the faculty of The University of North Carolina. Cobb's second wife was Ann DeLise Fennell of Sampson County, to whom he was married 3 Sept. 1891. They had three children.

The last ten years of Cobb's life were spent on his Sampson County farm, where he died.

SEE: Biography File (Baptist Historical Collection, Wake Forest University, Winston-Salem [photograph]); "The History of Shorthand Writing in North Carolina," *Biennial Report of the Superintendent of Public Instruction*, 1898–99; Weymouth T. Jordan, Jr., comp., *North Carolina Troops, 1861–1865: A Roster*, vol. 5 (1975); *North Carolina Baptist State Convention Annual*, 1905; Raleigh *Biblical Recorder*, 1861–65; Thomas J. Taylor, *A History of the Tar River Association* (ca. 1924).

JOHN R. WOODARD, JR.

Cochran, James (1761–13 Apr. 1817), planter and congressman, was born in or near the community of Mount Tirzah, Orange (now Person) County. He attended local schools and engaged in farming near the present Timberlake. At the time of his death he owned over six thousand acres of land. He represented Person County in the House of Commons in 1802–6 and in the senate in 1807. Elected as a Democrat to Congress, he served from March 1809 until March 1813. He was elected in 1814 and in 1815 to a seat on the council of state.

On 14 Jan. 1793, Cochran married Annis McNeill; they were the parents of Susanna, who married William A. Lea; Annis, who married John Dobbin and was the mother of James Cochran Dobbin, secretary of the navy from 1853 to 1857; and Addison, a minor at the time of his father's death, who entered The University of North Carolina in 1820.

Cochran died intestate, perhaps unexpectedly, and was buried in the cemetery at Lea's Chapel west of Roxboro. An obituary notice in the *Raleigh Register* of 25 Apr. 1817 referred to him as Major James Cochran, indicating perhaps a rank in the local militia.

SEE: *Biog. Dir. Am. Cong.* (1971); Cochran Estate Papers, Person County Records (North Carolina State Archives, Raleigh).

WILLIAM S. POWELL

Cocke, Norman Atwater (20 Nov. 1884–4 Nov. 1974), attorney and industrialist, was born in Prince George County, Va., the son of John James Cocke and grandson of Nathaniel Colley and Virginia Peterson Cocke of Aberdeen in eastern Prince George. His mother, Sarah Atwater, was a native of Coxsackie, N.Y. Cocke was reared in Petersburg, Va., where his father was an attorney. He began his education at the local schools, finishing at the Petersburg Academy. In 1905 he was graduated from the New York Law School, and from 1902 to 1906 he was a clerk in the law firm of Atwater and Cruikshank in New York City. He was licensed to practice law in New York in 1906 and in North Carolina in 1907. He became attorney in 1906 for the Southern Power Company and later for its successor, the Duke Power Company, continuing this association for over fifty years and making his home in Charlotte. After joining the company, he conceived and directed the

concern's extensive forestry and land management program. In 1927 he became a director and vice-president of Duke Power, and he was president from 1947 until his retirement on 1 Jan. 1959.

Cocke early gained the confidence of James B. Duke, who in 1925 appointed him one of the original trustees of the Duke Endowment. He played a large role in the work of the endowment as first trustee and later as vice-chairman and chairman of the board. He served Duke University in many capacities and was chairman of its board of trustees from 1954 to 1959.

Cocke was interested in other phases of the industrial development of Piedmont North Carolina and was appointed director of the Piedmont and Northern Railway in 1927. At the time of his death he was a director of the textile concern J. P. Stevens and Company.

When the four major power companies in the two Carolinas and Virginia organized the Carolinas-Virginia Nuclear Power Associates in 1956, to construct the first atomic power plant in the Southeast, Cocke became its first president. At about the same time he was elected to the board of directors of the Edison Electric Institute.

Cocke served as a trustee of Converse College and was an original trustee of the Morehead Scholarship Foundation of The University of North Carolina; he was elected chairman of the Morehead trustees in 1965. A member of Christ Church, Charlotte, he was an active layman and a trustee of the Episcopal Foundation of the Diocese of North Carolina.

During the course of his life, Cocke was the recipient of many honors. In 1951 he was awarded the Degree of Industry from Clemson University. He was later honored with doctoral degrees from Davidson College, Furman University, and Duke University. Duke Power Company's largest power impoundment, located on the Catawba River near Charlotte, was named Lake Norman in recognition of his services to the company. In 1959 he was selected Citizen of the Year by the North Carolina Citizen's Association.

He was married on 28 Nov. 1911 to Mary Sommers Booth of Petersburg, Va., and was the father of three sons, Norman, Jr., William Booth, and John.

SEE: J. B. Boddie, *Southside Virginia Families* (1955); Gary Trawick and Paul Wyche, *One Hundred Years, One Hundred Men* (1971); *Who's Who in America*, 1959.

CLAIBORNE T. SMITH, JR.

Coffin, Addison (22 Jan. 1822–16 Apr. 1897), abolitionist and educational, temperance, and agricultural leader, was born at New Garden (now Guilford College), son of Vestal and Alethea Fluke Coffin. The Coffins were descendants of Nantucket Friends who settled in Guilford County before the Revolution. Coffin was educated at the New Garden Brick School under Horace Cannon and at New Garden Boarding School. Owing to the death of his father in 1826, he was much under the influence of his cousin, Levi Coffin, and early became active in the abolition movement, in the establishment of Sabbath school and temperance societies, and in the promotion of women's rights.

A lifelong traveler, Coffin in 1843 walked five hundred miles to Cincinnati, Ohio, from which vantage point he visited settlements of North Carolina emigrants and attended the first National Abolition Convention. In 1843–44 he taught school. Returning briefly to North Carolina, he then removed permanently to Indiana in February 1845.

During his maturity, Coffin farmed, taught school in

winters, and yet found time to engage actively in the religious and political activities of the day and especially in the abolition movement. Owing to the necessary secrecy involved, few details are known of the means by which runaway slaves were assisted to reach free territory, but Coffin was a conductor of the Underground Railroad and made many secret journeys with hairbreadth escapes. During the Civil War he suffered much criticism for holding strictly to the Friends' tenets of peace, though he engaged actively in alleviating the suffering caused by the war. His home was a center for the protection of conscientious objectors, widows, orphans, and other victims of the times.

In 1866, in cooperation with the railways stretching through the west, Coffin organized emigrant trains from North Carolina and South Carolina, known as Coffin's trains, which bore people from the war-stricken Carolinas to the rich lands of middle America, where many of their relatives had gone during the prewar migration. In the decade following the war he led thousands from North Carolina, depopulating whole communities. These bewildered groups, passing through Baltimore to the distributing point in Cincinnati, excited the interest of the Baltimore Association of Friends, who thought that the problem should be attacked at its source and the people taught to be self-supporting where they were. The Quaker interest resulted in the establishment of a model farm near High Point, demonstrating improved conservation methods and development of natural resources. The Friends established schools, taught by volunteers of the association, and teacher training institutes designed to aid the educational process until the states could take over the effort.

In 1891, Coffin returned to North Carolina for the funeral of his mother, who had wished to be buried by her husband. For several years he remained largely in the New Garden area, lecturing on temperance, education, agriculture, and women's rights and interspersing tales of his extensive travels. In 1892, accompanied by J. Van Lindley, he made a nine-month tour of Egypt, Palestine, Asia Minor, and all the countries of Europe. In 1895 the inveterate traveler made his last long journey, to Mexico, in company with Julia Ballinger, a niece who was a missionary there. He returned as usual to lecture on the wonders of the world. At seventy-five, Coffin retired to the home of his daughter in Amo, Ind., where he died. He was buried near Hadley, his home in Indiana.

Coffin's first wife was Emily Hadley, whom he married 25 June 1845 and who died 2 Jan. 1851. Of their four sons, only one survived infancy: Trenmor, lawyer and banker of Carson, Nev. Coffin's second wife, a cousin of Emily, was Ruth Hadley; they were married 13 May 1854. She died 5 Mar. 1889, leaving one daughter, Ida (Mrs. Joseph John Doan, of Amo, Ind.).

SEE: Addison Coffin, *Life and Travels of Addison Coffin* (1897); William Wade Hinshaw, comp., *Encyclopedia of American Quaker Genealogy*, 6 vols. (1936–50); Quaker Collection (Guilford College Library, Greensboro); Stephen B. Weeks, *Southern Quakers and Slavery* (1896).

MARY KATHERINE HOSKINS

Coffin, Levi (28 Oct. 1789–16 Sept. 1877), abolitionist, temperance leader, and philanthropist, was born in New Garden, Guilford County, a descendant of Tristam Coffin, who came to America in 1642 and was one of nine purchasers of Nantucket from the Indians. Only son and seventh child of Levi and Prudence Williams Coffin,

whose families had removed from Nantucket to New Garden before the American Revolution, Levi was taught largely by his father in their pioneer home. At twenty-one he studied briefly in some unknown school, and thereafter he taught and studied alternately for several years. In spite of the opposition of the elders, he joined the young Quakers of New Garden in 1818 in establishing a Sunday school in the new brick school adjoining the meeting house. This endeavor met with such success that he assisted in organizing other Sunday schools wherever he went. At about this time he joined the first manumission society in Guilford County, remaining an active member throughout its existence. In 1821 he and his cousin, Vestal Coffin, organized a school for slaves; there, on Sunday afternoons, with permission of the masters, they taught the elements of Christianity and reading of the Bible. The slaves were so interested that some of the masters became opposed, and the school was forbidden.

On 28 Oct. 1824, Coffin married Catherine White at Hopewell Church, Guilford County. In 1826 they moved to Newport (now Fountain City), Wayne County, Ind., where they opened a store. Finding themselves on a route along which escaped slaves passed to free territory, they joined the movement known as the Underground Railroad, helping to shelter such people and arrange transportation to Canada and elsewhere. Maintaining two teams, Coffin journeyed at night over secret roads, carrying fugitives to hiding places from which others carried them on to safety. Among those so rescued from slavery was a nameless woman who carried her infant across the broken ice of the Ohio River while pursued by bloodhounds, eventually reaching the Coffin home. She was described as Eliza Harris in the Harriet Beecher Stowe novel *Uncle Tom's Cabin*, and the phrase "Eliza crossing the ice" became a synonym for a narrow escape.

Coffin, known as president of the Underground Railroad, was a member of the Committee on Concerns of People of Color to Consider Their Education and was treasurer of funds to aid the poor and destitute. He was also active in the temperance movement. Feeling it wrong to use goods made by slave labor, he removed to Cincinnati, Ohio, in 1847, where for five years he operated a wholesale store selling products of free labor. He began work for the freedmen at the outbreak of the Civil War and devoted the rest of his life to that cause. In May 1864 he went to the British Isles; there he was instrumental in organizing the English Freedmen's Aid Society, which sent over one hundred thousand dollars in money and supplies to America in a single year. He was delegate to the International Anti-Slavery Society in Paris in 1867. The last years of his life he spent in writing his autobiography, *Reminiscences of Levi Coffin*, published in 1876 by the Western Tract Society of Cincinnati, Ohio.

SEE: *Cincinnati Enquirer*, 18 Sept. 1878; Laura Haviland, *A Woman's Life Work* (1882); *Historical Magazine* 14 (Sept. 1868); *New England Historical and Genealogical Register* 2 (Oct. 1848); Quaker Collection (Guilford College Library, Greensboro); W. H. Seibert, *Underground Railroad from Slavery to Freedom* (1898); Stephen B. Weeks, *Southern Quakers and Slavery* (1896).

MARY KATHERINE HOSKINS

Coffin, Oscar Jackson (4 Feb. 1887–29 Oct. 1956), newspaperman, professor, and dean of the School of Journalism, The University of North Carolina, was born at Carter's Mill in Moore County on a farm within the present city limits of Robbins, the son of Alexander Horney Coffin and Ida Elizabeth Moring Coffin. The home once served as a toll house along the old plank road between Salem and Fayetteville, and his grandfather, Bethuel Coffin, served as tollkeeper. Coffin attended public school in Asheboro, where Dr. N. C. Newbold described him as "the brightest, most mischievous student I had." He entered The University of North Carolina in 1905 and was graduated in 1909. He reported news for the *Asheboro Courier* in 1910 and was sports editor of the *Winston-Salem Journal* in 1911. In early 1911 he was Abbotsburg High School principal.

Coffin and Gertrude Wilson of Haywood County were married 5 Sept. 1912 and had one son, Edwin Wilson.

Coffin served as news editor of the *Charlotte Observer* from 1912 to 1916 and also worked briefly for the Roanoke Rapids newspaper. As city editor (1916–18) and editor (1918–26) of the *Raleigh Times*, he wrote penetrating editorials that increased the *Times* readership and kept capitol officials uneasy. His barbed wit often pricked thin skins. An itinerant evangelist whom he termed an "immigrant ignoramus" sued him for twenty-five thousand dollars, but Coffin won the suit. Other than millions of words in newspapers, his only published writing was a seventy-nine-page pamphlet of humorous blank verse about state legislators, entitled *A State House Anthology* (1917).

Coffin's iconoclasm prompted the charge that he was atheist; he countered, "I was flushed in an August revival and have been a member of the Methodist church ever since."

He returned to Chapel Hill in 1926 to succeed Gerald W. Johnson as teacher of journalism and was designated dean when the department achieved the status of a school. Professorial contemporaries often viewed him as an academic maverick and noted especially his irreverence for textbooks. He never referred to a journalism text, preferring that his staff teach from actual experience. He tried to employ former newsmen "who had met a payroll." If he had one text, it was the Bible, which he said "every good newspaperman should know"; his own speech was sprinkled with scriptural quotations. He also spiced his lectures with salty observations from real life: his "ten commandments" to aspiring newsmen always began, "Thou shalt not take thyself too damn seriously." When a student asked his opinion of a post-prohibition beverage known as "near beer," his reply was, "Whoever named it was a helluva judge of distance." Yet if a student used slang or profanity he was chastised for his "laziness" and urged to employ the King's English. Coffin's discipline taught many writers to use precise linguistic discrimination and a wide variety of styles.

Coffin urged an interest in government from city hall upward and counted the growing complexity of public administrations a challenge to newspapermen. He discouraged "sewage" in media reports and, to the irritation of publishers, emphasized his wariness of newspaper monopolies.

His sense of the obligations of citizenship led him into political activity in his community and state. When the Democratic executive committee for the Sixth Congressional District became deadlocked in search of a candidate, Coffin advanced the name of Carl T. Durham, little known outside the circle of young friends he had made as Chapel Hill druggist, and succeeded in winning the nomination of this representative from the least populous county in the district. Durham served with distinction and ultimately headed the trail-blazing Joint Committee on Atomic Energy during the era from which peacetime nuclear industry emerged. Politicians who

first scoffed at Coffin's choice lived to praise him for his judgment.

Coffin was buried in the old Chapel Hill Cemetery.

SEE: *Asheville Citizen-Times*, 28 Oct. 1951; *Charlotte Observer*, 23 Apr. 1950, 30 Aug. 1953; *Durham Morning Herald*, 16 Aug. 1953; *State* 21 (13 June 1953); *University of North Carolina Alumni Review*, April 1929; *Winston-Salem Journal-Sentinel*, 30 June 1956.

JACK RILEY

Cogdell, Richard *(8 July 1724–10 May 1787)*, merchant, planter, and politician, was born in Beaufort, the eldest of fourteen children of George and Margaret Bell Cogdell. Contrary to the popular assumption that the Cogdells were Swiss who arrived with the De Graffenried expedition, the family probably emigrated from Virginia's Eastern Shore. John Cogdell, grandfather of Richard and founder of the North Carolina branch of the family, died in Bath in 1712. His sons, Charles and George, acquired landed estates in several counties and served as justices of the peace in Carteret County. Charles Cogdell also represented Carteret in the provincial assembly and held a commission as captain in the Carteret militia.

Richard Cogdell remained in the Beaufort area of Cartaret County until 1748. He served as an ensign in the militia during the Spanish invasion of Beaufort in 1747 and as deputy sheriff of the county in 1748. He subsequently migrated to Johnston County, where he opened a mercantile business. In 1756 he moved to New Bern to continue his mercantile trade and operate an ordinary from 1757 to 1763. While in New Bern he worshipped regularly at Christ Church, acted as town alderman, and helped to establish a free school in the town. He served as sheriff of Craven County from 1761 through 1764. Cogdell retained close ties with Carteret, however, and represented that county in the assembly in 1766. While a member of the legislature, he proposed bills to replace the New Bern district jail, which had burned, and to improve the navigation of the Neuse River by constructing a canal to join Old Topsail Inlet to the river. Upon the passage of these bills, he was appointed one of several commissioners to supervise the implementation of the projects.

In January 1767, Cogdell resumed his duties as justice of the peace for Craven County, in which capacity he served diligently until his ardent Whig sympathies occasioned his exclusion from the Craven commission of the peace in 1774. During his years as justice, he attended every quarterly session of the Craven County court; he was one of the magistrates who complained to the governor and council that too many justices neglected to attend the court meetings, thereby placing the burden of public business on the conscientious few. While justice of the peace, he advanced money to the county for sundry public expenses and served on committees to inspect guardians' accounts, to examine accounts of the commissioners responsible for building the courthouse, and to superintend the constructing of a temporary jail for the county. Although once accused of partiality in the execution of his magistrate's office, he was "fully and honorably acquitted" by an investigation of the governor and council.

Cogdell relinquished his seat in the assembly in 1767 upon his appointment by the Craven County court as inspector of commodities for the port of New Bern, a post he retained through 1775. In 1772 several charges were advanced against him for neglect of his office as inspector. The court thoroughly examined the allegations and by a split decision continued him as inspector. One of the dissenting justices then moved to impeach Cogdell for misfeasance as magistrate. The court also rejected that proposal, but it is significant that the charge of neglect as inspector and the attempt to impeach Cogdell were rarely duplicated in the county court records of colonial North Carolina.

Cogdell renewed his military endeavors in 1771 by participating in the expedition against the Regulators. As lieutenant colonel of the Craven militia he saw action in the Battle of Alamance. He was subsequently rewarded for his exertions by a promotion to colonelcy. Thereafter he manifested his sympathy for the colony in its struggle to preserve its political integrity in the face of overbearing British authority. He served as one of the Craven County representatives in the first three provincial congresses held at New Bern and Halifax in 1774 and 1775, but he evinced his radicalism most strongly as chairman of the safety committee at New Bern during 1775 and 1776. Under his guidance the committee enforced the Continental association, vigorously suppressed Tory sentiment, and supported the North Carolina war effort. In 1776 the fourth provincial congress appointed Cogdell a member of the state council of safety from the District of New Bern.

During the Revolution, Cogdell served the state as postmaster in New Bern and as judge of the admiralty court at Beaufort in 1776 and 1777. While sitting on the bench, he appointed his eighteen-year-old son, Richard, Jr., marshal of the court, but the boy's age evoked protests that, as a minor, he was ineligible for the office. The state legislature invalidated the appointment and thereafter arrogated to itself the power to determine marshals of the admiralty courts in North Carolina. Cogdell represented the town of New Bern in the House of Commons from 1778 until 1779, when he resigned his seat to accept an appointment by the legislature as treasurer of the District of New Bern. He retained that office until declining health forced him to retire from public life in 1783.

Cogdell married Lydia Duncan of Massachusetts on 8 July 1752. The couple had ten children, five of whom lived to maturity: Ann, who married John Wright Stanly; Margaret, who married James Green; Richard, married to Nancy Ormand; Susannah, married first to Wright Stanly and then to Bela Badger; and Lydia, married to Thomas Badger.

SEE: Samuel A. Ashe, ed., *Biographical History of North Carolina*, vol. 2 (1905); M. Delamar, *Early Cogdells of North Carolina* (1946); North Carolina State Archives (Raleigh), for Richard Cogdell Papers and Minutes of the Craven County Court of Pleas and Quarter Sessions (1756–75); William L. Saunders and Walter Clark, eds., *Colonial and State Records of North Carolina*, vols. 6–25 (1888–1905).

ALAN D. WATSON

Coke, Octavius (4 Oct. 1840–30 Aug. 1895), North Carolina secretary of state, was born in Williamsburg, Va., the son of John Coke and his wife, Eliza Hawkins. His uncle, Richard Coke, Jr. (16 Nov. 1791–16 Mar. 1851), served two terms in the U.S. House of Representatives (1829–33) as a Jacksonian Democrat from Virginia. One brother, Richard (13 Mar. 1829–14 May 1897), became a Democratic governor of Texas (1873–77) and a U.S. senator (1877–95); two others, George, a physician, and Lucius, later moved to North

Carolina and settled in Perquimans and Martin counties, respectively.

Coke studied at the College of William and Mary (1857–58) but apparently did not graduate; he then read law and opened practice in Williamsburg just before the outbreak of the Civil War. On 31 Aug. 1861 he enlisted in the Williamsburg Junior Guards, later incorporated as Company C, Thirty-second Virginia Infantry; advancing rapidly through the ranks, he was elected captain on 11 May 1862, with his commission to date from 23 Oct. 1861. He was wounded several times, most seriously during the Seven Days' and at Five Forks.

After the war, Coke emigrated to Edenton, where he again practiced law and almost immediately involved himself in politics. In 1868 he ran unsuccessfully as a Conservative for a seat in the state constitutional convention; in 1872 he was the Greeley elector for the First District; and in 1876, despite the Republicans' county-wide edge in voter registration, Chowan elected him as a Democrat to one term in the state senate, where he quickly established himself as one of the party's main floor leaders.

Moving permanently to Raleigh in 1880, Coke maintained a strong interest in Democratic party affairs. That same year he served as chairman of the party's state executive committee and as such was considered by his contemporaries largely responsible for the Democrats' decisive victory in the fall elections. At the state convention of 1884, he was narrowly defeated for the gubernatorial nomination by Alfred M. Scales. In 1889, Governor Daniel G. Fowle appointed him to the board of directors of the state insane asylum to assist in the investigation of a scandal that resulted in the forced resignation of Dr. Eugene Grissom, an old political enemy, as director. In 1891, on the death of Secretary of State William L. Saunders, Coke was appointed by Governor Thomas M. Holt to fill the unexpired term; he was elected in his own right the next year by a large majority.

Coke died at his home in Raleigh and was buried in Oakwood Cemetery. The Raleigh *News end Observer*'s obituary lauded him for his forthright avowal of principle (Coke, an Episcopalian, was an outspoken opponent of prohibition, especially during the Raleigh referendum of 1886); and Josephus Daniels, a sometime political opponent, described him as "a gallant Confederate soldier, and an eloquent orator and advocate, with personal charm."

Coke married twice, in 1867 to Caroline Wood of Edenton, who died in 1876, and in 1879 to Kate Fisher of Raleigh. There were two children by his first marriage, Caroline Wood and Octavius, Jr., and four by his second, Kate, Julia, Jeff Fisher, and Richard.

SEE: Josephus Daniels, *Tar Heel Editor* (1939); John Wheeler Moore, *History of North Carolina*, vol. 2 (1880); Raleigh *News and Observer*, esp. 31 Aug. 1895 (obit. [drawing]); Virginia State Library (Richmond), for information on Coke's war record; John H. Wheeler, *Reminiscences and Memoirs of North Carolina* (1883–84).

BENNETT L. STEELMAN

Coker, Robert Ervin (4 June 1876–2 Oct. 1967), Kenan Professor of Zoology at The University of North Carolina, founder of the Institute of Fisheries Research at Morehead City, and a pioneer in the development of marine sea-life conservation in American coastal waters, was born at Society Hill, S.C., the son of William Caleb and Mary Ervin McIver Coker. William Caleb Coker was a captain in the Confederate Army and later president of the first cotton mill in northeastern South Carolina. Coker's brothers were Francis W., professor of political science and chairman of the department at Yale, and Edward C., professor of mathematics and astronomy at the University of South Carolina. A cousin, William C. Coker, was professor of botany at The University of North Carolina.

Coker was educated at St. David's Academy in Darlington, S.C., and spent a year at South Carolina College (1892–93). From The University of North Carolina, he earned his bachelor's degree and Phi Beta Kappa honors in 1896 and his M.S. in 1897, serving as an assistant in biology from 1895 to 1897. He taught in South Carolina for a year and from 1898 until 1901 served as principal of the Goldsboro public school, where he instituted a plan of student government.

Beginning his scientific studies of oysters and the diamond-back terrapin in 1902, Coker put together a plan to develop North Carolina's coastal fisheries. In 1905 he submitted the plan, asking that state laws be changed so that private individuals could lease oyster beds. He felt that oysters could be grown at a profit under well-defined conditions that maintained a balance of all factors involved. During the years he worked on this study (1902–4), he was custodian of the U.S. Fisheries Biological Laboratory in Beaufort, N.C., and biologist of the North Carolina Geologic and Economic Survey Center.

After completing his Ph.D. at Johns Hopkins in 1906, he turned down the offer of the prestigious Bruce Fellowship for postdoctoral study and instead accepted a position from the government of Peru to develop the country's nitrate industry and marine fisheries. From 1906 to 1908, by balancing all factors, he and his associates boosted the guano bird population 300 percent and raised the fertilizer output from 25,000 tons to 125,000 tons annually.

Coker served as the official representative of the Peruvian government and as vice-president for the Fourth International Fisheries Congress in Washington in 1908. Remaining in the United States, he joined the U.S. Bureau of Fisheries Biological Laboratory at Fairport, Iowa, in 1909, as a scientific assistant. During his years there he studied fish and mussels in the Mississippi basin, trying to determine under what conditions mussels, then the basis of the button industry, could survive and increase. From 1915 to 1922 he was chief of the Division of Scientific Inquiry of the Bureau of Fisheries, and from 1920 to 1922 he served as chairman of the International Marine Fisheries Commission.

In 1922, Coker accepted a position as a professor of zoology at Chapel Hill. Generations of the university's biology and premedical students took his general survey of vertebrate zoology. He pioneered the courses in hydrobiology in the 1920s and, later, introductory courses in oceanography. From 1935 until 1944 he served as chairman of his department, and during the same period he was chairman of the Division of Natural Sciences. He was on the Chancellor's Advisory Committee from 1945 to 1947 and also served on the Advisory Board of the School of Medicine (1930–47) and on the University Research Council (1936–47). In 1939 he was awarded a Kenan Professorship.

During the twenties and thirties, Coker spent summers at Biological stations at Mountain Lake, Va.; Beaufort, N.C.; and Woods Hole, Mass. Between 1927 and 1935 he directed and taught summer sessions at the Allegheny School of Natural Science at Quaker Bridge, N.Y.

In 1947, at the time of his retirement from teaching, he accepted Dr. Frank Porter Graham's offer to organize an Institute of Fisheries Research. In 1946 he was chairman of the Survey of Marine Fisheries; he served as director of the institute in 1947 and 1948 and as chairman of the executive committee from 1948 until 1953. The institute building was named in his honor, and in 1950 he received the O. Max Gardner Award for service in the organization of the fisheries survey and the institute.

From 1954 until 1963, Coker served as visiting professor and consultant in marine biology at the University of Puerto Rico, playing a leading role in the founding of a new laboratory, the Institute of Marine Biology at Mayaguez, and in the organizing of the International Association of Island Marine Laboratories in the Caribbean.

From 1926 to 1929, Coker was chairman of the Committee on Aquiculture of the National Research Council. Out of the committee grew the Limnological Society of America, which he served as vice-president in 1935 and president in 1938. During his career he was president of two other national societies, the American Society of Zoologists in 1941 and the Ecological Society of America in 1937. In 1939 he was elected president of the American Biological Society but resigned because of university and National Research Council responsibilities. He was president from 1929 to 1930 of the Elisha Mitchell Scientific Society and in 1941 of the North Carolina Academy of Science.

In addition to the Aquiculture committee, Coker was chairman of the Division of Biology and Aquiculture of the National Research Council from 1936 to 1940. He was a fellow of the American Association for the Advancement of Science and a member of its Council on Human Relations. He worked with the U.S. Forest Service and the U.S. Public Health Service and from 1940 to 1942 served as a member of the National Advisory Committee on Gerontology. He was a member of the Chicago Academy of Science of the American Fisheries Society and the Association of Southeastern Biologists. He also belonged to Sigma Xi, Phi Beta Kappa, and Chi Psi.

Coker published extensively. His major contributions to scientific research dealt with life in fresh and salt water, especially with the oyster, freshwater mussels, and small freshwater crustacea. Two of his books are basic to the field of zoology, *This Great and Wide Sea* (for which he received the Mayflower Cup in 1947) and *Streams, Lakes and Ponds*.

In 1948, Coker was awarded an honorary Sc.D. from the University of South Carolina; in 1959 he received an honorary LL.D. from The University of North Carolina. A Commemorative dinner was given by The University of North Carolina on 4 June 1966 to celebrate Coker's ninetieth birthday, which coincided with commencement and with the seventieth reunion of his class.

Coker was an Episcopalian. On 11 Oct. 1910 he married Jennie Louise Coit (24 Mar. 1883–9 June 1972) of Cheraw, S.C. There were two children, Robert Ervin (3 Aug. 1911–31 July 1966) and Coit McLean (11 Jan. 1914–19 Mar. 1960). Coker died in Chapel Hill and was buried in the old Chapel Hill Cemetery. The Institute on Fisheries has an oil portrait by Isabel Bowen.

SEE: *Chapel Hill Weekly*, 15 June 1966, 11 Jan. 1967, 4 Oct. 1967; Mrs. R. E. Coker (Chapel Hill), personal contact; Drawing by William Meade Prince and photographs (possession of Mrs. R. E. Coker); *Durham Morning Herald*, 3 Oct. 1967; *Greensboro Daily News*, 12 Dec. 1954; Almonte Charles Howell, *The Kenan Professorships* (1956); H. Eugene Lehman, "Robert Ervin Coker," *Journal of the Elisha Mitchell Scientific Society* 84 (1968); Library, University of North Carolina, Chapel Hill, for bibliography of Coker's publications; *North Carolina Authors* (1952); *Who Was Who in America*, vol. 5 (1973).

MARTHA B. CALDWELL

Coker, William Chambers *(24 Oct. 1872–27 June 1953)*, university professor, was born in Hartsville, S.C. His father, Major James Lide Coker, born at nearby Society Hill, was educated at the Citadel in Charleston and spent one year at Harvard working with Asa Gray and Louis Agassiz. The major, one of South Carolina's most successful businessmen, was also a leader in education, helping in the establishment of the public school system in South Carolina and founding Coker College for Women at Hartsville. William's mother, Susan Armstrong Stout, was the daughter of the Reverend Platt Stout, a Baptist minister of Carlowville, Ala.

From Coker's early childhood, his interest in nature was shared and encouraged by his father. His early schooling was given by a governess in the Coker home, and later he attended a small college preparatory school in Hartsville. He entered the University of South Carolina in 1891, being graduated in 1894. That year he began working as a runner in the Atlantic National Bank at Wilmington, N.C., where he rose to become one of the vice-presidents in 1896. In 1897 he decided to give up banking and do graduate work at Johns Hopkins University. After receiving the Ph.D. with high distinction in 1901, he spent a semester in Eduard Strasburger's laboratory at Bonn-am-Rhine, Germany. In the fall of 1902 he joined the faculty of The University of North Carolina as associate professor of botany, and there he served continuously until his retirement in 1945.

In the Chapel Hill area, Coker found a region rich botanically but largely unexplored. He began work on the local flora and published within a year a list of the woody plants of Chapel Hill. This interest, continued and expanded with the help of H. R. Totten, led to the publication of *Trees of North Carolina* in 1916 and of *Trees of the Southeastern States* in 1934 (3rd ed., 1945). Coker's other important publications on the higher plants were *Vegetation of the Bahama Islands* (1905) and *The Plant Life of Hartsville, S.C.* (1912). In its ecological treatment, the latter was significantly ahead of its time. His papers on teaching science in the high schools, the Venus flytrap, algae, bryophytes, and ferns, as well as several exceedingly interesting sketches of the lives of southern botanists, show the great diversity of his interests.

During a period of about 51 years, Coker produced 137 publications. As a botanist, however, he will be remembered longest for his researches on fungi. Out of 58 publications on fungi, the most noteworthy are "The Amanitas in the Eastern United States", *The Clavarias of the United States and Canada*, "The Gasteromycetes of the United States and Canada" (with J. N. Couch), *The Boletaceae of North Carolina* and *The Stipitate Hydnums of the Eastern United States* (the last two with Alma Holland Beers). In spite of his prodigious researches on the higher fungi, Coker's reputation as a mycologist rests largely on his work on the *Saprolegniaceae*, begun in 1908 and reaching its climax in the 1923 publication of *The Saprolegniaceae*, a work that has had world-wide influence in stimulating researches on the aquatic fungi.

All five of Coker's books were first published by The University of North Carolina Press, and all were later reprinted by commercial houses.

Coker's eminence as a botanist brought him honors too numerous to list. Briefly, he was elected chairman of the Mycological Section of the Botanical Society of America in 1927; in 1950 he was vice-president of the Mycological Section of the Sixth International Plant Congress at Stockholm, Sweden; and he was the first chairman of the Southeastern Section of the Botanical Society of America.

Coker also had a remarkable talent in landscape architecture, which he constantly improved by study and practice. Soon after he arrived in Chapel Hill he obtained permission of the university authorities to develop about six acres of boggy wasteland on what was then the eastern edge of the campus, the present Coker Arboretum. This unsightly area was gradually transformed into a natural garden featuring mostly native shrubs and trees. For thirty years, Coker was chairman and the inspiration of the Building and Grounds Committee, and his good judgment and taste were reflected in dignified, uncrowded buildings softened by informal plantings. For several years he carried on experiments with grasses in an attempt to find a mixture of seed suitable to keep the lawns of Chapel Hill green throughout the year. When finally a mixture was selected, a pamphlet was published telling in great detail how to prepare and fertilize the ground and plant the seed.

Coker's major interest in teaching was the course in general botany, and as an undergraduate instructor he ranked high. The excellence of the laboratories was due mainly to his insistence that the students have plenty of fresh and interesting plant material with which to work, and field trips were used to supplement lectures and the laboratory.

Coker's advanced classes rarely had more than three or four students, each of whom had a table in the research laboratory along with the professor. Such small classes were conducted informally, the students doing the lecturing by giving reports of research papers related to the work being done in the laboratory. Coker was never too hurried to look at something of interest a student had found, and he had a rare ability to stimulate the student to want to find out more for himself and to believe in the importance of what he was doing. This inspirational power derived partly from Coker's own sense of his work as important. Until his health began to fail, he devoted himself almost entirely to it, and one of his most distinctive characteristics was his single-minded devotion to his work.

Coker remained a bachelor until 28 Oct. 1934, when he married Louise Manning Venable, daughter of President Francis P. Venable.

SEE: *Chapel Hill Weekly*, 3 July 1953; Helen K. Hennig, *Great South Carolinians* (1949); A. C. Howell, *The Kenan Professorships* (1956); *Journal of the New York Botanical Garden*, 21 (1920); Raleigh *News and Observer*, 18, 28 June 1953, 14 Aug. 1953; George Lee Simpson, *The Cokers of Carolina* (1956); Gary E. Trawick and Paul B. Wyche, *100 Years, 100 Men* (1971); *Who Was Who in America* (1960); *Who's Who in the South and Southwest* (1950).

JOHN N. COUCH

Colburn, Burnham Standish *(10 Dec. 1872–26 Dec. 1959)*, banker, bridge builder, and real estate developer, was born in Detroit, Mich., to William Cullen Colburn and his wife, Mary Augusta Standish Colburn. A Mayflower ancestor was Myles Standish.

Colburn was educated at the University of Michigan, receiving a B.S. in civil engineering in 1896. He joined the Detroit Bridge and Iron Works as a draftsman that same year. In 1898 he became resident engineer for the Victoria Jubilee Bridge in Montreal, and in 1900 he was one of the organizers of the Canadian Bridge Company of Walkerville, Ont., of which he was secretary-treasurer until 1911. From 1911 until 1913 he was vice-president of the People's State Bank of Detroit. During the First World War he served as a field director (major) in the American Red Cross in Pensacola, Fla.

In 1920 the Colburns moved to North Carolina. One of Colburn's first projects was to assist in organizing the Biltmore Estate Company, of which he served as vice-president and treasurer until 1936; this company developed Biltmore Forest. From 1933 to 1953 he was president of the First National Bank and Trust Company in Asheville, and after his retirement in 1953 he retained his position as chairman of the board of directors. At the time of the merger with the Union National Bank of Charlotte, forming the First Union National Bank of North Carolina, Colburn was named honorary chairman of the board of the new organization.

Colburn was instrumental in the founding of the Southern Appalachian Mineral Society, the Society of Mayflower Descendants of North Carolina, and the Archaeological Society of North Carolina. He brought to all his activities a warm, genial personality, a liveliness of mind, an energetic temperament, and frequent extensions of the hospitality of his home.

Colburn's interest in mineralogy dated from child-hood, his father having owned a large iron mine. Roaming throughout the Southern Appalachian region in North Carolina, he acquired a collection of North Carolina minerals rated as the finest of its kind in the country. He reopened at great personal expense of both time and money the Hiddenite Mine near Stony Point. Most of his collection was purchased in 1945 by friends and alumni of the University of South Carolina and presented to the university for permanent exhibition in the geology department. The remainder of the collection has been donated by Colburn's family to form the nucleus of the Burnham S. Colburn Memorial Mineral Museum in Asheville, sponsored by the Southern Appalachian Mineral Society.

Throughout his life, Colburn did all he could to foster knowledge of and interest in the mineral world. He became a member of the Mineralogical Society of America in 1930, and in December 1936, in recognition of his lifelong interest in minerals and his great kindness and generosity to amateurs and professionals alike, he was elected a fellow. He served as vice-president for the year 1939.

Colburn initially joined the Mayflower Society in Detroit, Mich., in 1905; he served as governor of the Michigan society from 1909 to 1911 and as deputy governor general for several years. In 1927 he joined the Massachusetts society as a life member, and he was also a member of the Francis Cooke Colony of the Florida Society, for he was a winter resident of Ormond Beach, Fla. The organization of the North Carolina Society in 1924 was the result of the efforts of Addison Pierce Munroe, Macon Rush Dunnagan, and Colburn. Colburn served as governor from 1924 until 1933, and under his leadership the society grew rapidly. He continued as historian of the society and remained an active member for the rest of his life, enjoying the genealogical work associated with the society. His valuable collection of genealogical books is at Duke, with duplicates in the society's library in Plymouth. Colburn also contributed to the society and to North Carolina assistance in the establishment of the prestigious Mayflower Cup,

presented to a North Carolina writer of nonfiction each year.

Colburn's activity in the Mayflower Society culmi-nated with his service as governor general of the national society for two terms, from 1933 until 1939. Despite the depression, the society grew under Colburn's leader-ship, with three new state societies added. During his tenure in office the *Mayflower Quarterly* was begun, with the first edition dated 15 Oct. 1935. Colburn served as editor until July 1939.

After his death, the Society of Mayflower Descendants of North Carolina established a memorial to him, which took the form of furnishings for the Myles Standish House in Plymouth and a tablet there to Colburn's memory. The dedicatory service of the Standish House was held on 22 May 1965.

Colburn was active in the Archaeological Society of North Carolina—indeed, the organizational meeting was held in his home in 1934. His fine collection of Cherokee artifacts was sold to Samuel Beck of Asheville and through his generosity has come to form a part of the museum of the Cherokee Indians in Cherokee, N.C.

Colburn held membership in Psi Upsilon, the Asheville Civitan Club, Pen and Plate, and the Biltmore Forest Country Club. He served as president of the board of trustees of the Asheville School. He was a deacon of the First Presbyterian Church and a Republican. Interest in the Pack Memorial Library of Asheville led him to donate a rare Bible, an ancient map of the British colonies, and an 1875 circular promoting a bond issue to finance a railroad in Buncombe County.

On 21 Nov. 1900, Colburn married Elizabeth Grosvenor Pierce of Sturgeon Point, N.Y. The couple had five children, William Cullen, Elizabeth G. (Mrs. E. Wrayford Willmer), Burnham Standish, Mrs. Evelyn Colburn Thorn, and Mary Louise (Mrs. J. Frazier Glenn, Jr.). Colburn died in Asheville and was buried in the cemetery there. A portrait is in the home of Mrs. J. Frazier Glenn, Jr., of Asheville.

SEE: Waldo Morgan Allen, "In Memoriam: Burnham Standish Colburn," *Mayflower Quarterly*, 25 Feb. 1960; *Asheville Citizen*, 22 Nov. 1931, 16 and 17 Jan. 1959, 27 and 28 Dec. 1959, 24 July 1960, 20 Sept. 1971; *Asheville Times*, 29 Dec. 1959; *Charlotte Observer*, 11 Nov. 1934; Sturgis E. Leavitt, *A History of the Society of Mayflower Descendants in the State of North Carolina* (1966), and "Tribute—North Carolina Society," *Mayflower Quarterly*, 25 Feb. 1960; Waldemar T. Schaller, "Memorial of Burnham Standish Colburn," *American Mineralogist* 46 (1961); *Who's Who in Commerce and Industry*, vol. 5 (1936); *Who Was Who in America*, vol. 3 (1960).

MARTHA B. CALDWELL

Cole, Stephen William *(1 Jan. 1813–19 Sept. 1889),* planter and banker, son of William Terry and Judith Moseley Leake Cole, was born in Fayetteville. His father, a soldier of the War of 1812, was a member of the Fayetteville Light Infantry stationed at Wilmington. He died of yellow fever there at the age of twenty-six. Stephen's mother removed to Rockingham, a town built on a site donated by Stephen's great-grandfather, who came from Pennsylvania in about 1750.

At eighteen, Stephen Cole married Tabitha Randall Ledbetter, a daughter of a Methodist minister. Soon afterward they purchased a large plantation, Rural Retreat, six miles from Wadesboro. Inheritance of a large estate and devotion to business helped Cole to secure a prominent position in the community. He became a major in the county militia, and friends thereafter called him Major Cole. Appointed chairman of the county court and of the board of county commissioners, he also organized the first bank of Wadesboro in 1850. In 1852, a new home was built for him four miles from Rural Retreat in Ansonville, where he helped in establishing a college for young women, Carolina Female College. It was in operation from 1850 until 1867, when war and fever resulted in its decline.

Cole bought land in Florida and Arkansas with the idea of establishing colonies for his slaves. Florida proved undesirable, but one of his servants remained in Arkansas twenty-five years after the Civil War. Cole was overage for any military service in the war but gave aid to the needy and held his local positions. Although the war left him poor, his rare business tact and good judgment helped him to renew his old pursuits.

On 17 Sept. 1858, Cole's wife died. He returned to Rural Retreat with one daughter, while the other two married and moved to Salisbury. He joined them there eleven years later with a new bride, Sallie Farrer Shelton of Louisa County, Va. With his past financial experience, Cole founded the First National Bank of Salisbury in 1883. He was named president and held that position until his death. In 1887 he aided in the establishment of a cotton factory in Salisbury.

Cole was deeply interested in helping young men get a start in the business world. He was a consistent member of the Methodist church and spent many of his leisure hours reading. The bank, to which he gave untiring attention, was the pride of his later days.

SEE: Samuel A. Ashe, ed., *Biographical History of North Carolina*, vol. 4 (1906); James S. Brawley, *The Rowan Story* (1953).

KATHLEEN M. REA

Cole, Willard Glover (*24 Aug. 1906–28 May 1965*), newspaper editor, was born in Wilkes County, the son of Maria Dumgarner and Thomas H. Cole. He graduated from high school in North Wilkesboro and began his journalistic career at the age of twenty, when he joined the staff of the *Journal-Patriot* in North Wilkesboro. Soon he was editor of the *Ashe County Journal*. He returned home briefly to serve as editor of the *Journal-Patriot* before becoming a reporter for the *Winston-Salem Journal*. He then spent five years in Panama working for a road construction company; in the 1930s he returned to North Carolina to become secretary of the Tabor City Merchants Association. In 1948 he became editor of the Whiteville *News-Reporter*, a Columbus County weekly.

In 1950, Cole and editor Horace Carter of the *Tabor City Tribune* began a crusade against the Ku Klux Klan, which had recently become active in Columbus County. In response to many acts of terrorism and intimidation, the two newspapers published incessant attacks on the nightriders. Regularly threatened by the Klan, Cole carried a gun when he answered his door at night. His anti-Klan editorials assailed the organization for its secrecy and its vigilante violence. One Klansman said of him: "I guessed we despised the editor of the Whiteville *News-Reporter* most. . . . His criticism never ceased for one moment against the KKK." In the aftermath of Klan violence, over eighty Klansmen were arrested on kidnapping and assault charges; nearly all were convicted with sentences ranging up to six years. The two editors, Cole and Carter, shared the Pulitzer Prize for Meritorious Public Service in 1953 and also received various other service awards. In their successful efforts against the KKK, editors Cole and Carter ably

demonstrated the potential of small-town journalism as a positive, amelioristic force in the community. Cole, the older of the two and controller of the larger newspaper, led the fight.

Cole left Whiteville shortly after the Klan crusade and became editor of the *Lumberton Post* in Robeson County. In 1963 he founded and became editor of the *Robeson County Enterprise*, a semiweekly with offices in Lumberton. He was working in this capacity when he became fatally ill in 1965.

Cole was survived by his widow, Mary Frances Donnelly, whom he had divorced but remarried several years later; by a son, Willard John; and by a daughter, Mrs. Jean Burnette. He was buried in the Donnelly family cemetery in Ashe County.

SEE: Hamlet *News-Messenger*, 8 Oct. 1958; Raleigh *News and Observer*, 5 May 1952, 10 May 1953, 11 June 1953, 29 May 1965; *Time*, 11 May 1953.

JERRY LANIER

Coleman, Mary Channing (*11 July 1883–1 Oct. 1947*), educator, was born near South Boston, Va. Her grandfathers were Ethelbert Algernon Coleman, a physician and planter, and Frederick Winslow Page, librarian of the University of Virginia. Her father was John Mabrey Coleman and her mother, Evelyn Byrd Page. She grew up in the town of South Boston and at age fifteen entered the state Female Normal School of Farmville, Va. On completing the two-year teacher's course, she taught two years at the one-room Birch School near South Boston. In 1902 she moved to New York City, where she was employed until 1908 as a secretary and later as an office assistant to Dr. Walter Truslow, an orthopedic surgeon. Truslow encouraged her to continue her college training.

In 1908 she entered the Boston Normal School of Gymnastics, where she was much influenced by Amy Morris Homans, the school's director and a pioneer in American women's physical education. The BNSG became affiliated with Wellesley College in 1909, and Mary Coleman finished her two-year course at Wellesley. After completion of this training, she was head of the department of physical education at Winthrop College, Rock Hill, S.C., from 1910 to 1913; supervisor of the public schools of Detroit, Mich., from 1913 to 1916; teaching assistant in the Practical Arts School, Columbia University, 1916–17; and head of the physical education department at Margaret Morrison College of the Carnegie Institute of Technology, Pittsburgh, Pa., from 1917 to 1920. In 1917 she received the B.S. degree from Teachers College, Columbia University.

In September 1920, Miss Coleman became director of physical education at the state Normal and Industrial School of North Carolina (now The University of North Carolina at Greensboro). For twenty-seven years she administered the physical education program there, accomplishing during her tenure the first program for professional preparation of physical education teachers in North Carolina, the construction of two gymnasiums, and the organization, with Guy B. Phillips, of the North Carolina High School Girls Athletic Association. She wrote the first book on physical education published in North Carolina, *Lessons in Physical Education for Elementary Grades*, and in 1921 organized and became president of the first physical education society in the state.

During her years at the Woman's College, Mary Channing Coleman was active and also highly respected in the organizations of her profession. She was a program participant in many state, regional, and national conventions. In 1932 she was the first woman president of the Southern Section of the American Physical Education Association; she was vice-president and then second woman president of the American Physical Education Association in 1933 and 1934; and she was a member of the Greensboro Recreation Commission from 1933 to 1946.

As a teacher she was knowledgeable, stimulating, inspiring, and strict. Her general aloofness was tempered by kindness and sympathy. Her chief concern in her profession was to emphasize physical education as an integral part of the education of all children.

Miss Cole enriched her life and teaching by travel through most of the Western world. She was a member of the Episcopal church. She died in Greensboro but was buried at Ware Episcopal Church, Va. There is a portrait in the Coleman Memorial Library in the Coleman Gymnasium, constructed in 1952 and named in her honor, at The University of North Carolina, Greensboro.

SEE: Elizabeth C. Umstead, "Mary Channing Coleman" (Ph.D. diss., University of North Carolina, 1967).

ELIZABETH C. UMSTEAD

Coleman, Thaddeus Charles (15 Jan. 1837–21 Jan. 1895), Confederate Army engineer colonel and resident engineer for the completion of the Western North Carolina Railroad, was born on his father's farm seven miles north of Asheville near Weaverville. He was the son of William Coleman, a native of Cabarrus County, and of Ann Evelyn Baird of Buncombe County. His father for a time was postmaster at Asheville; Thaddeus and his brothers became Confederate officers and professional men. Thaddeus was prepared for college by Colonel Stephen Lee, a West Point graduate, and entered the junior class at The University of North Carolina. After his graduation he remained as a tutor in mathematics in 1856–57, but shortly afterward he became a civil engineer with the Western North Carolina Railroad, then under construction from Morganton to Asheville.

At the beginning of the Civil War, Coleman became a first lieutenant in the Tenth North Carolina Regiment; by the end of the war he was a lieutenant colonel with the Fifty-eighth Regiment. He served in 1862 under Confederate chief engineer Brigadier General Jeremy F. Gilmer in building defense earthworks near Petersburg, Richmond, Charleston, and Savannah. On General D. H. Hill's transfer to North Carolina, Coleman saw combat duty near Goldsboro and Washington. When he served on Hill's staff at Chickamauga, his gentle manner coupled with bravery under fire drew favorable comment. He supervised construction of earthworks for the retreat of General Albert S. Johnston's army and later at Bentonville led one of the last gallant charges as a combat colonel.

At the end of the war, Coleman returned home, married Mary Elizabeth Sloan of Greensboro, and continued living on the family farm north of Asheville. The Colemans' daughter Sarah married William Sydney Porter of Greensboro, better known as the writer O. Henry. Other children were Evelyn, who married William Coleman, and James Sloan, who remained on the family farm and reared a family of three children.

In 1866, Coleman was assistant engineer on the Charleston, Cleveland, and Cincinnati Railroad, with headquarters at Morristown, Tenn. In 1868 he returned to North Carolina as assistant engineer for the Western

North Carolina Railroad's Blue Ridge section. In 1871 he became chief engineer for this project, charged with changing the intricate location on the face of the Blue Ridge east of Swannanoa Tunnel. In 1874 he was chosen chief engineer of the Spartanburg-Asheville line and surveyed locations for climbing the Blue Ridge. He advised a longer route around Tryon Mountain, but shortage of funds dictated the steeper grade over Saluda Mountain.

Under the pseudonym Winstanley, Coleman published a volume of poems, *The Land of the Sky*, which he inscribed to Christian Reid. This twenty-two-page pamphlet, with no indication of its date, was printed in Asheville.

A few years before his death, Coleman retired to his birthplace; he was buried in the family cemetery there.

SEE: Sondley Collection (Public Library, Asheville), for statement of A. C. Avery and quotations from Asheville and Greensboro newspapers.

GEORGE MYERS STEPHENS

Coleman, Warren Clay (28 Mar. 1849–31 Mar. 1904), manufacturer, was the illegitimate son of Rufus Clay Barringer, afterward a Confederate general, and Roxanna Coleman, a slave owned by Daniel Coleman, Sr., of Concord. Prior to her marriage to John F. Young, a household slave and blacksmith, Roxanna had two sons, Thomas Clay and Warren Clay, by Barringer. A third illegitimate son, Joseph Smith, followed Roxanna's break with Barringer. When slaves married, it was generally accepted that the man's master would purchase the woman; contrary to this usual practice, Roxanna's husband became a slave on the Coleman estate, and the black family was maintained there as a unit. Barringer was the descendant of French Huguenots who migrated from France during the early seventeenth century to England and Germany. His grandfather, John Paul Barringer, settled in Dutch Buffalo Creek, now a part of Cabarrus County. Rufus Barringer attended The University of North Carolina, read law under Chief Justice Richmond M. Pearson, and represented Cabarrus County in the House of Commons from 1848 to 1850. He provided inspiration and financial assistance in Coleman's early business ventures and in his establishment of a cotton mill. He also guided Coleman's early development.

Coleman's first twenty-one years were consumed by a dull routine of slavery and farm work that constrained his highly motivated personality. During the Civil War, he worked for the Confederacy, making boots and shoes. With emancipation, he was bound to William M. Coleman, a Cabarrus planter-lawyer who later became North Carolina's attorney general. Coleman educated and trained young Warren until 28 Mar. 1870, when Warren was released. Warren went to Alabama for a year, seeking economic opportunity. He returned to Concord in 1871 and began his business career, starting as a collector of rags, bones, and junk and becoming one of Concord's richest merchants. From 1873 to 1874 he attended Howard University as a student in the Model School, preparing himself for business opportunities.

Coleman's first business was a combination barber shop and cake and candy store. Under his father's guidance, he bought land in the black areas of Concord and erected cheap frame rental houses. Between 1875 and 1904 he developed nearly one hundred rentals; he purchased four farms and a substantial number of city lots, thereby becoming one of Cabarrus County's largest property owners and most influential citizens.

In 1875, Coleman married Jane E. Jones. In 1879 he combined his two shops into a large general store that became one of Concord's major retail establishments. A proud and frugal man who sought wealth and fame, he extended his influence into North Carolina's black community. He was a member of the North Carolina Industrial Association, a Negro group seeking to develop black-owned businesses. He subsequently became the association's vice-president, treasurer, and president.

By 1895, Coleman was considered one of the South's richest blacks. He helped found the National Negro Protective Association and assisted black education at Howard University, Livingstone College, and Shaw University. He supported the North Carolina Oxford Orphans' Home and aided Professor R. M. Alexander in developing the Coleman School in Welford, S.C. His philanthropy extended to the Zion Hill Church and Price Memorial Temple in Concord.

Coleman's major contribution was his organization of Coleman Manufacturing Company, the nation's first black-owned and operated textile factory. In mid-June 1896 he tested the climate for a black-owned mill. Prominent white textile leaders, spearheaded by Washington Duke, supported his efforts. Coleman initially sought to raise stock subscriptions from black supporters, but they lacked the economic base to sustain such a venture, and he was forced to borrow from the Duke family. Initially, Coleman's venture enjoyed some success, but basic financial frailties and external market conditions overwhelmed the mill. The mill was underfinanced and opened with secondhand machinery. The ensuing results were predictable and were accelerated by Coleman's sudden death. Duke's notes matured, and the cotton mill was forced into bankruptcy. Coleman's dream, which had included plans for a black community to surround the manufacturing facility, generating black political power out of black capitalism, had ended. The mill operated for a brief period under white supervision but was sold at auction in late June 1904.

SEE: Marvin Krieger, "Warren Clay Coleman" (M.A. thesis, Wake Forest University, 1969).

MARVIN KRIEGER

Coley, Henry D. *(1819?–1887),* North Carolina state librarian, was a native of Connecticut. He was appointed state librarian in 1868 and held the position until February 1871. For thirty years prior to his appointment he worked in some of the largest bookstores of the South, including the North Carolina Bookstore operated in Raleigh by Henry D. Turner. Coley married Eleanor Stuart in 1845 and the union produced seven children.

SEE: Jerry Cross, "Historical Research Report for the Andrew Johnson Birthplace, Part 2," Appendix L (North Carolina State Archives, Raleigh); *Fourth Annual Report of the Auditor of Public Accounts* (Document No. 4, *Executive and Legislative Documents, 1871–1872*); Jonathan Worth Papers (North Carolina State Archives, Raleigh).

MAURY YORK

Collet (Collett), John Abraham *(fl. 1756–89),* a Swiss military engineer, map maker, captain in the British army, and governor of Fort Johnston, N.C., was probably from Geneva, where his widowed mother, a Moravian, was living in 1768. In the French service during the Seven Years' War (1756–63), Collet served in

six campaigns; for the next four years he studied mathematics, drawing, and fortification. He was recommended to Earl Shelburne, secretary of state for the Southern Department, and Viscount William Barrington, secretary at war, by Mr. and Mrs. Henry Grenville as of an "extreme good character and of a very honest, prudent disposition." In May 1767, George III appointed him an army captain and governor of Fort Johnston, at the mouth of the Cape Fear River.

On 4 Nov. Collet presented his credentials to Governor William Tryon at Brunswick. Collet was, with justification, dismayed by what he found. The fort was in "ruinous condition"; no salary was attached to his army commission; and the North Carolina assembly was in no mood, then or later, to vote pay to a British officer or to expend funds on the fort. The only emolument was a nominal health tax on shipping entering the Cape Fear River, a pittance amounting to less than thirty pounds a year. Captain John Dalrymple, the former army commandant, had died suddenly the year before, and Tryon had appointed a wealthy nearby planter, Robert Howe, to succeed him. At Tryon's suggestion, in order to mollify Howe's resentment at his replacement, Collet appointed him second in command and allowed him to retain the shipping tax and quarters in the fort. Before the end of the year, Collet drew a plan of the fort and made a detailed report on the repairs needed to make the fortification defensible. By the end of December, Tryon sent him to New York with the old great seal of the province, which by the royal warrant had to be returned upon receipt of the new seal. Tryon also wrote letters to Thomas Gage and Shelburne, recommending that Collet be made engineer of the Southern Department, with orders to make needed surveys of the coastal areas of the Carolinas. Collet returned from New York disappointed; Gage had neither authority nor funds to establish such a post. In February 1768, Collet wrote a long letter to Shelburne outlining the situation and his financial distress. In September 1768, Tryon appointed him an aide-de-camp on his expedition against the Regulators at Hillsborough, and Collet filled the position with such gallantry and merit that Tryon recommended him for higher service and, upon Collet's return to London early in December, entrusted him with a report on the conditions in the province.

With him, Collet took a manuscript map of North Carolina that extended to the recently established Indian boundary line and delineated the rivers, roads, and settlements in the western frontiers of the province. British authorities had for years urged the colonial governors to send them maps of their provinces, and North Carolina had not previously responded, although problems raised by frontier settlements were pressing. Collet's draft was basically a copy of an unfinished map willed to Tryon by William Churton, surveyor of the Granville District. Churton had died before its completion while surveying the Outer Banks in December 1768. Years before, Churton had contributed the information for the Granville District to Joshua Fry and Peter Jefferson's 1751 [1753] map of Virginia, adding information for its 1755 revision; he had continued to improve his map and enlarge the area it covered until the time of his death. Upon reaching London, Collet presented his manuscript to the king, who sponsored the engraved version that Collet published in 1770 at an actual loss, he wrote later, of five hundred pounds. "A Compleat Map of North-Carolina," 28⅝ × 43½ inches on a scale of 13¾ miles to an inch, was beautifully engraved by I. Bayly and published by S. Hooper. One of the finest provincial maps of the colonial period, it became the basis for the northern half of Henry Mouzon's "North and South Carolina" (1775) and of all other maps of North Carolina until the Price-Strother map of 1808. Although Collet's map of 1770 shows that he had made some surveys, added new details of the western frontiers, and assiduously collected information for the coastal area from Wimble's 1738 map and other sources, the map is essentially Churton's, compiled from twenty years of surveying.

In 1769, while in London, Collet wrote a description of Anson County, reporting on its roads, commerce, and potential agricultural opportunities; later, probably after his return to the province, he sold twenty-five thousand acres that had been granted to him in the center of that county. There is later evidence that he had ambitious plans for land development in North Carolina and South Carolina. In London, although George III employed him personally as a draftsman, Collet waited in vain to receive an appointment commensurate with his training and ability. In the summer of 1772, with disturbing reports from America, the secretary of war, Lord Barrington, ordered him back to resume his post at Fort Johnston.

Reaching North Carolina early in 1773, Collet found the fort in worsened condition. With the approval of Tryon's successor, Governor Josiah Martin, he undertook to improve and strengthen the fortifications. He showed more zeal than caution and diplomacy, and Dartmouth, Lord Privy Seal, refused government aid for repairs made only "for the security and convenience of commerce of the colony." Unwisely, Collet went ahead; he had expended his own patrimony, and he went heavily into debt. He recruited in New York and transported to the fort fifty men for garrison; he improved the ramparts, built officers' quarters and two barracks for soldiers, bought timber and flagging, and made a hundred thousand bricks. The colonists looked upon these activities with growing suspicion and anger. Although Martin pressured the house of assembly into voting for part of Collet's expenditures, the money was not paid.

By 1775, Collet was "harassed by every means the Americans could devise." They bribed his garrison to desert, finally leaving him with only three or four on whom he could rely of a remaining twelve, and they hindered him from obtaining food and provisions. Infuriated and goaded into rashness, he confiscated the grain on a vessel wrecked nearby, Captain Alexander McGregor's snow. Despite Martin's advice, he kept the grain and contemptuously tore up a writ served on him from the office of the attorney general of the province. These incidents formed the chief accusations in an inflammatory "Letter of the People" to Governor Martin, published 10 July 1775. Since March, increasing rumors of a planned attack on the fort came to the ears of the governor and of Collet; by 15 July the patriot Robert Howe, Collet's predecessor at the fort, was on the way with a troop of militia to take the fort. The governor had taken refuge on the armed sloop *Cruizer* offshore from the fort; he ordered the removal of the fort's cannon, sent by General Gage, as the ammunition had not yet arrived. Collet hastily loaded all the military supplies onto a small transport; on 19 July he saw from the transport a large rebel force enter the fort and destroy all the buildings. They burned his house and stables adjacent to the fort and looted his horses, cattle, carriages, furniture, and other property at a loss, he later claimed, of fifty-nine hundred pounds.

Collet sailed on 21 July to Boston, where he delivered his military cargo to Gage's headquarters. He was immediately assigned to the recruitment and command of "several companies of Volunteers and Light Infantry"; within a month he had enlisted, paid bounty money for, clothed, and drilled 145 men, going into debt a further £1732. But by "an unforseen and cruel circumstance," a new arrival from England, Lieutenant Colonel Joseph Goreham, came with orders to raise a regiment, the Royal American Fencibles, into which Collet and his men were absorbed.

Collet obtained revenge in North Carolina, however, in the southern campaign of 1776 under Sir Henry Clinton: he returned to the Cape Fear on 12 Mar. aboard the armed vessel *General Gage* and, landing with troops, "that pert little scoundrel" burned the mansion of William Dry in Brunswick; of his unfinished home three miles below Wilmington, William Hooper said, "That hopeful youth made a Bonfire of a country house of mine." On 12 May two regiments under Clinton and Cornwallis landed and destroyed the house of Continental General William Howe, leader of the rebels who had burned the fort and Collet's house.

Sailing north to Nova Scotia under Goreham, Collet returned to New York with Sir William Howe and took part in the attacks on Long Island, the taking of New York, and skirmishes in the Jerseys and at Knightsbridge that fall. Again in Nova Scotia, he was in command of Fort Edward and then cabinet engineer of the general at Halifax. In 1778 he was appointed chief engineer, but rumors of his extravagance apparently prevented confirmation. He was at Fort Cumberland (1777–80) and Fort Howe (1781) in Nova Scotia and made a short campaign in Canada under General Frederick Haldimand.

After his return to England, records of Collet's activities become increasingly sparse. In 1782 he submitted a lengthy proposal for recruiting a regiment of French and German soldiers and officers, with himself as colonel. In the same year, and again later, he submitted memorials to the Treasury for debts incurred in military expenditures in North Carolina and Boston; because an endorsement, dated 6 Nov. 1789, notes that Collet's demand is denied "for expenditures at the fort before the war and is chargeable to the province," it is doubtful that he ever received much compensation. In 1786 he wrote to Lord Shelburne requesting support for a map of Nova Scotia that he was dedicating to the king with royal permission; such a map has not been identified. Thereafter Collet fades from view.

Captain J. A. Collet's identity and career have been erroneously confused with those of two other John Collet(t)s. In 1776, George III appointed his "Trusty and wel beloved" John Collet as British consul at Genoa; from there the consul made reports during and after the war on French and Spanish naval actions in the Mediterranean. More confusing is the American career of John Collet, for twenty years a Philadelphia trader, who joined Lord Dunmore as lieutenant colonel of the Virginia Rangers, served in Browne's Florida Rangers and Carolina Rangers (1777–82), married a Mary Dupont of South Carolina in 1781, wrote memorials to the Loyalist Commission, and died in 1818, survived by his widow.

Collet had excellent qualities; he was energetic, ambitious, capable, and experienced as an officer and engineer. "Amiable and deserving," Governor Martin thought him, echoing the opinions of all earlier officials from Shelburne to Tryon. But he proved extravagant and arrogant at a time when restraint and conciliation were needed. His actions gave an opportunity for inflammatory and exaggerated accusations by patriot agitators;

later, Governor Martin also vigorously condemned his conduct as not based on "principles of justice, equity, and charity." Collet's very success in repairing Fort Johnston and his own unwise actions under stress in the spring of 1775 were the catalysts that precipitated the first rebellious military action in the province. His chief and most permanent achievement was his map of North Carolina.

SEE: E. W. Andrews and C. M. Andrews, eds., *Journal of a Lady of Quality* (1921); William L. Clements Library (University of Michigan, Ann Arbor), for Clinton Papers, Foreign Courts, Gage Papers (American and English Series), Manchester Papers, and Shelburne Papers; William P. Cumming, *North Carolina in Maps* (1966), and *The Southeast in Early Maps* (1958, 1962); Adelaide L. Fries, ed., *Records of the Moravians in North Carolina*, vol. 1 (1922); Historical Manuscripts Commission, *American MSS in the Royal Institution*, 4 vols. (1904–9); Lansdowne MSS 1219, ff. 83–86 (British Museum); Manuscript Division, Library of Congress, Washington, D.C., for sundry papers; North Carolina State Archives (Raleigh), for P.R.O. Sainsbury Transcripts; P.R.O. (London), A.O. 12/76, 101, 102; ibid., A.O. 13/118, ff. 204–8 (Collet Memorial); ibid., A.O. 118/118; ibid., A.O. Bundle 87; ibid., C.O. 324/15; ibid., Misc. Corr. 154/23–6; Hugh F. Rankin, *The North Carolina Continentals* (1971); William L. Saunders, ed., *Colonial Records of North Carolina*, 10 vols. (1886–90); Treasury (London), 1/646, ff. 212–13 (Collet Memorial); ibid., 52/65; ibid., 79/121.

WILLIAM P. CUMMING

Collins, Josiah, Sr. *(August 1735–14 May 1819)*, merchant, politician, manufacturer, and land speculator, was born in Taunton, Somersetshire, England, the son of Joan and David Collins. Little is known of his early life until he married Ann Lewis of Staffordshire in April 1761. The couple produced three children, Josiah II (b. 1763), Ann (b. 1764), and Elizabeth (b. 1769), before Mrs. Collins's death in 1770. Her death became the pivotal point in Collins's life. Leaving the young Elizabeth with relatives, the rest of the family sailed to Boston in 1773. After living in Providence, R.I., for a year, Collins relocated in Halifax, N.C. In 1777, Collins, apparently a nonparticipating Whig during the Revolution, moved to the scene of his success, the port of Edenton.

Collins quickly established himself as one of the foremost merchants of the new state. From 1777 to 1785 he was senior partner in the commercial and shipping firm of Collins, Stewart and Muir, before setting out on his own. He engaged in the export of tobacco, lye, and staves to Europe and the West Indies, in return for sugar, molasses, and rum. A rope manufacturing establishment fell into his hands in 1783; he turned its management over to his son, who built it into one of the nation's finest rope-making industries. Collins's shipping interests spread to the Mediterranean and the Orient. His employees included Captain Edward Preble, of Barbary War fame.

Despite his commercial success, Collins never remarried. His longing for England was demonstrated by a visit there of one year in 1791–92. Elizabeth Collins never came to America, having married a lawyer named Cook of Hatch, Beauchamp. Josiah II married Ann Rebecca Daves of New Bern, and this union produced Josiah III. The most important marriage was that of Ann to James Blount of Pitt County, which linked two of the most prominent families of late eighteenth- and early nineteenth-century North Carolina.

Collins had lived only a short time in North Carolina

before he began to assume various political offices. On 30 July 1779 he was appointed judge of the admiralty court for the Port of Edenton. During the Revolution he served the American cause on commissions for cannon, coast navigation, magazines, and other projects. In 1788 the state senate nominated him unsuccessfully for governor, and in November of that year he became a member of the council of state. He was elected to the same post in 1795. He was also a Federalist delegate to the 1788 Hillsborough convention.

Collins achieved his greatest fame as a land speculator. In 1755 hunters discovered Lake Phelps in Tyrrell County. The land surrounding the lake was deep in "the Great Alligator Dismal" swamp and attracted little interest. Eventually, a company to develop Lake Phelps was formed by W. R. Davie, Allen Jones, Nathaniel Allen, and others. This group received authorization from the legislature in 1784 to drain the seventeen-hundred-acre lake, but, although a preliminary survey was made, the project never materialized. In 1784, Collins entered into a verbal agreement with Allen and Dr. Samuel Dickinson, a minor partner in the enterprise, to acquire and develop land near Lake Phelps. It appears that the partnership, which came to be known as the Lake Company, was intended to coexist rather than compete with the original company; that group died out, however, and the legislature authorized the Lake Company to drain Lake Phelps in 1787. Collins and his partner apparently made no move in that direction. Instead they outfitted a Guineaman, which sailed to Africa to procure slaves for ditchdigging. By 1788 a six-mile-long canal, twenty feet wide, had been completed at a cost of thirty thousand dollars. Through grant and purchase, the company acquired 109,978 acres between the Scuppernong River and Lake Phelps. The 113 slaves the company owned by 1790 were employed building mills one quarter mile up the canal from the lake, and by 1794 two sawmills, a rice machine, and a gristmill were completed. Besides providing water power for the mills, the canals served for drainage, transportation, and irrigation for the rice culture. Originally producing rice and wheat, the Lake Company soon turned to corn as the primary crop, and the firm also produced lumber, staves, and shingles. The company flourished, owning in 1800 22 adult male slaves, 31 adult women, and "upwards of 20 boys and girls born in or since the year 1784." In 1816 the early North Carolina historian Hugh Williamson estimated the value of a third share of the Lake Company property at two hundred thousand dollars.

Despite this success, things did not go well for the partners. Allen and Dickinson became increasingly indebted to Collins, and Collins filed a suit of equity in 1794. Although the court ruled that Dickinson owed £4,000 and Allen £50, it did not order a settlement. This decision hastened Collins's desire to buy his partners' holdings, against the advice of such astute friends as Williamson. His task was eased in 1798, when Dickinson "made over to" Francis Peyrinnaut one half of his Lake Company holding. By November 1800, Peyrinnaut's lawyers advertised the sale of his sixth share, and Collins acquired it in early 1800 for $7764.50. After Dickinson's death, Collins in 1800 purchased the remainder of his portion from the estate for $5000. With the purchase of Allen's third in 1816 at a cost of $10,000, the land became Somerset Plantation, now a state historic site.

Collins had, of course, other landholdings besides the Lake Company. He lived and held property in Chowan County. In 1788 he owned 650 acres in what soon became

Tennessee, and after 1790 he acquired over 25,000 acres there. Collins's interest in accumulating landholdings far from North Carolina expressed itself in a desire to make a voyage to the "North-West of America" in 1790.

Although he amassed a large personal fortune, Collins was also a philanthropist. He was instrumental in the establishment of the Edenton Academy in 1800 and then helped restore St. Paul's Church in Edenton, then dangerously deteriorated. Among bequests of large landholdings and over sixty-five thousand dollars in cash, his will included a thousand dollars for St. Paul's and the same amount for the poor of Chowan County.

In 1805, Collins was the successful defendant in a test case in which the devisees of the Earl Granville attempted to regain the land of the old Granville tract.

SEE: Walter Clark, ed., *State Records of North Carolina*, 20 vols. (1895–1914); Josiah Collins Papers (North Carolina State Archives, Raleigh); *Edenton Gazette*, 19 Nov. 1800; Alice B. Keith, ed., *The John Gray Blount Papers*, vol. 1 (1952); William C. Poole, "An Economic Interpretation of the Ratification of the Federal Constitution in North Carolina," *North Carolina Historical Review* 27 (1950); Henry Potter, *Charge of Judge Potter to the Jury . . . Earl Granville against Josiah Collins* (1806); W. S. Tarlton, *Somerset Place and Its Restoration* (1954).

A. C. MENIUS III

Collins, Josiah, II (10 Nov. 1763–10 Feb. 1839), planter, merchant, and banker, the son of Josiah Collins, Sr., and his wife, Ann Lewis, was born at Islington, London. In 1773 he came with his father to America, where they lived for a year in Rhode Island and afterward in Halifax and Edenton, N.C. Somerset Plantation was left by Josiah, Sr., to Josiah III, but Josiah II operated the plantation for his son until he came of age. At Somerset, Josiah II built for himself a small house, known as the Colony House, and used it when he was there on business.

From 1788 or 1789, Collins lived at the Homestead in Edenton, where he was a merchant. He also operated a rope factory there and made superior cordage for shipbuilders. At a meeting in New Bern on 23 Apr. 1817, he was one of six laymen and three clergymen who organized the Episcopal Diocese of North Carolina.

In 1803, Collins married Ann Rebecca Daves, daughter of Major John Daves of New Bern. They were the parents of Anne Daves (1804–48), who married William Biddle Shepard of Elizabeth City; Mary Matilda (1806–37), who married Mathew Page, M.D., of Clark County, Va.; Josiah III (1808–63), married to Mary Riggs; Henrietta Elizabeth (1810–68), married to Mathew Page; Hugh Williamson (1812–54); John Daves (1815–ca. 1847); Louisa McKinley (b. 1817), who married first Thomas Harrison, M.D., of Brandon, Va., and second the Reverend William Stickney of Faunsdale, Ala.; and Elizabeth Alethea (b. 1824), who married Thomas Davis Warren, M.D., of Edenton.

Collins was buried in St. Paul's churchyard, Edenton.

SEE: John Gray Blount Papers (North Carolina State Archives, Raleigh); Robert Brent Drane Papers (Southern Historical Collection, University of North Carolina, Chapel Hill); William H. Masterson, ed., *The John Gray Blount Papers*, vol. 3 (1965); *Raleigh Register*, 25 Feb. 1839; William S. Tarlton, *Somerset Place and Its Restoration* (1954).

WILLIAM S. POWELL

Collins, Josiah, III (March 1808–17 June 1863), planter, the son of Josiah Collins II and his wife, Ann Rebecca Daves, was born probably in Edenton. Growing up with almost every conceivable advantage available to a youth in North Carolina at that time, the young Collins studied at Harvard and then read law at Litchfield, Conn. The completion of his education was signaled by his marriage to Mary Riggs of Newark, N.J., on 9 Aug. 1829. Ebenezer Pettigrew described the new Mrs. Collins as a "very amiable woman." Josiah Collins II spent some time preparing for the arrival of the newlyweds at Somerset Place on 5 Jan. 1830. Not satisfied with the two-story Colony House, the young Collins soon began construction of the large mansion that now constitutes the focal point of the Somerset Place State Historic Site.

Upon completion, the house became the setting for Collins's "aggressive type of hospitality," which some guests considered rather ludicrous. It was reported that "during a typical winter there were fourteen long-staying guests." Music, dances, and other sorts of entertainment were common during these periods. In the spring of 1857, for example, there were quadrilles every night. Despite their active social life, acquaintances described Mrs. Collins as reticent and her husband as increasingly moody and "domineering."

Collins quickly became politically active, though he apparently had little desire for public office. He served in the state senate for two sessions and was a member of the 1835 convention from Washington County. At the latter he was credited for being a "ready, skillful debator" and held the chair of the committee to arrange senatorial districts. He was a Harrison elector in 1840 and ran unsuccessfully for the House of Commons as a Whig from Washington County in 1850. The coming of the Civil War found Collins more than willing to defend his strongly antiabolitionist stance.

The Collinses traveled north in the spring of 1830 for the birth of their first child, Josiah IV. Of their six sons only three, Josiah IV, Arthur, and George, survived their childhood at Somerset Place: Edward and Hugh drowned in the canal in front of the house on 2 Feb. 1843, and William Kent died in a riding accident some years later. The survivors all served the South during the Civil War.

Wintering at the lake and touring the springs in the summer, the Collinses considered themselves rather cultured. Indeed, in 1845 they attempted to adopt French as the household language. Collins enjoyed reading aloud to his children so much that he organized a Monday night reading club that was active from about 1855 to 1860.

As had been the case with his father, religion occupied an important part of Collins's life. He was especially interested in the religious activities of his slaves, frequently reading the services to them. In 1836 he erected a chapel on the plantation and engaged E. M. Forbes to convert the slaves from Methodism to his own Episcopal church, a three-year process. In 1857 the Reverend George Patterson read the services of morning and evening prayer at Somerset Place.

At first, things apparently did not go particularly well at Lake Phelps. The crops were badly damaged during 1835 and 1836, causing Ebenezer Pettigrew to criticize Collins for neglecting the farm and playing the role of absentee planter. However, after converting to corn as the main crop, Collins became one of the three largest slaveholders in North Carolina: in 1860 his more than 4,000 acres were worked by 328 slaves. Collins did not appear to distinguish himself in other business activities. In 1836 he attempted to produce silk with Pettigrew on

Pea Ridge in the Albemarle Sound, but in 1842, after a deal with the Maryland Silk Company did not materialize, they began to liquidate their silk holdings.

The approach of the Civil War was an unhappy time for the Collins family. Collins became troubled by increasingly frequent headaches that served to make him more and more moody and erratic. Mrs. Collins suffered a stroke in 1860. Despite Collins's efforts to finance Washington County troops, the family and slaves were forced to flee Somerset Place, which fell in August 1862, for Hillsborough. The deserted plantation was frequently plundered throughout the duration of the hostilities. Collins died in Hillsborough shortly before the end of the war, and the efforts of Mrs. Collins and her sons to revitalize Somerset Place were unsuccessful. In 1870, two years before her death, Mrs. Collins sold the 4,428-acre holding to W. B. Shepard.

SEE: Elizabeth City *Economist*, 16 Apr. 1872; J. G. deRoulhac Hamilton, ed., *The Papers of William A. Graham*, 4 vols. (1957–61); Guion Johnson, *Ante-Bellum North Carolina* (1937); W. S. Tarlton, *Somerset Place and Its Restoration* (1954); John H. Wheeler, *Historical Sketches of North Carolina* (1851).

A. C. MENIUS III

Collins, Mordecai (22 Mar. 1785–25 July 1864), cabinetmaker, was born probably in Virginia, of unknown ancestry. His name first appears in Rowan County records on 3 Dec. 1809, in an entry stating that Collins purchased from John Scott 103 1/2 acres of land at a price of $200. This land lay on both sides of Reedy Branch, a prong of the Brushy Fork of Abbotts Creek in what is now Davidson County. The next entry regarding Collins, which establishes his trade, is in the Rowan court minutes of 6 Nov. 1810, recording that he took as apprentice John Swisegood "to learn the Cabinet and Joiners trade." Five entries in the Salem Community Store Journal of 1814–15 list accounts with Collins and purchases of locks, handles, glass, stain—articles used in cabinetmaking. This store was located in the Moravian community of Salem only a few miles from Collins's land.

To date, there have been six pieces of furniture—all corner cupboards—attributed to Collins. No known signed Collins piece has been found.

By 1816, Collins and his wife, Christina, had moved to Floyd County, Ind., and had purchased three tracts of land in the Greenville township. These purchases were made on 14 Apr., 9 May, and 25 June 1817. Additional transactions were recorded in Floyd County through 1843. There are no indications that Collins continued his cabinetmaking in Indiana; his land transactions indicate that he was primarily farming.

On 25 Aug. 1816, the Rowan County records show that Collins sold the 103 1/2 acres he purchased in 1809 to William Ledford for $450, a 125 percent profit. Land inherited by Christena from her father, David Byerly, was deeded to Lucy Byerly on 26 Nov. 1825, and this transaction finalized the relocation from North Carolina. A late North Carolina reference to Collins appeared in Salem's *Weekly Gleaner*, 6 Jan. 1829: "Collins, Mordecai" appeared in a list of names on letters unclaimed at the post office.

Collins and his wife, Christena Byerly of Davidson County, had at least six children. The family was among the organizers of St. John's Lutheran Church in Floyd County, Ind., and Collins was buried there in the churchyard.

SEE: Museum of Early Southern Decorative Arts (Winston-Salem), for references from research files; *The Swisegood School of Cabinetmaking* (1973).

WHALEY W. BATSON

Collins (Collens, Collings), William (d. ca. July 1709), justice of the general court and of Pasquotank Precinct Court, came to North Carolina before 1693. He was probably the son of William and Alice Collins, who at some earlier date settled in Perquimans Precinct with their three sons, Thomas, James, and William.

Collins was a justice of the Pasquotank Precinct Court in 1694 and 1697. The surviving records of that court do not show the length of his tenure, but he probably served at least in the intervening years.

On 20 Mar. 1699/1700, Collins was appointed justice of the North Carolina General Court. He held that office through November 1705.

Collins owned five hundred or more acres of land in Pasquotank Precinct. He died before 19 July 1709, when his will was probated. He apparently left no descendants. His widow, Elizabeth, later married Jonathan Jacocks.

SEE: J. Bryan Grimes, ed., *Abstract of North Carolina Wills* (1910); *North Carolina Historical and Genealogical Register*, 3 vols. (1900–1903); North Carolina State Archives (Raleigh), for Albemarle Book of Warrants and Surveys (1681–1706), Estate Papers of William Collins, and Will of William Collins; Mattie Erma E. Parker, ed., *North Carolina Higher-Court Records, 1670–1696* and *1697–1701* (1968, 1971); William S. Price, Jr., ed., *North Carolina Higher-Court Records, 1702–1708* (1974); William L. Saunders, ed., *Colonial Records of North Carolina*, vol. 1 (1886).

MATTIE ERMA E. PARKER

Colton, Elizabeth Avery (30 Dec. 1872–24 Aug. 1924), college professor and educational crusader, was born in the Choctaw nation of Indian Territory, the eldest of eight children of James Hooper Colton and Eloise Avery Colton, Presbyterian missionaries in the territory. Elizabeth's paternal grandfather, Simeon Baldwin Colton, a minister and teacher, moved to North Carolina from Massachusetts. On her mother's side, she was a direct descendant of Waightstill Avery, one of the leaders in North Carolina government in the early days of the state. He was a delegate to the third provincial congress and a member of a commission of four who, together with a commission from Virginia, effected a treaty with the Cherokee Indians, and of another that codified the laws brought over from the colonial courts. He became the state's first attorney general in 1778. Keenly interested in education, he was active in the efforts leading to the establishment of a state university. When the state capitol burned in 1831, the only complete collection of the proceedings of the General Assembly known to be extant was in the Avery library. This religious and educational heritage was carried on by the children of James and Eloise Colton: Susanne was a missionary in Korea and Moulton A., a teacher in the Naval Academy in Annapolis; the heritage was especially marked in the eldest daughter, Elizabeth Avery.

In 1877, when ill health forced the Coltons to give up their mission work in Indian Territory, they returned to the home of Mrs. Colton's mother in Morganton. James Colton's work in various small North Carolina towns as interim pastor, evangelist, teacher, or colporteur made life for his family financially difficult. Therefore, in obtaining an education, Elizabeth had to alternate study with teaching. She began teaching immediately after her graduation at sixteen from Statesville Female College. Two years (1891–93) in Mt. Holyoke College in Massachusetts were followed by the death of her father, which brought her back to North Carolina as a teacher at Queens College in Charlotte. After six years at Queens she went to Columbia University, where she received the B.S. degree from Teachers College in 1903 and the M.A. in 1905. For three years she was an instructor at Wellesley College; then in 1908 she began to teach at the Baptist University for Women (now Meredith College) in Raleigh, as head of the department of English. An excellent teacher, she was as deeply concerned for the whole college as for her own department. The year after she started at Meredith, she introduced the reckoning of entrance requirements in units, and she was largely responsible for the increase within four years of the required number of entrance units from 11.5 to 14. She also contributed to a marked improvement in the quality of the college work.

Thus began the work that gave Elizabeth Colton a nationwide reputation as the foremost authority on the education of women in the South. A dismaying experience when she went to Mt. Holyoke—she found her A.B. from Statesville Female College virtually worthless and had to spend a year in preparation before she could enter the freshman class—had opened her eyes to the deplorable state of most colleges for women in the South. For the rest of her life she worked unceasingly to improve their standards. She was a charter member of the Southern Association of College Women, organized in 1903, and was appointed chairman of the committee on college standards in 1910; elected as secretary in 1912 and president in 1914, she continued in the latter office so long as she was physically able. She was chosen in 1915 to be a member of the executive committee of the Association of Colleges and Secondary Schools of the Southern States. Beginning early in her stay at Meredith, she made for the Southern Association of College Women (later merged with the American Collegiate Association to form the American Association of University Women) a painstaking, detailed study of colleges for women in the South. The study was based on the results of questionnaires sent from time to time to the presidents of the colleges, supplemented where possible by information from state department and denominational boards of education, accrediting agencies, and investigators for the Carnegie Foundation. The results of the surveys appeared in a series of ten candid pamphlets, the most important of which were *Standards of Southern Colleges for Women* (1911), *The Approximate Value of Recent Degrees from Southern Colleges* (1912), and *The Various Types of Southern Colleges for Women* (1916). Gathering the material, with only a little volunteer secretarial help, was a colossal undertaking; publishing it took heroic courage. *The Various Types*, which Chancellor James Kirkland of Vanderbilt referred to as "the latest of Miss Colton's high explosive pamphlets," divided the 124 women's colleges that were studied into six classes: seven standard colleges, eight approximate colleges (which at that time included the college in which she taught), six normal and industrial colleges, thirty junior colleges, twenty-one unclassifiable colleges, and fifty-two nominal and imitation colleges (including a list of twenty that had disregarded repeated requests for catalogs but appeared, from the last catalog received and from other sources, to belong to the final class) Her

statements were not mere generalities; she gave the general nature of the work done by each group and then gave specific information about specifically named colleges. The Southern Association of College Women sent copies of this bulletin to four thousand girls graduating in 1916 from accredited high schools.

This widespread publicity brought a flood of outraged protests. There were several threats of lawsuits, not one of which ever materialized, for she could prove every syllable she wrote. Blustering, indignant college presidents who insisted on interviewing her were sometimes disarmed by her appearance—dainty, slender, and distinctly feminine. *The History of the American Association of University Women* records an especially dramatic interview. "An enraged president of a bogus school threatened to shoot Miss Colton, and thrust his hand in his pocket, apparently to make good his threat. Miss Colton looked calmly at him; he dropped his eyes and retired before her steady, honest gaze. Shortly afterward he closed his so-called college." These surveys were more effective than the 1918 proposal her joint committee of the Southern Association of College Women and the Association of Colleges and Secondary Schools of the Southern States presented to the legislative assembly of every southern state. The bill, proposing certain minimum standards a college must meet before being granted a charter, passed only in North Carolina and only with modifications greatly lessening its effectiveness.

The influence of Miss Colton's work is incalculable. *The History of the American Association of University Women* says that her publications began a new era in the education of women. Both B. E. Young, Vanderbilt professor, and Edward Kidder Graham, president of The University of North Carolina, called them epoch-making. For many years they had users all over the nation, including the U.S. government, the Carnegie Foundation, the Association of Colleges and Secondary Schools of the Southern States, the General Education Board, the Association of Medical Colleges, the Federation of Women's Clubs, departments of education, denominational boards of education, field secretaries of the YWCA, managers of teachers' agencies, educational directories of magazines, and leading colleges and universities.

The magnitude of her work is the more remarkable in that it was accomplished in so short a time, only about ten years. A malignancy in the spine from which she suffered acutely during the last two years of her teaching made her a complete invalid from 1920 until her death in Clifton Springs, N.Y. She was buried in Forest Hill Cemetery in Morganton.

SEE: Mary Lynch Johnson, *Elizabeth Avery Colton* (n.d.), and *A History of Meredith College* (1956); Meredith College publications, 1908–20; Minutes of the board of trustees and of the faculty of Meredith College, 1908–20 (Meredith College, Raleigh); *Notable American Women*, vol. 1 (1971); Personal association with Elizabeth Avery Colton; Martha Talbot and L. K. M. Rosenberry, *The History of the American Association of University Women* (1931); *Who's Who in America*, 1922–23.

MARY LYNCH JOHNSON

Colton, Henry Elliott (*26 Dec. 1836–8 Jan. 1892*), naturalist, geologist, and author, was born in Fayetteville, the son of the Reverend Simeon Colton, a native of Somers, Conn., and an 1806 graduate of Yale who moved to Fayetteville in 1833 as headmaster of Donaldson Academy, and his wife, Susan Chapman of

Connecticut. Where Colton received his early education is not known, but he clearly was quite well educated. His most famous and most widely circulated book was published in Raleigh by W. L. Pomeroy in 1859. This book, by the 22-year-old Colton, was *Mountain Scenery: The Scenery of the Mountains of Western North Carolina and Northwestern South Carolina*. The preface is dated from Asheborough, February 1859, where Colton's father had moved in 1854 to head an academy. Here, as well as elsewhere in the book, Colton expresses his indebtedness to Major J. C. Turner, chief engineer of the Western North Carolina Railroad, to one "Harry Hall" (perhaps a pseudonym), a Greensboro lawyer, and to several newspapers and periodicals from which he drew information: the *Asheville Spectator*, the *North Carolina Standard*, the *Southern Quarterly Review*, and the *North Carolina Presbyterian*. This work clearly indicates a thorough and detailed familiarity with the region. An earlier work, published when the author was just twenty, concerned Hillsborough and appeared in the *Southern Literary Messenger* for September 1856. In 1860 the *Western Advocate* in Asheville published his sixteen-page *Guide Book to the Scenery of Western North Carolina*.

On 27 Apr. 1862, Colton enlisted in New Hanover County as a private in the Thirty-sixth Regiment of North Carolina Troops. He was detailed for service in the Signal Corps at Smithville at the mouth of the Cape Fear River; in November 1863 he was transferred to the Thirteenth Battalion, North Carolina Light Artillery, but he was discharged on 1 Jan. 1864. When he was quite young, perhaps before his Confederate service, he worked in a printing office, possibly in Wilmington or in Asheville, and in 1858 was editor and proprietor of the *Asheville Spectator*. He also for a period was a legislative clerk in Raleigh. Shortly after the Civil War he was employed on the editorial staff of the *New York Tribune* while Horace Greeley was editor. He also served on the editorial staff of the *New York World* and was a contributor to a number of the leading monthlies of the time. In a series on picturesque America, *Appleton's Journal* between November 1870 and May 1871 published his five-part article on the French Broad River.

Exactly when Colton left North Carolina is not known, but he was a resident of Chattanooga, Tenn., in 1884–85 and was in Cleveland, Tenn., in 1889. At the time of his death in 1892 he was described as having lived in Knoxville for many years. Obituaries in the *Knoxville Daily Tribune* referred to him as Professor Colton. His most distinguished work, the paper reported, was as a geologist and metallurgist. He was state geologist of Tennessee during the administrations of several governors, but that of Governor Alvin Hawkins was mentioned specifically. Colton was credited with "developing a vast amount of crude mineral wealth" and also with the compilation of mineral and geological statistics. It was noted that he had contributed frequently to the *Tradesman*, of which he was described as associate editor, and to the *Iron Age*. The title page of *Hand-book of Tennessee* (Knoxville, 1882), a publication of the state bureau of agriculture, statistics, and mines, indicated that Colton, "practical geologist and mining engineer," assisted in its preparation. The same state agency also published *Coal: Report of Henry E. Colton, Geologist and Inspector of Mines, on the Coal Mines of Tennessee, and Other Minerals* (Nashville, 1883). In 1890, in the introduction to *The East Tennessee, Virginia and Georgia Railway System: Mineral Wealth, Agricultural and Timber Resources of the Main Line and Branches from Bristol to the Atlantic at Brunswick, to the Gulf at Mobile, to the*

Mississippi at Memphis. Embracing the Steel Ore Region of the South, Colton identified himself as "Henry E. Colton, Geologist."

Colton's knowledge of the mineral resources of the whole South was mentioned in the Knoxville paper at the time of his death. "His labors for the South were without pecuniary reward," it was reported, "for he died a poor man, but his fame is a sacred heritage which will be fondly cherished by the people among whom he cast his lot." In a rather enigmatic manner, one account concluded: "His faults, if any he had, were of the flesh and not of the spirit."

Colton was married to Sophia Daniels of Fayetteville, daughter of a Presbyterian clergyman; they had no children. His funeral was held at the Second Presbyterian Church, Knoxville, and he was buried in that city.

SEE: Colton's published writings; Franklin B. Dexter, *Biographical Sketches of the Graduates of Yale College*, vol. 4 (1907); *Knoxville Daily Tribune*, 10 and 12 Jan. 1892; McClung Room, Knoxville-Knox County Public Library (Knoxville, Tennessee), for a Colton letter.

HENRY E. COLTON
GEORGE STEPHENS

Colton, Simeon (*8 Jan. 1785–27 Dec. 1868*), minister and educator, the son of Jabez and Mary Baldwin Colton, was born at Somers, Conn. After his graduation from Yale in 1806, he became pastor of the Congregational church at Palmer, Mass. He was married in 1812 to Lucretia Colton, who died in 1821.

Although he was an ordained minister, Colton devoted most of his life not to the ministry but to education. He was principal of the Monson and Amherst academies in Massachusetts before he moved to Fayetteville in 1832 to be principal of the newly established Donaldson Academy and Manual Labor School on Hay Street. This academy, partially endowed by the Donaldson family, drew its students from the whole southeastern section of the state, and ten of the first sixteen trustees were residents of seven counties other than Cumberland. The curriculum was comparable to that of the Presbyterian classical schools, and old-fashioned discipline prevailed. The school was not for incorrigible or dissolute boys but for the education of youth of good habits in preparation for additional schooling at universities. The manual labor system was found to be impractical and was abandoned in a few years, when funds for necessary equipment could not be found.

In 1836 the trustees of the academy requested aid from the state literary fund, primarily on the grounds that the academy was preparing teachers for the common schools. The academy needed a library, science equipment (Colton's special desire), and manual arts equipment. The committees in both houses of the legislature replied that the literary fund would, of necessity, be used only for free and common schools.

Colton was considered an excellent teacher, learned in many subjects and especially so in the sciences. The trustees reported to the state legislature that they had "opened under the superintendence of an able, efficient and experienced Instructor." The remarkable success of the school was interrupted in 1838 when Colton was discovered to be the author of an anonymous pamphlet, consisting of six letters signed by "Presbyteros," of which the church disapproved. Colton was called before Fayetteville Presbytery in 1839 to answer charges about its offensiveness and the mischief it had caused. He denied the right of the presbytery to question him. No decision was made concerning the accusations; because of the esteem in which the author was held and because he and others considered that he had been prejudged, the presbytery preferred to refer the matter to a larger body.

The Synod of North Carolina agreed to hear the case, and the synod minutes of 10–12 Oct. 1839 record the proceedings. After the officers of Fayetteville Presbytery presented the facts, Colton was asked to speak in his defense; he declined to make a formal statement, stating instead his opinion that there was irregularity in the mode of proceeding, that the charge was not supported by the evidence, and that the process placed a restriction on liberty of speech and press. Members of the synod voted unanimously to sustain the charges against him. The minutes included the requirement that he make a full confession of guilt before he be restored to good standing.

Colton gave notice that he would appeal to the general assembly and obtained leave of absence for the rest of the meeting of the synod. On the last day, 12 Oct., however, he asked leave to appear before the synod and read a paper he had prepared. He stated that he had written the pamphlet under the "full conviction that I was doing my duty. It was written, without the least intention of wounding the feelings of my brethren, of doing harm to the cause of religion, or to the interests of the church. . . . Since Synod have viewed this in a different light, I do now, in this public manner . . . sincerely and cordially ask their forgiveness. . . . And, while I reserve to myself the right of private opinion, and of expressing that opinion, I do promise, that it shall be done in such manner as comports with the spirit of the gospel." The synod accepted his statement and united in prayers of thanksgiving.

During this period the Old School-New School division in the Presbyterian church was causing differences of opinion concerning church organization, ritual, and doctrine. Colton was opposed to the action of the 1837 general assembly in voting out many of the presbyteries in the west, charging them with irregularity in church government. Since he was of New England and Congregational church background, he no doubt saw church discipline from a point of view other than that of the members of Fayetteville Presbytery. The relationship with the presbytery and synod show that, in spite of differences of opinion, he was held in high esteem and in affection.

In 1846, Colton left Fayetteville to become president of a college in Clinton, Miss. After two years he returned to North Carolina to be principal of the Cumberland Academy at Summerville near present-day Lillington. His second wife, Susan Chapman of Connecticut, whom he had married in 1823, died in 1850 while he was at Summerville. She was the mother of his children: Alexander, James Hooper, Henry E., Jane, and Susan Maria. Women of the Presbyterian church contributed funds for a monument to her memory.

Colton's diary covering the years 1851–61 expresses gratitude at finding three companions in marriage who shared his interests and work and who were compatible in every way. His 1851 courtship of Mrs. Catherine Fuller, widow of Thomas Fuller, and his marriage to her in December of that year are described.

The Coltons moved in August 1854 to Asheboro, where he was principal of the Male Academy until the war closed its doors. Mrs. Colton assisted with instruction at the Female Academy. Both were recognized as outstanding teachers by the people of Asheboro and had the reputation of being so strict as to hold the students in awe. Here again Colton combined the ministry with education, for he was the second minister of the Asheboro Presbyterian Church, organized in 1850, serving from 1854 to 1862. He apparently retired from all active service in 1862 at the age of seventy-seven. Mrs. Colton continued as principal of the Female Academy until 1867.

Colton's diary reveals a man of many talents devoted to the Christian faith, which sustained him through all discouragements. To his adopted state he gave twenty-eight years of unselfish, conscientious, and able service. His education exceeded that of most of the adults in the communities in which he lived in North Carolina, but he contributed through his teaching to the preparation of leadership for another generation. He was a great supporter of The University of North Carolina, from which his son James Hooper was graduated in 1855. Faced with indifference, sham, feuds, poverty, unkept promises, and despair, he daily turned to his diary to express his reliance on his faith as a source of strength. On one occasion he commented: "I have commenced school this day with two pupils and I think it is doubtful whether I shall have any more from town during the session. Some do not like my government. They want their children to do well, but to be indulged in every humor."

For several months in 1840, Colton acted as agent of the board of internal improvement in soliciting subscriptions for the Fayetteville and Western Railroad. This service meant travel in some sixteen counties west of Fayetteville that might be touched by the railroad. His report to the board of 10 June 1840 not only covers the results of the solicitations but also provides a comprehensive summary of the values of an east-west railroad in the state. Although his well-organized report proposed immediate action, the board delayed a decision; it was ten years before the railroad was approved.

Colton left a lasting impression wherever he lived. In July 1854, as he was preparing to move to Asheboro, friends in Monson, Mass., among them E. W. Storrs, Charles Merriam, and William Grosvenor, sent him one hundred dollars for expenses so that he could attend the semicentennial anniversary of Monson Academy. While he was there, Merriam asked him to sit for a portrait to be hung at the academy.

Colton was buried at Summerville beside his second wife, Susan. The Cornelius Harnett Chapter of the DAR erected a monument at the grave.

SEE: Asheboro Presbyterian Church early records; Simeon Colton Papers (Southern Historical Collection, University of North Carolina, Chapel Hill), for 1851–61 diary; Charles Coon, *Beginnings of Public Education in North Carolina* (1908); William Henry Foote, *Sketches of North Carolina, Historical and Biographical* (1846); Historical Foundation of the Presbyterian Church, U.S. (Montreat, N.C.); *North Carolina Historical Review* 11 (1934); John A. Oates, *The Story of Fayetteville and the Upper Cape Fear* (1950); Presbyterian Church in the U.S., *Minutes of the Sessions*, Fayetteville Presbytery and North Carolina Synod; Frances R. Ross, *Summerville Presbyterian Church* (1949).

CHARLESANNA L. FOX

Coltrane, Daniel Branson (25 Dec. 1842–16 Jan. 1937), banker, industrialist, religious and educational leader, and Confederate veteran, was born in Randolph County in a two-room log house near Ebenezer Methodist

Church and Coltrane's Mill on Deep River, not far from Trinity and the Guilford County line. His father was Kelly Coltrane, a descendant of the first Coltrane (David) to come from Scotland to America; David settled in Edenton and married Mary Wallace. Kelly, one of the family members who called Randolph County home, married Mary Gossett in 1839.

Coltrane's first schooling was in a private home in the neighborhood. Later he attended school in a one-room school some two miles away, walking in good weather and riding in his father's wagon in bad. A typical school of that time, it was open during the winter months when there was no planting or harvesting to be done. When he was thirteen years of age, the family moved to a home in the community where Braxton Craven, president of Trinity College from 1859 to 1892, was both student and teacher.

His father's death in 1858, when Branson was sixteen, meant that his formal schooling was ended, for he became head of the family. His father was an industrious farmer, slave owner, and good provider; he left to his family a farm and a few slaves. His mother was a strong and courageous woman who carried on the duties and responsibilities of the farm and made a home for eight children.

At the age of nineteen, Coltrane began his service with the Confederate Army. His memoirs, written when he was ninety-three, reveal a young man of courage, strength, loyalty, and perception. Humorous circumstances balance accounts of the dangers encountered and the sorrow experienced in the loss of companions: very few members of the company starting with him in 1862 were mustered out with him in 1865.

Enlisting in 1861 in the Trinity Guards, an infantry company organized by Braxton Craven, Coltrane served in the forces of the South until the end of the war. After six months the company of Trinity Guards was disbanded. He then enlisted with a cavalry company organized by N. P. Rankin in Greensboro in 1862. He was with this company (Company I, Sixty-third Regiment, North Carolina Cavalry) for the rest of his service.

Following the war, Coltrane farmed as best he could with the resources left to the family that first year. In the fall of 1865, his brother, Dr. Wesley, who had moved to Cave Springs, Mo., in the 1850s, came home to visit his mother. His stories of opportunities in the West led Branson to leave for Missouri, where he worked in Arrow Rock, Miami, and Marshall. Another Confederate veteran taught him elementary photography, and he invested in a jewelry store; succeeding with both ventures, he with other investors established a bank. In Missouri, he married Ella Van Ice, who died in 1882. Of this marriage two children were born. Later Coltrane married Mariam Winslow, who died in 1915 in Concord; four children were born to them. One daughter, Ruth Louise, married Charles A. Cannon.

In 1886, Coltrane sold his interest in the Missouri bank and decided to settle elsewhere. He debated North Carolina and California, but visits to his mother brought about a decision to move to Concord. There he became one of the incorporators of a new bank, the Concord National Bank, which opened its doors on 5 July 1888. He was president of the bank from its opening until his death, and his son L. D. became cashier, remaining with the bank until his death in 1948.

In addition to his interest in the bank, Coltrane engaged also in textile manufacturing and other industries. He was president of the Kerr Bleaching and Finishing Works (1910 to 1937), the Norwood Manufacturing Company, Norwood, the Linn Mills

Company, Landis, and the Poplar Tent Gin Company; he was vice-president of the Locke Cotton Mills.

His interest in the community was pronounced throughout his lifetime. Church responsibilities and service to others through the church had priority over everything else. Of his church affiliation he said, "I attribute my success, whatever that is, to my fidelity to my church." When he left North Carolina for Missouri in 1865, he took his church letter with him. One of the accomplishments that gave him great satisfaction was the consolidation of the publications of the Methodist Episcopal Church, South, beginning in 1901; he also helped to strengthen the *North Carolina Christian Advocate*. He was chairman of the board of publications for thirty-five years. In Concord he was chairman of the board of stewards of the Central Methodist Church for twenty-five years and a Sunday school teacher or superintendent for fifty-eight years.

Next to his church, education was Coltrane's special concern. When he moved to Concord in 1888, he was astonished to find that many depositors at the bank could not write their names; he had known only one person in Missouri who could not do so. He launched a drive for better schools in Concord and nurtured the new school system for sixteen years. When Governor Robert Glenn appointed him a trustee of the Stonewall Jackson Training School, he resigned from the Concord School Board. He was elected treasurer of the training school board and served in that capacity until his death.

Coltrane died in Concord at the age of ninety-four.

SEE: Walter Clark, ed., *Histories of the Several Regiments and Battalions from North Carolina in the Great War, 1861–1865*, vol. 3 (1901); *Concord Daily Tribune*, 8 Feb. 1926, 26 Dec. 1930 and undated 1935 clipping in the Concord Public Library; Concord *Herald-Observer*, 25 Dec. 1935; Robert H. Frazier, comp., *Descendants of David Coltrane and James Frazier of North Carolina* (1961); Louis H. Manarin, comp., *North Carolina Troops, 1861–1865: A Roster*, vol. 2 (1968); *Memoirs of Daniel Branson Coltrane* (1956).

CHARLESANNA L. FOX

Coltrane, John William (23 Sept. 1926–17 July 1967), modern jazz saxophonist and composer, was born in Hamlet, the son of Alice Blair and John W. Coltrane, Sr. By the time of his death, he had achieved international eminence as one of the most talented, creative, and controversial figures in the history of jazz. His training in music began in high school, where he studied the E-flat alto horn, clarinet, and saxophone. He continued his musical training at the Granoff Studios and Ornstein School of Music in Philadelphia, making his professional debut in 1945 as a member of a cocktail party combo. He served in Hawaii with the U.S. Navy Band in 1945–46 and, upon returning to civilian life, toured as a sideman with Eddie Vinson's rhythm and blues band in 1947–48. He played in Dizzie Gillespie's big band from 1949 to 1951 and then with Earl Bostic in 1952–53 and Johnny Hodges in 1953–54.

In 1955, Coltrane joined the Miles Davis Quintet, which was to become the outstanding jazz group of its day. With Davis's group, Coltrane first attracted public and critical attention for his distinctive style of saxophone jazz. In the summer and fall of 1957 he worked with Theolonious Monk at the Five Spot in New York City. In January 1958 he rejoined Davis's quintet, remaining with the band until April 1960, when he organized his own quartet. The Coltrane band was one of the most original and influential groups in jazz during the period 1961 to 1965. Coltrane reached the peak of his public acclaim in 1965, winning the *Down Beat* award as America's best tenor saxophonist, Hall of Fame selection, and Jazzman of the Year, while his composition and recording of *A Love Supreme* was voted Record of the Year. From 1965 to 1967, he experimented broadly in the instrumentation of his group and developed a growing predilection for modality and multihorn group improvisation. Coltrane's music, although influenced by Indian, Oriental, and African forms, was unique in its development and exploration of sixteenth notes as a rhythmic base for jazz. His superb technical skill on the saxophone enabled him to experiment freely with the broadest improvisation in avant-garde jazz, thus making him a central and controversial figure in the field.

Coltrane recorded for numerous companies, including Columbia, Riverside, Blue Note, Prestige, Atlantic, and Impulse. Among his important recordings are *Straight, No Chaser, Blue Train, Kind of Blue, Giant Steps, My Favorite Things, Impressions, Chasin' the Trane, Crescent, A Love Supreme, Ascension, Naima, Locomotion, In a Sentimental Mood, Expressions, Soultrane,* and *Kulu Se Mama.*

He was married to Alice McLeod, a jazz pianist who performed with his group on many occasions. He died in Huntington, N.Y., with memorial services at St. Peter's Lutheran Church in New York City.

SEE: *Down Beat*, Aug. 1967 (portrait), 14 Dec. 1967; L. Feather, *The Encyclopedia of Jazz* (1960); *New York Times*, 18 July 1967; *Saturday Review*, 16 Sept. 1967; J. C. Thomas, *Chasin' the Trane* (1975).

MARCUS B. SIMPSON, JR.

Comberford, Nicholas *(d. 1673),* chartmaker in London and a central figure in the group now designated the "Thames School," claimed to have been born in Ireland and was quoted as saying that his father "was Nicholas the King's gaoler at Kilkenny." Comberford, in various spellings, was a fairly common name among the Anglo-Irish families of Kilkenny and other parts of southern Ireland, but efforts to connect Nicholas the chartmaker with Nicholas the king's gaoler have not been successful.

The Thames School group is so called because of similarities in the style of the members' hand-drawn sea charts, the fact that their residences were clustered in the hamlets east of the Tower along the Thames, and the common experience of most of them in a century-long series of master-apprentice connections within the Drapers' Company. The first firm dates for Nicholas are his eight-year apprenticeship, 1612–20, to John Daniel, a chartmaker of the Drapers' Company whose charts date from 1612 to 1642. Comberford took the freedom in the Drapers' Company, and we know of twenty-seven charts dated from 1626 to 1670 signed by him, usually with the address "neare unto the West Ende of the Schoole House in Ratcliff." Comberford was buried at St. Dunstans, Stepney, on 6 Dec. 1673.

There is no indication that Comberford ever visited the New World, but among his known charts are two of the North Carolina coast, one preserved at the National Maritime Museum in London, the other at the New York Public Library. Both charts are hand drawn on vellum, in color, with decorations, and mounted on two wooden panels hinged to close like a book—a style and format followed by all Thames School practitioners of the period. Both have a title across the top of the map (an unusual feature), "The South Part of Virginia," and bear signature and date " . . . By Nicholas Comberford . . . 1657." Both show the Carolina Banks centering on Cape

Hatteras with the adjacent mainland coast and estuaries as far south as Cape Lookout in considerable and nearly identical detail. There are some differences in decoration, but more importantly the example at the New York Public Library carries a subtitle, below the main title and in a different seventeenth-century hand, which reads "Now the North Part of Carolina."

Professor William Cumming has made a detailed study of Comberford's map of the Carolina coast and finds it more detailed and accurate than previous maps—better, in fact, than any map printed before the establishment of Carolina as a colony. Comberford was the first to use English place names, some of which have survived, and he also locates, at the mouth of the Roanoke River, "Batts House," apparently the home of Nathaniel Batts, the most prominent settler of the area. Cumming believes that the map was probably based on surveys made as late as 1656 but is unable to identify specific map sources that may have been used. He concludes that the map "deserves special attention because of its evident use of original contemporary source material, the excellence of its composition and the historical importance of the information it gives."

Little biographical information has been uncovered regarding the chartmakers of the Thames School, but three useful bits have turned up on Comberford. Samuel Pepys visited Comberford's shop but left only a frustratingly brief comment in his diary entry for 22 July 1663: " . . . and so by water to Ratcliffe and there went to speak with Comberford, the platt-maker and there saw his manner of working which is very fine and laborious." No other references have been found in Pepys, despite his long-continued interest in the state of English chartmaking and the comparative accuracy of hand-drawn as against printed charts.

A more enlightening account of a visit to Comberford comes from W. Dobbyns's "Narrative of a Deceiving of Expectations" in December 1655. The motivation for the visit was not cartographic, and Dobbyns had some difficulty in finding Comberford's house, "the ways beyond the houses at Wapping being very deep." Arriving at the house he was met by a woman (apparently the wife of Comberford's son) whom he described as "an ill-favored dirty slut." Comberford showed him some charts, and Dobbyns's account continued "upon debate of the price of what a map was worth, 25 shillings was the lowest, and he (Comberford) swore that he could make but one in three weeks . . . and that he and his son had much ado to maintain themselves and their family . . ."; the account then turned to other matters. By this account, chartmaking appears to have been laborious, ill-paid, and not held in very high regard, although Dobbyns, who had come with the expectation of finding a rich relative of friends in Ireland, may be a biased witness.

The third and most important item is the notice of Comberford's wedding in 1624, which identifies him as "Nicholas Comberford, of the precincts of St. Katherine, draper." The discovery that Comberford had been a member of the Drapers' Company, a totally unexpected association, led to the voluminous records at the Drapers' Hall and the further discovery that a series of master apprentice connections extending from 1590 into the early eighteenth century linked thirty-seven individuals, many of whom were identified as chartmakers. Twelve of these produced signed charts still in existence, within a total corpus, including a considerable number of anonymous charts, of at least fifteen hundred manuscript charts and maps in Thames School style. Comberford occupied a central place in this sequence and probably had at least indirect influence on other manuscript maps of the Carolina coast drawn (more likely copied) in the years after 1657. He had six apprentices of record, including his son, Thomas (fl. 1655–57), from whose hand no signed chart has yet been identified. Two other of Comberford's apprentices, Andrew Welch (fl. 1649–77) and John Burston (fl. 1628–65), took the freedom in the company, produced signed charts, and trained apprentices who themselves produced charts of the Carolina coast.

William Hack (fl. 1670–ca. 1700) began an apprenticeship with Welch in 1670 and is chiefly known for numerous copies, made during the two decades after ca. 1682, of an elaborate Spanish *Derrotero*, with many charts of the coasts and harbors on the Pacific side of the Americas. He also produced an atlas of the Atlantic coast of North America, without dedication or date, which contains a map of Carolina. In the British Museum there is also a separate map of Carolina, signed and dated 1684, as well as others that may also be by Hack.

Four other contemporary manuscript maps of the Carolina coast are found in the *Blathwayt Atlas*, an assemblage of forty-eight maps put together ca. 1682–83 by William Blathwayt, secretary to the Committee of Lords for Trade and Plantations. Long in possession of the Blathwayt family, the *Atlas* is now one of the treasures of the John Carter Brown Library, which has recently sponsored a handsome facsimile reproduction of the maps and also a brilliant commentary by Jeannette Black, curator of maps. The four Carolina maps are beautifully reproduced in color and are among ten manuscript maps in the *Blathwayt Atlas* done in the style of the Thames School. One map (no. 21) is of Albemarle Sound and dated 1679 and is the only known work signed by James Lancaster (fl. 1656–79), an apprentice of John Burston and, like Hack, "once removed" in the master-apprentice sequence from Comberford. The other three are similar in style and format to Lancaster's map but are not by his hand and are unsigned and undated. Miss Black believes one of the maps to be by the same draftsman who produced several other maps of the Carolina coast now preserved in the British Museum and the Public Record Office. The other two Carolina maps, nos. 18 and 19 in the *Blathwayt*, show the results of Hilton's two voyages in 1662 and again in 1663–64 but are by two different draftsmen of the Thames School. Like Comberford, the Thames School copyists of these four and the other six Thames School charts in the *Blathwayt Atlas* appear to have used up-to-date information, although Miss Black, like Cumming, cannot identify actual cartographic sources. Nor can she identify the draftsmanship of the unsigned maps as identical to Comberford's or to that of any member of the group whose signed work is known. Comberford's maps of 1657 were, however, the first indication of interest and participation in the detailed mapping of the Carolina coast by the Thames School chartmakers, although the degree of his involvement with the work, only some of which could have been accomplished before his death, remains unclear.

SEE: Jeannette D. Black, *The Blathwayt Atlas*, vols. 1–2 (1970–75); British Museum, K. Mar. VII 3; Tony Campbell, "The Drapers' Company and Its School of Seventeenth Century Chartmakers," in *My Head Is a Map*, ed. Helen Wallis and Sarah Tyacke (1973); William P. Cumming, "The Earliest Permanent Settlement in Carolina: Nathaniel Batts and the Comberford Map," *American Historical Review* 45 (1939), and *The Southeast in Early Maps* (1958, 1962); W. Dobbyns, "A Narrative of a

Deceiving of Expectations," in Historical Manuscripts Commission, *Egmont Papers*, vol. 1, pt. 2 (1905); G. W. Hill and W. H. Frere, eds., *Memorials of Stepney Parish . . . 1572–1662* (1890–91); P. L. Phillips, *Virginia Cartography* (1896); Thomas R. Smith, "Manuscript and Printed Sea Charts in Seventeenth Century London—The Case of the Thames School," in *The Compleat Plattmaker: Essays on Chart, Map, & Globe-Making in England in the 17th & 18th Centuries* (1978), Norman J. W. Thrower, ed.; *The Diary of Samuel Pepys*, ed. Henry B. Wheatley, vol. 3 (1904–5).

THOMAS R. SMITH

Cone, Ceasar *(22 Apr. 1859–1 Mar. 1917)*, industrialist and philanthropist, was born in Jonesboro, Tenn., the son of Herman and Helen Guggenheimer Cone. The parents were natives of Bavaria, born about ten miles apart but unacquainted until they met in Richmond, Va., where they were married in 1856. Herman Cone came to the United States in 1847, establishing a mercantile business near Richmond; he soon removed to Jonesboro and established there the same kind of business. In 1870 he moved his family to Baltimore, Md., and established a wholesale grocery business.

Cone attended the public schools of Baltimore until he was fourteen and then worked briefly in a stationery store and with his father. He and his brother, Moses (whose sketch provides further information), invested in the C. E. Graham Manufacturing Company in Asheville in 1887. Herman Cone's wholesale grocery firm closed in 1890 after twenty years, and Ceasar and Moses the next year established the Cone Export and Commission Company with offices in New York. It soon became the largest textile selling organization in the world, and in due time offices were opened in Atlanta, Baltimore, Nashville, St. Louis, Dallas, Chicago, Philadelphia, Boston, San Francisco, and Los Angeles. The two brothers began acquiring land in and around Greensboro and in 1895–96 opened a large cotton mill, the Proximity Manufacturing Company, with Ceasar serving as acting and active president. The original mill had only 240 looms, but in less than ten years the company had enlarged its capital stock and built another very large plant, the White Oak Mill. This second mill soon became the largest cotton mill in the South and the largest denim manufacturing plant in the world. The Cones' denim mill provided a durable, dependable, and lasting cloth for work clothes; and by reducing the cost of production, the Cones lowered the cost of clothes and helped to stabilize the world market. Within a short period, the Cones' various mills were consuming thirty-five million pounds of cotton yearly and producing more than seventy-five million yards of cloth.

Cone married Jeanette Siegel in 1894; they were the parents of three sons, Herman, Benjamin, and Ceasar. In addition to the family home in Greensboro, they maintained a summer home on Lake Placid in New York. Cone served as president of the American Cotton Manufacturers Association, the Greensboro Chamber of Commerce, and the Central Carolina Fair Association. He contributed a large sum of money to the Guilford County Tuberculosis Sanitarium and supported other public causes. He was also a trustee of the Stonewall Jackson Training School near Concord. Both the Cones actively supported Jewish affairs and interested themselves in the work of the YMCA. The brothers established model villages around their mills and generously supported the schools and churches there.

The Cone family has continued to render valuable

support to worthwhile public and private causes in North Carolina and elsewhere. Dr. Claribel and Miss Etta Cone, sisters of Moses and Ceasar, early appreciated the work of Picasso and Matisse and also collected Cezanne, Modigliani, Rouault, Chagall, Braque, and Van Gogh. As a result of their interest and generosity, one of the most complete collections of modern art in the world may be seen in the Cone Wing of the Baltimore Museum of Art.

SEE: American Jewish Historical Society, *Publications* 26 (1918); Samuel A. Ashe, ed., *Biographical History of North Carolina*, vol. 8 (1917); *American Wool and Cotton Reporter, Ceasar Cone: An Appreciation* (n.d.); Bettie D. Caldwell, *Founders and Builders of Greensboro* (1925); Cone Export and Commission Company, *Half Century Book, 1891–1941* (1941); *Greensboro Daily News*, 2 Mar. 1917; William P. Jacobs, *The Pioneer* (1935); *Orphans' Friend and Masonic Journal*, 1 July 1941.

WILLIAM S. POWELL

Cone, Laura Weil *(19 Sept. 1888–3 Feb. 1970),* civic leader and humanitarian, was born in Wilmington, the daughter of Solomon Weil and Ella Fishblatt. Solomon Weil, a graduate of The University of North Carolina, was a lawyer who practiced in Wilmington and later in New York City. Laura attended public school in Wilmington and prepared for college at Dana Hall, Wellesley, Mass. After the death of Solomon Weil, his family returned to Wilmington. In 1907, Laura Weil entered the North Carolina State Normal and Industrial School as a sophomore. Outstanding academically and in every phase of college life, she was graduated in 1910 with honors, serving as permanent president of her class. She taught in high school in Wilmington in 1911–12 and then returned to Greensboro, where she resided the rest of her life. Her first marriage was to David Stern, a lawyer. After his death, she married Julius W. Cone, president of the Cone Export Commission Company (a division of Cone Mills).

As a courageous civic leader, Laura Weil Cone exerted great influence in her community throughout her life. At the time of her death the Greensboro *Daily Record* paid her tribute, saying that she was "a volunteer in many a community cause, and a civic worker who put her strength, her energies and philanthropy at the service of her community and its people, rich or poor, black or white."

It was said at the time of her death that she had brought to the halls of education "a clear and precise intelligence, a broad compassion and hard nosed judgment." These rare talents she applied for twenty-two years as a member of the board of trustees of The University of North Carolina, as a member of its executive committee from 1934 until 1953, and as one of the chief builders of The Consolidated University of North Carolina. She was an active participant in the progress of Women's College, and repeatedly the college honored her service. Elliott Hall, the student union building, is in some measure a memorial to her, because it was made possible by her gifts and those of the Cone family. A high-rise dormitory was named in her honor and a portrait, presented by her daughter, Mrs. Edward Loewenstein, hangs in its halls. She served for nearly thirty years as a member of the board of Bennett College; in 1961 a residence hall on its campus was dedicated in her honor. She made substantial contributions to Bennett College, and a library furnished with monies she contributed is named for her.

She was a member of the board of trustees of the

Moses Cone Memorial Hospital where she died at the age of eighty-one after an illness of two weeks. She was survived by her daughter; a son, Edward T., a professor at Princeton University; and three grandchildren, F. Sand Hetherington, Laura Loewenstein Freedlander, and Jane Loewenstein Delisle.

SEE: *Alumni News of The University of North Carolina–Greensboro*; Mrs. Edward Loewenstein, personal contact.

GLADYS AVERY TILLETT

Cone, Moses Herman *(29 June 1857–8 Dec. 1908),* industrialist and philanthropist, was born in Jonesboro, Tenn., the son of Herman and Helen Guggenheimer Cone, natives of Bavaria. For further details of the life of Moses Herman Cone, see the sketch of his brother, Ceasar.

Cone was educated in Baltimore, Md., where his father operated a wholesale grocery business from 1870 until 1890. Moses and his brother bought the C. E. Graham Manufacturing Company in Asheville in 1887, and Moses reorganized it in 1892 as the Asheville Cotton Mills. Moses was in large measure responsible for the construction of the Southern Finishing and Warehouse Company in Greensboro, which was an early part of the brothers' plans for their textile enterprise in that city. In 1899 he built at Greensboro the Revolution Mill, which soon became the world's largest flannel mill. He was president of the Cone enterprises.

Cone married Bertha Lindau in 1888, but they had no children. In about 1900 he bought a large tract of land near Blowing Rock, and in 1950, after Mrs. Cone's death in 1947, the 3,500-acre estate with its magnificent mansion was given to the federal government as a Blue Ridge Parkway recreational area. The Moses H. Cone Memorial Park contains fine stands of balsam, dense forests of pine, and a deer park; there are bridle paths and wooded walks and trails around two lakes. Mountain crafts are exhibited and sold there, and demonstrations of various crafts are presented during the summer season. Moses Cone was buried on a nearby mountain slope.

The Moses H. Cone Memorial Hospital occupies a sixty-seven-acre site in Greensboro and is only one of his benefactions. He left a trust fund of $15 million from which support has been given to a wide variety of worthwhile causes. He served on the first board of trustees of the Appalachian Training School for Teachers at Boone, near his mountain home, and aided that institution, now Appalachian State University, in a very generous way.

SEE: American Cotton Manufacturers Association, *Lest We Forget* (1946); Samuel A. Ashe, ed., *Biographical History of North Carolina*, vol. 8 (1917); *North Carolina Biography*, vol. 4 (1919); William P. Jacobs, *The Pioneer* (1935); Raleigh *News and Observer*, 24 Aug. 1930, 8 July 1947.

WILLIAM S. POWELL

Conigland, Edward *(22 Apr. 1819–4 Dec. 1877),* lawyer, teacher, writer, orator, and Catholic layman, was born in Ireland, the fifth son of Dr. Patrick and Margaret Brison Conigland. Following the death of Dr. Conigland, Margaret B. Conigland emigrated with her children in 1834 to New York, where Edward began his law studies.

In 1844, Conigland removed to Halifax County to teach school and continue his study of law. He obtained a license to practice law in the North Carolina courts in

1846 and established a law office in Halifax. He represented Halifax County in the constitutional convention of 1865, and in 1871, although suffering from defective hearing, he served as a defense counsel in the Governor W. W. Holden impeachment proceedings. He formed a law partnership with Robert O. Burton in 1875 in Halifax, where he practiced law until his death.

Conigland was a close personal friend of Father (later Cardinal) James Gibbons, Bishop Patrick N. Lynch of Charleston, S.C., and Father (later Bishop) Harry P. Northrop.

He was married three times: to Mary E. Tillery on 7 Feb. 1849 in Halifax County; to Mary Wyatt Ezell on 16 Apr. 1855 in Northampton County; and to Emily Long on 18 Sept. 1867, also in Northampton County.

Conigland was struck and killed by a train on the south edge of Halifax town and was buried in the Conigland family cemetery overlooking Quankey Creek at the family home, Glen Ivey, in Halifax.

His portrait hangs in the main hallway of the Halifax County courthouse.

SEE: W. C. Allen, *History of Halifax County* (1918); Conigland family cemetery (Halifax); Edward Conigland Papers (Southern Historical Collection, University of North Carolina, Chapel Hill); James Gibbons Papers (Archives of the Archdiocese of Baltimore, Baltimore, Md.); Halifax County Marriage Bond Book (Office of the Register of Deeds, Halifax County courthouse, Halifax); P. N. Lynch Papers (Diocesan Archives, Diocese of Charleston, Charleston, S.C.); Northampton County Index to Marriages (Office of the Register of Deeds, Northampton County courthouse, Jackson); *Raleigh Register*, 6 Dec. 1877.

MARGARET M. HOFMANN

Connecorte (Old Hop) *(fl. 1740–60)*, the First Man or Ulustuli of Overhill Chota and therefore of the Cherokee nation, was sometimes referred to as the "Fire King" but was called "Old Hop" by the traders because of his lameness, said to have been caused by a childhood accident. Before 1751, South Carolina's official contacts with the Cherokees were made through the "Emperor" of Great Tellico, an office created by Sir Alexander Cuming, who on his own initiative visited the restive Cherokees in 1730 and induced them to send a delegation with him to England to make a treaty of trade and alliance with the Crown. The "Emperor" proved a convenient tool for exercising English control over the Cherokees. Presumably Connecorte, little known to the English, came to the headship of Chota, the true capital of the Cherokees, before 1740, and in true nativist tradition was willing that other men, notably his right-hand man, Attakullakulla or the Little Carpenter, should front for him. The extent to which he initiated policy is uncertain. As first man he was expected to subordinate his will to that of his council and to be the impartial arbiter of disputes and the upholder of traditional ways. He was the symbol of Cherokee nativist independence and as such was jealous of the "Emperor" of Great Tellico, upon whom the English showered favors.

In the 1740s, Chota, under Connecorte and the Little Carpenter, extricated the Cherokees from wars with the northern Indians and developed an intercourse with the French. At the end of the decade, French influence was channeled into the Cherokees through a French agent whom the English called "French John." Lame as Connecorte was lame, French John reputedly had been taken prisoner in a Cherokee raid on French Mississippi

convoys and had been adopted into Connecorte's household. However, Connecorte and the Little Carpenter did not desire to alienate the English, merely to establish a bargaining position. During disorders in the Cherokee nation occasioned by northern Indians summoned to help the Cherokees in their war on the Creek Indians, Connecorte himself disciplined those Indians who looted the Chota trader's store. Nevertheless, South Carolina embargoed the Cherokee trade, and the embargo, as intended, crippled the Cherokee defense against the Creeks. Chota then sought to increase its power and to undermine Great Tellico by gathering defeated Lower Towns to itself. Connecorte accepted the Little Carpenter's determination to seek a French or Virginia trade, or both, sending a message to the French at Fort Toulouse in Alabama and the Little Carpenter himself to Virginia. South Carolina's Governor James Glen then looked upon Connecorte and Chota as hostile to the English.

Chota, bent on its own policies, did not send deputies to the November 1751 meeting at Charlestown with Glen, arranged by the headmen of Tellico and Hiwassee. The inability of the Tellico-Hiwassee to implement the treaty made there and to get Glen to halt the Creek war, which he continued to tolerate in order to discipline the Cherokees, bankrupted the Tellico "Emperorship." Chota and Connecorte took over and in April 1752 sent a conciliatory message to Glen, suggesting that South Carolina should treat only with them and arguing that the embargo violated the Treaty of 1730 with the Crown. When Glen learned that the Tellico "Emperor" himself had been dallying with Virginia, he turned to Chota. Connecorte and the Little Carpenter took advantage of the situation; in June 1753 the Little Carpenter at Charlestown, with talk of going to the French and going to Virginia, forced Glen to agree to a Creek peace and to make trade concessions. Glen, seeing that he had formidable powers to deal with in Chota and Connecorte, decided to build a fort in the Lower Cherokee towns near Keowee, which as the center of English power could undercut Chota's influence. Connecorte and the Little Carpenter continued to negotiate with the French and Virginia.

Certain non-English headmen among the Overhills, perhaps instigated by South Carolina traders, then decided to pressure Connecorte and the Little Carpenter into giving up their French and Virginia negotiations. They accused Connecorte of taking English presents on false pretenses and the Little Carpenter of having violated his sacred word, given when he was in England to make the Treaty of 1730. Connecorte threatened to resign and even to commit suicide, but his relatives dissuaded him. The Little Carpenter, who had been severely beaten, became strongly pro-Carolina.

In May 1755 the Little Carpenter persuaded Connecorte to meet Glen at the conference of Saluda, S.C., where in return for favorable trade concessions and Glen's promise to build a fort among the Overhills, he joined the Little Carpenter in ceding overlordship of all Cherokee lands to the English Crown. For this latter act, both he and the Little Carpenter fell into the bad graces of Cherokee nativists, but the two chiefs expected the benefits derived from the treaty to overcome opposition. Connecorte's position became difficult when Glen failed to implement his promises. Nevertheless, though embittered, he refused a Shawnee invitation for the Cherokees to join the French in their war upon the English. He and his councilor now sought to play off Virginia against South Carolina by sending warriors to Virginia to help in the frontier war and sending the Little

Carpenter to Charlestown to demand action.

Hampered by a parsimonious assembly, Glen moved slowly. The Overhills turned again to Virginia and at the Treaty of Broad River with Virginia commissioners, March 1756, obtained a promise of a Virginia fort at Chota and a Virginia trade, in return for a promise that more warriors would go to Virginia. But Virginia, too, moved slowly, and Connecorte once again, with the aid of Shawnee visitors and French John, opened correspondence with the French, seeking peace and trade at New Orleans and Detroit. The Little Carpenter then confronted Connecorte, forcing him to promise that he meant no harm to the English and that the Little Carpenter could continue to treat with South Carolina.

When, late in 1756, Glen's successor, William Henry Lyttleton, succeeded in having Fort Loudon built near Chota, planning eventually to liquidate Shawnee missions to the Cherokees, Connecorte enabled French John to escape from the Cherokee country.

In 1759, after the murder of Cherokee warriors in Virginia by Virginia frontiersmen, the Cherokees demanded war on the English. Connecorte supported the belligerents and plotted to have the Little Carpenter, who was pursuing a peace policy, assassinated. Learning of this plan, the Little Carpenter moved to have Connecorte deposed and declared himself the head of the Cherokees. The nativists would not follow the Little Carpenter's lead but, although Connecorte remained first man, his death occurred before the Cherokees actually went to war with South Carolina.

SEE: David H. Corkran, *The Cherokee Frontier* (1962); Lyttleton Papers (Clements Library, Ann Arbor, Mich.); South Carolina Council Records (South Carolina Department of Archives and History, Columbia).

D. H. CORKRAN

Conner, Andrew Jackson *(1 Sept. 1860–25 Oct. 1931)*, teacher, county and city school superintendent, newspaper publisher, farmer and businessman, was born at Rich Square, Northampton County, the son of Elijah W. and Barbara (Powell) Conner. His ancestors had been important residents of Northampton County for several generations. His grandfather, Joel Conner, born there in 1783, operated a large plantation throughout his life. He had attended college and worked as a teacher and county surveyor. Andrew Jackson Conner's father, Elijah W., also worked as county surveyor for over forty years and farmed as well.

Conner grew up on his father's farm near Rich Square and attended school there until age twenty-one. In 1881 he began teaching at a school in adjoining Bertie County. At the close of the term he took a position at the Grange High School (private) in Lasker, Northampton County, and taught there until 1887. During summer vacations he also taught district school, and this added burden lead to a decline of his health which forced him to give up teaching temporarily. He returned to the school system in 1890 as the county superintendent of public instruction for Northampton County and continued in that position until his appointment as county examiner in 1895, a post newly created under state law. It was in this post that he first gained statewide attention as an educator.

In 1892 he began publishing the *Gleaner*, a monthly educational journal at Lasker. Three months later the State Grange ceased publication of its weekly paper, the Potecasi (N.C.) *Roanoke Patron*, and offered the press to Conner on the condition that he begin publishing the

Gleaner on a weekly basis. In July 1892 he began publishing the *Patron and Gleaner* (later named the Lasker *Roanoke-Chowan Times*) weekly, and he continued to publish and edit the paper until his death in 1931. At the time of its publication, the *Patron and Gleaner* was the only newspaper in North Carolina to devote the majority of its space to the promotion of education.

As a school superintendent and then county examiner, Conner made a statewide reputation for himself. In a time when the appointed county examiner was viewed as the only person checking the effects of partisan politics in the schools, he spoke concerning that problem at the Teachers Assembly at Morehead City, June 1896. As the editor and publisher of the only weekly paper in North Carolina devoted to the promotion of public and private education, Conner was noted for his strong editorials supporting schools and for his coverage of school and college news from all over the state. He gave specially strong support to the Woman's College at Greensboro (now The University of North Carolina at Greensboro).

He was appointed a trustee of the Woman's College when it was founded in 1892 and served until his death in 1931. He also served as secretary to the board for twenty-eight years.

On 10 Apr. 1931 the General Assembly appointed Conner to the board of trustees of the newly created Consolidated University of North Carolina. Sadly he died before the first meeting of the Board.

In addition to his activities on behalf of education, Conner, throughout most of his life, owned and operated a thousand-acre farm as well as a cotton gin, a saw mill, and a plant for manufacturing building materials. He served in several county elective positions, as a magistrate and as the food administrator for Northampton County in 1918.

Though Conner claimed that he maintained a non-partisan policy in his newspaper, as was the policy of "friends of education" in North Carolina around the turn of the century, he leaned heavily toward the Democrats in his editorials.

In his paper he supported larger appropriations for schools, local tax for schools, higher qualifications for teachers, free books for students, and an expanded curriculum. He also devoted considerable space to the news of black schools and lavishly praised black teachers who he thought taught exceptionally well.

Conner married Ella Parker at Lasker, 30 Nov. 1886. He was active in the Methodist church and he founded a Masonic Lodge. He died at Rocky Mount and was buried at Rich Square. Portraits of Conner exist in the Raleigh *North Carolinian*, 21 May 1896, and in *North Carolina: Rebuilding an Ancient Commonwealth*.

SEE: *The Alumnae News* (Woman's College, University of North Carolina, Greensboro); *House Journal, Session 1931*; *North Carolina: Rebuilding an Ancient Commonwealth*, vol. 3 (1928); Raleigh *North Carolinian*, 21 May 1896; Lasker *Patron and Gleaner*, 1892–1896; Raleigh *News and Observer*, 27 Oct. 1931.

WAYNE K. DURRILL

Connor, George Whitfield *(24 Oct. 1872–23 Apr. 1938)*, lawyer, legislator, and judge, was born in Wilson to Henry Groves and Kate Whitfield Connor. He was the first of twelve children, one of whom, Robert D. W. Connor, became a noted historian and first archivist of the United States. His father was a member of the state legislature, serving as speaker during the 1901 session, and was also a superior court judge and an associate justice of the North Carolina Supreme Court.

In many ways, George Connor's life followed that of his father. As a child, Connor attended the Wilson graded schools. In preparation for college, he was tutored by the Reverend B. S. Bronson, rector of Saint Timothy's Episcopal Church. Connor entered The University of North Carolina in the fall of 1888, not yet sixteen years old and the youngest member of his class, and was graduated *cum laude* in June 1892. He then served as principal of Goldsboro High School from September 1892 until June 1894. On 30 May 1894 he married Bessie Hadley, daughter of John C. Hadley of Wilson. They had four children, a son who died in infancy, another who died of an accidental gunshot wound, and two daughters, who grew up and married.

From 1894 until 1897, Connor served as superinten-dent of the Wilson public schools, and from the latter date until 1899 he was chairman of the Wilson County Board of Education. He also studied law, being admitted to the bar in February 1899 and thereafter practicing until his 1913 appointment by Governor Locke Craig as judge of the superior court, second district. Connor maintained a business partnership with J. C. Hadley and Company in Wilson from 1899 to 1912. He served as a trustee of The University of North Carolina from 1905 to 1909. From 1909 to 1911 he served in the state house of representatives and in his last year there was speaker of the house and a member of the Commission on Constitutional Amendments.

Connor served from 1913 to 1924 as superior court judge; in the latter year he was appointed by Governor Cameron Morrison associate justice of the supreme court. He held this position until his death in 1938. During his tenure as supreme court justice, he was a lecturer in the Law School of The University of North Carolina from 1925 until 1929. In 1928 he was awarded an honorary LL.D. degree from the university. He served as chairman of the Committee for the Improvement of the Laws of North Carolina in 1931.

Connor was a conservative, states' rights Democrat. As a legislator he opposed the Federal Income Tax Amendment as long as there was hope of defeating it. He was active in the Episcopal church and several civic organizations in Wilson.

Though in ill health several months before his death of a heart attack, Connor had been active on the bench as late as the previous week. Survived by his wife and two daughters, he was buried in the Connor family plot at the Good Shepard Episcopal Church in Wilson.

SEE: *North Carolina Manual* (1929); *North Carolina: Rebuilding an Ancient Commonwealth*, vol. 3 (1929); North Carolina State Bar *Proceedings*, vol. 36 (1936); *North Carolina: The Old North State and the New*, vol. 4 (1941); Raleigh *News and Observer*, 24 Apr. 1938 (photograph), 4 Sept. 1940; *Who Was Who in America*, vol. 1 (1943).

DARRYL TRAYWICK

Connor, Henry Groves (3 July 1852–23 Nov. 1924), judge, was born in Wilmington, where his parents, David and Mary Catherine Groves Connor, had moved from their native Florida. In 1855, David Connor, a carpenter described as a "master craftsman in woodworking," moved with his family to Wilson to work on the construction of a new county courthouse. He died there in 1867, leaving his widow with married daughters and several school-age children. The son, Henry Groves, who was always called Groves by his family and friends, left school to support himself and assist his mother and

her younger children. He went first to Tarboro to clerk in a store, planning a career in merchandising, but soon, probably through the influence of George Howard of Tarboro, returned to Wilson as clerk and student of law in the office of George W. Whitfield, who was associated in practice with Howard. Whitfield died in 1871, but for the remainder of his life, Howard was one of Connor's closest friends.

Connor completed his legal education by a few months of concentrated study with William T. Dortch of Goldsboro and received his license in 1871 at the age of nineteen. It was later said of him that the only rule he ever broke was the one requiring a practicing lawyer to be twenty-one years of age. In the same year he married Whitfield's daughter Katherine and established a home in Wilson for her, his mother, and a younger sister. In the meantime he had left the Roman Catholic church of his parents to affiliate with the Protestant Episcopal church, which was also that of his wife; the couple became and remained staunch members of St. Timothy's Episcopal Church in Wilson. In 1872 the Connors had a son, the first of twelve children, nine of whom lived to maturity. Connor was a devoted husband and father, and he and his wife shared a long and compatible marriage, dying in the same year.

Early responsibilities made the young man seem older than his years, and his personality, industry, and character soon won for him the respect and regard of his community. He became known as a hard-working and competent lawyer and in 1877 established a partnership with Frederick A. Woodard. His local political popularity was injured by his support of the Prohibition movement, and for several years he was content to work within the Democratic party without seeking office. In 1884 he ran for a seat in the North Carolina Senate as a Cleveland Democrat and was elected to represent the district of Wilson, Nash, and Franklin counties.

In spite of youth and legislative inexperience, Connor was appointed in the senate of 1885 chairman of the Judiciary Committee, a position of great prestige. His most significant service as a senator was his successful sponsorship of the Connor Act, requiring the registration of deeds and thus contributing greatly to the stabilization of land titles in the state.

Connor's contemporaries recognized that he was more interested in professional than in political advancement, and after the creation of additional superior court districts in 1885, on the recommendation of a joint legislative committee of which he was not a member, he was appointed by the governor to one of the new positions. At the next election in 1886 he was elected to the court for a term of eight years; he became widely known as a judge of ability and humanity. His popularity in his community grew to such an extent that when his home burned in 1888, at a time when temporary financial hardship had caused him to allow his insurance to lapse, his neighbors and friends provided the funds to rebuild it.

In 1893 the needs of his growing family caused Connor to resign his position on the bench and return to private practice in order to increase his income and have more time at home. As one of the coexecutors of the estate of Alpheus Branch, founder of the private Branch Banking Company of Wilson, he became closely associated with the legal affairs of the bank; in 1896, on the death of his coexecutor, he became bank president. This was not for him a full-time position, and he continued his other activities while serving until 1907 as nominal president of the bank.

Although Connor was a firm Democrat, in 1894 he was

nominated for a position on the North Carolina Supreme Court by the Populist party. He later wrote that it was the aspiration of his life to serve on the court, but he refused to run as the candidate of the Populists and was so embarrassed by their nomination that he also declined to seek the support of his own party.

When the Democrats lost control of the state as a result of the fusion of Republicans and Populists in 1896, Connor accepted his party's view that the safety and well-being of North Carolina required the return of the Democrats to power. He was an active participant in the campaign of 1898 led by his friend Charles B. Aycock, although he deplored the strong appeal to racial prejudice that marked the campaign. He was elected a representative of Wilson County to the North Carolina House of Representatives, and with Aycock's endorsement received the unusual honor of being chosen speaker in his first term in the house. He was thus a leader in the General Assembly that drafted the constitutional amendment establishing an educational qualification for voting, at the same time protecting the votes of illiterate whites by a "grandfather" clause. Connor's views of suffrage were those of his race and generation, but he was anxious that any restrictions be established openly and constitutionally, and one of his primary motivations was to secure honest elections.

After the adoption of the amendment, Connor was again elected to the legislature in a campaign that returned the state to Democratic control with the election of Aycock as governor. Connor was made chairman of the house Committee on Education and used his influence in opposing proposals to base the allocation of funds to white and black schools on the proportion of taxes paid by each race. He was also influential in effecting a compromise solution to the problem of railroad taxation and regulation, which had become a major issue in the state. It was neither education nor railroads, however, but impeachment that dominated the legislature of 1901, and on this controversy Connor was in a minority in his party and in the house.

The Fusionist legislature had established or altered positions to make places for Republican and Populist appointees, and the Democrats in turn in 1899 had made changes in an enfort to oust these and other officeholders appointed during the Fusion period. The Republican and Populist judges who made up the majority of the Supreme Court of North Carolina declared a number of the changes unconstitutional, basing their decisions largely on *Hoke* v. *Henderson*, a precedent in North Carolina since 1833. Democrats in the house sought to impeach the judges for having ordered the payment of a salary for which there was no legislative appropriation. Connor agreed that the judges had been politically biased and that the legal principle on which they had acted was wrong, but he insisted that no one believed the judges personally dishonest and that a reprimand, rather than impeachment, was the wise remedy. He was able to secure only twelve votes in favor of his position; at the end of the session he left the legislature feeling that his public career was ended, but he was gratified when the senate did not vote to convict the judges.

In 1902, friends encouraged Connor to seek the Democratic nomination to the supreme court in spite of his unpopular stand on impeachment, and he was chosen by the party convention after a close contest. His election was therefore a matter of course, and he began service on the court in February 1903. In that session he delivered the majority opinion in *Mial* v. *Ellington*, overruling a decision of a lower court similar to that which had led to the impeachment trial, and also

specifically overruling *Hoke* v. *Henderson*, thus establishing the ruling that a position created by the legislature could be altered or abolished only by the legislature.

Connor's six years of service on the North Carolina Supreme Court were ended when he was nominated by President William H. Taft and confirmed in May 1909 by the Senate to serve as judge of the U.S. Court for the Eastern District of North Carolina. Taft's choice offended Republican leaders in the state but proved a popular one with most North Carolinians, doing much to alleviate the antagonism toward federal courts then prevalent. Connor left the North Carolina Supreme Court reluctantly, feeling that he could not refuse the unusual honor of Taft's nomination and responding to the urging of friends who thought his service would benefit the state. He held the position for the remainder of his life, even though in some ways he found the work of the federal court less congenial than his service in the state courts had been. He was troubled by the Department of Justice's insistence that the suspended sentence, which he thought a useful device in rehabilitating first offenders, was not permitted by federal law, and he was made particularly uncomfortable by trials relating to the enforcement of World War I draft laws. Among his last work as a federal judge was the settlement of cases growing out of the condemnation of land for the establishment of Fort Bragg. Although some of his decisions were appealed to the Supreme Court of the United States, he had the unusual record of never having one reversed.

Connor was always conscious of his lack of formal education, which he felt rendered him unfit for service as a university trustee or professor, but in reality his devotion to his work, thorough study, and wide reading gave him a superior education that brought him respect as a scholar of law and of history. He was awarded the LL.D. degree by The University of North Carolina in 1908. He wrote a number of articles on lawyers and legal history and a biography of John Archibald Campbell published in 1902. He planned a biography of William Gaston, for which he undertook extensive investigation, but he completed only articles. He refused a professorship of law at The University of North Carolina in 1899 and again in 1922, when the trustees created the Thomas Ruffin Professorship of Law especially for him. He lectured in the Law School in the summer of 1923 and was in Chapel Hill for the same purpose in 1924 when he became ill. He died in Wilson and was buried there in Maplewood Cemetery.

Although Connor was a conservative in his political and economic views, opposed to sudden or drastic change, he was also open-minded and impersonal in considering new ideas and opposing viewpoints. He deplored intolerance in others and in 1923 devoted an entire grand jury charge to a discussion of the dangers inherent in such organizations as the Ku Klux Klan. He was so devoted to individual rights that he was far in advance of most of his contemporaries in his opposition to all corporal and capital punishment. He was known as a kindly and merciful judge but did not permit his sympathies to interfere with his judgment on the merits of a case. His personal dignity and calm were great assets in his profession.

Connor was a fine conversationalist with a great deal of humor, and his wide correspondence was marked by thoughtful consideration of many aspects of public affairs. His personal sweetness of disposition and his integrity of character made him one of the most loved and respected North Carolinians of his generation.

Portraits of Connor were presented to the three courts

with which he was most closely associated: to the superior court of Wilson County went one painted by Irene Price; to the Supreme Court of North Carolina one by Mary Arnold Nash; and to the U.S. Court for the Eastern District of North Carolina, Raleigh, one by Math Van Salk.

SEE: Josiah William Baily, *Henry Groves Connor Address* (1929); Vidette Bass, *Branch: A Tradition with a Future* (1962); Henry Groves Connor, "The Convention of 1835," *North Carolina Booklet*, vol. 8 (1908), "The Granville Estate of North Carolina," *University of Pennsylvania Law Review* 62 (1913), *John A. Campbell* (1920), "William Gaston," in William Draper Lewis, *Great American Lawyers*, vol. 3 (1908); Henry Groves Connor and Joseph B. Cheshire, Jr., *Constitution of the State of North Carolina, Annotated* (1911); Frank A. Daniels, *Henry Groves Connor, An Address* (1926); Josephus Daniels, *Henry Groves Connor, Address* (1929); *North Carolina General Assembly Journals*; N.C. *Reports*; Southern Historical Collection (University of North Carolina, Chapel Hill), for Henry Groves Connor Papers and Robert D. W. Connor Papers; R. H. Wettach, "Henry Groves Connor," *North Carolina Law Review* 2 (1923); Robert W. Winston, *Judge Henry Groves Connor, Memorial Address* (1925).

CAROLYN A. WALLACE

Connor, Henry William (5 Aug. 1793–6 Jan. 1866), planter and congressman, was born near Amelia Court House, Prince George County, Va., and was graduated from South Carolina College, Columbia, in 1812. In 1814 he served as major and as aide-de-camp to Brigadier General Joseph Graham in the expedition against the Creek Indians. After the war he settled as a planter near Sherrill's Ford on the Catawba River.

Connor first ran for Congress against two Federalists in 1819; he was defeated by William Davidson. He defeated Davidson two years later and served in Congress for ten consecutive terms, from 1821 to 1841, seldom facing serious opposition. In February of 1825, when the House selected John Quincy Adams as president, most of the North Carolina delegation supported W. H. Crawford; Connor and Robert B. Vance cast their ballots for Andrew Jackson. For the rest of his political career, Connor was a loyal Democrat. His votes generally opposed centralization of power in Washington. During his first terms on Capitol Hill he was assigned to the Committee on Manufactures, and later he served on the Post Office and Post Roads Committee, of which he was chairman for several years. In his last session he was a member of the powerful Ways and Means Committee. After he retired from Congress, his seat was taken by Green W. Caldwell, a fellow Democrat.

Connor was suggested as the Democratic candidate for governor in 1839. He was president of the Democratic State Convention in Salisbury in 1842 and was elected a councilor of state by the assembly in December of that year. Catawba County sent him to the state senate from 1848 to 1850. He died at Beattie's Ford soon after the end of the Civil War and was buried at Rehoboth Methodist Cemetery in Catawba County.

SEE: *Biog. Dir. Am. Cong.* (1971); J. G. deR. Hamilton, *Party Politics in North Carolina, 1835–1860* (1916); W. S. Hoffmann, *Andrew Jackson and North Carolina Politics* (1971).

DANIEL M. MCFARLAND

Connor, Robert Digges Wimberly (26 Sept. 1878– 25 Feb. 1950), historian and archivist, was born in Wilson, the fourth child and third son of the twelve children of Henry Groves and Kate Whitfield Connor. His father, an attorney, served as a member of the state senate and the house of representatives, of which he was speaker in 1899, and was a judge of the superior court, associate justice of the Supreme Court of North Carolina, and judge of the U.S. District Court.

Connor attended the public schools of Wilson and in 1899 received his Ph.B. degree from The University of North Carolina, where, in his senior year, he was editor-in-chief of all three student publications—the newspaper, the literary magazine, and the yearbook. From 1899 to 1903 he was engaged in public school work at Winston, Oxford, and Wilmington, and from 1904 to 1907 he served as secretary of the educational campaign committee in the office of the superintendent of public instruction.

In 1903, Connor was appointed by Governor Charles B. Aycock to membership on the newly established North Carolina Historical Commission; for four years he served as the unsalaried secretary of the commission. Recognizing that a larger appropriation and more comprehensive legislation were needed for the historical commission to become an effective historical agency, Connor prepared and had published in 1906 an ambitious plan providing the basis for a new legislative act the following year. He then accepted the salaried secretaryship of the historical commission and during the next fourteen years was primarily responsible for the development of one of the nation's outstanding state historical agencies. In 1943 the commission became the North Carolina State Department of Archives and History, characterized by Connor's long-time friend and colleague Waldo Gifford Leland as "a model historical agency, and a living monument to Robert Connor." In addition to his official duties, Connor was secretary of the North Carolina Teachers' Assembly from 1906 to 1912; president (1912) and secretary (1913–20) of the North Carolina Literary and Historical Association; member (1913–20) and secretary (after 1915) of The University of North Carolina Board of Trustees; president of the General Alumni Association of the university from 1917 to 1921; and, during World War I, member of the National Board of Historical Service.

During the academic year 1920–21, Connor was on leave for graduate study at Columbia University. Shortly after his return to North Carolina he resigned as secretary of the historical commission, noting that he had "seen the Commission grow from nothing but an idea and a hope to its present position of importance and influence among its kind in the United States." He accepted the Kenan Professorship in History and Government at The University of North Carolina, where he soon became identified as one of the university's most popular teachers and most productive scholars. A colleague wrote, "Careful preparation of lectures, systematic organization of materials, clarity and wit in presentation were characteristic of his teaching."

Connor's contributions to the field of archival administration were not forgotten, however, for when the position of archivist of the United States was created in 1934, the executive committee of the American Historical Association asked to be permitted to recommend his name to President Franklin D. Roosevelt. At first Connor declined but, upon prodding by J. Franklin Jameson and other leaders of the association, he yielded; on 14 July 1934, Jameson wrote President Roosevelt that Connor was "a man of great administrative capacity, a man of force and character who would wish and would be able to place the new institution on a high level and maintain it there, a man of affairs and action, yet one of quiet and agreeable ways, who has shown by his success in dealing with the North Carolina Legislature the tact and considerate spirit which a novel institution like the National Archives will require. . . . " Three months later the chief executive offered and Connor accepted the position.

The tasks confronting the first archivist of the United States were monumental: the building was not yet finished; a staff had to be employed and trained; a 150-year backlog of records had to be assembled, arranged, and made available to researchers; and both government officials and the public had to be educated to the meaning of what to most of them was a vague word—"archives." That Connor succeeded was attested by Roosevelt, who, upon Connor's resignation in 1941, wrote, "As the first Archivist of the United States you have not only laid the foundation but have built the actual structure of an extremely important and permanent repository for American historical source material. Your record is one which will always be acclaimed with well-deserved appreciation." Connor later recounted some of his vicissitudes in an article, "Adventures of an Amateur Archivist," in the 1943 *American Archivist*.

Connor thus earned the distinction of being the first archivist of both his native state and his nation. But his desire to return to the classroom drew him back to Chapel Hill in 1941, in the newly established Craige Professorship of Jurisprudence and History. He continued his teaching until his retirement in 1949, but his archival interests led him to the presidency of the Society of American Archivists (1941–43) and to the chairmanship of the North Carolina Historical Commission (1942–43) and of the executive board of its successor, the Department of Archives and History (1943 until his death).

An inspiring teacher and pioneering archivist, Connor made yet another contribution to scholarship through his many writings. His first major work, *Cornelius Harnett: An Essay in North Carolina History* (1909) won the Patterson Memorial Cup, and his *Makers of North Carolina History* (1911) was for many years a basic public school textbook. In 1919 he joined with two other outstanding North Carolina historians, J. G. deRoulhac Hamilton and William K. Boyd, in a three-volume *History of North Carolina*; Connor furnished the first volume, covering the colonial and revolutionary periods. His most ambitious work, however, was the two-volume *North Carolina: Rebuilding an Ancient Commonwealth* (1929), the best standard state history published to that time. His bibliography was extensive, including dozens of articles. He also edited numerous issues of the *North Carolina Manual*, including the one for 1913, which was perhaps the most frequently used book published in North Carolina before the middle of the twentieth century. Connor has been characterized by a colleague as "amongst that small group which in the twentieth century for the first time began the literary production by North Carolinians that attracted more than local distinction in quantity and quality."

Connor, an Episcopalian and Democrat, was married on 23 Dec. 1902 to Sadie Hanes of Mocksville. They had no children. He was buried in the Chapel Hill Cemetery. There are portraits in the National Archives, the North Carolina Division of Archives and History, and the North Carolina Collection at The University of North Carolina, Chapel Hill.

SEE: *Annual Reports of the Archivist of the United States*, 1934–42; *Biennial Reports of the North Carolina Historical Commission*, 1903–22; R. D. W. Connor, official

correspondence (National Archives, Washington, D.C.; North Carolina State Archives, Raleigh), and personal papers (Southern Historical Collection, University of North Carolina, Chapel Hill); James L. Godfrey, "Robert Digges Wimberly Connor" (typescript, 1973, files, secretary of the faculty, University of North Carolina, Chapel Hill); H. G. Jones, *The Records of a Nation* (1969); Hugh T. Lefler, "Robert Digges Wimberly Connor," in *Keepers of the Past*, ed. Clifford L. Lord (1965); Waldo Gifford Leland, "R. D. W. Connor, First Archivist of the United States," *American Archivist* 16 (1953); Mary L. Thornton, comp., *A Bibliography of North Carolina, 1589–1956* (1958), and *Official Publications of the Colony and State of North Carolina, 1749–1939* (1954).

H. G. JONES

Cook, Charles Alston (*7 Oct. 1848–21 Oct. 1916*), state legislator and judge, was the son of the Reverend Charles M. and Havana Alston Cook of Warrenton. He attended The University of North Carolina for two years and then enrolled at Princeton University, where he was granted an A.B. in 1870. After study under William Eaton of Warrenton, Cook received his license to practice law in January 1872.

Like most white men in Warren County, where a large majority of voters were black, Cook began his political career as a Democrat. He served as solicitor of the county inferior court from 1878 to 1880. In 1882 he left the Democratic party, declaring that it had deserted its democratic principles. Two years later, at the age of thirty-six, he was the Liberal-Republican candidate for state attorney general.

Cook was a member of the state senate in the session of 1887, representing the counties of Vance and Warren. Following the national Republican victory in 1888, President Benjamin Harrison appointed him U.S. attorney for the Eastern District of North Carolina, an office he held for four years, until 1893. Cook was a delegate to the national Republican convention of 1892. He served his second term as a state senator in the Fusion legislature of 1895. The next year, when his friend Daniel L. Russell won the governorship, Cook returned to the General Assembly as a member of the house of representatives.

Appointed by Governor Russell to fill a supreme court vacancy, Cook was an associate justice from 1901 to 1903. Thereafter he moved to Muskogee, Okla., where he returned to the private practice of law. He was a Republican member of the new state's second legislature in 1909 and an unsuccessful candidate for the state supreme court in 1912. In 1914, just two years before his death, he was defeated as the Republican nominee for Congress in Oklahoma's Second Congressional District.

Cook married Marina Williams Jones of Warren County on 11 Oct. 1871. He was a trustee of The University of North Carolina from 1887 to 1901 and an active member of the Methodist church.

SEE: *Directory of the State of Oklahoma* (1931); D. L. Grant, *Alumni History of the University of North Carolina* (1924); *Legislative Biographical Sketch Book, Session 1887*; *The Oklahoma Red Book*, vol. 2 (1912); *Who Was Who in America*, vol. 1 (1943).

ERIC D. ANDERSON

Cook, James P. (*12 Jan. 1863–22 Mar. 1928*), merchant and legislator, was born at Mt. Pleasant, Cabarrus County, the son of Matthew and Mary Costner Cook. His father (b. 1810) was a native of Baden, Germany, and came to America at the age of twenty, settling first in what is now Gaston County. Until his death at the age of eighty-four, he conducted an expansive mercantile business.

James Cook was educated at Mount Pleasant Collegiate Institute (then called North Carolina College) and was graduated in 1885. For four years he was principal of schools, first in southern Cabarrus County (1885–86), and later at the Boys' High School in Concord (1886–89). He established *The Daily Standard* in Concord and successfully operated it for six years (1890–96). Concurrently, he served as superintendent of schools for Cabarrus County. When he decided to sell his paper and become a special representative for educational publishers, he resigned as county superintendent but was elected chairman of the Cabarrus County Board of Education, serving from 1896 to 1912.

Cook was elected to the North Carolina Senate in 1913 and served one regular and one special session. During his tenure, his assignments included chairmanship of the important Finance Committee and of the Committee on Education. Governor Locke Craig appointed him to the board of directors of the state-owned North Carolina Railroad.

During his days as editor, Cook had promoted a vigorous attack on the treatment of juveniles in the local courts. That subject became the passion of his life. As editor, private citizen, and legislator, he continued his crusade, with little public approval or encouragement. His first major breakthrough came in 1907, when the legislature authorized promotion of a state reform institution for boys. Cook was appointed to its board by Governor Glenn and was named chairman on 3 Sept. 1907. He served as chairman for many years, and through his leadership and the cooperation of many friends in Cabarrus County, a site was provided, two buildings were erected, and the Stonewall Jackson Manual Training and Industrial School was opened 12 Jan. 1909. Cook and his associates ensured that the school's 120 boys were given good educational opportunities and that the "reformatory" angle was minimized. As untitled head of the school, Cook spent as much time as needed away from his vast and profitable farming interests to serve the institution. What the Stonewall Jackson School has become is a tribute to his work and leadership.

Cook was married to Margaret Jeannette Norfleet of Nansemond County, Va., whose parents were descended from prominent revolutionary and colonial Virginia families. The Cooks had no children but were continuously involved in multiple community affairs in Concord and that entire section of the state. They were active in the St. James Evangelical Lutheran Church; and for many years Cook was a trustee of the Mount Pleasant Collegiate Institute, itself under the aegis of the North Carolina Synod of the Evangelical Lutheran Church.

Cook died in Concord and was buried in a local cemetery.

SEE: S. G. Hawfield, *History of the Stonewall Jackson Manual Training and Industrial School* (1946); *History of North Carolina*, vol. 4 (1919).

C. SYLVESTER GREEN

Cook, Staley Albright (*6 Dec. 1895–8 May 1966*), newspaper editor and civic leader of Burlington, was born in southern rural Alamance County, the son of George Henry and Viola Albright Cook. His father was a merchant, public official, and highly respected citizen of Burlington. His uncle, Dr. W. W. Staley (for whom he was named) was the second president of Elon College

(1894–1905) and for many years a prominent minister of the Christian church in Suffolk, Va.

When Cook was three years old, his father moved the family into Burlington, and he attended elementary and secondary schools there. In his mid-teens he entered the U.S. Army and served on the Mexican border under General Donnell E. Scott, for whose company he was the official bugler. During World War I he was a member of the famous Thirtieth Division, brigaded with the British Second Army; he saw active service at the front in France and Belgium.

Following his military service, he enrolled in Northwestern University, Evanston, Ill., and earned a diploma in journalism through the U.S. Veterans Bureau. In 1931 he received a citation in journalism from the Illinois Press Association.

His career with the Burlington *Daily Times-News* began in 1920. He filled a succession of posts there until his retirement in 1963. He worked for fifteen years as a reporter; then became managing editor, chief editorial writer, and chief executive of the company; and in 1957 was named editor and general manager. Through his perceptive editorials and his fearless support of causes he believed right, Cook lifted the *Times-News* to a position of impressive leadership in the Piedmont area of the state. He also wrote occasional articles for *Sports Afield* and other journals and collaborated with Walter Whitaker and A. Howard White in the writing of *Centennial History of Alamance County* (Charlotte, 1949).

For many years, Cook was prominent in the activities of the North Carolina Press Association; he served one year as president of the Associated Press Club. He held memberships in several veterans groups, serving as state commander of Disabled American Veterans, commander of the Walter B. Ellis Post of the American Legion, and member of the Alamance Post of the Veterans of Foreign Wars. He attended many American Legion annual conventions and was tapped as the best bugler in 1934.

His political services to the state included one term in the house of representatives, where his committee assignments were wide-ranging and important: Appropriations, Conservation and Development, Insurance, Military Affairs, Manufacturing, Labor, and Printing. He was cosponsor of the original unemployment service law in North Carolina and, by gubernatorial appointment, became a member of the advisory committee of the Unemployment Compensation Commission. In that same session of the house he introduced a successful bill providing soil conservation practices and served as chairman of a joint subcommittee of the house and senate, for which he prepared the report that ultimately created the Western North Carolina Sanitorium. The Employment Security Commission was one of his successful projects in the house. He also served on the state ports authority in 1949–50, resigning in 1950 to accept an appointment to the board of conservation and development. There his leadership helped make the Alamance Battleground a state historic site.

In addition to all his state services, Cook made himself a valuable citizen of his community and region. He was a long-time chairman of the board of trustees of the Alamance General Hospital and for five years chairman of the trustees of the May Memorial Library. The location of the Burlington Mills in his home city is credited to his efforts, and he was instrumental in securing the Erwin A. Holt property as the site for the municipal building. In the early 1950s he addressed his editorial influence to the need for a new storage lake to vouchsafe the city's water supply; Lake Burlington was the result. He was chairman in 1958 of the Alamance Committee for Improved Courts. Through membership in the local Chamber of Commerce, the Kiwanis Club, and similar organizations, he was a dynamic and steady leader.

Cook was married to Grace Lillian Lane on 1 Aug. 1920. They had two daughters, Nora Lee (Mrs. Allen Drury Tate, Jr.) and Nancy Lane (Mrs. Stephen Irvin Moore, Jr.). Cook was a member of the Front Street Methodist Church for many years. He was buried in Pine Hill Cemetery, Burlington.

SEE: Files of the Burlington *Daily Times-News*.

C. SYLVESTER GREEN

Cooke, Charles Mather (*10 Mar. 1844–16 Jan. 1920*), state legislator, superior court justice, and North Carolina secretary of state, was born near Louisburg, the second son of Jones Cooke, a planter, and his third wife, Jane Ann Kingsbury. Charles's grandfather, Thomas Cooke (1700–1801), emigrated to the Louisburg area from Surry County, Va., and married Arabel Conyers, a Franklin County native. Charles's father, who at one time owned over eighteen hundred acres of land, commanded a company of Franklin County volunteers in the War of 1812 and served for many years as chief justice of the Franklin County Court of Pleas and Quarter Sessions. An active Baptist and moderator of the Tar River Baptist Association (1835–41), Jones Cooke reportedly exercised great influence in organizing the North Carolina State Baptist Convention and in founding Wake Forest College. Jane Cooke, a schoolteacher from New Hartford, Conn., was a daughter of Darius Kingsbury, whose wife, Esther Mather, was descended from Timothy Mather, brother of Cotton.

"Charlie" Cooke, as he was familiarly known, attended Louisburg Male Academy and in 1860 entered Wake Forest College, where he studied for two terms. On 12 May 1862 he enlisted in the Franklin County Farmers, a volunteer company later incorporated as Company I in the Fifty-fifth North Carolina Regiment. Commissioned second lieutenant on 11 Mar. 1863 and promoted to first lieutenant on 1 June that same year, he assumed active command of the company after its captain was captured at Gettysburg. He was detailed as regimental adjutant in June 1864 and served in that capacity until 31 Mar. 1865, when he was severely wounded in action at Hatcher's Run, near Petersburg, Va.

Paroled after Lee's surrender, Cooke returned to Louisburg, and began reading law. Admitted to the county bar (January 1867) and the state bar (January 1868), he entered practice first in partnership with Joseph J. Davis (1828–92) and then, after Davis's election to Congress in 1874, with W. H. H. Spencer. Cooke quickly gained a reputation as an effective and flamboyant trial lawyer with a particular talent for equity cases; throughout the 1880s and 1890s, he supposedly had the largest clientele of any practicing attorney in the Sixth Judicial District. For a time, he represented Patty D. B. Arrington, plaintiff in the celebrated "Peedybee cases," a long, bitter, and complex property suit that at various times involved Charles B. Aycock and Spier Whitaker as attorneys and that was finally investigated by a special committee of the General Assembly in 1895. In 1889, Cooke was counsel for Dr. Eugene Grissom, the superintendent of the state insane asylum, who was charged with mistreatment of inmates and mishandling of state funds. In 1901, Cooke was one of the attorneys representing Supreme Court Chief Justice David M. Furches and Associate Justice Robert M. Douglas in their impeachment trial before the state senate.

At the same time, Cooke, a Conservative/Democrat, pursued an active political career. In 1868 he ran unsuccessfully for the state senate from the seventh district. In 1872 he was a delegate to the Democratic National Convention. In 1874 he was elected to the senate, serving one term, and from 1877 to 1878 he was solicitor for the Sixth District. Appointed by Governor Thomas J. Jarvis to the state board of internal improvements in March 1879, he played a major role in the state's sale of the Western North Carolina Railroad, before resigning in August 1880. From 1884 to 1888 he was a member of the board of directors of the state prison.

Cooke's main political activity, however, was in the state house of representatives, in which he served three terms (1879–83, 1889–91). In 1879 he became chairman of the Judiciary Committee, and in 1881 he was elected speaker. In 1889, after reportedly declining the speakership, he served as chairman of the Committee on Internal Improvements and as vice-chairman of a conference committee on the establishment of a state railroad commission, becoming a central figure in that year's heated debate over railroad regulation. The original measure, establishing a state regulatory commission with far-reaching powers, was killed, and Cooke, who sided with the pro-regulation forces, introduced a bill requiring railroad companies to submit annual reports of their financial transactions. Cooke's bill passed the house, and although it failed in the senate, it established a precedent for much of the later regulatory legislation.

Cooke's lifelong ambition was election to the U.S. House of Representatives, a goal that always eluded him. In 1886 he was Franklin County's favorite-son candidate in a five-way race for the Democratic nomination in the Fourth Congressional District; he withdrew, however, in favor of John W. Graham of Orange County. His withdrawal caused a rift lasting for a generation between the Democratic organizations of Nash County, who saw it as a dirty deal against their candidate, and Franklin County. In 1894 he won the Democratic nomination but was defeated in that year's Fusionist landslide.

In September 1895, Governor Elias Carr appointed Cooke secretary of state to fill the unexpired term of Octavius Coke, who had died in office. In 1896, Cooke ran for a full term but was defeated by the Fusionist candidate, Dr. Cyrus Thompson. Two years later, in a campaign debate with Charles B. Aycock in Charlotte, Thompson claimed that Cooke, as secretary, had failed to disburse funds collected from certain seal taxes as required by law. A few days later, Aycock produced a canceled check, endorsed by Thompson, which purported to show that Cooke indeed had rightfully performed his duties. Thompson refused to accept the check as evidence, but the matter was not pursued further, and Cooke's reputation does not seem to have suffered as a result.

In 1902, in a closely contested convention in Rocky Mount, Cooke defeated Jacob Battle for the Democratic nomination to the state superior court from the Sixth Judicial District. That November he defeated the incumbent, E. W. Timberlake, in the general election. Reelected in 1910, Cooke remained on the bench for twelve years but resigned in 1915 because of poor health. He died at his home, Northfield, in Louisburg and was buried in Oaklawn Cemetery.

Originally a member of Flat Rock Baptist Church, Cooke was among the founders of Louisburg Baptist Church and served it for over twenty-five years as a deacon and Sunday school teacher. In 1876 he was moderator of the Baptist State Convention, and in 1885 he acted as moderator for the August meeting of the Tar River Baptist Association. A long-time member of the board of trustees of Wake Forest College (1871–1919) and The University of North Carolina (1892–1903), Cooke was also a member and past master of the Clinton Masonic Lodge, No. 124.

"The ablest man of his generation," in Josephus Daniels's words, Cooke was famed throughout the state for his speaking ability, wit, and personal charm. Late in his life, as he traveled the judicial circuit, he became legendary for his rotund figure, walrus mustache, and lenient and unconventional courtroom style.

In February 1868, Cooke married Elizabeth ("Bettie") Person (1843–1937), a Franklin County native. The couple had nine children, seven of whom survived to adulthood: Percy Henderson (1871–1912), a Louisburg attorney; Charles Mather, Jr.; Francis Neal (b. 11 Oct. 1875), a career army officer who graduated from the U.S. Military Academy in 1899 and rose to the rank of colonel before retiring to Florida; Frederick Kingsbury (12 Dec. 1877–8 Feb. 1910), a physician and first dean of Wake Forest's Bowman Grey Medical School; Wilbur Carter, a Spartanburg, S.C., cotton merchant; Edwin Mather (1884–1929), a journalist; and Elizabeth Kingsbury (1885–1906).

SEE: Samuel A. Ashe, ed., *Biographical History of North Carolina*, vol. 6 (1907), and *Cyclopedia of Eminent and Representative Men of the Carolinas of the Nineteenth Century*, vol. 2 (1892); "Charles M. Cooke," *North Carolina Bar Association Report*, 1920; Charles M. Cooke, "The Fifty-fifth Regiment," in *Histories of the Several Regiments and Battalions from North Carolina in the Great War, 1861–1865*, ed. Walter Clark, 5 vols. (1901), and *Speech Delivered by Charles M. Cooke in the Dr. Grissom Trial* (1889, North Carolina Collection, University of North Carolina, Chapel Hill); Josephus Daniels, *Editor in Politics* (1941), and *Tar Heel Editor* (1939); Edward Hill Davis, *Historical Sketches of Franklin County* (1948); Tom Henderson, *Judge Cooke* (1942), and "A Judge Cooke Story," *State* 18 (4 Feb. 1950); R. C. Lawrence, "Charles Mather Cooke," *State* 8 (22 June 1940); North Carolina State Archives (Raleigh), for Legislative Papers and Secretary of State Papers; Oliver H. Orr, Jr., *Charles Brantley Aycock* (1961); T. H. Pearce, *They Fought: Franklin County Men in the Years 1861–1865* (1969); Cecil B. Robbins Library, Louisburg College (Louisburg, N.C.), for genealogical material on the Cooke and Person families; Bill Sharpe, "Judge Cooke—They'll Never Forget This One," *State* 30 (19 Jan. 1963); Thomas H. Taylor, *A History of the Tar River Association* (ca. 1924); W. Buck Yearns, ed., *The Papers of Thomas Jordan Jarvis*, vol. 1 (1969).

BENNETT L. STEELMAN

Cooke, James Wallace (13 Aug. 1812–21 June 1869), Confederate naval officer and commander of the ironclad C.S.S. *Albemarle*, was born in Beaufort to Thomas and Esther Cooke. He was orphaned at the age of four years, and he and his sister, Harriet, were reared by their uncle, Henry M. Cooke, collector of customs at the Port of Beaufort. At the age of sixteen, James Cooke was appointed a midshipman in the U.S. Navy; he reported to his first station, the training ship *Guerriere*, on 1 Apr. 1828. Over the next thirty-three years he had extensive

sea duty and service in the naval observatory and commanded the U.S.S. *Relief*. He was promoted to the rank of lieutenant on 25 Feb. 1841.

Upon the secession of Virginia, Cooke resigned his commission in the U.S. Navy on 2 May 1861; two days later he was appointed to the same rank in the state navy of Virginia. His first assignment was with the construction of batteries on the James River. On 11 June 1861 he was appointed a lieutenant in the Confederate Navy and was ordered to duty at the naval batteries on Aquia Creek, which was part of the Potomac River defenses. In the latter part of the summer he was ordered to Norfolk, where he received command of the gunboat C.S.S. *Edwards*.

The surrender of the forts at Hatteras Inlet on 29 Aug. 1861 curtailed Confederate commerce raiding and threatened the entire eastern portion of the state. As a result of the Confederate military concentration in the area, Cooke was ordered to the command of the gunboat C.S.S. *Ellis*, which was a unit in Captain William F. Lynch's "mosquito fleet." Cooke took command of the former canal tugboat on 3 Oct. 1861.

When the Union forces attacked Roanoke Island on 7 Feb. 1862, the Confederate gunboats were engaged all day. The *Ellis* expended all its ammunition as well as that of the disabled *Curlew*. The Confederate fleet retired the next morning to Elizabeth City for repair and supply. The powerful Union flotilla, commanded by Commander Stephen Rowan, followed closely, and on 10 Feb., after a brief and devastating action at Cobb's Point near Elizabeth City, the Confederate fleet ceased to exist. Although beset by two superior Union vessels, Cooke refused to surrender and with his cutlass met the swarming boarders. After suffering two wounds he was finally overpowered. He received his parole at Roanoke Island on 12 Feb. 1862 and returned to his home in Portsmouth, Va., for recuperation.

Cooke was promoted to the rank of commander on 25 Aug. 1862, to date from 17 May, and following his exchange he was assigned to duty in North Carolina. He was ordered to proceed to Halifax to oversee the construction of an ironclad ram under contract by Gilbert Elliott. Under the resourceful leadership of the two men, the ram was built in a cornfield near Edward's Ferry on the Roanoke River. Constructed of yellow pine and armored with four inches of iron, the vessel was 152 feet in length, 45 feet wide, and drew 8 feet of water. The armament consisted of two 100-pound Brooke rifled cannon mounted in pivot. Christened the C.S.S. *Albemarle*, the new ship was destined to become one of the most famous and successful of the Confederate ironclads.

By April 1864 the *Albemarle* was so near completion that the Confederate command proposed a combined army-navy operation against Union-occupied Plymouth, a small port near the mouth of the Roanoke River. Cooke agreed to have the ironclad ready for action, and on the evening of 17 Apr. the vessel began its maiden voyage with portable forges and workmen aboard to fit the final layer of armor. With the aid of high water the *Albemarle* passed the Union river obstructions above Plymouth, and at 3:30 A.M. On 19 Apr. two Union ships, U.S.S. *Miami* and U.S.S. *Southfield*, steamed into view. In minutes the *Albemarle* rammed and sank the *Southfield* and drove the battered *Miami* past Plymouth. All day, shells from the ironclad rained on the Union fortifications, forcing their surrender on 20 Apr. to General Robert F. Hoke. In recognition of the crucial role of the *Albemarle* in the victory at Plymouth, the Confederate Congress presented a resolution of thanks to Cooke and his crew. Secretary of the Navy Stephen Mallory wrote, "The signal success of this brilliant naval engagement is due to the admirable skill and courage displayed by Commander Cooke, his officers and men, in handling and fighting his ship against a greatly superior force of men and guns."

The fall of Plymouth threatened the Union position in Eastern North Carolina, and a formidable fleet was gathered in Albemarle Sound to prevent further operations by the *Albemarle*. In an effort to cooperate with a Confederate move on New Bern, on 5 May 1864 the *Albemarle*, with two consorts, steamed down to Albemarle Sound to challenge the heavily armed Union fleet commanded by Captain Melancton Smith. For several hours seven of the Union ships engaged the *Albemarle* in a sustained and fierce battle in which the U.S.S. *Sassacus* unsuccessfully rammed the ironclad. That evening the lightly damaged *Albemarle* withdrew, leaving several disabled Union ships. The *Albemarle* did not attempt another sortie, and the balance of naval power remained stable in the area until 27 Oct. 1864, when Lieutenant William B. Cushing succeeded in sinking the ram *Albemarle* with a torpedo in one of the most daring acts of the war.

Cooke was promoted to captain on 10 June 1864 for "gallant and meritorious conduct." A week later he was detached from the *Albemarle* and given command of the inland waters of North Carolina, a post he held until his parole at Raleigh on 12 May 1863. His record in the Confederate Navy established him as one of America's great naval officers. Following the war, Cooke returned to Portsmouth, Va., where he lived in retirement.

In Norfolk, on 5 July 1848, Cooke married Mary E. A. Watts of Portsmouth. The Cookes made their home in Portsmouth and had a family of three sons.

SEE: Walter Clark, ed., *Histories of the Several Regiments and Battalions from North Carolina in the Great War, 1861–1865*, vol. 5 (1901 [photograph]); C. A. Evans, ed., *Confederate Military History*, vol. 4, *North Carolina*, by D. H. Hill, Jr. (1899); R. Johnson and C. Buel, eds., *The Way to Appomattox*, vol. 4 (n.d.); V. C. Jones, *The Civil War at Sea*, vol. 3 (1962); *Official Records of the Union and Confederate Navies*, scattered vols.; *Register of the Officers of the Confederate States Navy* (1931); J. T. Scharf, *History of the Confederate States Navy* (1887 [photographs]).

LINDLEY S. BUTLER

Cooke, John Rogers (*9 June 1833–10 Apr. 1891*), Confederate soldier, merchant, and civil administrator, was born at Jefferson Barracks, Mo. His father, Phillip St. George Cooke, then a first lieutenant in the First Dragoons, U.S. Army, was a native of Frederick County, Va. He was eventually to attain the rank of major general and retire from the army after fifty years of service. Young Cooke was educated at Harvard College as a civil engineer and in 1855 was commissioned directly into the U.S. Army as a second lieutenant serving in the Eighth Infantry. He saw service in Texas, New Mexico, and Arizona.

Upon the secession of Virginia from the Union at the outbreak of the Civil War in 1861, Cooke resigned his commission in the army and offered his services to General Theophilus Holmes, commander at Fredericksburg, Va., Cooke was accordingly made a first lieutenant. The horror of a family divided by a civil war was graphically illustrated with Cooke's family: he was in the Confederate Army; his father remained loyal to the Union and commanded cavalry in McClellan's Union army; one of Cooke's sisters, Flora, married James E. B.

("Jeb") Stuart, the famous Confederate cavalry leader, who was destined to fight against his father-in-law; another of Cooke's sisters, Maria, married a Confederate surgeon, Dr. Charles Brewer; and the third sister, Julia, married a Union general, Bvt. Brigadier General Jacob Sharpe.

Cooke raised a company of light artillery after the First Battle of Manassas and served with it along the Potomac. In February 1862 he was made a major and assigned to duty as chief of artillery of the Department of North Carolina under General Holmes. On 16 Apr., at the request of General Robert Ransom, Cooke was elected colonel of the Twenty-seventh North Carolina Regiment. He was to prove a most able commander and soon grew to be quite popular with his men, who found him firm in the enforcement of orders but not a martinet. A kind man, he looked after his troops, and they in turn responded with affection and a willingness to follow in battle equaled by few other regiments.

In the spring of 1862, McClellan's Union Army was advancing on Richmond, Va., in the Peninsula campaign, and Holmes's command was called to Virginia to help meet it. Cooke and the Twenty-seventh North Carolina Regiment accompanied Holmes there as a part of William Walker's brigade. During the great Seven Days' battles in front of Richmond (26 June–2 July 1862), Cooke's regiment was unengaged. It spent the remainder of the summer around Petersburg, seeing no action other than harassment of Union shipping in the James River. In September 1862, Cooke and the Twenty-seventh, now a part of a two-brigade division commanded by Walker, accompanied Lee's army northward into Maryland on the first invasion of the North. In the attack on Harper's Ferry, W. Va., Cooke's regiment participated in seizing Loudon Heights. When the town fell on 15 Sept., Walker's division hurried to join the rest of Lee's army at Sharpsburg, Md., on the bank of Antietam Creek.

During the battle of Sharpsburg, or Antietam, 17 Sept. 1862, Cooke commanded his regiment and the Third Arkansas in filling a crucial gap. General James Longstreet, commanding that part of the field, sent repeated messages to Cooke to hold his position at all costs, because it was the "key to the whole line." Though his ranks had heavy losses and were entirely without ammunition, Cooke did just that. For two and a half hours the men remained in their position without a cartridge, until the Union advance lost momentum and ceased. The stand made by Cooke's two resolute regiments held Lee's center together and saved the day, though it cost the Twenty-seventh North Carolina alone some 203 of its 325 men. Generals Jackson, Walker, Longstreet, and Lee all mentioned Cooke in their reports of the battle; he won the admiration of the entire army and earned a reputation as a hard fighter.

When the army returned to Virginia, Cooke, though he was junior colonel of his brigade, was appointed brigadier general on 1 Nov. 1862, to rank from the same date. His appointment was confirmed 22 Apr. 1863, and he was given command of a newly created brigade of North Carolina troops consisting of his own former regiment and the former Fifteenth, Forty-sixth, Forty-eighth, and Forty-ninth regiments. This brigade was a part of Ransom's (formerly Walker's) division. Not long afterward, Cooke got a chance to lead his new command in the Battle of Fredericksburg, Va., 13 Dec. 1862. There he was seriously wounded, but his brigade did admirable service throughout the battle.

In January 1863 the brigade was transferred to South Carolina, and Cooke resumed command in February.

The brigade remained in South Carolina until 26 Apr. 1863, when it was sent to North Carolina and aided in repelling Union forces following the Battle of Gum Swamp near Kinston. Early in June, Cooke's brigade was rushed to Richmond to join Lee's army once again, as a part of Henry Heth's division, for the Gettysburg campaign. At Richmond, however, the brigade was detained; Cooke and his men spent the summer there and around Fredericksburg, moving from place to place to repel threatening Union advances. In October it was finally assigned to Heth's division and participated in the pursuit of the Union Army from near Culpeper Court House. At Bristoe Station, over Cooke's protest, a hopeless attack was ordered. Cooke lost about 700 of his 1400 men in about thirty minutes of fighting and was himself severely wounded. He did not return to duty until the middle of April 1864.

Cooke led his brigade in the Wilderness campaign and was engaged in heavy fighting on the afternoon of 5 May 1864 (the first day of the Battle of the Wilderness), at the intersection of the Orange Plank Road. During the course of the afternoon's fighting, the brigade lost 1080 of its 1800 men but took a conspicuous part in the battle. From this day until the summer, it was almost constantly engaged; Cooke himself was again wounded.

During the early part of the siege of Petersburg, Cooke's brigade served in the trenches around the city. On 25 Aug. 1864 it took a conspicuous part in the Battle of Reams' Station on the Weldon Railroad, south of Petersburg. Lee himself highly complimented the efforts of Cooke and his men in this battle. During the fall of 1864 and the winter of 1864–65, the brigade took part in the operations of the right flank of Lee's army, southwest of Petersburg. On 25 Mar. 1865, Cooke was put in charge of two brigades of Heth's division to act as a support for General James B. Gordon's attack on Fort Stedman. The attack failed, however, and Cooke's two brigades were not used. In the days following this action, Cooke and his own men were engaged in the fighting on the extreme right of the Confederate line, beyond Hatcher's Run southwest of Petersburg. When at last, on 2 Apr. 1865, Union forces broke through Lee's lines around Petersburg, Cooke found himself senior officer in command of four small brigades cut off from the rest of the army by the Union attacks. This little command was overpowered at Sutherland's Station, west of Petersburg, by pursuing Union forces, but part of it escaped to rejoin the rest of Lee's army in its retreat to Appomattox. Cooke led his brigade in the retreat and on 9 Apr. 1865 surrendered his 560 officers and men, the largest brigade in Heth's division, along with the rest of the army.

Cooke's leadership throughout the war was sound. He was popular with and respected by his men and his superiors alike. In 1864, Colonel R. H. Chilton, Lee's chief of staff, transmitted to Cooke a letter in which Lee praised Cooke as the finest of his brigadier generals and his brigade as the finest of the army. Wounded a total of seven times during the war, Cooke missed promotion to the rank of major general only by the ending of the war.

After the war, Cooke entered the mercantile business in Richmond, Va., and later became prominent in the affairs of city and state. He served for several years as a member of the city committee of the Democratic party. He was also the director of the Chamber of Commerce and president of the board of directors of the state penitentiary. One of the founders of the Confederate Soldiers' Home in Richmond, he also served as manager. He was one of the first Confederate commanders of the Lee Camp, United Confederate Veterans, and acted as chief of staff at the laying of the cornerstone of the Lee Monument in Richmond.

Cooke was married to Nannie G. Patton, of Fredericksburg, Va., daughter of Dr. William F. Patton, surgeon, U.S.N. The couple had eight children. Cooke died in Richmond and was buried at Hollywood Cemetery.

SEE: Mrs. John H. Anderson, "The Confederate Generals of the Old North State," (typescript, North Carolina Collection, University of North Carolina, Chapel Hill); Walter Clark, ed., *Histories of the Several Regiments and Battalions from North Carolina in the Great War, 1861–1865,* 5 vols. (1901); C. A. Evans, ed., *Confederate Military History,* vol. 4, *North Carolina,* by D. H. Hill (1899); Douglas Freeman, *Lee's Lieutenants,* vols. 2–3 (1943–44); J. G. deRoulhac Hamilton, ed., *The Papers of Thomas Ruffin,* 2 vols. (1918–20); Ezra Warner, *Generals in Gray* (1959); Marcus J. Wright, *General Officers of the Confederate Army* (1911).

PAUL BRANCH

Cooke, William Dewey (27 May 1811–20 May 1885), educator of the deaf, editor, publisher, and cartographer, was born in Williston, Vt., to Milo and Harriet Bulkley Cooke. He was educated in Middlebury College, Middlebury, Vt., receiving the B.A. degree in 1832.

Cooke appears to have commenced his professional life by giving private instruction to students in Staunton, Va. After his marriage in 1834 he served jointly with his father-in-law, Lyttleton Waddell, as principal of Staunton Academy. Afterward he taught in Waynesville, Va., and was then briefly associated with his brothers H. B. and Robert L. in their Bloomfield (N.J.) Female Seminary. Though Cooke never lost interest in the New Jersey school, he soon gave up active participation in it in order to study for two years under Harvey Prindle Peet (1794–1873) in the New York Institution for the Instruction of the Deaf and Dumb, where he was awarded the M.A. degree.

In 1840, Cooke returned to Staunton; a school for the deaf, established there in the year of his marriage, was in the early 1840s entertaining plans of expansion both of physical plant and faculty. At the end of two years, in which he taught deaf students privately, it became apparent to him that delay in enlarging the school in Staunton would defer indefinitely the realization of his hope to be added to its faculty. In October 1843, consequently, he entered into correspondence with Governor John Motley Morehead on the subject of a private school for the deaf in North Carolina. The governor was receptive to the proposal and for the purpose offered Cooke the use of a tavern building he owned in Leakesville. Cooke considered Raleigh the proper location for such a school, however, and a visit to North Carolina in the winter of 1843–44 confirmed his opinion. Further correspondence with North Carolinians and appeals to various Presbyterian bodies suggested a public rather than a private school; as a result, Cooke sought public support for his proposal in a second visit to the state.

On 28 Dec. 1844, Cooke and his pupil Daniel M. Albright of Greensboro demonstrated to the General Assembly of North Carolina the method of teaching the deaf. The demonstration created a sensation. Eleven days later an act to establish the North Carolina Institution for the Deaf (now the Governor Morehead School) was ratified by the General Assembly. A few days after passage of the act, the literary board met and appointed Cooke principal, with instructions to open the school as soon as possible. The institution accepted its first students and opened on 1 May 1845. For the next fifteen years, Cooke served as head of the school and in this capacity made a lasting contribution to the state. In the fall of 1860 he resigned in order to accept the principalship of the Georgia Institution for the Education of the Deaf and Dumb, located at Cave Springs. After the Georgia school was closed during the Civil War, Cooke removed to Maryland, where he became principal of that state's school for the deaf. In 1871 he returned to Staunton to become principal teacher in Virginia's Institution for the Education of the Deaf, Dumb, and Blind; he remained there until his death.

As part of the curriculum of the North Carolina Institution for the Deaf, Cooke, characterized as possessing "a wonderful genius for mechanics," engaged a printer and established a press at the school. His brief experiment with the periodical the *Deaf Mute* (1849–51) appears to have led him into editing and publishing. His next venture was a literary newspaper, the *Southern Weekly Post* (6 Dec. 1851–24 Nov. 1855); Calvin Henderson Wiley originally coedited the newspaper but was forced to resign by the press of his duties as superintendent of common schools. Simultaneously with the newspaper, Cooke published and edited other periodicals. As a member and secretary of the executive committee of the Agricultural Society of North Carolina, he interested himself in agricultural developments in North Carolina and during 1853 and 1854 published John F. Tompkins's *Farmer's Journal*. When it failed, Cooke edited and published the *Carolina Cultivator* (March 1855–October 1857), with the assistance of Benjamin Sherwood Hedrick, professor of agricultural chemistry in The University of North Carolina. Through the university's Historical Society of North Carolina, of which he was a member, he became involved in the mounting movement to stir up public interest in the history of the state. From its revival in January 1852 through March 1857, Cooke published the *University of North Carolina Magazine* for the society, and in 1853 he compiled and published essays by Francis Lister Hawks, David Lowry Swain, and William Alexander Graham under the title *Revolutionary History of North Carolina*.

Cooke's brief association with Calvin H. Wiley led him into other fields. As early as 1852, Wiley and Cooke were joined by Samuel Pearce of Hillsborough in a joint effort to compile a gazetteer, natural history, and authoritative map of the state (the most recent predecessor, executed by Robert H. B. Brazier, was two decades old). Cooke immediately brought out a modest *Outline Map of North Carolina* (1852), and the three men set about gathering necessary data for their considerably more ambitious project. Though the General Assembly supported their proposal for a map, Wiley disengaged himself from the venture in 1854 in order to devote his total effort to common schools. Probably as a result of Wiley's withdrawal, Cooke and Pearce restricted their effort to the compilation of a map. They were successful, and in 1857 the map was published (presumably through the press of the Institution for the Deaf) under the title *Cooke's New Map of North Carolina*; Pearce's name was included in small letters in the lower right corner of the map, but with no statement of credit or explanation. In July 1858, Joseph Hutchins Colton of New York republished the map, still under date of 1857, using a newly engraved plate from which reference to Pearce had been excised. As an authority, this map was replaced within a decade by *Pearce's New Map of the State of North Carolina*. Cooke's experience with his and

Pearce's compilation apparently guided him in his subsequent *Map of the Routes to the Virginia Springs, Giving All Routes and Distances . . .* , lithographed in Richmond by Ritchie and Dunnavant in 1858.

A stockholder and director of the North Carolina Mutual Life Insurance Company, Cooke resigned his position as a member of its executive committee before leaving for Georgia. He maintained his membership and interest in the Presbyterian church and the Independent Order of Odd Fellows until his death of bronchitis in Staunton, Va.

Cooke was married to Lucy Ann Waddell on 2 Oct. 1834; the couple had nine children: Maria Elizabeth, Lyttleton Waddell, Mary St. Clair, William Latimer, Fanny Skinner, Harriet Latimer, Louisa Gordon, Charles Lyttleton, and James Addison.

SEE: North Carolina State Archives (Raleigh), for Governors' Papers (Morehead), William A. Graham Papers, Legislative Papers (1844–45), Map Collection, and Calvin H. Wiley Papers; *Our Living and Our Dead* 1 (1874); *Raleigh Register*, 3 Jan. 1845; Raleigh *Spirit of the Age*, 7 July 1858; Earl G. Swem, *Maps Relating to Virginia* (1914); Virginia State Archives (Richmond), for Augusta County Marriage Register (1813–50), Staunton City Death Register (1853–96), and Staunton *Valley Virginian*, 21 May 1885.

GEORGE STEVENSON

Cooley, Harold Dunbar (26 July 1897–15 Jan. 1974), lawyer, farmer, and congressman, was born in Nashville, Nash County, one of five children of Roger A. Pryor and Hattie Davis Cooley. He was educated in the public schools of Nash County. Cooley's father died when he was nine years old and his mother when he was sixteen; the five orphaned Cooley children decided to maintain their family home and "bring each other up," a decision that resulted in the formation of strong family ties among the four children surviving after one of them, Hubert, was killed in an automobile accident.

As a youth, Cooley showed little inclination to follow his father in the path of the law. When he was eighteen, however, he made the first of two decisions that were to have basic effects upon shaping his future, and decided to enter the legal profession. He attended the Law School of The University of North Carolina for two years and then, in the spring of 1918, applied to take the North Carolina Supreme Court's examination for admission to the bar, prior to graduating from law school and prior to attaining the minimum licensing age of twenty-one. He received his license to practice law on his twenty-first birthday.

After passing the bar examination, Cooley enlisted in the U.S. Navy. He was engaged in ground training with the Naval Aviation Flying Corps in Massachusetts at the conclusion of World War I. Before returning to North Carolina, he was accepted as a special student at the Yale University Law School, where he studied constitutional law under William Howard Taft. He returned to Nashville in 1919 and opened a law office. He soon developed a successful practice, being particularly adept at courtroom work; later he formed a partnership with Walter Bone.

Cooley first became active politically as an advocate for other candidates of the Democratic party; in the process, he became known for his oratorical ability. He was one of the chief advocates for the Democratic presidential and gubernatorial nominees in the election of 1928, and in 1932 he was one of the Democratic presidential electors in North Carolina. Two years later, following the death in

Cooley

April 1934 of Edward W. Pou, who had represented the Fourth Congressional District uninterruptedly for thirty-three years, Cooley decided to become a candidate. Although there were five candidates for the Democratic nomination, Cooley received a majority vote and was nominated in the first primary. In the general election he was elected for the first of seventeen successive terms in the U.S. House of Representatives.

Cooley's service in Congress was associated primarily with agricultural affairs and agricultural policy. His interest in agricultural matters stemmed from his early and close personal association with farming, in connection first with his father's farming activities and then with his own. Even while practicing law and serving in Congress, he continued to operate his farms, and visits to them were a regular part of his schedule when he returned home. During his first campaign for election he announced that he would seek membership on the House Committee on Agriculture if he were elected; and, in spite of the difficulty of securing membership on such an important committee as a first-year congressman, he succeeded. He joined the committee during the early stages of the development of the New Deal agricultural program, took an active part in the formulation of the program, and thereafter remained a lifelong advocate of its many features: production controls through acreage and marketing allotments, parity price supports for agricultural products, aids to farm credit, rural electrification, and soil conservation. Twice during his congressional career he opposed administration proposals for modifications of agricultural policy that he thought threatened the New Deal price support program. This opposition brought him into conflict with both a Democratic and Republican secretary of agriculture, each of whom had the support of the president. Cooley opposed the so-called Brannan Plan, proposed by Secretary of Agriculture Charles Brannan with the support of President Truman, to pay a direct government subsidy to producers of perishable farm products, the subsidy to equal the difference between parity price and the lower price on the open market when the goods were sold. This principle of maintenance of farm income by subsidy was to replace the program of government loans to maintain parity prices on the market, a program that produced large government-owned surpluses. The same policy was advocated by Ezra Benson, President Eisenhower's secretary of agriculture, for butter producers.

In 1949, in the Eighty-first Congress, Cooley's seniority on the House Agriculture Committee secured for him its chairmanship; the first North Carolina representative to hold this position in 104 years, he continued in it for the remainder of his congressional tenure, except during the Eighty-third Congress, when a Republican majority controlled the House. This important chairmanship consumed a large part of his time and energy, but it enabled him to wield a large influence in the House, particularly on matters dealing with agriculture. He utilized this influence in the early 1960s to secure approval of the Food for Freedom Program, which provided for the government's sale of surplus farm commodities in foreign nations. Cooley considered that this program would not only aid people in needy nations but would also help to solve a major problem of American agriculture, underconsumption of farm products, by helping to create a foreign market. His long tenure as committee chairman and his constant advocacy of agricultural welfare led him to be recognized as the outstanding representative of farm interests in the House.

Cooley's success in securing support in Congress for agricultural legislation was based partly on his skill in maintaining good working relationships with representatives of other interests; he exchanged support, for example, with proponents of urban programs. When opponents criticized him as too liberal for his constituency, he defended himself by maintaining that support of these so-called liberal measures enabled him to secure sufficient votes for his agricultural programs. As he told reporters after his defeat for reelection in 1966, "I voted for a lot of things I caught hell for, but I couldn't just vote for peanuts, popcorn, cotton, and tobacco and nothing else. I never betrayed my conscience, though."

Cooley's voting record and his clashes with Secretaries Brannan and Benson and Presidents Truman and Eisenhower were not the only controversial issues in which he became involved as chairman of the House Agricultural Committee. Because of the program of maintaining parity prices through loans to farm producers, the government held large stocks of surplus goods. This phenomenon and the charge that the program contributed to higher consumer prices made price supports increasingly controversial and especially unpopular in urban centers during the 1950s and 1960s. Another controversy in which Cooley became involved occurred during the Johnson administration. Liberal elements attacked Cooley, claiming that he used the influence of his chairmanship to put pressure on House Democratic leaders to prevent Adam Yarmolinsky's appointment as an important assistant to Sargent Shriver, head of President Johnson's antipoverty program. Cooley insisted he had no personal opposition to Yarmolinsky's appointment but that, in acting to block it, he was merely representing the wishes of the North Carolina House delegation. Another subject on which he became the target of criticism was his sponsorship of legislation establishing import quotas for foreign sugar producers. He was charged with being the tool of lobbyists for sugar interests and with accepting favors, particularly from the Dominican Republic, in return for favorable decisions concerning sugar quotas. His reply to these charges was that the sugar quota policy was in the nation's interest and that the whole question of sugar quotas was too complicated to explain to the layman. He acquired from his critics the nickname "sugar daddy."

Along with his interest in domestic agriculture, Cooley also developed strong interest in world agricultural affairs. In the post-World War II days he represented Congress on a number of committees that studied agricultural problems abroad, and in this connection he traveled in both Europe and in the Pacific area. He also attended meetings of the Inter-Parliamentary Union as an American delegate in Cairo in 1947, Rome in 1948, Stockholm in 1949, and Dublin in 1950, serving as president of the American delegation at some of the conferences. He was consultant and congressional adviser to the United Nations Educational, Scientific, and Cultural Organization.

After his success in the 1934 election, Cooley remained the representative of the Fourth North Carolina District until December 1966, with little opposition until 1964. His long record of political success was to a large degree based on his active advocacy of agricultural interests, particularly tobacco farming, in a district that until his later years was heavily rural, with a predominant interest in farming. His success was also, no doubt, facilitated by his personal characteristics: a rather large and somewhat debonair man, he was personally attractive; and to his appearance he added a basically sincere friendliness in his dealings with people.

In 1956 a Raleigh radio commentator, W. E. Debnam, opposed Cooley for the Democratic nomination, but Cooley easily turned back the challenge. In 1964 and 1966, however, both in the Democratic primaries and in the general elections, he faced formidable opposition. In 1964 a Raleigh attorney, Mayne Albright, who had unsuccessfully attempted to secure the Democratic gubernatorial nomination in 1948, contested his nomination; in 1966, Cooley faced primary opposition from William Creech, an attorney from Smithfield in Johnston County, who had moved to Raleigh in order to run for the office when Johnston County was separated from the Fourth District. Cooley succeeded in beating back both challenges, but only after strenuous campaigns and by rather narrow vote margins in each case.

In both 1964 and 1966, Cooley was offered strong opposition in the general election by his Republican challenger, James W. Gardner, a young Rocky Mount businessman. In 1964, Cooley defeated Gardner by about 5000 votes of some 140,000 cast. Immediately upon his defeat, Gardner announced that he would try again two years later and embarked upon a vigorous campaign of public appearances and work within the Republican party organization in the state. In his second effort, Gardner was successful, defeating Cooley after a bitter campaign, by approximately 12,000 votes of about 96,000 cast.

In 1923, Cooley married Madeline Matilda Strickland, whom he had known since boyhood; a graduate of the New England Conservatory, she was an accomplished pianist. They had two children, Roger A. Pryor II and Hattie Davis. Shortly after their marriage, the Cooleys purchased the Gassaway house on Nashville's Main Street, gratifying Cooley's desire to have the largest, whitest house in town. This remained their home, and they returned to it when he left his congressional seat in December 1966 and resumed his Nashville law practice.

Cooley died at Wilson Memorial Hospital, where he had been hospitalized for several months for treatment of emphysema. He was buried in Forest Hill Cemetery in Nashville.

SEE: *Biog. Dir. Am. Cong.* (1971); *Charlotte Observer*, scattered issues; *Congressional Directory* (1966); *Congressional Quarterly Almanac*, vol. 20 (1964); *Congressional Quarterly Weekly Report* 24 (11 Nov. 1966); *Durham Morning Herald*, scattered issues; Rowland Evans and Robert Novak, "The Yarmolinsky Affair," *Esquire* 63 (1965); William S. Powell, ed., *North Carolina Lives* (1962); Raleigh *News and Observer*, scattered issues; Paul A. Samuelson, *Economics*, 6th ed. (1964); Bland Simpson, "Barometer of Political Rebellion: The Fourth Congressional District of North Carolina, 1964–1966" (typescript, North Carolina Collection, University of North Carolina, Chapel Hill); Southern Historical Collection (University of North Carolina, Chapel Hill), for Cooley's papers.

L. WALTER SEEGERS

Coon, Charles Lee (*25 Dec. 1868–23 Dec. 1927*), educator and reformer, was born on a farm four miles west of Lincolnton, the first of nine children of Frances E. Hovis Coon (1842–1907) and David A. Coon (1834–1921). He was a descendant of Revolutionary and Civil War veterans and an inheritor of a rich Germanic culture (the family surname was originally spelled Kuhn). His father had risen to the rank of first lieutenant in the Confederate Army and on the third day of the Battle of Gettysburg had been wounded nine times, left for dead,

captured, and then imprisoned until the war's end. A respected leader in his community, David Coon served as an elder of Daniel's Evangelical Lutheran Church and as a member of the Lincoln County Board of Education.

As with his father, church and school were important forces in the life of young Charles Coon. A lifelong Lutheran, he joined Daniel's Evangelical Lutheran Church at age twelve, and his religious training influenced his views and rhetoric for the rest of his life. He attended the one-room school that met in Daniel's Church for ten years and then obtained additional education in the late 1880s at Concordia College in Conover, a coeducational college supported by the Lutheran church. While a student at Concordia, Coon spent a part of each year teaching in nearby rural public schools, and after graduation he became principal of Denver Academy in Lincoln County. He quickly earned recognition as a successful teacher and school organizer. In 1891 he returned to Concordia College as a teacher of English, history, and mathematics; before leaving Conover in the spring of 1896, he served as the town's mayor and began his editorship of the *Lincoln Democrat*, a four-page, weekly newspaper dedicated to the principles of the Democratic party. Coon published the paper from 27 Sept. 1895 until 1 Oct. 1896, gaining journalistic training, increased writing skill, and useful techniques for influencing public opinion.

After leaving the staff of Concordia College, Coon taught one year at Piedmont Seminary in Lincolnton and then was employed in 1897 by the Charlotte graded schools. Although he was becoming well known as a proficient teacher and a qualified conductor of teaching institutes, he was dismissed from his Charlotte job at the end of 1898 because he failed to conform to formalistic school practices. From November 1896 to June 1899, while his teaching career was in a state of flux, he supplemented his income by writing for the *Charlotte Observer*. Through numerous articles under the pseudonym "Teacher," he set forth his educational creed and his views on current school problems. By the end of the nineteenth century he had emerged as an active and well-informed educational critic and an avid campaigner for public school support. When The University of North Carolina's state funds were threatened by a denominational anti-state aid movement in 1896 and 1897, he championed the state university as the capstone of the public education system. In response to the 1897 legislative authorization of matching state funds for localities levying supplementary school taxes, Coon cooperated with State Normal President Charles D. McIver and State Superintendent of Public Instruction Charles H. Mebane in an unsuccessful attempt to create sentiment for district school taxation.

In June 1899, Coon was appointed superintendent of the Salisbury graded school system. During his term as superintendent, he reorganized the school administration, drew up a new course of study, sought out qualified teachers, tightened student discipline, and organized a school building program; as a result of his efforts, school enrollment rose, the term became longer, more diverse subjects were offered, and a high school level of education became available. Most importantly, Coon changed public attitudes and built up popular support for the public school system. In addition to his work in Salisbury, he took part in a state-wide movement to create public support for better schools. In February 1902, at the behest of Charles D. McIver and Governor Charles B. Aycock, a conference of state educational leaders met in Raleigh to rededicate themselves to the drive for universal education. Coon attended the meeting and was author of its educational manifesto, the "Declaration against Illiteracy." Described by historian R. D. W. Connor as "one of the most important documents in the history of education in the South," the declaration was widely circulated as the birth announcement of North Carolina's educational awakening.

In February 1903, Coon left his state to carry the fight for universal education to the rest of the South. He moved to Knoxville, Tenn., to become secretary and editor of the Bureau of Investigation and Information of the Southern Education Board. He served the board as chief propagandist, statistician, campaign organizer, and editor of its bulletin, *Southern Education*, which covered a broad range of educational topics and was frequently cited by the press. After the functions of his bureau were transferred North, Coon spent four months establishing a model rural school (Farragut School) near Concord, Tenn. He then returned to North Carolina and in July 1904 was appointed the first superintendent of Negro normal schools by State Superintendent of Public Instruction James Yadkin Joyner. For more than two years, Coon endeavored to upgrade the training of black teachers by revising the normal curriculum and consolidating school facilities. Then, from January to July 1907, he served as Joyner's chief clerk, devising new forms for school records and reports and compiling the first complete index to public school law. During his stay in Raleigh, Coon took part in the organization of the North Carolina Child Labor Committee and became its first secretary. For ten years he was active in the organization, fighting the arguments of the mill interests, supporting cooperation with the National Child Labor Committee, and organizing campaigns for needed state child labor legislation.

As a constructive critic of the established educational order of the early twentieth century, Coon presented teachers, legislators, and the public with a definite program of school reform. His fundamental goals were clarification of state and local educational responsibilities, a uniform system of school administration, larger units of local administration, an equitable system of local financial support, elimination of politics from school affairs, a respected and influential teaching profession, expertise in educational techniques, and professionally chosen textbooks. Coon insisted that teachers were both the core of the educational problem and potentially the chief element in its solution; he sought the creation of an organized profession with high academic and ethical standards. He was active in the North Carolina Teachers' Assembly, serving on committees on professional ethics and the history of education. In an address as outgoing president of the assembly in November 1911, he called for an end to haphazard, confused, inefficient school measures and for the creation of a well-defined and unified state school program. The address, entitled "The Need of a Constructive Educational Policy for North Carolina," became Coon's best-known and most debated denunciation of the state's education failings.

In the years following his 1911 address, Coon was involved in numerous legislative battles. He helped secure a special school for the retarded, Caswell Training School, and was active in campaigns for a strong compulsory attendance law and concomitant child labor regulations, for improved methods of teacher certification, and for longer school terms.

In addition to his influence on state school law, Coon created a modern consolidated school system at the county level that set a pattern for the rest of North Carolina. In his capacity as Wilson city school

superintendent (1907–27) and Wilson County superintendent (1913–27), he implemented a forward-looking program aimed at equalizing educational opportunities for urban and rural school children. His administration of the Wilson city schools brought higher quality teaching, a rise in teacher salaries, better student discipline, a growth in attendance, a broader course of study, increased local financial support, and more school buildings. The crowning achievement of his building program was a modern high school, which fittingly received his name in 1928 and his portrait in 1929. As county superintendent, he developed one of the earliest county-wide consolidated school systems in the state. He increased local financing through a county school tax and built central schools to which students were transported by county-owned buses. His consolidation plan resulted in the abolition of all one-room white schools and earned him local admiration as Wilson County's "father of education." School progress in Wilson County gained him recognition as the educational pacesetter for the rest of the state.

Black students in Wilson County received benefits from consolidation—new buildings, higher paid teachers, their own black school supervisor—but Coon's plans for improvement of black schools were still uncompleted at his death. During his lifetime, he served the cause of black education as propagandist, statistician, opponent of racial division of school funds, and proponent of increased opportunities. In his own state and elsewhere, he became known as a courageous spokesman for black education. His most notable speech was delivered in Atlanta in 1909 before the Twelfth Annual Conference for Education in the South. Entitled "Public Taxation and Negro Schools," the address stirred up controversy with statistics showing that black public schools were no "burden" for white taxpayers in North Carolina, Virginia, or Georgia. Misinterpretations of the address led to criticism of Coon in the *News and Observer*, to which friends responded with a defense of his right to free speech. According to participant and historian R. D. W. Connor, the Atlanta speech controversy helped widen the bounds of intellectual freedom in North Carolina.

Coon was president of the North Carolina School Peace League and a member of the editorial board of the *North Carolina Historical Review*. The year before his death, The University of North Carolina recognized his contributions with an LL.D. In 1960 his name was added to the North Carolina Educational Hall of Fame.

Coon was a very prolific writer and orator. Among his numerous articles and speeches were "The Beginnings of a County School System," *Addresses and Proceedings of the National Educational Association*, 1923; "The Beginnings of the North Carolina City Schools, 1867–1887," *South Atlantic Quarterly*, July 1913; "Charles Duncan McIver and His Educational Services, 1886–1906," *Report of the Commissioner of Education*, 1908; "The History of Textbook Adoption in North Carolina," *North Carolina Education*, November and December 1910; "The Next Step," *Southern Workman*, November 1903; and "School Support and Our North Carolina Courts, 1868–1926," *North Carolina Historical Review* 3 (July 1926). Also notable was Coon's *Public Schools of Wilson County, North Carolina* (1924), the record of consolidation progress. Of value to historians are his three volumes of educational documents: *The Beginnings of Public Education in North Carolina, 1790–1840*, 2 vols. (1908), and *North Carolina Schools and Academies, 1790–1840* (1915).

For the last two decades of his life, Coon made his home in the Eastern North Carolina town of Wilson. He had been married on 21 Oct. 1903 to Carrie Sparger (1882–1970), a native of Mount Airy, a graduate of the State Normal College, a teacher in Salisbury in 1902–3, first president of the Wilson Woman's Club, and a teacher and elementary school principal in Wilson. The Coons' children were Frances Elizabeth (b. 1905), Mary Moore (b. 1908), and Charles Lee, Jr. (1912–67).

Coon died after a two-day illness and was buried in the Wilson cemetery.

SEE: "Charles Lee Coon," *North Carolina Teacher*, February 1928; Charles L. Coon Papers (Manuscript Department, Library, Duke University, Durham), for Coon's research on North Carolina Germans; Southern Historical Collection (University of North Carolina, Chapel Hill), for an autobiographical sketch and bibliography; Charles D. McIver Papers (University of North Carolina, Greensboro); Southern Education Papers (Southern Historical Collection, University of North Carolina, Chapel Hill); State Superintendent of Public Instruction Papers (North Carolina State Archives, Raleigh); Charles L. Van Noppen Papers (Manuscript Department, Library, Duke University, Durham), for a biographical sketch by R. D. W. Connor; *Who's Who in America* (1926–27).

GEORGE-ANNE WILLARD

Cooper, David Young (21 Apr. 1847–20 Dec. 1920), tobacconist, industrialist, and financier, the son of Alexander Cooper and Harriet J. Young, was born in Granville County. His grandfather, James Cooper of Glasgow, Scotland, moved to Granville County from Virginia at the close of the eighteenth century and settled at Grassy Creek. Alexander Cooper resided throughout his life at Grassy Creek, where he became an elder in the Little Grassy Creek Presbyterian Church, a successful farmer and slaveowner, and a justice of the peace.

David Young Cooper received his early education at country schools near his home. From 1858 to 1863 he attended Horner Military School at Oxford, afterward serving a year in the Confederate Army. For five years after 1867 he operated the family farm.

In 1872, Cooper moved to Henderson, where he began the commercial and industrial career in which he became prominent. His first enterprise was the establishment of a tobacco auction warehouse in partnership with his uncle, James Crawford Cooper. The Cooper Warehouse made Henderson a leading tobacco market, and from 1875 to 1895, Cooper was one of the largest sellers of fine tobacco in the South. He purchased his uncle's interest in 1886 and personally directed the enterprise until 1902, when he relinquished operation to his sons Sydney Perry and Alexander. Cooper was also instrumental in organizing the Henderson Storage Warehouse. With this facility, it was no longer necessary to ship tobacco to Richmond and Petersburg for storage and certification, and therefore Henderson's position as a tobacco market was improved.

In 1895, Cooper organized the Henderson Cotton Mill. The mill opened with a capital of $90,000 and rapidly proved successful. In 1898 a second mill, the Harriet Cotton Mill, named in honor of Cooper's mother, was organized with a capital of $240,000. Until his death he presided over both mills, which soon became the largest employers in the region and the largest producers of hosiery yarn in the South. They continue to be a major force in the economy of Vance County.

Among his other financial endeavors, Cooper was a director of the Durham and Northern Railway, the Seaboard Airline Railway, the Commercial and Farmer's

Bank of Raleigh, and, from its formation in 1889, the Citizens Bank and Trust Company.

Cooper was active in civic and church affairs. He helped found the Henderson graded schools by organizing prominent citizens of Henderson to establish Central School in 1899. Operation of the school was undertaken by the General Assembly in 1901. Cooper was also prominent in the movement to establish Vance County from portions of Granville, Franklin, and Warren counties, a movement that succeeded in 1881. A member of the Episcopal church, he was active in acquiring St. Mary's School in Raleigh for the church and served as a trustee of the school from the date of its acquisition.

Cooper married Leah Hilliard Perry, daughter of Dr. Sydney Perry of the prominent Franklin County family, on 24 Feb. 1876. Four sons and a daughter were born of the marriage. Leah Cooper died in 1897, and in 1898, Cooper married Mrs. Florence Davis, daughter of Nicholas Chavasse of Henderson and granddaughter of Sir Thomas Chavasse, an eminent English surgeon.

Cooper was buried in Elmwood Cemetery in Henderson.

SEE: Samuel A. Ashe, ed., *Biographical History of North Carolina*, vol. 1 (1905); *History of North Carolina*, vol. 5 (1919); *North Carolina: The Old North State and the New*, vol. 3 (1941); Marjorie W. Young, *Textile Leaders of the South* (1963).

GEORGE T. BLACKBURN II

Cooper, John Downey (15 Mar. 1849–21 Jan. 1921), tobacconist, manufacturer, financier, and public servant, was born at Willow Hill in Granville County, the son of Alexander Cooper, a planter and county official, and Harriet Young Cooper. His brothers David Young and James Crawford became prominent in the economic development of Henderson; another brother, Madison Cooper, became a wealthy banker and capitalist in Waco, Tex.

Cooper received his primary education from his mother and supplementary instruction at the Horner Military School in Oxford. Following a brief attempt at farming, he journeyed to Texas, where he herded stock for Millet and Mabry, then the largest stock raisers in Texas. His travels continued, leading him to Kansas, California, Nebraska, and the Dakota Territory, where he prospected for gold. He was a member of the second party to explore the Black Hills region. In 1876 he returned to North Carolina and settled at Henderson, becoming a tobacco buyer for the Allen and Ginter Company of Richmond, Va. He continued as agent for the American Tobacco Company when that combination absorbed Allen and Ginter in 1914. The city council of Henderson appointed Cooper to fill a vacant mayoralty, and he was subsequently elected to a full term in 1883. As mayor and later as chairman of the Vance County Highway Commission, he was instrumental in developing improved roads and city streets for the area. His life of public service included vigorous support for the development of the Henderson public school system.

In 1890, Cooper organized the Cooper-Parham Supply Company, first of the many successful, independent enterprises he promoted. He joined with his brother David Y. to organize the Henderson Cotton Mill in 1895 and the Harriet Cotton Mill in 1898; together, they soon became the largest producers of hosiery yarn in the country. Cooper is chiefly noted as founder of the Carolina Bagging Company in 1908, for some time the largest manufacturer of cotton bagging in the United States. He was also president of the Farmers' and

Merchants' Bank in Henderson and of the Vance-Guano Company.

Seven sons and a daughter were born to Cooper and his wife, Fannie Spotswood Burwell, of a prominent Virginia family: George, John Downey, Jr., Lewis Ginter, James Wesley, David Alexander, Henry Burwell, Marshall Young, and Fannie Cooper Zollicoffer.

Cooper was a member of the Methodist Episcopal church and a Shriner. He was buried in Elmwood Cemetery in Henderson. A portrait by Mary Burwell is in the home of Mrs. John D. Cooper, Jr., Henderson.

SEE: *History of North Carolina*, vol. 4 (1919); *North Carolina: The Old North State and the New*, vol. 3 (1941).

GEORGE T. BLACKBURN II

Coor, James (*fl. 1737–1795*), naval architect, builder, and revolutionary leader, probably was born in England but apparently moved to North Carolina from the Eastern Shore of Maryland to serve as a naval architect at the invitation of Thomas Webber of Jones County, owner of land on Trent River as well as in New Bern. In New Bern Coor is said to have drawn plans for a house for Webber at 506 Craven St., as well as one for himself on the same street and for several other men. The Masonic Lodge and the New Bern Academy are also said to have been designed by him. Webber's and Coor's houses, the lodge and the academy still stand. His own house was built on a strong foundation of shell rock. A niece, Sarah Groendyke, stayed with Coor during his last years, and her husband, Benjamin Woods, joined her there after their marriage. In Apr. 1818 the dwelling was purchased from James Groedyke by William Gaston, who had his law office in the yard.

One James Coor was clerk of court in Craven County from 1737 to 1739, and by 1742 was married to Mary, youngest daughter of Thomas Smith of New River. The name of James Coor appears as witness to or executor of wills between 1743 and 1775, but it is not certain that this James Coor was the man of that name who was active during the Revolutionary War.

Coor was one of eighty-two subscribers to *A Collection of All the Acts of Assembly, of the Province of North-Carolina, in Force and Use, Since the Revisal of the Laws in 1751* published in 1764 by James Davis and one of fifty-seven subscribers in North Carolina to John Hawkesworth's *A New Voyage, Round the World, in the Years 1768, 1769, 1770, and 1771, under taken by . . . Captain James Cooke*, printed in New York in 1774.

Coor served three terms in the colonial assembly representing Craven County between 1773 and 1775. In 1775 and 1776 he served on the New Bern Council of Safety and during the same years on the provincial council. He was also one of the county's delegates to the second, third, fourth, and fifth provincial congresses that met between 1775 and 1776. He was present at the adoption of the Halifax Resolves and at the drafting and adoption of the first state constitution. Between 1777 and 1787 he represented Craven County in the state senate for twelve sessions, serving as speaker during the 1786–87 session. In 1791–92 when he was the New Bern borough representative in the House of Commons he voted to grant financial aid to the new University of North Carolina. In December 1775 he was one of two men designated by the council to receive money for the completion of a fort on the Neuse River. In July 1776 he was appointed commissioner for the port of New Bern and apparently continued to serve at least until 1781, when he was referred to by Governor Richard Caswell

as the Naval Officer of New Bern. Between 1792 and 1794 he was a member of the council of state and in 1792 was also a member of the New Bern town commission. He served the state as a commissioner of accounts and on one occasion in this connection he and his son Thomas were paid £144.9 for keeping accounts. The 1790 census records Coor living in a household that included two women and nine slaves. In October and November 1795 he advertised for a runaway slave who was described as "a good hand by water" and who might try to go to sea as he had done before. Coor presumably was dead by 1800 as his name does not appear in the census of North Carolina for that year.

SEE: John Cheney, *North Carolina Government, 1585–1974* (1975); Walter Clark, *State Records of North Carolina*, vols. 10, 12–13, 15–19, 22, 24 (1890–1905); R. D. W. Connor, ed., *A Documentary History of the University of North Carolina*, vol. 1 (1953); Craven County Records (North Carolina State Archives, Raleigh); *Newbern Gazette*, 31 Oct., 7 Nov. 1795; William S. Powell, *Patrons of the Press* (1962); John D. Whitford, "The Home Story of a Walking Stick—Early History of Baptist Church at New Bern, N.C." (North Carolina State Archives, Raleigh).

GERTRUDE CARRAWAY

Copeland, Oliver Perry (*23 Nov. 1816–?*), portrait artist, was born in Suffolk, Va., the son of Benjamin and Sophia Jones Copeland. He was still living at Suffolk in 1840, when he delivered a Fourth of July oration there, but soon afterward he moved to Northampton County, N.C., where he had married Sarah Hill in April 1839. For the next twelve years he supported himself as a portrait artist in Northampton and neighboring counties in Virginia and North Carolina. In 1850 he exhibited at Richmond, Va., a canvas entitled "The Death-Bed of Wesley"; in 1853 he toured various North Carolina towns with the same painting and three others, "Faith," "Hope," and "Charity." After showing these pictures in Hillsborough, Greensboro, and elsewhere, he took his works to the first North Carolina State Fair (1853) and won first prize for the Wesley scene.

After the fair closed, Copeland opened a studio in Raleigh and offered lessons in drawing and painting. In 1857 he moved to Oxford to take a position as drawing instructor at Oxford Female Academy. His wife died in Oxford on 16 Feb. 1858, and he soon afterward resigned his position. He found similar work at Louisburg Female Academy in the same year and also appears to have worked for a time at Warrenton. In February 1861 he married Henrietta C. Gambol of Warwick County, Va.; thereafter, he appears to have lived and worked at Norfolk, where he is known to have had a studio in 1871.

Copeland's North Carolina subjects included Samuel Wait, first president of Wake Forest College, and Mrs. Wait; the Reverend Charles Force Deems of Greensboro; Dr. W. R. Scott of Raleigh; and members of the Gray family of Northampton, the Gatling family of Hertford County, and the Ridley and Shands families of North Carolina and Virginia. A large canvas by Copeland, entitled "Old Rip Van Winkle Wide Awake," depicted North Carolina's progress in agriculture, industry, commerce, and so on and attracted a good deal of attention at the North Carolina State Fair in 1854.

Copeland was a lifelong supporter of the temperance movement and sometimes gave public readings of a long poem of his own composition entitled "Poetic Essay on Dram Drinking." He was also a professional daguerreotypist. The date of his death is not known. Of the ten children borne by his first wife, three survived their mother; the census of 1850 lists a son named Raphial and a daughter named Eumuke.

SEE: L. MacMillan, *North Carolina Portrait Index* (1963); Oxford *Leisure Hour*, 25 Feb. 1858; G. W. Paschal, *History of Wake Forest College*, vol. 1 (1834); Raleigh *Spirit of the Age*, 18 Jan. 1854, 1 Mar. 1854, 25 Oct. 1854; Suffolk (Va.) *Christian Sun*, 1 Sept. 1871.

THOMAS C. PARRAMORE

Coppridge, William Maurice *(24 July 1893–28 Aug. 1959)*, physician, teacher, statesman, pioneer urologist in North Carolina, clinical professor of urology at The University of North Carolina School of Medicine in Chapel Hill, and chief of urology and director of clinical laboratories at Watts Hospital in Durham, was born in Danville, Va., the son of William David Coppridge, an insurance man of Danville and Roanoke, Va., and Mary Ellen Ferguson Coppridge of Milton, N.C. He attended public schools in Danville and in Roanoke, when his family moved there in 1910. He entered St. Mary's College in Belmont, N.C., in 1911 and transferred from there in 1913 to The University of North Carolina; in 1916 he enrolled in the then two-year medical department, from which he earned a certificate of satisfactory accomplishment in 1916. He transferred to Jefferson Medical College, Philadelphia, receiving an M.D. degree in 1918 and spending a year of postgraduate work in the Philadelphia Polyclinic Hospital. There he came under the influence of Dr. B. A. Thomas, a distinguished teacher and professor of urology in the University of Pennsylvania School of Medicine. Coppridge's interest in the specialty of urology and in the chemical pathology of urinary tract disease began in this period.

Coppridge returned in 1919 to Chapel Hill, where he was appointed assistant professor of pathology to Dr. James B. Bullitt and, according to Bullitt, was indispensable to the pathology department while Bullitt himself served in the medical corps with the Sixty-fifth General Hospital during World War I. Coppridge also began the organization of a laboratory of clinical pathology in Watts Hospital in Durham. On 2 July 1919, he married the University of North Carolina Infirmary nurse, Ferrie Patterson Choate of Steele Creek, near Charlotte. Early in their married life they lived on Ward K in Watts Hospital, and Mrs. Coppridge was operating room supervisor. Their marriage was without issue but was enriched by the custody of Coppridge's nephews: Dr. Alton James Coppridge, a urologist in Durham, and the Reverend James Wendell Ligon, a Presbyterian minister who was a missionary in Indonesia and afterward a resident of Charlotte.

Coppridge practiced general surgery with Dr. Foy Roberson until his department of urology was certified for residency training in 1935 by the American Board of Urology. Coppridge was a founding member of the North Carolina Urological Society in 1930 and its first president; founding member of the Southeastern Branch of the American Urological Association and president from 1944 to 1946; founding fellow of the American Urological Association; member of the executive committee of the Southern Medical Association (1941–46); fellow of the American College of Surgeons; member of the Durham-Orange County Medical Society and president in 1925 and 1946; member of the North Carolina Medical Society and president in 1946–47; founding member of the Medical Care Commission in North Carolina, serving under five governors (1945–59); and a member of the American Medical Association, the

New York Academy of Science, the Tri-State Medical Society, the Durham County Board of Health (eight years), the North Carolina Board of Medical Examiners (1938–44), the Governor's Committee on Physicians' Needs in North Carolina (1937–38, 1944–45), and the Société Internationale d'Urologie. In World War I he served in the Medical Reserve Corps; in World War II he was chief of medical services for the North Carolina Office of Civil Defense and a member of the state Committee for Procurement and Assignment of Medical Personnel. He was given The University of North Carolina Medical School's Distinguished Service Award in 1955, and in May 1959 he was elected to the presidency of the American Urological Association, the highest professional honor an American urologist can attain.

Coppridge, author of fifty-seven scientific publications, was for forty years a member of the Watts Hospital staff. His interest in improved medical training and better health for all the citizens of the state is reflected in his wise and courageous leadership in the creation of the state Good Health Plan and the development of a four-year medical school and teaching hospital at the university in Chapel Hill.

Coppridge belonged to the Durham Pistol Club, the Democratic party, and the Presbyterian church. He died after four weeks in the New England Baptist Hospital. Funeral services were conducted in the First Presbyterian Church in Durham, and he was buried in Maplewood Cemetery. Ferrie Patterson Choate Coppridge died on 27 Feb. 1974 in Durham.

SEE: Coppridge Memorial Library Dedication, 6 June 1965, University of North Carolina Alumni Office (Chapel Hill); *Durham Herald-Sun*, 28 and 29 Aug. 1959; *Medicine in North Carolina*, 2 vols. (1972).

WARNER WELLS

Corbin, Francis *(d. 1767)*, council member, judge of the court of admiralty, associate justice of the general court, legislator, colonel of the militia, county justice, and agent and attorney to John Carteret, Earl Granville (proprietor of the northern counties of North Carolina), was born in Great Britain of unknown parentage. The rumor current in mid-eighteenth-century North Carolina that he was a natural son of Earl Granville appears to have been without foundation in fact. Corbin seems, however, to have had some claim to the earl's favor and patronage, and he remained intimately concerned in Granville's North Carolina proprietary affairs from 14 Nov. 1744 until 25 Apr. 1759.

The charter granting most of the northern half of the colony to Earl Granville (the only one of the Lords Proprietors of Carolina who declined to sell back to the Crown his share of the original 1663 grant) was perfected on 17 Sept. 1744. Two months later, Granville sent Corbin to America with the original of the new proprietary charter, an office copy of his surrender of claim to the remaining seven-eighths of the original territory of Carolina, printed exemplifications of each, packets for the governors of the two Carolinas, and instructions for Edward Moseley, who had since 1 Sept. 1740, served as the Earl's agent in revenues from quitrents. It was made clear in Granville's instructions to Moseley that Corbin was to be given responsibilities in the conduct of proprietary affairs, but the earl's intentions appear to have been ignored by Moseley, who preferred to share his duties with Robert Halton. In any event, Granville had provided Corbin with neither a commission nor a power of attorney. Consequently, Corbin found himself without immediate employment in North Carolina. Whether he is to be identified with the Francis Corbin who advertised himself as a teacher of reading, writing, and arithmetic in the 16 Dec. 1745 *South Carolina Gazette* remains doubtful.

A hiatus in the proprietary correspondence for this period prevents certain knowledge, but Corbin must have appealed to his patron. At any rate, when Granville named commissioners on 5 Sept. 1746 to act for him in surveying the extension of the southern boundary of the proprietary, Corbin was added to the list otherwise comprised of Moseley, his family connections, and his political associates: Robert Halton, Roger Moore, Matthew Rowan, James Hasell, James More, and John Swann. This association with political opponents of Governor Gabriel Johnston may account in part for Corbin's subsequent opposition to the governor. Shortly after the extension of the southern boundary was surveyed, Corbin returned to London and there, in 1748, joined anti-Johnstonian forces seeking the governor's removal. The strongest part of Johnston's London-based opposition was made up of Henry McCulloh, the land speculator, and his associates Arthur Dobbs, Jeremiah Joye, and Samuel Smith. Acting upon information received from Moseley, Corbin and his later associate in Granville's proprietary affairs, Thomas Child, added their testimony to charges against Johnston of maladministration and disloyalty to the Crown. By the summer of 1749 the charges had come to naught, Moseley and Halton had died, and Corbin and Child were still in London.

In October 1749, Granville commissioned Child and Corbin his proprietary agents and gave them powers of attorney for North Carolina; both men returned to the colony, set the proprietary affairs upon a business footing, and opened the land office in Edenton in October 1750. Shortly thereafter, Child returned to London. Though Corbin was joined in the performance of his commission successively by James Innes (1751–4), Benjamin Wheatley (1754–6), and Joshua Bodley (1756–59), he remained the principal proprietary agent resident in the colony during the following decade.

By virtue of his commission as proprietary agent, Corbin was given appointments in the colony's royal government. He was simultaneously a member of the governor's council, judge of the court of vice admiralty, an associate justice in the colony's general court system, colonel of the Chowan County militia, and a justice in Chowan's court of pleas and quarter sessions. Though he subsequently fell into disfavor with Governor Arthur Dobbs and was removed from his various offices, Corbin appears to have performed his governmental duties well. His proprietary duties, however, were allowed to suffer neglect.

Corbin's conduct as agent to Earl Granville came under contemporary fire, and as principal resident agent he probably should be held accountable for the abuses practiced on the earl's tenants. There is no evidence that Corbin defrauded the proprietor, but he was unhappy in his choice of proprietary underofficers. His lieutenants charged excessive fees and made illegal and arbitrary decisions regarding disputed land claims; business was so ill-attended that the procedure of granting the land to tenants, which should have taken from six to twelve months, was not infrequently dragged out for six to twelve years. The tenants' ill will toward the proprietary underofficers was eventually extended to Corbin. Moreover, Corbin came under the displeasure of persons of consequence in the colony. He incurred the wrath of

Governor Dobbs by reporting to Earl Granville (not only the proprietor but also one of the principal secretaries of state and a member of the Privy Council) that the governor had illegally granted proprietary lands. Corbin next greatly offended the colonial connections of the land speculator Henry McCulloh, by issuing patents for land situated on a tract of nearly three hundred thousand acres within the proprietary reserved to McCulloh by treaty with the earl. Matters came to a head in January 1759, when Colonel Alexander McCulloch, with an extralegal posse from Halifax, Edgecombe, and Granville counties, seized Corbin in Edenton and forcibly carried him off to Enfield; there he and his coagent, Joshua Bodley, were held under armed guard and obliged to give bond for the reformation of the proprietary land office. The Enfield Riot, as it came to be called, was fraught with disastrous results for Corbin. He was unsuccessful in his attempt to bring the ringleaders to justice and was, in addition, stripped by Dobbs of all Crown offices in the colony except his seat on the governor's council. After Earl Granville removed his protection and revoked his power of attorney to Corbin on 25 Apr. 1759, Dobbs removed him from the council as well.

That Corbin stood for election and was immediately returned a member of the General Assembly from Chowan County may serve as an indication that his reputation was not materially touched in his home county. As a member of the assembly he joined with principal proprietary agent Thomas Child, Robert Jones, proprietary collector of quitrents, and former proprietary collector Thomas Barker in opposing the administration of Governor Dobbs. From April 1760 through May 1765, Corbin represented Chowan County in the General Assembly. On 19 Mar. 1763 he was restored by Dobbs to his position as a justice in the colony's highest court of law, with a commission as associate justice on the bench of the Edenton District Superior Court. After the death of Dobbs, Governor William Tryon proposed in 1766 to readmit Corbin to the governor's council, but Corbin's death a few months later intervened.

In 1761, Corbin married Jean Innes, widow of Colonel James Innes; from about 1764, the couple appear to have lived mostly at the Innes plantation in New Hanover County. There Corbin died and was buried sometime between 16 Jan. and 7 Apr. 1767. He was survived by his widow and by a kinsman traditionally spoken of as his brother, Edmund Corbin. The widow's administration of Corbin's estate appears to have been unsatisfactory, and after her death further administration of his estate was granted first to Edmund Corbin in 1775 and subsequently to Thomas Craike in 1783.

Though the town originally called Corbinton in his honor was eventually renamed Hillsborough, Corbin is still memorialized in the name of Corbin Street, Salisbury. His town house in Edenton, the Cupola House, is a reminder of the elegant taste of this controversial colonial figure.

SEE: *Acts of the Privy Council of England*, vol. 4 (1911); Granville Proprietary Records (Longleat, Wiltshire, England); North Carolina State Archives (Raleigh), for Colonial Court Records, Governors' Papers, Granville Papers, and Secretary of State Records; William L. Saunders, *Colonial Records of North Carolina*, 10 vols. (1886–90).

GEORGE STEVENSON

Corbitt, David Leroy *(3 May 1895–12 Oct. 1967)*, archivist and historical editor, was born in Chicod

Township, Pitt County, the second of three children and only son of James Samuel and Mary Virginia Parkerson Corbitt. His father, a part-time Primitive Baptist preacher, was a farmer and small businessman in Pitt County.

"Roy" Corbitt as a child worked on the farm; at the age of eleven he took the first of several temporary jobs, this one in a textile mill in Greenville. Successive illnesses—typhoid fever, smallpox, and rheumatism—struck him by the time he was sixteen years of age. From the latter, subsequently diagnosed as arthritis, he never recovered; after three weeks in Johns Hopkins Hospital in Baltimore, he was sent home in 1912 with little hope for life. But, despite the crippling effects of the disease, he learned to use a wheelchair and later a cane and crutch. Largely restricted to his home, he spent most of his time reading, sewing, embroidering, and whittling. A carelessly lighted firecracker resulted in the loss of sight in his right eye. These misfortunes delayed his graduation from high school until he was twenty-four years old. He then took a job in the Greenville mayor's office, where for a year he served as justice of the peace and notary public.

On 13 Mar. 1920, Corbitt's mother died, leaving him in the care of his father and younger sister, Mary. Tragedy struck again in August when Mary died. Unable even to put on his socks and tie his shoes, Leroy was taken in by his uncle, Charles Parkerson.

With the help of friends, relatives, and summer jobs, Corbitt attended The University of North Carolina, where he received his A.B. degree in 1924. Shortly after graduation he secured employment with the North Carolina Historical Commission in Raleigh, where he was chief library assistant until 1926 and chief archivist from that year until 1945. In 1945 he became head of the division of publications of the agency, which by then had become the North Carolina Department of Archives and History. He was assistant editor of the *North Carolina Historical Review* from 1926 to 1935 and managing editor from then until his retirement in 1961.

During his thirty-seven years with the state's historical agency, Corbitt contributed significantly to the expansion of both the archival and the publications programs. In addition to his administrative work and editorial supervision over the *North Carolina Historical Review* and many documentary volumes and pamphlets, he compiled and edited nine volumes of public addresses and releases of North Carolina governors from Morrison through Umstead. His most widely used production, however, was *The Formation of the North Carolina Counties, 1663–1943* (1950). He wrote numerous articles and book reviews and also edited *Calendars of Manuscript Collections [in the State Archives]* (1926); *Handbook of County Records Deposited with the North Carolina Historical Commission* (1925); *Explorations, Descriptions, and Attempted Settlements of Carolina, 1584–1590* (1948, 1953); *Secretaries of the United States Navy: Brief Sketches of Five North Carolinians* (1948); and *Pictures of the Civil War Period in North Carolina* (1958).

Corbitt was a popular speaker on state and local history. On behalf of the North Carolina Literary and Historical Association, he assisted in organizing historical societies in thirty-eight counties and was a frequent participant in their meetings. In 1958–59 he was president of the Historical Society of North Carolina and vice-president of the North Carolina Society of County and Local Historians. He was elected an honorary life member of the Literary and Historical Association and a fellow of the Society of American Archivists, and he was an active participant in other professional organizations.

Following his retirement from the Department of Archives and History in 1961, Corbitt continued for two years as a part-time consultant, working primarily on records relating to the Granville grant. In the 1965 legislative session he was librarian for the General Assembly.

In an unpublished autobiography completed in 1966, Corbitt wrote, "A person who does not have difficulties or handicaps to overcome does not fully understand the real meaning of living a worthwhile life." He overcame his difficulties, and few persons of the twentieth century have contributed more to the preservation and dissemination of North Carolina history.

Corbitt married Alma Jordan of Chatham County on 10 Oct. 1927. They had no children but for many years gave a home to his niece, Dorothy Cox, who married Dr. Pierre Elias Awad of Egypt. Corbitt was buried in Montlawn Memorial Park in Raleigh.

SEE: David Leroy Corbitt, "This Is My Life: A Brief Autobiography" (typescript, David Leroy Corbitt Papers, North Carolina State Archives, Raleigh); *Directory of American Scholars*, 1959 ff.; "In Memoriam: David Leroy Corbitt," *Thirty-Second Biennial Report of the State Department of Archives and History*, 1966–68; William S. Powell, ed., *North Carolina Lives* (1962); *Who's Who and What*, 1949, 1954; *Who's Who in American Education*, 1959–60.

H. G. JONES

Corbitt, Richard Johnson (15 Feb. 1873–16 May 1961), founder and director of one of the few automotive manufacturing enterprises in the South, was born in Enfield. His father, Carr Bowers Corbitt, a Confederate veteran and native of Nansemond County, Va., was established as a merchant in Enfield but died when Richard was two years old.

Corbitt received early education at James R. Rodwell's school in Enfield. His study was terminated about ten years after his father's death, when his mother, Mary Lou Wilkins Corbitt, married Theophilus Stallings and moved with him to Macon in Warren County. The Stallings soon moved to Henderson in newly organized Vance County, and there Richard entered the employ of a local druggist, Edward L. Smith. A year and a half later, Corbitt engaged in the leaf tobacco business as an employee of J. P. Taylor. After a brief period of commercial study at the Oak Ridge Institute, he continued to represent the Taylor Tobacco Company in Henderson and Enfield.

In 1899, Corbitt established the Corbitt Buggy Company in Henderson, manufacturing buggies and surries. Advent of the horseless carriage did not end the enterprise: in 1905, Corbitt began conversion of his plant to the production of self-powered vehicles. A chain-driven horseless buggy drove off the assembly line in 1907, and by 1912 the Corbitt company was producing an identifiably modern automobile with a motor under a long hood, headlights, fenders, and pneumatic tires.

In 1913 the Corbitt company began to manufacture trucks, an enterprise that marked the company's major success in succeeding years. Custom-made trucks were manufactured for the army in World War I, and their use spread to twenty-three foreign countries. During the Second World War, over four thousand standard trucks were manufactured for the war effort at the Henderson plant. Furthermore, the company designed and manufactured specialty vehicles for military use both before and after the war. The T-33 military truck, designed and manufactured by the Corbitt company, was, upon production, the second largest truck in the world and the most versatile in range of power and speed. The truck weighed twenty-five tons and was powered by a radial, air-cooled aircraft engine.

Because of material shortages, postwar production levels were held at a maximum of 150 diesel truck tractors per month. The company was the largest truck manufacturer in the South. Corbitt continued as general manager and chairman of the board of the corporation throughout the war and for some time thereafter. The business was sold in 1952 and later disbanded. An independent parts department remained in operation in Henderson, supplying Corbitt trucks still in use.

Corbitt married Jennie Shaw, daughter of Captain William B. Shaw, on 12 Dec. 1894. Their family included three children, William Shaw, Elizabeth Mae (Mrs. F. L. Toepleman), and Richard J., Jr. Corbitt's wife and children all predeceased him.

A member of the Methodist Episcopal church, Corbitt was active in church affairs and especially in the construction of the First Methodist Church at Henderson, where he served as chairman of the board of stewards. His civic efforts included many years' service as chairman of the Vance County Board of Education. He was a member of Masonic Lodge 229 and of the Sudan Temple of the Shrine.

Corbitt was buried in Elmwood Cemetery, Henderson.

SEE: American Cotton Manufacturers Association, *Lest We Forget* (1946); Samuel T. Pearce, *"Zeb's Black Baby," Vance County, North Carolina* (1955); Raleigh *News and Observer*, 17 May 1961.

GEORGE T. BLACKBURN II

Cordon, Norman (20 Jan. 1904–1 Mar. 1964), operatic singer and music educator, son of Norman Cheshire and Betty Houghton Cordon, was born in Washington, N.C., but moved with his family to Charlotte early in his life. There he attended private elementary schools, completing his secondary education at Fishburne Military Academy, Waynesboro, Va., in 1920.

Described as having "a natural bent for music," Cordon sang in school choruses in Charlotte and at Fishburne and was for several years a boy soprano in the well-known boys' choir of St. Peter's Episcopal Church, Charlotte. He entered The University of North Carolina in 1920, studied both academic subjects and music there for two years, and gained an early reputation for performing ability. In 1922 he left Chapel Hill and enrolled at the Nashville Conservatory of Music, Nashville, Tenn., after spending the summer studying voice at Salem College, Winston-Salem. Gaetano de Luca was his teacher in Nashville; he continued his study under Hadley Outland in Chicago and later under William Thorner in New York. During those years of study, he sang in church choirs and was an early performer on radio, first in Nashville and later in Chicago and New York and on occasional visits to North Carolina.

His first major professional opportunity came in 1931, when at the age of twenty-seven he joined the Merrimen Vocal Quartet of the famous Paul Whiteman Orchestra as a bass-baritone. He sang with the quartet for three years and in his last year there sang also a number of minor parts with the San Carlo Opera Company. Through that contact, he sang a major role in *La Tosca* for the Chicago Opera Company's 1933–34 season.

That performance led to a three-year contract with the Chicago Opera Company, during which time he schooled himself in operatic parts, learning the complete scores of more than twenty major roles. For the Chicago company he performed the herculean job of doing twenty-two major roles, with few repeats, in thirty-two days. He supplemented his Chicago appearances by singing between seasons with opera companies in St. Louis, Detroit, Minneapolis, and Toronto; he was hailed as one of the truly great opera performers of the era.

The Metropolitan Opera Company of New York City offered him a contract in 1936, and for ten years he enjoyed one of the Metropolitan's top billings, a position he earned by hard work and superb performances. During those ten years he sang first in *Rigoletto* and, in more than six hundred appearances, played literally dozens of roles. He was most famous for his Mephistopheles in *Faust*, but many opera goers of that decade remember him in *Lohengrin* and *Carmen*. Supplementing his appearances with the Metropolitan in New York, he toured two continents with Metropolitan companies and later made individual appearances in Buenos Aires and in many cities in the United States, notably San Francisco and Cincinnati.

Cordon's operatic career was capped by two years of solo concert appearances all across the United States in a program of great variety including opera, spirituals, and livelier numbers. He did one Broadway musical, Rice's 1947 *Street Scene*. In addition, he made numerous recordings, again over a wide field that included opera, folk songs, spirituals, and popular hits of the day, plus the reading of Rudyard Kipling's poems and the telling of Joel Chandler Harris's inimitable stories of Uncle Remus.

Frequent visits to North Carolina and especially to Chapel Hill—the university awarded him an honorary Doctor of Music degree in 1946—inspired him to come back to the state in 1948 and devote himself to an innovative project of developing active cultural interest and participation in a state-wide program of music, with an emphasis on opera. Through his connection with the Extension Division of The University of North Carolina, he worked indefatigably at this task. For the next sixteen years he traveled all over the state speaking at schools and colleges and before civic clubs and community groups, making a persuasive plea for musical enhancement of the life of the state. He was a great believer in radio as a communications medium, and for thirteen years he did a very popular series over the university's station, WUNC, "Let's Listen to Opera." He appealed to the masses and especially to young people, with his intimate and personable manner and narratives.

Cordon held membership in Delta Kappa Epsilon and Phi Mu Alpha, the Actors' Equity Association, the American Guild of Musical Artists, and the American Federation of Radio Artists. He was a loyal Episcopalian and, although he took no major part in politics, a registered Democrat. He was an ardent spectator sportsman, and he enjoyed many social contacts, especially upon his return to Chapel Hill. He also had a reputation as a craftsman who created many beautiful pieces of furniture in his shop at home.

Cordon was married 17 May 1939 to Susan Dease Van Landingham of Charlotte. They had one daughter, Susan Harwood. Cordon died seven weeks after his sixtieth birthday and was buried in Chapel Hill.

SEE: Alumni Records, University of North Carolina (Chapel Hill); *Nat. Cyc. Am. Biog.*, vol. 52 (1970); North Carolina Collection (University of North Carolina, Chapel Hill); Raleigh *News and Observer*, 2 Mar. 1964.

C. SYLVESTER GREEN

Cornell, Samuel *(1730–81)*, member of the royal council, was a native of Long Island, N.Y., who settled in New Bern in about 1754 and established a mercantile business. Within ten years he had become the wealthiest man in the North Carolina colony, owning two plantations on the Trent River and a house in New Bern valued at £7,500 in 1779. His cellar could hold eighty hogsheads of rum, and in addition to several warehouses and a retail store, he possessed at least three trading vessels. In 1784 his realty in North Carolina was valued at £40,976 sterling. Thirteen years later, in a lawsuit brought by his executors, the indebtedness of North Carolinians to Cornell was said to exceed £44,000.

Because of his wealth, Cornell came to the attention of Governor William Tryon shortly after his arrival in North Carolina. In 1767 the merchant loaned the colony eight thousand pounds for the construction of the executive mansion in New Bern called Tryon Palace. Out of gratitude, the governor nominated Cornell to a seat on the royal council, and on 16 Oct. 1770 he was sworn in. Cornell attended council sessions with regularity and generally supported Tryon's programs. When the expedition to crush the Regulators was launched in the spring of 1771, Cornell underwrote it with the loan of six thousand pounds and served in the field as a general officer. He received a leg wound at the Battle of Alamance but recovered quickly.

After Tryon's 1771 departure from North Carolina to become governor of New York, Cornell continued to serve on the council. In the summer of 1775 he began to fear that Patriots might force him to underwrite currency issues of the provincial congresses, and he obtained permission from Governor Josiah Martin to move to New York. Hoping to block confiscation of his North Carolina holdings, Cornell sailed back to New Bern in December 1777. Initially, the local committee of safety refused to allow him to land until he swore allegiance to the revolutionary cause. Governor Richard Caswell intervened, however, permitting Cornell ashore to inventory his household effects and collect a few servants. In an unsuccessful effort to prevent confiscation, he deeded all his North Carolina property to three of his daughters.

Cornell returned to New York to sit out the war. Early in 1781 he joined an expedition sailing to relieve British troops in Virginia, but he became ill during the voyage and returned to New York. Shortly after arriving there he died. At the close of the Revolution, his heirs sued to recover his property in North Carolina in litigation that became the famous *Bayard* v. *Singleton* case of 1786–87.

SEE: Bayard-Campbell-Pearsall Collection (New York Public Library), for many of Cornell's business papers; North Carolina State Archives (Raleigh), for Cornell to Elias Debrosses, letter (original in C.O. 5/154), Loyalist Claims Commission Transcripts (claim filed by Henry Chad), and Miscellaneous Estates Papers (1746–1864, Craven County); William L. Saunders, *Colonial Records of North Carolina*, vols. 8–9 (1890).

WILLIAM S. PRICE, JR.

Cosby, Dabney *(ca. 1779–August 1862)*, architect and builder, who flourished in Virginia and North Carolina from the 1820s to his death, was born in Virginia. He resided in Raleigh from about 1840 until his death, and he is one of a small group of nineteenth-century North Carolina builders whose identity and works are known. Highly respected in his profession, he constructed a number of significant architectural monuments in Virginia and North Carolina during the early Victorian

period. His specialty was roughcasting—that is, the application of a rough exterior wall surface composed of mortar and fine pebbles—and many of his buildings have this finish. During his long and extremely productive career, he worked in a variety of architectural styles, including the Federal, the Greek Revival, the Classical Revival, the Italianate Revival, and the medieval revivals. He is said to have worked with Thomas Jefferson in the construction of the original buildings at the University of Virginia in the 1820s. His earliest documented work is the construction of the Sussex County, Va., Courthouse in 1825. In addition to several additional Virginia courthouses, Cosby built a large number of plantation houses in Halifax County, Va., between 1835 and 1850. He constructed a good part of Union Theological Seminary at Hampden-Sydney, Va., before 1845 and churches in Petersburg and Smithfield, Va.

In 1840, Cosby purchased a lot in Raleigh on Dawson Street; he remained a Raleigh resident until his death, although his letters indicate that he traveled almost continuously during this period. His earliest documented work in North Carolina was the construction in 1840–42 of a house for the Mordecai family in Raleigh, perhaps the Mary Lane Mordecai House, now demolished. At the same time he built a house in Wake County for Mrs. Rebecca J. Williams. From 1845 to 1847, Cosby was working under architect A. J. Davis as the subcontractor in charge of masonry on the additions to Old East and Old West buildings at The University of North Carolina. His next known project was the construction of a brick house for Dr. Beverly Jones near Bethania, in Forsyth County, in 1847. Cosby's Dawson Street residence, a now-demolished Italianate Revival villa, is attributed to him and was probably built during this period. Between 1847 and 1850 he built the residence and schoolhouse for the North Carolina Deaf and Dumb Institute on Caswell Square in Raleigh. In 1850 he constructed the mammoth Yarborough Hotel on Fayetteville Street, Raleigh. He designed the Caswell County Courthouse, which was built, not by him, between 1858 and 1861. His last known projects, in 1855, were additional work to the Governor's Palace, which was an early nineteenth-century building on South Street, Raleigh, and the construction of a residence for Professor W. M. Wingate of Raleigh. On both projects he acted as superintendent under James Saintsing, a Raleigh architect and builder.

Many of Cosby's Virginia buildings have been preserved, but of his identified North Carolina building projects, only the additions to Old East and Old West in Chapel Hill and the Beverly Jones House are still standing. It is likely that many more Cosby buildings will be discovered in North Carolina as research continues.

Cosby and his wife, Frances, had many children, including at least three sons. Two of these, Dabney, Jr., and John, continued in their father's profession. Both worked in Raleigh on the Deaf and Dumb Institute and later moved to Halifax County, Va.

SEE: *A Memorial to the General Assembly of North Carolina by Dabney and John W. Cosby* (1851); "The Late Dabney Cosby, Esq." (1862, North Carolina Collection, University of North Carolina, Chapel Hill); *Milton Chronicle*, 8 Jan. 1858; North Carolina State Archives (Raleigh), for Account Books of Thomas Briggs (1847–86), U.S. Census Records for Raleigh (1860), and Wake County Accounts, Deeds, and Tax Lists (1841–54); Southern Historical Collection (University of North Carolina, Chapel Hill), for Dabney Cosby Papers (vols. 1

and 2), Dr. Beverly Jones Papers, George W. Mordecai Papers, and David Lowry Swain Papers.

RUTH LITTLE-STOKES

Cotten, Bruce (*3 Mar. 1873–1 Apr. 1954*), collector, writer, and army officer, was a native of Pitt County. His father, Colonel Robert Randolph Cotten, a businessman and owner of Cottendale Plantation, was the son of John Llewellyn and Nancy Pennine Johnson Cotten. Bruce's mother, Sally Sims Southall Cotten, a widely known author and civic leader, was the daughter of Susanna Sims and Thomas James Southall. Cotten had five brothers and sisters, one of whom was Admiral Lyman Atkinson.

Cotten attended Horner's Military School at Oxford and, in 1891–92, The University of North Carolina. After a short business career, he went to Alaska during the gold rush, later describing his experiences in *An Adventure in Alaska, During the Gold Excitement of 1897–1898* (1922). Upon returning to Seattle, he volunteered for the Spanish-American War. He then joined the regular army, participating in the Boxer Campaign (1900) and the Philippine Insurrection (1901–2) and winning a commission in 1901. During World War I he served as chief of military intelligence of the second military intelligence division of the general staff (1918–19). At his discharge he held the rank of major. Cotten described this career in *Drills, Raids and Escapades* (1925).

While stationed at Fort McHenry, Cotten met Edith Johns, the widow of Jesse Tyson, a Baltimore industrialist who had made a fortune mining chrome. Cotten followed her to Europe, where they were married on 4 Aug. 1910. They lived at Cylburn, a mansion and showplace of some 180 acres that is now a Baltimore City Park, used as a wildflower display and garden center. Mrs. Cotten, as chairwoman of the assembly for a quarter of a century, was "Baltimore's social arbiter." She was also a patron of music and the theater. She died in 1942; they had no children.

Cotten was an avid collector of materials pertaining to North Carolina, amassing the largest known private assortment of materials on state history. Early inspiration to assemble the collection came from his mother, who had noted the paucity of materials available for the state exhibit at the 1892 Chicago World's Fair. His collection and experiences are described in his *Housed on the Third Floor* (1941). Upon his death, he willed the entire collection to The University of North Carolina, where it forms a significant part of the North Carolina Collection. He investigated his own family history, compiling *The Cotten Family of North Carolina* (reprinted in 1963), and related local legends and family reminiscences in *As We Were: A Personal Sketch of Family Life* (1935) and *The Mirrors of Bensboro* (1925).

He was buried in Baltimore.

SEE: Baltimore *Sun*, 2 Apr. 1954, 18 July 1954, 15 May 1960; *Durham Morning Herald*, 2 Apr. 1954; *Greensboro Daily News*, 18 May 1941; *History of North Carolina*, vol. 5 (1919).

WILLIAM T. MOYE

Cotten, Elizabeth Brownrigg Henderson (*4 Aug. 1875–3 Feb. 1975*), women's rights leader and librarian, was born at Salisbury, the daughter of John Steele and Elizabeth Brownrigg Cain Henderson. She was a direct descendant of Thomas Henderson, a Jamestown, Va., settler (1612), who came from Dumfries, Scotland. Her

paternal line included eminent lawyers and members of the U.S. Congress. Her father, during his service in Congress (1885–95), was the originator of the successful move to establish Rural Free Delivery throughout the United States. Archibald Henderson, scholar, litterateur, and mathematician of Chapel Hill, was her brother.

Elizabeth Henderson was educated in the private school of Salisbury and then attended St. Mary's School, Raleigh, from which she was graduated with honors. Before she was twenty-five she had become an active and outspoken member of the Daughters of the Confederacy and had dedicated herself to raising money to provide assistance to Confederate veterans of the Civil War. She appeared before the North Carolina General Assembly in 1901, pleading successfully for increased pensions for those veterans, in a speech received with great enthusiasm by the legislators. It is believed that she was the first woman ever to speak before the assembly.

As a civic and social leader in Salisbury, Miss Henderson was interested in amateur theatricals; her distinguished cousin, "Christian Reid" (Mrs. Frances Christine Tiernan), made her the central character in a play, *Under the Southern Cross*, and a novel, *Princess Nadine*. Miss Henderson used the play to raise money for the work of the Daughters of the Confederacy, reading it before many audiences throughout the state. Her interest in poor and struggling people led her to undertake many projects for social betterment in Salisbury and Rowan County. In addition to her membership in the Daughters of the Confederacy, she was an active member of the local chapter of the Daughters of the American Revolution and served for a term as its regent.

While her father was in Congress, she spent a great deal of time in Washington. In later years she recalled frequent visits to the White House and personal acquaintance with President and Mrs. Grover Cleveland; though she often revisited the White House in subsequent years, Mrs. Cleveland remained her "ideal White House hostess."

Miss Henderson was married on 16 July 1908 to Captain Lyman A. Cotten, U.S. Navy; they had two sons, Lyman Atkinson, Jr., and John Henderson. Married at the age of thirty-three, she had already established her position as "Charming Bessie Henderson" of Salisbury.

Although Salisbury remained her home, she spent many years of her married life at posts where her husband was stationed, principally China, Japan, and Turkey. As the wife of the chief of staff of the American Naval Representatives, she entertained extensively, receiving local personages and the leading ambassadorial, military, and missionary leaders. She was presented to royal and imperial princesses in Europe, and her life in Constantinople was "fascinating, the hours filled with gaieties." Yet she found time for social services. While Captain Cotten was chief of staff to Admiral Mark L. Bristol, U.S. high commissioner, she spent much of her time in relief work for Russian refugees. The six years the Cottens were in Japan were the most notable of her foreign residence. She was organizer and first president of the Woman's Club of Tokyo and a leader in the Woman's Auxiliary of Trinity Cathedral; she was active in the establishment of a library and a nursing association and in the support of St. Luke's Hospital (in 1930 she was chairman of the committee in the Diocese of North Carolina to raise funds for that hospital). Hostess for many formal occasions in Japan, she earned tribute as "the most admired and beloved American woman who has ever lived in Japan."

During the years of World War I, while her husband was at sea or on active war duty, Mrs. Cotten participated in Liberty Loan drives, supervised Red Cross work rooms, served as chairman of the Eighth Congressional District's Council of National Defense, and was the organizer of the local Navy League. During the dread influenza epidemic of 1918, she organized and supervised countless volunteer nursing units and diet kitchens. Through all the war years she diligently emphasized methods of conservation and organized and promoted canteens for military personnel.

On the death of Captain Cotten in 1926, his widow moved to Chapel Hill; she made her home there until her death. North Carolinians remember her best for these nearly fifty years of her life. She became an energetic member of the North Carolina Suffrage League and the League of Women Voters. An ardent Democrat, she was vice-chairman of the Eighth Congressional District party organization in 1928 and was a diligent worker in behalf of Al Smith's candidacy for the presidency. She made speeches all over the state and was lauded for her "convincing eloquence." She was renamed to the group in 1930.

In 1933 she was favorably considered for appointment to the U.S. Civil Service Commission, although the post went to the widow of Governor Benton McMillan of Tennessee. In the early 1940s, she was an original promoter of the restoration of Tryon Palace at New Bern, a project made possible in the early 1950s through the generosity of Mrs. J. E. Latham of Greensboro. During the Second World War, Mrs. Cotten carried on an extensive correspondence with friends in Europe, especially England, about the problems of peace after the war. Although in her late sixties, she found many ways to serve the war effort and encourage others working in civilian projects.

Mrs. Cotten began an entirely new career in 1932, which brought her great fame and praise. She became assistant to Dr. J. G. deRoulhac Hamilton in his successful effort to establish the Southern Historical Collection in the Library of The University of North Carolina; she was also the first curator. After promoting the organization of the Friends of the Library, she became its first secretary and used her position to solicit and secure thousands of items of Tar Heel memorabilia and historical data. She was particularly successful in obtaining records and papers of U.S. naval officers and private papers of prominent North Carolina families of the previous two hundred years. She was the production supervisor (1935–39) of the Works Progress Administration project that produced the *Guide to the Manuscripts in the Southern Historical Collection of the University of North Carolina* (1940). At its 1958 meeting, the Friends of the Library bestowed on her a laudatory citation for expansive and comprehensive work in behalf of the library. She was the author of *John Paul Jones–Willie Jones Tradition* and coeditor of the highly respected *Old Homes and Gardens of North Carolina*.

Throughout the years, Mrs. Cotten served the Episcopal Chapel of the Cross in Chapel Hill, of which she was a dedicated member. Her funeral service was held in that church on Thursday, 6 Feb. 1975, and several days later graveside services were held in Arlington National Cemetery; Captain Cotten had been buried there in 1926.

SEE: *Chapel Hill Newspaper*, 4 Feb. 1975; Chapel Hill *University Gazette*, 21 Feb. 1975; *Charlotte Observer*, 30 Nov. 1930; 23 Feb. 1936; *Nat. Cyc. Am. Biog.*, vol. A (1930); North Carolina Collection (University of North Carolina, Chapel Hill), for data file; Raleigh *News and Observer*, 3 Feb. 1975 (obit.); *University of North Carolina Library Notes*, 21 Feb. 1975.

C. SYLVESTER GREEN

Cotten, Lyman Atkinson (18 Dec. 1874–12 Jan. 1926), naval officer and diplomat, was born at Wilson but grew up at Cottendale, the family plantation, in Pitt County. He was the son of Colonel Robert Randolph Cotten and Sallie Sims Southall Cotten. After receiving early education from governesses, he attended Bronson's School in Warrenton and Horner's School in Oxford. He entered the U.S. Naval Academy at Annapolis, Md., in September 1894 and was graduated 6 Apr. 1898, two months early because of the impending war with Spain.

His first assignment was aboard the U.S.S. *Columbia*, which participated in the blockade of Cuba and the capture of Puerto Rico. He then traveled to the Philippines via the Suez Canal and served in a number of joint army-navy expeditions during the Philippine Insurrection. In April 1900 he was commissioned an ensign and, at captain's pay, assumed command of the U.S.S. *Zafiro*, a tender for the commander-in-chief of the Asiatic Station. During this period he first served in Japan and China. In the summer of 1900, during the Boxer Rebellion, the *Zafiro* relayed to Washington, D.C., from the Gulf of Pichili the news of the relief of the foreign legations in Peking.

During tours in South America and the West Indies, Cotten was promoted to lieutenant junior grade and given orders as instructor of ordnance at Annapolis. After his duty at Annapolis, he returned to the Philippines and the Far East for three years, with the rank of lieutenant. In the summer of 1908 he was assigned to the Naval War College at Newport, R.I., first as a student and then as a member of the staff. This seems to have been a significant event in his life, for thereafter he was an avid student of naval history and world affairs. His study was of benefit to his several diplomatic posts and contributed greatly to his successes. Following his promotion to lieutenant commander in 1910, he served from 1912 to 1915 as naval attaché at the American embassy in Tokyo and at the American legation in Peking, where he was remarkably successful in the discharge of his duties. He was in Japan at the beginning of World War I, and his reports to the Navy Department were so comprehensive that they were used for years afterward. He was promoted to commander in 1916 and assigned to the U.S.S. *Nebraska*. At Vera Cruz, Mexico, he once again distinguished himself in the rescue of American refugees.

In February 1918, following the entry of the United States into World War I, Cotten received orders to New London, Conn., where he outfitted and sent to England a number of submarine chasers. He received a temporary promotion to captain and was ordered to command the American Naval Base and the squadron of subchasers at Plymouth, England. The most important command held by any officer of his rank, it was considered an admiral's billet. Besides other larger vessels, there were thirty-six to seventy-two subchasers, and it was their duty to safeguard the English Channel and the approaches to England and France. Cotten had the responsibility for the training and operations of the subchasers and was responsible, too, for the American troops, often as many as a thousand, who were in Plymouth awaiting transfer to field units. Cotten ensured smooth relations with the Allies by keeping a firm control over all matters at the base. During his command of the subchaser squadron, not a single Allied merchant ship was sunk, and not a single mine was laid within the area of his responsibility.

In March 1919, Cotten was made a member of the General Board of the Navy, its highest policy-making body, where he served for one year. In 1920 he again went to sea, this time in command of the U.S.S. *Chattanooga*. He also served as chief of staff of the U.S. Naval Detachment in the Eastern Mediterranean, which was under the command of Rear Admiral Mark L. Bristol, U.S. high commissioner of Turkey. Cotten proved to be of great service during the turbulent times following the armistice, and he took a conspicuous part in many diplomatic negotiations. He was promoted permanently to captain in 1921. In 1922, because of his great success as naval attaché in Japan, he was offered his choice of several positions as attaché to important countries, all of which he refused. The Navy Department insisted that he take the vacancy that soon occurred in Tokyo—a vitally important post requiring great delicacy. During this service, Cotten made many close friends among the Japanese, many of them powerful and distinguished people. He may have been the only American to call Admiral Togo "friend."

In 1923, Cotten was detached from attaché duty with the Office of Naval Intelligence and was appointed a member of the Naval Examining and Naval Retirement boards. Following this service, he returned to sea in command of the U.S.S. *Richmond*, the flagship of the Light Cruiser Division under Admiral Thomas P. Magruder. Cotten was in Honduran waters during the Revolution of 1924. The division was then ordered to Scotland, from which it returned as the escort of the Army World Fliers. With the unit was an Italian plane piloted by a Lieutenant Locatelli, with a crew of three; the Italians went down at sea in a fog off the coast of Greenland, and the *Richmond* located them after a three-and-a-half day search. In April 1925, Cotten went with the division on a friendly visit to Australia, New Zealand, Tasmania, Samoa, Marquesas, and Galapagos, returning to the United States in November.

On 8 Jan. 1926, during the worst storm of the winter, the *Richmond*, with the Light Cruiser Division, sailed out of New York harbor en route to Guatemala for naval practice. Cotten, although already ill, personally took the flagship and the division through the channel and safely out to sea. Shortly after going below, he collapsed with a temperature of 106 degrees. The *Richmond* put in at the naval base in Norfolk, Va., where he was transferred to the naval hospital. He died of pneumonia shortly afterward and was buried in Arlington National Cemetery on 14 Jan.

Among his honors and decorations, Cotten counted the Spanish Campaign Medal, the Philippine Campaign Medal, the China Campaign Medal, the Mexican Service Medal, and the Distinguished Service Medal and Victory Medal from World War I. For the rescue of Lieutenant Locatelli and Italian plane and crew, he received the Commenda della Corona D'Italia from the king of Italy.

Cotten was a prolific writer and was the author of many articles, both professional and popular. "Safe Guarding the World Flyers" appeared in *World's Work*. He wrote several pieces for the *United States Naval Institute Proceedings*. In 1910 he won honorable mention from the institute for a study entitled "Naval Strategy of the Russo-Japanese War." In 1917 he won the gold medal, which carried with it life membership, for his study "Commerce Destroying in War." He was the author of many songs, still sung by Navy men, among them "Governor General or a Hobo," "Damn, Damn, Damn

the Philippinos," "Philippinitis," "Keep on the Target," and the "Sub-Chaser Song."

In testimony to the esteem in which Cotten was held by his country, a destroyer built at the Federal Shipbuilding and Drydock Company of Kearney, N. J., and launched 12 June 1942, was named *Cotten*. (A World War II Liberty Ship, launched at Wilmington, was named *Cotten* in honor of Cotten's mother, first president of the North Carolina Federation of Women's Clubs.)

Cotten was married on 16 July 1908 to Elizabeth Brownrigg ("Bessie") Henderson, daughter of John Steele Henderson and his wife, Elizabeth Brownrigg Cain. The Cottens had two sons: Lyman Atkinson (b. 25 Apr. 1909) was a member of the faculty of the English department at The University of North Carolina, and John Henderson (b. 28 June 1913) was a captain in the U.S. Navy. Captain Cotten was survived by his parents; two brothers, Major Bruce of Baltimore, Md., and Preston S. of Boston, Mass.; and three sisters, Mrs. Russell B. Wiggin of Brookline, Mass., Mrs. D. B. Wesson of Springfield, Mass., and Mrs. T. B. Timberlake of Raleigh.

SEE: C. S. Carr and Edwin T. Pollock papers (Manuscript Department, Library, Duke University, Durham); Library and Archives, U.S. Naval Academy (Annapolis, Md.); Naval History Division (Washington, D.C.); North Carolina Collection (University of North Carolina, Chapel Hill); Raleigh *News and Observer*, scattered issues.

CHARLES M. INGRAM

Cotten, Robert Randolph (*20 June 1839–14 Aug. 1928*), planter and businessman, was born on his father's farm near Whitakers in Edgecombe County. He was the oldest son of John Lewellyn Cotten and his wife, Nancy Bell Penine Tart Johnson. Cotten attended the public schools of Edgecombe County until the age of eighteen. At that time he left school to take a clerkship in the store of a man named Alston at Tarboro. After a year there he attended Baltimore Business College and became a traveling salesman for a year. He then entered into a partnership with Walter Gwynn to form Cotten and Gwynn, a firm of cotton brokers and commission merchants, which operated out of Baltimore for the next twenty-three years.

Upon the outbreak of the Civil War, the firm was dissolved and Cotten returned to North Carolina. Shortly thereafter he joined the Scotland Neck Mounted Riflemen under the command of Captain A. B. Hill. His unit was Company G, Third North Carolina Cavalry, Forty-first Regiment of North Carolina Troops, with Colonel A. M. Waddell of Wilmington commanding. Cotten's outfit did scout work and picket duty in Eastern Carolina and was especially active around New Bern, Washington, and the Wilmington and Weldon Railroad. On one occasion the company was deployed to Virginia, where it was a part of Wade Hampton's brigade on the left of Lee's army during the battle for Richmond. Company G was at Weldon at the end of the war, and Cotten made his way from there to his mother's home.

Immediately, he set to work to reclaim something from the aftermath of the war, opening a mercantile business at Tarboro. It proved such a successful venture that he opened a branch business at Wilson. In addition, he acquired two plantations in Pitt County, which he named Cottendale and Southwood.

In 1869, Cotten moved his business to Wilson, where he continued to operate a store for many years. He also opened a branch store at Falkland, where he moved his family in 1878. The following year he moved to Southwood, and in 1880 the family settled permanently at Cottendale. There he built a noted home and engaged in extensive farming interests for the rest of his life. Simultaneously, he relocated his store at Centre Bluff on the Tar River, where he operated a mercantile business in conjunction with his plantations for twenty-five years. In 1900 he moved his business again; abandoning the river site, he established a store and post office in Pitt County at a spot he named Bruce after an early business associate.

An active member of the Democratic party, Cotten served on the state executive committee. He represented Pitt County in the house of representatives in 1908 and the senate in 1910. Among other positions, Cotten held the chairmanship of the Pitt County Inferior Court, the directorship of the state penitentiary, and also that of the state Hospital for the Insane.

Devout Episcopalians, Cotten and his family were communicants at St. Paul's Church, Greenville, although poor roads often prevented the family's attending services there. Cotten read morning prayer daily at Cottendale and often entertained the bishops and other clergymen.

Cotten was married at Murfreesboro on 14 Mar. 1866 to Sallie Swepson Sims Southall, daughter of Thomas James Southall and his wife, Susannah Sims. The Cottens were the parents of nine children, Agnes, Robert Randolph, Jr., Frederick, Alla, Bruce, Lyman Atkinson, Sallie, Preston, and Elba. Cotten died at Cottendale and was buried in Pitt County.

SEE: Bruce Cotten, *As We Were* (1935), and *The Cotten Family of North Carolina* (1927).

JAMES ELLIOTT MOORE

Cotten, Sallie Swepson Sims Southall (*13 June 1846–4 May 1929*), writer and Woman's Club and civic leader, was born in Lawrenceville, Brunswick County, Va., the daughter of Susannah Sims and Thomas J. Southall. Of Irish descent, she had ancestors who were active in the early history of this country, including one who served in the Continental Congress and was a signer of the Declaration of Independence. As a young girl, Sallie Southall was sent to live with an uncle in Murfreesboro; there she attended public school and later Wesleyan Female College. She then went to Greensboro Female College, from which she was graduated in 1863. For the next two years, during the Civil War, she was a teen-age schoolteacher.

On 14 Mar. 1866, Sallie Southall married Robert Randolph Cotten, a Confederate veteran of Edgecombe County. They lived first in Tarboro, where he had a mercantile business; later they moved to Wilson. His desire was to be a planter, however, and it was not long before he purchased two plantations in Pitt County, Southwood and Cottendale. The family lived first at Southwood, where Cotten prospered as merchant and farmer. When his Wilson business needed his attention, he moved his family back to live in Wilson for ten years. A final move brought a return to Pitt County and Cottendale, where the Cottens spent the remaining years of their long and busy lives.

The first half of Mrs. Cotten's married life was largely domestic. Surrounded by children, she organized a school on the plantation and invited other neighborhood children to participate. She worked in the house and garden, visited friends, and was a leader in the Episcopal church. She found time also to read, think, and do some writing.

Her first opportunity for public service came in 1893,

when Governor Elias Carr appointed her one of North Carolina's managers for the Chicago World's Fair. She traveled over most of the state gathering materials and relics to exhibit. She prepared a collection of books written by North Carolina women and presented them to the International Library of books written by women, on exhibit at the fair. This collection won for her a World's Fair medal and diploma. She served the state again on the board of managers at the Atlanta and Charleston expositions.

In her travels, Mrs. Cotten met women from all parts of the country who were active in the budding "woman movement." Long interested in the status of women, she returned home and began work immediately in encouraging women to organize themselves on the local level. As a result, many clubs came into being. A principal leader in the organization of the North Carolina Federation of Women's Clubs in 1902, she was the fifth president and an active member for twenty-five years. Her leadership led women through many movements with far-reaching results: they achieved a law permitting women to sit on school boards; they worked for local civic reform, libraries, education, child labor reform, and improvement in institutions of correction; and they raised money to establish an educational loan fund for girls, naming it the Sallie Southall Cotten Loan Fund. Mrs. Cotten composed the federation song in 1910 and wrote *The History of the North Carolina Federation of Women's Clubs, 1901–1925* (1925). The federation made her honorary life president.

Mrs. Cotten was present at the organizational meeting of the National Congress of Mothers (later the Congress of Parents and Teachers) in Washington in 1897 and served from 1897 to 1906 as its recording secretary. She was active also in local clubs, the United Daughters of the Confederacy, the King's Daughters, the Pitt County Federation, and the End of the Century Book Club in Greenville.

In addition to her history of the Women's Clubs, Sallie Southall Cotten published a verse history of the Lost Colony, *The White Doe*, in 1901. She also wrote poetry and articles that appeared in the magazines of her day.

After her husband's death in 1928, Mrs. Cotten moved to Massachusetts and lived with a daughter. Her health was not good, but she made one final public appearance: she attended a gathering of women in Boston, where she was introduced as "the Julia Ward Howe of the South" and received a standing ovation. She died in Winchester, Mass., and was buried in the family plot in Greenville, N.C.

Two university dormitories are named for Mrs. Cotten, one at The University of North Carolina at Greensboro and the other at East Carolina University. In May of 1943 a Liberty Freighter was named for her and, at the launching ceremonies at Wilmington, was christened by her granddaughter.

The Cottens were the parents of nine children, Agnes, Robert Randolph, Jr., Frederick, Alla, Bruce, Lyman Atkinson, Sallie, Preston, and Elba.

SEE: Samuel A. Ashe, ed., *Biographical History of North Carolina*, vol. 8 (1917); Bruce Cotten, *As We Were* (1935); Sallie Southall Cotten, *History of the North Carolina Federation of Women's Clubs* (1925); *North Carolina Authors* (1952); *Notable American Women*, vol. 1 (1971); Lou Rogers, *Tar Heel Women* (1949).

ELIZABETH H. COPELAND

Cotton, James (*3 Aug. 1739–22 Dec. 1785*), colonial officeholder and Loyalist, was born in Hamlet Parish, Ipswich, Mass., son of Leonard and Mary Frieze Cotton.

He was the grandson of the Reverend Thomas and Bridget Hoar Cotton of London and of Jacob and Rachel Chase Frieze of Hampton, N.H. His great-grandfather, Dr. Leonard Hoar, was the third president of Harvard. Cotton's father was a teacher in the church under the pastorates of his cousins, John and Theophilus Cotton.

James Cotton received a thorough classical education. As a youth he removed with his parents to the Piedmont of Virginia and, upon his majority, to Rowan (now Anson) County. There, by the eve of the American Revolution, he had become Anson County's wealthiest and most prominent citizen. He was one of the advisers of colonial Governor Josiah Martin, a member of the assembly, lieutenant colonel in the provincial militia, magistrate of Anson County, deputy collector of his majesty's quitrents, surveyor and registrar of Anson County, ranger of woods and wastes, and keeper of the land office for the back counties. His wife, Margaret Williams, member of a well-known Loyalist family, bore him three children, James, Thomas, and Alicia Cotton.

Cotton recruited a company of Loyalists and took part in the Battle of Moore's Creek Bridge on 27 Feb. 1776. Proscribed by the provincial congress and the committee of safety, he went into hiding and eventually made his way to the British fort of St. Augustine in East Florida. After being re-outfitted by Governor Patrick Tonyn, he joined General Sir Henry Clinton at Charleston, S.C. After the British loss of Fort Moultrie in the Battle of Sullivan's Island later in the year, he went with Clinton to New York, by then the Loyalist and British capitol of the American colonies. After a year in the quartermaster department under General William Howe, Cotton went to England and lived in London until 1784. He successfully brought a claim before the Wilmot-Coke Commission for his confiscated property (over £12,000) and the loss of the offices he had enjoyed under the Crown (£250 annually). The final property settlement was the sum of £3,387 and an annual allowance of £100 for the loss of his offices. He then, with his second wife, Ann (daughter of a Lancaster clergyman), and two small children, removed to the British West Indies. He died at St. Jago de la Veyga, Jamaica. His wife went to North Carolina after his death and there received for many years a British pension as his widow; his oldest son, James (1765–1838), received an American pension for *his* services as a Patriot in the Revolution.

As his biographer has pointed out, Cotton's life and career, "against the background of an incipient and accomplished revolution, illustrates the dilemma of Colonial officials, the bases for their continued loyalty to Great Britain, the reasons for the exodus of many Loyalists from America, the losses of property and liberties suffered by loyal colonials, and finally the nature and methods of partial compensation for losses so incurred."

SEE: Frank E. Cotton manuscript records (New England Historic Genealogical Society, Boston); Robert M. McBride, *Portrait of an American Loyalist: James Cotton of Anson County, North Carolina* (1954); M. C. S. Noble, "The Battle of Moore's Creek Bridge," *North Carolina Booklet* 3 (1904); Bessie L. Whitaker, "The Provincial Council and the Committee of Safety in North Carolina," *James Sprunt Historical Monographs* 8 (1908).

ROBERT M. MCBRIDE

Council, Arthur *(1755–April 1777)*, Revolutionary War officer, is noted as one of the youngest and most active leaders of the early revolutionary movement in North Carolina. He was the son of Joanna Willis and Captain

James Council but whether he was born in Bladen or in Cumberland County is a matter of dispute, as his father owned much land in both. Captain James Council had moved to Bladen County in the 1750s from Virginia, where his family had been established since the early seventeenth century. He took up land granted to him for service in the French and Indian War, and he soon became active in the movement toward independence. He was a member of the provincial congress at Halifax in the spring of 1776, representing Campbellton; paymaster of militia troops in the Wilmington District; and holder of other local offices. Arthur Council first appears in the records of the region in November 1770, when he was made an ensign in the Sixth Company, Cross Creek Militia. His name also appears on the 1771 list of Cumberland County officers.

On 13 Mar. 1772, young Council was one of thirty-four residents of Campbellton who signed a petition to Governor Josiah Martin requesting a new charter for the town, "empowering . . . Freeholders within two miles of the Court-house of Cambellton or seized of an Estate of their own . . . to elect a Member to represent them in the General Assembly." Council was elected to represent Campbellton in the provincial congress at Halifax in April 1776; his father represented Bladen County, and both were active members. The younger man served on a number of committees, three of which were charged with investigating the activity of certain loyalists; he also served on a committee to investigate the availability of salt in the Cross Creek area and another to investigate the accounts of one Matthew Ramsey, public official. Council was present on 12 Apr. when the congress adopted the famous resolves calling on all the American colonies to join together in declaring independence from Great Britain.

Four days later, Council was commissioned captain in the Sixth Continental Regiment being raised in the Wilmington District; in June he was authorized to receive the arms for his company. In the spring of 1777 the regiment was in camp near Little River on the coast about thirty miles from the Cape Fear, where it was feared the British would attempt a landing. There Council, just twenty-two, died. A journal kept by Hugh McDonald, a volunteer in the regiment, recorded: "Not more than three weeks after the brigade was embodied, my Captain, Arthur Council, a young man who had been raised near Cross Creek, and whose father's house is yet known by the name of Council Hall, died. This young gentleman was distinguished in the regiment for modesty, gentility and morality. Shortly after the death of Council, his first lieutenant who was known by the name of Philadelphia Thomas White, became our Captain, and he was as immoral as Council was moral."

Council was buried in the Gause family tomb not far from Little River, by the wish of his sister, Margaret, who was married to William Gause, owner of the immense Gause plantation. During Reconstruction, the remnants of the Gause family moved to Louisiana and elsewhere, sealing the family tomb before they left. A rumor circulated that gold and jewels were buried in the mausoleum, and when, in the 1940s, a Gause descendant searched out the tomb, it was discovered that vandals had succeeded in breaking the walls. The visitor removed the remains of his relatives and took them away for reburial elsewhere.

In August 1784, Council's heirs were awarded 3,840 acres of land for his revolutionary service.

SEE: Judson Councill, *Hodges Councill of Virginia and Descendants* (1941); Kinchin Bascom Council papers (formerly in the possession of Clyde Council of Lake Waccamaw but now destroyed); Hugh F. Rankin, *The North Carolina Continentals* (1971); William L. Saunders and Walter Clark, eds., *Colonial and State Records of North Carolina*, 30 vols. (1886–1914).

PAUL A. ROCKWELL

Council, Carl C. [Carlyle Ceasar] *(26 Jan. 1895– 27 Jan. 1964)*, newspaper publisher and radio and television executive, son of William L. and Ida Herndon Council, was born in Chatham County. His family moved to Durham while he was in his early teens, and as a very small boy he carried a part of a newspaper delivery route for the *Durham Morning Herald*, working under a subcontract until he was old enough to have a route in his own right.

Council attended elementary and secondary public schools in Durham but, following the death of his father, left school to take a full-time job in the circulation department of the *Herald*. In 1918 he left the *Herald* for work with a Durham business firm, but within a few months, through his friendship with E. T. Rollins, he became co-owner of the *Herald*, purchasing the partnership holdings of Joe King.

In his new role, Council oriented himself in all phases of the work of the paper, assuming increasing responsibility for circulation and advertising and sharing the business management with Rollins. In 1927, Council was given the title of manager. Rollins had great respect and esteem for his young associate, and the business relationship of the two remained cordial. The circulation of the paper increased rapidly, advertising multiplied, and the business was an impressive success. In 1929 the Durham Herald Company bought the local afternoon paper, the *Durham Sun*, and soon produced both newspapers on an around-the-clock schedule in the same shop.

When Rollins died in 1931, Council assumed the presidency of the company and held it successfully until his death. He directed the growth in circulation of the papers, enhancing their status as advertising media, as opinion molders, and as communicators of news and opinions.

Council was an active churchman. He joined Temple Baptist Church, Durham, in his early youth and through the years served on many of the church's committees and boards, including the board of deacons, of which he was chairman for two terms.

He was equally active in civic affairs in Durham and earned two of the city's top honors: the annual civic award to the outstanding citizen, presented by the Chamber of Commerce in 1941; and the designation as Father-of-the-Year by the Durham Merchants Association in 1962. He was a member of the Durham County Board of Education for fourteen years (1942–56) and served twenty-five years (1939–64) as a member of the city planning and zoning commission. He was founder (1936), president, and treasurer of the Durham Radio Corporation, which was the operator of radio stations WDNC and WDNC-FM, and later of WTVD, until their sale to Capitol Cities Broadcasting Corporation, of which he was a director. He was also a director of the Home Savings and Loan Association, the Security Savings and Loan Association, and the Durham and Southern Railway and chairman of the local board of the North Carolina National Bank.

His civic connections included membership in and the presidency of the Chamber of Commerce, the Durham Community Chest (United Fund), the Durham

Merchants Association, and the Rotary Club of Durham and the directorship of the local YMCA.

From his early years with the paper, Council was a leader in various newspaper organizations: the North Carolina Press Association (president, 1936–37), the Southern Newspaper Publishers Association (director), the American Society of Newspaper Publishers, the state and regional organizations of the Associated Press, and other newsgathering organizations.

He served for a number of years, by gubernatorial appointment, as a board member and sometime chairman of the North Carolina Sanitoriums for the Treatment of Tuberculosis. In 1960 he was the state chairman of the Christmas Seal campaign.

Council was married to Mary Frances Stuart on 11 Aug. 1915; they had two children, Carl C., Jr., who lost his life on Anzio Beach in World War II, and Mary Frances (Mrs. Thomas S. White, Jr.), who survived her father. Council died at Duke Hospital, Durham, and was buried in Durham's Maplewood Cemetery.

SEE: *Durham Morning Herald*, 6 Mar. 1949, 1 Feb. 1964; *Who's Who in America*, 1962–63; *Who Was Who in America*, vol. 4 (1968).

C. SYLVESTER GREEN

Council, Commodore Thomas, Sr. *(31 Oct. 1886– 13 July 1960)*, pharmaceutical manufacturer, churchman, and civic leader, the son of John Lawrence and Glendora Burgess Council, was born in rural Chatham County. He went first to the local Piney Grove School and then to Trinity Park, the preparatory school adjunct to Trinity College (now Duke University). Following his graduation there in 1905, he entered the School of Pharmacy at The University of North Carolina and after one year passed the qualifying examination to become a registered pharmacist, satisfying an ambition developed during after-school work in a Durham drug store.

After leaving the university, Council first worked for the West Side Pharmacy, owned by R. Blacknall and Sons; two years later (1908), he formed a partnership with Germain Bernard, himself a pharmacist at Blacknall's. They established the Five Points Drug Company, with Council as its manager.

In 1910, Council began the manufacture of B.C. headache remedy: he compounded a prescription for a friend who complained of severe headaches; the remedy worked, and the friend told others about Council's medicine. From that simple beginning came the world-famous headache powders and later (1947) tablets. The name B.C. came from the names Bernard and Council. The first materials used in its manufacture were bought on the credit of the store, with the agreement that Bernard would get a share of any profit that might develop. Throughout the years, even after Council's death, the profits of the B.C. Remedy Company were shared with Bernard and his heirs, although he was never in any way affiliated with the actual manufacture and sales of the product. This allegiance to an early gentlemen's agreement made Bernard, as well as Council, a very wealthy man, each accruing a fortune high in seven figures.

For many years, Council did all the mixing of the formula for B.C., and its ingredients were not in writing anywhere. Eventually, it is believed, the formula was entrusted to one man, a lifetime associate of Council's in both the pharmacy and the B.C. Remedy Company.

The partnership of Bernard and Council continued. The Five Points Drug Company was merged in 1932 with the Blacknall Drug Company, becoming the Durham

Drug Company, in a new location near Five Points on lower West Main Street in Durham. Council continued as vice-president and director until 1949; he remained as president of the B.C. Remedy Company (incorporated 1937) until his death.

Council became a director of the Depositors National Bank, Durham, in 1932 and president in 1938, serving in that post until the bank became a branch of the North Carolina Bank and Trust Company, with headquarters in Charlotte. He then became chairman of the local board of the Durham branch and a member of the general board of the bank, serving in both capacities until his death. He was vice-president and chairman of the board of the Home Savings and Loan Association, Durham.

Council's state-wide activities included service as a trustee of The University of North Carolina and of Meredith College. He held active membership in the North Carolina Pharmaceutical Association, the North Carolina Pharmaceutical Research Foundation, the North Carolina Business Foundation, the Proprietary Association of America, the North Carolina Citizens Association, and the North Carolina Good Health Association.

Council was a loyal churchman and an avid supporter of city-wide activities. He was a charter member (1923) of the Watts Street Baptist Church and one of its most generous and faithful members. He was a long-time trustee of Wright Refuge, a haven for displaced children, and was a member and served on the advisory board of the YMCA. He served terms as a member of the Durham County Board of Health and of the School Board of the City of Durham. For all his professional years he held membership in the Durham Chamber of Commerce, serving as its president in 1937; also in 1937, he was awarded the organization's highest honor, its civic award to a distinguished citizen, for his part in implementing the Raleigh-Durham Airport. Politically, he called himself an independent. Though he was never a candidate for public office, he took an alert interest in all political activities.

On 23 Mar. 1910, Council was married to Elizabeth Frances Durham, daughter of Mr. and Mrs. William Durham of nearby rural Orange County. The Councils had two children: a son, Commodore Thomas, Jr., who died 2 Jan. 1960; and a daughter, Frances (Mrs. C. R. Yeager); Council's wife and daughter survived him. Council died at Watts Hospital, Durham, and was buried in the family plot in Maplewood Cemetery in that city.

SEE: *Durham Morning Herald*, 14 July 1960; *Nat. Cyc. Am. Biog.*, vol. 47 (1965); William S. Powell, ed., *North Carolina Lives* (1962).

C. SYLVESTER GREEN

Council, John Pickett (31 Jan. 1855–23 Dec. 1929), manufacturer and sportsman, was the son of Catherine Sykes and Kinchen Kitchen Council of Bladen County. He was the descendant of English settlers in Isle of Wight, Va., who came to North Carolina in the seventeenth century. An ancestor, James Council, represented Bladen County in the provincial congress in Halifax in 1776.

Council showed an early interest in machinery and, after ventures in contracting and in the mercantile business, went to Georgia to study the turpentine industry. Returning to Bladen County, he opened the Council Tool Company in a small blacksmith shop at Council Station in 1884. In about 1902 he moved the company to Lake Waccamaw, and the Atlantic Coast Line Railroad established a freight stop there. Council

continued to experiment with steel, sulphur, and carbon for an improved product, employing only local labor on a profit-sharing basis. By 1910 he was manufacturing an estimated 90 percent of the tools used in the turpentine industry in the United States.

A large landowner and farmer, Council developed Sunset Park in Wilmington. He was also an avid hunter and fisherman and founded the North Carolina Game Club, an organization that is still functioning. He was active in the game conservation movement, particularly in the passage of the doe law. His desire to retain hunting rights on land that he sold led him in 1922 to take the question to the North Carolina Supreme Court, where his right to do so was upheld in *Council* v. *Sanderlin* (*N.C. Reports* 183).

Council was married to John Anna Wooten (1859–1926), and they were the parents of six sons and two daughters: Edison B., Walter W., K. Clyde, James R., Jesse K., John M., Agnes Council Lytton, and Mary Council Parker.

SEE: Judson Councill, *Hodges Councill of Virginia and Descendants* (1941); Family papers in possession of Jane Council Gregg (Lake Waccamaw, N.C.).

JANE C. GREGG

Coupee, Francis (20 July 1773–12 Mar. 1814), printer, was of French origin. He moved to Salisbury in the 1790s to open the first printing shop in Western North Carolina. He and John M. Slump set up the German-English Printing Office in 1797 in Salisbury, using the printing types, tools, implements, and press Michael Brown had purchased in 1794 from Benjamin Shoe of Shenandoah County, Va. In this venture, Slump and Coupee were apparently printers hired by Michael Brown, a planter and millwright by profession; in 1798 a work by the Reverend Samuel E. McCorkle, pastor at Thyatira Presbyterian Church, Rowan County, appeared with the imprint of Coupee and Slump at "Michael Brown's German-English Printing Office."

The shop was opened in 1797, when McCorkle had one of his sermons printed by Coupee; Abraham Hodge, printer at Halifax, had printed McCorkle's earlier sermons. The Moravians at Salem took notice of the printshop and recorded in their diary under the date 23 Jan. 1798, "A book printery has been established in Salisbury and it is suggested that in future we might have our festival odes printed there." Coupee assumed control of the office by 1800, when Slump moved to Lincolnton and Brown's name ceased to appear on the title pages of books published in Salisbury. Coupee's printing office issued religious tracts by McCorkle, the Reverend James McRae, and the Reverend Robert Johnston Miller, besides a *Collection of Songs for the German Communities in North Carolina*. In 1799 and in 1800, Coupee published the *North Carolina Almanac* for 1800 and 1801, respectively.

In May 1798, Coupee began the first newspaper in his section of the state, printing the first issue of the *North Carolina Mercury and Salisbury Advertiser*. Slump was not connected with Coupee in this venture, though the two names appeared in the imprints of pieces from the office from 1797 to 1799. The newspaper was published weekly until 1802, when it was discontinued.

Coupee carried on the printing business alone from 1800 until 1811, when Jacob Krider, a native of Salisbury, became his associate. Together they published many books on religion, one of the last being *Poor Peter's Call to His Children* by Peter Clemmons (1812).

Coupee apparently made money in his venture, for by

1801 he purchased one third of lot 2 in the east square of Salisbury, one of the more desirable business lots in the town. He acquired in the same year fourteen acres on the main Yadkin River and in 1806 seventy acres on Grants Creek. In 1811 he purchased two more lots in Salisbury on the edge of the business section.

He was a prominent Mason in the old Cone Lodge in Salisbury and solicited help from a brother Mason, General John Steele, in winning an appointment as clerk for the county of Rowan. The printing business must have been slack at this time (1809): "Nothing but want of employment in my professional business . . . could have compelled me to address you," he wrote.

Coupee was buried in the old Lutheran Cemetery in Salisbury. He was survived by his widow, Margaret; three sons, Charles, Francis, and John; and three daughters, Evelena, Mary, and Sally (who married William Cooper on 12 Apr. 1827). His business partner, Jacob Krider, was appointed guardian for Coupee's orphaned children. His widow married Thomas Holton on 8 Aug. 1817.

SEE: Robert Elliott, "North Carolina Newspapers in the Federal Period, 1789–1800" (M.A. thesis, University of North Carolina, 1948); Adelaide L. Fries, ed., *Records of the Moravians in North Carolina*, 8 vols. (1922–54); D.'C. McMurtrie, *Eighteenth Century North Carolina Imprints* (1938); *North Carolina Mercury and Salisbury Advertiser*, scattered issues; William S. Powell, "Eighteenth-Century Imprints: A Revision and Supplement to McMurtrie," *North Carolina Historical Review* 35 (1958); *Raleigh Register and North Carolina State Gazette*, 25 Mar. 1814; Rowan County Deed Books, 13, 18, 21, 22 (North Carolina State Archives, Raleigh); Salisbury *Western Carolinian*, scattered issues; U.S. Census (1810); H. M. Wagstaff, ed., *The Papers of John Steele*, 2 vols. (1924).

JAMES S. BRAWLEY

Courts, Daniel William (26 Nov. 1800–April 1883), legislator and state treasurer, was born in Culpeper County, Va., and by 1806 moved with his father, George Courts, to Rockingham County. Reared in Rockingham County, Courts was graduated from The University of North Carolina with an A.B. degree in 1823; he received an A.M. degree in 1832. After reading law in his home county, he began practice there, serving a term as county attorney; but within a few years he moved to Surry County. He was appointed to the board of trustees of The University of North Carolina in 1832 and remained on the board a total of twenty-nine years in two terms: 1832–39 and 1846–68; he became a member of the board's executive committee.

Entering politics as a Jacksonian Democrat, Courts represented Surry County in the House of Commons for four terms in 1831–33 and in 1836. In the last session of the legislature he was elected state treasurer, a position he held for two years until 1839, when he resigned to take an appointment by President Martin Van Buren as U.S. consul at Matanzas, Cuba. Following a short tenure in this post, he returned to North Carolina and his home county, Rockingham. Reentering politics, he was elected from Rockingham County to the House of Commons in 1846 and 1848 and to the senate in 1850. While in the senate he was again elected state treasurer, serving ably from 1852 until January 1863. When North Carolina seceded from the United States, he became a member of the prosecession faction of the Democratic party. He was defeated in 1862 by Jonathan Worth, the nominee of the party led by the newly elected governor, Zebulon Vance.

From Raleigh, Courts returned to his substantial Rockingham County plantation, which had in 1860 over a thousand acres and forty-six slaves. His last political office was a term in the state senate in 1864. During the economic disruption of the postwar period, he sold his property in Rockingham County to satisfy debts and moved back to Raleigh, where he lived quietly until his death. He was buried in Rockingham County.

In 1828, Courts married Eliza Allen Waugh (1807–43) of Waughtown, Stokes County; they had a family of three daughters, M. E., J. J., and Eliza A., and two sons, William James and George Albert. After the death of his first wife, Courts married Martha Jones (1803–62) of White Plains, Wake County, on 16 Nov. 1847.

SEE: Kemp P. Battle, *Sketches of the History of the University of North Carolina* (1889); Daniel W. Courts Letters (North Carolina State Archives, Raleigh); D. L. Grant, *Alumni History of the University of North Carolina* (1924); Raleigh *Biblical Recorder*, 18 Apr. 1883; *Raleigh Register*, 3 Feb. 1843, 20 Nov. 1847; Rockingham County Deeds (North Carolina State Archives, Raleigh); Stokes County Marriage Bonds (North Carolina State Archives, Raleigh); Wake County Marriage Bonds and Wills (North Carolina State Archives, Raleigh); John H. Wheeler, *Historical Sketches of North Carolina* (1851); R. L. Zuber, *Jonathan Worth* (1965).

LINDLEY S. BUTLER

Coutanche, Michael (ca. 1720–ca. 1762), colonial official, was a native of the island of Jersey. On 5 Mar. 1739, as Captain Michael Coutanche of "Boston, in New England, Mariner," he bought lots 24 and 25 in Bath Town. He evidently soon removed to North Carolina; by January 1740 he was referred to in a deed on record in Beaufort County as "Merchant of Bath." Soon becoming prominent in his new home, Coutanche was made a justice of Beaufort County in 1745 and was elected to serve the borough of Bath in the colonial assembly the same year. With the exception of the year 1746, he represented Bath Town in this capacity continuously until 1760. In 1753 he was one of the commissioners appointed by the North Carolina colony to lay out a town on Core Banks near Ocracoke Inlet and to erect a fort, to be called Fort Granville, at the same place.

Soon after his arrival in Bath, Coutanche married Sarah Pilkington, daughter of Seth Pilkington and his wife, Sarah Porter, the daughter of John Porter and widow of John Lillington, who died in 1723. Coutanche made his will, dated 1762, in Beaufort County, mentioning therein his wife, Sarah, children Susanna, Michael, and Benjamin, and his small estate in the parish of St. John on the island of Jersey. Son-in-law Richard Evans was appointed executor. Benjamin Coutanche died young. Michael, Jr., styled of "Beaufort County" in June 1761, bought lots 105 and 106 in the new town of Tarboro; he evidently died childless, because his sister later sold this property. Prior to 1763, Sarah Pilkington Coutanche became the third wife of the Reverend Alexander Stewart, rector of St. Thomas Church, Bath, who is said to have come to North Carolina as chaplain to the household of Governor Arthur Dobbs.

Coutanche is best known for the fine house he built in Bath Town a few years after his arrival. It has been assigned the date of 1744 and is now one of the oldest houses in the state. On his death, the house was owned for a year by the brothers James and Lillington Lockhart, first cousins to Sarah Pilkington Coutanche. It was then bought by Robert Palmer, surveyor general of North Carolina. Familiarly known as the Palmer-Marsh house, it was restored and handsomely furnished in recent years by the Beaufort County Historical Society and is now maintained as a museum.

The Coutanche family exists on the island of Jersey today and is considered of ancient origin. Like other Jersey families, the Coutanches are of French descent; some early connection with the city of Coutances in Normandy may be inferred. In North Carolina the name has been subject to many variations in spelling. In Greenville, Cotanche Street commemorates the Evans-Coutanche connection.

SEE: Beaufort County Wills and Deeds (North Carolina State Archives, Raleigh); C. Wingate Reed, *Beaufort County* (1962); William L. Saunders, ed., *Colonial Records of North Carolina*, 10 vols. (1886–90).

CLAIBORNE T. SMITH, JR.

Cowles, Calvin Josiah (*6 Jan. 1821–1 Apr. 1907*), merchant, real estate and mine operator, union leader, and assayer, was born in Hamptonville, the son of Connecticut natives Deborah Sanford and Josiah Cowles. In describing his family's settlement in North Carolina, Cowles noted that his father, after spending a winter or two in the South, went home to Connecticut, married Deborah Sanford in 1815, "hitched up to some little peddling wagons taking a limited supply of furniture and came through to Hamptonville, Surry County, where they settled and went to work." Josiah Cowles was a tinsmith who became a prosperous merchant and active Whig, serving as chairman of the Surry County court and as a member of Governor William A. Graham's council of state (1846–49). Deborah Cowles died in 1827, leaving three children: Calvin; Abel Sanford, who was educated as a physician and died young; and Eliza Ann, who married Dr. Bilson B. Benham. In 1828, Cowles, Sr., married Mrs. Nancy Carson Duvall, who also had three children: Robert Carson, an 1841 graduate of the U.S. Naval Academy; Alvan Simpson, Jr.; and Martha Temperance.

Cowles's formal education was limited to the schools of Hamptonville, supplemented by a lifelong habit of home study, business travel, and wide-ranging personal associations. After an apprenticeship in his father's store in Hamptonville and marriage to his stepsister Martha Duvall, on 19 Sept. 1844, he set up in trade as J. and C. J. Cowles in Elkville near the Caldwell/Wilkes county line.

For thirteen years, 1846 to 1858, Cowles built a trade with the mountain people in furs and hides, dried fruits, wool, feathers, and wax, items that he sold to merchants in New York, Baltimore, Boston, and Philadelphia; there, on annual trips lasting several weeks, he purchased paint, books, guns, medicines, salt, ear trumpets, and dulcimer strings. By 1849 he had expanded his business to collecting roots and herbs; it was called a "risky business" by his father, but Calvin, charmed by the perfumes of his roots and herbs and listing their names like a litany—balm of Gilead, lady slipper, lobelia, gensing, mayapple—surmounted the hazard of getting them to market, over the mountains in wagons to railroads and rivers for shipment out of Wilmington and Charleston, S.C., at exorbitant freight rates. In three years, shipping his bales of sage to butchers, ginger to the beer makers, and sassafras root to the Shakers in Lebanon, N.H., and New Lebanon, Ohio, he could claim to have the largest root and herb business south of the Potomac.

While at Elkville, Cowles became infected with mining fever and began buying land on speculation, paying twenty-five cents to a dollar an acre, often buying at foreclosure sales or purchasing land warrants, sometimes from men who had served in the militia during the Cherokee Removal of 1838. He read textbooks on mining; corresponded with miners in Virginia and Tennessee; sent letters to the governor to be forwarded to peripatetic Ebenezer Emmons, the state geologist; sought investors; and sent minerals and Indian artifacts to the Crystal Palace at the New York World's Fair of 1853, to promote the western counties of North Carolina.

In 1858 he gave up his store and the postmastership he had held since 1852 and moved his wife and four sons to Wilkesboro, where he opened another store and continued to buy mineral lands. Although he was interested in many mines—Baker's in Caldwell County, Elk Knob in Watauga, Flint Knob in Wilkes, Martin's in Yadkin—Cowles's favorite was the Gap Creek Mine near Jefferson, Ashe County, which for forty years he tried to develop into a great copper mine.

On the eve of the Civil War, Cowles estimated that he owned 6,000 acres in Wilkes and adjoining counties, 1,100 in Kansas, and 400 in Missouri, in addition to three farms at Gap Creek (400 acres), one near Elkville called the Buck Dula lands (357 acres), and 200 acres at Wilkesboro.

Cowles was active in Whig politics in the antebellum period. As a determined Unionist, he opposed secession; by June 1861 he noted, "War sets upon me like a nightmare . . . with all enterprises falling to the ground." He continued as postmaster in Wilkesboro under the Confederacy, but his repeated refusals to take the loyalty oath finally resulted in removal of the post office from his store in 1863. In Hamptonville his postmaster father was in a similar political position, although after two years of Confederate rule, Cowles, Sr., signed the loyalty oath, believing by 1863 that the new government was stable.

During the war, Cowles channeled his trade to the markets in Charleston, New Orleans, and Mobile and began selling his roots and herbs to the Confederate medical purveyors in Charlotte and Goldsboro. He was exempt from military service because of a chronically infected leg, but three half brothers served the Confederacy: Miles Melmoth, a lawyer who died of wounds in Richmond in July 1862; William Henry Harrison, cavalry officer, lawyer, and U.S. representative (1885–93); and Andrew Carson, state legislator (1860–73). His stepbrother Robert Carson Duvall (1819–63) commanded the North Carolina naval steamer *Beaufort* at Oregon Inlet in July 1861.

By May 1865, Wilkesboro was cut off from the world without mail service and with most of the horses too worn out to travel. Cowles borrowed fifteen dollars to get to Charlotte to ship his roots, ruefully commenting that his coat was threadbare, yet he was considered a rich man. After several years of intermittent illness, his wife died on 3 Apr. 1866, leaving five sons: Arthur Duvall (1846–1902), merchant; Calvin Duvall (1849–1937), career army officer; Josiah Duvall (1853–80), surveyor; Andrew Duvall (1856–99), lawyer and adjutant general; and William Duvall (1862–1912), bank clerk.

During Reconstruction, Cowles became an active Republican. He was elected by the General Assembly to serve on the council of state for Provisional Governor William W. Holden (May–December 1865). In his bids for elective office, Cowles was defeated as a delegate to the constitutional convention of 1865, defeated by one vote for the state senate, and elected a delegate from Wilkes County to the 1868 constitutional convention, by a majority of 1,600 votes. He was chosen to preside at the convention, held 14 Jan.–17 Mar. in Raleigh. When the convention disbanded, he remained in Raleigh to see the constitution through its printing and then personally delivered a parchment copy to President Andrew Johnson.

On 23 July 1868, Cowles and Ida Holden, daughter of the governor, were married in the governor's private residence by the rector of Christ Church.

In the months and years directly after the constitutional convention, Cowles unsuccessfully sought the Republican nomination for Congress from his district; became Wilkes County's representative on the board of trustees of The University of North Carolina; and was appointed a director of the Eastern Division of the Western North Carolina Railroad Company and treasurer of the Wilmington, Charlotte, and Rutherfordton Railroad Company. In May 1869 he took an oath of allegiance to the federal government and became a pension agent for Union veterans or their survivors in Wilkes County. He was also a delegate to the National Immigration Convention in Indianapolis in 1870. When Governor Holden's impeachment trial was held in the senate chambers of the capitol in Raleigh, Cowles attended his father-in-law much of the time during the months of the trial, from January to March 1871. Like Holden, Cowles saw the trial as a struggle between an elected governor and a powerful, secretive Ku Klux Klan.

Cowles solicited the superintendency of the U.S. Branch Mint in Charlotte from a number of political friends, hoping that through the assay office, the only activity at the mint revived after the war, he could promote mining interests and establish contacts with men in the mineral business. Receiving the appointment in January 1869, he closed his house and store in Wilkesboro and moved his family into the living quarters at the mint. From then until he resigned in 1885, he battled to restore the South's only remaining branch mint to a permanent center for coinage. He wrote innumerable letters to the officials at the U.S. Mint and the Treasury Department, to North Carolina's congressmen, and to newspaper editors, arguing that the gold miners of North Carolina, Tennessee, and Georgia needed not only the assay office at Charlotte but the services of a full-scale mint.

After his return to Wilkesboro in 1885, Cowles set up an office and worked full-time on his land interests. His sons assisted him actively, looking up land grants, surveying tracts, raising money, and appearing in court to argue claims. He rented many acres as farm lands and worked to promote mining and railroad development in the area.

At this time he rediscovered a number of his earlier interests, one of which was service as a voluntary county statistician and weather observer for federal and state agricultural departments. In addition to his reports on county crops and physical conditions, he sent specimens for identification to the divisions of entomology, ornithology, botany, mammalology, and seeds at the U.S. Department of Agriculture. He nourished a long-time interest in family history and began to compile information with a view to publication. The work was completed by his son, Calvin D., who published a two-volume genealogy of the Cowles family in America in 1929.

Two of Cowles's children acquired more than local fame: Calvin Duvall (1839–1937), West Point graduate, fought Indians in the West and the Spanish in Cuba and compiled the atlas accompanying *The War of the Rebellion: A Compilation of the Official Records of the Union and Confederate Armies*; Charles Holden (1875–1957) was active in state Republican politics, served several terms in the state legislature, was U.S. congressman in 1908–10, and was editor-publisher of the *Wilkes Patriot*. Other children by Cowles's second marriage were Annie Laurie Holden, who married Hamilton V. Horton; Nellie Holden, who married Joseph C. Thomas; Ida Holden, married to Ralph S. Mott; and Joseph Sanford.

Cowles belonged to no religious denomination, but his son, Calvin D., wrote that his father "was deeply religious by nature, and would have gone to the stake for a principle or conscience's sake." Cowles was buried in Elmwood Cemetery in Charlotte, near the graves of three of his children, who died in infancy.

SEE: Susan Blosser, "Calvin J. Cowles's Gap Creek Mine," *North Carolina Historical Review* 51 (1974); Calvin D. Cowles, *Genealogy of the Cowles Family in America* (1929); Calvin J. Cowles Papers, 1817–85 (North Carolina State Archives, Raleigh); Calvin Josiah Cowles, 1773–1941, Papers (Southern Historical Collection, University of North Carolina, Chapel Hill); William S. Pearson, "Calvin Josiah Cowles (1821–1907), Politician," Charles L. Van Noppen Papers (Library, Duke University, Durham).

ELLEN MCGREW

Cowles, Charles Holden (16 July 1875–2 Oct. 1957), editor, deputy clerk of U.S. District Court, state legislator, and congressman, was born in Charlotte, the son of Calvin J. and Ida Augusta Holden Cowles. His father was at that time director of the U.S. assay office in Charlotte, and his mother was the daughter of former Governor William W. Holden.

Cowles moved with his parents in 1885 to Wilkesboro, where he received his early education and completed a commercial college course. Because of family tradition and close political ties, young Cowles was destined to lead an active life in the Republican party. Shortly after his twenty-first birthday he was elected to the board of aldermen in Wilkesboro (1897); he then was appointed deputy clerk, U.S. Court, Statesville and Charlotte, serving from 1899 to 1901. He was private secretary to Congressman Edmond Spencer Blackburn in 1901–3. He won election to the lower house of the state legislature in 1904 and was reelected in 1906, 1920, 1922, 1924, 1926, 1928, and 1932. In 1908 he was elected to the Sixty-first Congress (4 Mar. 1909–3 Mar. 1911), and in 1912 he was nominated for the U.S. Senate by the Progressive Republican (Bull Moose) party, though he declined to enter the race. He also served as a North Carolina delegate to the national Republican conventions from 1904 through 1916.

Cowles was founder, editor, and publisher of the *Wilkes Patriot* of Wilkesboro for many years but sold his interests in 1920. Like his newspaperman grandfather, W. W. Holden, he was a fearless and energetic reporter and always worked for the economic advancement of his section of the state, as well as the good of the Republican party. During World War I, he served as a member of the Council of Defense for Wilkes County and was chairman of the Wilkes County War Savings Committee; during World War II he was chairman of War Price and Rationing Board No. 1 for Wilkes. On 6 Sept. 1916 he married Louise S. Lunn, a teacher in the Wilkesboro High School and a daughter of L. L. and Lula Haliburton Lunn of Winston-Salem. The Cowleses had one daughter, Carolyn Louise. Cowles was buried in the St. Paul's Episcopal Church cemetery, Wilkesboro.

SEE: *Biog. Dir. Am. Cong.* (1950); Calvin D. Cowles, *Genealogy of the Cowles Families in America* (1929); Raleigh *News and Observer*, 4 Oct. 1957.

HORACE W. RAPER

Cowles, Henry Clay (17 June 1842–14 Jan. 1914), U.S. clerk of court at Salisbury, Charlotte, and Statesville, U.S. commissioner, and leading industrialist and banker, was born in Hamptonville, the son of Josiah and Nancy Carson Duvall Cowles. Like his brothers, Henry Cowles lived on the family farm and worked in his father's general merchandising store, attended the common schools, and was graduated from the Jonesville High School in Yadkin County. He did not serve in the Confederate Army because of ill health but was captain of the home guard; later he was called colonel to distinguish him from his nephew, Andrew Cowles, a captain in the State Guard, but the title was purely honorary, and Cowles never claimed it.

In the fall of 1865, Cowles moved to Statesville and served first as station agent and later as conductor on the Western North Carolina Railroad. During the presidency of Dr. J. J. Mott, he was appointed secretary-treasurer of the road and served until about 1877. In 1872, when the federal court was established, Cowles was appointed clerk at Statesville and Charlotte; he also acted as the clerk at Salisbury when the court was created there. Later, when the law was changed to provide one clerk for the entire judicial district, Cowles was made deputy clerk to J. M. Millikin of Greensboro but continued to supervise the court business in the same three cities. He held the position until his death. Cowles was active in Republican party activities, serving in many capacities at all levels. At various times he was member of the Statesville Board of Aldermen, U.S. commissioner, and member of the National Republican Committee.

In addition to his official positions, Cowles was active in many Statesville business enterprises. He helped organize the First National Bank in 1886, serving as director and vice-president. He also helped to organize the First Building & Loan Association in Statesville and was a director of the Statesville Furniture Company.

Cowles was married on 14 Dec. 1869 to Juliet Moore (27 Dec. 1845–13 Jan. 1918), daughter of Dr. James Madison and Mary Haggins Moore of Statesville. From this union there were three children, Mary Caroline, Henry Clay, Jr., and Eloise Irwin.

SEE: Calvin D. Cowles, *Genealogy of the Cowles Families in America* (1929); Cowles Manuscripts, Charles L. Van Noppen Papers (Manuscript Department, Library, Duke University, Durham).

HORACE W. RAPER

Cowles, Josiah (3 Apr. 1791–11 Nov. 1873), Western North Carolina merchant, manufacturer, and political leader, was born in Farmingbury (now Wolcott), Conn., the son of Calvin Cowles. Little is known of Josiah's early boyhood, except that he was orphaned at about ten years of age. Despite the insolvency of his father's estate, he acquired a good common school education and learned the tinner's trade, perhaps as an apprentice. Prior to marriage in 1815, he made a profitable trip to the Creek country in Georgia, peddling Yankee notions and buying animal skins: at that time it was considered unpatriotic to wear an English hat, and American hatters were forced to pay well for rabbit skins. He set up a tinner's shop later and worked one year near Kernersville, but he settled permanently in 1816 at Hamptonville, Yadkin County.

Cowles became one of the most successful businessmen in his section, engaging in general mercantile business and the manufacture of tinware for local and national markets. He acquired a large fortune in land and slaves, most of which was lost during the Civil War and Reconstruction periods; his losses were worsened by his refusal to press for collection of debts, lest he distress his debtors. He was known for his strict integrity, great benevolences, and hospitable and generous nature. Because of his strong leadership capabilities, he took an active role in local and state politics, serving as a justice of the peace and member of the court of pleas and quarter sessions for Surry and Yadkin counties for many years, as a member of the council of state to Governor William A. Graham (1845–49), and as a postmaster for nearly half a century. Cowles was an old-line Whig in politics, and although he bitterly opposed secession, he supported the Confederacy during the Civil War.

Cowles was twice married. First, on 20 Sept. 1815, he married Deborah Sanford (11 June 1795–9 Jan. 1827) of Woodbridge and Meriden, Conn., who was related to many prominent Connecticut families, including that of Henry Ward Beecher. On 25 July 1828, Cowles married Mrs. Nancy Caroline Carson Duvall (19 May 1802–3 July 1863), the widow of Alvin Simpson Duvall of Hamptonville. She was the daughter of Captain Andrew Carson of Revolutionary War fame and the niece of Lindsay Carson, father of Christopher ("Kit") Carson, the famous western scout, guide, and soldier. Cowles was the father of eleven children, several of whom distinguished themselves as outstanding business and political leaders of North Carolina. The eleven were Eliza Ann, who married Bilson Belzar Benham; Elviria Deborah; Calvin Joseph, an outstanding Republican leader in the state; Abel Sanford, a physician who died at the age of twenty-nine; Josiah; Andrew Carson; Miles Melmoth, lieutenant in the Thirty-eighth North Carolina Infantry, who died of wounds received at the Battle of Mechanicsville, Va.; Lewis Williams; William Henry Harrison, Democratic congressman; Henry Clay, federal court clerk at Statesville and Charlotte; and Caroline Mary.

Cowles was not a member of any religious denomination but regularly attended the local Presbyterian church. He was buried at the Flat Rock Cemetery, Hamptonville.

SEE: Calvin D. Cowles, *Genealogy of the Cowles Families in America* (1929).

HORACE W. RAPER

Cowles, William Henry Harrison (22 Apr. 1840–30 Dec. 1901), attorney and congressman, was born in Hamptonville in the southern part of the present Yadkin County. His father, Josiah Cowles, was a native of Connecticut who had come to the South and begun a mercantile business at Hamptonville in 1816. His mother, Nancy Carson, was a member of one of the earliest families to settle in the territory between the Yadkin and the Catawba rivers; she was a daughter of Andrew Carson of Hunting Creek in Iredell County and a first cousin of Kit Carson, well-known Indian scout of the West. Both Josiah Cowles and Nancy Carson had been married earlier, Nancy Carson to Alvin Simpson Duvall of Hamptonville. W. H. H. Cowles can be understood only as a part of a large clan composed of brothers, sisters, half-brothers, half-sisters, and their families.

Before the Civil War the Cowles clan was staunchly Whig, opposed to secession as the war approached but warm in the support of the Confederacy during the war. Josiah Cowles had risen to be a member of the council of state under Whig Governor William A. Graham; and one of his sons, Andrew Carson, was a perennial member of the legislature from Yadkin County during the Civil War and Reconstruction. After the war the Cowles clan split politically; Josiah, Andrew Carson, and William Henry Harrison became Democrats. Andrew C. barely missed the Democratic nomination for Congress from the Seventh North Carolina District in 1872. Henry Clay Cowles, on the other hand, was a prominent Republican in Statesville; and Calvin Josiah, older halfbrother of W. H. H., was a leading member of the Republican party during Reconstruction and president of the North Carolina Constitutional Convention in 1868. One of Calvin's sons, Andrew Duvall, became adjutant general of the North Carolina State Guard under Republican Governor Daniel Russell. Another son, Charles Holden, was elected to the U.S. House of Representatives in 1908 as a Republican but was defeated two years later by Democrat Robert L. Doughton.

William Henry Harrison Cowles's youth was spent in Hamptonville, where he attended the common schools and the academies of the county. When the Civil War broke out, he entered the Confederate Army as a private in Company A, First North Carolina Cavalry, in the spring of 1861 and served in Virginia until near the end of the war, being gradually promoted to lieutenant colonel of the regiment. He was badly wounded twice, once at Mine Run in 1862 and near the end of the war at Petersburg. There he was taken prisoner and as soon as he could travel was paroled by Major Senaca R. Cowles of New York.

Back home, he read law under Judge Richmond Pearson at Richmond Hill in Yadkin County, was licensed to practice, and moved to Wilkesboro to practice in 1868. There he became active in politics as a Democrat. He was appointed reading clerk of the North Carolina Senate from 1872 through 1874 and then was elected solicitor of the Tenth Judicial District, serving for four years. For eight years he was a member of the Democratic state executive committee, exercising considerable influence on the party.

Until 1884, Wilkes County was in the Seventh Congressional District, dominated largely by Statesville and Salisbury influences. Factionalism gradually developed in the Democratic party between two Statesville leaders, W. M. Robbins and R. F. Armfield. Armfield, who had moved from Wilkesboro to Statesville, usually had the backing of Wilkes and Yadkin counties, and W. H. H. Cowles was largely responsible for pushing Armfield to the front in 1878 and 1880 to win the Democratic nomination and the fall election. The factionalism was finally to cost the Democrats control of the district, when Robbins was defeated in 1882 by Dr. Tyre York of Wilkes.

Before the election of 1884 a new Eighth Congressional District had been formed, which placed Wilkes with such counties as Cleveland and Gaston, rather than Iredell and Rowan. From that district, Cowles was elected to Congress for four terms, serving in the House of Representatives from 4 Mar. 1885 until 3 Mar. 1893. He declined to run for a fifth term and retired to his country place on the Yadkin River, about a mile and a half below Wilkesboro. He was living there when he died of pneumonia. He and his family were active Presbyterians, and he was buried in the Presbyterian cemetery in Wilkesboro.

Cowles was married twice, on 1 June 1870 to Rosomond Corinna Worth, from Creston in Ashe County, and on 16 Oct. 1883 to Mary Lura Bost of Newton. From the two marriages came eleven children, most of whom lived to maturity. Two sons, Miles Andrew and Stuart Lee, were educated at West Point and became career army officers; Miles Andrew served with distinction during World War I and became a brigadier general in 1942, and Stuart Lee retired with the rank of colonel. Another son, William Henry Harrison, Jr., served in World War I and became professor of mathematics at Pratt Institute. Cowles's oldest daughter, Caroline Elizabeth, married Judge T. B. Finley of North Wilkesboro. Corinna Albina married Joseph A. Gaither, an industrialist of Newton; Sarah Sherrill married R. O. Self of Raleigh; Esther married the Reverend Sidney S. Bost, Episcopal priest of Durham; and Mary Loretz married Neely Kincaid of Statesville. The younger children were reared in Statesville, where Mrs. Cowles moved after her husband's death for the better education of her children.

SEE: *Biog. Dir. Am. Cong.* (1950); Calvin D. Cowles, *Genealogy of the Cowles Families in America* (1929).

HOMER M. KEEVER

Cox, Albert Lyman (*1 Dec. 1883–15 Apr. 1965*), attorney, state senator, judge, and major general, U.S. Army, was born in Raleigh. His father was Confederate general, judge, and U.S. congressman William Ruffin Cox, son of state senator Thomas Cox of Washington County and grandson of English-born Thomas Cox, a seafaring man, and of Margaret Cheshire Cox of Edenton. His mother, Fannie Augusta Lyman Cox, daughter of Right Reverend Theodore Benedict Lyman, Episcopal Bishop of North Carolina from 1881 to 1893, died about two years after Albert's birth. His only brother was Dr. Francis A. of Alexandria, Va.

While his father represented North Carolina in the Forty-seventh through Fiftieth Congresses and served as secretary of the Senate, Cox attended public schools in Washington, D.C.; later he entered Horner Military School in Oxford. A 1904 graduate of The University of North Carolina, with A.B. and A.M. degrees, he participated in varsity football, baseball, and track and was a member of the Phi Society, Sigma Alpha Epsilon, Golden Fleece, and Gimghouls. He was president and permanent president of his class and in 1921 was president of the General Alumni Association. He was admitted to both the Massachusetts and the North Carolina bar in 1907, following studies at Harvard Law School, where he was a member of Phi Delta Phi legal fraternity.

Representing Wake County in the North Carolina House of Representatives in 1909, Cox was chairman of the Public Buildings and Grounds Committee and a member of the Appropriations, Constitutional Amendment, Insurance, Judiciary I, and Military Affairs committees. Active in Democratic politics, he was a delegate to the Democratic National Conventions of 1912, 1932, 1940, 1944, and 1948 and was Democratic elector-at-large in 1920. He declined to enter the race for the 1932 gubernatorial nomination, although a 1927 movement encouraged him to do so.

With his brother, Francis Augustus, Cox practiced law in Raleigh from 1908 to 1919; afterward he practiced alone, largely in trial and corporate law. During these years he was president of the Raleigh Chamber of Commerce (1912); a charter member (1914) and the second president of the Raleigh Rotary Club, North Carolina's first; president of the Raleigh Baseball Club; vice-president and counsel for Boylan-Pearce Company and Jolly's Jewelers; director and counsel for Raleigh Building and Loan Association, Southern Coach Company, Merchants National Bank of Raleigh, and North State Electric Supply Company; director of Capital Construction Company, Colonial Life Insurance Company of High Point, and Rex Hospital, Raleigh; and trustee of the University of the South, Sewanee, Tenn. In 1916 he was appointed superior court judge for the Seventh Judicial District of North Carolina, which position he resigned in July 1917.

Cox saw Mexican border service in 1916 as captain of Company B, Third North Carolina Infantry. The following year, as colonel, he organized and commanded the 1st North Carolina Field Artillery, which he continued to command when it became the 113th Field Artillery, A.E.F.; the unit served in the St. Mihiel and Meuse-Argonne offensives and at other locations in France, including assignment in the Army of Occupation. Cox later received the Distinguished Service Medal. He became brigadier general in the Officers' Reserve Corps in 1922, commanding the 155th Field Artillery Brigade of the 80th Division, and he was president of the Third Corps Area advisory board of reserve officers. As commander-elect of the North Carolina Department of the American Legion in 1927, he and his predecessor in office led the state's contingent of some two hundred veterans to France as part of the pilgrimage of eighteen thousand American Legionnaires to comrades' graves and to the legion convention in Paris.

Moving to Washington in 1932, Cox was admitted to the District of Columbia bar in 1933 and became a director of the Potomac Electric Power Company. Military activities continued to deflect considerable time from his law practice. During World War II he served as District of Columbia Director of Selective Service, commanding general of the Washington Provisional Brigade and later of the Military District of Washington, and commander-in-chief of the Military Order of the World Wars. As provost marshal of Washington, D.C., he had custody of the Nazi saboteurs who landed from submarines on the Atlantic coast. As commanding general of the District of Columbia National Guard after 17 May 1938, he accomplished a reorganization of the unit and was instrumental in acquiring the armory building completed in Washington in 1941 and dedicated after the war, 20 June 1947. He continued to command the guard until his retirement on 6 Nov. 1949, with the rank of major general, U.S. Reserves.

Cox held memberships in the American, District of Columbia, North Carolina, and Wake County bar associations; Sons of the American Revolution; Carolina Country Club, Raleigh; Metropolitan Club and Metropolitan Police Boys' Club of Washington; Washington Board of Trade; U.S. Chamber of Commerce; National Press Club; North Carolina Society of Washington; National Guard Association; Reserve Officers Association; President's Cup Regatta Association; Masons; Rotary Club; and Knights of Pythias. An Episcopalian, he was a vestryman of the Church of the Good Shepherd in Raleigh and of St. John's Church, Washington, and served as trustee of the Diocese of North Carolina and executive councilor of the Diocese of Washington.

His retirement years were spent at his residence on Linwood Avenue, Goldsboro, where he continued his law practice, principally related to estates. He was active in Chamber of Commerce endeavors, chairing the committee on conventions and tourism, and was instrumental in promoting the Salvation Army locally. He participated in the local cancer society's drives to fight the disease that eventually claimed his own life. He died in Goldsboro and was buried in Willow Dale Cemetery with full military honors.

Cox was married on 1 Dec. 1909 in Tarboro to Arabel Parker Nash, daughter of Samuel Simpson and Annie Gray Cheshire Nash of Tarboro. The Cox's children included Rear Admiral William Ruffin, Ret., of New Hartford, N.Y.; Arabel Parker (Mrs. Murray Borden, Jr.) of Goldsboro; Colonel Albert Lyman, Jr., U.S.A.F., Ret., of Washington, D.C.; Annie Cheshire (Mrs. William Mayes Lively) of Denver, Colo.; and Frances Augusta (Mrs. Vincent Joseph Mancuso) of Goldsboro. A portrait of Cox painted by Clement Strudwick in 1922 is in the possession of Mrs. Murray Borden, Jr.

SEE: Samuel A. Ashe, ed., *Biographical History of North Carolina*, vol. 1 (1905); Cox papers (possession of Rear Admiral William R. Cox, Hartford, N.Y.); *Encyclopedia of American Biography*, vol. 37 (1968); A. L. Fletcher, *History of the 113th Field Artillery, 30th Division* (1920 [photograph]); *Goldsboro News-Argus*, 16 and 18 Apr. 1965; D. L. Grant, *Alumni History of the University of North Carolina* (1924); *A History of the Rotary Club of Raleigh* (1955 [photograph]); *Nat. Cyc. Am. Biog.*, vol. 51 (1969); *North Carolina Manual* (1909, 1913); North Carolina State Archives (Raleigh), for photographs; *New York Times*, 17 Apr. 1965; William S. Powell, ed., *North Carolina Lives* (1962); Raleigh *News and Observer*, 6 and 11 Mar. 1927, 21 Aug. 1927, 4 and 11 Sept. 1927, 23 Oct. 1927, 18 May 1938, 7 Dec. 1942, 6 Nov. 1949; *Raleigh Times*, 13 July 1912; *State 1* (22 July 1933 [photograph]), 15 (16 Aug. 1947); *University of North Carolina Alumni Review*, October 1921 (photograph); Elizabeth C. Waugh, *North Carolina's Capital, Raleigh* (1967); *Who's Who in America*, 1964–65; *Who's Who in the South*, 1927; *Who Was Who in America*, vol. 4 (1968).

ELIZABETH DAVIS REID

Cox, Francis Augustus (21 Aug. 1885–12 July 1978), clergyman, missionary, university administrator, was born in Raleigh, the son of Frances Lyman and William Ruffin Cox. He was the grandson of Bishop Theodore B. Lyman. Cox attended Horner Military School and was graduated from The University of North Carolina in 1905. After receiving a degree in law from the University of Virginia in 1907 he practiced in Raleigh until 1917. During World War I he served as a captain of field artillery with the Eighty-second Division, American Expeditionary Force, in France. After the war he prepared for the ministry at the Virginia Theological Seminary and upon graduation in 1921 was married to Mary Pemberton Moncure of Alexandria, Va., and left for China to serve as a missionary. He was ordained to the Episcopal priesthood the following year. Living first at Soochow, where he became archdeacon of the diocese, and afterward at Shanghai, where he was chancellor of St. John's University, Cox served for twenty-one years until he was imprisoned by the Japanese at the beginning of hostilities between their nation and the United States. Mrs. Cox returned to the United States in March 1941, but Cox was not permitted to leave until the summer of 1942. While he was in prison the Virginia Theological Seminary conferred upon him in absentia the degree of doctor of divinity. In China he served as chairman of the Diocesan Standing Committee, of the Board of Examining Chaplains, and the Board of Directors of St. John's University. After returning to the United States he served as rector of the church in Pittsburgh, Pa., and afterward of Fox Chapel Community Church which he helped to organize in a

Pittsburgh suburb. In 1960 he published *The Cross and the Dragon*, a volume dealing with his work between 1921 and 1942. After retirement he lived in Alexandria, Va., where he was buried at Ivy Hill Cemetery. Mrs. Cox died two years earlier and he was survived by two nephews and three nieces.

SEE: Daniel L. Grant, *Alumni History of the University of North Carolina* (1924); William S. Powell, ed., *North Carolina Lives* (1962); Raleigh *News and Observer*, 14 Sept. 1942, 2 Dec. 1945, 18 July 1978; *Who's Who in the South and Southwest*, 1961.

WILLIAM S. POWELL

Cox, Gertrude Mary (13 Jan. 1900–17 Oct. 1978), statistician and professor, was born in Dayton, Iowa, the daughter of Allen and Emma Cox. She received B.S. and M.S. degrees from Iowa State University in 1929 and 1931, respectively, and the degree of D.Sc. (hon.) in 1958. Following postgraduate study at the University of California, Berkeley, where she was a graduate assistant in psychological statistics, she returned to Iowa State as assistant in the newly organized statistical laboratory. In 1939 she was named a research assistant professor. The following year Miss Cox joined the faculty of North Carolina State College in Raleigh as the first woman to become a member of the regular teaching staff. In time she became a professor, head of the department of experimental statistics, and director of the Institute of Statistics, a joint program which she created, of The University of North Carolina and North Carolina State College. She also was instrumental in establishing the Research Triangle Institute and headed its statistical research division. Her work took her to Egypt, South Africa, Thailand, many countries in South America, and elsewhere; in many of these countries she served as statistical adviser and program specialist to the governments. Her work was often sponsored by the Rockefeller Foundation, various agencies of the United States government, and others. She conducted summer institutes at many colleges and universities. Miss Cox was a member of and an officer in numerous professional organizations and was named to the National Academy of Sciences in 1975. In addition to her teaching, research, and consulting she was the author of numerous research bulletins and publications and was co-author of a widely used textbook. In 1959 she received the O. Max Gardner Award for her contributions to the welfare of the human race. In 1960 she retired from the North Carolina State University faculty but continued to reside in Raleigh where her parents had also lived from 1947 until their death. She was buried in Montlawn Memorial Park. The seven-story physics and statistics building on the North Carolina State University campus was named in her honor.

SEE: Raleigh *News and Observer*, 29 Mar. 1959, 26 Nov. 1959, 4 May 1975, 18 Oct. 1978; *The Oliver Max Gardner Award* (1959); *Who's Who in America* (1978).

WILLIAM S. POWELL

Cox, Jonathan Elwood (1 Nov. 1856–29 Mar. 1932), banker and manufacturer, was born on his father's farm in Rich Square, Northampton County. He was the son of Jonathan Elliott and Elizabeth Hare Cox, who had met while students at New Garden Boarding School near Greensboro in Guilford County. The Cox family of Perquimans County and the Hares of Suffolk County, Va., were Quakers and had been in America since the early years of the eighteenth century. The elder Cox moved to Guilford County in 1859 to become superintendent of the New Garden School. His son attended classes there and then entered Earlham College, a Quaker college in Richmond, Ind. After two years at Earlham, he took a business course in Baltimore. Following a brief career as a rural schoolteacher and another as a traveling salesman of fruit trees, he settled in High Point in 1880 and remained there until his death. Shortly after his marriage in 1878, he entered into business with his father-in-law, William Henry Snow, and established the firm that eventually became the J. Elwood Cox Manufacturing Company, a firm engaged in manufacturing wooden shuttles and bobbins for the textile industry. The firm expanded rapidly and soon developed into a major producer for both domestic and foreign markets. After controlling the firm for nearly forty years, Cox incorporated it and turned it over to his nephew, Joseph D. Cox, who became its principal officer.

Cox contributed greatly to High Point's development from the rural community of seven hundred citizens he found when he moved there into one of the South's major industrial centers. In addition to his interests in manufacturing, he also achieved prominence in banking and established one of the principal financial institutions in High Point. In 1891 he founded the Commercial National Bank, remaining its president until it was forced to close in January 1932, at the height of the depression. He also served as president of the High Point Savings and Trust Company; as a director of the First National Bank of Thomasville, the Greensboro Loan and Trust Company, the Virginia Trust Company in Richmond, and the Jefferson Standard Life Insurance Company; and as an officer or director of numerous other manufacturing, commercial, and railroad companies in North Carolina and elsewhere. Active in the North Carolina State Bankers Association, he was also a member of the executive council of the American Bankers Association for fifteen years and in 1917 was elected president of the National Bank section of the organization. In 1923 he was elected treasurer of the national group for a term of two years. He was a director of the Southern Exposition Building and of the High Point Hotel for a number of years.

A loyal Quaker and an active member of the Central Friends Society, Cox was appointed in 1893 a trustee of Guilford College, the institution developed by the Society of Friends from the New Garden Boarding School, to which Cox's family had such close ties. He was chairman of the board of Guilford from 1903 until his death and chairman of the city school board in High Point for nineteen years. He served as a trustee of George Peabody College for Teachers in Nashville, Tenn., and was selected by James B. Duke, who with his brother, Benjamin N. Duke, had been Cox's schoolmates at New Garden School, as an original trustee of the Duke Endowment.

Cox ran as a Republican in the gubernatorial election of 1908 and through his unsuccessful campaign, substantially reduced the Democratic majority. He was appointed by Governor Cameron Morrison to the first state highway commission in 1921 and served as commissioner for the fifth district for ten years. He was also a representative from North Carolina on the War Finance Corporation.

On 23 Oct. 1878, Cox was married to Bertha Emily Snow, the daughter of William Henry Snow, a former captain in the Union army who had moved to North Carolina from Vermont after the Civil War. Snow successfully experimented with various woods for use in textile manufacturing equipment and was instrumental in organizing the Asheboro Railroad. The Coxes, who had been schoolmates at New Garden, had one daughter, Clara I., who with her mother spent the season at the family's winter home in St. Petersburg, Fla. In 1929, Cox built a handsome estate in the fashionable Emerywood section of High Point. He died after an illness of two months caused by a weak heart and was buried in the family mausoleum in Oakwood Memorial Park in High Point.

SEE: Jonathan Elwood Cox MSS (Manuscript Department, Library, Duke University, Durham); *Greensboro Daily News*, 29–31 Mar. 1932; *History of North Carolina*, vol. 5 (1919); Raleigh *News and Observer*, 29–31 Mar. 1932.

PAUL I. CHESTNUT

Cox, Joseph John (13 May 1845–17 July 1903), physician and furniture manufacturer, was born on a farm near Rich Square, Northampton County, of English ancestry. His father was Jonathan E. Cox, a farmer who became superintendent of New Garden Boarding School just before the Civil War and maintained it successfully through that troubled era. His mother was Elizabeth Hare of Nansemond County, Va.

While his father served as superintendent and his mother as matron of the New Garden School, young Joseph Cox applied himself studiously to his courses of study. In 1866, Allen Jay, on his first religious visit to North Carolina, held a service at New Garden School for young people desirous of a better life; Cox was among those confessing Christ publicly. That experience affected his course of life and caused him to decide to become a physician. His parents feared that the strain would be too much for his physical strength, but in the fall of 1868 he entered Miami College at Cincinnati, Ohio, and a year later Jefferson Medical College at Philadelphia, from which he was graduated in March 1871.

In 1872, Cox married Mary Hollowell, who died in 1874. In 1876 he married Mary Dundas, daughter of John and Sarah Dundas, who, seeking a climate milder than Canada's, had settled near New Garden. Cox's son, Joseph D., became prominent in the business, civic, and religious life of High Point.

Cox's large country practice so taxed his strength that he moved to the growing town of High Point to avoid the exposure and weariness incidental to rural practice. His health greatly improved, and after a few years he gave up the practice of medicine to become secretary and treasurer of the Home Furniture Company, with which he was actively identified until his death. He was active in the religious, civic, business, and political life of High Point. At the time of his death he was superintendent of the Friends Bible School, an elder in his church, treasurer of the Foreign Mission Board, president of the board of trustees of Guilford College, director of the Commercial National Bank and member of the High Point School Board.

Cox was buried at New Garden Cemetery.

SEE: Samuel A. Ashe, ed., *Biographical History of North Carolina*, vol. 4 (1906); *Greensboro Patriot*, 22 July 1903.

HOLT MCPHERSON

Cox, William Ruffin (11 Mar. 1832–26 Dec. 1919), lawyer, agriculturalist, Confederate general, congressman, and civic leader, was born in Scotland Neck, Halifax County, of English ancestry. His grandfather was John

Cox, whose London baptism was recorded in St. Paul's Cathedral; John Cox served in the British navy and settled in North Carolina early in the nineteenth century in time to sail as an American merchantman during the War of 1812. William's father was Thomas Cox; his mother, Olivia Norfleet, was the daughter of a wealthy Halifax County planter, Marmaduke Norfleet. As a young man, Thomas Cox engaged in an extensive trade with the West Indies, holding partnerships in companies based in Plymouth, N.C., and Philadelphia, Pa. A leading advocate of railroad building and other progressive improvements, he represented Washington County in the state senate. In 1825 he removed to Halifax County to become a planter. At the time of his death in 1836, he had three daughters and four sons, of whom William was the youngest.

William Ruffin Cox began his education in the Vine Hill Academy of Scotland Neck. After the death of Thomas Cox, his widow moved the family to Nashville, Tenn., in order to be near her eldest daughter. There young Cox's education continued, as he prepared to enter Franklin College, an institution from which he was graduated with distinction in 1850. After reading law at Lebanon College, he was admitted to the bar and practiced law for five years in Nashville as the partner of John C. Ferguson.

In 1857, upon his marriage to Penelope Battle, daughter of Edgecombe County planter James S. Battle, Cox returned to North Carolina and began to develop Penelo, the fine Edgecombe County plantation he retained all his life. He resettled in Raleigh in 1859 and opened a successful legal practice.

An ardent southern rights man, Cox became an enthusiastic secessionist. As preparation for military service he had studied military tactics; when war came, he organized and financed an artillery company. On 8 May 1861, Governor John W. Ellis appointed him to the rank of major in the Second North Carolina Regiment, launching him on a distinguished military career. Serving in the corps of Thomas J. ("Stonewall") Jackson and Richard Stoddert Ewell, he was successively promoted to lieutenant colonel (September 1862), colonel (March 1863), and, when he assumed command of Stephen D. Ramseur's old brigade, brigadier general (May 1864). Cox commanded a reorganized brigade of North Carolina troops, consisting of the First, Second, Third, Fourth, Fourteenth, and Thirtieth regiments. He fought in numerous battles and campaigns, including Malvern Hill, Antietam, Chancellorsville (where his regiment was so heavily engaged that half his men were killed or wounded), the Valley Campaign of 1864, and the defense of Petersburg. In the retreat to Appomattox, he led the last organized attack of the Army of Northern Virginia. He was noted for his intrepid spirit, his valor under fire, and his ability to keep his depleted and dispirited troops intact. Twice he was officially commended by Robert E. Lee. After the war, Governor Zebulon B. Vance took pleasure in publicly recalling Lee's satisfaction with Cox in the discouraging retreat from Petersburg: upon observing a small brigade that was especially orderly, obviously prideful, and well organized, Lee asked an aide, "What troops are those?" The reply was, "Cox's North Carolina brigade," whereupon Lee removed his hat, bowed his head, and said with feeling, "God bless gallant old North Carolina." Wounded eleven times, five at Chancellorsville, Cox emerged from the Civil War a popular and well-loved North Carolina military hero.

In 1865, Cox reopened his Raleigh law office. Soon thereafter he was elected president of the board of the

Chatham Coal Fields Railway Company. His military reputation opened many possibilities, and he eventually turned to politics. He was considered at one time as a gubernatorial alternative to the Conservative candidate Jonathan Worth, but he did not accept nomination; instead, he sided with those who opposed congressional Reconstruction. In 1868 he stood for the temporarily important post of solicitor in the Raleigh district. He was elected by twenty-seven votes, although the Republican majority in the district was approximately four thousand. He was an able solicitor for the next six years—at times the only prominent Democrat holding state office. A delegate to the 1868 Democratic National Convention, he became increasingly active in party affairs. He succeeded Daniel M. Barringer as state Democratic chairman in 1874 and invigorated the party by emphasizing grassroots organization and rigid party discipline. He was instrumental in "redeeming" North Carolina in the exciting elections of 1874, 1875, and 1876. He was a viable candidate for governor in 1876 but cheerfully withdrew when he learned that Zeb Vance was available. Vance, after his victory, appointed Cox to the judgeship of the Sixth Judicial District of North Carolina, a position he filled with courage and ability until 1880.

Cox represented the Raleigh-Durham district in the Forty-seventh, Forty-eighth, and Forty-ninth Congresses (4 Mar. 1881–3 Mar. 1887). His most notable and controversial role came in the Forty-ninth Congress when, as chairman of the Committee on Civil Service, he championed reform. His views were generally unpopular among politicians who favored the old patronage system. In one speech to the House, Cox characterized a civil service system based on merit as "the genius and essence of democracy." This stand apparently caused his party to drop him from the ticket in 1886, although 197 convention ballots were required to nominate someone else. Cox declined President Grover Cleveland's offer of a post in the Land Office amid allegations, which he vigorously denied, that he was being rewarded for his defense of the civil service system. He was elected secretary to the U.S. Senate in 1893 and served in that capacity until his resignation in 1900, when he returned to North Carolina to stay. In his later years he resided at Penelo or Raleigh and engaged in agricultural pursuits.

Cox was actively involved in the civic affairs of his state. In the 1870s he was chairman of the North Carolina Education Association and was instrumental in founding the *North Carolina Journal of Education*, a monthly publication devoted to promoting the common schools. Long a member of the executive committee of the North Carolina Agriculture Society, he became president in 1900. He was grand master of North Carolina Masons in 1878 and 1879 and a dedicated layman in the Protestant Episcopal church, frequently attending diocesan conventions and serving as trustee of the University of the South. His many public addresses, although without real distinction, were well received because of their source; most memorable of these was his 1891 address on the life and character of Major General Stephen D. Ramseur.

In 1857, Cox married Penelope Battle; their only child, Pierre B., died in early manhood. In 1883 Cox was married to Frances Augusta Lyman; their union produced two sons, Albert L. and Francis. In 1905, Cox married Mrs. Herbert A. Claiborne of Richmond, Va. He died at Richmond and was buried in Raleigh's Oakwood Cemetery, attended by Confederate veterans and by numerous Masons.

SEE: Samuel A. Ashe, ed., *Biographical History of North Carolina*, vol. 1 (1905), and *Cyclopedia of Eminent and*

Representative Men of the Carolinas of the Nineteenth Century, vol. 2 (1892 [portrait]); *Biog. Dir. Am. Cong.* (1961); *DAB*, vol. 4 (1930); Raleigh *News and Observer*, 27–29 Dec. 1919.

MAX R. WILLIAMS

Coxe, Franklin (2 Nov. 1839–2 June 1903), industrialist, banker, and railroad executive, was born in Rutherfordton, the son of Francis Sidney and Jane McBee Alexander Coxe. An ancestor, Daniel Coxe, had settled in New Jersey in the early years of the eighteenth century and held title to extensive grants of land in the Carolinas and elsewhere. Tench Coxe, Daniel's grandson and the grandfather of Franklin, was assistant secretary of the treasury under Alexander Hamilton and later commissioner of revenue by appointment of President Washington. Lands in the coal fields of Pennsylvania were a source of substantial wealth to the Coxes, and it was in the interest of their landholdings in the South that Francis Coxe moved to Rutherford County.

Frank Coxe, as he usually signed himself, was educated in the local schools of Rutherfordton and briefly at Furman University in Greenville, S.C., the locality from which his mother's family had come. At sixteen he entered the sophomore class of the University of Pennsylvania, receiving his degree in 1857. After graduation he began work as a civil engineer in the anthracite coal fields of Pennsylvania, where his family's firm was rapidly becoming one of the nation's largest coal operators.

With the outbreak of war, Coxe returned to Greenville and joined Joseph Kershaw's Brigade of South Carolina Volunteers. His stay in the Confederate service was short, because the State of Pennsylvania and the federal government both threatened confiscation of his property, along with that of his Pennsylvania associates. Coxe placed the matter before President Jefferson Davis, and upon Davis's advice left the army, went to Philadelphia, and then departed for an extended stay in Europe. As a measure of aid to the Confederacy he placed funds in trust to be spent for the relief of prisoners of war from the Carolinas and Virginia.

At the war's end, Coxe returned to the South. He lived in Rutherfordton for a time and then moved to Charlotte in 1877; there, within a few years, he became president of the Commercial National Bank. While living in Charlotte he developed an interest in railroads and in the mountain area around Asheville. He was a stockholder and officer in the Western North Carolina Railroad and later president of the Charleston, Cincinnati, and Chicago Railroad. In 1886 he built the Battery Park Hotel, a fashionable and elegant structure that was attractive to tourists; it was an immediate financial success and contributed to the development of Asheville as a resort center.

In 1861, Coxe married Mary Matilda Mills, the daughter of Dr. Otis P. Mills. Though Coxe retained business interests in Pennsylvania and with his family frequently spent time in Philadelphia, he always regarded North Carolina as home. He maintained a beautiful country estate, Green River, situated between the Green and Broad rivers in Polk and Rutherford counties, and there he and Mrs. Coxe entertained countless friends.

Politically, Coxe was a Democrat. He gave the party liberal financial support but resisted all suggestions that he run for office.

Coxe died at Green River. The funeral services were conducted in Rutherfordton in St. Francis Episcopal

Chapel, a church he had erected in memory of his parents, and burial was in the nearby cemetery.

SEE: Samuel A. Ashe, ed., *Biographical History of North Carolina*, vol. 1 (1905); *Prominent People of North Carolina* (1906); *Rutherfordton Tribune*, 4 June 1903; *Western North Carolina Historical and Biographical* (1890).

J. ISAAC COPELAND

Craig, David Irvin (*11 Feb. 1849–9 Feb. 1925*), Presbyterian minister and historian, was born in Orange County, the son of James Newton (14 Oct. 1816–12 Feb. 1879) and Emaline Strayhorn Craig. Craig received early education in the Hughes Academy, Cedar Grove; afterward, he farmed for several years before attending Davidson College during 1874–75. He was graduated from Columbia Theological Seminary, then in Columbia, S.C., in 1878 and was licensed to preach by Orange Presbytery on 31 May 1878. He was ordained by the same presbytery on 1 June 1879. He was stated supply of the First Presbyterian Church of Reidsville from 1878 to 1879 and was elected pastor of the church in the latter year. His ministry there began on 7 July and continued without cessation until his retirement on 7 July 1921, when he became pastor emeritus until his death in 1925. He filled the office of stated clerk of Orange Presbytery for thirty years and served as stated clerk of the Synod of North Carolina, Presbyterian Church in the U.S., from 1900 to 1925. He was a moderator of Orange Presbytery and of the Synod of North Carolina in 1918 and also served terms as a trustee of Davidson College and of Union Theological Seminary, Richmond, Va., and as a member of the board of regents of the Presbyterian Orphans' Home.

Craig married Isabell Gertrude Newman of Columbia, S.C., on 7 Sept. 1881. Of his four surviving children, one, the Reverend Carl Brackett (1890–1954), entered the Presbyterian ministry and served with his father for three years as copastor of the Reidsville church.

Craig was author of several brief histories of Presbyterian churches, including the New Hope Church near Chapel Hill; of the *Manual of Orange Presbytery*, containing historical sketches of the churches of the presbytery; and of *History of the Development of the Presbyterian Church in North Carolina*, dealing primarily with the missionary outreach of the church. He was awarded a D.D. degree by Davidson College in 1910.

SEE: D. I. Craig, *Historical Sketch of New Hope Church in Orange County* (1886); Memorial in Minutes of Orange Presbytery, 21–23 Apr. 1925; *Reidsville Review*, 13 Feb. 1925 (obit.); E. C. Scott, comp., *Ministerial Directory of the Presbyterian Church, U.S.* (1942).

H. J. DUDLEY

Craig, Locke (*16 Aug. 1860–9 June 1924*), governor and legislator, was born in Bertie County of Scottish heritage. His paternal ancestors had come in 1749 from Ireland to Orange County, where they played an active role in the Revolution and afterward. His father, Andrew Murdock Craig, was a Baptist minister and scholar known for his cultivated tastes; his mother, Clarissa Rebecca Gilliam, was of an influential Bertie County family.

Craig, who was named for the English philosopher John Locke, grew up on the family farm in Bertie County. His mother, widowed shortly after the Civil War, sold the farm and accompanied him to The University of North Carolina when he was only fifteen. Scholarly from boyhood, he blossomed at Chapel Hill into an active student leader. Upon graduation at nineteen he was the youngest person ever to have gained his degree there; he was chosen commencement speaker for his oratorical skills. Among his classmates at the university was Charles B. Aycock, with whom in later years he would often share the stage in Democratic party struggles.

After graduation, Craig taught chemistry at the university briefly and for a time was a teacher at a private Chapel Hill school. In 1883 he moved to Asheville to set up a law practice. Thereafter, his home would always be in the mountains, and he was destined to become, after Zebulon B. Vance, that section's most eloquent political spokesman. Though he was short in stature, his fine features and commanding voice were impressive; in later years he would be known throughout the state as the "Little Giant of the West."

As his law practice grew, Craig began to take an active part in the local Democratic party. In 1892 he was chosen Democratic elector for the Ninth Congressional (Cleveland) District; in 1896, as elector-at-large, he canvassed the state for William Jennings Bryan and drew many large crowds with his oratory. Throughout the late 1890s he was in the forefront of the Democratic fight to wrest state control from the Fusionists, who had gained power with a stunning upset in the 1894 elections. Before the 1898 elections, he took part, together with Aycock, Furnifold M. Simmons, and others, in a memorable speech-making campaign directed against the Fusionists. On 10 May 1898 at Laurinburg, a joint speech given by Aycock and Craig ignited the so-called white supremacy campaign. The Democrats, after a bitter struggle, won victory at the polls and regained control of both houses of the legislature. Craig was elected to the legislature from Buncombe County in 1898 with a seven-hundred-vote majority, reversing a previous Republican majority of six hundred.

In the 1899 legislature, Craig was one of a group of Democrats who formulated the "grandfather clause," a constitutional amendment proposing educational requirements for voters but exempting those whose ancestors (prior to 1867) were qualified voters. In the 1900 elections the amendment was passed by the voters, and the Fusionist governor, Daniel Russell, was defeated by Aycock.

Craig had been a firebrand in the fight to overthrow Fusionism, and thereafter his high status in the party was assured. He continued in the legislature but, though actively supported, lost two attempts at higher office. In 1903 he sought to become U.S. senator, but Lee S. Overman was chosen the party nominee. In 1908 he made a determined bid for the governorship, but a close, three-way race among Craig, W. W. Kitchin, and Ashley Horne resulted in a deadlock after three days of speeches and balloting. When Horne bowed out, Craig in turn conceded graciously to Kitchin. It became a foregone conclusion that Craig would be next in line for the governorship, and at the 1912 convention he was nominated by acclamation.

His administration, which began on 15 Jan. 1913 and comprised the four years immediately before World War I, carried forward the educational reforms of Aycock and initiated several programs of its own. Public school districts were consolidated; four months' attendance was made compulsory for children aged eight through twelve; and local taxation for school support was encouraged. Transportation advanced, with the appointment of the first highway commission. A program of road building, which led ultimately to North Carolina's national recognition as the "Good Roads State," was begun: five thousand miles of state-built roads in 1913 grew to fifteen thousand miles by 1917.

The problem of railroad freight rates was alleviated by reducing the rates to the level of the rest of the South. This move spurred manufacturing and economic development, as state merchants were saved an estimated $2 million in shipping charges. Industry was also helped by the harnessing of electric power from several of the state's rivers, including the Yadkin, Catawba, French Broad, and Cape Fear.

The Craig administration was noted for its humanitarianism. State-supported health and welfare institutions were founded, and private endeavors were encouraged. The prison system returned a net profit of four hundred thousand dollars after the state contracted to have prisoners perform road and railroad labor. A part of prisoners' earnings were returned to their families. Executive clemency was invoked often, and many pardons were issued.

The administration was particularly sensitive to the needs of the western part of the state. Road building through the difficult mountains was encouraged. The land around Mount Mitchell, the highest peak in eastern America, was purchased in 1915, and a state park was founded there. Craig served on the Appalachian Park Commission, which promoted Pisgah National Forest. In 1916, when great floods ravaged the western areas, he acted decisively; a state relief committee was formed, and through public and private contributions the effects of the disaster, the worst flooding the mountains had then seen, were brought under efficient control.

The Craig administration was in general prosperous and progressive, continuing the reforms begun under predecessors Aycock, Glenn, and Kitchin. It has been remarked that the state progressed more in the years 1900 to 1917 than in the previous hundred years, and Craig's governorship played a large part in that achievement.

When his term ended, he retired to his home on the Swannanoa River and to his law practice. In declining health, he was looked on as an elder statesman and treated almost reverentially by his mountain neighbors. He was buried in Asheville at Riverside Cemetery.

A lifelong Baptist, Craig was married in 1891 to Annie Burgin of McDowell County. The couple had four sons, Carlyle, George, Arthur, and Locke, Jr. On 16 Oct. 1944 a portrait by Asheville artist Cuthbert Lee was unveiled at presentation ceremonies in the senate chamber of the capitol at Raleigh.

SEE: Samuel A. Ashe, ed., *Biographical History of North Carolina*, vol. 6 (1907); *Asheville Citizen*, 10 June 1924, 15 Oct. 1944; Beth G. Crabtree, *North Carolina Governors, 1585–1958* (1958); Craig Portrait Committee, *Locke Craig* (1944); Josephus Daniels, *Editor in Politics* (1941); *History of North Carolina*, vol. 3, *North Carolina since 1860*, by J. G. deR. Hamilton (1919); May F. Jones, ed., *Public Letters and Papers of Locke Craig* (1916); Raleigh *News and Observer*, 10 June 1924, 17 Oct. 1944.

JAMES MEEHAN

Craige, Francis Burton (*13 Mar. 1811–30 Dec. 1875*), editor, lawyer, and congressman, the youngest son of David and Mary Foster Craige, was born on the south fork of the Yadkin River five miles from Salisbury. He attended classical school in Salisbury, was graduated from The University of North Carolina in 1829, studied law with David F. Caldwell, and was admitted to the bar in 1832 when he was barely twenty-one.

While reading law, Craige edited the Salisbury *Western Carolinian* (1830–33), making it the chief advocate of

Nullification in the state and suggesting full cooperation with South Carolina in the dispute with Andrew Jackson. Craige was also a leader in the campaign to revise the state constitution. He represented the borough of Salisbury and the County of Rowan in the House of Commons from 1832 to 1835, continually attacking those who upheld Jackson and supporting the call for a state constitutional convention.

Craige was decisively defeated by Abraham Rencher in 1835, when he challenged Rencher for his seat in Congress. The following year, Craige married Elizabeth Phifer Erwin (1815–81), daughter of Colonel James Erwin of Burke and granddaughter of General Matthew Locke of Revolutionary War fame. He settled down to practice law, farm, and raise a family. James Alexander was born in 1841, Kerr in 1843, Francis Burton, Jr., in 1846, Mary Elizabeth in 1848, and finally Annie Erwin in 1852. Craige was active in the Episcopal church. In 1847, The University of North Carolina awarded him a master's degree. But these were the years of the Mexican war, the abolitionist activity to the north, and the Compromise of 1850, and politics were never far from Craige's attention.

In 1853, as a Democrat, Craige opposed Whig James W. Osborne for the Seventh Congressional District seat, winning by 316 votes. He was returned in 1855 over Know-Nothing competitors, in 1857 without opposition, and in 1859 over S. H. Walkup, a Whig. In Congress he was an ardent defender of southern rights and opponent of compromise. After the election of 1860 he favored secession, and in March 1861 he attended the Goldsboro convention of the Southern Rights party, which called for North Carolina to leave the Union.

Craige left Congress in 1861 and was elected a delegate to North Carolina's Secession Convention in Raleigh. At the request of Governor John W. Ellis, Craige introduced the ordinance that repealed the state's ratification of the federal Constitution. He then became a delegate to the provisional Confederate Congress meeting in Richmond from July 1861 to February 1862. His three sons saw service in the Confederate Army.

After the war, Craige continued his farming activities and returned to the practice of law. He died at Concord while attending the Cabarrus County Superior Court. He was buried in Oak Grove Cemetery in Salisbury.

SEE: Samuel A. Ashe, ed., *Biographical History of North Carolina*, vol. 2 (1905); *Biog. Dir. Am. Cong.* (1971); J. C. Sitterson, *The Secession Movement in North Carolina* (1939).

DANIEL M. MCFARLAND

Craige, Kerr (*14 Mar. 1843–1 Sept. 1904*), attorney, assistant postmaster general, and banker, was the son of Burton and Elizabeth Phifer Erwin Craige. His father was born in Rowan County and represented Salisbury and Rowan County in the House of Commons; he introduced the Ordinance of Secession in the convention of May 1861. His mother was the daughter of Colonel James Erwin of Burke County.

Craige, prepared at Concord Academy and at Catawba College in Newton, entered The University of North Carolina but left at the age of eighteen to join the Confederate Army. He mustered in as sergeant of Company F, Ninth North Carolina State Troops (First Regiment of North Carolina Cavalry). He was transferred to Company I upon appointment as second lieutenant to rank from 1 Oct. 1861. He was promoted to first lieutenant 20 June 1863 and to captain 1 Mar. 1865. During the greater part of the war he served as aide-de-camp to General James B. Gordon. He was captured at Namozine Church, Va., on 3 Apr. 1865 and confined at Johnson's Island in Lake Erie until released after taking the Oath of Allegiance on 18 June 1865.

Following the war, Craige studied law under Judge Richmond Pearson and was admitted to the bar in 1867. In 1870 he was elected reading clerk of the North Carolina house, and in 1872 he was elected a member of the house from Rowan. He served until 1874. Nominated by the Democrats for the town board of Salisbury in 1881, he won the election and was reelected in 1882 and in 1887.

In August 1884 he was nominated for Congress by the Democratic convention of the Seventh District, but he withdrew from the race because of ill health. In 1887 he was appointed by President Cleveland collector of internal revenue for the new Fifth District; he served at Salisbury until March 1889 and then resigned to avoid serving under the next administration. In 1892, through the influence of his law partner, John S. Henderson, then chairman of the Committee on Post Offices in the House, he was appointed third assistant postmaster general. He held the position until 1894 and, in this capacity, was influential in having established out of China Grove the first rural mail route in the state and the second in the nation.

Craige was a prominent banker, and in 1881 he was appointed a director of the North Carolina Railroad.

He was married to Josephine, youngest daughter of General L. O'B. and Nancy Blount Branch of Raleigh, in November 1873. They were the parents of six children, three sons and three daughters. His wife predeceased him, in 1885. He and his family were buried in the Old English Cemetery in Salisbury.

SEE: John Preston Arthur, *Western North Carolina* (1914); Samuel A. Ashe, ed., *Biographical History of North Carolina*, vol. 1 (1905); Louis H. Manarin, comp., *North Carolina Troops, 1861–1865: A Roster*, vol. 1 (1966); Raleigh *News and Observer*, 16 July 1885; Salisbury *Carolina Watchman*, 15 Nov. 1877, 6 May 1881, 11 Aug. 1881, 4 May 1882, 14 and 21 Aug. 1884, 11 June 1885; W. Buck Yearns, ed., *The Papers of Thomas Jordan Jarvis*, vol. 1 (1969).

                                                JAMES S. BRAWLEY

Craighead, Alexander (*18 Mar. 1707–Mar. 1766*), maverick Presbyterian minister in Pennsylvania, Virginia, and North Carolina, was born the son of the Reverend Thomas and Margaret Craighead, near Donegal, Ireland. Arriving at Boston in October 1714, the Craigheads gradually drifted into Pennsylvania and joined the Donegal Presbytery and the Synod of Philadelphia. After studying the classics and theology under his father, Alexander was licensed to preach in 1734 and ordained in 1735. He then became minister to Middle Octorara Presbyterian Church in Lancaster County.

In 1740, Craighead was denounced from several quarters for meddling with the congregations of other ministers without an invitation; members of his own church accused him of reprehensible conduct. When hailed before a meeting of the presbytery in his own church, he heaped verbal abuse on the presbytery and charged a number of ministers, whose names he dared call, of various shortcomings in the performance of their duties. The presbytery suspended him, but he continued his ministry as if nothing had happened.

Craighead's zeal of 1740 may have been touched off by the evangelistic fervor that electrified the religious atmosphere of Pennsylvania after the visits of George Whitefield late in 1739. The Great Awakening, of which the controversial Whitefield was the central figure, received Craighead's approval and support. Whitefield referred to Craighead as a worthy minister, but he might more appropriately have described the eccentric Presbyterian as cantankerous. In the Old Side-New Side controversy that split the Presbyterians in 1741, Craighead naturally joined the New Sides and with them was excommunicated from the Synod of Philadelphia. After that experience, Craighead began to identify himself as a rigid Covenanter or Cameronian, meaning that he had adopted the views of Richard Cameron, a seventeenth-century Scottish Covenanter; the Cameronians refused to take the oath of allegiance to the British government or to hold office under it. Craighead also admired the teachings of Ebenezer Erskine, who formed the Scottish Secession church and denounced all secular control over the church.

By espousing Cameronian doctrines, which avowedly mixed theology and politics, Craighead soon precipitated a political disturbance. In 1743 there was published in Pennsylvania an anonymous pamphlet that everyone attributed to him. To the provincial authorities the pamphlet seemed "calculated to foment disloyal and rebellious practices, and disseminate principles of disaffection." Considering it most radical in tone, the governor complained to the Synod of Philadelphia. The synod, agreeing with the governor that the pamphlet was seditious, disavowed it and Craighead.

From 1743 to 1749, Craighead remained in Pennsylvania and presided over a group called the Covenanter Society. The year 1743 was an eventful one for him. To explain his withdrawal from the Donegal Presbytery during the preceding year, he wrote and published *The Reasons of Mr. Alexander Craighead's Receding from the Present Judicature's of This Church*. Benjamin Franklin printed the pamphlet at Philadelphia in the same year. In November 1743, Craighead called Covenanter Society members together at Middle Octorara and renewed the National and Solemn League Covenants that had once been adopted by the Presbyterian Church of Scotland. He then commemorated the event by writing *Renewal of the Covenants, Nov. 11, 1743*, a pamphlet printed by Franklin in 1744.

In 1749, Craighead moved to Augusta County, Va., and became minister of the Mossy Creek Presbyterian Church. His views seem to have disturbed Governor Robert Dinwiddie of Virginia even more than the officials of Pennsylvania, for on 10 June 1752, Craighead was arrested for proclaiming doctrines that smacked of treason. Making every effort to straighten matters out, the Presbyterian clergyman made a plea to the governor's council. He was permitted to preach again but only if he recanted all disloyal utterances and took a public oath of allegiance to the government. Whether Craighead ever met this condition is not clear, but he continued to live in Virginia for several more years, accumulating a considerable amount of property in the form of land and slaves. He also continued to be a member of the New-Side New York Synod.

Unsettled conditions in the back country during the French and Indian War prompted Craighead and some of his congregation to move to North Carolina in 1757. In November 1758 he was installed as pastor of the Rocky River and Sugaw Creek Presbyterian churches in Mecklenburg County. Presiding at the ceremonies was William Richardson, a New-Side Presbyterian, who was being sent by the New Hanover Presbytery of Virginia to serve as a missionary to the Cherokee Indians in South Carolina. Craighead's political views were as radical as ever, and he urged his congregations to resist, not cooperate with, the provincial government. In 1760, Craighead left Rocky River and devoted full-time to the Sugaw Creek Church, apparently because two officials of the Rocky River Church agreed to cooperate with the colonial government in working out the boundary line between North Carolina and South Carolina.

Craighead was married to a woman named Jane, whose surname is not known. He left to her his plantation and slaves. Their children were Margaret, Agness, Jane, Rachel, Mary, Elizabeth, Robert, and Thomas. Agness married the minister William Richardson, and Rachel married David Caldwell, who was also a minister. One of Craighead's sons, Thomas, entered the ministry and at one point in his career served the Sugaw Creek Presbyterian Church.

SEE: "Diary and Journal of William Richardson, South Carolina, 1758–1759" (Historical Foundation, Montreat); W. M. Engles, ed., *Records of the Presbyterian Church in the United States of America, 1706–1788* (1904); William Henry Foote, *Sketches of North Carolina, Historical and Biographical* (1846); W. M. Glasgow, *History of the Reformed Presbyterian Church in America* (1888); N. R. McGeachy, *A History of the Sugaw Creek Presbyterian Church* (1954); A. Nevin, ed., *Encyclopedia of the Presbyterian Church in the United States of America* (1884); J. K. Rouse, *Colonial Churches in North Carolina* (n.d.); William L. Saunders, ed., *Colonial Records of North Carolina*, vol. 5 (1887); J. A. Waddell, *Annals of Augusta County, Virginia* (1888).

DAVID T. MORGAN

Cramer, Stuart Warren (*31 Mar. 1868–2 July 1940*), leader in the development and improvement of textile mills, inventor, and leader in the Republican party in North Carolina, was born in Thomasville to John Thomas and Mary Jane Thomas Cramer.

Cramer's education at the U.S. Naval Academy, from which he was graduated in 1888, gave him a love of the navy that led him to promote its interests in his native state. He helped found and was the first commander of the North Carolina Naval Reserve in 1890. He also served on the board of visitors of the Naval Academy from 1912 to 1926.

Although Cramer studied naval engineering at the academy, he decided to turn to mining engineering to help with his family's many interests. He studied at Columbia University School of Mines from 1888 to 1889 and left to take a position as head of the U.S. Mint in Charlotte. Within four years he had shifted to a position as chief engineer and manager of D. A. Tompkins Company, which ran an iron foundry and distributed cotton mill machinery and supplies. After two years he left to establish his own engineering and contracting firm in Charlotte to build textile mills. Over the next ten years (1895–1905) he designed and/or equipped about one-third of the new cotton mills in the South. He turned his profits into his own textile mills, especially those at Cramerton, where, under the influence of a model plantation owned by his grandfather, he developed a model mill community. For Cramerton Village he built schools, churches, recreation centers, playgrounds, and other embellishments, to give his workers some of the best living conditions in the textile community.

One of Cramer's chief contributions to textile progress came through his engineering genius. He is credited with sixty patents, including an improvement in the humidification system for textile factories that became known as air conditioning. He also developed a system

of individually driven electric motors for machines, when he saw its advantages over the central power plant with belts and shafts. Cramer wrote on textile industrial engineering, industrial welfare, and related subjects. His best-known work was the four-volume *Useful Information for Cotton Manufactures*, published from 1904 to 1909.

Realizing the need to provide adequate power to supply textile mills, Cramer collaborated with James B. Duke in founding Duke Power Company, of which he became a director. To promote better cooperation among textile manufacturers, Cramer organized the American Cotton Manufacturers Association and served as its president from 1916 to 1917. He combined northern and southern textile interests in the National Council of American Cotton Textile Manufacturers, presiding over this new creation in 1917–18 and 1920–27. For his efforts in promoting the textile interest in tariff legislation, he was awarded a medal by the Association of Cotton Manufacturers in 1913.

Cramer was a leading member of the Republican party in a state where the party had lost its majority. A delegate to several national conventions, he was part of the official committee to notify Herbert Hoover of his nomination to the presidency by the party. In 1931, Hoover named him a member of the president's Organization on Unemployment Relief.

Cramer married three times. His first wife was Bertha Hobart Berry of Portland, Me.; they married in 1889 and had two children: Katherine Hobart, who later married James R. Angell, a president of Yale University; and Stuart Warren, Jr., who took control of many of his father's interests later in life. When Bertha Cramer died, Stuart Cramer in 1896 married her sister, fulfilling his first wife's deathbed wish. The second Mrs. Cramer died in 1897. In 1902, Cramer married Rebecca Warren Tinkham, sister of George Holden Tinkham, a congressman from Boston; their son was George Bennet.

Cramer died in Charlotte of a heart ailment and was buried there on 4 July 1940 in Elmwood Cemetery.

SEE: American Cotton Manufacturers Association, *Lest We Forget* (1946); Samuel A. Ashe, ed., *Biographical History of North Carolina*, vol. 7 (1919); *Charlotte Observer*, 3 July 1940, 23 Apr. 1943, 10 Jan. 1954; *Who Was Who in America*, vol. 1 (1943); Marjorie W. Young, *Textile Leaders of the South* (1963).

THOMAS S. MORGAN

Craven, Braxton (*26 Aug. 1822–7 Nov. 1882*), educator, Methodist minister, and Mason, was a native of Randolph County. His mother was Ann Craven and his father, according to the Reverend D. V. York, was Braxton York, a cousin of Brantley York, the founder of Union Institute and father of D. V. York. At the age of seven Craven was taken into the home of a Quaker neighbor, Nathan Cox, an enterprising man who combined several other occupations with farming. Craven lived with Cox for nine years, indicating later that he was "sorely oppressed" in his youth, but that he learned industry, thrift, and self-reliance and developed a spirit of faith, optimism, and cheerfulness.

At the age of sixteen, Craven struck out on his own. Although he had had little formal schooling, he chose to be a teacher and the following year started a subscription school. After two years of teaching and working during vacation, he was able to attend New Garden School (now Guilford College) for two academic years. Then he became assistant teacher at Union Institute, a school organized in his home county in 1838 by a group of Quakers and Methodists. Upon Brantley York's resignation in 1842 as the first principal of the school, Craven succeeded him. Wishing to upgrade the institute from an academy and recognizing that the first requirement for improved common schools in North Carolina was better-educated teachers, he started a program of teacher training.

In 1849, Craven improved his own academic standing by passing the examination on the entire course of study at Randolph-Macon College; he was awarded an honorary A.B. degree. Two years later both Randolph-Macon and The University of North Carolina conferred upon him an honorary A.M. degree, and later he received the D.D. degree from Andrew College in Tennessee and the LL.D. degree from the University of Missouri.

In 1850, Craven and Reuben H. Brown launched the *Southern Index* in Asheboro. This was an educational journal in which Craven set forth his ideas about the training of teachers and the common schools. After several months it became a literary magazine, with the title *Evergreen*. It ran for twelve issues and carried two novels by Craven that later appeared in book form as *Mary Barker* and *Naomi Wise*, under the pseunonym Charlie Vernon.

Having become acquainted with the normal school movement in the country, Craven decided that a normal college should be started in North Carolina. He succeeded in getting a bill passed in the General Assembly in 1851, incorporating Union Institute as Normal College. The bill provided for state support, but the legislature refused to vote the funds, although it did grant Normal College graduates the privilege of teacher certification without examintion. In another vain attempt to secure state support for Normal, Craven joined with Wake Forest and Davidson in asking the legislature to establish scholarships for training teachers at all three colleges. He succeeded in getting Normal's charter amended in 1853 to make it a state school, but the only financial support he received from the state was a loan of ten thousand dollars from the Literary Fund at 6 percent interest. This loan he ultimately paid back himself.

Little actually came of Craven's experiment in teacher training. Under the amended charter, Normal College could grant academic degrees, but after a few years of turning out poorly educated teachers and receiving widespread criticism for doing so, Craven decided to deemphasize the teacher-training program and concentrate on developing a regular collegiate curriculum. He never ceased, however, to lend assistance to the cause of public education.

Discouraged by the lack of tax support for Normal College and by the opposition of educational leaders of the state, Craven turned elsewhere for help. He persuaded the North Carolina Conference of the Methodist Episcopal Church, South, to adopt Normal in 1856 as its college. Three years later the name of the college was changed to Trinity, and, except for two years in the mid-1860s, Craven continued as its president until his death.

When the Civil War began, Craven organized a company of young men he called the Trinity Guard to prevent the total disruption of the college. He also instituted a course in military training for the summer of 1861. Later that year he and the guard were assigned to the Confederate prison at Salisbury. He retained the presidency of Trinity and returned there after about a month as commander of the prison.

Trinity College was on shaky financial grounds all during Craven's presidency, in part because of a schism in the North Carolina Conference that began in the late 1850s over support of the college and its administration. Criticism of Craven finally led to his resignation on 1 Jan. 1864. After the war, however, he was persuaded by the conference to return and reopen the college, which had closed in April 1865, in January 1866. Although financial crises, rivalries, and attacks upon his administration continued, Craven never lost faith in the future of Trinity or his belief that Christian education was the greatest gift to youth.

Although he became a college administrator and preacher, Craven never gave up teaching. The wide range of subject matter in his courses is indicative of the versatility of his mind. As a public speaker, preacher, and leader of Methodism in North Carolina, he became widely known. He was licensed to preach in 1840 and nineteen years later was admitted to full connection in the North Carolina Conference. He served the conference as secretary and in other ways, but he held only one pastorate, the Edenton Street Methodist Church in Raleigh in 1864 and 1865.

On 26 Sept. 1844, Craven married Irene Leach, the first female graduate of Union Institute and a teacher in the school. He found it necessary to operate a farm on the side to support his growing family, which came to include two daughters and two sons, Emma Lenora, James Lucius Melville, Willie Oscar, and Sallie Kate.

Despite a reserved manner, Craven had a kind and generous nature. He manifested charity toward his enemies in the North Carolina Conference, and immediately after the Civil War he began urging the reunification of the Methodist church.

Craven was buried in the village that grew up around Trinity College, which also took the name of Trinity.

SEE: Nora C. Chaffin, *Trinity College, 1839–1892* (1950); John F. Crowell, *Personal Recollections of Trinity College* (1939); Jerome Dowd, *The Life of Braxton Craven* (1939); Duke University Archives (Durham), for Braxton Craven Papers and various publications; Manuscript Department, Library, Duke University (Durham), for Craven-Pegram Family Papers and Charles Alexander Long Papers.

MATTIE U. RUSSELL

Craven, James (d. Oct. 1755), member of the royal council, was a native of Droughton in Yorkshire, England. Although the date of his immigration to North Carolina is unknown, he was serving as clerk of the court in Pasquotank Precinct in 1734. He was sworn in as clerk of the Chowan County court in January 1740, and the following month he was elected to the lower house of assembly from Edenton; he continued in that office for six years. In an effort to create a balance in the upper house between the northern and southern counties, Governor Gabriel Johnston in September 1751 nominated Craven, then serving as secretary of North Carolina, to the royal council. On 28 Mar. 1753, Craven presented his commission as a councilor and took the prescribed oaths. His attendance at council meetings was erratic, since he frequented only those sessions meeting in Edenton. By October 1755 he was dead.

A merchant, Craven married Penelope Hodgson of Chowan County; they had no children. He owned a farm called Pagett's Plantation in the county, and his handsome house in Edenton still stands.

SEE: J. Bryan Grimes, ed., *North Carolina Wills and Inventories* (1912); William S. Price, Jr., " 'Men of Good Estates': Wealth among North Carolina's Royal Councillors," *North Carolina Historical Review* 49 (1972);

William L. Saunders, ed., *Colonial Records of North Carolina*, vols. 4–5 (1886–87).

WILLIAM S. PRICE, JR.

Crawford, Leonidas Wakefield (5 Apr. 1842–21 Feb. 1908), Methodist minister, professor of theology at Trinity College, and editor of the *North Carolina Christian Advocate*, was born on the family plantation just east of Salisbury, the fifth son of William Dunlop Crawford and Christiana Mull Crawford. His father was an honor graduate of The University of North Carolina, a Salisbury attorney, and long-time legislator from Rowan County. His mother was a member of an old Rowan family and had attended Salem Academy.

When Leonidas was two years old, his father died, and when he was twelve, his mother remarried. He spent some of his formative years in Charlotte, a favorite of his stepfather, Peter Brown, Esq. When the Civil War broke out, he was sent to Olin High School, a Methodist Institution in northern Iredell County, in an attempt to get him away from secession enthusiasm. The plan did not succeed: six months later he was allowed to join the infantry company of one of his brothers as a junior officer in the Forty-second Regiment. He served with distinction until he was taken prisoner at Second Cold Harbor near Richmond.

His imprisonment until the end of the war gave him time to study, and after he was paroled, he went back to Olin and then to the University of Virginia, where he was graduated in English and Moral Philosophy and afterward received a master's degree. Later he received honorary D.D. degrees from Central College in Missouri and Weaverville College in North Carolina.

Crawford's family background was Methodist, and his training turned him to the ministry of the Methodist church. In 1867 he was licensed to preach, and in 1868 he joined the North Carolina Conference of the Methodist Episcopal Church, South. From the first his appointments were to the larger churches—Hillsborough, Salisbury, Fayetteville, Greensboro, New Bern—and he spent in each the four years allowed by Methodist policy.

Crawford's interest in education was strong. In 1883, while pastor of West Market Street Church in Greensboro, he headed a movement to save Greensboro Female College for the Methodist church, and he helped secure the state Normal and Industrial College at Greensboro. While editor of the *North Carolina Christian Advocate*, he established the small chapel that has grown to be College Place United Methodist Church, just off the campus of The University of North Carolina at Greensboro; he was its pastor for four years. He became professor of theology at Trinity College in 1890 and held that position for four years, while Trinity was being moved from Randolph County to Durham. Lack of funds caused his department to be abandoned, and he went back into the itinerancy. At about that time, John Crowell resigned as president of Trinity College, and there was considerable sentiment for Crawford to be made president in his stead. The trustees, however, chose John C. Kilgo of South Carolina.

After a year and a half as pastor in Reidsville, Crawford in mid-1896 purchased a controlling interest in the *North Carolina Christian Advocate*, established late in 1893 as a merger of the *Raleigh Christian Advocate* and the *Western Advocate* of Asheville, in order to give the two North Carolina Methodist conferences a single periodical. It was owned by a stock company and published in Greensboro. At the meeting of the Western North Carolina Conference that fall, Crawford was appointed

editor for that conference, while Thomas Neal Ivey was appointed coeditor for the North Carolina Conference.

Under such an arrangement, the periodical developed a two-edged editorial policy; Crawford and Ivey each filled two pages with editorials, often in direct conflict. It was the time of the Kilgo-Clark controversy over higher education and the Gattis-Kilgo lawsuit that grew out of it. Ivey used his pages to support Kilgo, and Crawford attacked Trinity College for accepting tobacco money, praising other Methodist colleges in the state to the exclusion of Trinity. After two years the North Carolina Conference withdrew its support of the *Advocate* and Ivey reestablished the *Raleigh Christian Advocate*. The controversy did not end there, however. Kilgo took exception to some of Crawford's statements, and the disagreement that followed led Crawford's son, R. B., a prominent Winston merchant, to a physical attack on Kilgo on 22 July 1901. Reaction strongly favored Kilgo; two months after the incident, L. W. Crawford made arrangements for the Western North Carolina Conference to buy his stock in the *Advocate* and withdrew from the paper to devote his time to the chapel he had established. In spite of the controversy that had attended his editorship and the withdrawal of the support of the North Carolina Conference, he had put the *Advocate* on a sound financial footing.

After finishing four years at the church on Spring Garden Street in Greensboro, Crawford went back to Reidsville as pastor; in 1907 he went to the Asheville District as presiding elder. Early the next year, while meeting appointments in Yancey County, he contracted pneumonia and died. His body was brought back to Greensboro and buried there.

On 12 Dec. 1872, Crawford was married to Mariemma Pullen of Raleigh, who had been educated at Louisburg College, under Dr. T. M. Jones, and at Vassar. At the time of her marriage she was teaching under Dr. Jones at Warrenton. The Crawfords had a family of five sons and one daughter. For two years, Mrs. Crawford assisted her husband in editing the *Advocate*; after he gave it up, she continued to edit the page of the Woman's Foreign Missionary Society for years. She died in 1925 at the age of seventy-five.

SEE: Samuel A. Ashe, ed., *Biographical History of North Carolina*, vol. 5 (1906); Paul Neff Garber, *John Carlisle Kilgo* (1937); Journals of the Western North Carolina Conference and North Carolina Conference of the Methodist Episcopal Church, South; *North Carolina Christian Advocate*, 1893ff.; Marion Timothy Plyler, *Thomas Neal Ivey* (1925).

HOMER M. KEEVER

Crawford (Crafford), William (ca. 1638–ca. 1700), council member and leader in Culpeper's Rebellion, came to the North Carolina colony, then called Albemarle, in his mid-twenties. A contemporary document calls him a New England man, but the reference may have arisen from his business and political interests, which were the same as those of the New Englanders who traded with the colony. Other sources suggest that he may have come to North Carolina from Virginia.

Crawford was associated with the North Carolina colony by 1665, in connection with the supply of livestock and goods to a plantation on Collington Island, operated as a private venture by several of the Carolina proprietors. The enterprise was then under the oversight of Captain John Whitty, who transported passengers and "commodities" between England, Virginia, and Albemarle. Crawford apparently continued his association with the venture after supervision was taken over in 1665 by Peter Carteret, then secretary and council member for Albemarle and later governor.

By 1670, Crawford had become a member of the Albemarle council. He was also on the council in 1673 and from 1679 until at least 1681, probably 1683. Crawford was one of the chief leaders in the uprising called Culpeper's Rebellion. He helped organize the revolt and was a member of both the assembly and the council in the rebel government. For a time his house was used as a prison for several of the ousted officials, including Thomas Miller, who had been acting as governor.

At the time of the uprising, Crawford lived in Pasquotank Precinct. He also lived for a time in Chowan Precinct, where he held a tract of land granted him by patent. He no doubt was a planter, but he seems also to have been engaged in shipping, either as a shipmaster or through investments. The title captain, seldom omitted in references to him, probably indicated his status as seaman, not as soldier.

Crawford, who made frequent trips to England, was given power of attorney over the Albemarle affairs of several Londoners. One of these was Peter Carteret, who had gone to London intending to return to Albemarle but had found it advisable to remain in England. In 1676, Carteret made Crawford his attorney, apparently for liquidation of his Albemarle interests.

About the middle of the 1680s, Crawford and his wife, Margaret, left Albemarle. They probably moved to Norfolk County, Va., where a William Crawford, whose wife was named Margaret, died about March 1699/1700. A William Crawford who represented Norfolk County in the Virginia assembly in 1688 and 1696 and was justice of the Norfolk County court in 1691 may have been the Albemarle Crawford.

The names of Crawford's children are not known. One of his grandsons was William Crawford of Chowan Precinct, who died about January 1735. A William Crawford who represented Norfolk County in the Virginia assembly from 1714 to 1747 may have been another grandson, or perhaps a son.

SEE: *North Carolina Historical and Genealogical Register*, 3 vols. (1900–1903); Edward W. James, ed., *Lower Norfolk County Antiquary*, vol. 1 (1895); Charles Fleming McIntosh, ed., *Brief Abstract of Lower Norfolk County and Norfolk County Wills* (1914); North Carolina State Archives (Raleigh), for Albemarle Book of Warrants and Surveys (1681–1706), Timothy Biggs, "A Narrative of The Transactions past in the Conty of Albemarle Sence Mr. Tho. Miller his Arrivall there" (original in Arents Tobacco Collection, New York Public Library, New York City), Council Minutes, Wills, Inventories (1677–1701), and Wills of Dorothy Harvey, Thomas Keile, and William Seares; Mattie Erma Edwards Parker, ed., *North Carolina Higher-Court Records, 1670–1696* (1968); William S. Powell, ed., *Ye Countie of Albemarle in Carolina* (1958); Hugh F. Rankin, *Upheaval in Albemarle: The Story of Culpeper's Rebellion* (1962); William L. Saunders, ed., *Colonial Records of North Carolina*, vol. 1 (1886); William G. Stanard and Mary Newton Stanard, comps., *The Colonial Virginia Register* (1902); Clayton Torrence, comp., *Virginia Wills and Administrations* (1972).

MATTIE ERMA E. PARKER

Crawford, William Thomas (*1 June 1856–16 Nov. 1913*), congressman and state legislator, was born near Waynesville in Haywood County. As a boy, he spent long hours tilling the soil of his family's mountain farm, but he managed to find time to attend local public schools and Waynesville Academy. Later he clerked in a local general store and read law at night.

Crawford soon entered local politics and won a seat as a Democrat in the North Carolina House of Representatives, where he sat in the sessions of 1885 and 1887. He then studied law at The University of North Carolina (1889–91), before being admitted to the bar in 1891. In the preceding year he had won his first term in the U.S. Congress from North Carolina's old Ninth District; he gained reelection in 1892 but lost in the Democratic catastrophe of 1894. After his defeat, Crawford remained very active in North Carolina politics: he served as a delegate to every Democratic State Convention from 1900 to 1912; he was a presidential elector in 1904; and he received the Democratic nomination for Congress several more times. In 1906 he won another term in Congress (from the new Tenth District), but he lost again in 1908 in a very close race. After his final defeat he practiced law in Waynesville as a member of the firm of Crawford and Hannah until his death and burial in 1913.

Crawford was a Democrat of the Grover Cleveland type: he believed in the gold standard and a low tariff and was unalterably opposed to a system of state-wide primary elections and to electing U.S. senators by direct popular vote.

Crawford married Inez Coman in 1892; they had four sons and three daughters. He was a Baptist.

SEE: *Biog. Dir. Am. Cong.* (1950); D. L. Grant, *Alumni History of the University of North Carolina* (1924); Julius C. Martin, "William Thomas Crawford," North Carolina State Bar, *Proceedings* 16 (1914); *North Carolina Manual* (1911, 1913); Raleigh *News and Observer*, 18 Nov. 1913.

K. RODABAUGH

Cray, William, Sr. (*1726–29 Nov. 1778*), councilor of state, legislator, county clerk, colonel of militia, merchant, and farmer, was of Scottish descent. He first appears in North Carolina records in 1746, when he recorded a power of attorney designating that he was from Charleston, S.C. In 1747 he proved another power of attorney in the Carteret County court, and in 1749 he bought land on the east side of New River in Onslow County. In 1750 he was granted land on New River at the mouth of Duck Creek, where he resided for the rest of his life. As early as 1753, he appears as clerk of court for Onslow County; he served in that capacity until he was replaced by his son, William, Jr., in 1774. Deed records of 1753 reveal that he was a merchant (importer), that he had a brick kiln on Duck Creek, and that he engaged in the naval stores trade.

In Onslow County, Cray held at one time or another the offices of clerk of the county court, register, colonel of the militia, and county coroner. He probably filled all these offices simultaneously during most of his public career, as one report to the assembly seems to indicate. His first twelve years as Onslow clerk of court—perhaps the most important formative period of his life—were spent in close association with Colonel John Starkey, whom Governor Arthur Dobbs considered the most dangerous exponent of democratic principles in the colony. Cray not only served the local court, which Starkey dominated, but also entered the House of Commons as Starkey's junior partner during the last session in which Starkey served; Starkey's ideals and principles no doubt profoundly influenced the young Cray and helped to prepare him for the role he would later play in the struggle for liberty.

Cray in 1761 was appointed by the assembly one of three commissioners to improve and promote the navigation of New River Inlet. Three years later, Onslow County sent Cray to the North Carolina House of Commons to serve in the sixth assembly under Governor Dobbs (1764–65). Cray was reelected to represent Onslow County in the first and second assemblies under William Tryon (1766–70), and he also served in the first, third, and fourth assemblies under Josiah Martin (1771, 1773–75). In 1774 and 1775 he represented Onslow County in the First and Second Provincial Congresses. In 1777 the county sent Cray to the North Carolina Senate, where he served until shortly after his election to the council of state on 18 Apr. 1777. He resigned his seat in the senate following his election to the council, and the council promptly elected him to serve as its president, succeeding Cornelius Harnett, who was elected to the Continental Congress. From then until Cray's death, the assembly kept him on the council of state, and the council kept him in its office of president—the second highest position in the state government of that time. His second election to the council came on 18 Apr. 1778, just slightly over seven months before his death.

In his career in the assembly, Cray rapidly advanced to some of its most influential committees and positions, gaining many of the places of prestige and honor that Starkey had held. Cray was one of the assemblymen most frequently sent as liaison between the commons and the council or senate, as well as between the assembly and the governors. He served on the Committee on Public Accounts throughout his career in the assembly and also sat on various committees to prepare special legislation. He was appointed, along with Cornelius Harnett and Joseph Hewes, to examine and settle the claims of the forces in the War of the Regulators. On occasions when the house resolved itself into a committee of the whole, Cray was unanimously chosen chairman. In 1769 he also served on a seven-member committee to prepare the reply to Governor Tryon's speech and on a committee investigating allegations against Thomas Person. In 1770 he was chairman of the Committee of Privileges and Elections.

Cray's military genius and administrative efficiency in the training of the Onslow militia earned him a place among the seven colonels chosen by Governor Tryon to participate in his council of war and to share the leadership in the campaign against the Regulators. Toward the end of April 1771, Cray marched the Onslow militiamen to a rendezvous in Johnston County, where they were reviewed by the governor. After the Battle of Alamance, Cray was appointed to sell the captured horses and to account to the public treasurer for the monies received. He was one of five colonels appointed by Governor Tryon to receive the expense accounts for the Regulator War and to make a full report and settlement to Tryon's successor as governor.

Not serving in the assembly of 1772, Cray had time for personal business pursuits and decided to invest in the new port town being developed in the southeastern corner of Onslow. In 1773 he bought one-twelfth of the lots comprising the original town of Swansboro; his son-in-law, Joseph French, bought almost as many. To what extent Cray was able to make commercial use of these lots before the revolutionary cause claimed his full attention, we do not know.

From the beginning of the movement for indepen-

dence, Cray was a thorough Patriot. He appears to have been head of the committee of safety for Onslow County from the beginning in 1775, and he was also appointed to the committee of safety for the Wilmington District that same year. In conjunction with the Battle of Moore's Creek Bridge in 1775, he led the Onslow minutemen in the strategy that prevented the passage of the Loyalists through Duplin County. He was reappointed colonel of the Onslow militia and minutemen in 1775 and 1776, and in 1776 and 1777 he was named on both commissions of the peace for Onslow County.

Cray's election to the senate in 1777 opened the door to his most significant public service. Moving from the senate to the council of state and thence to the presidency of the council, he reached one of the most powerful positions in the government, where he influenced the planning and directing of North Carolina's role in the American Revolution. In council and at home, he never wavered in his loyalty to the Patriot cause but seized every opportunity to strengthen that cause, expelling from Onslow any who sympathized with the enemy and executing five deserters from the ranks of the Continental Line.

Cray's last official function was presiding over the council session that opened on 9 Sept. 1778. His death shortly thereafter must have come unexpectedly. He was originally buried on his Duck Creek Plantation, but when the Camp Lejeune Marine Corps Base was established, Cray's gravestones and those of his family were moved to the Montford Point Cemetery near Jacksonville, N.C.

In 1746, Cray married Mary Magdalene de Gignilliatt (b. 3 June 1726) of Charleston, S.C. She was the daughter of Henry de Gignilliatt and Esther Marion; the famous Revolutionary general Francis Marion was her first cousin.

Cray apparently had three children who predeceased him: Gabriel, who died in 1767 at the age of twelve; Hester, who died in 1765, aged sixteen months; and one child whose gravestone is so eroded that only the first initial, "R," can now be read. Cray in his will refers to his wife and five children: William, Jr., who married Elizabeth Randall; Mary, who married first Joseph French, Jr., and second William Gibbs; Joseph Scott, who married Frances Howard; Henrietta, who was not twenty-one years old at the time of her father's will; and Charlotta, who married first James Davis and second Enoch Hancock.

SEE: J. P. Brown, *The Commonwealth of Onslow* (1960); William S. Powell, James K. Huhta, and Thomas J. Farnham, eds., *The Regulators in North Carolina* (1971); William L. Saunders and Walter Clark, eds., *Colonial and State Records of North Carolina*, 30 vols. (1886–1914).

TUCKER REED LITTLETON

Creech, Oscar, Jr. *(14 Nov. 1916–22 Dec. 1967),* surgeon, researcher, teacher, administrator, was born in Nashville, N.C., the son of Oscar Creech, Sr., Baptist minister, and Martha Gulley Creech. He finished high school in Ahoskie in 1933, received his bachelor's degree from Wake Forest College in 1937, and obtained an M.D. from Jefferson Medical College in 1941. He served his internship at Charity Hospital in New Orleans. Military service, however, interrupted his graduate training there.

From 1942 to 1946, Creech served in the Army Medical Corps, and was discharged from the army with the rank of major. On his way home to North Carolina, where he planned to enter general practice, he stopped in New

Orleans where during a chance encounter with a friend, he learned of the availability of a surgical residency at Tulane University. He applied for the position, was accepted, and began his serious pursuit of surgery.

When Dr. Michael DeBakey, one of his mentors at Charity, accepted the chair of surgery at Baylor Medical College in Houston in 1949, Creech joined the department there as a full-time faculty member. While at Baylor, he worked with Dr. DeBakey in the development of synthetic blood vessel grafts.

In 1956, Creech returned to New Orleans to accept the William Henderson Professorship of Surgery and to chair the Department of Surgery at Tulane Medical School. Dr. Alton Ochsner, Creech's former chief and outgoing chairman of the department, said, "I took it as one of the greatest compliments ever paid to me when he came back to succeed me."

The new Tulane department head was a pioneer in organ transplants and blood vessel grafts. His interests, however, ranged across a broad spectrum. He helped devise a new method of cancer chemotherapy (regional perfusion), a technique by which the diseased part of the body is isolated from the general circulation and a heart-lung machine pumps concentrations of antitumor drugs into the affected area. The Tulane transplant team under Dr. Creech's supervision made the first successful implantations of animal kidneys into humans. This team, illustrating Creech's interdisciplinary approach to medical treatment, included a urologist, a pediatrician, an immunologist, and an internist as well as surgeon.

Creech possessed an unusual interest in language. He was so concerned about the careless use of language in medicine that he became the first to appoint to his faculty a professor of scientific communications. This professor was enjoined to teach students, residents, and faculty how to present scientific material clearly and gracefully.

When Creech became dean of the medical school at Tulane on 1 July 1967, he realized that it was possibly the final step in his medical career. Both he and the university administration knew that he suffered from a disease—reticulum cell sarcoma—which could abruptly end his life as indeed it did six months later.

Creech's final contribution to medicine centered upon his efforts to shape medical education for the future. He looked ahead to 1990, forecasting that the traditional private practice of medicine would cease. He believed that physicians would eventually become full-time employees of community medical centers or of the federal government and that clinical associates—college graduates with one year of apprenticeship in a specialty —would assume most of the functions heretofore performed by practicing physicians. Under those circumstances, doctors would become system specialists. Thus, in an effort to help assure that the medical profession would dictate the broad terms of health care in the future, Creech worked in the field of medical education for the last six months of his life.

He pushed forward his proposals as chairman of the school's planning committee for an expanded medical complex with a university hospital at Tulane that would provide superior medical care, education, and research. According to President Herbert E. Longenecker of Tulane, "Dr. Creech accomplished more in his six months as dean before his untimely death than would have been considered possible. He has left his associates a legacy in the challenge to accomplish their mutual goals."

During Creech's years at Tulane, his weekly surgical amphitheater clinic was immensely popular. Many young physicians interested in surgical careers were attracted to that institution because of the opportunity to work under his personal tutelage. His former residents, as a token of their appreciation and respect, organized the Oscar Creech Surgical Society.

Among honors received by Oscar Creech during his medical career are two American Medical Association Hektoen gold medals for scientific exhibits, American Heart Association Citation for contributions to research, *Modern Medicine* Award for Distinguished Achievement, and an honorary Doctor of Science degree from Wake Forest College. In addition to membership in numerous medical and scientific organizations, including the International Society of Surgery, he served as president of the American Surgical Association and of the North American chapter of the International Cardiovascular Society, and vice-president of the Society of Clinical Surgery. He also served on numerous educational and research committees of national organizations, including the American Board of Surgery, and was a member of the Training Committee of the National Heart Institute at the time of his death. He contributed more than 125 articles to scientific and medical publications and was associate editor of *Archives of Surgery*.

Creech was married to the former Dorothy Browne and they had four children: Oscar, III, Diana, Archie, and Martha. He was buried in the Ahoskie Cemetery.

SEE: Lois DeBakey, "A Tribute: Oscar Creech, Jr., M.D." *Archives of Surgery* 96 (1968); "Lofty Career Cut Short at its Peak," *Medical World News*, 19 Jan. 1968; *New York Times*, 23 Dec. 1967.

RACHEL N. PITTMAN

Creecy, Richard Benbury *(19 Dec. 1813–22 Oct. 1908)*, author and newspaper editor, was born at Greenfield Plantation near Edenton, a son of Joshua S. and Mary Benbury Creecy. On his mother's side he was descended from Thomas Benbury, a commissary general in the American Revolution whom President Washington later appointed first collector of revenue for the Port of Edenton. His grandfather was Lemuel Creecy, a Chowan County farmer and a member of the state senate for many years. There was a tradition that the Creecys were descendants of five brothers of Huguenot origin who fled from France in the early 1600s, were shipwrecked on the Outer Banks, and later settled along Albemarle Sound. Other antecedents were Christopher Gale, first chief justice of North Carolina (1712), and General William Skinner of the Revolution.

Creecy attended the Edenton Academy and was graduated from The University of North Carolina in 1835. Receiving his license to practice law a year later, he moved to Elizabeth City, where he lived for the remainder of his life. On 7 Nov. 1844 he married Mary Brosher Perkins, daughter of Edmund Perkins, a Pasquotank County farmer. She died in 1867, leaving ten children. Soon after his marriage, Creecy gave up his law practice and went to live on his father-in-law's plantation, Cloverdale, eight miles below Elizabeth City. There, until after the Civil War, he devoted his entire time to farming, literature, philosophy, and the raising of his children. During this period he wrote and published *A Child's History for the Fireside*.

Impoverished by the aftermath of the war, he returned to Elizabeth City in 1870 and to his law practice. But like many other lawyers of his day, he was adept at doing other things and soon joined another attorney, E. F. Lamb, who did a large and profitable business in real estate. Financed by Lamb, with the backing of other prominent men in the Albemarle, he founded the *Economist*, a weekly newspaper, the first issue of which appeared on 14 Feb. 1872. Colonel Creecy (an honorary title bestowed on him later in life) had a way with words and was a relentless foe of Republicans and the corrupt northern carpetbaggers then infesting Elizabeth City. For more than thirty-five years he fought, through his newspaper, on the side of all those who favored better government and an end to northern tyranny over the prostrate South. He sought "to unite the opposition to the reckless tendency of the times," believing that the country's institutions were in dire peril and that the precious heritage of his forefathers was "in very grave danger of being swept away by the tide of corruption then sweeping the South."

In its early days, Creecy's *Economist* was printed by the editor of the rival weekly *North Carolinian*, which admitted strong northern ties and sympathies. Soon after July 1872 this disadvantage was eliminated, when an editorial committee made up of prominent men of the area decided to sponsor the *Economist*. They were all staunch Democrats who pledged themselves "to guarantee the integrity and success of the new enterprise"; Creecy set about "to administer to the literary tastes of his readers, to promote the agricultural, commercial, professional, mechanical and other industrial interests in Northeastern North Carolina with all the capacity, industry and zeal he could command."

By nature a quiet, conservative, and philosophic man, Creecy often found it necessary to comment caustically on political conditions as he saw them in North Carolina, especially in the 1870s, when a great battle for constitutional liberties was raging. "Let every man who is opposed to corruption, dishonest and bad government do what he can against the bayonet element in our elections," he urged in August 1872. He saw the Radical or Grant party paving the way "to bring Federal troops into North Carolina to carry the State election" and warned that, unless they were ousted from North Carolina politics, "our own and certainly our children's liberties will be crushed out forever."

Although he retired in 1904 at the age of ninety-one years, Creecy continued a frequent contributor to newspaper columns over the state. His book, *Grandfather's Tales of North Carolina History*, was published in 1901, and his "Stray Leaves of Our History" appeared in the *University of North Carolina Magazine* in January 1906.

Upon his death in 1908, Creecy was the oldest alumnus of The University of North Carolina and was said to be the oldest newspaper editor in the United States. A lifelong Episcopalian, he was buried in Hollywood Cemetery from Christ Church, Elizabeth City.

SEE: Samuel A. Ashe, ed., *Biographical History of North Carolina*, vol. 4 (1906), and *Cyclopedia of Eminent and Representative Men of the Carolinas of the Nineteenth Century*, vol. 2 (1892); Scrapbook of newspaper clippings dating to 1870 (possession of Betty Wales Silver); University of North Carolina, *University Magazine* 37 (Apr. 1907); 39 (Nov. 1908).

BETTY WALES SILVER

Crisp, Lucy Cherry (*4 Mar. 1899–25 Nov. 1977*), museum administrator and poet, was born in Crisp, Edgecombe County, the daughter of Sellers M. and Annie Gorham Crisp. She was graduated from the North Carolina College for Women in Greensboro with a degree in music and continued her education at Columbia and Boston universities and at Radcliffe College. She taught piano and was supervisor of music in the public schools of North Carolina for a time and for a number of years contributed a weekly folk column, "Byways and Hedges," and a Sunday column, "Tar Heel Art," to the Raleigh *News and Observer*. She also wrote feature articles for many state papers and was the author of two volumes of poetry, *Spring Fever*, in dialect, published in 1935, and *Brief Testament*, published in 1947. Other poems by her were published in periodicals and anthologies. She served briefly as religious counselor at the University of Illinois, Champaign-Urbana, and for a few years was director of the Museum of Art, Science, and History in Florence, S.C. During World War II she was director of the United Services Organization Club at Greenville, N.C. In 1947 she became the director of an art museum in Raleigh under the patronage of the North Carolina State Art Society and continued in that position until 1955. This museum was the forerunner of the North Carolina Museum of Art. While director of the museum, Miss Crisp edited *North Carolina News of Art*, a monthly bulletin, and in 1956 completed "A History of the North Carolina State Art Society." She served as secretary to a state art commission created in 1951 by the General Assembly to purchase art and to establish procedures for governing the North Carolina Museum of Art. She also assisted in assembling the staff, purchasing equipment, and training volunteers for the new museum that opened in 1956. After leaving Raleigh she served as director of the Greenville Art Center. She was a member of the Presbyterian church, of the American Association of Museums, and of the Society of Mayflower Descendants. She was buried in Falkland Cemetery, Pitt County, in the community where her family had lived for several generations.

SEE: Lucy Cherry Crisp MSS (East Carolina University Manuscript Collection, Greenville); Ola Maie Foushee, *Art in North Carolina* (1972); Greenville *Daily Reflector*, 27 Nov. 1977; William S. Powell, ed., *North Carolina Lives* (1962).

WILLIAM S. POWELL

Crittenden, Charles Christopher (*1 Dec. 1902– 13 Oct. 1969*), university professor, historian, author, and state agency head, was born in Wake Forest, the only child of Charles Christopher and Ethel Taylor Crittenden. His father was a teacher of pedagogy, and his mother was for many years librarian of Wake Forest College. His maternal grandfather, Charles E. Taylor, was president of the college from 1885 to 1905. Charles Christopher Crittenden, Sr., died when his son was less than a year old, and so the younger Crittenden never adopted the suffix "Jr." After about 1940 he ceased using his first name.

Crittenden attended the local public schools and received from Wake Forest College the B.A. degree in history in 1921 and the M.A. degree in 1922. During the school year 1922–23 he was principal of Roxobel School in Bertie County, after which he entered graduate school at Yale University. He was instructor of history at Yale in 1924–25 and received his Ph.D. degree from Yale in 1930. He was instructor of history from 1926 to 1929 and assistant professor of history from 1930 to 1935 at The University of North Carolina. In 1935 he was elected to succeed Albert Ray Newsome as secretary of the North Carolina Historical Commission in Raleigh. Except for a year's leave of absence (1946–47), when he was in

Washington, D.C., as assistant director of the World War II Records Project of the National Archives, Crittenden remained executive head of the historical commission (renamed the North Carolina Department of Archives and History in 1943) until 1968; he then stepped down to the assistant directorship, which position he held until his death. In 1936–37 he also served as state director of the Historical Records Survey and regional director of the Survey of Federal Archives.

During his thirty-three years as head of the state's historical agency, Crittenden transformed a respectable department into a model for other states. While demanding adherence to scholarly principles, he adopted the slogan "History for all the people" and put greater emphasis on historical markers and easy-to-read materials for use in the public schools. He expanded the archival program to encompass modern records management, promoted the publication of primary source materials, assumed administration of state historic sites, and encouraged the preservation of historic properties by nonstate groups. The agency staff grew from 8 people in 1935 to 135 in 1968. Crittenden also guided various history-related agencies and organizations, such as the Carolina Charter Tercentenary Commission, Confederate Centennial Commission, and North Carolina Society for the Preservation of Antiquities. At the height of his successful career in "selling" the history of North Carolina, he supervised the movement of the agency into the new Archives and History-State Library Building in 1968 and then stepped down as director.

Crittenden's innovative leadership of the state historical agency was matched by his varied national activities. He was a founding member and later president (1946–48) of the Society of American Archivists, chairman (1938–40) of the Conference of Historical Societies, and a founder and first president (1940–42) of its successor organization, the American Association for State and Local History. In 1946 he was one of three persons who met with David E. Finley and proposed the formation of an organization patterned after the National Trust of England. This proposal led to the organization of the National Council for Historic Sites and Buildings, which in turn led in 1949 to the creation of the National Trust for Historic Preservation, of which Crittenden served as a trustee.

From 1935 until his death, Crittenden was secretary-treasurer of the North Carolina Literary and Historical Association, in which capacity he was in charge of the state's annual "Culture Week," a unique gathering of cultural organizations with a state-wide mission. He also held offices in other professional organizations, including the presidency of the Archaeological Society of North Carolina (1948–50, 1955–56) and of the Historical Society of North Carolina (1956–57).

Crittenden was a prolific writer. From 1935 until his retirement he was editor of the *North Carolina Historical Review*. His first book, *North Carolina Newspapers before 1790*, was published in 1928, and *The Commerce of North Carolina, 1763–1789*, appeared in 1936. With Dan Lacy he compiled and edited *The Historical Records of North Carolina: The County Records* (3 vols.) in 1938–39. In 1944 he compiled and edited *Historical Societies in the United States and Canada: A Handbook*. For a time he was a member of the advisory editorial board of *American Heritage*. His articles and reviews were published in many scholarly journals, and for several years prior to his death he wrote a weekly column for the Associated Press, titled "The Light of History."

Two honorary degrees were conferred upon Crittenden, the Litt.D. from Wake Forest College in 1956 and the LL.D. from The University of North Carolina in 1961. In 1963 he received the Award of Distinction, the highest honor bestowed upon an individual by the American Association for State and Local History. He was a fellow of the Society of American Archivists, and in 1964 his department received the first Distinguished Service Award ever conferred by that society.

Crittenden was a Democrat and a Baptist, though he wore his religion lightly. A jovial man, he became something of a legend even during his lifetime because of his wisecracks, practical jokes, and attractions to the unusual.

Crittenden married Janet Quinlan of Waynesville on 6 Sept. 1930, and they had three children: Charles Christopher, Jr. (b. 11 Nov. 1933), Robert Hinton (b. 11 Mar. 1936), and Ann Lane (b. 23 June 1938).

Crittenden died after suffering a stroke and heart attack, and his body was cremated.

To commemorate Crittenden's service, the North Carolina Literary and Historical Association established the Christopher Crittenden Memorial Award, given annually to an individual, group, or organization for extraordinary contributions to the preservation of North Carolina history.

SEE: Biennial reports of the North Carolina Historical Commission (1934–42) and State Department of Archives and History (1942–68); Philip C. Brooks, "Christopher Crittenden," *American Archivist* 33 (1970); North Carolina State Archives (Raleigh), for Crittenden's personal papers, official records of his administration of the department, and photographs; William S. Powell, ed., *North Carolina Lives* (1962); Raleigh *News and Observer*, 15 Oct. 1969; *Washington* (N.C.) *Daily News*, 29 Oct. 1969; *Who's Who in America*, 1952–69; *Who's Who in North Carolina*, 1947.

H. G. JONES

Croom, Hardy Bryan (*8 Oct. 1797–9 Oct. 1837*), planter, politician, and naturalist, was born at his father's estate in Lenoir County. He was the son of Major General William Croom and his first wife, Mary Bryan, a daughter of Colonel Nathan Bryan, a prominent citizen and member of Congress from New Bern. Croom's early years were spent on his father's plantation with two brothers and a sister. His mother died when he was about seven years old, and his father married Elizabeth Whitfield, daughter of General Bryan Whitfield of White Hall, Wayne County. By Betsy Whitfield, General Croom had five children.

Croom is said to have attended a local academy. He received an A.B. degree at The University of North Carolina in 1817 and an M.A. there in 1820. He was considered a brilliant student. Along with his university classmate, Francis Lister Hawks, he read law with Judge William Gaston in New Bern. In 1821 he married Frances Henrietta Smith, the daughter of Nathan Smith, a wealthy citizen of New Bern; the Crooms had three children, Henrietta Mary, William Henry, and Justina Rosa.

Always an active and popular public figure, Croom delivered the Fourth of July address before a company of local militia at Kinston, Lenoir County, in 1825. No doubt he was preparing himself a place in local politics; in 1828 he was elected to represent Lenoir County in the state senate.

In 1826, Croom's father established planting interests in Gadsden County, Fla., though he never became a citizen of Florida. After General Croom's death in 1829, his son resigned his seat in the General Assembly to go to Florida in 1830 in the interest of the estate. He was succeeded in the state senate by William Dunn Moseley, who later moved to Florida and became that state's first governor (1845–49). On his first visit to Florida, Croom became so interested in the state that upon his return to Lenoir County in 1831 he sold his estate and removed his plantation slaves to Florida. His family moved to New Bern.

Croom had a keen interest in geology, mineralogy, and botany and was especially taken with the fauna and flora of Florida. In 1833 he and Dr. H. Loomis brought out the *Catalogue of Plants Observed in the Neighborhood of New Bern, North Carolina*, which was published by the *Spectator* office in New Bern. After Croom's untimely death, a new edition of this catalog was published by G. P. Scott and Company, with Croom's friend Dr. John Torrey, a botanist of New York City, seeing it through the press. Croom's writings were published in volumes 25, 26, and 28 of the *American Journal of Science and Arts* in 1834 and 1838. His most famous paper, the monograph "Observations on the Genus Sarracenia, with an Account of a New Species," appeared posthumously in the fourth volume of the *Annals of the New York Lyceum of Natural History*, of which he was a member. He also held membership in the Philosophical Society of South Carolina and was a corresponding member of the Academy of Natural Sciences of Philadelphia.

In the early 1830s, Croom began work on a biography of General Richard Caswell, the first governor of North Carolina after independence. Caswell was a resident of Lenoir County before his death in 1789, and Croom had a lively interest in him. The biography of Caswell was never completed, and the manuscript, which Croom was reported to have sent to New York publishers just before his death, has never been recovered.

In 1832, Croom purchased a plantation on the west side of the Apalachicola River, near Marianna, Fla., and another in Gadsden County, near Quincy, Fla. In 1834 he began to develop another plantation in Leon County. He hoped to establish a residence there, three miles from the territorial capital of Tallahassee.

While traveling from his Leon County plantation to his Gadsden County lands, Croom discovered one of the rarest coniferous trees, which he named *Torreya taxifolium* in honor of Dr. John Torrey. This tree has four species, each growing in widely separated locations: China, Japan, California, and Florida. Croom's discovery was the first of this species in the United States. Later Croom discovered another plant, which Dr. Torrey named *Croomia pauciflora* in his memory.

Each year from 1830 to 1837, Croom went annually to Florida; his family lived in New Bern, spending the summer months at Saratoga and New York City. In 1826, Bryan Croom, Hardy Bryan Croom's brother, moved from Lenoir County to Florida, and established a plantation in Gadsden County, named Rocky Comfort; later, he built Goodwood, a handsome antebellum mansion near Tallahassee in Leon County. Against Bryan's advice, Hardy Bryan decided to brave the bad economic conditions then prevailing in Florida and move his family from New Bern to Tallahassee. He decided first to establish a summer home in Charleston, S.C., in 1837, and then to move his family, who were on holiday in New York City, via Charleston to Florida.

Croom and his wife and children sailed from New York on the steamboat *Home* on 7 Oct. 1837. The next day, Croom's fortieth birthday, a bad storm was encountered, and the steamboat began having difficulties. On the ninth the boiler fire was put out by high water inside the ship, at which time the captain tried to put ashore south of Cape Hatteras. As night came on the passengers were ordered on deck to abandon ship. Many were swept away and drowned in the large waves that overcame the boat, and among those lost were all of the Croom family.

As a result of the disaster, one of the most interesting cases in legal history was filed in circuit court in Leon County, Fla., 24 Jan. 1839. Henrietta Smith, the maternal grandmother of the Croom children, and their maternal aunt, Elizabeth M. Armistead, filed a bill of complaint against the sister and two brothers of Hardy Bryan Croom, for the purpose of determining who would inherit the estate. Bryan Croom purchased the rights of his brother and sister and was represented by James Louis Pettigru of Charleston, one of the most able and noted attorneys in the South. The case was litigated for twenty years. In 1857 the Florida Supreme Court rendered a final decision, overturning the original decision, which had decided in favor of Bryan Croom. Mrs. Smith and Mrs. Armistead got all the personal property, which was the most valuable part of the estate, and two-eighths of the real estate; Bryan Croom received the rest. This case is recognized as a landmark in the United States on the question of survivorship in a common calamity.

A marble shaft in St. John's Episcopal churchyard in Tallahassee stands as a memorial to the Croom family. Only the bodies of Mrs. Croom, the son and the youngest daughter were ever recovered; they were taken to New Bern and buried in the vault of Croom's father-in-law, Nathan Smith, in Cedar Grove Cemetery.

SEE: Hardy Bryan Croom, *Catalogue of Plants Observed in the Neighborhood of New Bern* (1837); North Carolina Collection (University of North Carolina, Chapel Hill), for newspaper files and Mary Lindsay Thornton, "North Carolina Biographical and Historical Sketches" (typescript); D. H. Redfearn, "The Steamboat Home," *Florida Bar Journal* 37 (1963).

JOHN BAXTON FLOWERS III

Croom, William (*4 Jan. 1772–9 May 1829*), planter, politician, and militia officer, was born probably on his father's dwelling plantation on Lower Falling Creek in Dobbs (now Lenoir) County. His father, Major Croom, Sr., a son of Daniel Croom, Irish progenitor of the family in North Carolina, sold his patrimony in Virginia in 1743, when he was twenty-one, and settled a plantation on Lower Falling Creek. William Croom's mother was Olive Avery. In May 1771, Major Croom, Sr., and his eldest son, Joshua, were engaged to transport matériel for Governor William Tryon when he marched against the Regulators on the western frontier of the colony. Both Major and Joshua Croom served in the revolutionary militia; Major was a member of the committee of safety for the New Bern District in 1775 and 1776 and was appointed commissioner of magazines for that district in February 1779. Joshua Croom served in both the House of Commons and the state senate and was one of the outstanding public figures of Lenoir County.

It was in a home of public service that William Croom was reared. His early education is now obscure, but he was undoubtedly well educated. In 1793, when he was twenty-one years old, he succeeded his brother Joshua in the state senate. Reelected to the senate in 1794, 1795, 1805, 1806, and 1807, he manifested there a keen interest in agriculture.

Croom was an officer in the state militia, rising to the rank of major general. During the War of 1812 he was in command of the Second, Third, and Twelfth brigades of militia from Lenoir and Jones counties. During July 1814, when the British fleet under Admiral Sir George Cockburn landed and sacked Ocracoke and Portsmouth islands off the North Carolina coast, Croom rushed his three brigades to defend New Bern against what was prematurely reported to be an invasion of the mainland.

After the war, Croom retired to Newington, a large estate about three miles east of Kinston in Lenoir County that had formerly belonged to General Richard Caswell, first governor of the State of North Carolina. In 1826, Croom established planting interests in Gadsden County, Fla., though he never became a Florida citizen. Before his death he added to his landholdings the historic Tower Hill Plantation, established by royal Governor Arthur Dobbs, and the Rountree Plantation, both of which adjoined Newington.

Croom's first wife, Mary Bryan, was a daughter of Colonel Nathan Bryan and his wife, Winifred Bryan, of Jones County. The Crooms had four children: Hardy Bryan, who married Frances Henrietta Smith of New Bern; Susan Matilda, who married Edmond Whitfield of White Hall in Wayne County; Bryan, who married Eveline, sister of the Right Reverend Francis Lister Hawks; Richard, who married Winifred, daughter of General Bryan Whitfield of Spring Hill in Lenoir County and his second wife, Winifred Bryan.

On 20 Apr. 1809, Croom married Elizabeth Whitfield, a daughter of General Bryan Whitfield by his first wife, Nancy Bryan. Elizabeth Whitfield Croom was born 19 July 1787; she died at Kinston on 27 June 1831 and was buried beside her husband. Elizabeth and William Croom had six children: Nancy Bryan, who married Dr. Edward Croom Bellamy of Nash County; William Whitfield, who married Julia Stephens, a daughter of Cicero Stephens of New Bern; John Quincy, who died young; Betsy, who married Stephen Bellamy of Nash County; George Alexander, who married Julia Church of Athens, Ga.; and Anne.

SEE: S. M. Lemmon, *Frustrated Patriots: North Carolina and the War of 1812* (1973); Lenoir County Records (North Carolina State Archives, Raleigh); Emma Morehead Whitfield, *Whitfield, Bryan, Smith and Related Families* (1948); Lillian F. Wood, *Daniel Croom of Virginia, His Descendants in North Carolina* (1945).

JOHN BAXTON FLOWERS III

Cross, Tom Peete (*8 Dec. 1879–25 Dec. 1951*), scholar, folklorist, and friend of Tar Heel drama, was born in Nansemond County, Va. He was the son of Thomas Hardy and Eleanor Elizabeth Wright Cross and grandson of Hardy and Martha Peete Cross. His father was a planter.

Cross attended Norfolk (Va.) Academy and received the B.A. degree in 1899 (S.B. 1900) from Hampden-Sydney College. At Harvard University he received the M.A. in 1906 and the Ph.D. in 1909. During the summer of 1909 he studied at the School of Irish Learning, Dublin. After teaching stints at Norfolk Academy (1900–1905), Harvard and Radcliffe (1910–11), and Sweetbriar College (1911–12), Cross went to The University of North Carolina as professor of English during the 1912–13 term.

Cross maintained a lifelong interest in North Carolina folklore and folk drama. With Cross as a sponsor, a dramatic association was formed that year at the university, and a play, reportedly the first in several decades at the school, was performed and taken on tour to several towns in the state. The dramatic association

continued to function after Cross left the university; and in 1918, Professor Frederick Koch, a graduate student of drama at Harvard when Cross was there, arrived in Chapel Hill and formed the Carolina Playmakers. Articles by Cross about Tar Heel folklore influenced the subject matter of the Playmakers' first performances. In 1909 he had published an article about a Northampton County witch in the *Journal of American Folklore*, and in 1919 his article "Witchcraft in North Carolina" appeared in *Studies in Philology*, a scholarly journal published at The University of North Carolina. The first native folkplay produced by the Carolina Playmakers (1919) was Elizabeth Lay's "When Witches Ride," about a Northampton County witch. In 1922, Cross was asked by Professor Koch to write an appendix on the dialect of the North Carolina region for the first published collection of Carolina folkplays.

During his later career, Cross wrote articles for the *Review Celtique* of Paris and a book about the Celts, *Harper and Bard* (1931); he was a fellow of the American Irish Historical Society and of the American Council of the Irish Texts Society. He was a member from 1913 to 1945 of the English faculty of the University of Chicago, teaching English, Celtic, and comparative literature. Also an Arthurian scholar, he wrote special articles on folklore and superstition for the *Chicago Herald*. He was the author, with C. H. Slover, of *Ancient Irish Tales* (1933), but his best-known publication was the *Motif-Index of Early Irish Folk-Literature* (1952), which he spent twenty-five years compiling. He belonged to a number of professional and fraternal organizations; his religious affiliation was with the Methodist church.

Cross was married in 1914 to Elizabeth Douglas Weathers of Avon, Ky. They had two daughters, Ellen Elizabeth, who married Storm Bull, and Evelyn Douglas, who married Louis S. Baer. Cross died in Aylett, Va.

SEE: *Journal of American Folklore* 22 (1909); F. H. Koch, ed., *Carolina Folk-Plays*, 1st ser. (1922); *Nat. Cyc. Am. Biog.*, vol. 40 (1955); *Studies in Philology* 16 (1919).

E. T. MALONE, JR.

Crossan, Thomas Morrow (*14 May 1819–16 Oct. 1865*), naval officer, was born in Pittsburgh, Pa., the son of James C. and Nancy Morrow Crossan. He spent much of his childhood in Kentucky with a maternal uncle, Thomas Morrow, and was appointed to the U.S. Naval Academy from Kentucky. He was graduated with an acting midshipman's commission on 1 July 1836; passing through the various grades in the navy, he ultimately resigned his commission as lieutenant on 1 Sept. 1857. An officer for twenty-one years, his service at sea aggregated more than twelve years. He saw much active service in the Mexican War, attached to the *Albany*, under the command of Captain Isaac Mayo.

On 10 July 1854, Crossan married Rebecca Brehon, daughter of James Gloster Brehon of Warren County. Through this marriage he became connected with the socially prominent Somerville family. The Crossans had an only son, Brehon Somerville, who later moved to Pittsburgh.

When the Civil War began, Crossan was living in Warren County. Although he had many relatives in the North, he volunteered his services to North Carolina, which was establishing a small navy. This organization, under the titular command of former Governor Warren Winslow, secretary of the newly established military and naval board, slowly grew into a small fleet used to patrol the sounds and prey upon Federal shipping. The *Raleigh*

Weekly Register reported Crossan's appointment as a lieutenant in the North Carolina navy on 5 June 1861.

Winslow ordered William T. Muse, another former officer in the U.S. Navy, to purchase vessels in Norfolk and fit them out as gunboats at the Norfolk Navy Yard. One of these vessels, the *J. E. Coffee*, a 207-ton sidewheel steamer employed in the Chesapeake trade, was equipped with one short thirty-two-pounder cannon and a six-pounder brass rifled cannon and placed under Crossan's command. It was rechristened the *Warren Winslow* in honor of Secretary Winslow. In mid-June 1861, Crossan sailed the *Warren Winslow* to New Bern for friction primers and ammunition for his rifled cannon.

Crossan left New Bern in late June and proceeded to harass Federal shipping. On 25 June 1861, with "quite a number of soldiers on board," he captured the brig *Hannah Balch*, commanded by Sailing Master Albert Kautz of the U.S. Navy. Kautz tried to escape, he wrote, "by setting all sail and running free, but the steamer being a fast one and the brig a slow sailer I was soon overtaken and compelled to surrender." Kautz was sent to Raleigh in Crossan's custody. His captor soon took him to Warrenton, treating him more like a guest than a prisoner.

Crossan captured two more brigs and five schooners before relinquishing command of the *Warren Winslow* in August 1861. It is a certainty that his activities prompted the Federal attack on Forts Hatteras and Clark in late August.

Governor Henry T. Clark later commissioned Crossan a lieutenant colonel in the Coast Artillery. In January 1862, Brigadier General Richard C. Gatlin, commanding the Department of North Carolina, placed Crossan in command of all the forts on the Neuse River below New Bern, and Crossan greatly strengthened the fortifications at Fort Thompson and the other Neuse batteries. During the Battle of New Bern, 14 Mar. 1862, the Federals made a heavy attack upon Crossan's position at Fort Thompson. Crossan "opened on them with grape from three 32-pounders with such terrible effect that after about six shots they fell back; and though they kept up a constant and warm fire, they made no advance toward the work." As the main Confederate line fell back in great confusion, the fighting at Fort Thompson became desperate, with the fort's interior falling under heavy Federal artillery fire. Crossan spiked all his guns but, because "the enemy pressed on closely," had no time to blow up the magazine; he participated in the retreat to Kinston.

In November 1862, Crossan was ordered by Governor Zebulon B. Vance to accompany Special Commissioner John White to England. Crossan's specific duty was to purchase a British vessel that could be converted into a blockade-runner for North Carolina. He bought the passenger steamer *Lord Clyde* for thirty-five thousand dollars and quickly renamed it the *Ad-Vance*, presumably in honor of Governor Vance. With this vessel, Crossan made a number of trips through the blockade to Wilmington, bringing clothing and other military supplies from England and returning with between five hundred and seven hundred bales of cotton on each trip. In early September 1863, Vance seriously considered the sale of the *Ad-Vance*, with the proceeds to be deposited in England to the credit of North Carolina, but Crossan's success caused him to change his mind.

Blockade-running was a profitable business. Crossan received the monthly pay of a captain in the Confederate Navy and a thousand dollars for each round trip. The vessels' inward cargoes were also valuable, including large quantities of machinery supplies, arms, ammuni-

tion, cloth and clothing, food, medicine, and other goods.

Crossan retired to Warrenton late in the war because of ill health. He attempted to engage in business ventures in New York in the summer of 1865 but was unsuccessful, because, as he explained, "Commerce has not resumed its former channel as yet, and the inspirer (not King remember) Cotton is suffering from severe indisposition which I fear is somewhat chronic in its nature." He soon returned to Warrenton, where he died. He was buried in the Somerville Burial Ground, a family cemetery near Warrenton. Crossan named his wife the administratrix of his estate and left the modest sum of $5,300.57 to his family.

SEE: Walter Clark, ed., *Histories of the Several Regiments and Battalions from North Carolina in the Great War, 1861–1865*, vol. 5 (1901 [photograph]); Marshall DeLancey Haywood, "Thomas Morrow Crossan" (Manuscript Department, Library, Duke University, Durham); Albert Kautz to Gideon Welles, letter (20 Nov. 1861, in *Official Records of the Union and Confederate Navies in the War of the Rebellion*, ed. Richard Rush, 1st ser., vol. 5 1897); *New Bern Daily Progress*, 20 June 1861; North Carolina State Archives (Raleigh), for Miscellaneous Letters and Telegrams Received and Sent by Gov. Z. B. Vance, 1862–64 (Vance to Messrs. Power, Lowe, and Co., 1 Feb. 1864), Zebulon B. Vance Letter Book, 1862–63 (Thomas M. Crossan to John White, 30 July 1863; Vance to Crossan, 9 Sept. 1863), Z. B. Vance Papers (vol. 8, 1865, Thomas M. Crossan to Vance, 1 July 1865), and Warren County Estates Records (Collins-Burwell, Davis, 1768–1920), Graves Index (Warrenton), and Marriage Bonds (1779–1868, A–C); *Raleigh Weekly Register*, 5 June 1861; Robert D. Scott, ed., *War of the Rebellion: Official Records*, 1st ser., vol. 9 (Charles C. Lee to Lawrence O'B. Branch, 16 Mar. 1862; S. B. Spruill to Branch, 16 Mar. 1862), 1st ser., vol. 51 (Richard C. Gatlin to Henry T. Clark, 18 Jan. 1862, Gatlin to Branch, 1 Mar. 1862), 2nd ser., vol. 2 (Clark to Leroy Pope Walker, 6 Aug. 1861), 4th ser., vol. 2 (Zebulon B. Vance, Order, 19 Nov. 1862).

RICHARD W. IOBST

Crowell, John (*18 Sept. 1780–25 June 1846*), Indian agent, territorial delegate, and congressman, was born in Halifax County. His father, Edward, had left New Jersey to settle in North Carolina, where he married a Miss Rabun, an aunt of William Rabun, governor of Georgia from 1817 to 1819. The Crowells were of English descent, and various accounts agree that the name was originally Cromwell. Two brothers, relatives of Oliver Cromwell, fled to the American colonies and, fearing further persecution, changed their name.

In 1815, John Crowell was appointed agent to the Muscogee Indians; he moved to Alabama and lived in St. Stephens for a brief time. In 1818 he was elected by the territorial legislature as delegate to the Fifteenth U.S. Congress. In the following year he was elected to the Sixteenth Congress as Alabama's first representative. Little is known of his record during his one term in the House, except for a comment made by Governor John Dandridge Bibb: "John Crowel [sic] was not talented, but the Territory at that time had no one else to spare that would have done any better."

Following his retirement from Congress in 1821, Crowell was appointed agent to the Creek Indians of western Georgia and eastern Alabama; he held this office until 1836. He is reputed to have been a lover of horse-racing and to have enjoyed entering his own fine horses in the contests.

Crowell never married. He died at his home in Fort Mitchell in Russell County and was buried there in a private cemetery.

SEE: *Biog. Dir. Am. Cong.* (1961); "Governor Bibb and the Times," *Alabama Historical Quarterly* 19 (1957); "National Characters Associated with Treaties," ibid. 12 (1950); Thomas McAdory Owen, *History of Alabama and Dictionary of Alabama Biography*, vol. 3 (1921); John H. Wheeler, *Historical Sketches of North Carolina* (1851); *Who Was Who in America, 1607–1896*; "William Rabun," in Walter G. Cooper, *The Story of Georgia*, vol. 4 (1938).

J. ISAAC COPELAND

Crowell, John Franklin *(1 Nov. 1857–6 Aug. 1931)*, educator, economist, and journalist, was president of Trinity College from 1887 to 1894 and directed its move in 1892 from Randolph County to Durham. He was born in York, Pa., one of at least five children of Daniel and Sarah Ann Jacobs Craul. He attended Dartmouth College for a year and changed his name to Crowell about the time he left there. He transferred to Yale, where he was graduated with the B.A. degree in 1883. After serving as principal of Schuylkill Seminary at Reading, Pa., in 1883–84, he returned to Yale for a year in the Divinity School and another year in the Graduate School as Larned scholar in philosophy. He returned for the year 1886–87 to Schuylkill Seminary, which had been moved from Reading to Fredericksburg. This move from an urban environment to a rural one Crowell considered detrimental to the school, and he would later achieve the reverse for Trinity College.

Crowell married Laura Kistler Getz, the daughter of a prominent Reading manufacturer, in 1887. She died the following year, and in 1891 he married Caroline Haas Pascoe. No children were born of either marriage. An inheritance from his first wife largely financed the construction in her memory of the Crowell Science Hall on the Trinity campus in Durham.

A group of farsighted members of the Trinity board of trustees saw in Crowell the type of progressive educator and administrator that was needed to lift the college out of stagnation. There was opposition to his appointment, because he was northern and of another faith, but the opposition was overcome by arguments that the tenets of his church, the Evangelical, were similar to those of the Methodist church and that he had developed a special interest in the South.

When Crowell reached Trinity College and saw how meager its resources were, he was tempted to resign at once. Instead, he immediately announced changes in the curriculum. He gradually upgraded the faculty and improved the educational facilities of the college. He taught each year as well as administering the college and supervising the construction of its new campus and the move to Durham. A man of vision and tremendous energy, he also traveled widely over the state, speaking and preaching to different groups. In this way and through publication he sought to expand the reputation and influence of the college and to acquire students and financial support for it. He supervised the setting up of academies and gave advice to those already in operation. He dreamed of Trinity as a university, with the other Methodist colleges in the state in affiliation and preparatory schools serving as feeders for the whole system. One of Crowell's many innovations at Trinity was the introduction of intercollegiate football. The owners of the college, the two North Carolina conferences of the Methodist Episcopal Church, South,

came to oppose this and some other actions of his so strongly that he resigned.

After leaving Trinity, Crowell attended Columbia University for a year and received his Ph.D. degree there in 1897. From 1895 to 1897 he was head of the Department of Economics and Sociology at Smith College. In 1897–98 he studied at the University of Berlin. He had been awarded the Litt.D. degree by The University of North Carolina in 1889, and in 1917 he was awarded the LL.D. degree by Trinity College.

Crowell's second career as an economist and statistician in Washington and New York was a distinguished one. He was also, from 1906 to 1915, associate editor of the *Wall Street Journal*. He retired in 1925 after serving six years as director of the World Market Institute of New York. During his retirement years, much of his time was devoted to lecturing and writing, and his published works include studies on college training, taxation, industry, and commerce. His *Personal Recollections of Trinity College, North Carolina, 1887–1894*, is a Duke University Centennial Publication.

Before his death, Crowell became a member of the First Church of Christ, Scientist in Boston. He died in East Orange, N.J., and was buried in Red Mount Church cemetery, near his boyhood home. A portrait hangs in the William R. Perkins Library of Duke University.

SEE: Nora C. Chaffin, *Trinity College, 1839–1892* (1950); John Franklin Crowell Papers (Archives, Duke University, Durham); *New York Times*, 7 and 9 Aug. 1931; Earl W. Porter, *Trinity and Duke, 1892–1924* (1964); *Who Was Who in America*, vol. 1 (1943).

MATTIE U. RUSSELL

Cruden, John, Jr. *(d. ca. 1786)*, a Loyalist merchant, was in partnership with his uncle, John Cruden, and his brother James. They established stores in Wilmington and Cross Creek in 1774, using money the uncle had made in trade between Britain and the West Indies. Later they added a third store, in Guilford County.

As the head of the company, the elder Cruden hesitantly signed a nonimportation association in March 1775 and made small contributions to the Wilmington Committee of Safety. The Crudens provided supplies to the Loyalists who were defeated at Moore's Creek Bridge, however, and it was not until 1779 that they made their peace with the revolutionaries. The Crudens were not included in the 1779 Confiscation and Banishment Act.

The Cruden brothers took an openly Loyalist course following the British capture of Charles Town, and as a result the company lost its North Carolina holdings. The younger John Cruden was in Charles Town by the summer of 1780 and volunteered for Loyalist militia service. In September, Cornwallis appointed him a commissioner of sequestered estates, entrusting to him some administration of slaves taken from revolutionaries.

For the remainder of the war and even afterward, Cruden conscientiously tried to keep records on those sequestered slaves who were still in the hands of Loyalists. In East Florida after the war he discomfited some of his fellow Loyalist refugees by insisting that they return to the Americans the sequestered slaves in their possession; he hoped that the state governments would reciprocate by allowing the Loyalists to return to their homes and property. In the summer of 1783, James Cruden was driven from Wilmington by an arrest warrant, accompanied by the allegation that one or both of the brothers had sent American-owned slaves to Nova

Scotia. Some blacks from the Cape Fear area indeed were among former slaves in Nova Scotia after the war.

John Cruden's postwar behavior suggests that he had lost his sense of reality. For a while he headed a group of Loyalist refugees living between the St. Johns and St. Marys rivers in northern East Florida, who planned to take control of the province and forcibly prevent the Spanish cession for which the Treaty of Paris provided. Cruden abandoned the scheme after it attracted the robber bands who were molesting the area, but he pursued several visionary and incoherent schemes in East Florida and the Bahama Islands. His proceedings were one reason why some of the Loyalists who moved from East Florida to Nova Scotia delayed their departure until the summer of 1785.

Cruden died by 1788; he was survived by his brother James, who lived in the Bahamas.

SEE: Bahamas Registrar General, F/1 (microfilm in P. K. Yongs Library, University of Florida, Gainesville); Charleston *South-Carolina and American General Gazette*, 23 Aug. 1780; Joseph Bryne Lockey, *East Florida, 1783–1785*, ed. John Walton Caughey (1949); P.R.O., A.O. 12:37, 109; William L. Saunders and Walter Clark, eds., *Colonial and State Records of North Carolina*, vols. 9–11, 15–18 (1890–95, 1898–1900).

CAROLE WATTERSON TROXLER

Crudup, Josiah (*13 Jan. 1791–20 May 1872*), clergyman, legislator, and congressman, was born in Wakelon, Wake County, the youngest of the nine children of Josiah Crudup, a Baptist minister, and Elizabeth Battle, daughter of Elisha and Elizabeth Sumner Battle. Elisha Battle moved from Nansemond County, Va., to Edgecombe County before the Revolution; Elizabeth Sumner Battle was the granddaughter of William Sumner of Sumner Manor, Isle of Wight County, Va., and the cousin of General Jethro Sumner of the Continental Army.

Josiah Crudup, Jr., was educated at the Reverend Dr. William McPheeter's academy in Raleigh and at Columbian College (now George Washington University) in Washington, D.C. He studied theology and after his ordination continued in the ministry until his death. He was elected to the state senate in 1820 to represent Wake County, but soon after he took his seat it was declared vacant, because the Constitution of North Carolina prohibited ministers from holding office while still exercising ministerial functions. He was elected to Congress the next year and served one term, 1821–23. Defeated for reelection in 1823, he tried again in 1825 and lost in a close election to Willie P. Mangum. He resumed farming and preaching in Granville County, where he had settled. Although he remained interested in political affairs, he held no other elected office except representation of Granville County at the constitutional convention of 1835. He was a member of the Whig party and remained loyal to it throughout his career. Although a large slaveholder himself, he did not favor secession and opposed Lincoln in 1860 on the grounds that Lincoln's election would enable secessionists to further their cause throughout the South, his unpopularity bringing many into the secessionist fold.

Crudup was a more effective preacher and farmer than politician, and it was thought that he won more votes by his preaching than by his political expertise. Winning by only a few votes in 1825, Mangum attributed his victory to a heavy rainstorm, which prevented Crudup from attending a meeting at which the two candidates were to speak. Mangum was able to get to this meeting and thought that he won enough votes there to carry the election. Crudup's clerical status did not shield him from criticism, some arguing that he was more interested in the ministry than in politics and should not hold public office. A rumor circulated in 1821 charged him with plying voters with liquor to influence their choice at the ballot box.

A successful farmer, Crudup had extensive landholdings in North Carolina and Mississippi. A stallion he had bred placed second in the judging at the first North Carolina State Fair in 1853. In his petition for pardon, submitted following the Civil War, he estimated that he owned approximately 160 slaves, all of whom remained with him voluntarily after the war. He claimed to be worth about twenty thousand dollars in 1865.

Crudup was married on 16 Nov. 1813 to Mrs. Anne Maria Davis Brickell, daughter of Archibald Davis of Franklin County. The Crudups had four children, Archibald Davis, James Henry, Martha, and Edward Alston. Following the death of Anne Brickell Crudup on 27 Mar. 1822, Crudup married Mary E. Boddie, on 5 May 1825. Four children were born to this union, John Boddie, Lucy (Mrs. George Kittrell), Mary (Mrs. John Cannady), and William Boddie. Crudup died at his home near Kittrell and was buried in the family burial ground nearby.

SEE: *Biog. Dir. Am. Cong.* (1950); *Farmer's Journal*, November 1853; Ernest Haywood MSS (Southern Historical Collection, University of North Carolina, Chapel Hill); North Carolina State Archives (Raleigh), for Josiah Crudup MSS and Military Papers (Civil War Collection, Petitions for Pardon); Thomas Merritt Pittman MSS (Manuscript Department, Library, Duke University, Durham); H. T. Shanks, ed., *The Papers of Willie Person Mangum*, 5 vols. (1950–56); *Who Was Who in America, 1607–1896*.

PAUL I. CHESTNUT

Cruikshank, Margaret Mordecai Jones (*13 Oct. 1878–26 Dec. 1955*), teacher and college president, was born in Hillsborough, the daughter of Halcott Pride Jones and his wife, Olive Echols. She attended the Nash-Kollock School in Hillsborough and was graduated from St. Mary's Academy in Raleigh in 1896. She then taught at St. Mary's for three years before entering The University of North Carolina for the session of 1901–2. Returning to St. Mary's to teach for three more years, she also studied in Chapel Hill and at Teachers College, Columbia University, traveling in Europe in the summers. She was graduated from Columbia in 1911 and on 17 June married Ernest Cruikshank, business manager of St. Mary's.

Mrs. Cruikshank continued to teach at St. Mary's until 1921, when her husband became president of Columbia Institute in Tennessee. He died the following year, and she succeeded him as president. She held the position until 1932, when she was elected principal and academic head of St. Mary's Junior College, as the first woman to head the institution; the alumnae apparently played a significant role in her selection. In 1937 she earned a master's degree at Duke University. She continued to serve as head of St. Mary's until her death from a heart attack.

During her teaching career, Mrs. Cruikshank's specialties were mathematics, astronomy, German, and the Bible. She was a Democrat and an Episcopalian. She was survived by a son, Ernest, and two daughters, Mary Price (Mrs. Frank Clark) and Olive (Mrs. Robert T. Foss).

SEE: Daniel L. Grant, *Alumni History of the University of North Carolina* (1924); Raleigh *News and Observer*, 8 Apr. 1932, 27 Dec. 1955, 1 Jan. 1958; *Who Was Who in America* (1960).

WILLIAM S. POWELL

Crump, Earl Alexander (*4 Sept. 1900–3 Feb. 1960*), North Carolina state highway engineer and personnel director, was a native of Lumberton and the son of Solomon and Nannie Nance Crump. Orphaned by the death of both parents before he was one year old, he was raised by his father's brother, Columbus Crump. He attended the public schools of Lumberton until 1917 and studied civil engineering at Tri-State College in Indiana from 1923 to 1925 and at North Carolina State College in 1925–26.

Except for two years as repair foreman of the Townson Motor Company in Lumberton (1920–23), Crump's entire working career was spent in the service of the highway commission. This career paralleled the rapid growth of the highway commission, in response to a demand for government agencies to assume expanding responsibility in service to the state. Accordingly, just as the Good Roads Movement was gaining momentum in 1926, he returned to Robeson County and his first job as rodman. He worked in the period of unprecedented construction during the twenties and thirties as rodman and inspector on highway and bridge projects in Robeson, Bladen, and Cumberland counties; in 1929 he was promoted to instrumentman.

In 1931, when the state assumed responsibility of all public roads, Crump was transferred to much-needed projects in the western counties of Yadkin and Surry. In 1932 he became junior resident engineer, planning and directing projects in Wilson, Pitt, Greene, and Wayne counties. Promotion to senior resident engineer came in 1935, with work in Craven, Onslow, and Carteret counties and later Robeson, Vance, Johnston, and Wayne counties. In May 1939 he became senior claims engineer in the new Sixth Highway Division at Asheboro. In this essential position, he had the job of obtaining right-of-way agreements and negotiating settlements of damage claims. Promotion came again in 1941, when he assumed the position of assistant division engineer, headquartered at Wilson.

As he advanced in the highway commission, Crump retained an active interest in highway employees at all levels. He was a primary force in the creation of the North Carolina Highway Employees' Association, serving as its first vice-president in 1947 and as its president in 1948–49. While president of the employees' association, he left the Wilson territory to become highway engineer in the division including Wake County. In 1953, as a tribute to his outstanding work in employee welfare, he was appointed by Governor Kerr Scott as director of the highway commission's first personnel office. Three years later he was transferred to Durham as engineer of the fifth division; returning to Raleigh in 1957, he served in the newly created position of assistant chief engineer until his death.

Crump's career with the highway commission coincided with the modern era of road building in the state, from the Good Roads Movement to the advent of interstate highways. From rodman to engineer, he was a prominent figure in numerous construction projects across many counties. His work with highway personnel provided a valuable service to the employees and the highway commission as a whole. He was professionally active in the North Carolina Society of Engineers and the East Carolina Engineers Club and socially active as a

Thirty-second degree Mason and a member of the Sudan Temple. He maintained an abiding loyalty to his home church and often returned to Lumberton to attend services. He married Mary Euphemia Tyson in 1930 and after her death was married in 1952 to Sarah Ann Dillon of Wilson.

SEE: *History of North Carolina*, vol. 3 (1956); Raleigh *News and Observer*, 4 Feb. 1960; Capus Waynick, *North Carolina Roads and Their Builders*, vol. 1 (1952).

HARRIETTE CRUMP PARTIN

Cullen, Thomas (*d. ca. 1689*), colonial official, came to the North Carolina colony from Dover, England. He arrived before October 1669, when he was granted 660 acres of land. He had a plantation on Salmon Creek in Chowan Precinct and engaged in the Indian trade as well as planting.

Cullen was a member of the council in 1670, 1673, and 1675. He also served on the rebel council that governed the colony for about two years following the uprising called Culpeper's Rebellion, which occurred in December 1677. Cullen, who was one of the leaders of the uprising, had served as speaker of the assembly held in the fall of 1677 under Thomas Miller, then acting as governor. Cullen also was speaker of the rebel assembly elected after Miller's overthrow. In 1680, after reestablishment of a legally constituted government, Cullen was the presiding justice of the Chowan Precinct Court; in 1683 he was a justice of the county court of Albemarle.

Cullen and his wife, Sarah, had eight children, all of whom appear to have been born in England. The children were Thomas, Jr., John, Richard, Sarah, Anne, Mary, Christian, and Martha. In March 1678/79, Cullen executed a deed of gift conveying his Salmon Creek plantation to his wife for her lifetime and afterward to two of his daughters, Mary and Martha. Whether the other daughters were then living is not known. At the time of the deed, Cullen's daughter Mary was the wife of John Currer, who died a few years later. Martha was then unmarried, but she later became the wife of Robert West and after West's death married Thomas Pollock; she died 17 Mar. 1700/1701. Only one of Cullen's sons, Thomas, Jr., appears as an adult in North Carolina records. He witnessed a bill of sale in March 1683/84, but his later history is not known.

Cullen and his family, with the exception of Martha, appear to have left North Carolina in the late 1680s. They may have moved to Isle of Wight County, Va., where a Thomas Cullen died in 1689.

SEE: *The North Carolina Historical and Genealogical Register*, 3 vols. (1900–1903); North Carolina State Archives (Raleigh), for Albemarle Book of Warrants and Surveys (1681–1706), Timothy Biggs, "A Narrative of The Transactions past In the Conty of Albemarle Sence Mr. Tho. Miller his Arrivall there" (original in the Arents Tobacco Collection, New York Public Library, New York City), Minutes of Shaftesbury (Chowan) Precinct Court (1 Apr. 1680, in Colonial Court Records), W. H. Parker, "The Cullen Family of North Carolina" (typescript); Mattie Erma Edwards Parker, ed., *North Carolina Higher-Court Records, 1670–1696*, and *1697–1701* (1968, 1971); William L. Saunders, ed., *Colonial Records of North Carolina*, vol. 1 (1886); Annie Noble Sims, "Three Early Landowners of the County of Isle of Wight, Virginia," *William and Mary Quarterly* 27 (1918); Clayton Torrence, comp., *Virginia Wills and Administrations* (1972).

MATTIE ERMA E. PARKER

Cullom, Willis Richard *(15 Jan. 1867–20 Oct. 1963)*, clergyman and educator, was born in Halifax County, near Weldon. He was the fifth child and second son of Joseph Joel and Mary E. Johnson Cullom, who ultimately became the parents of fourteen children. He was taught to read by a maiden aunt, Amanda Cullom, and completed his education at various private schools in Halifax and Warren counties.

Joseph and Mary Cullom were pious Methodists with strong convictions concerning the importance of religion to the individual, and Willis early demonstrated an interest in church matters. In 1880 he came under the influence of the Reverend Albert G. Willcox, a young Baptist preacher who comforted the Cullom family in the long illness and the death from typhoid of Willis's older brother, Charles. In the summer of 1881, Willis Cullom was converted during a revival conducted in a brush arbor near the Cullom home by Willcox and Dr. James D. Hufham of Scotland Neck. On the following 1 Sept., Cullom and eleven fellow converts covenanted together to form the Quankie Baptist Church, which Cullom's parents soon joined. In the spring of 1883, sixteen-year-old Cullom became superintendent of the Quankie Church Sunday school.

Cullom's first employment away from his father's farm was as bookkeeper at the cotton gin of Burwell Davis in Warren County, where he worked in the fall of 1882 and again in 1883. In 1884 he took a job as clerk in J. L. Rodwell's store at Axtell, Warren County. There he remained until the fall of 1885, when he became the teacher of the elementary grades of a school at Yadkin Valley, Davie County; the school's principal, Gilbert L. Finch, who taught the higher grades, agreed to teach Cullom at night and on weekends in return for his assistance at the school during the weekdays. At the end of the school year, in June 1886, Cullom returned to Axtell, where he occupied his old room in Rodwell's store while teaching a six-week summer school nearby. There, at some time during July, he concluded that he was called to preach. Upon the invitation of the pastor of the Baptist church at Warrenton, the Reverend Thomas J. Taylor, Cullom conducted a prayer meeting at Warrenton and lost his lingering doubts of the genuineness of his call.

Cullom gave up the principalship of the school at Yadkin Valley, to which he had been named following Finch's resignation, and the following September entered the preparatory department of Wake Forest College. There, in addition to the regular course of study, he read widely in the college library in such varied areas as biography, history, philosophy, theology, economics, sociology, and literary criticism. His favorite periodical was apparently the *Edinburgh Review*. In the fall of 1887 he entered the freshman class of Wake Forest College, becoming an excellent student. In 1888 he was called to the pastorate of the Warren Plains Baptist Church, where he served while continuing his studies at Wake Forest. On 22 July 1888 he was ordained to the ministry by his home church, Quankie Baptist. As a devout Christian of conservative background, he, like many of his fellow students, was deeply disturbed by the implications for religious faith of the discussion of Darwinian evolution agitating the campus. Gradually, he was able to work out a reconciliation of Christian doctrine and evolutionary theory that satisfied his own mind and strongly influenced his later work as a pioneer teacher of religion at the college level.

In June 1892, after six years of study pursued despite financial difficulties, Cullom was graduated by Wake Forest College with the A.M. degree. The following

1 Oct. he was one of approximately two hundred young men who were enrolled at the Southern Baptist Theological Seminary, Louisville, Ky., to study under such giants of Baptist theological education as John A. Broadus, A. T. Robertson, and John R. Sampey. Cullom received the Th.M. degree in 1895 but remained at the seminary for doctoral studies during 1895–96. Although seriously ill with typhoid for several weeks, he managed to complete the school year. Following the approval of his dissertation, "The Final State of the Impenitent," by the seminary's board of examiners, he was awarded the Th.D. in 1904.

In the meantime he had become professor of the Bible in Wake Forest College in 1896. In addition to his teaching duties, he served over the years in a number of North Carolina pastorates, at Youngsville, Wakefield, Dunn, Forestville, Spring Hope, and elsewhere. He was also a frequent contributor to the press of his denomination, especially the *Biblical Recorder*, the official journal of the Baptist State Convention of North Carolina, and he directed and taught in a number of Bible and Pastors' Institutes, first at Wake Forest and later at Meredith College. He planned and taught correspondence courses to help the Baptist pastors of the state keep abreast of developments in their areas of professional interest. For fourteen years (1901–15) he served as executive secretary of the board of education of the Baptist State Convention of North Carolina, the predecessor of the present Council of Christian Higher Education. In the 1930s he served as the state representative on the Education Commission of the Southern Baptist Convention; in 1931 he was its chairman. His contributions to the religious and educational life of his denomination were recognized by the University of Richmond (Va.) in 1915, with the honorary D.D. degree. Cullom's interests, however, were in no sense narrowly denominational; his associates "caught a glimpse more than once of . . . his truly ecumenical Christian spirit."

From 1 June 1918 to 1 Sept. 1920, Cullom was on leave of absence from Wake Forest College to serve as a special fund-raiser for the Southern and North Carolina Baptist conventions and as director of the "Mobile Schools," a system of twenty-eight centers scattered over the state, at which North Carolina Baptists gathered on 19–23 July 1920 "to pray, to counsel, to think, to plan." During 1922–23 he served as acting dean of Wake Forest College. In December 1922 the Baptist State Convention meeting at Winston-Salem rejected a move to depose W. L. Poteat as president of Wake Forest College on a heresy charge growing out of his support of theistic evolution; Cullom's unobtrusive influence counted heavily in Poteat's favor. Though as much a theistic evolutionist as Poteat, Cullom was protected from a similar charge of heresy by his conservative appearance, his close friendship with many of the convention's more conservative leaders, and his less exalted position at the college.

After his mandatory retirement from teaching in 1938, Cullom continued to write pamphlets on various theological topics as well as articles for the *Biblical Recorder*, *Charity and Children*, the *Review and Expositor*, and *Christian Horizons*. Especially noteworthy was the series "Wayside Heroism," which he contributed during the 1940s to *Charity and Children*, the official organ of the North Carolina Baptist Children's homes; the series told the stories of "ordinary people who faced poverty, illness, misfortunes with heroic faith." He also followed a busy schedule of preaching and speaking, and for some years after his retirement from the faculty of Wake Forest College he continued to serve as the regular pastor of the

Spring Hope Baptist Church. In 1956, at age eighty-nine, he delivered the last commencement sermon of Wake Forest College prior to its removal from Wake Forest to Winston-Salem.

Cullom visited Europe and the Near East in 1914 and returned to Europe in 1924. His interest in the latest developments in the theological field and in world affairs continued almost to the moment of his death. After his eyesight failed, he was assisted by readers who came to his home each day.

Cullom married Fanny Farmer of Louisville, Ky., on 2 June 1897. They became the parents of five children, Edward, Nancy, Elizabeth, Sarah, and a son who died at birth. Cullom died at Wake Forest, and funeral services were held in the Wake Forest Baptist Church, where he had been a member for seventy-seven years. Burial was in the Wake Forest Cemetery.

SEE: James H. Blackmore, *The Cullom Lantern: A Biography of W. R. Cullom* (1963 [photograph]); *Charity and Children*, 1943–63; W. R. Cullom, *Summary of the Life of W. R. Cullom* (n.d.); S. C. Linder, *William Louis Poteat* (1966); W. A. Mueller, *History of Southern Baptist Theological Seminary* (1959); G. W. Paschal, *History of Wake Forest College*, vol. 2 (1843); Quankie Baptist Church (Halifax County) Records, 1881–87 (church office, Roanoke Rapids); Raleigh *Biblical Recorder*, 1895–1963, esp. 26 Oct. 1963; *Wake Forest Student* 6–12 (1887–95); *Who Was Who in America*, vol. 5 (1973).

W. CONARD GASS

Culpeper, Frances *(1634–90)*, proprietor of North Carolina and wife of three colonial governors, was born at Hollingbourne, Kent, England, the daughter of Thomas Culpeper and his wife, Katherine St. Leger. Her uncle was John, first Lord Culpeper; her brother was John, leader of Culpeper's Rebellion.

The year of her arrival in the New World is not known. She was married in Virginia in 1652 to Samuel Stephens of Warwick County, Va., "Commander of the Southern Plantation" in 1662–64 and governor of Albemarle in 1667–70. Upon his death in 1670, she married, later that same year, Sir William Berkeley, governor of Virginia. As first lady of Virginia, she lived in state. Green Spring, the governor's plantation home near Jamestown, was the first of the splendid James River plantation houses; it was built of brick with a large central hall and staircase, a refinement hitherto unknown in the colonies. A courtier of King Charles and one of the original proprietors of Carolina, Berkeley had been commissioned governor in 1642. His earlier years in office had been happy ones, but by the time of his marriage, his popularity had waned. He became an object of ridicule when, a bachelor of sixty-four, he chose a wife half his age.

Frances, "vigorous and energetic," became his staunch partisan, taking an active part in the political unrest that culminated in Bacon's Rebellion. To show her contempt for the commissioners sent to investigate her husband's activities, she had the "common hangman mounted as an improvised postillion," to conduct the commissioners away from their visit to Green Spring. Berkeley in his will spoke of her as his "dear and most virtuous wife." He died in 1677, deaf, senile, and discredited by his former adherents.

Three years later, Frances wed still another governor, Colonel Philip Ludwell of Rich Neck, a large estate near Green Spring. The year before, Ludwell had been commissioned "Governor of that part of our Province of Carolina that lyes North and east of Cape feare." Thus,

for the second time, Frances Culpeper was first lady of North Carolina.

In 1691, both Carolinas were put under Ludwell's jurisdiction, but by then Frances was dead and buried near the old church at Jamestown. Her tombstone reads, "Frances, Lady Berkeley," a title she was loath to relinquish and a choice indicative of her sometimes arbitrary nature.

Because she left no children, Green Spring was eventually inherited by Philip Ludwell, Jr., Colonel Ludwell's son by an earlier marriage. A portrait of Frances as Lady Berkeley, painted in London by an unknown artist, passed from the Ludwell family to the Lees, Ludwell descendants, and is now owned by a Lee in Connecticut.

As legatee of her second husband, Frances became a proprietor of Carolina, and "by a curious combination of circumstances . . . had the good fortune to sell this interest twice, in 1682 and again in 1684, and each time to be paid for it."

SEE: Virginius Dabney, *Virginia: The New Dominion* (1971); Fairfax Harrison, *The Proprietors of the Northern Neck* (1926); Lawrence Lee, *The Lower Cape Fear in Colonial Days* (1965); William L. Saunders, ed., *Colonial Records of North Carolina*, vol. 1 (1886); Alexander W. Weddell, *Memorial Volume of Virginia Portraiture* (1930); George F. Williston, *Behold Virginia, the Fifth Crown* (1951).

JAQUELIN DRANE NASH

Culpeper, John *(ca. 1633–ca. 1692)*, surveyor general and member of parliament in South Carolina, is known chiefly for his participation in the so-called Culpeper's Rebellion in North Carolina and for his subsequent trial in England on charge of treason.

The earliest certain record of Culpeper is dated 15 July 1670. It records his appearance in a North Carolina court, where he was identified as attorney for Sir William Berkeley, governor of Virginia and a proprietor of Carolina. Culpeper was in court to petition for administration on the estate of Samuel Stephens, recently deceased governor of the North Carolina colony, then called Albemarle. Stephens's widow, Frances, had married Berkeley the preceding month, but, for reasons not given in surviving records, the court departed from usual practice and, instead of naming Berkeley administrator, granted administration to Culpeper.

The appointment of Culpeper as Stephens's administrator has special significance in the light of a theory concerning Culpeper's identity: genealogists of the Culpeper family have concluded that the John Culpeper of Albemarle fame was a son of Thomas Culpeper of Feckenham, Worcestershire, England, whose son John was baptised 4 Apr. 1633; if the theory is correct, John Culpeper was Lady Berkeley's brother. Such a relationship would provide a plausible explanation for the court's otherwise puzzling choice. After Berkeley's death some years later, Lady Berkeley's brother, Alexander Culpeper, was appointed Berkeley's administrator in England "as natural and lawful brother of Dame Frances Berkeley, relict of the deceased." Although the Albemarle court was silent on the matter, its appointment of John Culpeper to administer Stephens's estate strongly indicates that he, too, was Lady Berkeley's brother.

Culpeper appears not to have been a resident of Albemarle when he was appointed Stephens's administrator although he was in the colony for the next few months, settling the estate. The following February he arrived in the newly established South Carolina colony and took up residence there. Within a month after his arrival, South Carolina officials were arranging for him to take over the work of the surveyor general, Florence O'Sullivan, of whose inadequacies as a surveyor they had complained to the proprietors. For some months, O'Sullivan nominally retained office and split the fees with Culpeper, who did the surveying. By the end of the year, however, Culpeper had officially replaced O'Sullivan: on 30 Dec. 1671, the London proprietors issued a commission appointing Culpeper surveyor general for South Carolina.

There is no documentary evidence that Sir William Berkeley arranged for Culpeper to receive the South Carolina position, but that appointment bears a striking parallel to one granted Alexander Culpeper through Berkeley's influence. Soon after John went to South Carolina, Berkeley wrote a series of letters to London officials urging that Alexander, whom he identified as his wife's brother, be appointed surveyor general for Virginia. Alexander was granted his post a few weeks before issuance of John's commission for the comparable post in South Carolina.

Culpeper remained in South Carolina more than two years, his wife, Judith, joining him in December 1671. The next year he was granted a lot in Charles Town and a plantation of 370 acres; also in that year, he served as a member of the South Carolina parliament. In addition to routine surveying, he mapped the Ashley River area for the proprietors and laid out the old Charles Town.

In about June 1673, Culpeper suddenly left South Carolina without notice. In leaving as he did, he violated a law that made it a felony, punishable by death, to leave the colony without obtaining permission three weeks in advance from the governor and council. The fact that he "ran away" placed him in an unfavorable light and probably gave rise to certain allegations, apparently without substance, later made against him. He was said to have instigated local disturbances and to have left because he was in danger of being hanged. In the opinion of a recent historian, he left because of a food shortage that plagued the colony. It is possible, however, that the reason for his departure was one that he was not at liberty to disclose. At the time he left, the proprietors were engaged in secret negotiations for a division of Carolina, whereby Sir William Berkeley was expected to receive sole possession of the Albemarle area and to relinquish his interest in the remainder of the province. Such a division, although never effected, appeared imminent in 1673. If Culpeper was indeed Berkeley's brother-in-law and held office in South Carolina through Berkeley's influence, he no doubt was confidentially informed of the intended division and of the seeming advisability of his prompt removal to Albemarle.

Whatever his reason, Culpeper had settled in Albemarle by November 1673. By that date he had become active in one of the political factions into which the colonists were divided. He supported the party of the leading early settlers, which was headed by the acting governor, John Jenkins. The opposing party, composed chiefly of later settlers, was led by the speaker of the assembly, Thomas Eastchurch. The uprising called Culpeper's Rebellion was a culmination of power struggles and animosities between those two factions. The dissension already existed when Culpeper arrived, and it continued several years. The rebellion took place in December 1677, a few months after one Thomas Miller, an outspoken supporter of Eastchurch, had assumed power as acting governor. The proprietors appointed Eastchurch, not Miller, governor of the

colony, but Eastchurch stopped for an extended stay in Nevis on his way home from London. He sent Miller, whom the proprietors had appointed council member, to govern Albemarle until his arrival.

On reaching Albemarle, Miller assumed office by armed force despite protests that Eastchurch lacked authority to appoint him acting governor. Miller and his supporters then barred their opponents from the assembly by imposing restrictions on voting, illegally fined and took other retaliatory measures against leaders of the party opposing them, and committed other abuses of power. As customs collector, for which position he had received a commission in London, Miller further antagonized the colonists by rigidly collecting the hated penny-per-pound tax on tobacco exports, which his predecessor had been lax in collecting. In their revolt, the colonists imprisoned Miller and several members of his council, elected a new assembly, chose a new council, and appointed a special court to try Miller and others for alleged offenses. The new assembly appointed Culpeper customs collector in place of Miller, who was then in prison.

Why the uprising is called Culpeper's Rebellion is not known. The name, which apparently is traditional, probably originated in popular misconceptions concerning the circumstances of Culpeper's trial in England. There is no evidence, even in the testimony produced at the trial, that Culpeper spearheaded the revolt against Miller. In fact, Culpeper was absent from Albemarle much, if not all, of the fall preceding the revolt, which occurred early in December. He was in Boston that September, and he returned to Albemarle, presumably from his New England trip, only a few days before the uprising. He may have been instrumental in procuring the arms that reached Albemarle on the eve of the revolt, and he may have performed other missions in New England or elsewhere, but he could not have been the chief instigator and organizer of the events in Albemarle without being in the colony during the months immediately preceding them.

The extant accounts of the uprising make it clear that the revolt was directed by a group of the colony's leaders, of whom Culpeper was only one. The chief actions attributed to Culpeper during the affair were drafting a "Remonstrance" sent to an outlying section of the colony to arouse support; drafting other "seditious libells"; "agitating" the people of Chowan; participating in the seizure and imprisonment of one of Miller's clerks; being in a group that seized Miller's papers and the official records of the colony; advising the prosecutors in Miller's trial and instructing the foreman of the jury of the proper form for returning the verdict; and other acts fitting the role ascribed to him as "their Secretary or Register and one of their Caball or Grand Council in matters of advise."

Tradition also is in error in the long-standing belief that the rebels made Culpeper governor in Miller's place; Culpeper replaced Miller only as customs collector. Indeed, so far as extant records show, Culpeper was not a member of either the council or the assembly chosen by the rebels. It was the post of customs collector that caused Culpeper to be charged with treason. The charge was lodged by Crown officials in England in December 1679, upon complaint of Thomas Miller, who had escaped from his Albemarle prison and gone to England. Miller, who hoped to regain the post of customs collector or at least secure compensation for its loss, reached London about the time that Culpeper was preparing to return to Albemarle, after spending most of that year in England. Miller had failed in an earlier effort to have

Culpeper prosecuted through a former subordinate in London. Crown officials, after investigating those charges, had dismissed them when Culpeper gave bond for payment of the customs alleged to be due. This time, however, with Miller himself in London persistently pressing his complaint, officials paid more attention. Eventually, Culpeper was brought to trial on the charge that he had seized the king's customs without authority, had conspired to defraud the king's customs, and had incited the people of Albemarle against the king and the proprietors.

Initially, the Carolina proprietors appeared to support the prosecution of Culpeper, but they reversed their position during the trial. Culpeper was acquitted on the basis of testimony given on behalf of the proprietors by Lord Shaftesbury, who testified that Thomas Miller took over the government of Albemarle without legal authority and that, consequently, his overthrow was not rebellion against the proprietors or the king. Upon Shaftesbury's assurance that the situation in Albemarle had been settled, that the customs due the king would be paid, and that in future the customs would be properly handled, the charges against Culpeper were again dismissed.

After his trial Culpeper returned to Albemarle. His wife, Judith, had died, probably some years earlier. Either before he went to England in 1679 or soon after his return in 1680, he married his second wife, Margaret Bird, widow of Valentine Bird. After Margaret's death in 1687 or early the next year, Culpeper married Sarah Mayo, who probably was the daughter of Edward Mayo, Sr. That marriage took place on 23 Aug. 1688.

At about the time of his second marriage, Culpeper took up a plantation in Pasquotank Precinct, where he lived the remainder of his life as a merchant-planter. So far as surviving records show, he took no further part in public affairs. In his business, however, he had widespread connections with merchants in New England, New York, and elsewhere.

Culpeper's death occurred at some date between 11 June 1691 and February 1693/94, by which time his widow had remarried. He left two or more minor children, designated in extant records only as "the orphans of John Culpeper." His widow married Patrick Henley and subsequently Matthew Pritchard. One of Culpeper's children probably was Sarah Culpeper, who married Benjamin Pritchard, brother of Matthew, in 1704. Sarah and the Pritchard family were Quakers.

SEE: Agnes Leland Baldwin, comp., *First Settlers of South Carolina* (1969); Langdon Cheves, ed., "The Shaftesbury Papers and Other Records Relating to Carolina . . . prior to 1676," *Collections of the South Carolina Historical Society*, vol. 5 (1897); Fairfax Harrison, *The Proprietors of the Northern Neck* (1926); *The North Carolina Historical and Genealogical Register*, 3 vols. (1900–1903); William Wade Hinshaw, comp., *Encyclopedia of American Quaker Genealogy*, vol. 1 (1936); North Carolina State Archives (Raleigh), for Albemarle Book of Warrants and Surveys (1681–1706), Council Minutes, Wills, Inventories (1677–1701), and Joshua Lamb Papers; Mattie Erma Edwards Parker, "Legal Aspects of 'Culpeper's Rebellion,'" *North Carolina Historical Review* 45 (1968), and *North Carolina Higher-Court Records, 1670–1696*, and *1697–1601* (1968, 1971); Hugh F. Rankin, *Upheaval in Albemarle: The Story of Culpeper's Rebellion* (1962); Alexander S. Salley, Jr., ed., *Warrants for Lands in South Carolina* (1973); William L. Saunders, ed., *Colonial Records of North Carolina*, vol. 1 (1886); M. Eugene Sirmans, Jr., *Colonial South Carolina* (1966); Henry A. M.

Smith, "Charleston: The Original Plan and the Earliest Settlers," *South Carolina Historical and Genealogical Magazine* 9 (1908), and "Old Charles Town and Its Vicinity," ibid. 16 (1915).

MATTIE ERMA E. PARKER

Culpepper (Culpeper), John *(1764–Jan. 1841)*, Baptist clergyman and Federalist congressman, son of Samson Culpepper, was born near Wadesboro in Anson County, in the area later made into Montgomery County. Nothing is known of his personal life, although one reference indicates that he may have served in the Revolutionary War, perhaps in Georgia where he lived for awhile before 1784. He said in 1820 that "he knew what it was to be a soldier himself, and to serve when a morsel of bread was a luxury." He attended local schools and was ordained in the Sandy Creek Association some time prior to 1812. It is probable that he preached at Meadow Branch Church in Union County, where he acquired a reputation as "a great evangelist." By 1815 the number of Baptist congregations had increased, and the new Pee Dee Association, to which Culpepper belonged for the remainder of his life, was created. At the 1816 meeting of the Sandy Creek Association, he was the guest preacher, using as his text for the opening discourse Hebrews 4:16.

Unconcerned over the issue of separation of church and state, Culpepper ran for the General Assembly of North Carolina and was elected as one of the two Anson County representatives in 1801. His service was not remarkable; he favored the calling of a constitutional convention for revision of the state constitution, and he favored stricter laws to regulate gambling. On the last day of the session, however, he and two other clerical members were challenged by the House of Commons on the basis of having violated Section 31 of the constitution, which forbade practicing clergy to hold office in the General Assembly. His seat was thereupon declared vacant, he was awarded all his back pay, and a new election in Anson County was called. This event did not discourage him, for in 1807 he ran for Congress as a Federalist against Duncan McFarland and won in a contested election. McFarland appealed to the House of Representatives, which, after taking testimony evidencing such irregularities as an insufficient number of judges and failure to administer proper oaths to election officials, declared the seat vacant but would not award it to McFarland. A new election returned Culpepper again, whereupon he took his seat and began the first of six terms in Congress (1807–9, 1813–17, 1819–21, 1823–25, 1827–29).

Philosophically, Culpepper was more nearly an Old Jeffersonian than a Federalist. As he himself stated, he "had always been independent enough to disregard precedents in his course, and he should continue to do so." He stood with the Federalists in opposition to the War of 1812, averring his willingness to support a defensive war but never a war "for the purpose of invasion of Canada." He voted against the Loan Bill of 1814 in a lengthy speech, referring to "this premature, this ill-advised, this miserably conducted war. . . ."

Culpepper did not follow the nationalist surge that ensued at the close of the war. He voted against the charter of the second Bank of the United States and aginst the protective tariffs of 1816, 1824, and 1828. Although he initially supported an appropriation for roads and canals, by 1824 he also opposed these expenditures, on the grounds of invasion of states' rights. He did not hesitate to vote for appropriations that would benefit the "little man," supporting pensions for all Revolutionary War soldiers, for instance, and salary increases for government clerks.

Although it is not known if he was a slaveholder, Culpepper supported the institution. During the 1820 struggle over the admission of Missouri, he voted consistently for slavery in the new state but was willing to support its prohibition north of 36 degrees 30 minutes. Further, he opposed an authorization for the president to negotiate with foreign countries to abolish the African slave trade, and he also objected to the use of resolutions in the House as vehicles for abolitionist propaganda.

To some, the country preacher was good only for "log-rolling or corn shucking." Indeed, once the members of the House walked off the floor in the midst of a Culpepper speech. To others, he "was deemed a man of sound sense, but not brilliant, useful rather than showy." Not a wealthy man, he did not consider himself able to serve in Congress without adequate compensation. "My family are to be provided for, and I shall vote for the compensation I deem just, and use my wages to support myself, to pay my debts, to support my family, etc., just as I would the avails of my labor on my farm, or any where else. . . ." His socioeconomic status and his views are generally Jeffersonian, and it must remain a mystery why he called himself a Federalist.

Following the end of his sixth term he retired; he died twelve years later, at the age of eighty, at the home of a son in Darlington County, S.C. He was buried in the Welch Neck Church cemetery at Society Hill, S.C.

SEE: *Biog. Dir. Am. Cong.* (1971); Catherine B. Matthews, "John Culpepper: A Biographical Sketch" (North Carolina Collection, University of North Carolina, Chapel Hill); "Minutes of North Carolina Baptist General Meeting of Correspondence, 1812," *Wake Forest Student* 27 (1907); *Report of the Committee of Elections*, 1807; John H. Wheeler, *Historical Sketches of North Carolina* (1851).

SARAH MCCULLOH LEMMON

Cumming, William (30 July 1724–ca. 1797), attorney, legislator, and member of the Continental Congress, was born in Annapolis, Md., the son of Elizabeth Coursey and William Cumming. Although he clearly was well educated and wrote extremely well, there is no evidence that he attended any of the leading colleges of the day. He studied law, however, and had been admitted to the bar before coming to North Carolina in 1762 or earlier. In his will, dated 11 July 1796, he observed that he had experienced financial stringency to the point of mortgaging his property to cover losses sustained by his father. He also commented with enthusiasm on his life in Edenton, "where I have experienced humanity, friendship, promotion, perhaps more than my merit." A William Cumming represented Currituck County in the assembly in 1762, 1764, and 1765, in the latter year serving as chairman of the committee of the whole. In 1766 one William Cumming presented a petition claiming that he had been chosen a representative from Nixonton in Pasquotank County, but a committee decided that he had been illegally returned. In 1773 a William Cumming complained of an irregular election in the same county, and a new one was ordered; two years later this man represented Pasquotank County in the Third Provincial Congress, which met in Hillsborough in August and September, but whether this William

Cumming was the one who served in the Continental Congress later cannot be determined.

Cumming was living in Edenton as a lawyer by January 1762 and apparently was well accepted locally. A letter of that date to his sister, Betty, in Maryland, told of the pending marriage of elderly Governor Arthur Dobbs to fifteen-year-old Justina Davis. Cumming represented Edenton in the House of Commons in 1783, 1784, and 1788. In 1784 he was elected to the Continental Congress, serving until 1786. He appears to have been the only North Carolina delegate present at the 1785 session of the Congress. In February 1786 he was named to another term, but the state's failure to pay funds due to him, and a subsequent debilitating illness (apparently a paralysis), made it impossible for him to serve; he so advised Governor Richard Caswell on 3 Aug. 1786.

Cumming was particularly active in the assembly of 1783, serving on various committees, notably on one appointed "to consider making a revisal of the laws of the State" and another, a joint committee, "to enquire into the present state and condition of the Public Revenue and to make a report thereon." During the session he also introduced several significant bills, including "a Bill of pardon, indemnity, and oblivion, and for restoring tranquility to the State" and another supporting roads, ferries, bridges, and the clearing of inland rivers and creeks. He joined fifty-five other men in petitioning the governor to "exercise mercy" toward two accused horse thieves of Hillsborough, insisting that the men had "otherwise good reputations."

In 1788, when he was the borough representative for Edenton in the assembly, he served on "the Committee on the State and Condition of the Public Revenue" and was the author of a "Bill to amend an Act to prevent Domestick Insurrection" and of another "to punish House Breaking and other crimes." Perhaps with an eye to conservation or perhaps merely to protect the interests of residents of the state against interlopers, he presented a "Bill to prevent the exportation of raw hides, of both cattle, and wild animals."

Cumming was nominated for a judgeship in 1790, but the records do not reveal whether he was actually named to the post. The federal census of the year records as members of his Edenton household Cumming himself, one white male under the age of sixteen (an apprentice, perhaps), and two slaves. In 1791, when he was a candidate for the General Assembly, Cumming noted that he had served his country sporadically for nearly twenty-eight years; he apparently was not elected.

Cumming was never married. The date and place of his death and burial are not known, but he was certainly dead by 29 June 1797, when James Hathaway was made administrator of his estate. In advertisements in the *State Gazette* of 29 June and 13 July 1797, Hathaway asked that books missing from Cumming's library be returned, as his estate was to be sold at Colonel John Hamilton's on 21 July.

SEE: Samuel A. Ashe, "William Cumming" (Manuscript Department, Library, Duke University, Durham); *Biog. Dir. Am. Cong.* (1971); William L. Saunders and Walter Clark, eds., *Colonial and State Records of North Carolina*, 30 vols. (1886–1914).

C. SYLVESTER GREEN

Cunningham, John Wilson (6 Feb. 1820–15 July 1889), planter, merchant, and political leader, was born in Petersburg, Va. His parents were Alexander Cunningham, a wholesale merchant of Petersburg, and Mattie

Wilson Cunningham; the Cunningham family was of Scottish origin. In 1796, Alexander purchased a large tract of land in northwestern Person County and established a branch of his mercantile business at what by 1821 had become a post office known as "Cunningham's Store." John Wilson attended the famous Bingham's School, whence he entered The University of North Carolina, being graduated in 1840. At Chapel Hill he shared a room in East Building with Calvin H. Wiley, the future first state superintendent of North Carolina common schools (1853–65). Although Cunningham was a lifelong Democrat and Wiley an antebellum Whig, Wiley became Cunningham's fast friend and later served as his political adviser and the actual but secret author of many of his speeches, reports to his constituents, and letters to important political personages.

Following his graduation from the university, Cunningham settled on his father's Person County plantation, where he was to reside for the remainder of his life. He was much interested in the latest and best farming methods and eventually exerted a strong influence for agricultural progress in Person and adjoining counties. He tried each year to add some improvement to his own farm and acquired in time the reputation of owning one of the best-managed plantations and most attractive residences in his section of the state. He was also a successful merchant and served for many years as the presiding justice of the Person County Court. In 1844 he was elected to the House of Commons, and he represented Person County in the state senate from 1852 to 1860. During his tenure in each house he was a member of the standing committee on education and an influential advocate of public schools.

Although he favored internal improvements, Cunningham generally objected to the use of public funds to finance them, except in those instances where, in his opinion, the state was practically guaranteed a profit on its investment. He was strongly opposed to the accumulation of a large public debt and insisted that the state meet on schedule the interest on its bonds, by increased taxation whenever necessary. Such, he insisted, was both good ethics and good business management. In the bitter political and economic conflicts between East and West that characterized the antebellum period of the state's history, Cunningham usually sided with the East, opposing especially the demand for the creation of new counties in the West. Regarding banks as at best a necessary evil, he advocated a strong currency and raised his voice and vote in the legislature against the "bank craze" that seemingly demanded a legislatively chartered bank at "every village and crossroads," with full authority to flood the state with "worthless rags."

Although Cunningham considered Lincoln's election in 1860 an affront to North Carolina, and argued that the state's interests could be protected only by leaving the Union and joining a southern confederacy, his justification for such a course of action was the age-old right of revolution rather than the doctrine of secession. A strong supporter of Governor John W. Ellis, he was named to the council of state under Ellis and remained a member during the administration of Henry T. Clark, who became governor upon Ellis's death in 1861. Cunningham represented Person County in the Secession Convention that met in Raleigh on 20 May 1861 and continued in existence, with four periods of adjournment, until 1 Nov. 1862. For a brief time after 31 Aug. 1861, he served as Confederate receiver for the property of "alien enemies" in the eastern district of North Carolina, but he was forced to resign by the pressure of other duties.

In 1864–65 he again served in the lower house of the legislature. An ardent follower of Governor Zebulon B. Vance, he supported wholeheartedly Vance's resistance to encroachment of Confederate civil and military authorities upon the state's sovereignty. He served in the state senate in 1866–68 and in the legislatures of 1872, 1877, and 1879. In 1875 he was a member of the convention that revised the North Carolina Constitution of 1868.

Cunningham was an Episcopalian. In 1860 he married Helen Somerville of Warrenton; they became the parents of John Somerville (b. 5 Sept. 1861), prominent Person County planter and agricultural leader. John W. Cunningham died eighteen months after the death of his wife.

SEE: Samuel A. Ashe, ed., *Cyclopedia of Eminent and Representative Men of the Carolinas of the Nineteenth Century*, vol. 2 (1892 [photograph]); John Wilson Cunningham Papers (Southern Historical Collection, University of North Carolina, Chapel Hill); J. G. McCormick, *Personnel of the Convention of 1861* (1900); *Milton Chronicle*, scattered issues; William S. Powell, *The North Carolina Gazetteer* (1968); Raleigh *North Carolina Standard*, scattered issues; Raleigh *North Carolina Star*, scattered issues; *Raleigh Register*, scattered issues; Calvin Henderson Wiley Papers (North Carolina State Archives, Raleigh; Southern Historical Collection, University of North Carolina, Chapel Hill).

W. CONARD GASS

Cupples, Charles (*d. ca. 1785*), Anglican clergyman, was born in Great Britain and sent to North Carolina as a missionary by the Society for the Propagation of the Gospel in 1766. Governor William Tryon assigned him to St. John's Parish, Bute County, and in 1768 Cupples was recorded as a member of the Blandford-Bute Masonic Lodge. In his earliest known letter to the secretary of the Society in London on 9 Apr. 1768, Cupples commented on his labors and stressed a need felt by many colonial clergy for a resident bishop. He further reported that he had baptized many slaves and in some cases had assigned them godparents of their own race. In the summer of 1770 Cupples visited Rowan County, then without a clergyman, and performed ministerial duties there.

Cupples arrived in the colony at a difficult time as the resentment of many settlers in the back country to excessive taxation and unfair local officials was ready to boil over into what became known as the Regulator Movement. As a clergyman, he was appalled at their violent reaction. As he wrote to his superiors in England on 25 Apr. 1771, some of these people had obstructed courts of justice, burned buildings, and whipped public officials. Sympathy for the Regulators was strong in Bute County, and Cupples observed that although the people there had a religious turn of mind, they did not agree when he preached the duty of a Christian to live in submission to government. Four years later, at the beginning of the Revolution, Cupples was obliged to appear before the Bute County committee of safety on complaint that he had said something favorable respecting Lord Dunmore, the royal governor of Virginia. After hearing him, the committee concluded that he was friendly to the country and the peace of society. As the war progressed Cupples became more fervent in his patriotism and at the revolutionary

Assembly in the spring of 1779, meeting in Smithfield, he served as chaplain, a post he was to fill again the following year in New Bern.

In December 1785 the assembly awarded Ann Cupples £17, probably indicating that the Rev. Mr. Cupples was then dead and this was payment for his service as chaplain. This undoubtedly was welcome relief as Cupples had mortgaged his personal property, including a library, in February 1774 to Dinwiddie and Craufurd, merchants in Glasgow, to secure a debt. The surname of Ann, his wife, is not known. In May 1777 the Bute County court had apprenticed a five-year-old orphan, Sarah Dudley, to Charles and Ann Cupples to learn the art of housewifery. The Cupples appear not to have had any children; the only person of this unusual name in the state at the time of the 1790 census was one Elizabeth Cupples of Iredell County.

In an early letter to the Society Cupples reported that he had held services at five stations. While they were not identified, it is probable that some were in neighboring Granville Parish which then had no clergyman. His main station probably was Trinity Church in the Parish of St. John; its traditional location is near the site of old Bute County courthouse. The parish had a glebe, or farm, for the use of its clergy and a house existed on it during Cupples's lifetime; he probably was residing there at the time of his death. It was identified as late as 1823 on Tanner's map of the state, located in what became northeastern Franklin County after the division of Bute in 1779 into two new counties.

SEE: Bute-Warren County records (Warren County courthouse, Warrenton); *Minutes Bute County Committee of Safety* (1978); Joseph B. Cheshire, *Sketches of Church History* (1892); Marshall DeLancey Haywood, *Lives of the Bishops of North Carolina* (1910); William L. Saunders, ed., *Colonial Records of North Carolina*, vols. 7–8 (1890).

CLAIBORNE T. SMITH, JR.

Curtis, Moses Ashley (11 May 1808–10 Apr. 1872), Episcopal priest, teacher, botanist, and mycologist, was born in Stockbridge, Mass., the son of Jared and Thankful Ashley Curtis. His earliest education was received under his father, who was principal of Stockbridge Academy; he was graduated from Williams College in 1827. The University of North Carolina in 1852 conferred upon him the D.D. degree.

For two years after college graduation, Curtis taught in local schools, but in 1830 he became a tutor in the family of Edward B. Dudley in Wilmington. As a college student, young Curtis had been interested in the natural sciences, and in Wilmington he joined Dr. James F. McRee in the study of local plants. In 1833, however, he returned to Massachusetts and in Boston began the study of theology under the rector of the Church of the Advent; this study was continued the following year in Wilmington, apparently under the direction of the Reverend Thomas F. Davis, rector of St. James's Church. On 3 Dec. 1834, Curtis and Mary Jane de Rosset of Wilmington were married. In due course, Curtis was ordained to the Episcopal priesthood and served various churches in North Carolina, including, in his early years, Lincolnton, Salisbury, Morganton, and Charlotte.

In January 1837, Curtis went to Raleigh to teach in the Episcopal School for Boys, a predecessor of St. Mary's Junior College. Financial conditions at the school were such that, instead of receiving proper compensation for his labors, it developed that he was in large measure supporting the school. In 1840, having sold many of his personal possessions to satisfy creditors of the school, he departed for service as a missionary in the vicinity of Washington, Beaufort County. He accepted a call to St. Matthew's Church, Hillsborough, in June 1841 and remained at the post for the remainder of his life, except for the years 1847–56, which were spent in Society Hill, S.C.

Curtis, through some strength of spirit almost beyond comprehension, led two nearly separate but equally full lives. He was a devout and unselfish priest and teacher on the one hand. On the other he was a knowledgeable scientist, and the judgment of those who followed him in his chosen field of mycology acclaim him as a keen observer and a pioneer discoverer of many American plants. These were not the only fields in which he excelled. As a musician he was appreciated by a wide circle of friends throughout the state, with whom he played on many occasions. The piano, flute, and organ were his principal instruments; but he also played the violin. He sometimes served as church organist and frequently trained his choir to sing such works as Handel's "Hallelujah Chorus," Mozart's "Gloria," and Haydn's *Creation*. Whenever possible he attended concerts, particularly when he happened to be in Philadelphia, New York, or Boston, and his comments on them indicate a cultivated appreciation of good music. He also composed hymns and anthems. One of his compositions, "How Beautiful upon the Mountains," was written for his own ordination. Curtis was also in demand as a lyceum speaker, and manuscripts of some of his lectures, a poster, and clippings of lecture advertisements from the years before the Civil War survive in his papers. As a linguist, he was unusually well trained. He is said to have known German, French, Greek, Hebrew, and Latin. For his own convenience he frequently made notes in shorthand, and he employed shorthand symbols in letters to members of his family.

The Curtis children were William White (1838–43), Armand de Rosset (1839–56), Moses Ashley (1842–1933), John Henry (1844–65), Katharine Fullerton (1845–1922), Charles Jared (1847–1931), Mary Louisa (1849–1929), Magdalen de Rosset (April–September 1851), Caroline (1852–62), and Elizabeth de Rosset (1854–1928). Curtis was a devoted husband and father and while away from home observed strict "writing days." He frequently took his children with him on trips through the state as well as to the North. Until the Civil War intervened, he wrote regularly to his father and even managed to get some communications to him under a flag of truce during the war. News of the death of the elder Curtis reached him in 1862, through the kindness of a Union chaplain in occupied New Bern. The war was a particularly sad occasion for Curtis for a number of reasons. Although born in New England, he came of a slaveholding family. His sympathies lay wholly with the South, and one of his sons was killed at the Battle of Bentonville in 1865. Curtis had a book almost ready for the press when the war began, but it was never published. His contact with fellow churchmen and scientists throughout the country and abroad was suddenly cut off.

Wherever Curtis was he was interested in local plants. His first parish in Lincolnton provided ample opportunity for collecting specimens, and from his missionary journeys he always returned with well-filled portfolios. Some of his parishioners even caught the spirit and began to collect and press plants for him. It may have been his familiarity with the mountain region that brought him an assignment to the committee charged with selecting a site for the University of the South in 1857. This was an undertaking of the church of which he heartily approved, and he took the lead in the mountaintop services when a site was chosen at Sewanee, Tenn.

Curtis was known at home as an Episcopal clergyman of unusual vigor, yet outside North Carolina he was known as a scientist. His interest may have been stirred at Williams College, where he knew Ebenezer Emmons and others with similar talent, but it flourished when he reached Wilmington, and from there he went botanizing into South Carolina and Georgia. His first report was published in the *Journal of the Boston Society of Natural History* in 1835, and in it he corrected much previous misinformation concerning the Venus's flytrap. In his expeditions into the mountains he studied the relation of plant life to geologic and climatic surroundings. It was Curtis who first brought to the attention of the whole country the unique position of North Carolina in climate, soil, and forest products. He pointed out "that North Carolina has a difference of elevation between the east and west which gives a difference of climate equal to 10 or 12 degrees of latitude." Curtis was in close and frequent communication with leading botanists at home and abroad, including Asa Gray, H. W. Ravenel, William S. Sullivant, Edward Tuckerman, and A. W. Chapman (whose *Flora of the Southern United States*, published in 1860, was dedicated to Curtis). His national reputation was such that specimens collected by U.S. exploring expeditions were sent to him for study, identification, and report.

By 1846, Curtis had begun to express particular interest in the study of fungi. By the time of the Civil War he had made such an extensive investigation that he was a recognized authority in the field of mycology. During the war he undertook to prepare a work on "Esculent Fungi," for which his son, Charles Jared, prepared colored drawings. The book was completed but never published. In 1869, Curtis made the unchallenged claim that he had eaten a greater variety of mushrooms than any one on the American Continent. By carefully testing one species after another, he learned their quality as food and discovered that the flavor varied with the type of material in which the mushroom grew. Mushrooms growing in hickory and mulberry wood, for example, were found especially desirable. At one time during the war he asserted that he believed it possible to "maintain a regiment of soldiers five months of the year upon mushrooms alone." In partial support of this theory, he reported that he had collected and eaten forty species found within two miles of his own house.

Curtis contributed scientific articles to a variety of American and British journals and was the author of several books, including *A Catalogue of the Plants of the State, With Descriptions and History of the Trees, Shrubs, and Woody Vines* (Raleigh, 1860); *A Catalogue of the Indigenous and Naturalized Plants of the State* (Raleigh, 1867); and *The Woods and Timbers of North Carolina* (Raleigh, 1883).

Herbaria collected by Curtis are now at The University of North Carolina, Harvard University, the University of Nebraska, and the New York State Museum.

Curtis was buried in the yard of St. Matthew's Church, Hillsborough.

SEE: *Charlotte Observer*, 12 Feb. 1928; *Mycologia* 11 (1919); William S. Powell, *Moses Ashley Curtis, 1808–1872, Teacher, Priest, Scientist* (1958); *Scientific Monthly* 9 (1919); Thomas F. Wood, *Sketch of the Botanical Work of the Rev. Moses A. Curtis* (1885).

WILLIAM S. POWELL

Cutten, George Barton (*11 Apr. 1874– 2 Nov. 1962*), clergyman, college president, and authority on early American silver, was born in Amherst, Nova Scotia, the son of William Freeman and Abbie Ann Trefry Cutten. After his preliminary education in local schools, he attended Acadia University, Wolfville, Nova Scotia, where he was graduated in 1896 with the B.A. degree. He then attended Yale University, New Haven, Conn., where he was graduated with a B.A. degree in 1897; that same year he was awarded the M.A. degree from Acadia University, on the basis of previously completed work. Subsequently, he continued his work at Yale. He received the Ph.D. in 1902 and the B.D. in 1903.

Having been ordained to the Baptist ministry during his undergraduate days at Acadia, Cutten held the pastorate of a Baptist church in New Haven during his student days there and later was pastor at Corning, N.Y., and then at Columbus, Ohio.

After thirteen years as a pastor, he was elected president of Acadia University in 1910. During World War I he was on leave from the Acadia presidency and served as a major in the Canadian Army. Following the 1918 munitions explosion that wrecked the city of Halifax, Nova Scotia, he was in charge of several phases of the rehabilitation of the harbor and the city. In connection with his military duties he served as chief recruiting officer for the Province of Nova Scotia.

In 1922, Cutten went to Colgate University, Ithaca, N.Y., as its president; there, for twenty years, he administered a program that doubled the physical equipment of the university, quadrupled the acreage of its campus, and doubled its endowment to a figure approximating ten million dollars. When he retired from the presidency of Colgate in 1942, he served one year as interim president of the Colgate-Rochester Divinity School, adjunct to Colgate University. In the next year the Cuttens moved to Chapel Hill, North Carolina, where they lived until 1960. They went then to Amherst and Northampton, Mass., and Cutten lived in Northampton until his death at the age of eighty-eight.

Cutten was a distinguished scholar in the fields of theology, psychology, and history. He served on many boards and committees and was active in numerous organizations connected with educational instruction and administration, as well as those interested in general culture.

Typical among the high civic posts Cutten held during his active career, he was at one time president of the National Council of the YMCA; an early president of the International Association of Torch Clubs, he was a charter member of the Durham-Chapel Hill Torch Club.

Cutten was the recipient of several honorary degrees: D.D., Colgate (1911), McMaster (1920); LL.D., Acadia wrote an article on education that appeared in *School and Society* and was widely quoted and reprinted. He wrote more than a dozen books on psychology, education, and religion.

North Carolinians are indebted to Cutten for his exhaustive study *The Silversmiths of North Carolina*. Before coming to North Carolina he had published similar studies of silversmiths in New York and Virginia, and the catalog of the Library of Congress credits him with the authorship of a small shelf of books on early American silver. He accumulated a vast and valuable collection of North Carolina silver and comprehensive data on the silversmiths themselves. That collection became the property of the State of North Carolina in 1956 through a special purchase arrangement; it may be seen at the North Carolina Museum of History, Raleigh.

Cutten was the recipient of several honorary degrees: D.D., Colgate (1911), McMaster (1920); LL.D., Acadia (1914); Ph.D., New York State College for Teachers (1932); Doctor of Humane Letters, Muhlenberg (1935);

and Sc.D., Alfred (1942). He also received the Goodrich
Award for Distinguished Service in Education.

Cutten was married to Minnie Warren Brown of Nova
Scotia, with whom he had four children, Muriel, Claire,
William F., and Sarah (d. 1926). Cutten died at
Cooley-Dickinson Hospital in Northampton, Mass., and
was buried in a local cemetery.

SEE: George Barton Cutten, *Silversmiths of North Carolina*
(1973); *New York Times*, 4 Nov. 1962 (obit.); *Who Was Who
in America*, vol. 4 (1968).

C. SYLVESTER GREEN